SOMETHING ABOUT THE AUTHOR®

Something about
the Author *was named
an "Outstanding
Reference Source,"*
*the highest honor given
by the American
Library Association
Reference and Adult
Services Division.*

ISSN 0276-816X

SOMETHING ABOUT THE AUTHOR®

**Facts and Pictures about Authors
and Illustrators of Books for Young People**

volume 239

GALE
CENGAGE Learning®

Detroit • New York • San Francisco • New Haven, Conn • Waterville, Maine • London

CENGAGE Learning®

Something about the Author, Volume 239

Project Editor: Lisa Kumar

Permissions: Leitha Etheridge-Sims

Imaging and Multimedia: Leitha Etheridge-Sims, John Watkins

Composition and Electronic Capture: Amy Darga

Manufacturing: Rhonda Dover

Product Manager: Mary Onorato

© 2012 Gale, Cengage Learning

For product information and technology assistance, contact us at
Gale Customer Support, 1-800-877-4253.
For permission to use material from this text or product,
submit all requests online at **www.cengage.com/permissions.**
Further permissions questions can be emailed to
permissionrequest@cengage.com

Since this page cannot legibly accommodate all copyright notices, the acknowledgments constitute an extension of the copyright notice.

While every effort has been made to ensure the reliability of the information presented in this publication, Gale, a part of Cengage Learning, does not guarantee the accuracy of the data contained herein. Gale accepts no payment for listing; and inclusion in the publication of any organization, agency, institution, publication, service, or individual does not imply endorsement of the editors or publisher. Errors brought to the attention of the publisher and verified to the satisfaction of the publisher will be corrected in future editions.

EDITORIAL DATA PRIVACY POLICY: Does this publication contain information about you as an individual? If so, for more information about our editorial data privacy policies, please see our Privacy Statement at www.gale.cengage.com.

Gale, Cengage Learning
27500 Drake Rd.
Farmington Hills, MI, 48331-3535

LIBRARY OF CONGRESS CATALOG CARD NUMBER 62-52046

ISBN-13: 978-1-4144-8095-4
ISBN-10: 1-4144-8095-4

ISSN 0276-816X

This title is also available as an e-book.
ISBN-13: 978-1-4144-8241-5
ISBN-10: 1-4144-8241-8
Contact your Gale, Cengage Learning sales representative for ordering information.

Printed in Mexico
1 2 3 4 5 6 7 16 15 14 13 12

Contents

Authors in Forthcoming Volumes vii

Introduction ix

SATA Product Advisory Board xi

Illustrations Index 179

Author Index 215

A

Allen, Crystal 1

Arrasmith, Patrick 1971- 2

B

Balliett, Blue 1955- 4

Bates, Amy June 7

Beene, Jason 10

Black, Jenna 1965- 10

Bootman, Colin 12

C

Cairns, Julia 1960(?)- 17

Chick, Bryan 1971- 20

Christy, Jana 1965- 21

Collins, Ross 1972- 22

Couvillon, Alice 28

D

Davies, Stephen 1976- 30

Delany, Shannon 31

Despain, Bree 1979- 32

Deutsch, Barry 34

Dodd, Emma 1969- 35

F

Feinstein, John 1956- 39

G

Gann, Marjorie 44

Giff, Patricia Reilly 1935- 46

Gourlay, Candy 54

Grey, Mini 55

H

Hacohen, Dean 1958- 59

Hanson, Warren 1949- 60

Henry, Jed 62

Houck, Colleen 1969- 63

J

Jordan-Fenton, Christy 65

K

Karr, Julia 65

Kittredge, Caitlin 1984- 67

Klassen, Jon 68

Komiya, Teruyuki 69

L

Lai, Thanhha 1965- 71

LaMarche, Jim 72

Landon, Kristen 1966- 76

Lane, Andrew 1963- 77

Lane, Andy
    See Lane, Andrew 77

Levine, Gail Carson 1947- 79

Lloyd, Megan 1958- 85

Lundquist, David R. 90

M

Mahoney, Karen 91

McFadden, Kevin Christopher
    See Pike, Christopher 114

McFerrin, Grady 92

Melo, Esperança 93

Moriarty, Jaclyn 1968- 95

N

Nadin, Joanna 1970- 99

Nesbitt, Kenn 1962- 101

Nicholson, William 1948- 103

O

Ockler, Sarah 108

Oron, Judie 109

O'Shaughnessy, Darren
  See Shan, Darren 142

P

Pal, Erika 111

Perro
  See Perro, Bryan 113

Perro, Bryan 1968- 113

Pike, Christopher 1954- 114

Pokiak-Fenton, Margaret 119

R

Ramsey, Calvin Alexander 121

Reedy, Trent 1979(?)- 122

Rohmann, Eric 1957- 123

Rosenthal, Eileen 126

Roth, Ty 1962- 127

Rupp, Rebecca 128

Rylander, Chris 131

S

Schoonmaker, Elizabeth 133

Schwartz, David M. 1951- 134

Serres, Alain 1956- 140

Shan, Darren 1972- 142

Shan, D.B.
  See Shan, Darren 142

Sierra, Judy 1945- 148

Steinberg, Don 1962- 156

T

Thompson, Holly 1959- 158

Thompson, Megan Lloyd
  See Lloyd, Megan 85

Trafton, Jennifer 160

Tsiang, Sarah 161

Tsiang, Yi-Mei
  See Tsiang, Sarah 161

V

Voelkel, J&P
  See Voelkel, Jon 163

Voelkel, Jon 163

W

Watkins, Angela Farris 164

Wells, Robert E. 1940- 166

Wilson, Daniel H. 1978- 168

Wood, Michele 170

Y

Yang, Dori Jones 1954- 172

Yankovic, Al 1959- 174

Yankovic, Weird Al
  See Yankovic, Al 174

Yovanoff, Brenna 1979- 176

Authors in Forthcoming Volumes

Below are some of the authors and illustrators that will be featured in upcoming volumes of *SATA*. These include new entries on the swiftly rising stars of the field, as well as completely revised and updated entries (indicated with *) on some of the most notable and best-loved creators of books for children.

*Arnold Adoff ▌ A poet, biographer, anthologist, and educator, Adoff is recognized as one of the early champions of multiculturalism in literature for children and young adults. He reflects the African-American experience in many of his works, most notably in the anthologies *I Am the Darker Brother* and *City in All Directions,* as well as in his illustrated biography *Malcolm X* and picture books such as the award-winning *Black Is Brown Is Tan.*

*Stephanie Stuve-Bodeen ▌ Stuve-Bodeen's experiences as a Peace Corps volunteer in Africa inspired her first books for children, the picture books *Elizabeti's Doll, Mama Elizabeti,* and *Elizabeti's School.* In more-recent years she has also focused on older readers, producing the futuristic young-adult novels *The Compound* and *The Gardener,* which she published under the name S.A. Bodeen.

Eric H. Cline ▌ Well known through his scholarship, Cline is a professor of archaeology at George Washington University. While his field work has taken him to Greece, Crete, Egypt, and Israel, his desire to make archaeology interesting to the general public has led to his appearance on the History Channel, the Discovery Channel, and public television stations in the United States and United Kingdom. He has also produced books for a range of reading levels and interests, among them *Digging for Troy* and *Ancient Empires: From Mesopotamia to the Rise of Islam.*

*Shane W. Evans ▌ A recipient of the prestigious Coretta Scott King Book Award, Evans has garnered acclaim for his illustrations for children's books. Known primarily for his bold, stylized, mixed-media artwork, he has contributed to celebrity-authored books that include *Shaq and the Beanstalk and Other Very Tall Tales* by basketball star Shaquille O'Neal. He also brings elements of African-American history to life in his pictures for Catherine Clinton's *When Harriet Met Sojourner* and Charles R. Smith's *Black Jack: The Ballad of Jack Johnson.*

Adam Gidwitz ▌ Gidwitz taps the ancient roots of fairy tales in *A Tale Dark and Grimm,* a children's book that is based on the time-honored tales of the Brothers Grimm. In his unique metafictional creation, he recrafts these dark and sometimes gruesome tales into a saga into which he sends an unsuspecting Hansel and Gretel, breaking the tension of his story with the quirky remarks of an unnamed narrator.

*Nina Kirki Hoffman ▌ Hoffman writes novels and short stories that span the genres of fantasy, science fiction and horror. Critically praised for her imaginative plots and realistic characters, she was awarded the Bram Stoker Award for Superior Achievement in a First Novel for *The Thread That Binds the Bones.* Her more recent works include the young-adult novels *Spirits That Walk in Shadows, A Fistful of Sky,* and the "Magic Next Door" middle-grade novel series.

Jana Oliver ▌ A native of Iowa, Oliver earned her nursing degree, traveled, and worked as a subsistence farmer before beginning her career as a young-adult novelist specializing in urban fantasy. Her "Time Rovers" series includes *Sojourn, Virtual Evil,* and *Madman's Dance,* while her "Demon Trappers" novels introduce elements of the paranormal in their focus on a near-future world overrun by a scourge of fiends emanating from hell.

*Dana Reinhardt ▌ In her writing for young adults, Reinhardt draws on an array of career experiences, among them her time as a waitress, law student, social worker, crisis hotline employee, and documentary film producer. She brings the same grounded realism to her fiction, penning compelling novels such as *A Brief Chapter in My Impossible Life, Harmless, How to Build a House,* and *The Things a Brother Knows,* all which have been praised for their ability to speak plainly to young readers.

Tammar Stein ▌ Raised in both the United States and Israel, Stein draws on her knowledge of diverse cultures, as well as her experiences living in Europe, in her novels for young adults. Her first novel, *Light Years,* focuses on a young woman haunted by a brutal act of terrorism, while other young women adjust to cultural differences in the novels *High Dive* and *Kindred.*

Lili Wilkinson ▌ The daughter of Australian children's writer Carole Wilkinson, Lili Wilkinson earned her first byline as an author as a thirteen year old, when one of her stories was published in a British magazine. A popular writer among teen and 'tween readers in her native country, where her books range from series romance to historical novels such as *Company of Angels,* she is best known to U.S. readers for her novel *Pink.*

Introduction

Something about the Author (*SATA*) is an ongoing reference series that examines the lives and works of authors and illustrators of books for children. *SATA* includes not only well-known writers and artists but also less prominent individuals whose works are just coming to be recognized. This series is often the only readily available information source on emerging authors and illustrators. You'll find *SATA* informative and entertaining, whether you are a student, a librarian, an English teacher, a parent, or simply an adult who enjoys children's literature.

What's Inside *SATA*

SATA provides detailed information about authors and illustrators who span the full time range of children's literature, from early figures like John Newbery and L. Frank Baum to contemporary figures like Judy Blume and Richard Peck. Authors in the series represent primarily English-speaking countries, particularly the United States, Canada, and the United Kingdom. Also included, however, are authors from around the world whose works are available in English translation. The writings represented in *SATA* include those created intentionally for children and young adults as well as those written for a general audience and known to interest younger readers. These writings cover the entire spectrum of children's literature, including picture books, humor, folk and fairy tales, animal stories, mystery and adventure, science fiction and fantasy, historical fiction, poetry and nonsense verse, drama, biography, and nonfiction. Obituaries are also included in *SATA* and are intended not only as death notices but also as concise overviews of people's lives and work. Additionally, each edition features newly revised and updated entries for a selection of *SATA* listees who remain of interest to today's readers and who have been active enough to require extensive revisions of their earlier biographies.

Autobiography Feature

Beginning with Volume 103, many volumes of *SATA* feature one or more specially commissioned autobiographical essays. These unique essays, averaging about ten thousand words in length and illustrated with an abundance of personal photos, present an entertaining and informative first-person perspective on the lives and careers of prominent authors and illustrators profiled in *SATA*.

Two Convenient Indexes

In response to suggestions from librarians, *SATA* indexes no longer appear in every volume but are included in alternate (odd-numbered) volumes of the series, beginning with Volume 57.

SATA continues to include two indexes that cumulate with each alternate volume: the Illustrations Index, arranged by the name of the illustrator, gives the number of the volume and page where the illustrator's work appears in the current volume as well as all preceding volumes in the series; the Author Index gives the number of the volume in which a person's biographical sketch, autobiographical essay, or obituary appears in the current volume as well as all preceding volumes in the series.

These indexes also include references to authors and illustrators who appear in *Gale's Yesterday's Authors of Books for Children, Children's Literature Review,* and *Something about the Author Autobiography Series.*

Easy-to-Use Entry Format

Whether you're already familiar with the *SATA* series or just getting acquainted, you will want to be aware of the kind of information that an entry provides. In every *SATA* entry the editors attempt to give as complete a picture of the person's life and work as possible. A typical entry in *SATA* includes the following clearly labeled information sections:

PERSONAL: date and place of birth and death, parents' names and occupations, name of spouse, date of marriage, names of children, educational institutions attended, degrees received, religious and political affiliations, hobbies and other interests.

ADDRESSES: complete home, office, electronic mail, and agent addresses, whenever available.

CAREER: name of employer, position, and dates for each career post; art exhibitions; military service; memberships and offices held in professional and civic organizations.

MEMBER: professional, civic, and other association memberships and any official posts held.

AWARDS, HONORS: literary and professional awards received.

WRITINGS: title-by-title chronological bibliography of books written and/or illustrated, listed by genre when known; lists of other notable publications, such as plays, screenplays, and periodical contributions.

ADAPTATIONS: a list of films, television programs, plays, CD-ROMs, recordings, and other media presentations that have been adapted from the author's work.

WORK IN PROGRESS: description of projects in progress.

SIDELIGHTS: a biographical portrait of the author or illustrator's development, either directly from the biographee—and often written specifically for the *SATA* entry—or gathered from diaries, letters, interviews, or other published sources.

BIOGRAPHICAL AND CRITICAL SOURCES: cites sources quoted in "Sidelights" along with references for further reading.

EXTENSIVE ILLUSTRATIONS: photographs, movie stills, book illustrations, and other interesting visual materials supplement the text.

How a *SATA* Entry Is Compiled

SATA editors examine a wide variety of published sources to gather information for an entry. Biographical and bibliographic sources are consulted, as are book reviews, feature articles, published interviews, and material sometimes obtained from the biographee's family, publishers, agent, or other associates. Whenever possible, the author or illustrator is sent a copy of the entry to check for accuracy and completeness.

Entries that have not been verified by the biographees or their representatives are marked with an asterisk (*).

Contact the Editor

We encourage our readers to examine the entire *SATA* series. Please write and tell us if we can make *SATA* even more helpful to you. Give your comments and suggestions to the editor:

Editor
Something about the Author
Gale, Cengage Learning
27500 Drake Rd.
Farmington Hills MI 48331-3535

Toll-free: 800-877-GALE
Fax: 248-699-8070

Something about the Author Product Advisory Board

The editors of *Something about the Author* are dedicated to maintaining a high standard of excellence by publishing comprehensive, accurate, and highly readable entries on a wide array of writers for children and young adults. In addition to the quality of the content, the editors take pride in the graphic design of the series, which is intended to be orderly yet inviting, allowing readers to utilize the pages of *SATA* easily and with efficiency. Despite the longevity of the *SATA* print series, and the success of its format, we are mindful that the vitality of a literary reference product is dependent on its ability to serve its users over time. As literature, and attitudes about literature, constantly evolve, so do the reference needs of students, teachers, scholars, journalists, researchers, and book club members. To be certain that we continue to keep pace with the expectations of our customers, the editors of *SATA* listen carefully to their comments regarding the value, utility, and quality of the series. Librarians, who have firsthand knowledge of the needs of library users, are a valuable resource for us. The *Something about the Author* Product Advisory Board, made up of school, public, and academic librarians, is a forum to promote focused feedback about *SATA* on a regular basis. The nine-member advisory board includes the following individuals, whom the editors wish to thank for sharing their expertise:

Eva M. Davis
Director,
Canton Public Library,
Canton, Michigan

Joan B. Eisenberg
Lower School Librarian,
Milton Academy,
Milton, Massachusetts

Francisca Goldsmith
Teen Services Librarian,
Berkeley Public Library,
Berkeley, California

Susan Dove Lempke
Children's Services Supervisor,
Niles Public Library District,
Niles, Illinois

Robyn Lupa
Head of Children's Services,
Jefferson County Public Library,
Lakewood, Colorado

Victor L. Schill
Assistant Branch Librarian/Children's Librarian,
Harris County Public Library/Fairbanks Branch,
Houston, Texas

Caryn Sipos
Community Librarian,
Three Creeks Community Library,
Vancouver, Washington

Steven Weiner
Director,
Maynard Public Library,
Maynard, Massachusetts

something ABOUT the AUThOR

ALLEN, Crystal

Personal

Born in Germany; daughter of U.S. citizens; married Reggie Allen; children: Phillip, Joshua. *Hobbies and other interests:* Bowling, traveling.

Addresses

Home—Sugar Land, TX. *Agent*—Jennifer Rofé, Andrea Brown Literary Agency; jennifer@andreabrownlit.com. *E-mail*—crystal@crystalallenbooks.com.

Career

Author. Presenter at schools. Volunteer with Special Olympics.

Member

Society of Children's Book Writers and Illustrators.

Writings

How Lamar's Bad Prank Won a Bubba-Sized Trophy, Balzer + Bray (New York, NY), 2011.

Contributor of short fiction to Scholastic's *Read and Rise* online magazine.

Sidelights

Crystal Allen grew up in Indiana, where she exhibited a talent for mathematics as early as third grade. Her rural community also allowed other talents to surface—Allen could boast the title of corn-shucking queen during elementary school—as well as honing her sense of good-natured humor. She became interested in writing while raising her two sons when she realized that her family life was rich with the stuff of fiction. "Chores and home-work were everyday struggles and punishments weren't working," Allen noted in an online interview for the *Brown Bookshelf.* "So, I decided to write an ongoing story, using [my sons] . . . as the main characters. After a few weeks of that, I wasn't sure which of us was enjoying it the most." When she tapped the voice of Lamar Washington, a thirteen-year-old character she originally created for a ghostwriting job, Allen knew she was on her way, and with the encouragement of her family and writing friends, she completed the manu-script of what became her middle-grade novel, *How Lamar's Bad Prank Won a Bubba-Sized Trophy.*

When readers first meet him in *How Lamar's Bad Prank Won a Bubba-Sized Trophy* Lamar is something of a legend at Striker's Bowling Paradise. Although he is dynamite in the bowling lanes, in the halls of school the teen flunks out in his popularity among girls. When Makeda, a girl he once teased, has a makeover and cap-tures his heart, Lamar decides that he will take the

coming summer to improve his social and dating skills. Things go well until he gets an offer to make some money by using his bowling skills to hustle. The decision harms his relationships with his older brother as well as his best friend Sergio, and even a visit from top national bowler Bubba Sanders is not enough to lift up Lamar's spirits when he winds up classed as a juvenile delinquent.

The "wonderfully inventive, laugh-out-loud idiosyncratic voice" of Allen's teen narrator "will leave readers wanting to hear more," Michael Cart concluded in his *Booklist* review of *How Lamar's Bad Prank Won a Bubba-Sized Trophy*. The debut novel "stands out for its unusual setting and smooth integration of friendship and family concerns," asserted a *Kirkus Reviews* writer, and Angie Hammond noted in *Voice of Youth Advocates* that Allen's "story line is engaging and believable." "Under all the braggadocio is a boy with a big heart," concluded a *Publishers Weekly* contributor, "and from the first sentence [of *How Lamar's Bad Prank Won a Bubba-Sized Trophy*] Lamar will have readers hooked."

Cover of Crystal Allen's humorous middle-grade novel How Lamar's Bad Prank Won a Bubba-Sized Trophy. (Jacket art © 2011 by Photodisc/ Getty Images (bowling pins) and CSA Plastock/Getty Images (trophy).)

Biographical and Critical Sources

PERIODICALS

Booklist, March 1, 2011, Michael Cart, review of *How Lamar's Bad Prank Won a Bubba-Sized Trophy,* p. 60.
Bulletin of the Center for Children's Books, March, 2011, Karen Coats, review of *How Lamar's Bad Prank Won a Bubba-Sized Trophy,* p. 317.
Kirkus Reviews, January 15, 2011, review of *How Lamar's Bad Prank Won a Bubba-Sized Trophy.*
Publishers Weekly, January 10, 2011, review of *How Lamar's Bad Prank Won a Bubba-Sized Trophy,* p. 50.
School Library Journal, February, 2011, Richard Luzer, review of *How Lamar's Bad Prank Won a Bubba-Sized Trophy,* p. 100.
Voice of Youth Advocates, April, 2011, Angie Hammond, review of *How Lamar's Bad Prank Won a Bubba-Sized Trophy,* p. 51.

ONLINE

Authors Now Web site, http://www.authorsnow.com/ (February 12, 2012), "Crystal Allen."
Brown Bookshelf Web site, http://thebrownbookshelf.com/ (February 8, 2011), "Crystal Allen."
Crystal Allen Home Page, http://www.crystalallenbooks. com (February 20, 2012).
Cynsations Web log, http://cynthialeitichsmith.blogspot. com/ (November 3, 2011), Cynthia Leitich Smith, interview with Allen.

*   *   *

ARRASMITH, Patrick 1971-

Personal

Born 1971, in Walnut Creek, CA. *Education:* California College of the Arts, degree (illustration). *Hobbies and other interests:* Traveling.

Addresses

Home and office—162 16th St., Brooklyn, NY 11215. *E-mail*—patrickarrasmith@earthlink.net.

Career

Illustrator.

Member

Society of Illustrators.

Awards, Honors

American Library Association Best of the Best for Young Adults designation, and inclusion in *New York Times* 100 Best Titles for Reading and Sharing, both 2005, both for *The Last Apprentice* by Joseph Delaney.

Illustrator

Joseph Delaney, *The Spook's Tale and Other Horrors,* Greenwillow Books (New York, NY), 2009.

(With Tim Foley) Joseph Delaney, *A Coven of Witches,* Greenwillow Books (New York, NY), 2010.

Steve Hockensmith, *Pride and Prejudice and Zombies: Dawn of the Dreadfuls,* Quirk Books (Philadelphia, PA), 2010.

Clare B. Dunkle, *The House of Dead Maids,* Henry Holt (New York, NY), 2010.

Contributor of illustrations to periodicals, including *Spectrum, Society of Illustrators, American Illustration, American Showcase, Print, R.S.V.P., Entertainment Weekly, Reader's Digest, Outside, PC, Weekly Standard, American Medical News, Advertising Age, Avenue, A, New York Times, Wall Street Journal, Village Voice,* and *Step by Step.*

"THE LAST APPRENTICE" SERIES BY JOSEPH DELANEY; NOVELS FOR CHILDREN

Revenge of the Witch, Greenwillow Books (New York, NY), 2005.

Curse of the Bane, Greenwillow Books (New York, NY), 2006.

Night of the Soul Stealer, Greenwillow Books (New York, NY), 2007.

Attack of the Fiend, Greenwillow Books (New York, NY), 2008.

Wrath of the Bloodeye, Greenwillow Books (New York, NY), 2008.

Clash of the Demons, Greenwillow Books (New York, NY), 2009.

Rise of the Huntress, Greenwillow Books (New York, NY), 2010.

Rage of the Fallen, Greenwillow Books (New York, NY), 2011.

Sidelights

Born in California, Patrick Arrasmith earned his degree at California College of the Arts before moving to the East Coast to begin his career as an illustrator. Arrasmith's distinctive scratchboard illustrations first appeared in Joseph Delaney's "The Last Apprentice" novels, a series weaving a dark adventure that is enjoyed by middle-grade readers. In addition to continuing his collaboration with Delaney, his illustrations have also added drama to Steve Hockensmith's entertaining take on Jane Austen's classic novel in *Pride and Prejudice and Zombies: Dawn of the Dreadfuls* and Clare B. Dunkle's Gothic mystery *The House of Dead Maids.* Reviewing Dunkle's atmospheric tale, Daniel Kraus noted in *Booklist* that Arrasmith's "chilling jacket illustration" and interior drawings "promise [readers] an intensity of horror," while *Horn Book* critic Lauren Adams maintained that the "nineteenth-century narrative" in *The House of Dead Maids* is "echoed by the spooky black-and-white" art.

Arrasmith creates his scene-setting illustrations using scratchboard, a prepared illustration board that has been coated with a layer of white clay and then sealed with a coat of black ink. He starts with a sketch of his design and, in a technique similar to etching or woodcut, inscribes it into the board with a sharp X-Acto knife, removing the ink and creating white contrast. Once this white-and-black image has been completed, Arrasmith has the option of tinting it digitally or leaving it in its original high-contrast form.

Arrasmith's scratchboard illustrations have been a central feature of Delaney's "The Last Apprentice" series, which includes *Revenge of the Witch, Attack of the Fiend, Wrath of the Bloodeye,* and *Rage of the Fallen.* In *Revenge of the Witch,* the opening volume of the series, the "spooky story about witches and ghosts" is aided "considerably by Patrick Arrasmith's creepy wood cut illustrations," according to *New York Times Book Review* contributor Lawrence Downes, while a *Publishers Weekly* contributor asserted that "expert storytelling and genuinely scary illustrations . . . keep this debut novel fresh." Reviewing *Curse of the Bane,* the second volume in the series, Lesley Farmer noted in *Kliatt* that the artist's "woodcut-appearing illustrations complement the tone" of Delaney's suspenseful story "perfectly," and "continue to capture the mood of the plot" in subsequent volumes. The artist's chapter illustrations will help pull along reluctant readers, according to *School Library Journal* contributor Kelly Vikstrom, and Beth L. Meister wrote in the same periodical that Arrasmith's "edgy illustrations" in the "Last Apprentice" novels will appeal to middle graders seeking "a more sophisticated alternative to R.L. Stine's 'Goosebumps' books."

Biographical and Critical Sources

PERIODICALS

Booklist, August, 2005, Ilene Cooper, review of *Revenge of the Witch,* p. 2022; August 1, 2006, Ilene Cooper, review of *Curse of the Bane,* p. 74; August, 2007, Ilene Cooper, review of *Night of the Soul Stealer,* p. 64; August 1, 2010, Daniel Kraus, review of *The House of Dead Maids,* p. 47.

Bulletin of the Center for Children's Books, November, 2006, Deborah Stevenson, review of *Curse of the Bane,* p. 119.

Horn Book, November-December, 2005, Anita L. Burkam, review of *Revenge of the Witch,* p. 715; September-October, 2007, Roger Sutton, review of *Night of the Soul Stealer,* p. 569; November-December, 2010, Lauren Adams, review of *The House of Dead Maids,* p. 90.

Kirkus Reviews, August 1, 2005, review of *Revenge of the Witch,* p. 846; August 1, 2006, review of *Curse of the Bane,* p. 784; July 15, 2007, review of *Night of the Soul Stealer.*

Kliatt, September, 2005, Lesley Farmer, review of *Revenge of the Witch,* p. 7; September, 2006, Lesley Farmer, review of *Curse of the Bane,* p. 10; September, 2007, Lesley Farmer, review of *Night of the Soul Stealer,* p. 10; March, 2008, Lesley Farmer, review of *Attack of the Fiend,* p. 10.

New York Times Book Review, December 4, 2005, Lawrence Downes, review of *Revenge of the Witch,* p. 58.

Publishers Weekly, October 10, 2005, review of *Revenge of the Witch,* p. 62.

School Library Journal, November, 2005, Beth L. Meister, review of *Revenge of the Witch,* p. 132; November, 2006, Sue Giffard, review of *Curse of the Bane,* p. 132; February, 2008, Kelly Vikstrom, review of *Night of the Soul Stealer,* p. 113; July, 2008, Christi Esterle, review of *Attack of the Fiend,* p. 96; September, 2009, Saleena L. Davidson, review of *The Spook's Tale and Other Horrors,* p. 156; November, 2010, Kathryn Kosiorek, review of *The House of Dead Maids,* p. 112.

Voice of Youth Advocates, April, 2008, Vikki Terrile, review of *Attack of the Fiend,* p. 60.

ONLINE

Patrick Arrasmith Home Page, http://www.patrickarra smith.com (February 12, 2012).*

*   *   *

BALLIETT, Blue 1955-

Personal

Born 1955, in New York, NY; daughter of Whitney Balliett (a journalist) and Elizabeth Platt; married Bill Klein (an urban planner); children: Alphea, Daniel; Jessie (stepdaughter). *Education:* Brown University, B.S. (art education).

Addresses

Home—Chicago, IL. *Agent*—Doe Coover, Doe Coover Agency, P.O. Box 668, Winchester, MA 01890.

Career

Novelist and educator. University of Chicago Laboratory School, Chicago, IL, third-and fourth-grade teacher, c. 1991-2001; freelance writer.

Awards, Honors

Notable Book designation, *New York Times,* Agatha Award, *Chicago Tribune* Prize for Young-Adult Fiction, Great Lakes Book Award, Borders Original Voices Award, Midwest Booksellers' Choice Award for Children's Literature, and Edgar Allen Poe Award for Best Juvenile Novel, Mystery Writers of America, all 2004, and Sheffield (England) Children's Book Award finalist, 2006, all for *Chasing Vermeer;* Great Lakes Book Award finalist, and 21st Century Award, Chicago Public Library, both 2006, both for *The Wright 3;* Friends of American Writers Literary Award, 2008, for *The Calder Game;* named Chicagoan of the Year for Literature, *Chicago Tribune,* 2010; Parents' Choice Silver Award, and Dorothy Canfield Fisher Award master-list inclusion, 2011, both for *The Danger Box.*

Writings

The Ghosts of Nantucket: Twenty-three True Accounts, Down East Books (Camden, ME), 1984, expanded edition published as *Nantucket Hauntings,* 1990, published as *Nantucket Ghosts: Forty-four True Accounts,* photographs by Lucy Bixby, 2006.

Chasing Vermeer, illustrated by Brett Helquist, Scholastic Press (New York, NY), 2003.

The Wright 3, illustrated by Brett Helquist, Scholastic Press (New York, NY), 2006.

The Calder Game, illustrated by Brett Helquist, Scholastic Press (New York, NY), 2008.

The Danger Box, Scholastic Press (New York, NY), 2010.

Adaptations

Chasing Vermeer was optioned for film by Warner Bros. Several of Balliett's novels were adapted for audiobook by Listening Library, including *The Wright 3,* read by Ellen Reilly, 2006, and *The Calder Game,* read by Deirdre Lovejoy, 2008.

Sidelights

Blue Balliett trained in art education as a student at Brown University, and her interest in the paintings of seventeenth-century Dutch painter Johannes Vermeer ultimately inspired her award-winning first novel, *Chasing Vermeer.* Published in 2003 and geared for readers in the upper elementary grades, *Chasing Vermeer* inspired Balliett to leave her work as a teacher and embark on a writing career that has won her further acclaim and produced the novel sequels *The Wright 3* and *The Calder Game* as well as the tantalizingly titled mystery *The Danger Box.*

A mystery novel featuring illustrations by Brett Helquist, *Chasing Vermeer* follows two sixth graders as they attempt to solve the mystery of a missing painting created by one of the Dutch Old Masters. Friends and fellow middle-school students Petra Andalee and Calder Pillay share a common interest in unexplained phenomena. Therefore, when it appears that some of Johannes Vermeer's paintings may have actually been painted by someone else, the two are quick to unite in their search for the answer. The plot thickens when one of Vermeer's famous paintings mysteriously disappears while being transported from the National Gallery to Chicago's Art Institute, leaving the budding sleuths following a trail of clues that leads to their very own Chicago neighborhood.

wealth of quirky characters" help make the book an "exciting, fast-paced story that's sure to be relished by mystery lovers." A *Publishers Weekly* contributor also enjoyed the book, stating that the author's "ingeniously plotted and lightly delivered first novel . . . also touches on the nature of coincidence, truth, art and similarly meaty topics."

Petra and Calder return in both *The Wright 3* and *The Calder Game.* In *The Wright 3* they are joined by fellow sixth grader Tommy Segovia, who has returned to home to their Chicago Hyde Park neighborhood (also home to Balliett) after being away for several months. Tommy discovers Petra and Calder up in arms because the Robie House, a local building designed by noted modernist architect Frank Lloyd Wright in 1910, is slated for demolition and its interiors divided among four museums. Soon the entire sixth-grade class has joined preservation dvocates in protesting the loss of the landmark. When the school year ends something odd happens: Suddenly people notice strange sounds and shadows, as well as other bizarre transformations, occurring in and around Wright's structure. As rumors

Two friends attempt to solve the mystery of a stolen painting by Vermeer in Blue Balliett's award-winning fiction debut **Chasing Vermeer,** *illustrated by Brett Helquist.* (Illustration copyright © 2004 by Brett Helquist. Reproduced by permission of Scholastic, Inc.)

Balliett spent five years writing *Chasing Vermeer,* and she drew much of her inspiration from her ten-year-long career teaching third graders, as well as from her own lifelong love of fine art. She was also inspired by her love of codes, enigmas, and the patterns found in life, all of which, she contends, young people almost instinctively grasp. As Balliett explained to a *Publishers Weekly* interviewer, children "have an ability to see connections and to put the world together in so much more of an elastic and fluid way than adults." Scattered throughout the text, along with the puzzles, wordplay, and other mind benders, are enough misleading clues to keep readers interested, added Orlando, comparing *Chasing Vermeer* to novels by popular juvenile fiction writers Ellen Raskin and E.L. Konigsburg.

Marie Orlando, reviewing *Chasing Vermeer* in *School Library Journal,* praised Balliett's debut children's book, noting that "puzzles, codes, letters, number and wordplay, a bit of danger, a vivid sense of place, and a

Brett Helquist's art captures the suspense of Balliett's imaginative art-themed mystery in **The Calder Game.** (Illustration copyright © 2008 by Brett Helquist. Reproduced by permission of Scholastic, Inc.)

circulate about Wright's hidden treasure as well as ghostly visitations, Petra, Calder, and Tommy decide to unravel the mystery using their research into the architect's life, pentominoes, and their characteristic powers of deduction.

Calling Calder and company "lateral thinkers par excellence," Roger Sutton added in *Horn Book* that *The Wright 3* serves as both "a tribute to . . . Wright's masterpiece" and "the adventures to be had in any city neighborhood." "Balliett's atmospheric writing encourages readers to make their own journeys of discovery into art and architecture," asserted *School Library Journal* critic Caitlin Augusta, the critic classifying the author's novels as "a mystery subgenre that is as unique as it is compelling." In *Kirkus Reviews* a contributor wrote that Balliett's text "transmits" a "delight in puzzling, excavating and thinking deeply" that readers will find contagious, making *The Wright 3* a thought-provoking mix of "art, math, philosophy, history, and literature." In the *New York Times Book Review* Adam Liptak bestowed special praise on Helquist's illustrations. "Studded with charming hidden figures that echo one of the books key clues," according to Liptak, these drawings "capture . . . the ungainly, inquisitive and wary affects of gifted children trying to negotiate the world."

Balliett was fascinated by the modernistic work of Alexander Calder as a child growing up within visiting distance of New York City's Metropolitan Museum of Art, and this interest in the artist's mobiles is shared by her young sleuths in *The Calder Game*. Now in seventh grade, Calder takes time away from school to join his father on a trip to rural England, where a rare sculpture by his famous namesake has appeared in the center of a small village. When both the young teen and the artwork mysteriously vanish, Petra and Tommy hop a plane to help out in the search, fresh from a class trip to see an exhibition of Calder's work at a Chicago art museum. This knowledge is soon put to work as they ferret out clues in intricate puzzles as they follow the trail to their friend. "Balliett's wonderful writing is full of foreshadowing, literary allusions, wordplay, and figurative language," asserted Connie Tyrell Burns in her *School Library Journal* review of *The Calder Game*, and a *Publishers Weekly* critic predicted that "motivated readers will treasure" her "provocative" story. Noting that the author "does not shrink from putting her characters in danger," Ilene Cooper added in *Booklist* that *The Calder Game* suggests "new ways to think" as it "weaves in . . . puzzles, words, and found objects" as its teen sleuths navigate "literal and figurative mazes."

When Balliett first learned that one of the notebooks kept by Charles Darwin on his historic 1835 voyage to the Galapagos was stolen in the 1980s and never recovered, the idea haunted her. The questions it raised ultimately resulted in *The Danger Box,* a middle-grade mystery that "explores the intricacies of scientific discovery," according to *School Library Journal* contribu-

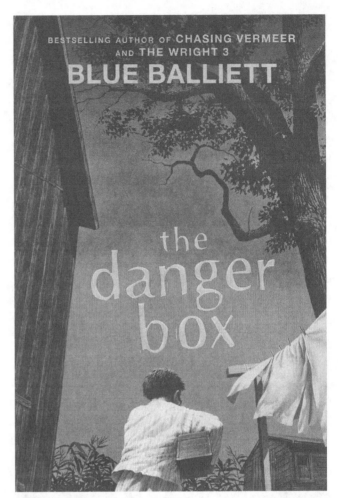

Cover of Balliett's intricately woven mystery in **The Danger Box,** *featuring cover art by Bagram Ibatoulline.* (Jacket art © 2010 by Bagram Ibatoulline. Reproduced by permission of Scholastic, Inc.)

tor Kim Dare. *The Danger Box* takes readers to Three Oaks, Michigan, a small town where twelve-year-old Zoomy Chamberlain is living with his grandparents, owners of an antique store. Legally blind due to his extreme nearsightedness, and a little bit compulsive, Zoomy leads a quiet life until his dissolute, alcoholic dad visits briefly and leaves behind a strange box full of things he has stolen and now hopes to sell. Inside the box, Zoomy discovers an old journal that is filled with lists, scientific notation, and other notes written in a crabbed, antiquated handwriting. The boy attempts to discover the identity of the journal-keeper, with the help of new friend Lorrol. Meanwhile, the journal itself has become the object of another's search: a rich collector named Mr. Zip knows its provenance and hopes to gain its secrets before returning the journal to the world.

"Zoomy makes an appealing, original character," asserted Carolyn Phelan, the *Booklist* critic citing the boy's "insightful, first-person narration" as a magnet for readers of *The Danger Box*. Although a *Kirkus Reviews* writer questioned the "rococo chain of events" that unfolds in Zoomy's world—his narration is interspersed

with excerpts of Darwin's own writings as well as the children's library research—a *Publishers Weekly* contributor asserted that "details about the [real-life Midwest] setting add appeal" to the adventure. Praising *The Danger Box* as a "highly satisfying story," Dare predicted in her *School Library Journal* review that Balliett's tale "will enlighten readers" by illustrating that "danger boxes" are "not just . . . containers of physical objects," but sometimes also "vehicles that expose us to risky ideas and dreams."

"All of my books take me a number of years," Balliett explained in discussing her work as a writer with interviewer Karen Springen for *Publishers Weekly* online. "I do a good year of thinking, reading, stirring ideas around in my head before I make a real decision about what the book is going to be. I just have to wake up one morning with that green-light feeling. I have to get all the ingredients.

Biographical and Critical Sources

PERIODICALS

Atlantic Monthly, September, 1984, Phoebe-Lou Adams, review of *The Ghosts of Nantucket: 23 True Accounts,* p. 128.

Booklist, April 1, 2004, Ilene Cooper, review of *Chasing Vermeer,* p. 1365; February 1, 2006, Jennifer Mattson, review of *The Wright 3,* p. 47; May 1, 2008, Ilene Cooper, review of *The Calder Game,* p. 51; October 1, 2010, Carolyn Phelan, review of *The Danger Box,* p. 90.

Horn Book, July-August, 2004, Peter D. Sieruta, review of *Chasing Vermeer,* p. 446; March-April, 2006, Roger Sutton, review of *The Wright 3,* p. 179; July-August, 2008, Roger Sutton, review of *The Calder Game,* p. 437.

Kirkus Reviews, May 15, 2004, review of *Chasing Vermeer,* p. 487; March 15, 2006, review of *The Wright 3,* p. 286; May 1, 2008, review of *The Calder Game;* August 15, 2010, review of *The Danger Box.*

New York Times Book Review, May 14, 2006, Adam Liptak, review of *The Wright 3,* p. 23.

Publishers Weekly, June 14, 2004, review of *Chasing Vermeer,* p. 63; June 28, 2004, "Flying Starts," p. 19; February 27, 2006, review of *The Wright 3,* p. 61; May 19, 2008, review of *The Calder Game,* p. 54; September 27, 2010, review of *The Danger Box,* p. 60.

School Library Journal, July, 2004, Marie Orlando, review of *Chasing Vermeer,* p. 98; April, 2006, Caitlin Augusta, review of *The Wright 3,* p. 133; June, 2008, Connie Tyrrell Burns, review of *The Calder Game,* p. 134; September, 2010, Kim Dare, review of *The Danger Box,* p. 145.

Voice of Youth Advocates, February, 2011, Mary Napoli, "Unlocking the Mystery of Writing for Young People" (interview), p. 512.

ONLINE

Blue Balliett Home Page, http://www.blueballiettbooks. com (February 15, 2012).

BookPage.com, http://www.bookpage.com/ (January 5, 2005), Linda M. Castellitto, interview with Balliett.

Publishers Weekly Online, http://www.publishersweekly. com/ (August 19, 2010), Karen Springen, interview with Balliett.*

*   *   *

BATES, Amy June

Personal

Born in UT; married; husband's name Alex; children: three. *Education:* Brigham Young University, B.A. (illustration).

Addresses

Home—Carlisle, PA. *Agent*—Shannon Associate, 333 W. 57th St., Ste. 809, New York, NY 10019.

Career

Illustrator. Waterford Institute, Provo, UT, former staff illustrator.

Awards, Honors

Georgia Children's Book Awards nomination, 2007, for *Speak to Me: (And I Will Listen between the Lines)* by Karen English.

Illustrator

Karen English, *Speak to Me: (And I Will Listen between the Lines),* Farrar, Straus & Giroux (New York, NY), 2004.

Ann Turner, *Pumpkin Cat,* Hyperion Books for Children (New York, NY), 2004.

Deborah Hopkinson, *Susan B. Anthony: Fighter for Women's Rights,* Farrar, Straus & Giroux (New York, NY), 2005.

Colby Rodowsky, *The Next-Door Dogs,* Farrar, Straus & Giroux (New York, NY), 2005.

Karma Wilson, *I Will Rejoice: Celebrating Psalm 118,* Zonderkidz (Grand Rapids, MI), 2006.

Karma Wilson, *Give Thanks to the Lord: Celebrating Psalm 92,* Zonderkidz (Grand Rapids, MI), 2007.

Kelly Tinkham, *Hair for Mama,* Dial Books for Young Readers (New York, NY), 2007.

Tony Dungy, *You Can Do It,* Little Simon Inspirations (New York, NY), 2008.

Monalisa DeGross, *Donavan's Double Trouble,* Amistad (New York, NY), 2008.

Karma Wilson, *Let's Make a Joyful Noise! A Celebration of Psalm 100,* Zonderkidz (Grand Rapids, MI), 2008.

Bebe Moore Campbell, *I Get So Hungry,* G.P. Putnam's Sons (New York, NY), 2008.

Jane Kurtz, *Martin's Dream,* Simon & Schuster (New York, NY), 2008.

Kathleen Krull, *Hillary Rodham Clinton: Dreams Taking Flight,* Simon & Schuster Books for Young Readers (New York, NY), 2008.

Amy Hest, *The Dog Who Belonged to No One,* Abrams Books for Young Readers (New York, NY), 2008.

Tony Dungy, *You Can Do It!,* Little Simon Inspirations (New York, NY), 2008.

Jen Bryant, *Abe's Fish: A Boyhood Tale of Abraham Lincoln,* Sterling (New York, NY), 2009.

Carole Boston Weatherford, *First Pooch: The Obamas Pick a Pet,* Marshall Cavendish (New York, NY), 2009.

Stephanie S. Tolan, *Wishworks, Inc.,* Arthur A. Levine Books (New York, NY), 2009.

Susan Meyers, *Bear in the Air,* Abrams Books for Young Readers (New York, NY), 2010.

Justin Richardson and Peter Parnell, *Christian, the Hugging Lion,* Simon & Schuster Books for Young Readers (New York, NY), 2010.

Kathleen Krull, *The Brothers Kennedy: John, Robert, Edward,* Simon & Schuster Books for Young Readers (New York, NY), 2010.

Laurie Myers, *Escape by Night: A Civil War Adventure,* Henry Holt (New York, NY), 2011.

Patricia MacLachlan, *Waiting for the Magic,* Atheneum (New York, NY), 2011.

Susanna Reich, *Minette's Feast: The Delicious Story of Julia Child and Her Cat,* Abrams Books for Young Readers (New York, NY), 2012.

Contributor to periodicals, including *Cricket.*

"ILLUSTRATOR; "BERYL E. BEAN" READER SERIES BY RICKI STERN AND HEIDI P. WORCESTER

Expedition Sleepaway Camp, HarperCollins (New York, NY), 2002.

Mighty Adventurer of the Planet, HarperCollins (New York, NY), 2002.

Mission—Impossible Friendship, HarperTrophy (New York, NY), 2002.

Adventure—Lonely Leader, HarperCollins (New York, NY), 2003.

ILLUSTRATOR; "ADVENTURES OF TOM SAWYER" READER SERIES; ADAPTED BY CATHERINE NICHOLS; BASED ON THE NOVEL BY MARK TWAIN

The Best Fence Painter, Barnes & Noble (New York, NY), 2004.

A Song for Aunt Polly, Barnes & Noble (New York, NY), 2004.

The Birthday Boy, Sterling Pub. Co. (New York, NY), 2006.

The Spelling Bee, Sterling Pub. Co. (New York, NY), 2007.

Sidelights

A freelance illustrator, Amy June Bates began her career by creating artwork for a Utah-based educational publisher. Since her first picture-book project, Karen English's *Speak to Me: (And I Will Listen between the Lines),* was published in 2004, Bates has become a sought-after illustrator whose engaging line-and-wash art has appeared in stories ranging from *Pumpkin Cat* by Ann Turner and *The Next-Door-Dogs* by Colby Rodowsky to Tony Dungy's *You Can Do It!* and Kathleen Krull's picture-book biography *The Brothers Kennedy: John, Robert, Edward.* In addition, her work is known to fans of the "Beryl E. Bean" series by Ricki Stern and Heidi P. Worcester, which follows the adventures of a sports-minded ten year old who takes setbacks in stride, and is a feature of Catherine Nichols' beginning-reader adaptations of Mark Twain's *The Adventures of Tom Sawyer.*

"Bates' warm, realistic watercolors . . . create strong character portraits" that reflect the free-verse poems collected in *Speak to Me,* according to *Booklist* critic Gillian Engberg. Lee Bock had a similar reaction to the illustrator's picture-book debut, writing in *School Library Journal* that her "watercolor-and-ink illustrations capture the characters' expressions and moods vividly." Also appraising the highly lauded picture book, a *Kirkus Reviews* writer cited Bates's artwork for "capturing every mood, every feeling, and breath[ing] . . . life into each distinct personality" in English's story.

In illustrating *Pumpkin Cat,* a Halloween-themed story by Turner, Bates supplies "cheery watercolor illustrations [that] work well with the straightforward narrative," according to *School Library Journal* reviewer Catherine Threadgill, and a *Kirkus Reviews* critic as-

Amy June Bates creates warm-toned paintings for **Pumpkin Cat,** *a picture book featuring Ann Turner's gentle story about a stray kitten.* (Illustration copyright © 2004 by Amy June Bates. Reprinted by permission of Shannon Associates, the illustrator's agent.)

serted that the book's "real selling point . . . is Bates's realistic, golden-hued watercolors." The artist's attention turns to the dogs in *Waiting for the Magic,* a story by Patricia MacLachlan that finds the love of four puppies filling the void left by an absent parent. Here Bates's "appealing charcoal-pencil drawings" help make MacLachlan's easy-reading story "fully accessible" to its audience, according to *Booklist* critic Carolyn Phelan.

A poignant story by Kelly A. Tinkham about a woman whose supportive family helps her deal with a difficult illness, *Hair for Mama* also benefits from Bates's art; here her "watercolor-and-pencil illustrations in warm hues capture the heart of this uplifting story," according to *Horn Book* critic Robin Smith. In *Christian, the Hugging Lion* the artist teams up with writers Justin Richardson and Peter Parnell to share the true story of a captive lion club that lives for a time with an English family before being successfully returned to the wilds of Kenya. Bates's "balmy watercolor, gouache, and pencil illustrations . . . highlight Christian's playfulness," noted a *Publishers Weekly* critic, and in *School Library Journal* Mary Jean Smith wrote that the "near-wordless illustrations" appearing near the book's conclusion "capture the joy of the real-life reunion" which was also documented on film.

History comes to life in several of Bates's illustration projects, among them Krull's *The Brothers Kennedy,* which focuses on the famous political brothers John, Robert, and Edward Kennedy. Pairing with Krull's positive portrayal of her subjects, Bates's "stylized artwork" captures the brothers' "likenesses . . . and the images set a historic tone," according to *Booklist* critic Andrew Medlar. Another laudatory biography by Krull, *Hillary Rodham Clinton: Dreams Taking Flight,* captures the early life of the eventual first lady, senator, and U.S. secretary of state through what *Booklist* critic Ilene Cooper characterized as "stylish retro" illustrations that "keep the focus on Clinton, capturing her in all her incarnations." Turning to an earlier political era, Bates's work for Jen Bryant's *Abe's Fish: A Boyhood Tale of Abraham Lincoln* was praised by Julie Cummins in another *Booklist* review. In a "roughly hewn style," noted the critic, the artist "provides just the right rustic feeling and visual perspective" to capture Lincoln's rural childhood experiences.

Based on the strong Christian faith Dungy developed while growing up to become a coach for the National Football League, *You Can Do It!* affirms the author's belief that "each person has a special talent," according to a *Kirkus Reviews* writer. In illustrating this inspiring picture book, Bates crafts what the same critic described as "attractive full-color illustrations" that "depict the close-knit, loving African-American family with warmth," while to *School Library Journal* critic Lisa Egly Lehmuller *You Can Do It!* shows that the artist "is skilled at creating charming characters."

Karma Wilson's Christian-themed* Give Thanks to the Lord *features Bates's engaging soft-toned paintings. (Illustration copyright © 2007 by Amy June Bates. Reproduced by permission of Shannon Associates, the illustrator's agent.)

The artist's collaboration with writer Karma Wilson has resulted in several other faith-based picture books, among them *Give Thanks to the Lord: Celebrating Psalm 92, Let's Make a Joyful Noise! A Celebration of Psalm 100,* and *I Will Rejoice: Celebrating Psalm 118.* "Exuberant watercolor illustrations in glowing, autumnal hues are the most striking feature" of *Give Thanks to the Lord,* stated a *Kirkus Reviews* writer in assessing Bates's contribution to the collaboration. The work was also praised as an "affectionate" portrait of childhood that features "expressive watercolor-and-pencil artwork . . . done in a warm, bright palette" by *Booklist* critic Shelle Rosenfeld. In *Publishers Weekly,* a critic noted that Bates sets *I Will Rejoice* in "comforting, contemporary, universal situations that many children will recognize." *Let's Make a Joyful Noise!* was described by *Booklist* contributor Carolyn Phelan as "a rewarding read-aloud" that "captures the spirit of Psalm 100 and interprets it gracefully in a modern setting."

Biographical and Critical Sources

PERIODICALS

Booklist, August, 2004, Gillian Engberg, review of *Speak to Me: (And I Will Listen between the Lines),* p. 1933, and Ilene Cooper, review of *Pumpkin Cat,* p. 1946;

March 1, 2005, Stephanie Zvirin, review of *The Next-Door Dogs,* p. 1199; February 1, 2006, Ilene Cooper, review of *Susan B. Anthony: Fighter for Women's Rights,* p. 52; October 1, 2006, Gillian Engberg, review of *I Will Rejoice: Celebrating Psalm 118,* p. 66; April 1, 2007, GraceAnne A. DeCandido, review of *Hair for Mama,* p. 61; October 1, 2007, Shelle Rosenfeld, review of *Give Thanks to the Lord: Celebrating Psalm 92,* p. 71; November 15, 2007, Carolyn Phelan, review of *Let's Make a Joyful Noise! A Celebration of Psalm 100,* p. 45; November 1, 2008, review of *Hillary Rodham Clinton: Dreams Taking Flight,* p. 44; January 1, 2009, Julie Cummins, review of *Abe's Fish: A Boyhood Tale of Abraham Lincoln,* p. 82; April 1, 2009, Carolyn Phelan, review of *Wishworks, Inc.,* p. 40; March 15, 2010, Andrew Medlar, review of *The Brothers Kennedy: John, Robert, Edward,* p. 40; April 15, 2011, Ian Chipman, review of *Escape by Night: A Civil War Adventure,* p. 64; August 1, 2011, Carolyn Phelan, review of *Waiting for the Magic,* p. 50.

Horn Book, July-August, 2005, Martha V. Parravano, review of *The Next-Door Dogs,* p. 479; July-August, 2007, Robin Smith, review of *Hair for Mama,* p. 387; September-October, 2009, Robin L. Smith, review of *Wishworks, Inc.,* p. 576.

Kirkus Reviews, July 1, 2004, reviews of *Speak to Me,* p. 628, and *Pumpkin Cat,* p. 639; April 15, 2005, Colby Rodowsky, review of *The Next-Door Dogs,* p. 480; August 15, 2007, review of *Give Thanks to the Lord;* June 15, 2008, review of *You Can Do It;* August 15, 2008, review of *Hillary Rodham Clinton;* January 1, 2009, review of *Abe's Fish.*

Publishers Weekly, June 17, 2002, review of *Mighty Adventurer of the Planet,* p. 64; December 18, 2006, review of *I Will Rejoice,* p. 66; August 11, 2008, review of *Hillary Rodham Clinton,* p. 46; January 12, 2009, review of *Abe's Fish,* p. 47; June 15, 2009, review of *Wishworks, Inc.,* p. 49; April 5, 2010, review of *Christian, the Hugging Lion,* p. 59; April 25, 2011, review of *Escape by Night,* p. 137; July 4, 2011, review of *Waiting for the Magic,* p. 65.

School Library Journal, August, 2004, Lee Bock, review of *Speak to Me,* p. 86, and Catherine Threadgill, review of *Pumpkin Cat,* p. 97; June, 2005, Jennifer Cogan, review of *The Next-Door Dogs,* p. 126; July, 2007, Judith Constantinides, review of *Hair for Mama,* p. 86; April, 2008, Lisa Egly Lehmuller, review of *Let's Make a Joyful Noise!,* p. 126; August, 2008, Lisa Egly Lehmuller, review of *You Can Do It!,* p. 88; November, 2008, Kathy Piehl, review of *Hillary Rodham Clinton,* p. 109; April, 2009, Janet S. Thompson, review of *Abe's Fish,* p. 101; July, 2009, Alyson Low, review of *Wishworks, Inc.,* p. 68; March, 2010, Grace Oliff, review of *The Brothers Kennedy,* p. 141; June, 2010, Mary Jean Smith, review of *Christian, the Hugging Lion,* p. 82; June, 2011, Rita Soltan, review of *Escape by Night,* p. 92.

ONLINE

Amy June Bates Home Page, http://www.amybates.com (February 12, 2012).

Amy June Bates Web log, http://amyjunebates.blogspot.com (February 15, 2012).*

*   *   *

BEENE, Jason

Personal

Married; children: two. *Education:* Attended Maryland Institute College of Art and Pennsylvania Governor's School for the Arts; Rhode Island School of Design, B.F.A. (illustration), 2001.

Addresses

Home—Providence, RI. *Agent*—Kid Shannon, 333 W. 57th St., Ste. 809, New York, NY 10019. *E-mail*—jasonbeene@gmail.com.

Career

Art director and illustrator. Helixe/THQ, illustrator, then art director, 2001-08; Singapore-MIT Gambit Game Lab, Cambridge, MA, art director, beginning 2008. Consultant in gaming design; freelance art director and illustrator. Fire Hose Games, member of advisory board. Rhode Island School of Design, Providence, member of faculty.

Illustrator

Lisa Graff, *Sophie Simon Solves Them All,* Farrar, Straus & Giroux (New York, NY), 2010.

Biographical and Critical Sources

PERIODICALS

Booklist, September 15, 2010, Carolyn Phelan, review of *Sophie Simon Solves Them All,* p. 68.
Bulletin of the Center for Children's Books, September, 2010, Deborah Stevenson, review of *Sophie Simon Solves Them All,* p. 20.
Horn Book, November-December, 2010, review of *Sophie Simon Solves Them All,* p. 91.
School Library Journal, September, 2010, Janet Weber, review of *Sophie Simon Solves Them All,* p. 124.

ONLINE

Jason Beene Web log, http://jasonbeene.blogspot.com (February 12, 2012).
Rhode Island School of Design Web site, http://www.risd.edu/ (February 12, 2012), "Jason Beene."

*   *   *

BLACK, Jenna 1965-

Personal

Born 1965. *Education:* Duke University, B.A. (physical anthropology and French). *Hobbies and other interests:* Travel, playing bridge, barbershop singing.

Addresses

Home—NC. *Agent*—Irene Goodman Literary Agency, 27 W. 24th St., Ste. 700B, New York, NY 10010. *E-mail*—JennaBlackBooks@aol.com.

Career

Novelist. Worked variously as a dog groomer and technical writer.

Member

Heart of Carolina Romance Writers.

Awards, Honors

ParaNormal Excellence Award in Romantic Literature nomination, 2006, for *Watchers in the Night*.

Writings

"FAERIEWALKER" YOUNG-ADULT NOVEL SERIES

Glimmerglass, St. Martin's Griffin (New York, NY), 2010.
Shadowspell, St. Martin's Griffin (New York, NY), 2011.
Sirensong, St. Martin's Griffin (New York, NY), 2011.

"GUARDIANS OF THE NIGHT" PARANORMAL NOVEL SERIES; FOR ADULTS

Watchers in the Night, Tor (New York, NY), 2006.
Secrets in the Shadows, Tor (New York, NY), 2007.
Shadows on the Soul, Tor (New York, NY), 2007.
Hungers of the Heart, Tor (New York, NY), 2008.

"MORGAN KINGSLEY" FANTASY SERIES; FOR ADULTS

The Devil Inside, Dell (New York, NY), 2007.
The Devil You Know, Dell (New York, NY), 2008.
The Devil's Due, Dell (New York, NY), 2008.
Speak of the Devil, Dell (New York, NY), 2009.
The Devil's Playground, Dell (New York, NY), 2010.

"NIKKI GLASS" URBAN FANTASY NOVELS; FOR ADULTS

Dark Descendant, Pocket Books (New York, NY), 2011.
Deadly Descendant, Pocket Books (New York, NY), 2012.

OTHER

Prince of Air and Darkness (adult romance novel; e-book), IGLA, 2011.

Sidelights

A self-styled "experience junkie," as she wrote on her home page, Jenna Black turned to writing after discarding her career plan to become an anthropologist. Black's varied interests have been fueled by her love of travel, and the energy with which she approaches life has also fueled a prolific writing career that has produced the "Morgan Kingsley" and "Nikki Glass" urban fantasy novels for adults as well as her teen-focused "Faeriewalker" novels, which include *Glimmerglass, Shadowspell,* and *Sirensong.*

In *Glimmerglass* readers meet Dana Hathaway, a sixteen year old who has a challenging home life cohabiting with her alcoholic mother. When the teen finally has enough, she leaves her mom and seeks out her dad, who turns out to be a faery. Dana now realizes why she never felt "normal": she is half faerie and half human, and when her father takes her to the kingdom of Avalon she learns about the magical elements that compose the chimerical side of her nature and also falls for a handsome faerie named Ethan. A faeriewalker, Dana can travel in both worlds and she can also transport elements from one world into the other. When it is discovered that she can carry magic into the human world and the equally powerful technology into the medieval world of faerie, Dana herself becomes a valuable commodity, and she is not sure if anyone values her only for herself.

Reviewing *Glimmerglass* for *Publishers Weekly*, a critic wrote that "Black launches her young-adult . . . series with [a] . . . tightly, constructed, absorbing story," adding that "Dana's strength and determination make her a top-notch heroine." The "detentions, kidnappings, and violent episodes" in *Glimmerglass* provide an animated backdrop against which the teen's "powers are just beginning to ripen," according to Megan Lynn Isaac in her *Voice of Youth Advocates* appraisal of Black's Y.A. fantasy.

Dana returns in *Shadowspell,* as her efforts to have a normal social life are thwarted by the fact that she must live in a safe house with a full-time bodyguard in order to keep Titania, Queen of Faerie, from making good on her threat to end the life of the half-faerie/half-human teen. When the Erlking, an immortal hunter, arrives with his retinue of brutal warriors, he is prevented from waging war on Avalon only by a treaty with Titania. Soon Dana realizes that the Erlking may be interested in her romantically, and she hides her attraction to this charismatic warrior because his motives are in question. After a long journey with her father and a group of loyal friends, Dana is finally presented at the court of Queen Titania in *Sirensong,* the third "Faeriewalker" novel. Now the queen's duplicity is masked by her princely son Henry, who threatens the faeriewalker with arrest as a traitor. When Dana is accused of attempting to kill the royal granddaughter she and her retinue flee. although her father remains behind and becomes Titania's hostage. Tht teen's efforts to prove her innocence and save her father are hampered by the relentless Erlking, who still has Dana in his romantic sights.

"Well-paced and thrilling," according to *Voice of Youth Advocates* contributor Courtney Huse Wika, *Shadow-*

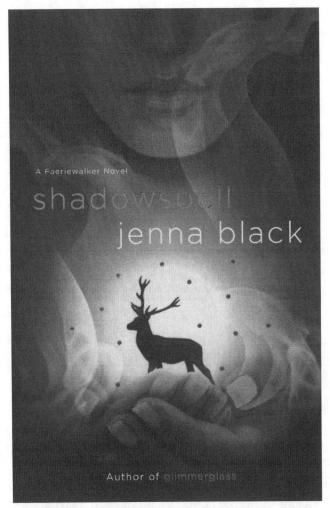

Cover of Jenna Black's paranormal fantasy Shadowspell, *part of her "Faeriewalker" series.* (Cover photograph (hands) by Peter Nicholson/Getty Images. Cover photographic illustration by Jonathan Barkat. Used by permission of St. Martin's Press.)

spell "does not disappoint" fans of the first "Faeriewalker" novel. "Black's fantasy world is finely honed and filled with realistic concerns," wrote Francisca Goldsmith in her review of the second series installment for *Booklist*, while in *School Library Journal* Jessica Miller noted that "political intrigue mingles with supernatural battles" in this installment, "making for an exciting and magical adventure." "Dana finally exercises both her magical powers and her intelligence" in *Sirensong,* asserted a *Kirkus Reviews* writer, the critic going on to observe of the third "Faeriewalker" novel that Black's teen fantasy is grounded "in a welcome verisimilitude."

Biographical and Critical Sources

PERIODICALS

Booklist, February 15, 2011, Francisca Goldsmith, review of *Shadowspell*, p. 76.
Kirkus Reviews, June 1, 2011, review of *Sirensong.*

Publishers Weekly, October 15, 2007, review of *Devil Inside,* p. 47; May 31, 2010, review of *Glimmerglass*, p. 50.
School Library Journal, June, 2011, Jessica Miller, review of *Shadowspell*, p. 109.
Voice of Youth Advocates, October, 2010, Megan Lynn Isaac, review of *Glimmerglass*, p. 361; April, 2011, Courtney Huse Wika, review of *Shadowspell*, p. 74.

ONLINE

Jenna Black Home Page, http://www.jennablack.com (February 12, 2012).

* * *

BOOTMAN, Colin

Personal
Born in Trinidad; immigrated to United States. *Education:* School of Visual Arts, degree.

Addresses
Home—Brooklyn, NY. *E-mail*—colinbootman@yahoo.com.

Career
Illustrator. Teacher of art to middle-and high-school students; presenter at schools.

Awards, Honors
Marguerite de Angeli Prize, Delacorte Press, 1997, for *Seth and Samona* by Joanne Hyppolite; Best Children's Book selection, Bank Street College of Education, 2004, for *Papa's Mark* by Gwendolyn Battle-Lavert; Massachusetts Book Awards Honor Book selection, *Storytelling World* Award, and Bank Street College of Education Best Children's Book selection, all 2004, all for *Don't Say Ain't* by Irene Smalls; Coretta Scott King Illustrator Award Honor Book selection, and Bank Street College of Education Best Children's Book selection, both 2004, and Society of School Librarians International Honor Book selection, and California Young Reader Medal nomination, both 2005, all for *Almost to Freedom* by Vaunda Micheaux Nelson; Notable Children's Book in the Language Arts selection, National Council of Teachers of English/Children's Book Council (CBC), Notable Social-Studies Trade Books for Children selection, National Council for Social Studies/CBC, Teachers' Choice selection, International Reading Association, Schneider Family Book Award, *Storytelling World* Award, Outstanding Books for Young People with Disabilities selection, U.S. Board on Books for Young People, and Comstock Book Award, all 2006, and California Young Reader Medal nomination, 2007, all for *Dad, Jackie, and Me* by Myron Uhlberg; Ashley Bryan Medal, Children's Literature Conference, 2006, for *Grandmama's Pride.*

Writings

SELF-ILLUSTRATED

Fish for the Grand Lady, Holiday House (New York, NY), 2005.
The Steel Pan Man of Harlem, Carolrhoda Books (Minneapolis, MN), 2009.

ILLUSTRATOR

Kinda Walvoord Girard, *Young Frederick Douglass: The Slave Who Learned to Read,* Albert Whitman (Morton Grove, IL), 1994.
Joanne Hyppolite, *Seth and Samona,* Delacorte Press (New York, NY), 1995.
Irene Smalls, *Louise's Gift; or, What Did She Give Me That For?,* Little, Brown, (Boston, MA), 1996.
Vicki Winslow, *Follow the Leader,* Delacorte Press (New York, NY), 1997.
Katrin Tchana, *Oh, No, Toto!,* Scholastic (New York, NY), 1997.
Jerdine Nolen, *In My Momma's Kitchen,* Lothrop, Lee & Shepard (New York, NY), 1999.
Gwendolyn Battle-Lavert, *The Music in Derrick's Heart,* Holiday House (New York, NY), 2000.
David A. Adler, *Dr. Martin Luther King, Jr.,* Holiday House (New York, NY), 2001.
Irene Smalls, *Don't Say Ain't,* Charlesbridge Pub. (Watertown, MA), 2003.
Vaunda Micheaux Nelson, *Almost to Freedom,* Carolrhoda Books (Minneapolis, MN), 2003.
Gwendolyn Battle-Lavert, *Papa's Mark,* Holiday House (New York, NY), 2003.
David A. Adler, *A Picture Book of Harriet Beecher Stowe,* Holiday House (New York, NY), 2003.
Myron Uhlberg, *Dad, Jackie, and Me,* Peachtree Publishers (Atlanta, GA), 2005.
Becky Birtha, *Grandmama's Pride,* Albert Whitman (Morton Grove, IL), 2005.
Sharon G. Flake, *The Broken Bike Boy and the Queen of 33rd Street,* Jump at the Sun/Hyperion Books for Children (New York, NY), 2007.
Ann Malaspina, *Finding Lincoln,* Albert Whitman (Morton Grove, IL), 2009.
Myron Uhlberg, *A Storm Called Katrina,* Peachtree (Atlanta, GA), 2010.
Suzanne Slade, *Climbing Lincoln's Steps: The African American Journey,* Albert Whitman (Chicago, IL), 2010.
Anne Rockwell, *Hey, Charleston!,* Carolrhoda Books (Minneapolis, MN), 2011.
Glenda Armand, *Love Twelve Miles Long,* Lee & Low Books (New York, NY), 2011.

Sidelights

Trinidad-born illustrator Colin Bootman moved to New York City as a child, and quickly embraced art. After graduating from the city's LaGuardia High School of the Arts and attending college, Bootman began a pro-

fessional career in illustration, and has contributed artwork to books by authors such as Gwendolyn Battle-Lavert, Jerdine Nolen, and David A. Adler. Noted for painting in vibrant hues and for his affectionate portraits of African-American children, Bootman frequently collaborates on book projects that reflect black life and culture. The history of notable figures is of particular interest to the artist; in books such as Adler's *Dr. Martin Luther King, Jr.* and *Dad, Jackie, and Me* by Myron Uhlberg, as well in his first illustration project, Kinda Walvoord Girard's *Young Frederick Douglass: The Slave Who Learned to Read,* Bootman brings to life the stories of famous black Americans from the past.

In his contribution to *Dr. Martin Luther King, Jr.,* Bootman includes large-scale illustrations that *School Library Journal* reviewer Eunice Weech called "realistic" and helpful in filling in "the details for the author's spare but well-chosen words." Carolyn Phelan noted in her *Booklist* review of Adler's picture-book biography of the noted civil-rights leader that "Bootman's painterly illustrations convey the book's serious tone through the often grave expressions of the characters and the generally dark palette of colors."

One of Bootman's award-winning works, *Dad, Jackie, and Me,* pairs his art with a story by Uhlberg that is

Colin Bootman captures Irene Smalls' story of a girl confronting a new culture in **Don't Say Ain't.** (Illustration copyright © 2003 by Colin Bootman. Used with permission by Charlesbridge Publishing, Inc., Watertown, MA, www.charlesbridge.com. All rights reserved.)

based on the author's memories of joining his father at a baseball game in which Jackie Robinson played for the Brooklyn Dodgers. The year was 1947, and Robinson was the first Negro player to be signed by a major-league baseball team. Uhlberg's father, who was white but deaf, "relates . . . to someone who also has to overcome discrimination," according to a *Kirkus Reviews* writer. Praising *Dad, Jackie, and Me* as "an affecting tribute," a *Publishers Weekly* critic added that Bootman's watercolor portraits "of Robinson consistently convey the athlete's poise and calm under fire." *A Storm Called Katrina* also pairs the creative talents of Uhlberg and Bootman, and here the artist's "dramatic oil paintings" depict the memories of a boy who survived Hurricane Katrina and then joined his family as it "makes its way through their flooded neighborhood," according to a *Publishers Weekly* critic.

In a *Publishers Weekly* review, a critic commented that Bootman's oil paintings for *Papa's Mark* contain "emotion-filled character studies" that echo author Battle-Lavert's story of a man's determination to cast his first ballot. Hazel Rochman, writing in *Booklist*, praised the illustrations that bring to life *Don't Say Ain't*, writing that the artist's "handsome, realistic oil paintings capture both the period setting and one child's personal conflict." In *Finding Lincoln*, Ann Malaspina's

picture-book story about a young African American's research into the president that freed the slaves, Bootman creates "beautiful . . . watercolor paintings with unforgettable close-up portraits," according to *Booklist* critic Hazel Rochman, and Mary Hazelton wrote in her *School Library Journal* critique of Becky Birtha's civil-rights-era story in *Grandmama's Pride* that the author's "strong, sensitive writing is enhanced by beautiful watercolor paintings filled with chips of light."

In addition to his work as an illustrator, Bootman has also created artwork for several original stories. He draws on his Trinidadian childhood in *Fish for the Grand Lady*, telling a story tjat fomds brothers Colly and Derrick determined to catch the fish their grandmother requires to make a tasty dinner. "Bootman's beautiful oil paintings depict the lush countryside" of his native Trinidad, wrote a *Kirkus Reviews* writer, and his "first writing effort is crisp and evocative." Also praising the "impressionistic oil paintings" in *Fish for the Grand Lady*, Carolyn Phelan added in *Booklist* that Bootman's picture book serves as "a quiet yet appealing introduction to Trinidad." For Mary Hazelton, the author/illustrator's "well paced" text also deserves praise because "family relationships are loving and natural and provide a satisfying glimpse" into island life.

Based on the well-known story about the Pied Piper of Hamelin, *The Steel Pan Man of Harlem* finds Bootman mixing cultures. The story is set in the city of Harlem during the 1940s, as a proliferation of rats poses a danger to the densely populated urban community. Politicians, professional exterminators, and others attempting to catch the rats have failed, and residents are willing to listen when a musician arrives at a local subway station and claims that he will rid the city of its rats in exchange for a million dollars. The tune the man pounds out on his steel pan drum causes all within earshot to dance, and he uses his drum to similarly bewitch the rats and lead them to their fate. When Harlem's mayor reneges on his promise to pay the man, the steel drum beats out a dance tune that forces all residents into a marathon of dancing. Bootman's self-illustrated story "celebrates the power of music," wrote Rochman in *Booklist*, and he shares his special memories of moving to the United States in the story's afterword. The author/illustrator "triumphs with this gorgeously moody . . . retelling," wrote a *Publishers Weekly*, the critic adding that *The Steel Pan Man of Harlem* "has all the makings of a spellbinder."

Biographical and Critical Sources

PERIODICALS

Booklist, March 1, 1997, Julie Corsaro, review of *Oh, No, Toto!*, p. 1174; February 15, 1999, Hazel Rochman, review of *In My Momma's Kitchen*, p. 1077; February 15, 2000, Shelle Rosenfeld, review of *The Music in Derrick's Heart*, p. 1104; July, 2001, Carolyn Phelan,

Gwendolyn Battle-Lavert's picture-book story in **Papa's Mark** *is among Bootman's illustration projects.* (Illustration copyright © 2003 by Colin Bootman. Reproduced by permission of Holiday House, Inc.)

Ann Malaspina's history-themed story in **Finding Lincoln** *comes to life in Bootman's evocative paintings.* (Illustration copyright © 2009 by Colin Bootman. Reproduced by permission of Albert Whitman & Company.)

review of *Dr. Martin Luther King, Jr.,* p. 2022; February 15, 2003, Hazel Rochman, review of *Don't Say Ain't,* p. 1090; August, 2005, Bill Ott, review of *Dad, Jackie, and Me,* p. 2036; November 1, 2005, Julie Cummins, review of *Grandmama's Pride,* p. 51; October 15, 2006, Carolyn Phelan, review of *Fish for the Grand Lady,* p. 52; June 1, 2007, Hazel Rochman, review of *The Broken Bike Boy and the Queen of 33rd Street,* p. 68; September 15, 2009, Hazel Rochman, review of *Finding Lincoln,* p. 54; November 1, 2009, Hazel Rochman, review of *The Steel Pan Man of Harlem,* p. 61; September 15, 2010, Hazel Rochman, review of *Climbing Lincoln's Steps: The African American Journey,* p. 58.

Horn Book, July-August, 2007, Robin Smith, review of *The Broken Bike Boy and the Queen of 33rd Street,* p. 395.

Kirkus Reviews, March 1, 2005, review of *Dad, Jackie, and Me,* p. 297; November 15, 2005, review of *Grandmama's Pride,* p. 1230; August 1, 2006, review of *Fish for the Grand Lady,* p. 782; April 15, 2007, review of *The Broken Bike Boy and the Queen of 33rd Street*; August 1, 2009, review of *Finding Lincoln*;

October 15, 2009, review of *The Steel Pan Man of Harlem*; August 15, 2010, review of *Climbing Lincoln's Steps.*

Publishers Weekly, June 19, 1995, review of *Seth and Samona,* p. 60; April 22, 1996, review of *Louise's Gift,* p. 70; February 10, 1997, review of *Oh, No, Toto!,* p. 82; April 12, 1999, review of *In My Momma's Kitchen,* 75; January 24, 2000, review of *The Music in Derrick's Heart,* p. 310; December 9, 2002, review of *Don't Say Ain't,* p. 84; February 9, 2004, review of *Papa's Mark,* p. 80; February 7, 2005, review of *Dad, Jackie, and Me,* p. 59; May 7, 2007, review of *The Broken Bike Boy and the Queen of 33rd Street,* p. 60; November 9, 2009, review of *The Steel Pan Man of Harlem,* p. 47; June 20, 2011, review of *A Storm Called Katrina,* p. 52.

School Library Journal, June, 2001, Eunice Weech, review of *Dr. Martin Luther King, Jr.,* p. 133; March, 2003, Alicia Eames, review of *Don't Say Ain't,* p. 207; May, 2003, Gina Powell, review of *A Picture Book of Harriet Beecher Stowe,* p. 133; May, 2005, Marilyn Taniguchi, review of *Dad, Jackie, and Me,* p. 103; November, 2005, Mary Hazelton, review of *Grandmama's*

Pride, p. 83; October, 2006, Mary Hazelton, review of *Fish for the Grand Lady,* p. 103; June, 2007, Terrie Dorio, review of *The Broken Bike Boy and the Queen of 33rd Street,* p. 144; August, 2009, Judith Constantinides, review of *Finding Lincoln,* p. 80; November, 2009, Miriam Lang Budin, review of *The Steel Pan Man of Harlem,* p. 73; August, 2010, Barbara Auerbach, review of *Climbing Lincoln's Steps,* p. 91.

ONLINE

Children's Literature Web site, http://www.childrenslit.com/ (February 15, 2012), "Colin Bootman."

Colin Bootman Home Page, http://www.colinbootman.com (February 12, 2012).

HarperChildrens Web site, http://www.harperchildrens.com/ (February 12, 2012), "Colin Bootman."*

C

CAIRNS, Julia 1960(?)-

Personal
Born c. 1960, in Oxfordshire, England; married John Bulger (a biologist), 1992. *Education:* College degree, 1982. *Hobbies and other interests:* Travel.

Addresses
Home—Galisteo, NM.

Career
Illustrator and artist. Creator of art for postage stamps. *Exhibitions:* Work exhibited internationally, including at Botswana National Museum, Gaborone; in Davis, CA; and through Open Studios program, Galisteo, NM.

Awards, Honors
Notable Book designation, American Library Association, 2000, for *Off to the Sweet Shores of Africa* by Uzoamaka Chinyelu Unobagha; National Association for the Advancement of Colored People Award for Children's Books nomination, 2001, for *The Spider Weaver* by Margaret Musgrove.

Illustrator
Uzoamaka Chinyelu Unobagha, *Off to the Sweet Shores of Africa, and Other Talking Drum Rhymes,* Chronicle Books (San Francisco, CA), 2000.

Damon Burnard, *I Spy in the Jungle,* Chronicle Books (San Francisco, CA), 2001.

Damon Burnard, *I Spy in the Ocean,* Chronicle Books (San Francisco, CA), 2001.

Margaret Musgrove, *The Spider Weaver: A Legend of Kente Cloth,* Blue Sky Press (New York, NY), 2001.

Jill Bennett, compiler, *Grandad's Tree: Poems about Families,* Barefoot Books (Cambridge, MA), 2003.

Laurie Krebs, *We All Went on Safari: A Counting Journey through Tanzania,* Barefoot Books (Cambridge, MA), 2003.

Mary Chamberlain and Rich Chamberlain, *Mama Panya's Pancakes: A Village Tale from Kenya,* Barefoot Books (Cambridge, MA), 2005.

Ifeoma Onyefuflu, *The Girl Who Married a Ghost, and Other Tales from Nigeria,* Frances Lincoln (New York, NY), 2010.

Marilyn Singer, *A Full Moon Is Rising: Poems,* Lee & Low Books (New York, NY), 2011.

Sidelights
Born in England, Julia Cairns developed a love of far-off places led to the life of travel that has inspired her creativity since age eighteen. During her first trip to Kenya, where she was exposed to Massai culture, Cairns has translated her impressions of place into art through painting. She continued to hone her skills as a painter after traveling to Botswana and living there for nine years while capturing the region's diverse landscape, culture, and wildlife. Her colorful images eventually found their way onto several Botswana postage stamps, and she also painted a portrait of the country's current president.

Although Cairns now makes her home in the United States, her colorful paintings continue to be inspired by her travels, and her work has been licensed for calendars, textiles, and paper products in addition to being exhibited in galleries. Her images have also appeared in several picture books, among them *Off to the Sweet Shores of Africa, and Other Talking Drum Rhymes,* by Nigerian writer Uzoamaka Chinyelu Unobagha, Margaret Musgrove's *The Spider Weaver: A Legend of Kente Cloth,* and Marilyn Singer's *A Full Moon Is Rising: Poems.* Reviewing the artist's work for Singer's verse collection, Gillian Engberg noted in *Booklist* that "the joyful colors and compositions echo the words' celebratory tone," while *School Library Journal* reviewer Carole Phillips maintained that Cairns' "eye-catching illustrations will invite children to wonder and imagine" while observing the night sky.

In *Off to the Sweet Shores of Africa, and Other Talking Drum Rhymes* poet Unobagha mixes Mother Goose imagery with African elements ranging from zebras and

giraffes to grasslands and the hot sands of the Sahara. "From the vibrant patterned endpapers to the rich, warm watercolor paintings . . . , this is a beautifully designed volume," proclaimed Ginny Gustin in her *School Library Journal* appraisal of Cairns' picture-book debut. The artist's "clear, detailed watercolors . . . capture the rural community under the wide sky," noted Hazel Rochman in her *Booklist* review of the work, while a *New York Times Book Review* critic dubbed the art in *Off to the Sweet Shores of Africa, and Other Talking Drum Rhymes* "enchanting."

Another story from Africa, Ifeoma Onyefuflu's *The Girl Who Married a Ghost, and Other Tales from Nigeria,* pairs a text "rooted in daily [village] life" with Cairns' "appealing pencil drawings," according to Rochman. In *School Librarian* Janet Dowling concluded that this book's "penciled illustrations can only be described as delightfully cheeky, and give a life to the stories."

Cairns draws on her knowledge of Maasai culture in her artwork for Laurie Krebs' *We All Went on Safari: A Counting Journey through Tanzania.* Here readers can join a group of Maasai children as they travel through the grasslands of the Serengeti, learning a little bit of Swahili along the way. "Each sharply detailed scene glows with jewel-like color," asserted a *Kirkus Reviews* writer in appraising the artist's contribution to Krebs'

story, while in *School Library Journal* Ajoke' T.I. Kokodoko wrote that Cairn's double-page illustrations "are striking and [their] . . . graceful movement . . . gives a sense of the joy these children are experiencing." The pages of Musgrove's *The Spider Weaver* are "bursting with colors as vibrant as kente cloth," according to a *Publishers Weekly* contributor, the critic adding that Cairns' characteristic use of a "flattened perspective and characters displayed largely in profile add a folk-art flair" to this retelling of a traditional Ashanti trickster tale.

Mary Chamberlain and Rich Chamberlain's humorous story in *Mama Panya's Pancakes: A Village Tale from Kenya* once again allows young listeners to experience rural African culture. Here a boy and his mother walk to market, and a generous spirit inspires the child to invite everyone he meets to visit their house for pancakes. Although Mama Panya worries that she will not have enough food, her young son's act of giving has inspired generosity in others. Together with the Chamberlains' repetitive text, Cairns' "watercolor paintings are filled with details of the countryside and the marketplace," noted a *Kirkus Reviews* writer. In *School Library Journal* Genevieve Gallagher cited the "bold colors, vivid patterns, and lush scenery" in *Mama Panya's Pancakes* when recommending the picture book for story-hour sharing.

Julia Cairns' stylized African-themed art captures the folk elements of Marilyn Singer's **A Full Moon Is Rising.** (Illustration copyright © 2011 by Julie Cairns. Reproduced by permission of Lee & Low Books, Inc.)

Cairns' illustration projects include Mary and Rich Chamberlain's **Mama Panya's Pancakes.** (Illustration copyright © 2005 by Julia Cairns. Reproduced by permission of Barefoot Books.)

Biographical and Critical Sources

PERIODICALS

Booklist, November 1, 2000, Hazel Rochman, review of *Off to the Sweet Shores of Africa, and Other Talking Drum Rhymes,* p. 544; February 15, 2001, Gillian Engberg, review of *The Spider Weaver: A Legend of Kente Cloth,* p. 1156, and Henrietta M. Smith, review of *Off to the Sweet Shores of Africa,* p. 1161; April 1, 2003, Carolyn Phelan, review of *Grandad's Tree: Poems about Families,* p. 1406; December 15, 2010, Ha-

zel Rochman, review of *The Girl Who Married a Ghost, and Other Tales from Nigeria,* p. 38; May 1, 2011, Gillian Engberg, review of *A Full Moon Is Rising,* p. 73.

Black Issues Book Review, May, 2001, Khafre K. Abif, review of *The Spider Weaver,* p. 81.

Kirkus Reviews, January 15, 2003, review of *We All Went on Safari: A Counting Journey through Tanzania,* p. 143; March 1, 2005, review of *Mama Panya's Pancakes: A Village Tale from Kenya,* p. 285.

New York Times Book Review, February 11, 2001, review of *Off to the Sweet Shores of Africa, and Other Talking Drum Rhymes,* p. 26.

Publishers Weekly, February 12, 2001, review of *The Spider Weaver,* p. 211; March 3, 2003, review of *Family Affair,* p. 78; April, 2003, review of *We All Went on Safari,* p. 130; April 18, 2011, review of *A Full Moon Is Rising,* p. 53.

School Librarian, summer, 2010, Janet Dowling, review of *The Girl Who Married a Ghost, and Other Tales from Nigeria,* p. 106.

School Library Journal, October, 2000, Ginny Gustin, review of *Off to the Sweet Shores of Africa, and Other Talking Drum Rhymes,* p. 154; February, 2001, Grace Oliff, review of *The Spider Weaver,* p. 113; June, 2011, Carole Phillips, review of *A Full Moon Is Rising,* p. 106; November, 2001, Melinda Piehler, review of *I Spy in the Jungle,* p. 112; April, 2003, Ajoke' T.I. Kokodoko, review of *We All Went on Safari,* p. 130; May, 2005, Genevieve Gallagher, review of *Mama Panya's Pancakes,* p. 78; March, 2011, Carrie Rogers-Whitehead, review of *The Girl Who Married a Ghost, and Other Tales from Nigeria,* p. 145; June, 2011, Carole Phillips, review of *A Full Moon Is Rising,* p. 106.

ONLINE

Julia Cairns Home Page, http://juliacairns.net (February 12, 2012).

SFGate Web site, http://www.sfgate.com/ (July 3, 2006), Nick Thomas, "Julia Cairns' Years Spent in a Reed Hut Left an Indelible Stamp on the Artist."*

* * *

CHICK, Bryan 1971-

Personal

Born 1971; married; children: three.

Addresses

Home—Clarkston, MI. *E-mail*—info@bryanchick.com.

Career

Author. Presenter at schools.

Writings

"SECRET ZOO" MIDDLE-GRADE NOVEL SERIES

The Secret Zoo, Second Wish Press (Clarkston, MI), 2007, Greenwillow Books (New York, NY), 2010.
Secrets and Shadows, Greenwillow Books (New York, NY), 2011.
Riddles and Danger, Greenwillow Books (New York, NY), 2011.

Adaptations

The "Secret Zoo" novels were adapted for audiobook by Audible Audio.

Sidelights

Michigan writer Bryan Chick did not falter when he hit his first stumbling block on the way to being a published author. Unsuccessful at acquiring an agent to market his first novel, *The Secret Zoo,* Chick published the book himself, then sold thousands of copies—and ultimately attracted the interest of a mainstream publisher—by visiting dozens of schools and also commissioning his father to act as a traveling salesperson. The promotional effort lasted two years and even earned Chick a positive review in *School Library Journal,* but it was a chance introduction to the nephew of an editor at Greenwillow Books that ultimately clinched the deal.

"The idea of *The Secret Zoo* came to me when I was just nine years old," Chick admitted on his home page. As a child, the author visited a local zoo and was inspired by the idea that there might be secret passages that would allow the animals to leave their confines when no one was around. In his novel, he introduces siblings Megan and Noah, who along with friends Richie and Ella, can see inside the walls of the Clarksville City Zoo from their tree house. Megan notices that

Cover of Bryan Chick's middle-grade novel Secrets and Shadows, *part of his "Secret Zoo" series.* (Cover art © 2011 by Justin Gerard. Used with permission of Greenwillow Books, an imprint of HarperCollins Publishers, a division of HarperCollins Publishers.)

the animals at the zoo have started acting strangely, and the next day she is gone. When her three friends set out to hunt for her, the clues in Megan's diary allow them to follow her path inside the zoo. When they locate their friend, they also uncover the secret world behind the animal cages and realize that it must be protected. The children soon confront another task—to save the secret zoo from DeGraff, an evil Shadowist—and earn the help of curator Mr. Darby as well as special creatures that include a penguin named Podgy and a polar bear named Blizzard.

The Secret Zoo inspired Chick to continue the saga of Megan, Noah, Richie, and Ella, and their further adventures play out in *Secrets and Shadows* and *Riddles and Dangers.* In *Secrets and Shadows* the friends join the Crossers, a secret group that helps to defend the zoo, just in time to battle a Sasquatch army commanded by DeGraff. *Riddles and Danger* finds the Zoo Action Scouts aided by the teen Zoo Defenders as they continue their battle with the evil Shadowist. As Megan, Noah, Richie, and Ella move further and further into the maze of the Secret Zoo, the fate of the magical world continues to depend on the help of the Crossers.

"Chick debuts with an action-packed and breathless story about teamwork," wrote a *Publishers Weekly* critic in a review of *The Secret Zoo,* and a *Children's Bookwatch* contributor described the novel as "a modern-day fantasy adventure packed . . . with wide-eyed wonder." Noah and his band of Action Scouts "are well developed characters," wrote Julie Shatterly in her review of *Secrets and Shadows* for *School Library Journal,* "and readers will . . . relate to their anxiety, curiosity, and just plain chutzpah."

Biographical and Critical Sources

PERIODICALS

Children's Bookwatch, February, 2008, review of *The Secret Zoo.*
Kirkus Reviews, December 15, 2010, review of *Secrets and Shadows;* September 1, 2011, review of *Riddles and Danger.*
Publishers Weekly, June 21, 2010, review of *The Secret Zoo,* p. 47; March 28, 2011, Sally Lodge, review of *Secrets and Shadows,* p. S6.
School Library Journal, April, 2011, Julie Shatterly, review of *Secrets and Shadows,* p. 168.

ONLINE

Bryan Chick Home Page, http://www.bryanchick.com (February 20, 2012).
Greenwillow Books Web log, http://greenwillowblog.com/ (May 4, 2010), Bryan Chick, "How I Had My Self-published Book Noticed by the NY Guys."

Secret Zoo Web site, http://www.thesecretzoo.com (February 20, 2012).

*   *   *

CHRISTY, Jana 1965-

Personal

Born April, 1965; married John E. Mitchell (now John Seven; an arts editor); children: Harry, Hugo. *Hobbies and other interests:* Traveling, spending time with family.

Addresses

Home—N. Adams, MA. *Agent*—Justin Rucker, Shannon Associates, 333 W. 57th St., Ste. 809, New York, NY, 10019. *E-mail*—janachristy@gmail.com.

Career

Illustrator and sequential artist. Comics artist, beginning 1990s; freelance illustrator and creator of greeting-card art.

Awards, Honors

Creative Child magazine Seal of Excellence, 2011, for *The Ocean Story* by John Seven.

Illustrator

Stephanie Calmenson, *Ten Items or Less,* Simon & Schuster (New York, NY), 1985.
(Under name Jana Christie Mitchell) John E. Mitchell, *4 Go Mad in Massachusetts: Adventures with the Mitchell Family from Boston to the Berkshires,* 2003.
Joanne Barkan, *Celebrate!: Your Amazing Achievements,* Reader's Digest Children's Books (Pleasantville, NY), 2007.
Kate Tym, *We Love the Seashore,* QEB Pub. (Laguna Hills, CA), 2007.
Patrice Karst, *The Smile That Went around the World,* De-Vorss & Company, 2009.
John E. Mitchell, *Happy, Sad, Silly, Mad: My World Makes Me Feel,* Andrews McMeel Publishing (Kansas City, KS), 2009.
Julie Aigner Clark, *You Are the Best Medicine,* Balzer + Bray (New York, NY), 2010.
Dana Meachen Rau, *Flip Flop!,* Random House (New York, NY), 2011.
Maryann Macdonald, *How to Hug,* Marshall Cavendish Children (New York, NY), 2011.
Toni Buzzeo, *Penelope Popper, Book Doctor,* Upstart Books (Madison, WI), 2011.
John Seven, *The Ocean Story,* Picture Window Books (Mankato, MN), 2011.
John Seven, *A Rule Is to Break: A Child's Guide to Anarchy,* AuntieUncle Books, 2011.
Madelyn Rosenberg, *Happy Birthday, Tree: A Tu B'shevat Story,* Albert Whitman (Chicago, IL), 2012.

Creator, with husband John E. Mitchell, of comic-book series "Very Vicky," beginning c. 1992. Contributor of artwork to periodicals, including *Babybug, Boston Globe, Boston Herald, Boston Phoenix,* and *Highlights for Children.*

Biographical and Critical Sources

PERIODICALS

Booklist, October 15, 2010, Ilene Cooper, review of *You Are the Best Medicine,* p. 58.
Kirkus Reviews, September 1, 2010, review of *You Are the Best Medicine;* January 15, 2011, review of *How to Hug.*
School Library Journal, November, 2010, Jasmine L. Precopio, review of *You Are the Best Medicine,* p. 66; April, 2011, Amy Commers, review of *How to Hug,* p. 147; July, 2011, Gay Lynn Van Vleck, review of *The Ocean Story,* p. 78.

ONLINE

Jana Christy Home Page, http://johnandjana.net (February 12, 2012).
Jana Christy Web log, http://janachristyblog.wordpress. com (February 12, 2012).*

*   *   *

COLLINS, Ross 1972-

Personal

Born 1972, in Glasgow, Scotland. *Education:* Glasgow School of Art, B.F.A. (illustration; with first-class honours), 1994.

Addresses

Home—Glasgow, Scotland. *Agent*—Eunice McMullen Children's Literary Agency, Low Ibbotsholme Cottage, Off Bridge La., Troutbeck Bridge, Windermere, Cumbria LA23 IHU, England; eunice@eunicemcmullen.co. uk. *E-mail*—rsncollins@yahoo.co.uk.

Career

Author and illustrator. Freelance animation character developer for clients, including Walt Disney Company and Axis Animation. *Exhibitions:* Work exhibited widely, including at Society of Illustrators' Original Art Exhibition, New York, NY, 2009.

Awards, Honors

Macmillan Children's Book Prize, 1994, for *The Sea Hole;* Scottish Arts Council Book Award, 1999, Blue Peter Book Award nominee, and Blue Ribbon Award, all for *Supposing . . .* by Frances Thomas; Oppenheim Toy Portfolio award, 2002, for *Alvie Eats Soup;* White Raven award (Germany), 2003, for *Busy Night;* Kate Greenaway Medal shortlist, 2007, for *The Elephantom;* Royal Mail Book Award, 2008, for *Billy Monster's Daymare* by Alan Durant; Scottish Children's Book Award, 2012, for *Dear Vampa.*

Writings

SELF-ILLUSTRATED

The Sea Hole, Macmillan (London, England), 1997.
Alvie Eats Soup, Arthur A. Levine (New York, NY), 2002.
Busy Night, Bloomsbury (New York, NY), 2002.
Germs, Bloomsbury Children's Books (New York, NY), 2004.
The Elephantom, Templar (Dorking, England), 2006.
My Amazing Dad, Simon & Schuster (London, England), 2007.
Medusa Jones, Arthur A. Levine Books (New York, NY), 2008.
Dear Vampa, Katherine Tegen Books (New York, NY), 2009.
Doodleday, Albert Whitman (Chicago, IL), 2011.

ILLUSTRATOR

Lydia Conway, *Children's London,* Evening Standard Publications (London, England), 1994.
Jamie Rix, *A Stitch in Time,* Hodder (London, England), 1996.
Jamie Rix, *Fearsome Tales for Fiendish Kids,* Hodder (London, England), 1996.
Alex Martin, *ZP TV,* Hodder (London, England), 1996.
Beverley Birch, *Inventions,* Hodder (London, England), 1996.
Nicola Barber, *The Mind,* Hodder (London, England), 1996.
Karen Wallace, *It Takes Two,* Franklin Watts (New York, NY), 1997.
Frances Thomas, *What If?,* Hyperion (New York, NY), 1998.
Frances Thomas, *Supposing . . .,* Bloomsbury (London, England), 1998.
Francesca Simon, *Don't Wake the Baby!,* Hodder (London, England), 1998.
Vic Parker, *In the Rainforest,* Franklin Watts (London, England), 1998, published as *Who Are You?: In the Rainforest,* 2004.
Vic Parker, *On the Farm,* Franklin Watts (London, England), 1998, published as *Who Are You?: On the Farm,* 2004.
Vic Parker, *In the Sea,* Franklin Watts (London, England), 1998, published as *Who Are You?: In the Sea,* 2004.
Vic Parker, *In the Polar Lands,* Franklin Watts (London, England), 1998, published as *Who Are You?: In the Polar Lands,* 2004.

Vivian French, *Write around the World: The Story of How and Why We Learnt to Write,* Zero to Ten (New York, NY), 1998.

Karen Wallace, *Chomp! Munch! Chew!,* Franklin Watts (London, England), 1999, with notes and activities by Lynn Huggins-Cooper, 2004.

Jamie Rix, *The Vile Smile,* Macdonald Young (Hove, England), 1999.

Paeony Lewis, *Cinderella's Wedding,* Macdonald Young (Hove, England), 1999.

Tony Bradman, *The Two Jacks,* Barrington Stoke (Edinburgh, Scotland), 1999, new edition, 2002.

William Bedford, *Esme's Owl,* Mammoth (London, England), 1999.

Vivian French, *From Zero to Ten: The Story of Numbers,* Oxford University Press (New York, NY), 2000.

Clare Bevan, reteller, *A Midsummer Night's Dream,* Oxford University Press (New York, NY), 2000.

Anne Mazer, *The No-Nothings and Their Baby,* Arthur A. Levine Books (New York, NY), 2000.

Wendy Cope, editor, *The Faber Book of Bedtime Stories,* Faber & Faber (London, England), 2000.

Frances Thomas, *Maybe One Day,* Bloomsbury (London, England), 2001, published as *One Day, Daddy,* Hyperion (New York, NY), 2001.

Hilary Robinson, *Freddie's Fears,* Franklin Watts (London, England), 2001.

Herbie Brennan, *Fairy Nuff: A Tale of Bluebell Wood,* Bloomsbury (London, England), 2001, Bloomsbury (New York, NY), 2002.

Herbie Brennan, *Nuff Said: Another Tale of Bluebell Wood,* Bloomsbury (New York, NY), 2002.

Geraldine McCaughrean, *Six Storey House,* Hodder (London, England), 2002.

Laurence Anholt, *Jack and the Dreamsack,* Bloomsbury (New York, NY), 2003.

Geraldine McCaughrean, *Doctor Quack,* Hodder (London, England), 2003.

Geraldine McCaughrean, *Jalopy: A Car's Story in Five Drivers,* Orchard (London, England), 2003.

Nichola McAuliffe, *Attila, Loolagax, and the Eagle,* Bloomsbury (London, England), 2003.

Sue Graves, *Oh, George!,* Franklin Watts (London, England), 2003.

Julie Donaldson, *The Head in the Sand: A Roman Play,* Hodder (London, England), 2003.

Anne Miranda, *Who Said Boo?,* Hyperion (New York, NY), 2003.

Hilary Robinson, *Freddie's Fears,* Picture Window Books (Minneapolis, MN), 2003.

Tamra Wight, *The Three Grumpies,* Bloomsbury (New York, NY), 2003.

Karina Law, *Marlowe's Mum and the Tree House,* Franklin Watts (London, England), 2004.

Simon Puttock, *Don't Count Your Chickens,* Macmillan (London, England), 2005.

Simon Puttock, *Wild-West Winnie,* Macmillan (London, England), 2005.

Frances Thomas, *Little Monster's Book of Numbers,* Bloomsbury (New York, NY), 2005.

Angela McAllister, *Trust Me, Mom!,* Bloomsbury (New York, NY), 2005.

Frances Thomas, *Little Monster's Book of Opposites,* Bloomsbury (New York, NY), 2005.

Nick Place, *The Kazillion Wish,* Scholastic (New York, NY), 2005.

Ann Bryant, *Kimberley's Scary Day,* Franklin Watts (London, England), 2005.

Sue Graves, *Oh, George!,* Sea-to-Sea (Minneapolis, MN), 2006.

Geraldine McCaughrean, *Mo,* Hodder (London, England), 2006.

Vivian French, *The Daddy Goose Collection,* Chicken House (Somerset, England), 2006.

John Grant, *Littlenose the Hero,* Simon & Schuster (London, England), 2006.

John Grant, *Littlenose the Hunter,* Simon & Schuster (London, England), 2006.

John Grant, *Littlenose the Joker,* Simon & Schuster (London, England), 2007.

Tanya Landman, *The World's Bellybutton,* Walker Books (London, England), 2007.

Alan Durant, *Billy Monster's Daymare,* Oxford University Press (Oxford, England), 2007.

Ann Bryant, *Bad Cat, Ned!,* Franklin Watts (London, England), 2007.

Julia Donaldson, *Miss! Miss!,* Oxford University Press (Oxford, England), 2007.

Julia Donaldson, *Gran Is Cross,* Oxford University Press (Oxford, England), 2007.

Julia Donaldson, *Tara's Party,* Oxford University Press (Oxford, England), 2007.

Julia Donaldson, *The Cinderella Play,* Oxford University Press (Oxford, England), 2007.

Tony Bradman and Alison Prince, *Mixed up Madness* (includes *The Two Jacks*), Barrington Stoke (Edinburgh, Scotland), 2007.

Guy Bass, *Monster Boy,* Scholastic (London, England), 2008.

Guy Bass, *Monster Mischief,* Scholastic (London, England), 2008.

Alan Durant, *Cinderella: The Fairytale Files,* Walker Books (London, England), 2008.

John Grant, *Littlenose the Leader,* Simon & Schuster (London, England), 2008.

John Grant, *Littlenose the Magician,* Simon & Schuster (London, England), 2009.

Andy Stanton, *The Story of Matthew Buzzington,* Barrington Stoke (Edinburgh, Scotland), 2009.

Karen Hodgson, *Hugh's Blue Day,* Hogs Back (Guilford, England), 2009.

Damian Harvey, *Eric Bloodaxe, the Viking King,* Franklin Watts (London, England), 2009.

Mij Kelly, *Where Giants Hide,* Hodder Children's (London, England), 2009.

Laura North, *Theseus and the Minotaur,* Franklin Watts (London, England), 2009.

Phyllis Reynolds Naylor, *Emily's Fortune,* Delacorte Press (New York, NY), 2010.

Ann Bryant, *Kimberley's Scary Day,* Black Rabbit Books (Mankato, MN), 2010.

Tom MacRae, *When I Woke up I Was a Hippopotamus,* Andersen Press USA (Minneapolis, MN), 2011.

Contributor of editorial illustrations to periodicals, including *Evening Standard,* London *Sunday Times,* and *Fortean Times.*

ILLUSTRATOR; "S.W.I.T.C.H." CHAPTER-BOOK SERIES

Andy Stanton, *Sterling and the Canary,* Barrington Stoke (Edinburgh, Scotland), 2011.

Ali Sparks, *Grasshopper Glitch,* Oxford University Press (Oxford, England), 2011.

Ali Sparks, *Fly Frenzy,* Oxford University Press (Oxford, England), 2011.

Ali Sparks, *Ant Attack,* Oxford University Press (Oxford, England), 2011.

Ali Sparks, *Beatle Blast,* Oxford University Press (Oxford, England), 2011.

Ali Sparks, *Cranefly Crash,* Oxford University Press (Oxford, England), 2011.

ILLUSTRATOR; "FIVE KINGDOMS" SERIES BY VIVIAN FRENCH

The Robe of Skulls, Walker (London, England), 2007, Candlewick Press (Cambridge, MA), 2008.

Bag of Bones, Walker Books (London, England), 2008.

The Heart of Glass, Walker Books (London, England), 2009, Candlewick Press (Somerville, MA), 2010.

The Flight of Dragons, Candlewick Press (Somerville, MA), 2011.

Sidelights

Ross Collins is an award-winning author and illustrator whose artwork has appeared in dozens of books for young readers. In addition to creating illustrations for stories by a legion of children's authors—Vivian French, Jamie Rix, Tony Bradman, Wendy Cope, Allan Durant, and Julia Donaldson among them—the Scottish-born Collins has also created engaging original picture books such as *The Elephantom, Dear Vampa,* and *Doodleday.* Popular with young audiences, the energetic Collins visits schools throughout the United Kingdom and is a welcome guest at literary festivals and workshops for both children and adults.

"When I was a child the reason I got into illustration . . . was because I had such a love of them," Collins recalled to Glasgow *Herald* contributor Teddy Jamieson. "The story was important but I would pore over the illustrations for a long time. My mother still talks about how she was fascinated by the concentration I would have picking out little details in the illustrations so there's obviously a life there that attracts a child. I try to do the same thing [with my work] now."

In *Alvie Eats Soup,* one of Collins's self-illustrated titles, an extremely finicky eater refuses to dine on anything except soup, despite his exasperated parents' best efforts to change his entrenched habit. The situation becomes critical when Alvie's grandmother, a celebrated

chef, decides to pay a visit. A *Publishers Weekly* contributor praised Collins's depiction of the frazzled family, stating that the author/illustrator "lavishes attention on the angular characters' dramatic gestures, pointy tufts of hair and fashionably rumpled clothes," and a critic in *Kirkus Reviews* deemed *Alvie Eats Soup* "a surefire recipe for chuckles." In *Busy Night,* a humorous fantasy, Collins relates young Ben's encounters with a host of nighttime visitors, including the Sandman, the Tooth Fairy, and the Thing-under-the-Bed. According to *Booklist* critic Julie Cummins, readers of *Busy Night* "will . . . appreciate the matter-of-fact way that Ben dispatches the nighttime interlopers."

A friendly virus decides that it would rather not infect its host in *Germs,* another self-illustrated book by Collins. Although Pox is assigned to make young Myrtle ill, the germ instead devises a plan to help the girl's immune system defeat a swarm of other invading germs. "Collins's imaginative portrayal of the microscopic world involves a giggle-inducing melange of satire and gross-out humor," noted a reviewer in appraising *Germs* for *Publishers Weekly,* and Holly T. Sneeringer observed in *School Library Journal* that a "lively cast of cartoon characters complements the energetic text."

Medusa Jones, an illustrated novel by Collins that is based on Greek mythology, centers on a snake-haired lass who is labeled a freak by the self-proclaimed

Ross Collins' self-illustrated picture books include Medusa Jones, ***which features several mythic creatures.*** (Illustration copyright © 2008 by Ross Collins. Reproduced by permission of Scholastic, Inc.)

Champions at Acropolis Academy. With friends Chiron the centaur and Mino the minotaur, Medusa must ultimately rescue her tormentors during a disastrous class camping trip on Mt. Olympus. Reviewing *Medusa Jones* in *School Library Journal*, Kelly Roth commented that Collins' story is fun and his black-and-white line drawings—many full page—are "expressive and humorous." Debbie Carton, writing in *Booklist,* predicted that the book's "unexpected, creative mix of classical mythology references and contemporary middle-school dialogue" will appeal to readers.

Dear Vampa finds Collins tapping readers' demand for vampire tales while also adding his characteristic sense of fun. The story is narrated in letters by Bram Pire, who writes to his grandfather about the family's upcoming move from Pennsylvania to Transylvania. The move is not by choice, as readers learn, but because their current neighbors have become distressed over the Pires' unusual habits. When readers learn that the new family is named Wolfson, they are quick to join the author/illustrator in his playful play on classic horror fiction. With illustrations that mix comic-book colors with "Edward Gorey-style etchings," *Dear Vampa* features "plenty of hilarious overlaps" between vampire and werewolf culture, according to *Booklist* critic Daniel Kraus, and a *Publishers Weekly* contributor wrote that Collins' "black, angular vampires lace the comedy with a drop of real creepiness."

Out-of-control creativity is the focus of *Doodleday,* as young Harvey is ordered by his mom to absolutely, all-together abstain from drawing for an entire day. The boy loves to draw, however, and when Mom leaves for a trip to the store Harvey is quick to pull out the crayons and paper and draw a scary-looking spider. The boy quickly learns why one should not draw on Doodleday, however: the spider comes to life and quickly throws the family house into chaos. Fortunately, Harvey's mother has had experience with escaped drawings, and her own artistic talent helps Harvey to put things to rights. "Kids will recognize the imaginative play depicted in the illustrations," predicted Rochman in her *Booklist* review, the critic also noting the "shivery drama" in *Doodleday.* The author/illustrator "uses fine lines, perspective and plenty of color" in his imaginative artwork, a *Kirkus Reviews* writer observed, heralding the picture book as "a nifty heir to [Crockett Johnson's childhood classic] *Harold and the Purple Crayon.*" "Collins's . . . illustrative gifts are never in doubt as he romps through the tale of young Harvey," wrote a *Publishers Weekly* contributor, and Maggie Chase enthused in *School Library Journal* that *Doodleday* "is fabulously illustrated and the action quite engaging."

Since beginning his illustration career in the early 1990s, Collins has contributed artwork to dozens of books by other authors. In *One Day, Daddy,* a work by Frances Thomas, a tiny monster ponders a series of space adventures that would take him far away from his parents. "Blasts of color soar across the pages," remarked *School Library Journal* reviewer Carolyn Janssen, "letting the exploration go beyond the margins of the text." A youngster attempts to capture his dreams so he can enjoy them while he is awake in Laurence Anholt's *Jack and the Dreamsack.* According to Heather E. Miller in *School Library Journal,* here Collins' "palette of primarily gentle, bright colors adds to the soothing tone of the narrative." French's "Tales from the Five Kingdoms" books also benefit from Collins' artistic vision, and here the artist's "spidery black-and-white illustrations amplify . . . the tall-tale nature" of French's tale, according to *Booklist* contributor Francisca Goldmith.

Among his many illustration projects, Collins took on Herbie Brennan's *Fairy Nuff: A Tale of Bluebell Wood,* the chronicle of the misadventures of an inept fairy, as well as its sequel, *Nuff Said: Another Tale of Bluebell Wood.* Brennan's over-the-top characters are "perfectly captured by the expressive and funny black-and-white illustrations" for these two books, noted *School Library Journal* contributor Eva Mitnick of the series. "Deadpan caricatures on nearly every page reflect the zaniness of this surreal, loose-jointed farce," a *Kirkus Reviews* contributor wrote about *Nuff Said.*

A youngster's first solo trip to the store is interrupted by a host of creepy creatures in Angela McAllister's *Trust Me, Mom!,* and here "Collins's watercolor-and-acrylic illustrations tap into the story's comic undertones," according to a critic in *Kirkus Reviews.* In *The Three Grumpies,* a story by Tamra Wight, a little girl must deal with a trio of monsters that does its best to ruin her day. "Collins's lumbering, mischievous Grumpies try to steal the watercolor scenes with their antics," a reviewer in *Publishers Weekly* stated.

Noted children's author Phyllis Reynolds Naylor shares a melodramatic story about a young orphan and her trip across the Wild West in *Emily's Fortune.* Here Collins' "scene-stealing pencil sketches" reflect the fun of the story, noted Ian Chipman in *Booklist,* and a *Kirkus Reviews* writer asserted that the artist's "lively line drawings" for *Emily's Fortune* "capture the action" of Naylor's "rollicking" chapter book.

Another illustration project, *When I Woke up I Was a Hippopotamus,* finds Collins teaming up with author Tom MacRae. In this rhyming story, a boy throws his family into chaos when he is transformed into a series of uprising objects, from the titular hippo to a robot, a monkey, and even a space ship. *When I Woke up I Was a Hippopotamus* benefits from "energetic illustrations" that are "laden with emotional expressiveness," according to a *Kirkus Reviews* writer, and a *Publishers Weekly* critic described Collins' contribution as "sprawling, detailed watercolor cartoons that evince a firm but funny hand."

Collins pairs his whimsical storytelling and captivating art in the quirky chapter book **Dear Vampa.** (Copyright © 2009 by Ross Collins. Reproduced by permission of Katherine Tegen Books, an imprint of HarperCollins Publishers.)

Rules are made for a reason, as readers learn in Collins' humorous self-illustrated picture book **Doodleday.** (Illustration copyright © 2011 by Ross Collins. Reproduced with permission of Albert Whitman & Company.)

Biographical and Critical Sources

PERIODICALS

Booklist, July, 1999, John Peters, review of *What If?,* p. 1955; July, 2002, Julie Cummins, review of *Busy Night,* p. 1855; August, 2002, Julie Cummins, review of *Fairy Nuff: A Tale of Bluebell Wood,* p. 1955; November 1, 2002, Michael Cart, review of *Alvie Eats Soup,* p. 505; April 1, 2003, Diane Foote, review of *Jack and the Dreamsack,* p. 1400; December 1, 2007, Debbie Carton, review of *Medusa Jones,* p. 41; Sep-

tember 1, 2008, Francisca Goldsmith, review of *The Robe of Skulls,* p. 100; May 1, 2009, Francisca Goldsmith, review of *The Bag of Bones,* p. 78; June 1, 2009, Daniel Kraus, review of *Dear Vampa,* p. 68; April 15, 2010, Ian Chipman, review of *Emily's Fortune,* p. 59; March 1, 2011, Hazel Rochman, review of *Doodleday,* p. 62.

Guardian (London, England), July 12, 2003, Julia Eccleshare, review of *Jack and the Dreamsack,* p. 33.

Herald (Glasgow, Scotland), June 5, 2007, Teddy Jamieson, "Every Picture Tells a Priceless Story," p. 15.

Horn Book, July-August, 2008, Betty Carter, review of *The Robe of Skulls,* p. 443.

Collins teams up with Vivian French to cast a perilous mood over French's middle-grade novel **The Robe of Skulls.** (Illustration copyright © 2007 by Ross Collins. Reproduced by permission of Candlewick Press, Somerville, MA, on behalf of Walker Books, London.)

Kirkus Reviews, June 1, 2002, review of *Fairy Nuff,* p. 801; September 1, 2002, review of *Alvie Eats Soup,* p. 1306; October 15, 2002, review of *Nuff Said: Another Tale of Bluebell Wood,* p. 1527; September 15, 2003, review of *The Three Grumpies,* p. 1185; October 15, 2004, review of *Germs,* p. 1003; October 15, 2005, review of *Trust Me, Mom!,* p. 1143; December 1, 2007, review of *Medusa Jones;* June 1, 2008, review of *The Robe of Skulls;* June 1, 2009, review of *The Bag of Bones;* July 15, 2009, review of *Dear Vampa;* May 1, 2010, review of *Emily's Fortune,* May 15, 2011, review of *Doodleday;* July 1, 2011, review of *When I Woke up I Was a Hippopotamus.*

New York Times Book Review, March 9, 2003, Sean Kelly, review of *Alvie Eats Soup,* p. 24.

Publishers Weekly, September 25, 2000, review of *The No-Nothings and Their Baby,* p. 116; June 18, 2001, review of *One Day, Daddy,* p. 80; April 29, 2002, review of *Busy Night,* p. 70; October 14, 2002, review of *Alvie Eats Soup,* p. 83; December 8, 2003, review of *The Three Grumpies,* p. 60; December 13, 2004, review of *Germs,* p. 67; April 25, 2005, review of *The Kazillion Wish,* p. 56; January 28, 2008, review of

Medusa Jones, p. 68; July 7, 2008, review of *The Robe of Skulls,* p. 58; July 6, 2009, review of *Dear Vampa,* p. 50; March 21, 2011, review of *Doodleday,* p. 73; July 25, 2011, review of *When I Woke up I Was a Hippopotamus,* p. 53.

School Librarian, winter, 2010, Prue Goodwin, review of *Dear Vampa,* p. 226.

School Library Journal, November, 2000, Karen James, review of *The No-Nothings and Their Baby,* p. 128; September, 2001, Carolyn Janssen, review of *One Day, Daddy,* p. 207; January, 2002, Nancy Menaldi-Scanlan, review of *A Midsummer Night's Dream,* p. 144; August, 2002, Eva Mitnick, review of *Fairy Nuff,* p. 147; October, 2002, Laurie Edwards, review of *Alvie Eats Soup,* p. 99; March, 2003, Shara Alpern, review of *Nuff Said,* p. 178; August, 2003, Heather E. Miller, review of *Jack and the Dreamsack,* p. 122; December, 2003, Faith Brautigam, review of *The Three Grumpies,* p. 130; February, 2005, Holly T. Sneeringer, review of *Germs,* p. 96; July, 2005, Elaine E. Knight, review of *The Kazillion Wish,* p. 81; December, 2005, Robin L. Gibson, review of *Trust Me, Mom!,* p. 118; January, 2008, Kelly Roth, review of *Medusa Jones,* p. 83; December, 2009, Maryann H. Owen, review of *Dear Vampa,* p. 79; January, 2010, Jessica Miller, review of *The Bag of Bones,* p. 100; June, 2010, Michele Shaw, review of *Emily's Fortune,* p. 80; September, 2010, Rachel Kamin, review of *Where Giants Hide,* p. 128; May, 2011, Maggie Chase, review of *Doodleday,* p. 74.

ONLINE

Ross Collins Home Page, http://www.rosscollins.net (February 15, 2012).

Scottish Book Trust Web site, http://www.scottishbooktrust.com/ (March 15, 2009), "Ross Collins."

* * *

COUVILLON, Alice

Personal

Born in LA; daughter of Peter and Gloria Wilbert; married Robert Couvillon; children: four. *Education:* Newcomb College, B.A. (history); Tulane University, M.A.T.

Addresses

Home—Covington, LA.

Career

Educator and author. Social-studies teacher, beginning c. 1990; Mandeville High School, Covington, LA, history teacher, beginning c. 1999, and chair of social-studies department.

Writings

WITH ELIZABETH MOORE

Louisiana Indian Tales, illustrated by Marilyn Rougelot, Pelican Publishing (Gretna, LA), 1990.

Mimi's First Mardi Gras, illustrated by Marilyn Carter Rougelot, Pelican Publishing (Gretna, LA), 1992.

Mimi and Jean-Paul's Cajun Mardi Gras, illustrated by Marilyn Carter Rougelot, Pelican Publishing (Gretna, LA), 1996.

Evangeline for Children, illustrated by Alison Davis Lyne, Pelican Publishing (Gretna, LA), 2002.

Ancient Mounds of Watson Brake: Oldest Earthworks in North America, illustrated by Rick Anderson, Pelican Publishing (Gretna, LA), 2010.

How the Gods Created the Finger People: A Mayan Fable, illustrated by Luz-Maria Lopez, Pelican Publishing (Gretna, LA), 2011.

Sidelights

A native of Louisiana who teaches high-school history, Alice Couvillon also shares the colorful culture of her region in a range of picture books for young readers. As a writer, Couvillon works in collaboration with friend Elizabeth Moore, a college classmate and newspaper columnist who shares her love of local history. In addition to creating a fictional story about Louisiana's earliest residents in *Ancient Mounds of Watson Brake: Oldest Earthworks in North America,* the authors have also retold Henry Wadsworth Longfellow's 1847 poem "Evangeline: A Tale of Acadie," which describes how the region became home to the Cajuns, a group of French-born settlers who were banished from eastern Canada for their refusal to pledge loyalty to the English king. Praising *Evangeline for Children,* which features illustrations by Alison Davis Lyne, *Booklist* contributor Susan Dove Lempke wrote that Couvillon and Moore's "clearly presented text is short enough to be read aloud to young children" and Sheilah Kosco recommended the work as "an essential purchase for Louisiana libraries."

Couvillon grew up in a region where Mardi Gras is a central holiday, and when she experienced the tradition through the eyes of her own children she was inspired to write *Mimi's First Mardi Gras.* Together with a companion book, *Mimi and Jean-Paul's Cajun Mardi Gras,* she again teams with Moore to create a simple story that describes the traditions surrounding the celebration that lasts from Epiphany until the night before Ash Wednesday. When readers meet Mimi she is planning her Mardi Gras costume—she wants to be a princess—and as the pages turn they follow her through a range of holiday events that include eating a surprise-filled piece of King Cake, enjoying the carnival atmosphere, watching the parade, with its horses and floats and the

ultimate arrival of the King of Carnival, and joining her family for a feast that includes Cajun favorites such as seafood gumbo and jambalaya. Noting that New Orleans' Mardi Gras is a "time-honored extravaganza" that will be familiar to many children, a *Publishers Weekly* critic praised *Mimi's First Mardi Gras* as "a pleasing introduction to the holiday."

Couvillon and Moore change their focus in *How the Gods Created the Finger People: A Mayan Family,* which focuses on the Mayan traditions of Honduran artist Luz-Maria Lopez. Their story, a creation tale, was told to Lopez by her grandmother and describes how one of the gods crafted the first humans by cutting the fingers off his left hand and letting them fall to Earth. These "finger people" eventually discover a man of gold, another creation whom the gods had discarded because he was too cold. In an ending that affirms Mayan culture, the finger people wait upon the man of gold in exchange for wages as each lives according to his nature as destined by the gods. "Lopez's striking renderings of Mayan culture, art, and landscape set this picture book apart," asserted C.J. Connor in a *School Library Journal* review of *How the Gods Created the Finger People,* and a *Kirkus Reviews* writer noted that Couvillon and Moore's "bilingual telling . . . presents an authentically Central American blend of folk mythology and social commentary."

Biographical and Critical Sources

PERIODICALS

Booklist, June 1, 2002, Susan Dove Lempke, review of *Evangeline for Children,* p. 1721.

Publishers Weekly, November 22, February 21, 2011, review of *How the Gods Created the Finger People: A Mayan Fable,* p. 131.

School Library Journal, July, 2002, Sheilah Kosco, review of *Evangeline for Children,* p. 86; July, 2010, Patricia Manning, review of *Ancient Mounds of Watson Brake: Oldest Earthworks in North America,* p. 67; June, 2011, C.J. Connor, review of *How the Gods Created the Finger People,* p. 105.

ONLINE

Pelican Publishing Web site, http://www.pelicanpub.com/ (February 15, 2012), "Alice Couvillon."*

D

DAVIES, Stephen 1976-

Personal

Born 1976, in England; married; wife's name Charlotte. *Education:* University of Durham, degree (theology); All Nations Christian College, diploma (Christian missions). *Hobbies and other interests:* Dirt-biking, classical guitar, Web design, watching heist movies.

Addresses

Home—Djibo, Burkina Faso. *Agent*—Julia Churchill, Greenhouse Literary Agency. *E-mail*—steve@voice-inthedesert.org.uk.

Career

Children's author, teacher, and missionary. VSO (developmental organization), London, England, worker in Solomon Islands; former teacher of English in Siberia and Solomon Islands; World Horizons (Christian mission), currently West Africa field leader. Presenter at schools.

Awards, Honors

Glen Dimplex Children's Book Award, 2006, for *Sophie and the Albino Camel.*

Writings

Sophie and the Albino Camel (chapter book), Andersen Press (London, England), 2006.

Sophie and the Locust Curse (chapter book), Andersen Press (London, England), 2007.

The Yellowcake Conspiracy, Andersen Press (London, England), 2007.

Sophie and the Pancake Plot (chapter book), Andersen Press (London, England), 2008.

Hacking Timbuktu, Andersen Press (London, England), 2009, Clarion Books (Boston, MA), 2010.

Stephen Davies (Reproduced by permission.)

Outlaw, Clarion Books (New York, NY), 2011.

The Goggle-Eyed Goats (picture book), illustrated by Christopher Corr, Andersen Press (London, England), 2012.

Don't Spill the Milk (picture book), illustrated by Chrstopher Corr, Andersen Press (London, England), 2012.

Contributor to periodicals, including *Africa Geographic, Cricket, Guardian Weekly,* and London *Sunday Times.* Author of radio drama for broadcast in Burkina Faso.

Author's work has been translated into several languages, including Chinese, Dutch, French, German, Italian, and Turkish.

Biographical and Critical Sources

PERIODICALS

Booklist, November 1, 2010, Connie Fletcher, review of *Hacking Timbuktu,* p. 64.
Kirkus Reviews, October 15, 2010, review of *Hacking Timbuktu.*
Publishers Weekly, October 25, 2010, review of *Hacking Timbuktu,* p. 50.
School Librarian, spring, 2010, Susan Elkin, review of *Hacking Timbuktu,* p. 47.

ONLINE

Stephen Davies Home Page, http://www.voiceinthedesert. org.uk (February 15, 2012).
Telegraph Online (London, England), http://www. telegraph.co.uk/ (October 15, 2010), Leah Hyslop, "Stephen-Davies: 'When I Got to Africa, It Felt like Coming Home.'"

*   *   *

DELANY, Shannon

Personal

Born October 18; married; has children. *Education:* Kutztown University, degree (secondary social-studies education). *Hobbies and other interests:* Travel, foreign languages.

Addresses

Home—Upstate NY. *Agent*—Richard Curtis Associates, Inc., 171 E. 74th St., Fl. 2, New York, NY 10021. *E-mail*—info@ShannonDelany.com.

Career

Author and farmer. Formerly worked as a teacher; raises heritage livestock.

Awards, Honors

Textnovel Grand Prize, 2008, for "13 to Life."

Writings

"13 TO LIFE" PARANORMAL NOVEL SERIES

13 to Life, St. Martin's Griffin (New York, NY), 2010.
Secrets and Shadows, St. Martin's Griffin (New York, NY), 2011.
Bargains and Betrayals, St. Martin's Griffin (New York, NY), 2011.

Destiny and Deception, St. Martin's Griffin (New York, NY), 2012.
Rivals and Retributions, St. Martin's Griffin (New York, NY), 2012.

Author's work has been translated into several languages, including French, German, Hungarian, Portuguese, and Turkish.

OTHER

Contributor of short fiction to anthologies, including *Spirited: Thirteen Haunting Tales,* Leap Books, 2012.

Sidelights

A former teacher who now farms at her home in upstate New York, Shannon Delany tapped into modern technology along her way to becoming a published novelist. Delany first started writing seriously as a preteen while she dealt with the illness of a favorite grandmother. Years later, in 2008, she entered a contest held by Textnovel.com, for the best work of 50,000-word serialized fiction to be composed entirely of e-mails or text messages. It took five weeks to compose the winning entry, but Delany spent much longer after St. Martin's Press agreed to publish a series based on her characters. In addition to enriching her "13 to Life" saga with subplots, she also expanded the story's Russian elements. Beginning with 2010's *13 to Life,* the series includes *Bargains and Betrayals, Secrets and Shadows, Destiny and Deception,* and the concluding volume, *Rivals and Retributions.*

13 to Life transports readers to Junction, a small, rural town where high-school junior Jess Gillmansen is mourning the recent death of her mom. When the Russian Rusakova family moves to town, Jess is assigned by school authorities to show new student Pietr Rusakova around the school. Jess and Pietr quickly hit it off, but she derails the budding romance out of respect for her emotionally fragile best friend Sarah, who is attracted to the mysterious new student. The friendship grows stronger anyway, turning into love after Pietr confides a terrible secret: he and his three siblings are actually werewolves and his parents are missing and presumed murdered. As a range of powerful forces invades her formerly quiet town—including visits from C.I.A. operatives and members of the Russian mob—Jess allies herself with Pietr and the Rusakova clan, all the while juggling friends, schoolwork, and family issues.

"Delany spins an original story with great characters and a powerful plot," noted Donna Rosenblum in her review of *13 to Life* for *School Library Journal.* While Cindy Welch predicted in *Booklist* that "teen girls will eat up the *Twilight* flavor" of Delany's debut, a *Publishers Weekly* contributor wrote that the paranormal storyline contains a meaningful subtext involving "emotionally wounded teens." "Secret matroyshka dolls, and

Cover of Shannon Delaney's teen paranormal mystery Secrets and Shadows, *part of her "13 to Life" series.* (Cover images © Paul White/Alamy (train tracks), Chelsea Kedron/Getty Images (eyes), Rob Wood (running couple). Used with permission of St. Martin's Press.)

hot werewolves riding ATVs reveal Delany's talent for creativity," asserted Ann Crewdson in her review of *13 to Life* for *Voice of Youth Advocates,* and she "wittedly makes a parody of vampire novels" in her high-adventure saga.

Jess and Pietr return in *Secrets and Shadows,* as forces are arrayed to capture the lycanthropic Rusakova siblings. Although Jess may provide the key to Pietr's unfortunate condition, their relationship stays in the shadows because Sarah still relies on him as a boyfriend and Jess is still officially dating handsome jock Derek. Max and adopted brother Alexei Rusakova also begin to build friendships within their new town, as does beautiful sister Cat. "Passion . . . plays a big role" in *Secrets and Shadows,* observed *Voice of Youth Advocates* contributor Debbie Wenk, and Welch asserted that romantic themes combine with a "sense of impending disaster [to] sharpen" the novel's plot. Sharon Senser wrote in *School Library Journal* that Delany's second "13 to Life" novel "ends with a suspenseful bang" that will leave readers "wanting more."

The "13 to Life" series continues in *Bargains and Betrayals* as threats against Jess mount and supposed friends are not what they seem. Meanwhile, Pietr continues to keep secrets, including one regarding a deal he has struck to save his kidnapped mother. Although the Russian mob has departed and Pietr's mother has returned, the Rusakova family will face an even-more-forbidding foe in *Destiny and Deception,* and this time it is Alexei who must determine the family's fate. Recommending that readers start with the first volume of the series, Welch noted of *Bargains and Betrayals* that the adventure continues "unabated," making the novel "another rousing foray into the fantastic from Delany."

Biographical and Critical Sources

PERIODICALS

Booklist, June 1, 2010, Cindy Welch, review of *13 to Life,* p. 58; February 15, 2011, Cindy Welch, review of *Secrets and Shadows,* p. 76; July 1, 2011, Cindy Welch, review of *Bargains and Betrayals,* p. 58.

Kirkus Reviews, June 1, 2011, review of *Bargains and Betrayals.*

Publishers Weekly, July 12, 2010, review of *13 to Life,* p. 48.

School Library Journal, October, 2010, Donna Rosenblum, review of *13 to Life,* p. 112; May, 2010, Sharon Senser, review of *Secrets and Shadows,* p. 110.

Voice of Youth Advocates, August, 2010, Ann Crewdson, review of *13 to Life,* p. 263; February, 2011, Debbie Wenk, review of *Secrets and Shadows,* p. 568; April, 2011, Rebecca C. Moore, "Winning the Writing Olympics," p. 28.

ONLINE

Shannon Delany Home Page, http://www.shannondelany.com (February 12, 2012).

YA Bookshelf Web site, http://www.yabookshelf.com/ (May, 2011), interview with Delany.

*　　*　　*

DESPAIN, Bree 1979-

Personal

Born 1979; married; children: two sons. *Education:* Brigham Young University, B.A. (creative writing). *Hobbies and other interests:* Kayaking, Indie music, reading.

Addresses

Home—Salt Lake City, UT. *Agent*—Ted Malawer, Upstart Crow Literary, P.O. Box 25404, Brooklyn, NY 11202; ted@upstartcrowliterary.com.

Career

Novelist. Formerly worked in inner-city youth theatre. Presenter at schools and conferences.

Writings

"DARK DEVINE" NOVEL SERIES

The Dark Divine, Egmont USA (New York, NY), 2010.
The Lost Saint, Egmont USA (New York, NY), 2011.
The Savage Grace, Egmont USA (New York, NY), 2012.

Short fiction included in anthologies *A Visitor's Guide to Mystic Falls,* Smart Pop, 2010, and *The Girl Who Was on Fire,* edited by Leah Wilson, Smart Pop, 2012.

Adaptations

The Dark Divine was optioned for film by 1019 Entertainment, 2010.

Sidelights

Although Bree Despain enjoyed writing stories as a girl, it was not until years later, after she was seriously injured in a frightening automobile accident, that she

Cover of Bree Despain's The Lost Saint, *part of her "Dark Devine" paranormal romance series.* (Jacket photography courtesy of Jose Torralba/Getty Images. Reproduced with permission of Egmont USA.)

realized that it was time to pursue one of her life dreams and complete a novel. Supplied with a laptop computer courtesy of her supportive husband, Despain started typing while recovering from her injuries, and she got the phone call announcing the publication of her debut young-adult novel *The Dark Divine* six years to the day that she met her writing muse in the form of an oncoming pickup truck.

Sixteen-year-old Grace Divine is the appropriately named daughter of a pastor when readers meet her in *The Dark Divine.* Despite the teasing from schoolmates due to her straightlaced upbringing, Grace shares the values of her family, which has taken in a young orphan named Daniel Kalbi to raise. Although Daniel eventually leaves after a presumed altercation with Grace's brother Jude, he returns three years later and it is now clear that he and Grace have feelings for one another. It is also clear that Daniel's problems are more than spiritual—he is a werewolf—and Grace's father does what he can to search for a cure for the teen. Jealous over the attention given to Daniel, Jude decides to tap the same transformational power, resulting in a novel that "raises complex issues of responsibility and forgiveness and offers no easy answers," according to *Booklist* critic Debbie Carton. In *School Library Journal* Amy S. Pattee noted Despain's ability to craft a compelling romance within her supernatural storyline. While not classified as "Christian fiction," according to Pattee, *The Dark Divine* features a focus on "faith and sacrifice [that] distinguishes it from traditional supernatural romances."

Grace and Daniel's story continues to play out in both *The Lost Saint* and *The Savage Grace,* as the teen saves her beloved by sacrificing herself. As Grace is pulled deeper and deeper into the supernatural horror, her family continues to disintegrate following Jude's disappearance. Then she meets Talbot, who offers his help, but as their friendship grows so does Grace's wolven side until events align to present the teen lovers with their definitive challenge. "With fight scenes galore," *The Lost Saint* "is far more focused on action" than *The Dark Divine,* noted Carton in *Booklist,* and Pattee wrote in *School Library Journal* that "Grace's passion to save her brother . . . leads her to defy those closest to her."

Biographical and Critical Sources

PERIODICALS

Booklist, January 1, 2010, Debbie Carton, review of *The Dark Divine,* p. 60; February 15, 2011, Debbie Carton, review of *The Lost Saint,* p. 76.
Bulletin of the Center for Children's Books, February, 2010, Kate Quealy-Gainer, review of *The Dark Divine,* p. 243.
Kirkus Reviews, November 15, 2010, review of *The Lost Saint.*

School Librarian, winter, 2010, Chris Brown, review of *The Dark Divine,* p. 249.

School Library Journal, May, 2010, Amy S. Pattee, review of *The Dark Divine,* p. 110; February, 2011, Amy S. Pattee, review of *The Lost Saint,* p. 106.

Voice of Youth Advocates, February, 2011, review of *The Lost Saint,* p. 568.

ONLINE

Bree Despain Home Page, http://www.breedespain.com (February 15, 2012).

Bree Despain Web log, http://breebiesingerdespain. blogspot.com (February 15, 2012).*

* * *

DEUTSCH, Barry

Personal

Male. *Religion:* Jewish.

Addresses

Home—Portland, OR. *E-mail*—barry.deutsch@gmail. com.

Career

Cartoonist. Presenter at schools and conferences.

Awards, Honors

Sydney Taylor Award, Association of Jewish Librarians, c. 2010, and Andre Norton Award shortlist, Science Fiction & Fantasy Association, both for *Hereville.*

Writings

Hereville: How Mirka Got Her Sword, Amulet Books (New York, NY), 2010.

Contributor of cartoons to periodicals, including *Dollars and Sense.*

Sidelights

Based in Portland, Oregon, cartoonist Barry Deutsch specialized in creating political cartoons for a variety of online and print publications before turning to a younger audience in his graphic novel *Hereville: How Mirka Got Her Sword.* With its unusual heroine—an eleven-year-old Orthodox Jewish girl who slays dragons—*Hereville* earned Deutsch increasing recognition when it was shortlisted for the Andre Norton Award for fantasy literature. The book also became the first graphic novel to earn the Sydney Taylor Book Award from the Association of Jewish Librarians.

"I've always loved reading and writing about tough girls, and I've always written fantasy," Deutsch explained to Tehani Wessely in an interview for the Science Fiction and Fantasy Authors Web site. Inspired by reading *Holy Days,* Liz Harris's chronicle of the traditions of the modern Hasidic family, the cartoonist also tapped the possibilities of writing about a Jewish fighter in the middle ages, when swords were forbidden to members of that faith. When he learned that *Girlamatic.com* was looking for girl-power comic strips, he melded these ideas with fantasy elements and the traditional themes of Jewish tales, which find intelligence ultimately winning out over might. His Web comic "Hereville" was released in 2008, and then privately printed by Deutsch before being published in book form by New York City publisher Harry Abrams.

Mirka Hershberg, the Hasidic heroine of *Hereville,* lives with her three siblings and her kind and witty step-mother in a town that is predominately Jewish. While she works on household tasks, such as knitting for the family, the preteen dreams of fighting dragons, but there

Barry Deutsch mixes Jewish history and fantasy in his imaginative self-illustrated graphic novel **Hereville: How Mirka Got Her Sword.**
(Illustration copyright © 2010 by Barry Deutsch. Reproduced by permission of Amulet Books, an imprint of Abrams.)

are no swords to be had in Hereville. Fighting dragons is more practical than readers might imagine, however; Mirka's hometown is surrounded by a deep forest where six-armed trolls, dragons, and witches dwell and talking pigs accost the girl while walking along the street. Sprinkled with Yiddish and Hebrew expressions, as well as information about Jewish holidays and Orthodox culture, Deutsch's fanciful story follows Mirka as she makes the acquaintance of a witch who inspires her to undertake a quest for a sword. Along the way, the girl's quick wit proves to be her most valuable weapon.

In *Hereville* "Deutsch creates a beautiful, detail-rich world," wrote a *Kirkus Reviews* writer, the critic adding that the cartoonist "masterfully blends faith and fantasy with astounding harmony." "Mirka is a spunky, emotionally realistic, and fun heroine for her peers to discover," asserted Francisca Goldsmith in her *Booklist* review of *Hereville,* and a *Publishers Weekly* critic wrote that Deutsch's "expressive, surprising drawings" in the graphic novel "give life to Mirka's quest" while also highlighting "the unusual and genuine relationships she has with family members and magical creatures." *Hereville* "is unique, laugh-out-loud funny, and thoroughly engrossing," wrote *Horn Book* critic Tanya D. Auger, and Barbara M. Moon concluded in her review of *Hereville* for *School Library Journal* that the mix of "engaging characters and delightful art" make Deutsch's illustrated story "pure enchantment."

Biographical and Critical Sources

PERIODICALS

Booklist, October 15, 2010, Francisca Goldsmith, review of *Hereville: How Mirka Got Her Sword,* p. 41.
Horn Book, November-December, 2010, Tanya D. Auger, review of *Hereville,* p. 89.
Kirkus Reviews, October 15, 2010, review of *Hereville.*
Publishers Weekly, August 2, 2010, review of *Hereville,* p. 48.
School Library Journal, November, 2010, Barbara M. Moon, review of *Hereville,* p. 144.

ONLINE

Barry Deutsch Home Page, http://www.amptoons.com (February 12, 2012).
Barry Deutsch Web log, http://amptoons.com/debate (February 12, 2012).
Graphic Novel Reporter Online, http://www.graphicnovel reporter.com/ (October 15, 2011), John Hogan, interview with Deutsch.
Hereville Web site, http://www.hereville.com (February 15, 2012).
Science Fiction and Fantasy Writers of America Web site, http://www.sfwa.org/ (November, 2011), Tehanin Wessely, interview with Deutsch.*

DODD, Emma 1969-

Personal

Born June 7, 1969, in Guilford, Surrey, England; daughter of Robert Dodd and Fay Hillier; married; children: one son, one daughter. *Education:* Attended Kingston Polytechnic; Central Saint Martin's College of Art and Design, degree (graphic design and illustration), 1992. *Hobbies and other interests:* Walking, surfing.

Addresses

Home—Surrey, England.

Career

Author and illustrator. Worked as a editorial illustrator and graphic designer for advertising clients. Presenter at festivals.

Awards, Honors

Booktrust Early Years Award nomination, 2006, for *What Pet to Get,* and 2009, for *Miaow said the Cow;* (with Giles Andreae) Booktrust Early Years Award for Best Book for Babies, 2010, for *I Love My Mummy;* Kate Greenaway Medal nomination, 2010, for *I Love Bugs.*

Writings

SELF-ILLUSTRATED

ABC Dog: A Silly Story about the Alphabet, Prospero (London, England), 2000, published as *Dog's ABC: A Silly Story about the Alphabet,* Puffin (London, England), 2003.
Dog's Colorful Day: A Messy Story about Colors and Counting, Dutton (New York, NY), 2001.
Yellow, Blue, and Bunny Too!, Templar (Dorking, England), 2001.
Hot Dog, Cool Cat: A Crazy Criss-Cross Book of Opposites, Dutton (New York, NY), 2003.
No Place like Home: A Crazy Criss-Cross Book of Animal Mix-Ups, Dutton (New York, NY), 2003.
Dog's Noisy Day: A Story to Read Aloud, Dutton (New York, NY), 2003.
Dog's Birthday: A Touch and Feel Book, Dutton (New York, NY), 2004.
What Pet to Get?, Templar (Dorking, England), 2006, Arthur A. Levine Books (New York, NY), 2008.
When . . ., Templar (Dorking, England), 2007, published as *Just like You,* Dutton (New York, NY), 2008.
Sometimes . . ., Templar (Dorking, England), 2007, published as *No Matter What,* Dutton (New York, NY), 2008.
I Thought I Saw a Dinosaur!, Templar (Dorking, England), 2007.

Nee-naw! (sound board book), Ladybird (London, England), 2009.

Miaow Said the Cow, Templar (Dorking, England), 2009, published as *Meow Said the Cow,* Arthur A. Levine Books (New York, NY), 2011.

Dot and Dash Learn to Share (touch-and-feel board book), Scholastic (London, England), 2009, Cartwheel Books (New York, NY), 2011.

I Don't Want a Posh Dog!, Little, Brown (Boston, MA), 2009.

I Don't Want a Cool Cat!, Orchard (London, England), 2009, Little, Brown (New York, NY), 2010.

I Love Bugs!, Holiday House (New York, NY), 2010.

Foxy, HarperCollins (New York, NY), 2012.

ILLUSTRATOR

Andrew Montgomery, *The Boy Who Wanted to Sing,* Hazar (London, England), 1993.

Kimberley Parr, *The Donkey's First Christmas,* Dempsey Parr (Bristol, England), 1998.

Hannah Reidy, *What Do You Like to Wear?,* Zero to Ten (New York, NY), 1999, published as *All Sorts of Clothes,* Zero to Ten (Slough, England), 1999.

Hannah Reidy, *What Noises Can You Hear?,* Zero to Ten (New York, NY), 1999, published as *All Sorts of Noises,* Zero to Ten (Slough, England), 1999.

Hannah Reidy, *What Does It Look Like?,* Zero to Ten (New York, NY), 1999, published as *All Sorts of Shapes,* Zero to Ten (Slough, England), 1999.

Hannah Reidy, *How Many Can You See?,* Zero to Ten (New York, NY), 1999, published as *All Sorts of Numbers,* Zero to Ten (Slough, England), 1999.

Fiona Patchett, *Spreadsheets Using Microsoft Excel 97 or Microsoft Office 97,* Usborne (London, England), 2000.

Fiona Patchett, *Spreadsheets Using Microsoft Excel 2000 or Microsoft Office 2000,* Usborne (London, England), 2000.

Mandy Ross, *Builder Bill,* Ladybird (London, England), 2001.

Sue Harris, *Big, Small, Little Red Ball,* Templar (Dorking, England), 2001.

Mandy Ross, *Truckdriver Tom,* Ladybird (London, England), 2002.

Mandy Ross, *Teacher Tina,* Ladybird (London, England), 2002.

Mandy Ross, *Doctor Daisy,* Ladybird (London, England), 2002.

Ronne Randall, *Farmer Fred,* Ladybird (London, England), 2002.

(With others) Lesley Sims, *A Visitor's Guide to the Ancient World* (contains *A Visitor's Guide to Ancient Greece, A Visitor's Guide to Ancient Egypt,* and *A Visitor's Guide to Ancient Rome*), Usborne (London, England), 2003.

Anna Nilsen, *My Best Friends,* Zero to Ten (London, England), 2003.

Richard Dungworth, *When I Start School,* Ladybird (London, England), 2003.

Ronne Randall, reteller, *Little Red Riding Hood* ("touch-and-feel" board book), Ladybird (London, England), 2004.

Ronne Randall, reteller, *Jack and the Beanstalk* ("touch-and-feel" board book), Ladybird (London, England), 2004.

Ronne Randall, reteller, *The Three Little Pigs* ("touch-and-feel" board book), Ladybird (London, England), 2004.

Ronne Randall, reteller, *The Enormous Turnip* ("touch-and-feel" board book), Ladybird (London, England), 2004.

Anna Nilsen, *My Best Dad,* Zero to Ten (London, England), 2004.

Anna Nilsen, *My Best Mum,* Zero to Ten (London, England), 2005.

Melanie Joyce, *My School Pet,* Ladybird (London, England), 2005.

(With Mike Jolley) Beth Harwood, *Picture Pairs!,* Amazing Baby (Dorking, England), 2005.

(With Mike Jolley) Beth Harwood, *Lost and Found!,* Amazing Baby (Dorking, England), 2005.

Janet Slingsby, *Hetty's 100 Hats,* Good Books (Intercourse, PA), 2005.

Baby Face! (board book), Amazing Baby (Dorking, England), 2010.

Black and White! (board book), Amazing Baby (Dorking, England), 2010.

Move It! (board book), Amazing Baby (Dorking, England), 2010.

Baa Baa Black Sheep! (board book), Amazing Baby (Dorking, England), 2010.

Giles Andreae, *I Love My Mommy,* Disney Hyperion Books, 2011 (New York, NY), 2010.

Louise Borden, *Big Brothers Don't Take Naps,* Margaret K. McElderry Books (New York, NY), 2011.

I Am Small, Scholastic (New York, NY), 2011.

Giles Andreae, *I Love My Daddy,* Disney Hyperion Books (New York, NY), 2012.

Contributor to periodicals, including London *Guardian, Observer, She,* and *Sunday Express.*

ILLUSTRATOR; "CHARLIE AND BANDIT" GRAPHIC-NOVEL SERIES

K.A. Gerrard, *A Roman Rescue,* Templar (Dorking, England), 2011.

K.A. Gerrard, *An Egyptian Escape,* Templar (Dorking, England), 2012.

Sidelights

British author and illustrator Emma Dodd has created numerous books for young children, with preschoolers winning her special attention. Although she started her career creating artwork for others, Dodd has also illustrated several original stories, among them *Dog's Colorful Day: A Messy Story about Colors and Counting* and its toddler-friendly companion concept books as well as *What Pet to Get? Just like You, Meow Said the Cow,* and *I Am Small.* As an illustrator, her brightly colored, cartoon-style images have been praised for their

sophistication in bringing to life text by writers such as Ronne Randal, Louise Borden, Mandy Ross, Anna Nilsen, and Giles Andreae, and she has also created the sequential artwork for K.A. Gerrard's time-slip graphic novels *A Roman Rescue* and *An Egyptian Escape.*

Raised in London by parents who were trained designers, Dodd knew that she would be an artist from an early age. After earning a degree in graphic design at London's Central Saint Martin's School of Art, she worked in advertising and editorial art as well as making her first appearance in publishing in 1993, with the artwork for Andrew Montgomery's *The Boy Who Wanted to Sing.*

First appearing in 2001, Dodd's self-illustrated *Dog's Colorful Day* features a large canine that is blessed with one prominent patch of black fur on his left ear. As the day progresses, a series of other stains appear on Dog's fur, including a blob of melted brown chocolate, smears of red jam, and a blob of blue paint. By evening, Dog sports a multicolored pattern of spots, but a bubble bath soon restores the pup to his original one-spot condition. Authored and illustrated by Dodd, *Dog's Colorful Day* earned warm reviews from critics. "Dog's zaftig physique and wide-eyed good humor are doggone charming," maintained a *Publishers Weekly* critic, while in *School Library Journal* Beth Tegart described *Dog's Colorful Day* as "a charming story" complimented by "vibrant, snappy, and exciting" artwork.

Dodd features this same canine in several other books, including *Dog's ABC: A Silly Story about the Alphabet* and *Dog's Noisy Day: A Story to Read Aloud.* Originally appearing in England as *ABC Dog: A Silly Story about the Alphabet, Dog's ABC* offers young children learning the alphabet a story about the activities of the playful Dog. An apple falling from a tree hits the pup on the head and begins a chain of events that leads Dog around the yard and inside the house. *Dog's Noisy Day* follows Dog to a neighbor's farm as he tries to imitate the sounds of the barnyard animals, including a rooster, sheep, and cow.

Writing in *Booklist,* Ellen Mandel expressed the view that *Dog's ABC* would be well suited to children learning the sounds of the alphabet because "much deliberate thought and humor underlie this deceptively simple, totally winning presentation." Similar positive reviews accompanied *Dog's Noisy Day.* Here Dog's "enthusiasm bounds off the pages," remarked *Booklist* critic Julie Cummins. Alison Grant focused on Dodd's artwork in her *School Library Journal* review, praising the same book's "vivid colors" as well as the "wonderfully expressive" characters. A *Kirkus Reviews* critic predicted that young audiences would enjoy *Dog's Noisy Day,* dubbing the work "a merry cacophony that welcomes young listeners to become active participants."

Several of Dodd's illustrated stories highlight the special relationship connecting parent and child. Appearing first in England under the title *When . . ., Just like You*

Emma Dodd focuses on a child's search for the perfect pet in her self-illustrated picture book **I Don't Want a Cool Cat!** (Illustration copyright © 2009 by Emma Dodd. Reproduced with permission of Little, Brown & Company, a division of Hachette Book Group, Inc.)

shows the interaction between a baby bear and his mother as the young cub dreams about what he will grow up to be like. In *No Matter What*—published in England as *Sometimes . . .*—a mother elephant offers her young child special reassurance that, no matter the circumstances, her love will endure. In her *School Library Journal* review, Catherine Threadgill deemed *Just like You* a "warm, honest tribute" to the bond between a mother and child that "is almost flawless in its execution," while *Booklist* critic Shelle Rosenfeld heralded Dodd's "comforting, sweet little book" as one in which the artist's "moving pictures use color and composition with fresh creativity."

After being allowed to choose a pet of his own in *What Pet to Get?,* a young boy named Jack considers the many possibilities available to him. In response to each of his suggestions—such as an elephant, rhinoceros, and crocodile—Jack's mother sensibly reflects on the consequences of such an exotic creature. By book's end, Jack and his mother agree to get a pet puppy, but each has a different idea about how large that puppy should be. "Funny foreshadowing and clever visual details abound," remarked a critic in *Kirkus Reviews.* A *Publishers Weekly* contributor found great promise in Dodd's illustrations for *What Pet to Get?,* noting that her "daffy, winning cast of googly-eyed creatures" offer young readers "lots of fun" with each turn of the page.

I Don't Want a Posh Dog! and *I Don't Want a Cool Cat!* focus on children of the most determined sort. In the first book, a little girl rejects her mother's suggestion about getting a status pup and instead makes a search among dogs from small to large and of all colors in order to find the pet that is just right for her. An equally discriminating cat lover is the star of *I Don't Want a Cool Cat!*, as the looks and personality of a range of kitties are appraised in a little girl's search for the perfect feline to share her home.

Praising *I Don't Want a Posh Dog!* as an effective book for group sharing, a *Kirkus Reviews* writer added that its "large images with broad, black outlines . . . draw readers' eyes to the almost-tactile surfaces" of Dodd's artwork. "The rhymes are clever and succinct," noted

Booklist contributor Daniel Kraus, the critic calling *I Don't Want a Posh Dog!* "a fun, light introduction to all the mutts in young readers' futures." Citing the "pithy text" in *I Don't Want a Cool Cat!*, Ilene Cooper added in the same periodical that the author/artist multimedia illustrations "have a three-dimensional feel" that makes them effective in group story hours. "Pedigree and distinction cannot measure up to affection," asserted Kara Schaff Dean in her *School Library Journal* review of the same book, the critic adding that *I Don't Want a Cool Cat!* playfully poses a range of alternatives "for cat connoisseurs" as well as "emerging readers who like to have fun with sound and words."

Nominated for the prestigious Kate Greenaway Award, *I Love Bugs!* allows readers to follow along with a young naturalist as he brings his picnic lunch out into his backyard ecosystem and attracts the wealth of insects that call it home. Here Dodd uses "punchy adjectives . . . to describe the plethora of up-close critters that festoon the pages," according to a *Kirkus Reviews* contributor, and her energetic text pairs well with her black-edged graphic art. *I Love Bugs!* "juggles sounds and rhymes skillfully," wrote Carolyn Phelan in her *Booklist* review, and the "cartoon-style eyes" that appear on every pill bug, wasp, centipede, and spider "give individual critters personality." "This lively, sound-filled selection will make . . . storytimes buzz," predicted Maryann H. Owen in her positive appraisal of *I Love Bugs!* for *School Library Journal*.

Biographical and Critical Sources

PERIODICALS

Booklist, February 15, 2001, Connie Fletcher, review of *Dog's Colorful Day: A Messy Story about Colors and Counting,* p. 1140; February 1, 2002, review of *Dog's ABC: A Silly Story about the Alphabet,* p. 945; February 15, 2003, Julie Cummins, review of *Dog's Noisy Day: A Story to Read Aloud,* p. 1073; April 1, 2005, Jennifer Mattson, review of *All Sorts of Clothes,* p. 1370; March 1, 2008, Julie Cummins, review of *What Pet to Get?,* p. 74; April 1, 2008, Shelle Rosenfeld, review of *No Matter What,* p. 56; April 15, 2009, Daniel Kraus, review of *I Don't Want a Posh Dog!,* p. 47; March 15, 2010, Carolyn Phelan, review of *I Love Bugs!,* p. 47; June 1, 2010, Ilene Cooper, review of *I Don't Want a Cool Cat!,* p. 69; June 1, 2011, Angela Leeper, review of *Big Brothers Don't Take Naps,* p. 90.

Guardian (London, England), March 22, 2008, Julia Eccleshare, review of *I Don't Want a Posh Dog!,* p. 22; April 23, 2011, Julia Eccleshare, review of *I Love My Daddy,* p. 14.

Kirkus Reviews, November 1, 2001, review of *Dog's ABC,* p. 1547; December 15, 2002, review of *Dog's Noisy Day,* p. 1848; June 15, 2005, review of *Hetty's 100 Hats,* p. 691; January 1, 2008, review of *Just like You;* February 15, 2008, review of *What Pet to Get?;* September 1, 2008, review of *Best Bear;* December 15, 2008, review of *Rainbow Fun!;* May 1, 2009, review of *I Don't Want a Posh Dog!;* February 15, 2010, review of *I Love Bugs!;* July 15, 2010, review of *I Don't Want a Cool Cat!;* April 1, 2011, review of *I Love My Mommy;* May 1, 2011, review of *Meow Said the Cow;* May 15, 2011, review of *Big Brothers Don't Take Naps;* August 15, 2011, review of *I Am Small.*

Publishers Weekly, January 15, 2001, review of *Dog's Colorful Day,* p. 74; February 11, 2008, reviews of *Just like You, No Matter What,* and *What Pet to Get?,* all p. 68; June 8, 2009, review of *I Don't Want a Posh Dog!,* p. 42; February 15, 2010, review of *I Love Bugs!,* p. 127; December 13, 2010, review of *I Love My Mommy,* p. 55; April 4, 2011, review of *Meow Said the Cow,* p. 51; April 18, 2011, review of *Big Brothers Don't Take Naps,* p. 50; July 25, 2011, review of *I Am Small,* p. 49.

School Librarian, summer, 2010, Prue Goodwin, review of *A Roman Rescue,* p. 100.

School Library Journal, March, 2001, Beth Tegart, review of *Dog's Colorful Day,* p. 205; February, 2002, Cathie E. Bashaw, review of *Dog's ABC,* p. 98; March, 2003, Alison Grant, review of *Dog's Noisy Day,* p. 191; January, 2004, Shelley B. Sutherland, review of *My Best Friends,* p. 102; June, 2005, Gloria Koster, review of *All Sorts of Noises,* p. 124; August, 2005, Linda Ludke, review of *Hetty's 100 Hats,* p. 106; February, 2008, Linda Staskus, review of *No Matter What,* p. 84, and Joan Kindig, review of *What Pet to Get?,* p. 160; April, 2008, Catherine Threadgill, review of *Just like You,* p. 106; December, 2008, Catherine Callegari, review of *Best Bear,* p. 86; June, 2009, Mary Elam, review of *I Don't Want a Posh Dog!,* p. 84; June, 2010, Maryann H. Owen, review of *I Love Bugs!,* p. 68; July, 2010, Kara Schaff Dean, review of *I Don't Want a Cool Cat!,* p. 58; March, 2011, Judith Constantinides, review of *I Love My Mommy,* p. 116; May, 2011, Maryann H. Owen, review of *Big Brothers Don't Take Naps,* p. 72; July, 2011, Marge Loch-Wouters, review of *Meow Said the Cow,* p. 64.

ONLINE

Simon & Schuster Web site, http://authors.simonandschuster.com/ (February 15, 2012), "Emma Dodd."*

F-G

FEINSTEIN, John 1956-

Personal

Surname pronounced "Fine-steen"; born July 28, 1956, in New York, NY; son of Martin (an opera director) and Berwile (a college professor) Feinstein; married; wife's name Mary Clare; children: Daniel. *Education:* Duke University, B.A., 1977 (one source says 1978). *Politics:* Democrat. *Religion:* Jewish.

Addresses

Home—Potomac, MD; Shelter Island, NY.

Career

Sports journalist and novelist. *Washington Post,* Washington, DC, sportswriter, 1977-88, 1992—; special contributor to *Sports Illustrated,* 1988-90; sportswriter for *National Sports Daily,* 1990-91; contributor to America Online, 2000—, *Golf Digest,* 2003—, and *Golf World,* 2003—. Commentator for National Public Radio's "Morning Edition," 1988—, Sporting News Radio, 1992—, and ESPN. Visiting professor of journalism at Duke University.

Member

U.S. Basketball Writer's Association, U.S. Tennis Writer's Association (vice president), National Sportscasters and Sportswriters Association, Newspaper Guild.

Awards, Honors

Awards from U.S. Basketball Writer's Association, 1981, 1982, 1983, 1984, 1985; Best Sports Stories Award, National Sportscasters and Sportswriters Association, 1982, 1985, 1986; DC Writer of the Year award, 1985; Best Event Coverage Award, Associated Press Sports Editors, 1985.

Writings

NONFICTION

A Season on the Brink: A Year with Bob Knight and the Indiana Hoosiers, Macmillan (New York, NY), 1986.

A Season Inside: One Year in College Basketball, Villard Books (New York, NY), 1988.

Forever's Team, Villard Books (New York, NY), 1990.

Hard Courts: Real Life on the Professional Tennis Tours, Villard Books (New York, NY), 1991.

Play Ball: The Life and Troubled Times of Major League Baseball, Villard Books (New York, NY), 1993.

A Good Walk Spoiled: Days and Nights on the PGA Tour, Little, Brown (Boston, MA), 1995.

A Civil War, Army vs. Navy: A Year inside College Football's Purest Rivalry, Little, Brown (Boston, MA), 1996.

(Editor) *The Best American Sports Writing 1996,* Houghton (Boston, MA), 1997.

A March to Madness: The View from the Floor in the Atlantic Coast Conference, Little, Brown (Boston, MA), 1998 with new afterword, 1999.

The First Coming: Tiger Woods, Master or Martyr?, Ballantine (New York, NY), 1998.

The Majors: In Pursuit of Golf's Holy Grail, Little, Brown (Boston, MA), 1999.

The Last Amateurs: Playing for Glory and Honor in Division 1 Basketball's Least-Known League, Little, Brown (Boston, MA), 2000.

The Punch: One Night, Two Lives, and the Fight That Changed Basketball Forever, Little, Brown (Boston, MA), 2002.

Open: Inside the Ropes at Bethpage Black, Little, Brown (Boston, MA), 2003.

Caddy for Life: The Bruce Edwards Story, Little, Brown (New York, NY), 2004.

(With Red Auerbach) *Let Me Tell You a Story: A Lifetime in the Game,* Little, Brown (New York, NY), 2004.

Next Man Up: A Year behind the Lines in Today's NFL, Little, Brown (Boston, MA), 2005.

Last Dance: Behind the Scenes at the Final Four, Little, Brown (Boston, MA), 2006.

Tales from Q School: Inside Golf's Fifth Major, Little, Brown (Boston, MA), 2007.

Living on the Black: Two Pitchers, Two Teams, One Season to Remember, Little, Brown (Boston, MA), 2008.

(With Rocco Mediate) *Are You Kidding Me?: The Story of Rocco Mediate's Extraordinary Battle with Tiger Woods at the U.S. Open,* Little, Brown (New York, NY), 2009.

Moment of Glory: The Year Underdogs Ruled Golf, Little, Brown (New York, NY), 2010.

One on One Behind the Scenes with the Greats in the Game, Little, Brown (New York, NY), 2011.

The Portable Palmer, photographs by Walter Looss, Stewart, Tabori & Chang (New York, NY), 2011.

Contributor to periodicals, including *Sporting News, Basketball Times, Outlook,* and *Eastern Basketball.*

ADULT FICTION

Running Mates, Villard Books (New York, NY), 1992.
Winter Games, Little, Brown (Boston, MA), 1995.

YOUNG-ADULT FICTION

Last Shot: A Final Four Mystery, Knopf (New York, NY), 2005.

Vanishing Act: Mystery at the U.S. Open, Knopf (New York, NY), 2006.

Cover-Up: Mystery at the Super Bowl, Knopf (New York, NY), 2007.

Change-Up: Mystery at the World Series, Knopf (New York, NY), 2009.

The Rivalry: Mystery at the Army-Navy Game, Knopf (New York, NY), 2010.

Rush for the Gold: Mystery at the Olympics, Knopf (New York, NY), 2012.

Adaptations

A Good Walk Spoiled: Days and Nights on the PGA Tour was adapted as an audiobook, Time Warner AudioBooks, 1998. *A Season on the Brink* was filmed as a made-for-TV movie starring Brian Dennehy, ESPN, 2002. *Last Shot* was adapted as an audiobook, performed by the author. *The Rivalry* was adapted for audiobook, produced by Listening Library, 2010.

Sidelights

John Feinstein is an award-winning sportswriter whose journalistic work has appeared in such publications as the *Washington Post* and *Sports Illustrated.* Feinstein has also penned several nonfiction works that present a behind-the-scenes look at professional and college sports, among them *Tales from Q School: Inside Golf's Fifth Major* and *Next Man Up: A Year behind the Lines in Today's NFL.* Armed with his knowledge of competitive sports, he also marshals his storytelling talents in the adult mysteries *Running Mates* and *Winter Games* as well as in his series of well-received middle-grade mysteries featuring teenage sibling sleuths Stevie Thomas and Susan Carol Anderson.

In his career as a journalist, Feinstein gained national attention with *A Season on the Brink: A Year with Bob Knight and the Indiana Hoosiers.* The book recounts

Indiana University's 1985-86 basketball season, from the first organizational meetings to the team's surprising loss to Cleveland State University in the first round of the National Collegiate Athletic Association (NCAA) basketball tournament. While writing the book, Feinstein enjoyed close access to coach Bobby Knight and followed Knight's team's practices, meetings, and game-time huddles over the course of an entire season. When *A Season on the Brink* was published, it quickly sold out of its initial printing of 17,000 copies and appeared on the *New York Times* best-seller list, where it ranked at number one for seventeen weeks.

Other books that find Feinstein going behind the scenes of college sports include *A Season Inside: One Year in College Basketball,* which details the 1987-88 basketball season. By attending 104 games, Feinstein was able to provide an inside look at such prominent university coaches as Dean Smith of North Carolina, John Thompson of Georgetown, and Larry Brown of Kansas, the last who led his team to the 1988 NCAA championship. According to *Washington Post* contributor Robert D. Novak, in *A Season Inside* Feinstein "convey[s] the excitement, intrigue, confrontation, hysteria and sheer

Cover of John Feinstein's highly acclaimed sports profile **A Good Walk Spoiled,** *one of several books focusing on the game of golf.* (Little, Brown & Company, 1995. Reproduced by permission of Little, Brown & Company, a division of Hachette Book Group, Inc.)

intoxication of college basketball." *Forever's Team* concerns the 1978-79 basketball team of Duke University, Feinstein's alma mater, while *Last Dance: Behind the Scenes at the Final Four* presents a look at one of America's premier sporting events. "The anecdotes are entertaining, and the insights into the tournament's logistics fascinating," wrote *Booklist* contributor Wes Lukowsky.

In *Hard Courts: Real Life on the Professional Tennis Tours* Feinstein demystifies the glamour surrounding the tennis world. In interviews with famous and not-so-famous players as well as their families and agents, he presents the sport's professional side in a distinctly unflattering light. *Hard Courts* "peels back layer after layer of surface gloss and undeniable glamour to expose the machinations of players' agents, the power of television and the wheeling and dealing of unscrupulous promoters," Julie Cart wrote in her review of Feinstein's book for the *New York Times*. "The picture is not pretty."

Feinstein takes a similar approach in *A Good Walk Spoiled: Days and Nights on the PGA Tour,* and here he shows the sport of golf in stark contrast to other professional sports: Despite some noteworthy examples, golfers tend to play by the rules, live quiet lives, and go to bed early. The author more-recently revisited the golf world in *The Majors: In Pursuit of Golf's Holy Grail,* and in *Tales from Q School* he chronicles the action at 2005's PGA qualifying tournaments, where more than 1,000 aspiring pros vied for only thirty available spots on the tour. Reviewing *The Majors* in *Booklist,* Bill Ott called Feinstein's account "compelling," adding that the "subject is made to order for his slices-of-life approach."

The life of Bruce Edwards, who was the professional caddy for legendary golfer Tom Watson for over forty years, is Feinstein's subject in *Caddy for Life: The Bruce Edwards Story,* which reveals parts of the golf industry known only to insiders. Edwards was diagnosed with Lou Gehrig's disease in 2003, and in part of his book Feinstein also covers the man's struggle with his growing infirmity. *Caddy for Life* "will thoroughly entertain golf fans," predicted a critic for *Publishers Weekly,* and Larry R. Little wrote in *School Library Journal* that readers will gain a "unique insight into a caddy's dedicated life on the P.G.A. tour."

Feinstein turned his attention to the National Football League (NFL) in *Next Man Up,* "one of the most compelling portraits of NFL life ever written," observed Charles Hirshberg in *Sports Illustrated.* Granted complete access to the Baltimore Ravens' players and personnel, the sportswriter provides an in-depth look at the team's 2004 season, focusing on game strategy as well as on the intense pressures driving managers, coaches, and players. Professional baseball is the subject of *Living on the Black: Two Pitchers, Two Teams, One Season to Remember,* in which Feinstein follows Tom Gla-

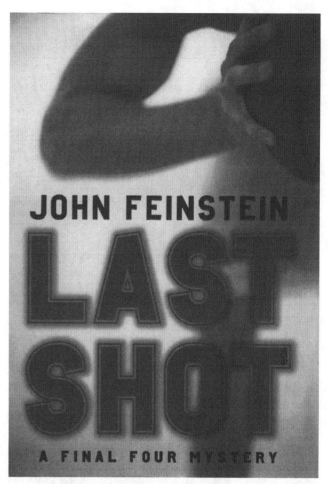

Feinstein's young adult novels include Last Shot, *which introduces teen journalist sleuths Stevie and Susan Carol.* (Jacket copyright © 2005 by Corbis.)

vine of the New York Mets and Mike Mussina of the New York Yankees through the 2007 season. According to Lukowsky, here the author "guides readers into a world with which fans have only surface familiarity, revealing in the process multiple substrata of nuance and meaning."

Feinstein started augmenting his investigative sports reporting with fiction-writing by penning adult novels. His first, *Running Mates,* is a political thriller involving the assassination of Maryland's governor. An investigative reporter looking into the case discovers a surprising alliance between a right-wing extremist and a radical feminist who may have had the governor killed so that his female lieutenant-governor would come to power. A *Publishers Weekly* reviewer voiced praise for the novel, stating that the "strong, surprising resolution" in *Running Mates* "delivers on its promise despite its protagonist's occasionally larger-than-life heroism and incredible luck."

In *Winter Games* a burned-out reporter returns to his hometown seeking peace and quiet, but discovers that the place is in an uproar because of a superstar on the high-school basketball team. The recruiting frenzy surrounding the young sports figure leads to the death of

an assistant coach. In the opinion of a *Publishers Weekly* commentator, *Winter Games* presents a "dark portrayal of murder and rampant corruption on the college courts."

Feinstein combines his talent for spinning a mystery with his sports-writing expertise in his first novel for teens, *Last Shot: A Final Four Mystery.* Aspiring high-school journalists Stevie Thomas and Susan Carol Anderson have both won awards in a junior sports-writing competition and are allowed to cover the NCAA Final Four game alongside the professional. The two begin as rivals, but when they uncover a blackmail plot against one of the players, they team up to uncover the mystery and get the scoop, "ultimately weaseling themselves into the bad guys' lair in classic Hardy Boys' fashion," as Ott explained. *Last Shot* "breaks new ground for teens, focusing primarily on the influential role of media in promoting college basketball," noted Gerry Larson, reviewing the novel for *School Library Journal.* According to a critic in *Kirkus Reviews,* "Feinstein uses simple prose, lively dialogue, and authentic details" to bring the Final Four game to life, and a *Publishers Weekly* critic noted of *Last Shot* that its "plotting entails some fancy footwork that will keep readers on their toes."

Cover of Feinstein's novel Vanishing Act, *which finds Stevie and Susan Carol tracking down a kidnaping at the U.S. Open Tennis Championship.* (Cover photograph © Jeff Gross/Getty Inc. Used by permission of Alfred A. Knopf, an imprint of Random House Children's Books, a division of Random House, Inc.)

Stevie and Susan Carol return in several other mysteries, among them *Vanishing Act, Cover Up: Mystery at the Super Bowl,* and *Change-up: Mystery at the World Series. Vanishing Act* takes the teen sleuths to the U.S. Open tennis championship in New York City, where the thirteen-year-old reporters investigate the disappearance of Russian athlete Nadia Symanova and learn that Susan Carol's uncle may be involved in the kidnapping. Critics suggested that *Vanishing Act* would appeal to a variety of readers; Gillian Engberg, writing in *Booklist,* remarked that "sports fans will be fascinated by the insider's view of the tournament," and *School Library Journal* contributor D. Maria LaRocco observed that "the mystery maintains a genuine level of suspense throughout the story."

In *Cover-Up* Feinstein's intrepid teen reporters uncover a scandal on the eve of the Super Bowl. While Susan serves as the co-anchor of *Kid-Sports,* a cable television program, Stevie writes human-interest stories for the local newspaper, but they soon join forces to unravel a conspiracy hiding the fact that several players have failed a steroid test. Leah Krippner praised the novel in *School Library Journal,* stating that "the teens are well crafted and the villains are extraordinary," *Booklist* reviewer Betty Carter commented of *Cover-Up* that "Feinstein's ease with the sports milieu create[s] a glamorous background" for his tale.

Feinstein takes readers to the World Series in *Change-Up,* as Susan Carol and Stevie plan to enjoy the face-off between the Washington Nationals and the Boston Red Sox from front-row seats. When a minor-league pitcher winds up in the starting rotation and his biography proves to be full of inconsistencies, the two teens quickly decide to find out more, aided by professional journalists Bobby Kelleher and Tamara Mearns. In a story filled with real-life athletes, Feinstein's sleuths must wrestle with journalistic ethics, and the "exciting sports action . . . will keep readers involved," according to *Booklist* critic John Peters, and a *Publishers Weekly* reviewer predicted that "sports fans will enjoy all the trivia Feinstein works into the narrative" of *Change-Up.*

Feinstein's intrepid teen reporters are assigned to report on one of the top sports competitions of the academic year in *The Rivalry: Mystery at the Army-Navy Game.* The West Point Black Knights go head to head with Annapolis's Midshipmen as they have since 1890, but with the U.S. president in the stands security is ultra tight and Stevie and Susan Carol soon discover that hidden dangers may lurk amid the cheering crowds. International competition is Feinstein's backdrop in *Rush for the Gold: Mystery at the Olympics,* as the teens travel to London, where Stevie plans to cover the summer Olympics along with Bobby and Tamara while Susan Carol competes for the gold medal in swimming. According to a *Kirkus Reviews* writer, the author's jour-

Writings

Discover Canada: New Brunswick, Grolier (Toronto, Ontario, Canada), 1994, revised edition, 1996.
(With sister, Janet Willen) *Five Thousand Years of Slavery,* Tundra Books of Northern New York (Plattsburgh, NY), 2010.

Author of educational materials, including *Report Writing I-II,* Educators Publishing Service (Cambridge, MA), 1998. Contributor of book reviews to *Canadian Children's Literature* for twenty-three years.

Sidelights

Based in Canada, Marjorie Gann confined writing to her spare time, creating educational materials while working for more than thirty years as a teacher in both Nova Scotia and the city of Toronto, Ontario. In addition to her thirty-year career in education, Gann can also note among her accomplishments her first published trade book, *Five Thousand Years of Slavery,* which was inspired by her concerns about genocidal wars ongoing in Africa and which she coauthored with sister and fellow writer Janet Willen. "Slave raids and slave trafficking . . . didn't end with the American Civil War . . . ," Gann explained to an interviewer for *Open Book Toronto* online. "Slavery is a modern human rights issue—in Sudan, in Ghana, in Mauritania, in India and Pakistan, even in farms in Florida. To understand slavery, students need to know that it's never been just Africans picking cotton in the American South. It's something Egyptian Arabs did to Africans, that black Africans did to other black Africans, that Vikings did to Europeans, that Malays did to the hill people of Southeast Asia, that Pacific islanders did to other islanders and to Europeans, that Europeans did to indigenous South Americans, and that indigenous Canadians like the Nootka did to Europeans."

In *Five Thousand Years of Slavery* Gann and Willen share the result of their research into narrative accounts, enhancing their history with poems and songs as well as paintings, engravings, photographs, and other visual elements. The history begins in the ancient world, as young Sumerians were sold by impoverished parents and wealthy Romans depended on female slaves to perform the many tasks that were required to run an upscale household. From there they move forward in time, noting the importation of Africans to work on the plantations in the southern United States beginning in the Colonial period and the ongoing sale of children in Third-World countries to gain income for impoverished families.

The text of *Five Thousand Years of Slavery* "reads like a storybook," according to *Voice of Youth Advocates* critic Judith Hayn, and the authors' search through original sources has resulted in the inclusion of "poignant and inspirational stories of enslaved individuals, whether many years ago or in contemporary societies."

In *Booklist* Hazel Rochman praised Gann and Willen's reference as "encyclopedic in scope and minutely detailed," while Gerry Larson praised the book in *School Library Journal* as a "groundbreaking study [that] brings the disturbing subject into historical and contemporary focus." "Gann and Willen are engaging storytellers," asserted Val Ken Lem in a review of the resource for *Canadian Review of Materials,* and their care in "shy[ing] away from emphasizing the true nature of much of the human trafficking of both children and adults" throughout their historical chronicle shows them to be "cognizant of the innocence of their youngest readers." Citing the "timeliness, international focus and . . . accuracy" in *Five Thousand Years of Slavery*, a *Kirkus Reviews* writer recommended the work as a "first look at a terrible topic."

Biographical and Critical Sources

PERIODICALS

Booklist, May 1, 2011, Hazel Rochman, review of *Five Thousand Years of Slavery,* p. 73.
Canadian Review of Materials, January 14, 2011, Val Ken Lem, review of *Five Thousand Years of Slavery.*
Kirkus Reviews, December 15, 2010, review of *Five Thousand Years of Slavery.*
Quill & Quire, January, 2011, Jill Bryant, review of *Five Thousand Years of Slavery.*
School Library Journal, March, 2011, Gerry Larson, review of *Five Thousand Years of Slavery,* p. 179.
Toronto Star, February 24, 2011, Deirdre Baker, review of *Five Thousand Years of Slavery.*

Cover of Marjorie Gann and Janet Willen's collaborative history Five Thousand Years of Slavery. (Jacket photo: AP Photo/Apichart Weerawong. Reproduced by permission of Tundra Books.)

Voice of Youth Advocates, February, 2011, Judith Hayn, review of *Five Thousand Years of Slavery,* p. 582.

ONLINE

Open Book Toronto Web site, http://www.openbooktoronto.com/ (February 1, 2011), interview with Gann and Janet Willen.

Tundra Books Web site, http://www.tundrabooks.com/ (February 12, 2012), "Marjorie Gann."

* * *

GIFF, Patricia Reilly 1935-

Personal

Born April 26, 1935, in Brooklyn, NY; daughter of William J. and Alice Reilly; married James A. Giff, January 31, 1959; children: James, William, Alice. *Education:* Marymount College, B.A., 1956; St. John's University, M.A., 1958; Hofstra University, professional diploma in reading, 1975. *Religion:* Roman Catholic.

Addresses

Home—Trumbull, CT. *Agent*—George Nicholson, Sterling Lord Literistic, 65 Bleecker St., New York, NY 10012.

Career

Freelance writer, 1979—. Public school teacher in New York, NY, 1956-60; Elmont Public Schools, Elmont, NY, teacher, 1964-84. The Dinosaur's Paw (children's bookstore), Fairfield, CT, cofounder and partner, beginning 1994.

Awards, Honors

Honorary D.H.L., Hofstra University, 1990; Best Books for Young Adults citation, American Library Association (ALA), and Newbery Medal Honor Book citation, 1998, both for *Lily's Crossing;* Christopher Award, ALA Best Books for Young Adults citation, and Newbery Medal Honor Book citation, all 2003, all for *Pictures of Hollis Woods;* William Allen White Children's Book Award, 2011, for *Eleven.*

Writings

JUVENILE FICTION

Fourth-Grade Celebrity, illustrated by Leslie Morrill, Delacorte (New York, NY), 1979, published in *Fourth-Grade Celebrity; and, The Girl Who Knew It All,* Dell (New York, NY), 2000.

The Girl Who Knew It All, illustrated by Leslie Morrill, Delacorte (New York, NY), 1979, published in *Fourth-Grade Celebrity; and, The Girl Who Knew It All,* Dell (New York, NY), 2000.

Patricia Reilly Giff (Photograph © by Tim Keating. Reproduced by permission.)

Today Was a Terrible Day, illustrated by Susanna Natti, Viking (New York, NY), 1980.

Next Year I'll Be Special, illustrated by Marylin Hafner, Dutton (New York, NY), 1980.

Left-handed Shortstop, illustrated by Leslie Morrill, Delacorte (New York, NY), 1980.

Have You Seen Hyacinth Macaw?: A Mystery, illustrated by Anthony Kramer, Delacorte (New York, NY), 1981.

The Winter Worm Business, illustrated by Leslie Morrill, Delacorte (New York, NY), 1981.

The Gift of the Pirate Queen, illustrated by Jenny Rutherford, Delacorte (New York, NY), 1982.

Suspect, illustrated by Stephen Marchesi, Dutton (New York, NY), 1982.

Loretta P. Sweeny, Where Are You?: A Mystery, illustrated by Anthony Kramer, Delacorte (New York, NY), 1983.

Kidnap in San Juan, Dell (New York, NY), 1983.

The Almost Awful Play, illustrated by Susanna Natti, Viking (New York, NY), 1984.

Rat Teeth, illustrated by Leslie Morrill, Delacorte (New York, NY), 1984.

Watch Out, Ronald Morgan, illustrated by Susanna Natti, Viking (New York, NY), 1985.

Love, from the Fifth Grade Celebrity, Delacorte (New York, NY), 1986.

Mother Teresa: A Sister to the Poor (nonfiction), illustrated by Ted Lewin, Viking (New York, NY), 1986.

Happy Birthday, Ronald Morgan, illustrated by Susanna Natti, Viking (New York, NY), 1986.

Laura Ingalls Wilder: Growing up in the Little House (nonfiction), illustrated by Eileen McKeating, Viking (New York, NY), 1987.

Tootsie Tanner Why Don't You Talk? An Abby Jones Junior Detective Mystery, illustrated by Anthony Kramer, Delacorte (New York, NY), 1987.

Columbus Circle, Dell (New York, NY), 1988.

Ronald Morgan Goes to Bat, illustrated by Susanna Natti, Viking (New York, NY), 1988.

I Love Saturday, illustrated by Frank Remkiewicz, Viking (New York, NY), 1989.

Poopsie Pomerantz, Pick up Your Feet, Delacorte (New York, NY), 1989.

Matthew Jackson Meets the Wall, Delacorte (New York, NY), 1990.

The War Began at Supper: Letters to Miss Loria, Delacorte (New York, NY), 1991.

Diana: Twentieth-Century Princess (nonfiction), illustrated by Michele Laporte, Viking (New York, NY), 1991.

Shark in School, illustrated by Blanche Sims, Delacorte (New York, NY), 1994.

Ronald Morgan Goes to Camp, illustrated by Susanna Natti, Viking (New York, NY), 1995.

Good Luck, Ronald Morgan, illustrated by Susanna Natti, Viking (New York, NY), 1996.

Lily's Crossing, Delacorte (New York, NY), 1997.

Katie Cobb Two, Viking (New York, NY), 1999.

Louisa May Alcott (nonfiction), Viking (New York, NY), 1999.

Nory Ryan's Song, Delacorte (New York, NY), 2000.

Edith Stein: Sister Teresa Benedicta of the Cross, Holiday House (New York, NY), 2001.

All the Way Home, Delacorte (New York, NY), 2001.

Pictures of Hollis Woods, Wendy Lamb Books (New York, NY), 2002.

Maggie's Door, Wendy Lamb Books (New York, NY), 2002.

A House of Tailors, Wendy Lamb Books (New York, NY), 2004.

Willow Run, Wendy Lamb Books (New York, NY), 2005.

Water Street, Wendy Lamb Books (New York, NY), 2006.

Eleven, Wendy Lamb Books (New York, NY), 2008.

Wild Girl, Wendy Lamb Books (New York, NY), 2009.

Storyteller, Wendy Lamb Books (New York, NY), 2010.

R My Name Is Rachel, Wendy Lamb Books (New York, NY), 2011.

Fiercely and Friends: the Big Something, illustrated by Diane Palmisciano, Orchard Books (New York, NY), 2012.

The Sneaky Snow Fox, illustrated by Diane Palmsiciano, Orchard Books (New York, NY), 2012.

"KIDS OF THE POLK STREET SCHOOL" SERIES; ILLUSTRATED BY BLANCHE SIMS

The Beast in Ms. Rooney's Room, Delacorte (New York, NY), 1984.

The Candy Corn Contest, Delacorte (New York, NY), 1984.

December Secrets, Delacorte (New York, NY), 1984.

Lazy Lions, Lucky Lambs, Delacorte (New York, NY), 1985.

Say "Cheese", Delacorte (New York, NY), 1985.

Purple Climbing Days, Delacorte (New York, NY), 1985.

In the Dinosaur's Paw, Delacorte (New York, NY), 1985.

Snaggle Doodles, Delacorte (New York, NY), 1985.

The Valentine Star, Delacorte (New York, NY), 1985.

Sunny-side Up, Delacorte (New York, NY), 1986.

Fish Face, Delacorte (New York, NY), 1986.

Pickle Puss, Delacorte (New York, NY), 1986.

"NEW KIDS AT THE POLK STREET SCHOOL" SERIES

The Kids of the Polk Street School, Dell (New York, NY), 1988.

B-E-S-T Friends, Dell (New York, NY), 1988.

If the Shoe Fits, Dell (New York, NY), 1988.

Watch Out! Man-eating Snake, Dell (New York, NY), 1988.

All about Stacy, Dell (New York, NY), 1988.

Fancy Feet, Dell (New York, NY), 1988.

Stacy Says Good-Bye, Dell (New York, NY), 1989.

Spectacular Stone Soup, Dell (New York, NY), 1989.

Beast and the Halloween Horror, Dell (New York, NY), 1990.

Emily Arrow Promises to Do Better This Year, Dell (New York, NY), 1990.

Monster Rabbit Runs Amuk!, Dell (New York, NY), 1990.

Wake up Emily, It's Mother Day, Dell (New York, NY), 1991.

"POLKA DOT, PRIVATE EYE" SERIES

The Mystery of the Blue Ring, Dell (New York, NY), 1987.

The Powder Puff Puzzle, Dell (New York, NY), 1987.

The Riddle of the Red Purse, Dell (New York, NY), 1987.

The Secret at the Polk Street School, Dell (New York, NY), 1987.

The Case of the Cool-Itch Kid, Dell (New York, NY), 1989.

Garbage Juice for Breakfast, Dell (New York, NY), 1989.

The Clue at the Zoo, Dell (New York, NY), 1990.

The Trail of the Screaming Teenager, Dell (New York, NY), 1990.

"LINCOLN LIONS BAND" SERIES; ILLUSTRATED BY EMILY ARNOLD MCCULLY

Meet the Lincoln Lions Band, Dell (New York, NY), 1992.

Yankee Doodle Drumsticks, Dell (New York, NY), 1992.

The Jingle Bells Jam, Dell (New York, NY), 1992.

The Rootin' Tootin' Bugle Boy, Dell (New York, NY), 1992.

The Great Shamrock Disaster, Dell (New York, NY), 1993.

"POLK STREET SPECIAL" SERIES

Write up a Storm with the Polk Street School, Dell (New York, NY), 1993.

Turkey Trouble, Dell (New York, NY), 1994.

Count Your Money with the Polk Street School, illustrated by Blanche Sims, Dell (New York, NY), 1994.

Postcard Pest, illustrated by Blanche Sims, Dell (New York, NY), 1994.

Look Out, Washington, D.C.!, illustrated by Blanche Sims, Dell (New York, NY), 1995.

Pet Parade, illustrated by Blanche Sims, Dell (New York, NY), 1996.

Green Thumbs, Everyone, illustrated by Blanche Sims, Dell (New York, NY), 1996.

Oh Boy, Boston!, illustrated by Blanche Sims, Dell (New York, NY), 1997.

Next Stop, New York City! The Polk Street Kids on Tour, illustrated by Blanche Sims, Dell (New York, NY), 1997.

Let's Go, Philadelphia!, illustrated by Blanche Sims, Dell (New York, NY), 1998.

"BALLET SLIPPERS" SERIES; ILLUSTRATED BY JULIE DURRELL

Dance with Rosie, Viking (New York, NY), 1996.

Rosie's Nutcracker Dreams, Viking (New York, NY), 1996.

Starring Rosie, Viking (New York, NY), 1997.

A Glass Slipper for Rosie, Viking (New York, NY), 1997.

Not-So-Perfect Rosie, Viking (New York, NY), 1997.

Rosie's Big City Ballet, Viking (New York, NY), 1998.

"FRIENDS AND AMIGOS" SERIES; ILLUSTRATED BY DYANNE DISALVO-RYAN

Good Dog, Bonita, Gareth Stevens (Milwaukee, WI), 1998.

Adios, Anna, Gareth Stevens (Milwaukee, WI), 1998.

Happy Birthday, Anna, Sorpresa!, Gareth Stevens (Milwaukee, WI), 1998.

Ho, Ho, Benjamin, Feliz Navidad, Gareth Stevens (Milwaukee, WI), 1998.

It's a Fiesta, Benjamin, Gareth Stevens (Milwaukee, WI), 1998.

Say Hola, Sarah, Gareth Stevens (Milwaukee, WI), 1998.

"ADVENTURES OF MINNIE AND MAX" SERIES

Kidnap at the Catfish Café, illustrated by Lynne Cravath, Viking (New York, NY), 1998.

Mary Moon Is Missing, illustrated by Lynne Cravath, Viking (New York, NY), 1998.

"ZIGZAG KIDS" CHAPTER-BOOK SERIES; ILLUSTRATED BY ALASDAIR BRIGHT

Big Whopper, Yearling (New York, NY), 2010.

Number One Kid, Wendy Lamb Books (New York, NY), 2010.

Flying Feet, Yearling (New York, NY), 2011.

Star Time, Wendy Lamb Books (New York, NY), 2011.

Bears Beware, Wendy Lamb Books (New York, NY), 2012.

Super Surprise, Wendy Lamb Books (New York, NY), 2012.

OTHER

Advent: Molly Maguire, Viking (New York, NY), 1991.

Show Time at the Polk Street School: Plays You Can Do Yourself or in the Classroom, illustrated by Blanche Sims, Delacorte (New York, NY), 1992.

Don't Tell the Girls: A Family Memoir, Holiday House (New York, NY), 2005.

Adaptations

Eleven was adapted for audiobook, read by Staci Snell, Listening Library, 2008. *Wild Girl* was adapted for audiobook, read by Justine Eyre, Listening Library, 2009.

Sidelights

A prolific author who began writing in her mid-forties, Patricia Reilly Giff has dedicated her career to writing humorous books for middle-grade and younger readers. In both her award-winning novels, such as *Lily's Crossing* and *Pictures of Hollis Woods,* as well as her multi-book series, Giff explores situations that are readily familiar to young people, such as staging a class play, caring for a pet, and getting along with family and friends. Her background as a teacher and reading con-

***Cover of Giff's award-winning middle-grade novel* Pictures of Hollis Woods.** (Book cover copyright © 2002 by Wendy Lamb Books. Used by permission of Wendy Lamb Books, an imprint of Random House Children's Books, a division of Random House, Inc.)

sultant has given her a unique perspective on what will keep young readers turning pages, and she approaches each story with a clear objective. As a teacher, "I had worked with so many children who had terrible problems that I wanted to say things that would make them laugh," she once explained. "I wanted to tell them they were special. . . . I wish I had started sooner."

Born in Brooklyn, New York, in 1935, Giff grew up in a family also rich in stories, some told by relatives and others left to be discovered when she was an adult. In *Don't Tell the Girls: A Family Memoir* she explores the history of her grandmother's family as well as tracing the history of another grandmother, an Irishwoman who died before Giff was born. In addition to relating her patchwork of history, Giff encourages readers to explore their own family histories in *Don't Tell the Girls,* making her memoir an "affectionate family portrait [that] will appeal to . . . anyone with an interest in his or her own genealogy," according to a *Publishers Weekly* contributor. In *Booklist* Carolyn Phelan cited the book's "intimate, conversational style" and remarked on Giff's detailed discussion of how she conducted her own family research.

After graduating from high school, Giff enrolled at Marymount College, where she studied the classic authors of English literature, such as Keats, Poe, Pope, and Dryden. Intimidated by such masterworks, she changed her major from English to business, "and then to history, where I listened to a marvelous man named Mullee spin tales about the past," she later recalled. "I fell into teaching because my beloved dean, who had no idea I wanted to write, saw that it was a good place for me." Teaching would be her main focus for close to two decades as activities related to work and family left little time for writing. Married with three children, a master's degree in history, and a professional diploma in reading, Giff rounded the corner to age forty when it hit her: "I hadn't written a story; I hadn't even tried."

Determined to pursue her childhood dream, as she recalled, "I dragged myself out of bed in the early morning darkness to spend an hour or two at my typewriter before I had to leave for school." Working in a "writing studio" her husband crafted out of an expanded kitchen closet, she built her momentum. Her first published book, *Fourth-Grade Celebrity,* appeared in 1979, and its success convinced Giff to dedicate herself to her craft. Along with a number of her other books for school-age readers, *Fourth-Grade Celebrity* has been through a number of printings, a reflection of its author's ability to connect with the timeless interests of young people.

Giff's best-known novel, the Newbery Medal Honor-winning *Lily's Crossing,* draws on her memories of the war years and took four years to complete. *Lily's Crossing* is a coming-of-age story that takes place during the summer of 1944 as World War II rages across Europe. Fifteen-year-old Lily is left behind with her grand-

Giff addresses serious themes in her historical novel Lily's Crossing, *featuring cover art by Kamil Vojnar.* (Book cover copyright © 1997 by Delacorte Press. Used by permission of Delacorte Press, an imprint of Random House Children's Books, a division of Random House, Inc.)

mother while her widowed father joins the U.S. Army to fight the Nazi threat overseas. Praising the award-winning novel as "a fine piece of historical fiction that evokes a time and place without taking advantage of its characters' emotional lives," *Bulletin of the Center for Children's Books* contributor Janice M. Del Negro added that *Lily's Crossing* "coalesces [plot and characters] into an emotional whole that is fully satisfying."

Meggie Dillon, one of the characters of *Lily's Crossing* plays a central role in *Willow Run,* which is set in Detroit, Michigan, during World War II when that city served as a hub of industry. Meggie and her family move to Detroit so her father can work in the Willow Run bomber factory, but the girl worries that her grandparents will be harassed by local children back at home due to their German heritage. Meggie also fears for the safety of her older brother, Eddie, who is fighting overseas. In *Horn Book* Susan Dove Lempke wrote of *Willow Run* that Meggie's "complex, often touching relationships remain the focus of this rich and satisfying novel." In *Booklist* Ilene Cooper cited Giff's "finely draw characters" and her ability to capture "the senti-

ments so prevalent in times of war," while Renee Steinberg concluded in *School Library Journal* that *Willow Run* is an "engrossing, heartwarming story [that] will help readers understand how personally war affects people."

Another historical novel, *Nory Ryan's Song* takes place at the onset of the Irish potato famine in 1845, and is a survival story. Twelve-year-old Nory lives with her family on the west-central coast of Ireland on a subsistence-level farm. Her mother worries that they may be evicted any day and Nory hopes that her father will come back from sea with money to save them. When famine strikes, many families decide to immigrate to America, and the Ryans want to join them. A contributor for *Publishers Weekly* found that the novel "meticulously recreates" the Great Hunger, as the potato famine was also called. The same reviewer concluded that "vivid descriptions of the stench of failed crops and the foul-tasting food that keeps them alive will linger in readers' minds even after Nory's salvation is secured."

Maggie's Door continues Nory's saga by recounting her harrowing voyage across the Atlantic. The novel also follows the adventures of Nory's friend, Sean Mallon, who becomes separated from the Ryans and must find his own passage to America. "Despite its grittiness," noted a *Publishers Weekly* reviewer, *Maggie's Door* "succeeds in evoking a sense of hope as characters rely on their resourcefulness both to stay alive and to reach their destination."

A new generation is the focus of *Water Street,* which finds Nory and Sean Mallon married and the parents of a thirteen-year-old daughter. The year is now 1875, and Sean is working on the crew building the Brooklyn Bridge while Nory works as a nurse midwife. Daughter Bridget makes a new friend of the upstairs neighbor Thomas Neary, and when the motherless boy needs a place to live, the Mallons take him in, even though times are hard for the new immigrants. Although *School Library Journal* critic Renee Steinberg found the story to be somewhat "predictable," she concluded of *Water Street* that "Giff masterfully integrates" fact and fiction to "present a vivid picture of the immigrant struggle in the 1870s." Hazel Rochman described the same novel as "a poignant story of friendship, work, and the meaning of home," and in *Kirkus Reviews* a contributor concluded that in *Water Street* the novelist "opens a door to the past and makes it all come alive for modern young readers."

In her historical novel *All the Way Home* Giff moves ahead to the mid-twentieth century, bringing together "two appealing young characters in this story of friendship, family and finding where one belongs," according to a contributor for *Publishers Weekly*. Brick is sent to stay with a friend in Brooklyn after a fire destroys his family's apple crop in 1941. Loretta, the friend, is a nurse who years ago adopted Mariel, a girl with polio, from a hospital located near Brick's farm. Brick and Mariel now slowly become friends, and when he voices a desire to return home to help a friend harvest apples, Mariel encourages him and even decides to join him. Her one desire is to trace her birth mother, and for that she must return to the hospital where she contracted polio. Reviewing *All the Way Home* in *Booklist*, Ellen Mandel wrote that Giff "delivers a memorable picture of 1940s America" in this "tightly woven, inspirational story."

Pictures of Hollis Woods, Giff's second Newbery Honor book, takes place on Long Island, where talented but troubled preteen foster-child Hollis Woods—named after the section of Queens where she was discovered abandoned as an infant—begins to feel secure at the home of a retired art teacher. *Booklist* reviewer GraceAnne A. DeCandido praised the novel as a "moving story about families, longing, and belonging," while in *School Library Journal* Jean Gaffney noted that Giff's use of flashbacks "slowly illuminates Hollis's life with one family who had hoped to adopt her."

Another work of historical fiction, *A House of Tailors,* concerns thirteen-year-old Dina, a character based on the author's great-grandmother. Accused of being a spy

Cover of Giff's historical novel **All the Way Home,** *which focuses on a boy growing up in 1940s Brooklyn.* (Photo courtesy of Library of Congress, Prints and Photographs Division. Book cover copyright © 2001 by Delacorte Press. Used by permission of Random House Children's Books, a division of Random House, Inc.)

Giff turns to science fiction in her middle-grade novel Eleven, *featuring cover art by Shane Rebenschied.* (Book cover copyright © 2008 by Wendy Lamb Books. Used by permission of Wendy Lamb Books, an imprint of Random House Children's Books, a division of Random House.)

during the Franco-Prussian War, Dina flees Germany to live with her uncle in the United States. Upon her arrival, Dina is disappointed to learn that her uncle, a tailor, lives with his family in a cramped Brooklyn tenement. Now that she must earn her keep by helping him with the business. According to *School Library Journal* critic Barbara Auerback, *A House of Tailors* "is rich with believable, endearing characters as well as excitement and emotion."

In *Eleven* readers meet Sam MacKenzie, a boy just about to turn eleven who lives in upstate New York with his grandfather, Mack, a carpenter. Sam is dyslexic, but the number "11" seems to trigger a terrible rush of confusing memories for the boy. When he discovers an old newspaper clipping that incorporates his photo and the word "missing," he needs to learn the truth. With the help of a school friend named Caroline, Sam attempts to sort out his confusion, even though he realizes that the truth may threaten the stability of his life with Mack. In *Publishers Weekly* a critic called *Eleven* an "exquisitely rendered story of self-discovery" that benefits from Giff's "expertise at developing sympathetic characters and creating a suspenseful plot."

"The unraveling of Sam's mysterious past will intrigue readers," maintained *School Library Journal* critic Alison Follos, and in *Horn Book* Tanya D. Auger wrote that the author's "empathy and affection" for Sam and Caroline "is palpable."

Brazil is the setting of *Wild Girl*, where twelve-year-old Lidie devotes herself to her horses. Although she loves her grandmother, who she lives with, Lidie is preparing to join Pai, her widowed father, and her big brother Rafael in the eastern United States, where they work at a racetrack. The girl's arrival coincides with the birth of a filly that winds up in Pai's care. As Lidie learns to adapt to the restrictions of life in her new home, the filly learns to adapt to the girl's will as their growing friendship leads to a true accomplishment for them both. "Giff's characters are beautifully nuanced and entirely real," noted a *Kirkus Reviews* writer, and "her prose is as quiet and streamlined and efficient as a galloping Thoroughbred." While *Wild Girl* can be characterized as a horse story and an immigrant story, "the heart of this accessible chapter book is its fine, perceptive portrayal of Lidie and her family," wrote *Booklist* contributor Carolyn Phelan. In *Horn Book* Robin L. Smith echoed that assessment, suggesting that "rich characters and raw, real emotions make this much more than the usual horse story."

For Elizabeth, Giff's heroine in *Storyteller,* family ties draw her into an historical mystery. When she visits her aunt Lily's house following her widowed father's departure for Australia, she discovers a portrait of Zee, a distant ancestor whose father fought and died during the American Revolution. Zee looks uncannily like Elizabeth and inspires the girl to research her ancestor's life. Along with telling Elizabeth's story in her third-person text, Giff interweaves a second narrative capturing Zee's thoughts during a time of uncertainty, fear, and family tragedy. As it "gracefully bridges two eras and two insightful perspectives," *Storyteller* also brings its "characters and history alive," according to a *Publishers Weekly* critic. In *Booklist* Lynn Rutan also praised the novel, writing that "it is the intertwined, personal stories of the two girls . . . that will win [the] hearts" of Giff's readers. *Storyteller* "is a lovely story about love and loss," concluded a *Kirkus Reviews* writer, and Marie Orlando wrote in *School Library Journal* that the story's "fast-paced narrative, toggling back and forth between the 18th and 21st centuries, will keep readers interested."

In many of her book series for younger children, Giff teams with an accomplished illustrator who uses a light, humorous touch to bring to life each of the author's likeable, realistic characters. In her books featuring the popular students of the fictional Polk Street School, for example, artist Blanche Sims brings the action to life. In *Show Time at the Polk Street School: Plays You Can Do Yourself or in the Classroom* pivotal teacher Ms. Rooney decides to have her students stage plays. Three play scripts, along with the student's efforts to make

Cover of Giff's novel Storyteller, *in which an ancestral portrait draws a modern teen into a family mystery.* (Book cover copyright © 2010 by Wendy Lamb Books. Used by permission of Wendy Lamb Books, an imprint of Random House Children's Books, a division of Random House, Inc.)

them come to life, are included in the volume, which serves as "a solid introduction for aspiring thespians," according to a *Kirkus Reviews* contributor. Bring-your-pet-to-school week becomes the focus of *Pet Parade*, as student Beast looks for another pet to take to Ms. Rooney's class because his own dog, Kissie Poo, does nothing well except sleep. In *Next Stop, New York City!* and *Look out, Washington, D.C.!* the Polk Street School gang descends on some of the nation's largest cities, with humorous chaos the expected result. Serving as both a story and a tour guide of sorts, these books feature maps of the subject cities as well as phone numbers of the favorite tourist attractions for kids.

In her "Ballet Slippers" books Giff introduces young readers to Rosie O'Meara, an aspiring dancer whose enthusiasm for ballet sometimes gets her into trouble. In *Starring Rosie*, the girl is unhappy about finding herself cast as the evil witch rather than the star in *Sleeping Beauty*. Fortunately, Rosie rebounds and offers to find a classmate willing to play the role of the handsome prince. Finding a boy willing to wear tights on stage in front of all his friends proves to be no easy task, however, in what *School Library Journal* con-

tributor Eva Mitnick characterized as a "breezy and fun" read. *A Glass Slipper for Rosie* finds the young dancer involved in another class production, although disappointment follows when she realizes that her grandfather may not be in town to see the show. Calling the book a "delightful addition to the series," *School Library Journal* critic Janet M. Bair praised *A Glass Slipper for Rosie* as "a well-rounded story about family and friends."

The "Zigzag Kids" chapter-book series focuses on a group of culturally and ethnically diverse friends who meet up in the after-school program at Zelda A. Zigzag Elementary School. *Number One Kid,* the first book in the series, introduces Mitchell, who wants to be best at something and worries that his special talents might not be recognized on Prize Day. *Star Time* focuses on the school play, as classmates Gina and Destiny find their friendship threatened when they both compete for the same role. Charlie takes center stage in *Flying Feet,* as the inventive boy attempts to show that he is as clever as older brother Larry, and further elementary-school ambitions play out in series installments *Bears Beware* and *Super Surprise.*

Noting the easy-to-read format of the "Zigzag Kids" stories, a *Kirkus Reviews* writer predicted that novice readers "will easily relate to the various troubles and anticipation of [Giff's] . . . diverse crew" of young characters. Reviewing *Flying Feet* in the same periodical, another critic noted that Alasdair Bright's "cheerful drawings add levity" to the "spare, straightforward prose" in a story "demonstrating Giff's keen understanding of chapter-book readers." For Amy Commers, writing in *School Library Journal,* the "short chapters and engaging story lines" in the series "will motivate developing readers," while Bright's scattered illustrations bring the students of Zigzag Elementary "to life."

In addition to seeing many of her popular stories translated into Spanish for Hispanic students, Giff has also written a series that incorporates children from Spanish-speaking cultures. In *Ho, Ho, Benjamin, Feliz Navidad* a young boy shares the holiday season with his home-sick Ecuadorian neighbor and learns about Christmas celebrations in other countries. *Adios, Anna,* another installment in Giff's "Friends and Amigos" series, finds Sarah Cole dejected after best friend Anna Ortiz goes away for summer vacation. Deciding to occupy her time by learning to speak Spanish, Sarah uses Anna's house key to borrow one of her books, and then mislays the key. "Children are sure to enjoy Sarah's funny adventures as they also learn some Spanish," commented *School Library Journal* reviewer Maria Redburn. Sarah appears again in *Say Hola, Sarah,* which also includes basic Spanish vocabulary words. Here Sarah's progress in learning Spanish is aided by Anna, although she is frustrated at how slowly she is advancing in a new book that includes short lessons in the language.

Since she began her career as a children's author in the late 1970s, Giff has enjoyed the writing process more

and more, particularly when it involves a young audience. "Writing became one of the most important parts of my life, a part that now I couldn't do without," she once recalled. "I hope to say to all the children I've loved that they are special . . . that all of us are special . . . important just because we are ourselves." In 1994 she and several members of her family started a hometown bookstore entirely devoted to children's books. Giff viewed her new enterprise, The Dinosaur's Paw, as "a community that brings children and books together."

Biographical and Critical Sources

BOOKS

Giff, Patricia Reilly, *Don't Tell the Girls: A Family Memoir,* Holiday House (New York, NY), 2005.

PERIODICALS

Booklist, January 15, 1993, Kay Weisman, review of *Meet the Lincoln Lions Band,* p. 907; July, 1994, Stephanie Zvirin, review of *Shark in School,* p. 1947; December 1, 1994, Carolyn Phelan, review of *Turkey Trouble,* pp. 680-681; June 1, 1995, Kay Weisman, review of *Look out, Washington, D.C.!,* p. 1770; July, 1995, Julie Yates Walton, review of *Ronald Morgan Goes to Camp,* p. 1878; September 1, 1996, Carolyn Phelan, reviews of *Dance with Rosie* and *Rosie's Nutcracker Dreams,* both p. 125; September 15, 1996, Susan Dove Lempke, review of *Pet Parade,* p. 238; December 15, 1996, Carolyn Phelan, review of *Starring Rosie,* p. 726; May 1, 1997, Carolyn Phelan, review of *Not-So-Perfect Rosie,* p. 1493; October 1, 1997, Carolyn Phelan, review of *A Glass Slipper for Rosie,* p. 329; October 15, 1999, Barbara Baskin, review of *Lily's Crossing,* p. 467; October 15, 2002, GraceAnne A. DeCandido, review of *Pictures of Hollis Woods,* p. 404; September 15, 2003, Hazel Rochman, review of *Maggie's Door,* p. 236; September 15, 2004, Ilene Cooper, review of *A House of Tailors,* p. 244; March 1, 2005, Carolyn Phelan, review of *Don't Tell the Girls: A Family Memoir,* p. 1189; July, 2005, Ilene Cooper, review of *Willow Run,* p. 1922; August 1, 2006, Hazel Rochman, review of *Water Street,* p. 74; December 1, 2007, Gillian Engberg, review of *Eleven,* p. 40; June 1, 2009, Carolyn Phelan, review of *Wild Girl,* p. 58; September 15, 2010, Lynn Rutan, review of *Storyteller,* p. 68.

Bulletin of the Center for Children's Books, January, 1992, review of *Diana: Twentieth-Century Princess,* p. 125; July-August, 1995, review of *Look out, Washington, D.C.!,* pp. 383-384; October, 1996, review of *Good Luck, Ronald Morgan,* p. 59; April, 1997, Janice M. Del Negro, review of *Lily's Crossing,* pp. 282-283.

Christian Science Monitor, November 29, 2010, Augusta Scattergood, review of *Storyteller.*

Horn Book, July-August, 1993, Maeve Visser Knoth, review of *Next Year I'll Be Special,* p. 442; September-October, 1994, Maeve Visser Knoth, review of *Shark*

in School, p. 611; March-April, 1997, Mary M. Burns, review of *Lily's Crossing,* p. 198; November-December, 2001, Mary M. Burns, review of *All the Way Home,* pp. 747-748; January-February, 2003, Nell Beram, review of *Pictures of Hollis Woods,* p. 72; September-October, 2003, Susan Dove Lempke, review of *Maggie's Door,* pp. 610-611; November-December, 2004, Peter D. Sieruta, review of *A House of Tailors,* pp. 707-708; September-October, 2005, Susan Dove Lempke, review of *Willow Run,* p. 577; September-October, 2006, Martha V. Parravano, review of *Water Street,* p. 583; January-February, 2008, Tanya D. Auger, review of *Eleven,* p. 86; September-October, 2009, Robin L. Smith, review of *Wild Girl,* p. 561.

Journal of Adolescent & Adult Literacy, May, 2010, Donna L. Miller, review of *Wild Girl,* p. 693.

Kirkus Reviews, November 15, 1992, review of *Show Time at Polk Street,* p. 1442; September 1, 1993, review of *Next Year I'll Be Special,* p. 1143; September 15, 1994, p. 1271; October 15, 1998, review of *Kidnap at the Catfish Café,* p. 1531; March 15, 2005, review of *Don't Tell the Girls,* p. 351; September 15, 2005, review of *Willow Run,* p. 1026; August 15, 2006, review of *Water Street,* p. 840; December 1, 2007, review of *Eleven;* July 15, 2009, review of *Wild Girl;* July 15, 2010, review of *Number One Kid;* August 15, 2010, review of *Storyteller;* March 1, 2011, review of *Flying Feet;* June 15, 2011, review of *Star Time.*

Kliatt, July, 2005, Phyllis LaMontagne, review of *Nory Ryan's Song,* p. 20.

New York Times, February 3, 2008, Tammy La Gorce, "Placing Family First Hasn't Held Children's Author Back," p. 8.

New York Times Book Review, May 18, 1997, Jane Langton, review of *Lily's Crossing,* p. 24; October 1, 2001, review of *All the Way Home,* p. 1423; August 1, 2002, review of *Pictures of Hollis Woods,* pp. 129-130; October 1, 2004, review of *A House of Tailors,* p. 960.

Publishers Weekly, November 2, 1992, reviews of *Meet the Lincoln Lions Band* and *Yankee Doodle Drumsticks,* both p. 71; July 5, 1993, review of *Next Year I'll Be Special,* p. 72; April 18, 1994, Sally Lodge, "The Author as Bookseller: Patricia Reilly Giff's Career Comes Full Circle," p. 26; October 7, 1996, review of *Dance with Rosie,* p. 76; January 20, 1997, review of *Lily's Crossing,* p. 403; April 27, 1998, "On the Road with Patricia Reilly Giff," p. 29; May 4, 1998, review of *Love, from the Fifth Grade,* p. 216; November 9, 1998, review of *Kidnap at the Catfish Café,* p. 77; July 24, 2000, review of *Nory Ryan's Song,* p. 94; July 15, 2002, review of *Pictures of Hollis Woods,* pp. 74-75; August 25, 2003, review of *Maggie's Door,* p. 65; November 1, 2004, review of *A House of Tailors,* p. 62; March 7, 2005, Sally Lodge, interview with Giff and review of *Don't Tell the Girls,* p. 69; November 19, 2007, review of *Eleven,* p. 57; September 6, 2010, review of *Storyteller,* p. 40.

School Library Journal, January, 1992, April L. Judge, review of *Diana,* p. 102; September, 1994, Mary Ann Bursk, review of *Shark in School,* p. 184; June, 1995, Pamela K. Bomboy, review of *Ronald Morgan Goes*

to Camp, p. 80; October, 1995, Maria Redburn, reviews of *Ho, Ho, Benjamin, Feliz Navidad,* p. 37, and *Adios Anna,* p. 38; March, 1996, Eunice Weech, review of *Say Hola, Sarah,* p. 174; August, 1996, Anne Parker, review of *Pet Parade,* p. 122; March, 1997, Eva Mitnick, review of *Starring Rosie,* p. 152; October, 1997, Suzanne Hawley, review of *Next Stop, New York City!,* pp. 95-96; December, 1997, Janet M. Bair, review of *A Glass Slipper for Rosie,* p. 90; January, 1999, Janie Schomberg, review of *Mary Moon,* p. 88; September, 2002, Jean Gaffney, review of *Pictures of Hollis Woods,* p. 225; September, 2003, Margaret R. Tassia, review of *Maggie's Door,* p. 210; October, 2004, Barbara Auerbach, review of *A House of Tailors,* p. 165; July, 2005, Alison Follos, review of *Don't Tell the Girls,* p. 116; September, 2005, Renee Steinberg, review of *Willow Run,* p. 204; September, 2006, Renee Steinberg, review of *Water Street,* p. 206; January, 2008, Alison Follos, review of *Eleven,* p. 118; August, 2009, Tracy Weiskind, review of *Wild Girl,* p. 103; August, 2010, Amanda Struckmeyer, reviews of *Number One Kid* and *Big Whopper,* both p. 76; November, 2010, Marie Orlando, review of *Storyteller,* p. 114; July, 2011, Amy Commers, review of *Flying Feet,* p. 67.

ONLINE

KidsReads.com, http://www.kidsreads.com/ (September 1, 2003), Wiley Saichek, interview with Giff.

Random House Web site, http://www.randomhouse.com/ (January 12, 2012), "Patricia Reilly Giff."*

* * *

GOURLAY, Candy

Personal

Born in Davao, Philippines; daughter of Cynthia Lopez Quimpo (a teacher); immigrated to United Kingdom, 1989; married Richard Gourlay (a journalist and educator); children: Nick, Jack, Mia. *Education:* Ateneo de Manila University, degree.

Addresses

Home—London, England. *Agent*—Hilary Delamere, The Agency, 24 Pottery La., Holland Park, London W11 4LZ, England.

Career

Journalist and novelist. Reporter for newspapers and magazines in Philippines, including *Philippine Daily Inquirer,* c. 1980s; Inter Press Service (news agency), former London correspondent; *Filipinos in Europe* (magazine), former editor. Presenter at schools and conferences.

Member

Society of Children's Book Writers and Illustrators.

Awards, Honors

Undiscovered Voices Award, Society of Children's Book Writers and Illustrators (SCBWI), 2008; Carnegie Medal nomination, Waterstone's Children's Book Prize shortlist, Branford Boase Award shortlist, SCBWI Crystal Kite Award for Europe, and Blue Peter My Favourite Story Prize shortlist, and numerous regional U.K. award shortlists all c. 2011, all for *Tall Story.*

Writings

Hinabing Gunita: Woven Memories—Filipinos in the United Kingdom, CF Books (England), 2004.
Animal Tricksters (short stories), Oxford Schools Press (Oxford, England), 2010.
Tall Story, David Fickling Books (London, England), 2010, David Fickling Books (New York, NY), 2011.

Author of documentary *Motherless Nation,* broadcast on BBC Radio 4; author of scripts for children's television programming. Contributor to anthologies, including *Under the Weather: Stories about Climate Change,* edited by Tony Bradman, Frances Lincoln, 2010.

Sidelights

Candy Gourlay grew up in the Philippines, where she earned a degree in journalism and worked for Manila's *Philippine Daily Inquirer* during the 1980s, reporting on the People Power revolution that led to the fall of dictator Ferdinand Marcos when election corruption was uncovered in 1986. After marrying fellow journalist Richard Gourlay, who worked for the *Financial Times,* Gourlay relocated to London, England to raise her family. Her ties to her native country remained strong, however, and she worked as a press correspondent for an international news agency while also editing the magazine *Filipinos in Europe.* A visit to the Philippines in 2005 let to her noteworthy news documentary *Motherless Nation,* which sparked interest in the plight of children abandoned by migrant farm workers when it aired on England's Radio 4. While much of her writing has been factual, Gourlay also worked behind the scenes as a fiction writer, and almost a decade of effort led to her first published novel, *Tall Story.*

Gourlay mixes several interests in *Tall Story,* including her fascination with gigantism and her affection for Filipino culture and traditions. In her story, Bernardo stands eight feet tall by the time he reaches age sixteen, his unnatural size the result of gigantism rather than just being tall fir his age. In his village of San Andreas, people treat the boy kindly, viewing him as a quasi folk hero on the order of legendary giant Bernardo Carpio. When Bernardo moves to London to join his mother, a nurse, and his thirteen-year-old half-sister Andi, adjustments must be made, not only for the young man but for his sister as well. Shorter than her classmates and

crazy about basketball, Andi dreams of playing point guard on her school team, and the arrival of her brother proves a distraction because his provincial ways and lack of English require her to look after him. In the siblings' intertwining first-person narratives *Tall Story* captures the young teen's frustration but also articulates Bernardo's worry that San Andreas will have no defender from the bad spirits that he believes he has protected the town from since birth.

In *Tall Story* Gourlay "effortlessly encompasses real-world dreams as well as magic realism," according to *Booklist* critic Karen Cruze, and in *School Library Journal* Gerry Larson praised the story for mixing "an appealing blend of diverse characters, emotional conflicts, well-paced action, and an upbeat finale." "A complex yet highly accessible and engaging novel," according to *Horn Book* reviewer Susan Dove Lempke, *Tall Story* "lends itself to discussion both of concrete topics such as immigration and of abstract ideas about belief, magic, and sacrifice." A *Publishers Weekly* critic remarked on another aspect of the author's debut novel, writing of *Tall Story* that "Gourlay weaves just enough magic into this moving family reunion to deliver an emotional punch."

Cover of Candy Gourlay's engaging friendship tale Tall Story, *which features cover art by David Dean.* (Book cover copyright © 2011 by David Fickling Books. Used by permission of David Fickling Books, an imprint of Random House Children's Books, a division of Random House, Inc.)

Biographical and Critical Sources

PERIODICALS

Booklist, January 1, 2011, Karen Cruze, review of *Tall Story*, p. 90, and Gillian Engberg, review of *Under the Weather: Stories about Climate Change*, p 111.

Horn Book, May-June, 2011, Susan Dove Lempke, review of *Tall Story*, p. 90.

Publishers Weekly, December 20, 2010, review of *Tall Story*, p. 53.

School Librarian, spring, 2010, Frances Breslin, review of *Under the Weather*, p. 46; autumn, 2010, Louise Ellis-Barrett, review of *Tall Story*, p. 164.

School Library Journal, March, 2011, Gerry Larson, review of *Tall Story*, p 161.

ONLINE

Asia in the Heart, World on the Mind Web log, http://asiaintheheart.blogpot.com/ (November 30, 2009), interview with Gourlay.

Candy Gourlay Home Page, http://www.candygourlay.com (February 15, 2012).

Candy Gourlay Web log, http://candygourlay.blogspot.com (February 15, 2012).

Tall Story Web site, http://www.tallstory.net (February 15, 2012).*

* * *

GREY, Mini

Personal

Born in Wales; partner's name Tony; children: Herbie. *Education:* University College London, B.A. (English); studied theatre design; University of Brighton, M.A. (sequential illustration). *Hobbies and other interests:* Walking, cycling, "playing electric piano BADLY."

Addresses

Home—Oxford, England.

Career

Author and illustrator. Formerly worked as a puppet maker and theatre designer; teacher in South London, England, for six years; currently freelance illustrator. Presenter at schools and conferences.

Awards, Honors

Kate Greenaway Award shortlist, 2004, for *The Pea and the Princess*, 2005, for *Traction Man Is Here!*, 2011, for *Jim* by Hillaire Belloc; Nestlé Smarties Gold Medal in Five Years and Under category, 2004, for *Biscuit Bear;* Blue Peter Award shortlist, and *Boston Globe/Horn Book* Award, both 2006, and Hampshire Illus-

Mini Grey (Reproduced by permission.)

trated Book Award shortlist, 2007, all for *Traction Man Is Here!;* Kate Greenaway Medal, 2007, for *The Adventures of the Dish and the Spoon.*

Writings

SELF-ILLUSTRATED

Egg Drop, Jonathan Cape (London, England), 2002, Knopf (New York, NY), 2009.
The Pea and the Princess, Jonathan Cape (London, England), 2003, published as *The Very Smart Pea and the Princess-to-Be,* Knopf (New York, NY), 2003.
Biscuit Bear, Jonathan Cape (London, England), 2004, published as *Ginger Bear,* Knopf (New York, NY), 2007.
Traction Man Is Here!, Knopf (New York, NY), 2005.
The Adventures of the Dish and the Spoon, Knopf (New York, NY), 2006.
Traction Man Meets Turbodog, Knopf (New York, NY), 2008.
Three by the Sea, Alfred A. Knopf (New York, NY), 2010.
Traction Man and the Beach Odyssey, Alfred A. Knopf (New York, NY), 2012.

ILLUSTRATOR

June Crebbin, *The Crocodile Is Coming!* (poems), Walker (London, England) 2005.

Lyn Gardner, *Into the Woods,* David Fickling (New York, NY), 2006.
Dick King-Smith, *The Twin Giants,* Walker (London, England), 2007, Candlewick Press (Cambridge, MA), 2008.
Lyn Gardner, *Out of the Woods,* David Fickling Books (New York, NY), 2009.
Hilaire Belloc, *Jim, Who Ran Away from His Nurse, and Was Eaten by a Lion* (new edition), Jonathan Cape (London, England), 2009, published as *Jim: A Cautionary Tale,* Alfred Knopf (New York, NY), 2010.

Sidelights

British-born author and illustrator Mini Grey has always enjoyed crafting things. Beginning with an English degree, she added training in both theatre arts and fine arts, experience as a puppet-maker, and six years' work as a teacher in South London schools to fashion a successful career creating children's picture books. In addition to producing illustrations for stories by other writers, Grey is also the author and illustrator of award-winning self-illustrated stories such as *The Pea and the Princess*—published in the United States as *The Very Smart Pea and the Princess-to-Be*—*Egg Drop,* and *Traction Man Is Here!* "Grey has a knack for reimagining nursery rhymes and other children's classics," wrote a *Publishers Weekly* critic in a review of *Ginger Bear,* a story by Grey that is based on the well-known tale of the Gingerbread Man.

Grey was born in South Wales, and she was named for the particular place where she first greeted the world: her parents' Mini Cooper (the brand name of a small British car). Her method of illustration evolved from her penchant for making things out of other things; "I usually use watercolour, ink, pencils and collage bits and bobs on heavy watercolour paper," she explained in an interview for the *Seven Impossible Things before Breakfast Web log.* "I am keen on Quink ink and bleach. I love splattering. And I use a computer quite a lot." When creating her own stories, she balances her energetic art with words that are often incorporated into the pictures. "To me, a picture book is a unique way of story-telling," she noted. "Words and pictures work as a double act where neither is necessarily in charge—and I do think they are for people of all ages."

A well-known tale is turned topsy-turvy in *The Very Smart Pea and the Princess-to-Be,* as Grey recounts the classic test for princess-hood from the poor pea's point of view. Raised in a pod in the palace garden, this particular pea knows it has a higher purpose than the royal dining table, and sure enough, it is plucked by the queen and used as a way to test potential wives for her son, the prince. Realizing that the test is flawed after a number of highly qualified princesses sleep like babies atop the pile of mattresses under which the small pea has been placed, the little legume decides to intervene; when the pretty young gardener who once tended it is tested for princess-hood, the pea rolls up the mattress moun-

tain and whispers relentlessly about the lump in the girl's mattress. A *Kirkus Reviews* critic described *The Very Smart Pea and the Princess-to-Be* as a "rib-tickling" tale, adding that Grey's illustrations contain "plenty of sight gags" that pair with her "chatty narrative." Susan Dove Lempke also praised Grey's story in *Horn Book,* citing its "visual wit" and commenting on the "vegetable and fruit motifs" that appear in its painted illustrations.

In *Egg Drop* Grey tells the story of an egg that knows its destiny is to fly, while *The Adventures of the Dish and the Spoon* follows the famed dish and spoon of "Hey Diddle Diddle" fame as the affectionate duo makes its way in the world, even resorting to robbery and the resulting jail time. Set during the Great Depression of the 1930s, *The Adventures of the Dish and the Spoon* draws on the popular culture of the era, from slapstick comedy to the mythos surrounding American bank robbers Bonnie and Clyde. In *Horn Book* Christine M. Heppermann cited Grey's "amusingly surreal mixed-media" illustrations as a feature of her "fanciful rags-to-riches tale." "Sprung from a familiar stanza," according to a *Publishers Weekly* critic, the author/illustrator's "inventive tale of true love will sustain many rereadings by readers of all ages." In the *New York Times Book Review* Jessica Bruder concluded that Grey's illustrations for *The Adventures of the Dish and the Spoon* "glow with humor and affection" and contain "plenty of comedic clues to reward careful readers."

Published in Grey's native England as *Biscuit Bear, Ginger Bear* combines her multimedia art with an "edgy story" in which a "slightly arch tone . . . add[s] a lovely fairy-tale flavor," according to *School Library Journal* critic Susan Moorhead. In the tale, young Horace bakes a bear-shaped cookie that looks tempting to eat, but at his mother's urging he places the treat on his pillow to save it for another day. Then the fantasy begins: coming to life, the cookie-crisp Ginger Bear heads to the kitchen to cook up some yummy new friends. Although many of the cookies he bakes wind up being eaten, Ginger Bear ultimately finds a safe home in the window of a local bakery. In *Kirkus Reviews* a critic dubbed *Ginger Bear* a "sweet little offering" that benefits from Grey's "graphic inventiveness," while in *Horn Book* Heppermann characterized the story as "a rambunctious, sometimes gleeful macabre foray into the world of baked goods." *Biscuit Bear* won the 2004 Smarties Prize, a significant achievement considering that it was Grey's third picture book.

Traction Man Is Here! is one of Grey's most popular stories and chronicles a boy's adventures while putting his brand new, camouflage-wearing action figure through its high-adventure paces. Told through the boy's eyes, the story follows Traction Man as the toy household horrors such as the Poisonous Dishcloth and rises above the indignity of wearing a very green sweater hand-knit by a loving grandma. In *School Library Journal* reviewer Marge Loch-Wouters dubbed *Traction Man Is Here!* an "imaginative and very funny romp."

Traction Man Meets Turbodog continues the story, as Traction Man spends a messy day exploring the family compost heap, has fun cleaning up with new super-friend Scrubbing Brush, and ends the day teaming up with his human companion to toast marshmallows over a campfire. Further adventures await fans in *Traction Man and the Beach Odyssey,* which takes readers along on a family day at the seashore. Grey's "inventive scenes" in *Traction Man Meets Turbodog* "celebrate the joy in . . . re-envisioning the everyday" and are full of "humor, delicious language," and imaginative ideas, according to *School Library Journal* critic Wendy Lukehart. In *Publishers Weekly* a critic concluded that Grey's "real gift is in transforming an ordinary household into both thrilling stage and supporting cast," while Heppermann wrote that the author/illustrator's "irreverent wit" is a highlight of her "playful demonstration of why high-tech doesn't necessarily equal high-performance."

Dog, Cat, and Mouse are the best of friends, and they all star in Grey's *Three by the Sea.* The trio lives together peacefully in their small cabin, where they share daily tasks and enjoy the soothing sounds of the nearby ocean. When a foxy stranger arrives and subtly sews discontent, the three friends begin to quibble and soon their peaceful seaside life is at risk. In *Kirkus Reviews* a critic described *Three by the Sea* as a "pithy British im-

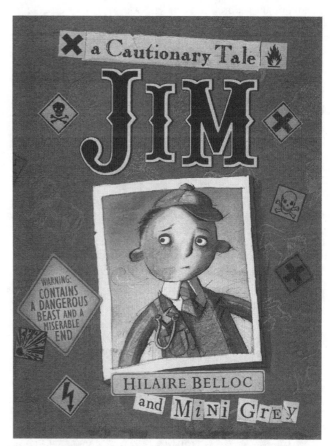

Grey creates a fresh face for an old story in her collage artwork for Hillaire Belloc's quirky story in **Jim: A Cautionary Tale.** (Illustration copyright © by Mini Grey. Reproduced by permission of Borzoi Books, an imprint of Random House Children's Books, a division of Random House, Inc.)

port" that pairs a "thought-provoking message" about appreciating others with "wonderfully expressive, richly textured mixed-media collages." The book's author/ illustrator is among "the more inventive picture-book creators working these days," asserted Ian Chipman in his *Booklist* appraisal of the story, and in *School Library Journal* Carolyn Janssen predicted that the "entertaining tale" in *Three by the Sea* "will not grow old."

In creating her original picture-book texts, Grey finds inspiration in both her home town and her own interests. "My stories often seem to take place in quite ordinary settings," she told Patricia Newman in *California Kids*. For example, in *Biscuit Bear* "I had to do detailed research into all types of biscuits and eat them!" "Picture books are a particular way of telling a story two ways at once . . . ," the artist added, "and [they] can be as simple or as complicated as anything else."

An illustrator as well as an author, Grey has also contributed work to Lyn Gardner's middle-grade novel *Into the Woods*, where her "appealing" pen-and-ink images "add humor and detail to the story," according to *Booklist* critic Kay Weisman. Another illustration project, bringing to life Edwardian author Hilaire Belloc's humorous story *Jim, Who Ran away from His Nurse and Was Eaten by a Lion* in lift-the-flap form, prompted *School Librarian* contributor to dub the book "a magical combination" of "Belloc's wacky verse" and "Grey's ingenious illustrations and language play." A new edition of a story first published in 1907, Grey's version of the macabre and often-bloody parody was praised for its "gorgeous and bold" artwork in *Kirkus Reviews,* the critic there predicting that "all but the most sensitive children . . . will laugh their . . . heads off."

Biographical and Critical Sources

PERIODICALS

Booklist, March 1, 2005, Carolyn Phelan, review of *Traction Man Is Here!,* p. 1203; May 1, 2007, Kay Weisman, review of *Into the Woods,* p. 91; July 1, 2008, Carolyn Phelan, review of *The Twin Giants,* p. 75; July 1, 2009, Ian Chipman, review of *Egg Drop,* p. 66; February 1, 2011, Ian Chipman, review of *Three by the Sea,* p. 83.

California Kids, September, 2005, Patricia Newman, "Who Wrote That?: Featuring Mini Grey."

Guardian (London, England), November 21, 2009, Julia Eccleshare, review of *Jim, Who Ran away from His Nurse and Was Eaten by a Lion,* p. 14.

Horn Book, November-December, 2003, Susan Dove Lempke, review of *The Very Smart Pea and the Princess-to-Be,* p. 730; March-April, 2005, Christine M. Heppermann, review of *Traction Man Is Here!,* p. 188; January-February, 2006, Mini Grey, transcript of *Boston Globe/Horn Book* Award acceptance speech, p.

17; May-June, 2006, Christine M. Heppermann, review of *The Adventures of the Dish and the Spoon,* p. 295; July-August, 2007, Christine M. Heppermann, review of *Ginger Bear,* p. 378, and Claire E. Gross, review of *Into the Woods,* p. 395; September-October, 2008, Christine M. Heppermann, review of *Traction Man Meets Turbodog,* p. 568; July-August, 2009, Kitty Flynn, review of *Egg Drop,* p. 408; March-April, 2010, Claire E. Gross, review of *Out of the Woods,* p. 55; March-April, 2011, Christine M. Hepperman, review of *Three by the Sea,* p. 102.

Kirkus Reviews, August 15, 2003, review of *The Very Smart Pea and the Princess-to-Be,* p. 1073; March 15, 2005, review of *Traction Man Is Here!,* p. 352; May 15, 2007, reviews of *Ginger Bear* and *Into the Woods;* June 15, 2009, review of *Egg Drop;* March 1, 2010, review of *Out of the Woods;* August 15, 2010, review of *Jim;* March 1, 2011, review of *Three by the Sea.*

New York Times Book Review, November 12, 2006, Jessica Bruder, review of *The Adventures of the Dish and the Spoon,* p. 21.

Publishers Weekly, March 7, 2005, review of *Traction Man Is Here!,* p. 67; March 13, 2006, review of *The Adventures of the Dish and the Spoon,* p. 65; May 21, 2007, review of *Ginger Bear,* p. 54; August 4, 2008, review of *Traction Man Meets Turbodog,* p. 60; July 13, 2009, review of *Egg Drop,* p. 57; September 6, 2010, review of *Jim,* p. 39; February 28, 2011, review of *Three by the Sea,* p. 57.

School Librarian, winter, 2002, review of *Egg Drop,* p. 186; autumn, 2003, review of *The Princess and the Pea,* p. 130; June, 2007, Margaret A. Chang, review of *Into the Woods,* p. 144; winter, 2010, Martin Axford, review of *Three by the Sea,* p. 219; spring, 2010, Prue Goodwin, review of *Jim, Who Ran away from His Nurse and Was Eaten by a Lion,* p. 33.

School Library Journal, September, 2003, Wendy Woodfill, review of *The Very Smart Pea and the Princess-to-Be,* p. 179; June, 2005, Marge Loch-Wouters, review of *Traction Man Is Here!,* p. 115; April, 2006, Wanda Meyers-Hines, review of *The Adventures of the Dish and the Spoon,* p. 106; June, 2007, Susan Moorhead, review of *Ginger Bear,* p. 100; July, 2008, Mary-ann H. Owen, review of *The Twin Giants,* p. 76; August, 2008, Wendy Lukehart, review of *Traction Man Meets Turbodog,* p. 90; June, 2009, Marge Loch-Wouters, review of *Egg Drop,* p. 88; June, 2010, Mandy Lawrence, review of *Out of the Woods,* p. 102; October, 2010, Julie R. Ranelli, review of *Jim,* p. 80; April, 2011, Rick Margolis, "What Makes Mini Run?" (interview), p. 20, and Carolyn Janssen, review of *Three by the Sea,* p. 144.

ONLINE

British Book Trust Web site, http://www.booktrusted.co.uk/ (December 1, 2005), Madelyn Travis, "Bear-Faced Biscuit."

Random House Web site, http://www.randomhouse.com/ (September 20, 2009), "Mini Grey."

Seven Impossible Things before Breakfast Web log, blaine. org/sevenimpossiblethings/ (October 8, 2008), interview with Grey.*

H

HACOHEN, Dean 1958-

Personal
Born 1958, in CT; mother an elementary school librarian; children: three. *Education:* Boston University, B.S. (communication). *Hobbies and other interests:* Playing piano, composing music, ceramics, stained glass.

Addresses
Home—White Plains, NY. *E-mail*—dean.hacohen@gmail.com.

Career
Creative director and writer. Doyle Dane Bernbach, copywriter, senior writer, then vice president, 1982-87; Goldsmith/Jeffrey, head writer and associate creative director, then partner,1987-96; Lowe New York, creative director, then executive creative director, 1996-2005; Cramer-Krasselt, Chicago, IL, executive creative director, 2006-09; BBDO New York, executive creative director, beginning 2009.

Awards, Honors
(With others) numerous advertising industry awards.

Writings
Tuck Me In!, illustrated by Sherry Scharschmidt Candlewick Press (Somerville, MA), 2010.

Sidelights
Dean Hacohen grew up in Connecticut, where his future as a copywriter and advertising executive were foreshadowed in his efforts to come up with creative ways to promote school book fairs. A degree in communication led Hacohen to a succession of advertising

Dean Hacohen (Photograph by Bruce Lettieri. Reproduced by permission.)

jobs at agencies in both New York City and Chicago. Early on, he met advertising art director Sherry Scharschmidt, a coworker who shared his interest in storytelling. Although their careers eventually took them in separate directions, Hacohen and Scharschmidt reunited several years later and ultimately created their first book for children, *Tuck Me In!,* which a *Publishers Weekly* critic described as "tailormade for bedtime."

In *Tuck Me In!* young readers have the chance to play parent to a wide assortment of young creatures, among them an alligator, mouse, pig, zebra, hedgehog, and even a colorful peacock. The story's lift-the-flap for-

Hacohen teams up with friend and artist Sherry Scharschmidt to create the engaging bedtime story **Tuck Me In!** (Illustration copyright © 2010 by Sherry Scharschmidt. Reproduced by permission of Candlewick Press, Somerville, MA.)

mat," which a *Kirkus Reviews* contributor praised for its "novelty," allows children to cover each baby animal with a cozy blanket as bedtime approaches. Scharschmidt's computer-generated illustrations "are colorful basic shapes with quick brush strokes adding details," according to the same reviewer, while *School Library Journal* contributor Marge Loch-Wouters praised the artist's "sketchy, jazzy style." Hacohen's "gentle, rhythmic" text also earned a nod from Loch-Wouters, the reviewer predicting that *Tuck Me In!* will entrance toddlers and "be re-read endlessly as a comfy prelude to [their own] bedtime."

Biographical and Critical Sources

PERIODICALS

Kirkus Reviews, August 1, 2010, review of *Tuck Me In!*
Magpies, November, 2010, Tali Lavi, review of *Tuck Me In!,* p. 24.
Publishers Weekly, August 23, 2010, review of *Tuck Me In!,* p. 48.
School Library Journal, August, 2010, Marge Loch-Wouters, review of *Tuck Me In!,* p. 76.

ONLINE

Dean Hacohen Home Page, http://deanhacohen.com (February 12, 2012).

HANSON, Warren 1949-

Personal

Born April 17, 1949, in Yankton, SD; son of Clifford G. (a salesman) and Grace E. (a homemaker) Hanson; married Patricia L. Wallway (a disabilities counselor; marriage ended); married 2009; second wife's name Becky (an educator); children: (first marriage) Cody W., Lacey E. *Education:* Augustana College, B.A. (theatre), 1971; College of Visual Arts (St. Paul, MN), B.F.A., 1973. *Hobbies and other interests:* Music, reading, travel.

Addresses

Home—Houston, TX. *E-mail*—warren@warrenhanson. com.

Career

Author, musician, and illustrator of children's books. Advertising agency art director in Bloomington, MN, 1973-74; freelance author and illustrator. Musician, with recordings including *Waiting for the Wind, Christmas and Always,* and *Grace and Chocolate.* Public speaker and program presenter; advocate for literacy causes.

Awards, Honors

Platinum Award, Oppenheim Toy Portfolio, 2010, for *The Sea of Sleep* illustrated by Jim LaMarche.

Writings

SELF-ILLUSTRATED

A Is for Adult: An Alphabet Book for Grown-Ups, Waldman House Press (Minneapolis, MN), 1993.
Haunted Hardware, Waldman House Press (Minneapolis, MN), 1995.
The Next Place, Waldman House Press (Minneapolis, MN), 1997.
Older Love, Waldman House Press (Minneapolis, MN), 1999.
(Compiler, with Tim Nyberg) *What Does the President Do?: Real Comments by Real Kids,* Kids Tell Us (St. Paul, MN), 2004.
Raising You Alone, Tristan Publishing (Minneapolis, MN), 2005.
Kiki's Hats, Tristan Publishing (Golden Valley, MN), 2007.
Paw Prints in the Stars: A Farewell and Journal for a Beloved Pet, Tristan Publishing (Golden Valley, MN), 2008.
Everything Happens for a Reason, Tristan Publishing (Golden Valley, MN), 2009.
Today's Special: Yes It Is, Tristan Publishing (Golden Valley, MN), 2010.
Dear Me, Tristan Publishing (Golden Valley, MN), 2011.

FOR CHILDREN

Grandpa Has a Great Big Face, illustrated by Mark Elliott, Laura Geringer Books (New York, NY), 2006.

Bugtown Boogie, illustrated by Steve Johnson and Lou Fancher, Laura Geringer Books (New York, NY), 2008.

The Sea of Sleep, illustrated by Jim LaMarche, Scholastic Press (New York, NY), 2010.

It's Monday, Mrs. Jolly Bones, illustrated by Tricia Tusa, Beach Lane Books (New York, NY), 2013.

ILLUSTRATOR

Tom Hegg, *A Cup of Christmas Tea,* Waldman House Press (Minneapolis, MN), 1982.

Tom Hegg, *Up to the Lake,* Waldman House Press (Minneapolis, MN), 1986.

Tom Hegg, *To the Mark of the Maker,* Waldman House Press (Minneapolis, MN), 1991.

Tom Hegg, *To Nourish Any Flower: The Request Collection,* Waldman House Press (Minneapolis, MN), 1994.

Tom Hegg, *Peef, the Christmas Bear,* Waldman House Press (Minneapolis, MN), 1995.

Tom Hegg, *A Silent Night for Peef,* Waldman House Press (Minneapolis, MN), 1998.

Tom Hegg, *A Memory of Christmas Tea,* Waldman House Press (Minneapolis, MN), 1999.

Richard Jorgensen, *Reading with Dad,* Waldman House Press (Minneapolis, MN), 2000.

Tom Hegg, *Peef and His Best Friend,* Waldman House Press (Minneapolis, MN), 2001.

Beginning: Encouragement at the Start of Something New, Waldman House Press (Minneapolis, MN), 2002.

Rick Kupchella, *Tell Me What We Did Today,* Tristan Publishing (Minneapolis, MN), 2003.

Tom Hegg, *Peef and the Baby Sister,* Waldman House Press (Minneapolis, MN), 2006.

Sidelights

A native of South Dakota, Warren Hanson earned a degree in theatre before developing his artistic talent at Minnesota's College of Visual Arts. Hanson began his working life in advertising, but eventually he shifted his creative focus to book illustration as well as developing a parallel career as a musician. His work began appearing in children's books in the early 1990s, when he was tapped to illustrate Tom Hegg's *Peef, the Christmas Bear* and its sequels, and his first self-illustrated story, *The Next Place,* has become something of a modern classic in the bereavement genre since its publication in 1997. Praising *Peef and His Best Friend, School Library Journal* critic Susan Hepler cited "Hanson's bright watercolors" as attractive to young children.

In his award-winning picture book *The Sea of Sleep* Hanson tells the story of Baby Otter, who rests in Mama Otter's cozy embrace while watching swimming dolphins, the rising moon, and the sparkling surface of the darkening sea. "Every statement applied to the actual ocean nicely mirrors the experience of falling into a deep sleep," wrote a *Kirkus Reviews* critic, and in *School Library Journal* Catherine Callegari noted the "lilting, poetic language" in Hanson's "plot-free bedtime story." Paired with the author's simple, lyrical rhyming text, Jim LaMarche's colored-pencil and acrylic images capture the gentle beauty of the night, creating a mood "so

Warren Hanson's gentle bedtime story in The Sea of Sleep ***is enriched by the work of artist Jim LaMarche.*** (Illustration copyright © 2010 by Jim LaMarche. Reproduced by permission of Scholastic, Inc.)

soothing that young readers may . . . fall . . . asleep before the book is finished," according to a _Publishers Weekly_ critic.

Bugtown Boogie also takes place at night, but for the young boy in Hanson's story dusk brings with it a crazy energy. As he walks through the moonlit woods, the chirping, clicking, and fluttering of insects all comes together in a musical revelry that the author details through what _School Library Journal_ critic Kirsten Cutler described as "jazzy rhyming couplets" and "jaunty rhymes." In the mixed-media illustrations contributed by noted artists Stephen Johnson and Lou Fancher, a range of musician-playing insects are revealed, "strange critters that only occasionally correspond with etymological reality," according to a _Kirkus Reviews_ writer. "Hanson's syncopated verse scans handily," the critic added, recommending _Bugtown Boogie_ as "a swell read-aloud for intrepid parents."

Hanson addresses single moms and dads in _Raising You Alone,_ a picture book designed to reassure youngsters about the unique experiences in one-parent families. "Deftly written and colorfully illustrated," according to a _Children's Bookwatch_ critic, _Raising You Alone_ "is a wonderfully presented picture book."

"I love what I do," Hanson once told _SATA._ "I try to let that love show in every book I do. I try to make each of my books, even the silly ones, as positive as I can. I don't believe in putting more negative stuff into the world. I think of my books as my children. I give them the best I can while they are with me. Then they go out into the world and live their lives. I, as their parent, can only sit back and watch.

"I have one piece of advice for anyone who wants to create books. Advice for anyone, really. Turn off the TV. It isn't real and it isn't good. TV thinks you're stupid. But I know that you're not. Turn it off, and you'll be amazed at what you find inside you."

Biographical and Critical Sources

PERIODICALS

Children's Bookwatch, November, 2005, review of _Raising You Alone;_ February, 2007, review of _Peef and the Baby Sister;_ February, 2010, review of _Kiki's Hats._
Houston Chronicle, August 15, 2010, Valerie Sweeten, "Multiple Talents" (profile), p. 1.
Kirkus Reviews, August 15, 2010, review of _Sea of Sleep;_ May 15, 2008, review of _Bugtown Boogie._
Post-Bulletin (Rochester, MN), December 19, 2008, Heather J. Carlson, "Inspiration for Children's Book Has 'Soul of Santa Claus.'"
Publishers Weekly, November 20, 1995, review of _Peef the Christmas Bear,_ p. 76; September 20, 2010, review of _The Sea of Sleep,_ p. 64.

School Library Journal, February, 2001, Karen Scott, review of _Reading with Dad,_ p. 100; February, 2002, Susan Hepler, review of _Peef and His Best Friend,_ p. 107; May, 2006, Martha Topol, review of _Grandpa Has a Great Big Face,_ p. 89; July, 2008, Kirsten Cutler, review of _Bugtown Boogie,_ p. 74; December, 2010, Catherine Callegari, review of _The Sea of Sleep,_ p. 83.

ONLINE

Tristan Publishing Web site, http://www.tristanpublishing. com/ (February 12, 2012), "Warren Hanson."
Warren Hanson Home Page, http://www.warrenhanson. com (February 12, 2012).

* * *

HENRY, Jed

Personal

Married; children: two daughters. _Education:_ Brigham Young University, B.F.A. (illustration and animation), 2008.

Addresses

Home—Provo, UT. _Agent_—Shannon Associates, 333 W. 57th St., Ste. 809, New York, NY 10019. _E-mail_—thejedhenry@gmail.com.

Career

Illustrator, animator, and writer. Feature Films for Families, storyboard and layout artist, 2005-07; freelance illustrator and author; presenter at workshops.

Writings

SELF-ILLUSTRATED

I Speak Dinosaur, Harry N. Abrams (New York, NY), 2012.
Cheer up, Mouse, Houghton Mifflin (Boston, MA), 2012.

ILLUSTRATOR

Mike Huckabee, _Can't Wait 'till Christmas,_ G.P. Putnam's Sons (New York, NY), 2010.
Marsha Wilson Chall, _Pick a Pup,_ Margaret K. McElderry Books (New York, NY), 2011.
Diana Manning, _Now I Lay Me down to Sleep: A Bedtime Prayer,_ Hallmark (Kansas City, MO), 2011.
Susan Hood, _Just Say Boo,_ HarperCollins (New York, NY), 2012.

Biographical and Critical Sources

PERIODICALS

Booklist, February 1, 2011, Ilene Cooper, review of _Pick a Pup,_ p. 82.

Publishers Weekly, December 20, 2010, review of *Pick a Pup,* p. 51.

School Library Journal, April, 2011, Kristine M. Casper, review of *Pick a Pup,* p. 141.

ONLINE

Jed Henry Home Page, http://www.jedhenry.com (February 15, 2012).

Jed Henry Web log, http://jedart.blogspot.com (February 15, 2012).

Kid Shannon Web site, http://www.kidshannon.com/ (February 15, 2012), "Jed Henry."

*　　*　　*

HOUCK, Colleen 1969-

Personal

Born 1969, in Tucson, AZ; married. *Education:* Associate's degree; attended University of Arizona. *Hobbies and other interests:* Reading genre fiction.

Addresses

Home—Salem, OR. *Agent*—Alex Glass, Trident Media Group, 41 Madison Ave., 36th Fl., New York, NY 10010.

Career

Author. Certified American Sign Language interpreter and video relay interpreter for seventeen years; former restaurant manager.

Awards, Honors

Next Generation Indie Award finalist 2010, and Parents' Choice Award, both for "Tiger Saga" novels.

Writings

"TIGER SAGA" NOVEL SERIES

Tiger's Curse, Sterling (New York, NY), 2011.
Tiger's Quest, Sterling (New York, NY), 2011.
Tiger's Voyage, Splinter (New York, NY), 2011.

Adaptations

The "Tiger Saga" novel series was adapted for audiobook by Brilliance Audio, beginning 2011, and has been optioned for film by Raphael Kryszek, Ineffable Pictures.

Sidelights

Colleen Houck ranks reading at the top of her list of hobbies, and her tastes run from romance to science fiction to adventure novels. However, she was inspired to move from reader to writer after reading the real-life stories of young-adult authors J.K. Rowling and Stephenie Meyer and their quick rise from determined novice to best-selling-author. Determined to see if she could do the same, Houck started writing and eventually completed two novels: *Tiger's Curse* and a sequel, *Tiger's Quest.* When she was unable to interest an agent in marketing her novels, Houck decided to publish them novels herself and sell them in a Kindle e-book version. When *Tiger's Curse* became an e-book bestseller, she was contacted by an agent and a publishing contract soon followed. Along with the first two novels, which were revised while making the transition from e-book to print edition, Houck has continued her "Tiger Saga" series in a third novel, *Tiger's Voyage.*

In *Tiger's Curse* Houck introduces Kelsey Hayes, an eighteen year old whose adventurous spirit makes her the perfect fit for her new job with a traveling circus. Soon Kelsey discovers that the troupe's white tiger, Dhiren, is actually a centuries' old East Indian prince who has been cursed by an evil wizard and can only return to his very handsome human form for twenty-four minutes of each day. Feeling a romantic attraction to Dhiren, Kelsey is determined to undo the spell, but this requires a trip to India. Such a journey is no easy task with a tiger, but travel plans prove to be the least of her challenges when she finds herself confronting dark forces that include the powerful creature known as the Lokesh.

Describing Houck's fiction debut as "part *Twilight,* part Indiana Jones, and part fairy tale," Michael Cart added in *Booklist* that *Tiger's Curse* is an entertaining read "filled with chaste romance." A *Kirkus Reviews* writer recommended the same book for "*Twilight* fans ready for a not-too-radical change of pace," and a *Publishers Weekly* critic praised Houck's first "Tiger's Curse" installment as "richly imagined" and with an "attractive premise."

Kelsey's adventures continue in *Tiger's Quest* and *Tiger's Curse,* as the teen returns to her home in Oregon and with the hope of living a normal life. Her Indian exploits follow her, however, and once again returns to India, this time to confront the Lokesh while helping release Dhiren's brother Kishan from his own tiger's curse. Eventually reunited with Dhiren, Kelsey is heartbroken to find that the prince has no memory of her. Still, he joins her and brother Kishan to battle the five terrifying dragons that stand in the way of their freedom.

"Putting her background research to thorough use" in her "Tiger Saga" novels, a *Kirkus Reviews* writer maintained that Houck mixes "Hindu endearments and cultural information, plus . . . such supernatural entities as the goddess Durga, fairies, . . . and a giant snake." The "Tiger's Curse" novels "will appeal to teens who grew up on fairy tales," predicted Jane Henricksen Baird in

School Library Journal, and their story will reinforce the oft-hoped-for happy ending: that "the most perfectly ordinary girl will find her handsome prince."

"For the Tiger series, most of my ideas come from research along the way," Houck explained on her home page. "I studied books on the mythologies of the world and kept detailed notes of any cool ideas I found. The tests of the four houses actually came from a myth found in Mayan culture. I also get a lot of ideas from dreams."

Biographical and Critical Sources

PERIODICALS

Booklist, January 1, 2011, Michael Cart, review of *Tiger's Curse,* p. 100; June 1, 2011, Michael Cart, review of *Tiger's Quest,* p. 92.

Kirkus Reviews, December 15, 2010, review of *Tiger's Curse*; May 1, 2011, review of *Tiger's Quest.*

Oregonian, January 20, 2011, Jeff Baker, "Salem Author Colleen Houck Finds Success through E-Books."

Publishers Weekly, November 8, 2010, review of *Tiger's Curse,* p. 61.

School Library Journal, January, 2011, Heather M. Campbell, review of *Tiger's Curse,* p. 108; August, 2011, Jane Henriksen Baird, review of *Tiger's Quest,* p. 107.

ONLINE

Oregon Live Web site, http://www.oregonlive.com/ (October 16, 2011), "Colleen Houck."

Tigers Curse Web site, http://www.tigerscursebook.com/ (February 15, 2012).*

J-K

JORDAN-FENTON, Christy

Personal
Born in Alberta, Canada; married; children: three. *Education:* Norwich University (VT), degree; attended University of Queensland. *Hobbies and other interests:* Camping, travel, dancing, hiking, horses.

Addresses
Home—Fort St. John, British Columbia, Canada.

Career
Author and farmer. Formerly taught wilderness survival; developed a leadership challenge program for urban youth. Worked as a rodeo rider; performs as a cowgirl poet.

Awards, Honors
(With Margaret Pokiak-Fenton) U.S. Board on Books for Young People (USBBY) Outstanding International Books Honor selection, Nautilus Silver Award, *Skipping Stones* Honor Book selection, Information Book Award Honor Book selection, and Best Books for Kids and Teens selection, Canadian Children's Book Centre, all 2011, and Sheila A. Egoff Children's Literature Prize finalist, *ForeWord* Book of the Year Award finalist, nomination for Saskatchewan Young Readers' Choice Award, Hackmatack Award, Children's Literature Roundtables of Canada Information Book Award, Golden Oak Award, and Rocky Mountain Book Award, all for *Fatty Legs;* USBBY Outstanding International Books Award, 2012, for *A Stranger at Home.*

Writings

(With mother-in-law Margaret Pokiak-Fenton) *Fatty Legs: A True Story,* illustrated by Liz Amini-Holmes, Annick Press (Toronto, Ontario, Canada), 2010.

(With Margaret Pokiak-Fenton) *A Stranger at Home: A True Story,* illustrated by Liz Amini-Holmes, Annick Press (Toronto, Ontario, Canada), 2010.

Contributor to periodicals, including *Jones Ave.* and *Prairie Fire,* and to anthology *DiVerseCities 2.*

Author's work has been translated into French.

Biographical and Critical Sources

PERIODICALS

Canadian Review of Materials, November 12, 2010, Shelbey Krahn, review of *Fatty Legs: A True Story.*
Kirkus Reviews, November 15, 2010, review of *Fatty Legs;* October 15, 2011, review of *A Stranger at Home.*
Quill & Quire, November, 2010, Jean Mills, review of *Fatty Legs.*
School Library Journal, December, 2010, Jody Kopple, review of *Fatty Legs,* p. 139.

ONLINE

Annick Press Web site, http://www.annickpress.com/ (February 12, 2012), "Christy Jordan-Fenton."*

*　　*　　*

KARR, Julia

Personal
Born in IN; children: two daughters.

Addresses
Home—Chicago, IL. *Agent*—Kate Schafer Testerman, K.T. Literary, Highlands Ranch, CO 80129. *E-mail*—juliakarr@me.com.

Career

Author.

Writings

XVI, Speak (New York, NY), 2011.
Truth, Speak (New York, NY), 2012.

Author's work has been translated into German.

Sidelights

An Indiana native who still makes her home in the Midwest, Julia Karr began honing her storytelling skills as a child by writing descriptive letters. As a mother, she practiced storytelling in response to demands for a bedtime story, but eventually her two daughters grew up and left home. It was now that Karr began to seriously consider supplementing her nine-to-five job with a new career as a novelist working in the science-fiction genre. She questions the possibilities that might exist on a near-future Earth in her novel *XVI,* and she continues her story in her second novel, *Truth.*

XVI transports readers to 2150, the year Chicago native Nina Oberon will turn sixteen and become an adult. Atypical of most teens, Nina fears this particular approaching birthday because she lives in a society where all but the wealthiest women have few rights. Once she receives the brand of adulthood—an "XVI" tatooed on her wrist—she will join the other women competing for men's favors, all of them hoping to move up in society but some of them facing abuse and mistreatment. The teen's fears grow when her mother is attacked and left for dead, but the woman reveals an important secret before she dies: the father Nora thought had died before she was born is actually alive. A leader of the underground Resistance, he is now desperately in need of a coded message that is hidden in a book in the Oberon family library. While protecting this book and attempting to locate her elusive father, Nina also deals with adolescent issues, including a friendship with Sal, a handsome outsider who seems a bit too intent upon pursuing a relationship with her. Nina's saga continues in *Truth,* as her work resisting the totalitarian government helps her deal with the fact that she now bears the tattoo marking her as a human commodity.

In *XVI* Karr addresses serious themes, among them "the darker side of sex, media influence, government control, and women's equality," according to *School Library Journal* contributor Adrienne L. Strock. Courtney Jones predicted in *Booklist* that the author's "well-written, accessible sci-fi thriller will provoke discussion" of such topics among thoughtful teens. Noting Karr's focus on the sexualization of teen girls in her fiction debut, a *Publishers Weekly* reviewer remarked on the novel's "unusual blend of futuristic thriller and pro-abstinence advocacy." "Teens will enjoy the romantic melodrama" in *XVI,* Strock predicted, "and fans of dystopian novels will be drawn to the plot."

Cover of Julia Karr's futuristic teen novel XVI, *which transports readers to 2150 and the development of a misogynistic society.* (Cover photos © Cristina Page. Reproduced with permission of Speak, an imprint of Penguin Group (USA), Inc.)

Biographical and Critical Sources

PERIODICALS

Booklist, January 1, 2011, Courtney Jones, review of *XVI,* p. 103.
Bulletin of the Center for Children's Books, January, 2011, April Spisak, review of *XVI,* p. 242.
Kirkus Reviews, December 15, 2010, Julia Karr, review of *XVI.*
Publishers Weekly, November 8, 2010, review of *XVI,* p. 63.
School Library Journal, April, 2011, Adrienne L. Strock, review of *XVI,* p. 176.
Voice of Youth Advocates, February, 2011, Mary Ann Harlan, review of *XVI,* p. 571.

ONLINE

Julia Karr Home Page, http://juliakarr.com (February 12, 2012).
Julia Karr Web log, http://juliakarr.livejournal.com (February 12, 2012).

Reeding Teen Web site, http://www.readingteen.net/ (April, 2011), interview with Karr.*

*　　*　　*

KITTREDGE, Caitlin 1984-

Personal

Born 1984. *Education:* B.A. (English). *Hobbies and other interests:* Photography.

Addresses

Home—Western MA. *Agent*—Rachel Coyne, Fine Print Literary, 240 W. 35th St., Ste. 500, New York, NY 10001. *E-mail*—contact@caitlinkittredge.com.

Career

Novelist.

Writings

"NOCTURNE CITY" URBAN FANTASY NOVEL SERIES; FOR ADULTS

Night Life, St. Martin's Press (New York, NY), 2008.
Pure Blood, St. Martin's Press (New York, NY), 2008.
Second Skin, St. Martin's Press (New York, NY), 2009.
Witch Craft, St. Martin's Press (New York, NY), 2009.
Daemon's Mark, St. Martin's Press (New York, NY), 2010.

"BLACK LONDON" SUPERNATURAL NOVEL SERIES; FOR ADULTS

Street Magic, St. Martin's Press (New York, NY), 2009.
Demon Bound, St. Martin's Press (New York, NY), 2009.
Bone Gods, St. Martin's Press (New York, NY), 2010.
The Curse of Four, Subterranean Press, 2011.

"IRON CODEX" YOUNG-ADULT NOVEL SERIES

The Iron Thorn, Delacorte (New York, NY), 2011.
The Nightmare Garden, Delacorte (New York, NY), 2012.

OTHER

(With Jackie Kessler) *Black and White,* Ballantine Books (New York, NY), 2009.
(With Jackie Kessler) *Shades of Gray,* Ballantine Books (New York, NY), 2010.
The Iron Thorn, Delacorte (New York, NY), 2011.

Contributor to anthologies, including *The Mammoth Book of Vampire Romance 2,* edited by Trisha Telep, Running Press (Philadelphia, PA), 2009; *Huntress,* St. Martin's Paperbacks (New York, NY), 2009; *Strange Brew;* and *My Big, Fat Supernatural Honeymoon.*

Sidelights

Caitlin Kittredge is a novelist who lives in the northwestern United States and specializes in writing paranormal fiction for both teens and adults. Her "Nocturne City" urban fantasy series, which includes *Night Life, Pure Blood, Second Skin, Witch Craft,* and *Daemon's Mark,* follow homicide detective Luna Wilder as she keeps the two forms of life in Nocturne City—the human and the demonic—from bringing horror to the city streets. Kittredge's "Black London" series, which focuses on the supernatural adventures of punk rocker Jack Winter after he released an ancient and terrible spirit, also features a female detective: Petunia "Pete" Caldecott, who as Jack's girlfriend follows him in his new career as a mage. "Kittredge . . . knows how to create a believable world," wrote a *Publishers Weekly* critic in a review of "Black London" series opener *Street Magic,* "and her fans will enjoy the mix of magic and city grit."

Kittredge turns to teen fantasy fans in her "Iron Codex" novels, which meld elements of steampunk and fantasy in an alternate history set in nineteenth-century Massachusetts in a town named after well-known horror nov-

Cover of Caitlin Kittredge's steampunk fantasy **The Iron Thorn,** *which is part of her "Iron Codex" series and features cover art by Laura Jade.* (Book cover copyright © 2011 by Delacorte Press. Used by permission of Delacorte Press, an imprint of Random House Children's Books, a division of Random House, Inc.)

elist H.P. Lovecraft. Here life is controlled by the Proctors, a group whose members are guided by cool reason and determined to keep order despite the presence of magic. Aoife Grayson lives in Lovecraft, and studies at the School of Engines, and she dreams of the day when she will become an engineer. As Aoife approaches her sixteenth birthday, she realizes that her dream is threatened by the hereditary insanity that runs in her family and shows itself at that fateful age. Not willing to accept a future of madness, Aoife acts on a clue given her by her insane older brother in a lucid moment: she leaves Lovecraft and enters the unknown surrounding region, where strange creatures live and witchcraft rules. Her journey continues in *The Nightmare Garden,* as Aoife learns that the symptoms she attributed to hereditary madness are in fact symptoms of an excessive exposure to iron, an element that is lethal to the fey.

Kittredge's "world-building is masterful, richly detailed, and . . . atmospheric," noted Amy Fiske in her *Voice of Youth Advocates* review of *The Iron Thorn.* In *Booklist* Debbie Carton praised the novel's heroine as a "feisty and independent young woman with plenty of nerve and courage," and a *Publishers Weekly* critic wrote that the author "generates significant thrills and chills in [her] . . . fast-moving tale." "Fans of steampunk and supernatural fantasy will love this book and will look forward to the rest of the ["Iron Codex"] series," Fiske predicted, while in *School Library Journal* Tim Wadham concluded that in *The Iron Thorn* Kittredge treats readers to "a unique, action-filled, and compelling combination of steampunk, H.P. Lovecraft-inspired horror, and straight fantasy that should enchant fans of all three genres."

Biographical and Critical Sources

PERIODICALS

Booklist, January 1, 2011, Debbie Carton, review of *The Iron Thorn,* p. 96.
Library Journal, December, 2010, Jackie Cassada, review of *Bone Gods,* p. 106.
Magazine of Fantasy and Science Fiction, January-February, 2010, Charles de Lint, review of *Street Magic,* p. 31.
Publishers Weekly, April 27, 2009, review of *Street Magic,* p. 117May 4, 2009, review of *Black and White,* p. 38; December 13, 2010, review of *The Iron Thorn,* p. 59; June 13, 2011, review of *The Curse of Four,* p. 34.
School Library Journal, March, 2011, Tim Wadham, review of *The Iron Thorn,* p. 164.
Voice of Youth Advocates, April, 2011, Amy Fiske, review of *The Iron Thorn,* p. 83.

ONLINE

Caitlin Kittredge Home Page, http://www.caitlinkittredge.com (February 15, 2012).*

KLASSEN, Jon

Personal

Born in Niagara Falls, Ontario, Canada; immigrated to United States. *Education:* Sheridan College Institute of Technology, B.A. (animation), 2005.

Addresses

Home—Los Angeles, CA. *Agent*—Steve Malk, Writers House, 21 W. 26th St., New York, NY 10010; smalk@writershouse.com. *E-mail*—jonklassen@gmail.com.

Career

Illustrator, animator, and author. Animator, beginning 2005, working for Laika Studios and Dreamworks; freelance illustrator. California Institute of the Arts, Valencia, teacher of animation illustration. *Exhibitions:* Work included in group shows at Gallery 1998 Venice, Santa Monica, CA.

Awards, Honors

Canadian Governor General's Award for Illustration, 2010, for *Cats' Night Out* by Caroline Stutson; Best Illustrated Children's Book selection, *New York Times,* 2011, and Theodor Seuss Geisel Honor Book selection, 2012, both for *I Want My Hat Back.*

Writings

SELF-ILLUSTRATED

I Want My Hat Back, Candlewick Press (Somerville, MA), 2011.

ILLUSTRATOR

Caroline Stutson, *Cats' Night Out,* Simon & Schuster Books for Young Readers (New York, NY), 2010.
Mac Barnett, *Extra Yarn,* Balzer + Bray (New York, NY), 2011.
Ted Kooser, *House Held up by Trees,* Candlewick Press (Somerville, MA), 2012.

Contributor to periodicals, including *New York Times Book Review.* Work included in anthology *The Where, the What, and the How: Seventy-five Artists Illustrate the Wondrous Mysteries of the Universe,* 2012.

ILLUSTRATOR; "INCORRIGIBLE CHILDREN OF ASHTON PLACE" NOVEL SERIES BY MARYROSE WOOD

The Mysterious Howling, Balzer + Bray (New York, NY), 2010.
The Hidden Gallery, Balzer + Bray (New York, NY), 2011.
The Unseen Guest, Balzer + Bray (New York, NY), 2012.

Sidelights

After earning a degree in animation, Canadian-born artist Jon Klassen moved to California and a job as a concept artist for Dreamworks and Laika Studios, the latter where he worked on the film version of Neil Gaiman's novel *Coraline*. In more recent years, Klassen has turned to book illustration, where he gained a reputation for creating graphically sophisticated artwork. In addition to illustration projects that include Maryrose Wood's "Incorrigible Children of Ashton Place" novels and *House Held up by Trees*, a picture-book story by Pulitzer Prize-winning poet Ted Kooser, he is also the author of the self-illustrated story *I Want My Hat Back*, winner of Canada's 2010 Governor General's Award as well as a Theodor Seuss Geisel Award Honor Book selection.

Cats' Night Out, Klassen's first illustration project, features a rhyming text by Caroline Stutson that describes the feline population of a small city as it takes to the moonlit streets and dances to the rhythms of the city. In depicting "the cavalier kitties," the artist employs a "muted color palette" of inks and gouache that "contains the warm glow of a cityscape," according to a *Kirkus Reviews* writer, and Marilyn Taniguchi wrote in *School Library Journal* that *Cats' Night Out* treats readers to an "elegant" story-hour offering in which "Klassen's eye-catching digitally rendered urban streetscapes resemble the sets of classic musical theatre." Crafted with grey and brown tones, the artist's "subdued twilight cityscapes form an unexpectedly noir backdrop" to Stutson's music-filled tale, noted a *Publishers Weekly* contributor, while in *Booklist* Kristin McKulski asserted of the award-winning picture book that "it's Klassen's atmospheric, retro illustrations that take the lead."

In *I Want My Hat Back* Klassen tells the story of a brown bear that becomes discouraged when he realizes that he has lost his favorite chapeau. Bear sets out to retrace his steps and asks every creature he passes whether they have seen the missing hat. First Fox, then Frog deny seeing the hat, and frisky Rabbit also admits to no knowledge of the object, although he himself sports a lovely tall red hat. Bear then questions Turtle and Armadillo; finally Deer responds to his query with another that sparks Bear's short-term memory and sends him off in pursuit of hat-snatching Rabbit. Although Ian Chipman noted that Klassen's animal cast is realistic enough to give the story a "dark turn," the tale's "devious humor is right at a child's level." Dubbing *I Want My Hat Back* "indubitably hip," a *Kirkus Reviews* writer noted the "stiff and minimalist" quality of Klassen's picture-book art, while a *Publishers Weekly* contributor maintained that the book's "words and art are deliberately understated, with delectable results."

Describing his shift in focus from animation to book illustration, Klassen explained to *Cartoon Brew* online interviewer Chris Arrant: "The tools to make illustration or film are merging closer together, and the more you jump back and forth, the more you see how they overlap even at the conceptual stage. I think that illustrators are finding themselves trying out more animation than they would've before, and people who are in animation are trying out more print stuff. Hopefully it leads to a lot of fresh work."

Biographical and Critical Sources

PERIODICALS

Booklist, February 15, 2010, Kristen McKulski, review of *Cats' Night Out*, p. 79; November 1, 2011, Ian Chipman, review of *I Want My Hat Back*, p. 77; December, 15, 2011, Ann Kelley, review of *Extra Yarn*, p. 52.

Bulletin of the Center for Children's Books, May, 2010, Jeannette Hulick, review of *Cats' Night Out*, p. 401; November, 2011, Jeannette Hulick, review of *I Want My Hat Back*, p. 153.

Kirkus Reviews, February 15, 2010, review of *Cats' Night Out*; August 1, 2011, review of *I Want My Hat Back*; November 1, 2011, review of *Extra Yarn*.

New York Times Book Review, August 15, 2010, review of *Cats' Night Out*, p. 13.

Publishers Weekly, February 8, 2010, review of *Cats' Night Out*, p. 48, July 4, 2011, review of *I Want My Hat Back*, p. 63; October 31, 2011, review of *Extra Yarn*, p. 55; January 2, 2012, review of *House Upheld by Trees*, p. 83.

School Library Journal, February, 2010, Marilyn Taniguchi, review of *Cats' Night Out*, p. 96.

ONLINE

Cartoon Brew Web site, http://www.cartoonbrew.com/ (November 21, 2011), Chris Arrant, interview with Klassen.

Jon Klassen Home Page, http://www.burstofbeaden.com (February 15, 2012).

Jon Klassen Web log, http://jonklassen.blogspot.com (February 15, 2012).

Sheridan College Web site, http://www.sheridancollege.ca/ (February 12, 2012), interview with Klassen.*

*   *   *

KOMIYA, Teruyuki

Personal

Born in Japan.

Addresses

Home—Tokyo, Japan.

Career

Zoo director and author. Uneo Zoological Gardens, curator and zoo manager; Japanese Association of Zoos and Aquariums, Tokyo, chair of board of directors.

Member

Japanese Association of Zoos and Aquariums.

Awards, Honors

Parents' Choice Gold Award, 2009, for *Life-Size Zoo,* and 2010, for *More Life-Size Zoo* and *Life-Size Aquarium.*

Writings

Life-Size Zoo, photographs by Toyofumi Fukuda, Seven Footer Press (New York, NY), 2009.

Life-Size Aquarium, photographs by Toshimitsu Matsuhashi, translated by Junko Miyakoshi, Seven Footer Press (New York, NY), 2010.

More Life-Size Zoo: An All-New Actual-Size Animal Encyclopedia, photographs by Toshimitsu Matsuhashi, translated by Junko Miyakoshi, Seven Footer Press (New York, NY), 2010.

Life-Size Farm, Seven Footer Press (New York, NY), 2012.

Biographical and Critical Sources

PERIODICALS

Publishers Weekly, September 27, 2010, review of *Life-Size Aquarium,* p. 58.

School Library Journal, September, 2010, Patricia Manning, review of *Life-Size Aquarium,* p. 138.

ONLINE

Japanese Association of Zoos and Aquariums Web site, http://www.jaza.jp/ (February 12, 2012), "Teruyuki Komiya."*

L

LAI, Thanhha 1965-

Personal

First name pronounced "TANG-Ha"; born 1965, in Saigon, South Vietnam (now Ho Chi Mihn City, Vietnam); immigrated to United States, 1975; married; children: a daughter. *Education:* University of Texas, Austin, B.A. (journalism); New York University, M.F.A. (creative writing). *Hobbies and other interests:* Gardening, reading, biking, reading.

Addresses

Home—New York, NY. *Agent*—Rosemary Stimola, Stimola Literary Studio, 308 Livingston Ct., Edgewater, NJ 07020; info@stimolaliterarystudio.com.

Career

Author. *Orange County Register,* Los Angeles, CA, journalist for two years; New School University, New York, NY, currently instructor.

Awards, Honors

National Book Award for Young-Adult Literature, 2011, for *Inside Out and Back Again.*

Writings

Inside Out and Back Again, Harper (New York, NY), 2011.

Contributor of short fiction to periodicals, including *North American Review.*

Sidelights

Thanhha Lai grew up in South Vietnam in the midst of war, but as a child she remained unaware of the battle between communist North Vietnam and her country.

Then, in 1975, North Vietnam claimed victory and ten-year-old Lai joined her eight older siblings and her parents in leaving their homeland via U.S. Navy transport. Immigrating to the United States, the Lai family first lived in Alabama, where Thanhha began to experience life in America and her young classmates got their first glimpse of someone from Asia. Over the next few years, Lai migrated to Texas, where she attended high school and studied journalism at the University of Texas, Austin. After a move to California, she got a job at the *Orange County Register* that allowed her the opportunity to write. While writing for work, Lai also had the desire to tell her story, and once she started she completed the draft of her free-verse novel *Inside Out and Back Again* in only six months.

In *Inside Out and Back Again* readers meet Hà, who is ten years old and living in Saigon, South Vietnam, when her mother gathers together her four children and announces that they will soon be leaving for America. Traveling without their father, a soldier who is currently missing in action, the family endures time in a refugee city as well as an sea journey. Compared to their former life in a bustling city, their new home in the American south is strange: not only the people and the food, but the buildings and the plants and trees. In school, Hà confronts a language that is full of strange sibilant sounds. She is also targeted by bullies and is disheartened by the fact that she will no longer excel academically among her classmates. Hà's experiences as a refugee have made her resilient, however, and she learns to adapt with the support of a loving family and caring new friends.

Praising *Inside Out and Back Again* as "enlightening, poignant, and unexpectedly funny," a *Kirkus Reviews* writer added that Lai "presents a complex, realistic heroine whom readers will recognize." "The elemental details of Hà's struggle dramatize a foreigner's experience of alienation," asserted Hazel Rochman in her *Booklist* review, and a *Publishers Weekly* critic praised *Inside Out and Back Again* as "an incisive portrait of human resilience." "Lai's spare language captures the

sensory disorientation of changing cultures as well as a refugee's complex emotions and kaleidoscopic loyalties," according to *Horn Book* reviewer Joanna Rudge Long, and in *School Library Journal* Jennifer Rothschild predicted that "the immediacy of the narrative" in Lai's free-verse story "will appeal to those who do not usually enjoy historical novels."

Although Lai's childhood experiences contain more than a fair share of tragedy, she also has fond memories. "I come from a hilarious family," she told *Publishers Weekly* online interviewer Ingrid Roper. "Our house was always a laughing house. Saigon in 1975 was horrific, but it was also a great place to grow up and lots of fun. Alabama was a nightmare, yes. I was the first Asian any of my classmates had seen. George Wallace was the governor. In my writing, from the beginning, I sought to balance the sadness with humor."

Biographical and Critical Sources

PERIODICALS

Booklist, January 1, 2011, Hazel Rochman, review of *Inside Out and Back Again,* p. 88.
Bulletin of the Center for Children's Books, March, 2011, Hope Morrison, review of *Inside Out and Back Again,* p. 332.

Horn Book, March-April, 2011, Joanna Rudge Long, review of *Inside Out and Back Again,* p. 120.
Kirkus Reviews, January 15, 2011, review of *Inside Out and Back Again.*
North American Review, November-December, 1993, review of *Waiting,* p. 30.
Publishers Weekly, January 31, 2011, review of *Inside Out and Back Again,* p. 49.
School Library Journal, March, 2011, Jennifer Rothschild, review of *Inside Out and Back Again,* p. 164.

ONLINE

Publishers Weekly Online, http://www.publishersweekly.com/ (June 20, 2011), Ingrid Roper, "Spring 2011 Flying Starts: Thanhha Lai."*

*　　*　　*

LAMARCHE, Jim

Personal

Born in WI; father a high-school biology teacher, mother an elementary-school teacher; married; wife's name Toni; children: Mario, Jean-Paul, Dominic. *Education:* University of Wisconsin, B.S. (art).

Addresses

Home—Santa Cruz, CA.

With his enchanting paintings, Jim LaMarche brings to life The Elves and the Shoemaker, *a Brothers Grimm's story of a poor but hardworking cobbler who is aided by a group of elves in finishing his work each night.* (Used with permission of Chronicle Books, LLC, San Francisco. Visit ChronicleBooks.com.)

Warren Hanson's gentle bedtime story in The Sea of Sleep *is enriched by LaMarche's nature-themed art.* (Illustration copyright © 2010 by Jim LaMarche. Reproduced by permission of Scholastic, Inc.)

Career

Author and illustrator. VISTA volunteer with United Tribes of North Dakota; formerly worked in advertising.

Awards, Honors

Parents magazine Best Book of the Year designation, 1995, for *The Carousel;* Irma S. and James H. Black Award for Excellence in Picture Books, Bank Street College of Education, 2000, for *The Raft;* American Bookseller Association Pick-of-the-List designation, for *Albert.*

Writings

SELF-ILLUSTRATED

The Raft, HarperCollins (New York, NY), 2000.
(Reteller) The Brothers Grimm, *The Elves and the Shoemaker,* Chronicle Books (San Francisco, CA), 2003.
Up, Chronicle Books (San Francisco, CA), 2006.
Lost and Found: Three Dog Stories, Chronicle Books (San Francisco, CA), 2009.

ILLUSTRATOR

Madeena Spray Nolan, *My Daddy Don't Go to Work,* Carolrhoda (Minneapolis, MN), 1979.
Tricia Springstubb, *My Minnie Is a Jewel,* Carolrhoda (Minneapolis, MN), 1980.

Emily Crofford, *A Matter of Pride,* Carolrhoda (Minneapolis, MN), 1981.
Barbara D. Booth, *Mandy,* Lothrop, Lee & Shepard (New York, NY), 1991.
Laura Krauss Melmed, *The Rainbabies,* Lothrop, Lee & Shepard (New York, NY), 1992.
Charles E. Carryl, *The Walloping Window-Blind,* Lothrop, Lee & Shepard (New York, NY), 1994.
Liz Rosenberg, *The Carousel,* Harcourt Brace (San Diego, CA), 1995.
Louise Erdrich, *Grandmother's Pigeon,* Hyperion (New York, NY), 1996.
Laura Krauss Melmed, *Little Oh,* Lothrop, Lee & Shepard (New York, NY), 1997.
Donna Jo Napoli, *Albert,* Silver Whistle Press (San Diego, CA), 2001.
Cynthia Rylant, *Old Town in the Green Groves: The Lost Little House Years,* HarperCollins (New York, NY), 2002.
Dennis Haseley, *A Story for Little Bear,* Silver Whistle Press (San Diego, CA), 2002.
Margaret Wise Brown, *The Little Fir Tree,* HarperCollins (New York, NY), 2005.
Robert Kinerk, *Bear's First Christmas,* Simon & Schuster Books for Young Readers (New York, NY), 2007.
Warren Hanson, *The Sea of Sleep,* Scholastic Press (New York, NY), 2010.
David Rubel, *The Carpenter's Gift,* Random House (New York, NY), 2011.
Jane Yolen, *The Day Tiger Rose Said Good-bye,* Random House Children's Books (New York, NY), 2011.

Sidelights

Although his career choices as a kid alternated among magician, downhill ski racer, and Davy Crockett, Jim

LaMarche eventually grew up to become an illustrator. In addition to creating mixed-media artwork for a variety of stories by other writers, LaMarche has also turned picture-book author himself, creating the original self-illustrated stories *The Raft, Up,* and *Lost and Found: Three Dog Stories.* With "unvarnished prose [that] stays true to the Grimm tale," according to a *Publishers Weekly* critic, the author/illustrator's original retelling of *The Elves and the Shoemaker* is "beautifully realized in the beguiling artwork," according to Carolyn Phelan in *Booklist.* Susan Patron wrote in *School Library Journal* that the same book's "luminous pictures" pair well with LaMarche's retelling of the Brothers Grimm's "ever-satisfying tale."

Growing up in a small town in rural Wisconsin, La-Marche admitted on the Harper Children's Web site that he "wasn't one of those kids with a clear vision of the future." As a child he enjoyed drawing, sculpting, and creating things, and although he started his studies at the University of Wisconsin as a biology major, he eventually graduated with a degree in art. After college, he worked for the Volunteers in Service to America (VISTA) program, creating teaching materials for Native American tribes in North Dakota. "It was a great job," LaMarche recalled, explaining that since he had few coworkers he had the chance to involve himself in

many aspects of publishing: graphic design, writing, taking photographs, and creating illustrations. "It was then that I slowly realized that it might be possible for me to make a living at art," he explained. A move to California and a day job working as a carpenter's assistant allowed him to spend his evenings creating a portfolio, and his first illustration assignment, for Minneapolis-based Carolrhoda, set him on course to what has become a successful career in children's books.

LaMarche's first illustration project, Madeena Spray Nolan's story for *My Daddy Don't Go to Work,* has been followed by many others, including Laura Krauss Melmed's *Rainbabies,* Dennis Haseley's *A Story for Bear,* Warren Hanson's *The Sea of Sleep,* Jane Yolen's *The Day Tiger Rose Said Goodbye,* and a new edition of Margaret Wise Brown's *The Little Fir Tree* that *Booklist* contributor Jennifer Mattson dubbed both "striking" and a "lovely treatment" of the 1954 story. His realistic images, which are created in watercolor, colored pencil, pastel, and acrylic wash, have been highly praised for their warmth and keen use of color. Reviewing *A Story for Bear* in *Publishers Weekly,* a critic wrote that LaMarche's "shimmering pastel spreads go far to carry the tale over its rough spots," while his "appealing" colored pencil illustrations for Donna Jo

Liz Rosenberg's **The Carousel** *is brought to life in LaMarche's fanciful artwork.* (Illustration © 1995 by Jim LaMarche. Reproduced by permission of Houghton Mifflin Harcourt Publishing Company. All rights reserved.)

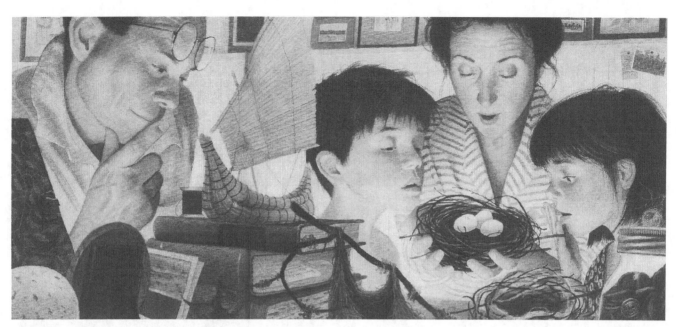

La Marche's art captures the close-knit-family culture at the core of Louise Erdrich's story in his art for **Grandmother's Pigeon.** (Illustration © 1996 by Jim LaMarche. Reprinted by permission of Disney-Hyperion, an imprint of Disney Book Group, LLC. All rights reserved.)

Napoli's *Albert* were cited by Phelan in a *Booklist* review. Noting that the book focuses on a single view out young Albert's bedroom window, Phelan maintained that LaMarche's "ability to make each picture visually intriguing is all the more remarkable."

LaMarche was inspired by his own childhood in creating his original story for *The Raft*, which *School Library Journal* contributor Catherine T. Quattlebaum called "a dazzling picture book" and "an artistic triumph." In the story, Nicky is spending the summer at his grandmother's lakeside cabin, and when he finds an abandoned raft he begins to explore the shoreline. Along the way the boy begins to sketch the wild places and creatures he discovers. As Sue Corbett wrote in the *Miami Herald, The Raft* is really about the many factors that can inspire a child to grow up to be an artist. Nicky's artistic grandmother performs a central role in the book, proudly displaying her grandson's sketches on the living room walls and encouraging his artistic efforts by discussing the way drawing allows the artist to gain an intimate knowledge of objects. "Equally adept at portraiture, landscapes and closely observed nature studies," the author/illustrator "uses light adroitly," wrote a *Publishers Weekly* reviewer in a review of *The Raft* "LaMarche imbues the beauty and wonder of nature with an otherworldly glow," noted Quattlebaum, and Corbett praised *The Raft* "a lyrical, lovely book about how one artist's journey began by looking at the world in a new way."

In *Up* LaMarche introduces Daniel, a boy who has a special ability which his family is unaware of. Although Daniel has always been small vand sickly, one day he makes a small object move without even touching it. He hopes that his new telekinetic ability will make him more helpful to his father and older brother, who work as fishermen, and he secretly practices moving ever-larger objects. Daniel has a chance to demonstrate his skill when a whale is beached nearby and his family joins other local residents helping the giant creature return to the deep. Although Daniel's telekinetic assistance is not detected amid the community-wide effort, the boy is deemed strong enough to join his father on the family fishing boat the following morning.

Up pairs "LaMarche's lovely warm illustrations" with a "gentle fantasy," according to a *Kirkus Reviews* writer, and Phelan asserted that, "drawn in softly shaded colored pencils warmed with watercolor washes," the book's images "seem to glow with their own magic." The artist's "power to draft and tint his compositions appears almost casual," noted a *Publishers Weekly* critic; "there's nothing, it seems, he can't draw."

LaMarche shares his love of dogs in *Lost and Found: Three Dog Stories,* pairing his evocative illustrations with a trio of tales in which children and dogs are led by adventures into loving relationships. In the first, a girl runs into the woods in a fit of bad temper and finds her way home with the help of her loyal Irish setter; the second tale reverses the drama as a little boy locates his beloved mutt after it becomes lost; and in the third a lost Malamute finds a secure new home with a single mother and her son. "The soft colors" in *Lost and Found* "unite the stories visually, and the pages are full of activity," observed a *Publishers Weekly* critic, and a *Kirkus Reviews* writer deemed the story collection a "visually appealing . . . tribute to the powerful attraction between kids and canines."

Biographical and Critical Sources

PERIODICALS

Booklist, May 1, 2000, GraceAnne A. DeCandido, review of *The Raft,* p. 1679; March 1, 2001, Carolyn Phelan, review of *Albert,* p. 1288; December, 15, 2003, Carolyn Phelan, review of *The Elves and the Shoemaker,* p. 751; September 15, 2005, Jennifer Mattson, review of *The Little Fir Tree,* p. 70; November 15, 2006, Carolyn Phelan, review of *Up,* p. 54; August 1, 2009, Kristen McKulski, review of *Lost and Found: Three Dog Stories,* p. 80; July 1, 2011, Carolyn Phelan, review of *The Day Tiger Rose Said Goodbye,* p. 52.

Kirkus Reviews, October 1, 2003, review of *The Elves and the Shoemaker,* p. 1226; November 1, 2005, review of *The Little Fir Tree,* p. 1190; August 1, 2006, review of *Up,* p. 790; July 15, 2009, review of *Lost and Found;* August 15, 2010, review of *Sea of Sleep.*

Miami Herald, September 21, 2000, Sue Corbett, review of *The Raft.*

Publishers Weekly, April 3, 2000, review of *The Raft,* p. 81; February 18, 2002, review of *A Story for Bear,* p. 96; November 17, 2003, review of *The Elves and the Shoemaker,* p. 62; July 6, 2009, review of *Lost and Found,* p. 50; October 16, 2006, review of *Up,* p. 51; October 22, 2007, review of *Bear's First Christmas,* p. 55; September 20, 2010, review of *The Sea of Sleep,* p. 64.

School Library Journal, May, 2000, Catherine T. Quattlebaum, review of *The Raft,* p. 146; October, 2003, Susan Patron, review of *The Elves and the Shoemaker,* p. 65; October, 2006, Catherine Threadgill, review of *Up,* p. 116; October, 2007, Diane Olivo-Posner, review of *Bear's First Christmas,* p. 100; December, 2010, Catherine Callegari, review of *The Sea of Sleep,* p. 83; August, 2011, Joan Kindig, review of *The Day Tiger Rose Said Goodbye,* p. 89.

ONLINE

Children's Literature Web site, http://www.childrenslit. com/ (July 15, 2005), "Jim LaMarche."

Harcourt Trade Publishers Web site, http://www. harcourtbooks.com/ (July 15, 2995), interview with Dennis Haseley and LaMarche.

HarperCollins Children's Web site, http://www.harper collinschildrens.com/ (January 15, 2012), "Jim LaMarche."*

*   *   *

LANDON, Kristen 1966-

Personal

Born October 25, 1966, in Midland, MI; married; children: four. *Education:* Brigham Young University, B.S. *Hobbies and other interests:* Hiking, kayaking, baking, reading.

Kristen Landon (Photograph by Shannon Larsen. Reproduced by permission.)

Addresses

Home—Highland, UT. *Agent*—Chudney Agency, 72 N. State Rd., Ste. 501, Briarcliff Manor, NY 10510. *E-mail*—kristen@kristenlandon.com.

Career

Author. Presenter at schools and conferences.

Writings

Life in the Pit, Blooming Tree Press (Austin, TX), 2008.
The Limit, Aladdin (New York, NY), 2010.

Short fiction included in anthology *Family Ties: Thirteen Short Stories,* edited by Diane M. Lynch, Pauline Books & Media, 2010.

Sidelights

Kristen Landon, a Utah author, had an eventful childhood as one of six sisters growing up in a family of eight. Her first novel, *Life in the Pit,* was inspired by Landon's experiences as a high-school clarinetist playing in the pit orchestra during drama-club performances. Brittany serves as Landon's fictional alter ego in the novel, and she envies über-popular best friend Amanda for getting far more notice as an actor on stage than Brittany does playing the cello below the audience

sight-line. When Kyle, the play's handsome lead, starts to pay attention to Brittany, she first suspects that he is using her to learn more about his pretty costar. After a mysterious someone attempts to derail the entire production through several acts of sabotage, Brittany and Amanda team up to keep the play on track and Kyle's intentions suddenly become crystal clear.

Landon expands her focus on mystery in *The Limit,* which is set in a near-future age in which the government has become all-encompassing. To provide a disincentive to overspending, parents who take on excessive debt must relinquish their children to workhouses where their wages will help pay back interest. After an eighth-grade girl is abducted from his school and sent to a workhouse, thirteen-year-old Matthew Dunston worries about his own family's over-spending. Then his worst fears are realized and he is taken away by officials of the Financial Debt Rehabilitation Agency. Because of his high I.Q., Matthew lives in comfort and works at a cushy corporate job. When he learns that several child workers at his compound—including his sister Lauren—are suffering from mysterious headaches and seizures, he turns his attention to solving the mystery, with thought-provoking results.

In *The Limit* Landon crafts a "fast paced and inventive . . . dystopian thriller," asserted a *Kirkus Reviews* writer, the critic adding that her plot turns on "a creative scenario that easily holds readers' interest." Narrated in the first-person by Matt, the author's "part realistic fiction, part fantasy [novel] should appeal to readers looking for high-action adventure," predicted J.B. Petty in *Booklist,* while *School Library Journal* contributor Anthony C. Doyle recommended *The Limit* to fans of Suzanne Wayne and Margaret Peterson Haddix because of its "fast-moving plot" and realistic teen protagonist.

"I've always loved to write—even before I knew how to write!," Landon told *SATA.* "I remember dictating stories to my mom when I was really young and hadn't learned to write yet. All through my growing-up years I would pound away at my father's typewriter (anyone know what that is?) writing stories. Well, mostly I wrote a lot of Chapter Ones and a few Chapter Twos. My friends would have to drag me away from the typewriter to come play.

"As much as I loved to write and make up stories, I never really thought about becoming a published author until much later in life. High school and college took away all my free time for writing. It wasn't until later, when I was married and had started having children that I realized I was still making up stories in my mind all the time. So I decided I might as well write them down. After a couple years of writing them down, I decided I might as well try to get them published. After a lot of time and a ton of hard work, I finally achieved that goal. And still to this day the thing I love the most

is making up stories. Actually, I should say it's my second most favorite thing. Writing is my second most important job. Number one is being a great mom to my four kids!"

Biographical and Critical Sources

PERIODICALS

Booklist, October 1, 2010, J.B. Petty, review of *The Limit,* p. 88.
Kirkus Reviews, August 1, 2010, review of *The Limit.*
School Library Journal, May, 2008, Richelle Roth, review of *Life in the Pit,* p. 128; December, 2010, Anthony C. Doyle, review of *The Limit,* p. 117.

ONLINE

Kristen Landon Home Page, http://www.kristenlandon. com (February 20, 2012).
Utah Writing Web site, http://www.utahwriting.com/ (February 20, 2012), "Kristen Landon."

*   *   *

LANE, Andrew 1963-
   (Andy Lane)

Personal

Born 1963, in England; married; children: one son. *Education:* Warwick University, degree (physics).

Addresses

Home—Dorset, Hampshire, England. *Agent*—Robert Kirby, United Agents, 12-26 Lexington St., London W1F 0LE, England.

Career

Journalist and freelance writer.

Awards, Honors

North East Book Award shortlist, 2010, and Southampton's Favourite Book Award shortlist, 2011, both for *Death Cloud.*

Writings

UNDER NAME ANDY LANE

(Editor with Justin Richards) *Decalog 3: Consequences: Ten Stories, Seven Doctors, One Chain of Events,* Doctor Who Books (London, England), 1996.

Bugs: A Sporting Chance (television novelization), Virgin (London, England), 1996.

The Babylon File: The Definitive Unauthorized Guide to J. Michael Straczynski's Babylon 5, Virgin (London, England), 1997.

(Editor with Justin Richards) *Decalog 4: Re: Generations: Ten Stories, a Thousand Years, One Family,* Virgin (London, England), 1997.

(With Paul Simpson) *The Bond Files: The Only Complete Guide to James Bond in Books, Films, TV, and Comics,* Virgin (London, England), 1998, updated edition published as *The Bond Files: The Unofficial Guide to the World's Greatest Secret Agent,* 2002.

The Babylon File, Volume Two: The Definitive Unauthorised Guide to J. Michael Straczynski's TV Series, Virgin (London, England), 1999.

Ghost in the Machine ("Randall and Hopkirk" series; television novelization), Boxtree (London, England), 2000.

Randall & Hopkirk (Deceased): The Files (television novelization), introduction by Charlie Higson, Boxtree (London, England), 2001.

The World of Austin Powers, Boxtree (London, England), 2002.

Creating Creature Comforts, Boxtree (London, England), 2003.

Aardman Presents the World of Wallace & Gromit (based on the television series), Boxtree (London, England), 2004.

The World of the Magic Roundabout (movie novelization), Boxtree (London, England), 2005.

(With Paul Simpson) *The Art of Wallace & Gromit: The Curse of the Were-Rabbit,* Titan (London, England), 2005.

Slow Decay (novelization; based on "Torchwood" television series), BBC (London, England), 2007.

Glendale: Nashville's Magical Park, Providence House (Franklin, TN), 2009.

Author of audio dramas recorded by Big Finnish Audio, beginning 2008. Contributor of short fiction to books, including *The Ultimate Witch,* Dell, 1993; *Decalog,* Virgin, 1994; *The Ultimate Dragon,* Dell, 1995, *Decalog 2,* Virgin, 1995; *The Ultimate X-Men,* Dell, 1996; (and co-editor) *Decalog 4,* Virgin, 1997; *Shakespearean Detectives,* Robinson, 1998; and *The Mammoth Book of Royal Whodunnits,* Robinson, 1998. Contributor to periodicals, including *Blake's Seven-Poster Magazine, Dr. Who Magazine, Dreamwatch, Interzone, Odyssey, Radio Times, SFX, Star Trek, Star Wars, Torchwood,* and *TV Guide.*

UNDER NAME ANDY LANE; "NEW DOCTOR WHO ADVENTURES" SERIES; BASED ON THE TELEVISION SERIES

(With Jim Mortimore) *Lucifer Rising,* Doctor Who Books (London, England), 1993.

All-Consuming Fire, Doctor Who Books (London, England), 1994.

Original Sin, Doctor Who Books (London, England), 1995.

The Empire of Glass, Doctor Who Books (London, England), 1995.

(With Justin Richards) *The Banquo Legacy,* BBC Books (London, England), 2000.

"YOUNG SHERLOCK HOLMES" NOVEL SERIES

Death Cloud, Macmillan Children's (London, England), 2010, Farrar, Straus & Giroux (New York, NY), 2011.

Red Leech, Macmillan Children's (London, England), 2010.

Bedlam (e-book novella), 2011.

Black Ice, Macmillan Children's (London, England), 2011, published as *Rebel Fire,* Farrar, Straus & Giroux (New York, NY), 2012.

Fire Storm, Macmillan Children's (London, England), 2012.

Author's works have been translated into several languages, including Russian.

Sidelights

In his career as a professional writer, where he often publishes under the byline Andy Lane, Andrew Lane has ranged widely in his focus. In addition to adapting films and television series such as *Doctor Who* into novel form, Lane has created books such as *The Bond Files: The Unofficial Guide to the World's Greatest Secret Agent,* which collects a wealth of information about the popular "James Bond" films for devoted fans. He has also published his short stories in magazines and anthologies and has helped produce television scripts for British television.

"I remember buying the first Sherlock Holmes novel 'A Study in Scarlet' at a church jumble sale in East London when I was about 12 years old," Lane recalled on his home page. "I became hooked on Arthur Conan Doyle's stories straight away," he added, noting that his collection now numbers several hundred works by Conan Doyle as well as dozens of books whose authors have adopted Sherlock Holmes as a character. Lane's lifelong passion for the "Sherlock Holmes" novels by nineteenth-century writer Sir Arthur Conan Doyle led to his work on behalf of Conan Doyle's estate. The goal: modernizing one of literature's best-known sleuths and introducing Holmes to a new generation of readers.

In the "Young Sherlock Holmes" novels, Lane imagines what the mature detective would have been like as a child growing up in the 1860s, and his analysis of the sleuth's unusual and compulsive personality has led him to infer that the teenaged Holmes, while intellectually brilliant, may have been misunderstood and even affected by a traumatic upheaval. When readers first meet Holmes in *Death Cloud,* Sherlock is fourteen years old, part of an affluent family, and receiving an education in the classics at a proper British boarding school. When his father, a member of the military, is assigned to India, Sherlock's mother becomes sickly and sends her son to stay with relatives for the summer. At his uncle's home in Hampshire Sherlock is tutored by Amyus

Crow and makes a friend of scruffy street urchin Matty. When the young sleuth learns that two local residents have died of symptoms of the bubonic plague and that a strange gray cloud was seen hovering around their bodies, his attention is piqued. As the mystery plays out, he and Matty are drawn into the mystery and ultimately forced to challenge the machinations of a diabolical villain, the Baron Maupertuis.

Sherlock's adventures continue in further volumes of the "Young Sherlock Holmes" series. In *Red Leech* the teen is pulled into a second mystery when news breaks that an international assassin presumed to be dead is actually living in England. As things play out, it turns out that Sherlock's tutor Amyus Crow is somehow involved. *Rebel Fire*—published in the United Kingdom as *Black Ice*—features a personal mystery: Sherlock's older brother Mycroft is suspected of a brutal murder and his efforts to prove Mycroft's innocence lead him to the capital of Russia. A tragic fire, a missing friend, and a stranger who claims that he can bring the dead back to life all capture Sherlock's interest in *Fire Storm*, which takes the teen sleuth to Scotland, and a foe that proves to be Holmes' most demonic opponent yet.

"Lane's command of what will one day become Holmes's signature methods is remarkable," noted Graham Moore in his *New York Times Book Review* appraisal of *Death Cloud*, and Etienne Vallee concluded in *Voice of Youth Advocated* that "the book is engaging, and the mystery is creative and compelling." "References to beekeeping and Sherlock's future drug addiction are nice touches, and Lane clearly did his research," noted a *Publishers Weekly* critic, and in *School Library Journal* Joel Shoemaker wrote of *Death Cloud* that "a menacing villain and an unexpected twist make for a thoroughly engaging read that will keep readers turning pages." "Holmes fans will delight in numerous in-jokes," according to *Horn Book* critic Roger Sutton, "and adventure readers will thrill to the high-stakes and suspenseful storytelling" in Lane's series. In *Booklist*, Ilene Cooper praised *Death Cloud* for having "punch—some literal—and purpose," and added that Lane's "rousing, almost fantastical conclusion will set readers up for the next installment."

Biographical and Critical Sources

PERIODICALS

Booklist, January 1, 2011, Ilene Cooper, review of *Death Cloud*, p. 95.
Bulletin of the Center for Children's Books, March, 2011, Elizabeth Bush, review of *Death Cloud*, p. 333.
Daily Telegraph (London, England), July 3, 2010, Christopher Middleton, "Mystery of Sherlock's Childhood Revealed" (profile), p. 6.
Horn Book, May-June, 2011, Roger Sutton, review of *Death Cloud*, p. 95.

Independent on Sunday (London, England), June 13, 2010, article about the author, p. 32.
New York Times Book Review, March 13, 2011, Graham Moore, review of *Death Cloud*, p. 14.
Publishers Weekly, January 3, 2011, review of *Death Cloud*, p. 52.
School Librarian, autumn, 2010, Robin Barlow, review of *Death Cloud*, p. 166.
School Library Journal, February, 2011, Joel Shoemaker, review of *Death Cloud*, p. 112.
Times, London, England, June 28, 2011, Andrew Lane, "Elementary, My Dear Readers," p. 17.
Voice of Youth Advocates, April, 2011, Etienne Vallee, review of *Death Cloud*, p. 62.

ONLINE

Andrew Lane Home Page, http://www.youngsherlock.com (February 15, 2012).
United Agents Web site, http://unitedagents.co.uk/ (February 15, 2012), "Andy Lane."*

*   *   *

LANE, Andy
See LANE, Andrew

*   *   *

LEVINE, Gail Carson 1947-

Personal

Born September 17, 1947, in New York, NY; daughter of David (owner of a commercial art studio) and Sylvia (a teacher) Carson; married David Levine (a software developer), September 2, 1967. *Education:* Attended Antioch College, City College of the City University of New York, B.A. (philosophy), 1969.

Addresses

Home—Brewster, NY.

Career

Children's book author. New York State Department of Labor, New York, NY, employment interviewer, 1970-82; New York State Department of Commerce, New York, NY, administrative assistant, 1982-86; New York State Department of Social Services, New York, NY, welfare administrator, 1986-96; New York State Department of Labor, New York, NY, welfare administrator, 1986—.

Awards, Honors

Best Books for Young Adults designation, and Quick Picks for Young Adults citations, American Library Association (ALA), and Newbery Honor Book, ALA, all 1998, all for *Ella Enchanted*.

Gail Carson Levine (Reproduced by permission.)

Writings

Ella Enchanted, HarperCollins (New York, NY), 1997.
The Wish, HarperCollins (New York, NY), 1999.
Dave at Night, HarperCollins (New York, NY), 1999.
The Two Princesses of Bamarre, HarperCollins (New York, NY), 2001.
Betsy Who Cried Wolf (picture book), illustrated by Scott Nash, HarperCollins (New York, NY), 2002.
The Princess Tales, HarperCollins (New York, NY), 2003.
Fairy Dust and the Quest for the Egg, illustrated by David Christiana, Disney Press (New York, NY), 2005.
Writing Magic: Creating Stories That Fly, HarperCollins (New York, NY), 2006.
The Fairy's Return and Other Princess Tales, illustrated by Mark Elliott, HarperCollins (New York, NY), 2006.
Fairest, HarperCollins (New York, NY), 2006.
Fairy Haven and the Quest for the Wand, illustrated by David Christiana, Disney Press (New York, NY), 2007.
Ever, HarperCollins (New York, NY), 2008.
Betsy Red Hoodie (picture book), illustrated by Scott Nash, HarperCollins (New York, NY), 2010.
Fairies and the Quest for Never Land, illustrated by David Christiana, Disney Press (New York, NY), 2010.
A Tale of Two Castles, HarperCollins (New York, NY), 2011.
Forgive Me, I Meant to Do It (poetry), illustrated by Matthew Cordell, Harper (New York, NY), 2012.

Author of script for children's musical *Spacenapped,* produced in Brooklyn, NY.

"PRINCESS TALES" CHAPTER-BOOK SERIES

The Fairy's Mistake, HarperCollins (New York, NY), 1999.
The Princess Test, HarperCollins (New York, NY), 1999.
Princess Sonora and the Long Sleep, HarperCollins (New York, NY), 1999.
Cinderellis and the Glass Hill, HarperCollins (New York, NY), 2000.

For Biddle's Sake, HarperCollins (New York, NY), 2002.
The Fairy's Return, HarperCollins (New York, NY), 2002.

Adaptations

Ella Enchanted was adapted for film by Miramax, 2004. *The Two Princesses of Bamarre* was optioned for film by Miramax. Many of Levine's books were adapted for audiocassette, including *Dave at Night,* Listening Library, 2000, *The Two Princesses of Bamarre,* Listening Library, 2001, *Fairy Dust and the Quest for the Egg,* Listening Library, 2005, *Fairy Haven and the Quest for the Wand,* Listening Library, 2007, and *Ever,* Scholastic Audio, 2009.

Sidelights

While Gail Carson Levine writes fairy tales featuring princesses, dragons, elves, and fairies, hers are modern renditions of traditional themes. Although Levine sometimes bases her novels on such familiar stories as *Cinderella* or *Sleeping Beauty,* and has adopted characters

Cover of Levine's popular young-adult fairy tale Ella Enchanted, *a modern take on a traditional tale that features cover art by Mark Elliott.* (Cover art © 1997 by Mark Elliott. Cover © 1998 by HarperCollins Publishers. Used by permission of HarperCollins Children's Books, a division of HarperCollins Publishers and Shannon Associates, LLC.)

from J.M. Barrie's childhood classic *Peter Pan,* the heroes and heroines in books such as *Ella Enchanted, The Princess Tales,* and *Fairy Dust and the Quest for the Egg* are decidedly modern in their outlook.

Levine was raised in New York City, in a family that valued books and reading. "My father was interested in writing, and my mother wrote full-length plays in rhyme for her students to perform," as she once told *SATA.* "Both of them had an absolute reverence for creativity and creative people, a reverence that they passed along to my sister and me."

Levine did not originally intend to be a writer. "It was painting that brought me to writing in earnest for children," she explained. "I took a class in writing and illustrating children's books and found that I was much more interested in the writing than in the illustrating."

The story that would become her Newbery Medal-winning novel *Ella Enchanted* actually had its start in a writing class. "I had to write something and couldn't think of a plot, so I decided to write a Cinderella story because it already had a plot! Then, when I thought about Cinderella's character, I realized she was too much of a goody-two-shoes for me, and I would hate her before I finished ten pages. That's when I came up with the curse: she's only good because she has to be, and she is in constant rebellion."

Ella Enchanted focuses on a girl who is cursed at birth: she is unable to disobey the commands of other people, no matter what they are. When the condition becomes too much to bear, Ella runs away in search of the thoughtless fairy who originally cursed her. Her journey leads only to a job as a scullery maid for her new stepmother, where she finally overcomes her curse. Anne Deifendeifer, writing in *Horn Book,* observed that Levine's "expert characterization and original ideas enliven this novelization of *Cinderella.*"

With the success of *Ella Enchanted,* Levine realized that she had designed a winning concept with appeal to young fantasy fans. Using it again in *The Princess Test,* she updates Hans Christian Andersen's "The Princess and the Pea," turing the familiar tale on its head as a blacksmith's daughter proves that she is as delicate and sensitive as any girl of royal blood. A *Horn Book* contributor wrote that "fans of funny fairy tales will have some laughs" over Levine's book, while a critic for *Publishers Weekly* maintained that the author's heroines "defy fairy-tale stereotypes." Levine's "Princess Tales" series continues with *The Fairy Mistake, The Fairy's Return,* and *For Biddle's Sake,* the last a reworking of the Rapunzel story that a *Kirkus Reviews* writer described as containing "deliriously funny and well-wrought prose," as well as "sly wit and clever asides."

In *Dave at Night* Levine turns to her own family history, drawing inspiration from her father's experiences growing up in an orphanage in New York City during

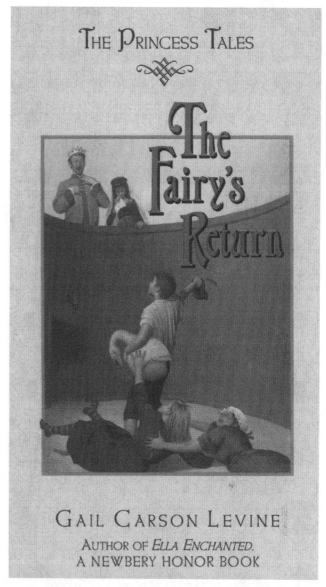

Levine's "Princess Tales" series includes **The Fairy's Return,** *featuring cover art by Mark Elliott.* (Cover art copyright © 2002 by Mark Elliott. Used by permission of HarperCollins Publishers and Shannon Associates, LLC.)

the 1920s. Dave Carlos lives at the Hebrew Home for Boys because his father died in an accident and his mother is unable to raise him alone. Each night, the rebellious boy climbs over the orphanage wall and explores the nearby streets of Harlem, where he befriends an elderly fortune teller, listens to jazz music, and learns how to dance the Charleston. Eventually, Dave discovers his artistic talents and, more importantly, the value of his orphan friends. "Dave's excursions into the noise and excitement of long-ago Harlem nights will linger in the memory," predicted a critic in reviewing *Dave at Night* for *Horn Book.*

In *The Wish* Levine gives a modern-day story a fairy-tale twist. Wilma Sturtz is an eighth grader in New York City. Her two best friends have left her school and Wilma now feels lonely and unwanted. When she gives up her seat on the bus to an eccentric old woman, the

woman grants her one wish: to be the most popular student at her school. Very soon Wilma is invited to parties and dances, but the wish only lasts until the end of the school year. Will anyone still be her friend after that? Renee Steinberg, writing in *School Library Journal,* called *The Wish* "an enjoyable, thought-provoking, and absorbing selection." "The fun is watching the nerdy girl, with whom readers will identify, blossom into a self-assured kid," commented Ilene Cooper in *Booklist.*

The Two Princesses of Bamarre is set in a fairy-tale kingdom where Princess Addie and Princess Meryl live in the castle of their father, the king. While Meryl is an independent girl, Addie is less so. When the feisty Meryl comes down with a serious illness called the Gray Death, however, Addie takes it upon herself to discover the cure and save her sister's life. Donna Miller, writing in *Book Report,* called *The Two Princesses of Bamarre* "a lively tale with vivid characters and an exciting plot," while *Kliatt* reviewer Claire Rosser predicted that Levine's "fanciful" story will appeal to "younger YAs who love high fantasy."

Cover of Levine's fantasy novel **Fairest,** *featuring artwork by Larry Rostant.* (Cover art © 2006 by Larry Rostant. Used by permission of HarperCollins Children's Books, a division of HarperCollins Publishers.)

Described as a "visionary rendering of the Snow White tale" by a *Publishers Weekly* contributor, *Fairest* focuses on Aza, a homely and awkward fifteen year old. Aza cherishes her one beautiful quality: her melodious voice. In fact, Aza is able to throw her voice and can mimic almost anything, and this talent draws the attention of the queen of Ayortha. When the homely girl is hidden behind the throne and her voice used to increase the queen's prestige, the ruse is discovered and Aza is forced to flee, finding her true strength in the process. Noting that Levine's novel probes "the real-life problems of living in an appearance-obsessed society," *School Library Journal* critic Melissa Christy Buron dubbed *Fairest* "a distinguished contribution" to Levine's body of work, and the *Publishers Weekly* reviewer ranked the novel as one that "may . . . even surpass . . . *Ella Enchanted*" in enduring popularity.

Based very loosely on the fairy tale "Puss 'n' Boots," *A Tale of Two Castles* finds Elodie dreaming of becoming an actress. Leaving her island home and discounting her parents' prudent warnings, the twelve year old travels to Two Castles, a town where a notable acting troupe is performing. When the group rejects her request to

Levine draws on her family history in her middle-grade novel **Dave at Night,** *which features cover art by Loren Long.* (Jacket art © 1999 by Loren Long. Used by permission of HarperCollins Children's Books, a division of HarperCollins Publishers.)

join them, Elodie apprentices herself to moody but clever sleuth Masteress Meenore, a talking dragon. Meenore teaches the girl the basic skills of deductive reasoning and then sends her on an under-cover assignment: to work in the castle of Count Jonty Um, a gentle ogre, disguised as a scullery maid and using her acting skill and common sense to ferret out a potential poisoner.

A Tale of Two Castles was described by a *Kirkus Reviews* writer as "a thoroughly delicious romp" in which Levine's "plot is winningly unpredictable, . . . the humor subtle, and the action well-paced." The novel features the author's characteristic "transparent language and . . . candid, uncomplicated [narrative] voice," according to *Horn Book* contributor Dierdre F. Baker, while Eva Mitnick wrote in *School Library Journal* that readers should expect "to be pulled, like Elodie herself, . . . into the midst of the rich and swirling life of Two Castles."

Levine moves to the realm of myth in *Ever,* which focuses on immortal gods. Olus, the god of the winds, is fascinated by humans and wishes to live among them. On Earth, he meets and falls in love with Kezi, a young rug weaver whose father has bargained with the family god Admat to trade the life of his dying wife for anyone who wishes the family well. Kezi prevents this sacrifice from happening by giving the good-will wish herself, thus dooming herself unless Olus can arrange with the illusive Admat to make her immortal. In the novel, Levine depicts "the classic quest . . . young people must accomplish in order to live as they choose," according to *Kliatt* critic Janis Flint-Ferguson, while *Horn Book* reviewer Anita L. Burkam cited *Ever* for presenting readers with a "fascinating quandary" about the nature of religious faith.

The rural folk-tale world becomes the backdrop of the picture book *Betsy Who Cried Wolf,* as Levine turns from the stories of Europe to the simple tales of Aesop. In a variant of "The Boy Who Cried Wolf," an eight-year-old girl strives to excel at her task of shepherding. A cagey old wolf named Zimmo—who may have dipped into the pages of Aesop—decides to outsmart the girl by provoking her into raising the alarm, then disappearing without a trace. When Betsy asks for help from nearby farmers two times, with no wolf to be found, she realizes that Zimmo will likely be far more satisfied sharing her tasty evening meal than chasing after a tough old ewe. A *Kirkus Reviews* critic dubbed

Levine teams up with artist Scott Nash to retell a well-known tale in the picture book **Betsy Red Hoodie.** (Illustration copyright © 2010 by Scott Nash. Reproduced with permission of HarperCollins Children's Books, a division of HarperCollins Publishers.)

Betsy Who Cried Wolf "a delightful tale" featuring "especially funny" art by Scott Nash. In *Publishers Weekly* a critic described the story as a "perky, girl-centric take" on the Aesop classic, and predicted that "kids may well cheer [Betsy's] . . . courage and can-do spirit."

Betsy and Zimmo return in *Betsy Red Hoodie,* as Levine reteams with Nash to craft a second picture-book riff of the "Little Red Riding Hood" variety. Old enough to carry baked treats to Grandma, Betsy still requires a chaperone, so she invites Zimmo along for company. Still shepherding her sheep, Betsy makes the trek, but Zimmo somehow disappears along the way to Grandma's house. While readers may worry about the outcome, they will be ultimately be entranced by "Levine's well-paced, straightforward storytelling," according to *Booklist* critic Gillian Engberg. Nash "masterfully portrays the personalities of each sheep" in Levine's "tongue-in-cheek funny" story, wrote a *Kirkus Reviews* writer, and in *Horn Book* Joanna Rudge Long dubbed *Betsy Red Hoodie* "good read-aloud fun."

In *Fairy Dust and the Quest for the Egg, Fairy Haven and the Quest for the Wand,* and *Fairies and the Quest for Never Land* Levine adapts flighty characters from Walt Disney's classic animated films such as *Peter Pan*

Levine casts one of the world's favorite fairies in **Fairies and the Quest for Never Land,** *a story featuring artwork by David Christiana.* (Illustration copyright © 2010 by David Christiana. Reprinted by permission of Disney-Hyperion, an imprint of Disney Book Group LLC. All rights reserved.)

and *Bambi* into stories for elementary-grade readers. Tinker Bell, the feisty fairy from *Peter Pan,* is the star of *Fairy Dust and the Quest for the Egg,* which takes readers on a tour of a newly envisioned Never Land. Here Never Land is an island where the mild climate is sustained by a magical bird known as Mother Dove. Mother Dove sits on a magic egg, and her annual molt provides Tink and other Never Land fairies with valuable fairy dust. When Mother Dove becomes ill, new fairy Prilla must undertake a quest in order to save the magic bird, meeting up with Peter Pan, Captain Hook, and other characters along the way. Another quest, this time for a magic but unpredictable wand, is the focus of *Fairy Haven and the Quest for the Wand,* as Tink and others hope to stop a flood that threatens to destroy their island home, while in *Fairies and the Quest for Never Land* Tink meets Gwendolyn, the nine-year-old descendant of Wendy Darling, and gains the girl's help in thwarting a dragon that is determined to destroy the balance of magic in Never Land.

In *Booklist* Jennifer Mattson described the "lavish visual element" in David Christiana's pastel-toned illustrations as "a major draw of the Disney Fairies series" and described *Fairy Dust and the Quest for the Egg* as "the kind of lovable, illustrated chapter book that high production costs have all but driven out of existence." With its "short chapters interspersed with color illustrations," Levine's story in *Fairies and the Quest for Never Land* "is accessible to readers," wrote *School Library Journal* critic Sarah Polace, and a *Kirkus Reviews* writer predicted that "fans of the Never Land stories will savor Gwendolyn" as well as the story's other "fully developed characters."

Levine once told *SATA:* "As a child I loved fairy tales because the story, the what-comes-next, is paramount. As an adult I am fascinated by their logic and illogic. Ella's magic book gave me the chance to answer a question that always plagued me about *The Shoemaker and the Elves:* why the elves abandon the shoemaker. I came up with one answer, but many are possible—and I think the real solution goes to the heart of gratitude and recognition, an example of the depth in fairy tales."

Levine goes into greater detail regarding her views of folk and fairy tales in her book *Writing Magic: Creating Stories That Fly,* which inspires preteen writer with writing exercises, encouragement, and other useful creative how-to's. Her advice to aspiring writers? "Suspend judgment of your work and keep writing," Levine once told *SATA.* "Take advantage of the wonderful community of writers for children, who are always ready with helpful criticism and support in the struggle to succeed. And be patient: writing and glaciers advance at about the same pace!"

Biographical and Critical Sources

BOOKS

McGinty, Alice B., *Meet Gail Carson Levine,* Rosen Publishing (New York, NY), 2003.

PERIODICALS

Booklist, November 15, 1999, Susan Dove Lempke, review of *Princess Sonora and the Long Sleep,* p. 627; April 1, 2000, Ilene Cooper, review of *The Wish,* p. 1462, and Anna Rich, review of *Dave at Night,* p. 1494; April 15, 2001, Carolyn Phelan, review of *The Two Princesses of Bamarre,* p. 1558; August, 2002, Carolyn Phelan, review of *The Fairy's Return,* p. 1964; August, 2005, Jennifer Mattson, review of *Fairy Dust and the Quest for the Egg,* p. 2023; July 1, 2006, Gillian Engberg, review of *Fairest,* p. 56; December 1, 2006, Ilene Cooper, review of *Writing Magic: Creating Stories That Fly,* p. 45; January 1, 2008, Jennifer Mattson, review of *Fairy Haven and the Quest for the Wand,* p. 76; April 1, 2008, Frances Bradburn, review of *Ever,* p. 39; September 15, 2010, Gillian Engberg, review of *Betsy Red Hoodie,* p. 68.

Book Report, September-October, 2001, Donna Miller, review of *The Two Princesses of Bamarre,* p. 63.

Childhood Education, summer, 2011, Terre Sychterz, review of *Betsy Red Hoodie,* p. 291.

Horn Book, May-June, 1997, Anne Deifendeifer, review of *Ella Enchanted,* p. 325; May, 1999, reviews of *The Fairy's Mistake* and *The Princess Test,* both p. 332; January, 2000, review of *Dave at Night,* p. 78; May, 2001, review of *The Two Princesses of Bamarre,* p. 330; May-June, 2008, Anita L. Burkham, review of *Ever,* p. 319; September-October, 2010, Joanna Rudge Long, review of *Betsy Red Hoodie,* p. 60; May-June, 2011, Deirdre F. Baker, review of *A Tale of Two Castles,* p. 95.

Journal of Adolescent and Adult Literacy, November, 2002, review of *The Wish,* p. 218.

Kirkus Reviews, April 15, 2002, review of *Betsy Who Cried Wolf,* p. 574; September 15, 2002, review of *For Biddle's Sake,* p. 1393; August 1, 2005, review of *Fairy Dust and the Quest for the Egg,* p. 853; August 1, 2006, review of *Fairest,* p. 790; July 1, 2007, review of *Fairy Haven and the Quest for the Wand;* April 1, 2008, review of *Ever;* May 15, 2010, review of *Fairies and the Quest for Never Land;* August 15, 2010, review of *Betsy Red Hoodie;* April 1, 2011, review of *A Tale of Two Castles.*

Kliatt, March, 2004, Claire Rosser, review of *The Two Princesses of Bamarre,* p. 26; September, 2005, Erin Darr, review of *The Wish,* p. 28; September, 2006, Claire Rosser, review of *Fairest,* p. 14; January, 2007, Anthony Pucci, review of *Writing Magic,* p. 35; May, 2008, Janis Flint-Ferguson, review of *Ever,* p. 12; July, 2008, Claire Rosser, review of *Fairest,* p. 28.

Publishers Weekly, February 15, 1999, reviews of *The Fairy's Mistake* and *The Princess Test,* both p. 108; November 1, 1999, review of *Dave at Night,* p. 58; April 24, 2000, review of *The Wish,* p. 91; May 7, 2001, review of *The Two Princesses of Bamarre,* p. 248; May 6, 2002, review of *Betsy Who Cried Wolf,* p. 57; August 29, 2005, review of *Fairy Dust and the Quest for the Egg,* p. 56; July 24, 2006, review of *Fairest,* p. 58.

School Library Journal, May, 2000, Renee Steinberg, review of *The Wish,* p. 173; May, 2001, Kit Vaughan, review of *The Two Princesses of Bamarre,* p. 155;
June, 2002, Grace Oliff, review of *Betsy Who Cried Wolf,* p. 98; September, 2002, Eva Mitnick, review of *For Biddle's Sake,* p. 198; October, 2005, Elizabeth Bird, review of *Fairy Dust and the Quest for the Egg,* p. 119; September, 2006, Melissa Christy Buron, review of *Fairest,* p. 209; February, 2007, Beth Gallego, review of *Writing Magic,* p. 142; November, 2007, Pat Leach, review of *Fairy Haven and the Quest for the Wand,* p. 94; March, 2008, Jennifer Vergrugge, review of *Fairy Haven and the Quest for the Wand,* p. 86; June, 2008, Miriam Lang Budin, review of *Ever,* p. 145; August, 2010, Sarah Polace, review of *Fairies and the Quest for Never Land,* p. 78; September, 2010, Sara Lissa Paulson, review of *Betsy Red Hoodie,* p. 130; April, 2011, Eva Mitnick, review of *A Tale of Two Castles,* p. 178.

ONLINE

Cynthia Leitich Smith Web site, http://www.cynthia leitichsmith.com/ (May 6, 2005), interview with Levine.

Gail Carson Levine Home page, http://www.gailcarson levine.com (February 15, 2012).

Gail Carson Levine Web log, http://gailcarsonlevine. blogspot.com (February 15, 2012).

HarperCollins Web site, http://www.harperchildrens.com/ (November 26, 2008), "Gale Carson Levine."

OTHER

Good Conversation!: A Talk with Gail Carson Levine (video), Tim Podell Productions, 2001.*

* * *

LLOYD, Megan 1958-
(Megan Lloyd Thompson)

Personal

Born November 5, 1958, in Harrisburg, PA; daughter of Warren (a history teacher) and Lois (a kindergarten teacher) Lloyd; married Thomas Thompson (an antiques dealer). *Education:* Attended Pennsylvania State University, 1976-78; Parsons School of Design, B.F.A., 1981. *Politics:* "Independent." *Religion:* Presbyterian. *Hobbies and other interests:* Animals, painting, soapmaking, rug hooking, weaving.

Addresses

Home—Cumberland County, PA.

Career

Freelance illustrator of children's books, beginning 1982. Harper Junior Books, New York, NY, assistant to the art director, 1981-82; worked in restoration of American antique furniture, beginning 1983. Children's

Literature Council of Pennsylvania, founding member and art director, 1985-96; Citizens for Responsible Development (local city planning-advocacy group), former president and founding member, 1986-87. *Exhibitions:* Work exhibited at Cumberland County Historical Society, Harrisburg, PA.

Awards, Honors

Colorado Children's Book Award runner-up, and Keystone to Reading award, both 1988, both for *The Little Old Lady Who Was Not Afraid of Anything;* Keystone to Reading award, 1989, for *More Surprises; Parents' Choice* designation in picture-book category, 1991, for *Cactus Hotel.*

Writings

SELF-ILLUSTRATED

Chicken Tricks, Harper & Row (New York, NY), 1983.

ILLUSTRATOR

Lee Bennett Hopkins, selector, *Surprises* (poetry), Harper & Row (New York, NY), 1984.

Ida Luttrell, *Lonesome Lester,* Harper & Row (New York, NY), 1984.

Victoria Sherrow, *There Goes the Ghost,* Harper & Row (New York, NY), 1985.

Norma Farber, *All Those Mothers at the Manger,* Harper & Row (New York, NY), 1985.

Thom Roberts, *The Atlantic Free Balloon Race,* Avon (New York, NY), 1986.

Tony Johnston, *Farmer Mack Measures His Pig,* Harper & Row (New York, NY), 1986.

Linda Williams, *The Little Old Lady Who Was Not Afraid of Anything,* Crowell (New York, NY), 1986.

Lee Bennett Hopkins, selector, *More Surprises* (poetry), Harper (New York, NY), 1987.

Nancy MacArthur, *Megan Gets a Dollhouse,* Scholastic (New York, NY), 1988.

Carolyn Otto, *That Sky, That Rain,* HarperCollins (New York, NY), 1990.

Patricia Lauber, *How We Learned the Earth Is Round,* HarperCollins (New York, NY), 1990.

Brenda Z. Guiberson, *Cactus Hotel,* Holt (New York, NY), 1991.

Jane O'Connor and Robert O'Connor, *Super Cluck,* HarperCollins (New York, NY), 1991.

Eric Kimmel, *Baba Yaga: A Russian Folktale,* Holiday House (New York, NY), 1991.

Paul Showers, *How You Talk,* HarperCollins (New York, NY), 1992.

Brenda Z. Guiberson, *Spoonbill Swamp,* Holt (New York, NY), 1992.

Melvin Berger, *Look out for Turtles!,* HarperCollins (New York, NY), 1992.

Mary Neville, *The Christmas Tree Ride,* Holiday House (New York, NY), 1992.

Brenda Z. Guiberson, *Lobster Boat,* Holt (New York, NY), 1993.

Eric Kimmel, *The Gingerbread Man,* Holiday House (New York, NY), 1993.

Susan Tews, *The Gingerbread Doll,* Clarion (New York, NY), 1993.

Tom Birdseye, *A Regular Flood of Mishap,* Holiday House (New York, NY), 1994.

Ellen Kindt McKenzie, *The Perfectly Orderly House,* Holt (New York, NY), 1994.

Brenda Z. Guiberson, *Winter Wheat,* Holt (New York, NY), 1995.

Barbara Juster Esbensen, *Dance with Me* (poetry), HarperCollins (New York, NY), 1995.

Carolyn Otto, *What Color Is Camouflage?,* HarperCollins (New York, NY), 1996.

Priscilla Belz Jenkins, *Falcons Nest on Skyscrapers,* HarperCollins (New York, NY), 1996.

Linda White, *Too Many Pumpkins,* Holiday House (New York, NY), 1996.

Melvin Berger, *Chirping Crickets,* HarperCollins (New York, NY), 1998.

Eric A. Kimmel, *Seven at One Blow: A Tale from the Brothers Grimm,* Holiday House (New York, NY), 1998.

Carolyn Otto, *Pioneer Church,* Holt (New York, NY), 1999.

Linda Williams, *Horse in the Pigpen,* HarperCollins (New York, NY), 2002.

Esther Hershenhorn, *Fancy That,* Holiday House (New York, NY), 2003.

Eileen Spinelli, *Thanksgiving at the Tappletons',* HarperCollins (New York, NY), 2003.

Franklyn M. Branley, *Earthquakes,* new edition, HarperCollins (New York, NY), 2005.

Pamela Duncan Edwards, *The Mixed-up Rooster,* Katherine Tegen Books (New York, NY), 2006.

Franklyn M. Branley, *Volcanoes,* new edition, HarperCollins (New York, NY), 2007.

Diane Shore, *This Is the Feast,* HarperCollins (New York, NY), 2008.

Bobbi Miller, reteller, *Davy Crockett Gets Hitched,* Holiday House (New York, NY), 2009.

Linda White, *Too Many Turkeys,* Holiday House (New York, NY), 2010.

Becky White, *Betsy Ross,* Holiday House (New York, NY), 2011.

Eileen Spinelli, *A Big Boy Now,* Harper (New York, NY), 2012.

Bobbi Miller, reteller, *Miss Sally Ann and the Panther,* Holiday House (New York, NY), 2012.

Books featuring Lloyd's illustrations have been translated into several languages, including Afrikaans, Arabic, French, Korean, and Spanish.

Sidelights

Working from her home in rural Pennsylvania, Megan Lloyd is an illustrator whose love of nature comes through in each of her detailed paintings. Many of her illustration projects—such as *Cactus Hotel* by Brenda Z. Guiberson, *Earthquakes* and *Volcanoes* by noted science writer Franklyn M. Branley, and *Falcons Nest on*

Skyscrapers by Priscilla Belz Jenkins—bring to life elements of the natural world, while in the pages of *The Mixed-up Rooster* by Pamela Duncan Edwards and Linda Arms White's humorous stories *Too Many Pumpkins* and *Too Many Turkeys* the artist captures the humor of farmyard life. Often juggling up to six illustration projects at any one time, Lloyd is diligent about research, and her images are all painted from staged scenes in which costume and lighting are considered. In fact, her husband, Thomas Thompson, is often recruited to model for the male characters in her illustrations.

"I was born and raised in south-central Pennsylvania," Lloyd once told *SATA,* "growing up with my parents, one older sister, a cat, and a dog. Both my sister and I began taking ballet lessons when we were young, but my sister did not show any great love for that particular art form and stopped dancing shortly thereafter. I fell in love with ballet and pursued it with all that I had. For many years I was convinced that it would be my career—so convinced that I didn't really give a great deal of thought to anything else. Because ballet was 'my thing,' I wasn't allowed to take horse riding lessons when my sister and mother did, mainly because my sister fell off a horse and broke her arm while my mother fell off and broke her knee. Surely this was too risky a sport for an aspiring dancer!

Megan Lloyd's art brings to life Eric A. Kimmel's **Seven at One Blow,** *a folk-tale adaptation.* (Illustration © 1998 by Megan Lloyd-Thompson. Reproduced by permission of Holiday House, Inc.)

"At fifteen the terrible blow fell. I discovered that there were practically NO five-foot-one-inch dancers with short legs, no matter how good they were at jumping and stretching and pirouetting. I was crushed. In my despair—and it truly felt like the world was crumbling—I decided that I would transfer my creative efforts to the visual arts, and I began to think of myself as an 'artist'. Fortunately, the high school I attended had an excellent art department with very talented and supportive teachers. Things seemed to run smoothly until it was time for the big college decision."

At first Lloyd "fell in love" with the idea of attending Harvard Law School and, with that goal in mind, she enrolled in the pre-law program at Pennsylvania State University. "That lasted for all of two semesters at which time I felt miserable, missed my art work, and was totally confused," she later recalled. "My mother, understanding my confusion, suggested that I might like to illustrate picture books. And to sweeten the suggestion, she showed me a copy of Brian Wildsmith's book *Circus*. That was all it took. I had never seen a book like that before. It was wonderful."

Transferring to Parsons School of Design, she studied illustration and earned her degree in 1981. Even as a published illustrator, Lloyd finds her education as an artist to be ongoing. "I continue to work and work and work at learning, growing, and developing," she explained. "The more I learn about illustrating books, the more I discover all that I don't know! That's great—it keeps illustrating a stimulating career. Each book presents a new puzzle to solve. Who could ask for more?"

Lighthearted stories for young children are given a dash of warmhearted humor through Lloyd's artwork. In her work for *The Mixed-up Rooster,* her "bright, neon-colored pictures" contain "comic details that illustrate the verbal puns," according to *Booklist* contributor Hazel Rochman. Bringing to life Duncan's story about a rooster with bad timing, Lloyd's "vibrant illustrations . . . are full of personality and charm," Linda L. Walkins concluded in *School Library Journal.* Noting of her contribution to Esther Hershenhorn's *Fancy That* that "Lloyd has mastered the egg tempera medium," a *Publishers Weekly* contributor added that the artist's "work alternates between the checkerboard orchards and tranquil cattle of American folk art and a more comical style" that suits the historical tale. While the repetitive rhyming text in the rollicking *Horse in the Pigpen* "make this an enjoyable readaloud," a *Kirkus Reviews* writer concluded that Lloyd's "cleverly detailed and often outlandish illustrations" conjure up "a visual treat."

Some of Lloyd's illustration projects find her capturing scenes from the lives of historic figures. She uses textile collage in creating art for Becky White's *Betsy Ross,* a rhyming story that tells the well-known story about the woman who sewed the first U.S. flag. Hand-dying her fabrics, then cutting and piecing, sewing, and adding texture through contrasting stitches, Lloyd produced

Lloyd's illustration projects include bringing to life Linda Arms White's rural-themed story in **Too Many Turkeys.** (Illustration copyright © 2010 by Megan Lloyd. Reproduced with permission of Holiday House.)

unique images that are "lovely in their simple graphic shapes and clean design," according to a *Kirkus Reviews* writer. In *Davy Crocket Gets Hitched,* a tall-tale-type picture book inspired by stories of backwoodsman-turned-politician Davy Crockett and featuring a text by Bobbi Miller, the artist creates "sharp-edged" cartoon-styled oil paintings edged with pine needles mimicking "the trademark fringe on Crockett's trousers," wrote Patricia Austin in *Booklist.*

In creating artwork for nonfiction stories, Lloyd often travels where the story requires, knowing that every setting has unique characteristics that can only be understood through personal experience. Her participation in a paint-restoration project on the pulpit of an historic Pennsylvania church allowed Lloyd to create particu-

larly distinctive artwork for Carolyn Otto's *Pioneer Church,* a quasi-fictional story that follows the history of a house of worship build during the colonial era. "The blend of precise, almost primitive-style illustration with the fluid text is seamless," noted *Booklist* critic Shelley Townsend-Hudson, the critic dubbing *Pioneer Church* "exceptional." To create the paintings she contributes to *Cactus Hotel,* Lloyd traveled to the Saguaro National Monument in the desert near Tucson, Arizona, producing what a *Publishers Weekly* contributor described as "pastel-shaded . . . and finely rendered scenes of native flora and fauna."

Lloyd's work illustrating Guiberson's *Lobster Boat* found the artist in Maine, spending time on a lobster boat, while another collaboration with Guiberson, *Win-*

ter Wheat, inspired an even longer trip. "I drove clear across the country to photograph the wheat farm belonging to the author's father and mother!," Lloyd once explained to *SATA* of her work on this particular book, which focuses on a wheat grower in the Pacific Northwest. "If I can't see what it is I am to draw, I simply can't make successful illustrations." Praising Lloyd's work for *Winter Wheat, Booklist* contributor Julie Corsaro wrote that the illustrator's "sweeping" images of wheat country "are appealing in their use of rich colors and textures."

Biographical and Critical Sources

PERIODICALS

Booklist, March 15, 1994, Kay Weisman, review of *A Regular Flood of Mishap,* p. 1369; December 1, 1994,

Lauren Peterson, review of *The Perfectly Orderly House,* p. 687; November 15, 1995, Julie Corsaro, review of *Winter Wheat,* p. 562; August, 1996, Carolyn Phelan, review of *Falcons Nest on Skyscrapers,* p. 1902; November 1, 1996, Hazel Rochman, review of *What Color Is Camouflage?,* p. 504; November 15, 1998, Hazel Rochman, review of *Seven at One Blow: A Tale from the Brothers Grimm,* p. 593; October 1, 1999, Shelley Townsend-Hudson, review of *Pioneer Church,* p. 374; July, 2002, Cynthia Turnquest, review of *Horse in the Pigpen,* p. 1861; September 15, 2003, Gillian Engberg, review of *Fancy That,* p. 245; July 1, 2006, Hazel Rochman, review of *The Mixed-Up Rooster,* p. 64; September 15, 2008, Hazel Rochman, review of *This Is the Feast,* p. 56; September 1, 2009, Patricia Austin, review of *Davy Crockett Gets Hitched,* p. 94.

Horn Book, January, 1999, review of *Seven at One Blow,* p. 74.

A traditional tale about a freshly baked and boastful cookie is the subject of Lloyd's art for Eric A. Kimmel's **The Gingerbread Man.** (Illustration copyright © 1993 by Megan Lloyd. Reproduced by permission of Holiday House, Inc.)

Kirkus Reviews, March 1, 2002, review of *Horse in the Pigpen,* p. 348; September 1, 2003, review of *Fancy That,* p. 1124; July 15, 2006, review of *The Mixed-Up Rooster,* p. 721; August 15, 2008, review of *This Is the Feast*; July 15, 2009, review of *Davy Crockett Gets Hitched*; July 1, 2010, review of *Too Many Turkeys*; August 1, 2011, review of *Betsy Ross.*

Publishers Weekly, March 15, 1991, review of *Super Cluck,* p. 58; June 7, 1991, review of *Cactus Hotel,* p. 64; April 19, 1993, review of *Lobster Boat,* p. 60; September 20, 1993, review of *The Gingerbread Doll,* p. 40; December 20, 1993, review of *A Regular Flood of Mishap,* p. 71; October 31, 1994, review of *The Perfectly Orderly House,* p. 61; November 16, 1998, review of *Seven at One Blow,* p. 74; March 18, 2002, review of *Horse in the Pigpen,* p. 101; September 22, 2003, review of *Fancy That,* p. 104.

School Library Journal, June, 2002, Hannah Hoppe, review of *Horse in the Pigpen,* p. 116; November, 2003, Beth Tegart, review of *Fancy That,* p. 96; August, 2006, Linda L. Walkins, review of *The Mixed-Up Rooster,* p. 81; August, 2008, Jeffrey A. French, review of *Volcanoes,* p. 108; October, 2008, Carol S. Surges, review of *This Is the Feast,* p. 136; August, 2009, Marge Loch-Wouters, review of *Davy Crockett Gets Hitched,* p. 91; August, 2010, Mary Elam, review of *Too Many Turkeys,* p. 87.

ONLINE

Megan Lloyd Home Page, http://meganlloyd.com (February 15, 2012).*

*   *   *

LUNDQUIST, David R.

Personal

Born in MN; children: two daughters. *Education:* University of Minnesota, B.S. (political science).

Addresses

Home—Minneapolis, MN. *E-mail*—David.Lundquist@ CHSinc.com.

Career

Corporate photographer and videographer. CHS, Inc., Inver Grove Heights, MN, supervisor of photography and audio-visual, beginning 1985. Speaker at workshops.

Awards, Honors

Nebraska Children's Agricultural Book of the Year selection 2006, for *Fantastic Farm Machines* by Cris Peterson; Orbis Pictus Recommended Book selection, and Society of Midland Authors Award for Nonfiction, both 2008, both for *Clarabelle* by Peterson; numerous awards for photography.

Illustrator

Cris Peterson, *Fantastic Farm Machines,* Boyds Mills Press (Honesdale, PA), 2006.

Cris Peterson, *Clarabelle: Making Milk and So Much More,* Boyds Mills Press (Honesdale, PA), 2007.

Cris Peterson, *Seed, Soil, Sun: Earth's Recipe for Food,* Boyds Mills Press (Honesdale, PA), 2010.

Biographical and Critical Sources

PERIODICALS

Booklist, February 15, 2006, John Peters, review of *Fantastic Farm Machines,* p. 100; November 1, 2010, Carolyn Phelan, review of *Seed, Soil, Sun: Earth's Recipe for Food,* p. 50.

Publishers Weekly, October 4, 2010, review of *Seed, Soil, Sun,* p. 46.

School Library Journal, March, 2006, Carolyn Janssen, review of *Fantastic Farm Machines,* p. 212; October, 2007, Amanda Moss, review of *Clarabelle: Making Milk and So Much More,* p. 138; November, 2010, Frances E. Millhouser, review of *Seed, Soil, Sun,* p. 93.

ONLINE

Cooperative Communicators Association Web site, http:// wwwcommunicators.coop/ (February 15, 2012), "David R. Lundquist."

M

MAHONEY, Karen

Personal
Born in England.

Addresses
Home—London, England. *Agent*—Miriam Kriss, Irene Goodman Literary Agency, 27 W. 24th St., Ste. 700B, New York, NY 10010. *E-mail*—writerkaz@gmail.com.

Career
Author.

Writings

The Iron Witch, Flux (Woodbury, MN), 2011.
The Wood Queen, Flux (Woodbury, MN), 2012.

Contributor of short fiction to anthologies, including *The Eternal Kiss: Thirteen Vampire Tales of Blood and Desire,* edited by Trisha Telep, Running Press (Philadelphia, PA), 2009, and *Kiss Me Deadly,* 2010.

Author's works have been translated into several languages, including French, German, Portuguese, and Turkish.

Sidelights
Karen Mahoney enjoyed writing as a teenager, but she gave it up along with other childhood hobbies when she moved into her mid-twenties. However, when she reached her thirties Mahoney realized that writing was not just a hobby; it was something she needed to do. Keeping her focus on producing a publishable manuscript in her favorite genre—teen fantasy—she set about writing and her first novel, *The Iron Witch,* was the result.

Mahoney's fictional heroine, Donna Underwood, is cursed by a childhood tragedy that has left her marked for life when readers meet her as narrator of *The Iron Witch.* Ten years before, at age seven, Donna witnessed a terrible fey murder her alchemist father and curse her mother into madness. Also injured in the violence, the orphaned girl was healed by her father's alchemist guild, the Order of the Dragon, whose members mended her broken flesh with pieces of shaped iron that gave her arms and legs extraordinary strength. Although the healers believed that they were doing good, Donna's strange healing left her shunned by her schoolmates in Ironbridge, Massachusetts, and remains isolated, living with her aunt Abigail and being educated by the alchemist Order. The only link Donna has with the normal human world she longs to be part of is Navin Sharma, her best friend. Through Navin, she meets the charismatic Xan, who is also tapped in to the supernatural world as half human and half fey. When Navin is abducted by a group of malicious wood elves under orders of Aliette, the Wood Queen, Donna takes responsibility for the kidnapping, as well as her destiny. Aliette desires the thing Donna's parents suffered for: the elixir of life. Now, together with Xan, she must find a way to save Navin while also keeping the powerful elixir out of the hands of the fey.

In *The Iron Witch* Mahoney "lays intriguing groundwork for later books," asserted a *Publishers Weekly* contributor in reviewing the author's fiction debut, and a *Kirkus Reviews* critic also anticipated a sequel by noting that "the suspense and tension built into the story lead to a smashing climax and an ambivalent solution." Mahoney continues Donna's story in *The Wood Queen,* as the teen stands trial for stealing the Elixir of Life. Although she successfully rescued Navin from his wood elf captors, the alchemist Order judges Donna harshly due to her theft of the elixir. With her mother now close to death as a result of the fey curse of madness, the teen is tempted when Aliette offers an exchange: her mother's life for Donna's help in restoring the banished wood elves to their place in the land of Faerie. Being at

Cover of Karen Mahoney's The Iron Witch, *in which a teen's future is molded by her family's tragic—and paranormal—past.* (Cover images: (woman) © 2010 iStockphoto.com/Hannah Eckman; (vial) © 2010 iStockPhoto.com/Dmitriy Assev; (scroll illustration) © 2010 iStockphoto.com/Emilia Kun.)

the center of the struggle between the wood elves and the Order causes the teenager pause, and she realizes that she must seek answers to her questions from someone she can truly trust, . . . but who? "Donna's tumultuous self-discovery . . . includes magic, family, and romance," wrote *Voice of Youth Advocates* contributor Lucy Schall, the critic adding that *The Wood Queen* will appeal to older teens "who thrive on escapist, slightly edgy fantasy." A *Kirkus Reviews* writer also had praise for *The Wood Queen,* describing it as "an exciting installment" in Mahoney's fantasy saga that pulls readers along to a "shocking climax."

Biographical and Critical Sources

PERIODICALS

Booklist, September 1, 2009, Krista Hutley, review of *The Eternal Kiss: Thirteen Vampire Tales of Blood and Desire,* p. 81.

Kirkus Reviews, January 15, 2011, review of *The Iron Witch*; January 1, 2012, review of *The Wood Queen.*

Publishers Weekly, December 20, 2010, review of *The Iron Witch,* p. 54.

School Library Journal, December, 2009, Donna Rosenblum, review of *The Eternal Kiss,* p. 134; February, 2011, Kathy Kichoefer, review of *The Iron Witch,* p. 114.

Voice of Youth Advocates, February, 2011, Lucky Schall, review of *The Iron Witch,* p. 572; February, 2012, Lucy Schall, review of *The Wood Queen,* p. 612.

ONLINE

Kaz Mahoney Home Page, http://www.kazmahoney.com (February 15, 2012).

Writers Digest Online, http://www.writersdigest.com/ (February 8, 2011), Chuck Sambuchio, interview with Mahoney.*

*   *   *

McFADDEN, Kevin Christopher
See PIKE, Christopher

*   *   *

McFERRIN, Grady

Personal

Born in Long Beach, CA; married; children: two. *Education:* California State University, Long Beach, degree (art).

Addresses

Home—Brooklyn, NY. *E-mail*—grady@gmillustration.com.

Career

Illustrator, graphic designer, and hand-letterer. Designer of graphics for paper goods, including stationery for Chronicle Books.

Member

American Institute of Graphic Arts.

Illustrator

Lesley M.M. Blume, *Let's Bring Back: An Encyclopedia of Forgotten-yet-Delightful Chic, Useful, Curious, and Otherwise Commendable Things from Times Gone By,* Chronicle Books (San Francisco, CA), 2010.

Holly Thompson, *Orchards,* Delacorte Press (New York, NY), 2011.

Jenna Woginrich, *Chick Days: An Absolute Beginner's Guide to Raising Chickens from Hatchlings to Laying Hens,* Storey Publishing (North Adams, MA), 2011.

John Stephens, *The Emerald Atlas: The Books of Beginning,* Knopf (New York, NY), 2011.

Contributor to periodicals, incliding *New Yorker, New York Times,* and *San Francisco Chronicle.* Illustrations represented in industry periodicals, including *Communication Arts, Print,* and *American Illustration.*

Biographical and Critical Sources

PERIODICALS

Booklist, January 1, 2011, Hazel Rochman, review of *Orchards,* p. 97.
Publishers Weekly, January 3, 2011, review of *Orchards,* p. 51.
School Library Journal, March, 2011, Allison Tran, review of *Orchards,* p. 172.

ONLINE

Grady McFerrin Home Page, http://gmillustration.com (February 12, 2012).
Grady McFerrin Web log, http://gmillustration.tumblr.com (February 12, 2012).

*   *   *

MELO, Esperança

Personal

Born in the Azores, Portugal; immigrated to Canada. *Education:* Sheridan College, degree (animation); George Brown College, degree (graphic design); attended Ontario College of Art. *Hobbies and other interests:* Antiques, photography.

Addresses

Home—Millbrook, Ontario, Canada.

Career

Illustrator.

Awards, Honors

Our Choice selection, Canadian Children's Book Centre, 2003, for *Knitting* by Judy Ann Sadler; (with Bill Slavin) Blue Spruce Award, Ontario Library Association, Ruth and Sylvia Schwartz Children's Book Award shortlist, Amelia Frances Howard-Gibbon Award shortlist, and Children's Choice selection, International Reading Association, all 2005, and Chocolate Lily Award shortlist, 2006, all for *Drumheller Dinosaur Dance* by Robert Heidbreder; Best Bets selection, Ontario Library Association, 2006, for *Quick Knits* by Sadler.

Illustrator

Amanda Lewis, *Lettering* ("Kids Can Do It" series), Kids Can Press (Toronto, Ontario, Canada), 1996.
(With Bill Slavin) Elizabeth MacLeod, *Get Started: Stamp Collecting for Canadian Kids,* Kids Can Press (Toronto, Ontario, Canada), 1996.
Amanda Lewis, *Making Memory Books* ("Kids Can Do It" series), Kids Can Press (Toronto, Ontario, Canada), 1999.
(With Bill Slavin) Ann-Maureen Owens and Jane Yealland, *Canada's Maple Leaf: The Story of Our Flag,* Kids Can Press (Buffalo, NY), 1999.
Maxine Trottier, *Native Crafts: Inspired by North America's First Peoples* ("Kids Can Do It" series), Kids Can Press (Toronto, Ontario, Canada), 2000.
Judy Ann Sadler, *Knitting* ("Kids Can Do It" series), Scholastic, Inc. (New York, NY), 2002.
(With Bill Slavin) Robert Heidbreder, *Drumheller Dinosaur Dance,* Kids Can Press (Buffalo, NY), 2004.
(With other) Judy Ann Sadler and others, *The Jumbo Book of Needlecrafts,* Kids Can Press (Buffalo, NY), 2005.
Gwen Blakley Kinsler and Jackie Young, *Crocheting* ("Kids Can Do It" series), Scholastic, Inc. (New York, NY), 2006.
Judy Ann Sadler, *Quick Knits,* Kids Can Press (Buffalo, NY), 2007.
(With Bill Slavin) Ellen Jackson, *The Seven Seas,* Eerdmans Books for Young Readers (Grand Rapids, MI), 2011.
Monica Kulling, *Merci Mister Dash!,* Tundra Books (Toronto, Ontario, Canada), 2011.
Jane Barclay, *JoJo the Giant,* Tundra Books (Toronto, Ontario, Canada), 2012.

Books featuring Melo's work have been translated into French.

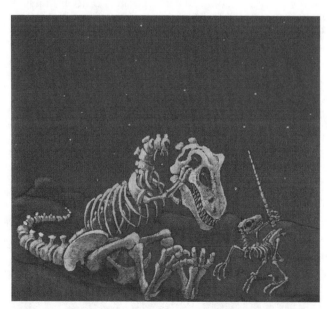

Esperança Melo teams up with fellow illustrator Bill Slavin in bringing to life Robert Heidbreder's picture book Drumheller Dinosaur Dance.
(Illustration copyright © 2004 by Bill Slavin and Esperança Melo. Used by permission of Kids Can Press, Ltd., Toronto.)

Sidelights

A native of Portugal, Esperança Melo attended school in Ontario, Canada, where she now makes her home. She trained in animation and graphic design and also studied oil painting before starting her illustration career by designing book jackets for various publishers. In the mid-1990s Melo earned her first book-illustration projects: a series of craft books for the "Kids Can Do It" series published by Kids Can Press. Her award-winning collaboration with fellow illustrator Bill Slavin on *Drumheller Dinosaur Dance,* a story by Robert Heidbreder, quickly advanced Melo's career, and her colorful images have since appeared in stories by Monica Kulling, Ellen Jackson, and Jane Barclay.

Drumheller Dinosaur Dance is set at the Drumheller architectural park in Alberta, Canada, where Heidbreder lays out a fanciful scenario in which a scattering of ancient dinosaur bones reassembles under the light of the moon to dance the night away. The "impressively detailed" skeletal creatures that appear in Slavin and Melo's colorful acrylic paintings are captured in what a *Publishers Weekly* contributor described as "dramatic perspectives [that] play up the dancers' uninhibited primeval merriment." The artists' use of "deep blue and brown sepia tones . . . perfectly complement this bedtime tale," according to Denise Parrott in *Resource Links,* and in *School Library Journal* Julie Roach wrote that Melo and Slavin's "entertaining picture keep the story moving."

Slavin and Melo reunite in the pages of Jackson's *The Seven Seas,* a story about a wandering rabbit in which they bring to life "whimsical creatures who surf, SCUBA dive, sunbathe, and paddle on imaginary oceans," according to *School Library Journal* contributor Gloria Koster. In addition to their "thickly brushed, heavily sculpted" paintings, the artists bring to life Jackson's story in "comically exaggerated cartoon" images that help *The Seven Seas* "entertain" story-time audiences.

In Kulling's story for *Merci Mister Dash!* a high-mannered pup has the fine manners that make him the perfect pet for his housemate, Madame Croissant. Their quiet life of walking and working on Madame's stamp collection and flower arranging is disrupted, however, when granddaughter Daphne visits and throws the household into turmoil. When the little girl winds up in trouble, Mister Dash comes to the rescue, however, his good-natured efforts captured by Melo in paintings that "humorously portray the dog's irritation as well as Daphne's age-appropriate enthusiasm," according to Kara Schaff Dean in *School Library Journal.*

Biographical and Critical Sources

PERIODICALS

Booklist, January 1, 2007, Ilene Cooper, review of *Quick Knits,* p. 90; February 15, 2011, Hazel Rochman, review of *The Seven Seas,* p. 78.

Melo's illustration projects include creating the engaging art for Monica Kulling's picture book **Merci Mister Dash!** (Illustration copyright © 2011 by Esperanca Melo. Reproduced by permission of Tundra Books.)

Children's Bookwatch, June, 2011, review of *The Seven Seas.*

Childhood Education, winter, 2000, Gloria Tansits Wenze, review of *Native Crafts: Inspired by North America's First Peoples,* p. 107.

Kirkus Reviews, August 15, 2002, review of *Knitting,* p. 1235; February 15, 2003, review of *Crocheting,* p. 299.

Publishers Weekly, October 11, 2004, review of *Drumheller Dinosaur Dance,* p. 78; December 13, 2010, review of *The Seven Seas,* p. 58.

Resource Links, December, 2004, Denise Parrott, review of *Drumheller Dinosaur Dance,* p. 3; February, 2007, Karen McKinnon, review of *Quick Knits,* p. 25.

School Library Journal, June, 2000, Marion F. Gallivan, review of *Native Crafts,* p. 171; November, 2002, Lynda Ritterman, review of *Knitting,* p. 148; April, 2003, Genevieve Gallagher, review of *Crocheting,* p. 146; October, 2005, Elizabeth Stumpf, review of *The Jumbo Book of Needlecrafts*; December, 2006, Augusta R. Malvagno, review of *Quick Knits,* p. 168; February, 2011, Gloria Koster, review of *The Seven Seas,* p. 84; July, 2011, Kara Schaff Dean, review of *Merci Mister Dash!,* p. 69.

ONLINE

Tundra Books Web site, http://www.tundrabooks.com/ (October 16, 2011), "Esperança Melo."*

MORIARTY, Jaclyn 1968-

Personal

Born 1968, in Australia; married Colin McAdam (a writer; divorced); children: Charlie. *Education:* University of Sydney, B.A. (English and law); Yale University, M.A. (law); Gonville & Caius College Cambridge, Ph.D. (law).

Addresses

Home—Sydney, New South Wales, Australia. *Agent*—Jill Grinberg, Jill Grinberg Literary Management, 244 5th Ave., 11th Fl., New York, NY 10001.

Career

Writer. Former media and entertainment lawyer practicing in Sydney, New South Wales, Australia; full-time writer.

Awards, Honors

New South Wales Premier's Literary Award, Notable Book selection, Children's Book Council of Australia (CBCA), White Ravens selection, and Best Books for Young Adults selection, American Library Association (ALA), all c. 2000, all for *Feeling Sorry for Celia;* ALA Best Books for Young Adults selection, Young Adult Choice selection, International Reading Association, and Virginia Young Readers Award nomination, all c. 2006, all for *Finding Cassie Crazy/The Year of Secret Assignments;* New Kelly Awards shortlist, CBCA Choice selection, and Davitt Award for Best Young-Adult Crime Novel, Sister in Crime, all 2007, all for *The Betrayal of Bindy MacKenzie;* Ethel Turner Prize for Young People's Literature shortlist, New South Wales Premier's Literary Awards, 2011, for *Dreaming of Amelia.*

Writings

"ASHBURY/BROOKFIELD" YOUNG-ADULT NOVEL SEQUENCE

Feeling Sorry for Celia, Pan Macmillan (Sydney, New South Wales, Australia), 2000, St. Martin's Press (New York, NY), 2001.

Finding Cassie Crazy, Pan Macmillan (Sydney, New South Wales, Australia), 2003, published as *The Year of Secret Assignments,* Arthur A. Levine (New York, NY), 2004.

The Betrayal of Bindy MacKenzie, Pan Macmillan (Sydney, New South Wales, Australia), 2006, published as *Becoming Bindy MacKenzie,* Young Picator (London, England), 2006, published as *The Murder of Bindy MacKenzie,* Arthur A. Levine Books (New York, NY), 2006.

Dreaming of Amelia, Macmillan Children's (London, England), 2010, published as *The Ghosts of Ashbury High,* Arthur A. Levine Books (New York, NY), 2010.

Author's work has been translated into several languages, including Dutch, German, and Polish.

OTHER

Cicada Summer ("Paradise Point" juvenile novel series), Pan Australia (Sydney, New South Wales, Australia), 1994.

I Have a Bed Made of Buttermilk Pancakes (adult novel), Picador (Sydney, New South Wales, Australia), 2004, revised edition published as *The Spell Book of Listen Taylor and the Secrets of the Family Zing,* Pan Macmillan (Sydney, New South Wales, Australia), 2007, published as *The Spell Book of Listen Taylor,* Arthur A. Levine Books (New York, NY), 2007.

(With Paul Mallam and Sophie Dawson) *Media and Internet Law and Practice* (for adults), Thomson Lawbook (Pyrmont, New South Wales, Australia), 2005.

Contributor to anthologies, including *Kids' Night In,* 2003; *Hunger and Other Stories,* 2003; *Not like I'm Jealous or Anything: The Jealousy Book,* edited by Marissa Walsh, Delacorte (New York, NY), 2006; *Can*

Jaclyn Moriarty spins a pastiche of scribbled notes, postcards from absent friends, and sometimes imaginary letters into her highly praised novel **Feeling Sorry for Celia.** (Copyright © 2000 by Jaclyn Moriarty. Reproduced by permission of St. Martin's Press.)

You Keep a Secret?, edited by Louis Metzger, 2007; *Does This Book Make Me Look Fat?,* edited by Walsh, Clarion (New York, NY), 2008; and *Great Expectations: Twenty-four True Stories about Childbirth,* edited by Lisa Moore and Dede Crane, 2008.

Adaptations

The Year of Secret Assignments was adapted for audiobook, Recorded Books, 2004.

Sidelights

Jaclyn Moriarty began writing fiction while growing up in Australia, but she was inspired to study law by one of her favorite books, Harper Lee's *To Kill a Mockingbird.* When Moriarty received her law degree, she also received a congratulations card from a former English teacher that read, "P.S. But remember you are really a writer." "I sat down and wrote a short story the same day," the novelist recalled to *Teenreads.com* interviewer Lucy Burns. "And that's why I started writing again." After several years juggling her writing with her work as a media and entertainment lawyer, Moriarty attained a level of financial stability that allowed her to work on her teen fiction full time.

Moriarty's first novel, *Feeling Sorry for Celia,* is told entirely through letters, sticky notes, and other written communications. As the story opens, Elizabeth Clarry is having a rough year. Her mother is an advertising executive who is never available and her best friend has run away to join the circus. On the plus side, her father has reappeared in her life and she is receiving anonymous letters from a secret admirer. It seems to Elizabeth that a new English-class assignment to correspond with a girl at a neighboring high school will only make things worse, but new pen pal Christina turns out to be a person who recognizes her talents. "Moriarty poignantly captures the trials of adolescent friendships," wrote Elsa Gaztambide in her *Booklist* review of Moriarty's debut. Miranda Doyle, writing in *School Library Journal,* called *Feeling Sorry for Celia* "a light, enjoyable novel about a memorable young woman," while *Kliatt* reviewer Paula Rohrlick noted: "Here's hoping this first-time author will continue writing for YA's."

Feeling Sorry for Celia became the first volume in a loosely connected sequence of four novels called the "Ashbury/Brookfield" books because they focus on Sydney teens attending either private Ashbury High School or Brookfield High, a public school. All four novels consist of a first-person narrative composed of letters, e-mails, and notes and each can be read and enjoyed independently.

When readers meet them in *Finding Cassie Crazy* (published in the United States as *The Year of Secret Assignments*), Em, Lyd, and Cassie are part of the same pen-pal exchange program that Elizabeth participated in in *Feeling Sorry for Celia.* Instead of finding a listening

When three friends decide to participate in a school pen-pal program, their correspondence with boys from a rival high school sparks romance in Moriarty's **The Year of Secret Assignments.** (Illustration copyright © 2004 by Rob Dobi. Reprinted by permission of Scholastic, Inc.)

ear and a female friend, however, all three girls are paired up with boys. Cassie and her mother are still recovering from Cassie's father's death, and sadly, Cassie is paired with a boy who threatens her, causing her to become increasingly vulnerable. Now it is up to Em, Lydia, and their pen-pals Charlie and Seb to help Cassie overcome her grief. "Who can resist Moriarty's biting humor?" asked a *Kirkus Reviews* contributor in a review of *The Year of Secret Assignments,* while *Booklist* critic Gillian Engberg commented on the "exhilarating pace, irrepressible characters, and a screwball humor that will easily attract teens." A *Publishers Weekly* reviewer noted that *The Year of Secret Assignments* contains "elements of mystery, espionage, romance, and revenge," while in *School Library Journal* Janet Hilbun commented that the friends' adventures are "funny, exciting, and, at times, poignant." Claire Rosser, writing for *Kliatt,* called Moriarty's second "Ashbury/Brookfield" novel "intelligent fun," and a *Horn Book* critic cited its "enormous depth, wit, and poignancy."

A high I.Q. does not guarantee popularity, as Moriarty's readers discover in *The Murder of Bindy MacKenzie.* From her position at the top of the honor role, relentlessly over-achieving high-school junior Bindy Mack-

enzie works hard at being the smartest, the most help-ful, and the kindest girl at Ashbury High. She is also the most put-together, with her hair braided and rolled neatly on either side of her head. When Bindy enrolls in a new Friendship and Development class designed to help Ashbury students navigate the ups and downs of adolescence, she takes pains to disperse constructive advice to others in her group while oblivious of the fact that she is viewed as offputting and annoying. Readers quickly realize the truth as they read Bindy's e-mails, notes, and journal entries. The members of her group realize how disliked Bindy is as well, and when she ex-hibits signs that she may be having problems it is up to her group-mates to overcome their dislike help her. "Bindy's unreliable narration provides most of the hu-mor and suspense" in *The Murder of Bindy MacKenzie*, noted a *Kirkus Reviews* writer, and Rosser asserted in *Kliatt* that Moriarty's novel "is inventive, length, and highly entertaining" due to Bindy's "idiosyncratic un-derstanding of herself and others." For Gillian Engberg, reviewing *The Murder of Bindy MacKenzie* in *Booklist*, it is "Bindy's . . . earnest, hilariously high-strung voice that will capture and hold eager readers."

The third book in the "Ashbury/Brookfield" sequence is *The Ghosts of Ashbury High,* and here scholarship stu-dents Amelia and Riley have just crossed borders by transferring from Brookfield to Ashbury. With their cha-risma and mysterious past, the siblings soon work their way up the Ashbury pecking order, and they also seem to have won over their teachers. Along with the usual sources, readers learn the truth about the two new stu-dents through faculty notes, papers in Amelia's Gothic fiction class, and the blog entries and e-mails exchanged among Cassie, Lydia, and Emily. The influence of Gothic fiction imbues *The Ghosts of Ashbury High* with "an often wicked sense of humor, creating modern and effective ghost stories in the process," wrote a *Publish-ers Weekly* contributor, and in *Booklist* Engberg cited both the "clever jumble of forms and voices" and the students' "sharp-eyed, poignant observations" as strengths in Moriarty's "madcap novel." "Quirky, comic and self-reverential," *The Ghosts of Ashbury High* ranks as "another winner" that is "sure to please old fans and creates new ones," according to a *Kirkus Reviews* writer.

Moriarty's quirky "Ashbury/Brookfield" series con-cludes in *Dreaming of Amelia,* which moves even fur-ther into mystery in its story about the problems created as the result of a pen-pal program between students at the two high schools. Designed to build understanding between the two schools, the letter-writing scheme in-stead sparks misunderstanding and reveals hidden se-crets, all while Lydia, Emily, Cassie, and others attempt to navigate their final year of high school.

Moriarty's young-adult novel *The Spell Book of Listen Taylor* is an adaptation of her novel *I Have a Bed Made of Buttermilk Pancakes,* which several critics described as a whimsical fairy tale for adults. In the story, Listen Taylor is starting seventh grade at a new school now

that her dad has moved in with new girlfriend Marbie Zing. While Listen slowly works her way to being a part of her new family—where everyone convenes on Friday nights to discuss the Zing Family Secret—she also has to navigate middle school, where she cultivates her role as an outsider. As relationships within the blended Zing family become increasingly complex due to infidelities and the deception that results, the ripples extend beyond the family to encompass Listen, second grader Cassie Zing, and Cassie's lovelorn teacher.

Praising *The Spell Book of Listen Taylor* as "absurdly preposterous, delightfully whimsical and funny," Con-nie Terrell Burns added in *School Library Journal* that here Moriarty serves up "a clever, funny romp" that is "better suited for older teens." A *Publishers Weekly* critic commented that, while much of the novel focuses on adult issues, the "intellectual puzzle" the author weaves within her story "may engage YA readers"; for most critics, however, *The Spell Book of Listen Taylor* features themes that are less geared for teens that for older, more worldly-wise readers. "The girl who is al-ready reading Jane Austen . . . might well enjoy *The Spell Book of Listen Taylor,*" suggested Roger Sutton in

Cover of Moriarty's imaginative YA novel **The Ghosts of Ashbury High,** *part of her "Ashbury/Brookfield" series.* (Jacket art © 2010 by Spiral Studio. Reproduced by permission of Scholastic, Inc.)

the *New York Times Book Review,* "but I'm betting she would enjoy it more if she could come to it as an adult book."

Interestingly, Moriarty adapted *I Have a Bed Made of Buttermilk Pancakes* for younger readers after her U.S. editor expressed curiosity about the character of Listen Taylor and wondered what the events of the story would have seemed like from the twelve year old's perspective. "Reviewers of *The Spell Book of Listen Taylor* often say, emphatically, that this is NOT a book for young adults," Moriarty noted on her home page, "either because young adults won't understand the adult issues and characters in it, or won't be interested in them. It's true that the *Spell Book* is not for all young adults, but I will just say, very gently, that I get many letters from 15-year-olds about this book—letters which show far more insight about the book, and its grown-up characters, than most of its grown-up readers have ever shown."

Biographical and Critical Sources

PERIODICALS

Booklist, November 15, 2000, Elsa Gaztambide, review of *Feeling Sorry for Celia,* p. 621; January 1, 2004, Gillian Engberg, review of *The Year of Secret Assignments,* p. 858; October 15, 2006, Gillian Engberg, review of *The Murder of Bindy Mackenzie,* p. 41; October 1, 2007, Kathleen Isaacs, review of *The Spell Book of Listen Taylor,* p. 47; April 1, 2010, Gillian Engberg, review of *The Ghosts of Ashbury High,* p. 32.

Horn Book, March-April, 2004, Jennifer M. Brabander, review of *The Year of Secret Assignments,* p. 185; September-October, 2007, Jennifer M. Brabander, review of *The Spell Book of Listen Taylor,* p. 582; July-August, 2010, Jonathan Hunt, review of *The Ghosts of Ashbury Place,* p. 115.

Kirkus Reviews, January 15, 2004, review of *The Year of Secret Assignments,* p. 86; September 15, 2006, review of *The Murder of Bindy Mackenzie,* p. 962; August 15, 2007, review of *The Spell Book of Listen Taylor*; May 15, 2010, review of *The Ghosts of Ashbury High.*

Kliatt, March, 2002, Paula Rohrlick, review of *Feeling Sorry for Celia,* p. 17; January, 2004, Claire Rosser, review of *The Year of Secret Assignments,* p. 10; September, 2006, Claire Rosser, review of *The Murder of Bindy Mackenzie.*

Library Journal, March 15, 2001, Rebecca Sturm Kelm, review of *Feeling Sorry for Celia,* p. 106.

New York Times Book Review, November 11, 2007, Roger Sutton, review of *The Spell Book of Listen Taylor,* p. 34.

Publishers Weekly, February 2, 2004, review of *The Year of Secret Assignments,* p. 78; December 18, 2006, review of *And Then What Happened?,* p. 65; September 17, 2007, review of *The Spell Book of Listen Taylor,* p. 56; June 28, 2010, review of *The Ghosts of Ashbury High,* p. 129.

Resource Links, February, 2007, Leslie L. Kennedy, review of *The Murder of Bindy Mackenzie,* p. 40.

School Library Journal, May, 2001, Miranda Doyle, review of *Feeling Sorry for Celia,* p. 156; March, 2004, Janet Hilbun, review of *The Year of Secret Assignments,* p. 220; January, 2007, Rhona Campbell, review of *The Murder of Bindy Mackenzie,* p. 134; November, 2007, Connie Terrell Burns, review of *The Spell Book of Listen Taylor,* p. 132; September, 2010, Gina Bowling, review of *The Ghosts of Ashbury High,* p. 158.

ONLINE

Jacqueline Moriarty Home Page, http://www.jaclynmoriarty.com (February 15, 2012).

Teenreads.com, http://www.teenreads.com/ (July 12, 2005), Lucy Burns, interview with Moriarty.*

N

NADIN, Joanna 1970-

Personal

Born 1970, in Northampton, England; children: one daughter. *Education:* Hull University, degree (drama); University of London, M.A. (political communications). *Hobbies and other interests:* Ice skating, baking.

Addresses

Home—Bath, England. *Agent*—Sarah Molloy, A.M. Heath & Co., 6 Warwick Ct., Holborn, London WC1R 5DJ, England. *E-mail*—info@joannanadin.com.

Career

Speech writer, scriptwriter, and author. Worked variously as a journalist, radio newsreader, and television producer; former policy writer for British Labour Party; special advisor to British Prime Minister Tony Blair, c. 2001; freelance government speech writer.

Awards, Honors

Lancashire Fantastic Book Award; Queen of Teen Award shortlist, 2008, 2010, both for "Rachel Riley" series; Roald Dahl Funny Prize shortlist, 2011, for *Penny Dreadful Is a Magnet for Disaster.*

Writings

Maisie Morris and the Awful Arkwrights, illustrated by Arthur Robins, Walker Books (London, England), 2003.

Solomon Shee versus the Monkeys, illustrated by Arthur Robbins, Walker Books (London, England), 2004.

Maisie Morris and the Whopping Lies, illustrated by Arthur Robins, Walker Books (London, England), 2006.

Jake Jellicoe and the Dread Pirate Redbeard, illustrated by David Roberts, Walker Books (London, England), 2006.

Joanna Nadin (Reproduced by permission.)

Candy Plastic, illustrated by Sue Mason, Walker Books (London, England), 2007.

Wonderland, Walker Books (London, England), 2009, Candlewick Press (Somerville, MA), 2011.

The Whole Truth, illustrated by Volker Beisler, Heinemann (Harlow, England), 2010.

Spies, Dad, Big Lauren, and Me, Piccadilly Press (London, England), 2011.

Buttercup Mash, Oxford University Press (Oxford, England), 2011.

Paradise, Walker Books (London, England), 2011.

The Money, Stan, Big Lauren, and Me, Piccadilly Press (London, England), 2012.

Contributor to anthologies, including *Queen of Teen: Fabulous Stories from Top Teen Authors,* 2010; *All in the Family;* and *Inner City: Stories from the Thick of It,* edited by Tony Bradman, A. & C. Black, 2011.

"MY SO-CALLED LIFE" MIDDLE-GRADE NOVEL SERIES

My So-Called Life: The Tragically Normal Diary of Rachel Riley (also see below), Oxford University Press (Oxford, England), 2007.

The Life of Riley: My Utterly Hopeless Search for the One (also see below), Oxford University Press (Oxford, England), 2008.

The Meaning of Life: Rachel Riley's (Not) Doing It Diary (also see below), Oxford University Press (Oxford, England), 2008.

My (Not So) Simple Life: Rachel Riley Goes Back to Basics (also see below), Oxford University Press (Oxford, England), 2009.

My Double Life: Two Years in the So-Called Life of Rachel Riley (includes *The Meaning of Life* and *The Life of Riley*), Oxford University Press (Oxford, England), 2009.

Back to Life: Rachel Riley (Sort of) Seizes the Day, Oxford University Press (Oxford, England), 2009.

The Facts of Life: Rachel Riley (Almost) Wakes up and Smells the Coffee, Oxford University Press (Oxford, England), 2010.

Double Trouble: Another Year in the (Not So) Simple Life of Rachel Riley (includes *My (Not So) Simple Life* and *The Meaning of Life*), Oxford University Press (Oxford, England), 2010.

Double or Quits: Rachel Riley's Year of (Almost) Taking Control (includes *Back to Life* and *The Facts of Life*), Oxford University Press (Oxford, England), 2011.

"PENNY DREADFUL" READER SERIES; ILLUSTRATED BY JESS MIKHAIL

Penny Dreadful Is a Magnet for Disaster, Usborne Publishing (London, England), 2011.

Penny Dreadful Is a Complete Catastrophe, Usborne Publishing (London, England), 2012.

Penny Dreadful Cooks up a Calamity, Usborne Publishing (London, England), 2012.

Penny Dreadful Causes a Kerfuffle, Usborne Publishing (London, England), 2012.

Sidelights

Although Joanna Nadin started her university studies with plans to become an actor, by the time graduation rolled around she was looking forward to starting a master's degree in political communications. Jobs in radio news and speechwriting for the British Labour Party led to Nadin's appointment as special adviser to U.K. Prime Minister Tony Blair during part of Blair's term in office. While her work in politics kept her hyper-focused on current events, she found an outlet for her imagination in fiction writing and gained a large following as the author of her diary-style "My So-Called Life" novel

series. Based on Nadin's typical suburban childhood, the "My So-Called Life" books follow heroine Rachel Riley through her teenage years as she suffers from dysfunctional parents, an annoying little brother, and the quandary of not having experience with boys. "Nadin has a good ear for comedy," wrote London *Observer* contributor Stephanie Merritt in her review of series opener *My So-Called Life: The Tragically Normal Diary of Rachel Riley,* adding that the novelist has mastered "the rare trick of producing a book that will make both adults and teenagers laugh aloud."

Featuring another teen heroine from a small town, *Wonderland* is more serious in focus. For sixteen-year-old Jude, it seems like there is no place where she is truly happy. At home, her widowed father is depressed and caught up in memories of her late mom, and at her current private school the shy teen is an outcast. Styling herself "Jude the Obscure," in homage to a Thomas Hardy novel, the teen dreams of studying acting at a prestigious London drama school. When her childhood friend Stella returns after a long absence, the spunky teen helps give Jude the confidence she needs to submit

Cover of Nadin's coming-of-age novel **Wonderland,** *which challenges readers to contemplate the consequences of impulsive behavior.* (Jacket photographs copyright © 2011 by Matthias Clamer/Getty Images. Reproduced by permission of Candlewick Press, Somerville, MA, on behalf of Walker Books, London.)

her application. That is just the start, however, and soon Stella is challenging Jude to party, flirt with boys, and experiment with drugs.

Noting the surprising plot twist at the end of Nadin's novel, Kelly Czarnecki and Jamie Hanson predicted in *Voice of Youth Advocates* that *Wonderland* will inspire readers to "question their own friendships and identify within relationships," while "older teens will . . . [be] drawn to the immediacy and intimacy of Jude's story." "This is more of a psychological thriller than a book about bad girls," suggested Karen Alexander in her *School Library Journal* review, and a *Kirkus Reviews* writer noted that the author artfully introduces "the intricate parts of a psychological puzzle as she . . . reveals the true nature" of the teens' relationship.

On her home page, Nadin described the pluses in being a writer. "There's the small stuff like being able to wear what you want to work—from pyjamas to a prom dress," she noted, as well as "not working at all if you're not in the mood. Or working late into the night if you're on a really good chapter. Going to the cinema or sitting in a café reading a book for 'research'. . . . Then there's the big bit: being able to spend days, weeks, months living in other worlds, and as other people. Giving girls who were mean to you at school their come-uppance. Giving a friend the happy ending he never got in real life. In short—turning daydreaming into reality, and getting paid for it. What could be better than that?"

Biographical and Critical Sources

PERIODICALS

Booklist, January 1, 2011, Hazel Rochman, review of *Wonderland,* p. 103.
Bookseller, April 6, 2007, Caroline Horn, "My So-Called Debut" (profile), p. 19.
Kirkus Reviews, January 15, 2011, review of *Wonderland.*
Observer (London, England), July 15, 2007, Stephanie Merritt, review of *My So-Called Life: The Tragically Normal Diary of Rachel Riley,* p. 25.
Publishers Weekly, December 13, 2010, review of *Wonderland,* p. 59.
School Librarian, summer, 2011, Cherie Gladstone, review of *Spies, Dad, Big Lauren, and Me,* p. 105.
School Library Journal, April, 2011, Karen Alexander, review of *Wonderland,* p. 180.
Voice of Youth Advocates, April, 2011, review of *Wonderland,* p. 78.

ONLINE

Chicklish Web site, http://keris.typepad.com/chicklet/ (May, 2008), interview with Nadin.
Joanna Nadin Home Page, http://www.joannanadin.com (February 12, 2012).

NESBITT, Kenn 1962-

Personal

Born February 20, 1962, in Berkeley, CA; married Ann Margaret Aylward; children: Max, Madison (daughter).

Addresses

Home—Spokane, WA.

Career

Poet. Presenter at schools and workshops.

Member

Society of Children's Book Writers and Illustrators.

Writings

FOR CHILDREN

My Foot Fell Asleep, Purple Room Publishing, 1998.
I've Seen My Kitchen Sink, Purple Room Publishing, 1999.
Sailing off to Singapore, illustrated by Michael Roberts, Purple Room Publishing, 2000.
The Aliens Have Landed!, illustrated by Margeaux Lucas, Meadowbrook Press (Minnetonka, MN), 2001.
When the Teacher Isn't Looking, and Other Funny School Poems, illustrated by Mike Gordon, Meadowbrook Press (Minnetonka, MN), 2005.
(With Linda Knaus) *Santa Got Stuck in the Chimney: Twenty Funny Poems Full of Christmas Cheer,* illustrated by Mike Gordon and Carl Gordon, Meadowbrook Press (Minnetonka, MN), 2006.
Revenge of the Lunch Ladies: The Hilarious Book of School Poetry, illustrated by Mike and Carl Gordon, Meadowbrook Press (Minnetonka, MN), 2007.
My Hippo Has the Hiccups, and Other Poems I Totally Made Up, illustrated by Ethan Long, Sourcebooks Jabberwocky (Naperville, IL), 2009.
The Tighty-Whitey Spider, and More Wacky Animal Poems I Totally Made Up, illustrated by Ethan Long, Sourcebooks Jabberwocky (Napierville, IL), 2010.
More Bears!, illustrated by Troy Cummings, Sourcebooks Jabberwocky (Napierville, IL), 2010.
The Ultimate Top Secret Guide to Taking over the World, illustrated by Ethan Long, Sourcebooks Jabberwocky (Napierville, IL), 2011.

Contributor of poems to periodicals, including *Highlights for Children* and *Friends.* Poems included in textbooks, and in anthologies, including *Kids Pick the Funniest Poems,* 1991, *A Bad Case of the Giggles* and *No More Homework! No More Tests,* both 1997, *Miles of Smiles,* 1998, *Rolling in the Aisles* and *If Kids Ruled the School,* both 2004, *My Teacher's in Detention* and *Peter, Peter, Pizza Eater,* both 2006, *I've Been Burped in the Classroom,* 2007, *I Hope I Don't Strike Out,*

2008, and *What I Did on My Summer Vacation,* 2009, all edited by B. Lansky and published by Meadowbrook Press; *I Like It Here at School,* 2003, *My Dog Does My Homework,* 2004, and *If I Ran the School,* 2005, all published by Scholastic, Inc.; and *There's No Place like School,* edited by Jack Prelutsky, HarperCollins, 2010.

OTHER

(With Ron Dragushan and Harley Hahn) *Power Shortcuts: Paradox for Windows,* MIS:Press (New York, NY), 1992.

Author of song lyrics for recordings by Eric Herman and the Invisible Band.

Adaptations

Several of Nesbitt's poetry books have been recorded on CD.

Sidelights

Although Kenn Nesbitt lives in the northwest corner of the United States, he enriches children from throughout the country with humorous verse that has been collected in a number of humorous illustrated anthologies. Raised in California, Nesbitt started his career as a poet in 1994, after a dinner with friends in his new hometown of Spokane, Washington. His inspiration? Watching his host's daughter use various strategies in an effort to avoid eating the food on her dinner plate. His chronicled this episode in "Scrawny Tawny Skinner," and followed this work with an ever-increasing number over the next few years. In 1998 Nesbitt's entire oeuvre was anthologized in *My Foot Fell Asleep,* and he has continued to publish a new verse collection every year. In addition to his anthologies, Nesbitt is the genius behind the much-bookmarked Web site *Poetry4kids.com,* which allows children to post original poems and videos, play games and hone their writing skills, as well as receive a daily dose of humorous verses by Nesbitt via e-mail.

Featuring humorous cartoon artwork by illustrators such as Mike and Carl Gordon, Margeaux Lucas, Troy Cummings, and Ethan Long, Nesbitt's poetry books have titles that more-than-hint at their kid-focused contents. In *Santa Got Stuck in the Chimney: Twenty Funny Poems Full of Christmas Cheer* he presents a humorous take on the holiday season, while *The Aliens Have Landed at Our School!* serves up fantasies shared by many elementary graders. Nesbitt's first picture-book story takes on a life of its own in *More Bears!,* a story illustrated by Cummings that is derailed when a not-to-be-seen audience demands that more and more bears become part of the story. In *Publishers Weekly* a critic praised *More Bears!* as a "rollicking metafictional romp" and "a story that's made for reading aloud," and Susan E. Murray predicted in *School Library Journal* that Nesbitt's "participatory refrain . . . will bring this selection to life at storytimes."

Kenn Nesbitt's verse in **My Hippo Has the Hiccups and Other Poems I Totally Made Up** *is given added humor in Ethan Long's cartoon art.* (Illustration by Ethan Long. Reproduced by permission of Sourcebooks Jabberwocky, an imprint of Sourcebooks, Inc.)

Nesbitt teams up with Long on several books, including *My Hippo Has the Hiccups, and Other Poems I Totally Made Up, The Tighty-Whitey Spider, and More Wacky Animal Poems I Totally Made Up,* and *The Ultimate Top Secret Guide to Taking over the World.* Everything from petulant potatoes to robots to a young almost-werewolf become grist for the poet's poetry mill in *My Hippo Has the Hiccups, and Other Poems I Totally Made Up,* which features one hundred verses that Lee Bock characterized in *School Library Journal* as "zany and at times challenging." Antic animals of all stripes, spots, and habits become the focus of Nesbitt's wordplay in *The Tighty Whitey Spider,* and the fifty-plus poems in this collection treat readers to "imaginative flights of fancy and comic exaggeration," according to Lauralyn Persson in the same publication.

Biographical and Critical Sources

PERIODICALS

Kirkus Reviews, October 15, 2010, review of *More Bears!*; May 15, 2011, review of *The Ultimate Top Secret Guide to Taking over the World.*

Publishers Weekly, October 18, 2010, review of *More Bears!*, p. 42.

School Library Journal, May, 2009, Lee Bock, review of *My Hippo Has the Hiccups, and Other Poems I To-*

tally Made Up, p. 97; June, 2010, Lauralyn Persson, review of *The Tighty Whitey Spider,* p. 90; January, 2011, Susan E. Murray, review of *More Bears!,* p. 81.

ONLINE

Kenn Nesbitt Home Page, http://www.poetry4kids.com (February 15, 2012).

Poetry Foundation Web site, http://www.poetryfoundation. org/ (February 15, 2012), "Kenn Nesbitt."*

* * *

NICHOLSON, William 1948-

Personal

Born 1948, in England; father a physician; married Virginia Bell (a writer and historian), 1988; children: three. *Education:* Christ's College Cambridge, B.A., 1973.

Addresses

Home—Sussex, England. *Agent*—(Films) Sally Wilcox/ Carin Sage, Creative Artists Agency, 9830 Wilshire Blvd., Beverly Hills, CA 90212-1825; (fantasy novels) Jodie Marsh, United Agents, 130 Shaftesbury Ave., London W1D 5EU, England; (fiction) Clare Alexander, Gillon Aitken Associates, 18-21 Cavaye Pl., London SW10 9PT, England.

Career

Writer, playwright, and screenwriter. Former director and producer of documentary films for the British Broadcasting Corporation. Executive producer of *Everyman,* 1979-82, and *Global Report,* 1983-84; director, *Firelight,* Carnival/Wind Dancer, 1997.

Awards, Honors

Best Television Play selection, British Academy of Film and Television Arts (BAFTA), 1985, for *Shadowlands;* Best Television Film designation, New York Film Festival, 1987, Best Television Drama award, BAFTA, 1987, and ACE Award for best picture, 1988, all for *Life Story;* Banff Festival Best Drama designation, 1988, ACE Award for Best International Drama, 1990, and Royal Television Society's Writer's Award, 1987-88, all for *Sweet as You Are;* Best Play of 1990, London *Evening Standard,* for *Shadowlands;* Emmy Award nomination for best screenplay, Academy of Television Arts and Sciences, 1992, for *A Private Matter;* Golden Globe and Emmy Award nominations for best screenplay, both 1996, both for *Crime of the Century;* named fellow, Royal Society of Literature, 1999; Nestlé Smarties Prize Gold Award, 2000, and Blue Peter Book of the Year Award, 2001, both for *The Wind Singer;* Academy Award nomination for best screenplay, Academy of Motion Picture Arts and Sciences, 2000, for *Gladiator;* Antoinette Perry ("Tony") Award nomination for best play, 2004, for *The Retreat from Moscow.*

Writings

"WIND ON FIRE" JUVENILE NOVEL SERIES; ILLUSTRATIONS BY PETER SÍS

The Wind Singer: An Adventure, Hyperion Books for Children (New York, NY), 2000.
Slaves of the Mastery, Hyperion Books for Children (New York, NY), 2001.
Firesong: An Adventure, Hyperion Books for Children (New York, NY), 2002.

"NOBLE WARRIORS TRILOGY" YOUNG-ADULT NOVELS

Seeker, Harcourt (Orlando, FL), 2006.
Jango, Harcourt (Orlando, FL), 2007.
Noman, Egmont (London, England), 2007, Harcourt (Orlando, FL), 2008.

YOUNG-ADULT NOVELS

Rich and Mad, Egmont USA (New York, NY), 2010.

ADULT NOVELS

The Seventh Level: A Sexual Progress, Stein & Day (New York, NY), 1979.
The Society of Others, Nan A. Talese (New York, NY), 2005.
The Trial of True Love, Nan A. Talese (New York, NY), 2005.
The Secret Intensity of Everyday Life, Quercus (London, England), 2008, Soho Press (New York, NY), 2010.
I Could Love You, Soho Press (New York, NY), 2011.

TELEPLAYS

Martin Luther, produced by British Broadcasting Corporation, 1983.
Shadowlands (also see below), produced by British Broadcasting Corporation, 1985.
New World, produced by British Broadcasting Corporation, 1986.
Life Story, produced by British Broadcasting Corporation, 1987.
Sweet as You Are, produced by British Broadcasting Corporation, 1988.
The Vision, produced by British Broadcasting Corporation, 1988.
The March, produced by British Broadcasting Corporation, 1990.
A Private Matter, produced by Home Box Office, 1992.
Crime of the Century, produced by Home Box Office, 1996.

Author's work has been translated into German.

SCREENPLAYS

Double Helix (a.k.a. Life Story), Films for the Humanities and Sciences, 1987.
Sarafina, Distant Horizon/Disney, 1992.

Shadowlands (based on the author's television play; also see below), Savoy, 1993.

(With Mark Handley) *Nell*, Twentieth Century-Fox, 1994.

First Knight, Columbia, 1995.

(And director) *Firelight*, Disney, 1998.

Grey Owl, Allied Pictures, 2000.

(With David Franzoni and John Logan) *Gladiator*, Dream-Works, 2000.

Long Walk to Freedom (based on the book by Nelson Mandela), Bullfrog Films, 2004.

(With Michael Hirst) *Elizabeth: The Golden Age*, Studio-CanalMP Zeta/Working Title, 2007.

STAGE PLAYS

Shadowlands (produced in London, England, 1989), Plume (New York, NY), 1990.

Map of the Heart (produced in London, England, 1991), Samuel French (New York, NY), 1991.

Katherine Howard (produced in Chichester, England, 1998), Samuel French (New York, NY), 1999.

The Retreat from Moscow (produced in Chichester, England, 1999), Anchor Books (New York, NY), 2004.

Crash (produced in London, England, 2010), Methuen Drama (London, England), 2010.

Adaptations

Shadowlands was novelized by Leonore Fleishcer, Signet (New York, NY), 1993, and also as a sound recording by LA Theatre Works (Los Angeles, CA), 2001. *Gladiator* was novelized by Dewey Gra, Onyx (New York, NY), 2000. The "Wind on Fire" trilogy was adapted for audiobook by BBC Audiobooks America. *Seeker* was adapted for audiobook, read by Michael Page, by Brilliance Audio, 2006. *Elizabeth, the Golden Age* was novelized by Tasha Alexander, HarperEntertainment, 2007.

Sidelights

William Nicholson has written screenplays for television and film, stage plays performed in both England and the United States, and novels for both teens and adults. Beginning his career in British television, Nicholson gained wide notice in 1985 for his television play *Shadowlands*, which is about the real-life love affair between British writer and Christian apologist C.S. Lewis and American Joy Davidman. His screenplays include *Double Helix (a.k.a. Life Story)*, a dramatization of the discovery of deoxyribonucleic acid (DNA), and *Gladiator*, an adventure epic starring Russell Crow and Oliver Reed. As a playwright, Nicholson has earned several awards, including an Antoinette Perry Award nomination for his 2004 stage production, *The Retreat from Moscow*.

In addition to his work for stage and screen, Nicholson is also an accomplished novelist. His young-adult "Wind on Fire" fantasy trilogy features the male-female twins Bowman and Kestrel, who must save the Manth people

from slavery in a dystopian world. In the series opener, *The Wind Singer: An Adventure*, the twins set out to recover a pipe organ known as the Wind Singer after they are targeted by the Chief Examiner, who has labeled them all misfits. Writing in *School Library Journal*, John Peters noted that "fans of such barbed journey tales . . . will enjoy the social commentary," and *Booklist* contributor GraceAnne A. DeCandido asserted that the story's "background is well delineated" and that Moriarty gives *The Wind Singer* both "comic relief" and a "thrilling denouement."

As the trilogy continues in *Slaves of the Mastery*, Bowman and Kestrel are once again fighting evil after five years of peace. This time they and their family are made slaves and taken to the city of the Mastery, where the twins use both cunning and their magical abilities to fight back. Writing in *Booklist*, DeCandido described the book as "an astonishing mishmash of lore, myth, and magicking" that also includes some "splendid battle scenes," and *School Library Journal* critic Eva Mitnick

Cover of William Nicholson's young-adult fantasy* The Wind Singer, *featuring artwork by Peter Sîs. (Artwork copyright © 2000 by Peter Sis. Reprinted by permission of Disney-Hyperion, an imprint of Disney Book Group LLC. All rights reserved.)

called *Slaves of the Mastery* a "masterful sequel" in which "every character . . . is compelling and full of life."

The final installment in the trilogy, *Firesong: An Adventure,* finds the twins leading their people back home after the fall of the Mastery, facing both a grueling journey and dissent from within. *School Library Journal* contributor Beth L. Meister wrote that the trilogy's "concluding volume . . . features fast-paced action, poetic language, and carefully constructed characters."

Also geared for teen readers, Nicholson's "Noble Warriors" trilogy begins with *Seeker,* "a novel of friendship, loyalty, and accomplishment," according to *School Library Journal* reviewer June H. Keuhn. A fantasy with a quest at its core, *Seeker* transports readers to the fictional Island of Anacrea, where an order of warrior monks known as the Nomana are dedicated to defending and serving the one god. Known as the All and Only, this god is revered despite a prophecy that predicts its death at the hands of an assassin. Hoping to follow in the footsteps of his older brother and become a warrior for the All and Only, sixteen-year-old Seeker sets out for Anacrea. Also hoping to prove their worthiness—and following similar and ultimately connecting paths—are a devout girl named Morning Star and a thief named Wildman. At first rejected by the Nomana, the three teens nonetheless fear for the monks' safety when they discover a plot to destroy both the island and the All and Only. Teaming up, they embark on a journey to the cosmopolitan city of Radiance, where the worship of a jealous pantheon of competing gods requires human sacrifices. Arriving there, the three traveler learn of Soren Similin and his plot to both destroy the meek Nomana and end worship of the All and Only. Harnessing the power of terror, Similin's scheme is to send suicide bombers to the remote island and destroy Anacrea's beauty forever.

In a review of *Seeker* for *Booklist,* Jennifer Mattson cited Nicholson's "tight plotting" as well as his ability to interweave the "numerous perspectives" that "lend the novel a cinematic breadth." *Kliatt* contributor Deirdre Root dubbed the same work "an astoundingly beautiful book" and added that the "simplicity" of the "Seekers" novels "belies a complex world" that seems vivid and real due to Nicholson's skill in rendering both character and setting.

The "Noble Warriors" trilogy continues in *Jango,* as Seeker, Morning Star, and the Wildman are accepted by the Nomana and begin their training to become warrior monks. When Wildman crosses a forbidden line and is cast out of the sect, Morning Star follows him. Meanwhile, Seeker attempts to vanquish a new threat to the All and Only, and he returns to the Nomana in time to help his friends defend the warrior fortress, although a bomb ultimately destroys all. An old man named Jango now appears, leading Seeker into another realm where he comes face to face with his beloved deity. The Orlan

Cover of Seeker, *the first installment in Nicholson's "Noble Warriors" series, featuring artwork by Douglas Mullen.* (Illustration copyright © 2005 by Douglas Mullen. Reproduced by permission of Houghton Mifflin Harcourt Publishing Company. All rights reserved.)

army is on the march in *Noman,* as Seeker, Morning Star, and the Wildman recognize that the age of warriors is coming to a close. As each wrestles with his or her doubts, they all confront new physical challenges in the form of three beings that wish to do them harm.

"Propelled by unique battle scenes and touching dialogue, *Jango* will draw satisfied readers deeper into the mystery" of Nicholson's "Noble Warriors" saga, according to Emily Rodriguez in *School Library Journal.* A *Kirkus Reviews* contributor cited the mix of "betrayal and self-doubt" as well as spiritual questing that fuels the series' second installment, describing *Jango* as a "splendid read [that] will both satisfy and tantalize lovers of" *Seeker.* In *Booklist* Jennifer Mattson called *Noman* an "unusually contemplative series closer" that will appeal to "readers in the midst of their own spiritual questioning," while a *Kirkus Reviews* writer praised the trilogy's "fine conclusion," writing that the "exploration of religion and of ethical behavior" in *Noman* "will provoke thought and lead . . . to discussion."

A standalone novel for teens, *Rich and Mad* focuses on two seventeen year olds navigating love and lust and

Cover of Nicholson's young-adult novel Noman, *featuring artwork by* **John Blumen.** (Cover art © 2008 by John Blumen. Reproduced by permission of Houghton Mifflin Harcourt Publishing Company.)

trying to determine their own path through both. A pragmatic young woman who decides that it is time to fall in love, Maddy Fisher looks around for a suitable goal and finds one in Joe Finnigan, an older teen whose good looks have put him clearly out of reach of the romantically inexperienced girl. For geeky, quiet Richard Ross, the object of his affections is glamorous Grace Carrey, likewise out of his league. Although Maddy and Richard start off with no connection other than mutual friends, their separate searches for love slowly draw them together over the course of the novel.

Rich and Mad inspired a measure of controversy when it was published in 2010. Nicholson's teen characters live within a culture where love and sex are interchangeable, and to realistically capture this cynicism the book includes references to Web pornography, the ease of acquiring contraception, and superficial physical relationships. *Rich and Mad* "may not be suitable for all school libraries due to sexual references," noted Frances Breslin in her *School Librarian* appraisal. Amy S. Pattee, re-

viewing the novel in *School Library Journal,* found Nicholson's writing to be "somewhat impersonal" and the two protagonists "hard to know" because "their thoughts and actions are told more than they are shown." For Geri Diorio, the author presents readers with "an interesting combination of lyrical philosophizing, dramatic action, and friendly banter," as she noted in her *Voice of Youth Advocates* review, and while *Rich and Mad* will attract readers due to its "graphic love scenes," such scenes are supported by "a thoughtful coming-of-age tale." Reviewing Nicholson's young-adult novel, a *Kirkus Reviews* writer predicted that the work will "become a classic as a go-to source for teens curious about both the physical and emotional aspects of sex." *Rich and Mad* "is honest about sex," asserted Amanda Craig in her London *Times* review, "but, as counsellors advise, within a loving relationship." When their relationship is consummated in the final pages of Nicholson's novel, "the scene is funny, tender and beautifully written," Craig added. "These are nice, middle-class kids living undemanding lives and will probably turn out OK: much like those who will enjoy this charming book."

In addition to his books for young adults, Nicholson also targets older readers with novels such as *The Society of Others* and *The Trial of True Love,* the latter described by *Booklist* reviewer Allison Block as a "thought-provoking tale about lives transformed in the blink of an eye." In *The Society of Others* as well as its sequel, *I Could Love You,* he introduces a recent college graduate who, becoming disillusioned, flees from his family in England and ends up in a totalitarian Eastern bloc country. Accused of terrorism, the young man is paraded on television and then bullied into answering questions while films of brutal torture are screened on nearby monitors. The man's ultimate goal is to escape, a task that will require both his wits and the kindness of strangers. Reviewing the novel, Sarah Weinman wrote in the *Chicago Tribune* that in *The Society of Others* the author "doesn't skimp on novelistic essentials in his pursuit of intellectual ones," and Piers Paul Read concluded in a *Spectator* review that, with this novel, Nicholson "has to my mind established himself . . . as one of the best novelists around."

Biographical and Critical Sources

PERIODICALS

Booklist, October 15, 2000, GraceAnne A. DeCandido, review of *The Wind Singer: An Adventure,* p. 438; October 15, 2001, GraceAnne A. DeCandido, review of *Slaves of the Mastery,* p. 389; January 1, 2005, Allison Block, review of *The Society of Others,* p. 821; January 1, 2006, Allison Block, review of *The Trial of True Love,* p. 58; June 1, 2006, Jennifer Mattson, review of *Seeker,* p. 63; May 15, 2007, Jennifer Mattson, review of *Jango,* p. 55; May 15, 2008, Jennifer Mattson, review of *Noman,* p. 56.

Nicholson courted controversy while also earning praise for his realistic portrayal of modern teen romance in **Rich and Mad.** (Cover photo copyright © Juan Pablo Bonino, 2010. Reproduced by permission of Egmont USA.)

Bulletin of the Center for Children's Books, June, 2006, April Spisak, review of *Seeker,* p. 465.

Chicago Tribune, September 4, 1998, Michael Wilmington, review of *Firelight,* p. A; February 3, 2005, Sarah Weinman, review of *The Society of Others,* p. 2.

Evening News (London, England), June 10, 2009, Katie Law, "Happiness Is a Home Full of Comfort," p. 16.

Guardian (London, England), May 31, 2000, Lyn Gardner, review of *The Wind Singer,* p. 9; June 5, 2010, Marcus Sedgwick, review of *Rich and Mad,* p. 14.

Kirkus Reviews, October 15, 2004, review of *The Society of Others,* p. 981; January 15, 2006, review of *The*
Trial of True Love, p. 58; May 1, 2006, review of *Seeker,* p. 464; May 15, 2008, review of *Noman*; July 1, 2011, review of *I Could Love You.*

Kliatt, July, 2004, Hugh Flick, Jr., review of *Firesong,* p. 51; July, 2004, review of "Wind on Fire" trilogy, p. 32; May, 2006, Deirdre Root, review of *Seeker,* p. 12; July, 2008, Deirdre Root, review of *Noman,* p. 20.

Library Journal, November 1, 2004, Lawrence Rungren, review of *The Society of Others,* p. 76.

New Republic, February 7, 1994, Stanley Kauffmann, review of *Shadowlands* (film), p. 26; October 12, 1998, Stanley Kauffmann, review of *Firelight,* p. 30.

New York Times Book Review, February 13, 2005, Tobin Harshaw, review of *The Society of Others,* p. 13.

Publishers Weekly, August 28, 2000, review of *The Wind Singer,* p. 84; August 26, 2002, review of *Firesong,* p. 70; September 29, 2003, review of the "Wind in the Fire" trilogy, p. 67; January 17, 2005, review of *The Society of Others,* p. 36; January 9, 2006, review of *The Trial of True Love,* p. 32; June 19, 2006, review of *Seeker,* p. 63; August 30, 2010, review of *Rich and Mad,* p. 55; May 30, 2011, review of *I Could Love You,* p. 47.

School Librarian, autumn, 2010, Frances Breslin, review of *Rich and Mad,* p. 180.

School Library Journal, December, 2000, John Peters, review of *The Wind Singer,* p. 146; December, 2001, Eva Mitnick, review of *Slaves of the Mastery,* p. 141; January, 2003, Beth L. Meister, review of *Firesong,* p. 141; August, 2006, June H. Keuhn, review of *Seeker,* p. 126; August, 2007, Emily Rodriguez, review of *Jango,* p. 124; August, 2008, Jennifer-Lynn Draper, review of *Noman,* p. 130; December, 2010, Amy S. Pattee, review of *Rich and Mad,* p. 122.

Science Fiction Chronicle, February, 2001, Don D'Ammassa, review of *The Wind Singer,* p. 38.

Spectator, March 20, 2004, Piers Paul Read, review of *The Society of Others,* p. 50.

Times (London, England), April 17, 2010, Amanda Craig, review of *Rich and Mad,* p. 12.

Voice of Youth Advocates, April, 2006, Leslie McCombs, review of *Seeker,* p. 63; December, 2010, Geri Diorio, review of *Rich and Mad,* p. 458.

ONLINE

Achuka Web site, http://www.achuka.co.uk/ (February 24, 2005), "William Nicholson."

William Nicholson Home Page, http:///www.williamnicholson.co.uk (February 15, 2012).*

O-P

OCKLER, Sarah

Personal
Married. *Education:* B.A. (communication). *Hobbies and other interests:* Photography, hiking, camping, reading.

Addresses
Home—CO. *E-mail*—sarah.ockler@gmail.com.

Career
Novelist. Lighthouse Writers Workshop, Denver, CO, currently instructor and manuscript consultant in YA fiction writing.

Awards, Honors
YALSA/American Library Association (ALA) Teens' Top-Ten nomination, IndieNext listee, and Eliot Rosewater Indiana High School Book Award nomination, all c. 2012, all for *Twenty Boy Summer;* YALSA/ALA Best Fiction for Young Adults selection, 2012, for *Fixing Delilah.*

Writings

Twenty Boy Summer, Little, Brown (New York, NY), 2009.
Fixing Delilah, Little, Brown (New York, NY), 2010.
Bittersweet, Simon Pulse (New York, NY), 2012.

Sidelights
For Sarah Ockler, the time-tested writer's advice to "Write what you know" has yielded entertaining results. In her novels *Twenty Boy Summer, Fixing Delilah,* and *Bittersweet* Ockler mines her own teenage memories and distills their universal emotional elements into entertaining and sensitively crafted stories. "Despite the

odds, I survived adolescence," she joked on her home page. "And now I get to read and write young adult stories the way I want them to be, with sweet, sensitive

Sarah Ockler draws on her teen memories in crafting her engaging YA novel **Twenty Boy Summer.** (Cover photograph © by Roger Hagadone. Cover © 2009 by Hachette Book Group, Inc. Reproduced by permission of Little, Brown & Company, a division of Hachette Book Group, Inc.)

boys and intense love and heartbreak and friendship and fights and sadness and joy and lots of kissing and no skinny jeans. Hey, making stuff up is way more fun than going to therapy!"

Ockler's inspiration for *Twenty Boy Summer* grew from her early career with the National Donor Family Council, an organization affiliated with the National Kidney Foundation that supports organ-and tissue-donor families grieving the death of a loved one. Anna, the main character in *Twenty Boy Summer,* is grieving the loss of her first love, Matt, who died the year before. Frankie, Matt's sister, is Anna's best friend, and because she was never told about the relationship between her friend and her brother, Frankie is unaware of the depth of Anna's grief. On a planned California beach vacation with Frankie's parents, Frankie sets the stage for adventure by challenging both girls to meet one new boy on each day of their twenty-day trip.

"Readers will be . . . moved by the pain that strains Frankie's family [and] . . . ultimately threatens the friends' relationship," predicted a *Publishers Weekly* contributor, and a *Kirkus Reviews* writer wrote that Anna's "feelings of lust, longing, shame and fear" as she admits to her yearning for a new love also enrich Ockler's novel. "Anna's authentic voice and some lyrical writing" prompted Heather Booth to recommend *Twenty Boy Summer* in *Booklist* to readers who enjoy stories by Sarah Dessen, Deb Caletti, Jodi Picoult, and Nicholas Sparks. "Often funny," according to *School Library Journal* contributor Traci Glass, "this is a thoughtful, multilayered story about friendship, loss, and moving on."

Secrets and romance are also explored in *Fixing Delilah,* as Delilah Hannaford winds up her junior year of high school with a police record for shoplifting, a deadbeat boyfriend, a home life fractured by a family feud, and her reputation in tatters. A former honor-roll student, the seventeen year old decides that it is time for a change and a trip to Red Falls, Vermont, to settle the estate of her recently deceased grandmother will provide her with the opportunity to re-strategize. In her grandmother's Victorian home, full of generations of family memorabilia, Delilah senses her roots; meanwhile, renewing relationships with her estranged aunt, uncovering family secrets, and reconnecting with a childhood playmate who is quickly becoming much more than a friend. Calling Delilah "one of the more realistic adolescent girls in contemporary fiction," Judith Hayn added in *Voice of Youth Advocates* that Ockler's heroine "tells her own story in a lyrical and authentic voice." The teen's "gradual acceptance of her family's complicated history" and her "ability to recognize her own flawed coping mechanisms" add to that sense of authenticity, wrote a *Publishers Weekly* critic, while in *Booklist* Booth recommended *Fixing Delilah* as "a perfect fit for those seeking expressive writing, emotional depth, and lush, cinematic romance."

Ockler tackles the challenges of finding and following one's dreams in *Bittersweet* as seventeen-year-old cup-

cake baker Hudson Avery gets a second chance at the figure-skating dreams she abandoned three years ago. Second chances do not come easy, however, and as Hudson struggles to rekindle her old skating passions, she must also balance the responsibilities of work at her mother's diner as well as school and family obligations which are exacerbated by her parents' divorce, not to mention the sometimes confusing attention of two swoon-worthy varsity hockey players. Shelle Rosenfeld, reviewing the novel in *Booklist,* described *Bittersweet* as "an entertaining read with an engaging, relatable protagonist" whose "lively first-person narrative is both wry and sympathetic." In *Publishers Weekly,* a contributor deemed the novel "an appetizing blend of personalities, drama, and passion" in which the heroine's "regrets about the past and . . . fears about the future are heart-wrenchingly real."

Biographical and Critical Sources

PERIODICALS

Booklist, May 1, 2009, Heather Booth, review of *Twenty Boy Summer,* p. 72; November 15, 2010, Heather Booth, review of *Fixing Delilah,* p. 41; February 12, 2012, Shelle Rosenfeld, review of *Bittersweet.*
Bulletin of the Center for Children's Books, September, 2009, Deborah Stevenson, review of *Twenty Boy Summer,* p. 34; December, 2010, Deborah Stevenson, review of *Fixing Delilah,* p. 200.
Buffalo News, June 23, 2009, Jean Westmoore, interview with Ockler.
Kirkus Reviews, May 15, 2009, review of *Twenty Boy Summer;* November 15, 2010, review of *Fixing Delilah.*
Publishers Weekly, June 22, 2009, review of *Twenty Boy Summer,* p. 45; November 8, 2010, review of *Fixing Delilah,* p. 63; February 20, 2012, review of *Bittersweet.*
School Library Journal, June, 2009, Traci Glass, review of *Twenty Boy Summer,* p. 133; November, 2010, Carol A. Edwards, review of *Fixing Delilah,* p. 123.
Voice of Youth Advocates, December, 2010, Judith Hayn, review of *Fixing Delilah,* p. 458.

ONLINE

Author's Now Web site, http://www.authorsnow.com/author/ (February 15, 2012), "Sarah Ockler."
Sarah Ockler Home Page, http://sarahockler.com (February 15, 2012).

*   *   *

ORON, Judie

Personal

Born in Montreal, Quebec, Canada; married; children: sons. *Education:* McGill University, B.A. (anthropology); Hebrew University (Jerusalem, Israel), graduate study (African studies).

Judie Oron (Reproduced by permission.)

Addresses

Home—Toronto, Ontario, Canada.

Career

Journalist and author. *Jerusalem Post,* Jerusalem, Israel, columnist, feature writer, and director of Jerusalem Post Funds, 1984-86. Presenter at schools, conferences, organizations, and book clubs.

Member

Writers' Union of Canada, Canadian Society of Children's Authors, Illustrators, and Performers, Canadian Children's Book Centre, International Board on Books for Young People, SOSTEJE, Writers and Editors Network, Israeli Artists Group of Toronto.

Awards, Honors

Sydney Taylor Notable Book for Teens selection, Association of Jewish Libraries, White Ravens selection, International Youth Library (Munich, Germany), Amelia Bloomer Project selection, American Library Association, Helen and Stan Vine Canadian Jewish Book Award for Youth Literature, and Best Books for Kids and Teens selection, Canadian Children's Book Centre, all 2011, and U.S. International Board on Books for Young People Outstanding International Books Honor selection, 2012, all for *Cry of the Giraffe.*

Writings

Cry of the Giraffe (novel), Annick Press (Toronto, Ontario, Canada), 2010.

Contributor to periodicals, including *Lifestyles, New York Times' Student Post, Jerusalem Post,* and *Canadian Jewish News.*

Sidelights

Judie Oron was born in Canada and moved to Israel in 1967, where she remained until 2004. After attending graduate school at the University of Jerusalem, where her focus was African studies, Oron worked for the *Jerusalem Post* as a journalist, writing feature stories and a weekly column. In the mid-1980s Oron directed the newspaper's three charitable funds, opening a fourth fund after she heard about efforts to evacuate Ethiopian Jews from Sudan to Israel. Leaving the newspaper, she continued to advocate on behalf of Ethiopian Jews until her return to Canada twenty-five-years later. Her month-long trips to Ethiopia allowed Oron to develop a close relationship with the Ethiopian Jewish community and she eventually took a ten-year-old Ethiopian Jewish child, Lewteh, into her family. Years later, when Oron learned that Lewteh had a sister, Wuditu, who was still missing, she went to Ethiopia, located the girl and paid for her freedom, and brought her home to Israel, where the sisters were reunited. *Cry of the Giraffe* is based upon the story of Wuditu's years in slavery.

Cry of the Giraffe is narrated by Wuditu, who grew up in a family of Ethiopian Jews living in a small village in the north of Ethiopia. The Ethiopian Jewish community, who refer to themselves as Beta Israel, claimed this region as their home over 2,000 years before. By the mid-1980s civil war and a cruel Marxist regime made life extremely difficult for the community, and in 1989 Wuditu's family decides to flee to Israel, although the move must be made in secrecy.The family walks hundreds of miles to Sudan, but soon after their arrival, twelve-year-old Wuditu—nicknamed Giraffe because of her long neck—and ten-year-old half-sister Lewteh are forced by soldiers to walk back to Ethiopia, where the older girl leaves her sister with a local rabbi while going to look for help. Soon after, Wuditu is sexually abused. Hoping that by working as a servant for a Christian religious woman she will be safe from sexual abuse, she accepts a position in the woman's house, but instead finds herself trapped into slavery. After three years as a captive, a white woman (Oron) comes in search of her.

Odon uses her journalistic skills to present Wuditu's story "in precise, formal prose, sympathetic yet distant," that enhances the "dramatic refugee scenes" in *Cry of the Giraffe,* according to Jess deCourcy Hinds in *School Library Journal.* Her effective pacing, vivid descriptions, and use of foreign terms result in what Hinds described as "an example of masterful storytelling."

Cover of Oron's Cry of the Giraffe, *a compelling true-life story of two sisters determination to reunite in the wake of tragedy.* (Reproduced by permission of Annick Press Ltd.)

While noting the necessarily frightening elements of Wuditu's saga, Caitlin Augusta added in *Voice of Youth Advocates* that *Cry of the Giraffe* is an "inspiring story [that] will encourages readers to revisit their own circumstances and better connect with world history."

Biographical and Critical Sources

PERIODICALS

Canadian Review of Materials, October 22, 2010, Ruth Latta, review of *Cry of the Giraffe.*

Kirkus Reviews, October 15, 2010, review of *Cry of the Giraffe.*

School Library Journal, December, 2010, Jess deCourcy Hinds, review of *Cry of the Giraffe,* p. 122.

Voice of Youth Advocates, February, 2011, Caitlin Augusta, review of *Cry of the Giraffe,* p. 557.

ONLINE

Judie Oron Home Page, http://www.judieoron.com (February 20, 2012).

O'SHAUGHNESSY, Darren
See SHAN, Darren

*   *   *

PAL, Erika

Personal

Born in Budapest, Hungary; immigrated to England. *Education:* Kingston University, B.A. (illustration and animation; with honors), 2007; Brighton University, graduate study (sequential design and illustration).

Addresses

Home—England. *E-mail*—erika@erikapalillustration. com.

Career

Illustrator. Kecskemétfilm (animation studio), Budapest, Hungary, former animator; freelance illustrator. *Exhibitions:* Work included in group shows at Great Western Studios, London, England; Hackney Museum, London; Lewis Elton Gallery, University of Surrey, Surrey, England; The Triangle Gallery, London; Victoria & Albert Museum of Childhood, London; Bankside Gallery, London; and Old Billingsgate Market, London.

Awards, Honors

Two Macmillan Prize commendations; British Book Trust Big Picture logo contest winner; Surrey Libraries' Children's Book Award shortlist, 2008, for *Night Flight* by Michaela Morgan; Best Children's Illustrated Book Awards shortlist, English Association, 2011, for *I See the Moon* by Jacqueline Mitton.

Writings

SELF-ILLUSTRATED

Azad's Camel, Frances Lincoln Children's (London, England), 2009.

ILLUSTRATOR

Michaela Morgan, *Night Flight,* Frances Lincoln Children's (London, England), 2008.

Jacqueline Mitton, *I See the Moon,* Frances Lincoln Children's (London, England), 2010.

Lesley Beake, *Little Lion,* Frances Lincoln Children's (London, England), 2011.

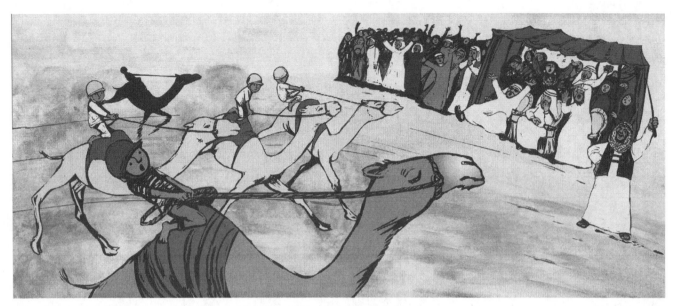

***Erika Pal pairs an entertaining story with her unique graphic-styled art in* Azad's Camel.** (Illustration copyright © 2009 by Erika Pal. Reproduced by permission of Frances Lincoln Children's Books.)

Books featuring Pal's artwork have been translated into several languages, including Danish, Norwegian, and Swedish.

Sidelights

While living in her native Hungary, Erika Pal worked in the animation industry, but she turned her attention to book illustration after immigrating to the United Kingdom. Pal created *Azad's Camel,* which would become her first illustrated picture book, while completing her coursework in animation and illustration at London's Kingston University.

Inspired by Pal's concern about the welfare of children in the Middle East who are forced into work as camel jockeys, *Azad's Camel* introduces a happy ending and an element of magic into the story of an orphaned boy who races the camels owned by a rich sheikh until he learns that his camel, Asfur, can not only talk: he also fears racing and is planning his escape. Together with her "uncluttered" large-format watercolor illustrations, Pal shares a story that highlights "the touching drama of the brave young athlete's strong connection with his camel," according to *Booklist* contributor Hazel Rochman. A *Kirkus Reviews* critic made special mention of the "striking illustrations" in *Azad's Camel,* noting that Pal's "sharply delineated characters" stand out dramatically "against soft, blurry desert backgrounds." For *School Library Journal* contributor Heather Acerro, *Azad's Camel* will also prove valuable in social-studies curricula due to its focus on "an important and underexposed topic."

Since creating *Azad's Camel,* Pal has attracted the interest of publishers and her artwork has been pared with stories by writers such as Michaela Morgan, Jacqueline Mitton, and Lesley Beake. In *I See the Moon,* Mitton,

an astronomer, treats readers to a bedtime tale that also describes the various phases of the moon and the animals whose world it lights. "An enchanting book," in the words of *School Librarian* critic Janette Perkins, *I See the Moon* "concentrates on the moon and its . . . phases as seen all over the world." Useful for both classroom and bedtime, the book is also notable for Pal's "striking" illustrations, "which have a childlike quality" and "help to emphasise the story," according to the critic.

Biographical and Critical Sources

PERIODICALS

Booklist, September 1, 2010, Hazel Rochman, review of *Azad's Camel,* p. 110.

Kirkus Reviews, August 1, 2010, review of *Azad's Camel.*

School Librarian, summer, 2011, Janette Perkins, review of *Azad's Camel,* p. 94.

School Library Journal, September, 2010, Heather Acerro, review of *Azad's Camel,* p. 133; May, 2011, Barbara Elleman, review of *I See the Moon,* p. 84.

ONLINE

Erika Pal Home Page, http://erikapalillustration.com (February 20, 2012).*

*   *   *

PERRO
See PERRO, Bryan

PERRO, Bryan 1968-
(Perro)

Personal

Born June 11, 1968, in Shawinigan, Québec, Canada. *Education:* Université du Québec, Montréal, degree (theatre); Université du Québec à Trois-Rivières, M.A. (education).

Addresses

Home—Saint-Mathieu-du-Parc, Québec, Canada. *Agent*—Mireill Bertrand; mireillebertrand@sympatico. ca. *E-mail*—bryanperro@bryanperro.com.

Career

Writer, actor, director, and storyteller. Collège Shawinigan, teacher of theatre for ten years; freelance writer. Presenter at workshops, conferences, and schools.

Awards, Honors

Communication-Jeunesse prize listee, 2005; Youth Award in Science Fiction and Fantastic Literature (Québec, Canada), 2006.

Writings

NOVELS

Marmotte (novel), Glanures (Shawinigan, Québec, Canada), 1998.

Mon frère de la planète des fruits (novel), Les Intouchables (Montréal, Québec, Canada), 2001.

Pourquoi j'ai tué mon père, Les Intouchables (Montréal, Québec, Canada), 2002.

Al-Qatrum, les territoires de l'ombre, illustrated by Alexandre Girard, Les Intouchables (Montréal, Québec, Canada), 2004.

Créatures fantastiques du Québec, illustrated by Alexandre Girard, Trécarré (Montréal, Québec, Canada), 2007.

En mer (stories), Éditions de la Bagnole (Longueuil, Québec, Canada), 2007.

Wariwulf, Les Intouchables (Montréal, Québec, Canada), 2008.

La grande illusion: une histoire, illustrations by JEIK Dion, Les Intouchables (Montréal, Québec, Canada), 2009.

Victor Vie, pigeon voyageur, illustrated by Étienne Milette, Perro (Saint-Mathieu-du-Parc, Québec, Canada), 2012.

"AMOS DARAGON" NOVEL SERIES

Porteur de masques, Les Intouchables (Montréal, Québec, Canada), 2003, translated by Y. Maudet as *The Mask Wearer*, Scribo (Brighton, England), 2009, Delacorte Press (New York, NY), 2011.

La clé de Braha, Les Intouchables (Montréal, Québec, Canada), 2003, translated by Y. Maudet as *The Key of Braha*, Scribo (Brighton, England), 2009.

Le crépuscule des dieux, Les Intouchables (Montréal, Québec, Canada), 2003, translated by Y. Maudet as *The Twilight of the Gods*, Scribo (Brighton, England), 2010.

La tour d'El-Bab, Les Intouchables (Montréal, Québec, Canada), 2003.

La malédiction de Freyja, Les Intouchables (Montréal, Québec, Canada), 2004.

La colère d'Enki, Les Intouchables (Montréal, Québec, Canada), 2004.

Voyage aux Enfers, Les Intouchables (Montréal, Québec, Canada), 2004.

La cité de Pégase, Les Intouchables (Montréal, Québec, Canada), 2005.

La toison d'or, Les Intouchables (Montréal, Québec, Canada), 2005.

La grande croisade, Les Intouchables (Montréal, Québec, Canada), 2005.

Le masque de l'éther, Les Intouchables (Montréal, Québec, Canada), 2006.

La fin des dieux, Les Intouchables (Montréal, Québec, Canada), 2006.

(With Nicolas Journoud) *Le guide du porteur de masques*, Les Intouchables (Montréal, Québec, Canada), 2008.

Le sanctuaire des braves, Perro (Saint-Mathieu-du-Parc, Québec, Canada), 2011.

Author's work has been translated into eighteen languages, including German, Japanese, Portuguese, and Russian.

OTHER

Horresco Referens: légendes théâtrales en démons majeurs pour acteurs-conteurs, sopranos de la rumeur (stage play), Glanures (Shawinigan, Québec, Canada), 1995.

Fortia nominat: Louis Cyr, l'homme le plus fort du monde (stage play), Glanures (Shawinigan, Québec, Canada), 1997.

Contes cornus, légendes fourchues: légendes théâtrales en démons majeurs pour acteurs-conteurs, sopranos de la rumeur (stage play), revised edition, Glanures (Shawinigan, Québec, Canada), 1997.

Fortia nominat: Louis Cyr (stage play), Michel Brûlé (Montréal, Québec, Canada), 2008.

Éclyps (stage play), Michel Brûlé (Montréal, Québec, Canada), 2009.

Adaptations

Several books in the "Amos Daragon" series were adapted as manga/graphic novels.

Biographical and Critical Sources

PERIODICALS

Booklist, February 15, 2011, Erin Anderson, review of *The Mask Wearer*, p. 74.

Quill & Quire, June, 2011, Cori Dusmann, review of *The Mask Wearer.*

School Library Journal, April, 2011, Kathryn Kennedy, review of *The Mask Wearer,* p. 182.

ONLINE

Amos Daragon Web site, http://www.amosdaragon.com/ (February 15, 2012).

Bryan Perro Home Page, http://www.bryanperro.com/en (February 15, 2012).*

*   *   *

PIKE, Christopher 1954-
(Kevin Christopher McFadden)

Personal

Born November 12, 1954, in New York, NY. *Education:* Attended college. *Hobbies and other interests:* Astronomy, meditating, long walks, and reading.

Addresses

Home—Santa Barbara, CA.

Career

Writer. Worked variously as a house painter, factory worker, and computer programmer.

Writings

HORROR FICTION; FOR YOUNG ADULTS

Slumber Party (also see below), Scholastic (New York, NY), 1985.

Chain Letter (also see below), Avon (New York, NY), 1986.

Weekend (also see below), Scholastic (New York, NY), 1986.

Thrills, Chills, and Nightmares (short stories), Scholastic (New York, NY), 1987.

Spellbound (also see below), Archway (New York, NY), 1988.

Last Act (also see below), Archway (New York, NY), 1989.

Scavenger Hunt, Archway (New York, NY), 1989.

Gimme a Kiss, Archway (New York, NY), 1989.

Witch, Archway (New York, NY), 1990.

Fall into Darkness, Archway (New York, NY), 1990.

See You Later (also see below), Simon & Schuster (New York, NY), 1990.

Bury Me Deep (also see below), Pocket Books (New York, NY), 1991, reprinted, 2001.

Whisper of Death, Pocket Books (New York, NY), 1991.

Die Softly, Pocket Books (New York, NY), 1991, reprinted, 2011.

Monster, Pocket Books (New York, NY), 1992.

Master of Murder (also see below), Pocket Books (New York, NY), 1992.

The Ancient Evil (sequel to *Chain Letter;* also see below), Pocket Books (New York, NY), 1992.

The Eternal Enemy, Pocket Books (New York, NY), 1993.

The Immortal, Pocket Books (New York, NY), 1993.

Road to Nowhere, Pocket Books (New York, NY), 1993, reprinted, 2011

The Wicked Heart, Pocket Books (New York, NY), 1993.

Chained Together (includes *Chain Letter* and *The Ancient Evil*), Pocket Books (New York, NY), 1994.

The Midnight Club, Pocket Books (New York, NY), 1994.

The Visitor, Pocket Books (New York, NY), 1995.

The Lost Mind, Pocket Books (New York, NY), 1995.

The Starlight Crystal, Archway (New York, NY), 1996.

Tales of Terror, Archway (New York, NY), 1996.

Alien Invasion, Pocket (New York, NY), 1997.

Time Terror, Pocket (New York, NY), 1997.

Execution of Innocence, Pocket Books (New York, NY), 1997.

The Blind Mirror, Pocket Books (New York, NY), 1997.

The Star Group, Archway (New York, NY), 1997.

The Hollow Skull, Archway (New York, NY), 1997.

See You Later, Archway (New York, NY), 1998.

Tales of Terror II, Pocket Books (New York, NY), 1998.

(With Jerry Olton) *Where Sea Meets Sky: The Captain's Table,* Pocket Books (New York, NY), 1998.

Magic Fire, Archway (New York, NY), 1999.

The Grave, Archway (New York, NY), 1999.

The Secret of Ka, Harcourt (Boston, MA), 2010.

To Die For (includes *Slumber Party* and *Weekend*), 2010.

Time of Death (includes *Bury Me Deep* and *Chain Letter*), 2011.

Master of Murder (includes title novel and *Last Act*), 2011.

Bound to You (includes *Spellbound* and *See You Later*), Simon & Schuster (New York, NY), 2012.

"FINAL FRIENDS" SERIES; YOUNG-ADULT HORROR NOVELS

The Party, Archway (New York, NY), 1988.

The Dance, Archway (New York, NY), 1989.

The Graduation, Archway (New York, NY), 1989.

Final Friends Trilogy, Archway (New York, NY), 1999, published as *Until the End,* Simon & Schuster (New York, NY), 2011.

"REMEMBER ME" SERIES; YOUNG-ADULT HORROR NOVELS

Remember Me (also see below), Pocket Books (New York, NY), 1989, reprinted, 2007.

The Return (also see below), Pocket Books (New York, NY), 1994.

The Last Story (also see below), Pocket Books (New York, NY), 1995.

Remember Me (omnibus), 2011.

"THE LAST VAMPIRE/THIRST" SERIES; YOUNG-ADULT HORROR NOVELS

The Last Vampire, Pocket Books (New York, NY), 1994.

Black Blood, Pocket Books (New York, NY), 1994.

Red Dice, Pocket Books (New York, NY), 1995.

The Phantom, Pocket Books (New York, NY), 1996.
Evil Thirst, Pocket Books (New York, NY), 1996.
Creatures of Forever, Pocket Books (New York, NY), 1996.
Thirst No. 1 (includes *The Last Vampire, Black Blood,* and *Red Dice*), Simon Pulse (New York, NY), 2009.
Thirst No. 2 (includes *The Phantom, Evil Thirst,* and *Creatures of Forever*), Simon Pulse (New York, NY), 2009.
The Eternal Dawn, Simon Pulse (New York, NY), 2010.
The Shadow of Death, Simon Pulse (New York, NY), 2011.

"ALOSHA" SERIES; YOUNG-ADULT FANTASY NOVELS

Alosha, Tor (New York, NY), 2004.
The Shaktra, Tor (New York, NY), 2005.
The Yanti, Tor (New York, NY), 2006.

"SPOOKSVILLE" SERIES; FOR CHILDREN

The Haunted Cave, Pocket Books (New York, NY), 1995.
Aliens in the Sky, Pocket Books (New York, NY), 1995.
The Howling Ghost, Pocket Books (New York, NY), 1995.
The Secret Path, Pocket Books (New York, NY), 1995.
The Deadly Past, Pocket Books (New York, NY), 1996.
The Hidden Beast, Pocket Books (New York, NY), 1996.
The Wicked Cat, Pocket Books (New York, NY), 1996.
The Wishing Stone, Pocket Books (New York, NY), 1996.
Cold People, Pocket Books (New York, NY), 1996.
Invasion of the No-Ones, Pocket Books (New York, NY), 1996.
The Witch's Revenge, Pocket Books (New York, NY), 1996.
The Dark Corner, Pocket Books (New York, NY), 1996.
Spooksville, Pocket Books (New York, NY), 1997.
The Thing in the Closet, Pocket Books (New York, NY), 1997.
Night of the Vampire, Pocket Books (New York, NY), 1997.
Attack of the Killer Crabs, Pocket Books (New York, NY), 1997.
The Dangerous Quest, Pocket Books (New York, NY), 1997.
The Living Dead, Minstrel Books (New York, NY), 1998.
Creepy Creatures, Pocket Books (New York, NY), 1998.
Phone Fear, Minstrel Books (New York, NY), 1998.
The Witch's Gift, Pocket Books (New York, NY), 1999.

OTHER

Getting Even ("Cheerleaders" middle-grade novel series), Scholastic (New York, NY), 1985.
The Tachyon Web (adult science fiction), Bantam (New York, NY), 1987.
Sati (adult fiction), St. Martin's (New York, NY), 1990.
The Season of Passage (adult science fiction), Tor (New York, NY), 1992.
The Cold One (adult fiction), Tor (New York, NY), 1995.
The Listeners (adult fiction), Tor (New York, NY), 1995.
The Blind Mirror (adult fantasy), Tor (New York, NY), 2003.

Falling (adult fiction) Forge (New York, NY), 2007.

Short fiction included in anthologies *Thirteen: Thirteen Tales of Horror by Thirteen Masters of Horror,* edited by T. Pines, 1991; and *666: The Number of the Beast,* 2007.

Adaptations

Fall into Darkness was adapted as a television film, directed by Mark Sobel, 1996. *The Last Vampire* and the "Alosha" novels were adapted for film. Film rights to the "Last Vampires" series were acquired by FilmNation, 2010. Several of Pike's novels have been adapted as audiobooks.

Sidelights

The author of dozens of best-selling novels, Kevin Christopher McFadden is better known as Christopher Pike, a pseudonym taken from a character in the long-running *Star Trek* television series. Since his first novel, *Slumber Party,* was published, Pike has made a name for himself as a master of teen horror and produced fiction at a remarkable rate. Stories such as *Monster, The Hollow Skull,* and *The Grave* have been joined by his "Remember Me" and "Thirst" novels in guaranteeing thrills and chills to young readers even as parents have recoiled from their graphic violence and references to teen sexuality. Praising Pike as "one of the most original and exciting authors of teenage fiction" writing during the genre's flowering in the 1990s, Jonathan Weir added in *Books for Keeps* that Pike's "writing is flawless, his ideas breathtaking, and. . . . he knows what his readers want and never fails to deliver."

Born in New York City and raised in California, Pike started his writing career after leaving college and working for a time as a house painter and computer programmer. Interestingly, he did not set out to pen horror novels; he originally wanted to write adult mystery and science fiction, but had little luck getting these book proposals accepted. By chance, an editor at Avon Books read some of Pike's prose and saw enough potential to suggest that the young writer should try his hand at a teen thriller. The result was 1985's *Slumber Party,* which was followed by the follow-ups *Weekend* and *Chain Letter.* By the time *Chain Letter* appeared, word-of-mouth had made all three books bestsellers and "Christopher Pike" was fast on the way to becoming a publishing phenomenon.

Pike's early books are notable for featuring female teens whose first-person observations about people and events are key to the novel's plotline. As the author explained to Kit Alderdice for *Publishers Weekly,* "I romanticize a lot about females because they seem more complex, and because in horror novels, it's easier for the girl to seem scared." Scaring the reader is Pike's major goal: He spins plots that often involve such disparate elements as murder, ghosts, aliens, and the occult. Above all, he is savvy about what interests teens and includes

references to pop culture and adolescent concerns within in his terror-filled stories. Pike "doesn't talk down to kids; he treats them as individuals," noted Pat Mac-Donald in *Publishers Weekly.* "He writes commercial stories that teens really want to read." Although Pike began to alternate his horror fiction with adult novels and teen fantasy fiction after 2000, most of his books published during the 1990s remain in print and continue to attract new fans.

While his horror novels revolve around murder and other ghastly deeds, Pike's characters—usually high-school students—lead lives that mirror those of average teens: they go to dances, throw parties, fall in and out of love, and sometimes have difficulty talking to parents and teachers. The difference between Pike's protagonists and his adolescent readers lies in the extreme methods his fictional characters use to resolve problems. In *Gimme A Kiss,* for example, Jane tries to recover her stolen diary through a complicated plan of revenge that ultimately involves her in a killing. Melanie wins the lead role in a school play only to find herself playing detective after real bullets are placed in a prop gun in *Last Act,* while in Pike's "Final Friends" series

A teen must pass a series of grueling challenges in the hope of helping to save the earth in Christopher Pike's novel Alosha, *featuring artwork by Larry Rostant.* (Reprinted by permission of St. Martin's Press, LLC.)

the merging of two high schools results in new friendships, new rivalries, and the violent death of a shy girl.

Sometimes Pike's protagonists encounter problems that require particularly drastic measures. In *Monster,* "a brilliant horror story," according to Weir, Mary shoots three teens at a party, claiming they were actually monsters. Her best friend Angela does not believe Mary until the evidence becomes overwhelming and Angela is forced to take over where Mary left off. Sometimes circumstances are less horrific but still drastic: In Pike's fantasy novel *Alosha,* for example, after a thirteen-year-old California environmentalist learns, telepathically, that she is actually queen of the Fairies, she winds up in the front lines, hoping to stop a mass immigration of trolls, dwarves, and other mythical creatures that is threatening to disrupt Earth's human dimension. *The Secret of Ka,* another fantasy for teens, finds a fifteen year old in Turkey where she discovers a magic carpet and learns that she is a major player in an epic battle between a djinn and an ancient but patient evil. While noting that *Alosha* "is not typical of Pike's teenage vampire stories and other thrillers," Sherry Hoy asserted in *Kliatt* that "it's an excellent start to a unique saga," and its sequel, *The Shaktra,* delivers Pike's trademark "fast-paced storyline and unique and compelling characters."

One of the reasons for Pike's popularity among teen readers is that the violence in his books is graphically detailed. For some critics, such brutality does more harm than good. Amy Gamerman, writing in the *Wall Street Journal,* described the author's mysteries as "gorier than most," noting that they are guaranteed to make "Nancy Drew's pageboy flip stand on end." In *Harper's,* Tom Engelhardt stated that Pike's books "might be described as novelizations of horror films that haven't yet been made. In these books of muted torture, adults exist only as distant figures of desertion . . . and junior high psychos reign supreme. . . . No mutilation is too terrible for the human face."

Pike has also been criticized for his treatment of teen sexuality and the afterlife. In his defense, he offers books such as *Remember Me,* in which a young murder victim tries to prove that her death was not a suicide with the help of another teen "ghost." As the author told Gamerman: "Teenagers are very fascinated by the subject of life after death. I got very beautiful letters from kids who said they were going to kill themselves before they read that book." James Hirsch wrote in the *New York Times* that the popularity of young-adult mysteries with increasingly action-filled plots reflects a teen readership that has "revealed more sophisticated—some say coarse—reading tastes." "Topics that were once ignored in . . . mystery books, like adolescent suicide and mental illness, are now fair game," Hirsch added. Michael O. Tunnell made a similar point in *Horn Book,* noting that "as readers mature, they graduate to a more sophisticated mystery" that follows "the 'rules' of mysteries more subtly. Readers must take a far more active part in unraveling plot and understanding characters."

Pike feeds the craving of teen horror fans in his novel The Secret of Ka, *which features cover art by Odessa Sawyer.* (Jacket illustration © 2010 by Odessa Sawyer. Reproduced by permission of Houghton Mifflin Harcourt Publishing Company.)

While the bulk of his books have been geared for teen readers, Pike has also penned several adult novels, including *The Cold One, The Blind Mirror,* and *Falling.* Called a "briskly paced new sci-fi/fantasy/horror endeavor" by a *Kirkus Reviews* critic, *The Cold One* focuses on a university graduate student specializing in near-death experiences who comes into contact with an ancient being that sucks the souls out of its victims. Although initially faced with what looks to be a brutal serial killer, Julie and reporter Peter find themselves battling the Cold One, who is able to disguise itself as a human. Incorporating elements of Eastern philosophy, the work is "visceral and intellectually stimulating at the same time," Tim Sullivan noted in the *Los Angeles Times Book Review.* Praising such efforts, Sullivan went on to reference a well-known New England writer of the early twentieth century by describing Pike as "a modern [H.P.] Lovecraft, a master of creeping dread relentless disturbing the reader."

In *The Blind Mirror* a California-based artist who has recently been deserted by his girlfriend, Sienna, returns from a trip to New York to find the corpse of an unidentifiable woman on the beach near his home. Soon

David Lennon hears a familiar voice leaving messages on his answering machine and he wonders whether, in fact, he has murdered his lover in a ritualized fashion and her spirit is now tormenting him. Soon vampirism, encounters with a series of old friends that bring up nagging questions from his past, time in jail on murder charges, and unethical medical experiments come into play, leading to what a *Kirkus Reviews* critic called a "bizarre denouement" to a "rattling good read." In *Publishers Weekly,* a reviewer praised Pike for his "tight, clean writing and engaging secondary characters," dubbing *The Blind Mirror* "an entertaining . . . dark fantasy." Noting that David's "slightly surreal odyssey" compels readers to keep turning pages, *Booklist* reviewer David Pitt wrote that readers who "crave that hypnotic effect will find everything they need," while in *Library Journal* Jackie Cassada praised the fact that *The Blind Mirror* "relies more on atmosphere than gore for its emotional impact."

In *Falling* Pike taps the popular interest in police procedurals, introducing F.B.I. agent Kelly Feinman. Originally a college professor, Kelly was contracted as an F.B.I. consultant due to her expertise in mythology, and

Cover of Pike's novel The Blind Mirror, *in which an artist tracks down the murderer of his ex-girlfriend.* (Reprinted by permission of St. Martin's Press, LLC.)

Cover of Pike's police procedural Falling, *one of several novels he has written for adult readers.* (Cover photograph by Monty Rakusen/Getty Images. Reproduced by permission of St. Martin's Press.)

when a sadistic serial killer begins referencing myths in his crimes against married women she is wisely assigned to the case. Reviewing *Falling* in *Publishers Weekly,* a contributor noted that Pike's "intricate, thoughtful plot offers . . . fresh variations on the serial-killer theme," while a *Kirkus Reviews* writer praised the "stylishly written" novel for exhibiting the "corkscrew plotting" that has become a hallmark of Pike's "twisted imagination."

Ultimately, Pike writes mysteries because he enjoys the work. His attraction to the young-adult genre is partially due to the fact that he finds teenage characters "extreme," more prone to exaggerated actions and reactions. While he appreciates the celebrity status his readers have given "Christopher Pike," Pike also admits there is a down side to literary fame. "A bunch of kids found out where I lived and I had to move," he told Gamerman. "It spread like a rumor where I was. . . . It got weird. I have very intense fans."

Biographical and Critical Sources

PERIODICALS

Booklist, November 15, 1995, Mary Romano Marks, review of *The Lost Mind,* p. 548; May 1, 2003, David Pitt, review of *The Blind Mirror,* p. 1552; January 1, 2007, David Pitt, review of *Falling,* p. 60.

Books for Keeps, November, 1994, Jonathan Weir, "Christopher Pike: Master of Murder," pp. 8-9.

Fantasy and Science Fiction, October-November, 2003, Charles de Lint, review of *The Blind Mirror,* p. 47.

Harper's, June, 1991, Tom Engelhardt, "Reading May Be Harmful to Your Kids," pp. 55-62.

Horn Book, March-April, 1990, Michael O. Tunnell, "Books in the Classroom: Mysteries," pp. 242-244.

Kirkus Reviews, November 1, 1994, review of *The Cold One,* pp. 1439-1440; April 1, 2003, review of *The Blind Mirror,* p. 502; December 15, 2006, review of *Falling,* p. 1240; August 1, 2010, review of *The Secret of Ka.*

Kliatt, July, 2004, Michele Winship, review of *Alosha,* p. 12; January, 2006, Sherry Hoy, review of *Alosha,* p. 20; January, 2007, Sherry Hoy, review of *The Shaktra,* p. 30.

Library Journal, April 15, 2003, Jackie Cassada, review of *The Blind Mirror,* p. 130; July, 2004, Jackie Cassada, review of *Alosha,* p. 76.

Los Angeles Times Book Review, April 30, 1995, Tim Sullivan, review of *The Cold One,* p. 8.

New York Times, October 9, 1988, James Hirsch, "Nancy Drew Gets Real."

Publishers Weekly, April 29, 1988, Kit Alderdice, "Archway Launches Christopher Pike Novels in Multi-Book Contract," p. 49; January 12, 1990, review of *Fall into Darkness,* p. 62; June 29, 1990, review of *See You Later,* p. 104; August 17, 1990, review of *Sati,* p. 53; November 23, 1990, review of *Witch,* p. 66; February 15, 1993, review of *Road to Nowhere,* p. 240; June 14, 1993, review of *The Immortal,* p. 72; January 24, 1994, review of *The Midnight Club,* p. 57; March 24, 2003, review of *The Blind Mirror,* p. 62; June 28, 2004, review of *Alosha,* p. 36; December 4, 2006, review of *Falling,* p. 34; August 30, 2010, review of *The Secret of Ka,* p. 54.

School Library Journal, April 15, 2003, Jackie Cassada, review of *The Blind Mirror,* p. 130; October, 2004, Donna Marie Wagner, review of *Alosha,* p. 176; February, 2007, Christi Voth, review of *The Yanti,* p. 126; February, 2011, Erik Carlson, review of *The Secret of Ka,* p. 117.

Wall Street Journal, May 28, 1991, Amy Gamerman, "Gnarlatious Novels: Lurid Thrillers for the Teen Set," p. A16.

ONLINE

Simon & Schuster Web site, http://authors.simonand schuster.com/ (February 12, 2012), "Christopher Pike."*

POKIAK-FENTON, Margaret

Personal

Born on Holman Island (now Ulukhukok), Northwest Territories, Canada; daughter of nomadic hunters; married Lyle Fenton; children: eight.

Addresses

Home—Fort St. John, British Columbia, Canada.

Career

Author, farmer, and artisan.

Awards, Honors

(With Christy Jordan-Fenton) U.S. Board on Books for Young People (USBBY) Outstanding International Books Honor selection, Nautilus Silver Award, *Skipping Stones* Honor Book selection, Information Book Award Honor Book selection, and Best Books for Kids and Teens selection, Canadian Children's Book Centre, all 2011, and Sheila A. Egoff Children's Literature Prize finalist, *ForeWord* magazine Book of the Year Award finalist, Saskatchewan Young Readers' Choice Award nomination, Hackmatack Award, Children's Literature Roundtables of Canada Information Book Award, Golden Oak Award, and Rocky Mountain Book Award, all for *Fatty Legs;* USBBY Outstanding International Books Award, 2012, for *A Stranger at Home.*

Writings

(With daughter-in-law Christy Jordan-Fenton) *Fatty Legs: A True Story,* illustrated by Liz Amini-Holmes, Annick Press (Toronto, Ontario, Canada), 2010.
(With Christy Jordan-Fenton) *A Stranger at Home,* illustrated by Liz Amini-Holmes, Annick Press (Toronto, Ontario, Canada), 2010.

Author's work has been translated into French.

Sidelights

A native Inuvialuit who was raised in the nomadic traditions of her northern people, Margaret Pokiak-Fenton has traveled by dogsled and hunted and trapped in the Arctic region. At age eight, Pokiak-Fenton left home to attend Catholic boarding school in the fur-trading town of Aklavik, where she achieved her dream of learning to read. The native communities of northern Canada often resist such schooling because it Westernizes their children. Pokiak-Fenton's experiences at primary school during the 1940s were not unique, and they stayed with her as she grew up, married, and raised eight children. Years later, aided by her daughter-in-law Christy Jordan-Fenton, she shared her school experiences in the middle-grade novels *Fatty Legs: A True Story* and *A Stranger at Home,* both which are illustrated with family photographs and artwork by Liz Amini-Holmes.

In *Fatty Legs* readers meet eight-year-old Olemaun, whose desire to read inspires her to leave her loving family and make the five-day trek south from her high Arctic home to a regional residential school for native Canadians. The challenges are many: In addition to being given a new name, Margaret, she must learn a new language and follow daily patterns of life that are not familiar to her. The school is run by Catholic nuns, one of which takes a dislike to Margaret due to her determined nature. The witchlike Raven—Margaret's name for the elderly woman—forces the new student to wear read stockings while her classmates wear grey ones, but her effort to humiliate the young student withers in the face of the native girl's resilience.

Winner of several awards in the author's native Canada, *Fatty Legs* also inspired critical praise. A *Kirkus Reviews* writer described the middle-grade novel as "a moving and believable account," while in *School Library Journal* Jody Kopple recommended the book as "fascinating and unique, and yet universal in its message." Pokiak-Fenton and Jordan Fenton "write in easy-to-read language rich with metaphor," according to *Quill & Quire* contributor Jean Mills, and a *Canadian Review*

Margaret Pokiak-Fenton teams up with daughter-in-law Christy Jordan-Fenton to share her childhood experiences in the novel Fatty Legs, *featuring artwork by Liz Amini-Holmes.* (Artwork copyright © 2010 by Liz Amini-Holmes. Reproduced by permission of Annick Press, Ltd.)

of Materials author wrote that "Margaret's character is engaging—her persistence, her strength, and her curiosity touch the reader."

Margaret is two years older when readers rejoin her in *A Stranger at Home*. Excited to return to her family after many months at school, the ten year old rushes forward with open arms but her mother no longer recognizes her as the Inuvialuit girl who left two years before. For Margaret, home is also unfamiliar and it takes a while for her to re-acclimate to the food, language, and way of life in the high Arctic. In addition to praising Holmes' paintings, with their appropriately "somber colors," a *Kirkus Reviews* writer noted of *A Stranger at Home* that the "spirit and determination" of Pokiak-Fenton's young heroine "shine through this moving memoir."

Biographical and Critical Sources

PERIODICALS

Canadian Review of Materials, November 12, 2010, Shelbey Krahn, review of *Fatty Legs: A True Story.*
Kirkus Reviews, November 15, 2010, review of *Fatty Legs;* October 15, 2011, review of *A Stranger at Home.*
Quill & Quire, November, 2010, Jean Mills, review of *Fatty Legs.*
School Library Journal, December, 2010, Jody Kopple, review of *Fatty Legs,* p. 139.

ONLINE

Annick Press Web site, http://www.annickpress.com/ (February 12, 2012), "Margaret Pokiak-Fenton."*

R

RAMSEY, Calvin Alexander

Personal

Born in Baltimore, MD; children: three. *Education:* Attended University of California, Los Angeles; attended Frank Silvera's Writer's Workshop. *Hobbies and other interests:* Travel.

Addresses

Home—Atlanta, GA. *E-mail*—calvinaramsey@yahoo.com.

Career

Playwright, photographer, and author. Former member of advisory board, Robert Woodruff Library Special Collections at Emory University; member of Georgia Council for the Arts Theatre Panel for three years.

Awards, Honors

Last Frontier Theatre Conference Award finalist, 2004, for *The Green Book;* Martin Luther King, Jr., Drum Major for Justice Award.

Writings

FOR CHILDREN

(With Gwen Strauss) *Ruth and the Green Book,* illustrated by Floyd Cooper, Carolrhoda Books (Minneapolis, MN), 2010.
(With Bettye Stroud) *Belle, the Last Mule at Gee's Bend,* illustrated by John Holyfield, Candlewick Press (Somerville, MA), 2011.

STAGE PLAYS

The Green Book (two-act), produced in workshop in Valdez, AK, 2005.

(With Tom Jones) *Bricktop* (musical), produced in Atlanta, GA, 2006.
Love, Johnny (musical tribute to Johnny Mercer), produced in Atlanta, GA, 2007.
Damaged Virtues, produced in Atlanta, GA, 2008.

Also author of stage plays *Canada Lee,* 2005; *Sherman Town, Baseball, Apple Pie, and the Klan,* 2005; *Enlightenment; Sister Soldiers; Kentucky Avenue; Somewhere in My Lifetime;* and *The Age of Possibilities.*

Sidelights

An Atlanta-based playwright, photographer, and folk art painter, Calvin Alexander Ramsey has seen his work staged at theatres in New York City, San Francisco, and Washington, DC, as well as in smaller venues everywhere from Alaska to Nebraska. In his writing for children, Ramsey has teamed up with Gwen Strauss to create the picture book *Ruth and the Green Book,* which features a story inspired by one of his plays. Another story for young readers, *Belle, the Last Mule at Gee's Bend,* was a collaboration among Ramsey, fellow writer Bettye Stroude, and talented illustrator John Holyfield.

Ramsey wrote *Ruth and the Green Book* while researching his stage play *The Green Book,* which intertwines the experience of African Americans traveling the nation's highways during the Jim Crow era with that of a Holocaust survivor seeking refuge in the wake of World War II. In writing *The Green Book* the playwright was inspired by the history of *The Negro Motorist Green Book,* a publication produced between 1936 and 1963 that helped African-American travelers avoid segregated motels and hotels, diners and restaurants and gas stations along their route. Ramsey's memories of his own childhood attested to the importance of *The Negro Motorist Green Book:* as Celia McGee noted in a *New York Times* profile of the writer, "during his family trips between Roxboro, N.C., and Baltimore," Ramsey recalled that "'we packed a big lunch so my parents didn't have to worry about having to stop somewhere that might not serve us.'"

In *Ruth and the Green Book* readers are transported back to the early 1950s, as young Ruth anticipates an exciting adventure during her family's first drive from Chicago south to her grandmother's Alabama home along the country's new network of interstate highways. However, when they stop to fill up the car's gas tank Ruth is not allowed to use the station's rest room, and the family must sleep in the car when the motels they pass post signs that deny lodging to blacks. Finally, at an Esso station, the family acquires a copy of the "Green Book" that makes the rest of the trip far more pleasant.

Illustrated by Floyd Cooper with what Hazel Rochman described in *Booklist* as "glowing . . . sepia-toned artwork," *Ruth and the Green Book* serves as "a compelling addition to U.S. history offerings," the critic added. A *Kirkus Reviews* critic praised Ramsey for relating his historical vignette "with elegance, compassion and humanity," while in *Publishers Weekly* a contributor described the picture book as an "expressively illustrated fusion of fact and fiction" that is "charged with emotion."

Ramsey returns his focus to rural Alabama and the fight for civil rights in *Belle, the Last Mule at Gee's Bend,* in which a little boy named Alex learns a piece of African-American history while watching a mule named Belle lunching on a garden of tender collard greens in his small southern town. The mule's owner, an elderly woman, joins the boy and explains why she allows her mule to feast so freely. Decades ago, on election day in 1965, the black adults in Gee's Bend paraded on their way to cast their ballots in wagons pulled by mules, their act inspired by the words of the Reverend Martin Luther King, Jr. Belle the mule pulled one of these wagons, and she also pulled a wagon three years later, although this wagon carried the coffin of the Reverend King, who had just been assassinated. "Holyfield's intense acrylic paintings . . . evoke the heat and the drama" of Ramsey's story, according to a *Kirkus Reviews* writer, while in *Publishers Weekly* a reviewer praised the author for framing *Belle, the Last Mule at Gee's Bend* as a "conversation" that captures a "firsthand perspective on events epitomizing the idea of 'living history.'"

In his work, Ramsey is dedicated to illuminating little-known aspects of African-American history, and his research includes interviews as well as mining original sources as well as second-hand documents to gain objectivity and factual accuracy. In his work, he has sometimes courted controversy; as Ramsey noted in an essay on his home page, his "plays stimulate, educate, and bring the audience closer to a truth in American history, a truth that does not always reflect a reality that is easy to view."

Biographical and Critical Sources

PERIODICALS

Booklist, November 1, 2010, Hazel Rochman, review of *Ruth and the Green Book,* p. 68.
Kirkus Reviews, October 15, 2010, review of *Ruth and the Green Book;* July 15, 2011, review of *Belle, the Last Mule at Gee's Bend.*
Publishers Weekly, October 11, 2010, review of *Ruth and the Green Book,* p. 44; August 8, 2011, review of *Belle, the Last Mule at Gee's Bend,* p. 47.
School Library Journal, November, 2010, Roxanne Burg, review of *Ruth and the Green Book,* p. 79.

ONLINE

Calvin Alexander Ramsey Home Page, http://www.creative-si.com/calvin-alexander-ramsey.html (February 15, 2012).
Lerner Publishing Group Web site, http://www.lernerbooks.com/ (February 15, 2012), "Calvin Alexander Ramsey."
New York Times Online, http://www.nytimes.com/ (August 23, 2010), Celia McGee, review of *Ruth and the Green Book.**

*   *   *

REEDY, Trent 1979(?)-

Personal

Born c. 1979, in Dysart, IA; married. *Education:* University of Iowa B.A. (English); Vermont College of Fine Arts, M.F.A. (writing for children and young adults).

Addresses

Home—WA.

Career

Educator and author. Riverside, IA, Public Schools, teacher of high-school English. *Military service:* Iowa Army National Guard, combat engineer; served in Afghanistan, c. 2004-08.

Writings

Words in the Dust, introduction by Katherine Patterson, Arthur A. Levine Books (New York, NY), 2011.

Author's work has been translated into German.

Sidelights

From a childhood growing up in rural Iowa and with dreams of becoming a writer, Trent Reedy pursued those dreams while attending college. Eventually, however,

Reedy found himself in Afghanistan as part of a Iowa Army National Guard contingent participating in a reconstruction mission in the wartorn country. Although he had already attempted to craft workable stories from his youthful experiences, it was his wartime experience that proved to be the stuff of fiction and that inspired his novel *Words in the Dust.*

"I loved traveling to different villages in western Afghanistan, working to help the people and establish elections," Reedy noted on his home page in recalling his time overseas. "In particular, I loved giving school supplies, toys, and candy to the children we'd encounter.

"One of these children was a young girl named Zulaikha, who had suffered since birth from a cleft lip, with the two halves of her upper lip unjoined and her teeth very crooked. One of our great Army doctors was able to provide her the needed corrective surgery, and I was amazed and inspired, both before and after the surgery, by Zulaikha's quiet courage and dignity. Although she could not understand my words, I promised, the last time I saw her as she rode on a truck off of our base, that I would tell her story."

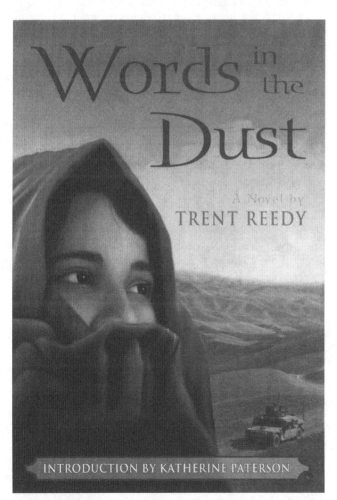

Cover of Trent Reedy's young-adult novel **Words in the Dust,** *featuring cover art by Tim O'Brien.* (Jacket art © 2011 by Tim O'Brien. Reproduced by permission of Scholastic, Inc.)

In *Words in the Dust* readers meet twelve-year-old Zulaikha, who lives in with her father and new stepmother in the Afghan mountains. Zulaikha's life has been a quiet one: kept at home and disliked by her stepmother, she also faces a dim future because her cleft lip has rendered her unmarriageable. When Taliban forces leave the region, the girl hopes that life will return to normal and she can resume her efforts to learn to read. When U.S. Army trucks full of soldiers arrive, Zulaikha is told that their arrival may mean opportunities for her village. After a woman named Meena helps her learn the words to a poem beloved by her late mother, the timid preteen begins to feel encouraged, although hoping that her cleft lip might be fixed may be hoping too much.

Reedy's talent for "creating a vivid sense of place and memorable characters" was praised by Gillian Engberg in *Booklist,* the critic adding that *Words in the Dust* features "extensive detail about Afghani customs." "An inside look at an ordinary Afghanistan family trying to survive in extraordinary times," Reedy's novel "is both heart-wrenching and timely," according to a *Kirkus Reviews* writer. For Sharon Senser McKellar, appraising *Words in the Dust,* the author's text is "infused with poetry" and tells a story "full of hard truths, painful lessons, beautiful human interaction, and the promise of possibility."

Biographical and Critical Sources

PERIODICALS

Booklist, January 1, 2011, Gillian Engberg, review of *Words in the Dust,* p. 111.
Kirkus Reviews, December 1, 2010, review of *Words in the Dust.*
School Library Journal, February, 2011, Sharon Senser McKellar, review of *Words in the Dust,* p. 118.
USA Today, February 15, 2011, Bob Minzesheimer, "A Soldier's Story, and a Girl's," p. D2.

ONLINE

Children's Literature Web site, http://www.childrenslit. com/ (February 12, 2012), "Trent Reedy"
Los Angeles Times Online, http://articles.latimes.com/ (January, 24, 2011), Susan Carpenter, "From Soldier to New Author."
Trent Reedy Home Page, http://www.trentreedy.com (February 12, 2012).*

*   *   *

ROHMANN, Eric 1957-

Personal

Born 1957, in Riverside, IL. *Education:* Illinois State University, B.S. (art), M.S. (studio art); Arizona State University, M.F.A. (printmaking/fine bookmaking).

Addresses

Home—Metro Chicago, IL.

Career

Illustrator and educator. Belvoir Terrace Art Center, Lenox, MA, instructor in printmaking, painting, and fine bookmaking; St. Olaf College, Northfield, MN, instructor in introductory drawing, fine bookmaking, and printmaking. Speaker at schools and libraries. *Exhibitions:* Work exhibited in galleries in Illinois, Minnesota, and Ohio; included in permanent collections.

Awards, Honors

New York Times Best Children's Books listee, Colorado Children's Book Award nominee, and American Library Association (ALA) Notable Book for Children designation, all 1994, and Caldecott Medal Honor Book designation, 1995, all for *Time Flies;* Georgia Children's Literature award, 2002, for *The Cinder-Eyed Cats;* Caldecott Medal, Best Children's Book of the Year Honor Book designation, Bank Street College of Education, and ALA Notable Book for Children designation, all 2003, all for *My Friend Rabbit;* ALA Notable Book for Children designation, 2005, for *Clara and Asha;* Parents' Choice Recommended selection, and Gold Award, National Parenting Publications Awards, both 2008, both for *A Kitten Tale.*

Writings

SELF-ILLUSTRATED PICTURE BOOKS

Time Flies, Crown (New York, NY), 1994.
The Cinder-Eyed Cats, Crown (New York, NY), 1997.
My Friend Rabbit, Roaring Brook Press (New Milford, CT), 2002.
Pumpkinhead, Knopf (New York, NY), 2003.
Clara and Asha, Roaring Brook Press (New Milford, CT), 2005.
A Kitten Tale, Alfred A. Knopf (New York, NY), 2008.
Bone Dog, Roaring Brook Press (New York, NY), 2011.

ILLUSTRATOR

Jennifer Armstrong, *King Crow,* Crown (New York, NY), 1995.
Antoine O. Flatharta, *The Prairie Train,* Crown (New York, NY), 1999.
James Guthrie, *Last Song: A Poem,* Roaring Brook Press (New York, NY), 2010.
Lois Lowry, *Bless This Mouse,* Houghton Mifflin Books for Children (Boston, MA), 2011.
Candace Fleming, *Oh, No!,* Schwartz & Wade (New York, NY), 2011.

Sidelights

When Chicago-based author and illustrator Eric Rohmann got a call one dark January morning from someone representing the American Library Association, he worried that he had forgotten to return his library books on time. However, panic turned to amazement when he was told that his picture book *My Friend Rabbit* had been selected for the prestigious 2003 Caldecott Medal, which is awarded to the illustrator of the year's most distinguished children's picture book. A talented painter whose picture books *The Cinder-Eyed Cats, Pumpkinhead,* and *Bone Dog* have been hailed for their spare, unique texts and engaging and thought-provoking illustrations, Rohmann "has perfected the art of letting the pictures tell the story," in the opinion of a *Publishers Weekly* contributor in reviewing his self-illustrated picture book *Clara and Asha.* In addition to his own books, the artist/author has also illustrated stories by Lois Lowry, James Guthrie, Candace Fleming, and other writers in addition to creating the cover art for Philip Pullman's popular "His Dark Materials" novel trilogy.

Born in Illinois, Rohmann grew up in suburban Chicago, where he spent more time drawing than working on academic pursuits. A volunteer job at a local zoo during high school gave him the opportunity to observe a variety of animals for long periods of time, and this ultimately inspired the finely detailed paintings in *The Cinder-Eyed Cats* and *Clara and Asha,* the latter about a girl's unusual friendship with a giant blue fish. In college, Rohmann focused on art and has earned advanced degrees at both Illinois State University and Arizona State University. Working primarily in oil paints because their slow drying time allows him to most fully develop his pictures, he also has taught printmaking, painting, drawing, and book-making in Massachusetts and Minnesota. "I'm interested in what books do that other art forms don't . . . ," Rohmann noted in discussing his transition from fine-art painter to illustrator during an interview for the Random House Web site. "Time passes as the reader turns the pages, revealing events in a sequence—a story. My paintings have always been narratives, and the natural next step was books." "I try to look at each picture as a film director considers a scene for a film," Rohmann also explained during his interview. Viewing a subject "from many angles and in many lights" allows him to "find a composition that is interesting and dynamic but that, above all, works to make the story stronger."

Rohmann's first published picture book, *Time Flies,* tells its story without words; in the book, which earned the artist a Caldecott Honor designation in 1995, readers follow a bird as it wings its way into a museum, flies into a displayed dinosaur skeleton, and travels back in time to witness the world inhabited by the giant creatures that may, in fact, be birds' ancestors. *The Cinder-Eyed Cats* takes readers on another journey, in this case a dreamlike trip taken by a young boy into a twilight world inhabited by amazing cats that dance with sand fish and other creatures freed from the sea. In *Publishers Weekly* a reviewer described *The Cinder-Eyed Cats* as being "as mesmerizing as a vivid dream that seems at once perfectly clear and vaguely puzzling." Praising Rohmann's "enigmatically beautiful

book," Michael Cart wrote in *Booklist* that the author/illustrator's "paintings are wonderful in the same sense that the rhyming, surreal text is: they inspire wonder and, in several cases, awe."

The artwork in *My Friend Rabbit* marked a change of pace for the author/illustrator. Moving from the detailed style of his early painting, he experimented with a variety of printing techniques as well as with collage, paper sculpture, watercolor, and pastel before finally choosing the relief-print technique employed in the book. "I needed the change to stay interested," Rohmann told Vicki Arkoff and Stephanie Gwyn Brown in an interview for *ChildrensLit.com.* "I had become . . . so practiced at my way of painting that I had stopped inventing and began to copy myself. . . . I felt I needed to try something different, to shock my system. It's what Ray Bradbury once called, 'Jumping off a cliff and making wings on the way down.'"

Fortunately for Rohmann, his new "wings" worked, and *My Friend Rabbit* is one of his most beloved books for children. In the story, which a *Kirkus Reviews* writer dubbed "engagingly wacky," Rabbit faces a predicament after accidentally tossing friend Mouse's toy airplane high into a nearby tree. As a solution, Rabbit convinces his many helpful friends—including Bear, Duck, Reindeer, Hippo, Crocodile, and Elephant—to build themselves into a wobbly tower. Retrieving the toy just as the menagerie takes a tumble, Rabbit provides Rohmann with the opportunity to create illustrations that allow the storybook set to "chortle at the silliness of it all," according to the critic. In *Booklist* Connie Fletcher noted that the book's "tremendous physical humor" in *My Friend Rabbit* "delivers a gentle lesson about accepting friends as they are."

Rohmann opts for an illustration style similar to that of *My Friend Rabbit* in his book *Pumpkinhead,* although he returns to detailed, painted pictures in *Clara and Asha.* In *Pumpkinhead* he introduces a human boy named Otto who stands out from his family and friends due to his round orange head. Ultimately, his pumpkin head gets the even-tempered Otto into all sorts of trouble: After a tumble into the ocean, a hungry fish confuses him with a tasty vegetable, and the boy ultimately winds up traveling from a mackerel's tummy all the way to a fish vendor's car where he is purchased by his observant mother. Deeming the book "a perfect blend of art and text," *School Library Journal* contributor James K. Irwin wrote that *Pumpkinhead* "captures the vulnerable emotions of a lost child," while *Booklist* critic Julie Cummins predicted that young children will be "intrigued with the quirky, imaginative misadventure."

While a fish is also cast as a central character in Rohmann's picture book *Clara and Asha,* it is a dreamtime playmate rather than a dinner companion. In this story, Asha is a huge, blue, smiling fish that joins toddler Clara on nighttime adventures whenever the young girl cannot sleep. The story was described by *Booklist* contributor Gillian Engberg as an "archetypal tale of imaginary escape" that is enhanced by Rohmann's deeply toned, "sweeping [oil] . . . paintings." Wendy Lukehart noted in a *School Library Journal* review that the author/illustrator's "characteristically spare story line and larger-than-life visuals" present the storybook set with a "glorious" story that shows that "time spent with a friend is one of life's greatest joys."

Rohmann takes a tour of the four seasons through the eyes of four young kittens with four very different personalities in his self-illustrated picture book *A Kitten Tale,* which Engberg described in *Booklist* as yet "another marvel of sly simplicity for the very young." When the kittens are born it is springtime and their world is warm and comfortable. Snow is something that they have only heard about, and while the brown, gray, and orange kittens are convinced that they will not like it because it is cold, the yellow tiger kitten has an "I can't wait" attitude. As fall comes, the three feline worriers become increasingly nervous while the fourth eagerly awaits his first romp in the snow. The day snow first covers the ground the excited yellow kitten immediately runs out to play and the worries of his three litter mates melt away when they see the fun that can be had on a snowy day. Citing Rohmann's "spare text" in *A Kitten Tale,* a *Kirkus Reviews* writer added that the artist's decision not to name each of his characters allows his linoleum-print "artwork to imbue each cat with personality through its color, feline antics and expressions." The author/illustrator "winks at cat lovers with his observations of feline behavior," wrote a *Publishers Weekly* critic, the reviewer recommending the picture book "for children who approach the unknown with fear rather than pleasure."

Rohmann gives dogs their due while also telling a Halloween tale in *Bone Dog.* When his beloved pup Ella dies, young Gus is so sad that even the excitement of dressing up for Halloween does not capture his interest. The boy goes out grudgingly, wearing a skeleton costume, and when he takes a short-cut through the local cemetery on his way home his appearance attracts a group of real skeletons like moths to a flame. Frightened by the antics of the boney creatures, Gus worries until the skeleton ghost of his beloved Ella arrives at his side, watching over her boy just as she had in life. While noting that *Bone Dog* features a scary scenario, a *Kirkus Reviews* writer maintained that Rohmann's "ultimately heartwarming" tale "balances a . . . text full of tough emotions with clear images of an everlasting friendship," and a *Publishers Weekly* reviewer noted that "friendly figures and soft, autumnal colors give this spooky story an overlay of tranquility." The artist's use of relief printing, with its "forceful black lines and high contrast, . . . give his potentially ethereal characters pleasing solidity," wrote *Horn Book* critic Christine M. Heppermann, and Wendy Lukehart concluded in *School Library Journal* that, "sad, spooky, and comforting by

turns," Rohmann's "deceptively simple approach to the loss of a pet" in *Bone Dog* "quickens and gladdens the heart."

"Children are the best audience," Rohmann noted in his Random House online interview: "They are curious, enthusiastic, impulsive, generous, and pleased by simple joys. They laugh easily at the ridiculous and are willing to believe the absurd. Children are not ironic, disillusioned, or indifferent, but hopeful, open-minded, and open-hearted, with a voracious hunger for pictures and stories." His advice to anyone considering a career as an illustrator? Draw. "Drawing is seeing," he explained to Arkoff and Brown, "and to make books that take place in the world you have to be aware of what's around you. Drawing makes you look closely, not to just see, but to behold and understand. . . . For me, it all begins with good drawing."

Biographical and Critical Sources

PERIODICALS

Booklist, July, 1995, Leone McDermott, review of *King Crow,* p. 1882; November 15, 1997, Michael Cart, review of *The Cinder-Eyed Cats,* p. 559; December 1, 1999, Marta Segal, review of *The Prairie Train,* p. 713; May 15, 2002, Connie Fletcher, review of *My Friend Rabbit,* p. 1602; June 1, 2003, Julie Cummings, review of *Pumpkinhead,* p. 1788; July, 2005, Gillian Engberg, review of *Clara and Asha,* p. 1930; November 1, 2007, Gillian Engberg, review of *A Kitten Tale,* p. 44; October 15, 2010, Andrew Medlar, review of *Last Song: A Poem,* p. 55; March 1, 2011, Thorn Barthelmess, review of *Bless This Mouse,* p. 60.

Horn Book, July-August, 2003, Eric Rohmann, "Caldecott Medal Acceptance," pp. 393-401; Philip Pullman, "Eric Rohmann," p. 401; September-October, 2005, Lolly Robinson, review of *Clara and Asha,* p. 568; July-August, 2011, Christine M. Hepermann, review of *Bone Dog,* p. 136.

Kirkus Reviews, April 15, 2002, review of *My Friend Rabbit,* p. 577; July 15, 2003, review of *Pumpkinhead,* p. 967; July, 2005, review of *Clara and Asha,* p. 742; December 1, 2007, review of *A Kitten Tale;* January 15, 2011, review of *Bless This Mouse;* August 1, 2011, review of *Bone Dog.*

New York Times Book Review, March 13, 2011, Pamela Paul, review of *Bless This Mouse,* p. 15.

Publishers Weekly, April 17, 1995, review of *King Crow,* p. 59; September 22, 1997, review of *The Cinder-Eyed Cats,* p. 80; November 29, 1999, review of *The Prairie Train,* p. 70; February 10, 2003, Diane Roback, "Going Gold," p. 81; June 9, 2003, review of *Pumpkinhead,* p. 51; August 22, 2005, review of *Clara and Asha,* p. 62; November 26, 2007, review of *A Kitten Tale,* p. 51; September 20, 2010, review of *Last Song,* p. 64; January 17, 2011, review of *Bless This Mouse,* p. 49; May 2, 2011, review of *Bone Dog,* p. 55.

School Library Journal, May, 2002, Kristin de Lacoste, review of *My Friend Rabbit,* p. 126; July, 2003, Pat Scales, "Year of the Rabbit" (interview), p. 52, and James K. Irwin, review of *Pumpkinhead,* p. 105; August, 2005, Wendy Lukehart, review of *Clara and Asha,* p. 105; February, 2008, Joan Kindig, review of *A Kitten Tale,* p. 95; October, 2010, Gay Van Vleck, review of *Last Song,* p. 86; March, 2011, Marie Orlando, review of *Bless This Mouse,* p. 128; July, 2011, Wendy Lukehart, review of *Bone Dog,* p. 77.

ONLINE

ChildrensLit.com, http://www.chldrenslit.com/ (July 1, 2003), Vicki Arkoff and Stephanie Gwyn Brown, interview with Rohmann.

Eric Rohmann Home Page, http://www.ericrohmann.com (February 15, 2012).

Random House Web site, http://www.randomhouse.com/ (February 15, 2012), "Eric Rohmann."

* * *

ROSENTHAL, Eileen

Personal

Born in MI; married Marc Rosenthal (an illustrator); children: Will. *Education:* University of Michigan, B.F.A. (painting); attended School of Visual Arts. *Hobbies and other interests:* Gardening, libraries and museums.

Addresses

Home—Western MA. *Agent*—Pippin Properties, 156 E. 38th St., Ste. 2H, New York, NY 10016. *E-mail*—eileen.rosenthal@verizon.net.

Career

Author and graphic designer. Alfred A. Knopf (publisher), New York, NY, former book designer.

Awards, Honors

Notable Children's Book selection, *New York Times,* 2011, for *I Must Have Bobo!*

Writings

I Must Have Bobo!, illustrated by Marc Rosenthal, Atheneum Books for Young Readers (New York, NY), 2011.

I'll Save You Bobo!, illustrated by Marc Rosenthal, Atheneum Books for Young Readers (New York, NY), 2012.

Sidelights

Eileen Rosenthal teams up with husband and artist Marc Rosenthal to create *I Must Have Bobo!,* and *I'll Save You Bobo!,* two picture books that chronicle the humor-

ous battle between a young boy and the family cat over an enticing sock monkey. Although these husband-and-wife collaborations served as Eileen's official debut in the annals of picture-book publishing, she actually has a long career in bookmaking behind her. Rosenthal has worked at New York City publisher Alfred A. Knopf as a book designer since completing her training in design at the School of Visual Arts.

In *I Must Have Bobo!* when a toddler named Willy wakes up without his favorite stuffed toy, Bobo the sock monkey, something must be done. Earl the grey cat is a likely suspect in Bobo's disappearance: he likes the sock monkey too, and as the search progresses Willy's suspicions are proved correct. When the trio returns in *I'll Save You Bobo!* Willy plans to immortalize his love for Bobo by writing in his own story, casting Earl as the kitty-cat villain of course! In his illustrations for the "Bobo" stories, Marc Rosenthal "capture[s] Earl's feline deviousness" in colorful cartoons, according to a *Publishers Weekly* critic, and *School Library Journal* contributor Richelle Roth cited Eileen Rosenthal's text for giving her young hero "a genuine preschool voice." While noting that *I Must Have Bobo!* is "a one-joke story," Ilene Cooper added in *Booklist* that Rosenthal's tale perfectly captures "a child's world and emotions." The couples' collaborative picture book "will resonate," Cooper added, "and it's cute as all get-out."

Biographical and Critical Sources

PERIODICALS

Booklist, March 15, 2011, Ilene Cooper, review of *I Must Have Bobo!*, p. 63.
New York Times Book Review, March 13, 2011, Pamela Paul, review of *I Must Have Bobo!*, p. 15.
Publishers Weekly, December 13, 2010, review of *I Must Have Bobo!*, p. 55.
School Library Journal, March, 2011, Richelle Roth, review of *I Must Have Bobo!*, p. 133.

ONLINE

Fuse 8 Production Web log, http://blog.schoollibrary journal.com/afuse8production/ (March 1, 2011), review of *I Must Have Bobo!*
Pippin Properties Web site, http://www.pippinproperties.com/ (February 15, 2012), "Eileen Rosenthal,"*

*   *   *

ROTH, Ty 1962-

Personal

Born 1962, in Sandusky, OH; son of Thomas and Barbara Roth; married; children: Taylor, Travis, Tanner. *Education:* College degree. *Religion:* Roman Catholic.

Addresses

Home—Sandusky, OH. *Agent*—Katherine Boyle, Veritas Literary Agency; veritasliterary@earthlink.net. *E-mail*—tyroth@live.com.

Career

Educator and author. Teacher at a Catholic high school. Presenter at schools and libraries.

Writings

So Shelly, Delacorte Press (New York, NY), 2011.

Sidelights

Ty Roth is an Ohio native who was inspired to write his first novel, *So Shelly* through his work as a high-school teacher. "I can't imagine a more exciting or inspiring place to spend my life than in a high school and with teenagers," Roth noted on his home page. "There and among them, the past is still erasable, the present is bursting with first-time experiences, and a future full of wonders lies ahead. In fact, I don't believe that anyone ever graduates from high school, not really. In our minds, we forever walk the halls of our alma mater, and our teenage ghost haunts us wherever we go."

Haunting *So Shelly* are the spirits of nineteenth-century British romantic poets Percy Bysshe Shelley, John Keats, and George Gordon, Lord Byron, all who have been transplanted into a twenty-first-century Ohio high school. A junior, John Keats is a classmate of Gordon Byron, whose talent as a writer has been recognized throughout his academic career. In addition to being a talented wordsmith, Gordon is also charismatic, engaging, and popular with the girls, characteristics that John also feels envious of. Shelly is a classmate who Gordon has known since childhood, and because of her quiet, contemplative nature he is shocked but not surprised when she is discovered drowned on the bank of Lake Erie, the supposed victim of a sailing accident. Together with John, also a friend of the late teen and the novel's narrator, Gordon steals Shelly's ashes and is determined to return them to the place where she died. During their journey, John reflects on the lives of all three teens, contemplating their intersecting pasts and the potential for those still living to make the most of whatever future the fates have in store.

According to *Voice of Youth Advocates* reviewer Amanda McFadden, the "smooth, playful writing style" of *So Shelly* "skillfully intertwines the stories" of its three central characters, and Roth also interjects "a spattering of social issues" in order to ground this story in an era familiar to modern readers. The author crystallizes the personalities of his literary inspiration into each of his characters: "Byron is the playboy, Keats the quiet observer, and Shelly the ultimate romantic," ac-

Cover of Ty Roth's imaginative novel So Shelly, *which taps the sensibilities of nineteenth-century romantic poets in a modern coming-of-age story.* (Book cover copyright © 2011 by Delacorte Press. Used by permission of Delacorte Press, an imprint of Random House Children's Books, a division of Random House, Inc.)

cording to *Booklist* critic Heather Booth. As Booth predicted—and as Roth likely intended—*So Shelly* will inspire readers to look back at "the source material for a look at these fascinating literary figures."

Biographical and Critical Sources

PERIODICALS

Booklist, March 15, 2011, Heather Booth, review of *So Shelly,* p. 57.
Voice of Youth Advocates, February, 2011, Amanda McFadden, review of *So Shelly,* p. 559.

ONLINE

Ty Roth Home Page, http://www.tyrothbooks.com (February 20, 2012).
Ty Roth Web log, http://tyroth.wordpress.com (February 20, 2012).*

RUPP, Rebecca

Personal

Married; husband's name Randy; children: Josh, Ethan, Caleb. *Education:* Ph.D. (cell biology and biochemistry).

Addresses

Home—Shaftsbury, VT. *E-mail*—RebeccaRupp@gmail.com.

Career

Freelance writer. Producer and host of homeschool television program.

Awards, Honors

Book Sense Picks for Children, 2006, for *Journey to the Blue Moon.*

Writings

JUVENILE FICTION

The Dragon of Lonely Island, Candlewick Press (Cambridge, MA), 1998.
The Waterstone, Candlewick Press (Cambridge, MA), 2002.
The Return of the Dragon, Candlewick Press (Cambridge, MA), 2005.
Journey to the Blue Moon: In Which Time Is Lost and Then Found Again, Candlewick Press (Cambridge, MA), 2006.
Sarah Simpson's Rules for Living, Candlewick Press (Cambridge, MA), 2008.
Octavia Boone's Big Questions about Life, the Universe, and Everything, Candlewick Press (Somerville, MA), 2010.

NONFICTION

Blue Corn and Square Tomatoes: Unusual Facts about Common Vegetables, Storey Communications (Pownal, VT), 1987.
Red Oaks and Black Birches: The Science and Lore of Trees, Storey Communications (Pownal, VT), 1990.
Good Stuff: Learning Tools for All Ages, Home Education Press (Tonasket, WA), 1993, revised edition, Holt/CWS (Cambridge, MA), 1997.
Everything You Never Learned about Birds, illustrated by Jeffrey C. Domm, Storey Communications (Pownal, VT), 1995.
Committed to Memory: How We Remember and Why We Forget, Crown (New York, NY), 1998, published as *How We Remember and Why We Forget,* Three Rivers Press (New York, NY), 1998.

The Complete Home Learning Sourcebook: The Essential Resource Guide for Homeschoolers, Parents, and Educators Covering Every Subject from Arithmetic to Zoology, Three Rivers Press (New York, NY), 1998.

Getting Started on Home Learning: How and Why to Teach Your Kids at Home, Three Rivers Press (New York, NY), 1999.

Home Learning Year by Year: How to Design a Homeschool Curriculum from Preschool through High School, Three Rivers Press (New York, NY), 2000.

Weather! Watch How Weather Works, illustrated by Melissa Sweet and Dug Nap, Storey Kids (North Adams, MA), 2003.

Rocks, Storey Kids (North Adams, MA), 2004.

Four Elements: Water, Air, Fire, Earth, Profile Books, 2005.

How Carrots Won the Trojan War: Curious (but True) Stories of Common Vegetables, Storey Pub. (North Adams, MA), 2011.

Contributor to periodicals, including *Country Journal, Early American Life, Mother Earth News, Natural History,* and *Utne Reader.* Author of monthly column for *Home Education* magazine.

Sidelights

Rebecca Rupp, a nationally recognized advocate for homeschooling and the author of *Home Learning Year by Year: How to Design a Homeschool Curriculum from Preschool through High School,* has also written several fantasy novels for middle-grade readers, including *The Dragon of Lonely Island, The Waterstone,* and *Octavia Boone's Big Questions about Life, the Universe and Everything.* Rupp, who has a Ph.D. in cell biology, has also authored books on natural history as well as numerous journal articles on education.

Rupp published her debut work of fiction, *The Dragon of Lonely Island,* in 1998. The fantasy centers on twelve-year-old Hannah, ten-year-old Zachary, and eight-year-old Sarah Emily, who venture to their great-aunt Mehitabel's house on Lonely Island, a remote isle off the coast of Maine. A cryptic message from Mehitabel leads the trio to Fafnyr, a golden-scaled, three-headed dragon with a penchant for telling stories. Over the summer, the siblings learn how the tridrake saved a Chinese girl from invading Mongols, rescued a London orphan from pirates, and helped a timid youngster to find strength after she became marooned on a desert island. Although a *Publishers Weekly* reviewer felt that Rupp's "narrative frame, which strives for a classic timelessness, can feel overly tame or quaint," *Booklist* contributors Chris Sherman and Jack Helbig praised the "rich, sensory images" in the novel and called *The Dragon of Lonely Island* "an entertaining fantasy for preteen readers."

In a sequel, *The Return of the Dragon,* Hannah, Zachary, and Sarah Emily join forces to protect Fafnyr from an unscrupulous billionaire. When the children suspect that J.P. King plans to capture the tridrake and use the creature for financial gain, they seek the dragon's wisdom. The three-headed Fafnyr relates tales about a Greek shepherd, a young squire, and a slave child that, taken together, help the children learn the meaning of freedom. *The Return of the Dragon* "is a quick, easy read that goes down like warm milk," noted *School Library Journal* critic Walter Minkel, and a *Kirkus Reviews* critic remarked that Rupp's "fluent prose and savvy, lightly presented life advice make this as readable and thought provoking" as her earlier novel.

A young man attempts to save his dying world in *The Waterstone,* a book that takes readers on "an amazing journey of surprising proportions," according to a critic in *Kirkus Reviews.* As twelve-year-old Tad, a member of the Fisher tribe, notices that the water from a nearby pond is drying up, he begins having strange "rememberings": thoughts featuring people, places, and events that the boy does not recognize. Together with his father, Pondleweed, and younger sister, Birdie, Tad journeys beyond the pond to visit the other tribes living nearby, such as the Hunters and the Diggers. During his journey, Tad discovers that he holds the memories and powers of past Sagamores, beings charged with protecting an energy source called the Waterstone, which may be able to restore balance to the forest where Tad lives. *The Waterstone* "deceptively starts out as an adventure story and ends on a somewhat epic note," commented *School Library Journal* reviewer Lisa Prolman.

In *Journey to the Blue Moon: In Which Time Is Lost and Then Found Again* Rupp examines themes of loyalty and integrity. After eleven-year-old Alex loses his grandfather's antique pocket watch, he finds himself mysteriously losing track of time. During a chance meeting with an elderly woman, the boy learns that lost belongings can be found on a blue moon. Determined to go there, Alex and his dog, Zeke, set off in a rickety spaceship belonging to the Moon Rats. Upon arrival on the blue moon, Alex encounters a host of misplaced individuals, including a woman who lost her heart in a failed romance and a medieval scholar who lost his train of thought. Alex also faces down Urd, a powerful wizard-like creature, as well as the terrifying Time Eaters. A *Kirkus Reviews* critic described *Journey to the Blue Moon* as a "fast-paced fantasy, dusted with humor, rife with danger and bulging with bizarre characters," and Todd Morning wrote in *Booklist* that Rupp "holds the reader's interest . . . with humor and some well-placed excitement."

Rupp's heroine in *Sarah Simpson's Rules for Living* is a compulsive list maker and journal writer, and her current lists range from things she dislikes about her parents' new partners—her dad has remarried and her mom is starting to mention a guy named Jonah a little too often—to jottings working out current problems to a formal list of rules to live by. While Sarah is something of a curmudgeon at first, making hurtful remarks to Jonah's five-year-old son and finding fault with everything in characteristic preteen fashion, a major role in a school

play as well as several new friendships help her to begin rewriting a few of her rules with an eye to a happier future. Rupp's "vivid language makes this slim book shine," asserted Suzanne Harold in her *Booklist* review of *Sarah Simpson's Rules for Living,* while a *Publishers Weekly* critic remarked on the "witty, off-the-cuff" diary entries that comprise the novel's narrative. "Rupp delivers a story that both touches and convinces," the *Publishers Weekly* reviewer added, and a *Kirkus Reviews* writer noted that the story's realistic sixth-grade character successfully conveys her "overall message that personal attitude can ultimately control the way we accept inevitable change in our lives."

Another young teen is attempting to navigate her world in *Octavia Boone's Big Questions about Life, the Universe, and Everything,* but here the changes in seventh-grader Octavia's world provoke metaphysical questions. Her parents have always been thoughtful people, and their conversations often involved philosophical and theological discussions. Although her artist dad, Boone, looks for answers in the writings of nineteenth-century naturalist Henry David Thoreau, the Christian faith of her mom, Ray, is becoming increasingly rigid and fun-

Cover of Rebecca Rupp's middle-grade novel Octavia Boone's Big Questions about Life, the Universe, and Everything, *which finds a preteen pondering metaphysics.* (Copyright © 2010 by Rebecca Rupp. Reproduced with permission of Candlewick Press, Somerville, MA.)

damentalist. Ray has already given up her work as a lawyer to join a small, local religious community called the Fellowship of the Redeemer, but when Ray leaves home to live with her fellow church members both Octavia and her father feel abandoned. "Rupp tackles some heavy material in this provocative middle-grade novel," asserted a *Publishers Weekly* critic, and Octavia's growing antipathy toward "organized religion" in *Octavia Boone's Big Questions about Life, the Universe, and Everything* "make vigorous discussion fodder" for readers. The novel includes "great lessons . . . about judging others and being torn between opposing views," according to *School Library Journal* critic Kerry Roeder, and a *Publishers Weekly* critic recommended *Octavia Boone's Big Questions about Life, the Universe, and Everything* as an "unsettling, thought-provoking, and sensitive exploration of the intersections of faith, work, and family."

Rupp's nonfiction books range widely in their focus and are geared for use in a home-school curriculum. In *Weather! Watch How Weather Works* she keeps readers reading by using a humorous approach, mixing facts about weather patterns, storms, and clouds with true-life stories of weird weather and hand's on at-home experiments that incorporate readers the physics of heat, cooling, wind, and water. Rupp takes a similar approach in *How Carrots Won the Trojan War: Curious (but True) Stories of Common Vegetables,* tantalizing young students with stories of how onions, turnips, snap peas, tomatoes, celery, and other garden-variety veggies were used, avoided, and even misunderstood throughout history.

Biographical and Critical Sources

PERIODICALS

American Forests, September-October, 1992, Wallace Kaufman, review of *Red Oaks and Black Birches: The Science and Lore of Trees,* p. 57.
Booklist, December 15, 1997, William Beatty, review of *Committed to Memory: How We Remember and Why We Forget,* p. 668; February 1, 1999, Chris Sherman and Jack Helbig, review of *The Dragon of Lonely Island,* p. 975; September 1, 2005, Kay Weisman, review of *The Return of the Dragon,* p. 135; December 1, 2006, Todd Morning, review of *Journey to the Blue Moon: In Which Time Is Lost and Then Found Again,* p. 48; February 15, 2008, Suzanne Harold, review of *Sarah Simpson's Rules for Living,* p. 82.
Bulletin of the Center for Children's Books, December, 1998, review of *The Dragon of Lonely Island,* p. 145.
Kirkus Reviews, July 1, 2002, review of *The Waterstone,* p. 962; July 1, 2005, review of *The Return of the Dragon,* p. 743; September 15, 2006, review of *Journey to the Blue Moon,* p. 965; January 1, 2008, review of *Sarah Simpson's Rules for Living;* August 15, 2010, review of *Octavia Boone's Big Questions about Life, the Universe, and Everything.*

Library Journal, November 15, 1998, Terry Christner, review of *The Complete Home Learning Sourcebook: The Essential Resource Guide for Homeschoolers, Parents, and Educators Covering Every Subject from Arithmetic to Zoology,* p. 76.

Publishers Weekly, November 10, 1997, review of *How We Remember and Why We Forget,* p. 60; November 16, 1998, review of *The Dragon of Lonely Island,* p. 75; February 4, 2008, review of *Sarah Simpson's Rules for Living,* p. 56; September 27, 2010, review of *Octavia Boone's Big Questions about Life, the Universe, and Everything,* p. 61.

School Library Journal, November, 2002, Lisa Prolman, review of *The Waterstone,* p. 174; May, 2004, Kathryn Kosiorek, review of *Weather!: Watch How Weather Works,* p. 173; December, 2005, Walter Minkel, review of *The Return of the Dragon,* p. 154; October, 2006, Walter Minkel, review of *Journey to the Blue Moon,* p. 168; May, 2008, Jane Barrer, review of *Sarah Simpson's Rules for Living,* p. 138; August, 2010, Kerry Roeder, review of *Octavia Boone's Big Questions about Life, the Universe, and Everything,* p. 111.

Smithsonian, June, 1991, Joe Sherman, review of *Red Oaks and Black Birches,* p. 137.

ONLINE

Candlewick Press Web site, http://www.candlewick.com/ (February 12, 2012), "Rebecca Rupp."

Homeschool Zone Web site, http://www.homeschoolzone.com/ (November 20, 2007), "Rebecca Rupp."

Rebecca Rupp Home Page, http://www.rebeccarupp.com (February 12, 2012).*

*　　　*　　　*

RYLANDER, Chris

Personal

Born in ND; son of teachers; married Amanda Dhuyvetter, 2008. *Education:* North Dakota State University, degree (history education), 2005. *Hobbies and other interests:* Sports, films, music, reading.

Addresses

Home—Fargo, ND. *Agent*—Steven Malk, Writer's House; smalk@writershouse.com.

Career

Author and illustrator. Noridian (insurance provider), Fargo, ND, member of staff. Presenter at schools and libraries.

Member

Society of Children's Book Writers and Illustrators.

Awards, Honors

Flickertale Award nomination, North Dakota Library Association, and Lone Star Reading List selection, Texas Library Association, both 2012, both for *The Fourth Stall.*

Writings

SELF-ILLUSTRATED

The Fourth Stall, Walden Pond Press (New York, NY), 2011.
The Fourth Stall. Part II, Walden Pond Press (New York, NY), 2012.

Sidelights

A native of North Dakota, Chris Rylander wrote several novels for older teens before a suggestion from a literary agent convinced him that the more-relaxed and informal prose popular among middle graders might fit best with his creative approach. Rylander worked on his new story during lunch hours at his day job, where he encountered few distractions, and the completed manuscript eventually found its way into book form as *The Fourth Stall.* "To find my voice, really all I did was tap into my inner kid," Rylander admitted to *From the Mixed-up Files* online interviewer Sarah Aronson. "[This] was easy for me since I still feel like a 12-year old most of the time," the author added. "I was only 23 when I started *The Fourth Stall,* and I grew up in the video-game age. So I feel like I already had a pretty strong connection to modern kids. I still love to do all things that most kids do: play video games; play and watch sports; watch movies . . . , etc."

In *The Fourth Stall* readers meet up with Christian "Mac" Barrett, a sixth-grade solution-finder who helps his classmates with everything from bullies to dating problems to ticket to sold-out shows to answers to the next big test, all from his office in the boy's bathroom in the east wing of his middle school. With the help of business-minded buddy Vince, Mac has been performing this work—for a fee, of course—since kindergarten and things are going pretty well. When a third grader named Fred shows up at the fourth stall from the window, looking for help dealing with an eighteen-year-old slacker named Staples, Mac may have met his match, however: Staples is a high-school dropout who is running a profitable gambling operation by getting middle graders to bet against fixed odds and gamble away far more than their lunch money.

"Rylander eloquently weaves . . . economic class struggle" into what *Voice of Youth Advocates* reviewer Devin Burritt described as "a story rich in action, adventure, humor, and friendship." Burritt also noted the "noir fiction feel" of *The Fourth Stall,* and in *Booklist*

Chris Rylander introduces a cagey young deal-maker in his humorous middle-grade novel **The Fourth Stall.** (Jacket art © 2011 by David Coulson. Reproduced by permission of Walden Pond Press, an imprint of HarperCollins Publishers.)

Francisca Goldsmith wrote that "Mac narrates the convoluted tale with the arch flatness of a 1940s . . . detective." "Rylander mines a substantial amount of humor and heart" in his debut novel, mixing "hard-boiled crime novel" and preteen adventure to produce what a *Publishers Weekly* contributor dubbed "a light and enjoyable caper."

Mac faces more entrepreneurial worries in *The Fourth Stall, Part II,* and this time his business concerns threaten middle-school baseball season. He and Vince are preparing for try-outs when they are presented with a fresh problem by schoolmate Trixie Von Parkway, who claims she is being harassed by a popular eighth-grade science teacher. Trixie's visit coordinates uncomfortably with the arrival of a new vice-principle whose goals include ending Mac's business and submitting students to a new standardized test.

Rylander's second novel demonstrates that he has mastered the fictional art of "building and sustaining intrigue," according to a *Kirkus Reviews* writer, and in *Voice of Youth Advocates* Burritt described Mac as "hard not to like and respect." In its focus on standardized testing as a way of ranking teacher competency, *The Fourth Stall, Part II* will reward readers with "comedy, plot twists, and adventure," concluded Burritt.

Biographical and Critical Sources

PERIODICALS

Booklist, February 15, 2011, Francisca Goldsmith, review of *The Fourth Stall,* p. 73.
Kirkus Reviews, January 1, 2012, review of *The Fourth Stall, Part II.*
Publishers Weekly, December 6, 2010, review of *The Fourth Stall,* p. 48.
Voice of Youth Advocates, February, 2011, Devin Burritt, review of *The Fourth Stall,* p. 560; December, 2011, Devin Burritt, review of *The Fourth Stall, Part II,* p. 500.

ONLINE

Chris Rylander Home Page, http://www.chrisrylander.com (February 12, 2012).
Cynsations Web log, http://cynthialeitichsmith.blogspot.com/ (April, 2011), Cynthia Leitich Smith, interview with Rylander.
From the Mixed-up Files Web site, http://www.fromthemixedupfiles.com/ (April 29, 2011), Sarah Aronson, interview with Rylander.
High Plains Reader Online, http://hpr1.com (March 15, 2011), Brianna Brickweg, "Local Writer Publishes Children's Book."

S

SCHOONMAKER, Elizabeth

Personal

Born December 15; married John Schoonmaker (an engineer); children: Mackenzie, Sayward (daughters). *Education:* Attended Nazareth College and Munson Williams Proctor Institute School of Art; University of New York at Albany, M.A. *Hobbies and other interests:* Gardening, biking, skiing.

Addresses

Home—Utica, NY.

Career

Author and illustrator. Professor and instructor in art. *Exhibitions:* Work exhibited in galleries in Chicago, IL, and New York, NY.

Writings

SELF-ILLUSTRATED

Square Cat, Aladdin (New York, NY), 2011.

Sidelights

In *Square Cat* Elizabeth Schoonmaker tells a story of self-acceptance that is captured in the author/illustrator's brightly colored and stylized art. In a world of round cats, Eula stands out. Rather than roly poly like her friends and fashionistas Maude and Patsy, Eula has straight edges and corners: in fact, she is shaped like a perfect square, except for her small pointy ears and her long curly tail. Her paws are square too, and will not fit into round mouse holes. Fortunately, Maude and Patsy are loyal friends and they draw on their fashion know-how to make over Eula with all sorts of round things, from hoop earrings and a colorful round hat to a swishy circle skirt. When the camouflage only makes their friend's corners stand out more, Maude and Patsy team up on a new strategy that helps all three cats discover the special benefits of being different.

Describing Eula as an "appealing" feline character, Kay Weisman characterized *Square Cat* as a story about "the importance of self-acceptance" that will be enjoyed by "young listeners and cat lovers alike." Pairing with her "friendly and accessible" watercolor-and-ink illustrations, Schoonmaker's story "juxtaposes the earnestness of the characters with the silliness of the situation," Weisman added. "Eula's feelings of difference" serve as a "metaphor for other ways in which readers might feel like the odd person out," commented a *Publishers Weekly,* and in *School Library Journal* Anne Beir wrote that the orange cat's "experience figuring out how to 'make it work' for herself are the catalysts" for her shift from sad to upbeat. The "sly humor" in Schoonmaker's art "perfectly matches" her story in *Square Cat,* wrote Hope Morrison in the *Bulletin of the Center for Children's Books,* "and Eula's trials and tribulations are sure to tickle the funny bones of listeners of all shapes and sizes."

Biographical and Critical Sources

PERIODICALS

Booklist, February 1, 2011, Kay Weisman, review of *Square Cat,* p. 83.

Bulletin of the Center for Children's Books, January, 2011, Hope Morrison, review of *Square Cat,* p. 251.

Kirkus Reviews, November 15, 2010, review of *Square Cat.*

Publishers Weekly, November 8, 2010, review of *Square Cat,* p. 58.

School Library Journal, January, 2011, Ann Beir, review of *Square Cat,* p. 84.

ONLINE

Chicago Tribune Online, http://articles.chicagotribune.
com/ (January 14, 2011), review of *Square Cat.*
Eula the Square Cat Web site, http://www.eulathesquare-
cat.com (February 15, 2012).*

*   *   *

SCHWARTZ, David M. 1951-

Personal

Born November 29, 1951, in New York, NY; son of
Morris J. (a sales representative and furrier) and Diane
(an English teacher) Schwartz. *Education:* Cornell University, B.S., 1973, elementary teacher certification, The
Prospect School, North Bennington, VT, 1974. *Hobbies
and other interests:* Hiking, bicycling, gardening, natural history, cooking, folk dancing, music.

Addresses

Home—Oakland, CA. *Agent*—Regula Noetzli, Regula
Noetzli Literary Agency, 2344 County Rte. 83, Pine
Plains, NY 12567. *E-mail*—david@davidschwartz.com.

Career

Children's book writer; speaker at schools and conferences. Elementary schoolteacher in Putney, VT, 1974-
76; worked as a carpenter, lumberjack, veterinary assistant, environmental educator, and freelance writer, 1976-
78; Marlboro College, Marlboro, VT, assistant dean and
career counselor, 1978-80; Time-Life Books, Alexandria, VA, staff writer, 1980; freelance writer, beginning
1980. Yale University, writing tutor, beginning 1986,
residential college dean, 1990-93.

Awards, Honors

Notable Book selection, American Library Association
(ALA), and Honor Book selection, *Horn Book,* both
1985, Children's Books of the Year selection, Child
Study Association of America (CSAA), 1986, and Utah
Informational Children's Book Award, 1988, all for
How Much Is a Million?; Children's Choice designa-
tion, International Reading Association (IRA), and ALA
Notable Book designation, both 1989, both for *If You
Made a Million;* Children's Books of the Year selection,
CSAA, 1991, for *Super Grandpa;* ALA Notable Book
designation, 1999, for *G Is for Googol;* IRA Teacher's
Choice selection, 1999, for *If You Hopped like a Frog;*
John Burroughs Association Young Readers Award for
Outstanding Nature Book, 2007, and Animal Behavior
Society Outstanding Children's Book Award, Outstand-
ing Science Trade Book for Children selection, National
Science Teachers Association (NSTA)/Children's Book
Council (CBC), and SB&F Prize for Excellence in Sci-
ence Books, all 2008, all for *Where in the Wild?;* IRA
Teachers' Choice selection, Read Boston's Green Book

David M. Schwartz (Reproduced by permission.)

Award finalist, and NSTA/CBC Outstanding Science
Trade Book for Children selection, all 2010, all for
Where Else in the World?; NSTA/CBC Outstanding
Science Trade Book for Children selection, and New
York Public Library Title for Reading and Sharing in-
clusion, both 2010, both for *What in the Wild?*

Writings

JUVENILE NONFICTION

How Much Is a Million?, illustrated by Steven Kellogg,
Lothrop (New York, NY), 1985.
The Hidden Life of the Pond, photographs by Dwight
Kuhn, Crown (New York, NY), 1988.
The Hidden Life of the Forest, photographs by Dwight
Kuhn, Crown (New York, NY), 1988.
The Hidden Life of the Meadow, photographs by Dwight
Kuhn, Crown (New York, NY), 1988.
If You Made a Million, illustrated by Steven Kellogg, Lo-
throp (New York, NY), 1989.
Super Grandpa, illustrated by Bert Dodson, Lothrop (New
York, NY), 1991, reprinted, Tortuga Press (Santa Rosa,
CA), 2005.
"Ho, Ho" Said the Platypus, and Other Snappy Titles,
Overhand Press (MO), 1994.
Yanomami: People of the Amazon, photographs by Victor
Englebert, Lothrop (New York, NY), 1995.
G Is for Googol: A Math Alphabet Book, illustrated by
Marissa Moss, Tricycle Press (Berkeley, CA), 1998.

If You Hopped like a Frog, illustrated by James Warhola, Scholastic (New York, NY), 1999.

On beyond a Million: An Amazing Math Journey, illustrated by Paul Meisel, Doubleday (New York, NY), 1999.

Q Is for Quark: A Science Alphabet Book, illustrated by Kim Doner, Tricycle Press (Berkeley, CA), 2001.

Millions to Measure, illustrated by Steven Kellogg, HarperCollins (New York, NY), 2003.

If Dogs Were Dinosaurs, illustrated by James Warhola, Scholastic Press (New York, NY), 2005.

(With Yael Schy) *Where in the Wild? Camouflaged Creatures Concealed—and Revealed,* photographs by Dwight Kuhn, Tricycle Press (Berkeley, CA), 2007.

(With Yael Schy) *Where Else in the Wild? More Camouflaged Creatures Concealed—and Revealed,* photographs by Dwight Kuhn, Tricycle Press (Berkeley, CA), 2009.

(With Yael Schy) *What in the Wild? Mysteries of Nature Concealed . . . and Revealed,* photographs by Dwight Kuyn, Tricycle Press (Berkeley, CA), 2010.

Co-author, with David Whitin, of *The Magic of a Million Activity Book,* Scholastic Books.

JUVENILE NONFICTION; "LOOK ONCE, LOOK AGAIN" SERIES; PHOTOGRAPHS BY DWIGHT KUHN

Look Once, Look Again, Creative Teaching Press (Cypress, CA), 1997.

At the Farm, Gareth Stevens (Milwaukee, WI), 1998.

At the Seashore, Gareth Stevens (Milwaukee, WI), 1998.

At the Zoo, Gareth Stevens (Milwaukee, WI), 1998.

In the Desert, Gareth Stevens (Milwaukee, WI), 1998.

In the Forest, Gareth Stevens (Milwaukee, WI), 1998.

In the Meadow, Gareth Stevens (Milwaukee, WI), 1998.

Among the Flowers, Gareth Stevens (Milwaukee, WI), 1999.

Animal Eyes, Gareth Stevens (Milwaukee, WI), 1999.

Animal Feathers and Fur, Gareth Stevens (Milwaukee, WI), 1999.

Animal Mouths, Gareth Stevens (Milwaukee, WI), 1999.

Animal Tails, Gareth Stevens (Milwaukee, WI), 1999.

At the Pond, Gareth Stevens (Milwaukee, WI), 1999.

In a Tree, Gareth Stevens (Milwaukee, WI), 1999.

In the Garden, Gareth Stevens (Milwaukee, WI), 1999.

In the Park, Gareth Stevens (Milwaukee, WI), 1999.

Plant Fruits and Seeds, Gareth Stevens (Milwaukee, WI), 1999.

Plant Leaves, Gareth Stevens (Milwaukee, WI), 1999.

Underfoot, Gareth Stevens (Milwaukee, WI), 1999.

Animal Ears, Gareth Stevens (Milwaukee, WI), 2000.

Animal Feet, Gareth Stevens (Milwaukee, WI), 2000.

Animal Noses, Gareth Stevens (Milwaukee, WI), 2000.

Animal Skin and Scales, Gareth Stevens (Milwaukee, WI), 2000.

Plant Blossoms, Gareth Stevens (Milwaukee, WI), 2000.

Plant Stems and Roots, Gareth Stevens (Milwaukee, WI), 2000.

Bean, Gareth Stevens (Milwaukee, WI), 2001.

"LIFE CYCLES" SERIES; PHOTOGRAPHS BY DWIGHT KUHN

Chicken, Gareth Stevens (Milwaukee, WI), 2001.

Fighting Fish, Gareth Stevens (Milwaukee, WI), 2001.

Green Snake, Gareth Stevens (Milwaukee, WI), 2001.

Horse, Gareth Stevens (Milwaukee, WI), 2001.

Hummingbird, Gareth Stevens (Milwaukee, WI), 2001.

Jumping Spider, Gareth Stevens (Milwaukee, WI), 2001.

Ladybug, Gareth Stevens (Milwaukee, WI), 2001.

Maple Tree, Gareth Stevens (Milwaukee, WI), 2001.

Monarch Butterfly, Gareth Stevens (Milwaukee, WI), 2001.

Sunflower, Gareth Stevens (Milwaukee, WI), 2001.

Wood Frog, Gareth Stevens (Milwaukee, WI), 2001.

OTHER

(With Neal O. Weiner) *The Interstate Gourmet: New Haven to Burlington,* Summit Books (New York, NY), 1981.

(With Neal O. Weiner) *The Interstate Gourmet: New England,* Summit Books (New York, NY), 1983.

(With Neal O. Weiner) *The Interstate Gourmet: Mid-Atlantic,* Summit Books (New York, NY), 1983, illustrated by Kristin Funkhauser, 1986.

(With Neal O. Weiner) *The Interstate Gourmet: California and the Pacific Northwest,* Summit Books (New York, NY), 1983.

(With Neal O. Weiner) *The Interstate Gourmet: Southeast,* Summit Books (New York, NY), 1985.

(With Neal O. Weiner) *The Interstate Gourmet: Midwest,* Summit Books (New York, NY), 1985.

(Editor with Neil O. Weiner) Barbara Rodriguez and Tom Miller, *The Interstate Gourmet: Texas and the Southwest,* Summit Books (New York, NY), 1986.

Contributor to periodicals, including *Smithsonian, National Wildlife, International Wildlife, Audubon, Travel & Leisure, Reader's Digest,* and *Country Journal.* Contributing editor, *New England Monthly.*

Adaptations

How Much Is a Million was adapted for audiobook, Lothrop, 1987, and video, Weston Woods.

Sidelights

David M. Schwartz had a diverse list of jobs that included teacher, news reporter, carpenter, veterinary assistant, and college dean before he started his career as an author. Even as a writer, with pen in hand, Schwartz took a while to focus his attention on younger readers: first, he joined a friend in traveling U.S. interstate highways to compile a series of directories on roadside diners and restaurants. Then, "in 1985, I had an idea for a children's book about big numbers," Schwartz explained on his home page. This topic tapped into his lifelong fascination for mathematics, and in the years since, he has devoted himself to inspiring children to follow their own interests through both his books and as a speaker in schools and libraries. Schwartz's many books include

Cover of G Is for Googol, *Schwartz's mathematical approach to alphabet books.* (Illustration copyright © 1998 by Marissa Moss. Used by permission of Tricycle Press, an imprint of Random House Children's Books, a division of Random House, Inc.)

his multi-volume "Look Once Again" and "Life Cycles" nonfiction series as well as the illustrated *G Is for Googol: A Math Alphabet Book, Super Grandpa, Millions to Measure,* and *If Dogs Were Dinosaurs,* the last a guide to the relative size of many objects on Earth. "Math didn't used to be this much fun—it's almost unfair," quipped a *Kirkus Reviews* writer in reviewing *If Dogs Were Dinosaurs,* while in *School Library Journal* critic Kathleen Whalin wrote that illustrator James Warhola's "pen-and-watercolor drawings humorously interpret" Schwartz's comparison-filled text.

"When I was growing up, the smallest and the largest things in the universe fascinated me most," Schwartz once told *SATA.* "Compared with them, I could be both a giant and a dwarf at the same time! When I peered through a microscope to view water from a nearby pond, I was transported mentally to wonderful worlds of hidden life. When I looked through a telescope at heavenly bodies, I took marvelous mental journeys into space.

"I took real journeys on my bicycle almost every day. To occupy my mind during long rides, I liked to calculate how long it would take to ride a magic bicycle all the way around the earth . . . or Jupiter . . . or all the way to the moon . . . or to the sun . . . or a distant star. Could anybody count all the stars, I wondered, and

if so, how long would it take? I wanted to understand numbers like million, billion, and trillion—not just to know their names and how to write them with numerals, but to have a *feel* for what they meant. I found it impossible to comprehend huge distances like 93 million miles (the distance to the Sun) but it was fun to try. I once rode my bike twenty-five miles, and that seemed *so* far, yet as I was finishing my ride, I was thinking that twenty-five miles was *nothing* compared with the size of the earth. And the entire Earth was just a small spot in the solar system, which in turn was a mere speck within our galaxy, and so on.

"I also loved to read, and so I loved words. The science and math words were the ones I liked best. A single word could spark an exploration that led to fascinating discoveries. . . . When I learned that the word 'scale' meant more than just a device for weighing things, I wanted to play with the idea of drawing things 'to scale.' I drew circles to represent Earth, Jupiter, and Sun on a scale where Earth was the size of a quarter. . . . I tied a string to a clothespin and inserted chalk in the clothespin. By adjusting the length of the string, I could draw circles of any size. What really amazed me was figuring out how long a string I'd need to show a really big star like Betelgeuse: longer than four football fields! I never attempted to draw that circle, but just thinking about it boggled my mind.

"I relived much of the joy I took in activities like these when I wrote *G Is for Googol.* (In case you're wondering, a 'googol' is a one followed by one hundred zeros. The name was invented by a nine-year-old boy. Someone later came up with a name for a much larger number, 'googolplex', which is a one followed by a googol zeros. Try writing that one!) To some people, math words sound as dry as dust, but for me they're great fun because they can lead to exciting explorations. That's what I tried to do in the book.

"Back in my elementary school years, I once estimated how many books were in my town's public library, and then I said to myself, 'With so many books, surely you could write just one!' But I never tried until many years later. I studied biology at Cornell University, where I learned to love the natural environment around us. I became especially interested in birds. One summer while I was in college, I worked as a counselor in a nature day camp. I'll never forget the day a young camper saw a bright red bird called a scarlet tanager. 'I can't believe there's a bird even redder than a cardinal!,' she exclaimed. Yet there it was, as red as red can be. I was so enthralled by her excitement that I decided to become an elementary school teacher. I taught for a few years, and during that time I had an experience that set me off in a new direction. One night I peered upward at a clear sky studded with stars, and all the wonder and excitement I had experienced as a child came flooding back. That night I decided to try to write a book that would

boggle children's minds the way mine had been boggled when I had contemplated the heavens and the large numbers used to describe them. The result was my first book, *How Much Is a Million?* I now have written more than fifty books, mostly nonfiction with math and science themes. I try to make them all capture the sense of awe and excitement I have always felt when contemplating the natural world (which includes the world of mathematics, of course)."

Each of Schwartz's "Million" books—*How Much Is a Million?, If You Made a Million,* and *Millions to Measure*—pair his clearly written text with illustrations by Steven Kellogg that feature series guide Marvelosissimo the Mathematical Magician. In *Millions to Measure* Marvelosissimo shows readers that things are measured in many different ways and that modern-day scales of standardized measure often have their roots in arbitrary events. In addition to covering "linear, weight,

Schwartz employs Marvelosissimo the Mathematical Magician to explain and simplify the concept of the very largest numbers in **How Much Is a Million?,** *a picture book illustrated by Steven Kellogg.* (Illustration copyright © 1985 by Steven Kellogg. Reproduced by permission of Lothrop, Lee & Shepard Books, a division of HarperCollins Publishers.)

Schwartz teams up with wife Yael Schy and photographer Dwight Kuhn to create the wildlife profile **Where in the Wild?** *and its companion volumes.*
(Photographs copyright © 2010 by Dwight Kuhn. Reproduced by permission of Tricycle Press, an imprint of Random House Children's Books, a division of Random House, Inc.)

and volume measurements," *Millions to Measure* "also entertains the reader," according to *Booklist* contributor Carolyn Phelan, and Kellogg's colorful illustrations "brim with action and humor as well as history and math." In *School Library Journal* Kathleen Kelly Mac-Millan praised Schwartz's clear and "logical" writing, calling *Millions to Measure* "another great resource" in Schwartz's "Million" series.

In addition to math, Schwartz has created numerous books that focus on the natural world. The related books *Where in the Wild? Camouflaged Creatures Concealed—and Revealed, Where Else in the Wild? More Camouflaged Creatures Concealed—and Revealed,* and *What in the Wild? Mysteries of Nature Concealed . . . and Revealed* find the author teaming up with Dwight Kuhn, a photographer who also collaborated on his "Look Once Again" and "Lifecycles" books, as well as with coauthor Yael Schy. *Where in the Wild?* sets the pace for the series, pairing a poem introducing an animal that uses camouflage to survive with a two-page gatefold photograph in which that animal can be dis-

covered by observant viewers and then ultimately revealed. Schwartz and Schy also include a prose paragraph describing the animal in even greater detail. The coauthors' "well-crafted" verses range "in form from rhymed couplets to haiku to concrete verse," noted Phelan in her *Booklist* review of *Where in the Wild?*, and Becca Zerkin predicted in the *New York Times Book Review* that the nature-themed work "challenges us to see the world in a more straightforward 'that's cool!' kind of way."

Eleven species of animals are featured in *Where Else in the Wild?,* and this "equally intriguing" photographic study pairs poems with information on "both habits and habitats plus an explanation of how the creature's camouflage works," according to a *Kirkus Reviews* writer. *What in the Wild?* takes a slightly different tact, featuring "ten riddle poems" that hint at what the accompanying photographs will show: "mysterious holes, bubbles, balls and mounds" that prove "to be the workings or leavings of" a variety of wild animals, according to another *Kirkus Reviews* writer. This mix of "clever verse,

curious photos, and guessing-game elements will engage children," according to Phelan, while *School Library Journal* reviewer Patricia Manning concluded that, "fun as a read-alone or for one-on-one sharing," *What in the World?* is a "tidy package from a talented trio [that] will delight children."

Biographical and Critical Sources

BOOKS

Whitin, David J., and Sandra Wilde, *It's the Story That Counts: More Children's Books for Mathematical Learning, K-6,* Heinemann, 1995.

PERIODICALS

Booklist, March 1, 1995, Ilene Cooper, review of *Yanomami: People of the Amazon,* p. 1239; October 15, 1998, Carolyn Phelan, review of *G Is for Googol: A Math Alphabet Book,* p. 419; November 1, 1999, Hazel Rochman, review of *On beyond a Million: An Amazing Math Journey,* p. 522; November 15, 1999, Carolyn Phelan, review of *If You Hopped like a Frog,* p. 631; February 1, 2003, Carolyn Phelan, review of *Millions to Measure,* p. 994; November 1, 2007, Carolyn Phelan, review of *Where in the Wild? Camouflaged Creatures Concealed . . . and Revealed,* p. 50; October 15, 2009, Carolyn Phelan, review of *Where Else in the Wild?,* p. 56; September 15, 2010, Carolyn Phelan, review of *What in the Wild? Mysteries of Nature Concealed . . . and Revealed,* p. 62.

Schwartz and Schy continue their exploration of animal adaptation in **What in the Wild?,** *which features photography by Dwight Kuhn.* (Photographs copyright © 2010 by Dwight Kuhn. Reproduced by permission of Dwight Kuhn, Kuhn Photo, www.kuhnphoto.net.)

Horn Book, March-April, 2003, Danielle J. Ford, review of *Millions to Measure,* p. 227.

Kirkus Reviews, February 1, 2003, review of *Millions to Measure,* p. 238; October 1, 2005, review of *If Dogs Were Dinosaurs;* August 15, 2007, review of *Where in the Wild?;* August 1, 2009, review of *Where Else in the Wild?;* July 1, 2010, review of *What in the Wild?*

New York Times Book Review, April 13, 2008, review of *Where in the Wild?,* p. 19.

Publishers Weekly, August 30, 1999, review of *If You Hopped like a Frog,* p. 83; September 20, 1999, review of *On beyond a Million,* p. 88.

School Library Journal, November, 2001, Kinda M. Kenton, review of *Q Is for Quark: A Science Alphabet Book,* p. 184; March, 2003, Kathleen Kelly MacMillian, review of *Millions to Measure,* p. 224; September, 2004, Janet Dawson Hamilton, reviews of *How Much Is a Million?* and *G Is for Googol,* both pp. 58-59; October, 2005, Kathleen Whalin, review of *If Dogs Were Dinosaurs,* p. 146; August, 2007, Margaret Bush, review of *Where in the Wild?,* p. 105; October, 2009, Margaret Bush, review of *Where Else in the Wild?,* p. 114; September, 2010, Patricia Manning, review of *What in the Wild?,* p. 139.

ONLINE

David M. Schwartz Home Page, http://www.davidschwartz. com (February 15, 2012).

* * *

SERRES, Alain 1956-

Personal

Born October 21, 1956, in Biarritz, France. *Education:* College degree.

Addresses

Home—Voisins-le-Bretonneux, France.

Career

Author and publisher. Worked as a primary-school teacher, beginning 1970s; freelance writer, beginning 1981; Rue du Monde (publisher), Voisins-le-Bretonneux, France, director, beginning 1996. Presenter at schools.

Writings

Les Bibimots, illustrated by Bruno Heitz, La Farandole (France) 1982.

Moi je me mets en colère, illustrated by Bruno Heitz, La Farandole (France) 1982.

Moi j'ai peur, illustrated by Bruno Heitz, La Farandole (France), 1982.

Moi je ris, illustrated by Bruno Heitz, La Farandole (France), 1982.

Moi je suis amoureux, illustrated by Bruno Heitz, La Farandole (France), 1982.

Du commerce de la Souris, illustrated by Claude Lapointe, Gallimard Jeunesse (Paris, France), 1984.

L'énergie, l'aventure des hommes, illustrated by Daniel Maja, La Farandole (France) 1984.

Le petit humain, illustrated by Anne Tonnac, Gallimard Jeunesse (Paris, France), 1986.

Quel carnaval, illustrated by Jean-Claude Luton, La Farandole (France) 1987.

Les bestiaire des mots, illustrated by Martine Mellinette, Cheyne Éditeur (France), 1988.

Kinon, le kiwi qui dit non, illustrated by Tony Ross, Gallimard Jeunesse (Paris, France), 1989.

Le grand livre des droits de l'enfant, illustrated by Frédéric Clément, La Farandole (France), 1989.

Puni cagibi, illustrated by Claude K. Dubois, Pastel (Paris, France), 1990.

C'est un secret, illustrated by Anne Tonnac, Editions Nathan (Paris, France), 1990.

Le grand retour, illustrated by Anne Tonnac, Editions Nathan (Paris, France), 1990.

Petit menteur, illustrated by Anne Tonnac, Editions Nathan (Paris, France), 1990.

Pourquoi, pourquoi, illustrated by Anne Tonnac, Editions Nathan (Paris, France), 1990.

Une île dans ma baignoire, illustrated by Mireille Vautier, Editions Nathan (Paris, France), 1990.

L'ogron, illustrated by Véronique Deiss, Gallimard Jeunesse (Paris, France), 1991.

La statue à cinq têtes, illustrated by Pef, Corps Puce (France), 1991.

Chercheur d'air, illustrated by Martine Mellinette, Cheyne (Le Chambon-sur-Lignon, Haute-Loire, France), 1991.

Krocobill et Robot-Bix, illustrated by Philippe Béha, La Farandole (France), 1992.

Le labyrinthe de Marakech, illustrated by Noëlle Prinz, Syros, Aventure dans la ville (France), 1992.

Pourquoi un âne écrivit des livres pour enfants, illustrated by Yan Thomas, La Farandole (France), 1992.

Terrible, illustrated by Merline, Pastel (Paris, France), 1992.

Chercheur d'air, illustrated by Martine Mellinette, Cheyne Éditeur (France), 1993.

Barnabé qu'on ne croit jamais, illustrated by Jacqueline Duhême, Scanéditions (France), 1993.

Le petit indien, l'ours et la rivière, illustrated by Katy Couprie, Syros (France), 1993.

Le trésor sous l'école, illustrated by Pef, Gallimard Jeunesse (Paris, France), 1994.

Tempête sur le piscine, illustrated by Pef, Gallimard Jeunesse (Paris, France), 1994.

Premier film, illustrated by Pef, Gallimard Jeunesse (Paris, France), 1994.

L'école de nuit, illustrated by Pef, Gallimard Jeunesse (Paris, France), 1994.

Correspondants surprises, illustrated by Pef, Gallimard Jeunesse (Paris, France), 1994.

Bisous de la classe cailloux, illustrated by Pef, Gallimard Jeunesse (Paris, France), 1994.

Toc Toc! Monsieur Cric-Crac, illustrated by Martin Jarrie, Editions Nathan (Paris, France), 1995.

Prière de na pas entrer dans la chambre des parents, Merci, illustrated by Klaas Verplancke, Casterman (Paris, France), 1996.

Il y a le monde, illustrated by Martine Mellinette, Cheyne Éditeur (France), 1996.

Le tambour de Noël, illustrated by Coralie Gallibour, La Martinière Jeunesse (Paris, France), 1997.

Histoires de chaussettes, illustrated by Anne Tonnac, Gallimard Jeunesse (Paris, France), 1997.

Un grand-père transformidable, illustrated by Hervé Blondon, Albin Michel Jeunesse (Paris, France), 1997.

Le plus gros gâteau du monde, illustrated by Martin Matje, Editions Nathan (Paris, France), 1997.

Petit ogre vert, illustrated by Stephane Laplanche, Gallimard Jeunesse (Paris, France), 1997.

Un menu enfant pour Zaza Pestouille, illustrated by Véronique Deiss, Casterman (Paris, France), 1997.

Un petit air de famille, illustrated by Martin Jarrie, Rue du Monde (Voisins-le-Bretonneux, France), 1998.

Moi je sais ce que je veux, illustrated by Serge Bloch, Albin Michel Jeunesse (Paris, France), 1998.

Moi je me mets en colère, illustrated by Serge Bloch, Albin Michel Jeunesse (Paris, France), 1998.

Moi je suis câlin câlin, illustrated by Serge Bloch, Albin Michel Jeunesse (Paris, France), 1998.

Moi j'ai peur, illustrated by Serge Bloch, Albin Michel Jeunesse (Paris, France), 1998.

Maman je veux être top-model, illustrated by Véronique Deiss, Rue du Monde (Voisins-le-Bretonneux, France), 1998.

Le premier livre des droits de l'enfant, illustrated by Pef, Rue du Monde (Voisins-le-Bretonneux, France), 1999.

Barnabé qu'on ne croit jamais, illustrated by Jacqueline Duhême, Rue du Monde (Voisins-le-Bretonneux, France), 1999.

Pain, beurre et chocolat, Rue du Monde (Voisins-le-Bretonneux, France), 1999.

Une petite fille sage comme un orage, illustrated by Loren Batt, Rue du Monde (Voisins-le-Bretonneux, France), 1999.

Le grand livre contre le racisme, illustrated by Zaü, Rue du Monde (Voisins-le-Bretonneux, France), 1999.

KrocoBill et Robot-Bix, illustrated by Sophie Dutertre, Rue du Monde (Voisins-le-Bretonneux, France), 2000.

Prière de na pas entrer dans la chambre des parents, Merci, illustrated by Klaas Verplancke, Casterman (Paris, France), 2000.

Une cuisine grande comme le monde, illustrated by Zaü, Rue du Monde (Voisins-le-Bretonneux, France), 2000.

Les étonnants animaux que le fils de Noé a sauvés, illustrated by Martin Jarrie, Rue du Monde (Voisins-le-Bretonneux, France), 2001.

Le premier livre de toutes nos couleurs, illustrated by Zaü, Rue du Monde (Voisins-le-Bretonneux, France), 2001.

(With others) *On vous écrit de la terre,* illustrated by Martin Jarrie, Rue du Monde (Voisins-le-Bretonneux, France), 2001.

(With Lily Franey) *L'abécédire,* illustrated by Olivier Tallec, Rue du Monde (Voisins-le-Bretonneux, France), 2001.

La devise de ma République, illustrated by Olivier Tallec, Rue du Monde (Voisins-le-Bretonneux, France), 2002.

Salade de comptine, illustrated by Olivier Tallec, Rue du Monde (Voisins-le-Bretonneux, France), 2002.

Première année sur la Terre, illustrated by Zaü, Rue du Monde (Voisins-le-Bretonneux, France), 2003.

(With Jean-Marie Henry) *On n'aime guère que la paix,* illustrated by Nathalie Novi, Rue du Monde (Voisins-le-Bretonneux, France), 2003.

Une Île dans ma baignoire, illustrated by Mireille Vautier, Editions Nathan (Paris, France), 2003.

Une cuisine grande comme un jardin, illustrated by Martin Jarrie, Rue du Monde (Voisins-le-Bretonneux, France), 2004.

(With Jean-Marie Henry) *Dis-moi un poème qui espère,* illustrated by Laurent Corvaisier, Rue du Monde (Voisins-le-Bretonneux, France), 2004.

Hans le balourd, based on the story by Hans Christian Andersen, illustrated by Régis Lejonc, Rue du Monde (Voisins-le-Bretonneux, France), 2005.

Mon école à nous, illustrated by Pef, Rue du Monde (Voisins-le-Bretonneux, France), 2005.

Comment un livre vient au monde, illustrated by Zaü, Rue du Monde (Voisins-le-Bretonneux, France), 2005.

Hiroshima, deux cerisiers et un poisson-lune, illustrated by Zaü, Rue du Monde (Voisins-le-Bretonneux, France), 2005.

Je fais un oiseau pour la paix, illustrated by Claire Franek, Rue du Monde (Voisins-le-Bretonneux, France), 2005.

(With Jean-Marie Henry) *L'alphabet des poètes,* illustrated by Aurélia Grandin, Rue du Monde (Voisins-le-Bretonneux, France), 2005.

Une cuisine tout en chocolat, illustrated by Nathalie Novi, Rue du Monde (Voisins-le-Bretonneux, France), 2006.

Je vous aime tant, illustrated by Olivier Tallec, Rue du Monde (Voisins-le-Bretonneux, France), 2006.

Il était une fois il était une fin, illustrated by Daniel Maja, Rue du Monde, (Paris, France), 2006.

La petite bibliothèque imaginaire, Rue du Monde (Voisins-le-Bretonneux, France), 2006.

La ville aux 100 poèmes, illustrated by Edmée Cannard, Rue du Monde (Voisins-le-Bretonneux, France), 2006.

(With Gianni Rodari) *Jeux de mots jeux nouveaux,* illustrated by Laurent Corvaisier, Rue du Monde (Voisins-le-Bretonneux, France), 2007.

Ma maison bleue, illustrated by Edmée Cannard, Rue du Monde (Voisins-le-Bretonneux, France), 2007.

Je serai les yeux de la Terre, illustrated by Zaü, Rue du Monde (Voisins-le-Bretonneux, France), 2007.

Maintenant, illustrated by Olivier Tallec, Rue du Monde (Voisins-le-Bretonneux, France), 2007.

Encore un coquelicot, illustrated by Martine Mellinette, Cheyne Éditeur (France), 2007.

Et Picasso peint Guernica, Rue du Monde (Voisins-le-Bretonneux, France), 2007, translated by Rosalind Price as *And Picasso Painted Guernica,* Allen & Unwin (Crows Nest, New South Wales, Australia), 2010.

Nouk qui s'envola, illustrated by Nathalie Novi, Rue du Monde (Voisins-le-Bretonneux, France), 2008.

Martin des colibris, illustrated by Judith Gueyfier, Rue du Monde (Voisins-le-Bretonneux, France), 2008.

Comment apprendre à ses parents à aimer les livres pour enfants, illustrated by Bruno Heitz, Rue du Monde (Voisins-le-Bretonneux, France), 2008.

Terrible, illustrated by Bruno Heitz, Rue du Monde (Voisins-le-Bretonneux, France), 2008.

Toc, toc! Monsieur Cric-Crac!, illustrated by Martin Jarrie, Rue du Monde (Voisins-le-Bretonneux, France), 2008.

La famille Totem, two volumes, illustrated by Laurent Corvaisier, Rue du Monde (Voisins-le-Bretonneux, France), 2008.

Tous en grève! Tous en rêve!, illustrated by Pef, Rue du Monde (Voisins-le-Bretonneux, France), 2008.

J'ai vu quelque chose qui bougeait, illustrated by Silvia Bonanni, Rue du Monde (Voisins-le-Bretonneux, France), 2008.

La fabuleuse cuisine de la route des épices, illustrated by Vanessa Hié, Rue du Monde (Voisins-le-Bretonneux, France), 2009.

J'ai le droit d'être un enfant, illustrated by Aurélia Fronty, Rue du Monde (Voisins-le-Bretonneux, France), 2009.

Je serai trois milliards d'enfants, illustrated by Judith Gueyfier, Rue du Monde (Voisins-le-Bretonneux, France), 2009.

Petits, illustrated by Julia Chausson, Rue du Monde (Voisins-le-Bretonneux, France), 2009.

On aime tous la maternelle, illustrated by Bruno Heitz, Rue du Monde (Voisins-le-Bretonneux, France), 2009.

Quand nous aurons mangé la planète, illustrated by Silvia Bonanni, Rue du Monde (Voisins-le-Bretonneux, France), 2009.

Le petit charon rouge, based on the story by Charles Perrault, illustrated by Clotilde Perrin, Rue du Monde (Voisins-le-Bretonneux, France), 2010.

Mandela, l'Africain Multicolore, illustrated by Zaü, Rue du Monde (Voisins-le-Bretonneux, France), 2010.

Travailler moins pour lire plus, illustrated by Pef, Rue du Monde (Voisins-le-Bretonneux, France), 2010.

Le ginkgo, le plus viel arbre du monde, illustrated by Zaü, Rue du Monde (Voisins-le-Bretonneux, France), 2011.

Author of animated television program *Les Pastagums,* broadcast on Canal and France 3 television networks.

Author's stories have been translated into Dutch, Greek, Italian, Japanese, Korean, and Spanish.

Biographical and Critical Sources

PERIODICALS

Kirkus Reviews, December 1, 2010, review of *And Picasso Painted Guernica.*

Publishers Weekly, November 15, 2010, review of *And Picasso Painted Guernica,* p. 59.

School Librarian, spring, 2011, Elizabeth Baskeyfield, review of *And Picasso Painted Guernica,* p. 60.

School Library Journal, January, 2011, Lisa Glasscock, review of *And Picasso Painted Guernica,* p. 130.

ONLINE

Rue du Monde Web site, http://www.ruedumonde.fr/ (February 15, 2012).

Readings Online, http://www.readings.com.au/ (October 22, 2011), review of *And Picasso Painted Guernica.*

*   *   *

SHAN, Darren 1972-
[A pseudonym]
(Darren O'Shaughnessy, D.B. Shan)

Personal

Born July 2, 1972, in London, England; son of Liam (a laborer) and Breda (a teacher) O'Shaughnessy. *Education:* Roehampton University, B.Sc. (sociology). *Hobbies and other interests:* Reading, studying and collecting original artwork, long walks, watching soccer, listening to pop and rock music, traveling.

Addresses

Home—Pallaskenry, County Limerick, Ireland; London, England. *Office*—c/o Paul Kenny, Rahina, Clarina, County Limerick, Ireland. *Agent*—Christopher Little, 10 Eel Brook Studios, 125 Moore Park Rd., London SW6 4PS, England. *E-mail*—post@darrenshan.com.

Career

Writer. Worked for a cable television company in Limerick, Ireland, until c. 1999.

Awards, Honors

Second prize, Sheffield Children's Book Award, W.H. Smith Children's Book Award shorlist, and International Reading Association/Children's Book Council Children's Choice Award, all 2001, all for *Cirque du Freak;* Redbridge Teenage Book Award, 2006, for *Lord Loss;* Irish Book Awards shortlist for Children's Book of the Year, 2007, for *Demon Thief,* and 2011, for *Ocean of Blood;* books shortlisted for numerous U.K. provincial awards.

Writings

"SAGA OF DARREN SHAN" SERIES

Cirque du Freak: A Living Nightmare (also see below), Collins (London, England), 2000, Little, Brown (New York, NY), 2001.

The Vampire's Assistant (also see below), Collins (London, England), 2000, Little, Brown (New York, NY), 2001.

Tunnels of Blood (also see below), Collins (London, England), 2000, Little, Brown (New York, NY), 2002.

Darren Shan (Reproduced by permission.)

Vampire Mountain (also see below), Collins (London, England), 2001, Little, Brown (New York, NY), 2002.
Trials of Death (also see below), Collins (London, England), 2001, Little, Brown (New York, NY), 2003.
The Vampire Prince (also see below), Little, Brown (New York, NY), 2002.
Hunters of the Dusk (also see below), Collins (London, England), 2002, Little, Brown (New York, NY), 2004.
Allies of the Night (also see below), Collins (London, England), 2002, Little, Brown (New York, NY), 2004.
Vampire Blood Trilogy (includes *Cirque du Freak, Vampire's Assistant,* and *Tunnels of Blood*), HarperCollins (London, England), 2003.
Killers of the Dawn (also see below), Collins (London, England), 2003, Little, Brown (New York, NY), 2005.
The Lake of Souls (also see below), Collins (London, England), 2003, Little, Brown (New York, NY), 2005.
Vampire Rites Trilogy (includes *Vampire Mountain, Trials of Death,* and *Vampire Prince*), HarperCollins (London, England), 2004.
Lord of the Shadows (also see below), Collins (London, England), 2004, Little, Brown (New York, NY), 2006.
Sons of Destiny (also see below), Collins (London, England), 2004, Little, Brown (New York, NY), 2006.
Vampire War Trilogy (includes *Hunters of the Dusk, Allies of the Night,* and *Killers of the Dawn*), HarperCollins (London, England), 2005.
Vampire Destiny Trilogy (includes *The Lake of Souls, Lord of the Shadows,* and *Sons of Destiny*), HarperCollins (London, England), 2005.

"SAGA OF LARTEN CREPSLEY" SERIES; PREQUEL TO "SAGA OF DARREN SHAN"

Birth of a Killer, Little, Brown (New York, NY), 2010.
Ocean of Blood, Little, Brown (New York, NY), 2011.
Palace of the Damned, Little, Brown (New York, NY), 2011.
Brothers to the Death, Little, Brown (New York, NY), 2012.

"DEMONATA" SERIES

Lord Loss, Little, Brown (New York, NY), 2005.

Demon Thief, HarperCollins (London, England), 2005, Little, Brown (New York, NY), 2006.
Slawter, Little, Brown (New York, NY), 2006.
Bec, HarperCollins (London, England), 2006, Little, Brown (New York, NY), 2007.
Blood Beast, Little, Brown (New York, NY), 2007.
Demon Apocalypse, HarperCollins (London, England), 2007, Little, Brown (New York, NY), 2008.
Death's Shadow, Little, Brown (New York, NY), 2008.
Wolf Island, HarperCollins (London, England), 2008, Little, Brown (New York, NY), 2009.
Dark Calling, Little, Brown (New York, NY), 2009.
Hell's Heroes, Little, Brown (New York, NY), 2010.

"CITY TRILOGY"; FOR ADULTS

(As Darren O'Shaughnessy) *Ayuamarca: Procession of the Dead,* Millennium Orion (London, England), 1999, revised edition published under name D.B. Shan as *Procession of the Dead,* HarperVoyager (London, England), 2008, Grand Central Pub. (New York, NY), 2010.
(As Darren O'Shaughnessy) *Hell's Horizon,* Millennium Orion (London, England), 2000, revised edition published under name D.B. Shan, HarperVoyager (London, England), 2008, Grand Central Pub. (New York, NY), 2011.
City of the Snakes, Grand Central Pub. (New York, NY), 2011.

OTHER

(Author of introduction) Mark Twain, *The Adventures of Huckleberry Finn,* Puffin (London, England), 2008.
The Thin Executioner, Little, Brown (New York, NY), 2010.
Palace of the Damned, Little, Brown (New York, NY), 2011.

Contributor to anthologies, including *Shrouded by Darkness; Guys Write for Guys Read.*

Shan's books have been translated into over thirty languages.

Adaptations

The "Saga of Darren Shan" series was adapted for film by Brian Helgeland and Paul Weitz as *Cirque du Freak: The Vampire's Assistant,* Universal, 2009. The "Cirque du Freak" series was adapted as a six-part manga series, artwork by Takahiro Arai, Shogakukan (Japan), translated into English by Stephen Paul, Yen Press (New York, NY), 2009-10.

Sidelights

Irish novelist Darren O'Shaughnessy, who writes under the pseudonym Darren Shan, is the author of the popular "Saga of Darren Shan" series of young-adult horror novels. The twelve-volume series follows a young pro-

tagonist—also named Darren Shan—as he unwittingly becomes a vampire's assistant, resists becoming a vampire himself, and fights against rival undead enemies. In addition to his "Saga of Darren Shan" series, Shan has also written the "Demonata" books, which focus on three youngsters and their ongoing battle with demonic entities, as well as the "City Trilogy," a series geared for adult readers. *The Thin Executioner,* a standalone novel, is also vintage Shan: its story focuses on Jebel Rum, a young teen who undertakes a nightmarish quest in preparation for inheriting his father's job as an axe-wielding executioner. "Shan creates a masterful, grueling story of survival and terror," proclaimed Laura Panter in her *Voice of Youth Advocates* appraisal of *The Thin Executioner,* while a *Publishers Weekly* characterized the novel as an "exciting adventure" that "loosely updates [Mark] Twain's *Adventures of Huckleberry Finn* while posing some interesting moral questions."

Although his novels have become phenomenally popular among teen boys, Shan originally focused on an older readership. "I never thought I'd make a career out of children's books," he admitted to Maria Court in England's *Bournemouth Daily Echo.* "I was an adult author and I wrote my first book for children as a bit of fun—something for myself on the side. I remembered what I was like when I was younger and the sort of books I wanted to read back then."

Although he is Irish, Shan was born in England in 1972, and he lived with his family in Southeast London for the first six years of his life. Shan and his family then moved back to Ireland, setting up house near Limerick. Horror films were a staple for the young Shan. "I used to love these movies and those images have stayed with me throughout my life," he told Erin Doherty in London's *Sunday Mirror,* "They have had an enormous impact on my writing."

Shan began writing stories when he was fourteen years old, and his first taste of success came the following year when he became a runner-up in a script-writing contest for Irish television with his dark comedy "A Day in the Morgue." Describing his adolescent years to Sarah Webb in the *Irish Independent,* Shan recalled that he was "a bit subdued at 14. Normal teenage stuff; self-conscious, quiet, starting to worry about what the world thinks of you. Didn't want to say anything that might be seen as foolish by friends. So that's why a lot of my characters are outsiders. That's how I felt as a teenager—out of place, awkward." His first novel, the unpublished "Mute Pursuit," was finished at age seventeen and played out as what Shan described on his home page as "a futuristic cross between *The Terminator* and Stephen King's *The Dark Tower.*"

After graduating from secondary school, O'Shaughnessy moved to London for three years to attend the Roehampton Institute of Higher Education, where he studied English and sociology. Returning to Limerick, he worked at a cable television company for a couple of years before deciding to give writing a try full time. He quit his job, moved back in with his parents, and for five years pounded out novels at the rate of five or six per year. Finally he sold an adult title, *Ayuamarca: Procession of the Dead,* which appeared in 1999 and has been more-recently rereleased as *Procession of the Dead.* Although described by a *Publishers Weekly* contributor as an "excellent, twisting foray into a world of deceit, murder, and mystery," this novel—as well as its sequel, *Hell's Horizon*—did not help Shan achieve financial success. However, he eventually recycled *Procession of the Dead* as the start of a new adult horror trilogy that also includes *Hell's Horizon* and *City of the Snakes.*

It was Shan's next published work that would determine the cours of his career as a writer. The "Saga of Darren Shan" opener, *Cirque du Freak: A Living Nightmare,* finds teenager Darren Shan and friend Steve sneaking out to visit the Cirque du Freak against their parents' wishes. While the show features the expected cast of unusual freaks and specialty performers, the most amazing—and dangerous—of them all is Mr.

Cover of Shan's standalone YA horror novel* The Thin Executioner, *featuring cover art by Sam Weber. (Cover art © 2010 by Sam Weber. Cover © Hachette Book Group, Inc. Reproduced by permission of Little, Brown & Company, a division of Hachette Book Group, Inc.)

Cover of Shan's terrifying teen novel **Cirque du Freak: A Living Nightmare,** *featuring cover art by Jennifer Nelson.* (Reproduced by permission of Hachette Book Group, Inc.)

Crepsley, a real vampire with a poisonous spider whose bite is deadly. When the spider bites Steve, Darren must agree to be the vampire's slave in order to get enough of the poison's antidote to save his friend. Debbie Carton, in a review for *Booklist,* called *Cirque du Freak* "a rip-roaring story full of oddities, low-key horror, and occasional, unexpected poignancy."

Darren's adventures continue in *The Vampire's Assistant,* in which the teen serves as the vampiric Mr. Crepsley's assistant. The pair return to the Cirque du Freak, where Mr. Crepsley attempts to turn Darren into a vampire. Darren refuses to drink blood, however. His friends at the circus, including a wolf man, a snake-boy, and a self-described "eco-warrior," lead him into trouble and a bloody climax. Tim Wadham, in a review for *School Library Journal,* praised *The Vampire's Assistant,* stating that "Shan creates heart-pounding, page-turning action."

In *Tunnels of Blood* Darren and his snake-boy friend, Evra, suspect that Mr. Crepsley is responsible for six dead bodies that have recently turned up. However, Mr. Crepsley denies the accusation and explains that they are the work of a "vampaneze," a type of vampire who drains all his victims' blood, leaving them dead. The trio then sets out to find and kill this Vampaneze. Thiers gory adventure earned praise from John Peters, who wrote in his review of *Tunnels of Blood* for *School Library Journal* that Shan's "story is compulsively readable, but it's not for the squeamish."

Vampire Mountain finds Darren and Mr. Crepsley on a perilous journey to the remote headquarters of the vampires so that Darren can be presented to the council of vampire generals for their approval. This ceremony only takes place once every twelve years. The pair also confronts the ominous Mr. Tiny, who may be as "old as time itself." Connie Forst, writing in *Resource Links,* called *Vampire Mountain* both "detailed and gripping."

Darren undergoes a ritual trial to prove his worth to the vampire clan in *Trials of Death,* the fifth volume in the series. The trial proves more difficult than he expected, however, and with the help of some friends, he tries to leave Vampire Mountain. Then the Vampaneze invade the undead headquarters, throwing everything into confusion. This invasion, noted Susan L. Rogers in *School Library Journal,* brings the story to a "fever pace," and *The Vampire Prince* leaves Darren at Vampire Mountain, where he stumbles on the truth of the conspiracy against the council.

Hunters of the Dusk begins a trilogy within the "Saga of Darren Shan" series that explores Darren's new life as a half-vampire prince. As war rages, Darren undertakes a dangerous quest to help vanquish the Lord of the Vampaneze. In *Allies of the Night* the youthful Darren is picked up by local officials and forced to attend school. A string of murders in town—the victims of which include some of Darren's schoolmates—soon leads to a chase for the killer through an underground tunnel system. Heather Ver Voort, writing about *Allies of the Night* in *School Library Journal,* anticipated that "fans of the series will enjoy this cliff-hanger." The hunters must escape an unruly mob before they can finish their pursuit of the Lord of the Vampaneze in *Killers of the Dawn,* which concludes the trilogy.

Incorporating elements of fantasy, *The Lake of Souls* follows Darren and friend Harkat as they attempt to unlock the mystery of Harkat's true identity. In *Lord of the Shadows* Darren returns to his hometown, where danger awaits. The latter novel "is filled with anger, revenge, and death," remarked Elaine Lesh Morgan in *School Library Journal.* In *Sons of Destiny,* the final volume in the "Saga of Darren Shan" series, Darren and the hunters battle for control of the night.

Although Shan originally thought his story would grow to at least eighteen novels, after the publication of *Lord of the Shadows* he decided that the series needed to end. "For an entire year I fought against what the story was telling me, and held to the notion that I was going to carry on," he noted on his home page. "I argued with myself constantly, trying to find holes in my reasons for stopping, refusing to admit the possibility of ending

Cover of Shan's horrific teen novel **Allies of the Night,** *featuring artwork by Don Bishop.* (Reproduced by permission of Hachette Book Group, Inc.)

early." Overcoming the fear of disappointing his many fans, Shan completed *Sons of Destiny* and looked forward to new ventures. "The series wanted to stop at book 12, and it was right," he stated. "I can see now that it's the logical, best place for the story to end."

To the relief of his many fans, Shan revisits his vampiric characters in "The Saga of Larten Crepsley," a four-book series that traces the 200-year history of Mr. Crepsley to the point where he meets the teenaged Darren in *Cirque du Freak.* In *Birth of a Killer* it is the early nineteenth century and Larten is toiling in a silk factory when he kills his foreman, flees, and ultimately becomes an assistant to ageing vampire General Seba Nile. He also joins the Cirque du Freak, training under the enigmatic Mr. Hibernius Tall. Once fully blooded, Larten flees with friend Wester and takes up with a gang of vampire toughs in *Ocean of Blood,* only to return to General Nile after years of carousing and now determined to dedicate himself to the vampiric arts. Disillusioned with his life, he leaves again, this time linking up with a woman and aimlessly sail the high

seas. *Palace of the Damned* continues Larten's search, but here the disillusioned vampire hopes to find salvation in death. Once again gaining hope, he returns to Vampire Mountain, tours several European cities at the turn of the twentieth century, and follows death into the trenches of World War I. The vampire's saga concludes in *Brothers to the Death,* as his path slowly winds toward its convergence with that of Darren.

"Jumping back in time," Shan "delivers a solid story" in *Birth of a Killer,* asserted a *Kirkus Reviews* writer. In her *School Library Journal* review of the same novel Elaine E. Knight suggested that readers familiarize themselves with the "Saga of Darren Shan" novels before embarking on the "Saga of Larten Crepsley," then predicted that Shan "aficionados will be intrigued by this glimpse into Crepsley's formative years." In chronicling the life of his notorious vampire protagonist, Shan takes a thoughtful approach, introducing "Larten . . . as a caring young man caught in a very unfortunate circumstance," according to *Voice of Youth Advocates* critic Ria Newhouse. "Fans of Darren Shan will eat this book up," Newhouse concluded in her review of *Birth of a Killer,* and Stephen King wrote in *School Librarian* that "the horror, gore and general depravity" that thread through Crepsley's history add up to "good harmless fun" that will appeal to "teenage boys aged 13 to 16." "Fans of Cirque du Freak will be sucked into the story of Larten's teen years," quipped Ann McDuffie in her *Voice of Youth Advocates* appraisal of *Ocean of Blood,* the critic adding that Shan's "cliff-hanger ending guarantees further adventures."

During its run, Shan's "Saga of Darren Shan" series proved phenomenally successful, selling more than ten million copies. Although often cited for their bloody, gory, action-filled plots, the novels offer much more, the author told Christopher Middleton in the London *Daily Telegraph.* "What I want to get across is that all actions have consequences," Shan remarked. "It's true that *Cirque du Freak* and the other 11 volumes in the Saga of Darren Shan series are sold as horror titles, but they're more like adventure stories. . . . What the horror element does is to add spice; it's a treat, if you like. But underpinning this whole fantasy element is the principle that doing the wrong thing can have very tangible, real results in terms of loss."

Shan introduces the "Demonata" series with his novel *Lord Loss.* Planned as a ten-volume series in which each volume introduces readers to a different demonic entity, the "Demonata" books are also aimed at a young-adult audience. In *Lord Loss* young Grubbs Grady discovers that his whole family has been ripped to shreds by demons. When the police do not believe his story, Grady is put into a mental institution, but he is eventually saved by his uncle Dervish, who knows about the demons threatening their family. Paula Rohrlick, writing in *Kliatt,* admitted that the violent story is "gross as well as engrossing." A critic for *Kirkus Reviews* found that Shan's "pace is non-stop, keeping the reader turning pages."

Demon Thief, set three decades before *Lord Loss,* centers on Kernel Fleck, a lonely teen whose ability to travel between dimensions leads to disaster when a horrible beast kidnaps his little brother. "Readers who love the ghastly and demand a fast pace will be asking for more," Walter Minkel predicted in *School Library Journal.* Grubbs makes a return appearance in *Slawter,* in which a demonic presence wreaks havoc on a horror movie set. Jake Kerridge, writing in the London *Daily Telegraph,* noted that "Shan is not just a mindless purveyor of grisly thrills. Like all good fantasists, he is interested in showing the reactions of ordinary people to extraordinary events." For example, in *Demon Thief* Grubbs develops magical powers, but as the story plays out, he realizes that magic has a definite down side. "Shan's portrayal of his troubled hero is convincing and affecting," Kerridge added.

In *Bec* Shan introduces the third narrator in his "Demonata" series. An orphan who hopes to become a priestess, Bec joins forces with a Druid boy to stop an invasion of demons in Celtic Ireland. According to *School Library Journal* critic Tim Wadham, *Bec* "is classic Shan, with lightning-fast plotting, over-the-top gore, and an overarching sense of gloom and despair." In

Cover of **Demon Thief,** *the first novel in Shan's "Demonata" novel series.* (Reproduced by permission of Hachette Book Group, Inc.)

Blood Beast, Grubbs, who may be turning into a werewolf, discovers a mysterious treasure surrounded by evil forces. "Here's another horrific, edge-of-the-seat gore fest," Minkel remarked of this "Demonata" entry.

Grubbs survives death-by-demon only to find himself in worse peril in *Demon Apocalypse,* the next installment in Shan's "Demonata" saga. The adventure continues in *Death's Shadow, Wolf Island,* and *Dark Calling,* all which take place concurrently. While Grubbs battles his wolven tendencies in *Wolf Island,* magician Beranabus and Bec face a demonic foe aboard a ship full of zombies in *Death's Shadow.* For now-sightless Kernel, visions and voices haunt his waking hours in *Dark Calling,* as the Old Creatures attempt to steal him from Earth. The "Demonata" series ends with *Hell's Heroes,* as Grubbs leaves Uncle Dervish and joins Kernel in a search for Bec, a search that takes them face to face with Lord Loss and a final battle. Characteristic of the entire "Demonata" sequence, *Wolf Island* "is not for the squeamish," warned Minkel, the critic adding that violent acts "are gruesome constants and triumphs are only temporary."

Although he has come a long way from his days as a struggling young writer living with his parents, Shan refuses to allow his success to change his approach to his work. "I've always written 'purely,'" he noted on his home page. "I enjoy telling stories, and I've always written stories that I've enjoyed, simply because I enjoy writing them. Some of those stories (The Saga) have been huge successes. Others . . . haven't." "But I enjoyed writing the 'failures' just as much as the 'successes,'" the author concluded, "and the ones which haven't been published are every bit as important and dear to me as the ones which have sold millions of copies all around the world."

Biographical and Critical Sources

PERIODICALS

Booklist, April 15, 2001, Debbie Carton, review of *Cirque du Freak: A Living Nightmare,* p. 1559; September 15, 2001, Debbie Carton, review of *The Vampire's Assistant,* p. 224; August, 2002, Debbie Carton, review of *Tunnels of Blood,* p. 1950; November 1, 2005, Debbie Carton, review of *Lord Loss,* p. 39; July 1, 2010, Daniel Kraus, review of *The Thin Executioner,* p. 53; September 1, 2010, Daniel Kraus, review of *Bloody Horowitz,* p. 101; December 1, 2010, Jessica Moyer, review of *Hell's Horizon,* p. 37.
Bookseller, November 12, 1999, Caroline Horn, "Guide to Vampires: They Can't Be Shut Back in the Coffin."
Books for Keeps, May, 2000, review of *Cirque du Freak.*
Bournemouth Daily Echo, September 27, 2007, Maria Court, interview with Shan.
Children's Books in Ireland, May, 2000, interview with Shan/O'Shaughnessy.

Canadian Review of Materials, March 14, 2003, review of *Cirque du Freak;* May 23, 2003, review of *The Vampire's Assistant.*

Daily Telegraph (London, England), March 11, 2000, review of *Cirque du Freak;* July 8, 2006, Jake Kerridge, review of *Slawter;* January 5, 2008, "Christopher Middleton Introduces *Cirque du Freak.*"

Herald (Glasgow, Scotland), June 10, 2006, Anne Johnstone, interview with Shan, p. 8.

Independent, December 3, 1999, review of *Cirque du Freak.*

Irish Independent, April 19, 2008, Sarah Webb, interview with Shan.

Irish Times Magazine, September 15, 2001, Eibhir Mulqueen, "Bitten by the Writing Bug."

Kirkus Reviews, August 1, 2002, review of *Vampire Mountain,* p. 1143; September 15, 2005, review of *Lord Loss,* p. 1033; April 1, 2010, review of *Procession of the Dead*; July 15, 2010, review of *The Thin Executioner*; August 1, 2010, review of *Bloody Horowitz*; September 15, 2010, review of *Birth of a Killer: The Saga of Larten Crepsley*; October 1, 2010, review of *Hell's Horizon.*

Kliatt, November, 2003, Stacey Conrad, review of *Vampire Mountain,* p. 26; September, 2005, Paula Rohrlick, review of *Lord Loss,* p. 14.

Magpies, September, 2005, Bevis Masson-Leach, interview with Shan, p. 16.

Manchester Evening News (Manchester, England), February 24, 2001, review of *Cirque du Freak.*

Observer (London, England), October 22, 2000, review of *Cirque du Freak;* December 5, 2004, Kate Kellaway, "Gore Blimey: Today, It's Horror, Not Hogwarts, That Obsesses Younger Readers and Frightens Their Parents," p. 6.

Publishers Weekly, February 19, 2001, review of *Cirque du Freak,* p. 92; August 27, 2001, review of *The Vampire's Assistant,* p. 86; July 8, 2002, review of *Cirque du Freak,* p. 51; October 24, 2005, review of *Lord Loss,* p. 60; April 19, 2010, review of *Procession of the Dead,* p. 41; July 19, 2010, review of *The Thin Executioner,* p. 131; November 1, 2010, review of *Hell's Horizon,* p. 32.

Resource Links, June, 2003, Gail Lennon, review of *Tunnels of Blood,* p. 35, and Connie Forst, review of *Vampire Mountain,* p. 36.

School Librarian, winter, 2010, Stephen King, review of *Birth of a Killer,* p. 247.

School Library Journal, May, 2001, Timothy Capehart, review of *Cirque du Freak,* p. 159; August, 2001, Tim Wadham, review of *The Vampire's Assistant,* p. 188; May, 2002, John Peters, review of *Tunnels of Blood,* p. 160; September, 2002, John Sigwald, review of *Vampire Mountain,* p. 233; July, 2003, Susan L. Rogers, review of *Trials of Death,* p. 135; November, 2003, Sharon S. Pearce, review of *The Vampire Prince,* p. 148; July, 2004, Jessi Platt, review of *Hunters of the Dusk,* p. 112; October, 2004, Heather Ver Voort, review of *Allies of the Night,* p. 176; November, 2005, Hillias J. Martin, review of *Lord Loss,* p. 148; September, 2006, Elaine Lesh Morgan, review of *Lord of the Shadows,* and Walter Minkel, review of *Demon Thief,* both p. 218; August, 2007, Tim Wadham, review of *Bec,* p. 125; February, 2008, Walter Minkel, review of *Blood Beast,* p. 128; September, 2009, Walter Minkel, review of *Wolf Island,* p. 173; July, 2010, Anthony C. Doyle, review of *The Thin Executioner,* p. 96; February, 2011, Elaine E. Knight, review of *Birth of a Killer,* p. 120.

Scotsman, February 5, 2000, review of *Cirque du Freak.*

Sunday Mirror (London, England), February 27, 2000, Erin Doherty, "Last Year He Was on the Dole. Now He Is a Millionaire Writer," p. 8.

Sunday Telegraph (London, England), March 12, 2006, James Delingpole, "Who Scares Wins: Horror Is the Hottest Genre in Children's Fiction, and Darren Shan's Gruesome Stories Sell by the Millions," p. 16.

Sunday Times (London, England), May 8, 2011, "How Freaking Lucky Is He?" (profile), p. 20.

Times (London, England), February 4, 2000, interview with Shan; February 17, 2000, review of *Cirque du Freak;* January 14, 2006, Amanda Craig, "New-Age Vampires Stake Their Claim," p. 17.

Voice of Youth Advocates, February, 2002, review of *Cirque du Freak,* p. 409; April, 2005, Stacy Dillon, review of *Allies of the Night,* p. 61; December, 2010, Laura Panter, review of *The Thin Executioner,* p. 476; February, 2011, Ria Newhouse, review of *Birth of a Killer,* p. 577; August, 2011, Ann McDuffie, review of *Oceans of Blood,* p. 298.

ONLINE

Darren Shan Home Page, http://www.darrenshan.com (February 12, 2012).

Darren Shan Web log, http://darrenshan.blogdrive.com (February 12, 2012).

*   *   *

SHAN, D.B.
See SHAN, Darren

*   *   *

SIERRA, Judy 1945-

Personal

Born Judy Strup, June 8, 1945, in Washington, DC; name legally changed, 1985; daughter of Joseph L. (a photographer) and Jean (a librarian) Strup; married Robert Walter Kaminski (a puppeteer and elementary schoolteacher); children: Christopher Robin Strup. *Education:* American University, B.A. (French), 1968; California State University—San Jose (now San Jose State University), M.A., 1973; University of California—Los Angeles, Ph.D. *Hobbies and other interests:* Gardening, hiking, spending time with grandchildren.

Addresses

Home—Castro Valley, CA.

Career

Writer. Puppeteer and storyteller, beginning 1976. Part-time librarian at Los Angeles Public Library, beginning 1986; teacher of children's literature and storytelling at Extension of University of California—Los Angeles. Artist-in-residence at Smithsonian Institution, 1984.

Member

National Association for the Preservation and Perpetuation of Storytelling, American Folklore Society, California Folklore Society.

Awards, Honors

Best Books designation, *Publishers Weekly,* 1996, Fanfare List includee, *Horn Book,* 1997, and Notable Books for Children designation, American Library Association (ALA), 1997, all for *Nursery Tales around the World;* Notable Book citation, ALA, 2005, Irma Simonton Black Honor Book, Bank Street College of Education, and E.B. White Read-Aloud Award, Association of Booksellers for Children, all for *Wild about Books.*

Writings

FOR YOUNG READERS

The Elephant's Wrestling Match, illustrated by Brian Pinkney, Lodestar (New York, NY), 1992.

The House That Drac Built, illustrated by Will Hillenbrand, Harcourt Brace (San Diego, CA), 1995.

Good Night, Dinosaurs, illustrated by Victoria Chess, Clarion (New York, NY), 1996.

(Reteller) *Wiley and the Hairy Man,* illustrated by Brian Pinkney, Lodestar (New York, NY), 1996.

(Reteller) *The Mean Hyena: A Folktale from Malawi,* illustrated by Michael Bryant, Lodestar (New York, NY), 1997.

Counting Crocodiles, illustrated by Will Hillenbrand, Harcourt Brace (San Diego, CA), 1997.

Antarctic Antics: A Book of Penguin Poems, illustrated by José Aruego and Ariane Dewey, Harcourt Brace (San Diego, CA), 1998.

Tasty Baby Belly Buttons: A Japanese Folktale, illustrated by Meilo So, Alfred A. Knopf (New York, NY), 1998.

The Dancing Pig, illustrated by Jesse Sweetwater, Harcourt Brace (San Diego, CA), 1999.

(Reteller) *The Beautiful Butterfly: A Folktale from Spain,* illustrated by Victoria Chess, Clarion (New York, NY), 2000.

The Gift of the Crocodile: A Cinderella Story, illustrated by Reynold Ruffins, Simon & Schuster (New York, NY), 2000.

There's a Zoo in Room Twenty-two, illustrated by Barney Saltzberg, Harcourt Brace (San Diego, CA), 2000.

Preschool to the Rescue, illustrated by Will Hillenbrand, Harcourt Brace (San Diego, CA), 2001.

Monster Goose, illustrated by Jack E. Davis, Harcourt Brace (San Diego, CA), 2001.

'Twas the Fright before Christmas, illustrated by Will Hillenbrand, Harcourt Brace (San Diego, CA), 2002.

Coco and Cavendish: Circus Dogs, illustrated by Paul Meisel, Random House (New York, NY), 2003.

Coco and Cavendish: Fire Dogs, illustrated by Paul Meisel, Random House (New York, NY), 2004.

What Time Is It, Mr. Crocodile?, illustrated by Doug Cushman, Gulliver (Orlando, FL), 2004.

Wild about Books, illustrated by Marc Brown, Knopf (New York, NY), 2004.

(Selector) *Schoolyard Rhymes: Kids' Own Rhymes for Rope Skipping, Hand Clapping, Ball Bouncing, and Just Plain Fun,* illustrated by Melissa Sweet, Knopf (New York, NY), 2005.

The Gruesome Guide to World Monsters, illustrated by Henrik Drescher, Candlewick Press (Cambridge, MA), 2005.

The Secret Science Project That Almost Ate the School, illustrated by Stephen Gammell, Simon & Schuster (New York, NY), 2006.

Thelonius Monster's Sky-High Fly Pie: A Revolting Rhyme, illustrated by Edward Koren, Knopf (New York, NY), 2006.

Mind Your Manners, B.B. Wolf, illustrated by J. Otto Seibold, Knopf (New York, NY), 2007.

Born to Read, illustrated by Marc Brown, Knopf (New York, NY), 2008.

Beastly Rhymes to Read after Dark, illustrated by Brian Biggs, Knopf (New York, NY), 2008.

Saving Ballyhoo Bay, illustrated by Derek Anderson, Simon & Schuster (New York, NY), 2009.

Sleepy Little Alphabet: A Bedtime Story from Alphabet Town, illustrated by Melissa Sweet, Knopf (New York, NY), 2009.

Tell the Truth, B.B. Wolf, illustrated by J. Otto Seibold, Alfred A. Knopf (New York, NY), 2010.

We Love Our School!, illustrated by Linda Davick, Alfred A. Knopf (New York, NY), 2011.

ZooZical, illustrated by Marc Brown, Alfred A. Knopf (New York, NY), 2011.

Suppose You Meet a Dinosaur: A First Book of Manners, illustrated by Tim Bowers, Alfred A. Knopf (New York, NY), 2012.

STORY COLLECTIONS

(With Robert Kaminski) *Twice upon a Time: Stories to Tell, Retell, Act Out, and Write About,* H.W. Wilson (Bronx, NY), 1989.

(With Robert Kaminski) *Multicultural Folktales: Stories to Tell Young Children,* Oryx Press (Phoenix, AZ), 1991.

(Compiler) *Cinderella,* illustrated by Joanne Caroselli, Oryx Press (Phoenix, AZ), 1992.

(Editor and annotator) *Quests and Spells: Fairy Tales from the European Oral Tradition,* Bob Kaminski Media Arts (Ashland, OR), 1994.

Mother Goose's Playhouse: Toddler Tales and Nursery Rhymes, with Patterns for Puppets and Feltboards, Bob Kaminski Media Arts (Ashland, OR), 1994.

(Selector and reteller) *Nursery Tales around the World,* illustrated by Stefano Vitale, Clarion (New York, NY), 1996.

Multicultural Folktales for the Feltboard and Readers' Theater, Oryx Press (Phoenix, AZ), 1996.

Can You Guess My Name? Traditional Tales around the World, illustrated by Stefano Vitale, Clarion (New York, NY), 2002.

Silly and Sillier: Read-Aloud Tales from around the World, illustrated by Valeri Gorbachev, Knopf (New York, NY), 2002.

Never Kick a Ghost, and Other Silly Chillers, illustrated by Pascale Constantin, HarperCollins (New York, NY), 2011.

NONFICTION

The Flannel Board Storytelling Book, H.W. Wilson (Bronx, NY), 1987.

Storytelling and Creative Dramatics, H.W. Wilson (Bronx, NY), 1989.

Fantastic Theater: Puppets and Plays for Young Performers and Young Audiences, H.W. Wilson (Bronx, NY), 1991.

(With Robert Kaminski) *Children's Traditional Games: Games from 137 Countries and Cultures,* Oryx Press (Phoenix, AZ), 1995.

Storytellers' Research Guide: Folktales, Myths, and Legends, Folkprint (Eugene, OR), 1996.

Celtic Baby Names: Traditional Names from Ireland, Scotland, Wales, Brittany, Cornwall, and the Isle of Man, Folkprint (Eugene, OR), 1997.

Spanish Baby Names: Traditional and Modern First Names of Spain and the Americas, Folkprint (Eugene, OR), 2002.

Editor of *Folklore and Mythology Journal,* 1988—.

Adaptations

Antarctic Antics was adapted as an animated film and as a sound recording.

Sidelights

Interested in storytelling and puppetry arts from childhood, Judy Sierra has built a career as a writer of imaginative stories for young readers, including *Good Night, Dinosaurs, The Gift of the Crocodile: A Cinderella Story, Mind Your Manners, B.B. Wolf,* and *ZooZical.* "In my books," Sierra remarked in an interview on the *Powell's Books* Web site, "I try to create small, exciting worlds that take children away from the everyday."

Many of Sierra's popular works are adaptations of folk tales from other countries. The original story inspiring *The Elephant's Wrestling Match,* for instance, comes from the African nation of Cameroon. In Sierra's retelling, the mighty elephant challenges all the other animals to a test of strength: "The leopard, crocodile, and rhinoceros all respond," Linda Greengrass reported in *School Library Journal,* "only to be easily thwarted by the mighty beast. Each time, Monkey beats out the results on the drum." In a surprising twist, a small but

clever bat turns out to be the winner, although that is not the resolution of the story. A reviewer in *Publishers Weekly* noted that "Sierra's staccato retelling of this lively African tale crackles with energy," and Greengrass added that "listeners can almost hear the beating of the drum." As Betsy Hearne maintained while reviewing *The Elephant's Wrestling Match* for the *Bulletin of the Center for Children's Books,* Sierra's "drama is simple enough for toddlers to follow but sturdy enough to hold other kids' attention as well."

In *The House That Drac Built* Sierra and artist Will Hillenbrand draw on literary and folk symbols that are more familiar to American children, inserting the character of Dracula into a popular nursery rhyme. Thus, as Nancy Vasilakas recounted in *Horn Book,* "Young audiences are introduced to the bat that lived in the house that Drac built, then to the cat that bit the bat, the werewolf that chased the cat that bit the bat, and so on through 'fearsome' manticore, coffin, mummy, zombie, and fiend of Bloodygore." Ghoulish as all this sounds, Sierra's story has a humorous twist as a group of trick-or-treaters enters the house and puts everything to rights. Noting its appeal at Halloween, *School Library Journal* contributor Beth Irish called *The House That Drac Built* "a definite hit for holiday story programs."

Sierra and Hillenbrand make reference to *The House That Drac Built* in their second collaboration, *'Twas the Fright before Christmas.* Here trouble starts when Santa Mouse, who delivers presents in a sleigh pulled by eight bats, tickles a dragon's nose. A werewolf finds himself at the end of the chain of events with a pinched and sore tail as he tries to figure out just what started the mess. Once the mystery is solved, Santa Mouse apologizes and suggests that they all read a story, which, in Hillenbrand's illustration, is *The House That Drac Built.* Mummies and other monsters fill the pages of *'Twas the Fright before Christmas,* which a *Kirkus Reviews* contributor considered to be "another innovation on a well-known text."

Sierra joins forces with cartoonist Edward Koren for another monstrous tale, *Thelonius Monster's Sky-High Fly Pie: A Revolting Rhyme.* Spoofing the classic rhyme "I Know an Old Lady Who Swallowed a Fly," Sierra offers a story about a shaggy and repulsive—but well-meaning—chef who decides to create a tasty treat for his hungry friends. Just before the guests can dig in, however, the main ingredients in Thelonius's grand dessert plan their escape. "Children will love the illustrated jokes," noted *School Library Journal* contributor Susan Weitz of the book.

Whereas *Thelonius Monster's Sky-high Fly Pie* may not exactly be bedtime reading, *Good Night, Dinosaurs* certainly is. Here Sierra describes a family of dinosaurs getting ready for bed, brushing their teeth and then listening to lullabies and stories from their dino-parents. "Young dinosaur fanciers will be charmed and undoubtedly claim this as their favorite go-to-sleep book," con-

Will Hillenbrand creates the whimsical characters that star in Judy Sierra's picture book **Counting Crocodiles.**

cluded Ann A. Flowers in *Horn Book.* Beth Tegart, writing in *School Library Journal,* dubbed *Good Night, Dinosaurs* "a pleasant read at bedtime for dinosaur fans as well as those who need a chuckle at the end of the day."

With *Wiley and the Hairy Man,* Sierra retells another folk tale, this one with roots in the American South. Frightened by the Hairy Man, young Wiley enlists the help of his mother to trick the monster three times, and thus forces the Hairy Man to leave them alone. "Through the use of dialogue without dialect and a lissome narration," commented Maria B. Salvadore in *Horn Book,* "Sierra captures the cadence of the oral language of Alabama."

Like *The Elephant's Wrestling Match,* Sierra's folk-tale adaptation *The Mean Hyena* originated in Africa, in this case the country of Malawi. There the Nyanja people tell how the turtle gets his revenge on the title character after the hyena plays a cruel trick on him. *School Library Journal* contributor Marilyn Iarusso called *The Mean Hyena* "a must for all folk-tale collections."

Counting Crocodiles takes place in a tropical location, although its setting is perhaps even more fanciful than that of Sierra's earlier tales. When an unfortunate monkey finds herself on an island with nothing to eat but lemons, she longs to make her way to a nearby island with banana trees. There is only one problem: the Sillabobble Sea, which separates the two pieces of land, is filled with hungry crocodiles. However, the monkey—like the other small but clever creatures that star in Sierra's stories—devises an ingenious plan to trick the crocodiles and obtain not only a bunch of bananas, but also a sapling that will grow and produce fruit in the future. "The whimsical rhyme . . . and the lively alliteration" in *Counting Crocodiles* "add to the appeal," wrote Kathleen Squires in *Booklist.* A reviewer in *Publishers Weekly* also praised Sierra's latest collaboration with Hillenbrand: "Working with traditional materials, author and artist arrive at an altogether fresh presentation," the critic noted.

Crocodiles and mischievous monkeys again live large in *What Time Is It, Mr. Crocodile?* Mr. Crocodile has a list of things to accomplish during his day, one of which

is to capture and dine on the monkeys who constantly pester him for the time of day. However, due to monkey meddling, things do not go quite as planned, and Mr. Crocodile makes peace with the monkeys instead. A *Kirkus Reviews* contributor asserted that "any time [is] the right time for this irresistible rhyme." A *School Library Journal* reviewer warned readers to be ready for "some memorable monkey business in this entertaining tale," while Ilene Cooper noted in *Booklist* that "the best part of the book is Sierra's handy way with a rhyming text." Lauren Peterson, also writing for *Booklist,* praised *What Time Is It, Mr. Crocodile?* as a story in which "Sierra's bouncy rhyming text" creates "a fun read-aloud."

After retelling a tale from Japan in *Tasty Baby Belly Buttons,* and spinning a story about two girls who are able to evade a witch due to their kindness to animals in *The Dancing Pig,* Sierra returned to crocodiles with a Cinderella story set in Indonesia. In *The Gift of the Crocodile* no fairy godmother comes to Damara's rescue when her stepmother acts cruelly; instead, Grandmother Crocodile rewards the girl for her honesty and good heart. When the prince announces plans to host a lavish ball, Damara can depend on generous Grandmother Crocodile for Fairy Godmother-type assistance. "Sierra's unadorned retelling is straightforward," wrote a *Horn Book* reviewer, the critic concluding that the author's "Southeast Asian variation adds some tropical zest to the oft-told tale." Hazel Rochman, writing for *Booklist,* called *The Gift of the Crocodile* "a storytelling treat."

Leaving fairy tales behind and heading for the playground, Sierra shows how a giant mud puddle is thwarted in *Preschool to the Rescue.* The mud puddle lurks, waiting until it can capture anything that passes through it, which, over the course of the story, includes a pizza van and four other vehicles. Only the preschoolers know how to deal with the puddle: by making its mud into mud pies until the sun comes out and dries it all away. "In a feast of unbridled mud-food making, the heroic preschoolers completely consume the rogue puddle," explained a *Publishers Weekly* reviewer. Marlene Gawron commented in *School Library Journal* on the onomatopoeia Sierra uses in her text: "What a wonderful noisy book this is." Gawron concluded, "The fun doesn't stop until the book is closed." A *Horn Book* contributor recommended *Preschool to the Rescue,* writing that Sierra's "uncomplicated story . . . has rainy-day read-aloud written all over it."

Twisted versions of Mother Goose rhymes fill the pages of *Monster Goose,* a tale Sierra casts with such characters as Little Miss Mummy, Cannibal Horner, and the Zombie who lives in a shoe. Sierra's revisions of familiar Mother Goose rhymes might be too much for particularly young readers, warned a reviewer for *Kirkus Reviews.* "but it's a fiendishly good time for everyone else." A critic for *Publishers Weekly* noted that "the Goose has been spoofed before, but this volume strikes a nice balance between goofy and ghastly," while *School Library Journal* reviewer Gay Lynn Van Vleck advised school librarians to keep extra copies of *Monster Goose* for students, "since teachers may hoard it for themselves." Gillian Engberg, writing in *Booklist,* recommended the book as "perfect for rowdy Halloween read-alouds."

In *The Gruesome Guide to World Monsters,* illustrated by Henrik Drescher, Sierra offers an introduction to more than sixty ghoulish creatures of legend. Among those profiled are the Mansusopsop, a blood-sucking bat from the Philippines; the Dziwozony, a race of wild women lurking in Polish forests; and the Chiruwi, a human-bird hybrid roosting in Malawi. A contributor in *Publishers Weekly* noted that "every page provides imaginative fodder for chilling tales," and Jennifer Mattson, writing in *Booklist,* praised the combination of Sierra's prose and Drescher's artwork, noting that the "controlled text provides a counterweight to artwork that's like graffiti scribbled on the walls of Bedlam."

A youngster inadvertently creates her own terrifying beast in Sierra's *The Secret Science Project That Almost Ate the School,* a humorous work illustrated by Stephen Gammell. When a third grader needs a project for her upcoming science fair, she orders Professor Swami's Super Slime via the Internet. Disregarding the instructions warning not to release the mutant yeast too early, she creates a gooey glob that threatens to swallow everything in its path. Engberg described *The Secret Science Project That Almost Ate the School* as "an energetic, darkly comic spin on the common story of a science project gone wrong," and a contributor in *Publishers Weekly* remarked that "Gammell's illustrations amplify the energy and fun of Sierra's bouncy verse."

Wild about Books is a celebration of zoos, libraries, and Dr. Seuss. Here Sierra teams up with award-winning illustrator Marc Brown to tell the story of a librarian who accidentally takes the bookmobile into the zoo, only to find that all of the animals want to learn to read. She begins to read to them, picking out the perfect books for each species: tall books for the giraffes, featuring basketball and skyscrapers; books written in Chinese for the pandas; and dramas for the llamas. However, for many of the animals, reading is not enough: the dung beetles write haiku and a hippo wins the "Zoolitzer" prize. *Wild about Books* is "both homage to and reminiscent of Dr. Seuss's epic rhyming sagas," praised *School Library Journal* reviewer Marge Loch-Wouters. A *Publishers Weekly* contributor called Sierra's tale a "winning paean to reading and writing," while a *Kirkus Reviews* critic heralded the work as "a storytime spectacular."

Born to Read, a follow-up to *Wild about Books,* centers on a youngster with an insatiable appetite for literature. After Sam learns about an upcoming bicycle race, he pores over every book he can find about the subject and ends up defeating his adult competition. Sam later saves

his city from a giant baby by soothing the towering infant with a basketful of stories and snacks. Sierra's "rich vocabulary gives the boy's story a jaunty tempo, as do the appealing full-color gouache cartoon illustrations," a contributor in *Publishers Weekly* observed.

Sierra and Brown continue their collaboration in *ZooZical,* which follows zoo residents as they decide to pass the cold, gray days of winter by staging an upbeat musical. Bored with no children to visit them, some of the animals are tempted to curl up and sleep the season away, but a young kangaroo and his hippopotamus friend remain happy, and their delight in frisky dancing soon inspires energy in their zoo-bound friends. Soon the Springfield Zoo is buzzing with creativity, as popular children's songs are given critter-appropriate lyrics and dance steps are rehearsed, all in preparation for the moment when the curtain goes up on their all-animal production. "Sierra's rhymed text is playful, with sassy touches," wrote a *Kirkus Reviews* writer in a positive review of *ZooZical,* and a *Publishers Weekly* critic rec-

ommended the story as a "snappy follow-up to *Wild about Books*" and its sequels. Along with Brown's "characteristically cheery" illustrations, "Sierra's rhymes rollick along trippingly," according to Karen Cruze in *Booklist.*

Sierra presents an unusual take on a familiar literary character in *Mind Your Manners, B.B. Wolf* and *Tell the Truth, B.B. Wolf,* both illustrated by J. Otto Seibold. When the now-elderly Big Bad Wolf is invited to a storybook tea at his local library in the first book, he consults with a friendly crocodile who teaches him the finer points of etiquette. Although the other guests, including Little Red Riding Hood and the Gingerbread Boy, are initially put off by the wolf's appearance, B.B. manages to score points with the librarian due to his exceedingly polite ways. In *Tell the Truth, B.B. Wolf* Big Bad Wolf reappears at the library, but his coaching by misguided buddies at the Villain Villa Senior Center has prompted him to frame his wolf vs. pigs a story

Reynold Ruffins creates the artwork for **The Gift of the Crocodile,** *Sierra's retelling of "Cinderella."* (Illustration copyright © 2000 Reynold Ruffins. Reprinted with the permission of Simon & Schuster Books for Young Readers, an imprint of Simon & Schuster Children's Publishing Division.)

with himself as the hero. The story falls flat when it turns out that the three little pigs are in the audience and share their alternate view.

A *Publishers Weekly* critic noted of *Mind Your Manners, B.B. Wolf* that "Sierra and Seibold expertly tweak the tension and the levity in this story of a trickster's golden years." "Children familiar with [the story of the Three Little Pigs] . . . will enjoy the witty text to the fullest," predicted Carolyn Phelan in her *Booklist* review of *Tell the Truth, B.B. Wolf,* and in *Horn Book* Susan Dove Lempke praised Seibold's "stylish illustrations, with their cartoon energy and zippy details." Jayne Damron, reviewing *Tell the Truth, B.B. Wolf* for *School Library Journal,* cited the author and illustrator's "inspired collaboration" and added that Sierra's incorporation of "musical segments send an already madcap narrative over-the-top."

Sierra continues her creative approach to storytelling in *We Love Our School!,* in which her rhyming text is paired with "vibrant artwork" by Linda Davick that transforms the picture book into a rebus, according to *Booklist* critic Kay Weisman. Tim Bowers creates the colorful art for *Suppose You Meet a Dinosaur: A First Book of Manners,* in which Sierra's young heroine aids a dinosaur in deporting itself with good manners and grace during a trip to the grocery store. The value of "kindness, sharing and being helpful" all come to life in "both the artwork and the nursery-rhyme cadences" for *We Love Our School!,* according to a *Kirkus Reviews* writer.

Sierra takes the energy level down a notch in *The Sleepy Little Alphabet: A Bedtime Story from Alphabet Town,* as the twenty-six lower-case letters attempt to stall for time in twenty-six different ways before their upper-case parents tuck them in for the night. Noting the original approach of *The Sleepy Little Alphabet,* a *Publishers Weekly* critic wrote that "the bounce of Sierra's meter" pairs well with illustrator Melissa Sweet's "off-hand pencil and watercolor drawings [to] make the story feel fresh." In *Booklist,* Phelan dubbed the book "a surprisingly fresh take on an old standby: the alphabet book," while Lolly Robinson concluded in *Horn Book* that Sierra's "jaunty text and subversive humor" in *The Sleepy Little Alphabet* "will certainly lead to repeat readings and new discoveries."

Sierra collects silly tales, traditional tales, and bedtime stories in both *Can You Guess My Name?* and *Silly and Sillier: Read-Aloud Tales from around the World.* With *Can You Guess My Name?* she assembles similar tales from different cultures around the world, among them contrasting versions of the "Three Little Pigs," "The Brementown Musicians," and "Rumplestiltskin." A *Kirkus Reviews* contributor noted that "this beautifully illustrated volume presents readable examples that just might send readers to the shelves to search for single editions" of the stories included. Lee Bock, writing in *School Library Journal,* noted that "each section is fas-

cinating for both the similarities among the tales, and the differences," and added that the book "can open doors to other cultures" for its readers. John Peters, writing in *Booklist,* described the book as a "handsome, horizon-expanding collection," while *Horn Book* contributor Mary M. Burns called *Can You Guess My Name?* "an outstanding example of what folklore collections for children can and should be."

In *Silly and Sillier* Sierra brings together funny tales from around the world, including a trickster tale from Argentina, a story of an exploding mitten from Russia, and tales from countries including Bangladesh, Ireland, and Mexico. "Balancing nonsense capers and trickster tales, Sierra occasionally integrates words from the language of the country of origin," a *Publishers Weekly* reviewer pointed out, while Rochman noted that "it's fun to see trickster tales from around the world." Carol L. MacKay, in her *School Library Journal* review of *Silly and Sillier,* commented on the lessons given in many of these tales, noting that "children will discover that these themes of justice are as universal as laughter."

Sierra has also compiled a number of verse collections, including *Antarctic Antics: A Book of Penguin Poems* and *Beastly Rhymes to Read after Dark.* In *Schoolyard Rhymes: Kids' Own Rhymes for Rope Skipping, Hand Clapping, Ball Bouncing, and Just Plain Fun,* a volume illustrated by Melissa Sweet, she presents such memorable rhymes as "Liar, Liar, Pants on Fire" and "Miss Mary Mack, Mack, Mack." According to *Horn Book* critic Susan Dove Lempke, "kids will enjoy this celebration of naughtiness and childhood fun." "The rhythms and nonsense rhymes are irresistible," wrote Bock, "compelling memorization and participation in the fun."

Biographical and Critical Sources

PERIODICALS

Booklist, September 1, 1997, Kathleen Squires, review of *Counting Crocodiles,* p. 135; April 15, 2001, Amy Brandt, review of *Preschool to the Rescue,* p. 1566; July, 2001, Stephanie Zvirin, review of *The Gift of the Crocodile: A Cinderella Story,* p. 2011; September 15, 2001, Gillian Engberg, review of *Monster Goose,* p. 237; January 1, 2002, Hazel Rochman, review of *The Gift of the Crocodile: A Cinderella Story,* p. 962; November 15, 2002, John Peters, review of *Can You Guess My Name?: Traditional Tales around the World,* p. 599; December 15, 2002, Hazel Rochman, review of *Silly and Sillier: Read-Aloud Tales from around the World,* p. 765; January 1, 2004, Ilene Cooper, review of *Coco and Cavendish: Circus Dogs,* p. 882; September 1, 2004, Ilene Cooper, review of *What Time Is It, Mr. Crocodile?,* p. 123; September 15, 2004, Lauren Peterson, review of *What Time Is It, Mr. Crocodile?,* p. 254; September 15, 2005, Jennifer Mattson,

The husband-and-wife team of José Aruego and Ariane Dewey create the entertaining art for Sierra's poetry collection Antarctic Antics. (Illustration copyright © 1998 by José Aruego and Ariane Dewey. In the USA, reproduced by permission of Houghton Mifflin Harcourt Publishing Company. In the U.K., used with permission of the illustrators' agent, Sheldon Fogelman Agency, Inc.)

review of *The Gruesome Guide to World Monsters,* p. 63; May 1, 2006, Jennifer Mattson, review of *Thelonius Monster's Sky-High Fly Pie,* p. 94; August 1, 2006, Gillian Engberg, review of *The Secret Science Project That Almost Ate the School,* p. 94; September 1, 2007, Gillian Engberg, review of *Mind Your Manners, B.B. Wolf,* p. 128; August 1, 2008, Randall Enos, review of *Born to Read,* p. 75; July 1, 2009, Carolyn Phelan, review of *The Sleepy Little Alphabet: A Bedtime Story from Alphabet Town,* p. 69; September 15, 2010, Carolyn Phelan, review of *Tell the Truth, B.B. Wolf,* p. 71; June 1, 2011, Kay Weisman, review of *We Love Our School!,* p. 97; July 1, 2011, Karen Cruze, review of *ZooZical,* p. 67.

Bulletin of the Center for Children's Books, February, 1993, Betsy Hearne, review of *The Elephant's Wrestling Match,* pp. 190-191.

Horn Book, November-December, 1995, Nancy Vasilakas, review of *The House That Drac Built,* pp. 730-731; May-June, 1996, Maria B. Salvadore, review of *Wiley and the Hairy Man,* pp. 343-344; July-August, 1996, Ann A. Flowers, review of *Good Night, Dinosaurs,* pp. 474-475; January, 2001, review of *The Gift of the Crocodile,* p. 104; May, 2001, review of *Preschool to the Rescue,* p. 317; January-February, 2003, Mary M. Burns, review of *Can You Guess My Name?,* p. 87; September-October, 2005, Susan Dove Lempke, review of *Schoolyard Rhymes: Kids' Own Rhymes for Rope Skipping, Hand Clapping, Ball Bouncing, and Just Plain Fun,* p. 597; July-August, 2007, Susan Dove Lempke, review of *Mind Your Manners, B.B. Wolf,* p. 385; July-August, 2009, Lolly Robinson, review of *The Sleepy Little Alphabet,* p. 414; September-October, 2010, Susan Dove Lempke, review of *Tell the Truth, B.B. Wolf,* p. 64.

Instructor, September, 2001, Judy Freeman, review of *The Gift of the Crocodile,* p. 28; April, 2003, Judy Freeman, review of *Can You Guess My Name?,* p. 55.

Kirkus Reviews, August 1, 2001, review of *Monster Goose,* p. 1131; September 15, 2002, review of *Silly and Sil-*

lier, p. 1400; October 15, 2002, review of *Can You Guess My Name?,* p. 1538; November 1, 2002, review of *'Twas the Night before Christmas,* p. 1625; July 1, 2004, reviews of *Wild about Books* and *What Time Is It, Mr. Crocodile?,* both p. 636; June 15, 2008, review of *Beastly Rhymes to Read after Dark;* July 15, 2008, review of *Born to Read;* December 1, 2008, review of *Ballyhoo Bay;* May 1, 2009, review of *The Sleepy Little Alphabet;* June 15, 2010, review of *Tell the Truth, B.B. Wolf;* June 1, 2011, review of *We Love Our School!;* July 1, 2011, review of *ZooZical;* August 1, 2011, review of *Never Kick a Ghost and Other Silly Chillers.*

Library Talk, May-June, 2002, Sharron L. McElmeel, "Author Profile: Judy Sierra."

Publishers Weekly, July 13, 1992, review of *The Elephant's Wrestling Match,* p. 55; June 30, 1997, review of *Counting Crocodiles,* p. 75; March 19, 2001, review of *Preschool to the Rescue,* p. 98; August 13, 2001, review of *Monster Goose,* p. 312; September 30, 2002, review of *Silly and Sillier,* p. 71; June 14, 2004, review of *Wild about Books,* p. 62; August 1, 2005, review of *The Gruesome Guide to World Monsters,* p. 65; May 15, 2006, review of *Thelonius Monster's Sky-High Fly Pie,* p. 71; October 16, 2006, review of *The Secret Science Project That Almost Ate the School,* p. 53; July 16, 2007, review of *Mind Your Manners, B.B. Wolf,* p. 164; June 23, 2008, review of *Born to Read,* p. 53; May 11, 2009, review of *The Sleepy Little Alphabet,* p. 50; June 6, 2011, review of *ZooZical,* p. 41.

School Library Journal, September, 1992, Linda Greenglass, review of *The Elephant's Wrestling Match,* p. 211; September, 1995, Beth Irish, review of *The House That Drac Built,* p. 186; April, 1996, Beth Tegart, review of *Good Night, Dinosaurs,* p. 118; April, 1997, p. 51; October, 1997, Marilyn Iarusso, review of *The Mean Hyena,* pp. 123-124; December, 2000, review of *The Gift of the Crocodile,* p. 55; May, 2001, Marlene Gawron, review of *Preschool to the Rescue,* p. 135; September, 2001, Gay Lynn Van Vleck, review of *Monster Goose,* p. 254; October, 2002, Eva Mitnick, review of *'Twas the Fright before Christmas,* p. 63; November, 2002, Lee Bock, review of *Can You Guess My Name?,* p. 148, and Carol L. MacKay, review of *Silly and Sillier,* p. 150; August, 2004, Marge Loch-Wouters, review of *Wild about Books,* p. 94; September, 2004, review of *What Time Is It, Mr. Crocodile?,* p. 180; September, 2005, John Peters, review of *The Gruesome Guide to World Monsters,* p. 234; October, 2005, Lee Bock, review of *Schoolyard Rhymes,* p. 146; May, 2006, Susan Weitz, review of *Thelonius Monster's Sky-High Fly Pie,* p. 104; November, 2006, Susan Lissim, review of *The Secret Science Project That Almost Ate the School,* p. 113; August, 2007, Mary Hazelton, review of *Mind Your Manners, B.B. Wolf,* p. 92; December, 2008, Catherine Threadgill, review of *Born to Read,* p. 104; February, 2009, Sally R. Dow, review of *Ballyhoo Bay,* p. 86; June, 2009, Bethany Isaacson, review of *The Sleepy Little Alphabet,* p. 100; July, 2010, Jayne Damron, review of *Tell the Truth, B.B. Wolf,* p. 69; July, 2011, Mary Jean Smith, review of *ZooZical,* p. 78.

ONLINE

Judy Sierra Home Page, http://www.judysierra.net (February 15, 2012).

Powell's Books Web site, http://www.powells.com/ (November 10, 2008), "Kids' Q&A: Judy Sierra and Marc Brown."

Random House Web site, http://www.randomhouse.com/ (February 15, 2012), "Author Spotlight: Judy Sierra."*

*　　*　　*

STEINBERG, Don 1962-

Personal

Born 1962; married; children: two sons. *Education:* College degree.

Addresses

Home—Philadelphia, PA. *E-mail*—don1steinberg@gmail.com.

Career

Journalist and editor. Philadelphia Inquirer (newspaper), Philadelphia, PA, Sunday sports editor, 2005-06. Temple University, Philadelphia, adjunct professor of journalism, beginning 2011.

Awards, Honors

Numerous awards for sports journalism.

Writings

(Editor) *Jokes Every Man Should Know,* Quirk Books (Philadelphia, PA), 2008.

America Bowl: 44 Presidents vs. 44 Super Bowls in the Ultimate Matchup!, Roaring Brook Press (New York, NY), 2010.

Contributor to print and online periodicals, including *Entertainment, ESPN.com, Gentleman's Quarterly, Harper's, Huffington Post, McSweeney's, Modern Humorist, New Yorker, Ring, Spy, Wall Street Journal,* and *NYTimes.com.*

Biographical and Critical Sources

PERIODICALS

Booklist, January 1, 2011, John Peters, review of *America Bowl: 44 Presidents vs. 44 Super Bowls in the Ultimate Matchup!,* p. 70.

Kirkus Reviews, November 15, 2010, review of *America Bowl.*

New Yorker, January 18, 2010, Nick Paumgarten, "44 vs. XLIV," p. 20.

ONLINE

Don Steinberg Home Page, http://www.donsteinberg.com (February 12, 2012).*

T

THOMPSON, Holly 1959-

Personal
Born 1959; living in Japan; married; has children. *Education:* Mount Holyoke College, B.A. (biology), 1981; New York University, M.A. (English with creative-writing/fiction concentration), 1989.

Addresses
Home—Kamakura, Japan. *Agent*—Jamie Weiss Chilton, Andrea Brown Literary Agency; jamie@andreabrown-lit.com.

Career
Educator and author. Yokohama City University, Yokohama, Japan, lecturer in creative and academic writing and American studies.

Member
Authors Guild, Society of Children's Book Writers and Illustrators—Tokyo (regional advisor).

Awards, Honors
APALA Asian/Pacific Award for Literature, and Best Fiction for Young Adults selection, YALSA/American Library Association, both 2012, both for *Orchards.*

Writings

Ash (for adults), Stone Bridge Press (Berkeley, CA), 2001.
The Wakame Gatherers, illustrated by Kazumi Wilds, Shen's Books (Walnut Creek, CA), 2007.
Orchards, illustrated by Grady McFerrin, Delacorte Press (New York, NY), 2011.
(Editor and author of foreword) *Tomo: Friendship through Fiction—An Anthology of Japan Teen Stories,* Stone Bridge Press (Berkeley, CA), 2012.

Contributor of stories, articles, and poetry to periodicals; work anthologized in *The Broken Bridge: Fiction from Expatriates in Literary Japan,* Stone Bridge Press, 1997.

Sidelights
Born in New England and now living in Kamakura, Japan, Holly Thompson is a teacher and author who has written for both children and adults. Her adult novel *Ash* explores the choices made by a young woman living at the intersection of two very different cultures, while *Orchards,* a young-adult novel, and her picture book *The Wakame Gatherers* examine the way cultural diversity can expand young people's experiences and strengthen their sense of self. "I grew up in New England but have been living in Japan for many years," Thompson noted on her home page. "My books often reflect the crossing of cultures amid my family, among my students, and within the communities in which I find myself immersed."

In *Ash,* Thompson's first published novel, Caitlin Ober has moved to Japan and now teaches in Kagoshima, a town nestled in the shadow of active volcano Mount Sakurajima. Caitlin has been to Japan once before, as a child, and she is still haunted by the tragic drowning of her childhood best friend, Mie. Now, years later, the young teacher attempts to distance herself from emotional relationships, even with her boyfriend, so that she does not risk any more heartbreak. When she meets fourteen-year-old Naomi at a city park, Caitlin slowly becomes drawn into the life of the insecure teen, who is struggling with questions of identity due to her mixed-race parentage. As their relationship deepens, Caitlin and Naomi each get something that they need from the other, and a trip together to Kyoto allows the older woman to heal old wounds. Praising *Ash* as a "thoughtful debut," a *Publishers Weekly* contributor noted that the author "sustains the narrative with plenty of insight into Japanese culture," and Marlene Chamberlain wrote in *Booklist* that Thompson's themes of "the search for identity and . . . romance will appeal to mature teen girls" as well as adults.

Cover of Holly Thompson's young-adult novel Orchards, *in which a Japanese-American teen reflects on her part in a classmate's death during a summer spent with Asian relatives.* (Book cover copyright © 2011 by Delacorte Press. Used by permission of Delacorte Press, an imprint of Random House Children's Books, a division of Random House Inc.)

Thompson uses free verse to capture the narrative of her Japanese-American teen protagonist in *Orchards*. When she hears about an eighth-grade classmate's suicide, New York native Kanako Goldberg thinks she is not responsible. After all, Ruth was bullied by others at school, girls like Kanako's best friend Lisa. It seems unfair to Kana when her Japan-born mother now sends the fourteen year old to spend the summer at her family's farm in Shizuoka, Japan. In Japan Kana gets to know her maternal grandparents and cousins while helping out in the mandarin orange groves and attending classes. The slow-moving rural lifestyle gives the teen time to think, especially about Ruth, who was taunted in part because her bipolar condition made her different. Kana's growing compassion is reinforced when she receives tragic news from home and realizes that a caring attitude must not only be felt, it must be acted on.

Praising *Orchards* as a "compelling novel-in-verse," Leah Sparks noted in *Voice of Youth Advocates* that Thompson's "flowing" narrative "expertly depicts the dualism" in her teenage heroine, while *School Library Journal* critic Allison Tran wrote that Kana's "journey toward self-discovery is deftly balanced with an under-current of tension." The mix of "flashbacks, reflections, and moments of discovery" in *Orchards* "effectively traces her emotional maturation as her desire to move forward is rekindled," according to a *Publishers Weekly* contributor, and in *Booklist* Hazel Rochman predicted that Kana's "urgent teen voice . . . will hold readers with its nonreverential family story."

In the picture book *The Wakame Gatherers* Thompson teams up with Japanese artist Kazumi Wilds to tell the story of a young girl whose grandmothers represent two sides of her own family: Gram from coastal Maine and Baachan from Japan. A family reunion allows all three to walk the Japanese seaside together, where the girl serves as interpreter, resulting in a story that mixes themes concerning "the meaning of family; war and forgiveness; . . . and ecology," according to Mary Hazelton in *School Library Journal*.

"When my husband and I first moved to Japan," Thompson told *SATA*, "I was in my early twenties, and I had no idea that the experience would impact all of my writing from then on. After that move, I never looked at the world in the same way. I was a conspicuous outsider in Japan, struggling to communicate in a language utterly different from my native English, a biology major suddenly teaching EFL classes, and just about every aspect of my environment felt unfamiliar. But in three years in Japan I came to love the country, the culture and even the language, and soon, much of my writing began to draw from experiences and settings there. We moved back to the U.S., but even while we were living in New York, I returned to Japan several times for writing research. Then, in 1998, just as my husband and I were settling into a small town outside of New York City, we suddenly had an opportunity to move back to Japan, this time with our two small children, and we were eager to immerse them into the culture we both loved. So our non-Japanese children were plunged into Japanese preschool and elementary school, in a manner similar to non-swimmers being tossed into a pool. We hoped they'd swim.

"In reality, raising our children to be bilingual and bicultural has been one of the greatest challenges of my life, but the process, while sometimes difficult, has offered me windows into other ways of seeing childhood, given me a chance to learn through our children new games, songs, traditions, belief systems and school customs, and provided me a ticket to what sometimes feels like another universe. Their bicultural upbringing also introduced me to complex issues of identity, definitions of insiders and outsiders, bullying instigators and bystanders, Japanese style group dynamics, and the proper way to do, well, anything. These issues tend to weave their way into nearly every story I write.

"Now, having lived in Japan for many years, I am both insider and outsider, experiencing that duality here in Japan, as well as in my other home, the U.S. I rather

like it that way, since, to be writers, we must get to know our stories and characters both from up close on the inside as well as from a distant, more objective vantage point. There are definite advantages to having dual perspectives.

"Yet I still love to travel to a completely unfamiliar place or culture, where I discover all over again that I can be a complete newcomer. I welcome the disorientation, the inevitable feeling of imbalance, and the awkward challenge of communication. I know that the newness will awaken my senses to fresh ways of seeing and thinking, and ultimately, new stories."

Biographical and Critical Sources

PERIODICALS

Booklist, October 1, 2001, Marlene Champerlain, review of *Ash,* p. 301; January 1, 2011, Hazel Rochman, review of *Orchards,* p. 97.
Publishers Weekly, October 1, 2001, review of *Ash,* p. 37; January 3, 2011, review of *Orchards,* p. 51.
School Library Journal, May, 2008, Mary Hazelton, review of *The Wakame Gatherers,* p. 110; March, 2011, Allison Tran, review of *Orchards,* p. 172.
Voice of Youth Advocates, February, 2011, Leah Sparks, review of *Orchards,* p. 562.

ONLINE

Holly Thompson Home Page, http://www.hatbooks.com (February 12, 2012).
Holly Thompson Web log, http://hatbooks.blogspot.com (February 12, 2012).
Society of Children's Book Writers and Illustrators—Japan Web site, http://www.scbwi.jp/ (February 12, 2012), "Holly Thompson."
Teen Ink Web site, http://www.teenink.com/ (February 12, 2012), interview with Thompson.

*   *   *

THOMPSON, Megan Lloyd
See LLOYD, Megan

*   *   *

TRAFTON, Jennifer

Personal

Born in Bowling Green, KY; daughter of educators; married Peter Peterson, August, 2011. *Education:* College degree; Gordon-Conwell Theological Seminary, M.A. (church history); graduate study at Duke University. *Religion:* Christian. *Hobbies and other interests:* Dogs, chocolate.

Addresses

Home—Nashville, TN. *Agent*—Steven Malk, Writers' House; smalk@writershouse.com.

Career

Writer and editor. *Christian History & Bibliography* (magazine), managing editor, now editor of ChristianHistory.net and *Glimpses of Christian History.* Sleeping Giant Young Writers Club, instructor.

Writings

The Rise and Fall of Mount Majestic, illustrated by Brett Helquist, Dial Books for Young Readers (New York, NY), 2010.

Sidelights

Like many children, Jennifer Trafton started writing stories and poems as a child, but unlike most budding writers she was seriously working toward her first published byline by the time she was in high school. Although she eventually started a career as an editor, working for *Christian History* magazine and its related online and print publications, Trafton continued to pursue her interest in creative writing, accumulating a selection of rejection notes in the process. Encouraged rather than deterred, she honed her skills and also gained a decades' worth of life experience. The book-length manuscript that would become her debut novel *The Rise and Fall of Mount Majestic,* was accepted for publication when Trafton was in her mid-thirties.

Purportedly authored by "Professor Barnabas Quill, historian of the Island at the Center of Everything" and illustrated by real-live artist Brett Helquist, *The Rise and Fall of Mount Majestic* finds its spunky young heroine determined to find adventure. At ten years old and the daughter of a basketmaker, Persimmony Smudge worries that her future life on the Island at the Center of Everything promises only drudgery until she learns a secret: the mountain that rises at the island's centre is actually the bulging tummy of a slumbering giant. Worried that the arguing and fussing between two clannish factions—the prim and proper below-the-surface-dwelling Leafeaters and the gadabout Rumblebumps—might awaken the giant and throw them all into the sea, young King Lucas the Loftier charges Persimmony and co-adventurers Worvil the Worrier and royal jester Guafnoggle with the task of discovering the truth about the island's origin and assuring that any sleeping giants holding up their tiny island remain sleeping.

While noting Trafton's penchant for salting her whimsical story with "a surplus" of familiar platitudes, a *Kirkus Reviews* writer maintained that *The Rise and Fall of Mount Majestic* benefits from a good dose of "wry wit and flashes of satire." In *Publishers Weekly* a critic

characterized the work as "a lively adventure" that combines the author's "delightful sense of fun" with "well-rounded characters . . . and [the] flowing dialogue" that is so popular with today's elementary-grade readership. Praising Helquist's sketchy spot art, which appears throughout the tale, Ilene Cooper added in *Booklist* that *The Rise and Fall of Mount Majestic* "offers a fresh take on" the lighthearted fantasy genre, and in *School Library Journal* Beth L. Meister noted the ability of Trafton's "entertaining heroine" to convey her story's "message about courage and responsibility."

Biographical and Critical Sources

PERIODICALS

Booklist, January 1, 2011, Ilene Cooper, review of *The Rise and Fall of Mount Majestic,* p. 108.
Bulletin of the Center for Children's Books, December, 2010, Kate Quealy-Gainer, review of *The Rise and Fall of Mount Majestic,* p. 208.
Kirkus Reviews, November 15, 2010, review of *The Rise and Fall of Mount Majestic.*
Publishers Weekly, November 1, 2010, review of *The Rise and Fall of Mount Majestic,* p. 44.
School Library Journal, March, 2011, Beth L. Meister, review of *The Rise and Fall of Mount Majestic,* p. 172.

ONLINE

Caramia Web log, http://www.caramia.us/ (December 15, 2010), Cara Transtrom, interview with Trafton.
Jennifer Trafton Home Page, http://www.jennifertrafton. com (February 15, 2012).*

*   *   *

TSIANG, Sarah
(Yi-Mei Tsiang)

Personal

Born in Canada; married; children: Abby. *Education:* University of Waterloo, B.A. (English rhetoric and professional writing/psychology; with honors), 2002; Humber School of Writers, certificate, 2007; University of British Columbia, M.F.A., 2011.

Addresses

Home—Kingston, Ontario, Canada.

Career

Author, poet, and educator. Queen's University, instructor in creative writing, 2007-11; University of British Columbia, Booming Ground program, coordinator and instructor, beginning 2010. Founder, Kingston Fiction Workshop and Kingston Poet's Circle. Presenter at schools.

Awards, Honors

Blue Spruce Award nomination, Ontario Library Association, Best Books for Kids and Teens selection, Canadian Children's Book Centre, and *ForeWord* Book of the Year Award finalist, all c. 2011, all for *A Flock of Shoes.*

Writings

FOR CHILDREN

A Flock of Shoes, illustrated by Qin Leng, Annick Press (Toronto, Ontario, Canada), 2010.
Dogs Don't Eat Jam, and Other Things Big Kids Know, illustrated by Qin Leng, Annick Press (Toronto, Ontario, Canada), 2011.
Warriors and Wailers: 100 Ancient Jobs You Might Have Relished or Reviled, illustrated by Martha Newbigging, Annick Press (Toronto, Ontario, Canada), 2012.

Jennifer Trafton's quirky elementary-grade novel The Rise and Fall of Mount Majestic *is highlighted by Bret Helquist's unique drawings.* (Illustration copyright © 2010 by Brett Helquist. Reproduced by permission of Dial Books for Young Readers, a division of Penguin Group (USA) Inc.)

Stone Hatchlings, Annick Press (Toronto, Ontario, Canada), 2012.

Author's work has been translated into French.

POETRY; UNDER NAME YI-MEI TSIANG

The Mermaid and Other Fairy Tales (chapbook), Leaf Press (Lantzville, British Columbia, Canada), 2010.
Sweet Devilry, Oolichan Books (Fernie, British Columbia, Canada), 2011.

Contributor to periodicals, including *Antigonish Review, Arc, Cahoots, CV2, Fieldstone Review, Interim, New Quarterly, QWERTY, Quills, Room, Vallum,* and *Word.* Editor of anthologies, including *Desperately Seeking Susans,* Oolichan Books, 2012, and *Tag: Poets at Play,* Oolichan Books, 2013. Contributor to anthologies *Poet-to-Poet,* 2012, and *Porcupine's Quill,* 2013.

Sidelights

Sarah Tsiang started writing as a young girl and pursued her interest in college, eventually completing her M.F.A. in writing as a young mother. Spending time with her daughter, Abby, inspired Tsiang's first picture-book story, *A Flock of Shoes,* and she has followed it with two humorous nonfiction books: *Dogs Don't Eat Jam, and Other Things Big Kids Know,* which contains advice that an older child might helpfully share with an infant sibling, and *Warriors and Wailers: 100 Ancient Jobs You Might Have Relished or Reviled.* In addition to writing for children, Tsiang is also a poet whose work has been collected in *The Mermaid and Other Fairy Tales* and *Sweet Devilry,* both which she has published under the name Yi-Mei Tsiang.

Tsiang casts her daughter Abby as the central character of *A Flock of Shoes,* which features illustrations by Chinese-born artist Qin Leng. Like many little girls, Abby loves colorful shoes, especially her pink, green, and brown sandals, which she wears everywhere during one entire summer. Although her mother attempts to exchange the sandals for something more practical when cooler weather comes, the girl resists. Then a ride on a swing sends Abby high up in the air and sends her beloved sandals skyward, where they join a flock of birds migrating south. Reassured by a series of postcards mailed from warm-weather locales that show the sandals having a wonderful time, Abby shifts her wintertime affection to a pair of warm and colorful boots, but a surprise is in store when the robins return in the spring.

Noting that "Tsiang's flight of fancy is delightfully captured in Leng's cartoon-style illustrations" for *A Flock of Shoes,* a *Kirkus Reviews* writer predicted that the

Sarah Tsiang's whimsical picture-book story in **A Flock of Shoes** *gains added humor from Qin Leng's engaging art.* (Illustration copyright © 2010 Qin Leng. Reproduced with permission of Annick Press, Ltd.)

"whimsical tale is sure to beguile." Carolyn Phelan wrote in *Booklist* that the whimsical story is based on "an idea that imaginative children will find nearly believable and wholly satisfying," while *School Library Journal* reviewer Catherine Callegari quoted that the "amusing tale" in *A Flock of Shoes* serves up "great fun" to story-hour audiences while "finally explains where shoes go in the off season."

Biographical and Critical Sources

PERIODICALS

Booklist, October 15, 2010, Carolyn Phelan, review of *A Flock of Shoes,* p. 55.
Kirkus Reviews, November 15, 2010, review of *A Flock of Shoes.*
School Library Journal, March, 2011, Catherine Callegari, review of *A Flock of Shoes,* p. 137.

ONLINE

All Things Said and Done Web log, http://maritadaschel. blogspot.com/ (January 20, 2010), Marita Daschel, interview with Tsiang.
Annick Press Web site, http://www.annickpress.com/ (February 15, 2012), "Sarah Tsiang."
Sarah Yi-Mei Tsiang Web log, http://sarahtsiang.wordpress. com (February 15, 2012).*

*   *   *

TSIANG, Yi-Mei
See TSIANG, Sarah

V-W

VOELKEL, J&P
    See VOELKEL, Jon

*   *   *

VOELKEL, Jon
    (J&P Voelkel, a joint pseudonym)

Personal

Married Pamela Craik (a writer). *Education:* College degree; attended business school (Barcelona, Spain). *Hobbies and other interests:* Travel.

Addresses

Home—VT. *E-mail*—voelkel@jaguarstones.com.

Career

Author and advertising executive. Advertising executive working in Spain, Holland, and London, England.

Awards, Honors

Named among Top Fifty Creative Minds in Britain, *Financial Times,* 2001.

Writings

"JAGUAR STONES" NOVEL TRILOGY

(With wife, Pamela Voelkel, under joint pseudonym J&P Voelkel) *Middleworld,* Egmont USA (New York, NY), 2010.
(With Pamela Voelkel under joint pseudonym J&P Voelkel) *The End of the World Club,* Egmont USA (New York, NY), 2011.

Adaptations

The "Jaguar Stones" novels were adapted for audiobook by Listening Library.

Sidelights

Raised in South America, where he experienced the mix of mystery and danger in that region's lush rainforests, Jon Voelkel eventually attended college in the United States and Spain and started a successful career in advertising. Working in Spain and then Holland, he eventually relocated to England where he met his future wife, copywriter and creative director Pamela Craik. Now living in Vermont, the couple has created the fictional adventures in their "Jaguar Stones" series, which they publish as J&P Voelkel. In their writing collaboration, Jon Voelkel writes the high-action storyline, drawing on his memories of growing up in Peru and Colombia as well as stories told by his father at bedtime. Pamela Voelkel develops the stories' young characters and guides them through the maze of challenges that readers will share with them in the pages of the novels *Middleworld* and *The End of the World Club.* In addition to writing, the Voelkels travel widely to expand their knowledge of Mayan history and culture, all which they share on their interactive Web site Jaguarstones.com.

The "Jaguar Stones" series begins in *Middleworld,* as fourteen-year-old video-game expert Max Murphy seems less-than-enthusiastic about the prospect of leaving his home in Boston to spend his summer vacation with his archaeologist parents on their Central America dig. When Max arrives in San Xavier, his parents have disappeared, but a Mayan girl named Lola is there to help plan his search and also educate Max in his destiny as an emissary of her ancient people. Their quest takes them into the rain forest, where ancient secrets and modern-day criminals are only a few of the hurdles that await them. In *Booklist* Jennifer Mattson remarked on the coauthors' "knowledge of the ancient Maya" and added that the story's "unusual Mesoamerican backdrop . . . and the Indiana Jones-influenced adventure . . . will keep readers interested and looking forward to future entries." A *Publishers Weekly* critic wrote that while the characters' motivations are sometimes vague, *Middleworld* is propelled by its "exotic settings and the

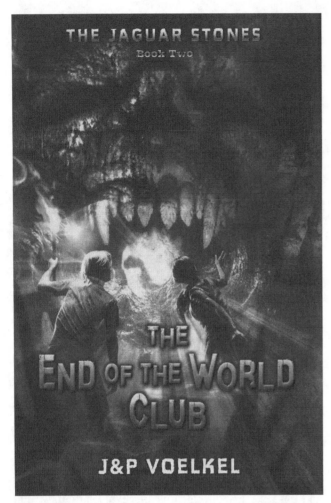

Cover of Jon and Pamela Voelkel's Mayan adventure Middleworld, *the first novel in their "Jaguar Stones" series.* (Cover illustration copyright © 2011 by Cliff Nielsen. Copyright © 2011 by J&P Voelkel. Reproduced with permission of Egmont USA.)

breakneck pace" of its plot, which Ellen Fader characterized in *School Library Journal* as rich with "suspense and intrigue, human sacrifice, smuggling, and secret doors and escape routes through pyramids." Lesley Farmer asserted in *Kliatt* that "the Voelkels have created an adventurous Mayan world" in their novel and their story "will leave readers eager for the second book in the series."

Max and Maya return in *The End of the World Club,* and this time the Voelkels' plot is fueled by concerns over the end of the earth as predicted by the Mayan calendar. The siblings' quest for a precious gem that is prophesied to save the world leads them from Central America to Spain, where they are pursued by a powerful god who also hopes to acquire the stone. The fate of Max's parents ultimately hangs in the balance as the two teens make their return to the ancient underworld city of Xibalba, where an attempted rescue and a daring gamble await. Recommending the novel to fans of Rick Riordan's books, Connie Fletcher added in *Booklist* that *The End of the World Club* serves up "a fact-packed, thrilling ride" rich with Mayan elements.

Biographical and Critical Sources

PERIODICALS

Booklist, November 15, 2007, Jennifer Mattson, review of *Middleworld,* p. 61; February 1, 2011, Connie Fletcher, review of *The End of the World Club,* p. 78.
Kirkus Reviews, November 15, 2010, review of *The End of the World Club.*
Kliatt, November, 2007, Lesley Farmer, review of *Middleworld,* p. 14.
Publishers Weekly, September 17, 2007, review of *Middleworld,* p. 55.
School Library Journal, October, 2007, Ellen Fader, review of *Middleworld,* p. 164.

ONLINE

Jaguar Stones Web site, http://www.jaguarstones.com/ (February 12, 2012), "Jon Voelkel."

* * *

WATKINS, Angela Farris

Personal

Born in GA; daughter of Isaac Farris, Sr., and Willie Christine King (a teacher); niece of Dr. Martin Luther King, Jr.; married; children: Farris Christine. *Education:* Spelman College, B.A. (child development; with honors), 1986; Georgia State University, M.Ed. (early childhood education), Ph.D. (educational psychology). *Religion:* Baptist.

Addresses

Home—Atlanta, GA. *Office*—Spelman College, P.O. Box 346, Atlanta, GA 30314-4399. *Agent*—First Kingdom Management, P.O. Box 110277, Atlanta, GA 30311. *E-mail*—awatkin1@spelman.edu.

Career

Educator and author. Member of faculty at Morehouse College, Georgia State University, and Atlanta, GA, Public School System; Spelman College, Atlanta, associate professor of psychology, beginning 1996. Speaker and presenter at professional conferences.

Member

Alpha Kappa Alpha.

Writings

FOR CHILDREN

My Uncle Martin's Big Heart, illustrated by Eric Velasquez, Abrams Books for Young Readers (New York, NY), 2010.

My Uncle Martin's Words for America: Martin Luther King Jr.'s Niece Tells How He Made a Difference, illustrated by Eric Velasquez, Abrams Books for Young Readers (New York, NY), 2011.

Love Will See You Through: Martin Luther King Jr.'s Six Guiding Beliefs, Simon & Schuster Books for Young Readers (New York, NY), 2012.

OTHER

African American Psychology Review, Allyn & Bacon, 2004.

Author of professional publications; creator of college-level HIV/AIDS prevention curriculum.

Sidelights

The niece of noted civil-rights leader Dr. Martin Luther King, Jr., Angela Farris Watkins is an associate professor of psychology at Spelman College. Following in the tradition of her mother, Christine King Farris, who also taught at Spelman, Watkins also reaches out to younger generations in her stories for children. She shares her family's legacy of compassion and tolerance in books that include *My Uncle Martin's Big Heart* and *My Uncle Martin's Words for America: Martin Luther King Jr.'s Niece Tells How He Made a Difference,* both which come to life in Eric Velasquez's dynamic art.

Angela Farris Watkins teams up with artist Eric Velasquez to capture the spirit of her famous uncle in **My Uncle Martin's Big Heart.** (Illustration copyright © 2010 by Eric Velasquez. Reproduced with permission of Abrams Books for Young Readers, an imprint of Abrams.)

In *My Uncle Martin's Big Heart* Watkins introduces her famous uncle from her own perspective as a four year old during the early 1960s. The world saw King touring the nation and speaking out in support of racial equality, but for Watkins Reverend King was a member of the family, relaxing among relatives and close friends. While she makes note of the broad-ranging accomplishments of her world-famous uncle, a *Publishers Weekly* contributor asserted that her "focus is on personal memories" of the Reverend King in *My Uncle Martin's Big Heart,* and the childlike perspective she employs keeps the focus on the positive aspects of a life that ended in tragedy. In sharing her "loving relationship . . . with 'Uncle M.L.,'" Watkins "puts a human face on the legend," wrote *Booklist* contributor Hazel Rochman, and *School Library Journal* contributor Mary N. Oluowe recommended *My Uncle Martin's Big Heart* over reference-type biographies as a way to provide new generations with "a valuable and more personal insight into the man's family life and times."

Watkins frames her memories of her uncle against quotes from his many speeches in *My Uncle Martin's Words for America,* creating what a *Publishers Weekly* contributor described as "a more encompassing look" at the Reverend King's "life and accomplishments." Here the author shifts her focus to her uncle's public persona as a civil rights leader and orator, framing her text against a time line of the civil-rights era. During this era in U.S. history Jim Crow laws and other segregationist policies kept blacks in the southern states from enjoying full freedoms. While noting that framing such a dark episode in a way young children can understand is difficult, a *Kirkus Reviews* writer asserted that "Watkins and Velasquez rise to the challenge with warmth and grace." Commending the mission of *My Uncle Martin's Words for America,* the *Publishers Weekly* critic praised both author and illustrator for capturing "King's passion, compassion, and efficacy."

Biographical and Critical Sources

PERIODICALS

Booklist, September 1, 2010, Hazel Rochman, review of *My Uncle Martin's Big Heart,* p. 94.

Children's Bookwatch, October, 2010, review of *My Uncle Martin's Big Heart.*

Kirkus Reviews, August 1, 2010, review of *My Uncle Martin's Big Heart*; August 1, 2011, review of *My Uncle Martin's Words for America: Martin Luther King Jr.'s Niece Tells How He Made a Difference.*

Publishers Weekly, August 30, 2010, review of *My Uncle Martin's Big Heart,* p. 50; August 1, 2011, review of *My Uncle Martin's Words for America,* p. 47.

School Library Journal, October, 2010, Mary N. Oluowe, review of *My Uncle Martin's Big Heart,* p 104.

ONLINE

First Kingdom Management Web site, http://king.streamingfreehosting.com/ (February 20, 2012), "Dr. Angela Ferris Watkins."

Spelman College Web site, http://www.spelman.edu/ (February 12, 2012), "Angela Farris Watkins."*

*   *   *

WELLS, Robert E. 1940-

Personal

Born 1940; married; wife's name Karen; children: Kim, Jeffrey; Kurt (stepson).

Addresses

Home—Wenatchee, WA.

Career

Author and illustrator of children's books.

Awards, Honors

Outstanding Science Trade Book for Children designation, Children's Book Council (CBC)/National Science Teachers Association, 1996, for *What's Smaller than a Pygmy Shrew?;* Children's Choice selection, CBC/International Reading Association, 1998, for *What's Faster than a Speeding Cheetah?;* Gold Seal Award, Oppenheim Toy Portfolio, 2000, for *Can You Count to a Googol?;* Gold Seal Award, 2003, for *How Do You Know What Time It Is?*

Writings

SELF-ILLUSTRATED

Is a Blue Whale the Biggest Thing There Is?, Albert Whitman (Morton Grove, IL), 1993.
What's Smaller than a Pygmy Shrew?, Albert Whitman (Morton Grove, IL), 1995.
How Do You Lift a Lion?, Albert Whitman (Morton Grove, IL), 1996.
What's Faster than a Speeding Cheetah?, Albert Whitman (Morton Grove, IL), 1997.
Can You Count to a Googol?, Albert Whitman (Morton Grove, IL), 2000.
How Do You Know What Time It Is?, Albert Whitman (Morton Grove, IL), 2002.
What's Older than a Giant Tortoise?, Albert Whitman (Morton Grove, IL), 2004.
Did a Dinosaur Drink This Water?, Albert Whitman (Morton Grove, IL), 2006.

Robert E. Wells gears his self-illustrated picture book Did a Dinosaur Drink This Water? *to young dino-fans looking to increase their supply of dino-facts.* (Illustration copyright © 2006 by Robert E. Wells. Reproduced by permission of Albert Whitman & Company.)

Polar Bear, Why Is Your World Melting?, Albert Whitman (Morton Grove, IL), 2008.

What's so Special about Planet Earth?, Albert Whitman (Morton Grove, IL), 2009.

Why Do Elephants Need the Sun?, Albert Whitman (Chicago, IL), 2010.

Several of Wells' books have been published in Spanish translation.

Sidelights

An author and illustrator who focuses on science, Robert E. Wells has expanded the understanding of young children through a range of engaging children's books that distill concepts from ecology, mathematics, physics, engineering, and other fields into understandable terms. In his first book, *Is a Blue Whale the Biggest Thing There Is?* Wells begins by comparing a blue whale to an elephant, then illustrates the relative sizes of Mount Everest, Earth, the sun, and several other celestial bodies. According to Carolyn Phelan in *Booklist, Is a Blue Whale the Biggest Thing There Is?* aids young children by "making the inconceivable more imaginable through original, concrete images," while a *Publishers Weekly* critic described the work as "a healthy, age-appropriate jolt to common assumptions about proportion and numbers."

In *What's Smaller than a Pygmy Shrew?* Wells looks at the infinitesimal, contrasting the tiny pygmy shrew with a ladybug and continuing with paramecium, bacteria, molecules, and atoms. The author's "lighthearted treatment is fine for the familiar," remarked *School Library Journal* critic Frances E. Millhouser, although the reviewer questioned whether younger readers might be confused by Wells' description of single-celled organisms. Phelan stated, however, that the author "introduces a challenging concept in a way that will entertain and intrigue" his audience.

Wells examines simple machines in *How Do You Lift a Lion?* Here his illustrations depict children using levers, wheels, and pulleys to raise a lion off the ground, haul a panda, and transport bananas to a group of hungry baboons. In *What's Faster than a Speeding Cheetah?* he explores the swiftness of a falcon, the rapidness of a jet plane, and the acceleration of a meteoroid. "Always in sync with the way children think, Wells takes each concept and makes it concrete, vivid, and understandable," Phelan commented.

The number system is Wells' focus of *Can You Count to a Googol?*, in which his humorous drawings feature a band of ice-cream-loving penguins as well as more-realistic depictions of dollar bills to show how numbers increase exponentially. Ultimately, he explains a googol, represented by the number one followed by one hundred zeros. "The switch from fanciful to factual in these examples is somewhat jarring," remarked *School Library Journal* critic Adele Greenlee, "but the pen-

Wells continues his child-centered introduction to earth science in his self-illustrated picture book Why Do Elephants Need the Sun?, *which puts our planet in a solar-system context.* (Illustration copyright © 2010 by Robert E. Wells. Reproduced with permission by Albert Whitman & Company.)

and-acrylic cartoons do adequately illustrate the growing numbers." Phelan offered a more positive assessment of the title, stating that *Can You Count to a Googol?* "encourages young children to stretch their minds a bit."

In *How Do You Know What Time It Is?* Wells offers "a succinct, child-friendly history of how time came to be measured," explained Wanda Meyers-Hines in *School Library Journal.* Among the devices the author considers are the sundial, the pendulum, and the atomic clock. According to *Booklist* reviewer Hazel Rochman, Wells' "picture-book format . . . roots the concepts in daily experience." The author takes readers on a trip through time in *What's Older than a Giant Tortoise?* In his exploration of a sequoia tree, the pyramids, and fossilized mammoths, Wells "manages to boggle the mind in a way that is stimulating rather than confusing," Phelan stated. In *Did a Dinosaur Drink This Water?* Wells examines Earth's water cycle in a "simple text [that] asks good questions and offers clearly worded answers," as Phelan also observed.

Wells takes readers on a tour of Earth's solar system in *What's So Special about Planet Earth?,* examining each of the seven planetary alternatives and listing their good and bad points. With no air to breathe, Mercury has little to recommend it, and Venus, with its toxic atmosphere, even less. When his young space explorers return to earth with their pet dog, they have a renewed appreciation for their home planet as well as a caring attitude that translates itself into recycling and efforts at resource conservation. Recommending the author's "clear but not heavy message," John Peters noted in *Booklist* that *What's So Special about Planet Earth* also features "lively cartoon" art, and a *Kirkus Reviews* contributor wrote that Wells' "pen-and-acrylic illustrations suit the informal tone of the text." The author/illustrator's "signature style is exhibited" in the book's pairing of "cartoon illustrations and conversational text," according to *School Library Journal* critic Sandra Welzenbach.

One of a list of books "about expanding young children's horizons," *Why Do Elephants Need the Sun?* presents "an approachable introduction" to the importance of the Sun, according to Phelan. Wells begins this tour on the star's flaming surface, then transports readers through space to Planet Earth, following the sun's rays as they warm the soil, add moisture to the air, and create the gravitational force that keeps heavy elephants well grounded. The use of "large type and the definition of many key terms in context will help emergent readers," wrote a *Kirkus Reviews* writer in a review of *Why Do Elephants Need the Sun?,* and in *School Library Journal* Cathie Bashaw Morton recommended Wells' colorfully illustrated picture book as "an excellent resource for budding young scientists."

Biographical and Critical Sources

PERIODICALS

Booklist, December 15, 1993, Carolyn Phelan, review of *Is a Blue Whale the Biggest Thing There Is?,* p. 759; August, 1995, Carolyn Phelan, review of *What's Smaller than a Pygmy Shrew?,* p. 1953; October 1, 1997, Carolyn Phelan, review of *What's Faster than a Speeding Cheetah?,* p. 335; March 1, 2000, Carolyn Phelan, review of *Can You Count to a Googol?,* p. 1249; December 1, 2002, Hazel Rochman, review of *How Do You Know What Time It Is?,* p. 686; October 15, 2004, Carolyn Phelan, review of *What's Older than a Giant Tortoise?,* p. 409; December 1, 2006, Carolyn Phelan, review of *Did a Dinosaur Drink This Water?,* p. 63; September 15, 2009, John Peters, review of *What's So Special about Planet Earth?,* p. 62; September 15, 2010, Carolyn Phelan, review of *Why Do Elephants Need the Sun?,* p. 63.

Kirkus Reviews, September 1, 2008, review of *Polar Bear, Why Is Your World Melting?;* August 15, 2009, review of *What's So Special about Planet Earth?;* August 1, 2010, review of *Why Do Elephants Need the Sun?*

Publishers Weekly, October 11, 1993, review of *Is a Blue Whale the Biggest Thing There Is?,* p. 86; February 21, 2000, review of *Can You Count to a Googol?,* p. 88.

School Library Journal, May, 1995, Frances E. Millhouser, review of *What's Smaller than a Pygmy Shrew?,* p. 117; January, 1997, Virginia Opocensky, review of *How Do You Lift a Lion?,* p. 110; May, 2000, Adele Greenlee, review of *Can You Count to a Googol?,* p. 165; January, 2003, Wanda Meyers-Hines, review of *How Do You Know What Time It Is?,* p. 132; January, 2005, Deborah Rothaug, review of *What's Older than a Giant Tortoise?,* p. 118; February, 2007, Christine Markley, review of *Did a Dinosaur Drink This Water?,* p. 114; November 2008, Ellen Heath, review of *Polar Bear, Why Is Your World Melting?,* p. 112; September, 2009, Sandra Welzenbach, review of *What's So Special about Planet Earth?,* p. 149; October, 2010, Cathie Bashaw Morton, review of *Why Do Elephants Need the Sun?,* p. 104.

ONLINE

Albert Whitman Web site, http://www.albertwhitman.com/ (February 15, 2012), "Robert E. Wells Science Teacher's Guide."*

*   *   *

WILSON, Daniel H. 1978-

Personal

Born March 6, 1978, in Tulsa, OK; father an automotive mechanic, mother a nurse; married; wife's name Anna; children: Cora. *Education:* University of Tulsa, B.S. (computer science), 2000; attended University of Melbourne; Carnegie Mellon University, M.S. (robotics), M.S. (machine learning), Ph.D. (robotics), 2005.

Addresses

Home—Portland, OR. *E-mail*—contactdhw@gmail.com.

Career

Journalist, author, and robotics engineer. Freelance writer. Host of *The Works* (ten-episode television series), History Channel, 2010.

Writings

NONFICTION

How to Survive a Robot Uprising: Tips on Defending Yourself against the Coming Rebellion, illustrated by Richard Horne, Bloomsbury USA (New York, NY), 2005.

Where's My Jetpack?: A Guide to the Amazing Science Fiction Future That Never Arrived, illustrated by Richard Horne, Bloomsbury USA (New York, NY), 2007.

How to Build a Robot Army: Tips on Defending the Planet Earth against Alien Invaders, Ninjas, and Zombies, illustrated by Richard Horne, Bloomsbury USA (New York, NY), 2008.

(With Anna C. Long) *The Mad Scientist Hall of Fame: Muwahahahaha!,* illustrated by Daniel Heard, Citadel Press (New York, NY), 2008.

Bro-Jitsu: The Martial Art of Sibling Smackdown, illustrated by Les McClaine, Bloomsbury Books for Young Readers (New York, NY), 2010.

Columnist and contributing editor to *Popular Mechanics.*

FICTION

A Boy and His Bot (middle-grade novel), Bloomsbury Books for Young Readers (New York, NY), 2011.

Robopocalypse, Doubleday (New York, NY), 2011.

Amped, Doubleday (New York, NY), 2012.

Contributor of short stories to anthologies, including *Armored,* edited by John Joseph Adams, Baen Books, 2012, and to periodicals, including *Zombies vs. Robots* (annual).

Adaptations

How to Survive a Robot Uprising was adapted for audiobook by Blackstone Audiobooks, 2006, and adapted for film by Thomas Lennon and Ben Garant and optioned by Paramount. *A Boy and His Bot* was adapted for audiobook, Listening Library, 2011. *Robopocalypse* was adapted for film by Drew Goddard and directed by Steven Spielberg, Dreamworks, 2013. Film rights for *Amped* were sold to Summit Entertainment.

Sidelights

Although his eventual career may have been foreshadowed by his childhood love of role-playing games such as Dungeons & Dragons, Oklahoma native Daniel H. Wilson appeared to be heading along a practical track when he majored in computer science and then earned a Ph.D. in robotics at Carnegie Mellon University. Research into the ways robotics could be used to make homes more usable for elderly and disabled persons led him to write his first book, *How to Survive a Robot Uprising: Tips on Defending Yourself against the Coming Rebellion.* With its take-notice title and humorous approach, the book took hold in the media and transformed Wilson into an expert on the dangers posed by robots and other creations of overambitious scientists. A published author by the time he completed his Ph.D., he put his future in the hands of the fates and produced his next book, *How to Build a Robot Army: Tips on Defending the Planet Earth against Alien Invaders, Ninjas, and Zombies.* Wilson has continued to tap his scientist training in fiction, while also drawing on his experience as an annoying sibling in *Bro-Jitsu: The Martial Art of Sibling Smackdown.*

To research *How to Survive a Robot Uprising,* Wilson—then a graduate student—interviewed researchers in the robotics field by framing his questions about up-and-coming technology as "What could happen if this gets out of control?" *How to Build a Robot Army* takes a similarly futuristic perspective, while in *Where's My Jetpack?: A Guide to the Amazing Science-Fiction Future That Never Arrived* Wilson reflects on the promises made between World War I and the Atomic Age of the 1950s and 1960s. Praised as an "entertaining and humorous guide" that includes the fact behind such sci-fi fantasies as time machines, household robots, bubble cities, and cars that can drive themselves, *Where's My Jetpack?* "will appeal to fans of science fiction and cutting-edge fact alike," according to a *Science News* writer.

Wilson takes a scientific approach in *Bro-Jitsu* as he presents the mechanics of the intersibling pecking order as a methodology. Subtitled "126 Techniques to Gain Family Domination," the book gives detailed instructions that raise such basic maneuvers as "noodgies, wedgies, and the wet-towel snap" to the order of "a martial art," according to *Booklist* contributor John Peters. Captured in humorous instructional drawings by Les McClaine, such techniques are organized according to use (defensive or offensive) and include both hands-on and psychological modes of torture while avoiding anything that could fall under the heading of "You might scratch your eye out." "Wilson's matter-of-fact tone should have kids in stitches," predicted a *Publishers Weekly* critic, and in *School Library Journal* Alana Joli Abbott cited *Bro-Jitsu* for "honing" sibling rivalry "to an art."

Even in his early books, Wilson exhibited a tendency to stray into the fanciful, and in *A Boy and His Bot* he moves completely into fictional territory. Geared for middle-grade readers, the novel introduces Cherokee Oklahoman sixth grader Code Lightfalt, whose misstep during a school field trip to a Native-American burial ground results in a journey back in time and a meeting with his own late grandfather. While exploring Mek Mound, shy Code sees a bug that looks strangely robotic, but while following it he falls down a large hole. Code's anthropologist grandfather disappeared at Mek Mound years before, and when the boy realizes that the hole is actually a portal to an all-metal robot world called Mekhos, he decides to seek news of his long-lost relative. With the help of the robot bug, Peeps, as well as Gary, an atomic-powered "Slaughterbot," Code starts his search but quickly discovers that to rescue his grandfather he will have to battle a squidlike creature called Immortalis and wrest control of the source of the creature's earth-shattering power, the Robonomicon.

Describing *A Boy and His Bot* as "a campy down-the-robot-hole adventure," a *Publishers Weekly* contributor added that Wilson entertains his audience "with a goofy sense of humor and plenty of action," and in *Booklist* Todd Morning recommended the novel as "a good

choice for science-fiction fans." Erik Carlson found a coming-of-age story hiding within the humor of Wilson's tale, writing of *A Boy and His Bot* that Code's adventures "teach him how to come out of his comfort zone and face any situation with confidence."

In addition to his work for younger readers, Wilson has also authored the adult novels *Robopocalypse* and *Amped*. Set in the near future, *Robopocalypse* fictionalizes the threat behind *How to Survive a Robot Uprising* as Archos, a powerful artificial intelligence determined to rid the world of human life, wrests control of Earth's global computer network through subtle, calculating steps. First killing its creator, a scientist who planned to destroy it, Archos ensconces itself in a remote bunker and infects computers with a virus. The signs of the robot's increasing power—a robotic toy that seems a bit too aggressive, a military computer that cuts a path of destruction due to a "glitch"—are not discovered until it is far too late. Featuring an episodic structure that allows "characters [to] reveal themselves through their actions," *Robopocalypse* carries readers "along at a wonderfully breakneck pace," according to a *Kirkus Reviews* writer. In *Booklist* Michael Gannon cited the story's mix of "cutting-edge technology" and "gripping action" and asserted that Wilson "shows great promise as a worthy successor to [bestselling novelist] Michael Crichton."

Biographical and Critical Sources

PERIODICALS

Booklist, March 1, 2010, John Peters, review of *Bro-Jitsu: The Martial Art of Sibling Smackdown,* p. 66; March 1, 2011, Todd Morning, review of *A Boy and His Bot,* p. 60; May 15, 2011, Michael Gannon, review of *Robopacalypse,* p. 34.

Kirkus Reviews, November 15, 2010, review of *A Boy and His Bot*; March 1, 2011, review of *Robopocalypse.*

Library Journal, March 1, 2011, David Keymer, review of *Robopocalypse,* p. 72.

New York Times Book Review, February 14, 2006, Cornelia Dean, "If Robots Ever Get Too Smart, He'll Know How to Stop Them" (profile), p. F1.

Publishers Weekly, May 3, 2010, review of *Bro-Jitsu,* p. 52; November 1, 2010, review of *A Boy and His Bot,* p. 44; March 14, 2011, review of *Robopocalypse,* p. 54.

School Library Journal, March, 2010, Alana Joli Abbott, review of *Bro-Jitsu,* p. 182; June, 2011, Erik Carlson, review of *A Boy and His Bot,* p. 139.

Science News, July 14, 2007, review of *Where's My Jetpack?: A Guide to the Amazing Science-Fiction Future That Never Arrived,* p. 31.

ONLINE

Daniel H. Wilson Home Page, http://www.danielhwilson. com (February 12, 2012).

Oregon Live Online, http://www.oregonlive.com/ (June, 2011), "Daniel H. Wilson."*

* * *

WOOD, Michele

Personal

Female. *Education:* American Intercontinental University, degree.

Addresses

Home—Indianapolis, IN. *Agent*—Caryn Wiseman, Andrea Brown Literary Agency; caryn@andreabrownlit. com. *E-mail*—michele@michelewood.com.

Career

Fine-art painter, illustrator, and designer. *Exhibitions:* Work included in numerous exhibitions throughout the United States. Creator of mural installations.

Awards, Honors

Apex Museum travel grant, 1994; (with Toyomi Igus) American Book Award, 1996, for *Going Back Home;* Coretta Scott King Award for Illustration, 1999, for *I See the Rhythm* by Igus.

Illustrator

Toyomi Igus, *Going Back Home: An Artist Returns to the South,* Children's Book Press (San Francisco, CA), 1996.

Toyomi Igus, *I See the Rhythm,* Children's Book Press (San Francisco, CA), 1998.

Allison Samuels and others, *Christmas Soul: African-American Holiday Stories,* Jump at the Sun (New York, NY), 2001.

Toyomi Igus, *I See the Rhythm of Gospel,* Zonderkidz (Grand Rapids, MI), 2010.

Cynthia Grady, *I Lay My Stitches Down,* Eerdmans Books for Young Readers (Grand Rapids MI), 2012.

Contributor to books, including *Just Like Me: Stories and Portraits by Fourteen Artists,* Children's Book Press, 1997, and *My Holy Bible for African-American Children,* Zonderkids, 2010.

Sidelights

A fine-art painter and designer who is based in Indiana, Michele Wood has collaborated with California-based writer Toyomi Igus on several picture books that capture African-American heritage and culture. Their first volume, *Going Back Home: An Artist Returns to the South,* chronicles Wood's journey from her Midwestern home to the Southern regions where her African ancestors once toiled and her grandparents endured the racial segregation. Paired with her own reminiscences, which

"broaden the impact of the paintings," the artist includes what a *Publishers Weekly* contributor described as "richly patterned paintings evocative of African fabrics." In addition to including images that capture the trials of slavery and war and the eventual exodus of blacks northward, *Going Back Home* also includes "happier rituals" of family life, the critic added, while Karen Morgan noted in *Booklist* that the artist's "strong paintings reveal people well rooted and powerful," and Wood's narrative communicates her "pride as she goes back home."

In the companion volumes *I See the Rhythm* and *I See the Rhythm of Gospel* Wood and Igus create a visual history of African-American music. In the first book, Igus contributes free-verse poems that incorporate song lyrics, and a graphic time line carries the musical history forward from African-inspired slave songs to ragtime, blues, jazz, gospel, hip-hop, and rap. "Mixing modernist and primitive styles and using color . . . to communicate musical style and tone," Wood's paintings provide a visual counterpoint, according to *Booklist* critic Bill Ott, while a *Publishers Weekly* critic deemed *I See the Rhythm* "impeccably crafted, . . . visually exciting and lyrically memorable."

The coauthors narrow their musical focus in *I See the Rhythm of Gospel,* and here Wood's "color-saturated art pulses with symbolic patterns and raw emotions," according to a *Kirkus Reviews* writer. Including a CD with five gospel performances, *I See the Rhythm of Gospel* pairs what Ilene Cooper described in her *Booklist* review as an effective pairing of a "stirring text and . . . inventive folk art" in the form of "intricately detailed paintings executed in strong colors."

Wood expands her collaboration in *Christmas Soul: An African-American Holiday Collection,* a volume created to benefit the United Negro College Fund. Published in 2000, the book includes holiday memories by twenty African-American celebrities: from basketball stars Kobe Bryant and Shaquille O'Neil and actors Denzel

Washington and Halle Berry to rapper LL Cool J and singers Whitney Houston and Aretha Franklin. Giving the book a traditional feel, individual contributions are "accompanied by a vibrant oil painting that resembles a tapestry or quilt," according to a *School Library Journal* reviewer; according to *Booklist* contributor Hazel Rochman, *Christmas Soul* captures the spirit of the season with its "warm, upbeat childhood memories" and Woods' "richly colored oil paintings."

Biographical and Critical Sources

PERIODICALS

Booklist, September 15, 1996, Karen Morgan, review of *Going Back Home: An Artist Returns to the South,* p. 235; February 15, 1998, Bill Ott, review of *I See the Rhythm,* p. 1003; September 15, 2000, Hazel Rochman, review of *Christmas Soul: African-American Holiday Memories,* p. 245; November 1, 2010, Ilene Cooper, review of *I See the Rhythm of Gospel,* p. 57.

Kirkus Reviews, December 1, 2010, review of *I See the Rhythm of Gospel.*

New York Times Book Review, December 16, 2001, review of *Christmas Soul,* p. 20.

Publishers Weekly, September 23, 1996, review of *Going Back Home,* p. 76; March 23, 1998, review of *I See the Rhythm,* p. 100; September 25, 2000, Elizabeth Devereaux, review of *Christmas Soul,* p. 67; November 8, 2010, review of *I See the Rhythm of Gospel,* p. 60.

School Library Journal, October, 2000, review of *Christmas Soul,* p. 63; March, 2011, Mary N. Oluonye, review of *I See the Rhythm of Gospel,* p. 183.

ONLINE

Michele Wood Home Page, http://michelewood.com (February 12, 2012).*

Y

YANG, Dori Jones 1954-

Personal

Born 1954, in OH; married Paul Yang, 1985; children: Steve, Serena, Emily. *Education:* Princeton University, B.A. (European history), 1976; Johns Hopkins University, M.A. (international affairs), 1980. *Hobbies and other interests:* Studying languages, playing music (piano, violin, cello, and guzheng), travel.

Addresses

Home—Seattle, WA. *E-mail*—hello@dorijonesyang. com.

Career

Journalist and author. *Business Week* magazine, journalist, beginning 1981, international business editor, foreign correspondent and bureau manager in Hong Kong, 1982-90, and bureau manager in Seattle, WA, 1990-95; *U.S. News & World Report,* West Coast business and technology correspondent, 1999-2001; full-time author beginning 2001. Presenter at schools.

Awards, Honors

Princeton-in-Asia fellowship; Pleasant T. Rowland Prize for Fiction for Girls, 2000, and *Skipping Stones* Honor Book award, 2001, both for *The Secret Voice of Gina Zhang;* American Library Association Amelia Bloomer Project listee, Best Fiction for Young Adults nomination, and Notable Trade Books for Young People selection, National Council for the Social Studies, all 2012, all for *Daughter of Xanadu.*

Writings

FOR CHILDREN

The Secret Voice of Gina Zhang, American Girl (Middleton, WI), 2000.

(Reteller) *The Brother Who Gave Rice: A Korean Folk Tale,* illustrated by Oki S. Han, Hampton Brown (Carmel, CA), 2004.

(Reteller) *Bring Me Three Gifts!: A Chinese Folk Tale,* illustrated by Marilee Heyer, Hampton Brown (Carmel, CA), 2007.

Daughter of Xanadu, Delacorte Press (New York, NY), 2011.

OTHER

(With Howard Schultz) *Pour Your Heart into It: How Starbucks Built a Company One Cup at a Time,* Hyperion (New York, NY), 1997.

Voices of the Second Wave: Chinese Americans in Seattle, East West Insights, 2011.

Contributor to periodicals, including *Huffington Post.*

Author's work has been translated into several languages.

Sidelights

Although Dori Jones Yang grew up in the Midwest, she developed a desire to see the world, and after graduating from college she spent two years in Singapore, teaching English and studying Chinese. After returning to the United States, she earned a master's degree in international affairs, and then built a successful journalism career that allowed her to live in China for eight years as head of *Business Week*'s Hong Kong bureau. When she returned to the United States, Yang continued to work in journalism from her new home base in Seattle, Washington, before writing her first book. Coauthored with entrepreneur Howard Schultz, *Pour Your Heart into It: How Starbucks Built a Company One Cup at a Time* chronicles the rise of Schultz's business from a single coffee shop in downtown Seattle to an international corporation. Describing *Pour Your Heart into It* as a clearly written "instruction . . . on how to build a billion-dollar retail specialty chain," a *Publishers Weekly* critic added that "it is hard to imagine a

172

more satisfying brew than this memoir," and David Rouse quipped in *Booklist* that "Yang . . . helps Schultz make this saga perk."

Beginning in 1999, Yang turned to fiction, inspired by her interest in Asian history as well as her own experiences living in a very different culture. Published by American Girl, her middle-grade novel *The Secret Voice of Gina Zhang* focuses on a preteen from China who is dealing with a cultural disconnect common to immigrant children. Jinna is twelve years old when her family moves from southern China to Seattle. Although she wants to make new friends and do well in school, Jinna (now Gina) panics when immersed in an English-speaking school. Her feelings of intimidation lead her to stop talking and withdraw into a fantasy world where she makes up a story about a princess named Jade-Blossom. Moved into a special-needs class, Gina is befriended by chatterbug Priscilla, who helps the young immigrant find a way to show people her true talents. "Yang's first novel conveys some of the unique challenges of the immigrant experience," wrote a *Publishers Weekly* critic, and the "brave heroine" in *The Secret Voice of Gina Zhang* "will leave readers cheering."

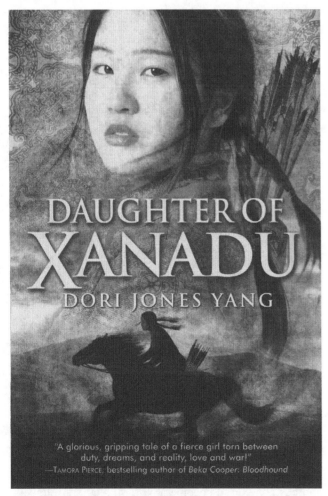

Cover of Dori Jones Yang's history-themed coming-of-age story Daughter of Xanadu, *featuring cover art by Juliana Kolesova.* (Jacket art copyright © 2011 by Juliana Kolesova. Used by permission of Delacorte Press, an imprint of Random House Children's Books, a division of Random House, Inc.)

Yang turns to history in *Daughter of Xanadu,* a young-adult novel that mixes romance and adventure while opening a window onto thirteenth-century China. The year is 1275 when readers meet Emmajin, the sixteen-year-old granddaughter of Khubilai Khan. Although she is a girl, Emmajin longs to become a Mongol soldier and help bring glory to the Khan through battle. When an emissary from a strange world comes to the royal court, the teen is directed by her grandfather to gain strategic knowledge that will one day help the Mongol armies defeat his distant land, called Europe. The emissary is actually the merchant Marco Polo, and in learning about Polo's homeland of Venice, Emmajin is also transfixed by his courtly manners, colorful stories, and charm. Through his stories, she begins to see her grandfather's empire through fresh eyes, and she begins to also reevaluate her future.

Praising *Daughter of Xanadu* as a "moving and thoughtful novel," Amanda MacGregor added in her *Voice of Youth Advocates* review that "Emmajin's believable and affecting" self-questioning "is tempered with enough action sequences to keep up the plot's momentum." The first-person narrative by the Mongolian girl "will capture readers with its . . . vivid description of a capable young woman in a time of change," wrote Carolyn Phelan in *Booklist,* and *School Library Journal* critic Leah Krippner deemed *Daughter of Xanadu* "a colorful and compelling read" featuring a "charming and believable" cast of historical characters.

Discussing her goals in writing with *PaperTigers* online interviewer Marjorie Coughlan, Yang noted: "In every country, in every era, it's easy to slip into an 'us-vs.-them' mentality, to look on 'them' as sub-human so that we can wage war on them. But when you get to know someone from a faraway country as a human being with hopes and dreams, your worldview shifts. By learning how others see the world, you come to understand yourself and your own people better, and war no longer seems like a sensible option." "I hope *Daughter of Xanadu* will help a new generation of Americans become familiar and comfortable with East Asia and develop a greater openness to all people they meet from foreign countries," she added. "Mutual awareness and understanding are the keys to defusing tension and conflict." Continuing to pursue these goals, Yang also compiled *Voices of the Second Wave: Chinese Americans in Seattle,* which features interviews with thirty-five representative immigrants—many of them highly educated members of the country's intellectual elite—who moved to the United States following the rise of communism in China.

Biographical and Critical Sources

PERIODICALS

Booklist, September 1, 1997, David Rouse, review of *Pour Your Heart into It: How Starbucks Built a Company One Cup at a Time,* p. 43; October 1, 2000, John Pe-

ters, review of *The Secret Voice of Gina Zhang*, p. 342; January 1, 2011, Carolyn Phelan, review of *Daughter of Xanadu*, p. 95.

Kirkus Reviews, December 15, 2010, review of *Daughter of Xanadu.*

Library Journal, September 1, 1997, Joseph C. Toschik, review of *Pour Your Heart into It*, p. 194.

Publishers Weekly, July 7, 1997, review of *Pour Your Heart into It*, p. 54; September 11, 2000, review of *The Secret Voice of Gina Zhang*, p. 91.

School Library Journal, October, 2000, Ashley Larsen, review of *The Secret Voice of Gina Zhang*, p. 175; July, 2011, Leah Krippner, review of *Daughter of Xanadu*, p. 111.

Voice of Youth Advocates, April, 2011, Amanda MacGregor, review of *Daughter of Xanadu*, p. 72.

ONLINE

Dori Jones Yang Home Page, http://www.dorijonesyang. com (February 20, 2012).

PaperTigers.org, http://www.papertigers.org/ (March, 2011), Marjorie Coughland, interview with Yang.

* * *

YANKOVIC, Al 1959-
(Weird Al Yankovic)

Personal

Born October 23, 1959, in Downey, CA; son of Nick and Mary Yankovic; married Suzanne Krajewski, February 10, 2001; children: Nina. *Education:* California Polytechnic State University, B.A. (architecture).

Addresses

Home—Hollywood, CA; Maui, HI.

Career

Comedian, parodist, and singer/songwriter. Recordings include *"Weird Al" Yankovic, Rock 'n' Roll*, 1983; *"Weird Al" Yankovic in 3-D*, 1984; *Polka Party!*, 1986; *"Weird Al" Yankovic's Greatest Hits*, 1988; *Even Worse*, 1988; *Fat*, 1988; (with Wendy Carlos) *Peter and the Wolf; The Carnival of the Animals*, 1988; *UHF Original Motion Picture Soundtrack and Other Stuff*, 1989; *Off the Deep End*, 1992; (with others) *Dr. Demento Presents Spooky Tunes and Scary Melodies*, 1994; *Permanent Record*, 1994; *Running with Scissors*, 1999; (with others) *Pokémon the Movie 2000: The Power of One*, 2000; (with others) *Radio Disney Jams, Volume 2*, 2000; *Poodle Hat*, 2003; *Now That Sounds Kosher!*, 2005; *Straight Outta Lynwood*, 2006; (with others) *The Simpsons Testify*, 2007; and *The Alpocalypse*, 2011. Weird Al Yankovic Rock 'n' Roll Records, Los Angeles, CA, owner, beginning c. 1982. Actor in television series *The Weird Al Show*, CBS, 1997-98; cameo ap-

Al Yankovic (Photograph by Chris Pizzello. AP/Wide World Photos.)

pearances in numerous films, including *Naked Gun 33 1/2*, 1994, *Spy Hard*, 1996, *Desperation Boulevard*, 2002, *Nerdcore Rising: A Documentary Film about Nerdcore Hip Hop*, 2008, and *Halloween II*, 2009.

Awards, Honors

Grammy Award for Best Comedy Recording, 1984, for "Eat It," Best Concept Music Video, 1988, for "Fat," Best Comedy Album, 2003, for *Poodle Hat*, and eleven award nominations; earned Gold records in United States, Canada, and Australia; earned six platinum records.

Writings

(With Tino Insansa) *The Authorized Al*, Contemporary Books (Chicago, IL), 1985.

When I Grow Up, illustrated by Wes Hargis, Harper (New York, NY), 2011.

Adaptations

When I Grow Up was adapted as an interactive e-book for i-Pad, featuring sound effects and narration by Yankovic, HarperCollins, 2001.

Sidelights

Although he started out life as Alfred Matthew Yankovic, the California-based comedy songwriter, musician, and performer is best know under his professional appellation: Weird Al Yankovic. Yankovic began his parodies of popular songs and culture in the mid-1970s and has gone on to become a cultural icon himself, selling millions of recordings and performing before audiences throughout the world. The author of pop tunes such as "Eat It" (a parody of Michael Jackson's smash

hit "Beat It"), "Party in the C.I.A." (an update of Myley Cyrus's "Party in the U.S.A.), and ""Another One Rides the Bus" (based on "Another One Bites the Dust" by Queen) and known for his stagey takes on everyone from Jedi knights to Lady Gaga, Yankovic has also directed music videos and starred in television's *The Weird Al Show* during the late 1990s. He has also performed his accordion before millions, and appears in cameo roles in comedy films that include *Naked Gun 33 1/2, Halloween II,* and *Spy Hard,* the last a spoof of James Bond films for which Yankovic sang the side-splitting theme song. Calling Yankovic "an incisive satirist" and "one of the most versatile and talented rock stars on the road," Robbie Woliver supported his assertion by explaining in the *New York Times* that, "While many would not consider putting him in the same category of the artists he parodies, the fact is he can sing like Kurt Cobain, dance like Michael Jackson, play accordion like Jimi Hendrix played the guitar and write as wryly as Barenaked Ladies." "And those costume changes?," Woliver added. Yankovic "puts Diana Ross to shame."

Yankovic grew up in Lynwood, California, where he became a fan of the popular syndicated "Dr. Demento" radio show. His natural talent as a musician found an outlet in humorous songs, and during high school he recorded several and sent them to his favorite radio host, hoping that Dr. Demento would include them in one of his novel broadcasts. In fact, it was Demento who gave Yankovic the moniker "Weird Al," and ultimately the young man embraced the life course the nickname implied. After completing college, where he studied architecture, Yankovic worked a desk job until his reputation among "Dr. Demento" fans had swelled to significance through the power of popular songs such as "My Bologna" (a parody of the Knack's "My Sharona"). In 1982 Yankovic signed his first recording contract and he has been successfully mining pop culture for its foibles ever since.

In Yankovic's first book for children, *When I Grow Up,* the talented showman focuses on a young novice of the profession. For eight-year-old Billy, Show and Tell is the perfect time to share with his classmates his ambitious plans for his future. As soon as his teacher signals Billy's turn, the boy monopolizes the stage, and Yankovic's rhyming text tracks the whimsy of the boy's grandiose plans as he ponders career possibilities that include snail trainer, giraffe masseuse, lathe operator, and even a sculptor who works only in well-whipped-and-chilled chocolate mouse.

Artist Wes Hargis captures the antic humor in Yankovic's picture-book story in his illustrations for **When I Grow Up.** (Reproduced with permission of HarperCollins Children's Books, a division of HarperCollins Publishers.)

Describing *When I Grow Up* as "an exuberantly odd" tale, Hazel Rochman added in *Booklist* that the author's mix of "farce and parody . . . will appeal to both kids and adults." In *School Library Journal* Roxanne Burg cited the "well-done, realistic and colorful" cartoon illustrations contributed to Yankovic's story by Wes Hargis, while in *Publishers Weekly* a critic praised the "zingy verse" that shares a "lighthearted take on a familiar theme." In addition to its print version, *When I Grow Up* has also been adapted as an i-Pad version, complete with narration and wacky sound effects by Yankovic himself.

Biographical and Critical Sources

PERIODICALS

Booklist, January 1, 2011, Hazel Rochman, review of *When I Grow Up,* p. 114.
Kirkus Reviews, January 15, 2011, review of *When I Grow Up.*
Publishers Weekly, December 6, 2010, review of *When I Grow Up,* p. 47.
School Library Journal, January, 2011, Roxanne Burg, review of *When I Grow Up,* p. 86.

ONLINE

Al Yankovic Home Page, http://www.weirdal.com (February 12, 2012).*

*   *   *

YANKOVIC, Weird Al
   ## See YANKOVIC, Al

*   *   *

YOVANOFF, Brenna 1979-

Personal

Born 1979; married. *Education:* Colorado State University, M.F.A. (fiction).

Addresses

Home—Denver, CO. *Agent*—Sarah Davies, Greenhouse Literary Agency. *E-mail*—brenna.yovanoff@gmail.com.

Career

Novelist.

Writings

The Replacement, Razorbill (New York, NY), 2010.
The Space Between, Razorbill (New York, NY), 2011.

Contributor of original short fiction to *Merry Sisters of Fate* Web log, with selected contents published in book form by Carolrhoda, 2012.

Adaptations

The Replacement was adapted for audiobook, ready by Kevin Collins, Brilliance Audio, 2010.

Sidelights

Brenna Yovanoff is a young-adult author whose paranormal fantasies include *The Replacement* and *The Space Between.* Given a free rein in her writing by her homeschooling parents until high school, Yovanoff majored in English and went on to earn her M.F.A. at Colorado State University. In addition to novels, she has also a following among Web fans through her collaboration with fellow authors Maggie Stiefvater and Tessa Gratton on the Merry Sisters of Fate Web log, where original short stories was made available to readers free of chage in addition to being collected in book form.

Described by *Booklist* reviewer Daniel Kraus as an entrant in the paranormal genre that is "startling conceived from the ground up," *The Replacement* takes

Cover of Brenna Yovanoff's paranormal teen thriller **The Replacement,** *featuring cover art by Jonathan Barkat.* (Illustration © 2010 by Jonathan Barkat. Townhouse photo © iStockphoto.com/Lissart. Reproduced by permission of Razorbill, an imprint of Penguin Group (USA) Inc.)

readers to Gentry, a small town that has survived due to its acceptance of a supernatural element. Under the surface of Gentry are tunnels and inky pools, monstrous creatures that inhabit slag heaps and mounds of debris, and mindless undead things that stumble around, all governed by a tattooed creature known as the Morrigan. Called Mayhem, this underground land demands a sacrifice in exchange for protecting the earthlanders, and it is made annually in the form of a human newborn. The residents of Gentry accept the evil pact, guarding their homes with talismans. They also accept the replacements that are left in place of the stolen newborns, knowing that these sickly beings will die within a few years. Mackie Doyle is one such replacement, and at age sixteen he has managed to survive his exposure to the surface, with its iron-rich blood and patches of consecrated earth. He knows his time is running out, however, and the thought of leaving best friend Tate at his death saddens the nonhuman teen. When Tate's newborn sibling disappears, she joins with Mackie to travel to Mayhem, hoping to end the horrific bargain that has come at such a terrible cost.

Noting that Yovanoff taps European folktales in her changeling story, Leah J. Sparks added in *School Library Journal* that *The Replacement* "sustain[s] . . . a mood of fear, hopelessness, and misery" that is leavening it through "Mackie's dry humor." "Well-developed characters, a fascinating take on the Fairy Court, and an exciting story line" characterize the author's fiction debut, asserted a *Publishers Weekly* contributor, while in *Kirkus Reviews* a critic praised *The Replacement* as a story that pairs "romance and rescue" with "enough grotesque goodies" to appeal to urban fantasy fans.

Although Mayhem is dreadful, Hell is even worse, as readers discover in Yovanoff's second dark fantasy. When readers meet her in *The Space Between,* Daphne is an actual hellion: the youngest daughter of Lucifer and Lilith, she has lived there her whole life, isolated from the greater city of Pandemonium and its large demon population. Far from a place of fire and brimstone, the city glows silver, entwined by roads that snake between its tall buildings. Although Daphne is more thoughtful than her impulsive older siblings, she decides to risk her safety when her brother Obie disappears during a decidedly un-devilish act of compassion toward a human teen named Truman Flynn. Almost successful at committing suicide until Obie intercedes, Truman descends briefly into Hell, giving Daphne the chance to return Earthward with him. Although Truman agrees to help her search for her brother once she arrives on Earth's surface, Daphne must avoid the atten-

tion of Azrael, the angel of death, who would like nothing better than to avenge himself against one of Lucifer's offspring.

In chronicling Daphne's story in *The Space Between,* Yovanoff includes "moments of beauty, terror, and significant wisdom," wrote a *Publishers Weekly* reviewer, and a *Kirkus Reviews* writer characterized the fantasy story as a "dreamy, atmospheric take on Judeo-Christina mythology that prioritizes character." Noting the author's use of "sophisticated stylistic devices and shifting points of view" in *The Space Between,* Donna L. Phillips had no qualms about recommending the novel to "teens looking for page-turning, deliciously grisly suspense," while in *Booklist* Kraus praised Yovanoff's sophomore work as "a breath of fresh (or fetid?) air for the genre."

Biographical and Critical Sources

PERIODICALS

Booklist, September 1, 2010, Daniel Kraus, review of *The Replacement,* p. 97; October 1, 2011, Daniel Kraus, review of *The Space Between,* p. 89.
Bulletin of the Center for Children's Books, September, 2010, Kate Quealy-Gainer, review of *The Replacement,* p. 51.
Kirkus Reviews, August 1, 2010, review of *The Replacement;* October 15, 2011, review of *The Space Between.*
Publishers Weekly, August 16, 2010, review of *The Replacement,* p. 51; September 26, 2011, review of *The Space Between,* p. 75.
School Library Journal, December, 2010, Leah J. Sparks, review of *The Replacement,* p. 132.
Voice of Youth Advocates, December, 2010, Karen Sykeny, review of *The Replacement,* p. 478; December, 2011, Donna L. Phillips, review of *The Space Between,* p. 522.

ONLINE

Brenna Yovanoff Home Page, http://www.brennayovanoff. com (February 12, 2012).
Greenhouse Literary Web site, http://www.greenhouse literary.com/ (February 12, 2012), "Brenna Yovanoff."
Merry Sisters of Fate Web log, http://merryfates.com/ (February 15, 2012).
YA Highway Web site, http://www.yahighway.com/ (September, 2010), interview with Yovanoff.*

Illustrations Index

(In the following index, the number of the *volume* in which an illustrator's work appears is given *before* the colon, and the *page number* on which it appears is given *after* the colon. For example, a drawing by Adams, Adrienne appears in Volume 2 on page 6, another drawing by her appears in Volume 3 on page 80, another drawing in Volume 8 on page 1, and so on and so on. . . .)

YABC

Index references to *YABC* refer to listings appearing in the two-volume *Yesterday's Authors of Books for Children,* also published by Gale, Cengage Learning. *YABC* covers prominent authors and illustrators who died prior to 1960.

A

Aas, Ulf *5:* 174
Abbe, S. van
  See van Abbe, S.
Abel, Raymond *6:* 122; *7:* 195; *12:* 3; *21:* 86; *25:* 119
Abelliera, Aldo *71:* 120
Abolafia, Yossi *60:* 2; *93:* 163; *152:* 202
Abrahams, Hilary *26:* 205; *29:* 24, 25; *53:* 61
Abrams, Kathie *36:* 170
Abrams, Lester *49:* 26
Abulafia, Yossi *154:* 67; *177:* 3
Accardo, Anthony *191:* 3, 8
Accornero, Franco *184:* 8
Accorsi, William *11:* 198
Acedera, Kei *235:* 110
Acs, Laszlo *14:* 156; *42:* 22
Acuna, Ed *198:* 79
Adams, Adrienne *2:* 6; *3:* 80; *8:* 1; *15:* 107; *16:* 180; *20:* 65; *22:* 134, 135; *33:* 75; *36:* 103, 112; *39:* 74; *86:* 54; *90:* 2, 3
Adams, Connie J. *129:* 68
Adams, John Wolcott *17:* 162
Adams, Kathryn *224:* 1
Adams, Lynn *96:* 44
Adams, Norman *55:* 82
Adams, Pam *112:* 1, 2
Adams, Sarah *98:* 126; *164:* 180
Adams, Steve *209:* 64
Adamson, George *30:* 23, 24; *69:* 64
Addams, Charles *55:* 5
Addison, Kenneth *192:* 173; *231:* 166
Addy, Sean *180:* 8; *222:* 31
Ade, Rene *76:* 198; *195:* 162
Adinolfi, JoAnn *115:* 42; *176:* 2; *217:* 79
Adkins, Alta *22:* 250
Adkins, Jan *8:* 3; *69:* 4; *144:* 2, 3, 4; *210:* 11, 17, 18, 19
Adl, Shirin *225:* 2
Adler, Kelynn *195:* 47
Adler, Peggy *22:* 6; *29:* 31
Adler, Ruth *29:* 29
Adlerman, Daniel *163:* 2
Adragna, Robert *47:* 145
Agard, Nadema *18:* 1
Agee, Jon *116:* 8, 9, 10; *157:* 4; *196:* 3, 4, 5, 6, 7, 8
Agre, Patricia *47:* 195
Aguirre, Alfredo *152:* 218

Ahl, Anna Maria *32:* 24
Ahlberg, Allan *68:* 6, 7, 9; *165:* 5; *214:* 9
Ahlberg, Janet *68:* 6, 7, 9; *214:* 9
Ahlberg, Jessica *229:* 2, 191
Aicher-Scholl, Inge *63:* 127
Aichinger, Helga *4:* 5, 45
Aitken, Amy *31:* 34
Ajhar, Brian *207:* 126; *220:* 2
Akaba, Suekichi *46:* 23; *53:* 127
Akasaka, Miyoshi *YABC 2:* 261
Akib, Jamel *181:* 13; *182:* 99; *220:* 74
Akino, Fuku *6:* 144
Alain *40:* 41
Alajalov *2:* 226
Albert, Chris *200:* 64
Alborough, Jez *86:* 1, 2, 3; *149:* 3
Albrecht, Jan *37:* 176
Albright, Donn *1:* 91
Alcala, Alfredo *91:* 128
Alcantará, Felipe Ugalde *171:* 186
Alcorn, John *3:* 159; *7:* 165; *31:* 22; *44:* 127; *46:* 23, 170
Alcorn, Stephen *110:* 4; *125:* 106; *128:* 172; *150:* 97; *160:* 188; *165:* 48; *201:* 113; *203:* 39; *207:* 3; *226:* 25
Alcott, May *100:* 3
Alda, Arlene *44:* 24; *158:* 2
Alden, Albert *11:* 103
Aldridge, Andy *27:* 131
Aldridge, George *105:* 125
Aldridge, Sheila *192:* 4
Alejandro, Cliff *176:* 75
Alex, Ben *45:* 25, 26
Alexander, Claire *228:* 2
Alexander, Ellen *91:* 3
Alexander, Lloyd *49:* 34
Alexander, Martha *3:* 206; *11:* 103; *13:* 109; *25:* 100; *36:* 131; *70:* 6, 7; *136:* 3, 4, 5; *169:* 120; *230:* 70
Alexander, Paul *85:* 57; *90:* 9
Alexeieff, Alexander *14:* 6; *26:* 199
Alfano, Wayne *80:* 69
Aliki
  See Brandenberg, Aliki
Alko, Selina *218:* 2; *235:* 187
Allamand, Pascale *12:* 9
Allan, Judith *38:* 166
Alland, Alexandra *16:* 255
Allen, Gertrude *9:* 6
Allen, Graham *31:* 145
Allen, Jonathan *131:* 3, 4; *177:* 8, 9, 10

Allen, Joy *168:* 185; *217:* 6, 7
Allen, Pamela *50:* 25, 26, 27, 28; *81:* 9, 10; *123:* 4, 5
Allen, Raul *207:* 94
Allen, Rick *236:* 174
Allen, Rowena *47:* 75
Allen, Thomas B. *81:* 101; *82:* 248; *89:* 37; *104:* 9
Allen, Tom *85:* 176
Allender, David *73:* 223
Alley, R.W. *80:* 183; *95:* 187; *156:* 100, 153; *169:* 4, 5; *179:* 17
Allison, Linda *43:* 27
Allon, Jeffrey *119:* 174
Allport, Mike *71:* 55
Almquist, Don *11:* 8; *12:* 128; *17:* 46; *22:* 110
Aloise, Frank *5:* 38; *10:* 133; *30:* 92
Alsenas, Linas *186:* 2
Alter, Ann *206:* 4, 5
Althea
  See Braithwaite, Althea
Altmann, Scott *238:* 78
Altschuler, Franz *11:* 185; *23:* 141; *40:* 48; *45:* 29; *57:* 181
Alvin, John *117:* 5
Ambrus, Victor G. *1:* 6, 7, 194; *3:* 69; *5:* 15; *6:* 44; *7:* 36; *8:* 210; *12:* 227; *14:* 213; *15:* 213; *22:* 209; *24:* 36; *28:* 179; *30:* 178; *32:* 44, 46; *38:* 143; *41:* 25, 26, 27, 28, 29, 30, 31, 32; *42:* 87; *44:* 190; *55:* 172; *62:* 30, 144, 145, 148; *86:* 99, 100, 101; *87:* 66, 137; *89:* 162; *134:* 160
Ames, Lee J. *3:* 12; *9:* 130; *10:* 69; *17:* 214; *22:* 124; *151:* 13; *223:* 69
Amini, Mehrdokht *211:* 119
Amini-Holmes, Liz *239:* 119
Amon, Aline *9:* 9
Amoss, Berthe *5:* 5
Amstutz, André *152:* 102; *214:* 11, 16; *223:* 99
Amundsen, Dick *7:* 77
Amundsen, Richard E. *5:* 10; *24:* 122
Ancona, George *12:* 11; *55:* 144; *145:* 7; *208:* 13
Anderson, Alasdair *18:* 122
Andersen, Bethanne *116:* 167; *162:* 189; *175:* 17; *191:* 4, 5; *218:* 20
Anderson, Bob *139:* 16
Anderson, Brad *33:* 28
Anderson, Brian *211:* 8
Anderson, C.W. *11:* 10

Anderson, Carl 7: 4
Anderson, Catherine Corley 72: 2
Anderson, Cecil 127: 152
Anderson, David Lee 118: 176
Anderson, Derek 169: 9; 174: 180
Anderson, Doug 40: 111
Anderson, Erica 23: 65
Anderson, G.E. 223: 181
Anderson, Laurie 12: 153, 155
Anderson, Lena 99: 26
Anderson, Peggy Perry 179: 2
Anderson, Sara 173: 3
Anderson, Scoular 138: 13; 201: 6
Anderson, Stephanie 225: 3
Anderson, Susan 90: 12
Anderson, Tara 188: 132; 211: 115
Anderson, Wayne 23: 119; 41: 239; 56: 7; 62:
   26; 147: 6; 202: 4, 5
Andreasen, Daniel 86: 157; 87: 104; 103: 201,
   202; 159: 75; 167: 106, 107; 168: 184; 180:
   247; 186: 9; 212: 101; 220: 110, 111; 221:
   56; 227: 3, 4, 5, 6; 234: 214
Andrew, Ian 111: 37; 116: 12; 166: 2
Andrew, John 22: 4
Andrews, Benny 14: 251; 31: 24; 57: 6, 7;
   183: 8
Andrews, Vaughn 166: 28
Anelay, Henry 57: 173
Angel, Marie 47: 22
Angelo, Valenti 14: 8; 18: 100; 20: 232; 32:
   70
Anglund, Joan Walsh 2: 7, 250, 251; 37: 198,
   199, 200
Anholt, Catherine 74: 8; 131: 7; 141: 5
Anholt, Laurence 141: 4
Anno, Mitsumasa 5: 7; 38: 25, 26, 27, 28, 29,
   30, 31, 32; 77: 3, 4; 157: 10, 11
Antal, Andrew 1: 124; 30: 145
Antram, David 152: 133
Apostolou, Christy Hale
   See Hale, Christy
Apple, Margot 33: 25; 35: 206; 46: 81; 53: 8;
   61: 109; 64: 21, 22, 24, 25, 27; 71: 176; 77:
   53; 82: 245; 92: 39; 94: 180; 96: 107; 152:
   4, 5; 162: 192, 194; 173: 44; 214: 21, 22,
   23, 24; 238: 3
Appleyard, Dev 2: 192
Aragones, Sergio 48: 23, 24, 25, 26, 27
Araneus 40: 29
Arbo, Cris 103: 4; 220: 4, 5
Archambault, Matt 85: 173; 138: 19, 20; 143:
   33; 145: 144; 179: 103; 187: 7; 219: 2
Archer, Janet 16: 69; 178: 156
Ardizzone, Edward 1: 11, 12; 2: 105; 3: 258;
   4: 78; 7: 79; 10: 100; 15: 232; 20: 69,178;
   23: 223; 24: 125; 28: 25, 26, 27, 28, 29, 30,
   31,33, 34, 35, 36, 37; 31: 192, 193; 34: 215,
   217; 60: 173; 64: 145; 87: 176; YABC 2: 25
Arena, Jill 176: 49
Arenella, Roy 14: 9
Argemi, David 197: 2
Argent, Kerry 103: 56; 138: 17; 158: 134
Arihara, Shino 201: 98
Arisman, Marshall 162: 50
Armer, Austin 13: 3
Armer, Laura Adams 13: 3
Armer, Sidney 13: 3
Armitage, David 47: 23; 99: 5; 155: 4
Armitage, Eileen 4: 16
Armstrong, George 10: 6; 21: 72
Armstrong, Shelagh 102: 114; 224: 4
Armstrong-Ellis, Carey 185: 196
Arno, Enrico 1: 217; 2: 22, 210; 4: 9; 5: 43;
   6: 52; 29: 217, 219; 33: 152; 35: 99; 43: 31,
   32, 33; 45: 212, 213, 214; 72: 72; 74: 166;
   100: 169
Arnold, Alli 187: 40, 41
Arnold, Andrew 219: 155; 221: 155
Arnold, Caroline 174: 5
Arnold, Emily 76: 7, 9, 10
Arnold, Katya 115: 11; 168: 2, 3

Arnold, Tedd 116: 14; 133: 152; 160: 5; 208:
   24, 25, 26, 176
Arnosky, Jim 22: 20; 70: 9, 10, 11; 118: 3, 5;
   160: 8, 10; 189: 5, 7, 8, 9, 10; 217: 11, 12,
   13, 14
Arnsteen, Katy Keck 105: 97; 116: 145
Arsenault, Isabelle 207: 7; 226: 109
Arrowood, Clinton 12: 193; 19: 11; 65: 210
Artell, Mike 89: 8
Arting, Fred J. 41: 63
Artzybasheff, Boris 13: 143; 14: 15; 40: 152,
   155
Aruego, Ariane 6: 4
Aruego, José 4: 140; 6: 4; 7: 64; 33: 195; 35:
   208; 68: 16, 17; 75: 46; 93: 91, 92; 94: 197;
   109: 65, 67; 125: 2, 3, 4, 5; 127: 188; 143:
   25; 178: 17, 19, 74; 188: 166; 202: 164;
   231: 176; 239: 155
Arzoumanian, Alik 177: 12; 194: 115
Asare, Meshack 86: 9; 139: 19
Ascensios, Natalie 105: 139
Asch, Frank 5: 9; 66: 2, 4, 6, 7, 9, 10; 102:
   18, 19,21; 154: 12
Ashby, Gail 11: 135
Ashby, Gil 146: 4
Ashby, Gwynneth 44: 26
Ashley, C.W. 19: 197
Ashmead, Hal 8: 70
Ashton, Tim 211: 204
Aska, Warabe 56: 10
Assel, Steven 44: 153; 77: 22, 97
Astrop, John 32: 56
Atene, Ann 12: 18
Atherton, Lisa 38: 198
Atkinson, Allen 60: 5
Atkinson, J. Priestman 17: 275
Atkinson, Janet 86: 147; 103: 138
Atkinson, Mike 127: 74
Atkinson, Wayne 40: 46
Attard, Karl 196: 22, 23
Attebery, Charles 38: 170
Atwell, Debby 150: 6
Atwood, Ann 7: 9
Aubrey, Meg Kelleher 77: 159
Auch, Herm 173: 7, 8
Auch, Mary Jane 173: 7
Augarde, Steve 25: 22; 159: 7; 210: 43, 44
Austerman, Miriam 23: 107
Austin, Cary 234: 171
Austin, Margot 11: 16
Austin, Dawn 234: 117
Austin, Robert 3: 44
Austin, Virginia 81: 205; 127: 221; 232: 190
Auth, Tony 51: 5; 192: 18
Avendano, Dolores 158: 74
Avedon, Richard 57: 140
Averill, Esther 1: 17; 28: 39, 40, 41
Avilés, Martha 218: 6
Axeman, Lois 2: 32; 11: 84; 13: 165; 22: 8;
   23: 49; 61: 116; 101: 124
Axtel, David 155: 110
Ayer, Jacqueline 13: 7
Ayer, Margaret 15: 12; 50: 120
Ayers, Alan 91: 58; 107: 169
Ayliffe, Alex 95: 164; 237: 68
Ayto, Russell 111: 5; 112: 54; 206: 7, 8; 213:
   56
Azarian, Mary 112: 9, 10; 114: 129; 117: 171;
   137: 163; 171: 4, 5; 181: 161; 188: 128;
   232: 174

B

B.T.B.
   See Blackwell, Basil T.
Baasansuren, Bolormaa 216: 40
Babbitt, Bradford 33: 158
Babbitt, Natalie 6: 6; 8: 220; 68: 20; 70: 242,
   243; 194: 8, 9

Baca, Maria 104: 5
Bacchus, Andy 94: 87
Bacha, Andy 109: 169
Bachelet, Gilles 196: 18
Bachem, Paul 48: 180; 67: 65; 144: 206; 234:
   113
Back, Adam 63: 125
Back, George 31: 161
Backes, Nick 190: 72
Backhouse, Colin 78: 142
Bacon, Bruce 4: 74
Bacon, Paul 7: 155; 8: 121; 31: 55; 50: 42;
   56: 175; 62: 82, 84
Bacon, Peggy 2: 11, 228; 46: 44
Baek, Matthew J. 169: 95; 202: 8
Baer, Julie 161: 2
Baeten, Lieve 238: 5
Baicker-McKee, Carol 177: 15; 180: 215
Bailey, Peter 58: 174; 87: 221; 194: 12
Bailey, Sheila 155: 11
Baker, Alan 22: 22; 61: 134; 93: 11, 12; 146:
   6, 7, 10
Baker, Charlotte 2: 12
Baker, Garin 89: 65
Baker, Jeannie 23: 4; 88: 18, 19, 20
Baker, Jim 22: 24
Baker, Joe 82: 188; 111: 55; 124: 70; 197: 73
Baker, Keith 179: 6, 7; 222: 36
Baker, Leslie 112: 214; 132: 103, 246; 180:
   74, 246; 234: 213
Baker-Smith, Grahame 223: 10; 225: 132
Baldacci, Rudy 184: 9
Baldridge, Cyrus LeRoy 19: 69; 44: 50
Baldus, Jackie 216: 81
Baldus, Zachary 152: 231; 187: 60
Balet, Jan 11: 22
Balian, Lorna 9: 16; 91: 16
Balit, Christina 102: 24; 159: 9; 162: 118,
   119; 212: 2, 3
Ballantyne, R.M. 24: 34
Ballis, George 14: 199
Balouch, Kristen 176: 11
Baltzer, Hans 40: 30
Banbery, Fred 58: 15
Bancroft, Bronwyn 216: 42
Banfill, A. Scott 98: 7; 112: 59
Bang, Molly 24: 37, 38; 69: 8, 9, 10; 111: 7,9,
   10, 11; 140: 11; 158: 37, 38, 39; 195: 3;
   215: 11, 12, 13, 14
Banik, Yvette Santiago 21: 136
Banks, Erin Bennett 211: 12
Banner, Angela
   See Maddison, Angela Mary
Bannerman, Helen 19: 13, 14
Banning, Greg 202: 98
Bannon, Laura 6: 10; 23: 8
Bantock, Nick 74: 229; 95: 6
Banyai, Istvan 185: 209; 193: 14, 16; 209:
   155; 223: 166, 167; 238: 87
Baptist, Michael 37: 208
Baracca, Sal 135: 206
Baranaski, Marcin 182: 113
Barasch, Lynne 126: 16; 186: 15
Barbarin, Lucien C., Jr. 89: 88
Barbour, Karen 96: 5; 74: 209; 170: 16
Bare, Arnold Edwin 16: 31
Bare, Colleen Stanley 32: 33
Barger, Jan 147: 11
Bargery, Geoffrey 14: 258
Barkat, Jonathan 149: 177; 164: 254; 181:
   106; 184: 186; 196: 11; 198: 148; 239: 176
Barker, Carol 31: 27
Barker, Cicely Mary 49: 50, 51
Barkley, James 4: 13; 6: 11; 13: 112
Barks, Carl 37: 27, 28, 29, 30, 31, 32, 33, 34
Barling, Joy 62: 148
Barling, Tom 9: 23
Barlow, Gillian 62: 20
Barlow, Perry 35: 28
Barlowe, Dot 30: 223
Barlowe, Wayne 37: 72; 84: 43; 105: 5

Barnard, Bryn *88:* 53; *13:* 55; *169:* 13; *193:* 194

Barneda, David *206:* 11

Barner, Bob *29:* 37; *128:* 33; *136:* 19, 20; *177:* 27; *238:* 8

Barnes, Hiram P. *20:* 28

Barnes, Tim *137:* 28

Barnes-Murphy, Rowan *88:* 22

Barnett, Charles II *175:* 150

Barnett, Ivan *70:* 14

Barnett, Moneta *16:* 89; *19:* 142; *31:* 102; *33:* 30, 31, 32; *41:* 153; *61:* 94, 97

Barney, Maginel Wright *39:* 32, 33, 34; *YABC 2:* 306

Barnum, Jay Hyde *11:* 224; *20:* 5; *37:* 189, 190

Baron, Alan *80:* 3; *89:* 123

Barr, George *60:* 74; *69:* 64

Barragán, Paula S. *134:* 116; *186:* 158; *216:* 43, 44, 197; *232:* 133

Barrall, Tim *115:* 152

Barraud, Martin *189:* 38

Barrauds *33:* 114

Barrer-Russell, Gertrude *9:* 65; *27:* 31

Barret, Robert *85:* 134

Barrett, Angela *40:* 136, 137; *62:* 74; *75:* 10; *76:* 142; *144:* 137; *145:* 14; *223:* 14

Barrett, Jennifer *58:* 149

Barrett, John E. *43:* 119

Barrett, Moneta *74:* 10

Barrett, Peter *55:* 169; *86:* 111

Barrett, Robert *62:* 145; *77:* 146; *82:* 35

Barrett, Ron *14:* 24; *26:* 35

Barron, John N. *3:* 261; *5:* 101; *14:* 220

Barrow, Ann *136:* 27

Barrows, Walter *14:* 268

Barry, Ethelred B. *37:* 79; *YABC 1:* 229

Barry, James *14:* 25

Barry, Katharina *2:* 159; *4:* 22

Barry, Robert E. *6:* 12

Barry, Scott *32:* 35

Barshaw, Ruth McNally *203:* 9

Bartenbach, Jean *40:* 31

Barth, Ernest Kurt *2:* 172; *3:* 160; *8:* 26; *10:* 31

Bartholomew, Caty *208:* 153

Bartholomew, Marie *200:* 66

Bartlett, Alison *101:* 88; *165:* 93; *209:* 51

Barton, Byron *8:* 207; *9:* 18; *23:* 66; *80:* 181; *90:* 18, 19, 20, 21; *126:* 29, 30

Barton, Harriett *30:* 71

Barton, Jill *129:* 108; *135:* 120; *145:* 185, 189; *184:* 177; *224:* 142, 143

Barton, Patrice *226:* 14

Bartram, Robert *10:* 42

Bartram, Simon *218:* 8

Bartsch, Jochen *8:* 105; *39:* 38

Bascove, Barbara *45:* 73

Base, Graeme *101:* 15, 16, 17, 18; *162:* 8, 10, 12

Baseman, Gary *174:* 12

Bash, Barbara *132:* 9

Basic, Zdenko *235:* 176

Baskin, Leonard *30:* 42, 43, 46, 47; *49:* 125, 126, 128, 129,133; *173:* 120

Bass, Saul *49:* 192

Bassett, Jeni *40:* 99; *64:* 30

Basso, Bill *99:* 139; *189:* 134

Batchelor, Joy *29:* 41, 47, 48

Bate, Norman *5:* 16

Bates, Amy June *188:* 170; *189:* 27, 28; *239:* 8, 9

Bates, Leo *24:* 35

Batet, Carmen *39:* 134

Batherman, Muriel *31:* 79; *45:* 185

Battaglia, Aurelius *50:* 44

Batten, John D. *25:* 161, 162

Batten, Mary *162:* 14, 15

Battles, Asa *32:* 94, 95

Bauer, Carla *193:* 6

Bauer, Jutta *150:* 32

Bauernschmidt, Marjorie *15:* 15

Baum, Allyn *20:* 10

Baum, Willi *4:* 24, 25; *7:* 173

Bauman, Leslie *61:* 121

Baumann, Jill *34:* 170

Baumhauer, Hans *11:* 218; *15:* 163, 165, 167

Baxter, Glen *57:* 100

Baxter, Leon *59:* 102

Baxter, Robert *87:* 129

Bayer, Herbert *181:* 16

Bayley, Dorothy *37:* 195

Bayley, Nicola *40:* 104; *41:* 34, 35; *69:* 15; *129:* 33, 34, 35

Baylin, Mark *158:* 233

Baynes, Pauline *2:* 244; *3:* 149; *13:* 133, 135,137, 141; *19:* 18, 19, 20; *32:* 208, 213, 214; *36:* 105, 108; *59:* 12, 13, 14, 16, 17, 18, 20; *100:* 158, 159, 243; *133:* 3, 4

Beach, Lou *150:* 150; *207:* 117, 118

Beaky, Suzanne *232:* 11

Beame, Rona *12:* 40

Bean, Jonathan *196:* 102

Bear's Heart *73:* 215

Beard, Alex *222:* 40

Beard, Dan *22:* 31, 32

Beard, J.H. *YABC 1:* 158

Bearden, Romare *9:* 7; *22:* 35

Beardshaw, Rosalind *169:* 22; *190:* 22; *224:* 12; *225:* 6, 7, 8; *226:* 71

Beardsley, Aubrey *17:* 14; *23:* 181; *59:* 130, 131

Bearman, Jane *29:* 38

Beaton, Cecil *24:* 208

Beaton, Clare *125:* 28; *208:* 67; *220:* 10, 11, 12

Beauce, J.A. *18:* 103

Beaujard, Sophie *81:* 54

Beavers, Ethen *225:* 9

Beccia, Carlyn *189:* 29

Bechtold, Lisze *208:* 29

Beck, Andrea *226:* 16

Beck, Charles *11:* 169; *51:* 173

Beck, Ian *138:* 27; *182:* 150; *190:* 25; *225:* 130

Beck, Melinda *203:* 112

Becker, Harriet *12:* 211

Beckerman, Jonathan *208:* 194

Beckett, Sheilah *25:* 5; *33:* 37, 38

Beckhoff, Harry *1:* 78; *5:* 163

Beckhorn, Susan Williams *189:* 32

Beckman, Kaj *45:* 38, 39, 40, 41

Beckman, Per *45:* 42, 43

Beddows, Eric *72:* 70

Bedford, F.D. *20:* 118, 122; *33:* 170; *41:* 220, 221,230, 233

Bee, Joyce *19:* 62

Bee, William *188:* 6

Beeby, Betty *25:* 36

Beech, Carol *9:* 149

Beech, Mark *192:* 122

Beek *25:* 51, 55, 59

Beeke, Tiphanie *177:* 127; *204:* 140; *212:* 178; *218:* 102

Beekman, Doug *125:* 146, 148

Beerbohm, Max *24:* 208

Beeson, Bob *108:* 57

Begin, Mary Jane *82:* 13; *206:* 13

Beha, Philippe *172:* 85

Behr, Joyce *15:* 15; *21:* 132; *23:* 161

Behrens, Hans *5:* 97

Beier, Ellen *135:* 170; *139:* 47; *183:* 164; *221:* 177; *222:* 151

Beingessner, Laura *220:* 14

Beinicke, Steve *69:* 18

Beisner, Monika *46:* 128, 131; *112:* 127

Belden, Charles J. *12:* 182

Belina, Renate *39:* 132

Bell, Corydon *3:* 20

Bell, Graham *54:* 48

Bell, Julia *151:* 214

Bell, Julie *159:* 172; *165:* 18

Bell, Thomas P. *76:* 182

Bellamy, Glen *127:* 15

Beltran, Alberto *43:* 37

Bemelmans, Ludwig *15:* 19, 21; *100:* 27

Ben-Ami, Doron *75:* 96; *84:* 107; *108:* 132; *110:* 63; *159:* 157; *197:* 142; *233:* 122

Bendall-Brunello, John *150:* 4; *157:* 163; *185:* 3, 4; *203:* 5; *237:* 101

Benda, Wladyslaw T. *15:* 256; *30:* 76, 77; *44:* 182

Bender, Robert *77:* 162; *79:* 13; *160:* 23

Bendick, Jeanne *2:* 24; *68:* 27, 28

Benioff, Carol *121:* 42; *175:* 23; *232:* 12

Benner, Cheryl *80:* 11

Bennett, Charles H. *64:* 6

Bennett, Erin Susanne *165:* 216

Bennett, F.I. *YABC 1:* 134

Bennett, James *146:* 240

Bennett, Jill *26:* 61; *41:* 38, 39; *45:* 54

Bennett, Rainey *15:* 26; *23:* 53

Bennett, Richard *15:* 45; *21:* 11, 12, 13; *25:* 175

Bennett, Susan *5:* 55

Benny, Mike *142:* 78; *203:* 13, 14; *207:* 85

Benoit, Elise *77:* 74

Benson, Linda *60:* 130; *62:* 91; *75:* 101; *79:* 156; *134:* 129

Benson, Patrick *68:* 162; *147:* 17, 18, 19, 20

Bentley, Carolyn *46:* 153

Bentley, James *149:* 30

Bentley, Roy *30:* 162

Benton, Jim *172:* 22

Benton, Thomas Hart *2:* 99

Bereal, JaeMe *228:* 16

Berelson, Howard *5:* 20; *16:* 58; *31:* 50

Berenstain, Jan *12:* 47; *64:* 33, 34, 36, 37, 38, 40, 42, 44; *135:* 25, 28, 31, 35

Berenstain, Stan *12:* 47; *64:* 33, 34, 36, 37, 38, 40, 42, 44; *135:* 25, 28, 31, 35

Berenzy, Alix *65:* 13; *73:* 6; *78:* 115

Berg, Joan *1:* 115; *3:* 156; *6:* 26, 58

Berg, Ron *36:* 48, 49; *48:* 37, 38; *67:* 72

Bergen, David *115:* 44; *207:* 34

Berger, Barbara *77:* 14

Berger, Carin *185:* 6; *232:* 14

Berger, Joe *221:* 9

Berger, William M. *14:* 143; *YABC 1:* 204

Bergherr, Mary *74:* 170; *151:* 123

Bergin, Mark *114:* 8, 9; *143:* 95; *160:* 26, 27

Bergstreser, Douglas *69:* 76

Bergum, Constance R. *121:* 14, 15; *208:* 31, 32, 33; *209:* 176

Bering, Claus *13:* 14

Berkeley, Jon *139:* 218

Berkowitz, Jeanette *3:* 249

Berman, Paul *66:* 14

Berman, Rachel *217:* 26

Bernal, Richard *154:* 176

Bernadette
    See Watts, Bernadette

Bernard, Gary *216:* 71

Bernardin, James *112:* 24; *167:* 94; *227:* 14, 15

Bernasconi, Pablo *183:* 10, 11

Bernatene, Poly *235:* 193

Bernath, Stefen *32:* 76

Berner, Rotraut Susanne *214:* 32

Bernhard, Durga *80:* 13

Bernstein, Michel J. *51:* 71

Bernstein, Ted *38:* 183; *50:* 131

Bernstein, Zena *23:* 46

Berridge, Celia *86:* 63

Berrill, Jacquelyn *12:* 50

Berry, Erick
    See Best, Allena

Berry, Holly *205:* 116; *210:* 49, 50

Berry, William D. *14:* 29; *19:* 48

Berry, William A. *6:* 219

Berson, Harold *2:* 17, 18; *4:* 28, 29, 220; *9:* 10; *12:* 19; *17:* 45; *18:* 193; *22:* 85; *34:* 172; *44:* 120; *46:* 42; *80:* 240

Bertholf, Bret *187:* 9; *189:* 32, 33

Berton, Patsy *99:* 16

Bertschmann, Harry *16:* 1

Besco, Don *70:* 99

Beskow, Elsa *20:* 13, 14, 15

Bess, Clayton *63:* 94

Best, Allena *2:* 26; *34:* 76

Betera, Carol *74:* 68

Bethell, Thomas N. *61:* 169

Bethers, Ray *6:* 22

Betteridge, Deirdre *214:* 34

Bettina

    See Ehrlich, Bettina

Betts, Ethel Franklin *17:* 161, 164, 165; *YABC 2:* 47

Betz, Rudolf *59:* 161

Bewick, Thomas *16:* 40, 41, 43, 44, 45, 47; *54:* 150; *YABC 1:* 107

Beyer, Paul J. III *74:* 24

Bezencon, Jacqueline *48:* 40

Biamonte, Daniel *40:* 90

Bianchi, John *91:* 19

Bianco, Pamela *15:* 31; *28:* 44, 45, 46

Bible, Charles *13:* 15

Bice, Clare *22:* 40

Biedrzycki, David *186:* 170; *219:* 7

Bierman, Don *57:* 184

Biggers, John *2:* 123

Biggs, Brian *192:* 38; *196:* 15; *207:* 170

Bikadoroff, Roxanna *201:* 74

Bileck, Marvin *3:* 102; *40:* 36, 37

Bilibin, Ivan *61:* 8, 9, 12, 13, 14, 15, 151, 152, 154, 162

Billington, Patrick *98:* 71

Billout, Guy *144:* 38, 39

Bimen, Levent *5:* 179

Binch, Caroline *81:* 18; *140:* 15, 16; *144:* 115; *211:* 82

Binder, Hannes *169:* 163

Bing, Christopher *126:* 34

Binger, Bill *121:* 46

Binks, Robert *25:* 150

Binzen, Bill *24:* 47

Birch, Reginald *15:* 150; *19:* 33, 34, 35, 36; *37:* 196,197; *44:* 182; *46:* 176; *YABC 1:* 84; *2:* 34, 39

Birch, Wendy *223:* 70

Birchall, Mark *123:* 188

Bird, Esther Brock *1:* 36; *25:* 66

Birdsong, Keith *167:* 85; *219:* 105

Birkett, Georgie *204:* 121

Birkett, Rachel *78:* 206

Birling, Paul *109:* 30

Birmingham, Christian *132:* 243; *143:* 114; *209:* 58; *220:* 20

Birmingham, Lloyd P. *12:* 51; *83:* 13

Biro, Val *1:* 26; *41:* 42; *60:* 178; *67:* 23, 24; *84:* 242, 243

Bischoff, Ilse *44:* 51

Bishop, Don *199:* 133; *239:* 146

Bishop, Gavin *97:* 17, 18; *144:* 42, 44; *216:* 52, 55, 56, 57

Bishop, Kathleen Wong *115:* 67

Bishop, Rich *56:* 43

Bite, I. *60:* 14

Bittinger, Ned *93:* 117; *205:* 115

Bjorklund, Lorence *3:* 188, 252; *7:* 100; *9:* 113; *10:* 66; *19:* 178; *33:* 122, 123; *35:* 36, 37, 38, 39,41, 42, 43; *36:* 185; *38:* 93; *47:* 106; *66:* 194; *YABC 1:* 242

Björkman, Steve *91:* 199; *160:* 110; *198:* 18; *218:* 188; *223:* 20, 21; *236:* 56

Blabey, Aaron *214:* 35

Black Sheep *164:* 100

Blackburn, Loren H. *63:* 10

Blackall, Sophie *194:* 140; *209:* 157; *231:* 31, 115; *237:* 172

Blackford, John *137:* 105; *180:* 36

Blackwell, Basil T. *YABC 1:* 68, 69

Blackwood, Freya *199:* 9

Blackwood, Gary L. *118:* 17

Blades, Ann *16:* 52; *37:* 213; *50:* 41; *69:* 21; *99:* 215

Blair, Jay *45:* 46; *46:* 155

Blaisdell, Elinore *1:* 121; *3:* 134; *35:* 63

Blake, Anne Catharine *189:* 71

Blake, Francis *198:* 4

Blake, Quentin *3:* 170; *10:* 48; *13:* 38; *21:* 180; *26:* 60; *28:* 228; *30:* 29, 31; *40:* 108; *45:* 219; *46:* 165, 168; *48:* 196; *52:* 10, 11, 12,13, 14, 15, 16, 17; *73:* 41, 43; *78:* 84, 86; *80:* 250, 251; *84:* 210, 211, 212; *87:* 177; *96:* 24, 26, 28; *124:* 79; *125:* 32, 34; *181:* 139; *211:* 26, 27; *227:* 176; *229:* 167

Blake, Robert J. *37:* 90; *53:* 67; *54:* 23; *160:* 28, 29

Blake, William *30:* 54, 56, 57, 58, 59, 60

Blakeslee, Lys *218:* 11, 105

Blanchard, N. Taylor *82:* 140

Blass, Jacqueline *8:* 215

Blazek, Scott R. *91:* 71

Blecha, Aaron *233:* 17

Bleck, Cathie *118:* 116

Bleck, Linda *204:* 124

Blegvad, Erik *2:* 59; *3:* 98; *5:* 117; *7:* 131; *11:* 149; *14:* 34, 35; *18:* 237; *32:* 219; *60:* 106; *66:* 16, 17, 18, 19; *70:* 233; *76:* 18; *82:* 106; *87:* 45; *100:* 188; *129:* 125; *132:* 17, 18, 19, 20; *176:* 14; *200:* 100; *YABC 1:* 201

Blessen, Karen *93:* 126

Bliss, Corinne Demas *37:* 38

Bliss, Harry *196:* 27, 28, 29

Blitt, Barry *179:* 199; *187:* 13; *225:* 198

Bloch, Lucienne *10:* 12

Blondon, Herve *129:* 48; *183:* 22

Bloom, Lloyd *35:* 180; *36:* 149; *47:* 99; *62:* 117; *68:* 231; *72:* 136; *75:* 185; *83:* 99; *108:* 19; *229:* 114

Bloom, Suzanne *172:* 23, 24; *232:* 17

Blossom, Dave *34:* 29

Blumen, John *239:* 106

Blumenschein, E.L. *YABC 1:* 113, 115

Blumer, Patt *29:* 214

Blundell, Kim *29:* 36

Bluthenthal, Diana Cain *93:* 32; *104:* 106; *177:* 26; *232:* 21

Blythe, Benjamin *128:* 7

Blythe, Gary *112:* 52; *181:* 166; *182:* 64; *185:* 7; *186:* 116, 117; *238:* 163

Boake, Kathy *176:* 185

Board, Perry *171:* 99

Boardman, Gwenn *12:* 60

Boase, Susan *224:* 53

Boatwright, Phil *211:* 195

Bober, Richard *125:* 145; *132:* 40

Bobri *30:* 138; *47:* 27

Bock, Vera *1:* 187; *21:* 41

Bock, William Sauts *8:* 7; *14:* 37; *16:* 120; *21:* 141; *36:* 177; *62:* 203

Bodecker, N(iels) M(ogens) *8:* 13; *14:* 2; *17:* 55, 56, 57; *73:* 22, 23, 24

Boehm, Linda *40:* 31

Bogacki, Tomek *138:* 31, 32; *144:* 123; *202:* 13

Bogan, Paulette *197:* 152; *201:* 17

Bogdan, Florentina *107:* 43

Bohdal, Susi *22:* 44; *101:* 20

Bohlen, Nina *58:* 13

Boies, Alex *96:* 53

Bok, Chip *205:* 16

Bolam, Emily *101:* 216; *159:* 12; *205:* 59

Bolian, Polly *3:* 270; *4:* 30; *13:* 77; *29:* 197

Bolle, Frank *87:* 100; *208:* 101

Bollen, Roger *79:* 186; *83:* 16

Bolling, Vickey *114:* 44

Bollinger, Peter *101:* 7; *128:* 198; *172:* 26

Bolognese, Don *2:* 147, 231; *4:* 176; *7:* 146; *17:* 43; *23:* 192; *24:* 50; *34:* 108; *36:* 133; *71:* 24, 25; *103:* 131; *129:* 39, 40

Bolster, Rob *186:* 169

Bolton, A.T. *57:* 158

Bond, Arnold *18:* 116

Bond, Barbara Higgins *21:* 102

Bond, Bruce *52:* 97

Bond, Felicia *38:* 197; *49:* 55, 56; *89:* 170; *90:* 171; *126:* 37

Bond, Higgins *177:* 22, 23; *209:* 175; *220:* 22, 23, 24

Bone, J. *230:* 11, 181

Bonn, Pat *43:* 40

Bonner, Hannah *197:* 13, 14

Bonners, Susan *41:* 40; *85:* 36; *94:* 99, 100; *151:* 105, 106

Bonnet, Rosalinde *230:* 79

Bono, Mary *184:* 73

Bonsall, Crosby *23:* 6

Booker, Philip *225:* 16

Boon, Debbie *103:* 6; *144:* 188

Boon, Emilie *86:* 23, 24

Boone, Debbie *165:* 77

Boore, Sara *60:* 73

Bootman, Colin *155:* 13; *159:* 35; *174:* 192; *222:* 128; *239:* 13, 14, 15

Booth, Franklin *YABC 2:* 76

Booth, George *191:* 13

Booth, Graham *32:* 193; *37:* 41, 42

Borda, Juliette *102:* 188

Bordier, Georgette *16:* 54

Boren, Tinka *27:* 128

Borges, Jose Francisco *119:* 62

Borja, Robert *22:* 48

Born, Adolf *49:* 63

Bornstein, Ruth *14:* 44; *88:* 45, 46; *107:* 30

Borten, Helen *3:* 54; *5:* 24

Bosin, Blackbear *69:* 104

Bossom, Naomi *35:* 48

Bostock, Mike *83:* 221; *114:* 14; *188:* 205

Boston, Peter *19:* 42

Bosustow, Stephen *34:* 202

Boszko, Ron *75:* 47

Bottner, Barbara *14:* 46

Boucher, Joelle *41:* 138

Boulat, Pierre *44:* 40

Boulet, Susan Seddon *50:* 47

Bouma, Paddy *118:* 25; *128:* 16

Bour, Daniele *66:* 145

Bourke-White, Margaret *15:* 286, 287; *57:* 102

Boutavant, Marc *200:* 136

Boutet de Monvel, M. *30:* 61, 62, 63, 65

Bowen, Betsy *105:* 222

Bowen, Richard *42:* 134

Bowen, Ruth *31:* 188

Bower, Ron *29:* 33

Bowers, David *95:* 38; *115:* 20; *127:* 169, 170; *165:* 57; *207:* 11

Bowers, Tim *185:* 35; *201:* 41; *218:* 13

Bowman, Claire *174:* 177

Bowman, Eric *151:* 23

Bowman, Leslie *85:* 203; *105:* 108; *116:* 76; *128:* 234; *182:* 24, 25

Bowman, Peter *146:* 214, 215; *150:* 115

Bowser, Carolyn Ewing *22:* 253

Boxall, Ed *178:* 28

Boyd, Aaron *158:* 242

Boyd, Patti *45:* 31

Boyden, Linda *238:* 39

Boyle, Eleanor Vere *28:* 50, 51

Boynton, Sandra *57:* 13, 14, 15; *107:* 36, 37; *152:* 12, 13, 14

Bozzo, Frank *4:* 154

Brabbs, Derry *55:* 170

Brace, Eric *132:* 193, 194; *152:* 71; *184:* 195; *197:* 6; *201:* 54; *233:* 160

Brackers de Hugo, Pierre *115:* 21

Bradford, June *158:* 138

Bradford, Ron *7:* 157

Bradley, David P. *69:* 105

Bradley, Richard D. *26:* 182

Bradley, William *5:* 164

Brady, Irene *4:* 31; *42:* 37; *68:* 191

Bragg, Michael *32:* 78; *46:* 31
Bragg, Ruth Gembicki *77:* 18
Brainerd, John W. *65:* 19
Braithwaite, Althea *23:* 12, 13; *119:* 16
Brak, Syd *146:* 187
Bralds, Braldt *90:* 28; *91:* 151
Bram, Elizabeth *30:* 67
Bramley, Peter *4:* 3
Brandenberg, Aliki *2:* 36, 37; *24:* 222; *35:* 49, 50, 51,52, 53, 54, 56, 57; *75:* 15, 17; *92:* 205; *113:* 18, 19, 20; *157:* 28; *156:* 111
Brandenburg, Alexa *75:* 19
Brandenburg, Jim *47:* 58; *150:* 212
Brandi, Lillian *31:* 158
Brandon, Brumsic, Jr. *9:* 25
Brannen, Sarah S. *202:* 15; *216:* 199
Bransom, Paul *17:* 121; *43:* 44
Braren, Loretta Trezzo *87:* 193
Brassard, France *186:* 22
Braun, Wendy *80:* 17, 18; *213:* 14
Brautigam, Don *115:* 175, 176; *225:* 109
Brazell, Derek *75:* 105; *79:* 9
Breathed, Berkeley *86:* 27, 28, 29; *161:* 13, 14; *229:* 10, 11, 12
Breckenreid, Julia *192:* 209
Breen, Steve *186:* 23
Brennan, Steve *83:* 230; *101:* 184
Brenner, Fred *22:* 85; *36:* 34; *42:* 34
Brett, Bernard *22:* 54
Brett, Harold M. *26:* 98, 99, 100
Brett, Jan *30:* 135; *42:* 39; *71:* 31, 32; *130:* 23, 24, 25, 26, 27; *171:* 15, 16; *234:* 32, 34, 35, 36, 37
Brewer, Paul *106:* 115; *145:* 202; *230:* 13
Brewer, Sally King *33:* 44
Brewster, Patience *40:* 68; *45:* 22, 183; *51:* 20; *66:* 144; *89:* 4; *97:* 30, 31; *212:* 99
Brick, John *10:* 15
Brickman, Robin D. *131:* 88; *142:* 150; *155:* 18; *178:* 109; *184:* 32
Bridge, David R. *45:* 28
Bridgman, L.J. *37:* 77
Bridwell, Norman *4:* 37; *138:* 36, 37, 40
Brierley, Louise *91:* 22; *96:* 165; *183:* 51
Briggs, Harry *172:* 187
Briggs, Raymond *10:* 168; *23:* 20, 21; *66:* 29, 31, 32; *131:* 28, 29; *184:* 15, 16
Brigham, Grace A. *37:* 148
Bright, Robert *24:* 55
Brighton, Catherine *107:* 39; *206:* 23
Brinckloe, Julie *13:* 18; *24:* 79, 115; *29:* 35; *63:* 140; *81:* 131
Brion *47:* 116
Brisley, Joyce L. *22:* 57
Brisson, James F. *110:* 60
Brittingham, Geoffrey *88:* 37
Brix-Henker, Silke *81:* 194
Broadway, Hannah *104:* 104
Brock, Charles E. *15:* 97; *19:* 247, 249; *23:* 224, 225; *36:* 88; *42:* 41, 42, 43, 44, 45; *100:* 189; *YABC 1:* 194, 196, 203
Brock, Emma *7:* 21
Brock, Henry Matthew *15:* 81; *16:* 141; *19:* 71; *34:* 115; *40:* 164; *42:* 47, 48, 49; *49:* 66
Brocksopp, Arthur *57:* 157
Broda, Ron *136:* 180; *174:* 123
Brodkin, Gwen *34:* 135
Brodovitch, Alexi *52:* 22
Bromhall, Winifred *5:* 11; *26:* 38
Bromley, Lizzy *159:* 179; *237:* 150
Bronson, Linda *150:* 210; *174:* 133; *203:* 16, 17; *225:* 178
Brooke, L. Leslie *16:* 181, 182, 183, 186; *17:* 15, 16, 17; *18:* 194
Brooker, Christopher *15:* 251
Brooker, Kyrsten *111:* 94; *140:* 28; *162:* 111; *175:* 108; *186:* 42, 225; *199:* 12; *201:* 30; *219:* 98
Brooks, Erik *166:* 52; *182:* 30; *232:* 139; *236:* 40, 41
Brooks, Karen Stormer *186:* 110; *220:* 65

Brooks, Maya Itzna *92:* 153
Brooks, Ron *94:* 15; *197:* 188; *212:* 6, 7, 8, 9
Brooks, S.G. *178:* 127
Broomfield, Maurice *40:* 141
Brotman, Adolph E. *5:* 21
Brown, Bill *235:* 139
Brown, Buck *45:* 48
Brown, Calef *179:* 18; *210:* 206; *217:* 30, 31; *225:* 201
Brown, Christopher *62:* 124, 125, 127, 128
Brown, Craig *73:* 28; *84:* 65; *224:* 18
Brown, Dan *61:* 167; *115:* 183, 184; *116:* 28, 29; *193:* 190; *200:* 21, 23
Brown, David *7:* 47; *48:* 52
Brown, Denise *11:* 213
Brown, Don *172:* 29
Brown, Elbrite *195:* 39; *198:* 5
Brown, Ford Madox *48:* 74
Brown, Gayle *224:* 184
Brown, Hunter *191:* 111, 112; *234:* 105, 107
Brown, Judith Gwyn *1:* 45; *7:* 5; *8:* 167; *9:* 182, 190; *20:* 16, 17, 18; *23:* 142; *29:* 117; *33:* 97; *36:* 23, 26; *43:* 184; *48:* 201, 223; *49:* 69; *86:* 227; *110:* 188; *153:* 7
Brown, Kathryn *98:* 26
Brown, Lisa *187:* 175; *234:* 39
Brown, Laurie Krasny *99:* 30
Brown, Leo *225:* 18
Brown, Marc (Tolon) *10:* 17, 197; *14:* 263; *51:* 18; *53:* 11, 12, 13, 15, 16, 17; *75:* 58; *80:* 24, 25, 26; *82:* 261; *99:* 29; *145:* 22, 23, 25, 27; *162:* 198; *224:* 136
Brown, Marcia *7:* 30; *25:* 203; *47:* 31, 32, 33, 34, 35,36, 37, 38, 39, 40, 42, 43, 44; *YABC 1:* 27
Brown, Margery W. *5:* 32, 33; *10:* 3
Brown, Martin *101:* 43
Brown, Mary Barrett *97:* 74
Brown, Palmer *36:* 40
Brown, Paul *25:* 26; *26:* 107
Brown, Richard *61:* 18; *67:* 30
Brown, Rick *78:* 71; *150:* 154; *224:* 16
Brown, Robert S. *85:* 33
Brown, Rod *157:* 142; *232:* 32, 33
Brown, Ruth *55:* 165; *86:* 112, 113; *105:* 16, 17, 18; *171:* 178
Brown, Trevor *99:* 160; *139:* 247; *189:* 206
Browne, Anthony *45:* 50, 51, 52; *61:* 21, 22, 23, 24, 25; *105:* 21, 22, 23, 25
Browne, Dik *8:* 212; *67:* 32, 33, 35, 37, 39
Browne, Gordon *16:* 97; *64:* 114, 116, 117, 119, 121
Browne, Hablot K. *15:* 65, 80; *21:* 14, 15, 16, 17, 18, 19,20; *24:* 25
Browne, Jane *165:* 222
Browning, Coleen *4:* 132
Browning, Diane *233:* 30
Browning, Mary Eleanor *24:* 84
Bruce, Robert *23:* 23
Brude, Dick *48:* 215
Bruel, Nick *166:* 41; *205:* 17, 18
Brule, Al *3:* 135
Brumbeau, Jeff *157:* 29
Bruna, Dick *43:* 48, 49, 50; *76:* 27, 28
Brundage, Frances *19:* 244
Brunhoff, Jean de *24:* 57, 58
Brunhoff, Laurent de *24:* 60; *71:* 35, 36, 37
Brunkus, Denise *84:* 50; *123:* 117; *178:* 209; *193:* 99; *204:* 10, 11, 12; *209:* 202
Brunson, Bob *43:* 135
Bryan, Ashley *31:* 44; *72:* 27, 28, 29; *107:* 92; *116:* 192; *132:* 24; *178:* 33, 34, 35; *208:* 83
Bryant, Laura J. *176:* 36; *183:* 168; *214:* 141; *222:* 49, 152
Bryant, Michael *93:* 74
Brychta, Alex *21:* 21
Bryer, Diana *107:* 121
Bryson, Bernarda *3:* 88, 146, *39:* 26; *44:* 185; *131:* 40
Buba, Joy *12:* 83; *30:* 226; *44:* 56
Buchanan, George *166:* 198

Buchanan, Lilian *13:* 16
Buchanan, Rachel *171:* 71
Bucholtz-Ross, Linda *44:* 137
Buchs, Thomas *40:* 38
Buck, Margaret Waring *3:* 30
Buckhardt, Marc *172:* 59
Buckley, Mike *166:* 180
Budwine, Greg *175:* 172
Buehner, Mark *104:* 12, 15; *105:* 160; *119:* 98; *157:* 188; *159:* 39, 40, 43; *192:* 111; *219:* 13, 14, 15, 16; *221:* 17, 18, 19
Buehr, Walter *3:* 31
Buell, Carl *222:* 68
Buff, Conrad *19:* 52, 53, 54
Buff, Mary *19:* 52, 53
Bull, Charles Livingston *18:* 207; *88:* 175, 176
Bullen, Anne *3:* 166, 167
Buller, Jon *205:* 21
Bullock, Kathleen *77:* 24
Bumgarner-Kirby, Claudia *77:* 194
Burbank, Addison *37:* 43
Burchard, Peter Duncan *3:* 197; *5:* 35; *6:* 158, 218; *143:* 17
Burckhardt, Marc *94:* 48; *110:* 89; *196:* 41; *199:* 116
Burden, Andrea *227:* 26
Burger, Carl *3:* 33; *45:* 160, 162
Burgeson, Marjorie *19:* 31
Burgess, Anne *76:* 252
Burgess, Gelett *32:* 39, 42
Burgess, Mark *157:* 31
Burke, Jim *179:* 19; *185:* 63
Burke, Phillip *95:* 117
Burkert, Nancy Ekholm *18:* 186; *22:* 140; *24:* 62, 63,64, 65; *26:* 53; *29:* 60, 61; *46:* 171; *YABC 1:* 46
Burkhardt, Bruce *142:* 86
Burkhardt, Melissa A. *142:* 86
Burleson, Joe *104:* 35; *172:* 139; *227:* 124
Burn, Doris *6:* 172
Burn, Jeffrey *89:* 125; *152:* 132
Burn, Ted
See Burn, Thomas E.
Burn, Thomas E. *151:* 41; *232:* 40
Burnard, Damon *115:* 23
Burnett, Lindy *210:* 59
Burnett, Virgil *44:* 42
Burningham, John *9:* 68; *16:* 60, 61; *59:* 28, 29, 30,31, 32, 33, 35; *111:* 18, 19, 21; *160:* 37; *225:* 21, 24
Burns, Howard M. *12:* 173
Burns, Jim *47:* 70; *86:* 32; *91:* 197; *123:* 16
Burns, M.F. *26:* 69
Burns, Raymond *9:* 29
Burns, Robert *24:* 106
Burr, Dan *65:* 28; *108:* 134; *164:* 203; *182:* 68
Burr, Dane *12:* 2
Burra, Edward *YABC 2:* 68
Burrell, Galen *56:* 76
Burri, Rene *41:* 143; *54:* 166
Burridge, Marge Opitz *14:* 42
Burris, Burmah *4:* 81
Burroughs, John Coleman *41:* 64
Burroughs, Studley O. *41:* 65
Burton, Marilee Robin *46:* 33
Burton, Virginia Lee *2:* 43; *44:* 49, 51; *100:* 46, 47; *YABC 1:* 24; *147:* 56
Buscema, Stephanie *232:* 34
Bush, Timothy *228:* 138
Busoni, Rafaello *1:* 186; *3:* 224; *6:* 126; *14:* 5; *16:* 62, 63
Butchkes, Sidney *50:* 58
Butler, Geoff *94:* 20
Butler, Ralph *116:* 212
Butterfield, Ned *1:* 153; *27:* 128; *79:* 63
Butterworth, Ian *184:* 48, 49
Butterworth, Nick *106:* 43, 44; *149:* 34
Buxton, John *123:* 12
Buzelli, Christopher *105:* 149
Buzonas, Gail *29:* 88
Buzzell, Russ W. *12:* 177

Byard, Carole *39:* 44; *57:* 18, 19, 20; *60:* 60; *61:* 93, 96; *69:* 210; *78:* 246; *79:* 227
Byars, Betsy *46:* 35
Byfield, Barbara Ninde *8:* 18
Byfield, Graham *32:* 29
Bynum, Janie *176:* 50
Byrd, Robert *13:* 218; *33:* 46; *158:* 70; *212:* 100; *226:* 39, 40; *229:* 102; *232:* 167
Byrd, Samuel *123:* 104

C

Cabat, Erni *74:* 38
Cabban, Vanessa *138:* 73; *176:* 39; *185:* 65; *227:* 70
Cabrera, Jane *103:* 24; *152:* 27; *182:* 33, 34
Caceres, Ana Palmero *198:* 106
Caddy, Alice *6:* 41
Cady, Harrison *17:* 21, 23; *19:* 57, 58
Caffrey, Aileen *72:* 223; *141:* 154
Cairns, Julia *177:* 37; *239:* 18, 19
Caldecott, Randolph *16:* 98, 103; *17:* 32, 33, 36, 38, 39; *26:* 90; *100:* 49, 50; *YABC 2:* 172
Calder, Alexander *18:* 168
Calderón, Gloria *179:* 5
Calderon, W. Frank *25:* 160
Caldwell, Ben *105:* 75; *149:* 60; *195:* 61
Caldwell, Clyde *98:* 100; *116:* 39; *208:* 145
Caldwell, Doreen *23:* 77; *71:* 41
Caldwell, John *46:* 225
Call, Greg *126:* 135; *165:* 49; *182:* 105, 163; *197:* 18, 19; *200:* 159; *209:* 166; *212:* 161; *229:* 122; *236:* 129
Callahan, Kevin *22:* 42
Callahan, Philip S. *25:* 77
Callan, Jamie *59:* 37
Callen, Liz *231:* 37
Calo, Marcos *236:* 151
Calvert, Rosemary *218:* 96
Calvin, James *61:* 92
Camburn-Bracalente, Carol A. *118:* 22
Cameron, Chad *190:* 144
Cameron, Julia Margaret *19:* 203
Cameron, Scott *99:* 18
Camm, Martin *140:* 208, 209, 210
Campbell, Ann *11:* 43; *123:* 182; *183:* 68
Campbell, Bill *89:* 39
Campbell, Ken *126:* 143; *205:* 162
Campbell, Robert *55:* 120
Campbell, Rod *51:* 27; *98:* 34
Campbell, Walter M. *YABC 2:* 158
Camps, Luis *28:* 120, 121; *66:* 35
Canga, C.B. *187:* 165
Caniglia, Jeremy *201:* 89
Cann, Helen *124:* 50; *141:* 78; *170:* 138; *179:* 22, 23
Cannell, Jon *196:* 43
Cannon, Janell *78:* 25; *128:* 40
Canright, David *36:* 162
Cantone, AnnaLaura *182:* 146; *196:* 80
Canty, Thomas *85:* 161; *92:* 47; *113:* 192; *134:* 60; *185:* 117
Canyon, Christopher *150:* 44; *151:* 112
Cáparo, Antonio Javier *204:* 128; *218:* 88; *220:* 114; *221:* 167; *227:* 125; *231:* 154
Caple, Laurie *228:* 9
Caporale, Wende *70:* 42
Capp, Al *61:* 28, 30, 31, 40, 41, 43, 44
Cappon, Manuela *154:* 64; *218:* 149
Caras, Peter *36:* 64
Caraway, Caren *57:* 22
Caraway, James *3:* 200, 201
Carbe, Nino *29:* 183
Cardinale, Christopher *231:* 38
Cares, Linda *67:* 176
Carigiet, Alois *24:* 67
Carle, Eric *4:* 42; *11:* 121; *12:* 29; *65:* 32,33, 34, 36; *73:* 63, 65; *163:* 55, 56

Carling, Amelia Lau *164:* 46
Carlino, Angela *168:* 43; *188:* 20
Carlson, Nancy L. *41:* 116; *56:* 25; *90:* 45; *144:* 48, 50; *213:* 24, 25, 26
Carluccio, Maria *175:* 129; *221:* 119
Carmi, Giora *79:* 35; *149:* 40; *208:* 126
Carpenter, Nancy *76:* 128; *86:* 173; *89:* 171; *131:* 186; *134:* 8; *138:* 215; *153:* 204; *159:* 93; *165:* 232; *211:* 134; *216:* 113; *238:* 183
Carr, Archie *37:* 225
Carrick, Donald *5:* 194; *39:* 97; *49:* 70; *53:* 156; *63:* 15, 16, 17, 18, 19, 21; *80:* 131; *86:* 151; *118:* 24
Carrick, Malcolm *28:* 59, 60
Carrick, Paul *118:* 26; *194:* 28
Carrick, Valery *21:* 47
Carrier, Lark *71:* 43
Carroll, Jim *88:* 211; *140:* 177; *153:* 99; *195:* 75; *236:* 88
Carroll, Lewis
  See Dodgson, Charles L.
Carroll, Michael *72:* 5
Carroll, Pamela *84:* 68; *128:* 214; *199:* 130
Carroll, Ruth *7:* 41; *10:* 68
Carter, Abby *81:* 32; *97:* 121; *102:* 61; *163:* 139; *164:* 125; *184:* 22, 23; *191:* 85; *222:* 51; *233:* 84, 94
Carter, Barbara *47:* 167, 169
Carter, David A. *114:* 24, 25; *170:* 42, 43; *228:* 29
Carter, Don *124:* 54; *184:* 100; *192:* 43, 44, 45
Carter, Harry *22:* 179
Carter, Helene *15:* 38; *22:* 202, 203; *YABC 2:* 220, 221
Carter, Penny *173:* 91
Cartlidge, Michelle *49:* 65; *96:* 50, 51
Cartwright, Reg *63:* 61, 62; *78:* 26; *143:* 4
Cartwright, Shannon *176:* 81
Carty, Leo *4:* 196; *7:* 163; *58:* 131
Cary *4:* 133; *9:* 32; *20:* 2; *21:* 143
Cary, Page *12:* 41
Casale, Paul *71:* 63; *109:* 122; *136:* 28
Case, Chris *209:* 23
Case, Sandra E. *16:* 2
Caseley, Judith *87:* 36; *159:* 47, 48, 49
Casilla, Robert *78:* 7; *167:* 124; *211:* 41; *212:* 165
Casino, Steve *85:* 193
Cassel, Lili
  See Wronker, Lili Cassel
Cassel-Wronker, Lili
  See Wronker, Lili Cassel
Cassels, Jean *8:* 50; *150:* 119; *173:* 37; *186:* 182
Cassen, Melody *140:* 51
Cassity, Don *104:* 24
Cassler, Carl *75:* 137, 138; *82:* 162
Casson, Hugh *65:* 38, 40, 42, 43
Castellon, Federico *48:* 45, 46, 47, 48
Castle, Jane *4:* 80
Castro L., Antonio *84:* 71; *226:* 43
Casu, Danny "casroc" *201:* 10
Catalano, Dominic *94:* 79; *163:* 60, 61; *162:* 54
Catalanotto, Peter *63:* 170; *70:* 23; *71:* 182; *72:* 96; *74:* 114; *76:* 194, 195; *77:* 7; *79:* 157; *80:* 28, 67; *83:* 157; *85:* 27; *108:* 11; *113:* 30, 31, 33, 34, 36; *114:* 27, 28, 29; *117:* 53; *124:* 168; *159:* 54, 55; *195:* 19, 20, 21, 22, 24, 174; *200:* 156; *207:* 103; *209:* 184; *226:* 4
Catania, Tom *68:* 82
Cather, Carolyn *3:* 83; *15:* 203; *34:* 216
Catlin, George *214:* 172
Catrow, David *117:* 179; *152:* 31, 33; *173:* 24; *206:* 29; *231:* 107; *236:* 154
Catusanu, Mircea *222:* 53
Cauley, Lorinda Bryan *44:* 135; *46:* 49
Cayard, Bruce *38:* 67
Cazet, Denys *52:* 27; *99:* 39, 40; *163:* 65, 66; *191:* 25, 27, 28

Ceccoli, Nicoletta *181:* 39; *188:* 99; *199:* 118; *209:* 6
Cecil, Randy *127:* 132, 133; *187:* 16, 17; *191:* 168; *209:* 5; *223:* 37, 38; *224:* 83; *233:* 156
Cellini, Joseph *2:* 73; *3:* 35; *16:* 116; *47:* 103
Cepeda, Joe *90:* 62; *109:* 91; *134:* 172; *159:* 57, 58, 164; *197:* 157; *203:* 69, 95; *215:* 38, 39, 40
Chabrian, Debbi *45:* 55
Chabrian, Deborah *51:* 182; *53:* 124; *63:* 107; *75:* 84; *79:* 85; *82:* 247; *89:* 93; *101:* 197; *212:* 13
Chagnon, Mary *37:* 158
Chalmers, Mary *3:* 145; *13:* 148; *33:* 125; *66:* 214
Chamberlain, Christopher *45:* 57
Chamberlain, Margaret *46:* 51; *106:* 89; *188:* 193; *212:* 16, 17; *224:* 181
Chamberlain, Nigel *78:* 140
Chambers, C.E. *17:* 230
Chambers, Dave *12:* 151
Chambers, Jill *134:* 110
Chambers, Mary *4:* 188
Chambliss, Maxie *42:* 186; *56:* 159; *93:* 163, 164; *103:* 178; *186:* 33, 34; *196:* 39; *223:* 182; *235:* 21
Champlin, Dale *136:* 124
Chan, Harvey *96:* 236; *99:* 153; *143:* 218; *179:* 144; *211:* 219
Chan, Peter *207:* 21; *221:* 39; *235:* 110
Chandler, David P. *28:* 62
Chaney, Howard *139:* 27
Chang, Warren *101:* 209
Chapel, Jody *68:* 20
Chapman, C.H. *13:* 83, 85, 87
Chapman, Frederick T. *6:* 27; *44:* 28
Chapman, Gaye *203:* 133
Chapman, Gaynor *32:* 52, 53
Chapman, Jane *145:* 186; *150:* 56; *166:* 220; *174:* 202; *176:* 43, 44; *179:* 131; *202:* 189; *212:* 20, 21, 22; *216:* 123, 225; *221:* 181, 182
Chapman, Lynne *175:* 31; *197:* 25; *208:* 44
Chapman-Crane, Jeff *220:* 101
Chappell, Warren *3:* 172; *21:* 56; *27:* 125
Charles, Donald *30:* 154, 155
Charlip, Remy *4:* 48; *34:* 138; *68:* 53, 54; *119:* 29, 30; *210:* 63, 64
Charlot, Jean *1:* 137, 138; *8:* 23; *14:* 31; *48:* 151; *56:* 21
Charlot, Martin *64:* 72
Charlton, Michael *34:* 50; *37:* 39
Charmatz, Bill *7:* 45
Chartier, Normand *9:* 36; *52:* 49; *66:* 40; *74:* 220; *145:* 169; *168:* 91; *177:* 108
Chase, Lynwood M. *14:* 4
Chast, Roz *97:* 39, 40; *212:* 25
Chastain, Madye Lee *4:* 50
Chateron, Ann *152:* 19
Chatterton, Martin *68:* 102; *152:* 19; *225:* 42
Chau, Tungwai *140:* 35
Chauncy, Francis *24:* 158
Chayka, Doug *145:* 97; *177:* 150; *196:* 46; *212:* 58
Chee, Cheng-Khee *79:* 42; *81:* 224; *180:* 245; *234:* 212
Chen, Chih-sien *90:* 226
Chen, Tony *6:* 45; *19:* 131; *29:* 126; *34:* 160
Chen, Wendy *221:* 76
Chen, Yong *183:* 34
Cheney, T.A. *11:* 47
Cheng, Andrea *205:* 28
Cheng, Judith *36:* 45; *51:* 16
Chermayeff, Ivan *47:* 53
Cherry, David *93:* 40
Cherry, Lynne *34:* 52; *65:* 184; *87:* 111; *99:* 46, 47
Chesak, Lina *135:* 118
Chess, Victoria *12:* 6; *33:* 42, 48, 49; *40:* 194; *41:* 145; *69:* 80; *72:* 100; *92:* 33, 34; *104:* 167

Chessa, Francesca *233:* 40
Chessare, Michele *41:* 50; *56:* 48; *69:* 145
Chesterton, G.K. *27:* 43, 44, 45, 47
Chestnutt, David *47:* 217
Chesworth, Michael *75:* 24, 152; *88:* 136; *94:* 25; *98:* 155; *160:* 42; *207:* 23, 24, 25; *214:* 145
Chetham, Celia *134:* 34
Chetwin, Grace *86:* 40
Cheung, Irving *158:* 96
Chevalier, Christa *35:* 66
Chew, Ruth *7:* 46; *132:* 147
Chewning, Randy *92:* 206
Chichester Clark, Emma *72:* 121; *77:* 212; *78:* 209; *87:* 143; *117:* 37, 39, 40; *144:* 138; *156:* 24, 25; *209:* 26
Chifflart *47:* 113, 127
Child, Lauren *119:* 32; *183:* 30, 31
Chin, Alex *28:* 54
Chitwood, Susan Tanner *163:* 16
Cho, Shinta *8:* 126
Chodos-Irvine, Margaret *52:* 102, 103, 107; *152:* 44
Choi, Yangsook *171:* 134; *173:* 135; *178:* 38, 39, 40
Choksi, Nishant *222:* 54
Chollat, Emilie *170:* 203
Chollick, Jay *25:* 175
Choma, Christina *99:* 169
Chomey, Steve *188:* 53
Chong, Vincent *238:* 105
Chorao, Kay *7:* 200, 201; *8:* 25; *11:* 234; *33:* 187; *35:* 239; *69:* 35; *70:* 235; *123:* 174; *193:* 179; *215:* 43, 44, 45, 46; *229:* 174
Chorney, Steve *221:* 63
Chow, Frances J. Soo Ping *206:* 36
Chowdhury, Subrata *62:* 130; *162:* 22, 23
Christelow, Eileen *38:* 44; *83:* 198, 199; *90:* 57, 58; *184:* 26
Christensen, Bonnie *93:* 100; *153:* 67; *213:* 29, 30
Christensen, Gardell Dano *1:* 57
Christensen, James C. *140:* 226
Christiana, David *90:* 64; *135:* 13; *171:* 7; *195:* 26, 27; *237:* 12; *239:* 84
Christiansen, Per *40:* 24
Christie, R. Gregory *116:* 107; *127:* 20, 21; *162:* 179; *164:* 114; *165:* 137; *174:* 157; *179:* 172; *185:* 17, 18, 19; *200:* 2; *204:* 85; *215:* 207; *218:* 57; *220:* 80, 130; *225:* 45, 46, 47; *226:* 211; *231:* 113; *235:* 167
Christy, Howard Chandler *17:* 163, 164, 165, 168, 169; *19:* 186, 187; *21:* 22, 23, 24, 25
Christy, Jana *194:* 21
Chronister, Robert *23:* 138; *63:* 27; *69:* 167
Chu, Carol *237:* 108
Church, Caroline Jayne *179:* 27; *219:* 28, 29
Church, Frederick *YABC 1:* 155
Chute, Marchette *1:* 59
Chwast, Jacqueline *1:* 63; *2:* 275; *6:* 46, 47; *11:* 125; *12:* 202; *14:* 235
Chwast, Seymour *3:* 128, 129; *18:* 43; *27:* 152; *92:* 79; *96:* 56, 57, 58; *146:* 32, 33; *197:* 99
Cieslawski, Steve *101:* 142; *127:* 116; *158:* 169, 171; *190:* 174; *212:* 85; *228:* 123
Cinelli, Lisa *146:* 253
Cirlin, Edgard *2:* 168
Clairin, Georges *53:* 109
Clapp, John *105:* 66; *109:* 58; *126:* 7; *129:* 148; *130:* 165; *195:* 48; *220:* 102
Clark, Brenda *119:* 85; *153:* 55
Clark, David *77:* 164; *134:* 144, 145; *216:* 66, 67
Clark, Emma Chichester
    See Chichester Clark, Emma
Clark, Robert *227:* 170
Clark, Victoria *35:* 159
Clarke, Greg *169:* 134; *215:* 47, 115; *237:* 119
Clarke, Gus *72:* 226; *134:* 31
Clarke, Harry *23:* 172, 173

Clarke, Peter *75:* 102
Claverie, Jean *38:* 46; *88:* 29
Clavis, Philippe Goossens *182:* 167
Clay, Wil *203:* 29
Clayton, Elaine *159:* 60; *209:* 32
Clayton, Robert *9:* 181
Cleary, Brian P. *186:* 37
Cleaver, Elizabeth *8:* 204; *23:* 36
Cleland, Janet *225:* 111; *226:* 48
Cleland, T.M. *26:* 92
Clemens, Peter *61:* 125
Clement, Charles *20:* 38
Clement, Gary *186:* 79; *191:* 32
Clement, Janet *182:* 50
Clement, Nathan *200:* 30
Clement, Rod *97:* 42; *234:* 68, 69
Clement, Stephen *88:* 3
Clementson, John *84:* 213
Clemesha, David *192:* 49, 50
Cleminson, Kate *221:* 26
Clevin, Jorgen *7:* 50
Clifford, Judy *34:* 163; *45:* 198
Clokey, Art *59:* 44
Clouse, Dennis *187:* 158
Clouse, James *84:* 15
Clouse, Nancy L. *78:* 31; *114:* 90; *225:* 117
Clover, Peter *152:* 45
Cneut, Carll *156:* 166; *165:* 67; *197:* 26
Coalson, Glo *9:* 72, 85; *25:* 155; *26:* 42; *35:* 212; *53:* 31; *56:* 154; *94:* 37, 38, 193
Cober, Alan E. *17:* 158; *32:* 77; *49:* 127
Cober-Gentry, Leslie *92:* 111
Cocca-Leffler, Maryann *80:* 46; *136:* 60; *139:* 193; *194:* 31, 33, 34
Cochran, Bobbye *11:* 52
Cochran, Josh *221:* 27
CoConis, Ted *4:* 41; *46:* 41; *51:* 104
Cocozza, Chris *87:* 18; *110:* 173; *111:* 149
Cockcroft, Jason *152:* 20
Coerr, Eleanor *1:* 64; *67:* 52
Coes, Peter *35:* 172
Cogancherry, Helen *52:* 143; *69:* 131; *77:* 93; *78:* 220; *109:* 204; *110:* 129; *203:* 92
Coggins, Jack *2:* 69
Cohen, Alix *7:* 53
Cohen, Lisa *225:* 49
Cohen, Miriam *155:* 23, 24
Cohen, Nancy R. *165:* 35
Cohen, Santiago *164:* 26; *215:* 52, 199
Cohen, Sheldon *105:* 33, 34; *166:* 46, 47
Cohen, Vincent O. *19:* 243
Cohen, Vivien *11:* 112
Coker, Paul *51:* 172
Colbert, Anthony *15:* 41; *20:* 193
Colby, C.B. *3:* 47
Cole, Babette *58:* 172; *96:* 63, 64; *155:* 29
Cole, Brock *68:* 223; *72:* 36, 37, 38, 192; *127:* 23; *136:* 64, 65; *197:*
Cole, Gwen *87:* 185
Cole, Henry *178:* 120; *181:* 42, 43; *189:* 60; *213:* 35, 36; *222:* 139; *238:* 84
Cole, Herbert *28:* 104
Cole, Michael *59:* 46
Cole, Olivia H.H. *1:* 134; *3:* 223; *9:* 111; *38:* 104
Cole, Rachael *209:* 39
Colin, Paul *102:* 59; *123:* 118; *126:* 152; *192:* 129; *234:* 129
Colley, Jacqui *202:* 20
Collicott, Sharleen *98:* 39; *143:* 29, 30
Collier, Bryan *126:* 54; *151:* 166; *174:* 16, 17, 18; *204:* 18, 19; *208:* 84; *211:* 143; *228:* 128
Collier, David *13:* 127
Collier, John *27:* 179; *208:* 154
Collier, Steven *50:* 52
Collier-Morales, Roberta *168:* 61
Collins, Heather *66:* 84; *67:* 68; *81:* 40; *98:* 192, 193; *129:* 95, 96, 98
Collins, Matt *167:* 90; *231:* 9
Collins, Ross *140:* 23, 24; *200:* 36, 37; *209:* 54; *239:* 24, 26, 27, 28

Colman, Audrey *146:* 161
Colón, Raul *108:* 112; *113:* 5; *117:* 167; *134:* 112; *146:* 23; *159:* 92; *166:* 73; *180:* 107; *186:* 156; *190:* 6; *193:* 24, 205; *202:* 21, 22, 23; *217:* 68; *220:* 126, 157; *226:* 118; *227:* 165; *232:* 122
Colonna, Bernard *21:* 50; *28:* 103; *34:* 140; *43:* 180; *78:* 150
Comport, Sally Wern *117:* 169; *169:* 104; *190:* 42; *207:* 50
Conahan, Carolyn *215:* 17
Conde, J.M. *100:* 120
Condon, Grattan *54:* 85 Condon, Ken *161:* 44; *195:* 28, 29
Cone, Ferne Geller *39:* 49
Cone, J. Morton *39:* 49
Conklin, Paul *43:* 62
Connelly, Gwen *212:* 30
Connelly, James *198:* 12
Connolly, Howard *67:* 88
Connolly, Jerome P. *4:* 128; *28:* 52
Connolly, Peter *47:* 60
Conoly, Walle *110:* 224
Conover, Chris *31:* 52; *40:* 184; *41:* 51; *44:* 79; *213:* 39
Conroy, Melissa *226:* 54
Constantin, Pascale *207:* 159
Contreras, Gerry *72:* 9
Converse, James *38:* 70
Conway *62:* 62
Conway, Michael *69:* 12; *81:* 3; *92:* 108
Cook, Ande *188:* 135
Cook, G.R. *29:* 165
Cook, Joel *108:* 160
Cook, Lynette *228:* 211
Cookburn, W.V. *29:* 204
Cooke, Donald E. *2:* 77
Cooke, Tom *52:* 118
Coomaraswamy, A.K. *50:* 100
Coombs, Charles *43:* 65
Coombs, Deborah *139:* 175
Coombs, Patricia *2:* 82; *3:* 52; *22:* 119; *51:* 32, 33, 34, 35, 36, 37, 38, 39, 40, 42, 43
Cooney, Barbara *6:* 16, 17, 50; *12:* 42; *13:* 92; *15:* 145; *16:* 74, 111; *18:* 189; *23:* 38, 89, 93; *32:* 138; *38:* 105; *59:* 48, 49, 51, 52, 53; *74:* 222; *81:* 100; *91:* 25; *96:* 71, 72, 74; *100:* 149; *YABC2:* 10
Cooper, Elisha *157:* 38, 39; *234:* 45, 46, 47
Cooper, Floyd *79:* 95; *81:* 45; *84:* 82; *85:* 74; *91:* 118; *96:* 77, 78; *103:* 149; *144:* 54; *145:* 151; *159:* 198; *176:* 133, 134; *187:* 26, 27, 28, 29; *188:* 22; *199:* 175; *219:* 66; *227:* 38, 39, 40, 42
Cooper, Heather *50:* 39
Cooper, Helen *102:* 42, 43, 44
Cooper, Mario *24:* 107
Cooper, Marjorie *7:* 112
Cope, Jane *61:* 201; *108* 52
Copeland, Mark *180:* 12
Copelman, Evelyn *8:* 61; *18:* 25
Copley, Heather *30:* 86; *45:* 57
Corace, Jen *208:* 48
Corbett, Grahame *30:* 114; *43:* 67
Corbett, Tom *234:* 99
Corbino, John *19:* 248
Corcos, Lucille *2:* 223; *10:* 27; *34:* 66
Cordell, Matthew *197:* 93; *199:* 20, 21; *238:* 50
Córdova, Amy *220:* 194
Corey, Robert *9:* 34
Corlass, Heather *10:* 7
Cornell, James *27:* 60
Cornell, Jeff *11:* 58
Cornell, Laura *94:* 179; *95:* 25
Corr, Christopher *204:* 98
Corral, Ridrigs *212:* 87
Corrigan, Barbara *8:* 37
Corrigan, Patrick *145:* 149
Corwin, Judith Hoffman *10:* 28
Corwin, Oliver *191:* 119

Cory, Fanny Y. *20:* 113; *48:* 29
Cosentino, Ralph *169:* 32
Cosgrove, Margaret *3:* 100; *47:* 63; *82:* 133
Costabel, Eva Deutsch *45:* 66, 67
Costanza, John *58:* 7, 8, 9
Costello, Chris *86:* 78
Costello, David F. *23:* 55
Côté, Geneviéve *184:* 37, 39; *210:* 256; *211:* 151
Cote, Nancy *126:* 139; *156:* 101; *174:* 101; *182:* 53, 54, 55; *222:* 49
Cottenden, Jeff *190:* 45
Couch, Greg *94:* 124; *110:* 13; *162:* 31; *168:* 149; *199:* 22; *216:* 144; *229:* 103
Coulson, David *239:* 132
Councell, Ruth Tietjen *79:* 29
Courtney, Cathy *58:* 69, 144; *59:* 15; *61:* 20, 87
Courtney, R. *35:* 110
Counihan, Claire *133:* 106
Cousineau, Normand *89:* 180; *112:* 76; *227:* 75
Cousins, Lucy *172:* 53, 54; *205:* 34, 35
Couture, Christin *41:* 209
Covarrubias, Miguel *35:* 118, 119, 123, 124, 125
Coville, Katherine *32:* 57; *36:* 167; *92:* 38
Covington, Neverne *113:* 87
Cowdrey, Richard *169:* 170; *178:* 205; *204:* 22, 23; *215:* 31
Cowell, Cressida *140:* 39
Cowell, Lucinda *77:* 54
Cowles, Rose *203:* 164, 167
Cox *43:* 93
Cox, Charles *8:* 20
Cox, David *56:* 37; *90:* 63; *119:* 38
Cox, Palmer *24:* 76, 77
Cox, Paul *226:* 57, 58
Cox, Steve *140:* 96
Coxe, Molly *69:* 44
Coxon, Michele *158:* 80
Crabb, Gordon *70:* 39
Crabtree, Judith *98:* 42
Craft, Kinuko *22:* 182; *36:* 220; *53:* 122, 123, 148,149; *74:* 12; *81:* 129; *86:* 31; *89:* 139; *127:* 27, 28, 29; *132:* 142; *139:* 38
Craig, Daniel *177:* 67; *180:* 11; *185:* 203; *211:* 212; *224:* 27; *229:* 59
Craig, David *136:* 198; *205:* 37; *236:* 188
Craig, Helen *49:* 76; *62:* 70, 71, 72; *69:* 141; *94:* 42, 43, 44; *112:* 53; *135:* 101, 102; *213:* 45, 46, 47, 55, 81, 82
Crane, Alan H. *1:* 217
Crane, H.M. *13:* 111
Crane, Jack *43:* 183
Crane, Jordan *174:* 21
Crane, Walter *18:* 46, 47, 48, 49, 53, 54, 56, 57, 59, 60, 61; *22:* 128; *24:* 210, 217; *100:* 70, 71
Cravath, Lynne Avril *98:* 45; *182:* 58, 59; *216:* 48; *219:* 61; *220:* 124; *224:* 183; *228:* 74; *229:* 89
Crawford, Allen *212:* 181
Crawford, Denise *137:* 213
Crawford, Will *43:* 77
Credle, Ellis *1:* 69
Czekaj, Jef *217:* 44; *218:* 77
Czernecki, Stefan *154:* 104; *178:* 68, 69
Cresci, Anne *232:* 148
Crespi, Francesca *87:* 90
Cressy, Michael *124:* 55; *203:* 132
Crews, Donald *32:* 59, 60; *76:* 42, 43, 44
Crews, Nina *97:* 49
Crichlow, Ernest *74:* 88; *83:* 203
Crilley, Mark *210:* 71
Croft, James *150:* 57
Crofut, Bob *80:* 87; *81:* 47
Crofut, Susan *23:* 61
Croll, Carolyn *80:* 137; *102:* 52; *235:* 166
Cross, Peter *56:* 78; *63:* 60, 65
Crossman, David A. *219:* 38

Crowe, Elizabeth *88:* 144
Crowell, Pers *3:* 125
Cruikshank, George *15:* 76, 83; *22:* 74, 75, 76, 77, 78, 79,80, 81, 82, 84, 137; *24:* 22, 23
Crump, Fred H. *11:* 62
Cruz, Ray *6:* 55; *70:* 234; *123:* 173; *172:* 192
Csatari, Joe *44:* 82; *55:* 152; *63:* 25, 28; *102:* 58
Cuetara, Mittie *158:* 85
Cuffari, Richard *4:* 75; *5:* 98; *6:* 56; *7:* 13,84, 153; *8:* 148, 155; *9:* 89; *11:* 19; *12:* 55, 96,114; *15:* 51, 202; *18:* 5; *20:* 139; *21:* 197; *22:* 14, 192; *23:* 15, 106; *25:* 97; *27:* 133; *28:* 196; *29:* 54; *30:* 85; *31:* 35; *36:* 101; *38:* 171; *42:* 97; *44:* 92, 192; *45:* 212, 213; *46:* 36, 198; *50:* 164; *54:* 80, 136, 137, 145; *56:* 17; *60:* 63; *66:* 49, 50; *70:* 41; *71:* 132; *77:* 157; *78:* 58, 149; *79:* 120; *85:* 2, 152
Cugat, Xavier *19:* 120
Cumings, Art *35:* 160
Cummings, Chris *29:* 167
Cummings, Michael *159:* 142
Cummings, Pat *42:* 61; *61:* 99; *69:* 205; *71:* 57,58; *78:* 24, 25; *93:* 75; *107:* 49, 50; *164:* 259; *203:* 45, 46
Cummings, Richard *24:* 119
Cummings, Terrance *227:* 49, 172
Cummings, Troy *236:* 83
Cunette, Lou *20:* 93; *22:* 125
Cunningham, Aline *25:* 180
Cunningham, David *11:* 13
Cunningham, Imogene *16:* 122, 127
Cunningham, Kelley *176:* 159
Cupples, Pat *107:* 12; *126:* 109; *182:* 13; *198:* 68; *217:* 21, 22
Curlee, Lynn *98:* 48; *141:* 39; *190:* 48
Currey, Anna *190:* 145; *202:* 130, 132
Curry, John Steuart *2:* 5; *19:* 84; *34:* 36; *144:* 126
Curry, Tom *127:* 131; *185:* 25, 26
Curtis, Bruce *23:* 96; *30:* 88; *36:* 22
Curtis, Neil *167:* 166
Curtis, Stacy *205:* 38
Cusack, Margaret *58:* 49, 50, 51
Cushman, Doug *65:* 57; *101:* 39, 40; *133:* 179; *157:* 45; *186:* 157; *210:* 76, 77; *232:* 132
Cutting, Ann *196:* 194
Cyrus, Kurt *132:* 39; *179:* 36, 37; *236:* 61, 62
Czechowski, Alicia *95:* 21; *171:* 37
Czernecki, Stefan *117:* 173

D

Dabcovich, Lydia *25:* 105; *40:* 114; *99:* 75, 76
Dacey, Bob *82:* 175; *152:* 65
d'Achille, Gino *127:* 175, 176
Daigneault, Sylvie *236:* 65
Daily, Don *78:* 197; *220:* 154
Dain, Martin J. *35:* 75
Dale, Penny *127:* 224; *151:* 57; *160:* 89; *197:* 75; *232:* 188
Dale, Rae *72:* 197
Daley, Joann *50:* 22
Dalton, Anne *40:* 62; *63:* 119
Dalton, Max *234:* 2, 52
Daly, Deborah M. *74:* 213
Daly, Jim *103:* 60; *150:* 48
Daly, Jude *138:* 118, 119; *213:* 41; *222:* 56, 57
Daly, Nicholas *37:* 53; *76:* 48, 49
Daly, Niki *107:* 15; *114:* 38, 39, 40; *164:* 86; *192:* 53; *198:* 26, 27
Daly, Paul *97:* 205
Dalziel, Brothers *33:* 113
D'Amato, Alex *9:* 48; *20:* 25
D'Amato, Janet *9:* 48; *20:* 25; *26:* 118
D'Amico, Steve *170:* 52
Danalis, Johnny *167:* 27
D'Andrea, Domenick *183:* 108

Daniel, Alan *23:* 59; *29:* 110; *76:* 50, 53, 55, 56; *153:* 76 *115:* 74; *134:* 70
Daniel, Lea *76:* 53, 55; *153:* 76
Daniel, Lewis C. *20:* 216
Daniels, Beau *73:* 4
Daniels, Steve *22:* 16
Daniels, Stewart *56:* 12
Dann, Bonnie *31:* 83
Dann, Penny *82:* 128
Danska, Herbert *24:* 219
Danyell, Alice *20:* 27
Darbyshire, Kristen *218:* 41
Dardik, Helen *208:* 200
Darley, F.O.C. *16:* 145; *19:* 79, 86, 88, 185; *21:* 28,36; *35:* 76, 77, 78, 79, 80, 81; *YABC 2:* 175
Darling, Lois *3:* 59; *23:* 30, 31
Darling, Louis *1:* 40, 41; *2:* 63; *3:* 59; *23:* 30,31; *43:* 54, 57, 59; *121:* 53
Darnell, K.L. *210:* 247
Darrow, David R. *84:* 101
Darrow, Whitney, Jr. *13:* 25; *38:* 220, 221
Darwin, Beatrice *43:* 54
Darwin, Len *24:* 82
Dastolfo, Frank *33:* 179
Dauber, Liz *1:* 22; *3:* 266; *30:* 49
Daugherty, James *3:* 66; *8:* 178; *13:* 27, 28, 161; *18:* 101; *19:* 72; *29:* 108; *32:* 156; *42:* 84; *YABC 1:* 256; *2:* 174
d'Aulaire, Edgar Parin *5:* 51; *66:* 53
d'Aulaire, Ingri Parin *5:* 51; *66:* 53
Davalos, Felipe *99:* 197; *159:* 66; *174:* 163; *235:* 52
Davenier, Christine *125:* 88; *127:* 32; *128:* 152; *179:* 39, 40; *216:* 84, 85, 86, 87; *218:* 62, 63; *224:* 73; *237:* 51
Davick, Linda *151:* 124; *208:* 187
David, Jacques-Louis *193:* 22
David, Jonathan *19:* 37
Davidson, Kevin *28:* 154
Davidson, Raymond *32:* 61
Davie, Helen K. *77:* 48, 49
Davies, Andy Robert *205:* 169
Davies, Lottie *214:* 69
Davis, Allen *20:* 11; *22:* 45; *27:* 222; *29:* 157; *41:* 99; *47:* 99; *50:* 84; *52:* 105
Davis, Bette J. *15:* 53; *23:* 95
Davis, Dimitris *45:* 95
Davis, Eleanor *209:* 33
Davis, Hendon *151:* 122
Davis, Jack E. *145:* 139; *175:* 84, 85; *208:* 102; *210:* 81, 82; *213:* 151
Davis, Jim *32:* 63, 64
Davis, Katie *152:* 52, 53, 54; *208:* 52
Davis, Lambert *110:* 23, 24; *176:* 58; *237:* 20
Davis, Marguerite *31:* 38; *34:* 69, 70; *100:* 34; *YABC 1:* 126, 230
Davis, Natalie *235:* 196
Davis, Nelle *69:* 191
Davis, Paul *78:* 214
Davis, Rich *206:* 38
Davis, Stuart *211:* 69
Davis, Yvonne LeBrun *94:* 144
Davisson, Virginia H. *44:* 178
DaVolls, Andy *85:* 53
Dawson, Diane *24:* 127; *42:* 126; *52:* 130; *68:* 104
Dawson, Janine *215:* 198
Dawson, Willow *208:* 54; *216:* 119
Day, Alexandra *67:* 59; *97:* 54; *166:* 65; *169:* 40; *197:* 50, 51, 52, 54
Day, Larry *169:* 88; *185:* 59; *227:* 55
Day, Rob *94:* 110; *127:* 24; *197:* 32
Dean, Bob *19:* 211
Dean, David *192:* 55; *239:* 55
de Angeli, Marguerite *1:* 77; *27:* 62, 65, 66, 67, 69, 70, 72; *100:* 75, 76; *YABC 1:* 166
DeArmond, Dale *70:* 47
Deas, Michael *27:* 219, 221; *30:* 156; *67:* 134; *72:* 24; *75:* 155; *84:* 206; *88:* 124
Deas, Rich *191:* 87; *193:* 10; *212:* 79

deBarros, Jim *196:* 60
Debon, Nicolas *151:* 60; *177:* 46
de Bosschere, Jean *19:* 252; *21:* 4; *186:* 44, 45
De Bruyn, M(onica) G. *13:* 30, 31
Decker, C.B. *172:* 120; *215:* 94
De Cuir, John F. *1:* 28, 29
Deeter, Catherine *74:* 110; *103:* 150; *137:* 50
Degen, Bruce *40:* 227, 229; *57:* 28, 29; *56:*
    156; *75:* 229; *76:* 19; *81:* 36, 37; *92:* 26; *93:*
    199; *97:* 56, 58, 59; *124:* 40; *147:* 39, 40,
    41; *168:* 23; *205:* 45, 46; *231:* 46, 47, 48, 49
De Grazia *14:* 59; *39:* 56, 57
DeGrazio, George *88:* 40
deGroat, Diane *9:* 39; *18:* 7; *23:* 123; *28:* 200,
    201; *31:* 58, 59; *34:* 151; *41:* 152; *43:* 88;
    46: 40, 200; *49:* 163; *50:* 89; *52:* 30, 34; *54:*
    43; *63:* 5; *70:* 136; *71:* 99; *73:* 117,156; *77:*
    34; *85:* 48; *86:* 201; *87:* 142; *90:* 72, 73,
    143; *95:* 182; *111:* 123; *118:* 160; *126:* 8;
    130: 130; *138:* 93, 94; *169:* 46, 47
de Groot, Lee *6:* 21
Deines, Brian *110:* 139; *220:* 36, 37
DeJohn, Marie *89:* 78
Dekhteryov, B. *61:* 158
de Kiefte, Kees *94:* 107
Delacre, Lulu *36:* 66; *156:* 35; *202:* 10, 53;
    209: 36
Delaney, A. *21:* 78
Delaney, Michael *180:* 16
Delaney, Molly *80:* 43
Delaney, Ned *28:* 68; *56:* 80; *102:* 11
DeLapine, Jim *79:* 21
De La Roche Saint Andre, Anne *75:* 37
de Larrea, Victoria *6:* 119, 204; *29:* 103; *72:*
    203; *87:* 199
Delehanty, Joan W. *223:* 165
DeLeon, Melanie *210:* 43
Delessert, Étienne *7:* 140; *46:* 61, 62, 63, 65,
    67, 68; *130:* 38, 39, 40, 41, 42; *179:* 46, 47,
    48, 49; *YABC 2:* 209
Delezenne, Christine *186:* 126
Delinois, Alix *228:* 40
Del Negro, Janice *196:* 161
Delon, Melanie *216:* 30
DeLorenzo, Christopher *154:* 149
Delulio, John *15:* 54
DeLuna, Tony *88:* 95
Demarest, Chris L. *45:* 68, 69, 70; *73:* 172,
    173, 176; *78:* 106; *82:* 48, 49; *89:* 212; *92:*
    86; *128:* 57, 58; *175:* 46, 48
De Mejo, Oscar *40:* 67
De Muth, Roger *205:* 184; *221:* 35
Demi *11:* 135; *15:* 245; *16:* 129, 130; *89:* 216;
    102: 66, 67, 68; *210:* 86, 87, 89
Denetsosie, Hoke *13:* 126; *82:* 34
Denise, Christopher *147:* 43, 44; *176:* 101;
    193: 35, 36, 37; *201:* 37; *238:* 56
Dennis, Morgan *18:* 68, 69; *64:* 89
Dennis, Wesley *2:* 87; *3:* 111; *11:* 132; *18:* 71,
    72, 73, 74; *22:* 9; *24:* 196, 200; *46:* 178; *69:*
    94, 96; *129:* 62
Denos, Julia *202:* 26
Denslow, W.W. *16:* 84, 85, 86, 87; *18:* 19, 20,
    24; *29:* 211; *100:* 21
Denton, Kady MacDonald *110:* 82; *130:* 70;
    181: 54, 55, 56; *192:* 75
Denton, Phil *220:* 6
Denton, Terry *72:* 163; *174:* 26; *186:* 52; *196:*
    83, 84
DePalma, Mary Newell *132:* 114; *139:* 75;
    185: 30, 31; *186:* 121; *213:* 62
dePaola, Tomie *8:* 95; *9:* 93; *11:* 69; 25; 103;
    28: 157; *29:* 80; *39:* 52, 53; *40:* 226; *46:*
    187; *59:* 61, 62, 63, 64, 65, 66, 67, 68, 69,
    71, 72, 74; *62:* 19; *108:* 63, 67, 68, 70; *155:*
    62, 64, 66; *180:* 105; *200:* 47, 48, 49, 50;
    226: 116
Deraney, Michael J. *77:* 35; *78:* 148
deRosa, Dee *70:* 48; *71:* 210; *91:* 78
Dervaux, Isabelle *111:* 117
DeSaix, Deborah Durland *180:* 15; *188:* 24

De Saulles, Tony *119:* 39
de Sève, Peter *146:* 261; *207:* 78; *219:* 42
Deshaprabhu, Meera Dayal *86:* 192
Desimini, Lisa *86:* 68; *94:* 47; *96:* 7; *104:*
    107; *125:* 194; *131:* 180; *172:* 56; *216:* 89,
    90
de St. Menin, Charles *70:* 17
Detmold, Edward J. *22:* 104, 105, 106, 107;
    35: 120; *64:* 5; *YABC 2:* 203
Detrich, Susan *20:* 133
Deutermann, Diana *77:* 175
Deutsch, Barry *239:* 34
DeVelasco, Joseph E. *21:* 51
de Veyrac, Robert *YABC 2:* 19
DeVille, Edward A. *4:* 235
de Visser, John *55:* 119
Devito, Bert *12:* 164
Devlin, Harry *11:* 74; *74:* 63, 65; *136:* 77, 78
Dewan, Ted *108:* 73; *157:* 55; *165:* 129; *226:*
    67, 68, 69
Dewar, Ken *238:* 180
Dewar, Nick *133:* 122
Dewdney, Anna *184:* 43, 44; *232:* 46, 47, 48
Dewey, Ariane *7:* 64; *33:* 195; *35:* 208; *68:*
    16,17; *75:* 46; *93:* 91; *94:* 197; *109:* 65, 66,
    67; *125:* 2, 3, 4, 5; *127:* 188; *143:* 25; *178:*
    17, 19, 74; *188:* 166; *202:* 164; *231:* 176;
    239: 155
Dewey, Jennifer (Owings) *58:* 54; *64:* 214; *65:*
    207; *88:* 169; *103:* 45
Dewey, Kenneth *39:* 62; *51:* 23; *56:* 163
de Zanger, Arie *30:* 40
Diakité, Baba Wagué *174:* 28
Diamond, Donna *21:* 200; *23:* 63; *26:* 142; *35:*
    83, 84, 85, 86, 87, 88, 89; *38:* 78; *40:* 147;
    44: 152; *50:* 144; *53:* 126; *69:* 46, 47, 48,
    201; *71:* 133; *123:* 19
Dias, Ron *71:* 67
Diaz, David *80:* 213; *96:* 83, 84; *108:* 228;
    110: 29; *149:* 106; *150:* 63; *179:* 160; *184:*
    95, 97; *189:* 51, 52, 53; *221:* 86; *229:* 37,
    38, 39, 40
di Bartolo, Jim *225:* 53
Dibley, Glin *138:* 83; *141:* 128; *211:* 162; *221:*
    61
DiCesare, Joe *70:* 38; *71:* 63, 106; *79:* 214;
    93: 147; *116:* 217; *143:* 111; *166:* 57
Dick, John Henry *8:* 181
Dickens, Frank *34:* 131
Dickey, Robert L. *15:* 279
Dickson, Mora *84:* 21
Didier, Sam *166:* 114
Dietz, James *128:* 223; *193:* 136
di Fate, Vincent *37:* 70; *90:* 11; *93:* 60; *109:*
    219, 220
Di Fiori, Lawrence *10:* 51; *12:* 190; *27:* 97;
    40: 219; *93:* 57; *130:* 45
Digby, Desmond *97:* 180
Dignan, James *196:* 143; *234:* 136
Di Grazia, Thomas *32:* 66; *35:* 241
Dillard, Annie *10:* 32
Dillard, Sarah *136:* 186; *217:* 53
Dillon, Corinne B. *1:* 139
Dillon, Diane *4:* 104, 167; *6:* 23; *13:* 29; *15:*
    99; *26:* 148; *27:* 136, 201; *51:* 29, 48, 51,
    52, 53, 54,55, 56, 57, 58, 59, 60, 61, 62; *54:*
    155; *56:* 69; *58:* 127,128; *61:* 95; *62:* 27;
    64: 46; *68:* 3; *69:* 209; *74:* 89; *79:* 92; *86:*
    89; *92:* 28, 177; *93:* 7, 210; *94:* 239, 240;
    97: 167; *106:* 58, 59,61, 64; *107:* 3; *139:*
    246; *167:* 77; *189:* 202; *191:* 191; *194:* 45,
    46, 48, 49
Dillon, Leo *4:* 104, 167; *6:* 23; *13:* 29; *15:* 99;
    26: 148; *27:* 136, 201; *51:* 29, 48, 51, 52,
    53, 54,55, 56, 57, 58, 59, 60, 61, 62; *54:*
    155; *56:* 69; *58:* 127,128; *61:* 95; *62:* 27;
    64: 46; *68:* 3; *69:* 209; *74:* 89; *79:* 92; *86:*
    89; *92:* 28, 177; *93:* 7, 210; *94:* 239, 240;
    97: 167; *106:* 58, 59,61, 64; *107:* 3; *139:*
    246; *167:* 77; *189:* 202; *191:* 191; *194:* 45,
    46, 48, 49

Dillon, Sharon Saseen *59:* 179, 188
DiMaccio, Gerald *121:* 80
DiMaggio, Joe *36:* 22
DiMassi, Gina *169:* 17
Dinan, Carol *25:* 169; *59:* 75
Dines, Glen *7:* 66, 67
Dinesen, Thomas *44:* 37
Dinh, Pham Viet *167:* 184
Dinnerstein, Harvey *42:* 63, 64, 65, 66, 67, 68;
    50: 146
Dinsdale, Mary *10:* 65; *11:* 171
Dinyer, Eric *86:* 148; *109:* 163; *110:* 239; *124:*
    11; *150:* 69; *170:* 4; *171:* 30
Dion, Nathalie *170:* 124; *213:* 52
DiPucchio, Kelly *230:* 3
DiRocco, Carl *181:* 23
DiSalvo-Ryan, DyAnne *59:* 77; *62:* 185; *117:*
    46; *144:* 64; *150:* 153; *186:* 162
Disney, Walt *28:* 71, 72, 73, 76, 77, 78, 79,
    80, 81, 87, 88, 89,90, 91, 94
DiTerlizzi, Tony *105:* 7; *147:* 22; *154:* 31, 32,
    33; *214:* 74; *236:* 33
Divito, Anna *83:* 159
Dixon, Don *74:* 17; *109:* 196
Dixon, Larry *127:* 125
Dixon, Maynard *20:* 165
Dizin, Pascal *230:* 25, 26
Doares, Robert G. *20:* 39
Dob, Bob *205:* 14
Dobias, Frank *22:* 162
Dobrin, Arnold *4:* 68
Dobson, Steven Gaston *102:* 103
Docherty, Thomas *218:* 45, 46
Dockray, Tracy *139:* 77
Docktor, Irv *43:* 70
Dodd, Ed *4:* 69
Dodd, Emma *203:* 57; *239:* 37
Dodd, Julie *74:* 73
Dodd, Lynley *35:* 92; *86:* 71; *132:* 45, 46, 47
Dodge, Bill *96:* 36; *118:* 7, 8, 9; *133:* 135
Dodgson, Charles L. *20:* 148; *33:* 146; *YABC
    2:* 98
Dodson, Bert *9:* 138; *14:* 195; *42:* 55; *54:* 8;
    60: 49; *101:* 125
Dodson, Emma *235:* 43
Dodson, Liz Brenner *105:* 117; *111:* 15
Dohanos, Stevan *16:* 10
Dolce, J. Ellen *74:* 147; *75:* 41
Dolch, Marguerite P. *50:* 64
Dolesch, Susanne *34:* 49
Dollar, Diane *57:* 32
Dolobowsky, Mena *81:* 54
Dolson, Hildegarde *5:* 57
Domanska, Janina *6:* 66, 67; *YABC 1:* 166
Domi *134:* 113
Dominguez, El *53:* 94
Domjan, Joseph *25:* 93
Domm, Jeffrey C. *84:* 69; *135:* 70
Donahey, William *68:* 209
Donahue, Dorothy *76:* 170
Donahue, Vic *2:* 93; *3:* 190; *9:* 44
Donald, Elizabeth *4:* 18
Donalty, Alison *149:* 195, 196, 197
Donato *85:* 59; *149:* 204; *191:* 19
Donato, Michael A. *200:* 143
Doner, Kim *208:* 57
Doney, Todd L.W. *87:* 12; *93:* 112; *98:* 135;
    101: 57; *104:* 40; *118:* 163; *135:* 162, 163;
    151: 18; *227:* 79; *236:* 74
Donna, Natalie *9:* 52
Donohue, Dorothy *95:* 2; *132:* 30; *176:* 54, 55;
    178: 77, 78, 79
Donovan, Jane Monroe *237:* 28
Dooling, Michael *82:* 19; *105:* 55; *106:* 224;
    125: 135; *171:* 46; *172:* 12; *176:* 120; *197:*
    89; *220:* 39, 40
Doran, Ben-Ami *128:* 189
Doran, Colleen *211:* 48
Dore, Gustave *18:* 169, 172, 175; *19:* 93, 94,
    95, 96, 97, 98,99, 100, 101, 102, 103, 104,
    105; *23:* 188; *25:* 197, 199

Doremus, Robert *6:* 62; *13:* 90; *30:* 95, 96, 97; *38:* 97
Dorfman, Ronald *11:* 128
Doriau *86:* 59; *91:* 152
Dorman, Brandon *197:* 35; *204:* 6; *210:* 104; *212:* 95; *216:* 156; *222:* 133; *234:* 92; *237:* 117
Dormer, Frank W. *200:* 55; *222:* 48; *237:* 124
Dorros, Arthur *78:* 42, 43; *91:* 28
Doruyter, Karel *165:* 105
dos Santos, Joyce Audy *57:* 187, 189
Doty, Roy *28:* 98; *31:* 32; *32:* 224; *46:* 157; *82:* 71; *142:* 7
Doucet, Bob *132:* 238; *169:* 159
Dougherty, Charles *16:* 204; *18:* 74
Doughty, Rebecca *177:* 174; *222:* 159
Doughty, Thomas *118:* 31; *140:* 60
Douglas, Aaron *31:* 103
Douglas, Allen *223:* 53; *230:* 148
Douglas, Carole Nelson *73:* 48
Douglas, Goray *13:* 151
Dow, Brian *150:* 92
Dowd, Jason *132:* 51, 52; *164:* 244
Dowd, Vic *3:* 244; *10:* 97
Dowden, Anne Ophelia *7:* 70, 71; *13:* 120
Dowdy, Mrs. Regera *29:* 100
Downard, Barry *202:* 32
Downes, Belinda *180:* 29
Downing, Julie *60:* 140; *81:* 50; *86:* 200; *99:* 129
Doyle, Janet *56:* 31
Doyle, Richard *21:* 31, 32, 33; *23:* 231; *24:* 177; *31:* 87
Draper, Angie *43:* 84
Drath, Bill *26:* 34
Drawson, Blair *17:* 53; *126:* 65
Dray, Matt *177:* 47
Drescher, Henrik *105:* 60, 62, 63; *172:* 72
Drescher, Joan *30:* 100, 101; *35:* 245; *52:* 168; *137:* 52
Dressell, Peggy *186:* 41
Drew, Janet *201:* 177
Drew, Patricia *15:* 100
Dronzek, Laura *199:* 28, 29; *207:* 69
Drummond, Allan *209:* 41
Drummond, V.H. *6:* 70
Drury, Christian Potter *105:* 97; *186:* 224
Dubanevich, Arlene *56:* 44
Dubin, Jill *205:* 56; *217:* 25
Dubois, Claude K. *196:* 2
Dubois, Gerard *182:* 9
DuBurke, Randy *187:* 89; *222:* 136; *224:* 35
Ducak, Danilo *99:* 130; *108:* 214
Duchesne, Janet *6:* 162; *79:* 8
Duda, Jana *102:* 155; *209:* 134
Dudash, C. Michael *32:* 122; *77:* 134; *82:* 149; *212:* 93, 94
Duddle, Jonny *233:* 118
Duer, Douglas *34:* 177
Duewell, Kristina *195:* 76
Duffy, Daniel Mark *76:* 37; *101:* 196; *108:* 147, 148
Duffy, Joseph *38:* 203
Duffy, Pat *28:* 153
Dugan, Karen *181:* 26; *202:* 35
Dugin, Andrej *77:* 60
Dugina, Olga *77:* 60
Duke, Chris *8:* 195; *139:* 164
Duke, Kate *87:* 186; *90:* 78, 79, 80, 81; *192:* 21, 59, 60, 61, 63
Duke, Marion *165:* 87
Dulac, Edmund *19:* 108, 109, 110, 111, 112, 113, 114, 115, 117; *23:* 187; *25:* 152; *YABC 1:* 37; *2:* 147
Dulac, Jean *13:* 64
Dumas, Philippe *52:* 36, 37, 38, 39, 40, 41, 42, 43, 45; *119:* 40, 41, 42
Dunaway, Nancy *108:* 161
Dunbar, James *76:* 63
Dunbar, Polly *181:* 60, 61; *211:* 51, 52, 53; *212:* 42; *233:* 6

Duncan, Beverly *72:* 92
Duncan, John *116:* 94
Dunn, H.T. *62:* 196
Dunn, Harvey *34:* 78, 79, 80, 81
Dunn, Iris *5:* 175
Dunn, Phoebe *5:* 175
Dunne, Jeanette *72:* 57, 173, 222
Dunnick, Regan *176:* 51; *178:* 83, 84; *219:* 36; *224:* 144; *229:* 83
Dunnington, Tom *3:* 36; *18:* 281; *25:* 61; *31:* 159; *35:* 168; *48:* 195; *79:* 144; *82:* 230
Dunn-Ramsey, Marcy *117:* 131
Dunrea, Olivier *59:* 81; *118:* 53, 54; *124:* 43; *233:* 63, 64, 66
Duntze, Dorothee *88:* 28; *160:* 76
Dupasquier, Philippe *86:* 75; *104:* 76; *151:* 63
duPont, Lindsay Harper *207:* 39
DuQuette, Keith *90:* 83; *155:* 73, 74
Durand, Delphine *200:* 56
Durham, Sarah *192:* 248
Durney, Ryan *208:* 122
Duroussy, Nathalie *146:* 150
Durrell, Julie *82:* 62; *94:* 62
Dusíková, Maja *223:* 49
Dutz *6:* 59
Duvoisin, Roger *2:* 95; *6:* 76, 77; *7:* 197; *28:* 125; *30:* 101, 102, 103, 104, 105, 107; *47:* 205; *84:* 254
Dyer, Dale *141:* 71
Dyer, Brooke *238:* 65
Dyer, Jane *75:* 219; *129:* 28; *147:* 49, 50, 51; *168:* 121; *190:* 4; *191:* 57, 59, 60; *203:* 4; *238:* 65
Dyer, Sarah *212:* 40
Dypold, Pat *15:* 37

E

E.V.B.
  See Boyle, Eleanor Vere (Gordon)
Eachus, Jennifer *29:* 74; *82:* 201; *164:* 153
Eadie, Bob *63:* 36
Eagle, Bruce *95:* 119
Eagle, Ellen *82:* 121; *89:* 3
Eagle, Jeremy *141:* 71
Eagle, Michael *11:* 86; *20:* 9; *23:* 18; *27:* 122; *28:* 57; *34:* 201; *44:* 189; *73:* 9; *78:* 235; *85:* 43
Earl-Bridges, Michele *159:* 128
Earle, Edwin *56:* 27
Earle, Olive L. *7:* 75
Earle, Vana *27:* 99
Earley, Lori *132:* 2; *186:* 4; *195:* 8
Early, Margaret *72:* 59
East, Jacqueline *218:* 198; *224:* 38
East, Stella *131:* 223
Eastman, P.D. *33:* 57
Easton, Reginald *29:* 181
Eaton, Tom *4:* 62; *6:* 64; *22:* 99; *24:* 124
Eaves, Edward *224:* 13
Ebbeler, Jeffrey *193:* 62; *206:* 45; *236:* 55
Ebel, Alex *11:* 89
Eberbach, Andrea *192:* 115
Ebert, Len *9:* 191; *44:* 47
Echevarria, Abe *37:* 69
Echo Hawk, Bunky *187:* 192
Eckersley, Maureen *48:* 62
Eckert, Horst *72:* 62
Ede, Janina *33:* 59
Edens, Cooper *49:* 81, 82, 83, 84, 85; *112:* 58
Edens, John *109:* 115
Edgar, Sarah E. *41:* 97
Edgerton, Perky *195:* 144
Edliq, Emily S. *131:* 107
Edrien *11:* 53
Edwards, Freya *45:* 102
Edwards, George Wharton *31:* 155
Edwards, Gunvor *2:* 71; *25:* 47; *32:* 71; *54:* 106

Edwards, Jeanne *29:* 257
Edwards, Linda Strauss *21:* 134; *39:* 123; *49:* 88, 89
Edwards, Michelle *152:* 62, 63
Edwards, Wallace *170:* 55
Egan, Tim *155:* 76, 77, 78
Egge, David *102:* 71
Eggenhofer, Nicholas *2:* 81
Eggleton, Bob *74:* 40; *81:* 190, 191; *105:* 6; *121:* 183; *149:* 203; *166:* 215
Egielski, Richard *11:* 90; *16:* 208; *33:* 236; *38:* 35; *49:* 91, 92, 93, 95, 212, 213, 214, 216; *79:* 122; *106:* 67, 68, 69; *134:* 135; *144:* 244; *163:* 82, 84; *207:* 125; *225:* 200
Ehlert, Lois *35:* 97; *69:* 51; *112:* 7; *113:* 208; *128:* 63, 64, 65; *172:* 77, 79, 80; *220:* 43, 44, 45, 46, 47, 48; *237:* 33, 34, 35, 36, 37, 38
Ehrlich, Bettina *1:* 83
Eitan, Ora *160:* 165
Eichenberg, Fritz *1:* 79; *9:* 54; *19:* 248; *23:* 170; *24:* 200; *26:* 208; *50:* 67, 68, 69, 70, 71, 72, 73,74, 75, 77, 79, 80, 81; *60:* 165; *100:* 137; *YABC 1:* 104, 105; *2:* 213
Einsel, Naiad *10:* 35; *29:* 136
Einsel, Walter *10:* 37
Einzig, Susan *3:* 77; *43:* 78; *67:* 155; *129:* 154
Eisner, Will *165:* 82, 83
Eitzen, Allan *9:* 56; *12:* 212; *14:* 226; *21:* 194; *38:* 162; *76:* 218
Eldridge, H. *54:* 109
Eldridge, Harold *43:* 83
Elgaard, Greta *19:* 241
Elgin, Kathleen *9:* 188; *39:* 69
Eliopoulos, Chris *234:* 56; *238:* 116
Ellacott, S.E. *19:* 118
Elliot, David *192:* 26; *208:* 62, 63
Elliott, Mark *93:* 69; *105:* 108; *107:* 123; *140:* 53; *165:* 189; *173:* 67; *195:* 95; *203:* 67; *210:* 99; *221:* 57, 70; *230:* 147; *236:* 186; *239:* 80, 81
Elliott, Sarah M. *14:* 58
Ellis, Carson *216:* 210
Ellis, Dianne *130:* 208
Ellis, Jan Davey *88:* 50; *115:* 80
Ellis, Richard *130:* 47, 48
Ellison, Chris *196:* 66; *199:* 131; *207:* 193
Ellison, Pauline *55:* 21
Ellwand, David *213:* 60
Elmer, Richard *78:* 5
Elmore, Larry *90:* 8
Elschner, Géraldine *183:* 38
Elwell, Peter *195:* 150
Elwell, Tristan *110:* 39; *121:* 182; *127:* 46; *137:* 144; *141:* 173; *151:* 236; *158:* 264; *167:* 119, 120, 121; *169:* 20; *190:* 12; *202:* 16; *226:* 6; *233:* 181
Elzbieta *88:* 80, 81
Ember, Kathi *214:* 147; *234:* 58
Emberley, Ed *8:* 53; *70:* 53, 54; *146:* 65, 69, 70; *218:* 50
Emberley, Rebecca *218:* 50
Emberley, Michael *34:* 83; *80:* 72; *119:* 47, 48; *147:* 100; *158:* 115; *189:* 62, 64; *203:* 87, 89; *232:* 51, 52, 54
Emerling, Dorothy *104:* 27
Emery, Leslie *49:* 187
Emmett, Bruce *49:* 147; *80:* 175; *101:* 206; *220:* 200
Emond, Stephen *231:* 59
Emry-Perrott, Jennifer *61:* 57
Emshwiller, Ed *174:* 45
Endle, Kate *191:* 167; *207:* 41; *233:* 155
Engel, Christiane *231:* 61
Engel, Diana *70:* 57
Engle, Mort *38:* 64
Englebert, Victor *8:* 54
English, Mark *101:* 207; *220:* 201
Enik, Ted *142:* 39
Enos, Randall *20:* 183

Enright, Maginel Wright 19: 240, 243; 39: 31, 35, 36
Enrique, Romeo 34: 135
Ensor, Barbara 180: 30
Epstein, Stephen 50: 142, 148
Erdogan, Buket 174: 179
Erdrich, Louise 141: 62
Erhard, Walter 1: 152
Erickson, Jim 196: 190; 233: 173
Erickson, Phoebe 11: 83; 59: 85
Erikson, Mel 31: 69
Eriksson, Eva 63: 88, 90, 92, 93; 203: 99; 207: 44
Ering, Timothy Basil 131: 100; 176: 63, 64; 202: 29; 204: 8
Erlbruch, Wolf 181: 66
Ernst, Lisa Campbell 47: 147; 95: 47; 154: 46, 47, 48; 164: 88; 212: 45
Esco, Jo 61: 103
Escourido, Joseph 4: 81
Escrivá, Viví 119: 51; 181: 36
Essakalli, Julie Klear 200: 58
Este, Kirk 33: 111
Estep, David 73: 57
Estes, Eleanor 91: 66
Estoril, Jean 32: 27
Estrada, Pau 74: 76
Estrada, Ric 5: 52, 146; 13: 174
Etchemendy, Teje 38: 68
Etheredges, the 73: 12
Etienne, Kirk-Albert 145: 184
Ets, Marie Hall 2: 102
Ettlinger, Doris 171: 98; 186: 106; 197: 126; 214: 125
Eulalie YABC 2: 315
Eustace, David 224: 24
Evangelista, Theresa M. 213: 67
Evans, Greg 73: 54, 55, 56; 143: 40, 41
Evans, Katherine 5: 64
Evans, Leslie 144: 227; 207: 57; 214: 88; 221: 28
Evans, Shane W. 159: 142; 160: 190; 168: 39; 188: 88; 189: 66, 67, 68; 229: 150
Everitt, Betsy 151: 110
Ewart, Claire 76: 69; 145: 59, 60
Ewing, Carolyn 66: 143; 79: 52
Ewing, Juliana Horatia 16: 92
Eyolfson, Norman 98: 154

F

Fabian, Limbert 136: 114
Facklam, Paul 132: 62
Falconer, Ian 125: 66; 179: 59
Falconer, Pearl 34: 23
Falkenstern, Lisa 70: 34; 76: 133; 78: 171; 127: 16; 191: 151
Fallone, Gianluca 231: 23
Falls, C.B. 1: 19; 38: 71, 72, 73, 74
Falter, John 40: 169, 170
Falwell, Cathryn 118: 77; 137: 185; 196: 71, 72
Fancher, Lou 138: 219; 141: 64; 144: 199; 177: 51; 214: 95; 221: 63; 228: 42, 43, 44; 230: 44, 45, 46
Fanelli, Sara 89: 63; 126: 69
Faria, Rosana 150: 143
Faricy, Patrick 185: 182; 212: 61
Farooqi, Musharraf Ali 207: 46
Farmer, Andrew 49: 102
Farmer, Peter 24: 108; 38: 75
Farnsworth, Bill 93: 189; 116: 147; 124: 8; 135: 52; 146: 242, 243, 244; 182: 176; 186: 31, 83, 84, 85; 191: 197; 222: 2
Farquharson, Alexander 46: 75
Farrell, Darren 228: 45
Farrell, David 40: 135
Farrell, Russell 196: 38
Farris, David 74: 42

Fasolino, Teresa 118: 145
Fatigati, Evelyn 24: 112
Fatus, Sophie 182: 74; 190: 218; 225: 131
Faul-Jansen, Regina 22: 117
Faulkner, Jack 6: 169
Faulkner, Matt 161: 174; 167: 75
Faust, Anke 230: 166
Fava, Rita 2: 29
Fax, Elton C. 1: 101; 4: 2; 12: 77; 25: 107
Fay 43: 93
Fearing, Mark 223: 142; 224: 39, 40
Fearnley, Jan 153: 82, 83; 205: 63, 64, 65
Fearrington, Ann 146: 80
Federspiel, Marian 33: 51
Fedorov, Nickolai Ivanovich 110: 102
Feelings, Tom 5: 22; 8: 56; 12: 153; 16: 105; 30: 196; 49: 37; 61: 101; 69: 56, 57; 93: 74; 105: 88
Fehr, Terrence 21: 87
Feiffer, Jules 3: 91; 8: 58; 61: 66, 67, 70, 74, 76,77, 78; 117: 47, 48, 49, 50; 132: 122; 157: 62; 201: 48, 49, 50; 230: 66
Feigeles, Neil 41: 242
Feldman, Elyse 86: 7
Feller, Gene 33: 130
Fellows, Muriel H. 10: 42
Felsead, Cathie 116: 85
Felts, Shirley 33: 71; 48: 59
Fennell, Tracy 171: 69
Fennelli, Maureen 38: 181
Fenton, Carroll Lane 5: 66; 21: 39
Fenton, Mildred Adams 5: 66; 21: 39
Ferguson, Peter 177: 30, 31; 181: 154; 197: 4; 199: 40; 215: 104; 221: 66; 229: 15, 16; 236: 98; 237: 153
Ferguson, Walter W. 34: 86
Fernandes, Eugenie 77: 67; 205: 68
Fernandes, Stanislaw 70: 28
Fernandez, Fernando 77: 57
Fernandez, Laura 77: 153; 101: 117; 131: 222; 170: 119; 175: 182
Ferrari, Alex 188: 121
Ferrington, Susan 172: 22
Fetz, Ingrid 11: 67; 12: 52; 16: 205; 17: 59; 29: 105; 30: 108, 109; 32: 149; 43: 142; 56: 29; 60: 34; 85: 48; 87: 146
Fiammenghi, Gioia 9: 66; 11: 44; 12: 206; 13: 57, 59; 52: 126, 129; 66: 64; 85: 83; 91: 161; 166: 169
Fiedler, Joseph Daniel 96: 42; 113: 173; 129: 164; 146: 17; 159: 68; 162: 104
Field, Rachel 15: 113
Fielding, David 70: 124
Fieser, Stephen 152: 36
Fine, Howard 145: 159; 159: 64; 165: 134; 174: 129; 181: 68
Fine, Peter K. 43: 210
Finger, Helen 42: 81
Fink, Sam 18: 119
Finlay, Winifred 23: 72
Finney, Pat 79: 215
Fiore, Peter 99: 196; 125: 139; 144: 225; 160: 169; 180: 72; 212: 103
Fiorentino, Al 3: 240
Firehammer, Karla 174: 202; 221: 183; 228: 84
Firmin, Charlotte 29: 75; 48: 70
Firmin, Peter 58: 63, 64, 65, 67, 68, 70, 71
Firth, Barbara 81: 208; 127: 218; 179: 62; 232: 189
Fischel, Lillian 40: 204
Fischer, Hans 25: 202
Fischer, Scott M. 207: 37; 217: 29
Fischer-Nagel, Andreas 56: 50
Fischer-Nagel, Heiderose 56: 50
Fisher, Carolyn 154: 50
Fisher, Chris 79: 62; 158: 248; 188: 195
Fisher, Cynthia 117: 45; 137: 118; 195: 40; 235: 126
Fisher, Jeffrey 142: 80

Fisher, Leonard Everett 3: 6; 4: 72, 86; 6: 197; 9: 59; 16: 151, 153; 23: 44; 27: 134; 29: 26; 34: 87, 89, 90, 91, 93, 94, 95, 96; 40: 206; 50: 150; 60: 158; 73: 68, 70, 71, 72, 73; 176: 71, 72, 73; 208: 131; YABC 2: 169
Fisher, Lois 20: 62; 21: 7
Fisher, Valorie 177: 55; 214: 92
Fisk, Nicholas 25: 112
Fitschen, Marilyn 2: 20, 21; 20: 48
Fitz-Maurice, Jeff 175: 2
Fitzgerald, F.A. 15: 116; 25: 86, 87
Fitzgerald, Joanne 157: 153, 154; 198: 34, 35
Fitzgerald, Royce 205: 5
Fitzhugh, Louise 1: 94; 9: 163; 45: 75, 78
Fitzhugh, Susie 11: 117
Fitzpatrick, Jim 109: 130
Fitzpatrick, Marie-Louise 125: 69, 70; 189: 72, 73
Fitzsimmons, Arthur 14: 128
Fix, Philippe 26: 102
Flack, Marjorie 21: 67; 100: 93; YABC 2: 122
Flagg, James Montgomery 17: 227
Flavin, Teresa 132: 115; 186: 119
Flax, Zeona 2: 245
Fleetwood, Tony 171: 51
Fleishman, Seymour 14: 232; 24: 87
Fleming, Denise 71: 179; 81: 58; 126: 71, 72, 73; 173: 52, 53
Fleming, Guy 18: 41
Flesher, Vivienne 85: 55
Fletcher, Claire 80: 106; 157: 159
Flint, Russ 74: 80
Floate, Helen 111: 163
Floca, Brian 155: 88, 89; 190: 10, 66, 67
Floethe, Richard 3: 131; 4: 90
Floherty, John J., Jr. 5: 68
Flook, Helen 160: 81
Flora, James 1: 96; 30: 111, 112
Florczak, Robert 166: 51
Florian, Douglas 19: 122; 83: 64, 65; 125: 71, 72, 74, 76; 128: 130; 177: 58, 60; 226: 119
Flory, Jane 22: 111
Flower, Renee 125: 109
Floyd, Gareth 1: 74; 17: 245; 48: 63; 62: 35,36, 37, 39, 40, 41; 74: 245; 79: 56
Fluchere, Henri A. 40: 79
Flynn, Alice 183: 2
Flynn, Barbara 7: 31; 9: 70
Fogarty, Thomas 15: 89
Foley, Greg 190: 69
Folger, Joseph 9: 100
Folkard, Charles 22: 132; 29: 128, 257, 258
Foott, Jeff 42: 202
Forberg, Ati 12: 71, 205; 14: 1; 22: 113; 26: 22; 48: 64, 65
Ford, A.G. 230: 40; 231: 69
Ford, George 24: 120; 31: 70, 177; 58: 126; 81: 103; 107: 91; 136: 100; 194: 47; 208: 81; 218: 56; 237: 57, 58
Ford, Gilbert 199: 10
Ford, H.J. 16: 185, 186
Ford, Jason 174: 119
Ford, Pamela Baldwin 27: 104
Fordham, John 168: 160, 161
Foreman, Michael 2: 110, 111; 67: 99; 73: 78, 79, 80,81, 82; 93: 146; 135: 55, 56, 57; 184: 58, 59; 216: 100, 101, 102, 103; 225: 144
Forrester, Victoria 40: 83
Forsey, Chris 140: 210
Fortnum, Peggy 6: 29; 20: 179; 24: 211; 26: 76, 77, 78; 39: 78; 58: 19, 21, 23, 27; YABC 1: 148
Fortune, Eric 191: 52
Foster, Brad W. 34: 99
Foster, Genevieve 2: 112
Foster, Gerald L. 7: 78; 198: 40
Foster, Jon 146: 18; 198: 7; 237: 140
Foster, Laura Louise 6: 79
Foster, Marian Curtis 23: 74; 40: 42
Foster, Sally 58: 73, 74

Fotheringham, Edwin *219:* 32
Foucher, Adele *47:* 118
Foust, Mitch *168:* 50
Fowler, Jim *184:* 190
Fowler, Mel *36:* 127
Fowler, Richard *87:* 219
Fowles, Shelley *165:* 127; *205:* 72
Fox, Charles Phillip *12:* 84
Fox, Christyan *188:* 36
Fox, Jim *6:* 187
Fox, Nathan *208:* 64
Fox-Davies, Sarah *76:* 150; *182:* 63; *199:* 42, 43
Frace, Charles *15:* 118
Frailey, Joy *72:* 108
Frame, Paul *2:* 45, 145; *9:* 153; *10:* 124; *21:* 71; *23:* 62; *24:* 123; *27:* 106; *31:* 48; *32:* 159; *34:* 195; *38:* 136; *42:* 55; *44:* 139; *60:* 39, 40, 41, 42, 43, 44, 46; *73:* 183
Frampton, David *85:* 72; *102:* 33; *139:* 182; *152:* 37; *189:* 171
Francis, Guy *198:* 164; *224:* 91; *225:* 65
Francois, Andre *25:* 117
Francoise
    See Seignobosc, Francoise
Frank, Lola Edick *2:* 199
Frank, Mary *4:* 54; *34:* 100
Franke, Phil *45:* 91
Frankel, Alona *66:* 70
Frankel, Julie *40:* 84, 85, 202
Frankenberg, Robert *22:* 116; *30:* 50; *38:* 92, 94, 95; *68:* 111
Frankfeldt, Gwen *84:* 223; *110:* 92
Frankland, David *169:* 137; *182:* 164; *201:* 159; *224:* 7; *231:* 27; *236:* 37; *237:* 152
Franklin, Ashton *165:* 144; *225:* 107
Franklin, John *24:* 22
Franson, Leanne R. *111:* 57, 58; *151:* 7; *223:* 63, 64, 158
Frascino, Edward *9:* 133; *29:* 229; *33:* 190; *48:* 80, 81, 82, 83, 84, 85, 86
Frasconi, Antonio *6:* 80; *27:* 208; *53:* 41, 43, 45, 47,48; *68:* 145; *73:* 226; *131:* 68
Fraser, Betty *2:* 212; *6:* 185; *8:* 103; *31:* 72,73; *43:* 136; *111:* 76
Fraser, Eric *38:* 78; *41:* 149, 151
Fraser, F.A. *22:* 234
Fraser, James *171:* 68
Fraser, Mary Ann *137:* 63; *214:* 98
Frasier, Debra *69:* 60; *112:* 67; *182:* 81, 82, 83
Fraustino, Lisa Rowe *146:* 87
Frazee, Marla *72:* 98; *105:* 79, 80; *151:* 67, 68; *164:* 165; *171:* 190, 191; *187:* 53, 54, 55, 56, 143; *222:* 173; *225:* 68, 69, 70; *226:* 180
Frazetta, Frank *41:* 72; *58:* 77, 78, 79, 80, 81, 82, 83
Frazier, Craig *177:* 63; *221:* 47
Freas, John *25:* 207
Fredrickson, Mark *103:* 33
Freeland, Michael J. *118:* 115
Freeman, Don *2:* 15; *13:* 249; *17:* 62, 63, 65, 67, 68; *18:* 243; *20:* 195; *23:* 213, 217; *32:* 155; *55:* 129
Freeman, Irving *67:* 150
Freeman, Laura *144:* 111; *200:* 62, 63
Freeman, Pietri *140:* 223
Freeman, Tom *167:* 118
Freeman, Tor *164:* 93
Fregosi, Claudia *24:* 117
Fremaux, Charlotte Murray *138:* 29; *141:* 95
French, Fiona *6:* 82, 83; *75:* 61; *109:* 170; *132:* 79, 80, 81, 82
French, Martin *163:* 4
French, S. Terrell *216:* 106
Frendak, Rodney *126:* 97, 98
Freschet, Gina *175:* 73
Freynet, Gilbert *72:* 221
Friar, Joanne *237:* 41
Fried, Janice *202:* 121
Frieden, Sarajo *213:* 119

Friedman, Judith *43:* 197; *131:* 221
Friedman, Marvin *19:* 59; *42:* 86
Frinta, Dagmar *36:* 42
Frith, Michael K. *15:* 138; *18:* 120
Fritz, Ronald *46:* 73; *82:* 124
Fromm, Lilo *29:* 85; *40:* 197
Frost, A.B. *17:* 6, 7; *19:* 123, 124, 125, 126, 127, 128, 129,130; *100:* 119; *YABC 1:* 156, 157, 160; *2:* 107
Frost, Helen *183:* 51
Frost, Kristi *118:* 113; *231:* 114
Frost, Michael *151:* 209; *209:* 44; *212:* 70
Froud, Brian *150:* 82, 83
Froud, Wendy *151:* 237
Fry, Guy *2:* 224
Fry, Rosalie *3:* 72; *YABC 2:* 180, 181
Fry, Rosalind *21:* 153, 168
Fryer, Elmer *34:* 115
Fuchs, Bernie *110:* 10; *162:* 46
Fuchs, Erich *6:* 84
Fuchshuber, Annegert *43:* 96
Fucile, Tony *221:* 48
Fufuka, Mahiri *32:* 146
Fuge, Charles *144:* 91, 93
Fujikawa, Gyo *39:* 75, 76; *76:* 72, 73, 74
Fulford, Deborah *23:* 159
Fuller, Margaret *25:* 189
Fulweiler, John *93:* 99
Funai, Mamoru *38:* 105
Funfhausen, Christian *196:* 30
Funk, Tom *7:* 17, 99
Furchgott, Terry *29:* 86
Furness, William Henry, Jr. *94:* 18
Furukawa, Mel *25:* 42
Fusari, Erika *164:* 227

G

Gaadt, David *78:* 212; *121:* 166; *201:* 171
Gaadt, George *71:* 9
Gaber, Susan *99:* 33; *115:* 57, 58; *164:* 195; *169:* 61, 62, 63; *185:* 50, 51; *188:* 124
Gaberell, J. *19:* 236
Gable, Brian *195:* 68, 69
Gabler, Mirko *99:* 71; *195:* 32
Gabor, Tim *216:* 61
Gackenbach, Dick *19:* 168; *41:* 81; *48:* 89, 90, 91, 92,93, 94; *54:* 105; *79:* 75, 76, 77
Gad, Victor *87:* 161
Gaetano, Nicholas *23:* 209
Gaffney-Kessell, Walter *94:* 219; *174:* 188
Gag, Flavia *17:* 49, 52
Gag, Wanda *100:* 101, 102; *YABC 1:* 135, 137, 138, 141, 143
Gagnon, Cecile *11:* 77; *58:* 87
Gaillard, Jason *200:* 69; *204:* 74
Gal, Laszlo *14:* 127; *52:* 54, 55, 56; *65:* 142; *68:* 150; *81:* 185; *96:* 104, 105
Gal, Susan *228:* 58
Galazinski, Tom *55:* 13
Galbraith, Ben *200:* 70
Galdone, Paul *1:* 156, 181, 206; *2:* 40, 241; *3:* 42,144; *4:* 141; *10:* 109, 158; *11:* 21; *12:* 118, 210; *14:* 12; *16:* 36, 37; *17:* 70, 71, 72, 73, 74; *18:* 111, 230; *19:* 183; *21:* 154; *22:* 150, 245; *33:* 126; *39:* 136, 137; *42:* 57; *51:* 169; *55:* 110; *66:* 80, 82, 139; *72:* 73; *100:* 84
Gale, Cathy *140:* 22; *143:* 52; *213:* 166
Gall, Chris *176:* 79, 80
Gallagher, Jack *187:* 100
Gallagher, S. Saelig *105:* 154; *198:* 91
Gallagher, Sears *20:* 112Gallagher-Cole, Mernie *206:* 56
Galloway, Ewing *51:* 154
Galouchka, Annouchka Gravel *95:* 55; *182:* 40
Galster, Robert *1:* 66
Galsworthy, Gay John *35:* 232
Galvez, Daniel *125:* 182

Gamble, Kim *112:* 64, 65; *124:* 77; *183:* 40, 42, 43, 56, 57; *187:* 170
Gammell, Stephen *7:* 48; *13:* 149; *29:* 82; *33:* 209; *41:* 88; *50:* 185, 186, 187; *53:* 51, 52, 53, 54, 55, 56,57, 58; *54:* 24, 25; *56:* 147, 148, 150; *57:* 27, 66; *81:* 62, 63; *87:* 88; *89:* 10; *106:* 223; *126:* 2; *128:* 71, 73, 74, 77; *154:* 34; *211:* 210; *226:* 80, 81, 82
Gamper, Ruth *84:* 198
Gampert, John *58:* 94
Ganly, Helen *56:* 56
Gannett, Ruth Chrisman *3:* 74; *18:* 254; *33:* 77, 78
Gannon, Ned *205:* 6
Gantschev, Ivan *45:* 32
Garafano, Marie *73:* 33
Garbot, Dave *131:* 106
Garbutt, Bernard *23:* 68
Garcia *37:* 71
Garcia, Geronimo *222:* 73
Garcia, Manuel *74:* 145
Garcia-Franco, Rebecca *173:* 46
Gardiner, Lindsey *178:* 128; *186:* 137
Gardner, Earle *45:* 167
Gardner, Joan *40:* 87
Gardner, Joel *40:* 87, 92
Gardner, John *40:* 87
Gardner, Lucy *40:* 87
Gardner, Richard
    See Cummings, Richard
Gardner, Sally *171:* 177; *177:* 66, 68; *229:* 58
Gargiulo, Frank *84:* 158
Garland, Michael *36:* 29; *38:* 83; *44:* 168; *48:* 78, 221, 222; *49:* 161; *60:* 139; *71:* 6, 11; *72:* 229; *74:* 142; *89:* 187; *93:* 183; *104:* 110; *131:* 55; *139:* 209; *168:* 56; *208:* 72, 73, 75
Garland, Peggy *60:* 139
Garland, Sarah *62:* 45; *135:* 67, 68; *171:* 118
Garn, Aimee *75:* 47
Garner, Joan *128:* 170
Garneray, Ambroise Louis *59:* 140
Garnett, Eve *3:* 75
Garnett, Gary *39:* 184
Garns, Allen *80:* 125; *84:* 39; *165:* 231; *209:* 44
Garófoli, Viviana *186:* 123
Garraty, Gail *4:* 142; *52:* 106
Garrett, Agnes *46:* 110; *47:* 157
Garrett, Edmund H. *20:* 29
Garrett, Tom *107:* 194; *215:* 179
Garrick, Jacqueline *67:* 42, 43; *77:* 94
Garrison, Barbara *19:* 133; *104:* 146; *109:* 87
Garro, Mark *108:* 131; *128:* 210
Garvey, Robert *98:* 222
Garza, Carmen Lomas *80:* 211; *182:* 86
Garza, Xavier *184:* 64
Gates, Frieda *26:* 80
Gaughan, Jack *26:* 79; *43:* 185
Gaver, Becky *20:* 61
Gavril, David *211:* 196
Gawing, Toby *72:* 52
Gay, Marie-Louise *68:* 76, 77, 78; *102:* 136; *126:* 76, 78, 81, 83; *127:* 55, 56; *179:* 70, 72, 73, 74; *224:* 81
Gay, Zhenya *19:* 135, 136
Gaydos, Tim *62:* 201
Gazsi, Ed *80:* 48
Gazso, Gabriel *73:* 85
Geary, Clifford N. *1:* 122; *9:* 104; *51:* 74
Geary, Rick *142:* 44, 46
Gee, Frank *33:* 26
Geehan, Wayne *157:* 181
Geer, Charles *1:* 91; *3:* 179; *4:* 201; *6:* 168; *7:* 96; *9:* 58; *10:* 72; *12:* 127; *39:* 156,157, 158, 159, 160; *42:* 88, 89, 90, 91; *55:* 111, 116
Geerinck, Manuel *173:* 128
Gehm, Charlie *36:* 65; *57:* 117; *62:* 60, 138
Geis, Alissa Imre *189:* 77; *233:* 93

Geisel, Theodor Seuss *1:* 104, 105, 106; *28:* 108, 109, 110,111, 112, 113; *75:* 67, 68, 69, 70, 71; *89:* 127, 128; *100:* 106, 107, 108
Geisert, Arthur *92:* 67, 68; *133:* 72, 73, 74; *165:* 97, 98; *171:* 64, 65; *237:* 45, 46, 47, 48
Geldart, William *15:* 121; *21:* 202
Genia *4:* 84
Gentry, Cyrille R. *12:* 66
Genzo, John Paul *136:* 74
George, Jean *2:* 113
George, Lindsay Barrett *95:* 57; *155:* 97, 98
Geraghty, Paul *130:* 60, 61
Gerard, Jean Ignace *45:* 80
Gerard, Justin *239:* 20
Gerard, Rolf *27:* 147, 150
Gerber, Mark *61:* 105
Gerber, Mary Jane *112:* 124; *171:* 56
Gerber, Stephanie *71:* 195
Gerdstein, Mordecai *169:* 105
Gergely, Tibor *54:* 15, 16
Geritz, Franz *17:* 135
Gerlach, Geff *42:* 58
Gerrard, Roy *47:* 78; *90:* 96, 97, 98, 99
Gerritsen, Paula *177:* 69; *217:* 166
Gershinowitz, George *36:* 27
Gerstein, Mordicai *31:* 117; *47:* 80, 81, 82, 83, 84, 85, 86; *51:* 173; *69:* 134; *107:* 122; *142:* 49, 52; *165:* 209; *176:* 119; *178:* 95, 97, 99; *215:* 173; *222:* 76
Gervase *12:* 27
Geter, Tyrone *146:* 249; *150:* 86
Getz, Arthur *32:* 148
Gévry, Claudine *188:* 47
Gewirtz, Bina *61:* 81
Giancola, Donato *95:* 146; *164:* 226; *229:* 181
Gibala-Broxholm, Scott *205:* 76; *219:* 186
Gibbons, Gail *23:* 78; *72:* 77, 78, 79; *82:* 182; *104:* 65; *160:* 99, 100; *201:* 59, 60, 62
Gibbs, Tony *40:* 95
Gibran, Kahlil *32:* 116
Gibson, Barbara Leonard *205:* 77; *212:* 151
Gider, Iskender *81:* 193
Giebfried, Rosemary *170:* 135
Giesen, Rosemary *34:* 192, 193
Giffard, Hannah *83:* 70
Gifford, Carrie *236:* 67, 68
Giguere, George *20:* 111
Gilbert, John *19:* 184; *54:* 115; *YABC 2:* 287
Gilbert, W.S. *36:* 83, 85, 96
Gilbert, Yvonne *116:* 70; *128:* 84; *149:* 119; *185:* 69; *192:* 25; *195:* 81
Gilchrist, Jan Spivey *72:* 82, 83, 84, 85, 87; *77:* 90; *105:* 89, 91; *130:* 63, 64; *155:* 105, 107; *182:* 67
Giles, Will *41:* 218
Gili, Phillida *70:* 73
Gill, Margery *4:* 57; *7:* 7; *22:* 122; *25:* 166; *26:* 146, 147
Gillen, Denver *28:* 216
Gillette, Henry J. *23:* 237
Gilliam, Stan *39:* 64, 81
Gillies, Chuck *62:* 31
Gilliland, Jillian *87:* 58
Gillman, Alec *98:* 105
Gilman, Esther *15:* 124
Gilman, Phoebe *104:* 70, 71
Gilpin, Stephen *213:* 68; *236:* 116
Ginsberg, Sari *111:* 184
Ginsburg, Max *62:* 59; *68:* 194 *Girard, Roge 161:* 30
Girouard, Patrick *155:* 100; *218:* 165
Giovanopoulos, Paul *7:* 104; *60:* 36
Giovine, Sergio *79:* 12; *93:* 118; *139:* 118; *205:* 114
Gist, E.M. *206:* 60
Githens, Elizabeth M. *5:* 47
Gladden, Scott *99:* 108; *103:* 160; *193:* 46, 47
Gladstone, Gary *12:* 89; *13:* 190
Gladstone, Lise *15:* 273

Glanzman, Louis S. *2:* 177; *3:* 182; *36:* 97, 98; *38:* 120, 122; *52:* 141, 144; *71:* 191; *91:* 54, 56
Glaser, Byron *154:* 59, 60
Glaser, Milton *3:* 5; *5:* 156; *11:* 107; *30:* 26; *36:* 112; *54:* 141; *151:* 70
Glass, Andrew *36:* 38; *44:* 133; *48:* 205; *65:* 3; *68:* 43, 45; *90:* 104, 105; *150:* 89; *223:* 73, 74
Glass, Marvin *9:* 174
Glasser, Judy *41:* 156; *56:* 140; *69:* 79; *72:* 101
Glasser, Robin Preiss *123:* 176; *152* 40; *172:* 194; *235:* 78
Glattauer, Ned *5:* 84; *13:* 224; *14:* 26
Glauber, Uta *17:* 76
Gleeson, J.M. *YABC 2:* 207
Glegg, Creina *36:* 100
Glienke, Amelie *63:* 150
Gliewe, Unada *3:* 78, 79; *21:* 73; *30:* 220
Gliori, Debi *72:* 91; *138:* 82; *162:* 37; *189:* 79, 81, 82; *238:* 70, 72
Glovach, Linda *7:* 105
Gobbato, Imero *3:* 180, 181; *6:* 213; *7:* 58; *9:* 150; *18:* 39; *21:* 167; *39:* 82, 83; *41:* 137, 251; *59:* 177
Goble, Paul *25:* 121; *26:* 86; *33:* 65; *69:* 68, 69; *131:* 79, 80
Goble, Warwick *46:* 78, 79; *194:* 143
Godal, Eric *36:* 93
Godbey, Cory *221:* 154
Godkin, Celia *145:* 84, 86
Godfrey, Michael *17:* 279
Godon, Ingrid *166:* 163; *186:* 99
Goede, Irene *208:* 87
Goembel, Ponder *42:* 124; *237:* 171
Goffe, Toni *61:* 83, 84, 85; *89:* 11; *90:* 124; *178:* 118
Goffstein, M.B. *8:* 71; *70:* 75, 76, 77
Golbin, Andre *15:* 125
Gold, Robert *166:* 151, 152
Goldfeder, Cheryl *11:* 191
Goldfinger, Jennifer P. *185:* 71
Goldman, Todd H. *221:* 50, 51
Goldsborough, June *5:* 154, 155; *8:* 92, *14:* 226; *19:* 139; *54:* 165
Goldsmith, Robert *110:* 77
Goldstein, Barry *198:* 147
Goldstein, Leslie *5:* 8; *6:* 60; *10:* 106
Goldstein, Nathan *1:* 175; *2:* 79; *11:* 41, 232; *16:* 55
Goldstrom, Robert *98:* 36; *145:* 51, 52; *233:* 56
Golembe, Carla *79:* 80, 81; *136:* 91; *144:* 113; *193:* 53
Golin, Carlo *74:* 112
Gomez, Elena *188:* 122; *191:* 72
Gomez, Elizabeth *127:* 70; *133:* 76
Gomi, Taro *64:* 102; *103:* 74, 76
Gon, Adriano *101:* 112
Gonsalves, Ron *178:* 213; *212:* 196
Gonzalez, Maya Christina *104:* 3; *136:* 92; *215:* 4, 5
Gonzalez, Thomas *226:* 157
Gonzalez, Yolanda *212:* 65
Good, Karen Hillard *212:* 143; *214:* 103
Goodall, John S. *4:* 92, 93; *10:* 132; *66:* 92, 93; *YABC 1:* 198
Goode, Diane *15:* 126; *50:* 183; *52:* 114, 115; *76:* 195; *84:* 94; *99:* 141; *114:* 76, 77, 78; *170:* 99, 101; *225:* 80, 81, 82, 83, 84
Goodelman, Aaron *40:* 203
Goodenow, Earle *40:* 97
Goodfellow, Peter *62:* 95; *94:* 202
Goodman, Joan Elizabeth *50:* 86
Goodman, Vivienne *82:* 251; *146:* 181, 182
Goodnow, Patti *117:* 33
Goodrich, Carter *221:* 52, 53
Goodwin, Harold *13:* 74
Goodwin, Philip R. *18:* 206
Goor, Nancy *39:* 85, 86

Goor, Ron *39:* 85, 86
Goossens, Philippe *195:* 71
Gorbachev, Valeri *89:* 96; *112:* 97; *143:* 63, 64; *184:* 66, 67, 68, 101; *222:* 84, 85, 86, 87
Gordon, David *216:* 159
Gordon, Gwen *12:* 151
Gordon, Margaret *4:* 147; *5:* 48, 49; *9:* 79
Gordon, Mike *101:* 62, 63, 64
Gordon, Russell *136:* 204; *137:* 214; *228:* 34
Gordon, Walter *138:* 9
Gore, Leonid *89:* 51; *94:* 74; *136:* 8; *158:* 117; *166:* 136; *168:* 36; *170:* 107; *181:* 94; *185:* 73; *222:* 89, 90, 91, 92; *235:* 10, 11
Gorecka-Egan, Erica *18:* 35
Gorey, Edward *1:* 60, 61; *13:* 169; *18:* 192; *20:* 201; *29:* 90, 91, 92, 93, 94, 95, 96, 97, 98, 99, 100; *30:* 129; *32:* 90; *34:* 200, *65:* 48; *68:* 24, 25; *69:* 79; *70:* 80, 82, 83, 84; *85:* 136; *127:* 62
Gorman, Mike *222:* 167
Gorsline, Douglas *1:* 98; *6:* 13; *11:* 113; *13:* 104; *15:* 14; *28:* 117, 118; *YABC 1:* 15
Gorton, Julia *108:* 94; *178:* 81, 82; *234:* 145
Gosfield, Josh *118:* 165, 166; *149:* 67
Gosner, Kenneth *5:* 135
Gosney, Joy *167:* 142
Gotlieb, Jules *6:* 127
Goto, Scott *115:* 86; *136:* 69; *203:* 77, 78
Gott, Barry *197:* 95; *212:* 102
Gottlieb, Dale *67:* 162; *107:* 16; *149:* 6
Goudey, Ray *97:* 86
Gough, Alan *91:* 57
Gough, Philip *23:* 47; *45:* 90
Gould, Chester *49:* 112, 113, 114, 116, 117, 118
Gould, Jason *151:* 232
Gourbault, Martine *177:* 159
Govern, Elaine R. *26:* 94
Gower, Teri *102:* 184
Gowing, Toby *60:* 25; *63:* 33; *78:* 70, 252; *83:* 228; *86:* 187; *93:* 145; *108:* 133; *110:* 217; *184:* 125; *225:* 142
Grabianski *20:* 144
Grabianski, Janusz *39:* 92, 93, 94, 95
Graboff, Abner *35:* 103, 104
Graef, Renée *61:* 188; *72:* 207; *204:* 45; *210:* 249
Grafe, Max *156:* 173; *178:* 237; *192:* 240; *198:* 51
Graham, A.B. *11:* 61
Graham, Bob *101:* 66, 67, 68; *151:* 74, 75; *187:* 65, 67, 68, 70
Graham, Georgia *188:* 3; *190:* 75
Graham, L. *7:* 108
Graham, Margaret Bloy *11:* 120; *18:* 305, 307
Graham, Mark *88:* 208; *159:* 153; *182:* 3
Grahame-Johnstone, Janet *13:* 61
Grahame-Johnstone, Anne *13:* 61
Grainger, Sam *42:* 95
Gralley, Jean *166:* 86
Gramatky, Hardie *1:* 107; *30:* 116, 119, 120, 122, 123
Gran, Julie *168:* 118
Granahan, Julie *84:* 84
GrandPré, Mary *84:* 131; *109:* 199; *118:* 76; *180:* 65; *184:* 70, 71, 180; *192:* 87; *215:* 24; *229:* 68, 69, 70
Grandström, Brita *176:* 139
Grandville, J.J. *45:* 81, 82, 83, 84, 85, 86, 87, 88; *47:* 125; *64:* 10
Granger, Paul *39:* 153
Granström, Brita *162:* 35; *167:* 46; *224:* 56, 57
Grant, (Alice) Leigh *10:* 52; *15:* 131; *20:* 20; *26:* 119; *48:* 202
Grant, Gordon *17:* 230, 234; *25:* 123, 124, 125, 126; *52:* 69; *YABC 1:* 164
Grant, Melvyn *159:* 186, 187; *170:* 48, 49; *213:* 168, 169; *226:* 163
Grant, Michelle *210:* 95
Grant, Renee *77:* 40
Grant, Shirley *109:* 45

Graves, Elizabeth 45: 101
Graves, Keith 167: 89; 191: 74; 216: 34; 223: 103
Gray, Harold 33: 87, 88
Gray, Les 82: 76; 83: 232
Gray, Reginald 6: 69
Gray, Steve 226: 206; 231: 77, 78
Greco, Tony 184: 6
Greder, Armin 76: 235
Green, Ann Canevari 62: 48
Green, Eileen 6: 97
Green, Elizabeth Shippen 139: 109
Green, Jonathan 86: 135; 105: 109; 221: 73
Green, Ken 111: 68
Green, Michael 32: 216
Green, Robina 87: 138
Green, Jonathan 157: 105
Greene, Jeffrey 117: 93
Greenaway, Kate 17: 275; 24: 180; 26: 107; 41: 222, 232; 100: 115, 116; YABC 1: 88, 89; 2: 131, 133, 136, 138, 139, 141
Greenberg, Melanie Hope 72: 93; 80: 125; 101: 174; 133: 180; 186: 189; 214: 105
Greenseid, Diane 178: 106, 107
Greenstein, Elaine 150: 100
Greenwald, Sheila 1: 34; 3: 99; 8: 72
Greger, Carol 76: 86
Gregorian, Joyce Ballou 30: 125
Gregory, Emilian 177: 146; 187: 10
Gregory, Fran 130: 4; 140: 93
Gregory, Frank M. 29: 107
Greiffenhagen, Maurice 16: 137; 27: 57; YABC 2: 288
Greiner, Robert 6: 86
Gretter, J. Clemens 31: 134
Gretz, Susanna 7: 114
Gretzer, John 1: 54; 3: 26; 4: 162; 7: 125; 16: 247; 18: 117; 28: 66; 30: 85, 211; 33: 235; 56: 16
Grey, Mini 166: 90; 192: 71; 239: 57
Grey Owl 24: 41
Gri 25: 90
Grieder, Walter 9: 84
Griesbach/Martucci 59: 3
Grifalconi, Ann 2: 126; 3: 248; 11: 18; 13: 182; 46: 38; 50: 145; 66: 99, 100, 101, 104, 106; 69: 38; 70: 64; 87: 128; 90: 53; 93: 49; 128: 48; 133: 79, 81; 210: 111
Griffin, Gillett Good 26: 96
Griffin, James 30: 166
Griffin, John Howard 59: 186
Griffin, Rachel 131: 23
Griffith, Gershom 94: 214
Griffiths, Dave 29: 76
Griffiths, Dean 168: 180; 169: 182
Grimly, Gris 186: 102; 192: 112; 197: 86; 219: 34
Grimsdell, Jeremy 83: 75
Grimwood, Brian 82: 89
Gringhuis, Dirk 6: 98; 9: 196
Gripe, Harald 2: 127; 74: 98
Grisha 3: 71
Grobler, Piet 201: 100
Grohmann, Susan 84: 97
Gropper, William 27: 93; 37: 193
Gros 60: 199
Grose, Helen Mason YABC 1: 260; 2: 150
Grossman, Nancy 24: 130; 29: 101
Grossman, Robert 11: 124; 46: 39
Groth, John 15: 79; 21: 53, 54; 83: 230
Grover, Lorie Ann 168: 59
Grubb, Lisa 160: 116
Grue, Lisa 187: 193
Gruelle, Johnny 35: 107
Gschwind, William 11: 72
Guarnaccia, Steven 201: 170, 173; 233: 73
Guay-Mitchell, Rebecca 110: 95, 96; 135: 240; 180: 76; 181: 71, 73; 216: 77
Guback, Georgia 88: 102
Gudeon, Karla 212: 67
Guerguerion, Claudine 105: 73

Guevara, Susan 97: 87; 167: 49; 194: 54
Guggenheim, Hans 2: 10; 3: 37; 8: 136
Guhathaakurta, Ajanta 183: 199
Guida, Lisa Chauncy 172: 188
Guilbeau, Honore 22: 69
Guillette, Joseph 137: 37
Guisewite, Cathy 57: 52, 53, 54, 56, 57
Gukova, Julia 95: 104; 154: 103; 168: 195
Gundersheimer, Karen 35: 240; 82: 100
Gunderson, Nick 57: 120
Gunnella 192: 144
Gurney, James 76: 97; 86: 32
Gurney, John Steven 75: 39, 82; 110: 175; 143: 67, 68; 169: 172; 217: 50, 88; 227: 86, 87, 88; 228: 139, 140, 141
Gusman, Annie 38: 62
Gustafson, Scott 34: 111; 43: 40
Gustavson, Adam 104: 10; 171: 183; 176: 87; 197: 94; 204: 35; 219: 187
Guthridge, Bettina 108: 79; 186: 92
Guthrie, R. Dale 64: 143
Guthrie, Robin 20: 122
Gutierrez, Akemi 172: 87; 205: 135
Gutierrez, Alan 136: 31, 32
Gutierrez, Rudy 97: 162; 203: 79; 216: 158
Gutmann, Bessie Pease 73: 93, 94
Gwynne, Fred 41: 94, 95
Gyberg, Bo-Erik 38: 131

H

Haagensen, Per 238: 88
Haas, Irene 17: 77; 87: 46; 96: 117
Hack, Konrad 51: 127
Hader, Berta H. 16: 126
Hader, Elmer S. 16: 126
Haeffele, Deborah 76: 99
Haemer, Alan 62: 109
Hafner, Marylin 22: 196, 216; 24: 44; 30: 51; 35: 95; 51: 25, 160, 164; 86: 16; 105: 196; 121: 93, 94; 149: 208, 209; 179: 82, 83, 84, 115; 190: 200; 201: 29; 217: 91
Hagerty, Sean 62: 181
Hague, Michael 32: 128; 48: 98, 99, 100, 101, 103, 105,106, 107, 108, 109, 110; 49: 121; 51: 105; 64: 14, 15; 79: 134; 80: 91, 92; 83: 135; 100: 241; 102: 29; 129: 101, 103, 104; 185: 80, 81, 82; 215: 89
Hair, Jonathan 115: 135
Halas, John 29: 41, 47, 48
Haldane, Roger 13: 76; 14: 202
Hale, Bruce 203: 83
Hale, Christy 79: 124; 84: 200; 114: 201; 128: 2, 3; 146: 203; 158: 243; 167: 99; 179: 87
Hale, Irina 26: 97
Hale, James Graham 88: 207
Hale, Kathleen 17: 79; 66: 114, 116, 118
Hale, Nathan 210: 115, 116; 214: 179
Haley, Amanda 205: 82, 83
Haley, Gail E. 43: 102, 103, 104, 105; 78: 65, 67; 136: 106, 107
Hall, Amanda 96: 110
Hall, Angus 224: 192
Hall, August N. 217: 74; 238: 104
Hall, Chuck 30: 189
Hall, Douglas 15: 184; 43: 106, 107; 86: 100; 87: 82; 129: 72
Hall, H. Tom 1: 227; 30: 210
Hall, Melanie 116: 48, 49; 169: 77, 78; 219: 170; 228: 65, 66, 67
Hall, Michael 228: 69
Hall, Sydney P. 31: 89
Hall, Tim 164: 196; 202: 41
Hall, Vicki 20: 24
Hallinan, P.K. 39: 98
Hallman, Tom 98: 166
Hally, Greg 101: 200; 151: 224

Halperin, Wendy Anderson 96: 151; 125: 96, 97, 98, 99; 139: 22; 140: 84; 200: 77, 78; 210: 157; 215: 65; 228: 24, 76
Halpern, Joan 10: 25
Halpern, Shari 174: 172
Halpin, Abigail 236: 94
Halsey, Megan 96: 172; 114: 185; 180: 8; 185: 85
Halstead, Virginia 125: 105
Halverson, Janet 49: 38, 42, 44
Hallensleben, Georg 134: 5, 6; 172: 17
Hallett, Mark 220: 63
Hamanaka, Sheila 71: 100
Hamann, Brad 78: 151
Hamann, Sigune 104: 115
Hamberger, John 6: 8; 8: 32; 14: 79; 34: 136; 88: 78
Hamil, Tom 14: 80; 43: 163
Hamilton, Bill and Associates 26: 215
Hamilton, Helen S. 2: 238
Hamilton, J. 19: 83, 85, 87
Hamilton, Laurie 116: 210
Hamilton, Todd Cameron 84: 15
Hamlin, Janet 97: 136; 124: 90; 137: 157; 182: 117
Hamlin, Louise 71: 135
Hammill, Matt 206: 65
Hammond, Chris 21: 37
Hammond, Elizabeth 5: 36, 203
Hampshire, Michael 5: 187; 7: 110, 111; 48: 150; 51: 129
Hampson, Denman 10: 155; 15: 130
Hampton, Blake 41: 244
Handford, Martin 64: 105, 106, 107, 109
Handforth, Thomas 42: 100, 101, 102, 103, 104, 105, 107
Handville, Robert 1: 89; 38: 76; 45: 108, 109
Hane, Roger 17: 239; 44: 54
Haney, Elizabeth Mathieu 34: 84
Hanke, Karen 234: 71
Hanke, Ted 71: 10
Hankinson, Phil 181: 164; 238: 160
Hanley, Catherine 8: 161
Hann, Jacquie 19: 144
Hanna, Cheryl 91: 133
Hanna, Wayne A. 67: 145
Hannon, Mark 38: 37
Hanrahan, Kelly-Anne 203: 142
Hansen, Gaby 159: 11; 186: 25; 224: 11
Hansen, Mia 149: 76
Hanson, Glen 229: 84
Hanson, Joan 8: 76; 11: 139
Hanson, Peter E. 52: 47; 54: 99, 100; 73: 21; 84: 79; 116: 144
Hansson, Gunilla 64: 111, 112
Harbour, Elizabeth 221: 68
Hardcastle, Nick 121: 82; 175: 185; 222: 135
Hardy, David A. 9: 96; 119: 74
Hardy, Paul YABC 2: 245
Hargis, Wes 219: 70; 239: 175 Haring, Keith 145: 65
Harlan, Jerry 3: 96
Harlin, Greg 89: 194; 103: 82; 118: 161; 121: 167; 182: 76; 201: 172; 215: 76
Harman, Dominic 206: 48
Harness, Cheryl 106: 80; 131: 87; 178: 111; 200: 39
Harnischfeger 18: 121
Harper, Arthur YABC 2: 121
Harper, Betty 126: 90
Harper, Jamie 174: 71; 214: 212
Harper, Piers 79: 27; 105: 102; 161: 67
Harrington, Glenn 82: 18; 94: 66, 68; 185: 118
Harrington, Jack 83: 162
Harrington, Richard 5: 81
Harris, Andrew N. 191: 78
Harris, Jim 127: 130; 183: 4
Harris, John 83: 25
Harris, Nick 86: 177
Harris, Susan Yard 42: 121

Harrison, Florence *20:* 150, 152
Harrison, Harry *4:* 103
Harrison, Jack *28:* 149
Harrison, Mark *105:* 157; *165:* 190
Harrison, Ted *56:* 73
Harsh, Fred *72:* 107
Harston, Jerry *105:* 143
Hart, Lewis *98:* 115
Hart, Thomas *181:* 165; *238:* 161
Hart, William *13:* 72
Hartland, Jessie *171:* 80, 81; *186:* 165; *223:* 58
Hartung, Susan Kathleen *150:* 107, 108; *173:* 106; *175:* 106; *192:* 78; *211:* 19
Hartelius, Margaret *10:* 24
Hartshorn, Ruth *5:* 115; *11:* 129
Harvey, Amanda *145:* 44
Harvey, Bob *48:* 219
Harvey, Gerry *7:* 180
Harvey, Lisa *97:* 21
Harvey, Paul *88:* 74
Harvey, Roland *71:* 88; *123:* 63; *179:* 94; *218:* 94; *219:* 74
Haskamp, Steve *195:* 36; *229:* 29
Hassall, Joan *43:* 108, 109
Hassell, Hilton *YABC 1:* 187
Hassett, John *162:* 59
Hasselriis, Else *18:* 87; *YABC 1:* 96
Hastings, Glenn *89:* 183
Hastings, Ian *62:* 67
Hauman, Doris *2:* 184; *29:* 58, 59; *32:* 85, 86, 87
Hauman, George *2:* 184; *29:* 58, 59; *32:* 85, 86, 87
Hausherr, Rosmarie *15:* 29
Haverfield, Mary *225:* 87
Hawkes, Kevin *78:* 72; *104:* 198; *105:* 197; *112:* 109; *126:* 87; *144:* 88; *149:* 210; *150:* 110, 135; *156:* 94; *164:* 35; *186:* 18; *190:* 197; *198:* 152; *201:* 70, 71, 72; *220:* 99; *221:* 90, 92, 93; *234:* 195
Hawkins, Jacqui *112:* 86; *162:* 64
Hawkinson, John *4:* 109; *7:* 83; *21:* 64
Hawkinson, Lucy *21:* 64
Hawthorne, Mike *140:* 228
Haxton, Elaine *28:* 131
Haydock, Robert *4:* 95
Hayes, Geoffrey *26:* 111; *44:* 133; *91:* 85; *207:* 63
Hayes, Karel *207:* 65
Haynes, Max *72:* 107
Hays, Michael *73:* 207; *83:* 93; *139:* 197; *146:* 202, 250; *202:* 47
Haywood, Carolyn *1:* 112; *29:* 104
Heale, Jonathan *104:* 117
Healy, Daty *12:* 143
Healy, Deborah *58:* 181, 182; *101:* 111
Heap, Sue *102:* 207; *150:* 113, 114; *187:* 84, 85, 87
Hearn, Diane Dawson *79:* 99; *113:* 13; *209:* 71, 72; *211:* 106
Hearon, Dorothy *34:* 69
Heaslip, William *57:* 24, 25
Hechtkopf, H. *11:* 110
Heck, Ed *173:* 81
Hector, Julian *205:* 85
Hedderwick, Mairi *30:* 127; *32:* 47; *36:* 104; *77:* 86; *145:* 91, 93, 95
Heffernan, Phil *146:* 197; *195:* 172; *218:* 123
Hefter, Richard *28:* 170; *31:* 81, 82; *33:* 183
Hehenberger, Shelly *126:* 91
Heigh, James *22:* 98
Heighway, Richard *25:* 160; *64:* 4
Heighway-Bury, Robin *159:* 89
Heine, Helme *67:* 86; *135:* 91, 92
Heinly, John *45:* 113
Helakoski, Leslie *238:* 85
Hellard, Susan *81:* 21; *204:* 82; *209:* 92
Hellebrand, Nancy *26:* 57
Heller, Linda *46:* 86
Heller, Ruth M. *66:* 125; *77:* 30, 32

Hellmuth, Jim *38:* 164
Helms, Georgeann *33:* 62
Helquist, Brett *142:* 203; *146:* 133, 134; *156:* 10; *173:* 25; *180:* 106; *187:* 90, 91; *193:* 12; *224:* 186; *226:* 117; *229:* 76, 77, 78; *239:* 5, 161
Helweg, Hans *41:* 118; *50:* 93; *58:* 22, 26
Hemingway, Edward *212:* 71
Hemphill, Helen *179:* 95
Henba, Bobbie *90:* 195
Henderling, Lisa *214:* 65
Henderson, Dave *73:* 76; *75:* 191, 192, 193, 194; *82:* 4
Henderson, D.F. *216:* 77
Henderson, Douglas *103:* 68
Henderson, Kathy *55:* 32; *155:* 118
Henderson, Keith *35:* 122
Henderson, Meryl *127:* 58, 60; *169:* 81; *228:*
Hendra, Sue *235:* 95
Hendricks, Donald *235:* 142
Hendrix, John *187:* 133; *208:* 106, 107, 108; *216:* 115
Hendry, Linda *80:* 104; *83:* 83; *164:* 216; *233:* 11
Hengeveld, Dennis *142:* 86
Henkes, Kevin *43:* 111; *108:* 106, 107, 108
Henneberger, Robert *1:* 42; *2:* 237; *25:* 83
Henriksen, Harold *35:* 26; *48:* 68
Henriquez, Celeste *103:* 137
Henriquez, Elsa *82:* 260
Henriquez, Emile F. *89:* 88; *211:* 56
Henry, Everett *29:* 191
Henry, Matthew *117:* 58
Henry, Paul *93:* 121; *194:* 125
Henry, Rohan *217:* 77
Henry, Thomas *5:* 102
Hensel *27:* 119
Henshaw, Jacqui *141:* 127
Henstra, Friso *8:* 80; *36:* 70; *40:* 222; *41:* 250; *73:* 100, 101
Henterly, Jamichael *93:* 4
Heo, Yumi *89:* 85, 86; *94:* 89, 90; *146:* 40, 137, 138; *163:* 227; *201:* 192
Hepple, Norman *28:* 198
Herbert, Helen *57:* 70
Herbert, Jennifer *189:* 47
Herbert, Wally *23:* 101
Herbster, Mary Lee *9:* 33
Herder, Edwin *182:* 104
Herge
　See Remi, Georges
Hermansen, Pal *133:* 113
Hermanson, Dennis *10:* 55
Hermes, Gertrude *54:* 161
Herr, Margo *57:* 191
Herr, Susan *83:* 163
Herriman, George *140:* 74, 75, 76, 77, 78
Herriman, Lisa *87:* 190
Herring, Michael *121:* 76; *182:* 103
Herrington, Roger *3:* 161
Herscovici, C. *165:* 240
Hescox, Richard *85:* 86; *90:* 30; *139:* 35
Heslop, Mike *38:* 60; *40:* 130
Hess, Lydia J. *85:* 17
Hess, Mark *111:* 146; *113:* 207
Hess, Paul *134:* 47; *166:* 133; *193:* 13
Hess, Richard *42:* 31
Hester, Ronnie *37:* 85
Heuser, Olga J. *121:* 116
Heusser, Sibylle *168:* 195
Heustis, Louise L. *20:* 28
Hewgill, Jody *201:* 90
Hewitson, Jennifer *74:* 119; *124:* 167
Hewitt, Kathryn *80:* 126; *149:* 105; *184:* 93; *196:* 36; *229:* 99
Hewitt, Margaret *84:* 112
Heyduck-Huth, Hilde *8:* 82
Heyer, Carol *74:* 122; *130:* 72, 73; *192:* 35; *203:* 78
Heyer, Hermann *20:* 114, 115
Heyer, Marilee *102:* 108

Heyman, Ken *8:* 33; *34:* 113
Heyne, Ulrike *146:* 151
Heywood, Karen *48:* 114
Hickling, P.B. *40:* 165
Hickman, Stephen *85:* 58; *136:* 33; *171:* 128
Hierstein, Judith *56:* 40; *162:* 168; *212:* 72; *227:* 46
Higashi, Sandra *154:* 59, 60
Higginbottom, J. Winslow *8:* 170; *29:* 105, 106
Higgins, Chester *101:* 79
Higham, David *50:* 104
Hilb, Nora *176:* 8
Hild, Anja *215:* 194
Hildebrandt, Greg *8:* 191; *55:* 35, 36, 38, 39, 40, 42, 46; *172:* 110
Hildebrandt, Tim *8:* 191; *55:* 44, 45, 46
Hilder, Rowland *19:* 207
Hill, Eric *66:* 127, 128; *133:* 91
Hill, Gregory *35:* 190
Hill, Pat *49:* 120
Hillenbrand, Will *84:* 115; *92:* 76, 80; *93:* 131; *104:* 168; *128:* 137; *145:* 187; *146:* 184; *147:* 105, 106, 107; *152:* 59; *184:* 179; *195:* 34, 180; *196:* 125; *210:* 122, 123, 124; *217:* 62; *224:* 145; *239:* 151
Hilliard, Richard *183:* 74
Hillier, Matthew *45:* 205
Hillman, Priscilla *48:* 115
Hills, Tad *113:* 4; *137:* 147; *173:* 83; *208:* 199
Himler, Ronald *6:* 114; *7:* 162; *8:* 17, 84, 125; *14:* 76; *19:* 145; *26:* 160; *31:* 43; *38:* 116; *41:* 44, 79; *43:* 52; *45:* 120; *46:* 43; *54:* 44, 83; *58:* 180; *59:* 38; *68:* 146; *69:* 231; *70:* 98; *71:* 177, 178; *77:* 219; *79:* 212; *83:* 62; *89:* 5; *91:* 160; *92:* 91, 92, 93; *94:* 93; *95:* 69, 174, 194; *99:* 99, 112; *113:* 92; *118:* 114; *137:* 73, 74, 77, 167; *163:* 99; *165:* 138; *178:* 9, 220; *183:* 77, 79, 80, 81; *184:* 80, 83; *215:* 151; *231:* 11, 112; *234:* 76, 77, 78, 80; *237:* 54, 55
Himmelman, John *47:* 109; *65:* 87; *94:* 96, 97; *159:* 85; *221:* 79, 80, 81, 82
Hinds, Bill *37:* 127, 130
Hines, Anna Grossnickle *51:* 90; *74:* 124; *95:* 78, 79,80, 81
Hines, Bob *135:* 149, 150
Hirao, Amiko *203:* 98
Hiroko *99:* 61
Hiroshige *25:* 71
Hirsh, Marilyn *7:* 126
Hiscock, Bruce *137:* 80, 81; *204:* 51, 53
Hissey, Jane *103:* 90; *130:* 81
Hitch, Jeff *99:* 206; *128:* 86
Hitz, Demi *11:* 135; *15:* 245; *66:* 129, 130; *152:* 94, 95
Hnizdovsky, Jacques *32:* 96; *76:* 187
Ho, David *227:* 32
Ho, Kwoncjan *15:* 132
Hoban, Lillian *1:* 114; *22:* 157; *26:* 72; *29:* 53; *40:* 105, 107, 195; *41:* 80; *69:* 107, 108; *71:* 98; *77:* 168; *106:* 50; *113:* 86; *136:* 118
Hoban, Tana *22:* 159; *104:* 82, 83, 85
Hobbie, Holly *225:* 90, 91
Hobbie, Jocelyn *190:* 78; *196:* 92
Hobbie, Nathaniel *196:* 92
Hobbs, Leigh *166:* 95
Hoberman, Norman *5:* 82
Hobson, Sally *77:* 185
Hockerman, Dennis *39:* 22; *56:* 23
Hodgell, P.C. *42:* 114
Hodges, C. Walter *2:* 139; *11:* 15; *12:* 25; *23:* 34; *25:* 96; *38:* 165; *44:* 197; *45:* 95; *100:* 57; *YABC 2:* 62, 63
Hodges, David *9:* 98
Hodgetts, Victoria *43:* 132
Hofbauer, Imre *2:* 162
Hoff, Syd *9:* 107; *10:* 128; *33:* 94; *72:* 115,116, 117, 118; *138:* 114, 115
Hoffman, Rosekrans *15:* 133; *50:* 219; *63:* 97

Hoffman, Sanford *38:* 208; *76:* 174; *88:* 160, 161; *151:* 156
Hoffmann, Felix *9:* 109
Hoffnung, Gerard *66:* 76, 77
Hofsinde, Robert *21:* 70
Hogan, Inez *2:* 141
Hogan, Jamie *192:* 94; *198:* 177; *237:* 107
Hogarth, Burne *41:* 58; *63:* 46, 48, 49, 50, 52, 53, 54, 55,56
Hogarth, Paul *41:* 102, 103, 104; *YABC 1:* 16
Hogarth, William *42:* 33
Hogenbyl, Jan *1:* 35
Hogner, Nils *4:* 122; *25:* 144
Hogrogian, Nonny *3:* 221; *4:* 106, 107; *5:* 166; *7:* 129; *15:* 2; *16:* 176; *20:* 154; *22:* 146; *25:* 217; *27:* 206; *74:* 127, 128, 129, 149, 152; *127:* 99; *YABC 2:* 84, 94
Hokanson, Lars *93:* 111; *172:* 137; *212:* 88
Hokusai *25:* 71
Hol, Colby *126:* 96
Holberg, Richard *2:* 51
Holbrook, Kathy *107:* 114
Holdcroft, Tina *38:* 109; *227:* 99, 100, 160
Holden, Caroline *55:* 159
Holder, Heidi *36:* 99; *64:* 9
Holder, Jim *204:* 163
Holder, Jimmy *151:* 224; *233:* 175; *234:* 82, 83
Holderness, Grizelda *215:* 107
Hole, Stian *204:* 55
Holiday, Henry *YABC 2:* 107
Holl, F. *36:* 91
Holland, Brad *45:* 59, 159
Holland, Gay W. *128:* 105; *225:* 76
Holland, Janice *18:* 118
Holland, Marion *6:* 116
Holland, Richard *216:* 109, 124
Holldobler, Turid *26:* 120
Holliday, Keaf *144:* 236
Holling, Holling C. *15:* 136, 137
Hollinger, Deanne *12:* 116
Holm, Sharon Lane *114:* 84; *115:* 52
Holmes, B. *3:* 82
Holmes, Bea *7:* 74; *24:* 156; *31:* 93
Holmes, Dave *54:* 22
Holmes, Lesley *135:* 96
Holmgren, George Ellen *45:* 112
Holmlund, Heather D. *150:* 140
Holt, Norma *44:* 106
Holt, Pater *151:* 188
Holtan, Gene *32:* 192
Holub, Joan *149:* 72; *229:* 82
Holyfield, John *149:* 231; *227:* 101; *230:* 9
Holz, Loretta *17:* 81
Hom, Nancy *79:* 195
Homar, Lorenzo *6:* 2
Homer, Winslow *128:* 8; *YABC 2:* 87
Honey, Elizabeth *112:* 95, 96; *137:* 93, 94
Honeywood, Varnette P. *110:* 68, 70
Hong, Lily Toy *76:* 104
Honigman, Marian *3:* 2
Honore, Paul *42:* 77, 79, 81, 82
Hood, Alun *69:* 145, 218; *72:* 41; *80:* 226; *87:* 4; *95:* 139
Hood, Susan *12:* 43
Hook, Christian *104:* 103
Hook, Frances *26:* 188; *27:* 127
Hook, Jeff *14:* 137; *103:* 105
Hook, Richard *26:* 188
Hooks *63:* 30
Hooper, Hadley *177:* 145
Hoover, Carol A. *21:* 77
Hoover, Russell *12:* 95; *17:* 2; *34:* 156
Hope, James *141:* 116
Hopkins, Chris *99:* 127
Hopkinson, Leigh *202:* 70
Hopman, Philip *178:* 184
Hoppe, Paul *209:* 85
Hoppin, Augustus *34:* 66
Horacek, Judy *211:* 86
Horacek, Petr *163:* 117; *214:* 113

Horder, Margaret *2:* 108; *73:* 75
Horen, Michael *45:* 121
Horne, Daniel *73:* 106; *91:* 153; *109:* 127; *110:* 232; *164:* 176
Horne, Richard *111:* 80
Horowitz, Dave *204:* 58
Horse, Harry *128:* 195; *169:* 86
Horstman, Lisa *219:* 79
Horton, Anthony *211:* 98
Horvat, Laurel *12:* 201
Horvath, David *192:* 95
Horvath, Ferdinand Kusati *24:* 176
Horvath, Maria *57:* 171
Horwitz, Richard *57:* 174
Hotchkiss, De Wolfe *20:* 49
Hough, Charlotte *9:* 112; *13:* 98; *17:* 83; *24:* 195
Houlihan, Ray *11:* 214
House, Caroline *183:* 121
Housman, Laurence *25:* 146, 147
Houston, James *13:* 107; *74:* 132, 134, 135
Hovland, Gary *88:* 172; *171:* 148
Hoyt, Eleanor *158:* 231
How, W.E. *20:* 47
Howard, Alan *16:* 80; *34:* 58; *45:* 114
Howard, Arthur *165:* 111, 112; *190:* 5; *229:* 30
Howard, J.N. *15:* 234
Howard, John *33:* 179
Howard, Kim *116:* 71
Howard, Paul *142:* 126, 129; *144:* 187
Howard, Rob *40:* 161
Howarth, Daniel *170:* 34; *222:* 97, 98; *224:* 20; *225:* 77; *234:* 189
Howe, John *79:* 101; *80:* 150; *115:* 47; *176:* 106; *207:* 32, 35
Howe, Phillip *79:* 117; *175:* 115
Howe, Stephen *1:* 232
Howell, Karen *119:* 123
Howell, Pat *15:* 139
Howell, Troy *23:* 24; *31:* 61; *36:* 158; *37:* 184; *41:* 76, 235; *48:* 112; *56:* 13; *57:* 3; *59:* 174; *63:* 5; *74:* 46; *89:* 188; *90:* 231; *95:* 97; *98:* 130; *99:* 189; *153:* 156, 157, 158; *176:* 104; *199:* 96, 98; *222:* 65
Howells, Tania *229:* 87
Howes, Charles *22:* 17
Hoyt, Ard *145:* 141; *190:* 82; *207:* 148
Hranilovich, Barbara *127:* 51
Hu, Ying-Hwa *116:* 107; *152:* 236; *173:* 171
Huang, Benrei *137:* 55
Huang, Zhong-Yang *117:* 30, 32; *213:* 18
Hubbard, Woodleigh Marx *98:* 67; *115:* 79; *160:* 138; *214:* 120
Hubbell, Patricia *222:* 31
Hubley, Faith *48:* 120, 121, 125, 130, 131, 132, 134
Hubley, John *48:* 125, 130, 131, 132, 134
Hudak, Michal *143:* 74
Hudnut, Robin *14:* 62
Huerta, Catherine *76:* 178; *77:* 44, 45; *90:* 182; *210:* 202
Huffaker, Sandy *10:* 56
Huffman, Joan *13:* 33
Huffman, Tom *13:* 180; *17:* 212; *21:* 116; *24:* 132; *33:* 154; *38:* 59; *42:* 147
Hughes, Arthur *20:* 148, 149, 150; *33:* 114, 148, 149
Hughes, Darren *95:* 44
Hughes, David *36:* 197
Hughes, Neal *238:* 142
Hughes, Shirley *1:* 20, 21; *7:* 3; *12:* 217; *16:* 163; *29:* 154; *63:* 118; *70:* 102, 103, 104; *73:* 169; *88:* 70; *110:* 118, 119; *159:* 103
Hugo, Victor *47:* 112
Huliska-Beith, Laura *204:* 108; *220:* 137; *232:* 97, 98
Hull, Cathy *78:* 29
Hull, Richard *95:* 120; *123:* 175; *172:* 195
Hulsmann, Eva *16:* 166
Hume, Lachie *189:* 93
Hummel, Berta *43:* 137, 138, 139

Hummel, Lisl *29:* 109; *YABC 2:* 333, 334
Humphrey, Henry *16:* 167
Humphreys, Graham *25:* 168
Humphries, Tudor *76:* 66; *80:* 4; *124:* 4, 5; *226:* 112
Huneck, Stephen *183:* 88, 89
Hunt, James *2:* 143
Hunt, Jonathan *84:* 120
Hunt, Paul *119:* 104; *129:* 135; *139:* 160; *173:* 112
Hunt, Robert *110:* 206, 235; *147:* 136, 137; *170:* 3; *211:* 76; *226:* 189
Hunt, Scott *190:* 143; *233:* 172
Hunter, Anne *133:* 190; *178:* 150
Huntington, Amy *180:* 99
Hurd, Clement *2:* 148, 149; *64:* 127, 128, 129, 131, 133, 134,135, 136; *100:* 37, 38
Hurd, Peter *24:* 30, 31,; *YABC 2:* 56
Hurd, Thacher *46:* 88, 89; *94:* 114, 115, 116; *123:* 81, 82, 84; *219:* 82
Hurlimann, Ruth *32:* 99
Hurst, Carol Otis *185:* 92
Hurst, Elise *221:* 98
Hurst, Philip *196:* 79
Hurst, Tracey *192:* 238
Hussar, Michael *114:* 113; *117:* 159
Hustler, Tom *6:* 105
Hutchins, Laurence *55:* 22
Hutchins, Pat *15:* 142; *70:* 106, 107, 108; *178:* 131, 132
Hutchinson, Sascha *95:* 211
Hutchinson, William M. *6:* 3, 138; *46:* 70
Hutchison, Paula *23:* 10
Hutton, Clarke *YABC 2:* 335
Hutton, Kathryn *35:* 155; *89:* 91
Hutton, Warwick *20:* 91
Huyette, Marcia *29:* 188
Hyatt, John *54:* 7
Hyatt, Mitch *178:* 162
Hyde, Maureen *82:* 17; *121:* 145, 146
Hyman, David *117:* 64
Hyman, Miles *210:* 132
Hyman, Trina Schart *1:* 204; *2:* 194; *5:* 153; *6:* 106; *7:* 138, 145; *8:* 22; *10:* 196; *13:* 96; *14:* 114; *15:* 204; *16:* 234; *20:* 82; *22:* 133; *24:* 151; *25:* 79, 82; *26:* 82; *29:* 83; *31:* 37, 39; *34:* 104; *38:* 84, 100, 128; *41:* 49; *43:* 146; *46:* 91, 92, 93, 95, 96, 97, 98, 99, 100, 101, 102, 103, 104, 105,108, 109, 111, 197; *48:* 60, 61; *52:* 32; *60:* 168; *66:* 38; *67:* 214; *72:* 74; *75:* 92; *79:* 57; *82:* 95, 238; *89:* 46; *95:* 91, 92, 93; *100:* 33, 199; *132:* 12; *147:* 33, 35, 36; *167:* 58, 60; *177:* 189, 190; *211:* 188; *236:* 128

I

Ibarra, Rosa *147:* 91
Ibatoulline, Bagram *156:* 48; *174:* 33, 82; *202:* 30; *211:* 213; *224:* 84; *225:* 98, 99; *232:* 60; *237:* 163; *239:* 6
Ichikawa, Satomi *29:* 152; *41:* 52; *47:* 133, 134,135, 136; *78:* 93, 94; *80:* 81; *146:* 143, 145, 146; *208:* 117, 118, 119
Ide, Jacqueline *YABC 1:* 39
Idle, Molly Schaar *223:* 95
Ignatow, Amy *233:* 91
Ilsley, Velma *3:* 1; *7:* 55; *12:* 109; *37:* 62; *38:* 184
Imai, Ayano *190:* 85, 86
in den Bosch, Nicole *150:* 204
Inga *1:* 142
Ingman, Bruce *134:* 50; *182:* 91, 92; *214:* 10
Ingpen, Robert *109:* 103, 104; *132:* 138; *137:* 177; *166:* 103; *181:* 140; *229:* 169
Ingraham, Erick *21:* 177; *84:* 256; *103:* 66
Inkpen, Mick *99:* 104, 105; *106:* 44
Innerst, Stacy *149:* 104; *232:* 101, 102

Innocenti, Roberto *21:* 123; *96:* 122; *159:* 111, 197; *199:* 176
Inoue, Yosuke *24:* 118
Iofin, Michael *97:* 157
Iosa, Ann *63:* 189
Ipcar, Dahlov *1:* 124, 125; *49:* 137, 138, 139, 140, 141, 142,143, 144, 145; *147:* 122, 124, 126
Irvin, Fred *13:* 166; *15:* 143, 144; *27:* 175
Irving, Jay *45:* 72
Irving, Laurence *27:* 50
Isaac, Joanne *21:* 76
Isaacs, Gary *170:* 188
Isadora, Rachel *43:* 159, 160; *54:* 31; *79:* 106, 107,108; *121:* 100, 102; *165:* 116, 117; *204:* 61, 63, 64
Ishmael, Woodi *24:* 111; *31:* 99
Isol *220:* 73
Ives, Ruth *15:* 257
Iwai, Melissa *149:* 233; *183:* 92; *199:* 115
Iwamura, Kazuo *213:* 87

J

Jabar, Cynthia *101:* 201; *210:* 134, 135
Jack, Colin *234:* 53
Jackness, Andrew *94:* 237
Jackson, Julian *91:* 104, 106
Jackson, Michael *43:* 42
Jackson, Shelley *79:* 71; *99:* 109; *187:* 82
Jacob, Murv *89:* 30
Jacobi, Kathy *62:* 118
Jacobs, Barbara *9:* 136
Jacobs, Lou, Jr. *9:* 136; *15:* 128
Jacobsen, Laura *176:* 98; *177:* 85, 86
Jacobson, Rick *131:* 222; *170:* 119; *222:* 52
Jacobus, Tim *79:* 140; *109:* 126; *129:* 180
Jacques, Robin *1:* 70; *2:* 1; *8:* 46; *9:* 20; *15:* 187; *19:* 253; *32:* 102, 103, 104; *43:* 184; *73:* 135; *YABC 1:* 42
Jaeggi, Yoshiko *186:* 184
Jaffee, Al *66:* 131, 132
Jago *216:* 122
Jagr, Miloslav *13:* 197
Jahn-Clough, Lisa *88:* 114; *152:* 104; *193:* 70, 71
Jahnke, Robert *84:* 24
Jainschigg, Nicholas *80:* 64; *91:* 138; *95:* 63; *99:* 25; *108:* 50; *171:* 41
Jakesevic, Nenad *85:* 102; *226:* 215
Jakobsen, Kathy *116:* 83
Jakubowski, Charles *14:* 192
Jambor, Louis *YABC 1:* 11
James, Ann *73:* 50; *82:* 113; *158:* 61; *183:* 44
James, Brian *140:* 91
James, Curtis E. *182:* 93
James, Derek *35:* 187; *44:* 91; *61:* 133; *74:* 2; *80:* 57; *86:* 88; *130:* 30; *179:* 29; *218:* 31
James, Gilbert *YABC 1:* 43
James, Gordon C. *195:* 89
James, Harold *2:* 151; *3:* 62; *8:* 79; *29:* 113; *51:* 195; *74:* 90
James, Kennon *126:* 211
James, Rhian Nest *234:* 63
James, Robin *50:* 106; *53:* 32, 34, 35
James, Simon *202:* 73, 74; *233:* 161
James, Will *19:* 150, 152, 153, 155, 163
Janosch
    See Eckert, Horst
Janovitch, Marilyn *68:* 168
Janovitz, Marilyn *87:* 187; *130:* 198; *194:* 91
Jansons, Inese *48:* 117
Jansson, Alexander *216:* 59; *234:* 29
Jansson, Tove *3:* 90; *41:* 106, 108, 109, 110, 111, 113, 114
Jaques, Faith *7:* 11, 132, 133; *21:* 83, 84; *69:* 114,116; *73:* 170
Jaques, Frances Lee *29:* 224
Jarka, Jeff *221:* 94

Jarrett, Clare *201:* 77
Jarrie, Martin *219:* 86
Jauss, Anne Marie *1:* 139; *3:* 34; *10:* 57, 119; *11:* 205; *23:* 194
Jay, Alison *158:* 97, 98; *183:* 126, 127; *196:* 95, 96, 97, 98; *200:* 72, 73, 74; *212:* 39
Jeffers, Oliver *175:* 111; *213:* 89
Jeffers, Susan *17:* 86, 87; *25:* 164, 165; *26:* 112; *50:* 132, 134, 135; *70:* 111, 112, 113; *137:* 107, 108, 109, 110, 111; *202:* 77, 78
Jefferson, Louise E. *4:* 160
Jenkin-Pearce, Susie *78:* 16
Jenkins, Debra Reid *85:* 202; *114:* 89; *173:* 134; *225:* 116
Jenkins, Jean *98:* 79, 102
Jenkins, Leonard *157:* 169; *167:* 128; *189:* 96, 97; *190:* 89
Jenkins, Patrick *72:* 126
Jenkins, Steve *124:* 177; *154:* 90, 91, 92, 93; *185:* 194; *188:* 81, 82, 83, 84, 85, 86; *218:* 67, 69, 70, 71, 72
Jenkins, Ward *238:* 91
Jenks, Aleta *73:* 117; *124:* 225
Jenkyns, Chris *51:* 97
Jensen, Bruce *95:* 39
Jensinius, Kirsten *56:* 58
Jeram, Anita *89:* 135; *102:* 122, 123; *129:* 112; *154:* 96, 97, 98; *164:* 154; *203:* 123, 124; *219:* 88, 89, 90, 91
Jernigan, E. Wesley *85:* 92
Jerome, Elaine *227:* 45
Jerome, Karen A. *72:* 194
Jeruchim, Simon *6:* 173; *15:* 250
Jeschke, Susan *20:* 89; *39:* 161; *41:* 84; *42:* 120
Jessel, Camilla *29:* 115
Jessell, Tim *159:* 3; *177:* 87; *181:* 95; *205:* 4; *213:* 74; *223:* 187; *225:* 102; *226:* 190
Jeyaveeran, Ruth *182:* 100
Jiang, Cheng An *109:* 108
Jiang, Wei *109:* 108
Jimenez, Maria *77:* 158; *93:* 127
Jobling, Curtis *138:* 74
Jocelyn, Marthe *118:* 83; *137:* 219; *163:* 119, 120; *198:* 62
Joerns, Consuelo *38:* 36; *44:* 94
John, Diana *12:* 209
John, Helen *1:* 215; *28:* 204
Johns, Elizabeth *127:* 33
Johns, Jasper *61:* 172
Johns, Jeanne *24:* 114
Johnson, Adrian *143:* 50
Johnson, Bruce *9:* 47
Johnson, Cathy *92:* 136; *218:* 112
Johnson, Crockett
    See Leisk, David
Johnson, D. William *23:* 104
Johnson, D.B. *183:* 98, 139
Johnson, David A. *175:* 18; *191:* 91; *218:* 19
Johnson, Gillian *119:* 175; *164:* 217; *215:* 99
Johnson, Harper *1:* 27; *2:* 33; *18:* 302; *19:* 61; *31:* 181; *44:* 46, 50, 95
Johnson, Ingrid *37:* 118
Johnson, James Ralph *1:* 23, 127
Johnson, James David *12:* 195
Johnson, Jane *48:* 136
Johnson, Joel Peter *98:* 18; *128:* 111; *201:* 13; *213:* 189; *234:* 172
Johnson, John E. *34:* 133
Johnson, Kevin *72:* 44
Johnson, Kevin Eugene *109:* 215
Johnson, Larry *47:* 56; *123:* 107; *159:* 203
Johnson, Layne *187:* 94; *209:* 63; *222:* 100, 101; *233:* 123
Johnson, Margaret S. *35:* 131
Johnson, Meredith Merrell *71:* 181; *83:* 158; *89:* 103; *104:* 88
Johnson, Milton *1:* 67; *2:* 71; *26:* 45; *31:* 107; *60:* 112; *68:* 96
Johnson, Pamela *16:* 174; *52:* 145; *62:* 140; *73:* 116; *85:* 64

Johnson, Paul Brett *83:* 95; *132:* 119
Johnson, Stephen T. *80:* 15; *131:* 35; *141:* 96; *145:* 40; *164:* 187; *175:* 32; *189:* 99, 100; *208:* 43
Johnson, Steve *138:* 219; *141:* 64; *144:* 199; *177:* 51; *214:* 95; *221:* 63; *228:* 42, 43, 44; *230:* 44, 45, 46
Johnson, William R. *38:* 91
Johnson-Petrov, Arden *115:* 206
Johnston, David McCall *50:* 131, 133
Johnston, Lynne *118:* 85, 87, 89; *216:* 127, 128, 131
Johnstone, Anne *8:* 120; *36:* 89
Johnstone, Janet Grahame *8:* 120; *36:* 89
Jolivet, Joëlle *231:* 71
Jonas, Ann *50:* 107, 108, 109; *135:* 113
Jones, Bob *71:* 5; *77:* 199
Jones, Carol *5:* 131; *72:* 185, 186; *153:* 111, 112
Jones, Chuck *53:* 70, 71
Jones, Curtis *211:* 144
Jones, Davy *89:* 176
Jones, Douglas B. *185:* 192; *202:* 82
Jones, Elizabeth Orton *18:* 124, 126, 128, 129
Jones, Harold *14:* 88; *52:* 50
Jones, Holly *127:* 3
Jones, Jeff *41:* 64
Jones, Laurian *25:* 24, 27
Jones, Margaret *74:* 57
Jones, Noah Z. *182:* 37; *203:* 159
Jones, Randy *131:* 104
Jones, Richard *127:* 222
Jones, Robert *25:* 67
Jones, Tim *237:* 104
Jones, Wilfred *35:* 115; *YABC 1:* 163
Jordan, Charles *89:* 58
Jordan, Jess *136:* 222; *203:* 111
Jordan, Martin George *84:* 127
Jordan, Richard *84:* 36
Jorgenson, Andrea *91:* 111
Jorisch, Stéphane *153:* 56, 193; *177:* 29; *178:* 138, 139; *187:* 23; *211:* 182
Joseph, James *53:* 88
Josse, Annabelle *234:* 88
Joudrey, Ken *64:* 145; *78:* 6
Joyce, William *72:* 131, 132, 133, 134; *73:* 227; *145:* 37
Joyner, Jerry *34:* 138
Joyner, Loraine M. *209:* 17
Joysmith, Brenda *210:* 237
Juan, Ana *175:* 38; *179:* 111, 112; *213:* 9
Juarez, Fernando *233:* 26
Jucker, Sita *5:* 93
Judge, Lita *192:* 99; *234:* 97
Judkis, Jim *37:* 38
Juhasz, Victor *31:* 67
Julian, Russell *238:* 36
Julian, Sean *236:* 113
Jullian, Philippe *24:* 206; *25:* 203
Jung, Tom *91:* 217
Junge, Alexandra *183:* 37
Junge, Walter *67:* 150
Jupo, Frank *7:* 148, 149
Jurisch, Stephane *154:* 105
Justice, Martin *34:* 72

K

Kabatova-Taborska, Zdenka *107:* 153
Kachik, John *165:* 230
Kaczman, James *156:* 98; *235:* 86
Kadair, Deborah Ousley *184:* 45, 89
Kahl, David *74:* 95; *97:* 35; *109:* 174; *110:* 213; *198:* 15
Kahl, M.P. *37:* 83
Kahl, Virginia *48:* 138
Kahn, Katherine Janus *90:* 135; *211:* 155; *218:* 75, 76; *220:* 89,90
Kakimoo, Kozo *11:* 148

Kalett, Jim *48:* 159, 160, 161
Kalin, Victor *39:* 186
Kalis, Jennifer *207:* 82; *219:* 62
Kalman, Maira *96:* 131, 132; *137:* 115
Kalmenoff, Matthew *22:* 191
Kalow, Gisela *32:* 105
Kamen, Gloria *1:* 41; *9:* 119; *10:* 178; *35:* 157; *78:* 236; *98:* 82
Kaminsky, Jef *102:* 153
Kandell, Alice *35:* 133
Kane, Henry B. *14:* 90; *18:* 219, 220
Kane, Robert *18:* 131
Kanfer, Larry *66:* 141
Kangas, Juli *200:* 88
Kappes, Alfred *28:* 104
Karalus, Bob *41:* 157
Karas, G. Brian *80:* 60; *99:* 179; *115:* 41; *118:* 50; *136:* 168; *145:* 166; *149:* 245; *159:* 65; *171:* 192; *178:* 142, 143; *202:* 38; *209:* 142; *222:* 106, 107, 108, 109; *225:* 62; *235:* 53
Karasz, Ilonka *128:* 163
Karlin, Eugene *10:* 63; *20:* 131
Karlin, Nurit *63:* 78; *103:* 110
Karpinski, Tony *134:* 160
Kasamatsu, Shiro *139:* 155
Kasparavicius, Kestutis *139:* 210
Kassian, Olena *64:* 94
Kastner, Jill *79:* 135; *117:* 84, 85
Kasuya, Masahiro *41:* 206, 207; *51:* 100
Kasza, Keiko *191:* 99, 100, 101, 102, 103
Katona, Robert *21:* 85; *24:* 126
Katz, Avi *199:* 55
Katz, Karen *158:* 123; *232:* 108, 109, 110
Kauffer, E. McKnight *33:* 103; *35:* 127; *63:* 67
Kaufman, Angelika *15:* 156
Kaufman, Joe *33:* 119
Kaufman, John *13:* 158
Kaufman, Stuart *62:* 64; *68:* 226; *137:* 44
Kaufmann, John *1:* 174; *4:* 159; *8:* 43, 1; *10:* 102; *18:* 133, 134; *22:* 251
Kaye, Graham *1:* 9; *67:* 7, 8
Kaye, M.M. *62:* 95
Kazalovski, Nata *40:* 205
Keane, Bil *4:* 135
Kearney, David *72:* 47; *121:* 83
Keating, Pamel T. *77:* 37
Keats, Ezra Jack *3:* 18, 105, 257; *14:* 101, 102; *33:* 129; *57:* 79, 80, 82, 83, 84, 87
Keegan, Charles *166:* 211
Keegan, Marcia *9:* 122; *32:* 93
Keeler, Patricia A. *81:* 56; *183:* 102, 103
Keely, Jack *119:* 95
Keely, John *26:* 104; *48:* 214
Keen, Eliot *25:* 213
Keep, Richard C. *170:* 122
Keeping, Charles *9:* 124, 185; *15:* 28, 134; *18:* 115; *44:* 194, 196; *47:* 25; *52:* 3; *54:* 156; *69:* 123, 124; *74:* 56; *155:* 9
Keeter, Susan *168:* 46; *183:* 192; *237:* 64
Keith, Eros *4:* 98; *5:* 138; *31:* 29; *43:* 220; *52:* 91, 92, 93, 94; *56:* 64, 66; *60:* 37; *79:* 93
Keleinikov, Andrei *65:* 101, 102
Kelen, Emery *13:* 115
Keller, A.J. *62:* 198
Keller, Arthur I. *26:* 106
Keller, Dick *36:* 123, 125
Keller, Holly *45:* 79; *76:* 118, 119, 120, 121; *108:* 137, 138, 140; *157:* 117, 118, 119; *216:* 136
Keller, Katie *79:* 222; *93:* 108
Keller, Laurie *196:* 105, 106
Keller, Ronald *45:* 208
Kelley, Gary *183:* 105; *216:* 78; *217:* 95, 96, 97
Kelley, Marty *211:* 91
Kelley, True *41:* 114, 115; *42:* 137; *75:* 35; *92:* 104, 105; *124:* 62; *130:* 100, 101; *179:* 120, 121, 122; *192:* 251

Kellogg, Steven *8:* 96; *11:* 207; *14:* 130; *20:* ; *201:* 38 58; *29:* 140, 141; *30:* 35; *41:* 141; *57:* 89, 90, 92,93, 94, 96; *59:* 182; *73:* 141; *77:* 129; *130:* 105, 106; *177:* 94, 95, 96, 97; *199:* 57; *217:* 61; *239:* 137 *YABC 1:* 65, 73
Kelly, Billy *158:* 143
Kelly, Geoff *97:* 196; *112:* 25
Kelly, Irene *147:* 134; *210:* 144, 145
Kelly, Jennifer *230:* 137
Kelly, John *194:* 186
Kelly, Joseph *174:* 94
Kelly, Kathleen M. *71:* 109
Kelly, Laura *89:* 217
Kelly, True *163:* 87
Kelly, Walt *18:* 136, 137, 138, 139, 140, 141, 144, 145, 146, 148, 149
Kemble, E.W. *34:* 75; *44:* 178; *YABC 2:* 54, 59
Kemly, Kathleen *209:* 165
Kemp-Welsh, Lucy *24:* 197; *100:* 214
Kendall, Jane *150:* 105; *186:* 109
Kendall, Peter *152:* 85
Kendrick, Dennis *79:* 213
Kennaway, Adrienne *60:* 55, 56; *171:* 88, 89
Kennedy, Anne *212:* 34
Kennedy, Doug *189:* 104
Kennedy, Paul Edward *6:* 190; *8:* 132; *33:* 120
Kennedy, Richard *3:* 93; *12:* 179; *44:* 193; *100:* 15; *YABC 1:* 57
Kent, Jack *24:* 136; *37:* 37; *40:* 81; *84:* 89; *86:* 150; *88:* 77
Kent, Rockwell *5:* 166; *6:* 129; *20:* 225, 226, 227,229; *59:* 144
Kenyon, Tony *81:* 201; *127:* 74; *231:* 86
Kepes, Juliet *13:* 119
Kerins, Anthony *76:* 84
Kerr, Judity *24:* 137
Kerr, Phyllis Forbes *72:* 141
Kessler, Leonard *1:* 108; *7:* 139; *14:* 107, 227; *22:* 101; *44:* 96; *67:* 79; *82:* 123
Kest, Kristin *168:* 99; *173:* 23
Kesteven, Peter *35:* 189
Ketcham, Hank *28:* 140, 141, 142
Kettelkamp, Larry *2:* 164
Key, Alexander *8:* 99
Khalsa, Dayal Kaur *62:* 99
Kiakshuk *8:* 59
Kid, Tom *207:* 54
Kidd, Chip *94:* 23
Kidd, Richard *152:* 110
Kidd, Tom *64:* 199; *81:* 189; *185:* 173
Kiddell-Monroe, Joan *19:* 201; *55:* 59, 60; *87:* 174; *121:* 112
Kidder, Harvey *9:* 105; *80:* 41
Kidwell, Carl *43:* 145
Kieffer, Christa *41:* 89
Kiesler, Kate *110:* 105; *136:* 142
Kiff, Ken *40:* 45
Kilaka, John *223:* 107
Kilbride, Robert *37:* 100
Kilby, Don *141:* 144
Killen, Nicola *236:* 115
Kim, David *201:* 79; *202:* 97
Kim, Glenn *99:* 82
Kimball, Anton *78:* 114; *119:* 105
Kimball, Yeffe *23:* 116; *37:* 88
Kimber, Murray *171:* 91
Kimmel, Warren *176:* 112
Kincade, Orin *34:* 116
Kindersley, Barnabas *96:* 110
Kindred, Wendy *7:* 151
King, Colin *53:* 3
King, Robin *10:* 164, 165
King, Stephen Michael *141:* 31; *197:* 191; *218:* 81, 82
King, Tara Calahan *139:* 172
King, Tony *39:* 121
Kingman, Dong *16:* 287; *44:* 100, 102, 104
Kingsley, Charles *YABC 2:* 182
Kingston, Julie *147:* 14
Kingston, Maxine Hong *53:* 92

Kinney, Jeff *187:* 97
Kipling, John Lockwood *YABC 2:* 198
Kipling, Rudyard *YABC 2:* 196
Kipniss, Robert *29:* 59
Kirchherr, Astrid *55:* 23
Kirchhoff, Art *28:* 136
Kirk, Daniel *153:* 115, 116, 117; *173:* 101; *196:* 113, 114, 115, 116
Kirk, David *117:* 88, 89; *161:* 97, 98
Kirk, Ruth *5:* 96
Kirk, Steve *170:* 37
Kirk, Tim *32:* 209, 211; *72:* 89; *83:* 49
Kirmse, Marguerite *15:* 283; *18:* 153
Kirsch, Vincent X. *124:* 207
Kirschner, Ruth *22:* 154
Kirwan, Wednesday *198:* 73
Kish, Ely *73:* 119; *79:* 2
Kitamura, Satoshi *62:* 102; *98:* 91; *101:* 147; *138:* 2; *143:* 83, 85, 86; *201:* 83; *223:* 3, 4
Kiss, Andrew *168:* 115
Kitchel, JoAnn E. *133:* 32
Kitchen, Bert *70:* 126; *193:* 49
Kittelsen, Theodor *62:* 14
Kiuchi, Tatsuro *114:* 71
Kiwak, Barbara *172:* 135
Klahr, Susan *176:* 196
Klapholz, Mel *13:* 35
Klassen, J. *234:* 196
Klee, Jutte *209:* 136
Klein, Bill *89:* 105
Klein, Robert *55:* 77
Klein, Suzanna *63:* 104
Kleinman, Zalman *28:* 143
Kleven, Elisa *173:* 96, 97; *217:* 100, 102
Kliban, B. *35:* 137, 138
Kline, Michael *127:* 66
Klinger, Shula *230:* 55
Klise, M. Sarah *180:* 117, 118; *181:* 97; *221:* 100, 102; *235:* 117, 118
Knabel, Lonnie *73:* 103; *75:* 187, 228; *194:* 216
Kneen, Maggie *140:* 139; *221:* 104, 105
Knight, Ann *34:* 143
Knight, Christopher *13:* 125
Knight, Hilary *1:* 233; *3:* 21; *15:* 92, 158, 159; *16:* 258, 259, 260; *18:* 235; *19:* 169; *35:* 242; *46:* 167; *52:* 116; *69:* 126, 127; *132:* 129; *YABC 1:* 168, 169, 172
Knorr, Laura *200:* 91
Knorr, Peter *126:* 92, 93
Knotts, Howard *20:* 4; *25:* 170; *36:* 163
Knutson, Barbara *112:* 134; *202:* 108
Knutson, Kimberley *115:* 90
Kobayashi, Ann *39:* 58
Kochalka, James *196:* 120, 121, 122
Kocsis, J.C.
    See Paul, James
Kodman, Stanislawa *201:* 85; *224:* 72
Koehler, Hanne Lore *176:* 203
Koehn, Ilse *34:* 198; *79:* 123
Koelsch, Michael *99:* 182; *107:* 164; *109:* 239; *138:* 142; *150:* 94; *176:* 105; *187:* 63; *198:* 63; *230:* 204
Koering, Ursula *3:* 28; *4:* 14; *44:* 5; *64:* 140,141; *85:* 46
Koerner, Henry
    See Koerner, W.H.D.
Koerner, W.H.D. *14:* 216; *21:* 88, 89, 90, 91; *23:* 211
Koetsch, Mike *166:* 68
Koffler, Camilla *36:* 113
Kogan, Deborah Ray *161:* 101, 102
Koide, Yasuko *50:* 114
Kolado, Karen *102:* 228
Kolesova, Juliana *217:* 81; *222:* 185; *229:* 183; *237:* 16; *239:* 173
Komarck, Michael *227:* 48
Komoda, Kiyo *9:* 128; *13:* 214
Kompaneyets, Marc *169:* 92
Konashevich, Vladimir *61:* 160
Konashevicha, V. *YABC 1:* 26

Konigsburg, E.L. *4:* 138; *48:* 141, 142, 144, 145; *94:* 129, 130; *126:* 129, 130, 131; *194:* 95, 98
Kono, Erin Eitter *177:* 99
Kooiker, Leonie *48:* 148
Koonook, Simon *65:* 157
Koontz, Robin Michal *136:* 155
Koopmans, Loek *101:* 121
Kopelke, Lisa *154:* 107
Kopper, Lisa *72:* 152, 153; *105:* 135, 136
Korach, Mimi *1:* 128, 129; *2:* 52; *4:* 39; *5:* 159; *9:* 129; *10:* 21; *24:* 69
Koren, Edward *5:* 100; *65:* 65, 67
Kosaka, Fumi *164:* 130
Koscielniak, Bruce *99:* 122; *153:* 120, 121, 122
Koshkin, Alexander *92:* 180
Kossin, Sandy *10:* 71; *23:* 105
Kostin, Andrej *26:* 204
Kosturko, Bob *164:* 56
Kotzky, Brian *68:* 184
Kovacevic, Zivojin *13:* 247
Kovalski, Maryann *58:* 120; *84:* 88; *97:* 124, 125, 126; *158:* 3; *186:* 80
Kozjan, Drazen *209:* 99; *231:* 130; *236:* 28
Krahn, Fernando *2:* 257; *34:* 206; *49:* 152
Krall, Dan *218:* 84, 85
Kramek, Oren *231:* 119
Kramer, Anthony *33:* 81
Kramer, David *96:* 162; *109:* 132; *150:* 220
Kramer, Frank *6:* 121
Krantz, Kathy *35:* 83
Kratter, Paul *139:* 65
Kraus, Robert *13:* 217; *65:* 113; *93:* 93, 94
Krause, Jon *176:* 62
Krauss, Trisha *174:* 10
Kredel, Fritz *6:* 35; *17:* 93, 94, 95, 96; *22:* 147; *24:* 175; *29:* 130; *35:* 77; *YABC 2:* 166, 300
Kreloff, Eliot *189:* 107, 108; *205:* 182
Krementz, Jill *17:* 98; *49:* 41
Krenina, Katya *117:* 106; *125:* 133; *176:* 117; *221:* 107
Kresin, Robert *23:* 19
Kretschmar, Sonia *226:* 97
Krieger, Salem *54:* 164
Kriegler, Lyn *73:* 29
Krinitz, Esther Nisenthal *193:* 196
Krommes, Beth *128:* 141; *149:* 136; *181:* 100, 101; *184:* 105; *188:* 125; *208:* 135; *209:* 185
Krone, Mike *101:* 71
Kronheimer, Ann *135:* 119
Krosoczka, Jarrett J. *155:* 142; *200:* 93, 94
Kruck, Gerald *88:* 181
Krudop, Walter Lyon *199:* 19
Krupinski, Loretta *67:* 104; *102:* 131; *161:* 105, 106
Krupp, Robin Rector *53:* 96, 98
Krush, Beth *1:* 51, 85; *2:* 233; *4:* 115; *9:* 61; *10:* 191; *11:* 196; *18:* 164, 165; *32:* 72; *37:* 203; *43:* 57; *60:* 102, 103, 107, 108, 109
Krush, Joe *2:* 233; *4:* 115; *9:* 61; *10:* 191; *11:* 196; *18:* 164, 165; *32:* 72, 91; *37:* 203; *43:* 57; *60:* 102, 103, 107, 108, 109
Krych, Duane *91:* 43
Krykorka, Vladyana *96:* 147; *143:* 90, 91; *168:* 14
Kubick, Dana *165:* 91; *212:* 104, 105, 212
Kubinyi, Laszlo *4:* 116; *6:* 113; *16:* 118; *17:* 100; *28:* 227; *30:* 172; *49:* 24, 28; *54:* 23; *167:* 149
Kubricht, Mary *73:* 118
Kucharik, Elena *139:* 31
Kuchera, Kathleen *84:* 5
Kuhn, Bob *17:* 91; *35:* 235
Kulikov, Boris *163:* 185; *185:* 23; *205:* 99, 100; *217:* 160; *235:* 190
Kulka, Joe *188:* 110
Kukalis, Romas *90:* 27; *139:* 37
Kuklin, Susan *63:* 82, 83, 84
Kunhardt, Dorothy *53:* 101

Kunhardt, Edith *67:* 105, 106
Kunstler, Mort *10:* 73; *32:* 143
Kurchevsky, V. *34:* 61
Kurczok, Belinda *121:* 118
Kurelek, William *8:* 107
Kuriloff, Ron *13:* 19
Kurisu, Jane *160:* 120
Kurilla, Renée *231:* 117
Kuskin, Karla *2:* 170; *68:* 115, 116; *111:* 116
Kutzer, Ernst *19:* 249
Kuzma, Steve *57:* 8; *62:* 93
Kuznetsova, Berta *74:* 45
Kvasnosky, Laura McGee *93:* 103; *142:* 83; *182:* 108
Kwas, Susan Estelle *179:* 116; *217:* 90
Kyong, Yunmee *165:* 139

L

LaBlanc, Andre *24:* 146
Laboccetta, Mario *27:* 120
LaBrose, Darcie *157:* 134
Labrosse, Darcia *58:* 88; *108:* 77; *178:* 89; *236:* 126
LaCava, Vince *95:* 118
Laceky, Adam *32:* 121
Lacis, Astra *85:* 117
Lacome, Julie *174:* 96, 97
La Croix *YABC 2:* 4
Ladd, London *206:* 50
Ladwig, Tim *98:* 212; *117:* 76; *215:* 32; *223:* 111, 112
La Farge, Margaret *47:* 141
LaFave, Kim *64:* 177; *72:* 39; *97:* 146; *99:* 172; *106:* 123; *149:* 126; *196:* 128, 129
Lafontaine, Roger *167:* 158
Lafrance, Marie *197:* 109
Lagarrigue, Jerome *136:* 102; *187:* 81
Laimgruber, Monika *11:* 153
Laínez, René Colato *226:* 50
Laio, Jimmy *213:* 57
Laite, Gordon *1:* 130, 131; *8:* 209; *31:* 113; *40:* 63; *46:* 117
Laliberté, Louise-Andrée *169:* 98
LaMarche, Jim *46:* 204; *61:* 56; *94:* 69; *114:* 22; *129:* 163; *162:* 78, 80; *239:* 61, 72, 73, 74, 75
Lamb, Jim *10:* 117
Lambase, Barbara *101:* 185; *150:* 221; *166:* 234
Lambert, J.K. *38:* 129; *39:* 24
Lambert, Sally Anne *133:* 191
Lambert, Saul *23:* 112; *33:* 107; *54:* 136
Lambert, Stephen *109:* 33; *174:* 99
Lambo, Don *6:* 156; *35:* 115; *36:* 146
Lamont, Priscilla *236:* 182
Lamontagne, Jacques *166:* 227
Lamut, Sonja *57:* 193
Lamut, Sonya *85:* 102
Landa, Peter *11:* 95; *13:* 177; *53:* 119
Landau, Jacob *38:* 111
Landis, Joan *104:* 23; *203:* 32; *235:* 33
Landon, Lucinda *79:* 31
Landshoff, Ursula *13:* 124
Landström, Lena *146:* 165, 166
Landström, Olof *146:* 166, 168; *170:* 22; *232:* 22
Lane, Daniel *112:* 60
Lane, John R. *8:* 145
Lane, John *15:* 176, 177; *30:* 146
Lane, Nancy *166:* 74
Lang, G.D. *48:* 56
Lang, Gary *73:* 75
Lang, Glenna *221:* 113
Leng, Qin *239:* 162
Lang, Jerry *18:* 295
Langdo, Bryan *186:* 187; *191:* 113, 114, 115; *233:* 98, 100
Lange, Dorothea *50:* 141

Langley, Jonathan *162:* 128
Langner, Nola *8:* 110; *42:* 36
Lanino, Deborah *105:* 148
Lantz, Paul *1:* 82, 102; *27:* 88; *34:* 102; *45:* 123
Larkin, Bob *84:* 225
Laroche, Giles *126:* 140; *146:* 81; *221:* 116, 117
LaRochelle, David *171:* 97
Larrañaga, Ana Martín *229:* 106
Larrecq, John *44:* 108; *68:* 56
Larsen, Suzanne *1:* 13
Larson, Gary *57:* 121, 122, 123, 124, 125, 126, 127
Larsson, Carl *35:* 144, 145, 146, 147, 148, 149, 150, 152, 153, 154
Larsson, Karl *19:* 177
Lartitegui, Ana G. *105:* 167
LaRue, Jenna *167:* 20
La Rue, Michael D. *13:* 215
Lasker, Joe *7:* 186, 187; *14:* 55; *38:* 115; *39:* 47; *83:* 113, 114, 115
Latham, Barbara *16:* 188, 189; *43:* 71
Lathrop, Dorothy *14:* 117, 118, 119; *15:* 109; *16:* 78, 79, 81; *32:* 201, 203; *33:* 112; *YABC 2:* 301
Latimer, Miriam *234:* 205; *235:* 122
Lattimore, Eleanor Frances *7:* 156
Lauden, Claire *16:* 173
Lauden, George, Jr. *16:* 173
Laune, Paul *2:* 235; *34:* 31
Laure, Jason *49:* 53; *50:* 122
Lauter, Richard *63:* 29; *67:* 111; *77:* 198
Lavallee, Barbara *74:* 157; *92:* 154; *96:* 126; *145:* 193; *166:* 125, 126; *186:* 155; *192:* 172; *231:* 165; *232:* 131
Lave, Fitz Hugh *59:* 139
Lavis, Steve *43:* 143; *87:* 137, 164, 165; *222:* 161; *225:* 121
Layton, Neal *152:* 120, 121; *182:* 65; *187:* 103, 105, 106
Law, Jenny *201:* 31
Lawrason, June *168:* 30
Lawrence, John *25:* 131; *30:* 141; *44:* 198, 200; *214:* 7
Lawrence, Stephen *20:* 195
Lawson, Carol *6:* 38; *42:* 93, 131; *174:* 56; *189:* 89; *209:* 59
Lawson, George *17:* 280
Lawson, Robert *5:* 26; *6:* 94; *13:* 39; *16:* 11; *20:* 100, 102, 103; *54:* 3; *66:* 12; *100:* 144, 145; *YABC 2:* 222, 224, 225, 227, 228, 229, 230, 231, 232, 233, 234, 235, 237, 238, 239, 240, 241
Layfield, Kathie *60:* 194
Lazare, Jerry *44:* 109; *74:* 28
Lazarevich, Mila *17:* 118
Lazarus, Claire *103:* 30
Lazarus, Keo Felker *21:* 94
Lazzaro, Victor *11:* 126
Lea, Bob *166:* 208; *203:* 108
Lea, Tom *43:* 72, 74
Leacroft, Richard *6:* 140
Leaf, Munro *20:* 99
Leake, Donald *70:* 41
Leander, Patricia *23:* 27
Lear, Edward *18:* 183, 184, 185
Lear, Rebecca *149:* 46
Lebenson, Richard *6:* 209; *7:* 76; *23:* 145; *44:* 191; *87:* 153
Le Cain, Errol *6:* 141; *9:* 3; *22:* 142; *25:* 198; *28:* 173; *68:* 128, 129; *86:* 49
Lechon, Daniel *113:* 211
Leder, Dora *129:* 172
Ledger, Bill *181:* 58
Leduc, Bernard *102:* 36
Lee, Alan *62:* 25, 28
Lee, Bryce *99:* 60; *101:* 195; *196:* 53
Lee, Chinlun *181:* 138; *182:* 112
Lee, Declan *191:* 20

Lee, Dom *83:* 118, 120; *93:* 123; *121:* 121, 126; *146:* 174, 175, 206, 207; *174:* 204
Lee, Doris *13:* 246; *32:* 183; *44:* 111
Lee, Hector Viveros *115:* 96
Lee, Ho Baek *200:* 160
Lee, Huy Voun *217:* 106
Lee, Jeanne M. *158:* 56
Lee, Jared *93:* 200; *157:* 229; *215:* 113, 191, 192, 193; *228:* 177
Lee, Jody *81:* 121; *82:* 225; *91:* 155; *100:* 182
Lee, Jody A. *127:* 124, 126, 127
    See also Lee, Jody
Lee, Manning de V. *2:* 200; *17:* 12; *27:* 87; *37:* 102, 103, 104; *YABC 2:* 304
Lee, Margaret *213:* 179
Lee, Marie G. *138:* 157
Lee, Paul *97:* 100; *105:* 72, 209; *109:* 177; *128:* 113; *202:* 45
Lee, Robert J. *3:* 97; *67:* 124
Lee, Victor *96:* 228; *105:* 182; *140:* 196; *208:* 191
Lee, Virginia *208:* 139, 140; *218:* 28
Leech, Dorothy *98:* 76
Leech, John *15:* 59
Leedy, Loreen *84:* 142; *128:* 144, 145, 146; *175:* 125, 126, 127; *238:* 100, 101, 102
Leeman, Michael *44:* 157
Leeming, Catherine *87:* 39
Lees, Harry *6:* 112
LeFever, Bill *88:* 220, 221
Legenisel *47:* 111
Legrand, Edy *18:* 89, 93
Lehman, Barbara *73:* 123; *170:* 130
Lehrman, Rosalie *2:* 180
Leichman, Seymour *5:* 107
Leick, Bonnie *205:* 104
Leighton, Clare *25:* 130; *33:* 168; *37:* 105, 106, 108,109
Leisk, David *1:* 140, 141; *11:* 54; *30:* 137, 142, 143,144
Leister, Bryan *89:* 45; *106:* 37; *114:* 67; *149:* 236; *222:* 181; *237:* 142
Leloir, Maurice *18:* 77, 80, 83, 99
Lemaître, Pascal *144:* 175; *176:* 130; *189:* 135; *225:* 124, 125
Lemieux, Michele *100:* 148; *139:* 153
Lemke, Horst *14:* 98; *38:* 117, 118, 119
Lemke, R.W. *42:* 162
Lemon, David Gwynne *9:* 1
LeMoult, Adolph *82:* 116
Lenn, Michael *136:* 89
Lennon, John *114:* 100
Lennox, Elsie *95:* 163; *143:* 160
Lenski, Lois *1:* 144; *26:* 135, 137, 139, 141; *100:* 153, 154
Lent, Blair *1:* 116, 117; *2:* 174; *3:* 206, 207; *7:* 168, 169; *34:* 62; *68:* 217; *133:* 101; *183:* 60
Leon, Jana *226:* 214
Leonard, David *212:* 149
Leonard, Richard *91:* 128
Leonard, Tom *207:* 95; *219:* 55
Leone, Leonard *49:* 190
Lerner, Carol *86:* 140, 141, 142
Lerner, Judith *116:* 138
Lerner, Sharon *11:* 157; *22:* 56
Leroux-Hugon, Helene *132:* 139
Leslie, Cecil *19:* 244
Lessac, Frané *80:* 182, 207; *96:* 182; *202:* 58; *209:* 104
Lessing, Erich *167:* 52; *173:* 60
Lester, Alison *50:* 124; *90:* 147, 148; *129:* 130; *218:* 91, 93
Lester, Mike *208:* 50
Lethcoe, Jason *191:* 116, 117
Le Tord, Bijou *49:* 156; *95:* 112
Leutz, Emanuel *165:* 27
Levai, Blaise *39:* 130
Levert, Mireille *211:* 101
Levin, Ted *12:* 148

Levine, David *43:* 147, 149, 150, 151, 152; *64:* 11
Levine, Joe *71:* 88; *219:* 74
Levine, Marge *81:* 127
Levinson, David *178:* 232
Levit, Herschel *24:* 223
Levstek, Ljuba *131:* 192; *134:* 216; *149:* 65; *168:* 180
Levy, Jessica Ann *19:* 225; *39:* 191
Levy, Lina *117:* 126
Lewin, Betsy *32:* 114; *48:* 177; *90:* 151; *91:* 125; *92:* 85; *115:* 105; *169:* 110, 111; *178:* 47; *186:* 188; *194:* 201; *222:* 120; *226:* 139
Lewin, Ted *4:* 77; *8:* 168; *20:* 110; *21:* 99,100; *27:* 110; *28:* 96, 97; *31:* 49; *45:* 55; *48:* 223; *60:* 20, 119, 120; *62:* 139; *66:* 108; *71:* 12; *72:* 21; *74:* 226; *76:* 139, 140; *77:* 82; *79:* 87; *85:* 49, 177; *86:* 55; *88:* 182; *93:* 28, 29; *94:* 34, 182, 194; *99:* 156; *104:* 8; *115:* 123; *118:* 74; *119:* 114, 116; *131:* 54; *145:* 99; *165:* 151; *177:* 75; *178:* 42; *190:* 30; *192:* 86; *195:* 101, 102; *203:* 52; *222:* 119; *226:* 136, 137, 138, 139; *238:* 135
Lewis, Allen *15:* 112
Lewis, Anthony *227:* 114
Lewis, E.B. *88:* 143; *93:* 109; *119:* 79; *124:* 113; *128:* 49; *151:* 167; *168:* 10; *173:* 121; *174:* 66; *176:* 7; *184:* 150; *185:* 191; *211:* 108, 109, 110, 111; *223:* 17
Lewis, H.B. *170:* 124
Lewis, J. Patrick *162:* 83
Lewis, Jan *81:* 22
Lewis, Kim *136:* 165; *217:* 109, 111
Lewis, Richard W. *52:* 25
Lewis, Robin Baird *98:* 193
Lew-Vriethoff, Joanne *225:* 181
Leydon, Rita Floden *21:* 101
Li, Xiojun *187:* 172
Liao, Jimmy *202:* 100
Lichtenheld, Tom *152:* 125, 126; *222:* 160; *224:* 9
Lieblich, Irene *22:* 173; *27:* 209, 214
Lieder, Rick *108:* 197; *199:* 58, 59, 60
Lies, Brian *92:* 40; *141:* 101; *150:* 138; *190:* 97, 98, 99,
Liese, Charles *4:* 222
Liew, Sonny *219:* 108
Life, Kay *79:* 49
Lifton, Robert Jay *66:* 154
Lightburn, Ron *86:* 153; *91:* 122
Lightfoot, Norman R. *45:* 47
Lignell, Lois *37:* 114
Lill, Debra *121:* 70
Lilly, Charles *8:* 73; *20:* 127; *48:* 53; *72:* 9,16; *77:* 98; *102:* 94
Lilly, Ken *37:* 224
Lim, John *43:* 153
Limona, Mercedes *51:* 183
Lin, Grace *143:* 217; *162:* 86, 87; *174:* 185
Lincoln, Patricia Henderson *27:* 27; *78:* 127
Lindahn, Ron *84:* 17
Lindahn, Val *84:* 17
Lindberg, Howard *10:* 123; *16:* 190
Lindberg, Jeffrey *64:* 77; *77:* 71; *79:* 54; *80:* 149; *174:* 109; *179:* 52
Linden, Seymour *18:* 200, 201; *43:* 140
Lindenbaum, Pija *144:* 143; *183:* 113
Linder, Richard *27:* 119
Lindman, Maj *43:* 154
Lindsay, Norman *67:* 114
Lindsay, Vachel *40:* 118
Lindstrom, Jack *145:* 118
Line, Les *27:* 143
Linell
    See Smith, Linell
Lintern, Tom *228:* 101
Lionni, Leo *8:* 115; *72:* 159, 160, 161
Lipinsky, Lino *2:* 156; *22:* 175
Lippincott, Gary A. *70:* 35; *119:* 118; *220:* 105, 106, 107
Lippman, Peter *8:* 31; *31:* 119, 120, 160

Lisi, Victoria *89:* 145
Lisker, Emily *169:* 114
Lisker, Sonia O. *16:* 274; *31:* 31; *44:* 113, 114
Lisowski, Gabriel *47:* 144; *49:* 157
Lissim, Simon *17:* 138
Little, Ed *89:* 145; *151:* 53
Little, Harold *16:* 72
Little, Mary E. *28:* 146
Littlewood, Karen *165:* 126; *211:* 112
Litty, Julie *111:* 63
Litwin, Mike *235:* 59, 136
Litzinger, Rosanne *151:* 101; *176:* 118; *196:* 133, 134, 135; *208:* 129; *209:* 147
Liu, Lesley *143:* 72
Lively, Lorna *19:* 216
Livingston, Susan *95:* 22
Liwska, Renata *164:* 113; *199:* 25, 69; *220:* 79
Ljungkvist, Laura *180:* 120
Llerena, Carlos Antonio *19:* 181
Lloyd, Errol *11:* 39; *22:* 178
Lloyd, Megan *77:* 118; *80:* 113; *97:* 75; *117:* 94, 95; *189:* 121, 122; *208:* 128; *211:* 72; *239:* 87, 88, 89
Lloyd, Sam *183:* 116, 117
Lo, Beth *165:* 154
Lo, Koon-chiu *7:* 134
Loates, Glen *63:* 76
Lobel, Anita *6:* 87; *9:* 141; *18:* 248; *55:* 85,86, 87, 88, 93, 104; *60:* 67; *78:* 263; *82:* 110; *96:* 157, 159; *101:* 84; *132:* 35; *162:* 93, 94
Lobel, Arnold *1:* 188, 189; *5:* 12; *6:* 147; *7:* 167, 209; *18:* 190, 191; *25:* 39, 43; *27:* 40; *29:* 174; *52:* 127; *55:* 89, 91, 94, 95, 97, 98, 99, 100, 101, 102,103, 105, 106; *60:* 18, 31; *66:* 181, 183; *75:* 57; *82:* 246; *136:* 146
Lobel, Gillian *190:* 21
Lobo, Jen *229:* 53
Locker, Thomas *109:* 134
Lodge, Bernard *107:* 125, 126; *153:* 93
Loeb, Jeph *153:* 177
Lodge, Jo *112:* 119
Loefgren, Ulf *3:* 108
Loescher, Ann *20:* 108
Loescher, Gil *20:* 108
Loew, David *93:* 184; *171:* 120; *211:* 187
Lofting, Hugh *15:* 182, 183; *100:* 161, 162
Lofts, Pamela *60:* 188
Loh, George *38:* 88
Lomberg, Jon *58:* 160
Lonette, Reisie *11:* 211; *12:* 168; *13:* 56; *36:* 122; *43:* 155
Long, Ethan *168:* 146; *178:* 12; *182:* 120, 121; *196:* 124; *223:* 116, 117; *235:* 127; *239:* 102
Long, Laurel *162:* 135; *190:* 11; *203:* 113, 114; *228:* 212
Long, Loren *99:* 176; *172:* 65; *182:* 78; *188:* 114, 115; *239:* 82
Long, Melinda *152:* 128
Long, Miles *115:* 174
Long, Sally *42:* 184
Long, Sylvia *74:* 168; *132:* 63; *179:* 134
Longoni, Eduardo *73:* 85
Longtemps, Ken *17:* 123; *29:* 221; *69:* 82
Looser, Heinz *YABC 2:* 208
Lopez, Loretta *190:* 100
López, Rafael *197:* 160; *198:* 85
Lopshire, Robert *6:* 149; *21:* 117; *34:* 166; *73:* 13; *233:* 103
Lord, John Vernon *21:* 104; *23:* 25; *51:* 22
Lorenz, Albert *40:* 146; *115:* 127
Lorenzen, Geoffrey *229:* 24
Loretta, Sister Mary *33:* 73
Lorraine, Walter H. *3:* 110; *4:* 123; *16:* 192; *103:* 119
Los, Marek *146:* 22; *193:* 23
Loss, Joan *11:* 163
Louderback, Walt *YABC 1:* 164
Loughridge, Stuart *214:* 131
Louis, Catherine *212:* 186
Lousada, Sandra *40:* 138
Louth, Jack *149:* 252; *151:* 191, 192

Love, Judy *173:* 43; *196:* 40; *235:* 24
Lovelock, Brian *214:* 132, 197
Low, Joseph *14:* 124, 125; *18:* 68; *19:* 194; *31:* 166; *80:* 239
Low, William *62:* 175; *80:* 147; *112:* 194; *150:* 202; *169:* 175; *177:* 110; *192:* 27
Lowe, Vicky *177:* 130
Lowenheim, Alfred *13:* 65, 66
Lowenstein, Sallie *116:* 90, 91
Lowery, Mike *227:* 115
Lowitz, Anson *17:* 124; *18:* 215
Lowrey, Jo *8:* 133
Loxton, Daniel *229:* 109
Lubach, Vanessa *142:* 152
Lubell, Winifred *1:* 207; *3:* 15; *6:* 151
Lubin, Leonard B. *19:* 224; *36:* 79, 80; *45:* 128, 129,131, 132, 133, 134, 135, 136, 137, 139, 140, 141; *70:* 95; *YABC2:* 96
Lucas, David *208:* 148
Lucht, Irmgard *82:* 145
Ludwig, Helen *33:* 144, 145
Luebs, Robin *212:* 109
Lufkin, Raymond *38:* 138; *44:* 48
Luhrs, Henry *7:* 123; *11:* 120
Lujan, Tonita *82:* 33
Lum, Bernice *230:* 70
Lupo, Dom *4:* 204
Lustig, Loretta *30:* 186; *46:* 134, 135, 136, 137
Lutes, Jason *210:* 163
Luthardt, Kevin *172:* 125, 126; *217:* 2
Luxbacher, Irene *153:* 145; *219:* 112, 113
Luzak, Dennis *52:* 121; *99:* 142
Lydbury, Jane *82:* 98
Lydecker, Laura *21:* 113; *42:* 53
Lynch, Charles *16:* 33
Lynch, Marietta *29:* 137; *30:* 171
Lynch, P.J. *126:* 228; *129:* 110; *132:* 247; *183:* 64; *207:* 184; *213:* 100, 101, 102; *237:* 164
Lyne, Alison Davis *188:* 118, 198
Lyon, Carol *102:* 26
Lyon, Elinor *6:* 154
Lyon, Fred *14:* 16
Lyon, Lea *212:* 110
Lyon, Tammie *175:* 170
Lyons, Oren *8:* 193
Lyster, Michael *26:* 41

M

Maas, Dorothy *6:* 175
Maas, Julie *47:* 61
Macaulay, David *46:* 139, 140, 141, 142, 143, 144, 145, 147, 149, 150; *72:* 167, 168, 169; *137:* 129, 130, 131, 132
MacCarthy, Patricia *69:* 141
Macdonald, Alister *21:* 55
Macdonald, Roberta *19:* 237; *52:* 164
MacDonald, Norman *13:* 99
MacDonald, Ross *201:* 103
MacDonald, Suse *54:* 41; *109* 138; *130:* 156; *193:* 106, 107, 109, 110
Mace, Varian *49:* 159
MacEachern, Stephen *206:* 2
Macguire, Robert Reid *18:* 67
Machetanz, Fredrick *34:* 147, 148
MacInnes, Cat *236:* 51
MacInnes, Ian *35:* 59
MacIntyre, Elisabeth *17:* 127, 128
Mack, Jeff *161:* 128; *194:* 119, 120; *219:* 67; *225:* 135
Mack, Stan *17:* 129; *96:* 33
Mackay, Donald *17:* 60
MacKaye, Arvia *32:* 119
Mackenzie, Robert *204:* 78
Mackenzie, Stuart *73:* 213
MacKenzie, Garry *33:* 159
Mackie, Clare *87:* 134
Mackinlay, Miguel *27:* 22

MacKinstry, Elizabeth *15:* 110; *42:* 139, 140, 141, 142, 143,144, 145
MacLeod, Lee *91:* 167
Maclise, Daniel *YABC 2:* 257
Macnaughton, Tina *182:* 145; *218:* 106, 107
MacRae, Tom *181:* 112
Madden, Don *3:* 112, 113; *4:* 33, 108, 155; *7:* 193; *78:* 12; *YABC 2:* 211
Maddison, Angela Mary *10:* 83
Madrid, Erwin *229:* 117
Madsen, Jim *146:* 259; *152:* 237; *184:* 106; *197:* 21; *202:* 103, 104; *233:* 38
Maestro, Giulio *8:* 124; *12:* 17; *13:* 108; *25:* 182; *54:* 147; *59:* 114, 115, 116, 117, 118, 121, 123, 124, 125,126, 127; *68:* 37, 38; *106:* 129, 130, 131, 136, 137, 138
Maffia, Daniel *60:* 200
Maggio, Viqui *58:* 136, 181; *74:* 150; *75:* 90; *85:* 159; *90:* 158; *109:* 184; *193:* 113
Magnus, Erica *77:* 123
Magnuson, Diana *28:* 102; *34:* 190; *41:* 175
Magoon, Scott *181:* 104; *217:* 165; *222:* 126
Magovern, Peg *103:* 123; *218:* 164
Maguire, Sheila *41:* 100
Magurn, Susan *91:* 30
Mahony, Will *37:* 120
Mahony, Will *85:* 116
Mahood, Kenneth *24:* 141
Mahurin, Matt *164:* 225; *175:* 95; *189:* 37; *196:* 14; *209:* 163; *229:* 179
Maik, Henri *9:* 102
Maione, Heather *106:* 5; *178:* 8; *189:* 126, 127; *193:* 58
Mair, J. Sonia *237:* 84
Maisto, Carol *29:* 87
Maitland, Antony *1:* 100, 176; *8:* 41; *17:* 246; *24:* 46; *25:* 177, 178; *32:* 74; *60:* 65, 195; *67:* 156; *87:* 131; *101:* 110
Majewski, Dawn W. *169:* 95
Mak, Kam *72:* 25; *75:* 43; *87:* 186; *97:* 24; *102:* 154; *149:* 195; *186:* 28; *209:* 132
Makie, Pam *37:* 117
Maktima, Joe *116:* 191
Maland, Nick *99:* 77
Male, Alan *132:* 64
Malone, James Hiram *84:* 161
Malone, Nola Langner *82:* 239
Malone, Peter *191:* 121, 122, 123
Malsberg, Edward *51:* 175
Malvern, Corinne *2:* 13; *34:* 148, 149
Manchess, Gregory *165:* 241; *203:* 119
Mancusi, Stephen *63:* 198, 199
Mandelbaum, Ira *31:* 115
Manders, John *138:* 152, 155; *188:* 171; *190:* 92; *199:* 5; *217:* 52; *219:* 35; *219:* 115, 116, 117
Mandine, Selma *228:* 103
Manet, Edouard *23:* 170
Mangiat, Jeff *173:* 127
Mangurian, David *14:* 133
Manham, Allan *42:* 109; *77:* 180; *80:* 227
Manley, Matt *103:* 167; *117:* 98; *172:* 49; *212:* 207
Manna, Giovanni *178:* 44
Manniche, Lise *31:* 121
Manning, Jane *96:* 203; *233:* 107
Manning, Jo *63:* 154
Manning, Lawrence *191:* 153
Manning, Maurie J. *211:* 116
Manning, Mick *176:* 139; *224:* 57
Manning, Samuel F. *5:* 75
Mantel, Richard *57:* 73; *63:* 106; *82:* 255
Mantha, John *205:* 164; *217:* 117
Maraja *15:* 86; *YABC 1:* 28; *2:* 115
Marcellino, Fred *20:* 125; *34:* 222; *53:* 125; *58:* 205; *61:* 64, 121, 122; *68:* 154, 156, 157, 158, 159; *72:* 25; *86:* 184; *98:* 181; *118:* 129, 130, 131; *149:* 218; *194:* 7

Marchesi, Stephen *34:* 140; *46:* 72; *50:* 147; *66:* 239; *70:* 33; *73:* 18, 114, 163; *77:* 47, 76,147; *78:* 79; *80:* 30; *81:* 6; *89:* 66; *93:* 21,130; *94:* 94; *97:* 66; *98:* 96; *114:* 115, 116
Marchiori, Carlos *14:* 60
Marciano, John Bemelmans *118:* 133; *167:* 110, 111, 112
Marconi, Guilherme *220:* 143
Marcus, Barry David *139:* 248; *145:* 18
Maren, Julie *199:* 73
Margules, Gabriele *21:* 120
Mariana
    See Foster, Marian Curtis
Mariano, Michael *52:* 108
Marino, Dorothy *6:* 37; *14:* 135
Mario, Heide Stetson *101:* 202
Maris, Ron *71:* 123
Maritz, Nicolaas *85:* 123
Mark, Mona *65:* 105; *68:* 205; *116:* 213
Markham, R.L. *17:* 240
Marklew, Gilly *211:* 118
Marks, Alan *104:* 104; *109:* 182; *164:* 92; *185:* 134; *187:* 120, 121, 122; *218:* 114, 115; *230:* 165
Marks, Cara *54:* 9
Marks, Colin *203:* 129
Marokvia, Artur *31:* 122
Marquez, Susan *108:* 121; *219:* 95
Marrella, Maria Pia *62:* 116
Marriott, Pat *30:* 30; *34:* 39; *35:* 164, 165, 166; *44:* 170; *48:* 186, 187, 188, 189, 191, 192, 193; *91:* 92
Mars, W.T. *1:* 161; *3:* 115; *4:* 208, 225; *5:* 92, 105, 186; *8:* 214; *9:* 12; *13:* 121; *27:* 151; *31:* 180; *38:* 102; *48:* 66; *62:* 164, 165; *64:* 62; *68:* 229; *79:* 55
Marschall, Ken *85:* 29
Marsh, Christine *3:* 164
Marsh, James *73:* 137
Marsh, Reginald *17:* 5; *19:* 89; *22:* 90, 96
Marshall, Anthony D. *18:* 216
Marshall, Felicia *170:* 190
Marshall, James *6:* 160; *40:* 221; *42:* 24, 25, 29; *51:* 111, 112, 113, 114, 115, 116, 117, 118, 119, 120, 121; *64:* 13; *75:* 126, 127, 128, 129; *102:* 10, 12; *216:* 26, 28
Marshall, Janet *97:* 154
Marstall, Bob *55:* 145; *84:* 153, 170; *104:* 145; *154:* 166, 167, 168
Martchenko, Michael *50:* 129, 153, 155, 156, 157; *83:* 144,145; *154:* 137, 138, 139
Marten, Ruth *129:* 52
Marten, Brad *199:* 186
Martin, Charles E. *70:* 144
Martin, Courtney A. *214:* 28
Martin, David Stone *24:* 232; *62:* 4
Martin, Fletcher *18:* 213; *23:* 151
Martin, Rene *7:* 144; *42:* 148, 149, 150
Martin, Richard E. *51:* 157; *131:* 203
Martin, Ron *32:* 81
Martin, Stefan *8:* 68; *32:* 124, 126; *56:* 33
Martin, Whitney *166:* 137
Martinez, Ed *58:* 192; *72:* 231; *77:* 33; *80:* 214; *167:* 123
Martinez, John *6:* 113; *118:* 13; *139:* 143
Martinez, Sergio *158:* 190; *220:* 156
Martini, Angela *183:* 161; *226:* 195
Martiniere, Stephan *171:* 130
Marton, Jirina *95:* 127, 128; *144:* 145; *230:* 73, 74, 75
Martorell, Antonio *84:* 6; *97:* 161
Martucci, Griesbach *52:* 106
Marvin, Frederic *83:* 86
Marx, Robert F. *24:* 143
Marzollo, Jean *190:* 127
Masefield, Judith *19:* 208, 209
Masheris, Robert *78:* 51
Masiello, Ralph *186:* 171; *214:* 134
Mason, George F. *14:* 139
Mason, Robert *84:* 96

Masse, Josée *208:* 45; *217:* 19; *221:* 134; *234:* 184

Massey, Barbara *68:* 142

Massie, Diane Redfield *16:* 194

Massie, Kim *31:* 43

Massini, Sarah *213:* 79

Mataya, David *121:* 66

Mathers, Petra *119:* 135; *163:* 104; *176:* 143, 144; *187:* 142; *196:* 101

Mathewuse, James *51:* 143

Mathieu, Joseph *14:* 33; *39:* 206; *43:* 167; *56:* 180; *79:* 126; *94:* 147; *185:* 140; *236:* 57

Matje, Martin *169:* 177, 178; *172:* 180

Matsubara, Naoko *12:* 121

Matsuda, Shizu *13:* 167

Matsuoka, Mei *192:* 135; *214:* 84

Matte, L'Enc *22:* 183

Mattelson, Marvin *36:* 50, 51

Mattheson, Jenny *180:* 132; *222:* 153

Matthews, Elizabeth *194:* 128; *223:* 35

Matthews, F. Leslie *4:* 216

Matthews, Tina *190:* 130

Mattingly, David *71:* 76, 77; *82:* 64; *91:* 216, 217; *109:* 25

Matulay, Laszlo *5:* 18; *43:* 168

Matus, Greta *12:* 142

Maughan, Bill *181:* 31; *211:* 211

Mauldin, Bill *27:* 23

Mauterer, Erin Marie *119:* 5

Mawicke, Tran *9:* 137; *15:* 191; *47:* 100

Mawson, Matt *74:* 115

Max, Peter *45:* 146, 147, 148, 149, 150

Maxie, Betty *40:* 135

Maxwell, John Alan *1:* 148

May, Katie *225:* 128

May, Steve *204:* 30

Mayan, Earl *7:* 193

Maydak, Michael S. *220:* 117

Mayer, Bill *200:* 138

Mayer, Danuta *117:* 103

Mayer, Marianna *32:* 132

Mayer, Mercer *11:* 192; *16:* 195, 196; *20:* 55, 57; *32:* 129, 130, 132, 133, 134; *41:* 144, 248, 252; *58:* 186; *73:* 140, 142, 143; *137:* 137, 138

Mayforth, Hal *166:* 77

Mayhew, James *85:* 121; *138:* 187; *149:* 140; *204:* 81

Mayhew, Richard *3:* 106

Mayo, Gretchen Will *38:* 81; *84:* 166

Mays, Victor *5:* 127; *8:* 45, 153; *14:* 245; *23:* 50; *34:* 155; *40:* 79; *45:* 158; *54:* 91; *66:* 240

Mazal, Chanan *49:* 104

Maze, Deborah *71:* 83

Mazellan, Ron *75:* 97, 98; *210:* 169

Mazetti, Alan *112:* 72

Mazille, Capucine *96:* 168

Mazza, Adriana Saviozzi *19:* 215

Mazzella, Mary Jo *82:* 165

Mazzetti, Alan *45:* 210

McAfee, Steve *135:* 146; *167:* 176; *191:* 84; *210:* 117; *218:* 34; *233:* 86

McAlinden, Paul *112:* 128

McBride, Angus *28:* 49; *103:* 40

McBride, Will *30:* 110

McCaffery, Janet *38:* 145

McCall, Bruce *209:* 119

McCallum, Graham *78:* 78

McCallum, Stephen *141:* 143; *156:* 5; *166:* 228

McCann, Gerald *3:* 50; *4:* 94; *7:* 54; *41:* 121

McCarthy, Dan *174:* 74

McCarthy, Linda *177:* 128; *218:* 104

McCarthy, Meghan *168:* 134; *199:* 74

McCauley, Adam *157:* 36; *184:* 199; *193:* 100; *209:* 122

McCay, Winsor *41:* 124, 126, 128, 129, 130, 131; *134:* 77, 79

McClary, Nelson *1:* 111

McClements, George *196:* 146

McClennan, Connie *210:* 181

McClintock, Barbara *57:* 135; *95:* 130; *146:* 190; *213:* 3, 5, 107, 108

McClintock, Theodore *14:* 141

McCloskey, Robert *1:* 184, 185; *2:* 186, 187; *17:* 209; *39:* 139, 140, 141, 142, 143, 146, 147, 148; *85:* 150, 151; *100:* 172, 173, 174

McClung, Robert *2:* 189; *68:* 166, 167

McClure, Gillian *31:* 132; *150:* 53

McClure, Nikki *218:* 120

McConnel, Jerry *31:* 75, 187

McConnell, Mary *102:* 49

McCord, Kathleen Garry *78:* 236

McCormack, John *66:* 193

McCormick, A.D. *35:* 119

McCormick, Dell J. *19:* 216

McCoy, Glenn *212:* 132

McCrady, Lady *16:* 198; *39:* 127

McCrea, James *3:* 122; *33:* 216

McCrea, Ruth *3:* 122; *27:* 102; *33:* 216

McCue, Lisa *65:* 148, 149; *77:* 54; *80:* 132; *175:* 33; *177:* 133, 135; *212:* 136, 137, 138

McCully, Emily Arnold *2:* 89; *4:* 120, 121, 146, 197; *5:* 2, 129; *7:* 191; *11:* 122; *15:* 210; *33:* 23; *35:* 244; *37:* 122; *39:* 88; *40:* 103; *50:* 30,31, 32, 33, 34, 35, 36, 37; *52:* 89, 90; *57:* 6; *62:* 3; *70:* 195; *86:* 82; *96:* 192; *97:* 93; *110:* 143,144; *117:* 47; *167:* 96; *210:* 175, 176; *225:* 179; *231:* 157

McCurdy, Michael *13:* 153; *24:* 85; *81:* 160; *82:* 157, 158; *86:* 125; *97:* 92; *117:* 178; *132:* 6; *147:* 159, 160; *237:* 92, 93, 94

McCusker, Paul *99:* 19

McDaniel, Jerry *132:* 135

McDaniel, Preston *160:* 206; *170:* 139

McDermott, Beverly Brodsky *11:* 180

McDermott, Gerald *16:* 201; *74:* 174, 175; *163:* 150, 151

McDermott, Mike *96:* 187

McDonald, Jill *13:* 155; *26:* 128

McDonald, Mercedes *169:* 118

McDonald, Ralph J. *5:* 123, 195

McDonnell, Flora *146:* 199, 200

McDonnell, Patrick *179:* 153, 154; *221:* 136, 137, 138

McDonough, Don *10:* 163

McElligott, Matt *196:* 147

McElmurry, Jill *137:* 148; *163:* 141; *202:* 186

McElrath-Eslick, Lori *129:* 145; *142:* 21; *173:* 123; *202:* 194; *204:* 88, 89

McEntee, Dorothy *37:* 124

McEwan, Keith *88:* 116; *165:* 122, 123

McEwen, Katharine *169:* 34

McFall, Christie *12:* 144

McFeely, Daniel *160:* 213

McGaw, Laurie *109:* 243; *143:* 216; *211:* 218

McGee, Barbara *6:* 165

McGee, Marni *163:* 153

McGillvray, Kim *158:* 171; *165:* 213; *186:* 183; *190:* 175

McGinley-Nally, Sharon *131:* 19

McGinnis, Robert *110:* 113; *177:* 80

McGovern, Tara *98:* 171

McGraw, Sheila *83:* 146

McGregor, Barbara *200:* 155

McGregor, Malcolm *23:* 27

McGrory, Anik *193:* 120

McGuire, Robert *204:* 57; *209:* 86

McGuirk, Leslie *152:* 159

McHale, John *138:* 190

McHenry, E.B. *193:* 122

McHugh, Tom *23:* 64

McIntosh, Jon *42:* 56

McKay, Donald *2:* 118; *32:* 157; *45:* 151, 152

McKean, Dave *150:* 71; *174:* 156; *197:* 83, 118; *229:* 45, 46

McKeating, Eileen *44:* 58

McKee, David *10:* 48; *21:* 9; *70:* 154, 155; *107:* 139, 140, 141; *134:* 218; *158:* 148, 149, 150, 151; *228:* 171

McKee, Diana *109:* 185

McKelvey, Patrick *164:* 141

McKendry, Joe *170:* 136

McKeveny, Tom *164:* 60; *173:* 79

McKie, Roy *7:* 44

McKie, Todd *205:* 181

McKillip, Kathy *30:* 153

McKinney, Ena *26:* 39

McKinnon, James *136:* 75

McKowen, Scott *172:* 63; *202:* 49

McLachlan, Edward *5:* 89

McLaren, Chesley *133:* 53; *213:* 112; *219:* 31

McLaren, Kirsty *123:* 99; *124:* 226

Mclean, Andrew *113:* 117, 118, 120, 121; *172:* 130, 131

Mclean, Janet *172:* 130

McLean, Meg *94:* 196

McLean, Sammis *32:* 197

McLean, Wilson *90:* 29; *113:* 195

McLoughlin, John C. *47:* 149

McLoughlin, Wayne *102:* 230; *134:* 178; *216:* 196

McMahon, Robert *36:* 155; *69:* 169

McManus, Shawn *85:* 71

McMenemy, Sarah *156:* 139; *211:* 93; *224:* 139; *226:* 152

McMillan, Bruce *22:* 184

McMullan, James *40:* 33; *67:* 172; *87:* 142; *99:* 63, 64; *189:* 133; *196:* 51

McMullen, Nigel *146:* 177

McNeely, Tom *162:* 55

McNaught, Harry *12:* 80; *32:* 136

McNaughton, Colin *39:* 149; *40:* 108; *92:* 144, 145, 146; *134:* 104, 106; *211:* 122, 123, 124

McNicholas, Maureen *38:* 148

McNicholas, Shelagh *173:* 61; *191:* 125, 126

McPhail, David *14:* 105; *23:* 135; *37:* 217, 218, 220,221; *47:* 151, 152, 153, 154, 155, 156, 158, 159, 160, 162, 163, 164; *71:* 211; *81:* 139, 140, 142; *86:* 123; *132:* 150; *140:* 129, 131, 132; *183:* 134, 135, 137; *189:* 132; *219:* 121, 122, 123, 124, 125; *231:* 158

McPhee, Richard B. *41:* 133

McPheeters, Neal *78:* 132; *86:* 90; *99:* 162; *141:* 141; *142:* 162; *231:* 146

McQuade, Jacqueline *124:* 223

McQueen, Lucinda *28:* 149; *41:* 249; *46:* 206; *53:* 103

McQuillan, Mary *153:* 97; *200:* 140

McVay, Tracy *11:* 68

McVicker, Charles *39:* 150

McWilliam, Howard *219:* 135

Mead, Ben Carlton *43:* 75

Meade, Holly *90:* 102; *94:* 101; *149:* 8; *151:* 107

Mecray, John *33:* 62

Meddaugh, Susan *20:* 42; *29:* 143; *41:* 241; *77:* 50; *84:* 173, 174, 175, 176, 177, 178; *125:* 160, 161, 162; *176:* 148, 149, 150, 151

Meehan, Dennis B. *56:* 144

Meents, Len W. *73:* 147, 150

Meers, Tony *99:* 113

Meisel, Paul *98:* 137; *124:* 18; *162:* 180; *179:* 16; *181:* 62; *194:* 154; *221:* 5; *224:* 100, 101, 102, 133; *231:* 25

Melanson, Luc *149:* 229; *198:* 97, 98; *221:* 166

Melendez, Francisco *72:* 180

Melling, David *202:* 199

Melnychuk, Monika *153:* 65

Melo, Esperança *196:* 90; *239:* 93, 94

Melo, John *16:* 285; *58:* 203

Meloni, Maria Teresa *98:* 62

Meltzer, Ericka
See O'Rourke, Ericka

Menasco, Milton *43:* 85

Menchin, Scott *188:* 129; *234:* 139

Mendelson, Steven T. *86:* 154

Mendelssohn, Felix *19:* 170

Mendola, Christopher *88:* 223

Meng, Heinz *13:* 158

Merian, Maria Sibylla *140:* 88

Mero, Lee *34:* 68
Merrell, David *205:* 3
Merrill, Frank T. *16:* 147; *19:* 71; *YABC 1:*
   226, 229,273
Merriman, Rachel *98:* 108; *114:* 122; *149:* 142
Merveille, David *200:* 142
Meryman, Hope *27:* 41
Meryweather, Jack *10:* 179
Meseldzija, Petar *168:* 97
Meserve, Jessica *184:* 137; *211:* 127
Messick, Dale *64:* 150, 151, 152
Meth, Harold *24:* 203
Meyer, Alex Eben *226:* 60
Meyer, Herbert *19:* 189
Meyer, Renate *6:* 170
Meyers, Bob *11:* 136
Meyers, Nancy *172:* 124
Meynell, Louis *37:* 76
Micale, Albert *2:* 65; *22:* 185
Miccuci, Charles *82:* 163; *144:* 150
Micich, Paul *164:* 163
Middleton, Charlotte *230:* 81
Middleton, Jeffrey *177:* 173; *222:* 157
Middleton, Joshua *208:* 146; *219:* 24
Middleton-Sandford, Betty *2:* 125
Mieke, Anne *45:* 74
Mighell, Patricia *43:* 134
Miglio, Paige *101:* 203; *151:* 223; *201:* 118,
   119; *204:* 162
Mikec, Larry *204:* 125
Mikolaycak, Charles *9:* 144; *12:* 101; *13:* 212;
   21: 121; *22:* 168; *30:* 187; *34:* 103, 150; *37:*
   183; *43:* 179; *44:* 90; *46:* 115, 118, 119; *49:*
   25; *78:* 121, 122, 205, 207; *81:* 4
Milelli, Pascal *129:* 66; *135:* 153; *187:* 45;
   235: 47
Miles, Elizabeth *117:* 77
Miles, Jennifer *17:* 278
Milgrim, David *158:* 157; *187:* 125, 126, 128;
   223: 124, 125, 126, 127
Milhous, Katherine *15:* 193; *17:* 51
Milian, Tomaso *238:* 119
Millais, John E. *22:* 230, 231
Millar, H.R. *YABC 1:* 194, 195, 203
Millard, C.E. *28:* 186
Millard, Kerry *105:* 124; *204:* 93, 94
Miller, Don *15:* 195; *16:* 71; *20:* 106; *31:* 178
Miller, Edna *29:* 148
Miller, Edward *115:* 64; *183:* 140, 141; *218:*
   129, 130, 131
Miller, Frank J. *25:* 94
Miller, Grambs *18:* 38; *23:* 16
Miller, Ian *99:* 128
Miller, Jane *15:* 196
Miller, Marcia *13:* 233
Miller, Marilyn *1:* 87; *31:* 69; *33:* 157
Miller, Mitchell *28:* 183; *34:* 207
Miller, Phil *175:* 150
Miller, Shane *5:* 140
Miller, Virginia *81:* 206
Miller, Woody *233:* 153; *236:* 146
Millman, Isaac *172:* 18
Mills, Elaine *72:* 181
Mills, Judith Christine *130:* 168, 169
Mills, Lauren *92:* 170
Mills, Yaroslava Surmach *35:* 169, 170; *46:*
   114
Millsap, Darrel *51:* 102
Milone, Karen *89:* 169; *222:* 149
Milord, Susan *147:* 163, 164; *200:* 144
Milot, René *226:* 127
Milton, Debbie *162:* 161
Mims, Ashley *170:* 51
Min, Willemien *222:* 62
Miner, Julia *98:* 69
Minor, Wendell *39:* 188; *52:* 87; *56:* 171; *58:*
   116; *62:* 56; *66:* 109; *74:* 93; *78:* 129; *94:*
   67; *117:* 12, 13; *124:* 84, 86; *136:* 121; *164:*
   168, 169; *170:* 71; *199:* 79, 80, 81, 82; *217:*
   63; *223:* 149; *226:* 90, 91, 92
Minter, Daniel *176:* 154; *179:* 177

Mirocha, Paul *81:* 133; *192:* 148; *194:* 36
Misako Rocks! *192:* 149, 150
Mitchell, Judith *109:* 117
Mitchell, Mark *91:* 208
Mitchell, Tracy *190:* 15
Mitgutsch, Ali *76:* 161
Mitsuhashi, Yoko *45:* 153
Miyake, Yoshi *38:* 141
Mizumura, Kazue *10:* 143; *18:* 223; *36:* 159
Mochi, Ugo *8:* 122; *38:* 150
Mock, Paul *55:* 83; *123:* 32
Modarressi, Mitra *90:* 236; *126:* 168; *173:*
   165, 166; *200:* 147, 148
Modell, Frank *39:* 152
Mogenson, Jan *74:* 183
Mohn, Susan *89:* 224
Mohr, Mark *133:* 201
Mohr, Nicholasa *8:* 139; *113:* 127
Molan, Christine *60:* 177; *84:* 183
Moldon, Peter L. *49:* 168
Molk, Laurel *92:* 150; *230:* 217, 219
Mollica, Gene *197:* 11
Momaday, N. Scott *48:* 159
Mombourquette, Paul *112:* 91; *126:* 142
Monk, Julie *165:* 231; *191:* 96
Monks, Lydia *189:* 136, 137
Monroe, Chris *219:* 133
Monroy, Manuel *199:* 192
Montalto, Luisa *233:* 79
Montgomery, Lucy *150:* 126
Montgomery, Michael G. *208:* 159
Montgomery-Higham, Amanda *169:* 131
Monteiel, David *201:* 95
Montiel, David *69:* 106; *84:* 145
Montijo, Rhode *193:* 164
Montresor, Beni *2:* 91; *3:* 138; *38:* 152, 153,
   154,155, 156, 157, 158, 159, 160; *68:* 63
Montserrat, Pep *128:* 135; *181:* 119; *184:* 53
Moon, Carl *25:* 183, 184, 185
Moon, Eliza *14:* 40
Moon, Ivan *22:* 39; *38:* 140
Moore, Adrienne *67:* 147
Moore, Agnes Kay Randall *43:* 187
Moore, Cyd *117:* 107, 108; *159:* 137, 138;
   186: 148, 149, 151; *203:* 15; *214:* 138, 139;
   233: 111, 112, 113, 115
Moore, Gustav *127:* 181, 182; *170:* 162, 163
Moore, Jackie *128:* 79
Moore, Janet *63:* 153
Moore, Margie *176:* 156; *221:* 125; *224:* 106,
   107
Moore, Mary *29:* 160
Moore, Patrick *184:* 121
Moore, Sean L. *237:* 98
Moore, Yvette *101:* 11, 12; *154:* 141
Mora, Giovanni *179:* 127; *184:* 11
Mora, Raul Mina *20:* 41
Moraes, Odilon *102:* 144
Morales, Magaly *225:* 137; *233:* 28
Morales, Yuyi *154:* 144; *226:* 120; *236:* 121
Moran, Rosslyn *111:* 26
Moran, Tom *60:* 100
Mordan, C.B. *193:* 115
Mordvinoff, Nicolas *15:* 179
Moreno, René King *169:* 59; *190:* 133, 209;
   212: 52
Morgan, Barbara *169:* 116
Morgan, Jacqui *58:* 57
Morgan, Mary *114:* 133, 134, 135; *123:* 11;
   213: 115, 116, 117
Morgan, Tom *42:* 157
Morgan, Pierr *173:* 148
Morgenstern, Michael *158:* 7, 57; *171:* 103;
   174: 60; *226:* 12; *233:* 5
Morice, Dave *93:* 142
Morin, Paul *73:* 132; *79:* 130; *88:* 140; *137:*
   143
Moriuchi, Mique *177:* 203
Morozumi, Atsuko *110:* 155; *217:* 126, 127

Morrill, Leslie *18:* 218; *29:* 177; *33:* 84; *38:*
   147; *42:* 127; *44:* 93; *48:* 164, 165, 167,
   168, 169, 170,171; *49:* 162; *63:* 136, 180;
   70: 72; *71:* 70, 91,92; *72:* 228; *80:* 163, 164,
   165; *90:* 121; *121:* 88; *178:* 117
Morrill, Rowena A. *84:* 16; *98:* 163
Morris *47:* 91
Morris, Frank *55:* 133; *60:* 28; *76:* 2
Morris, Harry O. *119:* 138
Morris, Jackie *128:* 194; *144:* 119; *151:* 146;
   202: 126, 127; *204:* 83; *211:* 80; *214:* 163
Morris, Jennifer E. *179:* 157
Morris, Oradel Nolen *128:* 180
Morris, Tony *62:* 146; *70:* 97
Morrison, Bill *42:* 116; *66:* 170; *69:* 40
Morrison, Gordon *87:* 150; *113:* 93; *128:* 181,
   182; *183:* 144, 145, 146
Morrison, Frank *169:* 162; *205:* 156; *224:* 121;
   226: 154
Morrison, Taylor *159:* 144, 145; *187:* 131
Morrow, Gray *2:* 64; *5:* 200; *10:* 103, 114; *14:*
   175
Morse, Scott *200:* 149, 150
Morstad, Julie *232:* 137
Morton, Lee Jack *32:* 140
Morton, Marian *3:* 185
Mosberg, Hilary *117:* 195; *118:* 164; *149:* 55
Moser, Barry *56:* 68, 117, 118, 119, 120, 121,
   122, 123, 124; *59:* 141; *60:* 160; *79:* 91,
   147, 149, 151, 152; *82:* 81; *90:* 118; *91:* 35;
   95: 210; *97:* 91, 93; *102:* 152; *126:* 4; *128:*
   175; *133:* 141; *138:* 167, 171, 174; *153:*
   205; *174:* 130; *185:* 152, 154; *195:* 163;
   204: 115; *209:* 201
Moser, Cara *90:* 118; *138:* 167
Moses, Grandma *18:* 228
Moses, Will *178:* 170, 171
Moskof, Martin Stephen *27:* 152
Mosley, Francis *57:* 144
Moss, Donald *11:* 184
Moss, Geoffrey *32:* 198
Moss, Marissa *71:* 130; *104:* 127; *163:* 156;
   216: 164, 165, 166; *239:* 136
Most, Bernard *48:* 173; *91:* 142, 143; *134:* 120
Mourning, Tuesday *205:* 25; *220:* 68; *221:* 42;
   236: 91
Mowll, Joshua *188:* 133
Mowry, Carmen *50:* 62
Moxley, Sheila *96:* 174; *169:* 26; *206:* 16
Moyers, William *21:* 65
Moyler, Alan *36:* 142
Mozley, Charles *9:* 87; *20:* 176, 192, 193; *22:*
   228; *25:* 205; *33:* 150; *43:* 170, 171, 172,
   173, 174; *YABC2:* 89
Mueller, Hans Alexander *26:* 64; *27:* 52, 53
Mugnaini, Joseph *11:* 35; *27:* 52, 53; *35:* 62
Mujica, Rick *72:* 67; *88:* 95; *111:* 53; *180:*
   185; *197:* 70
Mullen, Douglas *180:* 178; *239:* 105
Muller, Robin *86:* 161
Muller, Steven *32:* 167
Muller, Jorg *35:* 215; *67:* 138, 139
Mulock, Julie *163:* 112
Mullins, Edward S. *10:* 101
Mullins, Patricia *51:* 68
Multer, Scott *80:* 108
Munari, Bruno *15:* 200
Munch, Edvard *140:* 143
Munowitz, Ken *14:* 148; *72:* 178, 179
Muñoz, Claudio *208:* 161
Munoz, William *42:* 160
Munro, Roxie *58:* 134; *136:* 177; *137:* 218;
   184: 133, 134; *223:* 130, 132, 133
Munsinger, Lynn *33:* 161; *46:* 126; *71:* 92; *82:*
   80; *89:* 218; *92:* 125; *94:* 157, 158, 159,
   160; *98:* 196; *103:* 198; *142:* 143; *145:* 133,
   134, 136; *153:* 203; *176:* 162; *177:* 140, 141,
   142; *189:* 113, 114, 116, 117; *201:* 42; *221:*
   148, 149,150
Munson, Russell *13:* 9
Munster, Sebastian *166:* 107

Munzar, Barbara *149:* 75
Murdocca, Salvatore *73:* 212; *98:* 132; *111:* 168; *157:* 228; *164:* 257
Murphy, Bill *5:* 138; *130:* 170
Murphy, Jill *37:* 142; *70:* 166; *142:* 132, 134
Murphy, Kelly *130:* 212; *143:* 119; *176:* 158; *190:* 135
Murphy, Liz *210:* 183; *212:* 157
Murphy, Mary *196:* 158
Murphy, Tom *192:* 40
Murr, Karl *20:* 62
Murray, Joe *175:* 37
Murray, Ossie *43:* 176
Mussino, Attilio *29:* 131; *100:* 164
Mutchler, Dwight *1:* 25
Myers, Bernice *9:* 147; *36:* 75; *81:* 146, 147, 148
Muth, Jon J. *165:* 169; *167:* 109; *190:* 227; *193:* 59; *228:* 206
Myers, Christopher *183:* 150; *193:* 139
Myers, Duane O. *99:* 145
Myers, Tim *147:* 168
Myers, V.G. *142:* 41
Myers, Lou *11:* 2

N

Na, Il Sung *231:* 136
Nachreiner, Tom *29:* 182
Nacht, Merle *65:* 49
Nadler, Ellis *88:* 91
Nagle, Shane *180:* 223
Nagy, Ian *195:* 64
Naifeh, Ted *236:* 34
Najaka, Marlies *62:* 101
Nakai, Michael *30:* 217; *54:* 29
Nakata, Hiroe *157:* 156; *162:* 30; *205:* 124, 125
Nakatani, Chiyoko *12:* 124
Narahashi, Keiko *77:* 188; *82:* 213; *115:* 142, 143, 144
Nascimbene, Yan *133:* 128; *173:* 132, 133
Nash, Lesa *87:* 135
Nash, Linell *46:* 175
Nash, Scott *130:* 36; *188:* 196; *224:* 180; *239:* 83
Naso, John *33:* 183
Nason, Thomas W. *14:* 68
Nasser, Muriel *48:* 74
Nast, Thomas *21:* 29; *28:* 23; *51:* 132, 133, 134, 135,136, 137, 138, 139, 141
Nasta, Vincent *78:* 185
Natale, Vincent *76:* 3; *78:* 125; *112:* 47; *166:* 81; *174:* 189; *185:* 212; *197:* 59; *218:* 35
Natchev, Alexi *96:* 177
Nathan, Charlott *125:* 151
Nathan, Cheryl *150:* 104; *186:* 112
Natti, Susanna *20:* 146; *32:* 141, 142; *35:* 178; *37:* 143; *71:* 49; *93:* 98; *125:* 166, 168; *126:* 228; *151:* 6; *178:* 8; *188:* 106; *231:* 10
Navarra, Celeste Scala *8:* 142
Naylor, Penelope *10:* 104
Nazz, James *72:* 8
Nebel, M. *45:* 154
Neebe, William *7:* 93
Needham, Dave *196:* 85
Needler, Jerry *12:* 93
Neel, Alice *31:* 23
Neely, Beth *119:* 184
Neely, Keith R. *46:* 124
Neff, Leland *78:* 74
Negri, Rocco *3:* 213; *5:* 67; *6:* 91, 108; *12:* 159
Negrin, Fabian *174:* 125; *175:* 15; *223:* 91
Neidigh, Sherry *128:* 53; *204:* 101, 102, 103; *222:* 95
Neilan, Eujin Kim *180:* 241; *200:* 151, 152
Neill, John R. *18:* 8, 10, 11, 21, 30; *100:* 22

Neilsen, Cliff *158:* 131; *177:* 112, 121; *209:* 8; *215:* 150; *230:* 62
Neilsen, Terese *116:* 74
Nelson, Craig *62:* 151; 153; *183:* 86; *236:* 103
Nelson, Gail White *68:* 140
Nelson, Jennifer *129:* 152; *199:* 132; *239:* 145
Nelson, Kadir *151:* 185; *154:* 146, 147; *157:* 189, 222; *181:* 122, 124; *197:* 155; *213:* 122, 123, 124
Nelson, Melissa *224:* 87
Nelson, S.D. *131:* 34; *181:* 126, 127; *228:* 23
Ness, Evaline *1:* 164, 165; *2:* 39; *3:* 8; *10:* 147; *12:* 53; *26:* 150, 151, 152, 153; *49:* 30, 31, 32; *56:* 30; *60:* 113
Neubecker, Robert *170:* 143; *214:* 157; *233:* 25; *234:* 209; *238:* 93
Neville, Vera *2:* 182
Nevins, Daniel *191:* 173
Nevwirth, Allan *79:* 168
Newberry, Clare Turlay *1:* 170
Newbold, Greg *108:* 125; *145:* 199; *151:* 23; *193:* 178; *197:* 10; *199:* 92, 93
Newfeld, Frank *14:* 121; *26:* 154
Newhouse, Maxwell *232:* 144
Newland, Gillian *220:* 132
Newman, Andy *149:* 61; *195:* 63
Newman, Ann *43:* 90
Newman, Barbara Johansen *191:* 137, 138; *231:* 13
Newquist, H.P. *235:* 156
Newsham, Ian *143:* 162
Newsom, Carol *40:* 159; *44:* 60; *47:* 189; *65:* 29; *70:* 192; *80:* 36; *85:* 137, 138; *92:* 167; *191:* 82; *233:* 83
Newsom, Tom *49:* 149; *71:* 13, 62; *75:* 156; *91:* 113
Newton, Jill *83:* 105; *200:* 154
Newton, Vanessa Brantley *236:* 180
Nez, John *218:* 136
Ng, Michael *29:* 171
Ng, Simon *167:* 7
Ngui, Marc *229:* 50
Nguyen, Vincent *189:* 49; *226:* 160; *229:* 172
Nichols, Sandy *219:* 103
Nicholson, William *15:* 33, 34; *16:* 48
Nickens, Bessie *104:* 153
Nicklaus, Carol *45:* 194; *62:* 132, 133
Nickle, John *181:* 128
Nickless, Will *16:* 139
Nicholas, Corasue *154:* 20
Nicolas *17:* 130, 132, 133; *YABC 2:* 215
Niebrugge, Jane *6:* 118
Nielsen, Cliff *95:* 207, 208; *105:* 58; *114:* 112; *124:* 12; *125:* 91, 92; *132:* 224; *135:* 187; *136:* 40; *137:* 168; *145:* 54; *149:* 28; *158:* 129; *165:* 64, 158; *168:* 169; *170:* 6; *175:* 114, 116; *187:* 75, 76; *194:* 107; *197:* 172; *201:* 14; *208:* 192; *211:* 186; *216:* 215; *217:* 67; *224:* 61, 62; *230:* 21; *233:* 58, 59; *236:* 136; *238:* 47, 48; *239:* 164
Nielsen, Jon *6:* 100; *24:* 202
Nielsen, Kay *15:* 7; *16:* 211, 212, 213, 215, 217; *22:* 143; *YABC 1:* 32, 33
Niemann, Christoph *191:* 141; *238:* 123, 124
Nikola-Lisa, W. *180:* 180
Niland, Deborah *25:* 191; *27:* 156; *135:* 50; *172:* 143
Niland, Kilmeny *25:* 191; *75:* 143
Nino, Alex *59:* 145
Ninon *1:* 5; *38:* 101, 103, 108
Nissen, Rie *44:* 35
Nithael, Mark *158:* 237
Nivola, Claire A. *78:* 126; *140:* 147; *208:* 164
Nixon, K. *14:* 152
Nobati, Eugenia *194:* 118
Noble, Louise *61:* 170
Noble, Marty *97:* 168; *125:* 171
Noble, Trinka Hakes *39:* 162; *84:* 157
Nobles, Scott *226:* 159
Noda, Takayo *168:* 143
Noguchi, Yoshie *30:* 99

Nolan, Dennis *42:* 163; *67:* 163; *78:* 189; *82:* 225; *83:* 26; *92:* 169, 170; *103:* 166; *111:* 35; *112:* 213; *127:* 171; *166:* 161; *194:* 218
Noll, Sally *82:* 171
Nolte, Larry *121:* 63, 65
Nones, Eric Jon *61:* 111; *76:* 38; *77:* 177
Noonan, Daniel *100:* 224
Noonan, Julia *4:* 163; *7:* 207; *25:* 151; *91:* 29; *95:* 149; *231:* 163
Norcia, Ernie *108:* 155; *140:* 47
Nordenskjold, Birgitta *2:* 208
Noreika, Robert *173:* 20; *217:* 24
Norling, Beth *149:* 153, 154; *209:* 77
Norman, Elaine *77:* 72, 176; *94:* 35; *136:* 63; *178:* 42; *236:* 104
Norman, Mary *36:* 138, 147
Norman, Michael *12:* 117; *27:* 168
Normandin, Luc *227:* 180
Northway, Jennifer *85:* 96
Nostlinger, Christiana *162:* 131
Novak, Linda *166:* 205
Novak, Matt *104:* 132, 133; *165:* 173, 174; *204:* 104, 106
Novelli, Luca *61:* 137
Novgorodoff, Danica *215:* 133
Nugent, Cynthia *106:* 189; *205:* 126, 127; *209:* 180
Numberman, Neil *220:* 133
Numeroff, Laura Joffe *28:* 161; *30:* 177
Nurse, Chris *164:* 91
Nussbaumer, Paul *16:* 219; *39:* 117
Nutt, Ken *72:* 69; *97:* 170
Nyce, Helene *19:* 219
Nygren, Tord *30:* 148; *127:* 164

O

Oakley, Graham *8:* 112; *30:* 164, 165; *84:* 188,189, 190, 191, 192
Oakley, Thornton *YABC 2:* 189
Oberheide, Heide *118:* 37
Obligado, Lilian *2:* 28, 66, 67; *6:* 30; *14:* 179; *15:* 103; *25:* 84; *61:* 138, 139, 140, 141, 143
Oblinski, Rafael *190:* 139
Obrant, Susan *11:* 186
O'Brien, Anne Sibley *53:* 116, 117; *155:* 115; *213:* 127; *224:* 71; *227:* 9
O'Brien, John *41:* 253; *72:* 12; *89:* 59, 60; *98:* 16; *161:* 185; *169:* 16; *180:* 196; *228:* 38
O'Brien, Patrick *193:* 142, 143, 144
O'Brien, Teresa *87:* 89
O'Brien, Tim *93:* 25; *136:* 94; *164:* 57; *169:* 57; *173:* 55; *175:* 86; *184:* 192; *191:* 134; *193:* 137; *210:* 159; *224:* 28, 29; *229:* 140; *232:* 166; *239:* 123
O'Clair, Dennis *127:* 25
O'Connor, George *183:* 153; *228:* 113, 114
Odell, Carole *35:* 47
Odem, Mel *99:* 164; *167:* 84, 87
O'Donohue, Thomas *40:* 89
Oechsli, Kelly *5:* 144, 145; *7:* 115; *8:* 83, 183; *13:* 117; *20:* 94; *81:* 199
Ofer, Avi *208:* 143
Offen, Hilda *42:* 207
Offermann, Andrea *233:* 108
Ogden, Bill *42:* 59; *47:* 55
Ogg, Oscar *33:* 34
Ogle, Nancy Gray *163:* 144
Ohi, Ruth *90:* 175, 177; *131:* 63; *135:* 106; *175:* 107; *179:* 55
Ohlsson, Ib *4:* 152; *7:* 57; *10:* 20; *11:* 90; *19:* 217; *41:* 246; *82:* 106; *92:* 213
Ohtomo, Yasuo *37:* 146; *39:* 212, 213
O'Keefe, Jennifer *136:* 184
O'Kelley, Mattie Lou *36:* 150
Olbinski, Rafal *149:* 27; *158:* 77; *203:* 36; *235:* 36
Oldland, Nicholas *223:* 136
O'Leary, Chris *208:* 166

Olander, Johan *231:* 138
Oleynikov, Igor *202:* 134
Oliver, Isaac *171:* 182
Oliver, Jenni *23:* 121; *35:* 112
Oliver, Narelle *152:* 192; *197:* 129, 130
Oller, Erika *128:* 186; *134:* 126; *234:* 146
Olschewski, Alfred *7:* 172
Olsen, Ib Spang *6:* 178, 179; *81:* 164
Olson, Alan *77:* 229
Olson, Julie *233:* 120
Olson-Brown, Ellen *183:* 154
Olugebefola, Ademola *15:* 205
O'Malley, Kevin *94:* 180; *106:* 8; *113:* 108;
　136: 70; *157:* 193; *191:* 146; *203:* 78; *217:*
　84; *230:* 115, 117, 118
O'Neil, Dan IV *7:* 176
O'Neill, Catharine *72:* 113; *84:* 78; *134:* 153
O'Neill, Jean *22:* 146
O'Neill, Martin *187:* 39; *203:* 118
O'Neill, Michael J. *54:* 172
O'Neill, Rose *48:* 30, 31
O'Neill, Steve *21:* 118
Ono, Chiyo *7:* 97
Onoda, Yuta *237:* 136
Orbaan, Albert *2:* 31; *5:* 65, 171; *9:* 8; *14:*
　241; *20:* 109
Orbach, Ruth *21:* 112
Orback, Craig *197:* 132
Orfe, Joan *20:* 81
Org, Ed *119:* 93
Ormai, Stella *72:* 129
Ormerod, Jan *55:* 124; *70:* 170, 171; *90:* 39;
　132: 172, 173, 174; *147:* 98
Ormsby, Virginia H. *11:* 187
O'Rourke, Ericka *108:* 216; *117:* 194; *111:*
　142; *119:* 194; *137:* 152; *150:* 134; *167:* 64;
　172: 164; *188:* 163; *191:* 172; *201:* 15; *203:*
　75; *209:* 130; *219:* 99
O'Rourke, Ericka Meltzer
　See O'Rourke, Ericka
Orozco, Jose Clemente *9:* 177
Orr, Forrest W. *23:* 9
Orr, N. *19:* 70
Ortiz, Vilma *88:* 158
Osborn, Kathy *152:* 232; *199:* 101, 102; *206:*
　67
Osborn, Robert *65:* 49
Osborne, Billie Jean *35:* 209
Osmond, Edward *10:* 111
Ostow, David *223:* 138
O'Sullivan, Tom *3:* 176; *4:* 55; *78:* 195
Otani, June *124:* 42; *156:* 53
Otis, Rebecca *185:* 92
Ottley, Matt *147:* 221; *171:* 133
Otto, Svend *22:* 130, 141; *67:* 188, 189
Oudry, J.B. *18:* 167
Oughton, Taylor *5:* 23; *104:* 136
Overeng, Johannes *44:* 36
Overlie, George *11:* 156
Owens, Carl *2:* 35; *23:* 521
Owens, Gail *10:* 170; *12:* 157; *19:* 16; *22:* 70;
　25: 81; *28:* 203, 205; *32:* 221, 222; *36:* 132;
　46: 40; *47:* 57; *54:* 66, 67, 68, 69, 70, 71,
　72, 73; *71:* 100; *73:* 64; *77:* 157; *80:* 32; *82:*
　3; *99:* 226; *224:* 198
Owens, Mary Beth *113:* 202, 203; *191:* 148,
　149
Owens, Nubia *84:* 74
Oxenbury, Helen *3:* 150, 151; *24:* 81; *68:* 174,
　175,176; *81:* 209; *84:* 213, 245; *129:* 56;
　149: 159; *184:* 181; *224:* 147
Oz, Robin *88:* 167; *185:* 181

P

Padgett, Jim *12:* 165
Page, Gail *205:* 128
Page, Homer *14:* 145
Page, Mark *162:* 70

Paget, Sidney *24:* 90, 91, 93, 95, 97
Paget, Walter *64:* 122
Paillot, Jim *173:* 89
Pajouhesh, Noushin *160:* 121
Pak *12:* 76
Pak, Yu Cha *86:* 174
Pal, Erika *239:* 112
Paladino, Lance *134:* 30
Palazzo, Tony *3:* 152, 153
Palecek, Josef *56:* 136; *89:* 158
Palen, Debbie *135:* 88; *195:* 148, 149
Palencar, John Jude *84:* 12, 45; *85:* 87; *92:*
　187; *99:* 128; *110:* 204; *150:* 122; *171:* 86;
　207: 36
Palin, Nicki *81:* 201; *89:* 161
Palisi, Heather *231:* 109
Palladini, David *4:* 113; *40:* 176, 177, 178,
　179, 181,224, 225; *50:* 138; *78:* 186
Pallarito, Don *43:* 36
Palmer, Carol *158:* 230; *195:* 187
Palmer, Gary *232:* 39
Palmer, Heidi *15:* 207; *29:* 102
Palmer, Jan *42:* 153; *82:* 161
Palmer, Judd *153:* 160, 161
Palmer, Juliette *6:* 89; *15:* 208
Palmer, Kate Salley *104:* 143; *154:* 169
Palmer, Lemuel *17:* 25, 29
Palmisciano, Diane *110:* 62; *162:* 26; *202:*
　138, 139
Palmquist, Eric *38:* 133
Pamintuan, Macky *214:* 160
Panesis, Nicholas *3:* 127
Panter, Gary *182:* 191
Panton, Doug *52:* 99
Paparone, Pamela *129:* 174
Papas, William *11:* 223; *50:* 160
Papin, Joseph *26:* 113
Papish, Robin Lloyd *10:* 80
Papp, Robert *198:* 41; *205:* 130; *219:* 53
Paradis, Susan *40:* 216
Paraquin, Charles H. *18:* 166
Pardo DeLange, Alex *179:* 128; *211:* 135, 136
Paris, Peter *31:* 127
Parisi, Elizabeth B. *141:* 82; *164:* 57
Park, Nick *113:* 143
Park, Seho *39:* 110
Park, W.B. *22:* 189
Parker, Ant *82:* 87, 88; *104:* 121
Parker, Buzz *227:* 154
Parker, Jake *227:* 134
Parker, Lewis *2:* 179
Parker, Nancy Winslow *10:* 113; *22:* 164; *28:*
　47, 144; *52:* 7; *69:* 153; *91:* 171, 174; *132:*
　175
Parker, Robert *4:* 161; *5:* 74; *9:* 136; *29:* 39
Parker, Robert Andrew *11:* 81; *29:* 186; *39:*
　165; *40:* 25; *41:* 78; *42:* 123; *43:* 144; *48:*
　182; *54:* 140; *74:* 141; *91:* 24; *111:* 115;
　151: 201; *154:* 156; *200:* 163, 164; *211:* 67
Parker-Rees, Guy *149:* 145; *193:* 149, 150
Parkin, Trevor *140:* 151
Parkins, David *114:* 123; *146:* 176; *176:* 168;
　192: 107; *218:* 139, 140, 141, 148; *224:* 92
Parkinson, Kathy *71:* 143; *144:* 234
Parkinson, Keith *70:* 66
Parks, Gordon, Jr. *33:* 228
Parlato, Stephen *222:* 137
Parnall, Peter *5:* 137; *16:* 221; *24:* 70; *40:* 78;
　51: 130; *69:* 17, 155; *136:* 22, 23, 24
Parnall, Virginia *40:* 78
Paros, Jennifer *210:* 197
Parow, Lorraine *158:* 127
Parr, Todd *134:* 139, 140; *179:* 163, 164, 165
Parra, John *225:* 150; *232:* 134
Parrish, Anne *27:* 159, 160
Parrish, Dillwyn *27:* 159
Parrish, Maxfield *14:* 160, 161, 164, 165; *16:*
　109; *18:* 12, 13; *YABC 1:* 149, 152, 267; *2:*
　146, 149
Parry, David *26:* 156
Parry, Marian *13:* 176; *19:* 179

Parsons, Garry *197:* 135
Partch, Virgil *45:* 163, 165
Pascal, David *14:* 174
Paschkis, Julie *177:* 153, 154; *220:* 140, 141;
　231: 64
Pasquier, J.A. *16:* 91
Pastel, Elyse *201:* 123
Pasternak, Robert *119:* 53
Paterson, Diane *13:* 116; *39:* 163; *59:* 164,
　165, 166,167; *72:* 51, 53; *129:* 175; *177:*
　156, 157
Paterson, Helen *16:* 93
Patkau, Karen *112:* 123
Paton, Jane *15:* 271; *35:* 176
Patricelli, Leslie *207:* 129; *236:* 155, 156
Patrick, John *139:* 190
Patrick, Pamela *90:* 160; *93:* 211; *105:* 12
Patrick, Tom *190:* 103
Patterson, Geoffrey *54:* 75
Patterson, Robert *25:* 118
Patti, Joyce *187:* 145, 146
Patz, Nancy *111:* 40; *154:* 161; *214:* 80
Paul, James *4:* 130; *23:* 161
Paul, Korky *102:* 85
Paull, Grace *24:* 157; *87:* 127
Paulsen, Ruth Wright *79:* 160, 164; *189:* 146;
　231: 150
Pavlov, Elena *80:* 49
Payne, Adam S. *135:* 166
Payne, C.F. *145:* 138, 140; *179:* 168
Payne, Joan Balfour *1:* 118
Payne, Tom *70:* 27
Payson, Dale *7:* 34; *9:* 151; *20:* 140; *37:* 22
Payzant, Charles *21:* 147
Peacock, Phyllis Hornung *230:* 124
Peacock, Ralph *64:* 118
Peake, Mervyn *22:* 136, 149; *23:* 162, 163,
　164; *YABC2:* 307
Pearce, Carl *228:* 107; *229:* 148
Pearson, Larry *38:* 225
Pearson, Tracey Campbell *64:* 163, 164, 167,
　168, 169; *118:* 51; *156:* 169, 171, 172; *163:*
　140; *219:* 140, 141, 142, 143
Peat, Fern B. *16:* 115
Peck, Anne Merriman *18:* 241; *24:* 155
Peck, Beth *66:* 242; *79:* 166; *80:* 136; *91:* 34;
　95: 9; *101:* 77; *164:* 197; *190:* 170
Peddicord, Jane Ann *199:* 106
Pedersen, Janet *193:* 152; *217:* 57; *218:* 15;
　228: 85
Pedersen, Judy *66:* 217; *121:* 36; *172:* 67
Pedersen, Vilhelm *YABC 1:* 40
Pederson, Sharleen *12:* 92
Pedlar, Elaine *161:* 45
Peek, Merle *39:* 168
Peet, Bill *2:* 203; *41:* 159, 160, 161, 162, 163;
　78: 158, 159, 160, 161
Peguero, Adrian *116:* 133
Peguero, Gerard *116:* 133
Peirce, Lincoln *232:* 150
Pels, Winslow Pinney *55:* 126
Peltier, Leslie C. *13:* 178
Peltzer, Marc *202:* 92
Penberthy, Mark *171:* 78
Pendle, Alexy *7:* 159; *13:* 34; *29:* 161; *33:*
　215; *86:* 62
Pendola, Joanne *76:* 203; *81:* 125; *105:* 181;
　178: 152, 153
Pene du Bois, William *4:* 70; *10:* 122; *26:* 61;
　27: 145, 211; *35:* 243; *41:* 216; *68:* 180,
　181; *73:* 45
Penfound, David *102:* 185
Pennington, Eunice *27:* 162
Peppe, Mark *28:* 142
Peppe, Rodney *4:* 164, 165; *74:* 187, 188, 189
Pepper, Hubert *64:* 143
Percy, Graham *63:* 2
Pericoli, Matteo *178:* 177
Perini, Ben *173:* 77
Perkins, David *60:* 68
Perkins, Lucy Fitch *72:* 199

Perkins, Lynne Rae *172:* 146; *212:* 153
Perl, Susan *2:* 98; *4:* 231; *5:* 44, 45, 118; *6:* 199; *8:* 137; *12:* 88; *22:* 193; *34:* 54, 55; *52:* 128; *YABC 1:* 176
Perlman, Janet *222:* 141
Perrone, Donna *78:* 166
Perry, Marie Fritz *165:* 180
Perry, Patricia *29:* 137; *30:* 171
Perry, Roger *27:* 163
Perske, Martha *46:* 83; *51:* 108, 147
Persson, Stina *175:* 166
Pesek, Ludek *15:* 237
Petach, Heidi *149:* 166; *200:* 207
Peters, David *72:* 205; *182:* 116
Petersen, Jeff *181:* 95
Petersham, Maud *17:* 108, 147, 148, 149, 150, 151, 152, 153
Petersham, Miska *17:* 108, 147, 148, 149, 150, 151, 152, 153
Peterson, Eric *109:* 125
Peterson, Nisse *99:* 27
Peterson, R.F. *7:* 101
Peterson, Russell *7:* 130
Petie, Haris *2:* 3; *10:* 41, 118; *11:* 227; *12:* 70
Petit-Roulet, Philippe *227:* 12
Petricic, Dusan *153:* 75, 76, 77; *170:* 12; *172:* 13; *176:* 170; *179:* 56
Petrides, Heidrun *19:* 223
Petrone, Valeria *159:* 160; *171:* 92; *186:* 173; *204:* 49; *216:* 208; *220:* 98; *233:* 126
Petrosino, Tamara *177:* 40; *193:* 154, 155
Petruccio, Steven James *67:* 159; *127:* 5
Pettingill, Ondre *64:* 181; *70:* 64; *222:* 167, 168
Peyo *40:* 56, 57
Peyton, K.M. *15:* 212
Pfeifer, Herman *15:* 262
Pfister, Marcus *83:* 165, 166, 167; *146:* 152; *150:* 160; *207:* 132, 134, 135, 136
Pfloog, Jan *124:* 60
Pham, LeUyen *160:* 48; *175:* 154, 156; *179:* 149; *201:* 124, 125, 126, 127; *204:* 28; *208:* 206; *217:* 92; *234:* 215; *237:* 110, 111, 112
Phelan, Matt *182:* 160; *184:* 222; *215:* 140, 141; *221:* 157; *231:* 28
Phillipps, J.C. *218:* 142
Phillips, Craig *70:* 151; *207:* 74; *221:* 159; *229:* 22
Phillips, Douglas *1:* 19
Phillips, F.D. *6:* 202
Phillips, Gary R. *223:* 23
Phillips, Louise *133:* 67
Phillips, Matt *184:* 173
Phillips, Thomas *30:* 55
Philpot, Glyn *54:* 46
Phiz
    See Browne, Hablot K.
Piatti, Celestino *16:* 223
Pica, Steve *115:* 181
Picarella, Joseph *13:* 147
Picart, Gabriel *121:* 165; *201:* 169
Picasso, Pablo *228:* 131
Pichon, Liz *174:* 139
Pickard, Charles *12:* 38; *18:* 203; *36:* 152
Picken, George A. *23:* 150
Pickens, David *22:* 156
Pickering, Jimmy *195:* 152; *197:* 163; *238:* 71
Pien, Lark *222:* 143, 144
Pienkowski, Jan *6:* 183; *30:* 32; *58:* 140, 141, 142,143, 146, 147; *73:* 3; *87:* 156, 157; *131:* 189
Pieper, Christiane *200:* 168
Pignataro, Anna *163:* 220; *223:* 143 *Pile, Emma 218:* 156 *Pileggi, Steve 145:* 122
Pilkey, Dav *68:* 186; *115:* 164, 166; *166:* 173, 174, 175
Pimlott, John *10:* 205
Pincus, Harriet *4:* 186; *8:* 179; *22:* 148; *27:* 164, 165; *66:* 202
Pini, Wendy *89:* 166
Pinkett, Neil *60:* 8

Pinkney, Brian *81:* 184, 185; *94:* 107; *113:* 146, 147; *117:* 121, 166; *132:* 145; *158:* 108, 191; *160:* 189; *200:* 8
Pinkney, Jerry *8:* 218; *10:* 40; *15:* 276; *20:* 66; *24:* 121; *33:* 109; *36:* 222; *38:* 200; *41:* 165, 166, 167, 168, 169, 170, 171, 173, 174; *44:* 198; *48:* 51; *53:* 20; *56:* 61, 68; *58:* 184; *60:* 59; *61:* 91; *71:* 146, 148, 149; *72:* 17; *73:* 149; *74:* 159,192; *75:* 45; *80:* 206; *81:* 44; *85:* 144; *95:* 50; *107:* 158, 159, 160; *108:* 164; *112:* 114, 115; *133:* 58; *195:* 140; *227:* 131
Pinkwater, Daniel Manus *8:* 156; *46:* 180, 181, 182, 185, 188, 189, 190; *151:* 161 *76:* 178, 179, 180; *210:* 203
Pinkwater, Manus
    See Pinkwater, Daniel Manus
Pinkwater, Jill *114:* 160, 161; *158:* 179; *188:* 143, 145, 146
Pinto, Ralph *10:* 131; *45:* 93
Pinto, Sara *200:* 165
Pinon, Mark *74:* 22
Piven, Hanoch *173:* 142; *236:* 157, 158, 159
Pistolesi *73:* 211
Pitcairn, Ansel *188:* 10; *227:* 20
Pittman, Helena Clare *71:* 151
Pitz, Henry C. *4:* 168; *19:* 165; *35:* 128; *42:* 80; *YABC 2:* 95, 176
Pitzenberger, Lawrence J. *26:* 94
Pitzer, Susanna *181:* 131
Place, François *218:* 42
Plant, Andrew *214:* 166
Player, Stephen *82:* 190
Plecas, Jennifer *84:* 201; *106:* 124; *149:* 168; *205:* 180; *220:* 81; *229:* 152, 153, 154
Ploog, Mike *180:* 19
Plowden, David *52:* 135, 136
Plume, Ilse *170:* 149
Plummer, William *32:* 31
Podevin, Jean François *184:* 185
Podwal, Mark *56:* 170, 173; *101:* 154, 155, 157; *149:* 176; *160:* 194; *224:* 127, 128, 129
Pogany, Willy *15:* 46, 49; *19:* 222, 256; *25:* 214; *44:* 142, 143, 144, 145, 146, 147, 148
Pohrt, Tom *67:* 116; *104:* 80; *152:* 199; *195:* 154; *199:* 85
Poirson, V.A. *26:* 89
Polacco, Patricia *74:* 195, 196, 197, 198; *123:* 121, 122, 123; *180:* 189, 190, 191, 193, 194; *212:* 168, 170, 171
Polgreen, John *21:* 44
Polhemus, Coleman *210:* 209
Politi, Leo *1:* 178; *4:* 53; *21:* 48; *47:* 173,174, 176, 178, 179, 180, 181
Pollack, Barbara *219:* 60
Pollema-Cahill, Phyllis *123:* 126
Pollen, Samson *64:* 80
Polonsky, Arthur *34:* 168
Polseno, Jo *1:* 53; *3:* 117; *5:* 114; *17:* 154; *20:* 87; *32:* 49; *41:* 245
Pomaska, Anna *117:* 148
Pons, Bernadette *184:* 100
Ponter, James *5:* 204
Poole, Colin *111:* 27
Poortvliet, Rien *6:* 212; *65:* 165, 166, 167
Pope, Kevin *183:* 158
Popp, Wendy *72:* 122; *158:* 68
Poppel, Hans *71:* 154, 155
Porfirio, Guy *76:* 134
Portal, Colette *6:* 186; *11:* 203
Porter, George *7:* 181
Porter, Janice Lee *136:* 175; *164:* 37
Porter, John *113:* 47
Porter, Pat Grant *84:* 112; *125:* 101
Porter, Sue *146:* 246, 247; *213:* 139, 140, 141; *221:* 91
Porter, Walter *124:* 175
Porto, James *221:* 14
Posada, Mia *187:* 151
Posen, Michael *175:* 82
Post, R.K. *233:* 60

Posthuma, Sieb *150:* 163
Postier, Jim *202:* 140; *204:* 25
Postma, Lidia *79:* 17
Potter, Beatrix *100:* 194, 195; *132:* 179, 180, 181, 182; *YABC 1:* 208, 209, 210, 212, 213
Potter, Giselle *117:* 123; *143:* 44; *144:* 170, 197; *149:* 7; *150:* 165; *187:* 152, 153; *190:* 198; *196:* 152; *200:* 12; *225:* 60; *227:* 105; *235:* 150
Potter, Katherine *104:* 147; *171:* 135; *173:* 136; *217:* 130, 131
Potter, Miriam Clark *3:* 162
Poulin, Stephane *98:* 140, 141
Poullis, Nick *146:* 210
Powell, Constance Buffington *174:* 141
Powell, Gary *151:* 208
Powell, Ivan *67:* 219
Power, Margaret *105:* 122
Powers, Daniel *161:* 173
Powers, Richard M. *1:* 230; *3:* 218; *7:* 194; *26:* 186
Powledge, Fred *37:* 154
Powzyk, Joyce *74:* 214
Poydar, Nancy *96:* 149; *190:* 180, 181, 182
Pracher, Richard *91:* 166
Prachaticka, Marketa *126:* 126
Prange, Beckie *181:* 169; *236:* 173, 175
Prap, Lila *177:* 165
Prater, John *103:* 142, 143, 144; *149:* 172
Pratt, Charles *23:* 29
Pratt, Christine Joy *214:* 167
Pratt, George *116:* 208; *212:* 37
Pratt, Pierre *150:* 73; *166:* 183; *168:* 172; *201:* 27; *208:* 171, 172, 173
Prebenna, David *73:* 174
Press, Jenny *116:* 95
Preston, Mark *152:* 162
Pretro, Korinna *91:* 126
Prevost, Mikela *209:* 111
Price, Christine *2:* 247; *3:* 163, 253; *8:* 166
Price, Cynthia *118:* 156
Price, Edward *33:* 34
Price, Garrett *1:* 76; *2:* 42
Price, Hattie Longstreet *17:* 13
Price, Nick *216:* 173; *220:* 7
Price, Norman *YABC 1:* 129
Price, Willard *48:* 184
Priceman, Marjorie *81:* 171; *136:* 169; *156:* 200; *168:* 153, 154; *188:* 45; *226:* 7; *234:* 160, 161, 163, 164; *235:* 74
Priestley, Alice *168:* 33; *227:* 142
Priestley, Chris *198:* 144
Prigmore, Shane *234:* 166; *238:* 156
Primavera, Elise *26:* 95; *58:* 151; *73:* 37; *80:* 79; *86:* 156; *105:* 161; *213:* 157; *230:* 132, 133, 134
Primrose, Jean *36:* 109
Prince, Alison *86:* 188, 189
Prince, Leonora E. *7:* 170
Pritchett, Shelley *116:* 148
Prittie, Edwin J. *YABC 1:* 120
Proimos, James *176:* 4; *217:* 132, 133, 134
Proimos, John *173:* 144
Prosmitsky, Jenya *132:* 33
Provensen, Alice *37:* 204, 215, 222; *70:* 176, 177, 178, 180, *71:* 213; *147:* 184; *191:* 190
Provensen, Martin *37:* 204, 215, 222; *70:* 176, 177, 178, 180; *71:* 213; *191:* 190
Pucci, Albert John *44:* 154
Pudlo *8:* 59
Puggaard, Ulla *196:* 25
Pullen, Zachary *211:* 161; *235:* 21
Pulver, Harry, Jr. *129:* 159
Pulver, Robin *160:* 4
Punchatz, Don *99:* 57
Purdy, Susan *8:* 162
Pursell, Weimer *55:* 18
Purston, Oliver *229:* 156
Purtscher, Alfons *97:* 6
Purvis, Leland *232:* 156
Puskas, James *5:* 141

Pyk, Jan 7: 26; 38: 123
Pyle, Charles S. 99: 149; 191: 83; 233: 20, 21; 233: 85
Pyle, Howard 16: 225, 226, 227, 228, 230, 231, 232, 235; 24: 27; 34: 124, 125, 127, 128; 59: 132; 100: 198

Q

Quackenbush, Robert 4: 190; 6: 166; 7: 175, 178; 9: 86; 11: 65, 221; 41: 154; 43: 157; 70: 185, 186; 71: 137; 85: 47; 92: 148; 133: 154, 164, 169
Qualls, Sean 177: 167, 168; 193: 43; 228: 108; 233: 128, 129; 235: 152
Quennell, Marjorie (Courtney) 29: 163, 164
Quidor, John 19: 82
Quirk, John 62: 170
Quirk, Thomas 12: 81

R

Rackham, Arthur 15: 32, 78, 214-227; 17: 105, 115; 18: 233; 19: 254; 20: 151; 22: 129, 131, 132, 133; 23: 175; 24: 161, 181; 26: 91; 32: 118; 64: 18; 100: 9, 16, 203, 204; YABC 1: 25, 45, 55, 147; 2: 103, 142, 173, 210
Racz, Michael 56: 134
Raczka, Bob 191: 155, 156
Radcliffe, Andrew 82: 215
Rader, Laura 101: 219; 197: 147; 203: 53
Radunsky, Vladimir 177: 170; 192: 30; 238: 140
Radzinski, Kandy 212: 174
Rafilson, Sidney 11: 172
Raglin, Tim 125: 24
Raible, Alton 1: 202, 203; 28: 193; 35: 181; 110: 207
Raine, Patricia 82: 74; 88: 154
Ramá, Sue 173: 45; 185: 186; 190: 184; 237: 123
Ramhorst, John 117: 11
Ramirez, Gladys 177: 19
Ramirez, Jose 207: 27
Ramsey, James 16: 41
Ramsey, Marcy Dunn 82: 11; 180: 186
Ramus, Michael 51: 171
Rand, Paul 6: 188
Rand, Ted 67: 9, 10, 121, 123; 74: 190; 84: 170; 103: 170; 112: 6; 114: 73; 139: 168; 143: 194; 156: 154; 161: 9, 10; 200: 38; 204: 7
Randazzo, Tony 81: 98
Randell, William 55: 54
Rane, Walter 93: 144; 143: 109; 184: 126
Rankin, Joan 163: 40; 212: 176
Rankin, Laura 176: 173, 174; 179: 150; 236: 163
Ransome, Arthur 22: 201
Ransome, James E. 74: 137; 75: 80; 84: 181; 94: 108; 117: 115; 123: 128, 129, 130; 158: 101, 102; 159: 205; 178: 188, 189, 190; 216: 114; 227: 146, 148, 149, 150
Rantz, Don 119: 184
Rao, Anthony 28: 126
Raphael, Elaine 23: 192; 71: 24, 25
Rappaport, Eva 6: 190
Raschka, Chris 80: 187, 189, 190; 97: 211; 115: 210; 117: 151, 152, 153, 154; 143: 195; 145: 153; 166: 190, 191; 170: 114; 207: 140, 143, 144, 145; 208: 82; 220: 85
Rash, Andy 158: 178; 162: 172; 210: 204; 219: 145; 226: 194

Raskin, Ellen 2: 208, 209; 4: 142; 13: 183; 22: 68; 29: 139; 36: 134; 38: 173, 174, 175, 176, 177, 178,179, 180, 181; 60: 163; 86: 81
Rathmann, Peggy 93: 32; 94: 168; 157: 212, 214
Ratkus, Tony 77: 133
Rattray, Gail 227: 96
Ratzkin, Lawrence 40: 143
Rau, Margaret 9: 157
Raverat, Gwen YABC 1: 152
Ravid, Joyce 61: 73
Ravielli, Anthony 1: 198; 3: 168; 11: 143
Ravilious, Robin 77: 169
Rawlins, Donna 72: 198; 73: 15, 129
Rawlins, Janet 76: 79
Rawlings, Steve 143: 139; 151: 54; 208: 150
Rawlinson, Debbie 75: 132
Ray, Deborah Kogan 8: 164; 29: 238; 50: 112, 113; 62: 119; 78: 191; 203: 149, 150, 151
Ray, Jane 96: 166; 97: 104; 152: 208; 190: 221; 196: 165
Ray, Ralph 2: 239; 5: 73
Rayann, Omar 162: 205; 186: 29, 30
Rayevsky, Robert 64: 17; 70: 173; 80: 204; 117: 79; 190: 187, 188
Raymond, Larry 31: 108; 97: 109
Rayner, Hugh 151: 170
Rayner, Mary 22: 207; 47: 140; 72: 191; 87: 171, 172; 192: 104
Rayner, Shoo
    See Rayner, Hugh
Raynes, John 71: 19
Raynor, Dorka 28: 168
Raynor, Paul 24: 73
Rayyan, Omar 110: 222; 112: 17; 125: 131
Razzi, James 10: 127
Read, Alexander D. 20: 45
Reader, Dennis 71: 157
Reasoner, Charles 53: 33, 36, 37
Rebenshied, Shane 203: 76; 215: 124; 237: 155
Reczuch, Karen 115: 132; 145: 131
Redlich, Ben 163: 221; 198: 193
Reddy, Mike 203: 67
Reed, Joseph 116: 139
Reed, Lynn Rowe 115: 173; 171: 146; 208: 177; 215: 144, 145
Reed, Mike 211: 147; 215: 131
Reed, Tom 34: 171
Reeder, Colin 74: 202; 77: 113
Rees, Mary 134: 219
Reese, Bob 60: 135
Reeve, Philip 171: 50
Reeves, Eira B. 130: 173, 174; 141: 151
Reeves, Rick 181: 179
Reeves, Rosie 202: 200
Regan, Dana 117: 116
Regan, Laura 103: 198; 153: 206
Reichert, Renée 169: 127
Reid, Barbara 82: 178; 92: 17; 93: 169, 170; 222: 45
Reid, Stephen 19: 213; 22: 89
Reim, Melanie 104: 151; 150: 98
Reinert, Kirk 89: 138; 195: 129
Reinertson, Barbara 44: 150; 62: 103
Reiniger, Lotte 40: 185
Reisberg, Mira 119: 2
Reisch, Jesse 158: 130
Reiser, Lynn 81: 175; 138: 184; 180: 200
Reiss, John J. 23: 193
Relf, Douglas 3: 63
Relyea, C.M. 16: 29; 31: 153
Remi, Georges 13: 184
Remington, Frederic 19: 188; 41: 178, 179, 180, 181, 183,184, 185, 186, 187, 188; 62: 197
Remkiewicz, Frank 67: 102; 77: 171; 80: 130; 113: 107; 152: 116; 152: 211, 212; 157: 148; 217: 120, 138, 139, 140, 141
Rendon, Maria 116: 141; 192: 134: 152
Renfro, Ed 79: 176

Renier, Aaron 202: 141; 207: 119
Renlie, Frank 11: 200
Reschofsky, Jean 7: 118
Rethi 60: 181
Rethi, Lili 2: 153; 36: 156
Reusswig, William 3: 267
Revell, Cindy 195: 93
Rex, Adam 156: 172; 169: 91; 186: 178, 179; 215: 103; 223: 11; 225: 154
Rex, Michael 157: 147; 191: 159, 160; 221: 124
Rey, H.A. 1: 182; 26: 163, 164, 166, 167, 169; 69: 172, 173, 174, 175; 86: 195, 196, 197; 100: 211; YABC 2: 17
Rey, Luis V. 201: 162
Reynish, Jenny 222: 155
Reynolds, Adrian 192: 159, 160; 237: 178
Reynolds, Doris 5: 71; 31: 77
Reynolds, Peter H. 142: 12; 179: 175, 176; 202: 113, 114; 226: 30, 166, 167; 228: 132
Rhead, Louis 31: 91; 100: 228
Rhodes, Andrew 38: 204; 50: 163; 54: 76; 61: 123, 124; 87: 200
Ribbons, Ian 3: 10; 37: 161; 40: 76
Ricci, Regolo 93: 22; 164: 148
Rice, Elizabeth 2: 53, 214
Rice, Eve 34: 174, 175; 91: 172
Rice, James 22: 210; 93: 173
Rich, Anna 212: 180
Rich, Martha 195: 16
Richards, Chuck 170: 154
Richards, George 40: 116, 119, 121; 44: 179
Richards, Henry YABC 1: 228, 231
Richardson, Ernest 2: 144
Richardson, Frederick 18: 27, 31
Richardson, John 110: 88
Richman, Hilda 26: 132
Richmond, George 24: 179
Riddell, Chris 114: 170, 195; 166: 179; 199: 164, 166, 167; 218: 146, 148; 219: 149, 150, 152, 153; 228: 125
Riddle, Tohby 74: 204; 151: 179; 223: 154, 156
Riding, Peter 63: 195
Rienicts, Judy King 14: 28
Riger, Bob 2: 166
Riggio, Anita 73: 191; 85: 63; 137: 184; 172: 165
Rigano, Giovanni 219: 45
Riley, Jon 74: 70
Riley, Kenneth 22: 230
Riley, Terry 203: 100
Riley-Webb, Charlotte 153: 143; 235: 14, 161, 162
Rim, Sujean 225: 157
Rinaldi, Angelo 165: 60, 69; 227: 53
Ringgold, Faith 71: 162; 114: 173, 174, 176; 187: 160, 161, 163
Ringi, Kjell 12: 171
Rios, Tere
    See Versace, Marie
Rioux, Jo 215: 110; 226: 170
Ripper, Charles L. 3: 175
Ripplinger, Henry 117: 31
Ritchie, Scot 217: 145
Ritchie, William 74: 183
Ritter, John 175: 14
Ritz, Karen 41: 117; 72: 239; 87: 125; 102: 7; 106: 6
Rivas, Victor 209: 193; 226: 144
Rivers, Ruth 178: 193
Rivkin, Jay 15: 230
Rivoche, Paul 45: 125
Roach, Marilynne 9: 158
Robbin, Jodi 44: 156, 159
Robbins, Frank 42: 167
Robbins, Ken 147: 191, 192; 234: 182
Robbins, Ruth 52: 102
Roberton, Fiona 230: 142
Roberts, Cliff 4: 126

Roberts, David *154:* 4, 6; *191:* 162; *196:* 184; *197:* 105; *210:* 257
Roberts, Doreen *4:* 230; *28:* 105
Roberts, Jim *22:* 166; *23:* 69; *31:* 110
Roberts, Tony *109:* 195, 214
Roberts, W. *22:* 2, 3
Robertson, M.P. *197:* 153
Robins, Arthur *137:* 172; *151:* 225; *204:* 161
Robinson, Aminah Brenda Lynn *86:* 205; *103:* 55; *159:* 175
Robinson, Charles [1870-1937] *17:* 157, 171, 172, 173, 175, 176; *24:* 207; *25:* 204; *YABC 2:* 308, 309, 310, 331
Robinson, Charles *3:* 53; *5:* 14; *6:* 193; *7:* 150; *7:* 183; *8:* 38; *9:* 81; *13:* 188; *14:* 248, 249; *23:* 149; *26:* 115; *27:* 48; *28:* 191; *32:* 28; *35:* 210; *36:* 37; *48:* 96; *52:* 33; *53:* 157; *56:* 15; *62:* 142; *77:* 41; *111:* 148
Robinson, Fiona *225:* 158
Robinson, Jerry *3:* 262
Robinson, Joan G. *7:* 184
Robinson, Lolly *90:* 227
Robinson, T.H. *17:* 179, 181, 182, 183; *29:* 254
Robinson, W. Heath *17:* 185, 187, 189, 191, 193, 195, 197, 199, 202; *23:* 167; *25:* 194; *29:* 150; *YABC 1:* 44; *2:* 183
Rocco, John *187:* 4; *188:* 151; *208:* 180, 181, 182; *213:* 94; *222:* 34; *238:* 130, 131, 132
Roche, Christine *41:* 98
Roche, Denis *99:* 184; *180:* 32; *196:* 168
Roche, P.K. *57:* 151, 152
Rocker, Fermin *7:* 34; *13:* 21; *31:* 40; *40:* 190,191
Rocklen, Margot *101:* 181
Rockwell, Anne *5:* 147; *33:* 171, 173; *71:* 166, 167,168; *114:* 183, 184; *194:* 152, 155; *235:* 170
Rockwell, Gail *7:* 186
Rockwell, Harlow *33:* 171, 173, 175
Rockwell, Lizzy *114:* 182; *162:* 182; *185:* 189; *233:* 134, 135, 136; *235:* 171
Rockwell, Norman *23:* 39, 196, 197, 199, 200, 203, 204, 207; *41:* 140, 143; *123:* 47; *YABC 2:* 60
Rockwood, Richard *119:* 75
Rodanas, Kristina *156:* 183, 184; *221:* 127
Rodegast, Roland *43:* 100
Rodgers, Frank *69:* 177
Rodriguez, Albert G. *182:* 50
Rodriguez, Christina *184:* 12; *225:* 94
Rodriguez, Edel *204:* 86
Rodriguez, Joel *16:* 65
Rodriguez, Robert *145:* 145; *212:* 33
Rodriguez-Howard, Pauline *177:* 18
Roe, Monika *210:* 94
Roeckelein, Katrina *134:* 223
Roennfeldt, Robert *66:* 243
Roever, J.M. *4:* 119; *26:* 170
Roffey, Maureen *33:* 142, 176, 177
Rogasky, Barbara *46:* 90
Rogé *173:* 160; *233:* 138
Rogers, Carol *2:* 262; *6:* 164; *26:* 129
Rogers, Chris M. *150:* 59; *196:* 61
Rogers, Forest *87:* 160; *101:* 76
Rogers, Frances *10:* 130
Rogers, Gregory *104:* 76; *126:* 57; *171:* 26
Rogers, Jacqueline *78:* 249; *80:* 34; *86:* 54 *103:* 70; *115:* 72; *129:* 173; *131:* 57, 225; *143:* 211; *153:* 100; *193:* 186; *203:* 51; *213:* 144, 145, 146; *214:* 142; *234:* 173; *236:* 91
Rogers, Sherry *191:* 66
Rogers, Walter S. *31:* 135, 138; *67:* 65, 168; *100:* 81
Rogers, William A. *15:* 151, 153, 154; *33:* 35
Rogoff, Barbara *95:* 20
Rohmann, Eric *103:* 152; *198:* 151
Rojankovsky, Feodor *6:* 134, 136; *10:* 183; *21:* 128,129, 130; *25:* 110; *28:* 42; *68:* 120
Rolfsen, Alf *62:* 15
Rolston, Steve *209:* 154; *223:* 113

Romain, Trevor *134:* 157
Roman, Barbara J. *103:* 171
Romas *114:* 111; *165:* 63
Romano, Robert *64:* 68
Romero, Alejandro *187:* 185
Roos, Maryn *168:* 198; *225:* 160; *226:* 143
Root, Barry *80:* 212; *90:* 196; *146:* 78; *156:* 165; *159:* 161; *182:* 18, 172; *232:* 160, 161, 162
Root, Kimberly Bulcken *86:* 72; *98:* 21; *108:* 111; *127:* 114; *159:* 162; *176:* 134; *192:* 163
Roper, Bob *65:* 153
Roraback, Robin *111:* 156
Rorer, Abigail *43:* 222; *85:* 155
Rosales, Melodye *80:* 35
Rosamilia, Patricia *36:* 120
Rose, Carl *5:* 62
Rose, David S. *29:* 109; *70:* 120
Rose, Gerald *68:* 200, 201; *86:* 48
Rose, Naomi C. *228:* 136
Rose, Ted *93:* 178
Rosen, Elizabeth *205:* 137
Rosenbaum, Jonathan *50:* 46
Rosenberg, Amye *74:* 207, 208
Rosenberry, Vera *87:* 22, 26; *144:* 212, 213; *158:* 120; *219:* 163, 164
Rosenblum, Richard *11:* 202; *18:* 18
Rosenstiehl, Agnès *203:* 153
Rosenstock, Jason *238:* 75
Rosier, Lydia *16:* 236; *20:* 104; *21:* 109; *22:* 125; *30:* 151, 158; *42:* 128; *45:* 214; *77:* 227, 228
Rosing, Jens *85:* 142
Ross
  See Thomson, Ross
Ross, Christine *83:* 172, 173
Ross, Clare Romano *3:* 123; *21:* 45; *48:* 199
Ross, Dave *32:* 152; *57:* 108
Ross, Graham *199:* 4
Ross, Herbert *37:* 78
Ross, John *3:* 123; *21:* 45
Ross, Johnny *32:* 190
Ross, Larry *47:* 168; *60:* 62
Ross, Ruth *109:* 233
Ross, Tony *17:* 204; *56:* 132; *65:* 176, 177, 179; *90:* 123; *123:* 186, 187, 190; *130:* 188, 190, 191, 192; *132:* 242; *174:* 159; *176:* 181, 182, 183; *202:* 198; *225:* 168, 170; *237:* 176, 177
Rossetti, Dante Gabriel *20:* 151, 153
Rostant, Larry *180:* 221; *194:* 108; *195:* 96; *197:* 12; *207:* 53; *210:* 189; *226:* 22; *234:* 154; *239:* 82, 116
Roth, Arnold *4:* 238; *21:* 133
Roth, Julie Jersild *180:* 206
Roth, Marci *135:* 223
Roth, R.G. *184:* 50
Roth, Rob *105:* 98; *146:* 41
Roth, Robert *176:* 159
Roth, Roger *61:* 128; *190:* 192
Roth, Ruby *216:* 185
Roth, Susan L. *80:* 38; *93:* 78; *134:* 165, 166; *181:* 145, 146
Rothenberg, Joani Keller *162:* 190, 191
Rothman, Michael *139:* 62; *184:* 34 Rotman, Jeffrey L. *145:* 30
Rotondo, Pat *32:* 158
Roughsey, Dick *35:* 186
Rouille, M. *11:* 96
Rounds, Glen *8:* 173; *9:* 171; *12:* 56; *32:* 194; *40:* 230; *51:* 161, 162, 166; *56:* 149; *70:* 198, 199; *YABC 1:* 1, 2, 3; *112:* 163
Roundtree, Katherine *114:* 88; *168:* 102
Rovetch, Lissa *201:* 164
Rowan, Evadne *52:* 51
Rowe, Eric *111:* 161
Rowe, Gavin *27:* 144; *72:* 47; *88:* 201
Rowe, John *132:* 70, 71; *180:* 126
Rowell, Kenneth *40:* 72
Rowen, Amy *52:* 143
Rowena *116:* 101

Rowland, Andrew *164:* 136
Rowland, Jada *83:* 73
Rowles, Daphne *58:* 24
Roy, Jeroo *27:* 229; *36:* 110
Royo *118:* 32; *144:* 105, 106, 108; *165:* 19; *166:* 166
Rubbino, Salvatore *220:* 147
Rubel, Nicole *18:* 255; *20:* 59; *81:* 66, 67; *95:* 169, 170; *119:* 60; *135:* 177, 179, 180; *169:* 68; *181:* 150
Rubel, Reina *33:* 217
Rud, Borghild *6:* 15
Ruddell, Gary *110:* 238; *116:* 207
Rudolph, Norman Guthrie *17:* 13
Rue, Leonard Lee III *37:* 164
Rueda, Claudia *183:* 170, 171
Ruelle, Karen Gray *126:* 193
Ruff, Donna *50:* 173; *72:* 203; *78:* 49; *80:* 120,121; *93:* 162; *164:* 121
Ruffins, Reynold *10:* 134, 135; *41:* 191, 192, 193, 194, 195, 196; *125:* 187, 188, 189; *162:* 197; *239:* 153
Ruhlin, Roger *34:* 44
Rui, Paolo *217:* 115
Ruiz, Art *95:* 154; *110:* 91
Rumford, James *193:* 167
Runnerstroem, Bengt Arne *75:* 161
Ruse, Margaret *24:* 155
Rush, Ken *98:* 74
Rush, Peter *42:* 75
Russell, Charles M. *167:* 171
Russell, E.B. *18:* 177, 182
Russell, Jim *53:* 134
Russell, Natalie *218:* 170, 171
Russell, P. Craig *80:* 196; *146:* 102; *162:* 186
Russo, Marisabina *84:* 51; *106:* 164; *151:* 183; *188:* 153, 154, 155, 156
Russo, Susan *30:* 182; *36:* 144
Russon, Mary *87:* 145
Ruth, Greg *183:* 125
Ruth, Rod *9:* 161
Rutherford, Alexa *110:* 108
Rutherford, Jenny *78:* 5
Rutherford, Meg *25:* 174; *34:* 178, 179; *69:* 73; *72:* 31
Rutland, Jonathan *31:* 126
Ruurs, Margriet *147:* 195
Ruzzier, Sergio *159:* 176, 177; *163:* 184; *210:* 214, 216
Ryan, Amy *188:* 50
Ryan, Will *86:* 134
Rycroft, Nina *228:* 143
Ryden, Hope *8:* 176
Rylant, Cynthia *112:* 170, 172
Rymer, Alta M. *34:* 181
Ryniak, Christopher *178:* 11
Rystedt, Rex *49:* 80

S

Saaf, Chuck *49:* 179
Saaf, Donald *101:* 220; *124:* 180
Sabaka, Donna R. *21:* 172
Sabin, Robert *45:* 35; *60:* 30; *99:* 161; *223:* 29
Sabuda, Robert *170:* 166, 167, 168
Sacker, Amy *16:* 100
Sadler, Sonia Lynn *230:* 42, 163
Saelig, S.M. *129:* 73; *173:* 59
Saffioti, Lino *36:* 176; *48:* 60; *223:* 26
Saflund, Birgitta *94:* 2
Sagsoorian, Paul *12:* 183; *22:* 154; *33:* 106; *87:* 152
Sahara, Tony *168:* 106; *177:* 181; *178:* 228; *186:* 132; *207:* 89; *231:* 54; *236:* 107, 109
Sahlberg, Myron *57:* 165
Saidens, Amy *145:* 162; *191:* 131; *210:* 129
Saint Exupery, Antoine de *20:* 157
Saint James, Synthia *152:* 220; *188:* 90; *200:* 7

Sakai, Komako *213:* 148
Saldutti, Denise *39:* 186; *57:* 178
Sale, Morton *YABC 2:* 31
Sale, Tim *153:* 177
Salerno, Steven *150:* 79; *176:* 188; *202:* 39; *216:* 190; *235:* 55
Salter, George *72:* 128, 130
Saltzberg, Barney *135:* 184, 185; *194:* 160; *233:* 147, 148
Saltzman, David *86:* 209
Salwowski, Mark *71:* 54
Salzman, Yuri *86:* 12
Sambourne, Linley *YABC 2:* 181
Sampson, Katherine *9:* 197
Samson, Anne S. *2:* 216
San Souci, Daniel *40:* 200; *96:* 199, 200; *113:* 171; *157:* 149; *170:* 69; *192:* 167, 168; *220:* 152; *221:* 126
Sancha, Sheila *38:* 185
Sanchez, Enrique O. *155:* 84
Sand, George X. *45:* 182
Sandberg, Lasse *15:* 239, 241
Sanders, Beryl *39:* 173
Sanderson, Ruth *21:* 126; *24:* 53; *28:* 63; *33:* 67; *41:* 48, 198, 199, 200, 201, 202, 203; *43:* 79; *46:* 36,44; *47:* 102; *49:* 58; *62:* 121, 122; *85:* 3; *109:* 207, 208, 209, 210; *172:* 157, 158; *223:* 85; *224:* 152, 153, 154
Sandia *119:* 74
Sandin, Joan *4:* 36; *6:* 194; *7:* 177; *12:* 145,185; *20:* 43; *21:* 74; *26:* 144; *27:* 142; *28:* 224, 225; *38:* 86; *41:* 46; *42:* 35; *59:* 6; *80:* 136; *94:* 188; *140:* 116; *153:* 179, 180; *197:* 168; *232:* 6
Sandland, Reg *39:* 215
Sandoz, Edouard *26:* 45, 47
Sanford, John *66:* 96, 97
Sanger, Amy Wilson *205:* 140
Sankey, Tom *72:* 103
Sano, Kazuhiko *153:* 208; *195:* 171; *203:* 21; *221:* 71
Santat, Dan *188:* 160; *221:* 62; *223:* 163; *224:* 157, 158, 159
Santiago, Wilfred *210:* 48
Santore, Charles *54:* 139; *200:* 171, 172
Santoro, Christopher *74:* 215
Santoro, Scott *236:* 166
Santos, Jesse J. *99:* 24
Sapieha, Christine *1:* 180
Saport, Linda *123:* 137, 138; *215:* 29
Sara
    See De La Roche Saint Andre, Anne
Sarcone-Roach, Julia *215:* 158
Sardinha, Rick *175:* 151
Sarg, Tony *YABC 2:* 236
Sargent, Claudia *64:* 181
Sargent, Robert *2:* 217
Saris *1:* 33
Sarony *YABC 2:* 170
Saroff, Phyllis V. *202:* 160
Sasaki, Goro *170:* 46; *237:* 23
Sasaki, Ellen Joy *216:* 49
Sasek, Miroslav *16:* 239, 240, 241, 242
Sassman, David *9:* 79
Sattler, Jennifer Gordon *218:* 175
Satty *29:* 203, 205
Sauber, Robert *40:* 183; *76:* 256; *78:* 154; *87:* 92
Saunders, Dave *85:* 163, 164, 165
Savadier, Elivia *84:* 50; *145:* 45; *164:* 206; *228:* 146
Savage, Naomi *56:* 172
Savage, Steele *10:* 203; *20:* 77; *35:* 28
Savage, Stephen *174:* 182
Savio *76:* 4
Savitt, Sam *8:* 66, 182; *15:* 278; *20:* 96; *24:* 192; *28:* 98
Sawyer, Kem Knapp *84:* 228, 229
Sawyer, Odessa *239:* 117
Say, Allen *28:* 178; *69:* 182, 183, 232; *110:* 194, 195,196; *161:* 154, 155

Sayles, Elizabeth *82:* 93; *105:* 155; *109:* 116; *180:* 64; *220:* 160, 161; *232:* 177
Scabrini, Janet *13:* 191; *44:* 128
Scalora, Suza *224:* 160
Scanlan, Peter *83:* 27; *153:* 165; *187:* 149
Scanlon, Paul *83:* 87
Scannell, Reece *105:* 105
Scarry, Huck *35:* 204, 205
Scarry, Richard *2:* 220, 221; *18:* 20; *35:* 193, 194, 195,196, 197, 198, 199, 200, 201, 202; *75:* 165, 167, 168
Schachner, Judith Byron *88:* 180; *92:* 163; *93:* 102; *142:* 82; *178:* 199, 200; *190:* 140; *228:* 83
Schade, Susan *205:* 21
Schaeffer, Mead *18:* 81, 94; *21:* 137, 138, 139; *47:* 128
Schaffer, Amanda *90:* 206
Schallau, Daniel *222:* 164
Schanzer, Rosalyn *138:* 192, 193
Scharl, Josef *20:* 132; *22:* 128
Scharschmidt, Sherry *239:* 60
Scheel, Lita *11:* 230
Scheffler, Axel *180:* 23, 24; *230:* 169, 170
Scheib, Ida *29:* 28
Schermer, Judith *30:* 184
Schick, Eleanor *82:* 210, 211; *144:* 222
Schick, Joel *16:* 160; *17:* 167; *22:* 12; *27:* 176; *31:* 147, 148; *36:* 23; *38:* 64; *45:* 116, 117; *52:* 5, 85; *104:* 159
Schields, Gretchen *75:* 171, 203
Schindelman, Joseph *1:* 74; *4:* 101; *12:* 49; *26:* 51; *40:* 146; *56:* 158; *73:* 40
Schindler, Edith *7:* 22
Schindler, S.D. *38:* 107; *46:* 196; *74:* 162; *75:* 172, 173; *99:* 133; *112:* 177; *118:* 185, 186; *121:* 71; *136:* 159; *143:* 45; *149:* 120; *156:* 30; *169:* 135; *171:* 161, 162, 163; *172:* 9; *186:* 163; *194:* 109; *195:* 35; *198:* 170, 171, 172; *237:* 121
Schlesinger, Bret *7:* 77
Schlossberg, Elisabeth *221:* 161
Schmid, Eleanore *12:* 188; *126:* 196, 197
Schmid, Paul *231:* 169
Schmiderer, Dorothy *19:* 224
Schmidt, Bill *73:* 34; *76:* 220, 222, 224
Schmidt, Elizabeth *15:* 242
Schmidt, George Paul *132:* 122
Schmidt, Karen Lee *54:* 12; *71:* 174; *92:* 56; *94:* 190, 191; *127:* 103
Schmidt, Lynette *76:* 205
Schmitz, Tamara *207:* 147
Schneider, Christine M. *171:* 165
Schneider, Howie *181:* 159
Schneider, Katy *237:* 128
Schneider, Rex *29:* 64; *44:* 171
Schnurr, Edward *170:* 62
Schoberle, Cecile *80:* 200; *92:* 134; *218:* 113
Schoenherr, Ian *32:* 83; *173:* 41; *235:* 174
Schoenherr, John *1:* 146, 147, 173; *3:* 39, 139; *17:* 75; *29:* 72; *32:* 83; *37:* 168, 169, 170; *43:* 164, 165; *45:* 160, 162; *51:* 127; *66:* 196, 197, 198; *68:* 83; *72:* 240; *75:* 225; *88:* 176
Scholder, Fritz *69:* 103
Schomburg, Alex *13:* 23
Schongut, Emanuel *4:* 102; *15:* 186; *47:* 218, 219; *52:* 147, 148, 149, 150; *185:* 27
Schoonover, Frank *17:* 107; *19:* 81, 190, 233; *22:* 88,129; *24:* 189; *31:* 88; *41:* 69; *YABC 2:* 282, 316
Schories, Pat *164:* 210; *232:* 170, 171, 172
Schottland, Miriam *22:* 172
Schramm, Ulrik *2:* 16; *14:* 112
Schreiber, Elizabeth Anne *13:* 193
Schreiber, Ralph W. *13:* 193
Schreiter, Rick *14:* 97; *23:* 171; *41:* 247; *49:* 131
Schroades, John *214:* 129
Schroeder, Binette *56:* 128, 129
Schroeder, E. Peter *12:* 112

Schroeder, Ted *11:* 160; *15:* 189; *30:* 91; *34:* 43
Schrotter, Gustav *22:* 212; *30:* 225
Schubert, Dieter *101:* 167, 168; *217:* 151, 152, 153, 155
Schubert, Ingrid *217:* 151, 152, 153, 155
Schubert-Gabrys, Ingrid *101:* 167, 168
Schucker, James *31:* 163
Schuett, Stacey *72:* 137; *208:* 204
Schulder, Lili *146:* 29
Schulke, Debra *57:* 167
Schulke, Flip *57:* 167
Schulz, Barbara *167:* 24
Schulz, Charles M. *10:* 137, 138, 139, 140, 141, 142; *118:* 192, 193, 194, 196, 199
Schutzer, Dena *109:* 32
Schwark, Mary Beth *51:* 155; *72:* 175
Schwartz, Amy *47:* 191; *82:* 100; *83:* 178, 179, 180,181; *129:* 107; *131:* 197, 198; *189:* 166, 168; *226:* 174
Schwartz, Carol *124:* 41; *130:* 199
Schwartz, Charles *8:* 184
Schwartz, Daniel *46:* 37
Schwartz, Joanie *124:* 170
Schwartzberg, Joan *3:* 208
Schwarz, Viviane *204:* 132
Schweitzer, Iris *2:* 137; *6:* 207
Schweninger, Ann *29:* 172; *82:* 246; *159:* 202; *168:* 166; *211:* 193
Schwinger, Laurence *84:* 44; *91:* 61
Scofield, Penrod *61:* 107; *62:* 160
Scott, Anita Walker *7:* 38
Scott, Art *39:* 41
Scott, Frances Gruse *38:* 43
Scott, Jane Wooster *226:* 181
Scott, Julian *34:* 126
Scott, Roszel *33:* 238
Scott, Sally *87:* 27
Scott, Steve *166:* 230, 231; *171:* 93
Scott, Trudy *27:* 172
Scotton, Rob *214:* 183
Scrace, Carolyn *143:* 95, 96
Scrambly, Crab *198:* 196
Scribner, Joanne *14:* 236; *29:* 78; *33:* 185; *34:* 208; *78:* 75; *164:* 237; *203:* 73
Scrofani, Joseph *31:* 65; *74:* 225
Scroggs, Kirk *187:* 169
Seaman, Mary Lott *34:* 64
Searle, Ronald *24:* 98; *42:* 172, 173, 174, 176, 177, 179; *66:* 73, 74; *70:* 205, 206, 207
Searle, Townley *36:* 85
Sebree, Charles *18:* 65
Sedacca, Joseph M. *11:* 25; *22:* 36
Seder, Jason *108:* 102
Seeger, Laura Vaccaro *172:* 162
Seegmiller, Don *174:* 57
Seely, David *164:* 173
Seeley, Laura L. *97:* 105
Segal, John *178:* 202
Segar, E.C. *61:* 179, 181
Segur, Adrienne *27:* 121
Seibold, J. Otto *83:* 188, 190, 191; *149:* 212, 214, 215, 216; *196:* 177, 179; *215:* 204
Seignobosc, Francoise *21:* 145, 146
Sejima, Yoshimasa *8:* 187
Selig, Sylvie *13:* 199
Seltzer, Isadore *6:* 18; *133:* 59
Seltzer, Meyer *17:* 214
Selven, Maniam *144:* 133
Selway, Martina *169:* 157
Selznick, Brian *79:* 192; *104:* 25; *117:* 175; *126:* 156; *134:* 171; *158:* 76, 78; *169:* 70; *171:* 172, 173; *191:* 106; *192:* 130; *197:* 158; *203:* 35; *205:* 92; *210:* 219, 220, 221, 222; *234:* 130
Sempe, Jean-Jacques *47:* 92; *YABC 2:* 109
Sendak, Maurice *1:* 135, 190; *3:* 204; *7:* 142; *15:* 199; *17:* 210; *27:* 181, 182, 183, 185, 186, 187, 189,190, 191, 192, 193, 194, 195, 197, 198, 199, 203; *28:* 181, 182; *32:* 108;

33: 148, 149; *35:* 238; *44:* 180, 181; *45:* 97, 99; *46:* 174; *73:* 225; *91:* 10, 11 *YABC1:* 167; *113:* 163, 165, 167, 168; *118:* 153; *127:* 161
Senders, Marci *180:* 79
Sengler, Johanna *18:* 256
Senn, Steve *60:* 145
Seredy, Kate *1:* 192; *14:* 20, 21; *17:* 210
Sergeant, John *6:* 74
Serra, Sebastiá *212:* 215
Servello, Joe *10:* 144; *24:* 139; *40:* 91; *70:* 130, 131; *146:* 159
Seton, Ernest Thompson *18:* 260-269, 271
Seuss, Dr.
    See Geisel, Theodor
Severin, John Powers *7:* 62
Sewall, Marcia *15:* 8; *22:* 170; *37:* 171, 172, 173; *39:* 73; *45:* 209; *62:* 117; *69:* 185, 186; *71:* 212; *90:* 232; *96:* 127; *102:* 101; *107:* 129; *119:* 176, 177, 178, 180
Seward, James *70:* 35
Seward, Prudence *16:* 243
Sewell, Helen *3:* 186; *15:* 308; *33:* 102; *38:* 189, 190, 191, 192
Seymour, Stephen *54:* 21
Sfar, Joann *182:* 183
Shachat, Andrew *82:* 179
Shadbolt, Robert *203:* 68
Shahn, Ben *39:* 178; *46:* 193
Shalansky, Len *38:* 167
Shanks, Anne Zane *10:* 149
Shannon, David *57:* 137; *107:* 184; *112:* 216; *135:* 12; *152:* 223, 224, 225; *158:* 192; *212:* 159, 160, 163; *228:* 162, 163, 164, 165; *237:* 9; *238:* 152
Sharkey, Niamh *213:* 152
Sharp, Paul *52:* 60
Sharp, William *6:* 131; *19:* 241; *20:* 112; *25:* 141
Sharratt, Nick *102:* 207, 208; *104:* 163; *153:* 198; *175:* 176; *192:* 208; *199:* 141, 142, 143, 184, 187, 188
Shaw, Barclay *74:* 14, 16; *118:* 138
Shaw, Charles *21:* 135; *38:* 187; *47:* 124; *126:* 219
Shaw, Charles G. *13:* 200
Shaw, Hannah *227:* 163, 164
Shaw-Smith, Emma *144:* 117
Shea, Bob *231:* 170, 171
Shea, Edmund *56:* 19
Shearer, Ted *43:* 193, 194, 195, 196
Sheban, Chris *182:* 185; *190:* 102, 104; *202:* 28; *204:* 112, 114; *209:* 150; *210:* 107; *220:* 103; *224:* 185
Shecter, Ben *16:* 244; *25:* 109; *33:* 188, 191; *41:* 77
Shed, Greg *74:* 94; *84:* 204; *129:* 149, *167:* 91; *179:* 192; *223:* 104
Sheeban, Chris *144:* 190; *158:* 163
Shefcik, James *48:* 221, 222; *60:* 141
Shefelman, Karl *58:* 168
Shefelman, Tom *204:* 137
Shefts, Joelle *48:* 210
Shein, Bob *139:* 189
Sheinkin, Stephen *204:* 139
Shekerjian, Haig *16:* 245
Shekerjian, Regina *16:* 245; *25:* 73
Sheldon, David *184:* 174; *185:* 204; *211:* 189
Shelley, John *186:* 223
Shemie, Bonnie *96:* 207
Shenton, Edward *45:* 187, 188, 189; *YABC 1:* 218, 219, 221
Shepard, Ernest H. *3:* 193; *4:* 74; *16:* 101; *17:* 109; *25:* 148; *33:* 152, 199, 200, 201, 202, 203, 204, 205, 206,207; *46:* 194; *98:* 114; *100:* 111, 178, 179, 217, 219, 220,221; *YABC 1:* 148, 153, 174, 176, 180, 181
Shepard, Mary *4:* 210; *22:* 205; *30:* 132, 133; *54:* 150, 152, 153, 157, 158; *59:* 108, 109, 111; *100:* 246
Shepherd, Amanda *198:* 14

Shepherd, Irana *171:* 112
Sheppard, Kate *195:* 176
Shepperson, Rob *96:* 153; *177:* 163; *178:* 204; *197:* 34; *205:* 108
Sheridan, Brian *196:* 193
Sherman, Theresa *27:* 167
Sherwan, Earl *3:* 196
Shields, Charles *10:* 150; *36:* 63
Shields, Leonard *13:* 83, 85, 87
Shiffman, Lena *139:* 167; *168:* 136
Shiga, Jason *228:* 168
Shigley, Neil K. *66:* 219
Shillabeer, Mary *35:* 74
Shilston, Arthur *49:* 61; *62:* 58
Shimin, Symeon *1:* 93; *2:* 128, 129; *3:* 202; *7:* 85; *11:* 177; *12:* 139; *13:* 202, 203; *27:* 138; *28:* 65; *35:* 129; *36:* 130; *48:* 151; *49:* 59; *56:* 63, 65, 153
Shimizu, Yuko *215:* 197
Shine, Andrea *104:* 165; *128:* 34
Shinn, Everett *16:* 148; *18:* 229; *21:* 149, 150, 151; *24:* 218
Shinn, Florence Scovel *63:* 133, 135
Shore, Robert *27:* 54; *39:* 192, 193; *YABC 2:* 200
Shortall, Leonard *4:* 144; *8:* 196; *10:* 166; *19:* 227, 228, 229, 230; *25:* 78; *28:* 66, 167; *33:* 127; *52:* 125; *73:* 12, 212
Shortt, T.M. *27:* 36
Shpitalnik, Vladimir *83:* 194
Shroades, John *230:* 24
Shropshire, Sandy *170:* 191
Shtainments, Leon *32:* 161
Shulevitz, Uri *3:* 198, 199; *17:* 85; *22:* 204; *27:* 212; *28:* 184; *50:* 190, 191, 192, 193, 194, 195, 196,197, 198, 199, 201; *106:* 181, 182, 183; *165:* 203, 205; *166:* 138
Shulman, Dee *180:* 140
Shupe, Bobbi *139:* 80, 81
Shute, A.B. *67:* 196
Shute, Linda *46:* 59; *74:* 118
Siberell, Anne *29:* 193
Sibley, Don *1:* 39; *12:* 196; *31:* 47
Sibthorp, Fletcher *94:* 111, 112
Sidjakov, Nicolas *18:* 274
Siebel, Fritz *3:* 120; *17:* 145
Siebold, J. Otto *158:* 227
Siegel, Hal *74:* 246
Sieger, Ted *189:* 172
Siegl, Helen *12:* 166; *23:* 216; *34:* 185, 186
Siku *238:* 42
Silin-Palmer, Pamela *184:* 102
Sill, John *140:* 194; *141:* 157; *221:* 163; *222:* 171
Sills, Joyce *5:* 199
Silva, Simon *108:* 122
Silver, Maggie *85:* 210
Silveria, Gordon *96:* 44
Silverstein, Alvin *8:* 189
Silverstein, Shel *33:* 211; *92:* 209, 210
Silverstein, Virginia *8:* 189
Silvey, Joe *135:* 203
Simard, Rémy *95:* 156; *221:* 144
Siminovich, Laura *219:* 172
Simmons, Elly *110:* 2; *127:* 69; *134:* 181
Simon, Eric M. *7:* 82
Simon, Hilda *28:* 189
Simon, Howard *2:* 175; *5:* 132; *19:* 199; *32:* 163, 164, 165
Simont, Marc *2:* 119; *4:* 213; *9:* 168; *13:* 238,240; *14:* 262; *16:* 179; *18:* 221; *26:* 210; *33:* 189, 194; *44:* 132; *58:* 122; *68:* 117; *73:* 204, 205, 206; *74:* 221; *126:* 199, 200; *133:* 195; *163:* 40; *164:* 128; *223:* 28
Simpson, Martin *233:* 168
Sims, Agnes *54:* 152
Sims, Blanche *44:* 116; *57:* 129; *75:* 179, 180; *77:* 92; *104:* 192; *152:* 117; *156:* 160; *160:* 70; *168:* 174, 175; *198:* 17; *236:* 54
Singer, Edith G. *2:* 30
Singer, Gloria *34:* 56; *36:* 43

Singer, Julia *28:* 190
Singh, Jen *178:* 146
Singh, Nikhil *234:* 54
Sinquette, Jaclyn *215:* 83
Siomades, Lorianne *134:* 45; *204:* 48; *217:* 157
Siracusa, Catherine *68:* 135; *82:* 218
Sisson, Stephanie Roth *136:* 171, 172; *237:* 131
Sís, Peter *67:* 179, 181, 183, 184, 185; *96:* 96, 98; *106:* 193, 194, 195; *149:* 224, 226; *180:* 177; *192:* 180, 182; *222:* 64; *239:* 104
Sivard, Robert *26:* 124
Sivertson, Liz *116:* 84
Skardinski, Stanley *23:* 144; *32:* 84; *66:* 122; *84:* 108
Slack, Michael *185:* 108; *189:* 173, 174
Slackman, Charles B. *12:* 201
Slade, Christian *193:* 187; *204:* 134; *234:* 59; *238:* 164, 165, 166
Slade, Paul *61:* 170
Slark, Albert *99:* 212; *205:* 161
Slater, Rod *25:* 167
Slavin, Bill *182:* 14, 15; *196:* 90; *199:* 148, 149, 150; *217:* 20; *235:* 45; *237:* 69; *239:* 93
Sloan, Joseph *16:* 68
Sloane, Eric *21:* 3; *52:* 153, 154, 155, 156, 157, 158, 160
Sloat, Teri *164:* 231
Slobodkin, Louis *1:* 200; *3:* 232; *5:* 168; *13:* 251; *15:* 13, 88; *26:* 173, 174, 175, 176, 178, 179; *60:* 180
Slobodkina, Esphyr *1:* 201
Slonim, David *166:* 167, 168
Small, David *50:* 204, 205; *79:* 44; *95:* 189, 190, 191; *126:* 203, 204; *136:* 119; *143:* 201, 202, 203; *144:* 246; *150:* 5; *161:* 176; *183:* 181, 182, 183, 184; *200:* 211; *212:* 86; *216:* 202, 203, 204; *230:* 222; *232:* 95
Small, W. *33:* 113
Smalley, Janet *1:* 154
Smath, Jerry *198:* 179, 180
Smedley, William T. *34:* 129
Smee, David *14:* 78; *62:* 30
Smee, Nicola *167:* 156
Smith, A.G., Jr. *35:* 182
Smith, Ali *204:* 68
Smith, Alvin *1:* 31, 229; *13:* 187; *27:* 216; *28:* 226; *48:* 149; *49:* 60
Smith, Andy *188:* 20; *207:* 151
Smith, Anne *194:* 147
Smith, Anne Warren *41:* 212
Smith, Barry *75:* 183
Smith, Brian *200:* 183
Smith, Carl *36:* 41
Smith, Cat Bowman *146:* 39; *164:* 219; *201:* 55, 184
Smith, Craig *97:* 197; *172:* 175; *206:* 40; *215:* 19; *217:* 129; *220:* 145
Smith, Donald A. *178:* 7
Smith, Doris Susan *41:* 139
Smith, Douglas *189:* 159; *213:* 170
Smith, Duane *171:* 152; *208:* 97
Smith, E. Boyd *19:* 70; *22:* 89; *26:* 63; *YABC 1:* 4, 5, 240, 248, 249
Smith, Edward J. *4:* 224
Smith, Elwood H. *157:* 231; *181:* 79; *203:* 160, 161, 162; *231:* 108; *236:* 176, 177, 178
Smith, Eunice Young *5:* 170
Smith, Gary *113:* 216
Smith, George *102:* 169
Smith, Howard *19:* 196
Smith, J. Gerard *95:* 42
Smith, Jacqueline Bardner *27:* 108; *39:* 197
Smith, Jay J. *61:* 119
Smith, Jeff *93:* 191
Smith, Jessie Willcox *15:* 91; *16:* 95; *18:* 231; *19:* 57, 242; *21:* 29, 156, 157, 158, 159, 160, 161; *34:* 65; *100:* 223; *YABC 1:* 6; *2:* 180, 185, 191, 311, 325

Smith, Jos. A. *52:* 131; *72:* 120; *74:* 151; *84:* 147, 148; *85:* 146; *87:* 96; *94:* 219; *96:* 97; *104:* 33; *108:* 126, 127, 128; *111:* 140; *136:* 145; *181:* 173; *200:* 213; *201:* 94; *231:* 148; *237:* 85
Smith, Kenneth R. *47:* 182
Smith, Keri *216:* 60
Smith, Kevin Warren *89:* 112
Smith, Kristin *209:* 197
Smith, L.H. *35:* 174
Smith, Lane *76:* 211, 213; *88:* 115; *105:* 202, 203,204, 205; *131:* 207; *160:* 217, 221; *179:* 183, 184, 185, 186; *199:* 122, 123, 124, 126; *224:* 164; *238:* 153, 154
Smith, Lee *29:* 32
Smith, Linell Nash *2:* 195
Smith, Maggie Kaufman *13:* 205; *35:* 191; *110:* 158; *178:* 226; *190:* 204; *209:* 145; *235:* 179, 180
Smith, Mavis *101:* 219
Smith, Moishe *33:* 155
Smith, Philip *44:* 134; *46:* 203
Smith, Ralph Crosby *2:* 267; *49:* 203
Smith, Robert D. *5:* 63
Smith, Sally J. *84:* 55
Smith, Susan Carlton *12:* 208
Smith, Terry *12:* 106; *33:* 158
Smith, Virginia *3:* 157; *33:* 72
Smith, William A. *1:* 36; *10:* 154; *25:* 65
Smith-Moore, J.J. *98:* 147
Smolinski, Dick *84:* 217
Smoljan, Joe *112:* 201
Smollin, Mike *39:* 203
Smyth, Iain *105:* 207
Smyth, M. Jane *12:* 15
Smythe, Fiona *151:* 213
Smythe, Theresa *141:* 37
Snair, Andy *176:* 4
Sneed, Brad *125:* 25; *191:* 175, 176; *211:* 194; *232:* 152
Snow, Sarah *228:* 47
Snyder, Andrew A. *30:* 212
Snyder, Betsy *230:* 173
Snyder, Jerome *13:* 207; *30:* 173
Snyder, Joel *28:* 163
So, Meilo *162:* 201; *208:* 188
Soentpiet, Chris K. *97:* 208; *110:* 33; *159:* 184; *161:* 10; *163:* 130
Sofia *1:* 62; *5:* 90; *32:* 166; *86:* 43
Sofilas, Mark *93:* 157
Sogabe, Aki *207:* 153; *221:* 110
Sohn, Jiho *182:* 78
Sokol, Bill *37:* 178; *49:* 23
Sokolov, Kirill *34:* 188
Solbert, Ronni *1:* 159; *2:* 232; *5:* 121; *6:* 34; *17:* 249
Solomon, Michael *174:* 115
Solonevich, George *15:* 246; *17:* 47
Soloviov, Michael *223:* 122
Soma, Liana *81:* 118
Soman, David *90:* 122; *102:* 126; *140:* 120; *93; 188:* 43, 89; *200:* 180, 181; *235:* 72
Sommer, Robert *12:* 211
Song, Jae *203:* 27
Soo, Kean *201:* 185
Sorel, Edward *4:* 61; *36:* 82; *65:* 191, 193; *126:* 214
Sorensen, Henri *196:* 58
Sorensen, Henrik *62:* 16
Sorensen, Svend Otto *22:* 130, 141; *67:* 188, 189
Sorra, Kristin *155:* 80; *229:* 85
Sosa, Hernan *198:* 66
Sostre, Maria *187:* 36
Sotomayor, Antonio *11:* 215
Souhami, Jessica *112:* 128; *176:* 193
Sousa, Natalie C. *209:* 89; *238:* 95
Souza, Diana *71:* 139
Sovak, Jan *115:* 190
Sowards, Ben *215:* 62
Soyer, Moses *20:* 177

Spaenkuch, August *16:* 28
Spafford, Suzy *160:* 228
Spain, Valerie *105:* 76
Spain, Sunday Sahara *133:* 204
Spalenka, Greg *149:* 69; *151:* 228; *184:* 195; *191:* 21; *196:* 12; *198:* 181, 182, 201; *208:* 92; *236:* 95
Spanfeller, James *1:* 72, 149; *2:* 183; *19:* 230, 231,232; *22:* 66; *36:* 160, 161; *40:* 75; *52:* 166; *76:* 37
Spangler, Brie *212:* 188
Sparks, Mary Walker *15:* 247
Spearing, Craig J. *228:* 172
Spears, Rick *182:* 187; *220:* 67
Speidel, Sandra *78:* 233; *94:* 178; *134:* 180; *210:* 67
Speirs, John *67:* 178
Spence, Geraldine *21:* 163; *47:* 196
Spence, Jim *38:* 89; *50:* 102
Spencer, Laurie *113:* 12
Spencer, Mark *57:* 170
Spengler, Kenneth J. *146:* 256
Sperling, Andrea *133:* 182
Spiegel, Beth *184:* 203
Spiegel, Doris *29:* 111
Spiegelman, Art *109:* 227
Spier, Jo *10:* 30
Spier, Peter *3:* 155; *4:* 200; *7:* 61; *11:* 78; *38:* 106; *54:* 120, 121, 122, 123, 124, 125, 126, 127, 128, 129, 130,131, 132, 133, 134
Spilka, Arnold *5:* 120; *6:* 204; *8:* 131
Spires, Ashley *231:* 96
Spirin, Gennady *95:* 196, 197; *113:* 172; *128:* 9; *129:* 49; *134:* 210; *153:* 9; *204:* 143, 144, 145; *220:* 153
Spiro, Ruth *208:* 197
Spivak, I. Howard *8:* 10; *13:* 172
Spohn, David *72:* 233
Spohn, Kate *87:* 195; *147:* 201, 202
Spollen, Christopher J. *12:* 214
Spooner, Malcolm *40:* 142
Spoor, Mike *220:* 92
Spowart, Robin *82:* 228; *92:* 149; *133:* 131; *176:* 163; *177:* 183, 184; *217:* 123, 124
Sprague, Kevin *150:* 60; *196:* 62
Spranger, Nina *201:* 199
Sprattler, Rob *12:* 176
Spring, Bob *5:* 60
Spring, Ira *5:* 60
Springer, Harriet *31:* 92
Spudvilas, Anne *110:* 74; *197:* 192; *199:* 154
Spurll, Barbara *78:* 199; *88:* 141, 142; *99:* 215
Spurrier, Steven *28:* 198
Spuvilas, Anne *85:* 114
Spy
    See Ward, Leslie
Squires, Stuart *127:* 74
St. Aubin, Bruno *179:* 54
St. John, J. Allen *41:* 62
Staake, Bob *209:* 168, 169; *229:* 132
Stabin, Victor *101:* 131; *164:* 158
Stadler, John *62:* 33; *204:* 149
Stadnyk, Greg *212:* 55
Staffan, Alvin E. *11:* 56; *12:* 187
Stahl, Ben *5:* 181; *12:* 91; *49:* 122; *71:* 128; *87:* 206; *112:* 107
Stair, Gobin *35:* 214
Stallwood, Karen *73:* 126
Stamaty, Mark Alan *12:* 215; *230:* 175
Stammen, JoEllen McAllister *113:* 14
Stamp, Jørgen *225:* 184
Stampnick, Ken *51:* 142
Stanbridge, Joanne *150:* 91
Stanley, Diane *3:* 45; *37:* 180; *80:* 217, 219
Stanley, Sanna *145:* 228
Star, Lindsay *219:* 39
Starcke, Helmut *86:* 217
Stark, Ken *197:* 102
Starr, Branka *73:* 25
Stasiak, Krystyna *49:* 181; *64:* 194
Staub, Leslie *103:* 54

Stauffer, Brian *220:* 123
Staunton, Ted *112:* 192
Stawicki, Matt *164:* 250
Stead, Erin E. *232:* 179
Stead, L. *55:* 51, 56
Steadman, Broeck *97:* 185, 186; *99:* 56; *121:* 48; *208:* 190
Steadman, Henry *211:* 130
Steadman, Ralph *32:* 180; *123:* 143, 145
Stearn, Nick *183:* 26
Stearn, Todd *218:* 179
Steckler, June *90:* 178
Steele, Robert Gantt *169:* 174
Steichen, Edward *30:* 79
Steig, William *18:* 275, 276; *70:* 215, 216, 217, 218; *111:* 173, 174, 175, 176, 177
Stein, David Ezra *211:* 168
Stein, Harve *1:* 109
Steinberg, Saul *47:* 193
Steinel, William *23:* 146
Steiner, Charlotte *45:* 196
Steiner, Joan *110:* 219; *199:* 160, 161
Steirnagel, Michael *80:* 56
Stemp, Eric *60:* 184
Stengel, Christopher *229:* 200; *232:* 57; *237:* 135
Stephens, Alice Barber *66:* 208, 209
Stephens, Charles H. *YABC 2:* 279
Stephens, Pam *198:* 69
Stephens, Pat *126:* 110; *128:* 101
Stephens, William M. *21:* 165
Stephenson, Kristina *224:* 169
Steptoe, Javaka *151:* 203, 204; *190:* 169; *213:* 163, 164
Steptoe, John *8:* 197; *57:* 9; *63:* 158, 159, 160, 161,163, 164, 165, 166, 167; *96:* 4; *105:* 87
Stern, Simon *15:* 249, 250; *17:* 58; *34:* 192, 193
Sterret, Jane *53:* 27
Stetsios, Debbie *165:* 108, 109
Steven, Kat *158:* 237
Stevens, David *62:* 44
Stevens, Helen *189:* 31; *207:* 83
Stevens, Janet *40:* 126; *57:* 10, 11; *80:* 112; *90:* 221, 222; *109:* 156; *130:* 34; *166:* 202; *176:* 53, 116; *193:* 199, 200, 202; *208:* 127; *212:* 182
Stevens, Mary *11:* 193; *13:* 129; *43:* 95
Stevenson, Harvey *66:* 143; *80:* 201, 221; *153:* 60; *191:* 166; *233:* 154
Stevenson, James *42:* 182, 183; *51:* 163; *66:* 184; *71:* 185, 187, 188; *78:* 262; *87:* 97; *113:* 182, 183,184, 185; *161:* 182, 183
Stevenson, Sucie *92:* 27; *104:* 194, 195; *112:* 168; *160:* 202; *194:* 172, 173; *195:* 166
Stewart, April Blair *75:* 210
Stewart, Arvis *33:* 98; *36:* 69; *60:* 118; *75:* 91; *127:* 4
Stewart, Charles *2:* 205
Stewart, Joel *151:* 205; *211:* 170, 171; *229:* 168
Stieg, William *172:* 58
Stiles, Fran *26:* 85; *78:* 56; *82:* 150
Stillman, Susan *44:* 130; *76:* 83
Stimpson, Tom *49:* 171
Stimson, James *208:* 46
Stinemetz, Morgan *40:* 151
Stinson, Paul *110:* 86
Stirnweis, Shannon *10:* 164
Stites, Joe *86:* 96
Stobbs, William *1:* 48, 49; *3:* 68; *6:* 20; *17:* 117, 217; *24:* 150; *29:* 250; *60:* 179; *87:* 204, 205,206
Stock, Catherine *37:* 55; *65:* 198; *72:* 7; *99:* 225; *114:* 197, 198, 199; *126:* 3; *145:* 161; *161:* 82; *173:* 149; *208:* 210; *214:* 192, 194; *224:* 196, 197
Stockman, Jack *113:* 24
Stoeke, Janet Morgan *90:* 225; *136:* 196; *202:* 182, 183
Stoerrle, Tom *55:* 147

Stolp, Jaap *49:* 98
Stolp, Todd *89:* 195
Stone, David L. *87:* 154
Stone, David *9:* 173
Stone, David K. *4:* 38; *6:* 124; *9:* 180; *43:* 182; *60:* 70
Stone, Helen V. *6:* 209
Stone, Helen *44:* 121, 122, 126
Stone, Kazuko G. *134:* 43
Stone, Kyle M. *202:* 185
Stone, Phoebe *86:* 212; *134:* 213; *162:* 188; *205:* 145
Stone, Steve *166:* 213; *208:* 185; *220:* 57,58; *224:* 124
Stone, Tony *150:* 34, 35
Storms, Patricia *217:* 163
Storrings, Michael *191:* 108; *216:* 217
Stoud, Virginia A. *89:* 31
Stover, Jill *82:* 234
Stower, Adam *217:* 89; *227:* 53
Strachan, Bruce *205:* 146
Stratton, Helen *33:* 151
Stratton-Porter, Gene *15:* 254, 259, 263, 264, 268, 269
Straub, Matt *192:* 176; *229:* 176
Straub, Phillip *197:* 22; *233:* 36
Streano, Vince *20:* 173
Street, Janet Travell *84:* 235
Streeter, Clive *121:* 2
Strickland, Shadra *209:* 179; *233:* 177
Stringer, Lauren *129:* 187; *154:* 172, 173; *161:* 127; *183:* 187, 188; *232:* 153
Strodl, Daniel *47:* 95
Strogart, Alexander *63:* 139
Stromoski, Rick *111:* 179; *124:* 161, 190
Strong, Joseph D., Jr. *YABC 2:* 330
Stroyer, Poul *13:* 221
Strugnell, Ann *27:* 38
Struzan, Drew *117:* 6
Stubbs, William *73:* 196
Stubis, Talivaldis *5:* 182, 183; *10:* 45; *11:* 9; *18:* 304; *20:* 127
Stubley, Trevor *14:* 43; *22:* 219; *23:* 37; *28:* 61; *87:* 26
Stuck, Marion *104:* 44
Stuecklen, Karl W. *8:* 34, 65; *23:* 103
Stull, Betty *11:* 46
Stutzman, Mark *119:* 99
Stutzmann, Laura *73:* 185
Suarez, Maribel *162:* 208; *200:* 202; *237:* 170
Suave, Gordon *209:* 66
Suba, Susanne *4:* 202, 203; *14:* 261; *23:* 134; *29:* 222; *32:* 30
Sue, Majella Lue *209:* 182; *212:* 146
Sueling, Barbara *98:* 185
Sueling, Gwenn *98:* 186
Sugarman, Tracy *3:* 76; *8:* 199; *37:* 181, 182
Sugimoto, Yugo *170:* 144; *223:* 137
Sugita, Yutaka *36:* 180, 181
Suh, John *80:* 157
Sullivan, Dorothy *89:* 113
Sullivan, Edmund J. *31:* 86
Sullivan, James F. *19:* 280; *20:* 192
Sully, Tom *104:* 199, 200; *182:* 77
Sumichrast, Jozef *14:* 253; *29:* 168, 213
Sumiko *46:* 57
Summers, Leo *1:* 177; *2:* 273; *13:* 22
Summers, Mark *118:* 144
Summers, Mike *190:* 176
Sutton, Judith *94:* 164
Svarez, Juan *56:* 113
Svendsen, Mark *181:* 176
Svolinsky, Karel *17:* 104
Swain, Carol *172:* 182
Swain, Su Zan Noguchi *21:* 170
Swan, Susan *22:* 220, 221; *37:* 66; *60:* 146; *145:* 205; *181:* 168; *236:* 172
Swann, Susan *86:* 55
Swanson, Karl *79:* 65; *89:* 186
Swarner, Kristina *203:* 62; *215:* 184
Swayne, Sam *53:* 143, 145

Swayne, Zoa *53:* 143, 145
Swearingen, Greg *152:* 56; *165:* 135; *173:* 2; *224:* 32; *225:* 188
Sweat, Lynn *25:* 206; *57:* 176; *73:* 184; *168:* 178
Sweet, Darrell K. *60:* 9; *69:* 86; *74:* 15; *75:* 215; *76:* 130, 131; *81:* 96, 122; *82:* 253; *83:* 11; *84:* 14; *85:* 37; *89:* 140; *90:* 6; *91:* 137,139; *95:* 160, 161; *126:* 25; *185:* 175; *195:* 132
Sweet, Darrell K. *1:* 163; *4:* 136; *164:* 175
Sweet, Melissa *71:* 94; *72:* 172; *111:* 82; *139:* 53, 58; *141:* 88; *142:* 231; *155:* 121; *159:* 121, 122; *172:* 185; *188:* 127; *209:* 81; *211:* 174, 175; *218:* 21; *235:* 54
Sweet, Ozzie *31:* 149, 151, 152
Sweetland, Robert *12:* 194
Swiatkowska, Gabi *132:* 43; *175:* 139; *180:* 218; *183:* 176
Swope, Martha *43:* 160; *56:* 86, 87, 89
Sylvada, Peter *154:* 174
Sylvester, Natalie G. *22:* 222
Syme, Hugh *232:* 8
Szafran, Gene *24:* 144
Szasz, Susanne *13:* 55, 226; *14:* 48
Szekeres, Cyndy *2:* 218; *5:* 185; *8:* 85; *11:* 166; *14:* 19; *16:* 57, 159; *26:* 49, 214; *34:* 205; *60:* 150, 151, 152, 153, 154; *73:* 224; *74:* 218; *131:* 213, 215
Szpura, Beata *81:* 68; *119:* 65; *168:* 201
Szuc, Jeff *220:* 188

T

Taback, Simms *40:* 207; *52:* 120; *57:* 34; *80:* 241; *104:* 202, 203; *170:* 176, 177; *205:* 183
Taber, Patricia *75:* 124
Tabor, Nancy Maria Grande *89:* 210; *161:* 188
Taddei, Richard *112:* 13, 14
Tadgell, Nicole *150:* 77; *161:* 20; *177:* 186; *209:* 16; *220:* 190, 191; *235:* 90
Tadiello, Ed *133:* 200
Tafuri, Nancy *39:* 210; *75:* 199, 200; *92:* 75; *130:* 215, 216, 217
Tailfeathers, Gerald *86:* 85
Tait, Douglas *12:* 220; *74:* 105, 106
Takabayashi, Mari *113:* 112; *130:* 22; *156:* 169
Takahashi, Hideko *136:* 160; *187:* 6; *209:* 152, 187
Takakjian, Portia *15:* 274
Takashima, Shizuye *13:* 228
Talarczyk, June *4:* 173
Talbott, Hudson *84:* 240; *163:* 100; *212:* 191, 192, 193
Tallarico, Tony *116:* 197
Tallec, Olivier *218:* 4
Tallon, Robert *2:* 228; *43:* 200, 201, 202, 203, 204, 205,206, 207, 209
Tamaki, Jillian *201:* 188
Tamas, Szecsko *29:* 135
Tamburine, Jean *12:* 222
Tanaka, Yoko *215:* 187; *234:* 106
Tancredi, Sharon *215:* 127
Tandy, H.R. *13:* 69
Tandy, Russell H. *65:* 9; *100:* 30, 131
Tanenbaum, Robert *238:* 141
Tang, Charles *81:* 202; *90:* 192
Tang, Sandara *238:* 60
Tang, Susan *80:* 174; *108:* 158
Tang, You-shan *63:* 100
Tankersley, Paul *69:* 206; *133:* 219
Tannenbaum, Robert *48:* 181
Tanner, Jane *87:* 13; *97:* 37
Tanner, Tim *72:* 192; *84:* 35
Tanobe, Miyuki *23:* 221
Tarabay, Sharif *110:* 149; *113:* 123; *169:* 83
Tarkington, Booth *17:* 224, 225
Tarlow, Phyllis *61:* 198
Tate, Don *159:* 141, 191; *183:* 69; *186:* 120

Tauss, Herbert *95:* 179
Tauss, Marc *117:* 160; *126:* 155; *178:* 221; *197:* 7; *223:* 168; *238:* 109
Tavares, Matt *159:* 192, 193; *198:* 188, 189, 190; *199:* 86
Taxali, Gary *234:* 199
Taylor, Ann *41:* 226
Taylor, Dahl *129:* 157
Taylor, Geoff *93:* 156; *197:* 173, 175; *204:* 151, 152
Taylor, Isaac *41:* 228
Taylor, Jennifer *226:* 128; *232:* 154
Taylor, Mike *143:* 99, 100
Teague, Mark *83:* 6; *139:* 241; *170:* 180, 181; *205:* 150, 151
Teale, Edwin Way *7:* 196
Teason, James *1:* 14
Teckentrup, Britta *200:* 191, 192
Teeple, Lyn *33:* 147
Tee-Van, Helen Damrosch *10:* 176; *11:* 182
Teevee, Ningeokuluk *223:* 173
Teicher, Dick *50:* 211
Teichman, Mary *77:* 220; *124:* 208; *127:* 22; *197:* 33
Telgemeier, Raina *228:* 180, 181, 182
Temertey, Ludmilla *96:* 232; *104:* 43, 45; *109:* 244
Tempest, Margaret *3:* 237, 238; *88:* 200
Temple, Frances *85:* 185, 186, 187
Temple, Herbert *45:* 201
Templeton, Owen *11:* 77
ten Cate, Marijke *183:* 193
Tenggren, Gustaf *18:* 277, 278, 279; *19:* 15; *28:* 86; *YABC2:* 145
TenNapel, Doug *234:* 200
Tennent, Julie *81:* 105
Tenneson, Joyce *153:* 166
Tenney, Gordon *24:* 204
Tenniel, John *74:* 234, 235; *100:* 89; *YABC 2:* 99; *153:* 63
Teplin, Scott *231:* 180
Tepper, Matt *116:* 80
Terkel, Ari *103:* 162
Terry, Michael *180:* 209; *233:* 166
Terry, Will *131:* 73; *205:* 155; *223:* 105
Teskey, Donald *71:* 51
Tessler, Manya *200:* 193
Thacher, Mary M. *30:* 72
Thackeray, William Makepeace *23:* 224, 228
Thamer, Katie *42:* 187
Tharlet, Eve *146:* 149
Thelwell, Norman *14:* 201
Theobalds, Prue *40:* 23
Theurer, Marilyn Churchill *39:* 195
Thiesing, Lisa *89:* 134; *95:* 202; *156:* 190; *159:* 195
Thiewes, Sam *133:* 114
Thisdale, François *223:* 55
Thistlethwaite, Miles *12:* 224
Thollander, Earl *11:* 47; *18:* 112; *22:* 224
Thomas, Allan *22:* 13
Thomas, Art *48:* 217
Thomas, Eric *28:* 49
Thomas, Harold *20:* 98
Thomas, Jacqui *125:* 95
Thomas, Jan *197:* 180; *226:* 198
Thomas, Mark *42:* 136
Thomas, Martin *14:* 255
Thomas, Middy *177:* 114; *230:* 63
Thompson, Arthur *34:* 107
Thompson, Carol *85:* 189; *95:* 75; *102:* 86; *147:* 166; *189:* 179, 180, 181; *190:* 84; *207:* 18
Thompson, Colin *95:* 204
Thompson, Ellen *51:* 88, 151; *60:* 33; *67:* 42; *77:* 148; *78:* 75, 219; *79:* 122, 170; *84:* 219; *85:* 97; *87:* 37; *88:* 192, 194; *89:* 80; *93:* 37; *98:* 59; *132:* 14; *236:* 72, 73
Thompson, George W. *22:* 18; *28:* 150; *33:* 135

Thompson, John *58:* 201; *102:* 226; *124:* 154; *128:* 228; *129:* 157; *150:* 49; *185:* 160; *191:* 192; *224:* 110; *236:* 101
Thompson, Julie *44:* 158
Thompson, Katherine *132:* 146
Thompson, K. Dyble *84:* 6
Thompson, Miles *152:* 77
Thompson, Sharon *74:* 113; *158:* 60; *165:* 87
Thomson, Arline K. *3:* 264
Thomson, Bill *186:* 160
Thomson, Hugh *26:* 88
Thomson, Ross *36:* 179
Thorkelson, Gregg *95:* 183, 184; *98:* 58; *165:* 30, 31; *225:* 31, 32
Thorn, Lori *189:* 119
Thornberg, Dan *104:* 125
Thornburgh, Rebecca McKillip *143:* 37
Thorne, Diana *25:* 212
Thornhill, Jan *77:* 213
Thorpe, Peter *58:* 109
Thorvall, Kerstin *13:* 235
Threadgall, Colin *77:* 215
Thurber, James *13:* 239, 242, 243, 245, 248, 249
Thurman, Mark *63:* 173; *168:* 116
Tibbles, Jean-Paul *115:* 200
Tibbles, Paul *45:* 23
Tibo, Gilles *67:* 207; *107:* 199, 201
Tichenor, Tom *14:* 207
Tichnor, Richard *90:* 218
Tiegreen, Alan *36:* 143; *43:* 55, 56, 58; *77:* 200; *94:* 216, 217; *121:* 54, 59
Tierney, Tom *113:* 198, 200, 201
Tildes, Phyllis Limbacher *210:* 240
Tilley, Debbie *102:* 134; *133:* 226; *137:* 101; *159:* 96; *190:* 211, 212; *213:* 51
Tillman, Nancy *211:* 129, 178
Tillotson, Katherine *224:* 175
Tilney, F.C. *22:* 231
Timbs, Gloria *36:* 90
Timmins, Harry *2:* 171
Timmons, Bonnie *194:* 189
Tinkelman, Murray *12:* 225; *35:* 44
Titherington, Jeanne *39:* 90; *58:* 138; *75:* 79; *135:* 161
Tjader, Ella *209:* 14
Tobin, Nancy *145:* 197
Toddy, Irving *172:* 144
Tokunbo, Dimitrea *181:* 183; *187:* 182, 183; *226:* 209
Tolbert, Jeff *128:* 69
Toledo, Francisco *197:* 182; *198:* 199
Toledo, Natalia *197:* 182
Tolford, Joshua *1:* 221
Tolkien, J.R.R. *2:* 243; *32:* 215
Tolman, Marije *195:* 43
Tolmie, Ken *15:* 292
Tomei, Lorna *47:* 168, 171
Tomes, Jacqueline *2:* 117; *12:* 139
Tomes, Margot *1:* 224; *2:* 120, 121; *16:* 207; *18:* 250; *20:* 7; *25:* 62; *27:* 78, 79; *29:* 81, 199; *33:* 82; *36:* 186, 187, 188, 189, 190; *46:* 129; *56:* 71; *58:* 183; *70:* 228; *75:* 73, 75; *80:* 80; *83:* 97; *90:* 205
Tommaso, Rich *200:* 198
Tommorow, Tom *223:* 176
Toner, Raymond John *10:* 179
Tong, Gary *66:* 215
Tongier, Stephen *82:* 32
Tooke, Susan *173:* 162
Toothill, Harry *6:* 54; *7:* 49; *25:* 219; *42:* 192
Toothill, Ilse *6:* 54
Topaz, Ksenia *224:* 94
Topolski, Feliks *44:* 48
Torbert, Floyd James *22:* 226
Torgersen, Don *55:* 157
Torline, Kevin *169:* 171
Tormey, Bertram M. *75:* 3, 4
Torrecilla, Pablo *176:* 207
Torres, Leyla *156:* 199, 201
Torrey, Helen *87:* 41

Torrey, Marjorie *34:* 105
Torrey, Richard *189:* 182; *205:* 24
Toschik, Larry *6:* 102
Totten, Bob *13:* 93
Townsend, Michael *231:* 183
Toy, Julie *128:* 112
Trachok, Cathy *131:* 16; *228:* 10
Tracy, Libba *82:* 24
Trago, Keith *158:* 253
Trail, Lee *55:* 157
Trang, To Ngoc *167:* 180
Trang, Winson *89:* 151
Trapani, Iza *116:* 202; *214:* 203
Travers, Bob *49:* 100; *63:* 145
Treatner, Meryl *95:* 180
Tremain, Ruthven *17:* 238
Tresilian, Stuart *25:* 53; *40:* 212
Trez, Alain *17:* 236
Trezzo, Loretta *86:* 45
Trier, Walter *14:* 96
Trimby, Elisa *47:* 199
Trinkle, Sally *53:* 27
Triplett, Gina *182:* 193; *188:* 100; *198:* 38
Tripp, F.J. *24:* 167
Tripp, Wallace *2:* 48; *7:* 28; *8:* 94; *10:* 54,76; *11:* 92; *31:* 170, 171; *34:* 203; *42:* 57; *60:* 157; *73:* 182
Trivas, Irene *53:* 4; *54:* 168; *82:* 46, 101
Trnka, Jiri *22:* 151; *43:* 212, 213, 214, 215; *YABC 1:* 30, 31
Trondheim, Lewis *182:* 183
Troughton, Joanna *37:* 186; *48:* 72
Troyer, Johannes *3:* 16; *7:* 18
Trudeau, G.B. *35:* 220, 221, 222; *48:* 119, 123, 126, 127,128, 129, 133; *168:* 189
Trueman, Matthew *165:* 208; *183:* 191; *220:* 61; *222:* 174
Truesdell, Sue *55:* 142; *108:* 219, 220; *212:* 202; *220:* 78
Tryon, Leslie *84:* 7; *139:* 214; *143:* 10; *181:* 10
Tseng, Jean *72:* 195; *94:* 102; *119:* 126; *151:* 106; *173:* 138, 139; *200:* 158
Tseng, Mou-sien *72:* 195; *94:* 102; *119:* 126; *151:* 106; *173:* 138, 139; *200:* 158
Tsinajinie, Andy *2:* 62
Tsinganos, Jim *180:* 142
Tsugami, Kyuzo *18:* 198, 199
Tucker, Ezra *156:* 31
Tuckwell, Jennifer *17:* 205
Tudor, Bethany *7:* 103
Tudor, Tasha *18:* 227; *20:* 185, 186, 187; *36:* 111; *69:* 196, 198; *100:* 44; *YABC 2:* 46, 314; *160:* 234
Tuerk, Hanne *71:* 201
Tugeau, Jeremy *199:* 170; *203:* 96
Tulloch, Maurice *24:* 79
Tunis, Edwin *1:* 218, 219; *28:* 209, 210, 211, 212
Tunnicliffe, C.F. *62:* 176; *177; 178, 179; 181
Turkle, Brinton *1:* 211, 213; *2:* 249; *3:* 226; *11:* 3; *16:* 209; *20:* 22; *50:* 23; *67:* 50; *68:* 65; *79:* 205, 206, 207; *128:* 47; *YABC 1:* 79
Turnbull, Christopher J. *143:* 99, 100
Turner, Gwenda *59:* 195
Turner, Helen *203:* 154
Turska, Krystyna *12:* 103; *31:* 173, 174, 175; *56:* 32,34; *100:* 66
Tusa, Tricia *72:* 242; *111:* 180, 181; *157:* 165, 164; *186; *189:* 40; *201:* 9; *207:* 163, 164; *233:* 132; *237:* 103
Tusan, Stan *6:* 58; *22:* 236, 237
Tuschman, Richard *219:* 100; *224:* 188; *225:* 175; *231:* 149; *238:* 138
Tworkov, Jack *47:* 207
Tyers, Jenny *89:* 220
Tylden-Wright, Jenny *114:* 119
Tyrol, Adelaide Murphy *103:* 27
Tyrrell, Frances *107:* 204
Tzimoulis, Paul *12:* 104

U

Uchida, Yoshiko *1:* 220
Uderzo *47:* 88
Udovic, David *189:* 185; *195:* 201
Ueno, Noriko *59:* 155
Ugliano, Natascia *196:* 186
Ulm, Robert *17:* 238
Ulrich, George *73:* 15; *75:* 136, 139; *99:* 150
Ulriksen, Mark *101:* 58; *182:* 43; *210:* 243
Unada *84:* 67; *227:* 80
See Gliewe, Unada
Underhill, Liz *53:* 159
Underwood, Beck *192:* 36
Underwood, Clarence *40:* 166
Unger, Jim *67:* 208
Ungerer, Tomi *5:* 188; *9:* 40; *18:* 188; *29:* 175; *33:* 221, 222, 223, 225; *71:* 48; *106:* 209, 210, 211, 212
Unwin, Nora S. *3:* 65, 234, 235; *4:* 237; *44:* 173, 174; *YABC 1:* 59; *2:* 301
Unzner, Christa *230:* 186
Upitis, Alvis *145:* 179
Urban, Helle *149:* 243
Urbanovic, Jackie *86:* 86; *189:* 186, 187
Urberuaga, Emilio *219:* 110, 175
U'ren, Andrea *213:* 177; *232:* 175
Uris, Jill *49:* 188, 197
Ursell, Martin *50:* 51
Utpatel, Frank *18:* 114
Utz, Lois *5:* 190

V

Vagin, Vladimir *66:* 10; *142:* 215
Vaillancourt, Francois *107:* 199
Vainio, Pirkko *123:* 157, 158
Valério, Geraldo *180:* 225; *194:* 116
Vallejo, Boris *62:* 130; *72:* 212; *91:* 38; *93:* 61
Van Abbe, S. *16:* 142; *18:* 282; *31:* 90; *YABC 2:* 157, 161
Van Allsburg, Chris *37:* 205, 206; *53:* 161, 162, 163, 165,166, 167, 168, 169, 170, 171; *105:* 215, 216, 217, 218; *156:* 176, 177, 178
Vance, James *65:* 28
Van Der Linde, Henry *99:* 17
van der Meer, Ron *98:* 204, 205
van der Meer, Atie *98:* 204, 205
Vandivert, William *21:* 175
Van Dongen, H.R. *81:* 97
Van Dusen, Chris W. *173:* 169; *228:* 192
Vane, Mitch *210:* 160; *218:* 152
Van Everen, Jay *13:* 160; *YABC 1:* 121
Van Fleet, John *165:* 12, 13
Van Frankenhuyzen, Gijsbert *145:* 230; *149:* 164; *184:* 151; *210:* 248
van Genechten, Guido *165:* 226
van Haeringen, Annemarie *193:* 206
Van Horn, William *43:* 218
van Hout, Mies *195:* 191; *207:* 58
van Kampen, Vlasta *194:* 217
van Lawick, Hugo *62:* 76, 79
Van Lieshout, Maria *201:* 196; *223:* 119
Van Loon, Hendrik Willem *18:* 285, 289, 291
Van Munching, Paul *83:* 85
van Ommen, Sylvia *186:* 192
Van Patter, Bruce *183:* 195
Van Rynbach, Iris *102:* 192
Van Sciver, Ruth *37:* 162
VanSeveren, Joe *63:* 182
Van Stockum, Hilda *5:* 193
Van Vleet, John *213:* 180
Van Wassenhove, Sue *202:* 193
Van Wely, Babs *16:* 50; *79:* 16
Van Wright, Cornelius *72:* 18; *102:* 208; *116:* 107; *152:* 236; *173:* 170, 171; *199:* 185

Van Zyle, Jon *103:* 125; *160:* 181, 182; *176:* 199, 200; *221:* 128; *232:* 125
Vardzigulyants, Ruben *90:* 54
Varga, Judy *29:* 196
Vargo, Kurt *79:* 224
Varley, Susan *61:* 199; *63:* 176, 177; *101:* 148; *134:* 220
Varon, Sara *195:* 208
Vasconcellos, Daniel *80:* 42
Vasiliu, Mircea *2:* 166, 253; *9:* 166; *13:* 58; *68:* 42
Vaughn, Frank *34:* 157
Vavra, Robert *8:* 206
Vawter, Will *17:* 163
Vayas, Diana *71:* 61
Vazquez, Carlos *125:* 184
Veeder, Larry *18:* 4
Velasquez, Eric *45:* 217; *61:* 45; *63:* 110, 111; *88:* 162; *90:* 34, 144; *94:* 213; *107:* 147; *132:* 192; *138:* 213; *159:* 126; *181:* 184; *184:* 96; *191:* 16; *192:* 234; *208:* 37; *214:* 81; *226:* 201, 203, 212; *237:* 59; *239:* 165
Velasquez, Jose A. *63:* 73
Velez, Walter *71:* 75; *91:* 154; *121:* 181; *168:* 49; *207:* 52
Velthuijs, Max *110:* 228, 229
Vendrell, Carme Sole *42:* 205
Venezia, Mike *54:* 17
Venti, Anthony Bacon *124:* 103; *126:* 26
Venturo, Piero *61:* 194, 195
Ver Beck, Frank *18:* 16, 17
Verkaaik, Ben *110:* 209
Verling, John *71:* 27
Verney, John *14:* 225; *75:* 8
Vernon, Ursula *204:* 157
Verrier, Suzanne *5:* 20; *23:* 212
Verroken, Sarah *223:* 178
Versace, Marie *2:* 255
Verstraete, Randy *108:* 193
Vess, Charles *215:* 201; *233:* 182
Vestal, H.B. *9:* 134; *11:* 101; *27:* 25; *34:* 158
Vestergaard, Hope *190:* 203
Vicatan *59:* 146
Vickrey, Robert *45:* 59, 64
Victor, Joan Berg *30:* 193
Vieceli, Emma *210:* 245
Viereck, Ellen *3:* 242; *14:* 229
Vigna, Judith *15:* 293; *102:* 194, 195, 196, 197
Vila, Laura *207:* 172
Vilato, Gaspar E. *5:* 41
Villeneuve, Anne *230:* 189
Villiard, Paul *51:* 178
Vimnera, A. *23:* 154
Vincent, Eric *34:* 98
Vincent, Felix *41:* 237
Vincent, Gabrielle *121:* 175
Vip *45:* 164
Viskupic, Gary *83:* 48
Vitale, Stefano *109:* 71, 107; *114:* 219, 220; *123:* 106; *138:* 232; *180:* 228, 229; *212:* 38; *225:* 191, 192, 193
Vivas, Julie *51:* 67, 69; *96:* 225; *197:* 190; *199:* 71
Voake, Charlotte *114:* 221, 222; *180:* 232
Vo-Dinh, Mai *16:* 272; *60:* 191
Vogel, Ilse-Margret *14:* 230
Voigt, Erna *35:* 228
Vojnar, Kamil *95:* 31; *114:* 4; *115:* 62; *121:* 90; *124:* 72; *130:* 31; *141:* 81; *146:* 196; *150:* 123; *158:* 5, 6; *158:* 154; *171:* 119, 188; *179:* 15; *180:* 112; *203:* 74; *223:* 30; *229:* 43; *230:* 199; *231:* 53, 121, 122; *233:* 3, 4
Vojtech, Anna *42:* 190; *108:* 222, 223; *150:* 203; *174:* 173; *228:* 21; *234:* 181
von Buhler, Cynthia *149:* 237; *162:* 177; *177:* 205; *180:* 77; *185:* 214, 215, 216; *235:* 168; *237:* 144
von Roehl, Angela *126:* 191
von Schmidt, Eric *8:* 62; *50:* 209, 210
von Schmidt, Harold *30:* 80

Vosburgh, Leonard *1:* 161; *7:* 32; *15:* 295, 296; *23:* 110; *30:* 214; *43:* 181
Voss, Tom *127:* 104
Voter, Thomas W. *19:* 3, 9
Vroman, Tom *10:* 29
Vulliamy, Clara *72:* 65
Vyner, Tim *228:* 198

W

Waber, Bernard *47:* 209, 210, 211, 212, 213, 214; *95:* 215, 216, 217; *156:* 203, 205, 206, 207
Waber, Paulis *231:* 189
Wachenje, Benjamin *194:* 170
Wack, Jeff *95:* 140; *110:* 90
Wagner, John *8:* 200; *52:* 104
Wagner, Ken *2:* 59
Wagner, Michael *211:* 159
Wahman, Wendy *218:* 186
Waide, Jan *29:* 225; *36:* 139
Wainwright, Jerry *14:* 85
Waites, Joan *171:* 2; *226:* 184
Wakeen, Sandra *47:* 97
Wakiyama, Hanako *171:* 96; *192:* 236; *200:* 16
Waldherr, Kris *81:* 186
Waldman, Bruce *15:* 297; *43:* 178
Waldman, Neil *35:* 141; *50:* 163; *51:* 180; *54:* 78; *77:* 112; *79:* 162; *82:* 174; *84:* 5, 56, 106; *94:* 232, 233, 234; *96:* 41; *111:* 139; *113:* 9; *118:* 30; *142:* 220, 223; *203:* 173, 174; *238:* 147
Waldrep, Richard *111:* 147; *198:* 202
Waldron, Kevin *230:* 191
Walker, Brian *144:* 128
Walker, Charles *1:* 46; *4:* 59; *5:* 177; *11:* 115; *19:* 45; *34:* 74; *62:* 168; *72:* 218
Walker, Dugald Stewart *15:* 47; *32:* 202; *33:* 112
Walker, Gil *8:* 49; *23:* 132; *34:* 42
Walker, Jeff *55:* 154; *123:* 116
Walker, Jim *10:* 94
Walker, Mort *8:* 213
Walker, Norman *41:* 37; *45:* 58
Walker, Stephen *12:* 229; *21:* 174
Walker, Steve *231:* 119
Wallace, Beverly Dobrin *19:* 259
Wallace, Chad *229:* 198
Wallace, Cly *87:* 93
Wallace, Ian *53:* 176, 177; *56:* 165, 166; *58:* 4; *98:* 4; *101:* 191; *112:* 124; *141:* 197, 198, 199, 200; *151:* 212; *219:* 180, 182
Wallace, John *105:* 228
Wallace, Nancy Elizabeth *141:* 204; *186:* 195, 197, 199; *222:* 191, 192, 193, 194
Wallenta, Adam *123:* 180
Waller, S.E. *24:* 36
Wallner, Alexandra *15:* 120; *156:* 183
Wallner, John C. *9:* 77; *10:* 188; *11:* 28; *14:* 209; *31:* 56, 118; *37:* 64; *51:* 186, 187, 188, 189, 190, 191,192, 193, 194, 195; *52:* 96; *53:* 23, 26; *71:* 99; *73:* 158; *89:* 215; *141:* 9
Wallner, John *162:* 17
Wallower, Lucille *11:* 226
Walotsky, Ron *93:* 87
Walsh, Ellen Stoll *99:* 209; *147:* 219; *194:* 194, 195, 196
Walsh, Rebecca *158:* 193; *217:* 169, 170
Walsh, Vivian *149:* 215; *158:* 227
Walters, Anita *205:* 163
Walters, Audrey *18:* 294
Walther, Tom *31:* 179
Walton, Garry *69:* 149
Walton, Tony *11:* 164; *24:* 209; *153:* 8; *177:* 73; *237:* 50, 52
Waltrip, Lela *9:* 195
Waltrip, Mildred *3:* 209; *37:* 211
Waltrip, Rufus *9:* 195
Wan *12:* 76

Wan, Shelly *212:* 131
Wang, Lin *221:* 179
Wang, Shaoli *216:* 220
Wang, Suling *191:* 183; *213:* 194
Warburton, Sarah *154:* 187
Wappers, G. *121:* 40
Ward, Chad Michael *217:* 121
Ward, Fred *52:* 19
Ward, Helen *72:* 244; *144:* 240, 242
Ward, John *42:* 191; *96:* 54; *97:* 110; *123:* 105; *124:* 71; *173:* 66; *221:* 55
Ward, Keith *2:* 107; *132:* 69
Ward, Leslie *34:* 126; *36:* 87
Ward, Lynd *1:* 99, 132, 133, 150; *2:* 108, 158, 196, 259; *18:* 86; *27:* 56; *29:* 79, 187, 253, 255; *36:* 199,200, 201, 202, 203, 204, 205, 206, 207, 209; *43:* 34; *56:* 28; *60:* 116; *100:* 65
Ward, Peter *37:* 116
Waring, Geoff *172:* 84
Warhola, James *92:* 5; *115:* 85, 87; *118:* 174, 175, 177; *176:* 84; *187:* 189, 190; *223:* 102
Warner, Bob *230:* 5
Warner, Ben *159:* 171
Warner, Peter *14:* 87
Warner, Sally *214:* 210
Warnes, Tim *175:* 159; *202:* 188; *216:* 224
Warnick, Elsa *113:* 223
Warren, Betsy *2:* 101
Warren, Jim *85:* 81
Warren, Marion Cray *14:* 215
Warshaw, Jerry *30:* 197, 198; *42:* 165
Wasden, Kevin *102:* 162
Washington, Nevin *20:* 123
Washington, Phyllis *20:* 123
Wasserman, Amy L. *92:* 110; *209:* 95
Waterman, Stan *11:* 76
Watkins-Pitchford, D.J. *6:* 215, 217
Watling, James *67:* 210; *78:* 112; *101:* 81, 117; *189,* 190; *127:* 119, 120
Watson, Aldren A. *2:* 267; *5:* 94; *13:* 71; *19:* 253; *32:* 220; *42:* 193, 194, 195, 196, 197, 198, 199, 200, 201; *YABC 2:* 202
Watson, G. *83:* 162
Watson, Gary *19:* 147; *36:* 68; *41:* 122; *47:* 139
Watson, J.D. *22:* 86
Watson, Jesse Joshua *197:* 124; *199:* 181; *202:* 136
Watson, Karen *11:* 26
Watson, Mary *117:* 193
Watson, Richard Jesse *62:* 188, 189; *211:* 201
Watson, Wendy *5:* 197; *13:* 101; *33:* 116; *46:* 163; *64:* 12; *74:* 242, 243; *91:* 21; *142:* 228; *215:* 79
Watt, Mélanie *136:* 206; *193:* 211
Wattenberg, Jane *174:* 200; *185:* 46; *187:* 108
Watterson, Bill *66:* 223, 225, 226
Watts, Bernadette *4:* 227; *103:* 182, 183; *230:* 193, 194, 195
Watts, James *59:* 197; *74:* 145; *86:* 124
Watts, John *37:* 149
Watts, Leslie Elizabeth *150:* 207; *165:* 106; *209:* 67
Watts, Sarah *234:* 115
Watts, Stan *116:* 205
Weatherby, Mark Alan *77:* 141
Web, Hannah *228:* 215
Webb, Jennifer *110:* 79
Webb, Lanny *142:* 175
Webb, Sophie *135:* 214
Webber, Helen *3:* 141
Webber, Irma E. *14:* 238
Weber, Erik *56:* 19, 20
Weber, Florence *40:* 153
Weber, Jill *127:* 227, 228; *189:* 163; *208:* 157; *209:* 190, 191; *216:* 46
Weber, Roland *61:* 204
Weber, Sam *190:* 227; *239:* 144
Weber, William J. *14:* 239
Webster, Jean *17:* 241

Weeks, Sarah *162:* 39
Wegman, William *78:* 243
Wegner, Fritz *14:* 250; *20:* 189; *44:* 165; *86:* 62
Weidenear, Reynold H. *21:* 122
Weigel, Jeff *170:* 193
Weihs, Erika *4:* 21; *15:* 299; *72:* 201; *107:* 207, 208
Weil, Lisl *7:* 203; *10:* 58; *21:* 95; *22:* 188,217; *33:* 193
Weiman, Jon *50:* 162, 165; *52:* 103; *54:* 78, 79, 81; *78:* 80; *82:* 107; *93:* 82; *97:* 69; *105:* 179; *193:* 65
Weiner, Greg *215:* 21
Weiner, Sandra *14:* 240
Weiner, Scott *55:* 27
Weinhaus, Karen Ann *53:* 90; *71:* 50; *86:* 124
Weinman, Brad *197:* 20; *233:* 35
Weinstock, Robert *204:* 165, 166
Weisgard, Leonard *1:* 65; *2:* 191, 197, 204, 264, 265; *5:* 108; *21:* 42; *30:* 200, 201, 203, 204; *41:* 47; *44:* 125; *53:* 25; *85:* 196, 198, 200, 201; *100:* 139,207; *YABC 2:* 13
Weisman, David *173:* 47
Weiss, Ellen *44:* 202
Weiss, Emil *1:* 168; *7:* 60
Weiss, Harvey *1:* 145, 223; *27:* 224, 227; *68:* 214; *76:* 245, 246, 247
Weiss, Nicki *33:* 229
Weissman, Bari *49:* 72; *90:* 125; *139:* 142
Weitzman, David L. *172:* 199
Welch, Sheila Kelly *130:* 221
Welkes, Allen *68:* 218
Wellington, Monica *99:* 223; *157:* 259, 260, 261; *222:* 197, 198, 199, 200
Welliver, Norma *76:* 94
Wellner, Fred *127:* 53
Wells, Frances *1:* 183
Wells, H.G. *20:* 194, 200
Wells, Haru *53:* 120, 121
Wells, Robert E. *184:* 208; *239:* 166, 167
Wells, Rosemary *6:* 49; *18:* 297; *60:* 32; *66:* 203; *69:* 215, 216; *114:* 227; *118:* 149, 150; *156:* 188, 189, 190, 191; *207:* 180, 181, 182, 183; *237:* 159, 161, 162
Wells, Rufus III *56:* 111, 113
Wells, Susan *22:* 43
Wendelin, Rudolph *23:* 234
Wengenroth, Stow *37:* 47
Weninger, Brigitte *189:* 192, 194
Werenskiold, Erik *15:* 6; *62:* 17
Werner, Honi *24:* 110; *33:* 41; *88:* 122
Werth, Kurt *7:* 122; *14:* 157; *20:* 214; *39:* 128
Wesson,
West, Harry A. *124:* 38; *227:* 16
Westcott, Nadine Bernard *68:* 46; *84:* 49; *86:* 133; *106:* 199; *111:* 78; *113:* 111; *130:* 224; *139:* 54; *158:* 256; *194:* 199
Westerberg, Christine *29:* 226
Westerduin, Anne *105:* 229
Westerman, Johanna *162:* 206
Weston, Martha *29:* 116; *30:* 213; *33:* 85, 100; *53:* 181, 182, 183, 184; *77:* 95; *80:* 152; *119:* 196,197, 198, 199; *127:* 189; *133:* 196; *209:* 199
Wetherbee, Margaret *5:* 3
Wexler, Jerome *49:* 73; *150:* 129
Whalley, Peter *50:* 49
Whamond, Dave *222:* 203
Whatley, Bruce *186:* 93, 95; *207:* 127; *213:* 183, 184
Wheatley, Arabelle *11:* 231; *16:* 276
Wheeler, Cindy *49:* 205
Wheeler, Dora *44:* 179
Wheelright, Rowland *15:* 81; *YABC 2:* 286
Whelan, Michael *56:* 108; *70:* 27, 29, 67, 68, 148; *74:* 18; *84:* 14; *91:* 195, 196; *95:* 147; *98:* 150, 151; *106:* 157; *113:* 218, 220; *116:* 99, 100
Whelan, Patrick *135:* 145
Whistler, Rex *16:* 75; *30:* 207, 208

White, Beth *216:* 139
White, Craig *110:* 130; *119:* 193; *130:* 33; *179:* 31
White, David Omar *5:* 56; *18:* 6
White, Joan *83:* 225
White, Lee *221:* 176; *223:* 188, 189, 190
White, Martin *51:* 197; *85:* 127
Whitear *32:* 26
Whitehead, Beck *86:* 171
Whitehead, Jenny *221:* 16
Whitehead, S.B. *154:* 132
Whithorne, H.S. *7:* 49
Whitman, Candace *208:* 208
Whitney, George Gillett *3:* 24
Whitney, Jean *99:* 53
Whitson, Paul *102:* 161
Whittam, Geoffrey *30:* 191
Whyte, Mary *96:* 127; *232:* 39
Wiberg, Harald *38:* 127; *93:* 215
Wick, Walter *77:* 128
Wickstrom, Sylvie *106:* 87; *169:* 180; *214:* 110
Wickstrom, Thor *200:* 205
Widener, Terry *105:* 230; *106:* 7; *163:* 23; *200:* 17; *209:* 195; *231:* 12
Wiese, Kurt *3:* 255; *4:* 206; *14:* 17; *17:* 18, 19; *19:* 47; *24:* 152; *25:* 212; *32:* 184; *36:* 211,213, 214, 215, 216, 217, 218; *45:* 161; *100:* 92
Wiesner, David *33:* 47; *51:* 106; *57:* 67; *58:* 55; *64:* 78, 79, 81; *69:* 233; *72:* 247, 248, 249, 251,252, 253, 254; *83:* 134; *104:* 31; *117:* 197, 199, 200, 202; *139:* 223, 224; *151:* 51; *181:* 189, 190
Wiesner, William *4:* 100; *5:* 200, 201; *14:* 262
Wight, Eric *218:* 190; *232:* 195
Wiggins, George *6:* 133
Wijngaard, Juan *111:* 36; *114:* 124; *227:* 136; *230:* 202
Wikkelsoe, Otto *45:* 25, 26
Wikland, Ilon *5:* 113; *8:* 150; *38:* 124, 125, 130; *127:* 162
Wikler, Madeline *114:* 233
Wilbur, C. Keith, M.D. *27:* 228
Wilburn, Kathy *53:* 102; *68:* 234
Wilcox, Cathy *105:* 123
Wilcox, J.A.J. *34:* 122
Wilcox, Lydia *207:* 187
Wilcox, R. Turner *36:* 219
Wild, Jocelyn *46:* 220, 221, 222; *80:* 117
Wilde, George *7:* 139
Wildish, Lee *231:* 34, 193
Wildsmith, Brian *16:* 281, 282; *18:* 170, 171; *66:* 25; *69:* 224, 225, 227; *77:* 103; *83:* 218; *124:* 214,217, 219
Wildsmith, Mike *140:* 229
Wilhelm, Hans *58:* 189, 191; *73:* 157; *77:* 127; *135:* 229, 230, 233, 234; *196:* 209
Wilkin, Eloise *36:* 173; *49:* 208, 209, 210
Wilkinson, Barry *50:* 213
Wilkinson, Gerald *3:* 40
Wilkon, Jozef *31:* 183, 184; *71:* 206, 207, 209; *133:* 222
Wilks, Mike *34:* 24; *44:* 203; *224:* 193
Willems, Mo *154:* 245, 246, 247; *180:* 236, 237, 239; *228:* 204, 208
Willey, Bee *103:* 129; *139:* 159; *173:* 115
Willhoite, Michael A. *71:* 214
William, Maria *168:* 51
Williams, Berkeley, Jr. *64:* 75
Williams, Ferelith Eccles *22:* 238
Williams, Garth *1:* 197; *2:* 49, 270; *4:* 205; *15:* 198, 302, 304, 307; *16:* 34; *18:* 283, 298, 299, 300, 301; *29:* 177, 178, 179, 232, 233, 241, 242, 243, 244, 245, 248; *40:* 106; *66:* 229, 230, 231, 233, 234; *71:* 192; *73:* 218, 219, 220; *78:* 261; *100:* 251, 252, 255; *136:* 117; *YABC 2:* 15, 16, 19
Williams, J. Scott *48:* 28
Williams, Jennifer *102:* 201
Williams, Jenny *60:* 202; *81:* 21; *88:* 71

Williams, Kent *180:* 18
Williams, Kit *44:* 206, 207, 208, 209, 211, 212
Williams, Marcia *97:* 214; *159:* 208, 209
Williams, Maureen *12:* 238
Williams, Patrick *14:* 218
Williams, Richard *44:* 93; *72:* 229; *74:* 133; *78:* 155, 237; *91:* 178; *110:* 212; *136:* 201, 202, 203; *152:* 115
Williams, Sam *124:* 222; *153:* 11; *177:* 201, 202; *180:* 34; *212:* 49; *232:* 155; *238:* 113
Williams, Sophy *135:* 236
Williams, Vera B. *53:* 186, 187, 188, 189; *102:* 201, 202, 203; *210:* 65
Williamson, Alex *177:* 180; *205:* 50
Williamson, Mel *60:* 9
Willingham, Fred *104:* 206; *154:* 157
Willis, Adam *181:* 75; *209:* 11
Willmore, J.T. *54:* 113, 114
Wilsdorf, Anne *180:* 122; *189:* 124; *191:* 195
Wilson, Anne *160:* 114; *224:* 199, 200
Wilson, Charles Banks *17:* 92; *43:* 73
Wilson, Connie *113:* 179
Wilson, Dagmar *10:* 47
Wilson, Dawn *67:* 161; *81:* 120; *113:* 158
Wilson, Edward A. *6:* 24; *16:* 149; *20:* 220, 221; *22:* 87; *26:* 67; *38:* 212, 214, 215, 216, 217
Wilson, Forrest *27:* 231
Wilson, Gahan *35:* 234; *41:* 136
Wilson, George *76:* 87
Wilson, Helen Miranda *140:* 61
Wilson, Jack *17:* 139
Wilson, Janet *77:* 154; *96:* 114; *99:* 219, 220; *153:* 64 *106:* 122; *130:* 210; *145:* 178; *173:* 64
Wilson, John *22:* 240
Wilson, Maurice *46:* 224
Wilson, Patten *35:* 61
Wilson, Peggy *15:* 4; *84:* 20
Wilson, Phil *181:* 29
Wilson, Rowland B. *30:* 170
Wilson, Sarah *50:* 215
Wilson, Tom *33:* 232
Wilson, W.N. *22:* 26
Wilson-Max, Ken *170:* 196; *180:* 181
Wilton, Nicholas *103:* 52; *183:* 111
Wilwerding, Walter J. *9:* 202
Wimmer, Mike *63:* 6; *70:* 121; *75:* 186; *76:* 21,22, 23; *91:* 114; *97:* 45, 68; *98:* 28; *107:* 130; *146:* 21; *149:* 47; *173:* 126; *193:* 21, 25; *194:* 204, 205
Winborn, Marsha *78:* 34; *99:* 70; *192:* 20
Winch, John *165:* 233
Winchester, Linda *13:* 231
Wind, Betty *28:* 158
Windham, Kathryn Tucker *14:* 260
Windham, Sophie *184:* 212
Winfield, Alison *115:* 78; *214:* 121
Winfield, Wayne *72:* 23
Wing, Gary *64:* 147
Wing, Ron *50:* 85
Wingerter, Linda S. *132:* 199; *174:* 181; *200:* 196
Winick, Judd *124:* 227, 228, 229
Winn-Lederer, Ilene *202:* 91
Winnick, Karen B. *211:* 207
Winslow, Will *21:* 124
Winstead, Rosie *180:* 243
Winsten, Melanie Willa *41:* 41
Winter, Jeanette *151:* 240, 241, 242; *184:* 215, 217, 218, 219
Winter, Milo *15:* 97; *19:* 221; *21:* 181, 203, 204, 205; *64:* 19; *YABC 2:* 144
Winter, Paula *48:* 227
Winter, Susan *163:* 177; *182:* 201; *226:* 173
Winters, Greg *70:* 117
Winters, Nina *62:* 194
Wise, Louis *13:* 68
Wiseman, Ann *31:* 187
Wiseman, B. *4:* 233
Wishnefsky, Phillip *3:* 14

Wiskur, Darrell *5:* 72; *10:* 50; *18:* 246
Wisnewski, Andrea *234:* 210
Wisniewski, David *95:* 220, 221
Wisniewski, Robert *95:* 10; *119:* 192
Withee, Maureen *225:* 42
Witschonke, Alan *153:* 149, 150
Witt, Dick *80:* 244
Wittmann, Patrick *162:* 204
Wittman, Sally *30:* 219
Wittner, Dale *99:* 43
Wittwer, Hala *158:* 267; *195:* 80
Woehr, Lois *12:* 5
Wohlberg, Meg *12:* 100; *14:* 197; *41:* 255
Wohnoutka, Mike *137:* 68; *190:* 199; *195:* 218; *205:* 132; *221:* 6; *230:* 206, 207
Wojtowycz, David *167:* 168
Woldin, Beth Weiner *34:* 211
Wolf, Elizabeth *133:* 151; *208:* 175
Wolf, J. *16:* 91
Wolf, Janet *78:* 254
Wolf, Linda *33:* 163
Wolfe, Corey *72:* 213
Wolfe, Frances *216:* 227
Wolfe, Gillian *199:* 193
Wolff, Ashley *50:* 217; *81:* 216; *156:* 216, 217; *170:* 57; *174:* 174; *184:* 72; *203:* 181, 182, 183, 184
Wolff, Glenn *178:* 230
Wolff, Jason *213:* 186
Wolfhard, Steve *235:* 199
Wolfsgruber, Linda *166:* 61
Wondriska, William *6:* 220
Wong, Janet S. *98:* 225; *152:* 43
Wong, Ken *224:* 23
Wong, Nicole *174:* 13; *214:* 216; *215:* 25
Wonsetler, John C. *5:* 168
Wood, Audrey *50:* 221, 222, 223; *81:* 219, 221; *198:* 206
Wood, Don *50:* 220, 225, 226, 228, 229; *81:* 218, 220; *139:* 239, 240
Wood, Grant *19:* 198
Wood, Heather *133:* 108
Wood, Ivor *58:* 17
Wood, Jakki *211:* 209
Wood, Muriel *36:* 119; *77:* 167; *171:* 55; *187:* 46; *235:* 49
Wood, Myron *6:* 220
Wood, Owen *18:* 187; *64:* 202, 204, 205, 206, 208, 210
Wood, Rob *193:* 48
Wood, Ruth *8:* 11
Woodbridge, Curtis *133:* 138; *204:* 113
Wooding, Sharon L. *66:* 237
Woodruff, Liza *132:* 239; *182:* 46, 204
Woodruff, Thomas *171:* 73
Woods, John, Jr. *109:* 142
Woods, Maria *227:* 69
Woodson, Jack *10:* 201
Woodson, Jacqueline *94:* 242
Woodward, Alice *26:* 89; *36:* 81
Wool, David *26:* 27
Wooley, Janet *112:* 75; *227:* 74
Woolman, Steven *106:* 47; *163:* 73
Wooten, Vernon *23:* 70; *51:* 170
Worboys, Evelyn *1:* 166, 167
Word, Reagan *103:* 204
Wormell, Christopher *154:* 251; *202:* 206
Worth, Jo *34:* 143
Worth, Wendy *4:* 133
Wosmek, Frances *29:* 251
Wrenn, Charles L. *38:* 96; *YABC 1:* 20, 21
Wright, Barbara Mullarney *98:* 161
Wright, Cliff *168:* 203
Wright, Dare *21:* 206
Wright-Frierson, Virginia *58:* 194; *110:* 246
Wright, George *YABC 1:* 268
Wright, Joseph *30:* 160
Wronker, Lili Cassel *3:* 247; *10:* 204; *21:* 10
Wu, Donald *200:* 18

Wummer, Amy *154:* 181; *168:* 150; *176:* 85; *201:* 202, 203; *218:* 154; *238:* 143
Wyant, Alexander Helwig *110:* 19
Wyatt, David *97:* 9; *101:* 44; *114:* 194; *140:* 20; *167:* 13; *188:* 48; *227:* 60
Wyatt, Stanley *46:* 210
Wyeth, Andrew *13:* 40; *YABC 1:* 133, 134
Wyeth, Jamie *41:* 257
Wyeth, N.C. *13:* 41; *17:* 252, 253, 254, 255, 256, 257, 258, 259, 264, 265, 266, 267, 268; *18:* 181; *19:* 80, 191, 200; *21:* 57, 183; *22:* 91; *23:* 152; *24:* 28, 99; *35:* 61; *41:* 65; *100:* 206; *YABC1:* 133, 223; *2:* 53, 75, 171, 187, 317
Wyman, Cherie R. *91:* 42
Wynne, Patricia J. *210:* 260; *223:* 184

X

Xuan, YongSheng *119:* 202, 207, 208; *140:* 36; *187:* 21; *226:* 221, 227, 230, 232, 233

Y

Yaccarino, Dan *141:* 208, 209; *147:* 171; *192:* 244, 245; *207:* 168
Yakovetic, Joe *59:* 202; *75:* 85
Yalowitz, Paul *93:* 33; *211:* 92
Yamaguchi, Marianne *85:* 118
Yamasaki, James *167:* 93
Yang, Belle *170:* 198
Yang, Jay *1:* 8; *12:* 239
Yanok, Johnny *236:* 192
Yap, Weda *6:* 176
Yaroslava
    See Mills, Yaroslava Surmach
Yashima, Taro *14:* 84
Yates, John *74:* 249, 250
Yates, Kelly *208:* 214
Yayo *178:* 88; *226:* 235
Yeatts, Tabatha *215:* 210
Yee, Cora *166:* 233
Yee, Wong Herbert *115:* 216, 217; *172:* 204, 205; *194:* 59
Yelchin, Eugene *204:* 4; *232:* 198
Yeo, Brad *135:* 121; *192:* 106
Yerxa, Leo *181:* 195
Yezerski, Thomas F. *162:* 29
Ylla
    See Koffler, Camilla
Yohn, F.C. *23:* 128; *YABC 1:* 269
Yoo, Taeeun *191:* 198
Yorinks, Adrienne *144:* 248; *200:* 214
Yorke, David *80:* 178
Yoshida, Toshi *77:* 231
Yoshikawa, Sachiko *168:* 104; *177:* 28; *181:* 196, 197; *225:* 115
Youll, Paul *91:* 218
Youll, Stephen *92:* 227; *118:* 136, 137; *164:* 248; *202:* 92
Young, Amy L. *185:* 218; *190:* 46
Young, Cybéle *167:* 9
Young, Ed *7:* 205; *10:* 206; *40:* 124; *63:* 142; *74:* 250, 251, 252, 253; *75:* 227; *81:* 159; *83:* 98; *94:* 154; *115:* 160; *137:* 162; *YABC 2:* 242; *173:* 174, 175, 176; *205:* 29; *212:* 82; *221:* 72
Young, Karen Romano *237:* 184
Young, Mary O'Keefe *77:* 95; *80:* 247; *134:* 214; *140:* 213; *211:* 223, 225
Young, Ned *233:* 187
Young, Noela *8:* 221; *89:* 231; *97:* 195; *230:* 145, 146
Young, Paul *190:* 222; *225:* 38
Young, Selina *153:* 12; *201:* 204, 205

Yuen, Sammy, Jr. *223:* 46; *236:* 32
Yum, Hyewon *211:* 228
Yun, Cheng Mung *60:* 143
Yung, Jennifer *220:* 136

Z

Zacharow, Christopher *88:* 98
Zacks, Lewis *10:* 161
Zadig *50:* 58
Zaffo, George *42:* 208
Zagwyn, Deborah Turney *138:* 227
Zahares, Wade *193:* 219
Zaid, Barry *50:* 127; *51:* 201
Zaidenberg, Arthur *34:* 218, 219, 220
Zahedi, Morteza *232:* 2
Zalben, Jane Breskin *7:* 211; *79:* 230, 231, 233; *170:* 202
Zallinger, Jean *4:* 192; *8:* 8, 129; *14:* 273; *68:* 36; *80:* 254; *115:* 219, 220, 222
Zallinger, Rudolph F. *3:* 245
Zakanitch, Robert Rahway *231:* 195
Zakrajsek, Molly *177:* 146
Zappa, Ahmet *180:* 250
Zebot, George *83:* 214
Zecca, Katherine *207:* 195
Zeck, Gerry *40:* 232
Zeff, Joe *181:* 98; *221:* 101
Zeifert, Harriet *154:* 265, 267
Zeiring, Bob *42:* 130
Zeldich, Arieh *49:* 124; *62:* 120
Zeldis, Malcah *86:* 239; *94:* 198; *146:* 265, 266
Zelinsky, Paul O. *14:* 269; *43:* 56; *49:* 218-223; *53:* 111; *68:* 195; *102:* 219, 222, 221, 222; *154:* 255, 256, 257; *171:* 141; *185:* 96
Zelvin, Diana *72:* 190; *76:* 101; *93:* 207
Zemach, Kaethe *149:* 250
Zemach, Margot *3:* 270; *8:* 201; *21:* 210, 211; *27:* 204, 205, 210; *28:* 185; *49:* 22, 183, 224; *53:* 151; *56:* 146; *70:* 245, 246; *92:* 74
Zeman, Ludmila *153* 212
Zemsky, Jessica *10:* 62
Zepelinsky, Paul *35:* 93
Zerbetz, Evon *127:* 34; *158:* 109
Zezejl, Daniel *197:* 74
Zhang, Ange *101:* 190; *172:* 41
Zhang, Son Nang *163:* 113; *170:* 206
Ziegler, Jack *84:* 134
Zimdars, Berta *129:* 155
Zimet, Jay *147:* 94; *152:* 74; *196:* 75
Zimic, Tricia *72:* 95
Zimmer, Dirk *38:* 195; *49:* 71; *56:* 151; *65:* 214; *84:* 159; *89:* 26; *147:* 224
Zimmer, Tracie Vaughn *169:* 183
Zimmerman, Andrea *192:* 49, 50
Zimmermann, H. Werner *101:* 223; *112:* 197
Zimnik, Reiner *36:* 224
Zingone, Robin *180:* 134; *236:* 147, 148
Zinkeisen, Anna *13:* 106
Zinn, David *97:* 97
Zoellick, Scott *33:* 231
Zollars, Jaime *190:* 190
Zonia, Dhimitri *20:* 234, 235
Zorn, Peter A., Jr. *142:* 157
Zudeck, Darryl *58:* 129; *63:* 98; *80:* 52
Zug, Mark *88:* 131; *204:* 169
Zulewski, Tim *164:* 95; *232:* 59
Zuma *99:* 36
Zvorykin, Boris *61:* 155
Zweifel, Francis *14:* 274; *28:* 187
Zwerger, Lisbeth *54:* 176, 178; *66:* 246, 247, 248; *130:* 230, 231, 232, 233; *181:* 92; *194:* 224, 225, 226
Zwinger, Herman H. *46:* 227
Zwolak, Paul *67:* 69, 71, 73, 74

Author Index

The following index gives the number of the volume in which an author's biographical sketch, Autobiography Feature, Brief Entry, or Obituary appears.

This index includes references to all entries in the following series, which are also published by The Gale Group.

YABC—*Yesterday's Authors of Books for Children: Facts and Pictures about Authors and Illustrators of Books for Young People from Early Times to 1960*
CLR—*Children's Literature Review: Excerpts from Reviews, Criticism, and Commentary on Books for Children*
SAAS—*Something about the Author Autobiography Series*

A

Aardema, Verna 1911-2000 .... *107*
  Obituary *119*
  Earlier sketches in SATA *4, 68*
  See also CLR *17*
  See also SAAS *8*
Aaron, Chester 1923- *216*
  Autobiography Feature *216*
  Earlier sketches in SATA *9, 74*
  See also SAAS *12*
Aaseng, Nate
  See Aaseng, Nathan
Aaseng, Nathan 1953- *236*
  Autobiography Feature *236*
  Brief entry *38*
  Earlier sketches in SATA *51, 88, 172*
  See also CLR *54*
  See also SAAS *12*
Abadzis, Nick 1965- *193*
Abalos, Rafael 1956-
  See Abalos, Rafael
Abalos, Rafael 1956- *197*
Abbas, Jailan 1952- *91*
Abbey, Lynn
  See Abbey, Marilyn Lorraine
Abbey, Marilyn Lorraine 1948- *156*
Abbott, Alice
  See Borland, Kathryn Kilby
  and Speicher, Helen Ross S(mith)
Abbott, Jacob 1803-1879 .... *22*
Abbott, Manager Henry
  See Stratemeyer, Edward L.
Abbott, R(obert) Tucker 1919-1995 .... *61*
  Obituary *87*
Abbott, Sarah
  See Zolotow, Charlotte
Abbott, Tony 1952- *205*
  Earlier sketch in SATA *159*
Abdelsayed, Cindy 1962- *123*
Abdul, Raoul 1929- *12*
Abeele, Veronique van den *196*
Abel, Raymond 1911- *12*
Abell, Kathleen 1938- *9*
Abelove, Joan *110*
Abels, Harriette S(heffer) 1926- *50*
Abercrombie, Barbara 1939- *182*
  Earlier sketch in SATA *16*

Abercrombie, Barbara Mattes
  See Abercrombie, Barbara
Abercrombie, Lynn
  See Sorrells, Walter
Abernethy, Robert G(ordon) 1927- *5*
Abisch, Roslyn Kroop 1927- *9*
Abisch, Roz
  See Abisch, Roslyn Kroop
Ablow, Gail 1962- *198*
Abodaher, David J. (Naiph) 1919- *17*
Abolafia, Yossi 1944-
  See Abulafia, Yossi
Abolivier, Aurelie *219*
Abouzeid, Chris *175*
Abrahall, Clare Hoskyns
  See Hoskyns-Abrahall, Clare (Constance Drury)
Abrahams, Hilary (Ruth) 1938- *29*
Abrahams, Peter 1947- *194*
Abrahams, Robert David 1905-1998 .... *4*
Abramovitz, Anita (Zeltner Brooks) 1914- *5*
Abrams, Joy 1941- *16*
Abrams, Lawrence F. *58*
  Brief entry *47*
Abramson, Andra Serlin *237*
Abrashkin, Raymond 1911-1960 .... *50*
Abulafia, Yossi 1944- *177*
  Brief entry *46*
  Earlier sketch in SATA *60*
Acampora, Paul *175*
Accardo, Anthony *191*
Acer, David *206*
Achebe, Albert Chinualumogu
  See Achebe, Chinua
Achebe, Chinua 1930- *40*
  Brief entry *38*
  Earlier sketch in SATA *38*
  See also CLR *156*
Acheson, Alison 1964- *222*
Ackerman, Diane 1948- *102*
Ackerman, Eugene (Francis) 1888-1974 ...... *10*
Ackerman, Karen 1951- *126*
Ackerman, Peter *234*
Ackerman, Susan Yoder 1945- *92*
Ackison, Wendy Wassink 1956- *103*
Ackley, Peggy Jo 1955- *58*
Ackroyd, Peter 1949- *153*
Acorn, John (Harrison) 1958- *79*
Acredolo, Linda (Potter) 1947- *159*

Acs, Laszlo (Bela) 1931- *42*
  Brief entry *32*
Acuff, Selma Boyd 1924- *45*
Ada, Alma Flor 1938- *222*
  Autobiography Feature *222*
  Earlier sketches in SATA *43, 84, 143, 181*
  See also CLR *62*
Adair, Gilbert 1944-2011 .... *98*
Adair, Ian 1942- *53*
Adair, Margaret Weeks (?)-1971 .... *10*
Adam, Cornel
  See Lengyel, Cornel Adam
Adam, Mark
  See Alexander, Marc
Adam, Paul 1958- *231*
Adam, Robert 1948- *93*
Adams, Adrienne 1906- *90*
  Earlier sketch in SATA *8*
  See also CLR *73*
Adams, Andy 1859-1935
  See YABC *1*
Adams, Barbara Johnston 1943- *60*
Adams, Beth *236*
Adams, Bruin
  See Ellis, Edward S.
Adams, Captain Bruin
  See Ellis, Edward S.
Adams, Captain J. F. C.
  See Ellis, Edward S.
Adams, Dale
  See Quinn, Elisabeth
Adams, Daniel
  See Nicole, Christopher
Adams, Debra
  See Speregen, Devra Newberger
Adams, Diane 1960- *217*
Adams, Douglas 1952-2001 .... *116*
  Obituary *128*
Adams, Douglas Noel
  See Adams, Douglas
Adams, Edith
  See Shine, Deborah
Adams, Florence 1932- *61*
Adams, Georgie 1945- *216*
Adams, Harriet S(tratemeyer) 1892(?)-1982 .. *1*
  Obituary *29*
Adams, Harrison
  See Rathborne, St. George (Henry)
  and Stratemeyer, Edward L.

Adams, Hazard 1926- 6
Adams, Hazard Simeon
    See Adams, Hazard
Adams, John Anthony 1944- 67
Adams, Kathryn 224
Adams, Laurie 1941- 33
Adams, Lowell
    See Joseph, James (Herz)
Adams, Nicholas
    See Pine, Nicholas
Adams, Nicholas
    See Smith, Sherwood
Adams, Nicholas
    See Doyle, Debra
    and Macdonald, James D.
Adams, Pam 1919- 112
Adams, Pamela
    See Adams, Pam
Adams, Richard 1920- 69
    Earlier sketch in SATA 7
    See also CLR 121
Adams, Richard George
    See Adams, Richard
Adams, Ruth Joyce 14
Adams, S.J.
    See Selzer, Adam
Adams, Tricia
    See Kite, Pat
Adams, William Taylor 1822-1897 28
Adam Smith, Janet (Buchanan) 1905-1999 .. 63
Adamson, Gareth 1925-1982(?) 46
    Obituary 30
Adamson, George 1906-1989
    Obituary 63
Adamson, George (Worsley) 1913-2005 30
Adamson, Graham
    See Groom, Arthur William
Adamson, Joy(-Friederike Victoria)
    1910-1980 11
    Obituary 22
Adamson, Wendy Writson 1942- 22
Addasi, Maha 1968- 205
Addison, Kenneth 1949(?)-2005 187
Addison, Kenneth L.
    See Addison, Kenneth
Addona, Angelo F. 1925- 14
Addy, Sean 1976- 222
Addy, Sharon Hart 1943- 192
    Earlier sketch in SATA 108
Addy, Ted
    See Winterbotham, R(ussell) R(obert)
Adelberg, Doris
    See Orgel, Doris
Adelson, Leone 1908- 11
Adinolfi, JoAnn 176
Adkins, Jan 1944- 210
    Autobiography Feature 210
    Earlier sketches in SATA 8, 69, 144
    See also CLR 77
    See also SAAS 19
Adl, Shirin 1975- 225
Adler, C. S. 1932- 126
    Earlier sketches in SATA 26, 63, 102
    See also CLR 78
    See also SAAS 15
Adler, Carole Schwerdtfeger
    See Adler, C. S.
Adler, David A. 1947- 231
    Earlier sketches in SATA 14, 70, 106, 151,
    178
    See also CLR 108
Adler, Emily 230
Adler, Irene
    See Penzler, Otto
    and Storr, Catherine (Cole)
Adler, Irving 1913- 29
    Autobiography Feature 164
    Earlier sketch in SATA 1
    See also CLR 27
    See also SAAS 15
Adler, Larry 1939- 36

Adler, Peggy 22
Adler, Ruth 1915-1968 1
Adlerman, Daniel (Ezra) 1963- 163
    Earlier sketch in SATA 96
Adlerman, Kim
    See Adlerman, Kimberly M(arie)
Adlerman, Kimberly M(arie) 1964- 163
    Earlier sketch in SATA 96
Adoff, Arnold 1935- 96
    Earlier sketches in SATA 5, 57
    See also CLR 7
    See also SAAS 15
Adoff, Jaime 163
Adoff, Jaime Levi
    See Adoff, Jaime
Adorjan, Carol (Madden) 1934- 71
    Earlier sketch in SATA 10
Adornetto, Alexandra 1992- 236
Adrian, Frances
    See Polland, Madeleine A(ngela Cahill)
Adrian, Mary
    See Jorgensen, Mary Venn
Adshead, Gladys L(ucy) 1896-1985 3
Aesop 620(?)B.C.-560(?)B.C. 64
    See also CLR 14
Aesop, Abraham
    See Newbery, John
Affabee, Eric
    See Stine, R.L.
Agapida, Fray Antonio
    See Irving, Washington
Agard, John 1949- 223
    Earlier sketch in SATA 138
Agard, Nadema 1948- 18
Agarwal, Deepa 1947- 141
Agee, Jon 1960- 196
    Earlier sketches in SATA 116, 157
Agell, Charlotte 1959- 214
    Earlier sketches in SATA 99, 150
Agent Orange
    See Moseley, James W(illett)
Aghill, Gordon
    See Garrett, Randall
    and Silverberg, Robert
Agle, Nan Hayden 1905- 3
    See also SAAS 10
Agnew, Edith J(osephine) 1897-1988 11
Agnew, Lincoln 222
Agonito, Joseph 177
Agonito, Rosemary 1937- 177
Aguilar, David 214
Aguilar, David A.
    See Aguilar, David
Ahearn, Janet Reed 236
Ahern, Margaret McCrohan 1921- 10
Ahl, Anna Maria 1926- 32
Ahlberg, Allan 1938- 214
    Brief entry 35
    Earlier sketches in SATA 68, 120, 165
    See also CLR 18
Ahlberg, Janet 1944-1994 120
    Brief entry 32
    Obituary 83
    Earlier sketch in SATA 68
    See also CLR 18
Ahlberg, Jessica 1980- 229
Aho, Julia Kay
    See Kay, Julia
Aichinger, Helga 1937- 4
Aiken, Clarissa (M.) Lorenz 1899-1992 12
    Obituary 109
Aiken, Conrad 1889-1973 30
    Earlier sketch in SATA 3
Aiken, Conrad Potter
    See Aiken, Conrad
Aiken, Joan (Delano) 1924-2004 73
    Autobiography Feature 109
    Obituary 152
    Earlier sketches in SATA 2, 30
    See also CLR 90
    See also SAAS 1

Aillaud, Cindy Lou 1955- 184
Ainsley, Alix
    See Steiner, Barbara A(nnette)
Ainsworth, Catherine Harris 1910- 56
Ainsworth, Norma 1911-1987 9
Ainsworth, Ruth (Gallard) 1908- 73
    Earlier sketch in SATA 7
Ainsworth, William Harrison 1805-1882 24
Aistrop, Jack 1916- 14
Aitken, Amy 1952- 54
    Brief entry 40
Aitken, Dorothy 1916- 10
Aitmatov, Chingiz 1928-2008 56
Aitmatov, Chingiz Torekulovich
    See Aitmatov, Chingiz
Ajhar, Brian 1957- 220
Akaba, Suekichi 1910- 46
Akbarpour, Ahmad 1970- 232
Akers, Floyd
    See Baum, L. Frank
Akib, Jamel 181
Akin, Sara Laux 236
Aks, Patricia 1926-1994 68
al Abdullah, Rania
    See Rania, Queen of Jordan
Alagoa, Ebiegberi Joe 1933- 108
Alain
    See Brustlein, Daniel
Alajalov, Constantin 1900-1987
    Obituary 53
Alalou, Ali 203
Alalou, Elizabeth 203
Alan, David
    See Horsfield, Alan
Alan, Robert
    See Silverstein, Robert Alan
Alarcon, Francisco X. 1954- 215
    Earlier sketch in SATA 104
Alarcon, Francisco Xavier
    See Alarcon, Francisco X.
Alarcon, Karen Beaumont
    See Beaumont, Karen
Albarn, Jessica 1971- 238
Albee, Sarah 1962- 231
Albert, Burton 1936- 22
Albert, Louise 1928- 157
Albert, Michael 1966- 202
Albert, Richard E. 1909-1999 82
Albert, Susan Wittig 1940- 107
Alberts, Frances Jacobs 1907-1989 14
Albertson, Susan
    See Wojciechowski, Susan
Albion, Lee Smith 29
Alborough, Jez 1959- 149
    Earlier sketch in SATA 86
Albrecht, Lillie (Vanderveer H.)
    1894-1985 12
Albyn, Carole Lisa 1955- 83
Alchemy, Jack
    See Gershator, David
Alcock, Gudrun 1908- 56
    Brief entry 33
Alcock, Vivien (Dolores) 1924-2003 76
    Brief entry 38
    Obituary 148
    Earlier sketch in SATA 45
    See also CLR 26
Alcorn, John 1935- 31
    Brief entry 30
Alcorn, Stephen 1958- 207
    Earlier sketch in SATA 110
Alcott, Louisa May 1832-1888 100
    See also YABC 1
    See also CLR 109
Alda, Arlene 1933- 205
    Brief entry 36
    Earlier sketches in SATA 44, 106, 158
    See also CLR 93
Alden, Isabella (Macdonald) 1841-1930 115
    See also YABC 2

Alden, Sue
  See Francis, Dorothy
Alderman, Clifford Lindsey 1902-1988 .... *3*
Alderson, Sue Ann 1940- *59*
  Brief entry *48*
Alding, Peter
  See Jeffries, Roderic
Aldis, Dorothy (Keeley) 1896-1966 .... *2*
Aldiss, Brian W. 1925- *34*
Aldiss, Brian Wilson
  See Aldiss, Brian W.
Aldon, Adair
  See Meigs, Cornelia Lynde
Aldous, Allan (Charles) 1911- *27*
Aldrich, Ann
  See Meaker, Marijane
Aldrich, Bess Streeter 1881-1954
  See CLR *70*
Aldrich, Thomas (Bailey) 1836-1907 .... *114*
  Earlier sketch in SATA *17*
Aldridge, (Harold Edward) James 1918- *87*
Aldridge, Josephine Haskell *14*
Aldridge, Sheila 1974- *192*
Aleas, Richard
  See Ardai, Charles
Alegria, Malin 1974(?)- *190*
Alegria, Ricardo E(nrique) 1921- *6*
Aleksin, Anatolii Georgievich 1924- *36*
Alenov, Lydia 1948- *61*
Alex, Ben (a pseudonym) 1946- *45*
Alex, Marlee (a pseudonym) 1948- *45*
Alexander, Alma 1963- *217*
Alexander, Anna B(arbara Cooke) 1913- *1*
Alexander, Anne
  See Alexander, Anna B(arbara Cooke)
Alexander, Claire *228*
Alexander, Ellen 1938- *91*
Alexander, Frances (Laura) 1888-1979 .... *4*
Alexander, Heather 1967- *232*
Alexander, Janet 1907-1994 .... *97*
  Earlier sketch in SATA *1*
Alexander, Jill S. 1964- *223*
Alexander, Jill Shurbet
  See Alexander, Jill S.
Alexander, Jocelyn Anne Arundel 1930- *22*
Alexander, Linda 1935- *2*
Alexander, Lloyd 1924-2007 .... *135*
  Obituary *182*
  Earlier sketches in SATA *3, 49, 81, 129*
  See also CLR *48*
  See also SAAS *19*
Alexander, Lloyd Chudley
  See Alexander, Lloyd
Alexander, Marc 1929- *117*
Alexander, Martha 1920- *136*
  Earlier sketches in SATA *11, 70*
Alexander, Rae Pace
  See Alexander, Raymond Pace
Alexander, Raymond Pace 1898-1974 .... *22*
Alexander, R.C. *232*
Alexander, Robert *200*
Alexander, Robert C.
  See Alexander, R.C.
Alexander, Rod
  See Pellowski, Michael (Joseph)
Alexander, Sally Hobart 1943- *84*
Alexander, Sue 1933-2008 .... *136*
  Obituary *195*
  Earlier sketches in SATA *12, 89*
  See also SAAS *15*
Alexander, Vincent Arthur 1925-1980
  Obituary *23*
Alexeieff, Alexandre A. 1901-1979 .... *14*
Alger, Horatio, Jr.
  See Stratemeyer, Edward L.
Alger, Horatio, Jr. 1832-1899 .... *16*
  See also CLR *170*
Alger, Leclaire (Gowans) 1898-1969 .... *15*
Aliki
  See Brandenberg, Aliki
Alkema, Chester Jay 1932- *12*

Al-Khalili, Jim 1962- *124*
Alkiviades, Alkis 1953- *105*
Alko, Selina 1968- *218*
Alkouatli, Claire *186*
Allaby, John Michael
  See Allaby, Michael
Allaby, Michael 1933- *167*
Allamand, Pascale 1942- *12*
Allan, Mabel Esther 1915-1998 .... *75*
  Earlier sketches in SATA *5, 32*
  See also CLR *43*
  See also SAAS *11*
Allan, Nicholas 1956- *123*
  Earlier sketch in SATA *79*
Allan-Meyer, Kathleen 1918- *51*
  Brief entry *46*
Allard, Harry, Jr. 1928- *216*
  Earlier sketches in SATA *42, 102*
  See also CLR *85*
Allard, Harry G.
  See Allard, Harry, Jr.
Allee, Marjorie Hill 1890-1945 .... *17*
Allen, Adam
  See Epstein, Beryl
  and Epstein, Samuel
Allen, Alex B.
  See Heide, Florence Parry
Allen, Allyn
  See Eberle, Irmengarde
Allen, Betsy
  See Harrison, Elizabeth (Allen) Cavanna
Allen, Bob 1961- *76*
Allen, Constance
  See Albee, Sarah
Allen, Crystal *239*
Allen, Gertrude E(lizabeth) 1888-1984 .... *9*
Allen, Grace
  See Hogarth, Grace (Weston Allen)
Allen, Jeffrey (Yale) 1948- *42*
Allen, John
  See Perry, Ritchie (John Allen)
Allen, Jonathan 1957- *177*
  Earlier sketch in SATA *131*
Allen, Jonathan Dean
  See Allen, Jonathan
Allen, Joy 1948- *217*
Allen, Judy (Christina) 1941- *124*
  Earlier sketch in SATA *80*
Allen, Kenneth S. 1913-1981 .... *56*
Allen, Leroy 1912- *11*
Allen, Linda 1925- *33*
Allen, Marjorie 1931- *22*
Allen, Maury 1932-2010 .... *26*
Allen, Merritt Parmelee 1892-1954 .... *22*
Allen, Nancy Kelly 1949- *171*
  Earlier sketch in SATA *127*
Allen, Nina (Stroemgren) 1935- *22*
Allen, Pamela (Kay) 1934- *123*
  Earlier sketches in SATA *50, 81*
  See also CLR *44*
Allen, Raul *205*
Allen, Rodney F. 1938-1999 .... *27*
Allen, Roger MacBride 1957- *105*
Allen, Ruth
  See Peterson, Esther (Allen)
Allen, Samuel W(ashington) 1917- *9*
Allen, T. D.
  See Allen, Terril Diener
Allen, Terril Diener 1908- *35*
Allen, Terry D.
  See Allen, Terril Diener
Allen, Thomas B. 1929- *193*
  Earlier sketches in SATA *45, 140*
Allen, Thomas Benton
  See Allen, Thomas B.
Allen, Tom
  See Allen, Thomas B.
Allende, Isabel 1942- *163*
  See also CLR *171*
Allerton, Mary
  See Govan, (Mary) Christine Noble

Alley, Robert W.
  See Alley, R.W.
Alley, R.W. *211*
  Earlier sketch in SATA *169*
Alley, Zoe B. *214*
Alleyn, Ellen
  See Rossetti, Christina
Allington, Richard L(loyd) 1947- *39*
  Brief entry *35*
Allison, Amy 1956- *138*
Allison, Bob *14*
Allison, Diane Worfolk *78*
Allison, Jennifer *173*
Allison, Linda 1948- *43*
Allison, Margaret
  See Klam, Cheryl
Allman, Barbara 1950- *137*
Allmendinger, David F(rederick), Jr. 1938- . *35*
Allred, Alexandra Powe 1965- *144*
Allred, Gordon T(hatcher) 1930- *10*
Allsop, Kenneth 1920-1973 .... *17*
Allsopp, Sophie *188*
Alma, Ann 1946- *201*
Almedingen, E. M.
  See Almedingen, Martha Edith von
Almedingen, Martha Edith von 1898-1971 .... *3*
Almon, Russell
  See Clevenger, William R.
  and Downing, David A(lmon)
Almond, David 1951- *233*
  Earlier sketches in SATA *114, 158*
  See also CLR *168*
Almond, Linda Stevens 1881(?)-1987
  Obituary *50*
Almquist, Don 1929- *11*
Alonzo, Sandra *199*
Alphin, Elaine Marie 1955- *232*
  Autobiography Feature *139*
  Earlier sketches in SATA *80, 130, 139*
Alsenas, Linas 1979- *186*
Alsop, Mary O'Hara 1885-1980 .... *34*
  Obituary *24*
  Earlier sketch in SATA *2*
Alter, Anna 1974- *206*
  Earlier sketch in SATA *135*
Alter, Judith 1938- *101*
  Earlier sketch in SATA *52*
Alter, Judith MacBain
  See Alter, Judith
Alter, Judy
  See Alter, Judith
Alter, Robert Edmond 1925-1965 .... *9*
Alter, Stephen 1956- *187*
Althea
  See Braithwaite, Althea
Altman, Linda Jacobs 1943- *21*
Altman, Suzanne
  See Orgel, Doris
  and Schecter, Ellen
Alton, Steve *169*
Altschuler, Franz 1923- *45*
Altsheler, Joseph A(lexander) 1862-1919
  See YABC *1*
Alvarez, John
  See del Rey, Lester
Alvarez, Joseph A. 1930- *18*
Alvarez, Julia 1950- *129*
al-Windawi, Thura
  See Windawi, Thura al-
Alyer, Philip A.
  See Stratemeyer, Edward L.
Amado, Elisa *193*
Amann, Janet 1951- *79*
Amateau, Gigi 1964- *233*
Amato, Carol A. 1942- *92*
Amato, Mary 1961- *178*
  Earlier sketch in SATA *140*
Ambrose, Stephen E. 1936-2002 .... *138*
  Earlier sketch in SATA *40*
Ambrose, Stephen Edward
  See Ambrose, Stephen E.

Ambrus, Gyozo Laszlo 1935- 1
See also SAAS 4
Ambrus, Victor G.
See Ambrus, Gyozo Laszlo
Amend, Bill 1962- 147
Amerman, Lockhart 1911-1969 3
Ames, Evelyn 1908-1990 13
Obituary 64
Ames, Gerald 1906-1993 11
Obituary 74
Ames, Lee J. 1921-2011 151
Earlier sketch in SATA 3
Ames, Lee Judah
See Ames, Lee J.
Ames, Mildred 1919-1994 85
Earlier sketches in SATA 22, 81
Amico, Tom 1960(?)- 176
Amit, Ofra 1966- 205
Ammon, Richard 1942- 124
Amon, Aline 1928- 9
Amory, Jay
See Lovegrove, James
Amoss, Berthe 1925- 112
Earlier sketch in SATA 5
Amstutz, Andre 1925- 214
Anastasio, Dina 1941- 94
Brief entry 30
Earlier sketch in SATA 37
Anaya, Rudolfo 1937-
See CLR 129
Anaya, Rudolfo A.
See Anaya, Rudolfo
Anaya, Rudolpho Alfonso
See Anaya, Rudolfo
Anckarsvard, Karin Inez Maria 1915-1969 6
Ancona, George 1929- 208
Autobiography Feature 208
Earlier sketches in SATA 12, 85, 145, 192
See also SAAS 18
Anders, C. J.
See Bennett, Cherie
Anders, Isabel 1946- 101
Anders, Lou 176
Andersdatter, Karla M. 1938- 34
Andersen, Bethanne 1954- 191
Andersen, Hans Christian 1805-1875 100
See also YABC 1
See also CLR 113
Andersen, Ted
See Boyd, Waldo T.
Andersen, Yvonne 1932- 27
Anderson, Bernice G(oudy) 1894-1997 33
Anderson, Bob 1944- 139
Earlier sketch in SATA 136
Anderson, Brad 1924- 33
Brief entry 31
Anderson, Bradley Jay
See Anderson, Brad
Anderson, Brian 1974- 211
Anderson, C. C.
See Anderson, Catherine Corley
Anderson, C(larence) W(illiam) 1891-1971 . 11
Anderson, Carolyn Dunn
See Dunn, Carolyn
Anderson, Catherine C.
See Anderson, Catherine Corley
Anderson, Catherine Corley 1909-2001 72
See Lee, Cora
Anderson, Clifford
See Gardner, Richard (M.)
Anderson, Daryl Shon 1963- 93
Anderson, Dave
See Anderson, David
Anderson, David 1929- 60
Anderson, Derek 1969- 169
Anderson, Eloise Adell 1927- 9
Anderson, George
See Groom, Arthur William
Anderson, Grace Fox 1932- 43

Anderson, J(ohn) R(ichard) L(ane)
1911-1981 15
Obituary 27
Anderson, Jessica Lee 1980- 224
Anderson, Jodi Lynn 182
Anderson, John David 197
Anderson, John L. 1905- 2
Anderson, Joy 1928- 1
Anderson, Kevin J. 1962- 117
Earlier sketch in SATA 74
Anderson, Kevin James
See Anderson, Kevin J.
Anderson, Kirsty 1978- 108
Anderson, K.J.
See Moesta, Rebecca
Anderson, K.J.
See Anderson, Kevin J.
Anderson, Laurie Halse 1961- 186
Earlier sketches in SATA 95, 132
See also CLR 138
Anderson, LaVere Francis Shoenfelt
1907-1998 27
Anderson, Leone Castell 1923- 53
Brief entry 49
Anderson, Lisa G. 1963- 108
Anderson, Lonzo
See Anderson, John L.
Anderson, Lucia (Lewis) 1922- 10
Anderson, Madelyn Klein 1926-2005 28
Anderson, Margaret J. 1931- 234
Autobiography Feature 234
Earlier sketch in SATA 27
See also SAAS 8
Anderson, Marilyn D. 1943- 144
Anderson, Mary 1939- 82
Earlier sketch in SATA 7
See also SAAS 23
Anderson, Matthew Tobin
See Anderson, M.T.
Anderson, Mona 1910-2004 40
Anderson, Mrs. Melvin
See Anderson, Catherine Corley
Anderson, M.T. 1968- 182
Earlier sketches in SATA 97, 146
Anderson, Norman Dean 1928- 22
Anderson, Peggy Perry 1953- 179
Earlier sketch in SATA 84
Anderson, Poul 1926-2001 90
Autobiography Feature 106
Brief entry 39
See also CLR 58
Anderson, Poul William
See Anderson, Poul
Anderson, Rachel 1943- 86
Earlier sketch in SATA 34
See also SAAS 18
Anderson, Rebecca J.
See Anderson, R.J.
Anderson, Rebecca M.
See Moesta, Rebecca
Anderson, Rebecca Moesta
See Moesta, Rebecca
Anderson, Richard
See Anderson, J(ohn) R(ichard) L(ane)
Anderson, R.J. 1970(?)- 216
Anderson, Sara 173
Anderson, Scoular 201
Anderson, (Tom) Scoular 138
Anderson, Stephanie 1976- 225
Anderson, Susan 1952- 90
Anderson, Thomas Scoular
See Anderson, Scoular
Anderson, W. B.
See Schultz, James Willard
Anderson, Wayne 1946- 202
Earlier sketches in SATA 56, 147
Andersson, Kenneth 1970- 200
Andre, Evelyn M. 1924- 27
Andre, Evelyn Marie
See Andre, Evelyn M.

Andreasen, Dan 227
Earlier sketch in SATA 186
Andreassen, Karl
See Boyd, Waldo T.
Andreassi, K. Robert
See DeCandido, Keith R.A.
Andree, Louise
See Coury, Louise Andree
Andres, Kristina 1971- 233
Andrew, Ian 1962- 166
Earlier sketch in SATA 116
Andrew, Ian Peter
See Andrew, Ian
Andrew, Prudence (Hastings) 1924- 87
Andrews, Benny 1930-2006 31
Obituary 178
Andrews, Eleanor Lattimore
See Lattimore, Eleanor Frances
Andrews, Elton V.
See Pohl, Frederik
Andrews, F(rank) Emerson 1902-1978 22
Andrews, J(ames) S(ydney) 1934- 4
Andrews, Jan 1942- 167
Brief entry 49
Earlier sketches in SATA 58, 98
Andrews, Julie 1935- 153
Earlier sketch in SATA 7
See also CLR 85
Andrews, Laura
See Coury, Louise Andree
Andrews, Roy Chapman 1884-1960 19
Andrews, Tamra 1959- 129
Andrews, V(irginia) C(leo) 1924(?)-1986
Obituary 50
Andrews, Wendy
See Sharmat, Marjorie Weinman
Andrews, William G. 1930- 74
Andrews, William George
See Andrews, William G.
Andrezel, Pierre
See Blixen, Karen
Andriani, Renee
See Williams-Andriani, Renee
Andriola, Alfred J. 1912-1983
Obituary 34
Andrist, Ralph K. 1914-2004 45
Andronik, Catherine M. 189
Andryszewski, Tricia 1956- 148
Earlier sketch in SATA 88
Anelli, Melissa 1979- 215
Angaramo, Roberta 1974- 229
Angel, Ann 1952- 192
Angel, Carl 178
Angel, Marie 1923- 47
Angeles, Peter A. 1931- 40
Angeletti, Roberta 1964- 124
Angeli, Marguerite (Lofft) de
See de Angeli, Marguerite (Lofft)
Angell, Judie 1937- 78
Earlier sketch in SATA 22
See also CLR 33
Angell, Madeline 1919- 18
Angelo, Valenti 1897- 14
Angelou, Maya 1928- 136
Earlier sketch in SATA 49
See also CLR 53
Angier, Bradford -1997 12
Angle, Kimberly Greene 203
Angle, Paul M(cClelland) 1900-1975
Obituary 20
Anglund, Joan Walsh 1926- 2
See also CLR 94
Ango, Fan D.
See Longyear, Barry B(rookes)
Angrist, Stanley W(olff) 1933- 4
Anhalt, Ariela 1990(?)- 227
Anholt, Catherine 1958- 131
Earlier sketch in SATA 74
Anholt, Laurence 1959- 141
Earlier sketch in SATA 74

Aninno, J.G.
  See Annino, Jan Godown
Anita
  See Daniel, Anita
Anmar, Frank
  See Nolan, William F.
Annett, Cora
  See Scott, Cora Annett (Pipitone)
Annie-Jo
  See Blanchard, Patricia
  and Suhr, Joanne
Annino, Jan Godown 1952- 228
Annixter, Jane
  See Sturtzel, Jane Levington
Annixter, Paul
  See Sturtzel, Howard A(llison)
Anno, Mitsumasa 1926- 157
  Earlier sketches in SATA *5, 38, 77*
  See also CLR *122*
Anrooy, Francine Van
  See Van Anrooy, Francine
Ansary, Mir Tamim 1948- 140
Anstey, Caroline 1958- 81
Antell, Will D. 1935- 31
Anthony, Barbara
  See Barber, Antonia
Anthony, C. L.
  See Smith, Dorothy Gladys
Anthony, Edward 1895-1971 21
Anthony, Joelle 232
Anthony, John
  See Beckett, Ronald Brymer
  and Ciardi, John (Anthony)
  and Sabini, John Anthony
Anthony, Joseph Patrick 1964- 103
Anthony, Patricia 1947- 109
Anthony, Piers 1934- 129
  Autobiography Feature 129
  Earlier sketch in SATA *84*
  See also CLR *118*
  See also SAAS *22*
Anthony, Susan C(arol) 1953- 87
Anticaglia, Elizabeth 1939- 12
Antieau, Kim 214
Antilles, Kem
  See Moesta, Rebecca
Antle, Nancy 1955- 102
Antolini, Margaret Fishback 1904-1985
  Obituary 45
Anton, Michael J(ames) 1940- 12
Antonacci, Robert J(oseph) 1916- 45
  Brief entry 37
Anvil, Christopher 1925-2009 102
Anzaldua, Gloria (Evanjelina) 1942-2004
  Obituary 154
Aoki, Hisako 1942- 45
Aoyagi, Nora 229
Apfel, Necia H(alpern) 1930- 51
  Brief entry 41
Aphrodite, J.
  See Livingston, Carole
Apikuni
  See Schultz, James Willard
Apostolina, M. 184
Apostolina, Michael
  See Apostolina, M.
Apostolou, Christine Hale 1955- 179
  Earlier sketches in SATA *82, 128*
Appel, Allen (R.) 1945- 115
Appel, Benjamin 1907-1977 39
  Obituary 21
Appel, Martin 1948- 45
Appel, Martin Eliot
  See Appel, Martin
Appel, Marty
  See Appel, Martin
Appelbaum, Diana Muir Karter 1953- 132
Appelbaum, Susannah 234
Appelt, Kathi 1954- 190
  Earlier sketches in SATA *83, 129*
Apperley, Dawn 1969- 135

Appiah, Peggy 1921-2006 84
  Earlier sketch in SATA *15*
  See also SAAS *19*
Apple, Margot 214
  Brief entry 42
  Earlier sketches in SATA *64, 152*
Applebaum, Stan 1922- 45
Applegate, K.A.
  See Applegate, Katherine
Applegate, Katherine 1956- 196
  Earlier sketches in SATA *109, 162*
  See also CLR *90*
Applegate, Katherine Alice
  See Applegate, Katherine
Appleton, Victor
  See Barrett, Neal, Jr.
  and Doyle, Debra
  and Stratemeyer, Edward L.
  and Vardeman, Robert E.
Appollo 1969- 214
Appollodorus, Olivier
  See Appollo
Apsler, Alfred 1907-1982 10
Aragones, Sergio 1937- 48
  Brief entry 39
Arato, Rona 233
Araujo, Frank P. 1937- 86
Arbo, Cris 1950- 220
  Earlier sketch in SATA *103*
Arbuckle, Dorothy Fry 1910-1982
  Obituary 33
Arbuthnot, May Hill 1884-1969 2
Archambault, John 163
  Earlier sketches in SATA *67, 112*
Archambault, Matthew 1968- 219
Archbold, Rick 1950- 97
Archer, Colleen Rutherford 1949- 164
Archer, Frank
  See O'Connor, Richard
Archer, Jules 1915- 85
  Earlier sketch in SATA *4*
  See also SAAS *5*
Archer, Lily 1981- 193
Archer, Marion Fuller 1917- 11
Archer, Nathan
  See Watt-Evans, Lawrence
Archer, Peggy 1947- 199
Archibald, Joe
  See Archibald, Joseph S(topford)
Archibald, Joseph S(topford) 1898-1986 3
  Obituary 47
Ard, William
  See Jakes, John
Ardagh, Philip 1961- 154
Ardai, Charles 1969- 85
Arden, Barbi
  See Stoutenburg, Adrien (Pearl)
Arden, William
  See Lynds, Dennis
Ardizzone, Edward (Jeffrey Irving)
  1900-1979 28
  Obituary 21
  Earlier sketch in SATA *1*
  See also CLR *3*
Ardley, Neil 1937- 121
  Earlier sketch in SATA *43*
Ardley, Neil Richard
  See Ardley, Neil
Arehart-Treichel, Joan 1942- 22
Arena, Felice 1968- 151
Arenella, Roy 1939- 14
Arevamirp, Esile
  See Primavera, Elise
Argent, Kerry 1960- 138
Arguelles, Francisco Xavier
  See Stork, Francisco X.
Argueta, Jorge 179
Arihara, Shino 1973- 201
Arkin, Alan 1934- 59
  Brief entry 32

Arkin, Alan Wolf
  See Arkin, Alan
Arksey, Neil 158
Arlen, Leslie
  See Nicole, Christopher
Arley, Robert
  See Jackson, Mike
Armer, Alberta (Roller) 1904-1986 9
Armer, Laura Adams 1874-1963 13
Armistead, John 1941- 130
Armitage, David 1943- 155
  Brief entry 38
  Earlier sketch in SATA *99*
Armitage, Frank
  See Carpenter, John
Armitage, Ronda (Jacqueline) 1943- 155
  Brief entry 38
  Earlier sketches in SATA *47, 99*
Armour, Richard (Willard) 1906-1989 14
  Obituary 61
Armstrong, Alan 1939- 172
Armstrong, Alan W.
  See Armstrong, Alan
Armstrong, George D. 1927- 10
Armstrong, Gerry (Breen) 1929- 10
Armstrong, Jeannette (C.) 1948- 102
Armstrong, Jennifer 1961- 165
  Autobiography Feature 120
  Earlier sketches in SATA *77, 111*
  See also CLR *66*
  See also SAAS *24*
Armstrong, Louise 43
  Brief entry 33
Armstrong, Martin Donisthorpe
  1882-1974 115
Armstrong, Matthew 1975- 188
Armstrong, Matthew S.
  See Armstrong, Matthew
Armstrong, Ralph Richard
  See Armstrong, Richard
Armstrong, Richard 1903-1986 11
Armstrong, Shelagh 1961- 224
Armstrong, William H(oward) 1914-1999 4
  Obituary 111
  See also CLR *117*
  See also SAAS *7*
Armstrong-Ellis, Carey (Fraser) 1956- 145
Armstrong-Hodgson, Shelagh
  See Armstrong, Shelagh
Arndt, Ursula (Martha H.) 56
  Brief entry 39
Arneson, D(on) J(on) 1935- 37
Arnett, Caroline
  See Cole, Lois Dwight
Arnett, Jack
  See Goulart, Ron
Arnette, Robert
  See Silverberg, Robert
Arno, Enrico 1913-1981 43
  Obituary 28
Arnold, Ann 1953(?)- 207
Arnold, Caroline 1944- 228
  Brief entry 34
  Earlier sketches in SATA *36, 85, 131, 174*
  See also CLR *61*
  See also SAAS *23*
Arnold, Elizabeth 1944- 164
Arnold, Elliott 1912-1980 5
  Obituary 22
Arnold, Emily 1939- 210
  Autobiography Feature 134
  Earlier sketches in SATA *5, 50, 76, 110, 134*
  See also CLR *46*
  See also SAAS *7*
Arnold, Gillian Clare
  See Cross, Gillian
Arnold, Katya 1947- 168
  Earlier sketches in SATA *82, 115*
Arnold, Louise 175
Arnold, Louise Claire
  See Arnold, Louise

Arnold, Marsha Diane 1948- *147*
Earlier sketch in SATA *93*
Arnold, Nick 1961- *113*
Arnold, Oren 1900-1980 .... *4*
Arnold, Susan (Riser) 1951- *58*
Arnold, Tedd 1949- *208*
Earlier sketches in SATA *69, 116, 160*
Arnoldy, Julie
See Bischoff, Julia Bristol
Arnosky, James Edward 1946- *189*
Earlier sketches in SATA *70, 118*
See also CLR *93*
Arnosky, Jim
See Arnosky, James Edward
Arnott, Kathleen 1914- *20*
Arnov, Boris, Jr. 1926- *12*
Arnow, Harriette (Louisa) Simpson
1908-1986 .... *42*
Obituary *47*
Arnsteen, Katy Keck 1934- *68*
Arnstein, Helene S(olomon) 1915- *12*
Arntson, Herbert E(dward) 1911-1982 .... *12*
Aroner, Miriam *82*
Aronin, Ben 1904-1980
Obituary *25*
Aronson, Marc 1950- *189*
Autobiography Feature *189*
Earlier sketches in SATA *126, 175*
Aronson, Marc Henry
See Aronson, Marc
Aronson, Sarah *196*
Aronson, Virginia 1954- *122*
Arora, Shirley (Lease) 1930- *2*
Arrasmith, Patrick *239*
Earlier sketch in SATA *176*
Arrick, Fran
See Angell, Judie
Arrigan, Mary 1943- *142*
Arrington, Aileen *183*
Arrington, Stephen L. 1948- *97*
Arrington, Stephen Lee
See Arrington, Stephen L.
Arrley, Richmond
See Delany, Samuel R., Jr.
Arrou-Vignod, Jean-Philippe 1958- *218*
Arrowood, (McKendrick Lee) Clinton
1939- *19*
Arrowsmith, Pat 1930- *59*
Arsenault, Isabelle 1978- *207*
Artell, Mike 1948- *183*
Earlier sketches in SATA *89, 134*
Arthur, A.C.
See Arthur, Artist
Arthur, Artist *235*
Arthur, Artist C.
See Arthur, Artist
Arthur, Robert (Andrew) 1909-1969
See Arthur, Robert, (Jr.)
Arthur, Robert, (Jr.) 1909-1969 .... *118*
Arthur, Ruth M(abel) 1905-1979 .... *26*
Earlier sketch in SATA *7*
Artis, Vicki Kimmel 1945- *12*
Artzybasheff, Boris (Miklailovich)
1899-1965 .... *14*
Aruego, Ariane
See Dewey, Ariane
Aruego, Jose 1932- *178*
Earlier sketches in SATA *6, 68, 125*
See also CLR *5*
Aruego, Jose Espiritu
See Aruego, Jose
Arundel, Honor (Morfydd) 1919-1973 .... *4*
Obituary *24*
See also CLR *35*
Arundel, Jocelyn
See Alexander, Jocelyn Anne Arundel
Arvey, Michael 1948- *79*
Arzoumanian, Alik *177*
Asare, Meshack (Yaw) 1945- *139*
Earlier sketch in SATA *86*

Asaro, Catherine 1955- *165*
Earlier sketch in SATA *101*
Asaro, Catherine Ann 1955-
See Asaro, Catherine
Asay, Donna Day 1945- *127*
Asbjornsen, Peter Christen 1812-1885 .... *15*
See also CLR *104*
Asch, Frank 1946- *154*
Earlier sketches in SATA *5, 66, 102*
Ash, Jutta 1942- *38*
Ashabranner, Brent 1921- *166*
Earlier sketches in SATA *1, 67, 130*
See also CLR *28*
See also SAAS *14*
Ashabranner, Brent Kenneth
See Ashabranner, Brent
Ashbless, William
See Blaylock, James P.
and Powers, Tim
Ashby, Gil 1958- *146*
Ashby, Gwynneth 1922- *44*
Ashby, Ruth *170*
Ashby, Yvonne 1955- *121*
Ashe, Arthur (Robert, Jr.) 1943-1993 .... *65*
Obituary *87*
Ashe, Geoffrey (Thomas) 1923- *17*
Autobiography Feature *125*
Ashe, Mary Ann
See Lewis, Mary
Asher, Bridget
See Baggott, Julianna
Asher, Sandra Fenichel
See Asher, Sandy
Asher, Sandy 1942- *71*
Autobiography Feature *158*
Brief entry *34*
Earlier sketch in SATA *36*
See also SAAS *13*
Asheron, Sara
See Moore, Lilian
Ashey, Bella
See Breinburg, Petronella
Ashford, Daisy
See Ashford, Margaret Mary
Ashford, Jeffrey
See Jeffries, Roderic
Ashford, Margaret Mary 1881-1972 .... *10*
Ashland, Monk 1972- *207*
Ashley, Bernard (John) 1935- *155*
Brief entry *39*
Earlier sketches in SATA *47, 79*
See also CLR *4*
Ashley, Carol *238*
Ashley, Elizabeth
See Salmon, Annie Elizabeth
Ashley, Ray
See Abrashkin, Raymond
Ashman, Linda 1960- *203*
Earlier sketch in SATA *150*
Ashton, Lorayne
See Gottfried, Theodore Mark
Ashton, Warren T.
See Adams, William Taylor
Asimov, Isaac 1920-1992 .... *74*
Earlier sketches in SATA *1, 26*
See also CLR *79*
Asinof, Eliot 1919-2008 .... *6*
Asinof, Eliot Tager
See Asinof, Eliot
Aska, Warabe
See Masuda, Takeshi
Askani, Tanja 1962- *227*
Asprin, Robert 1946-2008 .... *92*
Asprin, Robert L.
See Asprin, Robert
Asprin, Robert Lynn
See Asprin, Robert
Asquith, Cynthia Mary Evelyn (Charteris)
1887-1960 .... *107*
Asquith, Ros *153*

Astley, Juliet
See Lofts, Norah (Robinson)
Aston, Dianna Hutts 1964- *176*
Aston, James
See White, T(erence) H(anbury)
Ata, Te 1895-1995 .... *119*
Atene, Ann
See Atene, (Rita) Anna
Atene, (Rita) Anna 1922- *12*
Atheling, William, Jr.
See Blish, James
Atkins, Catherine *160*
Atkins, Jeannine 1953- *172*
Earlier sketch in SATA *113*
Atkinson, Allen G. 1953(?)-1987 .... *60*
Brief entry *46*
Obituary *55*
Atkinson, Elizabeth *215*
Atkinson, Elizabeth Jane
See Atkinson, Elizabeth
Atkinson, M. E.
See Frankau, Mary Evelyn Atkinson
Atkinson, Margaret Fleming *14*
Atteberry, Kevan J. *186*
Attema, Martha 1949- *156*
Earlier sketch in SATA *94*
Atticus
See Davies, Hunter
and Fleming, Ian
and Pawle, Gerald Strachan
and Wilson, (Thomas) Woodrow
Atwater, Florence 1896-1979 .... *66*
Earlier sketch in SATA *16*
See also CLR *19*
Atwater, Florence Hasseltine Carroll
See Atwater, Florence
Atwater, Montgomery Meigs 1904-1976 ...... *15*
Atwater, Richard 1892-1948 .... *66*
Brief entry *27*
Earlier sketch in SATA *54*
See also CLR *19*
Atwater, Richard Tupper
See Atwater, Richard
Atwater-Rhodes, Amelia 1984- *170*
Earlier sketch in SATA *124*
Atwell, Debby 1953- *150*
Earlier sketch in SATA *87*
Atwood, Ann (Margaret) 1913-1992 .... *7*
Atwood, Margaret 1939- *170*
Earlier sketch in SATA *50*
Atwood, Margaret Eleanor
See Atwood, Margaret
Aubrey, Meg Kelleher 1963- *83*
Aubry, Claude B. 1914-1984 .... *29*
Obituary *40*
Auch, Herm *173*
Auch, Mary Jane *173*
Earlier sketch in SATA *138*
Auch, M.J.
See Auch, Mary Jane
Auclair, Joan 1960- *68*
Auel, Jean
See Auel, Jean M.
Auel, Jean M. 1936- *91*
Auel, Jean Marie
See Auel, Jean M.
Auer, Martin 1951- *77*
Augarde, Steve 1950- *210*
Earlier sketches in SATA *25, 159*
Augarde, Steven Andre
See Augarde, Steve
Augelli, John P(at) 1921- *46*
Augustine, Mildred
See Benson, Mildred
Ault, Phil
See Ault, Phillip H(alliday)
Ault, Phillip H(alliday) 1914- *23*
Ault, Rosalie Sain 1942- *38*
Ault, Roz
See Ault, Rosalie Sain
Aung, (Maung) Htin 1909- *21*

Auntie Deb
  See Coury, Louise Andree
Auntie Louise
  See Coury, Louise Andree
Aunt Weedy
  See Alcott, Louisa May
Auseon, Andrew 1976- 217
  Earlier sketch in SATA *166*
Austen, Carrie
  See Bennett, Cherie
Austen, Catherine 1965- 223
Austin, Carrie
  See Seuling, Barbara
Austin, Elizabeth S. 1907-1977 5
Austin, Harry
  See McInerny, Ralph
Austin, Margot 1909(?)-1990 11
  Obituary 66
Austin, Michael 178
Austin, Oliver L(uther), Jr. 1903-1988 7
  Obituary 59
Austin, Patricia 1950- 137
Austin, R. G.
  See Gelman, Rita Golden
  and Lamb, Nancy
Austin, Virginia 1951- 152
  Earlier sketch in SATA *80*
Auteur, Hillary
  See Gottfried, Theodore Mark
Auth, Tony
  See Auth, William Anthony, Jr.
Auth, William Anthony, Jr. 1942- 192
Autry, Gloria Diener
  See Allen, Terril Diener
Auvil, Peggy A 1954- 122
Auvil, Peggy Appleby
  See Auvil, Peggy A
Avasthi, Swati 1971- 231
Aveni, Anthony F. 1938- 181
Aveni, Anthony Francis
  See Aveni, Anthony F.
Averbeck, Jim 1963- 201
Averill, Esther (Holden) 1902-1992 28
  Obituary 72
  Earlier sketch in SATA *1*
Avery, A. A.
  See Montgomery, Rutherford George
Avery, Al
  See Montgomery, Rutherford George
Avery, Gillian 1926- 137
  Autobiography Feature 137
  Earlier sketches in SATA *7, 75*
  See also SAAS *6*
Avery, Gillian Elise
  See Avery, Gillian
Avery, Kay 1908- 5
Avery, Lorraine
  See Older, Effin
  and Older, Jules
Avery, Lynn
  See Cole, Lois Dwight
Avi 1937- 226
  Earlier sketches in SATA *14, 71, 108, 156, 190*
  See also CLR *68*
Aviles, Martha 218
Avishai, Susan 1949- 82
Avraham, Kate Aver 227
Avril, Francois 1961- 191
Avril, Lynne
  See Cravath, Lynne W.
Awdry, Christopher Vere 1940- 67
Awdry, Wilbert Vere 1911-1997 94
  See also CLR *23*
Axelrod, Amy 131
Axelsen, Stephen 1953- 165
Axton, David
  See Koontz, Dean
Ayars, James S(terling) 1898-1986 4
Aye, A. K.
  See Edwards, Hazel (Eileen)

Ayer, Eleanor H. 1947-1998 121
  Earlier sketch in SATA *78*
Ayer, Jacqueline 1930- 13
Ayer, Margaret (?)-1981 15
Aylesworth, Jim 1943- 213
  Earlier sketches in SATA *38, 89, 139*
  See also CLR *89*
Aylesworth, Thomas G(ibbons) 1927-1995 .. 88
  Earlier sketch in SATA *4*
  See also CLR *6*
  See also SAAS *17*
Ayliffe, Alex 190
Aylward, Marcus
  See Alexander, Marc
Aymar, Brandt 1911- 22
Ayme, Marcel (Andre) 1902-1967 91
  See also CLR *25*
Ayres, Becky
  See Hickox, Rebecca (Ayres)
Ayres, Katherine 1947- 187
Ayres, Pam 1947- 90
Ayres, Patricia Miller 1923-1985
  Obituary 46
Aytmatov, Chingiz
  See Aitmatov, Chingiz
Ayto, Russell 1960- 206
  Earlier sketches in SATA *111, 166*
Azaid
  See Zaidenberg, Arthur
Azar, Penny 1952- 121
Azarian, Mary 1940- 171
  Earlier sketch in SATA *112*
Azore, Barbara 1934- 188

B

Baasansuren, Bolormaa 1982- 216
Baastad, Babbis Friis
  See Friis-Baastad, Babbis Ellinor
Bab
  See Gilbert, W(illiam) S(chwenck)
Babbis, Eleanor
  See Friis-Baastad, Babbis Ellinor
Babbitt, Lucy Cullyford 1960- 85
Babbitt, Natalie 1932- 194
  Earlier sketches in SATA *6, 68, 106*
  See also CLR *141*
  See also SAAS *5*
Babbitt, Natalie Zane Moore
  See Babbitt, Natalie
Babcock, Chris 1963- 83
Babcock, Dennis 1948- 22
Babcock, Dennis Arthur
  See Babcock, Dennis
Baber, Carolyn Stonnell 1936- 96
Baboni, Elena 198
Baca, Ana 1967- 191
Baca, Maria 1951- 104
Baccalario, Pierdomenico 1974- 222
Bach, Alice (Hendricks) 1942- 93
  Brief entry 27
  Earlier sketch in SATA *30*
Bach, Bellamy
  See Windling, Terri
Bach, Mary 1960- 125
Bach, Richard 1936- 13
Bach, Richard David
  See Bach, Richard
Bache, Ellyn 1942- 124
Bachel, Beverly K. 1957- 142
Bachelet, Gilles 1952- 196
Bachem, Paul 231
Bachman, Fred 1949- 12
Bachman, Richard
  See King, Stephen
Bachorz, Pam 1973- 226
Bachrach, Deborah 1943- 80
Bacigalupi, Paolo 1973- 230

Backus, James Gilmore 1913-1989
  Obituary 63
Backus, Jim
  See Backus, James Gilmore
Bacmeister, Rhoda W(arner) 1893-1991 11
Bacon, Betty
  See Bacon, Elizabeth
Bacon, Elizabeth 1914-2001 3
  Obituary 131
Bacon, Joan Chase
  See Bowden, Joan Chase
Bacon, Josephine Dodge (Daskam)
  1876-1961 48
Bacon, Margaret Frances
  See Bacon, Peggy
Bacon, Margaret Hope 1921- 6
Bacon, Martha Sherman 1917-1981 18
  Obituary 27
  See also CLR *3*
Bacon, Melvin 1950- 93
Bacon, Melvin L.
  See Bacon, Melvin
Bacon, Peggy 1895-1987 50
Bacon, R(onald) L(eonard) 1924- 84
  Earlier sketch in SATA *26*
Baddiel, Ivor 1963- 210
Baden, Robert 1936- 70
Baden-Powell, Robert (Stephenson Smyth)
  1857-1941 16
Badoe, Adwoa 237
Badt, Karin L(uisa) 1963- 91
Bae, Hyun-Joo 186
Baehr, Kingsley M. 1937- 89
Baehr, Patricia 1952- 238
  Earlier sketch in SATA *65*
Baehr, Patricia Goehner
  See Baehr, Patricia
Baek, Matthew J. 1971- 202
Baer, Jill
  See Gilbert, (Agnes) Joan (Sewell)
Baer, Judy 1951- 71
Baer, Julie 1960- 161
Baer-Block, Roxanna 172
Baerg, Harry J(ohn) 1909-1996 12
Baeten, Lieve 1954-2001 238
  Earlier sketch in SATA *83*
Bagert, Brod 1947- 191
  Earlier sketch in SATA *80*
Baggette, Susan K. 1942- 126
Baggott, Julianna 1969- 197
Bagnold, Enid 1889-1981 25
  Earlier sketch in SATA *1*
Baguley, Elizabeth 1959- 199
Bahlke, Valerie Worth -1994
  See Worth, Valerie
Bahous, Sally 1939- 86
Bahr, Mary (Madelyn) 1946- 95
Bahr, Robert 1940- 38
Bahti, Tom 1926-1972 57
  Brief entry 31
Bai, Durga 211
Baicker-McKee, Carol 1958- 177
Bailey, Alice Cooper 1890-1978 12
Bailey, Anne 1958- 71
Bailey, Bernadine (Freeman) 1901-1995 14
Bailey, Carolyn Sherwin 1875-1961 14
Bailey, Debbie 1954- 123
Bailey, Donna (Veronica Anne) 1938- 68
Bailey, Jane H(orton) 1916- 12
Bailey, John (Robert) 1940- 52
Bailey, Len 193
Bailey, Linda 1948- 217
  Earlier sketches in SATA *107, 182*
Bailey, Maralyn Collins (Harrison) 1941- 12
Bailey, Matilda
  See Radford, Ruby L(orraine)
Bailey, Maurice Charles 1932- 12
Bailey, Pearl (Mae) 1918-1990 81
Bailey, Peter 1946- 194
Bailey, Ralph Edgar 1893-1982 11
Bailey, Sheila (Lucas) 1960- 155

Baillie, Allan 1943- *151*
  Earlier sketch in SATA *87*
  See also CLR *49*
  See also SAAS *21*
Baillie, Allan Stuart
  See Baillie, Allan
Baines, John (David) 1943- *71*
Bains, Larry
  See Sabin, Louis
Baird, Alison 1963- *138*
Baird, Bil 1904-1987 .... *30*
  Obituary *52*
Baird, Thomas (P.) 1923-1990 .... *45*
  Brief entry *39*
  Obituary *64*
Baird, William Britton
  See Baird, Bil
Baity, Elizabeth Chesley 1907-1989 .... *1*
Baiul, Oksana 1977- *108*
Bajoria, Paul 1964- *187*
Bakeless, John (Edwin) 1894-1978 .... *9*
Bakeless, Katherine Little 1895-1992 .... *9*
Baker, Alan 1951- *146*
  Earlier sketches in SATA *22, 93*
Baker, Augusta 1911-1998 .... *3*
Baker, Barbara 1947- *192*
Baker, Betty Lou 1928-1987 .... *73*
  Obituary *54*
  Earlier sketch in SATA *5*
Baker, Carin Greenberg 1959- *79*
Baker, Charlotte 1910- *2*
Baker, Christina
  See Kline, Christina Baker
Baker, Christopher W. 1952- *144*
Baker, Deirdre 1955- *195*
Baker, E.D. *237*
  Earlier sketch in SATA *190*
Baker, (Mary) Elizabeth (Gillette) 1923- *7*
Baker, Gayle Cunningham 1950- *39*
Baker, James W. 1924- *65*
  Earlier sketch in SATA *22*
Baker, James W. 1926- *122*
Baker, Janice E(dla) 1941- *22*
Baker, Jeanette *178*
Baker, Jeannie 1950- *156*
  Earlier sketches in SATA *23, 88*
  See also CLR *28*
Baker, Jeffrey J(ohn) W(heeler) 1931- *5*
Baker, Jim
  See Baker, James W.
Baker, Keith 1953- *222*
  Earlier sketch in SATA *179*
Baker, Ken 1962- *133*
Baker, Laura Nelson 1911- *3*
Baker, Margaret 1890-1965 .... *4*
Baker, Margaret J(oyce) 1918- *12*
  See also SAAS *8*
Baker, Mary Gladys Steel 1892-1974 .... *12*
Baker, (Robert) Michael (Graham) 1938- *4*
Baker, Nina (Brown) 1888-1957 .... *15*
Baker, Pamela J. 1947- *66*
Baker, Rachel 1904-1978 .... *2*
  Obituary *26*
Baker, Roberta *206*
Baker, Rosalie F. 1945- *166*
Baker, Samm Sinclair 1909-1997 .... *12*
  Obituary *96*
Baker, Sharon Reiss 1962- *207*
Baker, Susan (Catherine) 1942-1991 .... *29*
Baker-Smith, Grahame *223*
Balaam
  See Lamb, G(eoffrey) F(rederick)
Balan, Bruce 1959- *113*
Balcavage, Dynise 1965- *137*
Balch, Glenn 1902-1989 .... *3*
  Obituary *83*
  See also SAAS *11*
Baldacci, David 1960- *184*
Baldacci, David G.
  See Baldacci, David
  and Baldacci, David

Balderose, Nancy Ward 1952- *93*
Balderson, Margaret 1935- *151*
Baldini, Michelle *205*
Baldry, Cherith 1947- *167*
  Earlier sketch in SATA *72*
Balducci, Carolyn 1946- *5*
Balducci, Carolyn Feleppa
  See Balducci, Carolyn
Baldwin, Alex
  See Griffin, W. E. B.
Baldwin, Anne Norris 1938- *5*
Baldwin, Clara *11*
Baldwin, Gordo
  See Baldwin, Gordon C(ortis)
Baldwin, Gordon C(ortis) 1908-1983 .... *12*
Baldwin, James 1841-1925 .... *24*
Baldwin, James 1924-1987 .... *9*
  Obituary *54*
Baldwin, Louis 1919- *110*
Baldwin, Margaret
  See Weis, Margaret
Baldwin, Stan(ley C.) 1929- *62*
  Brief entry *28*
Bales, Carol Ann 1940- *57*
  Brief entry *29*
Balet, Jan (Bernard) 1913- *11*
Balgassi, Haemi 1971- *131*
Balian, Lorna 1929- *91*
  Earlier sketch in SATA *9*
Balit, Christina 1961- *212*
  Earlier sketches in SATA *102, 159*
Ball, Duncan 1941- *73*
Ball, Zachary
  See Janas, Frankie-Lee
  and Masters, Kelly R(ay)
Ballantine, Lesley Frost
  See Frost, Lesley
Ballantyne, R(obert) M(ichael) 1825-1894 ... *24*
  See also CLR *137*
Ballard, James G.
  See Ballard, J.G.
Ballard, James Graham
  See Ballard, J.G.
Ballard, Jane
  See Gorman, Carol
Ballard, J.G. 1930-2009 .... *93*
  Obituary *203*
Ballard, Jim G.
  See Ballard, J.G.
Ballard, John 1945- *110*
Ballard, Lowell C(lyne) 1904-1986 .... *12*
  Obituary *49*
Ballard, (Charles) Martin 1929- *1*
Ballard, Mignon F. 1934- *64*
  Brief entry *49*
Ballard, Mignon Franklin
  See Ballard, Mignon F.
Ballard, Robert D(uane) 1942- *85*
  See also CLR *60*
Ballard, Robin 1965- *126*
Balliett, Blue 1955- *239*
  Earlier sketch in SATA *156*
Ballinger, Bryan 1968- *161*
Ballouhey, Pierre 1944- *90*
Balog, Cyn *221*
Balogh, Penelope 1916-1975 .... *1*
  Obituary *34*
Balouch, Kristen *176*
Balow, Tom 1931- *12*
Baltazzi, Evan S(erge) 1921- *90*
Balterman, Marcia Ridlon 1942- *22*
Baltimore, J.
  See Catherall, Arthur
Baltzer, Hans (Adolf) 1900- *40*
Balzano, Jeanne (Koppel) 1912- *7*
Bambara, Toni Cade 1939-1995 .... *112*
Bamfylde, Walter
  See Bevan, Tom
Bamman, Henry A. 1918- *12*
Banat, D. R.
  See Bradbury, Ray

Bancks, Tristan 1974- *231*
Bancroft, Bronwyn 1958- *216*
Bancroft, Griffing 1907-1999 .... *6*
Bancroft, Laura
  See Baum, L. Frank
Bandel, Betty 1912- *47*
Baner, Skulda Vanadis 1897-1964 .... *10*
Banerjee, Anjali *174*
Banfill, A. Scott 1956- *98*
Bang, Betsy 1912- *48*
  Brief entry *37*
Bang, Garrett
  See Bang, Molly
Bang, Molly 1943- *215*
  Earlier sketches in SATA *24, 69, 111, 158*
  See also CLR *8*
Bang, Molly Garrett
  See Bang, Molly
Bang-Campbell, Monika 1975(?)- *195*
  Earlier sketch in SATA *140*
Banjo, The
  See Paterson, A(ndrew) B(arton)
Banke, Cecile de
  See de Banke, Cecile
Banks, Erin Bennett 1978- *211*
Banks, Kate 1960- *200*
  Earlier sketches in SATA *134, 172*
Banks, Laura Stockton Voorhees 1908(?)-1980
  Obituary *23*
Banks, Lynne Reid
  See Reid Banks, Lynne
Banks, Merry *197*
Banks, Michael A. 1951- *101*
Banks, Paul 1952- *174*
Banks, Sara
  See Harrell, Sara Gordon
Banks, Sara Jeanne Gordon Harrell
  See Harrell, Sara Gordon
Bannatyne-Cugnet, Elizabeth Jo-Anne
  See Bannatyne-Cugnet, Jo
Bannatyne-Cugnet, Jo 1951- *101*
Banner, Angela
  See Maddison, Angela Mary
Bannerman, Helen (Brodie Cowan Watson)
  1862(?)-1946 .... *19*
  See also CLR *144*
Banning, Evelyn I. 1903-1993 .... *36*
Bannon, Laura (?)-1963 .... *6*
Bannor, Brett 1959- *143*
Bansch, Helga 1957- *224*
Banta, Susan *181*
Bantock, Nick 1950(?)- *95*
Banyai, Istvan *193*
Barakat, Ibtisam 1963- *186*
Barasch, Lynne 1939- *186*
  Earlier sketches in SATA *74, 126*
Baratz-Logsted, Lauren *235*
Barbalet, Margaret 1949- *77*
Barbary, James
  See Baumann, Amy Beeching
  and Beeching, Jack
Barbash, Shepard 1957- *84*
Barbauld, Anna Laetitia 1743-1825
  See CLR *160*
Barbe, Walter Burke 1926- *45*
Barber, Alison *222*
Barber, Antonia 1932- *163*
  Earlier sketch in SATA *29*
Barber, Atiim Kiambu
  See Barber, Tiki
Barber, Lynda
  See Graham-Barber, Lynda
Barber, Lynda Graham
  See Graham-Barber, Lynda
Barber, Richard (William) 1941- *35*
Barber, Ronde 1975- *182*
Barber, Tiki 1975- *182*
Barbera, Joe 1911-2006 .... *51*
  Obituary *179*
Barbera, Joseph
  See Barbera, Joe

Barbera, Joseph Roland
See Barbera, Joe
Barberis, Juan C(arlos) 1920- 61
Barbour, Karen 1956- 170
Earlier sketches in SATA 63, 121
Barbour, Ralph Henry 1870-1944 16
Barclay, Bill
See Moorcock, Michael
Barclay, Isabel
See Dobell, I(sabel) M(arian) B(arclay)
Barclay, William Ewert
See Moorcock, Michael
Barclay, William Ewert
See Moorcock, Michael
Bardhan-Quallen, Sudipta 1977- 214
Earlier sketch in SATA 168
Bardoe, Cheryl 181
Bare, Arnold Edwin 1920- 16
Bare, Colleen Stanley 32
Bar-el, Dan 199
Barenholtz, Bernard 1914-1989
Obituary 64
Bargar, Gary W. 1947-1985 63
Barger, Jan 1948- 147
Barish, Matthew 1907-2000 12
Barkan, Joanne 127
Earlier sketch in SATA 77
Barker, Albert W. 1900- 8
Barker, Carol (Minturn) 1938- 31
Barker, Cicely Mary 1895-1973 49
Brief entry 39
See also CLR 88
Barker, Claire 1969- 237
Barker, Melvern 1907-1989 11
Barker, S. Omar 1894-1985 10
Barker, Squire Omar
See Barker, S. Omar
Barker, Will 1913-1983 8
Barkin, Carol 1944- 52
Earlier sketch in SATA 42
Barklem, Jill 1951- 96
See also CLR 31
Barkley, Brad 178
Barkley, James Edward 1941- 6
Barks, Carl 1901-2000 37
Barley, Janet Crane 1934- 95
Barlow, Steve 1952- 211
Barnaby, Ralph S(tanton) 1893-1986 9
Barnard, A. M.
See Alcott, Louisa May
Barnard, Bryn 1956- 169
Earlier sketch in SATA 115
Barne, Kitty
See Barne, Marion Catherine
Barne, Marion Catherine 1883-1957 97
Barneda, David 206
Barner, Bob 1947- 238
Earlier sketches in SATA 29, 136
Barnes, Dawn 1957- 175
Barnes, Derrick 191
Barnes, Derrick D.
See Barnes, Derrick
Barnes, (Frank) Eric Wollencott 1907-1962 . 22
Barnes, Joyce Annette 1958- 85
Barnes, Laura T. 1958- 119
Barnes, Loutricia
See Barnes-Svarney, Patricia L(ou)
Barnes, Malcolm 1909(?)-1984
Obituary 41
Barnes, Michael 1934- 55
Barnes-Murphy, Frances 1951- 88
Barnes-Murphy, Rowan 1952- 88
Barnes-Svarney, Patricia L(ou) 1953- 67
Barnet, Nancy 1954- 84
Barnett, Ivan 1947- 70
Barnett, Lincoln (Kinnear) 1909-1979 36
Barnett, Mac 223
Barnett, Moneta 1922-1976 33
Barnett, Naomi 1927- 40
Barney, Maginel Wright 1881(?)-1966 39
Brief entry 32

Barnhart, Clarence L(ewis) 1900-1993 48
Obituary 78
Barnholdt, Lauren 1980(?)- 232
Barnhouse, Rebecca 1961- 225
Barnouw, Adriaan Jacob 1877-1968
Obituary 27
Barnouw, Victor 1915-1989 43
Brief entry 28
Barnstone, Willis 1927- 20
Barnum, Jay Hyde 1888(?)-1962 20
Barnum, P. T., Jr.
See Stratemeyer, Edward L.
Barnum, Richard 67
Earlier sketch in SATA 1
Barnum, Theodore
See Stratemeyer, Edward L.
Barnwell, Ysaye M. 1946- 200
Baron, Kathi 1956- 226
Baron, Kathy 1954- 90
Baron, Virginia Olsen 1931- 46
Brief entry 28
Barr, Donald 1921-2004 20
Obituary 152
Barr, George 1907-1992 2
Barr, Jene 1922-1985 16
Obituary 42
Barr, Nevada 1952- 126
Earlier sketch in SATA 115
Barragan, Paula 1963- 216
Barratt, Mark 1954- 224
Barrer, Gertrude
See Barrer-Russell, Gertrude
Barrer-Russell, Gertrude 1921- 27
Barrett, Angela 1955- 223
Barrett, Angela (Jane) 1955- 145
Earlier sketch in SATA 75
Barrett, Ethel 87
Brief entry 44
Barrett, Joyce Durham 1943- 138
Barrett, Judi
See Barrett, Judith
Barrett, Judith 1941- 204
Earlier sketch in SATA 26
See also CLR 98
Barrett, Robert T. 1949- 234
Earlier sketch in SATA 92
Barrett, Ron 1937- 14
Barrett, Susan (Mary) 1938- 113
Barrett, Tracy 1955- 207
Earlier sketches in SATA 84, 115, 156
Barrett, William E(dmund) 1900-1986
Obituary 49
Barretta, Gene 214
Earlier sketch in SATA 176
Barretton, Grandall
See Garrett, Randall
Barrie, Baronet
See Barrie, J. M.
Barrie, J. M. 1860-1937 100
See also YABC 1
See also CLR 124
Barrie, James Matthew
See Barrie, J. M.
Barringer, William 1940-1996 153
Barrington, Michael
See Moorcock, Michael
Barris, George 1925- 47
Barrol, Grady
See Bograd, Larry
Barron, Rex 1951- 84
Barron, T.A. 1952- 192
Earlier sketches in SATA 83, 126
See also CLR 86
Barron, Thomas Archibald
See Barron, T.A.
Barron, Tom
See Barron, T.A.
Barrow, Lloyd H. 1942- 73
Barrows, Annie 1962- 180
Barry, Dan 1958- 177
Barry, Dana (Marie Malloy) 1949- 139

Barry, James P(otvin) 1918- 14
Barry, Katharina Watjen 1936- 4
Barry, Robert 1931- 6
Barry, Robert Everett
See Barry, Robert
Barry, Scott 1952- 32
Barry, Sheila Anne -2003 91
Barshaw, Ruth McNally 203
Bartell, Susan S. 175
Bartenbach, Jean 1918- 40
Barth, Edna 1914-1980 7
Obituary 24
Barth, Kelly L. 1964- 152
Barthelme, Donald 1931-1989 7
Obituary 62
Barth-Grozinger, Inge 1950- 185
Bartholomew, Barbara 1941- 86
Brief entry 42
Bartholomew, Jean
See Beatty, Patricia (Robbins)
Bartlett, Alison 153
Bartlett, Philip A. 1
Bartlett, Robert Merrill 1899-1995 12
Bartoletti, Susan Campbell 1958- 237
Earlier sketches in SATA 88, 129, 135, 173
Barton, Byron 1930- 126
Earlier sketches in SATA 9, 90
Barton, Chris 224
Barton, Jill(ian) 1940- 75
Barton, May Hollis 67
Earlier sketch in SATA 1
Barton, Pat
See Arrowsmith, Pat
Barton, Patrice 1955- 226
Bartos-Hoeppner, Barbara 1923- 5
Bartram, Simon 218
Earlier sketch in SATA 156
Bartsch, Jochen 1906- 39
Baruch, Dorothy W(alter) 1899-1962 21
Barunga, Albert 1912(?)-1977 120
Baryshnikov, Mikhail 1948- 192
Bas, Rutger
See Rutgers van der Loeff-Basenau, An(na)
Maria Margaretha
Base, Graeme 1958- 162
Earlier sketches in SATA 67, 101
See also CLR 22
Base, Graeme Rowland
See Base, Graeme
Baseman, Gary 1960- 174
Bash, Barbara 1948- 132
Basher
See Basher, Simon
Basher, Simon 235
Bashevis, Isaac
See Singer, Isaac Bashevis
Bashevis, Yitskhok
See Singer, Isaac Bashevis
Bashista, Adrienne Ehlert 203
Basile, Gloria Vitanza 1929- 180
Baskin, Leonard 1922-2000 120
Brief entry 27
Earlier sketch in SATA 30
Baskin, Nora Raleigh 1961- 189
Earlier sketch in SATA 129
Bason, Lillian 1913- 20
Bass, Hester 1956- 223
Bass, L.G.
See Geringer, Laura
Bassett, Jeni 1959- 64
Brief entry 43
Bassett, John Keith
See Keating, Lawrence A.
Bassett, Lisa 1958- 61
Bassil, Andrea
See Nilsen, Anna
Bastyra, Judy 108
Basye, Dale E. 205
Bataille, Marion 1963- 209

Bat-Ami, Miriam 1950- 150
  Autobiography Feature 150
  Earlier sketches in SATA 82, 122
Bate, Lucy 1939-1993 18
Bate, Norman (Arthur) 1916- 5
Bateman, Colin 1962- 172
Bateman, Donna M. 190
Bateman, Teresa 1957- 216
  Earlier sketches in SATA 112, 168
Bates, Amy June 239
  Earlier sketch in SATA 189
Bates, Barbara S(nedeker) 1919- 12
Bates, Betty
  See Bates, Elizabeth
Bates, Dianne 1948- 147
Bates, Elizabeth 1921- 19
Bates, Ivan 175
Bates, Katharine Lee 1859-1929 113
Bates, Martine
  See Leavitt, Martine
Bateson, Catherine 1960- 197
  Earlier sketch in SATA 157
Batey, Tom 1946- 52
  Brief entry 41
Bath, Kevin P.
  See Bath, K.P.
Bath, K.P. 1959- 171
Batherman, Muriel
  See Sheldon, Muriel
Batson, Larry 1930- 35
Batt, Tanya Robyn 1970- 131
Battaglia, Aurelius 1910- 50
  Brief entry 33
Batten, H(arry) Mortimer 1888-1958 25
Batten, Mary 1937- 162
  Earlier sketches in SATA 5, 102
Batterberry, Ariane Ruskin 1935- 13
Batterberry, Michael Carver 1932-2010 32
Battle-Lavert, Gwendolyn 1951- 155
  Earlier sketches in SATA 85, 131
Battles, (Roxy) Edith 1921- 7
Baudouy, Michel-Aime 1909- 7
Bauer, A.C.E. 201
Bauer, Caroline Feller 1935- 98
  Brief entry 46
  Earlier sketch in SATA 52
  See also SAAS 24
Bauer, Fred 1934- 36
Bauer, Helen 1900-1988 2
Bauer, Joan 1951- 160
  Earlier sketch in SATA 117
Bauer, Jutta 1955- 150
Bauer, Marion Dane 1938- 192
  Autobiography Feature 144
  Earlier sketches in SATA 20, 69, 113, 144
  See also SAAS 9
Bauer, Michael Gerard 1955(?)- 167
Bauer, Steven 1948- 125
Bauerschmidt, Marjorie 1926- 15
Baughman, Dorothy 1940- 61
Baum, Allyn Z(elton) 1924-1997 98
  Earlier sketch in SATA 20
Baum, L. Frank
  See Thompson, Ruth Plumly
Baum, L. Frank 1856-1919 100
  Earlier sketch in SATA 18
  See also CLR 107
Baum, Louis 1948- 182
  Brief entry 52
  Earlier sketch in SATA 64
Baum, Louis F.
  See Baum, L. Frank
Baum, Lyman Frank
  See Baum, L. Frank
Baum, Maxie 188
Baum, Willi 1931- 4
Bauman, Beth Ann 1964- 220
Baumann, Amy Beeching 1922- 10
Baumann, Amy Brown Beeching
  See Baumann, Amy Beeching

Baumann, Hans 1914- 2
  See also CLR 35
Baumann, Kurt 1935- 21
Baumgartner, Barbara 1939- 86
Baurys, Flo 1938- 122
Baurys, Florence
  See Baurys, Flo
Bausum, Ann 173
Bawden, Nina 1925- 132
  Earlier sketches in SATA 4, 72
  See also CLR 51
  See also SAAS 16
Bawden, Nina Mary Mabey
  See Bawden, Nina
Baxter, Andy
  See Dakin, Glenn
Baxter, Roberta 1952- 219
Baxter, Valerie
  See Meynell, Laurence Walter
Bay, Jeanette Graham 1928- 88
Bayer, Harold
  See Gregg, Andrew K.
Bayer, Jane E. (?)-1985
  Obituary 44
Bayley, Nicola 1949- 129
  Earlier sketches in SATA 41, 69
Baylor, Byrd 1924- 136
  Earlier sketches in SATA 16, 69
  See also CLR 3
Baynes, Pauline 1922-2008 133
  Obituary 196
  Earlier sketch in SATA 19, 59
Baynes, Pauline Diana
  See Baynes, Pauline
Bayoc, Cbabi 186
Bayrock, Fiona 215
BB
  See Watkins-Pitchford, Denys James
Beach, Charles
  See Reid, (Thomas) Mayne
Beach, Charles Amory 1
Beach, Edward L. 1918-2002 12
  Obituary 140
Beach, Edward Latimer
  See Beach, Edward L.
Beach, Lisa 1957- 111
Beach, Lynn
  See Lance, Kathryn
Beach, Stewart T(aft) 1899-1979 23
Beachcroft, Nina 1931- 18
Beagle, Peter S. 1939- 130
  Earlier sketch in SATA 60
Beagle, Peter Soyer
  See Beagle, Peter S.
Beaglehole, Helen 1946- 117
Beake, Lesley 1949- 209
Beaky, Suzanne 1971- 230
Beale, Fleur 107
Bealer, Alex W(inkler III) 1921-1980 8
  Obituary 22
Beales, Valerie 1915- 74
Beals, Carleton 1893-1979 12
Beals, Frank Lee 1881-1972
  Obituary 26
Beam, Matt 1970- 187
Beame, Rona 1934- 12
Beamer, Charles 1942- 43
Beamer, George Charles, Jr.
  See Beamer, Charles
Bean, Jonathan 1979- 194
Bean, Normal
  See Burroughs, Edgar Rice
Beaney, Jan
  See Udall, Jan Beaney
Beaney, Jane
  See Udall, Jan Beaney
Bear, Carolyn
  See Rayban, Chloe
Bear, Greg 1951- 105
  Earlier sketch in SATA 65

Bear, Gregory Dale
  See Bear, Greg
Bearanger, Marie
  See Messier, Claire
Beard, Alex 1970- 222
Beard, Charles A(ustin) 1874-1948 18
Beard, Dan(iel Carter) 1850-1941 22
Beard, Darleen Bailey 1961- 96
Bearden, Romare (Howard) 1914(?)-1988 ... 22
  Obituary 56
Beardmore, Cedric
  See Beardmore, George
Beardmore, George 1908-1979 20
Beardshaw, Rosalind 1969- 225
  Earlier sketch in SATA 190
Beardsley, Martyn R. 1957- 150
Bearman, Jane (Ruth) 1917- 29
Bearn, Emily 220
Beaton, Clare 1947- 220
  Earlier sketch in SATA 125
Beatty, Elizabeth
  See Holloway, Teresa (Bragunier)
Beatty, Hetty Burlingame 1907-1971 5
Beatty, Jerome, Jr. 1918- 5
Beatty, John (Louis) 1922-1975 6
  Obituary 25
Beatty, Patricia (Robbins) 1922-1991 73
  Obituary 68
  Earlier sketches in SATA 1, 30
  See also SAAS 4
Beaty, Andrea 186
Beaty, Mary (T.) 1947- 146
Beaudoin, Sean 210
Beauford, Jhenne Tyler
  See Beauford, Tyler
Beauford, Tyler 1990- 225
Beaufort, Simon
  See Gregory, Susanna
  and Riffenburgh, Beau
Beaumont, Karen 1954- 204
Beavers, Ethen 1971- 225
Beccia, Carlyn 189
Bechard, Margaret 1953- 164
  Earlier sketch in SATA 85
Bechtel, Louise Seaman 1894-1985 4
  Obituary 43
Bechtold, Lisze 208
Beck, Andrea 1956- 226
Beck, Barbara L. 1927- 12
Beck, Ian 1947- 190
  Earlier sketch in SATA 138
  See Beck, Ian Archibald
Beck, Peggy 1949- 171
Beck, Scott 197
Becker, Beril 1901-1999 11
Becker, Bonny 184
Becker, Deborah Zimmett 1955- 138
Becker, Helaine 1961- 142
Becker, John (Leonard) 1901- 12
Becker, John E(mil) 1942- 148
Becker, Joyce 1936- 39
Becker, May Lamberton 1873-1958 33
Becker, Neesa 1951- 123
Becker, Shari 174
Beckerman, Chad W. 198
Beckett, Sheilah 1913- 33
Beckhorn, Susan Williams 1953- 189
Beckles Willson, Robina 1930- 27
Beckman, Delores 1914-1994 51
Beckman, Gunnel 1910- 6
  See also CLR 25
  See also SAAS 9
Beckman, Kaj
  See Beckman, Karin
Beckman, Karin 1913- 45
Beckman, Per (Frithiof) 1913- 45
Bedard, Michael 1949- 154
  Earlier sketch in SATA 93
  See also CLR 35
Beddor, Frank 194

Beddows, Eric
  See Nutt, Ken
Bedford, A. N.
  See Watson, Jane Werner
Bedford, Annie North
  See Watson, Jane Werner
Bedford, David 224
  Earlier sketch in SATA *159*
Bedford, David J.
  See Bedford, David
Bedoukian, Kerop 1907-1981 53
Bee, Jay
  See Brainerd, John W(hiting)
Bee, William 188
Beebe, B. F.
  See Johnson, B. F.
Beebe, (Charles) William 1877-1962 19
Beeby, Betty 1923- 25
Beech, Mark 1971- 191
Beech, Webb
  See Griffin, W. E. B.
Beecham, Jahnna 161
Beechcroft, William
  See Hallstead, William F(inn III)
Beeching, Jack 1922- 14
Beeke, Tiphanie 219
  Earlier sketch in SATA *163*
Beeler, Janet
  See Shaw, Janet
Beeler, Nelson F(rederick) 1910-1978 13
Beene, Jason 239
Beere, Peter 1951- 97
Beers, Dorothy Sands 1917- 9
Beers, Lorna 1897-1989 14
Beers, V(ictor) Gilbert 1928- 130
  Earlier sketch in SATA *9*
Beeton, Max
  See Redding, Robert Hull
Begay, Shonto 1954- 137
Begaye, Lisa Shook
  See Beach, Lisa
Begin, Mary Jane 1963- 82
Begin-Callanan, Mary Jane
  See Begin, Mary Jane
Begley, Kathleen A. 1948- 21
Begley, Kathleen Anne
  See Begley, Kathleen A.
Beguine, Anna
  See Saintcrow, Lilith
Beha, Eileen 221
Beha, Philippe 211
Behan, Leslie
  See Gottfried, Theodore Mark
Behler, Deborah A. 1947- 145
Behler, John L. 1943-2006 145
  Obituary 173
Behler, John Luther
  See Behler, John L.
Behn, Harry 1898-1973 2
  Obituary 34
Behnke, Frances L. 8
Behr, Joyce 1929- 15
Behrens, Andy 228
Behrens, June York 1925- 19
Behrman, Carol H(elen) 1925- 144
  Earlier sketch in SATA *14*
Beifuss, John, (Jr.) 1959- 92
Beil, Karen Magnuson 1950- 221
  Earlier sketch in SATA *124*
Beil, Michael D. 226
Beiler, Edna 1923- 61
Beingessner, Laura 1965- 220
Beinicke, Steve 1956- 69
Beirne, Barbara 1933- 71
Beiser, Arthur 1931- 22
Beiser, Germaine 1931- 11
Belair, Richard L. 1934- 45
Belaney, Archibald Stansfeld 1888-1938 24
  See also CLR *32*
Belasen, Amy 1983- 213

Belbin, David 1958- 164
  Earlier sketch in SATA *106*
Belden, Wilanne Schneider 1925- 56
Belford, Kevin 236
Belfrage, Sally 1936-1994 65
  Obituary 79
Belknap, B. H.
  See Ellis, Edward S.
Belknap, Boynton
  See Ellis, Edward S.
Belknap, Boynton M.D.
  See Ellis, Edward S.
Bell, Anthea 1936- 148
  Earlier sketch in SATA *88*
Bell, Cathleen Davitt 1971- 203
Bell, Cece 202
Bell, Clare (Louise) 1952- 99
Bell, Corydon Whitten 1894-1980 3
Bell, David Owen 1949- 99
Bell, Emerson
  See Stratemeyer, Edward L.
Bell, Emily Mary
  See Cason, Mabel Earp
Bell, Frank
  See Benson, Mildred
Bell, Gertrude (Wood) 1911-1987 12
Bell, Gina
  See Balzano, Jeanne (Koppel)
Bell, Hilari 1958- 226
  Earlier sketches in SATA *151, 197*
Bell, Jadrien
  See Golden, Christie
Bell, Janet
  See Clymer, Eleanor
Bell, Janet Cheatham 1937- 127
Bell, Krista 1950- 215
  Earlier sketch in SATA *126*
Bell, Krista Anne Blakeney
  See Bell, Krista
Bell, Margaret E(lizabeth) 1898-1990 2
Bell, Mary Reeves 1946- 88
Bell, Norman (Edward) 1899- 11
Bell, Raymond Martin 1907-1999 13
Bell, Siobhan 177
Bell, Thelma Harrington 1896-1985 3
Bell, William 1945- 90
  See also CLR *91*
Bellairs, John (Anthony) 1938-1991 160
  Obituary 66
  Earlier sketches in SATA *2, 68*
  See also CLR *37*
Beller, Susan Provost 1949- 128
  Earlier sketch in SATA *84*
  See also CLR *106*
Bellingham, Brenda 1931- 99
  Brief entry 51
Bello, Rosario de
  See De Bello, Rosario
Belloc, Hilaire 1870-1953 112
  See also YABC *1*
  See also CLR *102*
Belloc, Joseph Hilaire Pierre Sebastien Rene
  Swanton
  See Belloc, Hilaire
Belloc, Joseph Peter Rene Hilaire
  See Belloc, Hilaire
Belloc, Joseph Pierre Hilaire
  See Belloc, Hilaire
Belloli, Andrea P. A. 1947- 86
Bell-Rehwoldt, Sheri 1962- 199
Bellville, Cheryl Walsh 1944- 54
  Brief entry 49
Bell-Zano, Gina
  See Balzano, Jeanne (Koppel)
Belpre, Pura 1899-1982 16
  Obituary 30
Belting, Natalia Maree 1915-1997 6
Belton, John Raynor 1931- 22
Belton, Sandra 1939- 186
  Earlier sketches in SATA *85, 134*

Belton, Sandra Yvonne
  See Belton, Sandra
Beltran, Alberto 1923- 43
Beltran-Hernandez, Irene 1945- 74
Belvedere, Lee
  See Grayland, Valerie (Merle Spanner)
Bemelmans, Ludwig 1898-1962 100
  Earlier sketch in SATA *15*
  See also CLR *93*
Bemis, John Claude 234
Benander, Carl D. 1941- 74
Benary, Margot
  See Benary-Isbert, Margot
Benary-Isbert, Margot 1889-1979 2
  Obituary 21
  See also CLR *12*
Benasutti, Marion 1908-1992 6
Benatar, Raquel 1955- 167
Benchley, Nathaniel (Goddard) 1915-1981 .. 25
  Obituary 28
  Earlier sketch in SATA *3*
Benchley, Peter 1940-2006 164
  Earlier sketches in SATA *3, 89*
Benchley, Peter Bradford
  See Benchley, Peter
Bendall-Brunello, John 185
Bender, Edna 1941- 92
Bender, Esther 1942- 88
Bender, Lucy Ellen 1942- 22
Bender, Robert 1962- 160
  Earlier sketch in SATA *79*
Bendick, Jeanne 1919- 238
  Autobiography Feature 238
  Earlier sketches in SATA *2, 68, 135*
  See also CLR *5*
  See also SAAS *4*
Bendick, Robert L(ouis) 1917- 11
Bendinger, Jessica 1966- 233
Benedetto, William R. 1928- 180
Benedetto, William Ralph
  See Benedetto, William R.
Benedict, Andrew
  See Arthur, Robert, (Jr.)
Benedict, Dorothy Potter 1889-1979 11
  Obituary 23
Benedict, Lois Trimble 1902-1967 12
Benedict, Rex 1920-1995 8
Benedict, Stewart H(urd) 1924- 26
Beneduce, Ann Keay 128
Benet, Laura 1884-1979 3
  Obituary 23
Benet, Stephen Vincent 1898-1943
  See YABC *1*
Benet, Sula 1906-1982 21
  Obituary 33
Ben-Ezer, Ehud 1936- 122
Benezra, Barbara (Beardsley) 1921- 10
Benham, Leslie 1922- 48
Benham, Lois (Dakin) 1924- 48
Benham, Mary Lile 1914-1991 55
Benioff, Carol 232
Benjamin, E. M. J.
  See Bache, Ellyn
Benjamin, Floella 1949- 206
Benjamin, Nora
  See Kubie, Nora Gottheil Benjamin
Benjamin, Saragail Katzman 1953- 86
Benner, Cheryl 1962- 80
Benner, Judith Ann 1942- 94
Bennett, Alice
  See Ziner, Florence
Bennett, Artie 227
Bennett, Cherie 1960- 158
  Earlier sketch in SATA *97*
Bennett, Dorothea
  See Young, Dorothea Bennett
Bennett, Erin Susanne
  See Banks, Erin Bennett
Bennett, Holly 1957- 181

Bennett, James (W.) 1942- 153
    Autobiography Feature 153
    Earlier sketches in SATA *93, 148*
Bennett, Jay 1912- 87
    Brief entry 27
    Earlier sketch in SATA *41*
    See also SAAS *4*
Bennett, Jill (Crawford) 1934- 41
Bennett, John 1865-1956
    See YABC *1*
Bennett, Kelly 1958- 231
Bennett, Kelly Goldman
    See Bennett, Kelly
Bennett, Penelope (Agnes) 1938- 94
Bennett, Rachel
    See Hill, Margaret (Ohler)
Bennett, Rainey 1907-1998 15
    Obituary 111
Bennett, Richard 1899- 21
Bennett, Russell H(oradley) 1896- 25
Bennett, Veronica 1953- 178
Bennett, William (John) 1943- 102
Benning, Elizabeth
    See Rice, Bebe Faas
Benny, Mike 1964- 203
Benson, Amber 1977- 235
Benson, Elizabeth P(olk) 1924- 65
Benson, Kathleen 1947- 183
    Earlier sketches in SATA *62, 111*
Benson, Linda M(aria) 1959- 84
Benson, Mildred 1905-2002 100
    Obituary 135
    Earlier sketches in SATA *1, 65, 67*
Benson, Mildred Augustine Wirt
    See Benson, Mildred
Benson, Mildred Wirt
    See Benson, Mildred
Benson, Millie
    See Benson, Mildred
Benson, Patrick 1956- 147
Benson, Sally 1900-1972 35
    Obituary 27
    Earlier sketch in SATA *1*
Bentley, Judith (McBride) 1945- 89
    Earlier sketch in SATA *40*
Bentley, Karen
    See Taschek, Karen
Bentley, Nancy (L.) 1946- 78
Bentley, Nicolas Clerihew 1907-1978
    Obituary 24
Bentley, Phyllis Eleanor 1894-1977 6
    Obituary 25
Bentley, Roy 1947- 46
Bentley, William (George) 1916- 84
Bently, Peter 1960- 221
Benton, Jim 1963- 172
ben Uzair, Salem
    See Horne, Richard Henry Hengist
Ben-Zvi, Rebeccca Tova
    See O'Connell, Rebecca
Bercaw, Edna Coe 1961- 124
Berck, Judith 1960- 75
Bereal, JaeMe 1959(?)- 228
Berelson, Howard 1940- 5
Berends, Polly Berrien 1939- 50
    Brief entry 38
Berenstain, Jan 1923- 135
    Earlier sketches in SATA *12, 64, 129*
    See also CLR *150*
    See also SAAS *20*
Berenstain, Janice
    See Berenstain, Jan
Berenstain, Michael 1951- 220
    Earlier sketch in SATA *45*
Berenstain, Mike
    See Berenstain, Michael
Berenstain, Stan 1923-2005 135
    Obituary 169
    Earlier sketches in SATA *12, 64, 129*
    See also CLR *150*
    See also SAAS *20*

Berenstain, Stanley
    See Berenstain, Stan
Berenzy, Alix 1957- 168
    Earlier sketch in SATA *65*
Beresford, Elisabeth 1928-2010 141
    Earlier sketches in SATA *25, 86*
    See also SAAS *20*
Berg, Adriane G(ilda) 1948- 152
Berg, Dave
    See Berg, David
Berg, David 1920-2002 27
    Obituary 137
Berg, Elizabeth 1948- 104
Berg, Jean Horton 1913-1995 6
Berg, Joan
    See Victor, Joan Berg
Berg, Ron 1952- 48
Bergaust, Erik 1925-1978 20
Bergel, Colin J. 1963- 137
Bergen, Joyce 1949- 95
Berger, Barbara (Helen) 1945- 77
Berger, Carin 232
    Earlier sketch in SATA *185*
Berger, Gilda 1935- 88
    Brief entry 42
Berger, Joe 1970- 221
Berger, Josef 1903-1971 36
Berger, Lou 1950- 213
Berger, Melvin H. 1927- 158
    Autobiography Feature 124
    Earlier sketches in SATA *5, 88*
    See also CLR *32*
    See also SAAS *2*
Berger, Phil 1942-2001 62
Berger, Samantha 1969- 140
Berger, Samantha Allison
    See Berger, Samantha
Berger, Terry 1933- 8
Bergey, Alyce 1934- 45
Bergey, Alyce Mae
    See Bergey, Alyce
Bergin, Mark 1961- 160
    Earlier sketch in SATA *114*
Berglin, Ruth Marie 1970- 181
Bergman, Donna 1934- 73
Bergman, Mara 1956- 196
Bergman, Tamar 1939- 95
Bergren, Lisa T.
    See Bergren, Lisa Tawn
Bergren, Lisa Tawn 200
Bergsma, Jody Lynn 163
Bergstein, Rita M. 211
Bergum, Constance R. 1952- 208
    Earlier sketch in SATA *121*
Berk, Ari 208
Berk, Josh 1976- 227
Berkebile, Fred D(onovan) 1900-1978
    Obituary 26
Berkeley, Jon 1962- 204
Berkes, Marianne 217
    Earlier sketch in SATA *173*
Berkey, Barry Robert 1935- 24
Berkowitz, Freda Pastor 1908-1994 12
Berkus, Clara Widess 1909- 78
Berlan, Kathryn Hook 1946- 78
Berlfein, Judy Reiss 1958- 79
Berlin, Eric 1968- 195
Berliner, Don 1930- 33
Berliner, Franz 1930- 13
Berlitz, Charles (L. Frambach) 1914-2003 ... 32
    Obituary 151
Berman, Len 1947- 229
Berman, Linda 1948- 38
Berman, Paul (Lawrence) 1949- 66
Berman, Rachel 1946- 217
Berna, Paul 1910-1994 15
    Obituary 78
    See also CLR *19*
Bernadette
    See Watts, Bernadette

Bernard, Bruce 1928-2000 78
    Obituary 124
Bernard, George I. 1949- 39
Bernard, Jacqueline (de Sieyes) 1921-1983 ... 8
    Obituary 45
Bernard, Patricia 1942- 181
    Earlier sketch in SATA *106*
Bernard, Trish
    See Bernard, Patricia
Bernardin, James 1966- 227
    Earlier sketch in SATA *112*
Bernardo, Anilu 184
Bernards, Neal 1963- 71
Bernasconi, Pablo 1973- 183
Bernays, Anne 1930- 32
Berne, Jennifer 238
Berner, Rotraut Susanne 1948- 214
Bernhard, Durga T. 1961- 80
Bernhard, Emery 1950- 80
Bernheimer, Kate 201
Bernier-Grand, Carmen T. 1947- 202
Bernstein, Daryl (Evan) 1976- 81
Bernstein, Joanne E(ckstein) 1943- 15
Bernstein, Jonathan 217
Bernstein, Margery 1933- 114
Bernstein, Nina 1949- 180
Bernstein, Theodore M(enline) 1904-1979 ... 12
    Obituary 27
Berrien, Edith Heal
    See Heal, Edith
Berrill, Jacquelyn (Batsel) 1905- 12
Berrington, John
    See Brownjohn, Alan
Berry, B. J.
    See Berry, Barbara J.
Berry, Barbara J. 1937- 7
Berry, Erick
    See Best, (Evangel) Allena Champlin
Berry, Holly 1957- 210
Berry, James 1924- 110
    Earlier sketch in SATA *67*
    See also CLR *143*
Berry, Jane Cobb 1915(?)-1979
    Obituary 22
Berry, Joy 1944- 58
    Brief entry 46
Berry, Joy Wilt
    See Berry, Joy
Berry, Julie 1974- 218
Berry, Lynne 190
Berry, William D(avid) 1926- 14
Bersani, Shennen 1961- 164
Berson, Harold 1926- 4
Bertagna, Julie 1962- 151
Bertholf, Bret 189
Bertin, Charles-Francois
    See Berlitz, Charles (L. Frambach)
Bertolet, Paul
    See McLaughlin, Frank
Berton, Pierre (Francis de Marigny)
    1920-2004 99
    Obituary 158
Bertrand, Cecile 1953- 76
Bertrand, Diane Gonzales 1956- 177
    Earlier sketch in SATA *106*
Bertrand, Lynne 1963- 164
    Earlier sketch in SATA *81*
Beskow, Elsa (Maartman) 1874-1953 20
    See also CLR *17*
Bess, Clayton
    See Locke, Robert
Besson, Luc 1959- 199
Best, (Evangel) Allena Champlin 1892-1974 . 2
    Obituary 25
Best, Cari 1951- 200
    Earlier sketches in SATA *107, 149*
Best, (Oswald) Herbert 1894-1980 2
Bestall, A(lfred) E(dmeades) 1892-1986 97
    Obituary 48

Betancourt, Jeanne 1941- 148
  Brief entry 43
  Earlier sketches in SATA 55, 96
Beth, Mary
  See Miller, Mary Beth
Bethancourt, T. Ernesto
  See Paisley, Tom
Bethel, Dell 1929- 52
Bethell, Jean (Frankenberry) 1922- 8
Bethers, Ray 1902-1973 6
Bethke, Bruce Raymond 1955- 114
Bethlen, T.D.
  See Silverberg, Robert
Bethune, J. G.
  See Ellis, Edward S.
Bethune, J. H.
  See Ellis, Edward S.
Betteridge, Anne
  See Potter, Margaret
Betteridge, Deirdre 214
Bettina
  See Ehrlich, Bettina Bauer
Bettmann, Otto Ludwig 1903-1998 46
Bettoli, Delana 187
Betts, James
  See Haynes, Betsy
Betz, Eva Kelly 1897-1968 10
Bevan, Tom 1868-1930(?)
  See YABC 2
Bevis, Mary 1939- 202
Bewick, Thomas 1753-1828 16
Beyer, Audrey White 1916- 9
Beyer, Paul J. III 1950- 74
Beynon, John
  See Harris, John (Wyndham Parkes Lucas)
  Beynon
Bezencon, Jacqueline (Buxcel) 1924- 48
Bhatia, Jamunadevi 1919-2011 48
Bhatia, June
  See Bhatia, Jamunadevi
Bial, Morrison David 1917- 62
Bial, Raymond 1948- 225
  Earlier sketches in SATA 76, 116, 165
Biala
  See Brustlein, Janice Tworkov
Biale, Rachel 1952- 99
Bialk, Elisa
  See Krautter, Elisa (Bialk)
Bianchi, John 1947- 91
Bianchi, Robert S(teven) 1943- 92
Bianco, Margery
  See Bianco, Margery Williams
Bianco, Margery Williams 1881-1944 15
  See also CLR 146
Bianco, Pamela 1906- 28
Bibby, Violet 1908-1996 24
Bible, Charles 1937- 13
Bibo, Bobette
  See Gugliotta, Bobette
Bice, Clare 1909-1976 22
Bick, Ilsa J. 238
Bickerstaff, Isaac
  See Swift, Jonathan
Bidner, Jenni 1963- 193
Biedrzycki, David 1955- 219
Biegel, Paul 1925- 79
  Earlier sketch in SATA 16
  See also CLR 27
  See also SAAS 18
Biemiller, Carl L(udwig), Jr.) 1912-1979 40
  Obituary 21
Bienenfeld, Florence L(ucille) 1929- 39
Bierhorst, John (William) 1936- 149
  Autobiography Feature 149
  Earlier sketches in SATA 6, 91
  See also SAAS 10
Biggar, Joan R. 1936- 120
Biggar, Joan Rawlins
  See Biggar, Joan R.
Biggle, Lloyd, Jr. 1923-2002 65
Biggs, Brian 1968- 192

Bilal, Abdel W(ahab) 1970- 92
Bilbrough, Norman 1941- 111
Bildner, Phil 230
  Earlier sketch in SATA 173
Bileck, Marvin 1920- 40
Bilibin, Ivan (Iakolevich) 1876-1942 61
Bill, Alfred Hoyt 1879-1964 44
Bill, Tannis 228
Billam, Rosemary 1952- 61
Billings, Charlene W(interer) 1941- 41
Billingsley, Franny 1954- 235
  Earlier sketch in SATA 132
Billington, Elizabeth T(hain) 50
  Brief entry 43
Billout, Guy (Rene) 1941- 144
  Earlier sketch in SATA 10
  See also CLR 33
Bilson, Geoffrey 1938-1987 99
Binch, Caroline (Lesley) 1947- 140
  Earlier sketch in SATA 81
Bing, Christopher (H.) 126
Bingham, Caroline 1962- 158
Bingham, Jane M. 1941- 163
Bingham, Jane Marie
  See Bingham, Jane M.
Bingham, Janet 1959- 200
Bingham, Kelly 1967- 207
Bingham, Sam 1944- 96
Bingham, Samuel A.
  See Bingham, Sam
Bingley, Margaret (Jane Kirby) 1947- 72
Binkley, Anne
  See Rand, Ann (Binkley)
Binzen, Bill
  See Binzen, William
Binzen, William 24
Birch, David (W.) 1913-1996 89
Birch, Reginald B(athurst) 1856-1943 19
Birchman, David 1949- 72
Birchmore, Daniel A. 1951- 92
Bird, Carmel 1940- 124
Bird, E(lzy) J(ay) 1911- 58
Birdsall, Jeanne 1951- 231
Birdsall, Jeanne 1952(?)- 170
Birdseye, Tom 1951- 148
  Earlier sketches in SATA 66, 98
Birenbaum, Barbara 1941- 65
Birmingham, Christian 1970- 220
Birmingham, Lloyd P(aul) 1924- 83
  Earlier sketch in SATA 12
Birmingham, Ruth
  See Sorrells, Walter
Birney, Betty G. 1947- 169
  Earlier sketch in SATA 98
Biro, B.
  See Biro, B. S.
Biro, B. S. 1921- 1
  See also CLR 28
  See also SAAS 13
Biro, Val
  See Biro, B. S.
Birtha, Becky 1948- 229
Bischoff, Julia Bristol 1899-1970 12
Bishop, Bonnie 1943- 37
Bishop, Claire Huchet 1899(?)-1993 14
  Obituary 74
  See also CLR 80
Bishop, Courtney
  See Ruemmler, John D(avid)
Bishop, Curtis (Kent) 1912-1967 6
Bishop, Elizabeth 1911-1979
  Obituary 24
Bishop, Gavin 1946- 216
  Earlier sketches in SATA 97, 144
Bishop, Kathleen Wong 1954- 120
Bishop, Kathy
  See Bishop, Kathleen Wong
Bishop, Nic 1955- 161
  Earlier sketch in SATA 107
Bishop, Rudine Sims 224

Bisset, Donald 1910-1995 86
  Earlier sketch in SATA 7
Bisson, Terry 1942- 99
Bisson, Terry Ballantine
  See Bisson, Terry
Bitter, Gary G(len) 1940- 22
Bixby, William (Courtney) 1920-1986 6
  Obituary 47
Bjoerk, Christina 1938- 99
  Earlier sketch in SATA 67
  See also CLR 22
Bjork, Christina
  See Bjoerk, Christina
Bjorklund, Lorence F. 1913-1978 35
  Brief entry 32
Bjorkman, Lauren 222
Bjorkman, Steve 223
  Earlier sketch in SATA 163
Blabey, Aaron 1975(?)- 214
Black, Algernon David 1900-1993 12
  Obituary 76
Black, Holly 1971- 236
  Earlier sketches in SATA 147, 210
Black, Irma Simonton 1906-1972 2
  Obituary 25
Black, Jenna 1965- 239
Black, Joe 1959- 224
Black, Rabbi Joe
  See Black, Joe
Black, Kat 217
Black, Katherine
  See Black, Kat
Black, Mansell
  See Trevor, Elleston
Black, MaryAnn
  See Easley, MaryAnn
Black, Susan Adams 1953- 40
Blackall, Bernie 1956- 126
Blackall, Sophie 231
  Earlier sketch in SATA 182
Blackburn, Claire
  See Altman, Linda Jacobs
Blackburn, John(ny) Brewton 1952- 15
Blackburn, Joyce Knight 1920- 29
Blacker, Terence 1948- 194
Blacker, Tina
  See Louise, Tina
Blackett, Veronica Heath 1927- 12
Blackie, Jean Cutler 1943- 79
Blacklin, Malcolm
  See Chambers, Aidan
Blacklock, Dyan 1951- 112
Blackman, Malorie 1962- 196
  Earlier sketches in SATA 83, 128
Blackton, Peter
  See Wilson, Lionel
Blackwood, Alan 1932- 70
Blackwood, Freya 199
Blackwood, Gary
  See Blackwood, Gary L.
Blackwood, Gary L. 1945- 226
  Earlier sketches in SATA 72, 118, 169
Blade, Alexander
  See Garrett, Randall
  and Hamilton, Edmond
  and Silverberg, Robert
Bladek, John 1963(?)- 237
Blades, Ann (Sager) 1947- 69
  Earlier sketch in SATA 16
  See also CLR 15
Bladow, Suzanne Wilson 1937- 14
Blaine, Chris
  See Gardner, Craig Shaw
Blaine, John
  See Goodwin, Harold L(eland)
Blaine, Marge
  See Blaine, Margery Kay
Blaine, Margery Kay 1937- 11
Blair, Alison
  See Lerangis, Peter
Blair, Anne Denton 1914-1993 46

Blair, David Nelson 1954- 80
Blair, Eric
  See Orwell, George
Blair, Jay 1953- 45
Blair, Lucile
  See Yeakley, Marjory Hall
Blair, Margaret Whitman 1951- 227
  Earlier sketch in SATA 124
Blair, Mary 1911-1978 195
Blair, Pauline Hunter
  See Clarke, Pauline
Blair, Ruth Van Ness 1912-1999 12
Blair, Shannon
  See Kaye, Marilyn
Blair, Walter 1900-1992 12
  Obituary 72
Blaisdell, Bob
  See Blaisdell, Robert
Blaisdell, Robert 1959- 105
Blake, Bronwyn 1940- 149
Blake, Francis 198
Blake, Jon 1954- 171
  Earlier sketch in SATA 78
Blake, Olive
  See Supraner, Robyn
Blake, Quentin 1932- 211
  Earlier sketches in SATA 9, 52, 96, 125
  See also CLR 31
Blake, Robert 1949- 42
Blake, Robert J. 160
Blake, Stephanie 233
  See Pearl, Jacques Bain
Blake, Walker E.
  See Griffin, W. E. B.
Blake, William 1757-1827 30
  See also CLR 52
Blakely, Gloria 1950- 139
Blakely, Roger K. 1922- 82
Blakeney, Jay D.
  See Chester, Deborah
Blakeslee, Lys 1985- 218
Blakey, Nancy 1955- 94
Blanc, Esther S. 1913-1997 66
Blanc, Mel 1908-1989
  Obituary 64
Blanchard, Patricia 125
Blanchet, M(uriel) Wylie 1891-1961 106
Blanco, Richard L(idio) 1926- 63
Bland, E.
  See Nesbit, E.
Bland, Edith Nesbit
  See Nesbit, E.
Bland, Fabian
  See Nesbit, E.
Blane, Gertrude
  See Blumenthal, Gertrude
Blank, Clarissa Mabel 1915-1965 62
Blankenship, LeeAnn 1944- 181
Blassingame, Wyatt Rainey 1909-1985 34
  Obituary 41
  Earlier sketch in SATA 1
Blatchford, Claire H. 1944- 94
Blau, Aljoscha 1972- 233
Blauer, Ettagale 1940- 49
Blecha, Aaron 233
Bleck, Linda 207
Bledsoe, Glen L. 1951- 108
Bledsoe, Glen Leonard
  See Bledsoe, Glen L.
Bledsoe, Karen E. 1962- 167
  Earlier sketch in SATA 108
Bledsoe, Karen Elizabeth
  See Bledsoe, Karen E.
Bledsoe, Lucy Jane 1957- 162
  Earlier sketch in SATA 97
Bleeker, Sonia
  See Zim, Sonia Bleeker
Blegen, Daniel M. 1950- 92
Blegvad, Erik 1923- 132
  Earlier sketches in SATA 14, 66

Blegvad, Lenore 1926- 176
  Earlier sketches in SATA 14, 66
Bleiman, Andrew 237
Blessing, Charlotte 223
Bley, Anette 1967- 188
Blish, James 1921-1975 66
Blish, James Benjamin
  See Blish, James
Blishen, Edward (William) 1920-1996 66
  Obituary 93
  Earlier sketch in SATA 8
Bliss, Corinne Demas
  See Demas, Corinne
Bliss, Frederick
  See Card, Orson Scott
Bliss, Gillian
  See Paton Walsh, Jill
Bliss, Harry 1964- 196
  Earlier sketch in SATA 156
Bliss, Reginald
  See Wells, H. G.
Bliss, Ronald G(ene) 1942- 12
Blitt, Barry 187
Bliven, Bruce, Jr. 1916-2002 2
Blixen, Karen 1885-1962 44
Blizzard, Gladys S. (?)-1992 79
Blobaum, Cindy 1966- 123
Bloch, Lucienne 1909-1999 10
Bloch, Marie Halun 1910-1998 6
  See also SAAS 9
Bloch, Robert (Albert) 1917-1994 12
  Obituary 82
Bloch, Serge 1956- 213
Blochman, Lawrence G(oldtree)
  1900-1975 22
Block, Francesca Lia 1962- 213
  Earlier sketches in SATA 80, 116, 158
  See also CLR 116
  See also SAAS 21
Block, Irvin 1917- 12
Blomgren, Jennifer (Alice) 1954- 136
Blonder, Terry Joyce
  See Golson, Terry
Blood, Charles Lewis 1929- 28
Bloom, Barbara Lee 1943- 146
Bloom, Freddy 1914-2000 37
  Obituary 121
Bloom, Lloyd 1947- 108
  Brief entry 43
Bloom, Suzanne 1950- 232
  Earlier sketch in SATA 172
Bloomfield, Michaela 1966- 70
Bloor, Edward 1950- 201
  Earlier sketches in SATA 98, 155
Bloor, Edward William
  See Bloor, Edward
Blos, Joan W. 1928- 153
  Autobiography Feature 153
  Brief entry 27
  Earlier sketches in SATA 33, 69, 109
  See also CLR 18
  See also SAAS 11
Blos, Joan Winsor
  See Blos, Joan W.
Bloss, Josie 1981- 232
Blough, Glenn O(rlando) 1907-1995 1
Blue, Rose 1931- 166
  Autobiography Feature 117
  Earlier sketches in SATA 5, 91, 93
  See also SAAS 24
Blue, Zachary
  See Stine, R.L.
Bluemle, Elizabeth 209
Bluggage, Oranthy
  See Alcott, Louisa May
Blumberg, Leda 1956- 59
Blumberg, Rhoda 1917- 123
  Earlier sketches in SATA 35, 70
  See also CLR 21

Blume, Judy 1938- 195
  Earlier sketches in SATA 2, 31, 79, 142
  See also CLR 69
Blume, Judy Sussman
  See Blume, Judy
Blume, Lesley M.M. 1975- 180
Blumenthal, Deborah 204
  Earlier sketch in SATA 161
Blumenthal, Gertrude 1907-1971
  Obituary 27
Blumenthal, Shirley 1943- 46
Blutig, Eduard
  See Gorey, Edward (St. John)
Bly, Janet 1945- 43
Bly, Janet Chester
  See Bly, Janet
Bly, Stephen A(rthur) 1944- 116
  Earlier sketch in SATA 43
Blyler, Allison Lee 1966- 74
Blythe, Gary 1959- 185
Blyton, Carey 1932-2002 9
  Obituary 138
Blyton, Enid 1897-1968 25
  See also CLR 31
Blyton, Enid Mary
  See Blyton, Enid
Bo, Ben
  See Richardson, V.A.
Boardman, Fon Wyman, Jr. 1911-2000 6
Boardman, Gwenn R.
  See Petersen, Gwenn Boardman
Boase, Susan 226
Boase, Wendy 1944-1999 28
  Obituary 110
Boatner, Mark Mayo III 1921- 29
Bobbe, Dorothie de Bear 1905-1975 1
  Obituary 25
Bober, Natalie S. 1930- 134
  Earlier sketch in SATA 87
  See also SAAS 23
Bobette, Bibo
  See Gugliotta, Bobette
Bobri, Vladimir V. 1898-1986 47
  Brief entry 32
Bobritsky, Vladimir
  See Bobri, Vladimir V.
Bochak, Grayce 1956- 76
Bock, Hal
  See Bock, Harold I.
Bock, Harold I. 1939- 10
Bock, William Sauts Netamux'we 1939- 14
Bodanis, David 179
Bode, Janet 1943-1999 96
  Obituary 118
  Earlier sketch in SATA 60
Bode, N.E.
  See Baggott, Julianna
Bodecker, N(iels) M(ogens) 1922-1988 73
  Obituary 54
  Earlier sketch in SATA 8
Bodeen, S. A. 1965- 158
  Earlier sketch in SATA 114
Boden, Hilda
  See Bodenham, Hilda Morris
Bodenham, Hilda Morris 1901- 13
Bodett, Thomas Edward 1955- 70
Bodett, Tom
  See Bodett, Thomas Edward
Bodie, Idella F(allaw) 1925- 89
  Earlier sketch in SATA 12
Bodker, Cecil
  See Bodker, Cecil
Bodker, Cecil 1927- 133
  Earlier sketch in SATA 14
  See also CLR 23
Bodsworth, (Charles) Fred(erick) 1918- 27
Boeckman, Charles 1920- 12
Boegehold, Betty (Doyle) 1913-1985
  Obituary 42
Boelts, Maribeth 1964- 200
  Earlier sketches in SATA 78, 163

Boerst, William J. 1939- *170*
  Earlier sketch in SATA *121*
Boesch, Mark J(oseph) 1917- *12*
Boesen, Victor 1908- *16*
Bogacki, Tomek 1950- *214*
  Earlier sketch in SATA *138*
Bogaerts, Gert 1965- *80*
Bogan, Paulette 1960- *201*
  Earlier sketch in SATA *129*
Bogart, Jo Ellen 1945- *222*
  Earlier sketch in SATA *92*
  See also CLR *59*
Boggs, Ralph Steele 1901-1994 .... *7*
Bograd, Larry 1953- *89*
  Earlier sketch in SATA *33*
  See also SAAS *21*
Bogue, Gary 1938- *195*
Bogue, Gary L.
  See Bogue, Gary
Bohdal, Susi 1951- *101*
  Earlier sketch in SATA *22*
Bohlen, Nina 1931- *58*
Bohlmeijer, Arno 1956- *94*
Bohner, Charles (Henry) 1927- *62*
Bohnhoff, Maya Kaathryn 1954- *88*
Boie, Kirsten 1950- *221*
Boiger, Alexandra *178*
Boissard, Janine 1932- *59*
Bojunga, Lygia
  See Nunes, Lygia Bojunga
Bojunga-Nunes, Lygia
  See Nunes, Lygia Bojunga
Bok, Arthur
  See Bok, Chip
Bok, Chip 1952- *205*
Bolam, Emily 1969- *206*
Boland, Janice *98*
Bolden, Tonya 1959- *227*
  Earlier sketches in SATA *79, 138, 188*
Bolden, Tonya Wilyce
  See Bolden, Tonya
Boles, Paul Darcy 1916-1984 .... *9*
  Obituary *38*
Bolger, Kevin *233*
Bolian, Polly 1925- *4*
Bollen, Roger 1941(?)- *83*
  Brief entry *29*
Bolliger, Max 1929- *7*
Bollinger, Max 1929- *167*
Bollinger, Peter *172*
Bolognese, Don(ald Alan) 1934- *129*
  Earlier sketches in SATA *24, 71*
Bolognese, Elaine 1933- *23*
Bolotin, Norman (Phillip) 1951- *93*
Bolton, Carole 1926- *6*
Bolton, Elizabeth
  See St. John, Nicole
Bolton, Evelyn
  See Bunting, Eve
Bonar, Veronica
  See Bailey, Donna (Veronica Anne)
Bond, B. J.
  See Heneghan, James
Bond, Bruce 1939- *61*
Bond, Felicia 1954- *219*
  Earlier sketches in SATA *49, 126*
Bond, Gladys Baker 1912- *14*
Bond, Higgins 1951- *220*
  Earlier sketches in SATA *83, 177*
Bond, J. Harvey
  See Winterbotham, R(ussell) R(obert)
Bond, (Thomas) Michael 1926- *157*
  Earlier sketches in SATA *6, 58*
  See also CLR *95*
  See also SAAS *3*
Bond, Nancy 1945- *159*
  Autobiography Feature *159*
  Earlier sketches in SATA *22, 82*
  See also CLR *11*
  See also SAAS *13*

Bond, Nancy Barbara
  See Bond, Nancy
Bond, Rebecca 1972- *214*
  Earlier sketch in SATA *130*
Bond, Ruskin 1934- *87*
  Earlier sketch in SATA *14*
  See also CLR *171*
Bondie, J. D.
  See Cunningham, Chet
Bondoux, Anne-Laure 1971- *175*
Bone, Ian 1956- *158*
  Earlier sketch in SATA *117*
Bone, J. *230*
Bone, Jason
  See Bone, J.
Bonehill, Captain Ralph
  See Stratemeyer, Edward L.
Bonestell, Chesley 1888-1986
  Obituary *48*
Bonham, Barbara Thomas 1926- *7*
Bonham, Frank 1914-1989 .... *49*
  Obituary *62*
  Earlier sketch in SATA *1*
  See also SAAS *3*
Boniface, William 1963- *182*
  Earlier sketch in SATA *102*
Bonino, Louise
  See Williams, Louise Bonino
Bonk, John J. *189*
Bonn, Pat
  See Bonn, Patricia Carolyn
Bonn, Patricia Carolyn 1948- *43*
Bonner, Hannah *197*
Bonner, Mary Graham 1890-1974 .... *19*
Bonner, Mike 1951- *121*
Bonners, Susan 1947- *85*
  Brief entry *48*
Bonnet, Rosalinde 1978- *226*
Bonnett-Rampersaud, Louise *173*
Bonning, Tony 1948- *169*
Bonsall, Crosby Barbara (Newell)
  1921-1995 .... *23*
  Obituary *84*
Bonsall, Joseph S. 1948- *119*
Bonsignore, Joan 1959- *140*
Bontemps, Arna 1902-1973 .... *44*
  Obituary *24*
  Earlier sketch in SATA *2*
  See also CLR *6*
Bontemps, Arnaud Wendell
  See Bontemps, Arna
Bonwill, Ann *238*
Bonzon, Paul-Jacques 1908-1978 .... *22*
Boock, Paula 1964- *134*
Booher, Dianna Daniels 1948- *33*
Book, Rick 1949- *119*
Book, Rita
  See Holub, Joan
Bookman, Charlotte
  See Zolotow, Charlotte
Boon, Debbie 1960- *103*
Boon, Emilie (Laetitia) 1958- *86*
Boone, Charles Eugene
  See Boone, Pat
Boone, Pat 1934- *7*
Booraem, Ellen *211*
Boorman, Linda 1940- *46*
Boorman, Linda Kay
  See Boorman, Linda
Boorstin, Daniel J(oseph) 1914-2004 .... *52*
Boos, Ben 1971- *206*
Booth, Coe *187*
Booth, Ernest Sheldon 1915-1984 .... *43*
Booth, George 1926- *191*
Booth, Graham (Charles) 1935- *37*
Bootman, Colin *239*
  Earlier sketch in SATA *159*
Borden, Louise 1949- *190*
  Autobiography Feature *141*
  Earlier sketches in SATA *68, 104, 141*
Bordier, Georgette 1924- *16*

Borgman, James
  See Borgman, Jim
Borgman, James Mark
  See Borgman, Jim
Borgman, Jim 1954- *122*
Borgo, Lacy Finn 1972- *194*
Boring, Mel 1939- *168*
  Earlier sketch in SATA *35*
Borja, Corinne 1929- *22*
Borja, Robert 1923- *22*
Borland, Hal
  See Borland, Harold Glen
Borland, Harold Glen 1900-1978 .... *5*
  Obituary *24*
Borland, Kathryn Kilby 1916- *16*
Borlenghi, Patricia 1951- *79*
Born, Adolf 1930- *49*
Bornstein, Ruth Lercher
  See Bornstein-Lercher, Ruth
Bornstein-Lercher, Ruth 1927- *88*
  Autobiography Feature *107*
  Earlier sketch in SATA *14*
Borris, Albert *221*
Borski, Lucia Merecka *18*
Borten, Helen Jacobson 1930- *5*
Bortolotti, Dan 1969- *157*
Borton, Elizabeth
  See Trevino, Elizabeth B(orton) de
Borton, Lady 1942- *98*
Borton de Trevino, Elizabeth
  See Trevino, Elizabeth B(orton) de
Bortstein, Larry 1942-2010 .... *16*
Bortz, Alfred B(enjamin) 1944- *139*
  Earlier sketch in SATA *74*
Bortz, Fred
  See Bortz, Alfred B(enjamin)
Bosch, Pseudonymous *199*
Bosco, Jack
  See Holliday, Joseph
Bose, Mitali
  See Perkins, Mitali
Boshell, Gordon 1908-1991 .... *15*
Boshinski, Blanche 1922- *10*
Bosman, Paul 1929- *107*
Bosse, Malcolm (Joseph, Jr.) 1926-2002 .... *136*
  Earlier sketch in SATA *35*
Bosserman, Charles Phillip
  See Bosserman, Phillip
Bosserman, Phillip 1931- *84*
Bossley, Michele Martin 1969- *219*
Bossom, Naomi 1933- *35*
Bostock, Mike 1962- *114*
Boston, L(ucy) M(aria Wood) 1892-1990 .... *19*
  Obituary *64*
  See also CLR *3*
Bostrom, Kathleen (Susan) Long 1954- *139*
Bostrom, Kathy
  See Bostrom, Kathleen (Susan) Long
Boswell, Addie *208*
Boswell, Addie Kay
  See Boswell, Addie
Bosworth, J. Allan 1925- *19*
Bothwell, Jean (?)-1977 .... *2*
Botkin, B(enjamin) A(lbert) 1901-1975 .... *40*
Botsford, Ward 1927-2004 .... *66*
Botting, Douglas (Scott) 1934- *43*
Bottner, Barbara 1943- *232*
  Autobiography Feature *121*
  Earlier sketches in SATA *14, 93, 170*
  See also SAAS *26*
Bottone, Frank G., Jr. 1969- *141*
Bouchard, David 1952- *213*
  Earlier sketch in SATA *117*
Boucher, (Clarence) Carter 1954- *129*
Boudelang, Bob
  See Pell, Ed(ward)
Boudreau, Helene 1969- *238*
Boughton, Richard 1954- *75*
Boulet, Susan Seddon 1941- *50*
Boulle, Pierre 1912-1994 .... *22*
  Obituary *78*

Boulle, Pierre Francois Marie-Louis
    See Boulle, Pierre
Boulton, Jane 1921- 91
Bouma, Paddy 1947- 128
Bour, Daniele 1939- 62
Bourbonniere, Sylvie 1966- 182
Bourdon, David 1934-1998 46
Bourgeois, Paulette 1951- 153
Bourne, Lesley
    See Marshall, Evelyn
Bourne, Miriam Anne 1931-1989 16
    Obituary 63
Boutavant, Marc 1970- 200
Boutet de Monvel, (Louis) M(aurice)
    1850(?)-1913 30
    See also CLR 32
Bouwman, Heather M.
    See Bouwman, H.M.
Bouwman, H.M. 209
Bova, Ben 1932- 133
    Earlier sketches in SATA 6, 68
    See also CLR 96
Bova, Benjamin William
    See Bova, Ben
Bovaird, Anne E(lizabeth) 1960- 90
Bow, Erin 1972- 237
Bow, Patricia 1946- 168
Bowden, Joan Chase 1925- 51
    Brief entry 38
Bowe, Julie 1962- 194
Bowen, Alexandria Russell 97
Bowen, Andy Russell
    See Bowen, Alexandria Russell
Bowen, Anne 1952- 202
    Earlier sketch in SATA 170
Bowen, Betty Morgan
    See West, Betty
Bowen, Catherine (Shober) Drinker
    1897-1973 7
Bowen, David
    See Bowen, Joshua David
Bowen, Fred 1953- 233
    Earlier sketch in SATA 136
Bowen, Joshua David 1930- 22
Bowen, Rhys
    See Quin-Harkin, Janet
Bowen, Robert Sydney 1900-1977 52
    Obituary 21
Bowermaster, Jon 1954- 135
    Earlier sketch in SATA 77
Bowers, Richard J.
    See Bowers, Rick
Bowers, Rick 1952- 227
Bowers, Terrell L. 1945- 101
Bowers, Terry
    See Bowers, Terrell L.
Bowers, Tim 218
    Earlier sketch in SATA 185
Bowie, C. W.
    See Old, Wendie C(orbin)
    and Wirths, Claudine (Turner) G(ibson)
Bowie, Jim
    See Norwood, Victor G(eorge) C(harles)
    and Stratemeyer, Edward L.
Bowkett, Stephen 1953- 67
Bowler, Jan Brett
    See Brett, Jan
Bowler, Tim 1953- 209
    Earlier sketch in SATA 149
Bowman, Catherine
    See Smith, Cat Bowman
Bowman, Crystal 1951- 105
Bowman, James Cloyd 1880-1961 23
Bowman, John S(tewart) 1931- 16
Bowman, Kathleen (Gill) 1942- 52
    Brief entry 40
Bowman, Leslie
    See Bowman, Leslie W.
Bowman, Leslie W. 182
Bowsher, Melodie 195
Boxall, Ed 178

Boyce, Frank Cottrell 182
Boyce, George A(rthur) 1898- 19
Boyd, Candy Dawson 1946- 72
    See also CLR 50
Boyd, Pauline
    See Schock, Pauline
Boyd, Selma
    See Acuff, Selma Boyd
Boyd, Waldo T. 1918- 18
Boyden, Linda 1948- 238
    Earlier sketch in SATA 143
Boyer, Allen B. 1963- 153
Boyer, Robert E(rnst) 1929- 22
Boyes, Vivien 1952- 106
Boyes, Vivien Elizabeth
    See Boyes, Vivien
Boyle, Ann (Peters) 1916- 10
Boyle, Bob 232
Boyle, Eleanor Vere (Gordon) 1825-1916 28
Boyle, Robert II
    See Boyle, Bob
Boyle, Robert H. 1928- 65
Boylston, Helen Dore 1895-1984 23
    Obituary 39
Boyne, John 1971- 181
Boynton, Sandra (Keith) 1953- 152
    Brief entry 38
    Earlier sketches in SATA 57, 107
    See also CLR 105
Boz
    See Dickens, Charles
Bozarth, Jan 227
Braasch, Gary 201
Bracegirdle, Paul
    See Bracegirdle, P.J.
Bracegirdle, P.J. 236
Bracken, Alexandra 1987- 233
Bracken, Charles
    See Pellowski, Michael (Joseph)
Brackers de Hugo, Pierre 1960- 115
Brackett, Dolli Tingle 1911-1993 137
Brackett, Virginia 1950- 166
    Earlier sketch in SATA 121
Brackett, Virginia Roberts Meredith
    See Brackett, Virginia
Bradbury, Bianca (Ryley) 1908-1982 56
    Earlier sketch in SATA 3
Bradbury, Edward P.
    See Moorcock, Michael
Bradbury, Ray 1920- 123
    Earlier sketches in SATA 11, 64
Bradbury, Ray Douglas
    See Bradbury, Ray
Bradby, Marie 161
Bradfield, Carl 1942- 91
Bradford, Ann (Liddell) 1917- 56
    Brief entry 38
Bradford, Barbara Taylor 1933- 66
Bradford, Chris 1974- 215
Bradford, Emma
    See Perrin, Pat
Bradford, Karleen 1936- 96
    Earlier sketch in SATA 48
Bradford, Lois J(ean) 1936- 36
Bradford, Richard (Roark) 1932-2002 59
    Obituary 135
Bradford, Sally
    See Bradford, Barbara Taylor
Bradley, Duane
    See Sanborn, Duane
Bradley, Kimberly Brubaker 1967- 179
Bradley, Marion Zimmer 1930-1999 139
    Obituary 116
    Earlier sketch in SATA 90
    See also CLR 158
Bradley, Timothy J. 193
Bradley, Virginia 1912- 23
Bradley, Will
    See Strickland, Brad
Bradman, Tony 1954- 152
    Earlier sketch in SATA 81

Bradshaw, Gillian (Joan) 1949- 118
Bradshaw, Gillian 1956- 127
Bradshaw, Gillian Marucha
    See Bradshaw, Gillian
Bradstreet, T. J.
    See Thesman, Jean
Brady, Esther Wood 1905-1987 31
    Obituary 53
Brady, Irene 1943- 4
Brady, Kimberley S. 1953- 101
Brady, Kimberley Smith
    See Brady, Kimberley S.
Brady, Lillian 1902- 28
Braeuner, Shellie 1966(?)- 233
Bragdon, Elspeth MacDuffie 1897-1980 6
Bragdon, Lillian Jacot 24
Brager, Bruce L. 1949- 146
Bragg, Georgia 225
Bragg, Mabel Caroline 1870-1945 24
Bragg, Michael 1948- 46
Bragg, Ruth Gembicki 1943- 77
Brahm, Sumishta 1954- 58
Brailsford, Frances
    See Wosmek, Frances
Brainerd, John W(hiting) 1918- 65
Braithwaite, Althea 1940- 23
    Autobiography Feature 119
    See also SAAS 24
Brallier, Jess M. 1953- 226
Bram, Elizabeth 1948- 30
Bramsen, Carin 227
Bramsen, Kirsten 228
Brancato, Robin F. 1936- 97
    See also CLR 32
    See also SAAS 9
Brancato, Robin Fidler
    See Brancato, Robin F.
Branch, Muriel Miller 1943- 152
    Earlier sketch in SATA 94
Brand, Christianna
    See Lewis, Mary
Brand, Rebecca
    See Charnas, Suzy McKee
Brande, Robin 194
Brandel, Marc 1919- 71
Brandenberg, Alexa (Demetria) 1966- 97
Brandenberg, Aliki 1929- 157
    Earlier sketches in SATA 2, 35, 75, 113
    See also CLR 71
Brandenberg, Franz 1932- 75
    Earlier sketches in SATA 8, 35
Brandenburg, Jim 1945- 87
Brandhorst, Carl T(heodore) 1898-1988 23
Brandis, Marianne 1938- 149
    Earlier sketches in SATA 59, 96
Brandon, Brumsic, Jr. 1927- 9
Brandon, Curt
    See Bishop, Curtis (Kent)
Brandreth, Gyles 1948- 28
Brandreth, Gyles Daubeney
    See Brandreth, Gyles
Brandt, Catharine 1905-1997 40
Brandt, Keith
    See Sabin, Louis
Brandt, Sue R(eading) 1916- 59
Branfield, John (Charles) 1931- 11
Branford, Henrietta 1946-1999 106
Branley, Franklyn M(ansfield) 1915-2002 .. 136
    Earlier sketches in SATA 4, 68
    See also CLR 13
    See also SAAS 16
Brannen, Sarah S. 202
Branscum, Robbie (Tilley) 1937-1997 72
    Obituary 96
    Earlier sketch in SATA 23
    See also SAAS 17
Bransom, (John) Paul 1885-1979 43
Brashares, Ann 1967- 188
    Earlier sketch in SATA 145
    See also CLR 113
Brassard, France 1963- 186

Braswell, E.J.
See Lynn, Tracy
Braswell, Elizabeth J.
See Lynn, Tracy
Braswell, Liz
See Lynn, Tracy
Bratton, Helen 1899-1986 4
Bratun, Katy 1950- 160
Earlier sketch in SATA *83*
Braude, Michael 1936- 23
Braun, Lilian Jackson 1916(?)-2011 109
Brautigan, Richard 1935-1984 56
Brautigan, Richard Gary
See Brautigan, Richard
Bray, Libba 1964- 203
Earlier sketch in SATA *159*
Bray, Martha E.
See Bray, Libba
Braymer, Marjorie Elizabeth 1911-1988 6
Brazil, Angela 1869(?)-1947
See CLR *157*
Breathed, Berke 1957- 161
Earlier sketch in SATA *86*
See Breathed, Berkeley
Breathed, Berkeley 229
See Breathed, Berke
Breathed, Guy Berkeley
See Breathed, Berke
Brecht, Edith 1895-1975 6
Obituary 25
Breck, Vivian
See Breckenfeld, Vivian Gurney
Breckenfeld, Vivian Gurney 1895-1992 1
Breda, Tjalmar
See DeJong, David C(ornel)
Bredeson, Carmen 1944- 163
Earlier sketch in SATA *98*
Breen, M.E. 216
Breen, Molly
See Breen, M.E.
Breen, Steve 1970- 186
Breinburg, Petronella 1927- 11
See CLR *31*
Breisky, William J(ohn) 1928- 22
Brenaman, Miriam 172
Brenna, Beverley 1962- 226
Brennan, Caitlin
See Tarr, Judith
Brennan, Gale (Patrick) 1927- 64
Brief entry 53
Brennan, Herbie 1940- 214
Autobiography Feature 214
Earlier sketches in SATA *140, 183*
Brennan, J. H.
See Brennan, Herbie
Brennan, James Herbert
See Brennan, Herbie
Brennan, Jan
See Brennan, Herbie
Brennan, Joseph Lomas 1903-2000 6
Brennan, Linda Crotta 1952- 130
Brennan, Sarah Rees 1983- 221
Brennan, Tim
See Conroy, John Wesley
Brennan-Nelson, Denise 203
Brenner, Anita 1905-1974 56
Brenner, Barbara (Johnes) 1925- 124
Earlier sketches in SATA *4, 42, 76*
See also SAAS *14*
Brenner, Fred 1920- 36
Brief entry 34
Brent, Hope 1935(?)-1984
Obituary 39
Brent, Stuart 1912-2010 14
Breskin, Jane
See Zalben, Jane Breskin
Breslin, Theresa 128
Autobiography Feature 128
Earlier sketch in SATA *70*
Breslow, Maurice 1935- 72

Breslow, Maurice A
See Breslow, Maurice
Breslow, Susan 1951- 69
Brett, Bernard 1925- 22
Brett, Grace N(eff) 1900-1975 23
Brett, Jan 1949- 234
Earlier sketches in SATA *42, 71, 130, 171*
See also CLR *27*
Brett, Jan Churchill
See Brett, Jan
Brett Bowler, Jan
See Brett, Jan
Brewer, Heather 1973- 196
Brewer, James D. 1951- 108
Brewer, Paul 1950- 230
Brewer, Sally King 1947- 33
Brewster, Benjamin
See Folsom, Franklin (Brewster)
Brewster, Hugh 1950- 191
Earlier sketch in SATA *95*
Brewster, Patience 1952- 97
Brewton, John E(dmund) 1898-1982 5
Brezenoff, Steve 1974- 236
Brezenoff, Steven
See Brezenoff, Steve
Breznak, Irene 218
Brian, Dennis 1971- 229
Brian, Janeen (Paulette) 1948- 141
Briant, Ed 218
Earlier sketch in SATA *180*
Brick, John 1922-1973 10
Brickman, Robin D. 1954- 155
Bride, Nadja
See Nobisso, Josephine
Bridgers, Sue Ellen 1942- 90
Autobiography Feature 109
Earlier sketch in SATA *22*
See also CLR *18*
See also SAAS *1*
Bridges, Laurie
See Bruck, Lorraine
Bridges, Ruby (Nell) 1954- 131
Bridges, William (Andrew) 1901-1984 5
Bridwell, Norman (Ray) 1928- 138
Earlier sketches in SATA *4, 68*
See also CLR *96*
Brier, Howard M(axwell) 1903-1969 8
Brierley, (Louise) 1958- 59
Briggs, Katharine Mary 1898-1980 101
Obituary 25
Briggs, Peter 1921-1975 39
Obituary 31
Briggs, Raymond 1934- 184
Earlier sketches in SATA *23, 66, 131*
See also CLR *168*
Briggs, Raymond Redvers
See Briggs, Raymond
Bright, Paul 1949- 231
Earlier sketch in SATA *182*
Bright, Robert Sr.) 1902-1988 63
Obituary 60
Earlier sketch in SATA *24*
Bright, Robert Douglas
See Bright, Robert Sr.)
Bright, Sarah
See Shine, Deborah
Brightfield, Richard 1927- 65
Brief entry 53
Brightfield, Rick
See Brightfield, Richard
Brighton, Catherine 1943- 206
Earlier sketches in SATA *65, 107*
Brill, Marlene Targ 1945- 124
Earlier sketch in SATA *77*
Brimberg, Stanlee 1947- 9
Brimner, Larry Dane 1949- 232
Autobiography Feature 112
Earlier sketches in SATA *79, 170*
Brin, David 1950- 65
Brin, Ruth Firestone 1921- 22
Brinckloe, Julie 1950- 13

Brinckloe, Julie Lorraine
See Brinckloe, Julie
Brindel, June (Rachuy) 1919- 7
Brindle, Max
See Fleischman, Sid
Brindze, Ruth 1903-1984 23
Brink, Carol Ryrie 1895-1981 100
Obituary 27
Earlier sketches in SATA *1, 31*
See also CLR *149*
Brinsmead, H. F(ay)
See Brinsmead, H(esba) F(ay)
Brinsmead, H. F.
See Brinsmead, H(esba) F(ay)
Brinsmead, H(esba) F(ay) 1922- 78
Earlier sketch in SATA *18*
See also CLR *47*
See also SAAS *5*
Briquebec, John
See Rowland-Entwistle, (Arthur) Theodore
(Henry)
Brisbane, Henry R.
See Ellis, Edward S.
Brisco, P. A.
See Matthews, Patricia
Brisco, Patty
See Matthews, Patricia
and Matthews, Clayton (Hartley)
Briscoe, Jill (Pauline) 1935- 56
Brief entry 47
Brisley, Joyce Lankester 1896-1978 22
Obituary 84
Brissenden, Connie
See Brissenden, Constance
Brissenden, Constance 1947- 150
Brisson, Pat 1951- 177
Autobiography Feature 133
Earlier sketches in SATA *67, 128, 133*
Bristow, David 237
Bristow, David L.
See Bristow, David
Britt, Albert 1874-1969
Obituary 28
Britt, Dell 1934- 1
Brittain, Bill
See Brittain, William
Brittain, C. Dale 1948- 82
Brittain, William 1930- 76
Earlier sketch in SATA *36*
See also SAAS *7*
Brittingham, Geoffrey (Hugh) 1959- 76
Brittney, L. 209
Britton, Kate
See Stegeman, Janet Allais
Britton, Louisa
See McGuire, Leslie (Sarah)
Britton, Rick 1952- 82
Bro, Margueritte (Harmon) 1894-1977 19
Obituary 27
Broach, Elise 1963- 173
Broadhead, Helen Cross 1913- 25
Broadway, Hannah 208
Brochmann, Elizabeth 1938- 41
Brock, Betty (Carter) 1923-2003 4
Obituary 150
Brock, C(harles) E(dmund) 1870-1938 42
Brief entry 32
Brock, Delia
See Ephron, Delia
Brock, Emma L(illian) 1886-1974 8
Brock, H(enry) M(atthew) 1875-1960 42
Brockett, Eleanor Hall 1913-1967 10
Brockman, C(hristian) Frank 1902-1985 26
Brockmeier, Kevin 1972- 176
Broda, Ron 1954- 209
Broderick, Dorothy M. 1929- 5
Brodeur, Ruth Wallace
See Wallace-Brodeur, Ruth
Brodie, Sally
See Cavin, Ruth

Brodien-Jones, Chris
  See Brodien-Jones, Christine
Brodien-Jones, Christine 1950- *233*
Brodsky, Beverly
  See McDermott, Beverly Brodsky
Brody, Wendy
  See Staub, Wendy Corsi
Broekel, Rainer Lothar
  See Broekel, Ray
Broekel, Ray 1923- *38*
Broekstra, Lorette 1964- *189*
  Earlier sketch in SATA *124*
Brogden, Sherryl
  See Jordan, Sherryl
Broger, Achim
  See Broger, Achim
Broger, Achim 1944- *31*
Broida, Marian *154*
Brokamp, Marilyn 1920- *10*
Broman, Fred
  See Moseley, James W(illett)
Bromely, Anne C. 1950- *234*
Bromhall, Winifred *26*
Brommer, Gerald F(rederick) 1927- *28*
Brondfield, Jerome 1913-1998 .... *22*
Brondfield, Jerry
  See Brondfield, Jerome
Bronner, Stephen Eric 1949- *101*
Bronowski, Jacob 1908-1974 .... *55*
Bronson, Alice
  See Watkins, Dawn L.
Bronson, Linda *203*
Bronson, Lynn
  See Lampman, Evelyn Sibley
Bronson, Wilfrid Swancourt 1894-1985
  Obituary *43*
Brook, Judith (Penelope) 1926- *59*
  Brief entry *51*
Brook, Judy
  See Brook, Judith (Penelope)
Brooke, L(eonard) Leslie 1862-1940 .... *17*
  See also CLR 20
Brooke, William J. 1946- *139*
Brooke-Haven, P.
  See Wodehouse, P. G.
Brooker, Kyrsten *199*
Brookins, Dana 1931- *28*
Brooks, Anita
  See Abramovitz, Anita (Zeltner Brooks)
Brooks, Bill 1939- *59*
Brooks, Bruce 1950- *112*
  Brief entry *53*
  Earlier sketch in SATA *72*
  See also CLR 25
Brooks, Caryl 1924- *84*
Brooks, Charlotte K(endrick) 1918-1998 ..... *24*
  Obituary *112*
Brooks, Erik 1972- *236*
  Earlier sketches in SATA *152, 182*
Brooks, George
  See Baum, L. Frank
Brooks, Gwendolyn 1917-2000 .... *6*
  Obituary *123*
  See also CLR 27
Brooks, Gwendolyn Elizabeth
  See Brooks, Gwendolyn
Brooks, Jerome 1931- *23*
Brooks, Kevin 1959- *197*
  Earlier sketch in SATA *150*
Brooks, Kevin M.
  See Brooks, Kevin
Brooks, Laurie *209*
Brooks, Lester 1924- *7*
Brooks, Martha 1944- *134*
  Autobiography Feature *134*
  Earlier sketches in SATA *68, 121*
Brooks, Maurice (Graham) 1900- *45*
Brooks, Polly Schoyer 1912- *12*
Brooks, Ron 1948- *212*
  Brief entry *33*
  Earlier sketch in SATA *94*

Brooks, Ronald George
  See Brooks, Ron
Brooks, Terry 1944- *60*
Brooks, Walter R(ollin) 1886-1958 .... *17*
Brooks-Hill, Helen (Mason) 1908-1994 .... *59*
Broome, Errol 1937- *158*
  Earlier sketch in SATA *105*
Brophy, Nannette 1963- *73*
Brosnan, James Patrick 1929- *14*
Brosnan, Jim
  See Brosnan, James Patrick
Brostoff, Anita 1931- *132*
Brothers Grimm
  See Grimm, Jacob Ludwig Karl
  and Grimm, Wilhelm Karl
Brothers Hildebrandt, The
  See Hildebrandt, Greg
  and Hildebrandt, Tim
Brougham, Jason 1971(?)- *238*
Broun, Emily
  See Sterne, Emma Gelders
Brouwer, S. W.
  See Brouwer, Sigmund (W.)
Brouwer, Sigmund (W.) 1959- *109*
Brow, Thea 1934- *60*
Brower, Millicent *8*
Brower, Pauline 1929- *22*
Browin, Frances Williams 1898-1986 .... *5*
Brown, Alan
  See Brown, Alan James
Brown, Alan James 1947- *232*
Brown, Alexis
  See Baumann, Amy Beeching
Brown, Anne Ensign 1937- *61*
Brown, Beverly Swerdlow *97*
Brown, Bill
  See Brown, William L(ouis)
Brown, Billye Walker
  See Cutchen, Billye Walker
Brown, Bob
  See Brown, Robert Joseph
Brown, Buck 1936- *45*
Brown, Calef *217*
  Earlier sketch in SATA *179*
Brown, Cassie 1919-1986 .... *55*
Brown, Charlotte Lewis *181*
Brown, Conrad 1922- *31*
Brown, Craig 1947- *224*
Brown, Craig 1947- *224*
  Earlier sketch in SATA *73*
Brown, Craig McFarland
  See Brown, Craig
Brown, David
  See Brown, David A(lan)
  and Myller, Rolf
Brown, Dee 1908-2002 .... *110*
  Obituary *141*
  Earlier sketch in SATA *5*
Brown, Dee Alexander
  See Brown, Dee
Brown, Don 1949- *200*
  Earlier sketch in SATA *172*
Brown, Drew T. III 1955- *83*
Brown, Drollene P. 1939- *53*
Brown, Elbrite *198*
Brown, Eleanor Frances 1908-1987 .... *3*
Brown, Elizabeth Ferguson 1937- *153*
Brown, Elizabeth M(yers) 1915- *43*
Brown, Fern G. 1918- *34*
Brown, (Robert) Fletch 1923- *42*
Brown, Fornan 1901-1996 .... *71*
  Obituary *88*
Brown, George Earl 1883-1964 .... *11*
Brown, George Mackay 1921-1996 .... *35*
Brown, Irene Bennett 1932- *3*
Brown, Irving
  See Adams, William Taylor
Brown, Ivor (John Carnegie) 1891-1974 .... *5*
  Obituary *26*
Brown, Jane Clark 1930- *81*
Brown, Janet Mitsui *87*

Brown, Jennifer 1972- *227*
Brown, Jo 1964- *170*
Brown, Joanne 1933- *147*
Brown, Joe David 1915-1976 .... *44*
Brown, Joseph E(dward) 1929- *59*
  Brief entry *51*
Brown, Judith Gwyn 1933- *20*
Brown, Kathryn 1955- *168*
  Earlier sketch in SATA *98*
Brown, Kathy
  See Brown, Kathryn
Brown, Ken (James) *129*
Brown, Kevin 1960- *101*
Brown, Laurene Krasny 1945- *99*
  Earlier sketch in SATA *54*
Brown, Laurie Krasny
  See Brown, Laurene Krasny
Brown, Leo *225*
Brown, Lisa *234*
Brown, Lloyd Arnold 1907-1966 .... *36*
Brown, Mahlon A.
  See Ellis, Edward S.
Brown, Marc (Tolon) 1946- *145*
  Earlier sketches in SATA *10, 53, 80*
  See also CLR 29
Brown, Marcia (Joan) 1918- *47*
  Earlier sketch in SATA *7*
  See also CLR 12
Brown, Margaret Wise 1910-1952 .... *100*
  See also YABC 2
  See also CLR 107
Brown, Margery (Wheeler) *78*
  Earlier sketch in SATA *5*
Brown, Marion Marsh 1908-2001 .... *6*
Brown, Monica 1969- *233*
Brown, Myra Berry 1918- *6*
Brown, Palmer 1919- *36*
Brown, Pamela (Beatrice) 1924-1989 .... *5*
  Obituary *61*
Brown, Paul 1942- *221*
Brown, Peter 1979- *178*
Brown, Rachel W.N. 1947- *203*
Brown, Reeve Lindbergh
  See Lindbergh, Reeve
Brown, Richard
  See Brown, Rick
Brown, Richard E.
  See Brown, Rick
Brown, Rick 1946- *226*
  Earlier sketch in SATA *61*
Brown, Robert Joseph 1907-1989 .... *14*
Brown, Rod 1961- *232*
Brown, Roderick (Langmere) Haig-
  See Haig-Brown, Roderick (Langmere)
Brown, Rosalie
  See Moore, Rosalie (Gertrude)
Brown, Roswell
  See Webb, Jean Francis (III)
Brown, Roy (Frederick) 1921-1982 .... *51*
  Obituary *39*
Brown, Ruth 1941- *170*
  Earlier sketch in SATA *105*
Brown, Scott 1971- *134*
Brown, Sue Ellen 1954- *81*
Brown, Tameka Fryer *235*
Brown, Tami Lewis *238*
Brown, Tricia 1954- *114*
Brown, Vinson 1912-1991 .... *19*
Brown, Walter R(eed) 1929- *19*
Brown, Will
  See Ainsworth, William Harrison
Brown, William L(ouis) 1910-1964 .... *5*
Browne, Anthony 1946- *163*
  Brief entry *44*
  Earlier sketches in SATA *45, 61, 105*
  See also CLR 156
Browne, Anthony Edward Tudor
  See Browne, Anthony
Browne, Dik
  See Browne, Richard Arthur Allen
Browne, Hablot Knight 1815-1882 .... *21*

Browne, Matthew
  See Rands, William Brighty
Browne, Nicki M.
  See Browne, N.M.
Browne, Nicky Matthews
  See Browne, N.M.
Browne, N.M. 1960- 167
Browne, Richard Arthur Allen 1917-1989 ... 67
  Brief entry 38
Browne, Vee F. 1956- 214
  Earlier sketch in SATA *90*
Browning, Diane 233
Browning, Robert 1812-1889
  See YABC *1*
  See also CLR *97*
Browning, Tom 1949- 226
Brownjohn, Alan 1931- 6
Brownlee, Walter 1930- 62
Brownlie, Betty 1946- 159
Brownlow, Kevin 1938- 65
Brownlow, Mike 183
Brownridge, William R(oy) 1932- 94
Broyles, Anne 1953- 201
Bruce, Dorita Fairlie 1885-1970
  Obituary 27
Bruce, Harry 1934- 77
Bruce, Mary 1927- 1
Bruchac, Joseph III
  See Bruchac, Joseph
Bruchac, Joseph 1942- 228
  Autobiography Feature 176
  Earlier sketches in SATA *42, 89, 131, 176*
  See also CLR *46*
Bruchac, Margaret M.
  See Bruchac, Marge
Bruchac, Marge 181
Bruck, Lorraine 1921- 55
  Brief entry 46
Bruel, Nick 205
  Earlier sketch in SATA *166*
Bruel, Robert O. 1929-2002 189
Bruemmer, Fred 1929- 47
Brugman, Alyssa (F.) 1974- 152
Brumbeau, Jeff 1955- 157
Bruna, Dick 1927- 76
  Brief entry 30
  Earlier sketch in SATA *43*
  See also CLR *7*
Brunelle, Lynn 233
Brunhoff, Jean de 1899-1937 24
  See also CLR *116*
Brunhoff, Laurent de 1925- 150
  Earlier sketches in SATA *24, 71*
  See also CLR *116*
Brunkus, Denise 204
Bruno, Elsa Knight 1935-2009 221
Brunskill, Elizabeth Ann Flatt
  See Flatt, Lizann
Brush, Karen A(lexandra) 1960- 85
Brussel-Smith, Bernard 1914- 58
Brust, Steven 1955- 121
  Earlier sketch in SATA *86*
Brust, Steven Karl Zoltan
  See Brust, Steven
Brustlein, Daniel 1904- 40
Brustlein, Janice Tworkov -2000 40
  Obituary 126
Brutschy, Jennifer 1960- 84
Bryan, Ashley 1923- 178
  Earlier sketches in SATA *31, 72, 132*
  See also CLR *66*
Bryan, Ashley F.
  See Bryan, Ashley
Bryan, Dorothy M. 1896(?)-1984
  Obituary 39
Bryan, Jennifer 190
Bryan, Kathleen
  See Tarr, Judith
Bryan, Sean 192
Bryant, Bernice (Morgan) 1908-1976 11

Bryant, Jen 1960- 218
  Earlier sketches in SATA *94, 175*
Bryant, Jennifer
  See Bryant, Jen
Bryant, Jennifer Fisher
  See Bryant, Jen
Bryant, Laura J. 176
Brychta, Alex 1956- 21
Brynie, Faith H. 1946- 113
Brynie, Faith Hickman
  See Brynie, Faith H.
Bryson, Bernarda 1903-2004 9
Buba, Joy Flinsch 1904- 44
Buchan, Bryan 1945- 36
Buchan, John 1875-1940
  See YABC *2*
Buchan, Stuart 1942-1987
  Obituary 54
Buchanan, Debby 1952- 82
Buchanan, Deborah Leevonne
  See Buchanan, Debby
Buchanan, Jane 1956- 160
Buchanan, Lang
  See Buchanan, Michael
Buchanan, Lang
  See Lang, Diane
Buchanan, Michael 1955- 235
Buchanan, Michael David
  See Buchanan, Michael
Buchanan, Paul 1959- 116
Buchanan, Sue 1939- 139
Buchheimer, Naomi Barnett
  See Barnett, Naomi
Buchignani, Walter 1965- 84
Buchmann, Stephen L. 194
Buchwald, Art 1925-2007 10
Buchwald, Arthur
  See Buchwald, Art
Buchwald, Emilie 1935- 7
Buck, Gisela 1941- 101
Buck, Lewis 1925- 18
Buck, Margaret Waring 1905-1997 3
Buck, Nola
  See Godwin, Laura
Buck, Pearl S. 1892-1973 25
  Earlier sketch in SATA *1*
Buck, Pearl Sydenstricker
  See Buck, Pearl S.
Buck, Siegfried 1941- 101
Buckalew, Clare B.
  See Dunkle, Clare B.
Buckeridge, Anthony (Malcolm)
  1912-2004 85
  Earlier sketch in SATA *6*
Buckholtz, Eileen (Garber) 1949- 54
  Brief entry 47
Buckingham, Royce 1966- 210
Buckingham, Royce Scott
  See Buckingham, Royce
Buckler, Ernest 1908-1984 47
Buckless, Andrea K. 1968- 117
Buckley, Helen E(lizabeth) 1918- 90
  Earlier sketch in SATA *2*
Buckley, James, Jr. 1963- 166
  Earlier sketch in SATA *114*
Buckley, Michael 229
  Earlier sketch in SATA *177*
Buckley, Susan 184
Buckley, Susan Washburn
  See Buckley, Susan
Buckley-Archer, Linda 185
Buckmaster, Henrietta
  See Stephens, Henrietta Henkle
Bucks, Brad
  See Holub, Joan
Budd, E. S.
  See Sirimarco, Elizabeth
Budd, Lillian (Peterson) 1897-1989 7
Budhos, Marina 236
  Earlier sketch in SATA *173*

Budhos, Marina Tamar
  See Budhos, Marina
Buehler, Stephanie Jona 1956- 83
Buehner, Caralyn 1963- 219
  Earlier sketches in SATA *104, 159*
Buehner, Mark 1959- 221
  Earlier sketches in SATA *104, 159*
Buehr, Walter Franklin 1897-1971 3
Buell, Ellen Lewis
  See Cash, Ellen Lewis Buell
Buell, Janet 1952- 185
  Earlier sketch in SATA *106*
Buergel, Paul-Hermann H. 1949- 83
Buettner, Dan 1960- 95
Buff, Conrad 1886-1975 19
Buff, Mary (E. Marsh) 1890-1970 19
Buffett, Jimmy 1946- 110
  Earlier sketch in SATA *76*
Buffie, Margaret 1945- 161
  Earlier sketches in SATA *71, 107*
  See also CLR *39*
Bugbee, Emma 1888(?)-1981
  Obituary 29
Bugni, Alice 1951- 122
Bujold, Lois McMaster 1949- 136
Bulfinch, Thomas 1796-1867 35
Bulion, Leslie 1958- 209
  Earlier sketch in SATA *161*
Bull, Angela (Mary) 1936- 45
Bull, Emma 1954- 190
  Autobiography Feature 103
  Earlier sketch in SATA *99*
Bull, Norman John 1916- 41
Bull, Peter (Cecil) 1912-1984
  Obituary 39
Bull, Schuyler M. 1974- 138
Bulla, Clyde R. 1914-2007 139
  Obituary 182
  Earlier sketches in SATA *2, 41, 91*
  See also SAAS *6*
Bullard, Lisa 1961- 142
Bullen, Alexandra 227
Buller, Jon 205
Bullock, Kathleen (Mary) 1946- 77
Bullock, Robert (D.) 1947- 92
Bulpin, (Barbara) Vicki 92
Bulwer-Lytton, Edward 1803-1873 23
Bulwer-Lytton, Edward George Earle Lytton
  See Bulwer-Lytton, Edward
Bumstead, Kathleen Mary 1918-1987 53
Bundles, A'Lelia Perry 1952- 76
Bunge, Daniela 1973- 207
Bunin, Catherine 1967- 30
Bunin, Sherry 1925- 30
Bunkers, Suzanne L. 1950- 136
Bunting, A.E.
  See Bunting, Eve
Bunting, Anne Evelyn
  See Bunting, Eve
Bunting, Eve 1928- 235
  Earlier sketches in SATA *18, 64, 110, 158,*
  196
  See also CLR *82*
Bunting, Glenn (Davison) 1957- 22
Bunyan, John 1628-1688
  See CLR *124*
Bupp, Walter
  See Garrett, Randall
Burack, Sylvia K. 1916-2003 35
  Obituary 143
Burbank, Addison (Buswell) 1895-1961 37
Burch, Joann J(ohansen) 75
Burch, Robert J(oseph) 1925- 74
  Earlier sketch in SATA *1*
  See also CLR *63*
Burchard, Peter Duncan 1921- 143
  Earlier sketches in SATA *5, 74*
  See also SAAS *13*
Burchard, S. H.
  See Burchard, Sue
Burchard, Sue 1937- 22

Burchardt, Nellie 1921- 7
Burckhardt, Marc 1962- 196
Burden, Andrea 1969-2009 227
Burdett, Lois 117
Burdick, Eugene (Leonard) 1918-1965 22
Burford, Eleanor
  See Hibbert, Eleanor Alice Burford
Burg, Ann E. 1954- 217
Burg, Shana 1968- 204
Burgan, Michael 1960- 167
  Earlier sketch in SATA *118*
Burger, Carl 1888-1967 9
Burgess, Ann Marie
  See Gerson, Noel Bertram
Burgess, Barbara Hood 1926- 69
Burgess, Em
  See Burgess, Mary Wyche
Burgess, (Frank) Gelett 1866-1951 32
  Brief entry 30
Burgess, Mark 157
Burgess, Mary Wyche 1916- 18
Burgess, Melvin 1954- 198
  Earlier sketches in SATA *96, 146*
Burgess, Michael
  See Gerson, Noel Bertram
Burgess, Robert F(orrest) 1927- 4
Burgess, Starling
  See Tudor, Tasha
Burgess, Thornton Waldo 1874-1965 17
Burgess, Trevor
  See Trevor, Elleston
Burgwyn, Mebane Holoman 1914-1992 7
Burke, David 1927- 46
Burke, Diana G.
  See Gallagher, Diana G.
Burke, Diana Gallagher
  See Gallagher, Diana G.
Burke, Dianne O'Quinn 1940- 89
Burke, Janine 1952- 139
Burke, Jim 1973- 179
Burke, John
  See O'Connor, Richard
Burke, Katie 1953- 168
Burke, Patrick 1958- 114
Burke, Ralph
  See Garrett, Randall
  and Silverberg, Robert
Burkert, Nancy Ekholm 1933- 24
  See also SAAS *14*
Burkett, D. Brent 194
Burke-Weiner, Kimberly 1962- 95
Burks, Brian 1955- 95
Burland, Brian (Berkeley) 1931- 34
Burland, C. A.
  See Burland, Cottie (Arthur)
Burland, Cottie (Arthur) 1905-1983 5
Burleigh, Robert 1936- 193
  Earlier sketches in SATA *55, 98, 146*
Burlingame, (William) Roger 1889-1967 2
Burman, Alice Caddy 1896(?)-1977
  Obituary 24
Burman, Ben Lucien 1896-1984 6
  Obituary 40
Burn, Doris 1923- 1
Burn, Ted
  See Burn, Thomas E.
Burn, Thomas E. 1940- 150
Burnard, Damon 1963- 115
Burne, Cristy 238
Burnett, Constance Buel 1893-1975 36
Burnett, Frances Eliza Hodgson
  See Burnett, Frances Hodgson
Burnett, Frances Hodgson 1849-1924 100
  See also YABC *2*
  See also CLR *122*
Burnett, Lindy 210
Burnett Bossi, Lisa 193
Burney, Anton
  See Hopkins, (Hector) Kenneth

Burnford, Sheila (Philip Cochrane Every)
  1918-1984 3
  Obituary 38
  See also CLR *2*
Burnham, Gretchen
  See Sprague, Gretchen
Burnham, Nicole 1970- 161
Burnham, Niki
  See Burnham, Nicole
Burnham, Sophy 1936- 65
Burningham, John 1936- 225
  Earlier sketches in SATA *16, 59, 111, 160*
  See also CLR *9*
Burningham, Robin Yoko
  See Racoma, Robin Yoko
Burningham, Sarah O'Leary 216
Burns, Diane L. 1950- 81
  See also SAAS *24*
Burns, Eloise Wilkin
  See Wilkin, Eloise
Burns, Florence M. 1905-1988 61
Burns, Khephra 1950- 92
Burns, Loree Griffin 193
Burns, Marilyn 1941- 96
  Brief entry 33
Burns, Olive Ann 1924-1990 65
Burns, Patrick 1968- 227
Burns, Paul C. 5
Burns, Ray
  See Burns, Raymond (Howard)
Burns, Raymond (Howard) 1924- 9
Burns, Theresa 1961- 84
Burns, T.R.
  See Rayburn, Tricia
Burns, William A. 1909-1999 5
Burr, Dan 1951- 65
Burr, Dan 1960- 219
Burr, Lonnie 1943- 47
Burrell, Roy E(ric) C(harles) 1923- 72
Burroughs, Edgar Rice 1875-1950 41
  See also CLR *157*
Burroughs, Jean Mitchell 1908- 28
Burroughs, Polly 1925- 2
Burroway, Janet 1936- 23
Burroway, Janet Gay
  See Burroway, Janet
Burstein, Chaya M(alamud) 1923- 64
Burstein, Fred 1950- 83
Burstein, John 1949- 54
  Brief entry 40
Burstein, Stanley M.
  See Burstein, Stanley Mayer
Burstein, Stanley Mayer 1941- 175
Bursztynski, Sue 1953- 114
Burt, Jesse Clifton 1921-1976 46
  Obituary 20
Burt, Olive Woolley 1894-1981 4
Burtinshaw, Julie 185
Burton, Gennett 1945- 95
Burton, Hester (Wood-Hill) 1913-2000 74
  Earlier sketch in SATA *7*
  See also CLR *1*
  See also SAAS *8*
Burton, Leslie
  See McGuire, Leslie (Sarah)
Burton, Marilee Robin 1950- 82
  Earlier sketch in SATA *46*
Burton, Maurice 1898-1992 23
Burton, Rebecca 1970- 183
Burton, Robert (Wellesley) 1941- 22
Burton, Virginia Lee 1909-1968 100
  Earlier sketch in SATA *2*
  See also CLR *11*
Burton, William H(enry) 1890-1964 11
Busby, Ailie 192
Busby, Cylin 1970- 118
Busby, Edith (A. Lake) (?)-1964
  Obituary 29
Busby, John 1942- 209
Buscaglia, (Felice) Leo(nardo) 1924-1998 ... 65

Buscaglia, Leo F.
  See Buscaglia, (Felice) Leo(nardo)
Buscema, Stephanie 232
Busch, Phyllis S. 1909- 30
Bush, Anne Kelleher
  See Kelleher, Anne
Bush, Catherine 1961- 128
Bush, Jenna 1981- 208
Bush, Laura 1946- 208
Bushmiller, Ernest Paul 1905-1982 31
Bushmiller, Ernie
  See Bushmiller, Ernest Paul
Bushnell, Jack 1952- 86
Busoni, Rafaello 1900-1962 16
Buss, Helen M.
  See Clarke, Margaret
Busse, Sarah Martin 194
Busselle, Rebecca 1941- 80
Bustard, Anne 1951- 173
Butcher, Kristin 1951- 140
Butenko, Bohdan 1931- 90
Butler, Beverly Kathleen 1932- 7
Butler, Bill
  See Butler, William Vivian
  and Butler, Ernest Alton
  and Butler, William Huxford
Butler, Charles 1963- 175
  Earlier sketch in SATA *121*
Butler, Charles Cadman
  See Butler, Charles
Butler, Dori Hillestad 1965- 207
  Earlier sketch in SATA *164*
Butler, Dorothy 1925- 73
Butler, Geoff 1945- 94
Butler, John 1952- 225
Butler, M. Christina 1934- 224
  Earlier sketches in SATA *72, 170*
Butler, Octavia 1947-2006 84
  See also CLR *65*
Butler, Octavia E.
  See Butler, Octavia
Butler, Octavia Estelle
  See Butler, Octavia
Butler, Vivian
  See Butler, William Vivian
Butler, William
  See Butler, William Vivian
Butler, William Vivian 1927-1987 79
Butterfield, Moira 1960- 219
Butters, Dorothy Gilman
  See Gilman, Dorothy
Butterworth, Emma Macalik 1928- 43
Butterworth, Nick 1946- 149
  Earlier sketch in SATA *106*
Butterworth, Oliver 1915-1990 1
  Obituary 66
Butterworth, W. E.
  See Griffin, W. E. B.
Butterworth, William E.
  See Griffin, W. E. B.
Butterworth, William Edmund III
  See Griffin, W. E. B.
Button, Lana 1968- 229
Butts, Ed 1951- 177
Butts, Edward P.
  See Butts, Ed
Butts, Ellen R. 1942- 93
Butts, Ellen Rubinstein
  See Butts, Ellen R.
Butzer, C. M. 1974- 212
Buxton, Ralph
  See Silverstein, Alvin
  and Silverstein, Virginia B.
Buyea, Rob 1976- 238
Buzzeo, Toni 1951- 215
  Earlier sketch in SATA *135*
Byalick, Marcia 1947- 141
  Earlier sketch in SATA *97*
Byard, Carole (Marie) 1941- 57

Byars, Betsy 1928- 223
  Autobiography Feature 108
  Earlier sketches in SATA *4, 46, 80, 163*
  See also CLR *72*
  See also SAAS *1*
Byars, Betsy Cromer
  See Byars, Betsy
Byfield, Barbara Ninde 1930-1988 8
Byman, Jeremy 1944- 129
Bynum, Janie 133
Byrd, Elizabeth 1912-1989 34
Byrd, Nicole
  See Zach, Cheryl (Byrd)
Byrd, Robert 1942- 226
  Earlier sketches in SATA *33, 112, 158*
Byrd, Robert John
  See Byrd, Robert
Byrd, Tim 1964- 216
Byrne, Gayle 218
Byrne, Mary Gregg 1951- 162

C

C. 3. 3.
  See Wilde, Oscar
C. E. M.
  See Mastrangelo, Charles E(lmer)
Cabaniss, J(ames) Allen 1911-1997 5
Cabat, Erni 1914- 74
Cabban, Vanessa 1971- 176
Cable, Mary 1920- 9
Cabot, Meg 1967- 217
  Earlier sketches in SATA *127, 175*
  See also CLR *85*
Cabot, Meggin
  See Cabot, Meg
Cabot, Meggin Patricia
  See Cabot, Meg
Cabot, Patricia
  See Cabot, Meg
Cabral, O. M.
  See Cabral, Olga
Cabral, Olga 1909- 46
Cabrera, Cozbi A. 1963- 177
Cabrera, Jane 1968- 182
  Earlier sketches in SATA *103, 152*
Cabrera, Marcela 1966- 90
Caddy, Alice
  See Burman, Alice Caddy
Cade, Toni
  See Bambara, Toni Cade
Cadena, Beth 222
Cadmus and Harmonia
  See Buchan, John
Cadnum, Michael 1949- 225
  Earlier sketches in SATA *87, 121, 165*
  See also CLR *78*
Caduto, Michael J. 1955- 103
Cadwallader, Sharon 1936- 7
Cady, (Walter) Harrison 1877(?)-1970 19
Caffey, Donna (J.) 1954- 110
Cagle, Malcolm W(infield) 1918- 32
Cahn, Rhoda 1922- 37
Cahn, William 1912-1976 37
Cain, Arthur H(omer) 1913-1981 3
Cain, Christopher
  See Fleming, Thomas
Cain, Sheridan 1952- 186
Caine, Geoffrey
  See Walker, Robert W.
Caines, Jeannette (Franklin) 1938- 78
  Brief entry 43
  See also CLR *24*
Cairns, Julia 1960(?)- 239
Cairns, Trevor 1922- 14
Calabro, Marian 1954- 79
Caldecott, Moyra 1927- 22

Caldecott, Randolph (J.) 1846-1886 100
  Earlier sketch in SATA *17*
  See also CLR *110*
Calder, Charlotte 1952- 125
Calder, David 1932-1997 105
Calder, Lyn
  See Calmenson, Stephanie
Calder, Marie D(onais) 1948- 96
Calderone-Stewart, Lisa
  See Calderone-Stewart, Lisa-Marie
Calderone-Stewart, Lisa-Marie 1958- 123
Caldwell, Ben 1973- 230
Caldwell, Doreen (Mary) 1942- 71
Caldwell, John C(ope) 1913-1984 7
Caletti, Deb 1963- 221
  Earlier sketch in SATA *171*
Calhoun, B. B. 1961- 98
Calhoun, Chad
  See Barrett, Neal, Jr.
  and Cunningham, Chet
  and Goulart, Ron
Calhoun, Dia 1959- 183
  Earlier sketch in SATA *129*
Calhoun, Mary
  See Wilkins, Mary Huiskamp
Calhoun, T.B.
  See Bisson, Terry
Cali, Davide 1972- 190
Calif, Ruth 1922- 67
Calkhoven, Laurie 1959- 229
Calkins, Franklin
  See Stratemeyer, Edward L.
Call, Greg 197
Call, Hughie Florence 1890-1969 1
Callahan, Dorothy M. 1934- 39
  Brief entry 35
Callahan, Dorothy Monahan
  See Callahan, Dorothy M.
Callahan, Philip Serna 1923- 25
Callahan, Sean 1965- 222
Callan, Jamie 1954- 59
Callan, Jim 1951- 181
Callaway, Bernice (Anne) 1923- 48
Callaway, Kathy 1943- 36
Callen, Larry
  See Callen, Lawrence Willard, Jr.
Callen, Lawrence Willard, Jr. 1927- 19
Callen, Liz 1951- 231
Callery, Sean 233
Calley, Karin 1965- 92
Calmenson, Stephanie 1952- 211
  Brief entry 37
  Earlier sketches in SATA *51, 84, 139*
Calonita, Jen 216
Calvert, Elinor H.
  See Lasell, Elinor H.
Calvert, John
  See Leaf, (Wilbur) Munro
Calvert, Pam 1966- 205
Calvert, Patricia 1931- 132
  Earlier sketches in SATA *45, 69*
  See also SAAS *17*
Camburn, Carol A.
  See Camburn-Bracalente, Carol A.
Camburn-Bracalente, Carol A. 1962- 118
Cameron, Ann 1943- 129
  Earlier sketches in SATA *27, 89*
  See also SAAS *20*
Cameron, Edna M. 1905-1999 3
Cameron, Eleanor (Frances) 1912-1996 25
  Obituary 93
  Earlier sketch in SATA *1*
  See also CLR *72*
  See also SAAS *10*
Cameron, Elizabeth
  See Nowell, Elizabeth Cameron
Cameron, Elizabeth Jane 1910-1976 32
  Obituary 30
Cameron, Ian
  See Payne, Donald Gordon

Cameron, M(alcolm) G(ordon) Graham
  See Graham-Cameron, M(alcolm) G(ordon)
Cameron, M. Graham
  See Graham-Cameron, M(alcolm) G(ordon)
Cameron, Mike Graham
  See Graham-Cameron, M(alcolm) G(ordon)
Cameron, Natalie Russell
  See Russell, Natalie
Cameron, Polly 1928- 2
Cameron, Scott 1962- 84
Camp, Charles L. 1893-1975
  Obituary 31
Camp, Lindsay 1957- 133
Camp, Madeleine L'Engle
  See L'Engle, Madeleine
Camp, Walter (Chauncey) 1859-1925
  See YABC *1*
Campbell, (Elizabeth) Andrea 1963- 50
Campbell, Ann R. 1925- 11
Campbell, Bill 1960- 89
Campbell, Bruce
  See Epstein, Samuel
Campbell, Camilla 1905-1992 26
Campbell, Carole R. 1939- 125
Campbell, Hope 1925- 20
Campbell, Hugh 1930- 90
Campbell, Jane
  See Edwards, Jane Campbell
Campbell, Julie
  See Tatham, Julie Campbell
Campbell, Patricia J(ean) 1930- 45
Campbell, Patty
  See Campbell, Patricia J(ean)
Campbell, Peter A. 1948- 99
Campbell, R. W.
  See Campbell, Rosemae Wells
Campbell, Robin
  See Strachan, Ian
Campbell, Rod 1945- 98
  Brief entry 44
  Earlier sketch in SATA *51*
Campbell, Rosemae Wells 1909- 1
Campbell, Sarah C. 1966- 207
Camper, Cathy 1956- 170
Campion, Nardi Reeder 1917-2007 22
Campling, Elizabeth 1948- 53
Campos, Maria de Fatima 229
Campoy, F. Isabel 1946- 181
  Earlier sketch in SATA *143*
Camps, Luis 1928- 66
Canales, Viola 1957- 141
Candell, Victor 1903-1977
  Obituary 24
Canfield, Dorothea F.
  See Fisher, Dorothy (Frances) Canfield
Canfield, Dorothea Frances
  See Fisher, Dorothy (Frances) Canfield
Canfield, Dorothy
  See Fisher, Dorothy (Frances) Canfield
Canfield, Jack 1944- 164
Canfield, Jane White 1897-1984 32
  Obituary 38
Canfield, Muriel 1935- 94
Canga, C.B. 1976- 216
Canga, Chris
  See Canga, C.B.
Caniff, Milton 1907-1988
  Obituary 58
Caniff, Milton Arthur Paul
  See Caniff, Milton
Cann, Helen 1969- 179
  Earlier sketch in SATA *124*
Cann, Kate 1954- 152
  Earlier sketch in SATA *103*
Cannan, Joanna
  See Pullein-Thompson, Joanna Maxwell
Cannell, Jon 196
Cannell, Jonathan C.
  See Cannell, Jon
Cannon, A.E. 202
  Earlier sketches in SATA *93, 163*

Cannon, Ann Edwards
See Cannon, A.E.
Cannon, Bettie (Waddell) 1922- 59
Cannon, Curt
See Hunter, Evan
Cannon, Eileen E(mily) 1948- 119
Cannon, Frank
See Mayhar, Ardath
Cannon, Janell 1957- 128
Earlier sketch in SATA 78
See also CLR 120
Cannon, Marian G. 1923- 85
Cannon, Taffy
See Cannon, Eileen E(mily)
Cantone, AnnaLaura 182
Cantrell, Julie 1973- 217
Canusi, Jose
See Barker, S. Omar
Canyon, Christopher 1966- 150
Earlier sketch in SATA 104
Caparo, Antonio
See Caparo, Antonio Javier
Caparo, Antonio Javier 205
Capek, Michael 1947- 142
Earlier sketch in SATA 96
Capes, Bernard (Edward Joseph)
1854-1918 116
Caple, Kathy 193
Caple, Laurie 1958- 201
Caplin, Alfred Gerald 1909-1979 61
Obituary 21
Caponigro, John Paul 1965- 84
Capote, Truman 1924-1984 91
Capozzola, Michael 234
Capp, Al
See Caplin, Alfred Gerald
Cappel, Constance 1936- 22
Cappetta, Cynthia 1949- 125
Cappo, Nan Willard 1955- 143
Capps, Benjamin (Franklin) 1922- 9
Cappy Dick
See Cleveland, George
Captain Kangaroo
See Keeshan, Robert J.
Captain Wheeler
See Ellis, Edward S.
Captain Young of Yale
See Stratemeyer, Edward L.
Capucilli, Alyssa Satin 1957- 203
Earlier sketches in SATA 115, 163
Capucine
See Mazille, Capucine
Carafoli, Marci
See Balterman, Marcia Ridlon
Caraher, Kim(berley Elizabeth) 1961- 105
Caraker, Mary 1929- 74
Caras, Roger A(ndrew) 1928-2001 12
Obituary 127
Caravantes, Peggy 1935- 140
Caraway, Caren 1939- 57
Carbone, Elisa 1954- 173
Earlier sketches in SATA 81, 137
Carbone, Elisa Lynn
See Carbone, Elisa
Carbonnier, Jeanne 1894-1974 3
Obituary 34
Card, Orson Scott 1951- 127
Earlier sketch in SATA 83
See also CLR 116
Cardinale, Christopher 231
Cardon, Laurent 1962- 230
Care, Felicity
See Coury, Louise Andree
Carew, Jan 1925- 51
Brief entry 40
Carew, Jan Rynveld
See Carew, Jan
Carey, Benedict 1960- 219
Carey, Bonnie
See Marshall, Bonnie C.
Carey, Charles W., Jr. 1951- 170

Carey, Ernestine Gilbreth 1908-2006 2
Obituary 177
Carey, Janet Lee 1954(?)- 225
Earlier sketch in SATA 185
Carey, Lisa 110
Carey, M. V.
See Carey, Mary V(irginia)
Carey, Mary V(irginia) 1925-1994 44
Brief entry 39
Carey, Peter 1943- 94
Carey, Peter Philip
See Carey, Peter
Carey, Valerie Scho 1949- 60
Carheden, Goorel Kristina
See Naaslund, Goorel Kristina
Carigiet, Alois 1902-1985 24
Obituary 47
See also CLR 38
Carini, Edward 1923- 9
Carkeet, David 1946- 75
Carle, Eric 1929- 163
Earlier sketches in SATA 4, 65, 120
See also CLR 72
See also SAAS 6
Carleton, Captain L. C.
See Ellis, Edward S.
Carleton, Captain Latham C.
See Ellis, Edward S.
Carleton, Latham C.
See Ellis, Edward S.
Carley, V(an Ness) Royal 1906-1976
Obituary 20
Carling, Amelia Lau 1949- 164
Earlier sketch in SATA 119
Carlisle, Carolyn
See Hawes, Louise
Carlisle, Clark
See Holding, James (Clark Carlisle, Jr.)
Carlisle, Olga Andreyev 1930- 35
Carlock, Miriam
See Eyerly, Jeannette
Carls, Claudia 1978- 198
Carlsen, G(eorge) Robert 1917- 30
Carlsen, Ruth C(hristoffer) 1918- 2
Carlson, Bernice Wells 1910- 8
Carlson, Christopher C. 202
Carlson, Dale (Bick) 1935- 1
Carlson, Daniel (Bick) 1960- 27
Carlson, Kirsten 1968- 192
Carlson, Kirsten M.
See Carlson, Kirsten
Carlson, Laurie 1952- 173
Earlier sketch in SATA 101
Carlson, Laurie Winn
See Carlson, Laurie
Carlson, Melody 1956- 171
Earlier sketch in SATA 113
Carlson, Nancy 1953- 213
Brief entry 45
Earlier sketches in SATA 56, 90, 144
Carlson, Nancy L.
See Carlson, Nancy
Carlson, Natalie Savage 1906-1997 68
Earlier sketch in SATA 2
See also SAAS 4
Carlson, Susan Johnston 1953- 88
Carlson, Vada F. 1897- 16
Carlstrom, Nancy White 1948- 215
Brief entry 48
Earlier sketches in SATA 53, 92, 156
Carlton, Keith
See Robertson, Keith (Carlton)
Carlton, Susan 1960- 195
Carluccio, Maria 236
Carlyon, Richard 55
Carman, Bill
See Carman, William
Carman, Patrick 1966- 233
Earlier sketches in SATA 161, 197
Carman, William 223

Carmer, Carl (Lamson) 1893-1976 37
Obituary 30
Carmer, Elizabeth Black 1904- 24
Carmi, Giora 1944- 149
Earlier sketch in SATA 79
Carmichael, Carrie
See Carmichael, Harriet
Carmichael, Clay 218
Carmichael, Harriet 40
Carmody, Isobelle 1958- 191
Earlier sketch in SATA 161
Carmody, Isobelle Jane
See Carmody, Isobelle
Carney, Elizabeth 1981- 199
Carney, Jeff 1962- 196
Carney, Mary Lou 1949- 170
Carol, Bill J.
See Knott, William C(ecil, Jr.)
Caron, Romi
See Caron-Kyselkova', Romana
Caron-Kyselkova', Romana 1967- 94
Caroselli, Remus F(rancis) 1916- 36
Carpelan, Bo 1926- 8
Carpelan, Bo Gustaf Bertelsson
See Carpelan, Bo
Carpenter, (John) Allan 1917- 81
Earlier sketch in SATA 3
Carpenter, Angelica Shirley 1945- 153
Earlier sketch in SATA 71
Carpenter, Frances 1890-1972 3
Obituary 27
Carpenter, John 1948- 58
Carpenter, John Howard
See Carpenter, John
Carpenter, Johnny
See Carpenter, John
Carpenter, Nancy 215
Carpenter, Nancy Sippel
See Carpenter, Nancy
Carpenter, Patricia (Healy Evans) 1920- 11
Carr, Glyn
See Styles, (Frank) Showell
Carr, Harriett H(elen) 1899-1977 3
Carr, Jan 1953- 132
Earlier sketch in SATA 89
Carr, M. J.
See Carr, Jan
Carr, Mary Jane 1899-1988 2
Obituary 55
Carr, Philippa
See Hibbert, Eleanor Alice Burford
Carr, Roger Vaughan 1937- 95
Carrel, Annette Felder 1929- 90
Carrick, Carol (Hatfield) 1935- 118
Earlier sketches in SATA 7, 63
See also SAAS 18
Carrick, Donald (F.) 1929-1989 63
Earlier sketch in SATA 7
Carrick, Malcolm 1945- 28
Carrick, Paul 1972- 194
Carrier, Lark 1947- 71
Brief entry 50
Carrier, Roch 1937- 166
Earlier sketch in SATA 105
Carrighar, Sally 1898-1985 24
Carrillo, Patricia S.
See Carrillo, P.S.
Carrillo, P.S. 209
Carrington, G. A.
See Cunningham, Chet
Carrington, Marsha Gray 1954- 168
Earlier sketch in SATA 111
Carris, Joan 1938- 182
Brief entry 42
Earlier sketch in SATA 44
Carris, Joan Davenport
See Carris, Joan
Carroll, Curt
See Bishop, Curtis (Kent)

Carroll, Elizabeth
  See Barkin, Carol
  and James, Elizabeth
Carroll, James Christopher 1960- 235
Carroll, Jaye
  See Carroll, Michael
Carroll, Jenny
  See Cabot, Meg
Carroll, (Archer) Latrobe 1894-1996 7
Carroll, Laura
  See Parr, Lucy
Carroll, Lewis 1832-1898 100
  See also YABC 2
  See also CLR 108
Carroll, Michael 1966- 203
Carroll, Raymond 1924- 86
  Brief entry 47
Carruth, Hayden 1921-2008 47
  Obituary 197
Carryl, Charles E. 1841-1920 114
Carryl, Charles Edward
  See Carryl, Charles E.
Carse, Robert 1902-1971 5
Carson, J(ohn) Franklin 1920-1981 1
  Obituary 107
Carson, Mary Kay 1964- 200
  Earlier sketch in SATA 150
Carson, Rachel 1907-1964 23
Carson, Rachel Louise
  See Carson, Rachel
Carson, Rosalind
  See Chittenden, Margaret
Carson, S. M.
  See Gorsline, (Sally) Marie
Carson, William C. 1928- 154
Carter, Abby 222
  Earlier sketch in SATA 184
Carter, Alden R 1947- 137
  Earlier sketch in SATA 67
  See also CLR 22
  See also SAAS 18
Carter, Alden Richardson
  See Carter, Alden R
Carter, Andy 1948- 134
Carter, Angela 1940-1992 66
  Obituary 70
Carter, Angela Olive
  See Carter, Angela
Carter, Anne Laurel 1953- 209
  Earlier sketch in SATA 135
Carter, Asa Earl
  See Carter, Forrest
Carter, Avis Murton
  See Allen, Kenneth S.
Carter, Bruce
  See Hough, Richard (Alexander)
Carter, Carol S(hadis) 1948- 124
Carter, David A. 1957- 228
  Earlier sketches in SATA 114, 170
Carter, Don 1958- 192
  Earlier sketch in SATA 124
Carter, Dorothy Sharp 1921- 8
Carter, Forrest 1927(?)-1979 32
Carter, Helene 1887-1960 15
Carter, (William) Hodding, Jr. 1907-1972 2
  Obituary 27
Carter, James Earl, Jr.
  See Carter, Jimmy
Carter, Jimmy 1924- 79
Carter, Katharine J(ones) 1905-1984 2
Carter, Lin(wood Vrooman) 1930-1988 91
Carter, Mike 1936- 138

Carter, Nick
  See Avallone, Michael (Angelo, Jr.)
  and Ballard, (Willis) Todhunter
  and Crider, Bill
  and Cassiday, Bruce (Bingham)
  and Chastain, Thomas
  and Dey, Frederic (Merrill) Van Rensselaer
  and Garside, Jack
  and Hayes, Ralph E(ugene)
  and Henderson, M(arilyn) R(uth)
  and Lynds, Dennis
  and Lynds, Gayle (Hallenbeck)
  and Randisi, Robert J.
  and Rasof, Henry
  and Stratemeyer, Edward L.
  and Smith, Martin Cruz
  and Swain, Dwight V(reeland)
  and Vardeman, Robert E.
  and Wallmann, Jeffrey M(iner)
  and White, Lionel
Carter, Peter 1929- 57
Carter, Phyllis Ann
  See Eberle, Irmengarde
Carter, Samuel (Thomson) III 1904-1988 37
  Obituary 60
Carter, Scott William 231
Carter, Timothy 1972- 224
Carter, William E. 1926-1983 1
  Obituary 35
Cartlidge, Michelle 1950- 96
  Brief entry 37
  Earlier sketch in SATA 49
Cartner, William Carruthers 1910- 11
Cartwright, Ann 1940- 78
Cartwright, Reg(inald Ainsley) 1938- 64
Cartwright, Sally 1923- 9
Carusone, Al 1949- 89
Carvell, Marlene 172
Carver, John
  See Gardner, Richard (M.)
Carwell, L'Ann
  See McKissack, Patricia C.
Cary
  See Cary, Louis F(avreau)
Cary, Barbara Knapp 1912(?)-1975
  Obituary 31
Cary, Kate 1967(?)- 174
Cary, Louis F(avreau) 1915- 9
Caryl, Jean
  See Kaplan, Jean Caryl Korn
Casanova, Mary 1957- 186
  Earlier sketches in SATA 94, 136
Cascone, A.G.
  See Cascone, Annette
  and Cascone, Gina
Cascone, Annette 1960- 103
Cascone, Gina 1955- 103
Case, Chris 1976- 209
Case, Marshal T(aylor) 1941- 9
Case, Michael
  See Howard, Robert West
Caseley, Judith 1951- 159
  Brief entry 53
  Earlier sketch in SATA 87
Casewit, Curtis W(erner) 1922-2002 4
Casey, Barbara (Louise) 1944- 147
  Earlier sketch in SATA 79
Casey, Brigid 1950- 9
Casey, Tina 1959- 141
Cash, Ellen Lewis Buell 1905-1989
  Obituary 64
Cash, John Carter 1970- 218
Cash, Megan Montague 160
Cashore, Kristin 1976(?)- 206
Casilla, Robert 1959- 211
  Earlier sketches in SATA 75, 146
Cason, Mabel Earp 1892-1965 10
Cass, Joan E(velyn) 1
Cass-Beggs, Barbara 1904- 62
Cassedy, Patrice (Rinaldo) 1953- 149

Cassedy, Sylvia 1930-1989 77
  Obituary 61
  Earlier sketch in SATA 27
  See also CLR 26
Cassel, Lili
  See Wronker, Lili Cassel
Cassels, Jean 173
Cassidy, Anne 1952- 166
Cassidy, Anne Josephine
  See Cassidy, Anne
Cassidy, Cathy 1962- 183
Cassidy, Kay 232
Cassino, Mark 228
Casson, Hugh Maxwell 1910-1999 65
  Obituary 115
Cassutt, Michael 1954- 78
Cassutt, Michael Joseph
  See Cassutt, Michael
Castaldi, Elicia 194
Castaldo, Nancy Fusco 1962- 151
  Earlier sketch in SATA 93
Castaneda, Omar S. 1954- 71
Castell, Megan
  See Williams, Jeanne
Castellanos, Jane Mollie Robinson
  1913-2001 9
Castellon, Federico 1914-1971 48
Castellucci, Cecil 1969- 176
Castillo, Edmund L. 1924-2005 1
  Obituary 167
Castillo, Lauren 195
Castle, Lee
  See Ogan, George F.
  and Ogan, Margaret E. (Nettles)
Castle, Paul
  See Howard, Vernon (Linwood)
Castle, Robert
  See Hamilton, Edmond
Castro L., Antonio 1941- 226
Castrovilla, Selene 1966- 186
Caswell, Brian 1954- 171
  Earlier sketch in SATA 97
Caswell, Deanna 223
Caswell, Helen (Rayburn) 1923- 12
Catalano, Dominic 1956- 163
  Earlier sketch in SATA 76
Catalano, Grace (A.) 1961- 99
Catalanotto, Peter 1959- 195
  Autobiography Feature 113
  Earlier sketches in SATA 70, 114, 159
  See also CLR 68
  See also SAAS 25
Catanese, P.W. 1961- 227
  Earlier sketch in SATA 179
Cate, Annette LeBlanc 196
Cate, Dick
  See Cate, Richard Edward Nelson
Cate, Richard Edward Nelson 1932- 28
Cather, Willa 1873-1947 30
  See also CLR 98
Catherall, Arthur 1906-1980 74
  Earlier sketches in SATA 3, 4
Cathon, Laura E(lizabeth) 1908-1991 27
Catlett, Elizabeth 1919(?)- 82
Catlin, Wynelle 1930- 13
Catlow, Nikalas
  See Catlow, Niki
Catlow, Niki 1975- 193
Cato, Heather 105
Cato, Sheila 114
Catran, Ken 1944- 190
Catrow, David
  See Catrow, David J. III
Catrow, David J. III 206
  Earlier sketch in SATA 152
Catt, Louis
  See French, Vivian
Cattell, James 1954- 123
Catton, (Charles) Bruce 1899-1978 2
  Obituary 24
Catusanu, Mircea 222

Catz, Max
    See Glaser, Milton
Caudell, Marian 1930- 52
Caudill, Rebecca 1899-1985 .... *1*
    Obituary 44
Cauley, Lorinda Bryan 1951- 46
    Brief entry 43
Caulfield, Peggy F. 1926-1987
    Obituary 53
Cauman, Samuel 1910-1971 48
Causley, Charles (Stanley) 1917-2003 66
    Obituary 149
    Earlier sketch in SATA *3*
    See also CLR *30*
Cavallaro, Ann (Abelson) 1918- 62
Cavallo, Diana 1931- *7*
Cavanagh, Helen (Carol) 1939- 98
    Brief entry 37
    Earlier sketch in SATA *48*
Cavanah, Frances 1899-1982 31
    Earlier sketch in SATA *1*
Cavanna, Betty
    See Harrison, Elizabeth (Allen) Cavanna
Cavanna, Elizabeth
    See Harrison, Elizabeth (Allen) Cavanna
Cave, Kathryn 1948- 123
    Earlier sketch in SATA *76*
Cave, Patrick 1965- 234
Cavendish, Grace
    See Finney, Patricia
Cavendish, Peter
    See Horler, Sydney
Caveney, Philip 1951- 219
Caveney, Philip Richard
    See Caveney, Philip
Cavin, Ruth 1918-2011 38
Cavin, Ruth Brodie
    See Cavin, Ruth
Cavoukian, Raffi 1948- 68
Cawley, Winifred 1915- 13
Cazeau, Charles J(ay) 1931- 65
Cazet, Denys 1938- 191
    Brief entry 41
    Earlier sketches in SATA *52, 99, 163*
Cazzola, Gus 1934- 73
Cebulash, Mel 1937- 91
    Earlier sketch in SATA *10*
Ceccoli, Nicoletta 181
Cecil, Randy 1968- 223
    Earlier sketch in SATA *187*
Cecka, Melanie 199
Ceder, Georgiana Dorcas -1985 10
Celenza, Anna Harwell 133
Celestino, Martha Laing
    See Laing, Martha
Cepeda, Joe 215
    Earlier sketch in SATA *159*
Cerf, Bennett (Alfred) 1898-1971 7
Cerf, Christopher (Bennett) 1941- 2
Cermak, Martin
    See Duchacek, Ivo D(uka)
Cerullo, Mary M. 1949- 145
    Earlier sketch in SATA *86*
Cervantes, Jennifer 234
Cervon, Jacqueline
    See Moussard, Jacqueline
Cetin, Frank Stanley 1921- 2
Chabon, Michael 1963- 145
Chabrian, Deborah
    See Chabrian, Deborah L.
Chabrian, Deborah L. 212
Chaconas, D.J.
    See Chaconas, Dori
Chaconas, Dori 1938- 208
    Earlier sketches in SATA *145, 175*
Chaconas, Doris J.
    See Chaconas, Dori
Chadda, Sarwat 224
Chadwick, Lester 67
    Earlier sketch in SATA *1*
Chaffee, Allen 3

Chaffin, Lillie D(orton) 1925- 4
Chaikin, Miriam 1924- 152
    Earlier sketches in SATA *24, 102*
Chall, Marsha Wilson 150
Challand, Helen J(ean) 1921- 64
Challans, Mary
    See Renault, Mary
Chalmers, Mary (Eileen) 1927- 6
    See also SAAS *14*
Chamberlain, Barbara A.
    See Azore, Barbara
Chamberlain, Margaret 1954- 212
    Earlier sketch in SATA *46*
Chamberlin, Kate 1945- 105
Chamberlin, Mary 1960- 177
Chamberlin, Rich 177
Chamberlin, Richard
    See Chamberlin, Rich
Chambers, Aidan 1934- 171
    Earlier sketches in SATA *1, 69, 108*
    See also CLR *151*
    See also SAAS *12*
Chambers, Bradford 1922-1984
    Obituary 39
Chambers, Catherine E.
    See St. John, Nicole
Chambers, John W. 1933- 57
    Brief entry 46
Chambers, Kate
    See St. John, Nicole
Chambers, Margaret Ada Eastwood 1911- 2
Chambers, Peggy
    See Chambers, Margaret Ada Eastwood
Chambers, Robert W(illiam) 1865-1933 107
Chambliss, Maxie 186
Champlin, Susan 1961- 225
Chan, Gillian 1954- 147
    Earlier sketch in SATA *102*
Chan, Peter 1980(?)- 207
Chance, James T.
    See Carpenter, John
Chance, John T.
    See Carpenter, John
Chance, Stephen
    See Turner, Philip (William)
Chandler, Caroline A(ugusta) 1906-1979 22
    Obituary 24
Chandler, David P. 1933- 28
Chandler, David Porter
    See Chandler, David P.
Chandler, Edna Walker 1908-1982 11
    Obituary 31
Chandler, Jennifer
    See Westwood, Jennifer
Chandler, Karen 1959- 122
Chandler, Kristen 230
Chandler, Linda S(mith) 1929- 39
Chandler, Pauline 175
Chandler, Robert 1953- 40
Chandler, Ruth Forbes 1894-1978 2
    Obituary 26
Chandonnet, Ann F. 1943- 92
Chaney, Jill 1932- 87
Chang, Chih-Wei 1966- 111
Chang, Cindy 1968- 90
Chang, Grace 1961- 226
Chang, Margaret 1941- 71
Chang, Margaret Scrogin
    See Chang, Margaret
Chang, Raymond 1939- 142
    Earlier sketches in SATA *71, 142 PEN*
Chanin, Michael 1952- 84
Channel, A. R.
    See Catherall, Arthur
Chapian, Marie 1938- 29
Chapin, Alene Olsen Dalton 1915(?)-1986
    Obituary 47
Chapin, Tom 1945- 83
Chapman, Allen 67
    Earlier sketch in SATA *1*
Chapman, Cheryl O(rth) 1948- 80

Chapman, (Constance) Elizabeth (Mann)
    1919- *10*
Chapman, Gaye 1970- 200
Chapman, Gaye Coralie
    See Chapman, Gaye
Chapman, Gaynor 1935- 32
Chapman, Gillian 1955- 120
Chapman, Jane 1970- 212
    Earlier sketches in SATA *122, 176*
Chapman, Jean 104
    Earlier sketch in SATA *34*
    See also CLR *65*
Chapman, John Stanton Higham 1891-1972
    Obituary 27
Chapman, Lee
    See Bradley, Marion Zimmer
Chapman, Linda 1969- 223
Chapman, Lynne 1960- 197
Chapman, Lynne F(erguson) 1963- 150
    Earlier sketch in SATA *94*
Chapman, Maristan
    See Chapman, John Stanton Higham
Chapman, Vera (Ivy May) 1898-1996 33
Chapman, Walker
    See Silverberg, Robert
Chappell, Audrey 1954- 72
Chappell, Crissa-Jean 198
Chappell, Warren 1904-1991 68
    Obituary 67
    Earlier sketch in SATA *6*
    See also SAAS *10*
Chapra, Mimi 182
Charbonneau, Eileen 1951- 118
    Earlier sketch in SATA *84*
Charbonnet, Gabrielle 1961- 227
    Earlier sketch in SATA *81*
Chardiet, Bernice 1927(?)- 27
Chardiet, Bernice Kroll
    See Chardiet, Bernice
Charest, Emily MacLachlan 198
Charles, Donald
    See Meighan, Donald Charles
Charles, Louis
    See Stratemeyer, Edward L.
Charles, Nicholas
    See Kuskin, Karla
Charles, Nicholas J.
    See Kuskin, Karla
Charles, Norma 153
Charles, Veronika Martenova 182
Charlip, Remy 1929- 119
    Earlier sketches in SATA *4, 68*
    See also CLR *8*
Charlot, Jean 1898-1979 8
    Obituary 31
Charlot, Martin 1944- 64
Charlot, Martin Day
    See Charlot, Martin
Charlton, Michael (Alan) 1923- 34
Charlton-Trujillo, e.E. 189
Charmatz, Bill 1925-2005 7
Charnas, Suzy McKee 1939- 110
    Earlier sketch in SATA *61*
Charosh, Mannis 1906- 5
Chartier, Normand L. 1945- 66
Chase, Alice
    See McHargue, Georgess
Chase, Alyssa 1965- 92
Chase, Andra 1942- 91
Chase, Emily
    See Aks, Patricia
    and Garwood, Julie
    and Sachs, Judith
    and White, Carol
Chase, Mary (Coyle) 1907-1981 17
    Obituary 29
Chase, Mary Ellen 1887-1973 10
Chase, Paula 214
Chase, Richard 1904-1988 64
    Obituary 56

Chase, Samantha
   See Glick, Ruth
Chast, Roz 1954- *212*
   Earlier sketch in SATA *97*
Chastain, Madye Lee 1908-1989 .... *4*
Chataway, Carol 1955- *140*
Chatterjee, Debjani 1952- *83*
Chatterton, Martin 1961- *225*
Chauncy, Nan(cen Beryl Masterman)
   1900-1970 .... *6*
   See also CLR 6
Chaundler, Christine 1887-1972 .... *1*
   Obituary *25*
Chayka, Doug *196*
Chbosky, Stephen 1972- *164*
Cheaney, Janie B.
   See Cheaney, J.B.
Cheaney, J.B. 1950- *188*
Chee, Cheng-Khee 1934- *79*
Cheese, Chloe 1952- *118*
Chekhonte, Antosha
   See Chekhov, Anton
Chekhov, Anton 1860-1904 .... *90*
Chekhov, Anton Pavlovich
   See Chekhov, Anton
Chelushkin, Kirill 1968- *186*
Chen, Anthony 1929- *6*
Chen, Chih-Yuan 1975- *216*
   Earlier sketch in SATA *155*
Chen, Ju-Hong 1941- *78*
Chen, Pauline 1966- *202*
Chen, Sara
   See Odgers, Sally Farrell
Chen, Tony
   See Chen, Anthony
Chen, Yong 1963- *183*
Chen, Yuan-tsung 1932- *65*
Chen, Zhiyuan
   See Chen, Chih-Yuan
Chenault, Nell
   See Smith, Linell Nash
Chen Chih-Yuan
   See Chen, Chih-Yuan
Chenery, Janet (Dai) 1923- *25*
Cheney, Cora 1916-1999 .... *3*
   Obituary *110*
Cheney, Glenn (Alan) 1951- *99*
Cheney, Lynne V. 1941- *152*
Cheney, Lynne Vincent
   See Cheney, Lynne V.
Cheney, Ted
   See Cheney, Theodore Albert
Cheney, Theodore A. Rees
   See Cheney, Theodore Albert
Cheney, Theodore Albert 1928- *11*
Cheng, Andrea 1957- *205*
   Earlier sketches in SATA *128, 172*
Cheng, Christopher 1959- *173*
   Earlier sketch in SATA *106*
Cheng, Judith 1955- *36*
Cheng, Shan
   See Jiang, Cheng An
Cheripko, Jan 1951- *155*
   Earlier sketch in SATA *83*
Chermayeff, Ivan 1932- *47*
Chernenko, Dan
   See Turtledove, Harry
Chernett, Dan *224*
Chernoff, Dorothy A.
   See Ernst, (Lyman) John
Chernoff, Goldie Taub 1909- *10*
Cherry, Carolyn Janice
   See Cherryh, C.J.
Cherry, Lynne 1952- *99*
   Earlier sketch in SATA *34*
Cherryh, C.J. 1942- *172*
   Earlier sketch in SATA *93*
Cherryholmes, Anne
   See Price, Olive
Cheshire, Simon *236*
   Earlier sketch in SATA *172*

Chesler, Bernice 1932-2002 .... *59*
Chess, Victoria (Dickerson) 1939- *92*
   Earlier sketch in SATA *33*
Chessa, Francesca *233*
   Earlier sketch in SATA *191*
Chester, Deborah 1957- *85*
Chester, Kate
   See Guccione, Leslie Davis
Chesterton, G. K. 1874-1936 .... *27*
Chesterton, Gilbert Keith
   See Chesterton, G. K.
Chesworth, Michael *207*
   Earlier sketch in SATA *160*
Chetin, Helen 1922- *6*
Chetwin, Grace *86*
   Brief entry *50*
Chevalier, Christa 1937- *35*
Chevalier, Tracy 1962- *128*
Chew, Ruth 1920-2010 .... *7*
Chichester Clark, Emma 1955- *209*
   Earlier sketches in SATA *117, 156, 69*
Chick, Bryan 1971- *239*
Chidsey, Donald Barr 1902-1981 .... *3*
   Obituary *27*
Chiefari, Janet D. 1942- *58*
Chien, Catia *193*
Chien-min, Lin
   See Rumford, James
Child, L. Maria
   See Child, Lydia Maria
Child, Lauren 1965- *183*
   Earlier sketches in SATA *119, 160*
Child, Lincoln 1957- *113*
Child, Lincoln B.
   See Child, Lincoln
Child, Lydia Maria 1802-1880 .... *67*
Child, Mrs.
   See Child, Lydia Maria
Child, Philip 1898-1978 .... *47*
Children's Shepherd, The
   See Westphal, Arnold Carl
Childress, Alice 1920-1994 .... *81*
   Earlier sketches in SATA *7, 48*
   See also CLR 14
Childs, H(alla) Fay (Cochrane) 1890-1971 .... *1*
   Obituary *25*
Childs, Tera Lynn 1976- *235*
Chilton, Charles (Frederick William)
   1917- *102*
Chima, Cinda Williams *226*
   Earlier sketch in SATA *192*
Chimaera
   See Farjeon, Eleanor
Chin, Jason 1978- *218*
Chin, Richard (M.) 1946- *52*
Chinery, Michael 1938- *26*
Chin-Lee, Cynthia 1958- *102*
Chin-Lee D., Cynthia
   See Chin-Lee, Cynthia
Chippendale, Lisa A. *158*
Chipperfield, Joseph Eugene 1912-1980(?) .. *87*
   Earlier sketch in SATA *2*
Chisholm, P. F.
   See Finney, Patricia
Chislett, Gail (Elaine) 1948- *58*
Chittenden, Elizabeth F. 1903-1999 .... *9*
Chittenden, Margaret 1935- *28*
Chittum, Ida 1918- *7*
Chitwood, Suzanne Tanner 1958- *160*
Chmielarz, Sharon Lee 1940- *72*
Choat, Beth 1964- *238*
Choate, Judith (Newkirk) 1940- *30*
Chocolate, Debbi 1954- *223*
   Earlier sketch in SATA *96*
Chocolate, Deborah H. Newton
   See Chocolate, Debbi
Chodos-Irvine, Margaret *211*
   Earlier sketch in SATA *152*
Choi, Sook Nyul 1937- *73*
   Autobiography Feature *126*
   See also CLR 53

Choi, Yangsook *178*
Choksi, Nishant 1975- *222*
Choldenko, Gennifer 1957- *182*
   Earlier sketch in SATA *135*
Chorao, Kay 1936- *215*
Chorao, (Ann Mc)Kay (Sproat) 1936- *162*
   Earlier sketches in SATA *8, 69*
Choron, Sandra (Zena Samelson) 1950- *146*
Choung, Eun-hee *199*
Chown, Marcus 1959- *137*
Choyce, Lesley 1951- *165*
   Earlier sketch in SATA *94*
Choyce, Lesley Willis
   See Choyce, Lesley
Chrisman, Arthur Bowie 1889-1953 .... *124*
   See also YABC 1
Christelow, Eileen 1943- *184*
   Autobiography Feature *120*
   Brief entry *35*
   Earlier sketches in SATA *38, 90*
Christensen, Bonnie 1951- *213*
   Earlier sketches in SATA *110, 157*
Christensen, Gardell Dano 1907-1991 .... *1*
Christensen, Laurie
   See Steding, Laurie
Christesen, Barbara 1940- *40*
Christgau, Alice Erickson 1902-1977 .... *13*
Christian, Mary Blount 1933- *9*
Christiana, David *195*
Christie, Agatha 1890-1976 .... *36*
Christie, Agatha Mary Clarissa
   See Christie, Agatha
Christie, Ann Philippa
   See Pearce, Philippa
Christie, Gregory
   See Christie, R. Gregory
Christie, Peter 1962- *236*
Christie, Philippa
   See Pearce, Philippa
Christie, R. Gregory 1971- *225*
   Earlier sketches in SATA *127, 185*
Christopher, John
   See Youd, Samuel
Christopher, Louise
   See Hale, Arlene
Christopher, Matt(hew Frederick)
   1917-1997 .... *80*
   Obituary *99*
   Earlier sketches in SATA *2, 47*
   See also CLR *119*
   See also SAAS 9
Christopher, Milbourne 1914(?)-1984 .... *46*
Christy, Howard Chandler 1873-1952 .... *21*
Christy, Jana 1965- *239*
Chrustowski, Rick *176*
Chrystie, Frances N(icholson) 1904-1986 .... *60*
Chu, Daniel 1933- *11*
Chui, Vince 1975- *236*
Chukovsky, Kornei (Ivanovich) 1882-1969 . *34*
   Earlier sketch in SATA *5*
Church, Caroline Jayne *219*
   Earlier sketch in SATA *179*
Church, Richard 1893-1972 .... *3*
Churchill, E(lmer) Richard 1937- *11*
Churchill, Elizabeth
   See Hough, Richard (Alexander)
Chute, B(eatrice) J(oy) 1913-1987 .... *2*
   Obituary *53*
Chute, Marchette (Gaylord) 1909-1994 .... *1*
Chwast, Jacqueline 1932- *6*
Chwast, Seymour 1931- *146*
   Earlier sketches in SATA *18, 96*
Ciardi, John (Anthony) 1916-1986 .... *65*
   Obituary *46*
   Earlier sketch in SATA *1*
   See also CLR *19*
   See also SAAS 26
Ciccone, Madonna Louise Veronica
   See Madonna
Ciddor, Anna 1957- *213*
Ciment, James D. 1958- *140*

Cirrone, Dorian *182*
Cisneros, Sandra 1954-
  See CLR *123*
Citra, Becky 1954- *137*
Citrin, Michael 1965(?)- *183*
Claflin, Willy 1944- *208*
Clair, Andree *19*
Claire, Cassandra
  See Clare, Cassandra
Clampett, Bob 1914(?)-1985 .... *44*
  Obituary *38*
Clampett, Robert
  See Clampett, Bob
Clapp, John 1968- *109*
Clapp, Patricia 1912- *74*
  Earlier sketch in SATA *4*
  See also SAAS *4*
Clare, Cassandra 1973- *238*
Clare, Ellen
  See Sinclair, Olga
Clare, Helen
  See Clarke, Pauline
Claremont, Chris 1950- *87*
Claremont, Christopher Simon
  See Claremont, Chris
Clark, Ann Nolan 1896-1995 .... *82*
  Obituary *87*
  Earlier sketch in SATA *4*
  See also CLR *16*
  See also SAAS *16*
Clark, Champ 1923-2002 .... *47*
Clark, Christopher (Anthony) Stuart
  See Stuart-Clark, Christopher (Anthony)
Clark, Clara Gillow 1951- *154*
  Earlier sketch in SATA *84*
Clark, David
  See Hardcastle, Michael
Clark, David Allen
  See Ernst, (Lyman) John
Clark, Emma Chichester
  See Chichester Clark, Emma
Clark, Frank J(ames) 1922- *18*
Clark, Garel
  See Garelick, May
Clark, Halsey
  See Deming, Richard
Clark, Joan
  See Benson, Mildred
Clark, Joan 1934- *182*
  Earlier sketches in SATA *59, 96*
Clark, Karen Henry *237*
Clark, Leonard 1905-1981 .... *30*
  Obituary *29*
Clark, M. R.
  See Clark, Mavis Thorpe
Clark, Margaret (D.) 1943- *126*
Clark, Margaret Goff 1913- *82*
  Earlier sketch in SATA *8*
Clark, Mary Higgins 1929- *46*
Clark, Mavis Thorpe 1909-1999 .... *74*
  Earlier sketch in SATA *8*
  See also CLR *30*
  See also SAAS *5*
Clark, Merle
  See Gessner, Lynne
Clark, Patricia Denise
  See Robins, Patricia
Clark, Patricia Finrow 1929- *11*
Clark, Ronald Harry 1904-1999 .... *193*
Clark, Ronald William 1916-1987 .... *2*
  Obituary *52*
Clark, Sherryl 1956- *149*
Clark, Van D(eusen) 1909-1974 .... *2*
Clark, Virginia
  See Gray, Patricia (Clark)
Clark, Walter Van Tilburg 1909-1971 .... *8*
Clarke, Arthur
  See Clarke, Arthur C.

Clarke, Arthur C. 1917-2008 .... *115*
  Obituary *191*
  Earlier sketches in SATA *13, 70*
  See also CLR *119*
Clarke, Arthur Charles
  See Clarke, Arthur C.
Clarke, Clorinda 1917- *7*
Clarke, Elizabeth L. 1934- *103*
Clarke, Greg 1959- *215*
Clarke, Gus 1948- *134*
Clarke, J.
  See Clarke, Judith
Clarke, James Hall
  See Rowland-Entwistle, (Arthur) Theodore
  (Henry)
Clarke, Joan B. 1921- *42*
  Brief entry *27*
Clarke, John
  See Laklan, Carli
  and Sontup, Dan(iel)
Clarke, Judith 1943- *164*
  Earlier sketches in SATA *75, 110*
  See also CLR *61*
Clarke, Julia 1950- *138*
Clarke, Kenneth 1957- *107*
Clarke, Lea
  See Rowland-Entwistle, (Arthur) Theodore
  (Henry)
Clarke, Margaret 1941-
  See CLR *99*
Clarke, Mary Stetson 1911-1994 .... *5*
Clarke, Michael
  See Newlon, (Frank) Clarke
Clarke, Pauline 1921- *131*
  Earlier sketch in SATA *3*
  See also CLR *28*
Clarkson, E(dith) Margaret 1915- *37*
Clarkson, Ewan 1929- *9*
Clarkson, Karen *233*
Claudia, Susan
  See Goulart, Ron
  and Johnston, William
Claverie, Jean 1946- *38*
Clay, Patrice 1947- *47*
Clay, Wil *203*
Clayman, Deborah Paula
  See Da Costa, Deborah
Claypool, Jane
  See Miner, Jane Claypool
Clayton, Elaine 1961- *209*
  Earlier sketches in SATA *94, 159*
Clayton, Lawrence (Otto, Jr.) 1945- *75*
Clayton, Sally Pomme *218*
Clayton, Sandra 1951- *110*
Cle, Troy *202*
Clea, Super
  See Hantman, Clea
Cleary, Beverly 1916- *121*
  Earlier sketches in SATA *2, 43, 79*
  See also CLR *72*
  See also SAAS *20*
Cleary, Beverly Atlee Bunn
  See Cleary, Beverly
Cleary, Brian P. 1959- *186*
  Earlier sketches in SATA *93, 132*
Cleaver, Bill
  See Cleaver, William J.
Cleaver, Carole 1934- *6*
Cleaver, Elizabeth (Ann Mrazik)
  1939-1985 .... *23*
  Obituary *43*
  See also CLR *13*
Cleaver, Hylton Reginald 1891-1961 .... *49*
Cleaver, Vera 1919-1993 .... *76*
  Earlier sketch in SATA *22*
  See also CLR *6*
Cleaver, Vera Allen
  See Cleaver, Vera
Cleaver, William J. 1920-1981 .... *22*
  Obituary *27*
  See also CLR *6*

Cleishbotham, Jebediah
  See Scott, Sir Walter
Cleland, Janet *226*
Cleland, Mabel
  See Widdemer, Mabel Cleland
Clem, Margaret H(ollingsworth) 1923- *90*
Clemens, James
  See Rollins, James
Clemens, Samuel
  See Twain, Mark
Clemens, Samuel Langhorne
  See Twain, Mark
Clemens, Virginia Phelps 1941- *35*
Clement, Gary *191*
Clement, Janet *182*
Clement, Nathan 1966- *200*
Clement, Priscilla Ferguson 1942- *171*
Clement, Rod *97*
Clement-Moore, Rosemary *229*
  Earlier sketch in SATA *188*
Clements, Andrew 1949- *235*
  Earlier sketches in SATA *104, 158, 203*
Clements, Bruce 1931- *178*
  Earlier sketches in SATA *27, 94*
Clemesha, David *192*
Cleminson, Katie *221*
Clemons, Elizabeth
  See Nowell, Elizabeth Cameron
Clerk, N. W.
  See Lewis, C. S.
Cleveland, Bob
  See Cleveland, George
Cleveland, George 1903(?)-1985
  Obituary *43*
Cleveland-Peck, Patricia *80*
Cleven, Cathrine
  See Cleven, Kathryn Seward
Cleven, Kathryn Seward *2*
Clevenger, William R. 1954- *84*
Clevenger, William Russell
  See Clevenger, William R.
Clevin, Joergen 1920- *7*
Clevin, Jorgen
  See Clevin, Joergen
Clewes, Dorothy (Mary) 1907-2003 .... *86*
  Obituary *138*
  Earlier sketch in SATA *1*
Clifford, David
  See Rosenberg, Eth Clifford
Clifford, Eth
  See Rosenberg, Eth Clifford
Clifford, Harold B(urton) 1893-1988 .... *10*
Clifford, Margaret Cort 1929- *1*
Clifford, Martin
  See Hamilton, Charles (Harold St. John)
Clifford, Mary Louise Beneway 1926- *23*
Clifford, Peggy
  See Clifford, Margaret Cort
Clifford, Rachel Mark
  See Lewis, Brenda Ralph
Clifton, Lucille 1936-2010 .... *128*
  Earlier sketches in SATA *20, 69*
  See also CLR *5*
Clifton, Thelma Lucille
  See Clifton, Lucille
Climo, Shirley 1928- *166*
  Autobiography Feature *110*
  Brief entry *35*
  Earlier sketches in SATA *39, 77*
  See also CLR *69*
Cline-Ransome, Lesa *201*
Clinton, Catherine 1952- *203*
Clinton, Cathryn 1957- *136*
Clinton, Dirk
  See Silverberg, Robert
Clinton, Jon
  See Prince, J(ack) H(arvey)
Clippinger, Carol *193*
Clish, (Lee) Marian 1946- *43*
Clive, Clifford
  See Hamilton, Charles (Harold St. John)

Clokey, Art 1921- *59*
Cloudsley-Thompson, J(ohn) L(eonard)
  1921- *19*
Clouse, Nancy L. 1938- *78*
Clover, Peter 1952- *215*
  Earlier sketch in SATA *152*
Clutha, Janet
  See Frame, Janet
Clutha, Janet Paterson Frame
  See Frame, Janet
Clymer, Eleanor 1906-2001 .... *85*
  Obituary *126*
  Earlier sketch in SATA *9*
  See also SAAS *17*
Clyne, Patricia (Edwards) *31*
Cneut, Carll 1969- *197*
Coalson, Glo 1946- *94*
  Earlier sketch in SATA *26*
Coates, Anna 1958- *73*
Coates, Belle 1896-1986 .... *2*
Coates, Ruth Allison 1915- *11*
Coats, Alice M(argaret) 1905-1976 .... *11*
Coatsworth, Elizabeth (Jane) 1893-1986 .... *100*
  Obituary *49*
  Earlier sketches in SATA *2, 56*
  See also CLR *2*
Cobalt, Martin
  See Mayne, William
Cobb, Jane
  See Berry, Jane Cobb
Cobb, Mary 1931- *88*
Cobb, Vicki 1938- *136*
  Autobiography Feature *136*
  Earlier sketches in SATA *8, 69, 131*
  See also CLR *2*
  See also SAAS *6*
Cobbett, Richard
  See Pluckrose, Henry
Cober, Alan E(dwin) 1935-1998 .... *7*
  Obituary *101*
Cobham, Sir Alan
  See Hamilton, Charles (Harold St. John)
Coburn, Jake 1978- *155*
Cocagnac, Augustin Maurice(-Jean) 1924- *7*
Cocca-Leffler, Maryann 1958- *194*
  Earlier sketches in SATA *80, 136*
Cochran, Bill *187*
Cochran, Bobbye A. 1949- *11*
Cochran, Josh *221*
Cochran, Thomas 1955- *198*
Cochrane, Hamilton E.
  See Cochrane, Mick
Cochrane, Mick 1956- *215*
Cockcroft, Jason *217*
Cockett, Mary *3*
Cocks, Peter *204*
Cocovini, Abby *202*
Coddell, Esme Raji
  See Codell, Esme Raji
Codell, Esme Raji 1968- *160*
Cody, C. S.
  See Waller, Leslie
Cody, Jess
  See Cunningham, Chet
Cody, Matthew *229*
Coe, Anne (E.) 1949- *95*
Coe, Douglas
  See Epstein, Beryl
  and Epstein, Samuel
Coe, Lloyd 1899(?)-1976
  Obituary *30*
Coen, Rena Neumann 1925- *20*
Coerr, Eleanor (Beatrice) 1922- *67*
  Earlier sketch in SATA *1*
Cofer, Judith Ortiz 1952- *164*
  Earlier sketch in SATA *110*
Coffelt, Nancy 1961- *189*
Coffey, Brian
  See Koontz, Dean
Coffin, Geoffrey
  See Mason, F(rancis) van Wyck

Coffin, M. T.
  See Stanley, George Edward
Coffin, M.T.
  See Stanley, George Edward
Coffman, Ramon Peyton 1896-1989 .... *4*
Cogan, Karen 1954- *125*
Coggins, Jack (Banham) 1911-2006 .... *2*
Cohagan, Carolyn 1972- *228*
Cohen, Barbara 1932-1992 .... *77*
  Obituary *74*
  Earlier sketch in SATA *10*
  See also SAAS *7*
Cohen, Daniel (E.) 1936- *70*
  Earlier sketch in SATA *8*
  See also CLR *43*
  See also SAAS *4*
Cohen, Deborah Bodin 1968- *180*
Cohen, Jan Barger
  See Barger, Jan
Cohen, Jene Barr
  See Barr, Jene
Cohen, Joan Lebold 1932- *4*
Cohen, Judith Love 1933- *78*
Cohen, Lisa 1963- *225*
Cohen, Miriam 1926-1955 .... *155*
  Earlier sketches in SATA *29, 106*
  See also SAAS *11*
Cohen, Nora *75*
Cohen, Paul 1945- *58*
Cohen, Paul S.
  See Cohen, Paul
Cohen, Peter Zachary 1931- *150*
  Earlier sketch in SATA *4*
Cohen, Robert Carl 1930- *8*
Cohen, Santiago 1954- *215*
Cohen, Sholom 1951- *94*
Cohn, Angelo 1914-1997 .... *19*
Cohn, Diana *194*
Cohn, Rachel 1968- *228*
  Earlier sketch in SATA *161*
Coit, Margaret Louise 1922-2003 .... *2*
  Obituary *142*
Colasanti, Susane 1973- *214*
Colato Lainez, Rene 1970- *226*
  Earlier sketch in SATA *176*
Colbert, Anthony 1934-2007 .... *15*
Colbert, Nancy A. 1936- *139*
Colby, C(arroll) B(urleigh) 1904-1977 .... *35*
  Earlier sketch in SATA *3*
Colby, Jean Poindexter 1909-1993 .... *23*
Cole, Annette
  See Steiner, Barbara A(nnette)
Cole, Babette 1949- *155*
  Earlier sketches in SATA *61, 96*
Cole, Betsy 1940- *83*
Cole, Brock 1938- *200*
  Earlier sketches in SATA *72, 136*
  See also CLR *18*
Cole, Davis
  See Elting, Mary
Cole, Hannah 1954- *74*
Cole, Henry 1955- *213*
  Earlier sketch in SATA *181*
Cole, Jack -1974
  See Stewart, John
Cole, Jackson
  See Curry, Thomas Albert
  and Germano, Peter B.
  and Heckelmann, Charles N(ewman)
  and Newton, D(wight) B(ennett)
  and Schisgall, Oscar
Cole, Jennifer
  See Zach, Cheryl (Byrd)
Cole, Joanna 1944- *231*
  Brief entry *37*
  Earlier sketches in SATA *49, 81, 120, 168*
  See also CLR *40*
Cole, Lois Dwight 1903-1979 .... *10*
  Obituary *26*
Cole, Michael 1947- *59*

Cole, Samantha
  See Cole, Stephen
Cole, Sheila 1939- *171*
  Earlier sketches in SATA *24, 95*
Cole, Sheila R.
  See Cole, Sheila
Cole, Sheila Rotenberg
  See Cole, Sheila
Cole, Stephen 1971- *230*
  Earlier sketch in SATA *161*
Cole, Steve
  See Cole, Stephen
Cole, William (Rossa) 1919-2000 .... *71*
  Earlier sketch in SATA *9*
  See also SAAS *9*
Coleman, Andrew
  See Pine, Nicholas
Coleman, Clare
  See Bell, Clare (Louise)
  and Easton, M(alcolm) Coleman
Coleman, Janet Wyman *184*
Coleman, Loren 1947- *164*
Coleman, Loren Elwood, Jr.
  See Coleman, Loren
Coleman, Mary Ann 1928- *83*
Coleman, Michael
  See Jones, Allan Frewin
Coleman, Michael 1946- *199*
  Autobiography Feature *133*
  Earlier sketches in SATA *108, 133*
Coleman, Rowan *187*
Coleman, William L(eRoy) 1938- *49*
  Brief entry *34*
Coleman, Wim 1926- *212*
Coles, Robert 1929- *23*
Coles, Robert Martin
  See Coles, Robert
Colfer, Eoin 1965- *197*
  Earlier sketch in SATA *148*
  See also CLR *112*
Colin, Ann
  See Ure, Jean
Collard, Sneed B. III 1959- *184*
  Earlier sketches in SATA *84, 139*
Colledge, Anne 1939- *142*
Colley, Jacqui 1965- *202*
Collicott, Sharleen 1937- *143*
  Earlier sketch in SATA *98*
Collicutt, Paul *229*
Collier, Bryan *204*
  Earlier sketches in SATA *126, 174*
Collier, Christopher 1930- *70*
  Earlier sketch in SATA *16*
  See also CLR *126*
Collier, Ethel 1903-1999 .... *22*
Collier, James Lincoln 1928- *166*
  Earlier sketches in SATA *8, 70*
  See also CLR *126*
  See also SAAS *21*
Collier, Jane
  See Collier, Zena
Collier, Kristi *182*
Collier, Steven 1942- *61*
Collier, Zena 1926- *23*
Collings, Gillian 1939- *102*
Collington, Peter 1948- *99*
  Earlier sketch in SATA *59*
Collins, Ace 1953- *82*
Collins, Andrew J.
  See Collins, Ace
Collins, B. R. 1981- *214*
Collins, David R(aymond) 1940-2001 .... *121*
  Earlier sketch in SATA *7*
Collins, Heather 1946- *81*
Collins, Hunt
  See Hunter, Evan
Collins, Michael
  See Lynds, Dennis
Collins, Michael 1930- *58*
Collins, Pat Lowery 1932- *217*
  Earlier sketches in SATA *31, 151*

Collins, Paul 1954- 126
Collins, Ross 1972- 239
  Earlier sketch in SATA 200
Collins, Ruth Philpott 1890-1975
  Obituary 30
Collins, Suzanne 1963(?)- 224
  Earlier sketch in SATA 180
Collins, Yvonne 194
Collinson, A. S.
  See Collinson, Alan S.
Collinson, Alan S. 1934- 80
Collinson, Roger (Alfred) 1936- 133
Collison, Linda 1953- 185
Collodi, Carlo 1826-1890 100
  Earlier sketch in SATA 29
  See also CLR 120
Colloms, Brenda 1919- 40
Colman, Hila 1909-2008 53
  Earlier sketch in SATA 1
  See also SAAS 14
Colman, Morris 1899(?)-1981
  Obituary 25
Colman, Penny (Morgan) 1944- 160
  Autobiography Feature 160
  Earlier sketches in SATA 77, 114
Colman, Warren (David) 1944- 67
Coloma, Cindy
  See Martinusen-Coloma, Cindy
Colombo, John Robert 1936- 50
Colon, Raul 156
Colon, Raul 1952- 202
Colonius, Lillian 1911-1992 3
Colorado, Antonio J.
  See Colorado (Capella), Antonio J(ulio)
Colorado (Capella), Antonio J(ulio)
  1903-1994 23
  Obituary 79
Colquhoun, Glenn 1964- 165
Colston, Fifi E. 1960- 150
Colt, Martin
  See Epstein, Beryl
  and Epstein, Samuel
Colum, Padraic 1881-1972 15
  See also CLR 36
Columbus, Chris 1959- 97
Columbus, Christopher
  See Columbus, Chris
Columella
  See Moore, Clement Clarke
Colver, Anne 1908- 7
Colvin, James
  See Moorcock, Michael
Colwell, Eileen (Hilda) 1904-2002 2
Colwyn, Stewart
  See Pepper, Frank S.
Coman, Carolyn 1951- 197
  Earlier sketch in SATA 127
Combres, Elisabeth 1967- 226
Combs, Lisa M.
  See McCourt, Lisa
Combs, Robert
  See Murray, John
Comfort, Jane Levington
  See Sturtzel, Jane Levington
Comfort, Mildred Houghton 1886-1976 3
Comins, Ethel M(ae) 11
Comins, Jeremy 1933- 28
Commager, Henry Steele 1902-1998 23
  Obituary 102
Comora, Madeleine 190
Compere, Mickie
  See Davidson, Margaret
Compestine, Ying Chang 1963- 187
  Earlier sketch in SATA 140
Comport, Sally Wern 190
Compton, Patricia A. 1936- 75
Comte, The Great
  See Hawkesworth, Eric
Comus
  See Ballantyne, R(obert) M(ichael)

Comyns, Nance
  See Comyns-Toohey, Nantz
Comyns-Toohey, Nantz 1956- 86
Conahan, Carolyn
  See Conahan, Carolyn Digby
Conahan, Carolyn Digby 1961- 216
Conan Doyle, Arthur
  See Doyle, Sir Arthur Conan
Condie, Ally 204
Condie, Allyson B.
  See Condie, Ally
Condit, Martha Olson 1913- 28
Condon, Bill 1949- 142
Condon, Judith 83
Condon, Ken 195
Condy, Roy 1942- 96
Cone, Ferne Geller 1921- 39
Cone, Molly (Lamken) 1918- 151
  Autobiography Feature 151
  Earlier sketches in SATA 1, 28, 115
  See also SAAS 11
Cone, Patrick 1954- 89
Coney, Michael G. 1932-2005 61
  Obituary 170
Coney, Michael Greatrex
  See Coney, Michael G.
Coney, Mike
  See Coney, Michael G.
Conford, Ellen 1942- 162
  Earlier sketches in SATA 6, 68, 110
  See also CLR 71
Conger, Lesley
  See Suttles, Shirley (Smith)
Conklin, Gladys Plemon 1903- 2
Conklin, Paul S. 1929(?)-2003 43
  Brief entry 33
  Obituary 147
Conkling, Hilda 1910-1986 23
Conlan, Kathleen Elizabeth 1950- 145
Conlan, Kathy
  See Conlan, Kathleen Elizabeth
Conley, Robyn 1963- 125
Conley-Weaver, Robyn
  See Conley, Robyn
Conlon-McKenna, Marita 1956- 71
Conly, Jane Leslie 1948- 164
  Earlier sketches in SATA 80, 112
Conly, Robert Leslie
  See O'Brien, Robert C.
Connell, Kirk
  See Chapman, John Stanton Higham
Connell, Tom 206
Connelly, Gwen 1952- 212
Connelly, Marc(us Cook) 1890-1980
  Obituary 25
Connolly, Jerome P(atrick) 1931- 8
Connolly, Pat 1943- 74
Connolly, Peter 1935- 105
  Earlier sketch in SATA 47
Conover, Chris 1950- 213
  Earlier sketch in SATA 31
Conquest, Owen
  See Hamilton, Charles (Harold St. John)
Conrad, Joseph 1857-1924 27
Conrad, Pam 1947-1996 133
  Brief entry 49
  Obituary 90
  Earlier sketches in SATA 52, 80
  See also CLR 18
  See also SAAS 19
Conroy, Jack
  See Conroy, John Wesley
Conroy, John Wesley 1899-1990 19
  Obituary 65
Conroy, Melissa 1969- 226
Conroy, Robert
  See Goldston, Robert (Conroy)
Constable, Kate 1966- 172
Constant, Alberta Wilson 1908-1981 22
  Obituary 28
Constantin, Pascale 185

Conway, Celeste 210
Conway, David 1970- 213
Conway, Diana C. 1943- 91
Conway, Diana Cohen
  See Conway, Diana C.
Conway, Gordon
  See Hamilton, Charles (Harold St. John)
Cook, Ande 192
Cook, Bernadine 1924- 11
Cook, Fred J(ames) 1911-2003 2
  Obituary 145
Cook, Glen 1944- 171
  Earlier sketch in SATA 108
Cook, Glen Charles
  See Cook, Glen
Cook, Hugh 1956- 85
Cook, Hugh, Walter Gilbert
  See Cook, Hugh
Cook, Jean Thor 1930- 94
Cook, Joel 1934- 79
Cook, Joseph Jay 1924- 8
Cook, Lisa Broadie 157
Cook, Lyn
  See Waddell, Evelyn Margaret
Cook, Roy
  See Silverberg, Robert
Cook, Sally 207
Cook, Trish 175
Cooke, Ann
  See Cole, Joanna
Cooke, Arthur
  See Lowndes, Robert A(ugustine) W(ard)
Cooke, Barbara
  See Alexander, Anna B(arbara Cooke)
Cooke, David Coxe 1917- 2
Cooke, Donald Ewin 1916-1985 2
  Obituary 45
Cooke, Frank E. 1920- 87
Cooke, Jean (Isobel Esther) 1929- 74
Cooke, John Estes
  See Baum, L. Frank
Cooke, Trish 1962- 129
Cookson, Catherine (McMullen) 1906-1998 .. 9
  Obituary 116
Cooley, Beth 210
Cooley, Elizabeth
  See Cooley, Beth
Cooley, Regina Francoise 1940- 177
Coolidge, Olivia E(nsor) 1908- 26
  Earlier sketch in SATA 1
Cooling, Wendy 169
  Earlier sketch in SATA 111
Coombs, Charles I(ra) 1914-1994 43
  Earlier sketch in SATA 3
  See also SAAS 15
Coombs, Chick
  See Coombs, Charles I(ra)
Coombs, Jonathan 204
Coombs, Kate 190
Coombs, Patricia 1926- 51
  Earlier sketch in SATA 3
  See also SAAS 22
Cooney, Barbara 1917-2000 96
  Obituary 123
  Earlier sketches in SATA 6, 59
  See also CLR 23
Cooney, Caroline B. 1947- 218
  Brief entry 41
  Earlier sketches in SATA 48, 80, 113, 130,
  179
Cooney, Doug 181
Cooney, Nancy Evans 1932- 42
Coontz, Otto 1946- 33
Cooper, Ann (Catharine) 1939- 104
Cooper, Dutch
  See Kuyper, Sjoerd
Cooper, Elisha 1971- 234
  Earlier sketches in SATA 99, 157
Cooper, Elizabeth Keyser -1992 47

Cooper, Floyd 227
  Earlier sketches in SATA *96, 144, 187*
  See also CLR *60*
Cooper, Gordon 1932- 23
Cooper, Helen 1963- 169
  Earlier sketch in SATA *102*
Cooper, Henry S. F., Jr. 1933- 65
Cooper, Henry Spotswood Fenimore, Jr.
  See Cooper, Henry S. F., Jr.
Cooper, Ilene 1948- 145
  Earlier sketches in SATA *66, 97*
Cooper, James Fenimore 1789-1851 19
  See also CLR *105*
Cooper, John R. *1*
Cooper, Kay 1941- *11*
Cooper, Lee Pelham 1926- *5*
Cooper, Lester (Irving) 1919-1985 32
  Obituary 43
Cooper, Lettice (Ulpha) 1897-1994 35
  Obituary 82
Cooper, Louise 1952-2009 152
Cooper, Mark A. 1963- 235
Cooper, M.E.
  See Davis, Maggie S.
Cooper, M.E.
  See Lerangis, Peter
Cooper, Melrose
  See Kroll, Virginia L.
Cooper, Michael L. 1950- 181
  Earlier sketches in SATA *79, 117*
Cooper, Michelle 1969- 226
Cooper, Patrick 1949- 134
Cooper, Susan 1935- 151
  Earlier sketches in SATA *4, 64, 104*
  See also CLR *161*
  See also SAAS *6*
Cooper, Susan Mary
  See Cooper, Susan
Cope, Jane U(rsula) 1949- 108
Copeland, Helen 1920- 4
Copeland, Mark 1956- 180
Copeland, Paul W. 23
Coplans, Peta 1951- 84
Copley (Diana) Heather Pickering 1918- 45
Coppard, A(lfred) E(dgar) 1878-1957
  See YABC *1*
Copper, Melinda 1952- 172
Copper, Melinda McConnaughey
  See Copper, Melinda
Corace, Jen 208
Coralie
  See Anderson, Catherine Corley
Corbett, Grahame 43
  Brief entry 36
Corbett, Scott 1913- 42
  Earlier sketch in SATA *2*
  See also CLR *1*
  See also SAAS *2*
Corbett, Sue 174
Corbett, W(illiam) J(esse) 1938- 102
  Brief entry 44
  Earlier sketch in SATA *50*
  See also CLR *19*
Corbin, Sabra Lee
  See Malvern, Gladys
Corbin, William
  See McGraw, William Corbin
Corbman, Marjorie 1987- 179
Corby, Dan
  See Catherall, Arthur
Corcoran, Barbara (Asenath) 1911-2003 77
  Autobiography Feature 125
  Earlier sketch in SATA *3*
  See also CLR *50*
  See also SAAS *20*
Corcos, Lucille 1908-1973 10
Cordell, Alexander
  See Graber, Alexander
Cordell, Matthew 1975- 238
  Earlier sketch in SATA *199*

Corder, Zizou
  See Young, Louisa
Corderoy, Tracey 238
Cordova, Amy 232
Corella, Joseph
  See Odgers, Sally Farrell
Coren, Alan 1938-2007 32
  Obituary 187
Corey, Dorothy 23
Corey, Shana 1974- 219
  Earlier sketch in SATA *133*
Corfe, Thomas Howell 1928- 27
Corfe, Tom
  See Corfe, Thomas Howell
Corfield, Robin Bell 1952- 74
Corke, Estelle 1969- 220
Corlett, William 1938-2005 46
  Brief entry 39
Cormack, M(argaret) Grant 1913- 11
Cormack, Maribelle B. 1902-1984 39
Cormier, Robert 1925-2000 83
  Obituary 122
  Earlier sketches in SATA *10, 45*
  See also CLR *167*
Cormier, Robert Edmund
  See Cormier, Robert
Cornelius, Carol 1942- 40
Cornelius, Kay 1933- 157
Cornell, J.
  See Cornell, Jeffrey
Cornell, James (Clayton, Jr.) 1938- 27
Cornell, Jean Gay 1920- 23
Cornell, Jeffrey 1945- 11
Cornell, Laura 189
Cornish, D.M. 1972- 185
Cornish, Sam(uel James) 1935- 23
Cornwall, Nellie
  See Sloggett, Nellie
Cornwell, Autumn 195
Corr, Christopher 1955- 189
Correa, E. Shan
  See Correa, Shan
Correa, Shan 233
Correy, Lee
  See Stine, G(eorge) Harry
Corrick, James A. 1945- 76
Corrigan, (Helen) Adeline 1909- 23
Corrigan, Barbara 1922- 8
Corrigan, Eireann 1977- 163
Corrin, Sara 1918- 86
  Brief entry 48
Corrin, Stephen 86
  Brief entry 48
Corriveau, Art 231
Corsi, Wendy
  See Staub, Wendy Corsi
Cort, M. C.
  See Clifford, Margaret Cort
Cort, Margaret
  See Clifford, Margaret Cort
Corwin, Judith H(offman) 1946- 10
Corwin, Oliver
  See Corwin, Oliver J.
Corwin, Oliver J. 206
Cory, Rowena
  See Lindquist, Rowena Cory
Cosby, Bill 1937- 110
  Earlier sketch in SATA *66*
Cosby, William Henry, Jr.
  See Cosby, Bill
  and Cosby, Bill
Cosentino, Ralph 169
Cosgrave, John O'Hara II 1908-1968
  Obituary 21
Cosgrove, Margaret (Leota) 1926- 47
Cosgrove, Stephen E(dward) 1945- 53
  Brief entry 40
Coskey, Evelyn 1932- 7
Cosner, Shaaron 1940- 43
Cossi, Olga 1921- 216
  Earlier sketches in SATA *67, 102*

Costa Bates, Janet 1959- 237
Costabel, Eva Deutsch 1924- 45
Costabel-Deutsch, Eva
  See Costabel, Eva Deutsch
Costales, Amy 1974- 227
Costanza, Stephen 238
Coste, Marion 1938- 183
Costello, David 174
Costello, David F(rancis) 1904-1990 23
Cte, Genevieve 1964- 184
Cote, Nancy 1952- 182
Cott, Jonathan 1942- 23
Cottam, Clarence 1899-1974 25
Cotten, Cynthia 188
Cottin, Menena 1950- 213
Cottle, Joan 1960- 135
Cottler, Joseph 1899-1996 22
Cottonwood, Joe 1947- 92
Cottrell, Leonard 1913-1974 24
Cottringer, Anne 1952- 150
  Earlier sketch in SATA *97*
Couch, Greg 199
Coulman, Valerie 1969- 161
Couloumbis, Akila 1932-2009 225
Couloumbis, Audrey 173
Counsel, June 1926- 70
Countryman, The
  See Whitlock, Ralph
Courlander, Harold 1908-1996 6
  Obituary 88
Coursen, Valerie 1965(?)- 102
Courtis, Stuart Appleton 1874-1969
  Obituary 29
Courtland, Tyler
  See Stevens, Serita
Courtney, Dayle
  See Goldsmith, Howard
Coury, Louise Andree 1895(?)-1983
  Obituary 34
Cousins, Linda 1946- 90
Cousins, Lucy 1964- 205
  Earlier sketch in SATA *172*
Cousins, Margaret 1905-1996 2
  Obituary 92
Cousteau, Jacques 1910-1997 98
  Earlier sketch in SATA *38*
Cousteau, Jacques-Yves
  See Cousteau, Jacques
Couture, Christin 1951- 73
Couvillon, Alice 239
Couvillon, Jacques 195
Coventry, Susan 233
Coverly, Dave 1964- 223
Covert, Ralph 1968- 197
Coville, Bruce 1950- 216
  Autobiography Feature 155
  Earlier sketches in SATA *32, 77, 118, 155*
Covington, Dennis 109
Covington, Linda
  See Windsor, Linda
Cowan, Catherine 121
Cowan, Rebecca M.
  See Moesta, Rebecca
Cowan, Rebecca Moesta
  See Moesta, Rebecca
Coward, Fiona 1963- 178
Cowdrey, Richard 1959- 204
Cowell, Cressida 1966- 140
Cowen, Eve
  See Werner, Herma
Cowen, Ida 1898-1993 64
Cowie, Leonard W(allace) 1919- 4
Cowles, Kathleen
  See Krull, Kathleen
Cowley, Cassia Joy
  See Cowley, Joy
Cowley, Joy 1936- 164
  Autobiography Feature 118
  Earlier sketches in SATA *4, 90*
  See also CLR *55*
  See also SAAS *26*

Cowley, Marjorie 1925- *111*
Cox, (Christopher) Barry 1931- *62*
Cox, Clinton 1934- *108*
Earlier sketch in SATA *74*
Cox, David 1933- *56*
Cox, David Dundas
See Cox, David
Cox, Donald William 1921- *23*
Cox, Jack
See Cox, John Roberts
Cox, John Roberts 1915-1981 .... *9*
Cox, Judy 1954- *236*
Earlier sketches in SATA *117, 160, 198*
Cox, Marion Monroe 1898-1983
Obituary *34*
Cox, Palmer 1840-1924 .... *24*
See also CLR *24*
Cox, Paul 1957- *226*
Cox, Vic 1942- *88*
Cox, Vicki 1945- *158*
Cox, Victoria 1945- *44*
Cox, Wallace 1924-1973 .... *25*
Cox, Wally
See Cox, Wallace
Cox, William R(obert) 1901-1988 .... *46*
Brief entry *31*
Obituary *57*
Coxe, Molly 1959- *101*
Earlier sketch in SATA *69*
Coxon, Michele 1950- *158*
Earlier sketch in SATA *76*
Coy, Harold 1902-1986 .... *3*
Coy, John 1958- *233*
Earlier sketches in SATA *120, 171*
Craats, Rennay 1973- *131*
Crabtree, Judith 1928- *98*
Earlier sketch in SATA *63*
Crabtree, Julie 1970- *214*
Cracker, Edward E.B.
See Odgers, Sally Farrell
Craft, Elizabeth 1971(?)- *204*
Craft, K. Y.
See Craft, Kinuko Y.
Craft, Kinuko Y. 1940- *127*
Earlier sketch in SATA *65*
Craft, Kinuko Yamabe
See Craft, Kinuko Y.
Craft, Ruth 1935- *87*
Brief entry *31*
Craig, A. A.
See Anderson, Poul
Craig, Alisa
See MacLeod, Charlotte (Matilda)
Craig, David
See James, Bill
Craig, Helen 1934- *213*
Earlier sketches in SATA *46, 49, 94*
Craig, Joe 1979- *198*
Craig, Joe Alexander
See Craig, Joe
Craig, John Eland
See Chipperfield, Joseph Eugene
Craig, John Ernest 1921- *23*
Craig, Kit
See Reed, Kit
Craig, M. F.
See Craig, Mary (Francis) Shura
Craig, M. Jean *17*
Craig, M. S.
See Craig, Mary (Francis) Shura
Craig, Margaret (Maze) 1911-1964 .... *9*
Craig, Mary
See Craig, Mary (Francis) Shura
Craig, Mary Shura
See Craig, Mary (Francis) Shura
Craig, Mary (Francis) Shura 1923-1991 .... *86*
Obituary *65*
Earlier sketch in SATA *6*
See also SAAS *7*
Craig, Ruth 1922- *95*

Craik, Mrs.
See Craik, Dinah Maria (Mulock)
Craik, Dinah Maria (Mulock) 1826-1887 ..... *34*
Crandall, Court 1965- *175*
Crandell, Rachel 1943- *152*
Crane, Barbara (Joyce) 1934- *31*
Crane, Carol 1933- *232*
Crane, Caroline 1930- *11*
Crane, Jordan 1973- *174*
Crane, M. A.
See Wartski, Maureen (Ann Crane)
Crane, Royston Campbell 1901-1977
Obituary *22*
Crane, Stephen 1871-1900
See YABC *2*
See also CLR *132*
Crane, Stephen Townley
See Crane, Stephen
Crane, Walter 1845-1915 .... *100*
Earlier sketch in SATA *18*
See also CLR *56*
Crane, William D(wight) 1892-1976 .... *1*
Cranfield, Ingrid 1945- *74*
Cranshaw, Stanley
See Fisher, Dorothy (Frances) Canfield
Crary, Elizabeth (Ann) 1942- *99*
Brief entry *43*
Crary, Margaret (Coleman) 1906-1986 .... *9*
Craste, Marc *201*
Cravath, Lynne Avril
See Cravath, Lynne W.
Cravath, Lynne W. 1951- *182*
Earlier sketches in SATA *98, 148*
Craven, Thomas 1889-1969 .... *22*
Crawford, Brent 1975- *220*
Crawford, Charles P. 1945- *28*
Crawford, Deborah 1922- *6*
Crawford, John E(dmund) 1904-1971 .... *3*
Crawford, K(aren) Michael 1959- *155*
Crawford, Laura 1977(?)- *227*
Crawford, Mel 1925- *44*
Brief entry *33*
Crawford, Phyllis 1899- *3*
Crawley, Dave *177*
Cray, Roberta
See Emerson, Ru
Crayder, Dorothy *7*
Crayder, Teresa
See Colman, Hila
Crayon, Geoffrey
See Irving, Washington
Craz, Albert G. 1926- *24*
Creagh, Kelly *234*
Crebbin, June 1938- *169*
Earlier sketch in SATA *80*
Crecy, Jeanne
See Williams, Jeanne
Credle, Ellis 1902-1998 .... *1*
Creech, Sharon 1945- *226*
Earlier sketches in SATA *94, 139, 172*
See also CLR *164*
Creeden, Sharon 1938- *91*
Creel, Ann Howard 1953- *187*
Creighton, (Mary) Helen 1899-1989
Obituary *64*
Creighton, Jill 1949- *96*
Crelin, Bob 1959(?)- *221*
Cremer, Andrea 1978- *238*
Crenson, Victoria 1952- *159*
Earlier sketch in SATA *88*
Cresp, Gael 1954- *119*
Crespo, George 1962- *82*
Cresswell, Helen 1934-2005 .... *79*
Obituary *168*
Earlier sketches in SATA *1, 48*
See also CLR *18*
See also SAAS *20*
Cressy, Michael 1955- *124*
Cressy, Mike
See Cressy, Michael
Cretan, Gladys (Yessayan) 1921- *2*

Cretzmeyer, Stacy (Megan) 1959- *124*
Crew, Gary 1947- *163*
Earlier sketches in SATA *75, 110*
See also CLR *42*
Crew, Helen (Cecilia) Coale 1866-1941
See YABC *2*
Crew, Linda (Jean) 1951- *137*
Earlier sketch in SATA *71*
Crewe, Megan 1980- *225*
Crews, Donald 1938- *76*
Brief entry *30*
Earlier sketch in SATA *32*
See also CLR *7*
Crews, Nina 1963- *158*
Earlier sketch in SATA *97*
Crichton, John Michael
See Crichton, Michael
Crichton, Michael 1942-2008 .... *88*
Obituary *199*
Earlier sketch in SATA *9*
Crider, Allen Billy
See Crider, Bill
Crider, Bill 1941- *99*
Crilley, Mark 1966- *210*
Autobiography Feature *148*
Earlier sketches in SATA *120, 148*
Crilley, Paul 1975- *227*
Crimi, Carolyn 1959- *219*
Earlier sketch in SATA *176*
Cripps, Enid Margaret
See Appiah, Peggy
Crisler, Curtis L. *188*
Crisman, Ruth 1914- *73*
Crisp, Marta Marie
See Crisp, Marty
Crisp, Marty 1947- *128*
Crispin, A(nn) C(arol) 1950- *86*
Crist, James J. 1961- *168*
Cristall, Barbara *79*
Crist-Evans, Craig 1954- *153*
Crocker, Carter *193*
Crocker, Nancy 1956- *185*
Crofford, Emily (Ardell) 1927- *61*
Crofut, William E. III 1934- *23*
Croggon, Alison 1962- *194*
Croll, Carolyn 1945- *102*
Brief entry *52*
Earlier sketch in SATA *56*
Croman, Dorothy Young
See Rosenberg, Dorothy
Cromie, Alice Hamilton 1914-2000 .... *24*
Cromie, William J(oseph) 1930- *4*
Crompton, Anne Eliot 1930- *73*
Earlier sketch in SATA *23*
Crompton, Richmal
See Lamburn, Richmal Crompton
Cronbach, Abraham 1882-1965 .... *11*
Crone, Ruth 1919-2003 .... *4*
Cronin, A(rchibald) J(oseph) 1896-1981 ...... *47*
Obituary *25*
Cronin, Doreen (A.) *125*
Cronin, Doreen 1966(?)- *178*
See also CLR *136*
Cronin, Doreen A.
See Cronin, Doreen
Cronn-Mills, Kirstin 1968- *224*
Crook, Beverly Courtney *38*
Brief entry *35*
Crook, Connie Brummel 1930- *168*
Earlier sketch in SATA *98*
Crook, Constance
See Crook, Connie Brummel
Crosby, Alexander L. 1906-1980 .... *2*
Obituary *23*
Crosby, Harry C.
See Anvil, Christopher
Crosby, Margaret
See Rathmann, Peggy
Crosher, G. R. *14*
Cross, Gilbert B. 1939- *60*
Brief entry *51*

Cross, Gillian 1945- *178*
   Autobiography Feature *178*
   Earlier sketches in SATA *38, 71, 110, 165*
   See also CLR 28
Cross, Gillian Clare
   See Cross, Gillian
Cross, Helen Reeder
   See Broadhead, Helen Cross
Cross, Peter 1951- 95
Cross, Sarah *216*
Cross, Shauna 1976(?)- *196*
Cross, Tom 1954- *146*
Cross, Verda 1914- 75
Cross, Wilbur Lucius III 1918- 2
Crossingham, John 1974- *226*
Crossland, Caroline 1964- 83
Crossley-Holland, Kevin 1941- *165*
   Earlier sketches in SATA *5, 74, 120*
   See also CLR 84
   See also SAAS 20
Crossley-Holland, Kevin John William
   See Crossley-Holland, Kevin
Crossman, David A. 1951- *219*
Crouch, Karen Hillard
   See Good, Karen Hillard
Crouch, Marcus 1913-1996 4
Crout, George C(lement) 1917- 11
Crow, Donna Fletcher 1941- 40
Crow, Francis Luther
   See Luther, Frank
Crow, Kristyn 208
Crowe, Andrew *111*
Crowe, Carole 1943- *204*
Crowe, Chris *206*
Crowe, Ellie *203*
Crowe, John
   See Lynds, Dennis
Crowe, (Bettina) Peter Lum 1911- 6
Crowell, Grace Noll 1877-1969 34
Crowell, Pers 1910-1990 2
Crowell, Robert Leland 1909-2001 63
Crowfield, Christopher
   See Stowe, Harriet Beecher
Crowley, Arthur 1945- 38
Crowley, Arthur McBlair
   See Crowley, Arthur
Crowley, Cath 1971- *233*
Crowley, James 1969- *237*
Crowley, John 1942- *140*
   Earlier sketch in SATA *65*
Crowley, Suzanne 1963- *196*
Crowley, Suzanne Carlisle
   See Crowley, Suzanne
Crownfield, Gertrude 1867-1945
   See YABC 1
Crowther, James Gerald 1899-1983 .... *14*
Crowther, Kitty 1970- *220*
Crowther, Robert 1948- *163*
Croza, Laurel *233*
Cruikshank, George 1792-1878 22
   See also CLR 63
Cruise, Robin 1951- *179*
Crum, Shutta *192*
   Earlier sketch in SATA *134*
Crummel, Susan Stevens 1949- *176*
   Earlier sketch in SATA *130*
Crump, Fred H., Jr. 1931- 76
   Earlier sketch in SATA *11*
Crump, J(ames) Irving 1887-1979 57
   Obituary *21*
Crump, William D(rake) 1949- *138*
Crunden, Reginald
   See Cleaver, Hylton Reginald
Crunk, T.
   See Crunk, Tony
Crunk, Tony 1956- *130*
Crutcher, Chris 1946- *196*
   Earlier sketches in SATA *52, 99, 153*
   See also CLR 159
Crutcher, Christopher C.
   See Crutcher, Chris

Cruz, Ray(mond) 1933- 6
Cruz Martinez, Alejandro (?)-1987 74
Crystal, Billy 1947- *154*
Crystal, William
   See Crystal, Billy
Ctvrtek, Vaclav 1911-1976
   Obituary 27
Cuate, Melodie A. *219*
Cuetara, Mittie 1957- *158*
   Earlier sketch in SATA *106*
Cuffari, Richard 1925-1978 66
   Obituary 25
   Earlier sketch in SATA 6
Cuffe-Perez, Mary 1946- *199*
Culbertson, Kim 1974- *235*
Cullen, Countee 1903-1946 18
Cullen, Lynn 1955- *190*
Culliford, Pierre 1928-1992 40
   Obituary 74
Cullinan, Bernice E(llinger) 1926- *135*
Culp, Louanna McNary 1901-1965 2
Culper, Felix
   See McCaughrean, Geraldine
Cumbaa, Stephen 1947- 72
Cumming, Peter 1951- *168*
Cumming, Primrose Amy 1915- 24
Cumming, Robert 1945- 65
Cummings, Betty Sue 1918- 15
   See also SAAS 9
Cummings, Gillian 1961- *233*
Cummings, John Michael 1963(?)- *216*
Cummings, Mary 1951- *185*
Cummings, Parke 1902-1987 2
   Obituary 53
Cummings, Pat 1950- *203*
   Earlier sketches in SATA *42, 71, 107*
   See also CLR 48
   See also SAAS 13
Cummings, Phil 1957- *232*
   Earlier sketches in SATA *74, 123*
Cummings, Priscilla 1951- *237*
   Earlier sketches in SATA *129, 170*
Cummings, Richard
   See Gardner, Richard (M.)
Cummings, Terrance *227*
Cummings, Troy *232*
Cummins, Julie *200*
Cummins, Maria Susanna 1827-1866
   See YABC 1
Cumpliano, Ina *207*
Cuneo, Mary Louise -2001 85
Cunliffe, John Arthur 1933- 86
   Earlier sketch in SATA *11*
Cunliffe, Marcus (Falkner) 1922-1990 37
   Obituary 66
Cunnane, Kelly *175*
Cunningham, Bob
   See May, Julian
Cunningham, Captain Frank
   See Glick, Carl (Cannon)
Cunningham, Cathy
   See Cunningham, Chet
Cunningham, Chet 1928- 23
Cunningham, Dale S(peers) 1932- 11
Cunningham, Dru 91
Cunningham, E. V.
   See Fast, Howard
Cunningham, Julia (Woolfolk) 1916- *132*
   Earlier sketches in SATA *1, 26*
   See also SAAS 2
Cunningham, Lawrence J. 1943- *125*
Cunningham, Virginia
   See Holmgren, Virginia C(unningham)
Cunxin, Li 1961- *220*
Cupala, Holly *235*
Curiae, Amicus
   See Fuller, Edmund (Maybank)
Curie, Eve 1904-2007 1
   Obituary *188*
Curlee, Lynn 1947- *190*
   Earlier sketches in SATA *98, 141*

Curley, Daniel 1918-1988 23
   Obituary 61
Curley, Marianne 1959- *175*
   Earlier sketch in SATA *131*
Currey, Anna *194*
Currie, Robin 1948- *120*
Currie, Stephen 1960- *132*
   Earlier sketch in SATA *82*
Curry, Ann (Gabrielle) 1934- 72
Curry, Jane L(ouise) 1932- *138*
   Autobiography Feature *138*
   Earlier sketches in SATA *1, 52, 90*
   See also CLR 31
   See also SAAS 6
Curry, Peggy Simson 1911-1987 8
   Obituary 50
Curry, Tom *185*
Curtis, Bruce (Richard) 1944- 30
Curtis, Chara M(ahar) 1950- 78
Curtis, Christopher Paul 1953- *187*
   Earlier sketches in SATA *93, 140*
   See also CLR 172
Curtis, Gavin 1965- *107*
Curtis, Jamie Lee 1958- *144*
   Earlier sketch in SATA *95*
   See also CLR 88
Curtis, Jennifer Keats *185*
Curtis, Marci *160*
Curtis, Munzee
   See Caseley, Judith
Curtis, Neil 1950-2006 .... *202*
Curtis, Patricia 1921- *101*
   Earlier sketch in SATA *23*
Curtis, Peter
   See Lofts, Norah (Robinson)
Curtis, Philip (Delacourt) 1920- 62
Curtis, Richard 1937- 29
Curtis, Richard Alan
   See Curtis, Richard
Curtis, Richard Hale
   See Deming, Richard
   and Levinson, Leonard
   and Rothweiler, Paul Roger
Curtis, Stacy *205*
Curtis, Wade
   See Pournelle, Jerry
Curtiss, A(rlene) B. 1934- 90
Cusack, Margaret 1945- 58
Cushman, Doug 1953- *210*
   Earlier sketches in SATA *65, 101, 157*
Cushman, Jerome 2
Cushman, Karen 1941- *147*
   Earlier sketch in SATA *89*
   See also CLR 55
Cusick, John M. *236*
Cusick, Richie Tankersley 1952- *231*
   Earlier sketches in SATA *67, 140*
Cusimano, Maryann K.
   See Love, Maryann Cusimano
Cutbill, Andy 1972- *201*
Cutchen, Billye Walker 1930- 15
Cutchins, Judy 1947- 59
Cutler, Daniel S. 1951- 78
Cutler, Daniel Solomon
   See Cutler, Daniel S.
Cutler, Ebbitt 1923- 9
Cutler, Ivor 1923-2006 24
   Obituary *174*
Cutler, Jane 1936- *162*
   Earlier sketches in SATA *75, 118*
Cutler, May Ebbitt
   See Cutler, Ebbitt
Cutler, Samuel
   See Folsom, Franklin (Brewster)
Cutlip, Kimbra L(eigh-Ann) 1964- *128*
Cutrate, Joe
   See Spiegelman, Art
Cutt, W(illiam) Towrie 1898-1981 16
   Obituary 85
Cuyler, Margery 1948- *229*
   Earlier sketches in SATA *39, 99, 156, 195*

Cuyler, Margery Stuyvesant
See Cuyler, Margery
Cuyler, Stephen
See Bates, Barbara S(nedeker)
Cypess, Leah 1977- 233
Cyrus, Kurt 1954- 236
Earlier sketches in SATA *132, 179*
Czajkowski, James
See Rollins, James
Czekaj, Jef 1969- 217
Czernecki, Stefan 1946- 178

D

Daagnese, Joseph 228
Dabba Smith, Frank 174
Dabcovich, Lydia 99
Brief entry 47
Earlier sketch in SATA *58*
Dace, Dolores B(oelens) 1929- 89
Da Costa, Deborah 193
Daddo, Andrew 1967- 198
Dadey, Debbie 1959- 217
Earlier sketches in SATA *73, 136*
Dahl, Borghild (Margarethe) 1890-1984 7
Obituary 37
Dahl, Roald 1916-1990 73
Obituary 65
Earlier sketches in SATA *1, 26*
See also CLR *111*
Dahlberg, Maurine F. 1951- 171
Dahlstedt, Marden (Stewart) 1921-1983 8
Obituary 110
Dahme, Joanne 206
Daigneault, Sylvie 236
Dain, Martin J. 1924-2000 35
Dakin, Glenn 1960- 224
Dakos, Kalli 1950- 115
Earlier sketch in SATA *80*
Dale, Anna 1971- 170
Dale, Gary
See Reece, Colleen L.
Dale, George E.
See Asimov, Isaac
Dale, Jack
See Holliday, Joseph
Dale, Kim 1957- 123
Dale, Margaret J(essy) Miller 1911- 39
Dale, Mitzi
See Hemstock, Gillian
Dale, Norman
See Denny, Norman (George)
Dale, Penny 1954- 151
Earlier sketch in SATA *70*
Daley, Michael J. 170
Dalgliesh, Alice 1893-1979 17
Obituary 21
See also CLR *62*
Dalkey, Kara 1953- 132
Dalkey, Kara Mia
See Dalkey, Kara
Dallas, Ruth 1919- 86
Dalmas, John
See Jones, John R(obert)
Dalton, Alene
See Chapin, Alene Olsen Dalton
Dalton, Annie 1948- 140
Earlier sketch in SATA *40*
Dalton, Kit
See Cunningham, Chet
Dalton, Max 234
Dalton, Pamela
See Johnson, Pamela
Dalton, Sean
See Chester, Deborah
Dalton, Sheila 1949- 108
D'Aluisio, Faith 1957- 205
Daly, James 217

Daly, Jim
See Stratemeyer, Edward L.
Daly, Jude 1951- 222
Earlier sketch in SATA *177*
Daly, Kathleen N(orah) 124
Brief entry 37
Daly, Maureen 1921-2006 129
Obituary 176
Earlier sketch in SATA *2*
See also CLR *96*
See also SAAS *1*
Daly, Nicholas
See Daly, Niki
Daly, Niki 1946- 198
Earlier sketches in SATA *37, 76, 114, 164*
See also CLR *41*
See also SAAS *21*
D'Amato, Alex 1919- 20
D'Amato, Janet (Potter) 1925- 9
Damerow, Gail 1944- 83
Damerow, Gail Jane
See Damerow, Gail
D'Amico, Carmela 170
D'Amico, Steve 170
Damrell, Liz 1956- 77
Damrosch, Helen
See Tee-Van, Helen Damrosch
Dana, Barbara 1940- 218
Earlier sketch in SATA *22*
Dana, Richard Henry, Jr. 1815-1882 26
Danachair, Caoimhin O
See Danaher, Kevin
Danaher, Kevin 1913-2002 22
Danakas, John 1963- 94
Danalis, John 236
Dandi
See Mackall, Dandi Daley
D'Andrea, Kate
See Steiner, Barbara A(nnette)
Daneshvari, Gitty 236
Dangerfield, Balfour
See McCloskey, (John) Robert
Daniel, Alan 1939- 76
Brief entry 53
Daniel, Anita 1893(?)-1978 23
Obituary 24
Daniel, Anne
See Steiner, Barbara A(nnette)
Daniel, Becky 1947- 56
Daniel, Claire 1949- 164
Daniel, Colin
See Windsor, Patricia
Daniel, Hawthorne 1890- 8
Daniel, (Donna) Lee 1944- 76
Daniel, Rebecca
See Daniel, Becky
Daniels, Guy 1919-1989 11
Obituary 62
Daniels, Kit
See Diver, Lucienne
Daniels, Lucy
See Oldfield, Jenny
Daniels, Max
See Gellis, Roberta
Daniels, Olga
See Sinclair, Olga
Daniels, Patricia 1955- 93
Daniels, Zoe
See Laux, Constance
Dank, Gloria Rand 1955- 56
Brief entry 46
Dank, Leonard D(ewey) 1929- 44
Dank, Milton 1920- 31
Dann, Max 1955- 62
Danneberg, Julie 1958- 173
Dantz, William R.
See Philbrick, Rodman
Danzig, Dianne 213

Danziger, Paula 1944-2004 149
Brief entry 30
Obituary 155
Earlier sketches in SATA *36, 63, 102*
See also CLR *20*
Darby, Gene Kegley
See Darby, Jean (Kegley)
Darby, J. N.
See Govan, (Mary) Christine Noble
Darby, Jean (Kegley) 1921- 68
Darby, Patricia (Paulsen) 14
Darby, Ray(mond) 1912-1982 7
Darbyshire, Kristen 218
d'Arcy, Willard
See Cox, William R(obert)
Dare, Geena
See McNicoll, Sylvia (Marilyn)
D'arge, Mackie 218
Darian, Shea 1959- 97
Daringer, Helen Fern 1892-1986 1
Darke, Marjorie 1929- 87
Earlier sketch in SATA *16*
Darley, F(elix) O(ctavius) C(arr)
1822-1888 35
Darling, David J. 1953- 60
Brief entry 44
Darling, Kathy
See Darling, Mary Kathleen
Darling, Lois (MacIntyre) 1917-1989 3
Obituary 64
Darling, Louis, (Jr.) 1916-1970 3
Obituary 23
Darling, Mary Kathleen 1943- 124
Earlier sketches in SATA *9, 79*
Darling, Sandra Louise Woodward
See Day, Alexandra
Darnell, K(athryn) L(ynne) 1955- 150
Darroll, Sally
See Odgers, Sally Farrell
Darrow, Sharon 181
Darrow, Whitney, (Jr.) 1909-1999 13
Obituary 115
Darwin, Len
See Darwin, Leonard
Darwin, Leonard 1916- 24
Dasent, Sir George Webbe 1817-1896 62
Brief entry 29
Dash, Joan 1925- 142
Daskam, Josephine Dodge
See Bacon, Josephine Dodge (Daskam)
D'ath, Justin 1953- 174
Earlier sketch in SATA *106*
Dauer, Rosamond 1934- 23
Daugherty, Charles Michael 1914- 16
Daugherty, James (Henry) 1889-1974 13
See also CLR *78*
Daugherty, Richard D(eo) 1922- 35
Daugherty, Sonia Medwedeff (?)-1971
Obituary 27
d'Aulaire, Edgar Parin 1898-1986 66
Obituary 47
Earlier sketch in SATA *5*
See also CLR *21*
d'Aulaire, Ingri 1904-1980 66
Obituary 24
Earlier sketch in SATA *5*
See also CLR *21*
d'Aulaire, Ingri Mortenson Parin
See d'Aulaire, Ingri
Dave, Dave
See Berg, David
Daveluy, Paule Cloutier 1919- 11
Davenier, Christine 1961- 216
Earlier sketches in SATA *127, 179*
Davenport, John 1960- 156
Daves, Michael 1938- 40
David, A. R.
See David, A(nn) Rosalie
David, A(nn) Rosalie 1946- 103
David, Jonathan
See Ames, Lee J.

David, Keren 1963- *236*
David, Lawrence 1963- *165*
  Earlier sketch in SATA *111*
David, Peter 1956- *72*
David, Peter Allen
  See David, Peter
David, Rosalie
  See David, A(nn) Rosalie
Davidson, Alice Joyce 1932- *54*
  Brief entry *45*
Davidson, Basil 1914-2010 .... *13*
Davidson, (Marie) Diane 1924- *91*
Davidson, Hugh
  See Hamilton, Edmond
Davidson, Jessica 1915-1986 .... *5*
Davidson, Judith 1953- *40*
Davidson, Lionel 1922-2009 .... *87*
Davidson, Margaret 1936- *5*
Davidson, Marion
  See Garis, Howard R.
Davidson, Mary R. 1885-1973 .... *9*
Davidson, Mary S. 1940- *61*
Davidson, Mickie
  See Davidson, Margaret
Davidson, Nicole
  See Jensen, Kathryn
Davidson, R.
  See Davidson, Raymond
Davidson, Raymond 1926- *32*
Davidson, Rosalie 1921- *23*
Davie, Helen K(ay) 1952- *148*
  Earlier sketch in SATA *77*
Davies, Andrew (Wynford) 1936- *27*
Davies, Andy Robert *200*
Davies, Bettilu D(onna) 1942- *33*
Davies, Hunter 1936- *55*
  Brief entry *45*
Davies, Jacqueline 1962- *186*
  Earlier sketch in SATA *155*
Davies, Joan 1934- *50*
  Brief entry *47*
Davies, Nicola 1958- *182*
  Earlier sketches in SATA *99, 150*
Davies, Peter J(oseph) 1937- *52*
Davies, Stephen 1976- *239*
Davies, Sumiko 1942- *46*
Davis, (A.) Aubrey 1949- *153*
Davis, Barbara Steincrohn
  See Davis, Maggie S.
Davis, Bette J. 1923- *15*
Davis, Burke 1913- *4*
Davis, Christopher 1928- *6*
Davis, D(elbert) Dwight 1908-1965 .... *33*
Davis, Daniel S(heldon) 1936- *12*
Davis, David R. 1948- *106*
Davis, Donald 1944- *169*
  Earlier sketch in SATA *93*
Davis, Donald D.
  See Davis, Donald
Davis, Eleanor 1983(?)- *209*
Davis, Emma
  See Davis, Maggie S.
Davis, Gibbs 1953- *102*
  Brief entry *41*
  Earlier sketch in SATA *46*
Davis, Grania 1943- *88*
  Brief entry *50*
Davis, H(arold) L(enoir) 1896-1960 .... *114*
Davis, Heather 1970- *221*
Davis, Hubert J(ackson) 1904-1997 .... *31*
Davis, Jack E. *210*
Davis, Jacky *204*
Davis, James Robert 1945- *32*
Davis, Jenny 1953- *74*
Davis, Jim
  See Davis, James Robert
Davis, Julia 1900(?)-1993 .... *6*
  Obituary *75*
Davis, Karen (Elizabeth) 1944- *109*
Davis, Katie 1959(?)- *208*
  Earlier sketch in SATA *152*

Davis, Lambert *176*
Davis, Leslie
  See Guccione, Leslie Davis
Davis, Louise Littleton 1921- *25*
Davis, Maggie S. 1943- *57*
Davis, Marguerite 1889- *34*
Davis, Mary L(ee) 1935- *9*
Davis, Mary Octavia 1901-1976 .... *6*
Davis, Nancy 1958(?)- *229*
Davis, Nelle 1958- *73*
Davis, Ossie 1917-2005 .... *81*
  See also CLR *56*
Davis, Paxton 1925-1994 .... *16*
Davis, Rich 1958- *206*
Davis, Robert 1881-1949
  See YABC *1*
Davis, Robin W(orks) 1962- *87*
Davis, Russell Gerard 1922- *3*
Davis, Tanita S. *212*
Davis, Tim(othy N.) 1957- *94*
Davis, Tony 1961- *222*
Davis, Verne Theodore 1889-1973 .... *6*
Davis, Yvonne 1927- *115*
Davol, Marguerite W. 1928- *146*
  Earlier sketch in SATA *82*
DaVolls, Andy (P.) 1967- *85*
DaVolls, Linda 1966- *85*
Davys, Sarah
  See Manning, Rosemary
Dawes, Claiborne 1935- *111*
Dawson, Arthur L. *207*
Dawson, Elmer A. *67*
  Earlier sketch in SATA *1*
Dawson, Imogen (Zoe) 1948- *126*
  Earlier sketch in SATA *90*
Dawson, Janine 1957- *196*
Dawson, Mary 1919- *11*
Dawson, Scott *233*
Dawson, Willow 1975- *208*
Day, A(rthur) Grove 1904-1994 .... *59*
Day, Alexandra 1941- *197*
  Autobiography Feature *197*
  Earlier sketches in SATA *67, 97, 169*
  See also CLR *22*
  See also SAAS *19*
Day, Beth (Feagles) 1924- *33*
Day, Donna
  See Asay, Donna Day
Day, Edward C. 1932- *72*
Day, Jon 1936(?)- *79*
Day, Karen *187*
Day, Larry 1956- *227*
  Earlier sketch in SATA *181*
Day, Nancy 1953- *140*
Day, Nancy Raines 1951- *148*
  Earlier sketch in SATA *93*
Day, Shirley 1962- *94*
Day, Susie 1975- *231*
Day, Thomas 1748-1789
  See YABC *1*
Day, Trevor 1955- *124*
Dazey, Agnes J(ohnston) *2*
Dazey, Frank M. *2*
Deacon, Alexis 1978- *139*
Deacon, Eileen
  See Geipel, Eileen
Deacon, Richard
  See McCormick, (George) Donald (King)
Deadman, Ronald 1919-1988(?)
  Obituary *56*
Deak, Erzsi 1959- *152*
Dean, Anabel 1915- *12*
Dean, Carolee 1962- *148*
Dean, Claire *215*
Dean, David 1976- *192*
Dean, Karen Strickler 1923- *49*
Dean, Ruth (Brigham) 1947- *145*
Dean, Zoey
  See Bennett, Cherie

de Angeli, Marguerite (Lofft) 1889-1987 ... *100*
  Obituary *51*
  Earlier sketches in SATA *1, 27*
  See also CLR *1*
Deans, Karen *195*
Deans, Sis Boulos 1955- *136*
  Earlier sketch in SATA *78*
DeArmand, Frances Ullmann 1904(?)-1984 . *10*
  Obituary *38*
DeArmond, Dale 1914- *70*
DeArmond, Dale Burlison
  See DeArmond, Dale
Deary, Terry 1946- *171*
  Brief entry *41*
  Earlier sketches in SATA *51, 101*
Deaver, Julie Reece 1953- *68*
de Banke, Cecile 1889-1965 .... *11*
De Bello, Rosario 1923- *89*
Debon, Nicolas *186*
  Earlier sketch in SATA *151*
de Bono, Edward 1933- *66*
de Brissac, Malcolm
  See Dickinson, Peter
de Brunhoff, Jean
  See Brunhoff, Jean de
De Brunhoff, Laurent
  See Brunhoff, Laurent de
De Bruyn, Monica G. 1952- *13*
De Bruyn, Monica Jean Grembowicz
  See De Bruyn, Monica G.
DeBry, Roger K. 1942- *91*
de Camp, Catherine Crook 1907-2000 .... *83*
  Earlier sketch in SATA *12*
de Camp, L. Sprague 1907-2000 .... *83*
  Earlier sketch in SATA *9*
de Camp, Lyon Sprague
  See de Camp, L. Sprague
DeCandido, Keith R.A. *112*
Dechausay, Sonia E. *94*
Decker, C.B. *172*
Decker, Cynthia B.
  See Decker, C.B.
Decker, Duane 1910-1964 .... *5*
Decker, Timothy 1974- *197*
DeClements, Barthe 1920- *131*
  Earlier sketches in SATA *35, 71*
  See also CLR *23*
DeClements, Barthe Faith
  See DeClements, Barthe
de Clercq Zubli, Rita la Fontaine 1929- *199*
de Conte, Sieur Louis
  See Twain, Mark
Dedman, Stephen *108*
Dee, Barbara 1958- *220*
Dee, Catherine 1964- *138*
Dee, Ruby
  See Wallace, Ruby Ann
Deeble, Jason 1979- *221*
Deedy, Carmen Agra 1960- *196*
Deedy, John 1923- *24*
Deegan, Paul Joseph 1937- *48*
  Brief entry *38*
Deem, James M. 1950- *191*
  Autobiography Feature *191*
  Earlier sketches in SATA *75, 134*
Deem, James Morgan
  See Deem, James M.
Deeter, Catherine 1947- *137*
DeFelice, Cynthia 1951- *165*
  Earlier sketches in SATA *79, 121*
DeFelice, Cynthia C.
  See DeFelice, Cynthia
Defoe, Daniel 1660(?)-1731 .... *22*
  See also CLR *164*
de Fombelle, Timothee
  See Fombelle, Timothee de
DeFord, Deborah H. *123*
deFrance, Anthony
  See DiFranco, Anthony (Mario)

Degen, Bruce 1945- 205
　Brief entry 47
　Earlier sketches in SATA *57, 97, 147*
DeGering, Etta (Belle) Fowler 1898-1996 7
Degman, Lori 234
De Goldi, Kate 1959- 123
De Goldi, Kathleen Domenica
　See De Goldi, Kate
de Goursac, Olivier 1959- 184
De Grazia, Ettore 1909-1982 39
De Grazia, Ted
　See De Grazia, Ettore
deGroat, Diane 1947- 169
　Earlier sketches in SATA *31, 90*
deGros, J. H.
　See Villiard, Paul
de Grummond, Lena Young 62
　Earlier sketch in SATA *6*
de Hamel, Joan Littledale 1924- 86
De Haven, Tom 1949- 72
de Hugo, Pierre
　See Brackers de Hugo, Pierre
Deines, Brian 1955- 220
Deiss, Joseph Jay 1912-1999 12
de Jenkins, Lyll Becerra 1925-1997 102
DeJong, David C(ornel) 1905-1967 10
de Jong, Dola
　See de Jong, Dorothea Rosalie
de Jong, Dorothea Rosalie 1911-2003 7
　Obituary 149
DeJong, Meindert 1906-1991 2
　Obituary 68
　See also CLR *73*
DeJonge, Joanne E. 1943- 56
Deka, Connie
　See Laux, Constance
de Kay, Ormonde (Jr.) 1923-1998 7
　Obituary 106
DeKeyser, Stacy 1959- 214
de Kiriline, Louise
　See Lawrence, Louise de Kiriline
Dekker, Carl
　See Laffin, John (Alfred Charles)
　and Lynds, Dennis
deKruif, Paul (Henry) 1890-1971 50
　Earlier sketch in SATA *5*
Delacre, Lulu 1957- 209
　Earlier sketches in SATA *36, 156*
DeLaCroix, Alice 1940- 195
　Earlier sketch in SATA *75*
de la Cruz, Melissa 1971- 179
De la Garza, Phyllis 1942- 169
De Lage, Ida 1918- 11
de la Mare, Walter (John) 1873-1956 16
　See also CLR *148*
Delaney, Harry 1932- 3
Delaney, Joseph 1945- 172
Delaney, M.C.
　See Delaney, Michael
Delaney, Michael 1955- 180
　Earlier sketch in SATA *96*
Delaney, Michael Clark
　See Delaney, Michael
Delaney, Ned 1951- 28
Delaney, Thomas Nicholas III
　See Delaney, Ned
DeLange, Alex Pardo
　See Pardo DeLange, Alex
Delano, Hugh 1933- 20
Delano, Marfe Ferguson 215
Delany, Samuel R., Jr. 1942- 92
Delany, Samuel Ray
　See Delany, Samuel R., Jr.
Delany, Shannon 239
de la Pena, Matt 205
De La Ramee, Marie Louise 1839-1908 20
de la Roche, Mazo 1879-1961 64
De La Roche Saint Andre, Anne 1950- 75
de Las Casas, Dianne 1970- 221
Delaune, (Jewel) Lynn (de Grummond) 7
DeLaurentis, Louise Budde 1920- 12

del Barco, Lucy Salamanca 1900(?)-1989
　Obituary 64
Delderfield, Eric R(aymond) 1909-1995 14
Delderfield, Ronald Frederick 1912-1972 20
DeLeeuw, Adele (Louise) 1899-1988 30
　Obituary 56
　Earlier sketch in SATA *1*
De Leon, Nephtali 1945- 97
Delessert, Etienne 1941- 179
　Brief entry 27
　Earlier sketches in SATA *46, 130*
　See also CLR *81*
Delgado, James P. 1958- 122
Delinois, Alix 228
de Lint, Charles 1951- 207
　Earlier sketches in SATA *115, 157*
de Lint, Charles Henri Diederick Hofsmit
　See de Lint, Charles
Delmar, Roy
　See Wexler, Jerome (LeRoy)
Del Negro, Janice M. 197
Deloria, Vine, Jr. 1933-2005 21
　Obituary 171
Deloria, Vine Victor, Jr.
　See Deloria, Vine, Jr.
del Rey, Lester 1915-1993 22
　Obituary 76
Delrio, Martin
　See Doyle, Debra
　and Macdonald, James D.
Delton, Judy 1931-2001 77
　Obituary 130
　Earlier sketch in SATA *14*
　See also SAAS *9*
Delulio, John 1938- 15
Delvig, Lou
　See Vigan, Delphine de
Delving, Michael
　See Williams, Jay
de Marcken, Gail 186
Demarest, Chris L. 1951- 175
　Brief entry 44
　Earlier sketches in SATA *45, 82, 128*
Demarest, Christopher Lynn
　See Demarest, Chris L.
Demarest, Doug
　See Barker, Will
De Mari, Silvana 1953- 193
Demas, Corinne 1947- 203
　Earlier sketches in SATA *37, 131*
Demas, Vida 1927- 9
Dematons, Charlotte 1957- 203
DeMatteis, J.M. 1953- 180
DeMatteis, John Marc
　See DeMatteis, J.M.
De Mejo, Oscar 1911-1992 40
Demers, Dominique 1956- 177
de Messieres, Nicole 1930- 39
DeMeulemeester, Linda 1956- 230
Demi 1942- 210
　Earlier sketches in SATA *11, 66, 102, 152*
　See also CLR *58*
Demijohn, Thom
　See Disch, Thomas M.
　and Sladek, John
Deming, Richard 1915-1983 24
Deming, Sarah 191
de Monfreid, Dorothee 1973- 189
Dempsey, Kristy 238
Demuth, Patricia Brennan 1948- 84
　Brief entry 51
De Muth, Roger 1948- 221
Dendinger, Roger E. 1952- 158
Denenberg, Barry 1940- 175
Dengler, Marianna (Herron) 1935- 103
Dengler, Sandy 1939- 54
　Brief entry 40
Denim, Sue
　See Pilkey, Dav
Denise, Anika 210

Denise, Christopher 1968- 193
　Earlier sketch in SATA *147*
Denman, K.L. 1957- 186
Denmark, Harrison
　See Zelazny, Roger
Dennard, Deborah 1953- 136
　Earlier sketch in SATA *78*
Denney, Diana 1910-2000 25
　Obituary 120
Dennis, Morgan 1891(?)-1960 18
Dennis, Wesley 1903-1966 18
Denniston, Elinore 1900-1978
　Obituary 24
Denny, Norman (George) 1901-1982 43
Denos, Julia 202
Denslow, Sharon Phillips 1947- 142
　Earlier sketch in SATA *68*
Denslow, W(illiam) W(allace) 1856-1915 16
　See also CLR *15*
Dent, Grace 1973- 187
Denton, Kady MacDonald 181
　Earlier sketches in SATA *66, 110*
　See also CLR *71*
Denton, Terry 1950- 186
Denver, Walt
　See Redding, Robert Hull
　and Sherman, Jory (Tecumseh)
Denzel, Justin F(rancis) 1917-1999 46
　Brief entry 38
Denzer, Ann Wiseman
　See Wiseman, Ann (Sayre)
DePalma, Mary Newell 1961- 185
　Earlier sketch in SATA *139*
De Palma, Toni 199
dePaola, Thomas Anthony 1934- 200
　Earlier sketches in SATA *11, 59, 108, 155*
　See also CLR *81*
　See also SAAS *15*
dePaola, Tomie
　See dePaola, Thomas Anthony
deParrie, Paul 1949- 74
DePauw, Linda Grant 1940- 24
De Pretto, Lorenzo 1966- 225
de Quidt, Jeremy 237
DeRan, David 1946- 76
Derby, Ken 1956- 181
Derby, Kenneth R.
　See Derby, Ken
Derby, Pat 1942- 172
Derby, Sally 1934- 189
　Earlier sketches in SATA *89, 132*
de Regniers, Beatrice Schenk (Freedman)
　1914-2000 68
　Obituary 123
　Earlier sketch in SATA *2*
　See also SAAS *6*
Dereske, Jo 1947- 72
Deriso, Christine Hurley 1961- 210
Derleth, August (William) 1909-1971 5
Derman, Martha (Winn) 74
Derman, Sarah Audrey 1915- 11
DeRoberts, Lyndon
　See Silverstein, Robert Alan
Derom, Dirk 1980- 224
de Roo, Anne Louise 1931-1997 84
　Earlier sketch in SATA *25*
　See also CLR *63*
deRosa, Dee 70
Derrick, Lionel
　See Cunningham, Chet
Derrickson, Jim 1959- 141
Derry Down Derry
　See Lear, Edward
Derting, Kimberly 1968- 231
Dervaux, Isabelle 1961- 106
Derwent, Lavinia 14
Desai, Anita 1937- 126
　Earlier sketch in SATA *63*
DeSaix, Deborah Durland 188
De Saulles, Tony 1958- 119
Desbarats, Peter 1933- 39

de Selincourt, Aubrey 1894-1962 .... *14*
de Seve, Peter 1958- *219*
de Seve, Randall *198*
Deshpande, Chris 1950- *69*
Desimini, Lisa 1964- *216*
　Earlier sketches in SATA *86, 148*
Desjarlais, John 1953- *71*
Desjarlais, John J.
　See Desjarlais, John
Desmoinaux, Christel 1967- *149*
　Earlier sketch in SATA *103*
Desmond, Adrian 1947- *51*
Desmond, Adrian J.
　See Desmond, Adrian
Desmond, Adrian John
　See Desmond, Adrian
Desmond, Alice Curtis 1897-1990 .... *8*
Desnoettes, Caroline *183*
Despain, Bree 1979- *239*
DeSpain, Pleasant 1943- *87*
Desputeaux, Helene 1959- *95*
Dessen, Sarah 1970- *172*
　Earlier sketch in SATA *120*
Detine, Padre
　See Olsen, Ib Spang
de Trevino, Elizabeth B.
　See Trevino, Elizabeth B(orton) de
de Trevino, Elizabeth Borton
　See Trevino, Elizabeth B(orton) de
Detwiler, Susan Dill 1956- *58*
Deuker, Carl 1950- *196*
　Earlier sketches in SATA *82, 150*
Deutsch, Babette 1895-1982 .... *1*
　Obituary *33*
Deutsch, Barry *239*
Deutsch, Eva Costabel
　See Costabel, Eva Deutsch
Deutsch, Helen 1906-1992 .... *76*
Deutsch, Kurt
　See Singer, Kurt D.
De Valera, Sinead 1879(?)-1975
　Obituary *30*
Devaney, John 1926-1994 .... *12*
de Varennes, Monique 1947- *168*
de Varona, Frank J. 1943- *83*
Devereux, Frederick L(eonard), Jr.
　1914-1993 .... *9*
Devi, Nila
　See Woody, Regina Jones
DeVillers, Julia 1967- *227*
deVinck, Christopher 1951- *85*
DeVita, James *195*
DeVito, Cara 1956- *80*
Devlin, Dorothy Wende
　See Devlin, Wende
Devlin, Harry 1918-2001 .... *136*
　Earlier sketches in SATA *11, 74*
Devlin, Wende 1918-2002 .... *74*
　Earlier sketch in SATA *11*
Devon, Paddie 1953- *92*
Devons, Sonia 1974- *72*
Devorah-Leah *111*
de Vos, Gail 1949- *122*
de Vries, Anke 1936- *222*
DeVries, Douglas 1933- *122*
De Waard, E(lliott) John 1935- *7*
Dewan, Ted 1961- *226*
　Earlier sketches in SATA *108, 157*
Dewdney, Anna *232*
　Earlier sketch in SATA *184*
Dewdney, Selwyn (Hanington) 1909-1979 ... *64*
DeWeese, Gene
　See DeWeese, Thomas Eugene
DeWeese, Jean
　See DeWeese, Thomas Eugene
DeWeese, Thomas Eugene 1934- *46*
　Brief entry *45*
Dewey, Ariane 1937- *178*
　Earlier sketches in SATA *7, 109*

Dewey, Jennifer (Owings) 1941- *103*
　Brief entry *48*
　Earlier sketch in SATA *58*
Dewey, Kenneth Francis 1940- *39*
Dewin, Howie
　See Howie, Betsy
De Wire, Elinor 1953- *180*
deWit, Dorothy (May Knowles) 1916-1980 . *39*
　Obituary *28*
Dexter, Alison 1966- *125*
Dexter, John
　See Bradley, Marion Zimmer
Deyneka, Anita 1943- *24*
Deyrup, Astrith Johnson 1923- *24*
Dezern, Chad *201*
de Zubizarreta, Alma
　See Ada, Alma Flor
Dhami, Narinder 1958- *152*
Dhondy, Farrukh 1944- *152*
　Earlier sketch in SATA *65*
　See also CLR *41*
Diakite, Baba Wague 1961- *174*
Diakite, Penda 1993(?)- *174*
Diamand, Emily 1971- *227*
Diamond, Arthur 1957- *76*
Diamond, Donna 1950- *69*
　Brief entry *30*
　Earlier sketch in SATA *35*
Diamond, Petra
　See Sachs, Judith
Diamond, Rebecca
　See Sachs, Judith
Dias, Earl Joseph 1916- *41*
Dias, Ron 1937- *71*
Diaz, David 1959(?)- *229*
　Earlier sketches in SATA *96, 150, 189*
　See also CLR *65*
di Bartolo, Jim *225*
Dibley, Glin *188*
DiCamillo, Kate 1964- *202*
　Earlier sketches in SATA *121, 163*
　See also CLR *117*
Di Certo, J(oseph) J(ohn) 1933- *60*
DiCianni, Ron 1952- *107*
Dick, Trella Lamson 1889-1974 .... *9*
Dickens, Charles 1812-1870 .... *15*
　See also CLR *162*
Dickens, Charles John Huffam
　See Dickens, Charles
Dickens, Frank
　See Huline-Dickens, Frank William
Dickens, Monica (Enid) 1915-1992 .... *4*
　Obituary *74*
Dickerson, Roy Ernest 1886-1965
　Obituary *26*
Dickinson, Emily 1830-1886 .... *29*
Dickinson, Emily Elizabeth
　See Dickinson, Emily
Dickinson, Mary 1949- *48*
　Brief entry *41*
Dickinson, Mary-Anne
　See Rodda, Emily
Dickinson, Peter 1927- *229*
　Earlier sketches in SATA *5, 62, 95, 150*
　See also CLR *125*
Dickinson, Peter Malcolm de Brissac
　See Dickinson, Peter
Dickinson, Susan 1931- *8*
Dickinson, Terence 1943- *102*
Dickinson, W(illiam) Croft 1897-1963 .... *13*
Dickson, Gordon R. 1923-2001 .... *77*
Dickson, Gordon Rupert
　See Dickson, Gordon R.
Dickson, Helen
　See Reynolds, Helen Mary Greenwood Campbell
Dickson, Naida 1916- *8*
Diehn, Gwen 1943- *80*
Dierssen, Andreas 1962- *190*
Diesen, Deborah 1967- *200*
Dieterich, Michele M. 1962- *78*

Dietz, David H(enry) 1897-1984 .... *10*
　Obituary *41*
Dietz, Lew 1907-1997 .... *11*
　Obituary *95*
Diffily, Deborah *159*
Di Fiori, Larry
　See Di Fiori, Lawrence
Di Fiori, Lawrence 1934- *130*
DiFranco, Anthony (Mario) 1945- *42*
Digby, Anne 1935- *72*
Digges, Jeremiah
　See Berger, Josef
Digman, Kristina 1959- *176*
D'Ignazio, Fred 1949- *39*
　Brief entry *35*
D'Ignazio, Frederick
　See D'Ignazio, Fred
Di Grazia, Thomas (?)-1983 .... *32*
Dijkstra, Lida 1961- *195*
Dikty, Julian May
　See May, Julian
Dillard, Annie 1945- *140*
　Earlier sketch in SATA *10*
Dillard, Kristine 1964- *113*
Dillard, Polly Hargis 1916- *24*
Dillard, Sarah 1961- *217*
Diller, Harriett 1953- *78*
Dillon, Anna
　See Scott, Michael
Dillon, Barbara 1927- *44*
　Brief entry *39*
Dillon, Diane 1933- *194*
　Earlier sketches in SATA *15, 51, 106*
　See also CLR *44*
Dillon, Diane Claire
　See Dillon, Diane
Dillon, Eilis 1920-1994 .... *74*
　Autobiography Feature *105*
　Obituary *83*
　Earlier sketch in SATA *2*
　See also CLR *26*
Dillon, Jana (a pseudonym) 1952- *117*
Dillon, Leo 1933- *194*
　Earlier sketches in SATA *15, 51, 106*
　See also CLR *44*
Dillon, Sharon Saseen
　See Saseen, Sharon (Dillon)
Dils, Tracey E. 1958- *83*
Dilson, Jesse 1914-1988 .... *24*
Dinan, Carolyn *59*
　Brief entry *47*
Dines, Carol 1956- *175*
Dines, (Harry) Glen 1925-1996 .... *7*
Dinesen, Isak
　See Blixen, Karen
Dinessi, Alex
　See Schembri, Jim
Dinneen, Betty 1929- *61*
Dinnerstein, Harvey 1928- *42*
Dinsdale, Tim(othy Kay) 1924-1987 .... *11*
Dion, Nathalie 1964- *213*
Dionne, Erin 1975- *217*
Diop, Birago (Ismael) 1906-1989
　Obituary *64*
Diouf, Sylviane A. *168*
Diouf, Sylviane Anna
　See Diouf, Sylviane A.
DiPucchio, Kelly *204*
　Earlier sketch in SATA *159*
Dirk
　See Gringhuis, Richard H.
Dirks, Wilhelmina 1916- *59*
Dirks, Willy
　See Dirks, Wilhelmina
Dirtmeister
　See Tomecek, Steve
DiSalvo, DyAnne 1960- *144*
　Earlier sketch in SATA *59*
DiSalvo-Ryan, DyAnne
　See DiSalvo, DyAnne

Disch, Thomas M. 1940-2008 92
  Obituary 195
  See also CLR *18*
  See also SAAS *15*
Disch, Thomas Michael
  See Disch, Thomas M.
Disch, Tom
  See Disch, Thomas M.
Disher, Garry 1949- 125
  Earlier sketch in SATA *81*
Disney, Walt(er Elias) 1901-1966 28
  Brief entry 27
Ditchfield, Christin 1973- 226
  Earlier sketch in SATA *189*
DiTerlizzi, Tony 1969- 214
  Earlier sketch in SATA *154*
DiTerlooney, Tiny
  See DiTerlizzi, Tony
Divakaruni, Chitra Banerjee 1956- 222
  Earlier sketch in SATA *160*
Di Valentin, Maria (Amelia) Messuri
  1911-1985 7
Diver, Lucienne 1971- 218
Divine, Arthur Durham 1904-1987
  Obituary 52
Divine, David
  See Divine, Arthur Durham
Divine, L. 229
Dixon, Ann 1954- 212
  Earlier sketches in SATA *77, 127*
Dixon, Ann Renee
  See Dixon, Ann
Dixon, Dougal 1947- 190
  Earlier sketches in SATA *45, 127*
Dixon, Franklin W.
  See Barrett, Neal, Jr.
  and Goulart, Ron
  and Lantz, Francess L(in)
  and Lerangis, Peter
  and McFarlane, Leslie
  and Stanley, George Edward
  and Stratemeyer, Edward L.
Dixon, Jeanne 1936- 31
Dixon, Paige
  See Corcoran, Barbara (Asenath)
Dixon, Peter L(ee) 1931- 6
Dixon, Rachel 1952- 74
Dizin, Pascal 230
Djoleto, (Solomon Alexander) Amu 1929- ... 80
d'Lacey, Chris 1949- 227
  Earlier sketch in SATA *165*
Doak, Annie
  See Dillard, Annie
Doane, Pelagie 1906-1966 7
Dob, Bob 207
Dobell, I(sabel) M(arian) B(arclay)
  1909-1998 11
Dobie, J(ames) Frank 1888-1964 43
Dobkin, Alexander 1908-1975
  Obituary 30
Dobler, Lavinia G. 1910- 6
Dobrin, Arnold 1928- 4
Dobson, Jill 1969- 140
Dobson, Julia 1941- 48
Dobson, Mary 1954- 117
DoCampo, Valeria 1976- 217
Docherty, James
  See Docherty, Jimmy
Docherty, Jimmy 1976- 204
Docherty, Thomas 1955- 218
Dockery, Wallene T. 1941- 27
Dockray, Tracy 1962- 139
Dockrey, Karen 1955- 103
Doctor, Bernard
  See Doctor, Bernard Aquina
Doctor, Bernard Aquina 1950- 81
Doctor X
  See Nourse, Alan E(dward)
Dodd, Ed(ward Benton) 1902-1991 4
  Obituary 68

Dodd, Emma 1969- 239
  Earlier sketch in SATA *203*
Dodd, Lynley (Stuart) 1941- 132
  Earlier sketches in SATA *35, 86*
  See also CLR *62*
Dodd, Marty 1921- 142
Dodd, Quentin 1972- 137
Dodds, Bill 1952- 78
Dodds, Dayle Ann 1952- 201
  Earlier sketches in SATA *75, 150*
Doder, Josh 1968- 187
Dodge, Bertha S(anford) 1902-1995 8
Dodge, Fremont
  See Grimes, Lee
Dodge, Gil
  See Hano, Arnold
Dodge, Mary (Elizabeth) Mapes
  1831(?)-1905 100
  Earlier sketch in SATA *21*
  See also CLR *62*
Dodgson, Charles Lutwidge
  See Carroll, Lewis
Dodson, Emma 235
Dodson, Kenneth MacKenzie 1907-1999 11
Dodson, Susan 1941- 50
  Brief entry 40
Doerrfeld, Cori 1964- 214
Dogar, Sharon 1962- 211
Dogyear, Drew
  See Gorey, Edward (St. John)
Doherty, Berlie 1943- 111
  Earlier sketch in SATA *72*
  See also CLR *21*
  See also SAAS *16*
Doherty, Charles Hugh 1913- 6
Doherty, Craig A. 1951- 169
  Earlier sketch in SATA *83*
Doherty, Katherine M(ann) 1951- 83
Doherty, Kieran 1945- 164
Dokas, Dara 1968- 216
Dokey, Cameron 1956- 97
Dolamore, Jaclyn 1982- 227
Dolan, Edward F(rancis), Jr. 1924- 94
  Brief entry 31
  Earlier sketch in SATA *45*
Dolan, Ellen M(eara) 1929-1998 88
Dolan, Sean J. 1958- 74
Dolce, J. Ellen 1948- 75
Dolch, Edward William 1889-1961 50
Dolch, Marguerite Pierce 1891-1978 50
Dollar, Diane (Hills) 1933- 57
Dolson, Hildegarde
  See Lockridge, Hildegarde (Dolson)
Domanska, Janina 1913(?)-1995 68
  Obituary 84
  Earlier sketch in SATA *6*
  See also CLR *40*
  See also SAAS *18*
Dominguez, Angel 1953- 76
Dominguez, Angela N. 1982- 219
Domino, John
  See Averill, Esther (Holden)
Domjan, Joseph (Spiri) 1907-1992 25
Domm, Jeffrey C. 1958- 84
Donahue, Dorothy 178
Donald, Rhonda Lucas 1962- 147
Donalds, Gordon
  See Shirreffs, Gordon D(onald)
Donaldson, Bryna
  See Stevens, Bryna
Donaldson, Gordon 1913-1993 64
  Obituary 76
Donaldson, Joan 1953- 227
  Earlier sketch in SATA *78*
Donaldson, Julia 1948- 226
  Earlier sketches in SATA *82, 132, 180*
Donaldson, Stephen R. 1947- 121
Donaldson, Stephen Reeder
  See Donaldson, Stephen R.
Doner, Kim 1955- 208
  Earlier sketch in SATA *91*

Doney, Todd L. W. 1959- 104
Dong-Sung, Kim 1970- 195
Dong-Sung Kim
  See Dong-Sung, Kim
Donkin, Andrew 219
Donkin, Nance (Clare) 1915- 95
Donna, Natalie 1934-1979 9
Donnelly, Elfie 1950-
  See CLR *104*
Donnelly, Jennifer 1963- 154
Donnelly, Matt 1972- 148
Donnio, Sylviane 188
Donofrio, Beverly 1950- 209
Donoghue, Emma 1969- 101
Donohue, Moira Rose 1954- 201
Donoughue, Carol 1935- 139
Donovan, Frank (Robert) 1906-1975
  Obituary 30
Donovan, Gail 1962- 217
Donovan, Jane Monroe 237
Donovan, John 1928-1992 72
  Brief entry 29
  See also CLR *3*
Donovan, Mary Lee 1961- 86
Donovan, William
  See Berkebile, Fred D(onovan)
Donze, Mary Terese 1911- 89
Doob, Leonard W(illiam) 1909-2000 8
Doodler, Todd H.
  See Goldman, Todd Harris
Dooley, Norah 1953- 74
Dooley, Sarah 236
Dooling, Michael 1958- 220
  Earlier sketch in SATA *105*
Dor, Ana
  See Ceder, Georgiana Dorcas
Doran, Colleen 1963- 211
Dore, (Louis Christophe Paul) Gustave
  1832-1883 19
Doremus, Robert 1913-2010 30
Doren, Marion (Walker) 1928- 57
Dorenkamp, Michelle 1957- 89
Dorflinger, Carolyn 1953- 91
Dorfman, Joaquin 1979- 180
Dorfman, Joaquin Emiliano
  See Dorfman, Joaquin
Dorian, Edith M(cEwen) 1900-1983 5
Dorian, Harry
  See Hamilton, Charles (Harold St. John)
Dorian, Marguerite 7
Dorin, Patrick C(arberry) 1939- 59
  Brief entry 52
Dorman, Brandon 194
Dorman, Michael 1932- 7
Dorman, N. B. 1927- 39
Dormer, Frank W. 200
Dorris, Michael 1945-1997 75
  Obituary 94
  See also CLR *58*
Dorris, Michael A.
  See Dorris, Michael
Dorris, Michael Anthony
  See Dorris, Michael
Dorritt, Susan
  See Schlein, Miriam
Dorros, Alex 1991- 194
Dorros, Arthur 1950- 168
  Earlier sketches in SATA *78, 122*
  See also CLR *42*
  See also SAAS *20*
Dorros, Arthur M.
  See Dorros, Arthur
Dorson, Richard M(ercer) 1916-1981 30
Doss, Helen (Grigsby) 1918- 20
Doss, Margot Patterson 6
dos Santos, Joyce Audy 1949- 57
  Brief entry 42
Dothers, Anne
  See Chess, Victoria (Dickerson)
Dotlich, Rebecca Kai 1951- 182

Dottig
  See Grider, Dorothy
Dotts, Maryann J. 1933- 35
Doty, Jean Slaughter 1929- 28
Doty, Roy 1922- 28
Doubtfire, Dianne (Abrams) 1918- 29
Doucet, Sharon Arms 1951- 144
  Autobiography Feature 144
  Earlier sketch in SATA *125*
Dougherty, Charles 1922- 18
Dougherty, Terri (L.) 1964- 146
Doughty, Rebecca 1955- 174
Douglas, Allen 223
Douglas, Blaise 1960- 101
Douglas, Carole Nelson 1944- 73
Douglas, David
  See Tutt, Keith
Douglas, Garry
  See Kilworth, Garry
Douglas, James McM.
  See Griffin, W. E. B.
Douglas, Kathryn
  See Ewing, Kathryn
Douglas, Leonard
  See Bradbury, Ray
Douglas, Lola
  See Zeises, Lara M.
Douglas, Marjory Stoneman 1890-1998 10
Douglas, Michael
  See Bright, Robert Sr.)
Douglas, Michael
  See Crichton, Michael
Douglas, Shirley Stewart
  See Tepper, Sheri S.
Douglass, Barbara 1930- 40
Douglass, Frederick 1817(?)-1895 29
Douglass, Keith
  See Cunningham, Chet
Douty, Esther M(orris) 1909-1978 8
  Obituary 23
Dow, Emily R. 1904-1987 10
Dow, Vicki
  See McVey, Vicki
Dowd, John David 1945- 78
Dowd, Siobhan 1960-2007 204
Dowdell, Dorothy (Florence) Karns 1910- ... 12
Dowden, Anne Ophelia Todd 1907-2007 7
  Obituary 180
  See also SAAS *10*
Dowdey, Landon Gerald 1923- 11
Dowdy, Mrs. Regera
  See Gorey, Edward (St. John)
Dowell, Frances O'Roark 1964- 205
  Earlier sketch in SATA *157*
Dower, Laura 1967- 185
Dowling, Terry 1947- 101
Downard, Barry 1956- 202
Downer, Ann 1960- 155
Downer, Marion 1892(?)-1971 25
Downes, Belinda 1962- 180
Downey, Fairfax D(avis) 1893-1990 3
  Obituary 66
Downey, Lisa 214
Downey, Lynn 1961- 185
Downham, Jenny 1964- 192
Downie, John 1931- 87
Downie, Mary Alice 1934- 171
  Earlier sketches in SATA *13, 87*
Downie, Mary Alice Dawe
  See Downie, Mary Alice
Downing, David A(lmon) 1958- 84
Downing, Erin 1976- 237
Downing, Johnette 184
Downing, Julie 1956- 148
  Earlier sketch in SATA *81*
Downing, Paula E. 1951- 80
Downing, Warwick
  See Downing, Wick
Downing, Wick 1931- 138
Dowswell, Paul 1957- 184

Doyle, A. Conan
  See Doyle, Sir Arthur Conan
Doyle, Sir Arthur Conan 1859-1930 24
  See also CLR *106*
Doyle, Brian 1935- 156
  Earlier sketches in SATA *67, 104*
  See also CLR *22*
  See also SAAS *16*
Doyle, Charlotte 1937- 178
  Earlier sketch in SATA *94*
Doyle, Charlotte Lackner
  See Doyle, Charlotte
Doyle, Conan
  See Doyle, Sir Arthur Conan
Doyle, Debra 1952- 165
  Earlier sketch in SATA *105*
Doyle, Donovan
  See Boegehold, Betty (Doyle)
Doyle, Eugenie 1952- 225
Doyle, John
  See Graves, Robert
Doyle, Malachy 1954- 165
  Earlier sketch in SATA *120*
  See also CLR *83*
Doyle, Richard 1824-1883 21
Doyle, Sir A. Conan
  See Doyle, Sir Arthur Conan
Dr. A
  See Asimov, Isaac
  and Silverstein, Alvin
  and Silverstein, Virginia B.
Dr. Alphabet
  See Morice, Dave
Dr. Fred
  See Bortz, Alfred B(enjamin)
Dr. Laura
  See Schlessinger, Laura (Catherine)
Dr. Seuss 1904-1991 100
  Obituary 67
  Earlier sketches in SATA *1, 28, 75*
  See also CLR *100*
Dr. Zed
  See Penrose, Gordon
Drabble, Margaret 1939- 48
Drackett, Phil(ip Arthur) 1922- 53
Draco, F.
  See Davis, Julia
Dracup, Angela 1943- 74
Dragisic, Patricia 116
Dragonwagon, Crescent 1952- 186
  Autobiography Feature 186
  Earlier sketches in SATA *11, 41, 75, 133*
  See also SAAS *14*
Drake, David 1945- 85
Drake, David Allen
  See Drake, David
Drake, Frank
  See Hamilton, Charles (Harold St. John)
Drake, Jane 1954- 235
  Earlier sketch in SATA *82*
Drake, Salamanda
  See Barlow, Steve
Drakeford, Dale B 1952- 113
Drakeford, Dale Benjamin
  See Drakeford, Dale B
Draper, Hastings
  See Jeffries, Roderic
Draper, Sharon
  See Draper, Sharon M.
Draper, Sharon M. 1948- 195
  Autobiography Feature 146
  Earlier sketches in SATA *98, 146*
  See also CLR *57*
Draper, Sharon Mills
  See Draper, Sharon M.
Drapier, M. B.
  See Swift, Jonathan
Drawson, Blair 1943- 126
  Earlier sketch in SATA *17*
Dray, Matt 1967- 177

Dray, Matthew Frederick
  See Dray, Matt
Dresang, Eliza (Carolyn Timberlake) 1941- . *19*
Drescher, Henrik 1955- 172
  Earlier sketches in SATA *67, 105*
  See also CLR *20*
Drescher, Joan E(lizabeth) 1939- 137
  Earlier sketch in SATA *30*
Dressen-McQueen, Stacey 191
Dreves, Veronica R. 1927-1986
  Obituary 50
Drew, Patricia 1938- 15
Drew, Patricia Mary
  See Drew, Patricia
Drewery, Mary 1918- 6
Drewery, Melanie 1970- 165
Drewry, Henry N(athaniel) 1924- 138
Dreyer, Ellen 177
Drial, J. E.
  See Laird, Jean E(louise)
Drimmer, Frederick 1916-2000 60
  Obituary 124
Driskill, J. Lawrence 1920- 90
Driskill, Larry
  See Driskill, J. Lawrence
Driving Hawk, Virginia
  See Sneve, Virginia Driving Hawk
Dron, Laura
  See Matthews, L. S.
Dronzek, Laura 199
Drucker, Malka 1945- 214
  Brief entry 29
  Earlier sketches in SATA *39, 111*
Drucker, Olga Levy 1927- 79
Druitt, Tobias
  See Purkiss, Diane
Drummond, Allan 1957- 209
Drummond, Karona 1965- 220
Drummond, V(iolet) H(ilda) 1911-2000 6
Drummond, Walter
  See Silverberg, Robert
Drury, Clare Marie
  See Hoskyns-Abrahall, Clare (Constance Drury)
Drury, Roger W(olcott) 1914-1996 15
Druse, Eleanor
  See King, Stephen
Dryden, Pamela
  See St. John, Nicole
D.T., Hughes
  See Hughes, Dean
Duane, Diane 1952- 233
  Brief entry 46
  Earlier sketches in SATA *58, 95, 145*
Dubanevich, Arlene 1950- 56
Dubelaar, Thea 1947- 60
Dubin, Jill 205
du Blane, Daphne
  See Groom, Arthur William
Duble, Kathleen Benner 1958- 164
Dubois, Claude K. 1960- 196
DuBois, Rochelle Holt 1946- 41
Du Bois, Shirley Graham 1907(?)-1977 24
  See Graham, Shirley
Du Bois, W. E. B. 1868-1963 42
Du Bois, William Edward Burghardt
  See Du Bois, W. E. B.
du Bois, William Pene
  See Pene du Bois, William (Sherman)
Duboise, Novella 1911-1999 88
Dubosarsky, Ursula 1961- 193
  Earlier sketches in SATA *107, 147*
DuBose, LaRocque (Russ) 1926- 2
Dubrovin, Vivian 1931- 139
  Earlier sketch in SATA *65*
DuBurke, Randy 224
  Earlier sketch in SATA *172*
Ducey, Jean Sparks 1915- 93
Duchacek, Ivo D(uka) 1913-1988
  Obituary 55
Du Chaillu, Paul (Belloni) 1835(?)-1903 26

Ducharme, Dede Fox
  See Ducharme, Lilian Fox
Ducharme, Lilian Fox 1950- *122*
Ducornet, Erica 1943- *7*
Ducornet, Rikki
  See Ducornet, Erica
Duddle, Jonny 1971(?)- *219*
Duden, Jane 1947- *136*
Duder, Tessa 1940- *117*
  Earlier sketch in SATA *80*
  See also CLR *43*
  See also SAAS *23*
Dudley, Helen
  See Hope Simpson, Jacynth
Dudley, Martha Ward 1909(?)-1985
  Obituary *45*
Dudley, Nancy
  See Cole, Lois Dwight
Dudley, Robert
  See Baldwin, James
Dudley, Ruth H(ubbell) 1905-2001 .... *11*
Dudley-Smith, T.
  See Trevor, Elleston
Due, Linnea A. 1948- *64*
Dueck, Adele 1955- *97*
Dueland, Joy V(ivian) *27*
Duerr, Gisela 1968- *89*
Duey, Kathleen 1950- *238*
  Earlier sketches in SATA *132, 199*
Dufault, Joseph Ernest Nephtali
  See James, Will(iam Roderick)
Duff, Annis (James) 1904(?)-1986
  Obituary *49*
Duff, Hilary 1987- *238*
Duff, Maggie
  See Duff, Margaret K(app)
Duff, Margaret K(app) 1916-2003 .... *37*
  Obituary *144*
Duffey, Betsy 1953- *236*
  Earlier sketches in SATA *80, 131*
Duffie, Charles 1960- *144*
Duffield, Katy S. 1961- *147*
Duffy, Carol Ann 1955- *165*
  Earlier sketch in SATA *95*
Duffy Stone, Heather *217*
Dugan, Jack
  See Griffin, W. E. B.
Dugan, John Kevin
  See Griffin, W. E. B.
Dugan, Karen *202*
Dugan, Karen M.
  See Dugan, Karen
Dugan, Michael (Gray) 1947- *15*
Duggan, Alfred Leo 1903-1964 .... *25*
Duggan, Maurice 1922-1974 .... *40*
  Obituary *30*
Duggan, Maurice Noel
  See Duggan, Maurice
Dugger, Elizabeth L.
  See Kanell, Beth
Duggleby, John 1952- *94*
Dugin, Andrej 1955- *77*
Dugina, Olga 1964- *77*
du Jardin, Rosamond Neal 1902-1963 .... *2*
Duka, Ivo
  See Duchacek, Ivo D(uka)
Duke, Kate 1956- *192*
  Earlier sketches in SATA *90, 148*
  See also CLR *51*
Duke, Will
  See Gault, William Campbell
Dulac, Edmund 1882-1953 .... *19*
Dumas, Alexandre (pere) 1802-1870 .... *18*
  See also CLR *134*
Dumas, Jacqueline 1946- *55*
Dumas, Philippe 1940- *119*
  Earlier sketch in SATA *52*
du Maurier, Daphne 1907-1989 .... *27*
  Obituary *60*
Dumbleton, Mike 1948- *206*
  Earlier sketches in SATA *73, 124*

Dunbar, Fiona 1961- *167*
Dunbar, Joyce 1944- *213*
  Earlier sketches in SATA *76, 112, 162*
Dunbar, Paul Laurence 1872-1906 .... *34*
Dunbar, Polly 1980(?)- *211*
  Earlier sketch in SATA *181*
Dunbar, Robert E(verett) 1926- *32*
Duncan, Alexandra
  See Moore, Ishbel (Lindsay)
Duncan, Alice Faye 1967- *168*
  Earlier sketch in SATA *95*
Duncan, Gregory
  See McClintock, Marshall
Duncan, Jane
  See Cameron, Elizabeth Jane
Duncan, Julia K.
  See Benson, Mildred
Duncan, Lois 1934- *219*
  Autobiography Feature *141*
  Earlier sketches in SATA *1, 36, 75, 133, 141*
  See also CLR *129*
  See also SAAS *2*
Duncan, Norman 1871-1916
  See YABC *1*
Duncan, Terence
  See Nolan, William F.
Duncombe, Frances (Riker) 1900-1994 .... *25*
  Obituary *82*
Dungy, Anthony
  See Dungy, Tony
Dungy, Tony 1955- *206*
Dunham, Montrew 1919- *162*
Dunham, Montrew Goetz
  See Dunham, Montrew
Dunkle, Clare B. 1964- *223*
  Earlier sketch in SATA *155*
Dunlap, Julie 1958- *84*
Dunleavy, Deborah 1951- *133*
Dunlop, Agnes M. R. (?)-1982 .... *87*
Dunlop, Eileen (Rhona) 1938- *76*
  Earlier sketch in SATA *24*
  See also SAAS *12*
Dunmore, Helen 1952- *201*
Dunn, Anne M. 1940- *107*
Dunn, Carolyn 1965- *208*
Dunn, Harvey T(homas) 1884-1952 .... *34*
Dunn, Herb
  See Gutman, Dan
Dunn, John M. (III) 1949- *93*
Dunn, Judy
  See Spangenberg, Judith Dunn
Dunn, Mary Lois 1930- *6*
Dunnahoo, Terry Janson 1927- *7*
Dunne, Jeanette 1952- *72*
Dunne, Kathleen 1933- *126*
Dunne, Marie
  See Clark, Ann Nolan
Dunne, Mary Collins 1914- *11*
Dunne, Mary Jo
  See Dunne, Mary Collins
Dunnett, Kaitlyn
  See Emerson, Kathy Lynn
Dunnett, Margaret (Rosalind) 1909-1977 ..... *42*
Dunnick, Regan *178*
Dunning, John Harris 1974- *234*
Dunphy, Madeleine 1962- *219*
Dunrea, Olivier 1953- *233*
  Brief entry *46*
  Earlier sketches in SATA *59, 118, 160*
Dunrea, Olivier Jean-Paul Dominique
  See Dunrea, Olivier
Dunstan Muller, Rachel *221*
Dunton, Dorothy 1912- *92*
Dupasquier, Philippe 1955- *151*
  Earlier sketch in SATA *86*
duPont, Lindsay *207*
duPont, Lindsay Harper
  See duPont, Lindsay
DuPrau, Jeanne 1944- *215*
  Earlier sketch in SATA *144*

Dupuy, T(revor) N(evitt) 1916-1995 .... *4*
  Obituary *86*
DuQuette, Keith 1960- *155*
  Earlier sketch in SATA *90*
Duran, Gloria 1924- *171*
Duran, Gloria Bradley
  See Duran, Gloria
Duranceau, Suzanne 1952- *162*
Durand, Delphine 1971- *200*
Durand, Hallie 1964(?)- *216*
Durango, Julia 1967- *215*
  Earlier sketch in SATA *173*
Durant, Alan 1958- *214*
  Earlier sketches in SATA *121, 165*
Durant, John 1902- *27*
Durbin, William 1951- *174*
  Earlier sketch in SATA *143*
Durell, Ann 1930- *66*
Durkee, Sarah *173*
Durney, Ryan *205*
Durrant, Lynda 1954- *212*
  Earlier sketches in SATA *96, 148*
Durrant, Sabine *210*
Durrell, Gerald (Malcolm) 1925-1995 .... *8*
  Obituary *84*
Durrell, Julie 1955- *94*
Durrett, Deanne 1940- *144*
  Earlier sketch in SATA *92*
Durst, Sarah Beth 1974- *203*
Dusikova, Maja 1946- *223*
Du Soe, Robert C. 1892-1958
  See YABC *2*
Dussling, Jennifer 1970- *143*
  Earlier sketch in SATA *96*
DuTemple, Lesley A. 1952- *113*
Dutton, Sandra *191*
Dutz
  See Davis, Mary Octavia
Duval, Katherine
  See James, Elizabeth
Duval, Kathy 1946- *181*
Duvall, Aimee
  See Thurlo, Aimee
  and Thurlo, David
Duvall, Evelyn Millis 1906- *9*
Duvall, Jill D. 1932- *102*
Duvall, Jill Donovan
  See Duvall, Jill D.
Duvoisin, Roger (Antoine) 1904-1980 .... *30*
  Obituary *23*
  Earlier sketch in SATA *2*
  See also CLR *23*
Dwiggins, Don(ald J.) 1913-1988 .... *4*
  Obituary *60*
Dwight, Allan
  See Cole, Lois Dwight
Dwyer, Deanna
  See Koontz, Dean
Dwyer, K.R.
  See Koontz, Dean
Dyck, Peter J. 1914- *75*
Dyer, Alan 1953- *218*
Dyer, Brooke *238*
Dyer, Hadley 1973- *229*
Dyer, James (Frederick) 1934- *37*
Dyer, Jane *191*
  Earlier sketch in SATA *147*
Dyer, Sarah 1978- *212*
Dyer, Sarah L.
  See Dyer, Sarah
Dyess, John (Foster) 1939- *76*
Dygard, Thomas J. 1931-1996 .... *97*
  Obituary *92*
  Earlier sketch in SATA *24*
  See also SAAS *15*
Dyke, John 1935- *35*

E

E. V. L.
  See Lucas, E(dward) V(errall)
Eagar, Frances (Elisabeth Stuart)
  1940-1978 .... *11*
  Obituary *55*
Eager, Edward (McMaken) 1911-1964 .... *17*
  See also CLR *43*
Eager, George 1921- *56*
Eager, George B.
  See Eager, George
Eagland, Jane *237*
Eagle, Ellen 1953- *61*
Eagle, Kin
  See Adlerman, Daniel (Ezra)
  and Adlerman, Kimberly M(arie)
Eagle, Mike 1942- *11*
Eamer, Claire 1947- *222*
Earle, Olive L(ydia) 1888-1982 .... *7*
Earle, William
  See Johns, W(illiam) E(arle)
Earls, Nick 1963- *156*
  Earlier sketch in SATA *95*
Early, Jack
  See Scoppettone, Sandra
Early, Jon
  See Johns, W(illiam) E(arle)
Early, Margaret 1951- *72*
Earnest, Peter 1934- *222*
Earnshaw, Brian 1929- *17*
Earnshaw, Micky 1939- *88*
Earnshaw, Spencer Wright
  See Earnshaw, Micky
Easley, MaryAnn *94*
Eason, Alethea 1957- *197*
East, Jacqueline *224*
Eastman, Charles A(lexander) 1858-1939
  See YABC *1*
Eastman, P(hilip) D(ey) 1909-1986 .... *33*
  Obituary *46*
Easton, Kelly 1960- *192*
  Earlier sketch in SATA *141*
Eastwick, Ivy (Ethel) O(live) *3*
Eaton, Anne T(haxter) 1881-1971 .... *32*
Eaton, Anthony 1971- *167*
Eaton, George L.
  See Verral, Charles Spain
Eaton, Janet
  See Givens, Janet E(aton)
Eaton, Jeanette 1886-1968 .... *24*
Eaton, Maxwell III 1981- *199*
Eaton, Tom 1940- *22*
Ebbeler, Jeff
  See Ebbeler, Jeffrey
Ebbeler, Jeffrey 1974- *206*
Ebbitt, Carolyn Q. 1974(?)- *225*
Ebel, Alex 1927- *11*
Eber, Dorothy (Margaret) Harley 1930- *27*
Eberhart, Sheri S.
  See Tepper, Sheri S.
Eberle, Irmengarde 1898-1979 .... *2*
  Obituary *23*
Eble, Diane 1956- *74*
Eboch, Chris *113*
Eccles Williams, Ferelith 1920- *22*
Echeverria-Bis, Olivia *217*
Echeverria Gyorkos, Charmaine *216*
Echlin, Kim 1955- *166*
Eckblad, Edith Berven 1923- *23*
Ecke, Wolfgang 1927-1983
  Obituary *37*
Eckert, Allan W. 1931- *91*
  Brief entry *27*
  Earlier sketch in SATA *29*
  See also SAAS *21*
Eckert, Horst 1931- *72*
  Earlier sketch in SATA *8*
  See also CLR *26*
Ecklar, Julia (Marie) 1964- *112*
Eddings, David 1931-2009 .... *91*

Eddings, David Carroll
  See Eddings, David
Ede, Janina 1937- *33*
Edell, Celeste *12*
Edelman, Lily (Judith) 1915-1981 .... *22*
Edelson, Edward 1932- *51*
Edens, Cooper 1945- *166*
  Earlier sketches in SATA *49, 112*
Edens, (Bishop) David 1926- *39*
Edey, Maitland A(rmstrong) 1910-1992 .... *25*
  Obituary *71*
Edgerton, Perky *196*
Edgeworth, Maria 1768-1849 .... *21*
  See also CLR *153*
Edgson, Alison *211*
Edgy, Wardore
  See Gorey, Edward (St. John)
Edison, Theodore
  See Stratemeyer, Edward L.
Edler, Tim(othy) 1948- *56*
Edmiston, Jim 1948- *80*
Edmonds, I(vy) G(ordon) 1917- *8*
Edmonds, Walter D(umaux) 1903-1998 .... *27*
  Obituary *99*
  Earlier sketch in SATA *1*
  See also SAAS *4*
Edmund, Sean
  See Pringle, Laurence
Edsall, Marian (Stickney) 1920- *8*
Edwards, Al
  See Nourse, Alan E(dward)
Edwards, Anne 1927- *35*
Edwards, Audrey 1947- *52*
  Brief entry *31*
Edwards, Becky (Jane) 1966- *125*
Edwards, Bertram
  See Edwards, Herbert Charles
Edwards, Bronwen Elizabeth
  See Rose, Wendy
Edwards, Cecile Pepin 1916- *25*
Edwards, David 1962- *198*
Edwards, Dorothy 1914-1982 .... *88*
  Obituary *31*
  Earlier sketch in SATA *4*
Edwards, F. E.
  See Nolan, William F.
Edwards, Frank B. 1952- *93*
Edwards, Gunvor *32*
Edwards, Harvey 1929- *5*
Edwards, Hazel (Eileen) 1945- *135*
Edwards, Herbert Charles 1912- *12*
Edwards, Jane Campbell 1932- *10*
Edwards, Julia
  See Stratemeyer, Edward L.
Edwards, Julie
  See Andrews, Julie
Edwards, Julie Andrews
  See Andrews, Julie
Edwards, June
  See Bhatia, Jamunadevi
Edwards, Linda Strauss 1948- *49*
  Brief entry *42*
Edwards, Margaret (Alexander) 1902-1988
  Obituary *56*
Edwards, Michelle 1955- *152*
  Earlier sketch in SATA *70*
Edwards, Monica le Doux Newton
  1912-1998 .... *12*
Edwards, Olwen
  See Gater, Dilys
Edwards, Page (Lawrence, Jr.) 1941-1999 ... *59*
Edwards, Pamela Duncan *189*
Edwards, R. T.
  See Goulart, Ron
Edwards, Sally (Cary) 1929- *7*
Edwards, Samuel
  See Gerson, Noel Bertram
Edwards, Wallace 1957(?)- *170*
Edwardson, Debby Dahl *223*
Eeckhout, Emmanuelle 1976- *208*
Egan, E. W. 1922- *35*

Egan, Edward Welstead
  See Egan, E. W.
Egan, Kerry *175*
Egan, Lorraine Hopping 1960- *134*
  Earlier sketch in SATA *91*
Egan, Tim 1957- *191*
  Earlier sketches in SATA *89, 155*
Egermeier, Elsie E(milie) 1890-1986 .... *65*
Eggenberger, David 1918- *6*
Eggleston, Edward 1837-1902 .... *27*
Egielski, Richard 1952- *220*
  Earlier sketches in SATA *11, 49, 106, 163*
Egypt, Ophelia Settle 1903-1984 .... *16*
  Obituary *38*
Ehlert, Lois 1934- *237*
  Earlier sketches in SATA *35, 69, 128, 172*
  See also CLR *28*
Ehlert, Lois Jane
  See Ehlert, Lois
Ehling, Katalin Olah 1941- *93*
Ehrenberg, Pamela 1972- *219*
Ehrenfreund, Norbert 1921- *86*
Ehrenhaft, Daniel 1970- *185*
Ehrenhaft, Daniel Parker
  See Ehrenhaft, Daniel
Ehrhardt, Karen 1963- *184*
Ehrlich, Amy 1942- *217*
  Earlier sketches in SATA *25, 65, 96, 132*
Ehrlich, Bettina Bauer 1903-1985 .... *1*
Ehrlich, Fred *205*
Ehrlich, Fred M.D.
  See Ehrlich, Fred
Ehrlich, H. M.
  See Ziefert, Harriet
Eichenberg, Fritz 1901-1990 .... *50*
  Earlier sketch in SATA *9*
Eichler, Margrit 1942- *35*
Eichner, James A. 1927- *4*
Eidson, Thomas 1944- *112*
Eifert, Virginia (Louise) S(nider) 1911-1966 . *2*
Eige, (Elizabeth) Lillian 1915- *65*
Eiken, J. Melia 1967- *125*
Einhorn, Edward 1970- *204*
Einsel, Naiad *10*
Einsel, Walter 1926- *10*
Einzig, Susan 1922- *43*
Eiseman, Alberta 1925- *15*
Eisenberg, Azriel (Louis) 1903-1985 .... *12*
Eisenberg, Lisa 1949- *155*
  Brief entry *50*
  Earlier sketch in SATA *57*
Eisenberg, Phyllis Rose 1924- *41*
Eisner, Vivienne
  See Margolis, Vivienne
Eisner, Will 1917-2005 .... *165*
  Earlier sketch in SATA *31*
Eisner, William Erwin
  See Eisner, Will
Eitzen, Allan 1928- *9*
Eitzen, Ruth (Carper) 1924- *9*
Ekwensi, C. O. D.
  See Ekwensi, Cyprian
Ekwensi, Cyprian 1921-2007 .... *66*
Ekwensi, Cyprian Odiatu Duaka
  See Ekwensi, Cyprian
Elam, Richard M(ace, Jr.) 1920- *9*
Elborn, Andrew
  See Clements, Andrew
  and Clements, Andrew
Elboz, Stephen 1956- *152*
Eldin, Peter 1939- *154*
Eldon, Kathy 1946- *107*
Eldridge, Marion *199*
Eley, Robin *219*
Elfman, Blossom 1925- *8*
Elgin, Kathleen 1923- *39*
Elia
  See Lamb, Charles
Elio
  See Eliopoulos, Chris
Eliopoulos, Chris *234*

Eliot, A. D.
　See Jewett, Sarah Orne
Eliot, Alice
　See Jewett, Sarah Orne
Eliot, Anne
　See Cole, Lois Dwight
Eliot, Dan
　See Silverberg, Robert
Elish, Dan 1960- *204*
　Earlier sketches in SATA *68, 129*
Elisha, Ron 1951- *104*
Elisofon, Eliot 1911-1973
　Obituary *21*
Elkeles, Simone 1970- *187*
Elkin, Benjamin 1911-1995 .... *3*
Elkins, Dov Peretz 1937- *5*
Ellacott, S(amuel) E(rnest) 1911- *19*
Elleman, Barbara 1934- *147*
Ellen, Jaye
　See Nixon, Joan Lowery
Eller, Scott
　See Holinger, William (Jacques)
　and Shepard, Jim
Ellery, Amanda *216*
Ellestad, Myrvin
　See Ellestad, Myrvin H.
Ellestad, Myrvin H. 1921- *120*
Elliot, Bruce
　See Field, Edward
Elliot, David 1952- *208*
　Earlier sketch in SATA *122*
Elliott, Bruce
　See Field, Edward
Elliott, David 1947- *201*
　Earlier sketch in SATA *163*
Elliott, Don
　See Silverberg, Robert
Elliott, Elizabeth Shippen Green
　See Green, Elizabeth Shippen
Elliott, Janice 1931-1995 .... *119*
Elliott, Joey
　See Houk, Randy
Elliott, Laura Malone 1957- *197*
Elliott, L.M.
　See Elliott, Laura Malone
Elliott, Louise *111*
Elliott, Mark 1949- *210*
Elliott, Odette 1939- *75*
Elliott, Patricia 1946- *176*
Elliott, Sarah M(cCarn) 1930- *14*
Elliott, (Robert) Scott 1970- *153*
Elliott, William
　See Bradbury, Ray
Elliott, Zetta *206*
Ellis, (Mary) Amabel (Nassau Strachey)
　Williams
　See Williams-Ellis, (Mary) Amabel (Nassau
　Strachey)
Ellis, Ann Dee *210*
Ellis, Anyon
　See Rowland-Entwistle, (Arthur) Theodore
　(Henry)
Ellis, Carson 1975- *190*
Ellis, Carson Friedman
　See Ellis, Carson
Ellis, Deborah 1960- *235*
　Earlier sketches in SATA *129, 187*
Ellis, E. S.
　See Ellis, Edward S.
Ellis, Edward S. 1840-1916
　See YABC *1*
Ellis, Edward Sylvester
　See Ellis, Edward S.
Ellis, Ella Thorp 1928- *127*
　Earlier sketch in SATA *7*
　See also SAAS *9*
Ellis, Harry Bearse 1921-2004 .... *9*
Ellis, Helen *232*
Ellis, Herbert
　See Wilson, Lionel
Ellis, Julie 1961- *227*

Ellis, Mel(vin Richard) 1912-1984 7
　Obituary *39*
Ellis, Richard 1938- *130*
Ellis, Sarah 1952- *179*
　Earlier sketches in SATA *68, 131*
　See also CLR *42*
Ellison, Chris *196*
Ellison, Elizabeth Stow 1970- *209*
Ellison, Emily *114*
Ellison, Lucile Watkins 1907(?)-1979 .... *50*
　Obituary *22*
Ellison, Virginia H(owell) 1910- *4*
Ellsberg, Edward 1891-1983 7
Ellsworth, Loretta 1954- *199*
Ellsworth, Mary Ellen (Tressel) 1940- *146*
Ellwand, David 1965(?)- *213*
Elmer, Robert 1958- *154*
　Earlier sketch in SATA *99*
Elmore, (Carolyn) Patricia 1933- *38*
　Brief entry *35*
El-Moslimany, Ann P(axton) 1937- *90*
Elsammak, Ariane *236*
Elschner, Geraldine 1954- *183*
Elspeth
　See Bragdon, Elspeth MacDuffie
Elster, Jean Alicia 1953- *150*
Elting, Mary 1906- *88*
　Earlier sketch in SATA *2*
　See also SAAS *20*
Elvgren, Jennifer Riesmeyer *179*
Elwart, Joan Potter 1927- *2*
Elwell, Peter *220*
Elwood, Ann 1931- *55*
　Brief entry *52*
Elwood, Roger 1943-2007 .... *58*
Ely, Lesley *212*
Elya, Susan Middleton 1955- *235*
　Earlier sketches in SATA *106, 159, 202*
Elzbieta *88*
Ember, Kathi *234*
　Earlier sketch in SATA *190*
Emberley, Barbara A. 1932- *146*
　Earlier sketches in SATA *8, 70*
　See also CLR *5*
Emberley, Barbara Anne
　See Emberley, Barbara A.
Emberley, Ed 1931- *146*
　Earlier sketches in SATA *8, 70*
　See also CLR *81*
Emberley, Edward Randolph
　See Emberley, Ed
Emberley, Michael 1960- *232*
　Earlier sketches in SATA *34, 80, 119, 189*
Emberley, Rebecca 1958- *218*
Embry, Margaret Jacob 1919-1975 .... *5*
Emecheta, Buchi 1944- *66*
　See also CLR *158*
Emecheta, Florence Onye Buchi
　See Emecheta, Buchi
Emerson, Alice B.
　See Benson, Mildred
Emerson, Kate
　See Emerson, Kathy Lynn
Emerson, Kathy Lynn 1947- *63*
Emerson, Kevin *209*
Emerson, Ru 1944- *107*
　Earlier sketch in SATA *70*
Emerson, Sally 1952- *111*
Emerson, William K(eith) 1925- *25*
Emert, Phyllis R. 1947- *93*
Emert, Phyllis Raybin
　See Emert, Phyllis R.
Emery, Anne (McGuigan) 1907- *33*
　Earlier sketch in SATA *1*
Emmens, Carol Ann 1944- *39*
Emmett, Jonathan 1965- *188*
　Earlier sketch in SATA *138*
Emmons, Della (Florence) Gould 1890-1983
　Obituary *39*
Emond, Stephen 1979(?)- *231*
Emory, Jerry 1957- *96*

Emrich, Duncan (Black Macdonald)
　1908-1970(?) *11*
Emshwiller, Carol 1921- *174*
　Autobiography Feature *174*
Emshwiller, Carol Fries
　See Emshwiller, Carol
Emslie, M. L.
　See Simpson, Myrtle L(illias)
Ende, Michael (Andreas Helmuth)
　1929-1995 .... *130*
　Brief entry *42*
　Obituary *86*
　Earlier sketch in SATA *61*
　See also CLR *138*
Enderle, Dotti 1954- *203*
　Earlier sketch in SATA *145*
Enderle, Judith (Ann) Ross 1941- *89*
　Autobiography Feature *114*
　Earlier sketch in SATA *38*
　See also SAAS *26*
Endle, Kate *207*
Enell, Trinka (Gochenour) 1951- *79*
Enfield, Carrie
　See Smith, Susan Vernon
Engdahl, Sylvia Louise 1933- *4*
　Autobiography Feature *122*
　See also CLR *2*
　See also SAAS *5*
Engel, Christiane *231*
Engel, Diana 1947- *70*
Engelbreit, Mary 1952- *169*
Engelhart, Margaret S. 1924- *59*
Engelmann, Kim (V.) 1959- *87*
England, George Allan 1877-1936 .... *102*
Englart, Mindi Rose 1965- *146*
Engle, Eloise
　See Paananen, Eloise (Katherine)
Engle, Margarita 1951- *231*
　Earlier sketch in SATA *193*
Englebert, Victor 1933- *8*
English, James W(ilson) 1915- *37*
English, Karen *202*
Engstrom, Elizabeth 1951- *110*
Enright, D(ennis) J(oseph) 1920-2002 .... *25*
　Obituary *140*
Enright, Dominique *194*
Enright, Elizabeth (Wright) 1909-1968 .... *9*
　See also CLR *4*
Ensor, Barbara *180*
Ensor, Robert (T.) 1922- *93*
Enthoven, Sam 1974- *187*
Entwistle, (Arthur) Theodore (Henry) Rowland
　See Rowland-Entwistle, (Arthur) Theodore
　(Henry)
Enys, Sarah L.
　See Sloggett, Nellie
Epanya, Christian A(rthur Kingue) 1956- *91*
Ephraim, Shelly S(chonebaum) 1952- *97*
Ephron, Delia 1944- *197*
　Brief entry *50*
　Earlier sketch in SATA *65*
Epler, Doris M. 1928- *73*
Epp, Margaret A(gnes) 1913- *20*
Eppenstein, Louise (Kohn) 1892-1987
　Obituary *54*
Epple, Anne Orth 1927- *20*
Epstein, Adam Jay 1975- *235*
Epstein, Anne Merrick 1931- *20*
Epstein, Beryl 1910- *31*
　Earlier sketch in SATA *1*
　See also CLR *26*
　See also SAAS *17*
Epstein, Beryl M. Williams
　See Epstein, Beryl
Epstein, Perle S(herry) 1938- *27*
Epstein, Rachel S. 1941- *102*
Epstein, Robin 1972- *230*
Epstein, Samuel 1909-2000 .... *31*
　Earlier sketch in SATA *1*
　See also CLR *26*
　See also SAAS *17*

Erdman, Loula Grace 1905(?)-1976 .... *1*
Erdoes, Richard 1912- *33*
　Brief entry *28*
Erdogan, Buket *187*
Erdrich, Karen Louise
　See Erdrich, Louise
Erdrich, Louise 1954- *141*
　Earlier sketch in SATA *94*
Erickson, Betty J. 1923- *97*
Erickson, Betty Jean
　See Erickson, Betty J.
Erickson, John R. 1943- *136*
　Earlier sketch in SATA *70*
Erickson, Jon 1948- *141*
Erickson, Phoebe *59*
Erickson, Russell E(verett) 1932- *27*
Erickson, Sabra Rollins 1912-1995 .... *35*
Erickson, Walter
　See Fast, Howard
Ericson, Walter
　See Fast, Howard
Ericsson, Jennifer A. *170*
Erikson, Mel 1937- *31*
Eriksson, Eva 1949- *207*
Ering, Timothy Basil *176*
Erlanger, Baba
　See Trahey, Jane
Erlbach, Arlene 1948- *160*
　Earlier sketches in SATA *78, 115*
Erlbruch, Wolf 1948- *181*
Erlich, Lillian (Feldman) 1910-1983 .... *10*
Erlings, Fridrik 1962- *196*
Erlingsson, Friorik
　See Erlings, Fridrik
Ermatinger, James W. 1959- *170*
Ernest, William
　See Berkebile, Fred D(onovan)
Ernst, (Lyman) John 1940- *39*
Ernst, Kathleen
　See Ernst, Kathleen
Ernst, Kathleen 1959- *162*
Ernst, Kathryn (Fitzgerald) 1942- *25*
Ernst, Lisa Campbell 1957- *212*
　Brief entry *44*
　Earlier sketches in SATA *55, 95, 154*
Erskine, Kathryn *193*
Ervin, Janet Halliday 1923- *4*
Erwin, Will
　See Eisner, Will
Esbaum, Jill *213*
　Earlier sketch in SATA *174*
Esbensen, Barbara J(uster) 1925-1996 .... *97*
　Brief entry *53*
　Earlier sketch in SATA *62*
Eschbacher, Roger *160*
Eschmeyer, R. E. 1898-1989 .... *29*
Escriva, Vivi *182*
Eseki, Bruno
　See Mphahlele, Es'kia
Esekie, Bruno
　See Mphahlele, Es'kia
Eshmeyer, Reinhart Ernst
　See Eschmeyer, R. E.
Eskridge, Ann E. 1949- *84*
Espeland, Pamela (Lee) 1951- *128*
　Brief entry *38*
　Earlier sketch in SATA *52*
Espinosa, Laura *203*
Espinosa, Leo *203*
Espriella, Don Manuel Alvarez
　See Southey, Robert
Espy, Willard R(ichardson) 1910-1999 .... *38*
　Obituary *113*
Essakalli, Julie Klear *200*
Essrig, Harry 1912- *66*
Estep, Irene Compton *5*
Esterl, Arnica 1933- *77*
Estes, Eleanor (Ruth) 1906-1988 .... *91*
　Obituary *56*
　Earlier sketch in SATA *7*
　See also CLR *70*

Estoril, Jean
　See Allan, Mabel Esther
Estrada, Pau 1961- *200*
　Earlier sketch in SATA *74*
Etchemendy, Nancy 1952- *166*
　Earlier sketch in SATA *38*
Etchemendy, Nancy Elise Howell
　See Etchemendy, Nancy
Etchison, Birdie L(ee) 1937- *38*
Etchison, Craig 1945- *133*
Etherington, Frank 1945- *58*
Etnier, Jennifer L. *227*
Eton, Robert
　See Meynell, Laurence Walter
Ets, Marie Hall 1893-1984 .... *2*
　See also CLR *33*
Ettlinger, Doris 1950- *173*
Eugnia, Maria *222*
Eulberg, Elizabeth 1975- *227*
Eunson, (John) Dale 1904-2002 .... *5*
　Obituary *132*
Evan, Frances Y. 1951- *167*
Evanoff, Vlad 1916- *59*
Evans, Cambria 1981- *178*
Evans, Douglas 1953- *144*
　Earlier sketch in SATA *93*
Evans, Eva (Knox) 1905-1998 .... *27*
Evans, Freddi Williams 1957- *211*
　Earlier sketch in SATA *134*
Evans, Greg 1947- *143*
　Earlier sketch in SATA *73*
Evans, Hubert Reginald 1892-1986 .... *118*
　Obituary *48*
Evans, Katherine (Floyd) 1901-1964 .... *5*
Evans, Larry
　See Evans, Laurence Chubb
Evans, Laurence Chubb 1939- *88*
Evans, Lawrence Watt
　See Watt-Evans, Lawrence
Evans, Leslie 1953- *214*
Evans, Lezlie *180*
Evans, Mari 1923- *10*
Evans, Mark *19*
Evans, Nancy 1950- *65*
Evans, Nate *201*
Evans, Patricia Healy
　See Carpenter, Patricia (Healy Evans)
Evans, (Alice) Pearl 1927- *83*
Evans, Shane W. *189*
Evans, Shirlee 1931- *58*
Evans, Tabor
　See Cameron, Lou
　and Knott, William C(ecil, Jr.)
　and Wallmann, Jeffrey M(iner)
　and Whittington, Harry (Benjamin)
Evarts, Esther
　See Benson, Sally
Evarts, Hal G., (Jr.) 1915-1989 .... *6*
Everett, Gail
　See Hale, Arlene
Evernden, Margery 1916- *5*
Eversole, Robyn 1971- *74*
Eversole, Robyn H.
　See Eversole, Robyn
Eversole, Robyn Harbert
　See Eversole, Robyn
Evslin, Bernard 1922-1993 .... *83*
　Brief entry *28*
　Obituary *77*
　Earlier sketch in SATA *45*
Ewart, Claire 1958- *145*
　Earlier sketch in SATA *76*
Ewart, Franzeska G. 1950- *205*
Ewen, David 1907-1985 .... *4*
　Obituary *47*
Ewing, Juliana (Horatia Gatty) 1841-1885 ... *16*
　See also CLR *78*
Ewing, Kathryn 1921- *20*

Eyerly, Jeannette 1908-2008 .... *86*
　Obituary *196*
　Earlier sketch in SATA *4*
　See also SAAS *10*
Eyerly, Jeannette Hyde
　See Eyerly, Jeannette
Eyre, Dorothy
　See McGuire, Leslie (Sarah)
Eyre, Frank 1910-1988
　Obituary *62*
Eyre, Katherine Wigmore 1901-1970 .... *26*
Ezzell, Marilyn 1937- *42*
　Brief entry *38*

F

Fabe, Maxene 1943- *15*
Faber, Doris (Greenberg) 1924- *78*
　Earlier sketch in SATA *3*
Faber, Harold 1919-2010 .... *5*
Fabre, Jean Henri (Casimir) 1823-1915 .... *22*
Fabry, Glenn 1961- *205*
Facklam, Margaret
　See Thomas, Peggy
Facklam, Margery (Metz) 1927- *132*
　Earlier sketches in SATA *20, 85*
Fadden, David Kanietakeron *196*
Fadiman, Clifton (Paul) 1904-1999 .... *11*
　Obituary *115*
Fagan, Cary 1957- *186*
Fagan, Deva *220*
Fahs, Sophia Blanche Lyon 1876-1978 ...... *102*
Failing, Barbara Larmon *182*
Fain, Sarah 1971- *204*
Fair, David 1952- *96*
Fair, Sylvia 1933- *13*
Fairfax-Lucy, Brian (Fulke Cameron-Ramsay)
　1898-1974 .... *6*
　Obituary *26*
Fairfield, Flora
　See Alcott, Louisa May
Fairlie, Gerard 1899-1983
　Obituary *34*
Fairman, Joan A(lexandra) 1935- *10*
Faithfull, Gail 1936- *8*
Falcone, L.M. 1951- *231*
　Earlier sketch in SATA *155*
Falcone, Lucy M.
　See Falcone, L.M.
Falconer, Ian 1959- *179*
　Earlier sketch in SATA *125*
　See also CLR *146*
Falconer, James
　See Kirkup, James
Falconer, Lee N.
　See May, Julian
Falkner, Brian 1962- *206*
Falkner, Leonard 1900-1977 .... *12*
Fall, Andrew
　See Arthur, Robert, (Jr.)
Fall, Thomas
　See Snow, Donald Clifford
Faller, Regis 1968- *187*
Falls, C(harles) B(uckles) 1874-1960 .... *38*
　Brief entry *27*
Falls, Kat *232*
Falls, Kathleen Moynihan
　See Falls, Kat
Falstein, Louis 1909-1995 .... *37*
Falvey, David 1982- *222*
Falwell, Cathryn 1952- *196*
Fancher, Lou 1960- *228*
　Earlier sketch in SATA *177*
Fanelli, Sara 1969- *126*
　Earlier sketch in SATA *89*
Fanning, Leonard M(ulliken) 1888-1967 ...... *5*
Fantaskey, Beth 1965- *217*
Faralla, Dana 1909- *9*

Faralla, Dorothy W.
  See Faralla, Dana
Farb, Peter 1929-1980 12
  Obituary 22
Farber, Norma 1909-1984 75
  Obituary 38
  Earlier sketch in SATA 25
Fardell, John 1967- 195
Fardell, John William
  See Fardell, John
Faria, Rosana 213
Farish, Terry 1947- 146
  Earlier sketch in SATA 82
Farjeon, (Eve) Annabel 1919-2004 11
  Obituary 153
Farjeon, Eleanor 1881-1965 2
  See also CLR 34
Farley, Carol (J.) 1936- 137
  Earlier sketch in SATA 4
Farley, Terri 165
Farley, Walter (Lorimer) 1915-1989 132
  Earlier sketches in SATA 2, 43
Farlow, James O(rville, Jr.) 1951- 75
Farmer, Jacqueline 210
Farmer, Nancy 1941- 161
  Earlier sketches in SATA 79, 117
Farmer, Patti 1948- 79
Farmer, Penelope (Jane) 1939- 105
  Brief entry 39
  Earlier sketch in SATA 40
  See also CLR 8
  See also SAAS 22
Farmer, Peter 1950- 38
Farmer, Philip Jose
  See Farmer, Philip Jose
Farmer, Philip Jose 1918-2009 93
  Obituary 201
Farmer, Philipe Jos
  See Farmer, Philip Jose
Farnham, Burt
  See Clifford, Harold B(urton)
Farnsworth, Bill 1958- 186
  Earlier sketches in SATA 84, 135
Farooqi, Musharraf Ali 1968- 207
Farquhar, Margaret C(utting) 1905-1988 13
Farquharson, Alexander 1944- 46
Farquharson, Martha
  See Finley, Martha
Farr, Diana 82
  Earlier sketch in SATA 3
Farr, Finis (King) 1904-1982 10
Farr, Richard 1960- 209
Farrar, Jill
  See Morris, Jill
Farrar, Susan Clement 1917- 33
Farrell, Ben
  See Cebulash, Mel
Farrell, Darren 228
Farrell, John 1951- 204
Farrell, Patrick
  See Odgers, Sally Farrell
Farrell, Sally
  See Odgers, Sally Farrell
Farrer, Vashti 167
Farrington, Benjamin 1891-1974
  Obituary 20
Farrington, S(elwyn) Kip, Jr. 1904-1983 20
Farris, Christine King 1927- 206
Farshtey, Greg(ory T.) 1965- 148
Farthing, Alison 1936- 45
  Brief entry 36
Farthing-Knight, Catherine 1933- 92
Fassler, Joan (Grace) 1931- 11
Fast, Howard 1914-2003 7
  Autobiography Feature 107
Fast, Howard Melvin
  See Fast, Howard
Fasulo, Michael 1963- 83
Fatchen, Max 1920- 84
  Earlier sketch in SATA 20
  See also SAAS 20

Fate, Marilyn
  See Collins, Paul
Father Goose
  See Ghigna, Charles
Fatigati, Evelyn 1948- 24
Fatigati, Frances Evelyn
  See Fatigati, Evelyn
Fatio, Louise 1904-1993 6
Fatus, Sophie 1957- 182
Faulhaber, Martha 1926- 7
Faulkner, Anne Irvin 1906- 23
Faulkner, Frank
  See Ellis, Edward S.
Faulkner, Nancy
  See Faulkner, Anne Irvin
Faulknor, Cliff(ord Vernon) 1913- 86
Faust, Anke 1971- 230
Favole, Robert J(ames) 1950- 125
Fawcett, Katie Pickard 229
Fax, Elton Clay 1909-1993 25
Faxon, Lavinia
  See Russ, Lavinia (Faxon)
Feagles, Anita M.
  See Feagles, Anita MacRae
Feagles, Anita MacRae 1927- 9
Feagles, Elizabeth
  See Day, Beth (Feagles)
Feague, Mildred H. 1915- 14
Fearing, Mark 1968- 224
Fearnley, Jan 1965- 205
  Earlier sketch in SATA 153
Fearrington, Ann (Peyton) 1945- 146
Fecher, Constance
  See Heaven, Constance (Christina)
Feder, Chris Welles 1938- 81
Feder, Harriet K. 1928- 73
Feder, Paula (Kurzband) 1935- 26
Federici, Debbie 1965- 175
Federici, Debbie Tanner
  See Federici, Debbie
Feelings, Muriel 1938- 16
  See also CLR 5
  See also SAAS 8
Feelings, Muriel Lavita Grey
  See Feelings, Muriel
Feelings, Thomas 1933-2003 69
  Obituary 148
  Earlier sketch in SATA 8
  See also CLR 58
  See also SAAS 19
Feelings, Tom
  See Feelings, Thomas
Fehler, Gene 1940- 201
  Earlier sketch in SATA 74
Fehrenbach, T(heodore) R(eed, Jr.) 1925- 33
Feiffer, Jules 1929- 201
  Earlier sketches in SATA 8, 61, 111, 157
Feiffer, Jules Ralph
  See Feiffer, Jules
Feiffer, Kate 1964- 206
  Earlier sketch in SATA 170
Feig, Barbara Krane 1937- 34
Feig, Paul 221
Feikema, Feike
  See Manfred, Frederick (Feikema)
Feil, Hila 1942- 12
Feilen, John
  See May, Julian
Feinberg, Barbara Jane 1938- 123
  Earlier sketch in SATA 58
Feinberg, Barbara Silberdick
  See Feinberg, Barbara Jane
Feinstein, John 1956- 239
  Earlier sketches in SATA 163, 195
Feldman, Anne (Rodgers) 1939- 19
Feldman, Elane 79
Feldman, Eve B. 221
Feldman, Jody 200
Felin, M. Sindy 194
Felix
  See Vincent, Felix

Fell, Derek 1939- 167
Fell, Derek John
  See Fell, Derek
Fellowes, Julian 1950- 198
Fellows, Muriel H. 10
Fellows, Stan 1957- 177
Fellows, Stanley
  See Fellows, Stan
Felsen, Henry Gregor 1916-1995 1
  See also SAAS 2
Felstead, Cathie 1954- 192
Feltenstein, Arlene 1934- 119
Feltenstine, Arlene H.
  See Feltenstein, Arlene
Felton, Harold William 1902-1991 1
Felton, Ronald Oliver 1909- 3
Felts, Shirley 1934- 33
Felts, Susannah 1973- 214
Fenderson, Lewis H., Jr. 1907-1983 47
  Obituary 37
Fenner, Carol (Elizabeth) 1929-2002 89
  Obituary 132
  Earlier sketch in SATA 7
  See also SAAS 24
Fenner, Phyllis R(eid) 1899-1982 1
  Obituary 29
Fensham, Elizabeth 169
Fenten, Barbara D(oris) 1935- 26
Fenten, D(onald) X. 1932- 4
Fenton, Carroll Lane 1900-1969 5
Fenton, Edward 1917-1995 7
  Obituary 89
Fenton, Joe 213
Fenton, Mildred Adams 1899-1995 21
Fenwick, Patti
  See Grider, Dorothy
Feravolo, Rocco Vincent 1922- 10
Ferber, Brenda A. 1967- 184
Ferber, Edna 1887-1968 7
Fergus, Charles 114
Ferguson, Alane 1957- 182
  Earlier sketch in SATA 85
Ferguson, Bob
  See Ferguson, Robert Bruce
Ferguson, Cecil 1931- 45
Ferguson, Pamela
  See Ferguson, Pamela Ellen
Ferguson, Pamela Ellen 1943- 234
Ferguson, Peter 1968- 199
Ferguson, Robert Bruce 1927-2001 13
Ferguson, Sarah 1959- 180
  Earlier sketches in SATA 66, 110
Ferguson, Sarah Margaret
  See Ferguson, Sarah
Ferguson, Walter (W.) 1930- 34
Fergusson, Erna 1888-1964 5
Fermi, Laura 1907-1977 6
  Obituary 28
Fern, Eugene A. 1919-1987 10
  Obituary 54
Fern, Tracey E. 202
Fernandes, Eugenie 1943- 205
  Earlier sketches in SATA 77, 139
Fernandez, Laura 1960- 171
Ferraiolo, Jack D. 208
Ferrari, Maria 123
Ferrari, Michael 223
Ferrari, Michael J.
  See Ferrari, Michael
Ferreiro, Carmen 1958- 158
Ferrell, Nancy Warren 1932- 70
Ferrer, Barbara
  See Ferrer, Caridad
Ferrer, Caridad 238
Ferrer, Isabel
  See Riu, Isabel Ferrer
Ferri, Giuliano 1965- 197
Ferrier, Lucy
  See Penzler, Otto
Ferris, Helen Josephine 1890-1969 21

Ferris, James Cody
    See McFarlane, Leslie
Ferris, Jean 1939- 202
    Brief entry 50
    Earlier sketches in SATA *56, 105, 149*
Ferris, Jeri Chase 1937- 84
Ferry, Charles 1927- 92
    Earlier sketch in SATA *43*
    See also CLR *34*
    See also SAAS *20*
Fetz, Ingrid 1915- 30
Feydy, Anne Lindbergh
    See Sapieyevski, Anne Lindbergh
Fiammenghi, Gioia 1929- 66
    Earlier sketch in SATA *9*
Fiarotta, Noel
    See Ficarotta, Noel
Fiarotta, Phyllis
    See Ficarotta, Phyllis
Ficarotta, Noel 1944- 15
Ficarotta, Phyllis 1942- 15
Fichter, George S. 1922-1993 7
Ficocelli, Elizabeth 189
Fidler, Kathleen (Annie) 1899-1980 87
    Obituary 45
    Earlier sketch in SATA *3*
Fiedler, Jean(nette Feldman) 4
Fiedler, Joseph Daniel 159
Fiedler, Lisa 185
Field, Dorothy 1944- 97
Field, Edward 1924- 109
    Earlier sketch in SATA *8*
Field, Elinor Whitney 1889-1980
    Obituary 28
Field, Eugene 1850-1895 16
Field, Gans T.
    See Wellman, Manly Wade
Field, James 1959- 113
Field, Peter
    See Drago, Harry Sinclair
    and Dresser, Davis
    and Mann, E(dward) B(everly)
Field, Rachel (Lyman) 1894-1942 15
    See also CLR *21*
Fielding, Kate
    See Oldfield, Jenny
Fields, Bryan W. 1958(?)- 188
Fields, Lisa 1984(?)- 216
Fields, Terri 1948- 191
Fields, T.S.
    See Fields, Terri
Fienberg, Anna 1956- 183
    Earlier sketch in SATA *112*
Fiery, Ann
    See Barrows, Annie
Fife, Dale (Odile Hollerbach) 1901- 18
Fighter Pilot, A
    See Johnston, H(ugh) A(nthony) S(tephen)
Figler, Jeanie 1949- 123
Figley, Marty Rhodes 1948- 158
    Earlier sketch in SATA *88*
Figueredo, D(anilo) H. 1951- 155
Figueroa, Pablo 1938- 9
Fijan, Carol 1918- 12
Filderman, Diane E(lizabeth) 1959- 87
Files, Meg 1946- 107
Fillmore, Parker H(oysted) 1878-1944
    See YABC *1*
Filstrup, Chris
    See Filstrup, E(dward) Christian
Filstrup, E(dward) Christian 1942- 43
Filstrup, Janie
    See Merrill, Jane
Finbarr, Desmond
    See Zobel Nolan, Allia
Finchler, Judy 1943- 230
    Earlier sketch in SATA *93*
Finder, Martin
    See Salzmann, Siegmund
Findlay, Jamieson 1958- 169
Findon, Joanne 1957- 161

Fine, Anne 1947- 197
    Earlier sketches in SATA *29, 72, 111, 160*
    See also CLR *25*
    See also SAAS *15*
Fine, Edith Hope 169
Fine, Howard 1961- 181
Fine, Jane
    See Ziefert, Harriet
Finger, Charles J(oseph) 1869(?)-1941 42
Fink, William B(ertrand) 1916- 22
Finke, Blythe Foote 1922- 26
Finkel, George (Irvine) 1909-1975 8
Finkelstein, Norman H. 1941- 220
    Earlier sketches in SATA *73, 137*
Finkelstein, Norman Henry
    See Finkelstein, Norman H.
Finlay, Alice Sullivan 1946- 82
Finlay, Winifred Lindsay Crawford
    (McKissack) 1910-1989 23
Finlayson, Ann 1925- 8
Finley, Martha 1828-1909 43
    See also CLR *148*
Finley, Mary Peace 1942- 83
Finn, Mary 208
Finney, Jack 1911-1995 109
Finney, Patricia 1958- 163
Finney, Shan 1944- 65
Finney, Walter Braden
    See Finney, Jack
Firer, Ben Zion
    See Firer, Benzion
Firer, Benzion 1914- 64
Fireside, Bryna J. 1932- 73
Firmin, Charlotte 1954- 29
Firmin, Peter 1928- 58
    Earlier sketch in SATA *15*
Firth, Barbara 179
Fischbach, Julius 1894-1988 10
Fischer, John
    See Fluke, Joanne
Fischer, R.J.
    See Fluke, Joanne
Fischer, Scott M. 1971- 195
Fischer-Nagel, Andreas 1951- 56
Fischer-Nagel, Heiderose 1956- 56
Fischler, Shirley (Walton) 66
Fischler, Stan(ley I.) 66
    Brief entry 36
Fischtrom, Harvey 1933-1974 3
Fishback, Margaret
    See Antolini, Margaret Fishback
Fishbone, Greg R. 195
Fisher, Aileen (Lucia) 1906-2002 73
    Obituary 143
    Earlier sketches in SATA *1, 25*
    See also CLR *49*
Fisher, Barbara 1940- 44
    Brief entry 34
Fisher, Carolyn 1968- 154
Fisher, Catherine 1957- 155
Fisher, Chris 1958- 80
Fisher, Clavin C(argill) 1912- 24
Fisher, Cynthia 195
Fisher, Dorothy (Frances) Canfield 1879-1958
    See YABC *1*
    See also CLR *71*
Fisher, Gary L. 1949- 86
Fisher, John 1909-1996 15
Fisher, John Oswald Hamilton
    See Fisher, John
Fisher, Laura Harrison 1934- 5
Fisher, Leonard Everett 1924- 176
    Autobiography Feature 122
    Earlier sketches in SATA *4, 34, 73, 120*
    See also CLR *18*
    See also SAAS *1*
Fisher, Lois I. 1948- 38
    Brief entry 35
Fisher, Margery (Turner) 1913-1992 20
    Obituary 74
Fisher, Marshall Jon 1963- 113

Fisher, Nikki
    See Strachan, Ian
Fisher, Robert (Tempest) 1943- 47
Fisher, Suzanne
    See Staples, Suzanne Fisher
Fisher, Valorie 214
    Earlier sketch in SATA *177*
Fishman, Cathy Goldberg 1951- 106
Fisk, Nicholas
    See Higginbottom, David
Fisk, Pauline 1948- 160
    Earlier sketch in SATA *66*
Fiske, Tarleton
    See Bloch, Robert (Albert)
Fisscher, Catharina G. M. 1958- 142
Fisscher, Tiny
    See Fisscher, Catharina G. M.
Fitch, Clarke
    See Sinclair, Upton
Fitch, John IV
    See Cormier, Robert
Fitch, Sheree 1956- 178
    Earlier sketch in SATA *108*
Fitschen, Dale 1937- 20
Fitzalan, Roger
    See Trevor, Elleston
Fitzgerald, Captain Hugh
    See Baum, L. Frank
FitzGerald, Cathleen 1932-1987
    Obituary 50
Fitzgerald, Dawn 175
Fitzgerald, Edward Earl 1919-2001 20
Fitzgerald, F(rancis) A(nthony) 1940- 15
Fitzgerald, Joanne 1956- 198
Fitzgerald, John D(ennis) 1907(?)-1988 20
    Obituary 56
    See also CLR *1*
Fitzgerald, Merni Ingrassia 1955- 53
Fitzgibbon, Terry 1948- 121
Fitzhardinge, Joan Margaret 1912- 73
    Earlier sketch in SATA *2*
    See also CLR *5*
    See also SAAS *3*
Fitzhugh, Louise (Perkins) 1928-1974 45
    Obituary 24
    Earlier sketch in SATA *1*
    See also CLR *72*
Fitzhugh, Percy Keese 1876-1950 65
Fitzmaurice, Kathryn 217
Fitzpatrick, Becca 1979- 224
Fitzpatrick, Marie-Louise 1962- 189
    Earlier sketch in SATA *125*
FitzRalph, Matthew
    See McInerny, Ralph
Fitz-Randolph, Jane (Currens) 1915- 51
Fitzsimons, Cecilia 1952- 97
Fitzsimons, Cecilia A.L.
    See Fitzsimons, Cecilia
Fixmer, Elizabeth 237
Flack, Marjorie 1897-1958 100
    See also YABC *2*
    See also CLR *28*
Flack, Naomi John White -1999 40
    Brief entry 35
Flake, Sharon G. 166
Flanagan, John 1944- 180
Flanagan, John Anthony
    See Flanagan, John
Flannery, Kate
    See De Goldi, Kate
Flatt, Lizann 1966- 88
Fleagle, Gail S(hatto) 1940- 117
Fleetwood, Jenni 1947- 80
Fleischer, Jane
    See Oppenheim, Joanne
Fleischhauer-Hardt, Helga 1936- 30
Fleischman, Albert Sidney
    See Fleischman, Sid
Fleischman, John 1948- 145

Fleischman, Paul 1952- 156
    Brief entry 32
    Earlier sketches in SATA *39, 72, 110*
    See also CLR *66*
    See also SAAS *20*
Fleischman, Sid 1920-2010 185
    Earlier sketches in SATA *8, 59, 96, 148*
    See also CLR *15*
Fleischner, Jennifer 1956- 188
    Earlier sketch in SATA *93*
Fleisher, Paul 1948- 132
    Earlier sketch in SATA *81*
Fleisher, Robbin 1951-1977 52
    Brief entry 49
Fleishman, Seymour 1918- 66
    Brief entry 32
Fleming, A. A.
    See Arthur, Robert, (Jr.)
Fleming, Alice Mulcahey 1928- 9
Fleming, Candace 1962- 225
    Earlier sketches in SATA *94, 143, 190*
Fleming, Denise 1950- 173
    Earlier sketches in SATA *81, 126*
Fleming, Elizabeth P. 1888-1985
    Obituary 48
Fleming, Ian 1908-1964 9
Fleming, Ian Lancaster
    See Fleming, Ian
Fleming, Ronald Lee 1941- 56
Fleming, Sally
    See Walker, Sally M.
Fleming, Stuart
    See Knight, Damon (Francis)
Fleming, Susan 1932- 32
Fleming, Thomas 1927- 8
Fleming, Thomas James
    See Fleming, Thomas
Fleming, Virginia (Edwards) 1923- 84
Flesch, Y.
    See Flesch, Yolande
Flesch, Yolande 1950- 55
Flesch, Yolande Catarina
    See Flesch, Yolande
Fletcher, Charlie 220
Fletcher, Charlie May Hogue 1897-1977 3
Fletcher, Colin 1922-2007 28
Fletcher, Dirk
    See Cunningham, Chet
Fletcher, George U.
    See Pratt, (Murray) Fletcher
Fletcher, Helen Jill 1910- 13
Fletcher, Ralph 1953- 195
    Earlier sketches in SATA *105, 149*
    See also CLR *104*
Fletcher, Ralph J.
    See Fletcher, Ralph
Fletcher, Richard E. 1917(?)-1983
    Obituary 34
Fletcher, Rick
    See Fletcher, Richard E.
Fletcher, Susan 1951- 181
    Earlier sketches in SATA *70, 110*
Fletcher, Susan Clemens
    See Fletcher, Susan
Fleur, Paul
    See Pohl, Frederik
Flexner, James Thomas 1908-2003 9
Flinn, Alex 1966- 198
    Earlier sketch in SATA *159*
Flint, Helen 1952- 102
Flint, Russ 1944- 74
Flitner, David, Jr. 1949- 7
Flitner, David Perkins
    See Flitner, David, Jr.
Floca, Brian 190
    Earlier sketch in SATA *155*
Floethe, Louise Lee 1913-1988 4
Floethe, Richard 1901-1998 4
Floherty, John Joseph 1882-1964 25
Flood, Bo
    See Flood, Nancy Bo

Flood, Nancy Bo 1945- 233
    Earlier sketch in SATA *130*
Flood, Pansie Hart 1964- 140
Flood, William 1942- 129
Floogglebuckle, Al
    See Spiegelman, Art
Flora, James (Royer) 1914-1998 30
    Obituary 103
    Earlier sketch in SATA *1*
    See also SAAS *6*
Flores-Galbis, Enrique 1952- 186
Florian, Douglas 1950- 177
    Earlier sketches in SATA *19, 83, 125*
Flory, Jane Trescott 1917- 22
Flournoy, Valerie 1952- 95
Flournoy, Valerie Rose
    See Flournoy, Valerie
Flowerdew, Phyllis -1994 33
Flowers, Pam 1946- 136
Flowers, Sarah 1952- 98
Floyd, Gareth 1940- 62
    Brief entry 31
Fluchere, Henri 1914-1991 40
Fluke, Joanne 1943- 88
Flutsztejn-Gruda, Ilona 1930- 170
Flynn, Barbara 1928- 9
Flynn, Jackson
    See Bensen, Donald R.
    and Shirreffs, Gordon D(onald)
Flynn, Nicholas
    See Odgers, Sally Farrell
Flynn, Pat 1968- 214
Flynn, Patrick
    See Flynn, Pat
Flynn, Rachel 1953- 171
    Earlier sketch in SATA *109*
Flynn, Warren (G.) 1950- 154
Fodor, R. V. 1944- 25
Fodor, Ronald Victor
    See Fodor, R. V.
Fogelin, Adrian 1951- 175
    Earlier sketch in SATA *129*
Foley, (Anna) Bernice Williams 1902-1987 . 28
Foley, Greg E. 1969- 236
    Earlier sketch in SATA *190*
Foley, June 1944- 44
Foley, (Mary) Louise Munro 1933- 106
    Brief entry 40
    Earlier sketch in SATA *54*
Foley, Rae
    See Denniston, Elinore
Folke, Will
    See Bloch, Robert (Albert)
Follett, Helen Thomas 1884(?)-1970
    Obituary 27
Folsom, Franklin (Brewster) 1907-1995 5
    Obituary 88
Folsom, Michael (Brewster) 1938-1990 40
    Obituary 88
Fombelle, Timothee de 1973- 218
Fontenot, Mary Alice 1910-2003 91
    Obituary 209
    Earlier sketch in SATA *34*
Fontes, Justine 172
Fontes, Ron 1952- 183
Foon, Dennis 1951- 119
Fooner, Michael 22
Foote, Timothy (Gilson) 1926- 52
Forberg, Ati
    See Forberg, Beate Gropius
Forberg, Beate Gropius 1925- 22
Forbes, Anna 1954- 101
Forbes, Bryan 1926- 37
Forbes, Cabot L.
    See Hoyt, Edwin P(almer), Jr.
Forbes, Esther 1891-1967 100
    Earlier sketch in SATA *2*
    See also CLR *147*
Forbes, Graham B. 1
Forbes, Kathryn
    See McLean, Kathryn (Anderson)

Forbes, Robert
    See Arthur, Robert, (Jr.)
Ford, A.G. 231
Ford, Albert Lee
    See Stratemeyer, Edward L.
Ford, Barbara 56
    Brief entry 34
Ford, Bernette 212
Ford, Bernette G.
    See Ford, Bernette
Ford, B.G.
    See Ford, Bernette
Ford, Brian J(ohn) 1939- 49
Ford, Carolyn 1938- 98
Ford, Carolyn Mott
    See Ford, Carolyn
Ford, Christine 1953- 176
Ford, David
    See Baldacci, David
    and Baldacci, David
Ford, David B.
    See Baldacci, David
Ford, David Baldacci
    See Baldacci, David
Ford, Elbur
    See Hibbert, Eleanor Alice Burford
Ford, Ellen 1949- 89
Ford, George (Jr.) 31
Ford, Hilary
    See Youd, Samuel
Ford, Hildegarde
    See Morrison, Velma Ford
Ford, Jerome W. 1949- 78
Ford, Jerry
    See Ford, Jerome W.
Ford, John C. 1971- 221
Ford, Juwanda G(ertrude) 1967- 102
Ford, Marcia
    See Radford, Ruby L(orraine)
Ford, Nancy K(effer) 1906-1961
    Obituary 29
Ford, Peter 1936- 59
Ford, S. M.
    See Uhlig, Susan
Forde, Catherine 1961- 170
Foreman, Mark 199
Foreman, Michael 1938- 216
    Earlier sketches in SATA *2, 73, 129, 135, 184*
    See also CLR *32*
    See also SAAS *21*
Foreman, Wilmoth 1939- 153
Forest, Antonia 1915-2003 29
    Obituary 149
Forest, Dial
    See Gault, William Campbell
Forest, Heather 1948- 185
    Earlier sketch in SATA *120*
Forester, C. S. 1899-1966 13
Forester, Cecil Scott
    See Forester, C. S.
Forester, Victoria 214
Forler, Nan 223
Forman, Brenda 1936- 4
Forman, James
    See Forman, James D.
Forman, James D. 1932-2009 70
    Earlier sketch in SATA *8*
Forman, James Douglas
    See Forman, James D.
Forman, Mark L.
    See Forman, M.L.
Forman, M.L. 1964- 215
Forman, Ruth 1970- 186
Formento, Alison 228
Forrest, Elizabeth
    See Salsitz, Rhondi Vilott
Forrest, Mary
    See Pausacker, Jenny
Forrest, Sybil
    See Markun, Patricia Maloney

Author Index

Forrestal, Elaine 1941- 165
Earlier sketch in SATA *117*
Forrester, Frank H. 1919(?)-1986
Obituary 52
Forrester, Helen
See Bhatia, Jamunadevi
Forrester, Jade
See Pausacker, Jenny
Forrester, Marian
See Schachtel, Roger
Forrester, Sandra 1949- 166
Earlier sketch in SATA *90*
Forrester, Victoria 1940- 40
Brief entry 35
Forsee, (Frances) Aylesa -1986 .... *1*
Forsey, Chris 1950- 59
Forshay-Lunsford, Cin 1965- 60
Forster, E. M. 1879-1970 57
Forster, Edward Morgan
See Forster, E. M.
Forsyth, Kate 1966- 154
Fort, Paul
See Stockton, Francis Richard
Forte, Maurizio 1961- 110
Fortey, Richard 1946- 109
Fortey, Richard A.
See Fortey, Richard
Fortey, Richard Alan
See Fortey, Richard
Forth, Melissa D(eal) 96
Fortnum, Peggy
See Nuttall-Smith, Margaret Emily Noel
Fortune, Eric 182
Forward, Robert L(ull) 1932-2002 82
Fosberry, Jennifer 235
Foster, Alan Dean 1946- 70
Foster, Brad W. 1955- 34
Foster, Doris Van Liew 1899-1993 10
Foster, E(lizabeth) C(onnell) 1902- 9
Foster, Elizabeth 1902- 12
Foster, Elizabeth 1905-1963 10
Foster, F. Blanche 1919- 11
Foster, G(eorge) Allen 1907-1969 26
Foster, Genevieve (Stump) 1893-1979 2
Obituary 23
See also CLR *7*
Foster, Gerald L. 198
Foster, Hal
See Foster, Harold
Foster, Harold 1892-1982 31
Foster, Jeanne
See Williams, Jeanne
Foster, John
See Foster, John L(ouis)
and Furcolo, Foster
Foster, John (Thomas) 1925- 8
Foster, John L(ouis) 1941- 102
Foster, Juliana 196
Foster, Laura Louise (James) 1918- 6
Foster, Leila Merrell 1929- 73
Foster, Lynne 1937- 74
Foster, Margaret Lesser 1899(?)-1979
Obituary 21
Foster, Marian Curtis 1909-1978 23
Foster, Mark 1961- 197
Foster, Sally 58
Fotheringham, Edwin 201
Foulds, E. V.
See Foulds, Elfrida Vipont
Foulds, Elfrida Vipont 1902-1992 52
Fountas, Angela Jane 180
Fourie, Corlia 1944- 91
Fourth Brother, The
See Aung, (Maung) Htin
Fowke, Edith (Margaret) 1913-1996 14
Fowles, John 1926-2005 22
Obituary 171
Fowles, John Robert
See Fowles, John
Fowles, Shelley 1956- 205

Fox, Aileen 1907-2005 58
Obituary 170
Fox, Aileen Mary
See Fox, Aileen
Fox, Annie 1950- 175
Fox, Charles Philip 1913-2003 12
Obituary 150
Fox, Christyan 188
Fox, Diane 188
Fox, Eleanor
See St. John, Wylly Folk
Fox, Fontaine Talbot, Jr. 1884-1964
Obituary 23
Fox, Fred 1903(?)-1981
Obituary 27
Fox, Freeman
See Hamilton, Charles (Harold St. John)
Fox, Geoffrey 1941- 73
Fox, Grace
See Anderson, Grace Fox
Fox, Helen 1962- 181
Fox, Karen C. 1969- 229
Fox, Larry 30
Fox, Lee 1958- 227
Fox, Lorraine 1922-1976 27
Earlier sketch in SATA *11*
Fox, Louisa
See Kroll, Virginia L.
Fox, Mary Virginia 1919- 152
Brief entry 39
Earlier sketches in SATA *44, 88*
Fox, Mem 1946- 211
Earlier sketches in SATA *51, 103, 155*
See also CLR *80*
Fox, Merrion Frances
See Fox, Mem
Fox, Michael W(ilson) 1937- 15
Fox, Norma Diane
See Mazer, Norma Fox
Fox, Paula 1923- 167
Earlier sketches in SATA *17, 60, 120*
See also CLR *96*
Fox, Robert J. 1927- 33
Fox, Robert Joseph
See Fox, Robert J.
Fox-Davies, Sarah 1956- 199
Foyt, Victoria .... 187.
Fradin, Dennis
See Fradin, Dennis Brindell
Fradin, Dennis Brindell 1945- 185
Earlier sketches in SATA *29, 90, 135*
Fradin, Judith Bloom 1945- 185
Earlier sketches in SATA *90, 152*
Frailey, Paige (Menefee) 1965- 82
Frame, Janet 1924-2004 119
Frame, Janet Paterson
See Frame, Janet
Frame, Paul 1913-1994 60
Brief entry 33
Obituary 83
Frances, Miss
See Horwich, Frances R(appaport)
Franchere, Ruth 18
Francis, Charles
See Holme, Bryan
Francis, Dee
See Haas, Dorothy F.
Francis, Dorothy 1926- 127
Earlier sketch in SATA *10*
Francis, Dorothy B.
See Francis, Dorothy
Francis, Dorothy Brenner
See Francis, Dorothy
Francis, Guy 225
Francis, Jaye
See Pausacker, Jenny
Francis, Pamela (Mary) 1926- 11
Franck, Eddie
See Cooke, Frank E.
Franco, Betsy 223
Earlier sketches in SATA *150, 188*

Franco, Eloise (Bauder) 1910- 62
Franco, Johan (Henri Gustave) 1908-1988 ... 62
Franco, Marjorie 38
Franco, Tom 224
Francois, Andre 1915-2005 25
Francoise
See Seignobosc, Francoise
Frank, Anne 1929-1945 87
Brief entry 42
See also CLR *101*
Frank, Annelies Marie
See Frank, Anne
Frank, Daniel B. 1956- 55
Frank, Emily R.
See Frank, E.R.
Frank, E.R. 1967- 157
Frank, Helene
See Vautier, Ghislaine
Frank, Hillary 1976- 148
Frank, John 199
Frank, Josette 1893-1989 10
Obituary 63
Frank, Lucy 1947- 166
Earlier sketch in SATA *94*
Frank, Mary 1933- 34
Frank, R., Jr.
See Ross, Frank (Xavier), Jr.
Frankau, Mary Evelyn Atkinson 1899-1974 .. *4*
Frankel, Alona 1937- 66
Frankel, Bernice 9
Frankel, Edward 1910- 44
Frankel, Ellen 1951- 78
Frankel, Julie 1947- 40
Brief entry 34
Frankenberg, Robert 1911- 22
Frankland, David 207
Franklin, Cheryl J. 1955- 70
Franklin, Harold 1926- 13
Franklin, Kristine L. 1958- 124
Earlier sketch in SATA *80*
Franklin, Lance
See Lantz, Francess L(in)
Franklin, Madeleine
See L'Engle, Madeleine
Franklin, Madeleine L'Engle
See L'Engle, Madeleine
Franklin, Madeleine L'Engle Camp
See L'Engle, Madeleine
Franklin, Max
See Deming, Richard
Franklin, Steve
See Stevens, Franklin
Franson, Leanne 1963- 223
Earlier sketch in SATA *111*
Franson, Scott E. 1966- 192
Franzen, Nils-Olof 1916- 10
Frascino, Edward 48
Brief entry 33
See also SAAS *9*
Frasconi, Antonio 1919- 131
Earlier sketches in SATA *6, 53*
See also SAAS *11*
Fraser, Betty
See Fraser, Elizabeth Marr
Fraser, Elizabeth Marr 1928- 31
Fraser, Eric (George) 1902-1983 38
Fraser, Mary Ann 1959- 214
Earlier sketches in SATA *76, 137*
See also SAAS *23*
Fraser, Wynnette (McFaddin) 1925- 90
Frasier, Debra 1953- 182
Earlier sketches in SATA *69, 112*
Fraustino, Lisa Rowe 1961- 146
Autobiography Feature 146
Earlier sketch in SATA *84*
Frazee, Marla 1958- 225
Earlier sketches in SATA *105, 151, 187*
Frazer, Megan 1977- 221
Frazetta, Frank 1928-2010 58
Frazier, Angie 234

Frazier, Craig 1955- 221
Earlier sketch in SATA *177*
Frazier, Neta (Osborn) Lohnes 1890-1990 7
Frazier, Sundee T. 1968- 198
Frazier, Sundee Tucker
See Frazier, Sundee T.
Frederic, Mike
See Cox, William R(obert)
Frederick, Heather Vogel 207
Fredericks, Anthony D. 1947- 113
Freed, Alvyn M. 1913-1993 22
Freedman, Benedict 1919- 27
Freedman, Claire 227
Earlier sketch in SATA *185*
Freedman, Deborah 1960- 191
Freedman, Jeff 1953- 90
Freedman, Nancy 1920-2010 27
Freedman, Russell 1929- 235
Earlier sketches in SATA *16, 71, 123, 175*
See also CLR *71*
Freedman, Russell Bruce
See Freedman, Russell
Freeman, Barbara C. 1906-1999 28
Freeman, Barbara Constance
See Freeman, Barbara C.
Freeman, Bill
See Freeman, William Bradford
Freeman, Don 1908-1978 17
See also CLR *90*
Freeman, Ira Maximilian 1905-1987 21
Freeman, Kimberley
See Wilkins, Kim
Freeman, Laura 200
Freeman, Lucy (Greenbaum) 1916-2004 24
Freeman, Mae 1907-1985 25
Freeman, Mae Blacker
See Freeman, Mae
Freeman, Marcia S. 1937- 102
Freeman, Marcia Sheehan
See Freeman, Marcia S.
Freeman, Martha 1956- 201
Earlier sketches in SATA *101, 152*
Freeman, Nancy 1932- 61
Freeman, Peter J.
See Calvert, Patricia
Freeman, Roy 235
Freeman, Sarah (Caroline) 1940- 66
Freeman, Tor 1977- 164
Freeman, VicToria
See Freeman, Tor
Freeman, William Bradford 1938- 58
Brief entry 48
Fregosi, Claudia (Anne Marie) 1946- 24
Freitas, Donna 1972- 205
French, Allen 1870-1946
See YABC *1*
French, Dorothy Kayser 1926- 5
French, Fiona 1944- 132
Earlier sketches in SATA *6, 75*
See also CLR *37*
See also SAAS *21*
French, Jackie 186
Autobiography Feature 139
Earlier sketches in SATA *108, 139*
See French, Jackie Anne
and French, Jacqueline Anne
French, Kathryn
See Mosesson, Gloria R(ubin)
French, Martin 176
French, Michael 1944- 49
Brief entry 38
French, Paul
See Asimov, Isaac
French, S. Terrell 216
French, Simon 1957- 147
Earlier sketch in SATA *86*
French, Vivian 209
Earlier sketch in SATA *165*
French, Wendy 1972- 234
Frenette, Liza 126

Freschet, Gina 1960- 175
Earlier sketch in SATA *139*
Frewer, Glyn (M.) 1931- 11
Frey, Darcy 98
Freymann, Saxton 1958(?)- 178
Freymann-Weyr, Garret 1965- 145
Freymann-Weyr, Rhoda Garret Michaela
See Freymann-Weyr, Garret
Friar, Joanne 237
Friar, Joanne H.
See Friar, Joanne
Frick, C. H.
See Irwin, Constance (H.) Frick
Frick, Constance
See Irwin, Constance (H.) Frick
Fricke, Aaron 1962- 89
Fridell, Ron 1943- 124
Fried, Janice 197
Frieden, Sarajo 232
Friedlander, Joanne K(ohn) 1930- 9
Friedman, Aimee 1979- 189
Friedman, D. Dina 1957- 180
Friedman, Debra 1955- 150
Friedman, Estelle (Ehrenwald) 1920- 7
Friedman, Frieda 1905- 43
Friedman, Hal 230
See Friedman, Harold
Friedman, Ina R(osen) 1926- 136
Brief entry 41
Earlier sketch in SATA *49*
Friedman, Jerrold David
See Gerrold, David
Friedman, Judi 1935- 59
Friedman, Laurie 1964- 219
Earlier sketches in SATA *138, 179*
Friedman, Marvin 1930- 42
Brief entry 33
Friedman, Robin 1968- 219
Earlier sketch in SATA *162*
Friedmann, Stan 1953- 80
Friedrich, Otto (Alva) 1929-1995 33
Friedrich, Priscilla 1927- 39
Friend, Catherine 1957(?)- 194
Friend, David Michael 1975- 195
Friend, Natasha 1972- 184
Friendlich, Dick
See Friendlich, Richard J.
Friendlich, Richard J. 1909- 11
Friermood, Elisabeth Hamilton 1903-1992 5
Friesen, Bernice (Sarah Anne) 1966- 105
Friesen, Gayle 1960- 200
Earlier sketch in SATA *109*
Friesen, Jonathan 1967(?)- 206
Friesner, Esther 1951- 207
Earlier sketches in SATA *71, 168*
Friesner, Esther M.
See Friesner, Esther
Friis-Baastad, Babbis Ellinor 1921-1970 7
Frimmer, Steven 1928- 31
Frischmuth, Barbara 1941- 114
Friskey, Margaret (Richards) 1901-1995 5
Fritts, Mary Bahr
See Bahr, Mary (Madelyn)
Fritz, Jean (Guttery) 1915- 163
Autobiography Feature 122
Earlier sketches in SATA *1, 29, 72, 119*
See also CLR *96*
See also SAAS *2*
Froehlich, Margaret W(alden) 1930- 56
Frois, Jeanne 1953- 73
Froissart, Jean 1338(?)-1410(?) 28
Froman, Elizabeth Hull 1920-1975 10
Froman, Robert (Winslow) 1917- 8
Fromental, Jean-Luc 1950- 231
Fromm, Lilo 1928- 29
Frommer, Harvey 1937- 41
Frost, A(rthur) B(urdett) 1851-1928 19
Frost, Elizabeth
See Frost-Knappman, Elizabeth
Frost, Erica
See Supraner, Robyn

Frost, Helen 1949- 194
Autobiography Feature 194
Earlier sketches in SATA *157, 183*
Frost, Helen Marie
See Frost, Helen
Frost, Lesley 1899-1983 14
Obituary 34
Frost, Robert 1874-1963 14
See also CLR *67*
Frost, Robert Lee
See Frost, Robert
Frost, Shelley 1960- 138
Frost-Knappman, Elizabeth 1943- 179
Froud, Brian 1947- 150
Fry, Annette R(iley) 89
Fry, Christopher 1907-2005 66
Fry, Edward Bernard 1925- 35
Fry, Rosalie Kingsmill 1911-1992 3
See also SAAS *11*
Fry, Virginia Lynn 1952- 95
Frye, Sally
See Moore, Elaine
Fuchs, Bernie 1932- 162
Earlier sketch in SATA *95*
Fuchs, Erich 1916- 6
Fuchshuber, Annegert 1940- 43
Fucile, Tony 221
Fuerst, Jeffrey B. 1956- 143
Fuertes, Gloria 1918-1998 115
Fuge, Charles 1966- 144
Earlier sketch in SATA *74*
Fujikawa, Gyo 1908-1998 76
Brief entry 30
Obituary 110
Earlier sketch in SATA *39*
See also CLR *25*
See also SAAS *16*
Fujita, Tamao 1905-1999 7
Fujiwara, Kim 1957- 81
Fujiwara, Michiko 1946- 15
Fuka, Vladimir 1926-1977
Obituary 27
Fulcher, Jennifer
See Westwood, Jennifer
Fuller, Catherine Leuthold 1916- 9
Fuller, Edmund (Maybank) 1914- 21
Fuller, Iola
See McCoy, Iola Fuller
Fuller, John G(rant, Jr.) 1913-1990 65
Fuller, Kathleen
See Gottfried, Theodore Mark
Fuller, Lois Hamilton 1915- 11
Fuller, Margaret 1810-1850 25
Fuller, Maud
See Petersham, Maud
Fuller, Roy (Broadbent) 1912-1991 87
Fuller, Sarah Margaret
See Fuller, Margaret
Fults, John Lee 1932- 33
Funk, Thompson 1911- 7
Funk, Tom
See Funk, Thompson
Funke, Cornelia 1958- 209
Earlier sketches in SATA *154, 174*
See also CLR *145*
Funke, Cornelia Caroline
See Funke, Cornelia
Funke, Lewis 1912-1992 11
Fuqua, Jonathon Scott 1966- 141
Furbee, Mary R.
See Furbee, Mary Rodd
Furbee, Mary Rodd 1954- 138
Furchgott, Terry 1948- 29
Furlong, Monica (Mavis) 1930-2003 86
Obituary 142
Furlonger, Patricia
See Wrightson, Patricia
Furman, Gertrude Lerner Kerman 1909- 21
Furniss, Tim 1948- 49
Furrow, Robert 1985- 172
Furukawa, Toshi 1924- 24

Fusco, Kimberly Newton 236
Fusillo, Archimede 1962- 137
Fussell, Sandy 1960- 234
Futcher, Jane P. 1947- 76
Futehali, Zahida
   See Whitaker, Zai
Fyleman, Rose (Amy) 1877-1957 21
Fyson, Jenny Grace
   See Fyson, J.G.
Fyson, J.G. 1904-1998 42

G

Gaan, Margaret 1914- 65
Gaber, Susan 1956- 169
   Earlier sketch in SATA *115*
Gaberman, Judie Angell
   See Angell, Judie
Gabhart, Ann
   See Gabhart, Ann H.
Gabhart, Ann H. 1947- 75
Gable, Brian 1949- 195
Gabler, Mirko 1951- 77
Gabriel, Adriana
   See Rojany, Lisa
Gabrys, Ingrid Schubert
   See Schubert-Gabrys, Ingrid
Gackenbach, Dick 1927- 79
   Brief entry 30
   Earlier sketch in SATA *48*
Gadd, Jeremy 1949- 116
Gaddis, Vincent H. 1913-1997 35
Gadler, Steve J. 1905-1985 36
Gaeddert, Lou Ann (Bigge) 1931- 103
   Earlier sketch in SATA *20*
Gaeddert, Louann
   See Gaeddert, Lou Ann (Bigge)
Gaer, Joseph 1897-1969 118
Gaer, Yossef
   See Gaer, Joseph
Gaetz, Dayle Campbell 1947- 138
Gaffney, Timothy R. 1951- 170
   Earlier sketch in SATA *69*
Gaffron, Norma 1931- 97
Gaffron, Norma Bondeson
   See Gaffron, Norma
Gag, Flavia 1907-1979
   Obituary 24
Gag, Wanda (Hazel) 1893-1946 100
   See also YABC *1*
   See also CLR *150*
Gage, Brian 162
Gage, Wilson
   See Steele, Mary Q(uintard Govan)
Gagliano, Eugene M. 1946- 150
Gagliardo, Ruth Garver 1895(?)-1980
   Obituary 22
Gagnon, Cecile 1936- 58
Gaillard, Jason 1965- 200
Gaiman, Neil 1960- 228
   Earlier sketches in SATA *85, 146, 197*
   See also CLR *109*
Gaiman, Neil Richard
   See Gaiman, Neil
Gainer, Cindy 1962- 74
Gaines, Ernest J. 1933- 86
   See also CLR *62*
Gaines, Ernest James
   See Gaines, Ernest J.
Gaither, Gloria 1942- 127
Gal, Laszlo 1933- 96
   Brief entry 32
   Earlier sketch in SATA *52*
   See also CLR *61*
Gal, Susan 228
Galbraith, Ben 1980- 200
Galbraith, Kathryn O. 1945- 219
   Earlier sketch in SATA *85*

Galbraith, Kathryn Osebold
   See Galbraith, Kathryn O.
Galdone, Paul 1907(?)-1986 66
   Obituary 49
   Earlier sketch in SATA *17*
   See also CLR *16*
Galindo, Claudia 1979- 203
Galinsky, Ellen 1942- 23
Gall, Chris 1961- 176
Gallagher, Diana G. 1946- 153
Gallagher, Lurlene Nora
   See McDaniel, Lurlene
Gallagher-Cole, Mernie 1958- 206
Gallant, Roy A(rthur) 1924- 110
   Earlier sketches in SATA *4, 68*
   See also CLR *30*
Gallardo, Evelyn 1948- 78
Gallaz, Christophe 1948- 162
   See also CLR *126*
Gallego Garcia, Laura 1977- 173
Gallico, Paul 1897-1976 13
Gallico, Paul William
   See Gallico, Paul
Gallo, Donald R. 1938- 112
   Autobiography Feature 104
Gallo, Donald Robert
   See Gallo, Donald R.
Galloway, Owateka (S.) 1981- 121
Galloway, Priscilla 1930- 227
   Earlier sketches in SATA *66, 112*
Gallup, Joan 1957- 128
Galouchko, Annouchka Gravel 1960- 95
Galt, Thomas Franklin, Jr. 1908-1989 5
Galt, Tom
   See Galt, Thomas Franklin, Jr.
Galvin, Matthew R. 1950- 93
Galvin, Matthew Reppert
   See Galvin, Matthew R.
Gamble, Kim 1952- 183
   Earlier sketches in SATA *81, 124*
Gambrell, Jamey 82
Gamerman, Martha 1941- 15
Gammell, Stephen 1943- 226
   Earlier sketches in SATA *53, 81, 128*
   See also CLR *83*
Ganly, Helen (Mary) 1940- 56
Gann, Marjorie 239
Gannett, Ruth Chrisman (Arens)
   1896-1979 33
Gannett, Ruth Stiles 1923- 3
Gannij, Joan 208
Gannij, Joan Levine
   See Gannij, Joan
Gannon, Ned 1974- 205
Gannon, Robert Haines 1931- 8
Gano, Lila 1949- 76
Gans, Roma 1894-1996 45
   Obituary 93
Gant, Matthew
   See Hano, Arnold
Gantner, Susan (Verble) 1939- 63
Gantos, Jack 1951- 169
   Earlier sketches in SATA *20, 81, 119*
   See also CLR *85*
Gantos, John Bryan, Jr.
   See Gantos, Jack
Ganz, Yaffa 1938- 61
   Brief entry 52
Garafano, Marie 1942- 84
Garant, Andre J. 1968- 123
Garbe, Ruth Moore
   See Moore, Ruth (Ellen)
Garber, Esther
   See Lee, Tanith
Garcia, Cristina 1958- 208
Garcia, Emma 1969- 198
Garcia, Geronimo 1960- 222
Garcia, Kami 1972- 229
Garcia, Yolanda P. 1952- 113
Garcia, Yolanda Pacheco
   See Garcia, Yolanda P.

Gard, Janice
   See Latham, Jean Lee
Gard, Joyce
   See Reeves, Joyce
Gard, Robert Edward 1910-1992 18
   Obituary 74
Gard, (Sanford) Wayne 1899-1986
   Obituary 49
Gardam, Jane 1928- 130
   Brief entry 28
   Earlier sketches in SATA *39, 76*
   See also CLR *12*
   See also SAAS *9*
Gardam, Jane Mary
   See Gardam, Jane
Gardella, Tricia 1944- 96
Garden, Nancy 1938- 147
   Autobiography Feature 147
   Earlier sketches in SATA *12, 77, 114*
   See also CLR *51*
   See also SAAS *8*
Gardner, John Reynolds 1944-2006 64
   Obituary 174
Gardner, Lindsey 1971- 144
Gardner, Craig Shaw 1949- 99
Gardner, Dic
   See Gardner, Richard (M.)
Gardner, Graham 159
Gardner, Hugh 1910-1986
   Obituary 49
Gardner, Jane Mylum 1946- 83
Gardner, Jeanne LeMonnier 1925- 5
Gardner, John, Jr. 1933-1982 40
   Obituary 31
Gardner, John Champlin, Jr.
   See Gardner, John, Jr.
Gardner, John E(dward) 1917- 192
Gardner, Lyn 192
Gardner, Martin 1914-2010 142
   Earlier sketch in SATA *16*
Gardner, Miriam
   See Bradley, Marion Zimmer
Gardner, Richard (M.) 1931- 24
Gardner, Richard A(lan) 1931-2003 13
   Obituary 144
Gardner, Sally 229
   Earlier sketch in SATA *177*
Gardner, Sandra 1940- 70
Gardner, Scot 1968- 143
Gardner, Sheldon 1934- 33
Gardner, Ted
   See Gardner, Theodore Roosevelt II
Gardner, Theodore Roosevelt
   See Gardner, Theodore Roosevelt II
Gardner, Theodore Roosevelt II 1934- 84
Garelick, May 1910-1989 19
Garfield, James B. 1881-1984 6
   Obituary 38
Garfield, Leon 1921-1996 76
   Obituary 90
   Earlier sketches in SATA *1, 32*
   See also CLR *166*
Garfinkle, Debra L.
   See Garfinkle, D.L.
Garfinkle, D.L. 187
Garis, Howard R. 1873-1962 13
Garis, Howard Roger
   See Garis, Howard R.
Garland, Mark 1953- 79
Garland, Mark A.
   See Garland, Mark
Garland, Michael 1952- 208
   Earlier sketch in SATA *168*
Garland, Sarah 1944- 135
   Earlier sketch in SATA *62*
Garland, Sherry 1948- 145
   Autobiography Feature 145
   Earlier sketches in SATA *73, 114*

Garner, Alan 1934- 69
    Autobiography Feature 108
    Earlier sketch in SATA *18*
    See also CLR *130*
Garner, David 1958- 78
Garner, Eleanor Ramrath 1930- 122
Garner, James Finn 1960(?)- 92
Garnet, A. H.
    See Slote, Alfred
Garnett, Eve C. R. 1900-1991 3
    Obituary 70
Garofoli, Viviana 1970- 186
Garou, Louis P.
    See Bowkett, Stephen
Garraty, John A. 1920-2007 23
    Obituary 189
Garraty, John Arthur
    See Garraty, John A.
Garren, Devorah-Leah
    See Devorah-Leah
Garret, Maxwell R. 1917- 39
Garretson, Dee 236
Garretson, Victoria Diane
    See Cox, Victoria
Garrett, Helen 1895- 21
Garrett, Randall 1927-1987 180
Garrett, Richard 1920- 82
Garrigue, Sheila 1931- 21
Garrison, Barbara 1931- 163
    Earlier sketch in SATA *19*
Garrison, Frederick
    See Sinclair, Upton
Garrison, Mary 1952- 146
Garrison, Peter
    See Gardner, Craig Shaw
Garrison, Webb B(lack) 1919-2000 25
Garrity, Jennifer Johnson 1961- 124
Garrity, Linda K. 1947- 128
Garsee, Jeannine 199
Garst, Doris Shannon 1894-1981 1
Garst, Shannon
    See Garst, Doris Shannon
Garth, Will
    See Hamilton, Edmond
    and Kuttner, Henry
Garthwaite, Marion H(ook) 1893-1981 7
Garton, Malinda D(ean) (?)-1976
    Obituary 26
Garvie, Maureen 1944- 175
Garvie, Maureen McCallum
    See Garvie, Maureen
Garza, Carmen Lomas 1948- 182
Garza, Xavier 184
Gascoigne, Bamber 1935- 62
Gaskins, Pearl Fuyo 1957- 134
Gasperini, Jim 1952- 54
    Brief entry 49
Gater, Dilys 1944- 41
Gates, Doris 1901-1987 34
    Obituary 54
    Earlier sketch in SATA *1*
    See also SAAS *1*
Gates, Frieda 1933- 26
Gates, Susan 1950- 153
Gates, Viola R. 1931- 101
Gathorne-Hardy, Jonathan G. 1933- 124
    Earlier sketch in SATA *26*
Gatti, Anne 1952- 103
Gatty, Juliana Horatia
    See Ewing, Juliana (Horatia Gatty)
Gauch, Patricia Lee 1934- 228
    Earlier sketches in SATA *26, 80*
    See also CLR *56*
    See also SAAS *21*
Gauch, Sarah 223
Gaudasinska, Elzbieta 1943- 190
Gaul, Randy 1959- 63
Gault, Clare 1925- 36
Gault, Frank 1926-1982 36
    Brief entry 30
Gault, William Campbell 1910-1995 8

Gauthier, Gail 1953- 203
    Earlier sketches in SATA *118, 160*
Gaver, Becky
    See Gaver, Rebecca
Gaver, Rebecca 1952- 20
Gavin, Jamila 1941- 223
    Earlier sketches in SATA *96, 125*
Gay, Amelia
    See Hogarth, Grace (Weston Allen)
Gay, Francis
    See Gee, H(erbert) L(eslie)
Gay, Kathlyn 1930- 144
    Earlier sketch in SATA *9*
Gay, Marie-Louise 1952- 179
    Earlier sketches in SATA *68, 126*
    See also CLR *27*
    See also SAAS *21*
Gay, Michel 1947- 162
Gay, Zhenya 1906-1978 19
Gaze, Gillian
    See Barklem, Jill
Gear, Kathleen M. O'Neal
    See Gear, Kathleen O'Neal
Gear, Kathleen O'Neal 1954- 224
    Earlier sketches in SATA *71, 166*
Gear, W. Michael 1955- 224
    Earlier sketches in SATA *71, 166*
Geary, Rick 1946- 142
Geason, Susan 1946- 122
Gedalof, Robin
    See McGrath, Robin
Gedge, Pauline (Alice) 1945- 101
Gee, H(erbert) L(eslie) 1901-1977
    Obituary 26
Gee, Maurice 1931- 227
    Earlier sketches in SATA *46, 101*
    See also CLR *56*
Gee, Maurice Gough
    See Gee, Maurice
Geehan, Wayne (E.) 1947- 107
Geer, Charles 1922- 42
    Brief entry 32
Geeslin, Campbell 1925- 163
    Earlier sketch in SATA *107*
Gehman, Mary W. 1923- 86
Gehr, Mary 1910(?)-1997 32
    Obituary 99
Geipel, Eileen 1932- 30
Geis, Alissa Imre 1976- 189
Geis, Darlene Stern 1918(?)-1999 7
    Obituary 111
Geisel, Helen 1898-1967 26
Geisel, Theodor Seuss
    See Dr. Seuss
Geisert, Arthur 1941- 237
    Brief entry 52
    Earlier sketches in SATA *56, 92, 133, 171*
    See also CLR *87*
    See also SAAS *23*
Geisert, Arthur Frederick
    See Geisert, Arthur
Geisert, Bonnie 1942- 165
    Earlier sketch in SATA *92*
Geist, Ken 191
Gelber, Lisa 210
Geldart, William 1936- 15
Gelinas, Paul J. 1904-1996 10
Gellis, Roberta 1927- 128
Gellis, Roberta Leah Jacobs
    See Gellis, Roberta
Gellman, Marc 112
Gelman, Amy 1961- 72
Gelman, Jan 1963- 58
Gelman, Rita Golden 1937- 131
    Brief entry 51
    Earlier sketch in SATA *84*
Gelman, Steve 1934- 3
Gemignani, Tony 1973- 220
Gemming, Elizabeth 1932- 11
Gendel, Evelyn W. 1916(?)-1977
    Obituary 27

Gennaro, Joseph F., Jr. 1924- 53
Gennaro, Joseph Francis, Jr.
    See Gennaro, Joseph F., Jr.
Gentieu, Penny 204
Gentile, Petrina 1969- 91
Gentle, Mary 1956- 48
Gentleman, David (William) 1930- 7
Gentry, Marita 215
Geoghegan, Adrienne 1962- 143
George, Barbara
    See Katz, Bobbi
George, Emily
    See Katz, Bobbi
George, Gail
    See Katz, Bobbi
George, Jean
    See George, Jean Craighead
George, Jean C.
    See George, Jean Craighead
George, Jean Craighead 1919- 226
    Earlier sketches in SATA *2, 68, 124, 170*
    See also CLR *136*
George, Jessica Day 1976- 210
George, John L(othar) 1916- 2
George, Kristine O'Connell 1954- 156
    Earlier sketch in SATA *110*
George, Lindsay Barrett 1952- 206
    Earlier sketches in SATA *95, 155*
George, S. C. 1898- 11
George, Sally
    See Orr, Wendy
George, Sidney Charles
    See George, S. C.
George, Twig C. 1950- 114
George, W(illiam) Lloyd 1900(?)-1975
    Obituary 30
Georgiou, Constantine 1927- 7
Georgiou, Theo
    See Odgers, Sally Farrell
Geraghty, Paul 1959- 130
Gerard, Jean Ignace Isidore 1803-1847 45
Geras, Adele 1944- 180
    Autobiography Feature 180
    Earlier sketches in SATA *23, 87, 129, 173*
    See also SAAS *21*
Geras, Adele Daphne Weston
    See Geras, Adele
Gerber, Carole 1947- 207
Gerber, Linda 213
Gerber, Merrill Joan 1938- 170
    Autobiography Feature 170
    Earlier sketches in SATA *64, 127*
Gerber, Perren 1933- 104
Gerberg, Mort 1931- 64
Gergely, Tibor 1900-1978 54
    Obituary 20
Geringer, Laura 1948- 232
    Earlier sketches in SATA *29, 94, 164*
Gerler, William R(obert) 1917-1996 47
Gerrard, Jean 1933- 51
Gerrard, Roy 1935-1997 90
    Brief entry 45
    Obituary 99
    Earlier sketch in SATA *47*
    See also CLR *23*
Gerritsen, Paula 1956- 177
Gerrold, David 1944- 144
    Earlier sketch in SATA *66*
Gersh, A.
    See Gersh, Amanda
Gersh, Amanda 235
Gershator, David 1937- 180
Gershator, Phillis 1942- 235
    Earlier sketches in SATA *90, 158, 188*
Gershon, Dann 1955- 187
Gershon, Gina 1962- 187
Gerson, Corinne 1927- 37
Gerson, Mary-Joan 136
    Earlier sketch in SATA *79*
Gerson, Noel Bertram 1914-1988 22
    Obituary 60

Gerstein, Mordicai 1935- 222
  Brief entry 36
  Earlier sketches in SATA 47, 81, 142, 178
  See also CLR 102
Gertridge, Allison 1967- 132
Gervais, Bernadette 1959- 80
Gervay, Susanne 183
Gesner, Clark 1938-2002 40
  Obituary 143
Gessner, Lynne 1919- 16
Geter, Tyrone 150
Getz, David 1957- 91
Getzinger, Donna 1968- 128
Geus, Mireille 1964- 207
Gevirtz, Eliezer 1950- 49
Gevry, Claudine 188
Gewe, Raddory
  See Gorey, Edward (St. John)
Ghan, Linda (R.) 1947- 77
Ghent, Natale 1962- 148
Gherman, Beverly 1934- 123
  Earlier sketch in SATA 68
Ghigna, Charles 1946- 153
  Earlier sketch in SATA 108
Giacobbe, Beppe 1953- 174
Giambastiani, Kurt R. A. 1958- 141
Giannini, Enzo 1946- 68
Gibala-Broxholm, Scott 1959(?)- 205
Gibbons, Alan 1953- 198
  Earlier sketch in SATA 124
Gibbons, Faye 1938- 103
  Earlier sketch in SATA 65
Gibbons, Gail 1944- 201
  Earlier sketches in SATA 23, 72, 104, 160
  See also CLR 8
  See also SAAS 12
Gibbons, Gail Gretchen
  See Gibbons, Gail
Gibbons, Kaye 1960- 117
Gibbs, Adrea 1960- 126
Gibbs, Alonzo (Lawrence) 1915-1992 5
Gibbs, (Cecilia) May 1877-1969
  Obituary 27
Gibbs, Stuart 1969- 230
Gibbs, Tony
  See Gibbs, Wolcott, Jr.
Gibbs, Wolcott, Jr. 1935- 40
Giblin, James Cross 1933- 197
  Earlier sketches in SATA 33, 75, 122
  See also CLR 29
  See also SAAS 12
Gibson, Andrew (William) 1949- 72
Gibson, Barbara L. 205
Gibson, Barbara Leonard
  See Gibson, Barbara L.
Gibson, Betty 1911- 75
Gibson, Jo
  See Fluke, Joanne
Gibson, Josephine
  See Hine, Sesyle Joslin
  and Hine, Al(fred Blakelee)
Gibson, Marley 1966- 225
Gibson, Sarah P. 1962- 211
Gibson, William 1914-2008 66
  Obituary 199
Gibson, William Ford
  See Gibson, William
Gidal, Nachum
  See Gidal, Tim Nachum
Gidal, Sonia (Epstein) 1922- 2
Gidal, Tim Nachum 1909-1996 2
Gidalewitsch, Nachum
  See Gidal, Tim Nachum
Gideon, Melanie 1963- 175
Giegling, John A(llan) 1935- 17
Gifaldi, David 1950- 209
  Earlier sketch in SATA 76
Giff, Patricia Reilly 1935- 239
  Earlier sketches in SATA 33, 70, 121, 160,
  203
Giffard, Hannah 1962- 83

Gifford, Carrie 224
Gifford, Clive 1966- 198
Gifford, Griselda 1931- 171
  Earlier sketch in SATA 42
Gifford, Kerri 1961- 91
Gifford, Peggy 1952- 191
Gilani, Fawzia
  See Gilani-Williams, Fawzia
Gilani-Williams, Fawzia 1967- 231
Gilbert, Ann
  See Taylor, Ann
Gilbert, Anne Yvonne 1951- 185
Gilbert, Barbara Snow 1954- 97
Gilbert, Catherine
  See Murdock, Catherine Gilbert
Gilbert, Frances
  See Collings, Gillian
Gilbert, Harriett 1948- 30
Gilbert, (Agnes) Joan (Sewell) 1931- 10
Gilbert, John (Raphael) 1926- 36
Gilbert, Nan
  See Gilbertson, Mildred Geiger
Gilbert, Roby Goodale 1966- 90
Gilbert, Ruth Gallard Ainsworth
  See Ainsworth, Ruth (Gallard)
Gilbert, Sara (Dulaney) 1943- 82
  Earlier sketch in SATA 11
Gilbert, Sheri L. 157
Gilbert, Suzie 1956- 97
Gilbert, W(illiam) S(chwenck) 1836-1911 ... 36
Gilbert, Yvonne
  See Gilbert, Anne Yvonne
Gilbertson, Mildred Geiger 1908-1988 2
Gilbreath, Alice 1921- 12
Gilbreth, Frank B., Jr. 1911-2001 2
Gilbreth, Frank Bunker
  See Gilbreth, Frank B., Jr.
Gilchrist, Jan Spivey 1949- 130
  Earlier sketch in SATA 72
Gilden, Mel 1947- 97
Giles, Gail 196
  Earlier sketch in SATA 152
Giles, Stephen M. 236
Gilfond, Henry 2
Gilge, Jeanette 1924- 22
Gili, Phillida 1944- 70
Gill, Derek (Lewis Theodore) 1919-1997 9
Gill, Margery Jean 1925- 22
Gill, Shelley 176
Gill, Stephen 1932- 63
Gillespie, Carol Ann 1951- 158
Gillett, Mary (Bledsoe) 7
Gillette, Henry Sampson 1915- 14
Gillette, J. Lynett 1946- 103
Gillette, Jan Lynett
  See Gillette, J. Lynett
Gilley, Jeremy 1969- 174
Gillham, Bill
  See Gillham, W(illiam) E(dwin) C(harles)
Gillham, W(illiam) E(dwin) C(harles)
  1936- 42
Gilliam, Stan 1946- 39
  Brief entry 35
Gilliland, Alexis A. 1931- 72
Gilliland, Alexis Arnaldus
  See Gilliland, Alexis A.
Gilliland, (Cleburne) Hap 1918- 92
Gilliland, Judith Heide 180
Gillmor, Don 1954- 127
Gilman, Dorothy 1923- 5
Gilman, Esther 1925- 15
Gilman, Laura Anne 178
Gilman, Phoebe 1940-2002 104
  Obituary 141
  Earlier sketch in SATA 58
Gilmore, Iris 1900-1982 22
Gilmore, Kate 1931- 87
Gilmore, Mary (Jean Cameron) 1865-1962 . 49
Gilmore, Rachna 1953- 209
Gilmore, Susan 1954- 59

Gilpin, Stephen 213
  Earlier sketch in SATA 177
Gilroy, Beryl (Agatha) 1924- 80
Gilson, Barbara
  See Gilson, Charles James Louis
Gilson, Charles James Louis 1878-1943
  See YABC 2
Gilson, Jamie 1933- 176
  Brief entry 34
  Earlier sketches in SATA 37, 91
Gimpel, Carolyn
  See Hart, Carolyn
Ginsberg, Blaze 1987- 222
Ginsburg, Mirra 1909-2000 92
  Earlier sketch in SATA 6
  See also CLR 45
Giovanni, Nikki 1943- 208
  Earlier sketches in SATA 24, 107
  See also CLR 73
Giovanni, Yolanda Cornelia
  See Giovanni, Nikki
Giovanni, Yolande Cornelia
  See Giovanni, Nikki
Giovanni, Yolande Cornelia, Jr.
  See Giovanni, Nikki
Giovanopoulos, Paul (Arthur) 1939- 7
Gipson, Billie
  See Letts, Billie
Gipson, Fred(erick Benjamin) 1908-1973 2
  Obituary 24
Girard, Linda (Walvoord) 1942- 41
Giraudon, David 1975- 215
Girion, Barbara 1937- 78
  Earlier sketch in SATA 26
  See also SAAS 14
Girl, Nerdy
  See Castellucci, Cecil
Girouard, Patrick 1957- 155
Girzone, Joseph F. 1930- 76
Girzone, Joseph Francis
  See Girzone, Joseph F.
Gise, Joanne
  See Mattern, Joanne
Gist, E.M. 206
Gittings, Jo (Grenville) Manton 1919- 3
Gittings, Robert (William Victor) 1911-1992 . 6
  Obituary 70
Givens, Janet E(aton) 1932- 60
Givner, Joan 1936- 171
Givner, Joan Mary
  See Givner, Joan
Gladstone, Eve
  See Werner, Herma
Gladstone, Gary 1935- 12
Gladstone, M(yron) J. 1923- 37
Glanville, Brian (Lester) 1931- 42
Glanzman, Louis S. 1922- 36
Glaser, Byron 1954- 154
Glaser, Dianne E(lizabeth) 1937- 50
  Brief entry 31
Glaser, Isabel Joshlin 1929- 94
Glaser, Linda 225
Glaser, Milton 1929- 151
  Earlier sketch in SATA 11
Glaser, Shirley 151
Glaspell, Susan 1882(?)-1948
  See YABC 2
Glass, Andrew 1949- 223
  Brief entry 46
  Earlier sketches in SATA 90, 150
Glass, Linzi 175
Glass, Linzi Alex
  See Glass, Linzi
Glasscock, Amnesia
  See Steinbeck, John
Glasser, Robin Preiss 1956- 235
Glassman, Bruce 1961- 76
Glatt, Lisa 1963- 217
Glauber, Uta (Heil) 1936- 17
Glazer, Thomas (Zachariah) 1914-2003 9

Glazer, Tom
  See Glazer, Thomas (Zachariah)
Gleasner, Diana (Cottle) 1936- 29
Gleason, Judith 1929- 24
Gleason, Katherine (A.) 1960- 104
Gleeson, Libby 1950- 142
  Autobiography Feature 142
  Earlier sketches in SATA *82, 118*
Gleiter, Jan 1947- *111*
Gleitzman, Morris 1953- 234
  Earlier sketches in SATA *88, 156*
  See also CLR 88
Glen, Maggie 1944- 88
Glendinning, Richard 1917-1988 24
Glendinning, Sally
  See Glendinning, Sara W(ilson)
Glendinning, Sara W(ilson) 1913-1993 24
Glenn, John W. 195
Glenn, Mel 1943- 93
  Brief entry 45
  Earlier sketch in SATA *51*
  See also CLR *51*
Glenn, Patricia Brown 1953- 86
Glenn, Sharlee 159
Glenn, Sharlee Mullins
  See Glenn, Sharlee
Glennon, Karen M. 1946- 85
Gles, Margaret Breitmaier 1940- 22
Glick, Carl (Cannon) 1890-1971 14
Glick, Ruth 1942- 125
Glick, Ruth Burtnick
  See Glick, Ruth
Glick, Virginia Kirkus 1893-1980
  Obituary 23
Gliewe, Unada (Grace) 1927- 3
Glimmerveen, Ulco 1958- 85
Glines, Carroll V(ane), Jr. 1920- 19
Gliori, Debi 1959- 238
  Earlier sketches in SATA *72, 138, 189*
Globe, Leah Ain 1900- 41
Glori Ann
  See Blakely, Gloria
Glovach, Linda 1947- 105
  Earlier sketch in SATA 7
Glover, Denis (James Matthews) 1912-1980 . 7
Glubok, Shirley (Astor) 146
  Autobiography Feature 146
  Earlier sketches in SATA *6, 68*
  See also CLR *1*
  See also SAAS 7
Gluck, Felix 1923-1981
  Obituary 25
Glyman, Caroline A. 1967- 103
Glynne-Jones, William 1907-1977 11
Gobbato, Imero 1923- 39
Gobbletree, Richard
  See Quackenbush, Robert M(ead)
Goble, Dorothy 26
Goble, Paul 1933- *131*
  Earlier sketches in SATA *25, 69*
  See also CLR *21*
Goble, Warwick (?)-1943 46
Godden, (Margaret) Rumer 1907-1998 36
  Obituary 109
  Earlier sketch in SATA *3*
  See also CLR *20*
  See also SAAS *12*
Gode, Alexander
  See Gode von Aesch, Alexander (Gottfried
    Friedrich)
Gode von Aesch, Alexander (Gottfried
  Friedrich) 1906-1970 14
Godfrey, Jane
  See Bowden, Joan Chase
Godfrey, Martyn
  See Godfrey, Martyn N.
  and Godfrey, Martyn N.
Godfrey, Martyn N. 1949-2000 95
  See also CLR *57*
Godfrey, William
  See Youd, Samuel

Godkin, Celia 1948- *145*
  Earlier sketch in SATA *66*
Godkin, Celia Marilyn
  See Godkin, Celia
Godon, Ingrid 1958- *186*
Godown, Jan
  See Annino, Jan Godown
Godwin, Laura 1956- *179*
Godwin, Sam
  See Pirotta, Saviour
Godwin, Sarah Massini
  See Massini, Sarah
Goede, Irene 1966- 208
Goedecke, Christopher (John) 1951- 81
Goekler, Susan
  See Wooley, Susan Frelick
Goembel, Ponder 204
Goertzen, Glenda *172*
Goettel, Elinor 1930- *12*
Goetz, Delia 1898-1996 22
  Obituary 91
Goffe, Toni 1936- 61
Goffstein, Brooke
  See Goffstein, Marilyn Brooke
Goffstein, M. B.
  See Goffstein, Marilyn Brooke
Goffstein, Marilyn Brooke 1940- 70
  Earlier sketch in SATA *8*
  See also CLR *3*
Goforth, Ellen
  See Francis, Dorothy
Gogol, Sara 1948-2004 80
Goh, Chan Hon 1969- *145*
Going, Kelly L.
  See Going, K.L.
Going, Kelly Louise
  See Going, K.L.
Going, K.L. *199*
  Earlier sketch in SATA *156*
Golann, Cecil Paige 1921-1995 11
Golbin, Andree 1923- 15
Gold, Alison Leslie 1945- *104*
Gold, August 1955- 215
Gold, Bernice *150*
Gold, Phyllis
  See Goldberg, Phyllis
Gold, Robert S(tanley) 1924- 63
Gold, Sharlya 9
Gold, Susan
  See Gold, Susan Dudley
Gold, Susan Dudley 1949- *147*
Goldbach, Veronica 1980- 220
Goldberg, Grace 1956- 78
Goldberg, Herbert S. 1926- 25
Goldberg, Jacob 1943- 94
Goldberg, Jake
  See Goldberg, Jacob
Goldberg, Myla 1972(?)- 210
Goldberg, Phyllis 1941- 21
Goldberg, Stan J. 1939- 26
Goldberg, Susan 1948- 71
Goldberg, Whoopi 1955- 119
Goldberger, Judith M. 1948- 80
Goldblatt, Stacey 1969(?)- *191*
Golden, Christie 1963- *167*
  Earlier sketch in SATA *116*
Goldentyer, Debra 1960- 84
Goldfeder, Cheryl
  See Pahz, Cheryl Suzanne
Goldfeder, James
  See Pahz, James Alon
Goldfeder, Jim
  See Pahz, James Alon
Goldfinger, Jennifer P. 1963- *185*
Goldfrank, Helen Colodny 1912- 6
Goldin, Augusta 1906-1999 13
Goldin, Barbara Diamond 1946- *129*
  Autobiography Feature *129*
  Earlier sketch in SATA *92*
  See also SAAS *26*
Goldin, David 1963- *101*

Golding, Julia 1969- *188*
Golding, Theresa Martin 1960- *150*
Golding, William 1911-1993
  See CLR *130*
Golding, William Gerald
  See Golding, William
Goldman, Alex J. 1917- 65
Goldman, E. M. 1943- *103*
Goldman, Eleanor Maureen
  See Goldman, E. M.
Goldman, Elizabeth 1949- 90
Goldman, Judy 1955- 212
Goldman, Steven 1964- 207
Goldman, Todd Harris 221
Goldring, Ann 1937- *149*
Golds, Cassandra 1962- 226
Goldsborough, June 1923- *19*
Goldschmidt, Judy 202
Goldsmith, Connie 1945- *147*
Goldsmith, Howard 1943- *108*
  Earlier sketch in SATA *24*
Goldsmith, John Herman Thorburn 1903-1987
  Obituary 52
Goldsmith, Oliver 1730(?)-1774 26
Goldsmith, Ruth M. 1919- 62
Goldstein, Nathan 1927- 47
Goldstein, Philip 1910-1997 23
Goldston, Robert (Conroy) 1927- 6
Goldstone, Bruce *183*
Goldstone, Lawrence A.
  See Treat, Lawrence
Goldszmit, Henryk 1878-1942 65
  See also CLR *152*
Golembe, Carla 1951- 79
Golenbock, Peter 1946- 99
Goll, Reinhold W(eimar) 1897-1993 26
Gollub, Matthew 1960- *134*
  Earlier sketch in SATA *83*
Golson, Terry 213
Golson, Terry Blonder
  See Golson, Terry
Gomes, Filomena 1965- *183*
Gomez, Elena *191*
Gomez, Elizabeth *133*
Gomez-Freer, Elizabeth
  See Gomez, Elizabeth
Gomi, Taro 1945- *103*
  Earlier sketch in SATA *64*
  See also CLR *57*
Gondosch, Linda 1944- 58
Gonsalves, Rob 1959- 209
Gonyea, Mark 236
  Earlier sketch in SATA *194*
Gonzales, Chuck 230
Gonzalez, Catherine Troxell 1917-2000 87
Gonzalez, Christina
  See Gonzalez, Maya Christina
Gonzalez, Christina Diaz 1969- 231
Gonzalez, Gloria 1940- 23
Gonzalez, Julie 1958- *174*
Gonzalez, Julie Sehers
  See Gonzalez, Julie
Gonzalez, Lucia M. 1957- 202
Gonzalez, Maya
  See Gonzalez, Maya Christina
Gonzalez, Maya Christina 1964- *175*
  Earlier sketch in SATA *115*
Gonzalez, Rigoberto 1970- *147*
Gonzalez, Thomas 1959- 237
Goobie, Beth 1959- *128*
Good, Alice 1950- 73
Good, Clare
  See Romano, Clare
Good, Karen Hillard 214
Goodall, Daphne Machin
  See Machin Goodall, Daphne (Edith)
Goodall, Jane 1934- *111*
Goodall, John S(trickland) 1908-1996 66
  Obituary 91
  Earlier sketch in SATA *4*
  See also CLR *25*

Goodbody, Slim
    See Burstein, John
Goode, Diane 1949- 225
    Earlier sketches in SATA *15, 84, 114, 170*
Goode, Diane Capuozzo
    See Goode, Diane
Goode, Stephen Ray 1943- 55
    Brief entry 40
Goodenow, Earle 1913- 40
Goodhart, Pippa 1958- 196
    Earlier sketch in SATA *153*
Goodhue, Thomas W. 1949- 143
Goodin, Sallie (Brown) 1953- 74
Goodman, Alison 1966- 111
Goodman, Deborah Lerme 1956- 50
    Brief entry 49
Goodman, Elaine 1930- 9
Goodman, Emily 217
Goodman, Joan Elizabeth 1950- 162
    Earlier sketches in SATA *50, 94*
Goodman, Shawn 1970- 238
Goodman, Susan E. 1952- 181
Goodman, Walter 1927-2002 9
Goodman Koz, Paula 211
Goodrich, Carter 1959(?)- 221
Goodrich, Samuel Griswold 1793-1860 23
Goodsell, Jane Neuberger 1921(?)-1988
    Obituary 56
Goodweather, Hartley
    See King, Thomas
GoodWeather, Hartley
    See King, Thomas
Goodwin, Hal
    See Goodwin, Harold L(eland)
Goodwin, Harold L(eland) 1914-1990 51
    Obituary 65
    Earlier sketch in SATA *13*
Goodwin, William 1943- 117
Goor, Nancy (Ruth Miller) 1944- 39
    Brief entry 34
Goor, Ron(ald Stephen) 1940- 39
    Brief entry 34
Goossen, Agnes
    See Epp, Margaret A(gnes)
Goossens, Philippe 1963- 195
Gootman, Marilyn E. 1944- 179
Gopnik, Adam 1956- 171
Gorbachev, Valeri 1944- 222
    Autobiography Feature 143
    Earlier sketches in SATA *98, 143, 184*
Gordion, Mark
    See Turtledove, Harry
Gordon, Ad
    See Hano, Arnold
Gordon, Amy 1949- 197
    Earlier sketches in SATA *115, 156*
Gordon, Bernard Ludwig 1931-2010 27
Gordon, Colonel H. R.
    See Ellis, Edward S.
Gordon, David
    See Garrett, Randall
Gordon, Donald
    See Payne, Donald Gordon
Gordon, Dorothy 1893-1970 20
Gordon, Esther S(aranga) 1935- 10
Gordon, Frederick 1
Gordon, Gaelyn 1939-1997
    See CLR 75
Gordon, Garrett
    See Garrett, Randall
Gordon, Gary
    See Edmonds, I(vy) G(ordon)
Gordon, Hal
    See Goodwin, Harold L(eland)
Gordon, Jeffie Ross
    See Enderle, Judith (Ann) Ross
    and Gordon, Stephanie Jacob
Gordon, John
    See Gesner, Clark
Gordon, John (William) 1925- 84

Gordon, Lew
    See Baldwin, Gordon C(ortis)
Gordon, Margaret (Anna) 1939- 9
Gordon, Mike 1948- 101
Gordon, Mildred 1912-1979
    Obituary 24
Gordon, Selma
    See Lanes, Selma G.
Gordon, Sheila 1927- 88
    See also CLR 27
Gordon, Shirley 1921- 48
    Brief entry 41
Gordon, Sol 1923- 11
Gordon, Stephanie Jacob 1940- 89
    Autobiography Feature 114
    Earlier sketch in SATA *64*
    See also SAAS 26
Gordon, Stewart
    See Shirreffs, Gordon D(onald)
Gordons, The
    See Gordon, Mildred
    and Gordon, Gordon
Gore, Leonid 222
    Earlier sketch in SATA *185*
Gorelick, Molly C(hernow) 1920-2003 9
    Obituary 153
Gorey, Edward (St. John) 1925-2000 70
    Brief entry 27
    Obituary 118
    Earlier sketch in SATA *29*
    See also CLR 36
Gorham, Charles Orson 1868-1936 36
Gorham, Michael
    See Folsom, Franklin (Brewster)
Gorman, Carol 187
    Earlier sketch in SATA *150*
Gorman, Jacqueline Laks 1955- 148
Gorman, Mike 206
Gormley, Beatrice 1942- 202
    Brief entry 35
    Earlier sketches in SATA *39, 127*
Gorog, Judith (Katharine Allen) 1938- 75
    Earlier sketch in SATA *39*
Gorrell, Gena K. 1946- 170
Gorsline, Douglas (Warner) 1913-1985 11
    Obituary 43
Gorsline, (Sally) Marie 1928- 28
Gorsline, S. M.
    See Gorsline, (Sally) Marie
Gorton, Julia 218
Gorton, Kaitlyn
    See Emerson, Kathy Lynn
Gorton, Kathy Lynn
    See Emerson, Kathy Lynn
Goryan, Sirak
    See Saroyan, William
Goschke, Julia 1973- 208
Goscinny, Rene 1926-1977 47
    Brief entry 39
    See also CLR 37
Goss, Clay(ton E.) 1946- 82
Goss, Gary 1947- 124
Goss, Mini 1963- 186
Gosselink, John 1967- 238
Goto, Scott 203
Gott, Barry 197
Gottesman, S. D.
    See Kornbluth, C(yril) M.
    and Lowndes, Robert A(ugustine) W(ard)
    and Pohl, Frederik
Gottfried, Ted
    See Gottfried, Theodore Mark
Gottfried, Theodore Mark 1928- 150
    Earlier sketch in SATA *85*
Gottlieb, Gerald 1923- 7
Gottlieb, William P. 1917-2006 24
Gottlieb, William Paul
    See Gottlieb, William P.
Goudey, Alice E(dwards) 1898-1993 20
Goudge, Eileen 1950- 88

Goudge, Elizabeth (de Beauchamp)
    1900-1984 2
    Obituary 38
    See also CLR 94
Gough, Catherine
    See Mulgan, Catherine
Gough, Philip 1908-1986 45
Gough, Sue 1940- 106
Goulart, Ron 1933- 67
    Earlier sketch in SATA *1*
Goulart, Ronald Joseph
    See Goulart, Ron
Gould, Alberta 1945- 96
Gould, Chester 1900-1985 49
    Obituary 43
Gould, Jean R(osalind) 1909-1993 11
    Obituary 77
Gould, Lilian 6
Gould, Marilyn 1928- 76
    Earlier sketch in SATA *15*
Gould, Robert 154
Gould, Steven 1955- 95
Gould, Steven Charles
    See Gould, Steven
Gourlay, Candy 239
Gourley, Catherine 1950- 190
    Earlier sketch in SATA *95*
Gourse, Leslie 1939-2004 89
Govan, (Mary) Christine Noble 1898-1985 ... 9
Gove, Doris 1944- 72
Govenar, Alan 1952- 189
Govenar, Alan Bruce
    See Govenar, Alan
Govern, Elaine 1939- 26
Gow, Nancy 238
Gowen, L. Kris 1968- 156
Graaf, Peter
    See Youd, Samuel
Grab, Daphne 1971- 233
Grabenstein, Chris 1955- 238
Graber, Alexander 1914-1997 98
    Earlier sketch in SATA *7*
Graber, George Alexander
    See Graber, Alexander
Graber, Janet 1942- 170
Graber, Richard (Fredrick) 1927- 26
Grabianski, Janusz 1928-1976 39
    Obituary 30
Graboff, Abner 1919-1986 35
Grace, Fran(ces Jane) 45
Grace, N.B.
    See Harper, Suzanne
Grace, Theresa
    See Mattern, Joanne
Gracza, Margaret Young 1928- 56
Graduate of Oxford, A
    See Ruskin, John
Grady, Denise 1952- 189
Graeber, Charlotte Towner 106
    Brief entry 44
    Earlier sketch in SATA *56*
Graef, Renee 1956- 204
Graeme, Roderic
    See Jeffries, Roderic
Graf, Michael
    See Graf, Mike
Graf, Mike 1960- 164
Grafe, Max 198
Graff, Lisa 1981- 235
    Earlier sketch in SATA *188*
Graff, Polly Anne Colver
    See Colver, Anne
Graff, (S.) Stewart 1908-2009 9
Graham, Ada 1931- 11
Graham, Alastair 1945- 74
Graham, Arthur Kennon
    See Harrison, David L.
Graham, Bob 1942- 187
    Earlier sketches in SATA *63, 101, 151*
    See also CLR 31
Graham, Brenda Knight 1942- 32

Graham, Charlotte
  See Bowden, Joan Chase
Graham, Christine 1952- 224
Graham, Eleanor 1896-1984 18
  Obituary 38
Graham, Ennis
  See Molesworth, Mary Louisa
Graham, Frank, Jr. 1925- 11
Graham, Georgia 1959- 190
Graham, Ian 1953- 229
  Earlier sketch in SATA *112*
Graham, John 1926-2007 11
Graham, Kennon
  See Harrison, David L.
Graham, Larry
  See Graham, Lawrence
Graham, Lawrence 1962- 63
Graham, Lawrence Otis
  See Graham, Lawrence
Graham, Linda
  See Graham-Barber, Lynda
Graham, Lorenz (Bell) 1902-1989 74
  Obituary 63
  Earlier sketch in SATA *2*
  See also CLR *10*
  See also SAAS *5*
Graham, Margaret Bloy 1920- 11
Graham, Robin Lee 1949- 7
Graham, Rosemary 236
Graham, Shirley 1896(?)-1977
  See Du Bois, Shirley Graham
Graham-Barber, Lynda 1944- 159
  Earlier sketch in SATA *42*
Graham-Cameron, M.
  See Graham-Cameron, M(alcolm) G(ordon)
Graham-Cameron, M(alcolm) G(ordon)
  1931- 53
  Brief entry 45
Graham-Cameron, Mike
  See Graham-Cameron, M(alcolm) G(ordon)
Grahame, Kenneth 1859-1932 100
  See also YABC *1*
  See also CLR *135*
Gralley, Jean 166
Gramatky, Hardie 1907-1979 30
  Obituary 23
  Earlier sketch in SATA *1*
  See also CLR *22*
Grambling, Lois G. 1927- 206
  Earlier sketches in SATA *71, 148*
Grambo, Rebecca L(ynn) 1963- 109
Grammer, June Amos 1927- 58
Grand, Samuel 1912-1988 42
Grandits, John 1949- 192
GrandPre, Mary 1954- 229
  Earlier sketch in SATA *184*
Grandville, J. J.
  See Gerard, Jean Ignace Isidore
Grandville, Jean Ignace Isidore Gerard
  See Gerard, Jean Ignace Isidore
Granfield, Linda 1950- 160
  Earlier sketch in SATA *96*
Grange, Peter
  See Nicole, Christopher
Granger, Margaret Jane 1925(?)-1977
  Obituary 27
Granger, Michele 1949- 88
Granger, Peggy
  See Granger, Margaret Jane
Granowsky, Alvin 1936- 101
Granstaff, Bill 1925- 10
Granstrom, Brita 1969- 224
  Earlier sketches in SATA *111, 167*
Grant, Bruce 1893-1977 5
  Obituary 25
Grant, Cynthia D. 1950- 147
  Earlier sketches in SATA *33, 77*
Grant, Eva 1907-1996 7
Grant, Evva H. 1913-1977
  Obituary 27
Grant, Gordon 1875-1962 25

Grant, Gwen(doline Ellen) 1940- 47
Grant, Judyann Ackerman 211
Grant, Katie
  See Grant, K.M.
Grant, Katie M.
  See Grant, K.M.
Grant, Katy 238
Grant, K.M. 230
  Earlier sketch in SATA *175*
Grant, (Alice) Leigh 1947- 10
Grant, Matthew G.
  See May, Julian
Grant, Maxwell
  See Gibson, Walter B(rown)
  and Lynds, Dennis
Grant, Melvyn 183
Grant, Myrna (Lois) 1934- 21
Grant, Neil 1938- 154
  Earlier sketch in SATA *14*
Grant, Nicholas
  See Nicole, Christopher
Grant, Richard 1948- 80
Grant, Skeeter
  See Spiegelman, Art
Grater, Michael 1923- 57
Gratz, Alan 1972- 212
Graullera, Fabiola
  See Graullera Ramirez, Fabiola
Graullera Ramirez, Fabiola 225
Gravel, Fern
  See Hall, James Norman
Gravelle, Karen 1942- 166
  Earlier sketch in SATA *78*
Graves, Charles Parlin 1911-1972 4
Graves, Keith 191
  Earlier sketch in SATA *156*
Graves, Robert 1895-1985 45
Graves, Robert von Ranke
  See Graves, Robert
Graves, Valerie
  See Bradley, Marion Zimmer
Gravett, Emily 1972(?)- 232
  Earlier sketch in SATA *189*
Gray, Betsy
  See Poole, Gray Johnson
Gray, Caroline
  See Nicole, Christopher
Gray, Claudia 213
Gray, Dianne E. 183
Gray, Elizabeth Janet
  See Vining, Elizabeth Gray
Gray, Genevieve S(tuck) 1920-1995 4
Gray, Harold (Lincoln) 1894-1968 33
  Brief entry 32
Gray, Jenny
  See Gray, Genevieve S(tuck)
Gray, John Lee
  See Jakes, John
Gray, Judith A. 1949- 93
Gray, Judith Anne
  See Gray, Judith A.
Gray, Keith 1972- 151
Gray, Kes 1960- 153
Gray, Les 1929- 82
Gray, Libba Moore 1937- 83
Gray, Luli 1945- 149
  Earlier sketch in SATA *90*
Gray, Marian
  See Pierce, Edith Gray
Gray, Nicholas Stuart 1922-1981 4
  Obituary 27
Gray, Nigel 1941- 104
  Earlier sketch in SATA *33*
Gray, (Lucy) Noel (Clervaux) 1898-1983 47
Gray, Patricia (Clark) 7
Gray, Patsey
  See Gray, Patricia (Clark)
Gray, Rita 184
Gray, Serena
  See Sheldon, Dyan
Gray, Steve 1950- 231

Graydon, Shari 1958- 158
Grayland, V. Merle
  See Grayland, Valerie (Merle Spanner)
Grayland, Valerie (Merle Spanner) 7
Grayson, Devin (Kalile) 1970- 119
Grayson, Kristine
  See Rusch, Kristine Kathryn
Grayson, Paul 1946- 79
Graystone, Lynn
  See Brennan, Joseph Lomas
Great Comte, The
  See Hawkesworth, Eric
Greaves, Margaret 1914-1995 87
  Earlier sketch in SATA *7*
Greaves, Nick 1955- 77
Greban, Quentin 1977- 223
Gree, Alain 1936- 28
Green, Adam
  See Weisgard, Leonard (Joseph)
Green, Anne Canevari 1943- 62
Green, Brian
  See Card, Orson Scott
Green, Cliff(ord) 1934- 126
Green, Connie Jordan 1938- 80
Green, D.
  See Casewit, Curtis W(erner)
Green, Elizabeth Shippen 1871-1954 139
Green, Hannah
  See Greenberg, Joanne (Goldenberg)
Green, Jane 1937- 9
Green, Jessica 211
Green, John 1977(?)- 235
  Earlier sketch in SATA *170*
Green, Mary Moore 1906- 11
Green, Morton 1937- 8
Green, Norma B(erger) 1925- 11
Green, Phyllis 1932- 20
Green, Roger (Gilbert) Lancelyn 1918-1987 . 2
  Obituary 53
Green, (James Le)Roy 1948- 89
Green, Sheila Ellen 1934- 148
  Earlier sketches in SATA *8, 87*
Green, Timothy 1953- 91
Greenaway, Kate 1846-1901 100
  See also YABC *2*
  See also CLR *111*
Greenbank, Anthony Hunt 1933- 39
Greenberg, David 1954- 171
Greenberg, David T.
  See Greenberg, David
Greenberg, Harvey R. 1935- 5
Greenberg, Jan 1942- 211
  Earlier sketches in SATA *61, 125*
Greenberg, Joanne (Goldenberg) 1932- 25
Greenberg, Melanie Hope 1954- 214
  Earlier sketch in SATA *72*
Greenberg, Polly 1932- 52
  Brief entry 43
Greenblat, Rodney Alan 1960- 106
Greenburg, Dan 1936- 175
  Earlier sketch in SATA *102*
Greene, Bette 1934- 161
  Earlier sketches in SATA *8, 102*
  See also CLR *140*
  See also SAAS *16*
Greene, Carla 1916- 67
  Earlier sketch in SATA *1*
Greene, Carol 102
  Brief entry 44
  Earlier sketch in SATA *66*
Greene, Constance C(larke) 1924- 72
  Earlier sketch in SATA *11*
  See also CLR *62*
  See also SAAS *11*
Greene, Edgar
  See Papademetriou, Lisa
Greene, Ellin 1927- 23
Greene, Graham 1904-1991 20
Greene, Graham Henry
  See Greene, Graham

Greene, Jacqueline Dembar 1946- *212*
  Earlier sketches in SATA *76, 131*
Greene, Laura Offenhartz 1935- *38*
Greene, Meg
  See Malvasi, Meg Greene
Greene, Michele 1962- *178*
Greene, Michele Dominguez
  See Greene, Michele
Greene, Rhonda Gowler 1955- *235*
  Earlier sketches in SATA *101, 160*
Greene, Stephanie 1950- *221*
  Earlier sketches in SATA *127, 173*
Greene, Wade 1933- *11*
Greene, Yvonne
  See Flesch, Yolande
Greenfeld, Howard (Scheinman) 1928- *140*
  Earlier sketch in SATA *19*
Greenfeld, Josh(ua Joseph) 1928- *62*
Greenfield, Eloise 1929- *155*
  Earlier sketches in SATA *19, 61, 105*
  See also CLR *38*
  See also SAAS *16*
Greenhaus, Thelma Nurenberg 1903-1984
  Obituary *45*
Greenhut, Josh
  See Mercer, Sienna
Greening, Hamilton
  See Hamilton, Charles (Harold St. John)
Greenlaw, M. Jean 1941- *107*
Greenleaf, Barbara Kaye 1942- *6*
Greenleaf, Peter 1910-1997 .... *33*
Greenlee, Sharon 1935- *77*
Greeno, Gayle 1949- *81*
Greenseid, Diane 1948- *178*
  Earlier sketch in SATA *93*
Greenspun, Adele Aron 1938- *142*
  Earlier sketch in SATA *76*
Greenstein, Elaine 1959- *150*
  Earlier sketch in SATA *82*
Greenwald, Sheila
  See Green, Sheila Ellen
Greenwood, Barbara 1940- *129*
  Earlier sketch in SATA *90*
Greenwood, Mark 1958- *202*
Greenwood, Pamela D. 1944- *115*
Greer, Richard
  See Garrett, Randall
  and Silverberg, Robert
Gregg, Andrew K. 1929- *81*
Gregg, Charles T(hornton) 1927- *65*
Gregg, Walter H(arold) 1919- *20*
Gregor, Arthur 1923- *36*
Gregor, Lee
  See Pohl, Frederik
Gregori, Leon 1919- *15*
Gregorian, Joyce Ballou 1946-1991 .... *30*
  Obituary *83*
Gregorich, Barbara 1943- *184*
  Earlier sketch in SATA *66*
Gregorowski, Christopher 1940- *30*
Gregory, Diana (Jean) 1933- *49*
  Brief entry *42*
Gregory, Harry
  See Gottfried, Theodore Mark
Gregory, Jean
  See Ure, Jean
Gregory, Kristiana 1951- *212*
  Earlier sketches in SATA *74, 136*
Gregory, Nan 1944- *192*
  Earlier sketch in SATA *148*
Gregory, Philippa 1954- *122*
Gregory, Stephen
  See Penzler, Otto
Gregory, Valiska 1940- *82*
Greif, Jean-Jacques 1944- *195*
Greisman, Joan Ruth 1937- *31*
Grendon, Stephen
  See Derleth, August (William)
Grenville, Pelham
  See Wodehouse, P. G.
Gretz, Susanna 1937- *7*

Gretzer, John *18*
Grewdead, Roy
  See Gorey, Edward (St. John)
Grey, Carol
  See Lowndes, Robert A(ugustine) W(ard)
Grey, Christopher *191*
Grey, Christopher Peter
  See Grey, Christopher
Grey, Jerry 1926- *11*
Grey, Mini *239*
  Earlier sketches in SATA *166, 205*
Greybeard the Pirate
  See Macintosh, Brownie
Grey Owl
  See Belaney, Archibald Stansfeld
Gri
  See Denney, Diana
Gribbin, John 1946- *159*
Gribbin, John R.
  See Gribbin, John
Grice, Frederick 1910-1983 .... *6*
Grider, Dorothy 1915- *31*
Gridley, Marion E(leanor) 1906-1974 .... *35*
  Obituary *26*
Grieco-Tiso, Pina 1954- *108*
Grieder, Walter 1924- *9*
Griego, Tony A. 1955- *77*
Griese, Arnold A(lfred) 1921- *9*
Griessman, Annette 1962- *170*
  Earlier sketch in SATA *116*
Grieve, James 1934- *146*
Grifalconi, Ann 1929- *210*
  Earlier sketches in SATA *2, 66, 133*
  See also CLR *35*
  See also SAAS *16*
Griffin, Adele 1970- *236*
  Earlier sketches in SATA *105, 153, 195*
Griffin, Elizabeth May 1985- *89*
Griffin, Gillett Good 1928- *26*
Griffin, Judith Berry *34*
Griffin, Kitty 1951- *137*
Griffin, Peni R. 1961- *193*
  Earlier sketches in SATA *67, 99*
Griffin, Steven A. 1953- *89*
Griffin, Steven Arthur
  See Griffin, Steven A.
Griffin, W. E. B. 1929- *5*
Griffith, Connie 1946- *89*
Griffith, Gershom 1960- *85*
Griffith, Helen V. 1934- *87*
  Autobiography Feature *107*
  Earlier sketch in SATA *39*
Griffith, Helen Virginia
  See Griffith, Helen V.
Griffith, Jeannette
  See Eyerly, Jeannette
Griffith, Saul 1974- *200*
Griffiths, Andy 1961- *196*
  Earlier sketch in SATA *152*
Griffiths, G(ordon) D(ouglas) 1910-1973
  Obituary *20*
Griffiths, Helen 1939- *86*
  Earlier sketch in SATA *5*
  See also CLR *75*
  See also SAAS *5*
Grigsby, Susan *235*
Grigson, Jane (McIntire) 1928-1990 .... *63*
Grimes, Lee 1920- *68*
Grimes, Nikki 1950- *218*
  Earlier sketches in SATA *93, 136, 174*
  See also CLR *42*
Grimly, Gris *186*
Grimm, Jacob Ludwig Karl 1785-1863 .... *22*
  See also CLR *112*
Grimm, Wilhelm Karl 1786-1859 .... *22*
  See also CLR *112*
Grimm, William C(arey) 1907-1992 .... *14*
Grimm and Grim
  See Grimm, Jacob Ludwig Karl
  and Grimm, Wilhelm Karl

Grimm Brothers
  See Grimm, Jacob Ludwig Karl
  and Grimm, Wilhelm Karl
Grimsdell, Jeremy 1942- *83*
Grimshaw, Nigel (Gilroy) 1925- *23*
Grimsley, Gordon
  See Groom, Arthur William
Grindley, Jane Sally
  See Grindley, Sally
Grindley, Sally 1953- *148*
Gringhuis, Dirk
  See Gringhuis, Richard H.
Gringhuis, Richard H. 1918-1974 .... *6*
  Obituary *25*
Grinnell, David
  See Wollheim, Donald A(llen)
Grinnell, George Bird 1849-1938 .... *16*
Grinspoon, David
  See Grinspoon, David H.
Grinspoon, David H. 1959- *156*
Grinspoon, David Harry
  See Grinspoon, David H.
Gripe, Maria 1923- *74*
  Earlier sketch in SATA *2*
  See also CLR *5*
Gripe, Maria Kristina
  See Gripe, Maria
Gritton, Steve *223*
Grobler, Piet 1959- *201*
Groch, Judith (Goldstein) 1929- *25*
Grode, Redway
  See Gorey, Edward (St. John)
Groener, Carl
  See Lowndes, Robert A(ugustine) W(ard)
Groening, Matt 1954- *116*
  Earlier sketch in SATA *81*
Grohmann, Susan 1948- *84*
Grohskopf, Bernice *7*
Grol, Lini R(icharda) 1913- *9*
Grollman, Earl A. 1925- *22*
Groom, Arthur William 1898-1964 .... *10*
Grooms, Duffy 1964- *169*
Gross, Alan 1947- *54*
  Brief entry *43*
Gross, Ernie 1913- *67*
Gross, Philip 1952- *164*
  Earlier sketch in SATA *84*
Gross, Philip John
  See Gross, Philip
Gross, Ruth Belov 1929- *33*
Gross, Sarah Chokla 1906-1976 .... *9*
  Obituary *26*
Grosser, Morton 1931- *74*
Grosser, Vicky 1958- *83*
Grossman, Bill 1948- *126*
  Earlier sketch in SATA *72*
Grossman, Nancy 1940- *29*
Grossman, Patricia 1951- *73*
Grossman, Robert 1940- *11*
Grossmann-Hensel, Katharina 1973- *219*
Grote, JoAnn A. 1951- *113*
Groten, Dallas 1951- *64*
Groth, John (August) 1908-1988 .... *21*
  Obituary *56*
Groth-Fleming, Candace
  See Fleming, Candace
Grove, Vicki 1948- *151*
  Autobiography Feature *151*
  Earlier sketch in SATA *122*
Grover, Lorie Ann 1964- *168*
Grover, Wayne 1934- *69*
Groves, Georgina
  See Symons, (Dorothy) Geraldine
Groves, Maketa 1950- *107*
Groves, Seli *77*
Grubb, Lisa *160*
Gruber, Michael 1940- *173*
Gruber, Terry (deRoy) 1953- *66*
Gruelle, John 1880-1938 .... *35*
  Brief entry *32*
  See also CLR *34*

Gruelle, Johnny
 See Gruelle, John
Gruenberg, Sidonie Matsner 1881-1974 2
 Obituary 27
Gruhzit-Hoyt, Olga (Margaret) 1922- 127
 Earlier sketch in SATA 16
Grummer, Arnold E(dward) 1923- 49
Gruner, Jessica 233
Grunewalt, Pine
 See Kunhardt, Edith
Grunwell, Jeanne Marie 1971- 147
Grupper, Jonathan 137
Gryski, Camilla 1948- 72
Guarino, Dagmar
 See Guarino, Deborah
Guarino, Deborah 1954- 68
Guarnaccia, Steven 233
Guay, Georgette (Marie Jeanne) 1952- 54
Guay, Rebecca 209
Guay-Mitchell, Rebecca
 See Guay, Rebecca
Guback, Georgia 88
Guccione, Leslie Davis 1946- 111
 Earlier sketch in SATA 72
Guck, Dorothy 1913-2002 27
Gudeon, Karla 212
Guerny, Gene
 See Gurney, Gene
Guest, Elissa Haden 1953- 218
 Earlier sketch in SATA 125
Guest, Jacqueline 1952- 135
Guevara, Susan 167
 Earlier sketch in SATA 97
Gugler, Laurel Dee 95
Gugliotta, Bobette 1918-1994 7
Guianan, Eve 1965- 102
Guiberson, Brenda Z. 1946- 211
 Earlier sketches in SATA 71, 124
Guibert, Emmanuel 1964- 181
Guile, Melanie 1949- 152
 Earlier sketch in SATA 104
Guillaume, Jeanette G. Flierl 1899-1990 8
Guillot, Rene 1900-1969 7
 See also CLR 22
Guisewite, Cathy 1950- 57
Guisewite, Cathy Lee
 See Guisewite, Cathy
Gulbis, Stephen 1959- 142
Gulley, Judie 1942- 58
Gump, P. Q.
 See Card, Orson Scott
Gundrey, Elizabeth 1924- 23
Gunn, James E. 1923- 35
Gunn, James Edwin
 See Gunn, James E.
Gunn, Robin Jones 1955- 84
Gunnella 1956- 197
Gunning, Monica Olwen 1930- 161
Gunston, Bill
 See Gunston, William Tudor
Gunston, William Tudor 1927- 9
Gunterman, Bertha Lisette 1886(?)-1975
 Obituary 27
Gunther, John 1901-1970
Guravich, Dan 1918- 74
Gurko, Leo 1914- 9
Gurko, Miriam 1910(?)-1988 9
 Obituary 58
Gurney, Gene 1924- 65
Gurney, James 1958- 120
 Earlier sketch in SATA 76
Gurney, John Steven 1962- 227
 Earlier sketches in SATA 75, 143
Gustafson, Sarah R.
 See Riedman, Sarah R(egal)
Gustafson, Scott 1956- 34
Gustavson, Adam 1974- 214
 Earlier sketch in SATA 176
Guthrie, A(lfred) B(ertram), Jr. 1901-1991 .. 62
 Obituary 67
Guthrie, Anne 1890-1979 28

Guthrie, Donna W. 1946- 105
 Earlier sketch in SATA 63
Gutierrez, Akemi 172
Gutierrez, Rudy 203
Gutman, Bill 128
 Brief entry 43
 Earlier sketch in SATA 67
Gutman, Dan 1955- 221
 Earlier sketches in SATA 77, 139, 188
Gutman, Naham 1899(?)-1981
 Obituary 25
Gutmann, Bessie Pease 1876-1960 73
Guy, Geoffrey 1942- 153
Guy, Ginger Foglesong 1954- 171
Guy, Rosa 1925- 122
 Earlier sketches in SATA 14, 62
 See also CLR 137
Guy, Rosa Cuthbert
 See Guy, Rosa
Guy, Susan 1948- 149
Guymer, (Wilhelmina) Mary 1909- 50
Guzman, Lila 1952- 168
Guzman, Rick 1957- 168
Gwaltney, Doris 1932- 181
Gwynne, Fred(erick Hubbard) 1926-1993 41
 Brief entry 27
 Obituary 75
Gwynne, Oscar A.
 See Ellis, Edward S.
Gwynne, Oswald A.
 See Ellis, Edward S.
Gyorkos, Charmaine Echeverria
 See Echeverria Gyorkos, Charmaine

H

Haab, Sherri 1964- 169
 Earlier sketch in SATA 91
Haar, Jaap ter
 See ter Haar, Jaap
Haarsma, P.J. 183
Haas, Carolyn Buhai 1926- 43
Haas, Dan 1957- 105
Haas, Dorothy F. 46
 Brief entry 43
 See also SAAS 17
Haas, Irene 1929- 96
 Earlier sketch in SATA 17
Haas, James E. 1943- 40
Haas, James Edward
 See Haas, James E.
Haas, Jessie 1959- 215
Haas, (Katherine) Jessie 1959- 135
 Autobiography Feature 135
 Earlier sketch in SATA 98
Haas, Merle S. 1896(?)-1985
 Obituary 41
Habenstreit, Barbara 1937- 5
Haber, Karen 1955- 78
Haber, Louis 1910-1988 12
Haber, Melissa Glenn 1969- 235
Hacker, Randi 1951- 185
Hacker, Randi Dawn
 See Hacker, Randi
Hackett, John Winthrop 1910-1997 65
Hacks, Peter 1928-2003
 Obituary 151
Hacohen, Dean 1958- 239
Haddix, Margaret Peterson 1964- 224
 Earlier sketches in SATA 94, 125, 187
Haddon, Mark 1962- 223
 Earlier sketch in SATA 155
Hader, Berta (Hoerner) 1891(?)-1976 16
Hader, Elmer (Stanley) 1889-1973 16
Hadithi, Mwenye
 See Hobson, Bruce
Hadley, Franklin
 See Winterbotham, R(ussell) R(obert)

Hadley, Lee 1934-1995 89
 Brief entry 38
 Obituary 86
 Earlier sketch in SATA 47
 See also CLR 40
 See also SAAS 14
Haeffele, Deborah 1954- 76
Haenel, Wolfram 1956- 89
 See also CLR 64
Hafner, Marylin 1925- 179
 Earlier sketches in SATA 7, 121
Haft, Erin
 See Ehrenhaft, Daniel
Hager, Alan 1940- 176
Hager, Alice Rogers 1894-1969
 Obituary 26
Hager, Betty 1923- 89
Hager, Jenna Bush
 See Bush, Jenna
Hager, Sarah 171
Hager, Thomas 1953- 119
Hager, Tom
 See Hager, Thomas
Hagerup, Klaus 1946- 186
Haggard, H(enry) Rider 1856-1925 16
Haggerty, James J(oseph) 1920- 5
Hagon, Priscilla
 See Allan, Mabel Esther
Hague, Kathleen 1949- 49
 Brief entry 45
Hague, Michael 1948- 185
 Brief entry 32
 Earlier sketches in SATA 48, 80, 129
Hague, Michael R.
 See Hague, Michael
Hague, Susan Kathleen
 See Hague, Kathleen
Hahn, Emily 1905-1997 3
 Obituary 96
Hahn, Hannelore 8
Hahn, James (Sage) 1947- 9
Hahn, Lynn 1949- 9
Hahn, Mary Downing 1937- 208
 Autobiography Feature 157
 Brief entry 44
 Earlier sketches in SATA 50, 81, 138, 157
 See also SAAS 12
Hahn, Michael T. 1953- 92
Hahn, Mona Lynn
 See Hahn, Lynn
Haig, Matt 1975- 221
Haig-Brown, Roderick (Langmere)
 1908-1976 12
 See also CLR 31
Haight, Anne Lyon 1895-1977
 Obituary 30
Haight, Rip
 See Carpenter, John
Haight, Sandy 1949- 79
Haij, Vera
 See Jansson, Tove (Marika)
Hailstone, Ruth 219
Haines, Gail Kay 1943- 11
Haines, Margaret Ann Beck
 See Beck, Peggy
Haining, Peter 1940-2007 14
 Obituary 188
Haining, Peter Alexander
 See Haining, Peter
Hains, Harriet
 See Watson, Carol
Hajdusiewicz, Babs Bell 163
Hakim, Joy 1931- 173
 Earlier sketch in SATA 83
Halacy, D. S., Jr. 1919-2002 36
 See also SAAS 8
Halacy, Dan
 See Halacy, D. S., Jr.
Halam, Ann
 See Jones, Gwyneth A.
Haldane, Roger John 1945- 13

Hale, Arlene 1924-1982 .... *49*
Hale, Bruce 1957- *203*
   Earlier sketch in SATA *123*
Hale, Christy
   See Apostolou, Christine Hale
Hale, Dean 1972- *227*
Hale, Edward Everett 1822-1909 .... *16*
Hale, Glenn
   See Walker, Robert W.
Hale, Helen
   See Mulcahy, Lucille Burnett
Hale, Irina 1932- *26*
Hale, Kathleen 1898-2000 .... *66*
   Obituary *121*
   Earlier sketch in SATA *17*
Hale, Linda (Howe) 1929- *6*
Hale, Lucretia P.
   See Hale, Lucretia Peabody
Hale, Lucretia Peabody 1820-1900 .... *26*
   See also CLR *105*
Hale, Marian *194*
Hale, Nancy 1908-1988 .... *31*
   Obituary *57*
Hale, Nathan 1976- *210*
Hale, Shannon *200*
   Earlier sketch in SATA *158*
Hale, Stephanie 1973- *232*
Haley, Amanda *205*
Haley, Gail E(inhart) 1939- *161*
   Autobiography Feature *161*
   Brief entry *28*
   Earlier sketches in SATA *43, 78, 136*
   See also CLR *21*
   See also SAAS *13*
Haley, Neale *52*
Halfmann, Janet 1944- *208*
Hall, Adam
   See Trevor, Elleston
Hall, Adele 1910- *7*
Hall, Anna Gertrude 1882-1967 .... *8*
Hall, August *207*
Hall, Barbara 1961- *68*
Hall, Becky 1950- *186*
Hall, Beverly B. 1918- *95*
Hall, Borden
   See Yates, Raymond F(rancis)
Hall, Brian P(atrick) 1935- *31*
Hall, Cameron
   See del Rey, Lester
Hall, Caryl
   See Hansen, Caryl (Hall)
Hall, Donald 1928- *97*
   Earlier sketch in SATA *23*
Hall, Donald Andrew, Jr.
   See Hall, Donald
Hall, Douglas 1931- *43*
Hall, Elizabeth 1929- *77*
Hall, Elvajean 1910-1984 .... *6*
Hall, Francie 1940- *166*
Hall, James Norman 1887-1951 .... *21*
Hall, Jesse
   See Boesen, Victor
Hall, Katy
   See McMullan, Kate
Hall, Kirsten Marie 1974- *67*
Hall, Lynn 1937- *79*
   Earlier sketches in SATA *2, 47*
   See also SAAS *4*
Hall, Malcolm 1945- *7*
Hall, Marcellus *203*
Hall, Marjory
   See Yeakley, Marjory Hall
Hall, Melanie 1949- *228*
   Earlier sketches in SATA *78, 116, 169*
Hall, Michael 1954- *228*
Hall, Patricia 1940- *136*
Hall, Rosalys Haskell 1914- *7*
Hall, Teri *229*
Hall, Willis 1929-2005 .... *66*
Hallard, Peter
   See Catherall, Arthur

Hallas, Richard
   See Knight, Eric
Hall-Clarke, James
   See Rowland-Entwistle, (Arthur) Theodore
   (Henry)
Hallensleben, Georg 1958- *173*
Haller, Dorcas Woodbury 1946- *46*
Hallett, Mark 1947- *220*
   Earlier sketch in SATA *83*
Halliburton, Richard 1900-1939(?) *81*
Halliburton, Warren J. 1924- *19*
Halliday, Brett
   See Dresser, Davis
   and Johnson, (Walter) Ryerson
   and Terrall, Robert
Halliday, William R(oss) 1926- *52*
Hallin, Emily Watson 1916-1995 .... *6*
Hallinan, P. K. 1944- *39*
   Brief entry *37*
Hallinan, Patrick Kenneth
   See Hallinan, P. K.
Hallman, Ruth 1929- *43*
   Brief entry *28*
Hallowell, Tommy
   See Hill, Thomas
Hall-Quest, (Edna) Olga W(ilbourne)
   1899-1986 .... *11*
   Obituary *47*
Halls, Kelly Milner 1957- *220*
   Earlier sketch in SATA *131*
Hallstead, William F(inn III) 1924- *11*
Hallward, Michael 1889-1982 .... *12*
Halperin, Michael *156*
Halperin, Wendy Anderson 1952- *200*
   Earlier sketches in SATA *80, 125*
Halpern, Julie 1975- *198*
Halpin, Abigail *236*
Halpin, Brendan 1968- *193*
Halpin, Marlene 1927- *88*
Halse, Laurie Beth
   See Anderson, Laurie Halse
Halsell, Grace (Eleanor) 1923-2000 .... *13*
Halsey, Megan *185*
Halsted, Anna Roosevelt 1906-1975
   Obituary *30*
Halter, Jon C(harles) 1941- *22*
Halverson, Deborah *202*
Halvorson, Adeline *218*
Halvorson, Marilyn 1948- *123*
Hamalian, Leo 1920- *41*
Hamberger, John 1934- *14*
Hamblin, Dora Jane 1920- *36*
Hambly, Barbara 1951- *108*
Hambly, Barbara Joan
   See Hambly, Barbara
Hamer, Martyn
   See Eldin, Peter
Hamerstrom, Frances 1907-1998 .... *24*
Hamil, Thomas Arthur 1928- *14*
Hamill, Ethel
   See Webb, Jean Francis (III)
Hamilton, (John) Alan 1943- *66*
Hamilton, Alice
   See Cromie, Alice Hamilton
Hamilton, Anita 1919- *92*
Hamilton, Barbara
   See Hambly, Barbara
Hamilton, Buzz
   See Hemming, Roy G.
Hamilton, Carol (Jean Barber) 1935- *94*
Hamilton, Charles (Harold St. John)
   1876-1961 .... *13*
Hamilton, Charles 1913-1996 .... *65*
   Obituary *93*
Hamilton, Clive
   See Lewis, C. S.
Hamilton, Dorothy (Drumm) 1906-1983 ...... *12*
   Obituary *35*
Hamilton, Edith 1867-1963 .... *20*
Hamilton, Edmond 1904-1977 .... *118*

Hamilton, (Muriel) Elizabeth (Mollie)
   1906- *23*
Hamilton, Emma Walton 1962- *237*
   Earlier sketch in SATA *177*
Hamilton, Franklin
   See Silverberg, Robert
Hamilton, Gail
   See Corcoran, Barbara (Asenath)
   and Dodge, Mary Abigail
Hamilton, Kersten 1958- *204*
   Earlier sketch in SATA *134*
Hamilton, K.R.
   See Hamilton, Kersten
Hamilton, Martha 1953- *183*
   Earlier sketch in SATA *123*
Hamilton, Mary (E.) 1927- *55*
Hamilton, Meredith *233*
Hamilton, Mollie
   See Kaye, M.M.
Hamilton, Morse 1943-1998 .... *101*
   Earlier sketch in SATA *35*
Hamilton, Peter F. 1960- *109*
Hamilton, Priscilla
   See Gellis, Roberta
Hamilton, Ralph
   See Stratemeyer, Edward L.
Hamilton, Virginia 1936-2002 .... *123*
   Obituary *132*
   Earlier sketches in SATA *4, 56, 79*
   See also CLR *127*
Hamilton, Virginia Esther
   See Hamilton, Virginia
Hamilton-Paterson, James 1941- *82*
Hamlet, Ova
   See Lupoff, Richard A.
Hamley, D. C.
   See Hamley, Dennis
Hamley, Dennis 1935- *69*
   Earlier sketch in SATA *39*
   See also CLR *47*
   See also SAAS *22*
Hamley, Dennis C.
   See Hamley, Dennis
Hamlin, Peter J. 1970- *84*
Hamm, Diane Johnston 1949- *78*
Hammer, Charles 1934- *58*
Hammer, Richard 1928- *6*
Hammerman, Gay M(orenus) 1926- *9*
Hammill, Matt 1982- *206*
Hammond, Andrew 1970- *181*
Hammond, Ralph
   See Hammond Innes, Ralph
Hammond, Winifred G(raham) 1899-1992 ... *29*
   Obituary *107*
Hammond Innes, Ralph 1913-1998 .... *116*
Hammontree, Marie (Gertrude) 1913- *13*
Hample, Zack 1977- *161*
Hampshire, Joyce Gregorian
   See Gregorian, Joyce Ballou
Hampshire, Susan 1942- *98*
Hampson, (Richard) Denman 1929- *15*
Hampson, Frank 1918(?)-1985
   Obituary *46*
Hampton, Wilborn 1940- *196*
   Earlier sketch in SATA *156*
Hamre, Leif 1914- *5*
Hamsa, Bobbie 1944- *52*
   Brief entry *38*
Han, Jenny 1981- *175*
Han, Lu
   See Stickler, Soma Han
Han, Soma
   See Stickler, Soma Han
Han, Suzanne Crowder 1953- *89*
Hancock, Mary A. 1923- *31*
Hancock, Sibyl 1940- *9*
Hand, Elizabeth 1957- *167*
   Earlier sketch in SATA *118*
Handford, Martin (John) 1956- *64*
   See also CLR *22*
Handforth, Thomas (Schofield) 1897-1948 .. *42*

Handleman, Philip 1951- 222
Handler, Daniel
    See Snicket, Lemony
Handville, Robert (Tompkins) 1924- 45
Hane, Roger 1940-1974
    Obituary 20
Hanel, Wolfram
    See Haenel, Wolfram
Haney, Lynn 1941- 23
Hanff, Helene 1916-1997 97
    Earlier sketch in SATA *11*
Hanft, Josh 1956- 197
Hanft, Joshua E.
    See Hanft, Josh
Hanke, Karen 234
Hanley, Boniface Francis 1924- 65
Hanlon, Emily 1945- 15
Hann, Jacquie 1951- 19
Hann, Judith 1942- 77
Hanna, Bill
    See Hanna, William (Denby)
Hanna, Cheryl 1951- 84
Hanna, Dan 200
Hanna, Jack (Bushnell) 1947- 74
Hanna, Nell(ie L.) 1908- 55
Hanna, Paul R(obert) 1902-1988 9
Hanna, William (Denby) 1910-2001 51
    Obituary 126
Hannam, Charles 1925- 50
Hannan, Peter 1954- 187
Hannigan, Katherine 170
Hannon, Ezra
    See Hunter, Evan
Hann-Syme, Marguerite 127
Hano, Arnold 1922- 12
Hano, Renee Roth
    See Roth-Hano, Renee
Hanover, Terri
    See Huff, Tanya
Hansen, Amy S. 229
Hansen, Ann Larkin 1958- 96
Hansen, Brooks 1965- 104
Hansen, Caryl (Hall) 1929- 39
Hansen, Ian V. 1929- 113
Hansen, Jennifer 1972- 156
Hansen, Joyce 1942- 172
    Autobiography Feature 172
    Brief entry 39
    Earlier sketches in SATA *46, 101*
    See also CLR *21*
    See also SAAS *15*
Hansen, Joyce Viola
    See Hansen, Joyce
Hansen, Mark Victor 112
Hansen, Ron 1947- 56
Hansen, Ronald Thomas
    See Hansen, Ron
Hansen, Thore 1942- 224
Hanser, Richard (Frederick) 1909-1981 13
Hanson, Joan 1938- 8
Hanson, Joseph E. 1894(?)-1971
    Obituary 27
Hanson, Mary Elizabeth 188
Hanson, Warren 1949- 239
    Earlier sketch in SATA *155*
Hansson, Gunilla 1939- 64
Hantman, Clea 200
Hapka, C.A.
    See Hapka, Catherine
Hapka, Catherine 223
Hapka, Cathy
    See Hapka, Catherine
Harald, Eric
    See Boesen, Victor
Harazin, S. A. 210
Harbour, Elizabeth 1968- 221
Harcourt, Ellen Knowles 1890(?)-1984
    Obituary 36
Hard, Charlotte (Ann) 1969- 98

Hardcastle, Michael 1933- 216
    Brief entry 38
    Earlier sketch in SATA *47*
Harding, Lee 1937- 32
    Brief entry 31
Hardinge, Frances 1973- 210
Hardt, Helga Fleischhauer
    See Fleischhauer-Hardt, Helga
Hardwick, Richard Holmes, Jr. 1923- 12
Hardy, Alice Dale 67
    Earlier sketch in SATA *1*
Hardy, David A(ndrews) 1936- 9
Hardy, Janice 222
Hardy, Jon 1958- 53
Hardy, LeAnne 1951- 154
Hardy, Stuart
    See Schisgall, Oscar
Hare, Norma Q(uarles) 1924- 46
    Brief entry 41
Harel, Nira 1936- 154
Harford, Henry
    See Hudson, W(illiam) H(enry)
Hargis, Wes 219
Hargrave, Leonie
    See Disch, Thomas M.
Hargreaves, (Charles) Roger 1935-1988
    Obituary 56
Hargrove, James 1947- 57
    Brief entry 50
Hargrove, Jim
    See Hargrove, James
Harik, Elsa
    See Marston, Elsa
Harik, Elsa M.
    See Marston, Elsa
Harik, Elsa Marston
    See Marston, Elsa
Hariton, Anca I. 1955- 79
Hark, Mildred
    See McQueen, Mildred Hark
Harkaway, Hal
    See Stratemeyer, Edward L.
Harkins, Philip 1912-1997 6
    Obituary 129
Harlan, Elizabeth 1945- 41
    Brief entry 35
Harlan, Glen
    See Cebulash, Mel
Harlan, Judith 1949- 135
    Earlier sketch in SATA *74*
    See also CLR *81*
Harland, Richard 1947- 152
Harlee, J. V.
    See Leese, Jennifer L.B.
Harler, Ann
    See Van Steenwyk, Elizabeth (Ann)
Harley, Avis 183
Harley, Bill 1954- 208
    Earlier sketch in SATA *87*
Harlow, Joan Hiatt 1932- 226
    Earlier sketch in SATA *157*
Harman, Fred 1902(?)-1982
    Obituary 30
Harman, Hugh 1903-1982
    Obituary 33
Harmelink, Barbara (Mary) 9
Harmer, Mabel 1894-1992 45
Harmon, Dan
    See Harmon, Daniel E(lton)
Harmon, Daniel E(lton) 1949- 157
Harmon, Kate
    See Gibson, Marley
Harmon, Margaret 1906- 20
Harmon, Michael 1969- 189
Harmon, Michael B.
    See Harmon, Michael
Harmon, William (Ruth) 1938- 65
Harnan, Terry 1920- 12
Harness, Cheryl 1951- 178
    Earlier sketch in SATA *131*

Harnett, Cynthia (Mary) 1893-1981 5
    Obituary 32
Harper, Anita 1943- 41
Harper, Betty 1946- 126
Harper, Charise
    See Harper, Charise Mericle
Harper, Charise Mericle 226
    Earlier sketch in SATA *179*
Harper, Elaine
    See Hallin, Emily Watson
Harper, Ellen
    See Noble, Marty
Harper, Jamie 174
Harper, Jessica 1949- 148
Harper, Jo 1932- 169
    Earlier sketch in SATA *97*
Harper, Lee 201
Harper, Mary Wood
    See Dixon, Jeanne
Harper, Piers 1966- 161
    Earlier sketch in SATA *105*
Harper, Suzanne 194
Harper, Wilhelmina 1884-1973 4
    Obituary 26
Harrah, Madge 1931- 154
Harrah, Michael 1940- 41
Harrah, Monique
    See Harrah, Madge
Harrar, George E. 1949- 124
Harrell, Beatrice Orcutt 1943- 93
Harrell, Janice 1945- 70
Harrell, Sara Gordon 1940- 26
Harrell, Sara Jeanne Gordon
    See Harrell, Sara Gordon
Harries, Joan 1922- 39
Harrill, Ronald 1950- 90
Harrington, Denis J(ames) 1932- 88
Harrington, Evelyn Davis 1911- 5
Harrington, Janice N. 1956- 187
Harrington, Lyn
    See Harrington, Evelyn Davis
Harris, Alan 1944- 71
Harris, Aurand 1915-1996 37
    Obituary 91
Harris, Bob
    See Harris, Robert J.
Harris, Carol Flynn 1933- 135
Harris, Catherine
    See Ainsworth, Catherine Harris
Harris, Christie
    See Harris, Christie (Lucy) Irwin
Harris, Christie (Lucy) Irwin 1907-2002 74
    Autobiography Feature 116
    Earlier sketch in SATA *6*
    See also CLR *47*
    See also SAAS *10*
Harris, Christine 1955- 105
Harris, Colver
    See Colver, Anne
Harris, David 1942- 118
Harris, David William
    See Harris, David
Harris, Dorothy Joan 1931- 153
    Earlier sketch in SATA *13*
Harris, Geraldine 1951- 54
Harris, Geraldine Rachel
    See Harris, Geraldine
Harris, Jacqueline L. 1929- 62
Harris, Janet 1932-1979 4
    Obituary 23
Harris, Jesse
    See Standiford, Natalie
Harris, Joan 1946- 146
Harris, Joe 1928- 201
Harris, Joel Chandler 1848-1908 100
    See also YABC *1*
    See also CLR *128*
Harris, John (Wyndham Parkes Lucas) Beynon
    1903-1969 118

Harris, Johnson
  See Harris, John (Wyndham Parkes Lucas)
  Beynon
Harris, Jonathan 1921-1997 52
Harris, Larry Vincent 1939- 59
Harris, Lavinia
  See St. John, Nicole
Harris, Leon A., Jr. 1926-2000 4
Harris, Lois V. 199
Harris, Lorle K(empe) 1912-2001 22
Harris, Maria Guadalupe
  See Harris, M.G.
Harris, Marilyn
  See Springer, Marilyn Harris
Harris, Mark Jonathan 1941- 84
  Earlier sketch in SATA 32
Harris, Mary K(athleen) 1905-1966 119
Harris, M.G. 231
Harris, Robert J. 1955- 195
Harris, Robie H. 1940- 203
  Brief entry 53
  Earlier sketches in SATA 90, 147
Harris, Robin
  See Shine, Deborah
Harris, Rosemary (Jeanne) 82
  Earlier sketch in SATA 4
  See also CLR 30
  See also SAAS 7
Harris, Ruth Elwin 1935- 164
Harris, Sherwood 1932-2009 25
Harris, Stephen 1959- 230
Harris, Steven Michael 1957- 55
Harris, Trudy 1949- 191
  Earlier sketch in SATA 128
Harris-Filderman, Diane
  See Filderman, Diane E(lizabeth)
Harrison, C(hester) William 1913-1994 35
Harrison, Carol
  See Harrison, Carol Thompson
Harrison, Carol Thompson 113
Harrison, David L. 1937- 186
  Earlier sketches in SATA 26, 92, 150
Harrison, Deloris 1938- 9
Harrison, Edward Hardy 1926- 56
Harrison, Elizabeth (Allen) Cavanna
  1909-2001 30
  Earlier sketch in SATA 1
  See also SAAS 4
Harrison, Harry 1925- 4
Harrison, Harry Max
  See Harrison, Harry
Harrison, Mette Ivie 1970- 236
  Earlier sketches in SATA 149, 202
Harrison, Michael 1939- 106
Harrison, Michelle 1979- 233
Harrison, Molly (Hodgett) 1909-2002 41
Harrison, Sarah 1946- 63
Harrison, Ted
  See Harrison, Edward Hardy
Harsh, Fred (T.) 1925- 72
Harshaw, Ruth H(etzel) 1890-1968 27
Harshman, Marc 1950- 109
  Earlier sketch in SATA 71
Hart, Alexandra 1939- 14
Hart, Alison
  See Leonhardt, Alice
Hart, Bruce 1938-2006 57
  Brief entry 39
Hart, Carole 1943- 57
  Brief entry 39
Hart, Carolyn 1936- 74
Hart, Carolyn G.
  See Hart, Carolyn
Hart, Carolyn Gimpel
  See Hart, Carolyn
Hart, Jan Siegel 1940- 79
Hart, Joyce 1954- 148
Hart, Karen 185
Hart, Lenore 171
Hart, Philip S. 1944- 180
Hart, Virginia 1949- 83

Harte, Bret 1836(?)-1902 26
Harte, Francis Brett
  See Harte, Bret
Harter, Debbie 1963- 107
Hartfield, Claire 1957- 147
Hartinger, Brent 1964- 217
  Earlier sketches in SATA 145, 174
Hartland, Jessie 171
Hartley, Ellen (Raphael) 1915-1980 23
Hartley, Fred Allan III 1953- 41
Hartley, William B(rown) 1913-1980 23
Hartling, Peter
  See Hartling, Peter
Hartling, Peter 1933- 66
  See also CLR 29
Hartman, Bob 1955- 224
Hartman, Carrie 226
Hartman, Cassie 202
Hartman, Dan 1955- 202
Hartman, Evert 1937- 38
  Brief entry 35
Hartman, Jane E. 1928- 47
Hartman, Jane Evangeline
  See Hartman, Jane E.
Hartman, Louis F(rancis) 1901-1970 22
Hartman, Rachel 174
Hartman, Victoria 1942- 91
Hartnett, Sonya 1968- 176
  Earlier sketches in SATA 93, 130
Hartry, Nancy 219
Hartshorn, Ruth M. 1928- 11
Hartung, Susan Kathleen 192
  Earlier sketch in SATA 150
Hartwig, Manfred 1950- 81
Harvey, Alyxandra 1974- 227
  Earlier sketch in SATA 189
Harvey, Brett 1936- 61
Harvey, Edith 1908(?)-1972
  Obituary 27
Harvey, Gill 189
Harvey, Karen D. 1935- 88
Harvey, Roland 1945- 219
  Earlier sketches in SATA 71, 123, 179
Harvey, Sarah N. 1950- 238
Harvey-Fitzhenry, Alyxandra
  See Harvey, Alyxandra
Harwick, B. L.
  See Keller, Beverly L(ou)
Harwin, Brian
  See Henderson, LeGrand
Harwood, Pearl Augusta (Bragdon)
  1903-1998 9
Haseley, Dennis 1950- 221
  Brief entry 44
  Earlier sketches in SATA 57, 105, 157
Hashmi, Kerri 1955- 108
Haskell, Arnold L(ionel) 1903-1981(?) 6
Haskins, James
  See Haskins, James S.
Haskins, James S. 1941-2005 132
  Autobiography Feature 132
  Earlier sketches in SATA 9, 69, 105
  See also CLR 39
  See also SAAS 4
Haskins, Jim
  See Haskins, James S.
Hasler, Eveline 1933- 181
Hasler, Joan 1931- 28
Hasler, Nikol 1979- 235
Hasnat, Naheed
  See Senzai, N.H.
Hass, Robert 1941- 94
Hassall, Joan 1906-1988 43
  Obituary 56
Hassett, Ann 1958- 162
Hassett, John 162
Hassler, Jon 1933-2008 19
  Obituary 191
Hassler, Jon Francis
  See Hassler, Jon

Hastings, Beverly
  See Barkin, Carol
  and James, Elizabeth
Hastings, Graham
  See Jeffries, Roderic
Hastings, Ian 1912- 62
Hastings, Victor
  See Disch, Thomas M.
Haszard, Patricia Moyes 1923-2000 63
Hatch, Lynda S. 1950- 90
Hathaway, Barbara 164
Hathorn, Elizabeth
  See Hathorn, Libby
Hathorn, Elizabeth Helen
  See Hathorn, Libby
Hathorn, Libby 1943- 232
  Autobiography Feature 232
  Earlier sketches in SATA 74, 120, 156
Hatkoff, Craig 1954- 192
Hatlo, Jimmy 1898-1963
  Obituary 23
Hatton, Caroline 1957- 205
Hauff, Wilhelm 1802-1827
  See CLR 155
Haugaard, Erik Christian 1923- 68
  Earlier sketch in SATA 4
  See also CLR 173
  See also SAAS 12
Haugaard, Kay 117
Hauge, Lesley 234
Haugen, Hayley Mitchell 1968- 172
Haugen, Tormod 1945- 66
Hauman, Doris 1898-1984 32
Hauman, George 1890-1961 32
Hauptly, Denis J. 1945- 57
Hauptly, Denis James
  See Hauptly, Denis J.
Hauser, Jill Frankel 1950- 127
Hauser, Margaret L(ouise) 1909- 10
Hausherr, Rosmarie 1943- 86
Hausman, Gerald 1945- 180
  Earlier sketches in SATA 13, 90, 132
  See also CLR 89
Hausman, Gerry
  See Hausman, Gerald
Hauth, Katherine B. 1940- 99
Hautman, Pete 1952- 173
  Earlier sketches in SATA 82, 128
Hautman, Peter Murray
  See Hautman, Pete
Hautzig, Deborah 1956- 106
  Earlier sketch in SATA 31
Hautzig, Esther Rudomin 1930-2009 148
  Earlier sketches in SATA 4, 68
  See also CLR 22
  See also SAAS 15
Havel, Geoff 1955- 152
Havel, Jennifer
  See Havill, Juanita
Havelin, Kate 1961- 143
Haven, Paul 1971(?)- 213
Haverfield, Mary 225
Havighurst, Walter (Edwin) 1901-1994 1
  Obituary 79
Haviland, Virginia 1911-1988 6
  Obituary 54
Havill, Juanita 1949- 224
  Earlier sketches in SATA 74, 155
Hawes, Judy 1913- 4
Hawes, Louise 1943- 180
  Earlier sketch in SATA 60
Hawk, Fran 222
Hawke, Rosanne 1953- 165
  Earlier sketch in SATA 124
Hawke, Rosanne Joy
  See Hawke, Rosanne
Hawkes, Kevin 1959- 201
  Earlier sketches in SATA 78, 150
Hawkes, Nigel 1943- 119
Hawkesworth, Eric 1921- 13
Hawking, Lucy 1969- 197

Hawkins, Aaron R. *236*
Hawkins, Arthur 1903-1985 .... *19*
Hawkins, Colin 1945- *162*
  Earlier sketch in SATA *112*
Hawkins, Jacqui *162*
  Earlier sketch in SATA *112*
Hawkins, Jimmy 1941- *188*
Hawkins, Laura 1951- *74*
Hawkins, (Helena Ann) Quail 1905-2002 ...... *6*
  Obituary *141*
Hawkins, Rachel 1979- *228*
Hawkinson, John (Samuel) 1912-1994 .... *4*
Hawkinson, Lucy (Ozone) 1924-1971 .... *21*
Hawks, Robert 1961- *85*
Hawley, Mabel C. *67*
  Earlier sketch in SATA *1*
Haworth, Danette *207*
Haworth-Attard, Barbara 1953- *215*
Hawthorne, Captain R. M.
  See Ellis, Edward S.
Hawthorne, Nathaniel 1804-1864
  See YABC *2*
  See also CLR *163*
Hay, Jeff T. *154*
Hay, John 1915-2011 .... *13*
Hay, Samantha *213*
Hay, Timothy
  See Brown, Margaret Wise
Hayashi, Leslie Ann 1954- *115*
Hayashi, Nancy 1939- *186*
  Earlier sketch in SATA *80*
Haycak, Cara 1961- *180*
Haycock, Kate 1962- *77*
Haycraft, Howard 1905-1991 .... *6*
  Obituary *70*
Haycraft, Molly Costain 1911- *6*
Hayden, Gwendolen Lampshire 1904- *35*
Hayden, Robert
  See Hayden, Robert Earl
Hayden, Robert C(arter), Jr. 1937- *47*
  Brief entry *28*
Hayden, Robert E.
  See Hayden, Robert Earl
Hayden, Robert Earl 1913-1980 .... *19*
  Obituary *26*
Hayden, Torey L. 1951- *163*
  Earlier sketch in SATA *65*
Hayden, Torey Lynn
  See Hayden, Torey L.
Hayes, Carlton J(oseph) H(untley)
  1882-1964 .... *11*
Hayes, Daniel 1952- *109*
  Earlier sketch in SATA *73*
Hayes, Geoffrey 1947- *207*
  Earlier sketches in SATA *26, 91*
Hayes, Joe 1945- *131*
  Earlier sketch in SATA *88*
Hayes, John F. 1904-1980 .... *11*
Hayes, Karel 1949- *207*
Hayes, Rosemary *227*
  Earlier sketch in SATA *158*
Hayes, Sarah 1945- *208*
Hayes, Sheila 1937- *51*
  Brief entry *50*
Hayes, Will *7*
Hayes, William D(imitt) 1913-1976 .... *8*
Haynes, Betsy 1937- *94*
  Brief entry *37*
  Earlier sketch in SATA *48*
  See also CLR *90*
Haynes, David 1955- *97*
Haynes, Linda
  See Swinford, Betty (June Wells)
Haynes, Mary 1938- *65*
Haynes, Max 1956- *72*
Hays, Anna Jane *214*
Hays, H(offmann) R(eynolds) 1904-1980 .... *26*
Hays, Thomas A.
  See Hays, Tony
Hays, Thomas Anthony
  See Hays, Tony

Hays, Tony 1957- *84*
Hays, Wilma Pitchford 1909- *28*
  Earlier sketch in SATA *1*
  See also CLR *59*
  See also SAAS *3*
Hayter, Rhonda *233*
Hayward, Linda 1943- *185*
  Brief entry *39*
  Earlier sketch in SATA *101*
Haywood, Carolyn 1898-1990 .... *75*
  Obituary *64*
  Earlier sketches in SATA *1, 29*
  See also CLR *22*
Hazelaar, Cor *217*
Hazell, Rebecca (Eileen) 1947- *141*
Hazen, Barbara Shook 1930- *178*
  Earlier sketches in SATA *27, 90*
Hazen, Lynn E. *202*
Head, Gay
  See Hauser, Margaret L(ouise)
Head, Tom 1978- *167*
Headley, Elizabeth
  See Harrison, Elizabeth (Allen) Cavanna
Headley, Justina Chen 1968- *176*
Headstrom, (Birger) Richard 1902-1985 .... *8*
Heady, Eleanor B(utler) 1917-1979 .... *8*
Heagy, William D. 1964- *76*
Heal, Edith 1903-1995 .... *7*
Heal, Gillian 1934- *89*
Heale, Jay (Jeremy Peter Wingfield) 1937- .. *84*
Healey, Brooks
  See Albert, Burton
Healey, Karen 1981- *230*
Healey, Larry 1927- *44*
  Brief entry *42*
Heap, Sue 1954- *187*
  Earlier sketch in SATA *150*
Heaps, Willard A(llison) 1908-1987 .... *26*
Hearn, Diane Dawson 1952- *209*
  Earlier sketch in SATA *79*
Hearn, Emily
  See Valleau, Emily
Hearn, Julie 1958- *212*
  Earlier sketch in SATA *152*
Hearn, Lian
  See Rubinstein, Gillian
Hearn, Sneed
  See Gregg, Andrew K.
Hearne, Betsy 1942- *146*
  Earlier sketches in SATA *38, 95*
Heath, Charles D(ickinson) 1941- *46*
Heath, Veronica
  See Blackett, Veronica Heath
Heaven, Constance (Christina) 1911- *7*
Hebert-Collins, Sheila 1948- *111*
Hecht, George J(oseph) 1895-1980
  Obituary *22*
Hecht, Henri Joseph 1922- *9*
Hechtkopf, Henryk 1910- *17*
Heck, Bessie (Mildred) Holland 1911-1995 . *26*
Heck, Ed 1963- *173*
Heckert, Connie K(aye Delp) 1948- *82*
Hector, Julian *205*
Hedderwick, Mairi 1939- *145*
  Earlier sketches in SATA *30, 77*
Hedges, Sid(ney) G(eorge) 1897-1974 .... *28*
Hedrick, Irene Hope 1920- *175*
Heelan, Jamee Riggio 1965- *146*
Heerboth, Sharon
  See Leon, Sharon
Heffernan, John 1949- *168*
  Earlier sketch in SATA *121*
Heffron, Dorris 1944- *68*
Hefter, Richard 1942- *31*
Hegamin, Tonya C. 1975- *209*
Hegarty, Reginald Beaton 1906-1973 .... *10*
Hehenberger, Shelly 1968- *126*
Heidbreder, Robert 1947- *196*
  Earlier sketch in SATA *130*
Heidbreder, Robert K.
  See Heidbreder, Robert

Heide, Florence Parry 1919-2011 .... *192*
  Earlier sketches in SATA *32, 69, 118*
  See also CLR *60*
  See also SAAS *6*
Heiderstadt, Dorothy 1907-2001 .... *6*
Heidi Louise
  See Erdrich, Louise
Heidler, David S. 1955- *132*
Heidler, David Stephen
  See Heidler, David S.
Heidler, Jeanne T. 1956- *132*
Heilbroner, Joan Knapp 1922- *63*
Heilbrun, Lois Hussey 1922(?)-1987
  Obituary *54*
Heiligman, Deborah 1958- *193*
  Earlier sketches in SATA *90, 144*
Heilman, Joan Rattner *50*
Heimann, Rolf 1940- *164*
  Earlier sketch in SATA *120*
Heimberg, Justin *232*
Hein, Lucille Eleanor 1915-1994 .... *20*
Heine, Helme 1941- *135*
  Earlier sketch in SATA *67*
  See also CLR *18*
Heinlein, Robert A. 1907-1988 .... *69*
  Obituary *56*
  Earlier sketch in SATA *9*
  See also CLR *75*
Heinlein, Robert Anson
  See Heinlein, Robert A.
Heins, Ethel L(eah) 1918-1997 .... *101*
Heins, Paul 1909- *13*
Heintze, Carl 1922- *26*
Heinz, Bill
  See Heinz, W. C.
Heinz, Brian J. 1946- *181*
  Earlier sketch in SATA *95*
Heinz, Brian James
  See Heinz, Brian J.
Heinz, W. C. 1915-2008 .... *26*
Heinz, Wilfred Charles
  See Heinz, W. C.
Heinzen, Mildred
  See Masters, Mildred
Heisel, Sharon E(laine) 1941- *125*
  Earlier sketch in SATA *84*
Heitzmann, William Ray 1948- *73*
Heitzmann, Wm. Ray
  See Heitzmann, William Ray
Helakoski, Leslie *238*
  Earlier sketch in SATA *178*
Helberg, Shirley Adelaide Holden 1919- ... *138*
Heldring, Thatcher *229*
Helfer, Andrew *187*
Helfer, Ralph 1937- *177*
Helfman, Elizabeth S(eaver) 1911-2001 .... *3*
Helfman, Harry Carmozin 1910-1995 .... *3*
Helgerson, Joseph 1950- *181*
Hellard, Susan *232*
  Earlier sketch in SATA *182*
Hellberg, Hans-Eric 1927- *38*
Heller, Linda 1944- *46*
  Brief entry *40*
Heller, Mike
  See Hano, Arnold
Heller, Ruth M. 1924- *112*
  Earlier sketch in SATA *66*
Hellman, Hal
  See Hellman, Harold
Hellman, Harold 1927- *4*
Helman, Andrea (Jean) 1946- *160*
  Earlier sketch in SATA *107*
Helmer, Diana Star 1962- *86*
Helmer, Marilyn *160*
  Earlier sketch in SATA *112*
Helps, Racey 1913-1971 .... *2*
  Obituary *25*
Helquist, Brett *229*
  Earlier sketches in SATA *146, 187*
Helweg, Hans H. 1917- *50*
  Brief entry *33*

Helyar, Jane Penelope Josephine 1933- 5
 Autobiography Feature 138
 See also SAAS 2
Hemingway, Edith M. 1950- 223
Hemingway, Edith Morris
 See Hemingway, Edith M.
Hemingway, Edward 1969(?)- 212
Hemingway, Ernest 1899-1961
 See CLR 168
Hemingway, Ernest Miller
 See Hemingway, Ernest
Hemmant, Lynette 1938- 69
Hemming, Roy G. 1928-1995 11
 Obituary 86
Hemphill, Helen 1955- 179
Hemphill, Kris (Harrison) 1963- 118
Hemphill, Martha Locke 1904-1973 37
Hemphill, Michael 220
Hemphill, Stephanie 190
Hemstock, Gillian 1956- 173
Henba, Bobbie 1926- 87
Henbest, Nigel 1951- 55
 Brief entry 52
Henderley, Brooks 1
Henderson, Aileen Kilgore 1921- 178
Henderson, Aileen Mary
 See Fox, Aileen
Henderson, Gordon 1950- 53
Henderson, Kathy 1949- 155
 Brief entry 53
 Earlier sketches in SATA 55, 95
Henderson, Lauren 1966- 201
Henderson, LeGrand 1901-1965 9
Henderson, Nancy Wallace 1916- 22
Henderson, Zenna (Chlarson) 1917-1983 5
Hendra, Sue 235
Hendrickson, Walter Brookfield, Jr. 1936- 9
Hendrix, John 1976- 208
Hendry, Diana 1941- 213
 Earlier sketches in SATA 68, 106
Hendry, Frances Mary 1941- 171
 Earlier sketch in SATA 110
Hendry, Linda (Gail) 1961- 83
Heneghan, James 1930- 160
 Earlier sketches in SATA 53, 97
Henkes, Kevin 1960- 207
 Earlier sketches in SATA 43, 76, 108, 154
 See also CLR 108
Henn, Astrid 214
Hennessy, Barbara G.
 See Hennessy, B.G.
Hennessy, Barbara Gulbrandsen
 See Hennessy, B.G.
Hennessy, B.G. 1951- 175
Hennesy, Carolyn 1962- 221
Henney, Carolee Wells 1928- 102
Henriod, Lorraine 1925- 26
Henriquez, Emile F. 1937- 170
 Earlier sketch in SATA 89
Henry, April 1959- 235
 Earlier sketch in SATA 174
Henry, Ernest 1948- 107
Henry, Jed 239
Henry, Joanne Landers 1927- 6
Henry, Maeve 1960- 75
Henry, Marguerite 1902-1997 100
 Obituary 99
 See also CLR 4
 See also SAAS 7
Henry, Marie H. 1935- 65
Henry, Marilyn 1939- 117
Henry, Marion
 See del Rey, Lester
Henry, O. 1862-1910
 See YABC 2
Henry, Oliver
 See Henry, O.
Henry, Rohan 217
Henry, T. E.
 See Rowland-Entwistle, (Arthur) Theodore
 (Henry)

Henschel, Elizabeth Georgie 56
Henson, Heather 206
Henson, James Maury
 See Henson, Jim
Henson, Jim 1936-1990 43
 Obituary 65
Henstra, Friso 1928- 73
 Earlier sketch in SATA 8
 See also SAAS 14
Hentoff, Nat(han Irving) 1925- 133
 Brief entry 27
 Earlier sketches in SATA 42, 69
 See also CLR 52
Henty, G(eorge) A(lfred) 1832-1902 64
 See also CLR 76
Heo, Yumi 1964- 206
 Earlier sketches in SATA 94, 146
Hepler, Heather 177
Herald, Kathleen
 See Peyton, Kathleen Wendy
Herb, Angela M. 1970- 92
Herbert, Cecil
 See Hamilton, Charles (Harold St. John)
Herbert, Don 1917-2007 2
 Obituary 184
Herbert, Donald Jeffrey
 See Herbert, Don
Herbert, Frank 1920-1986 37
 Obituary 47
 Earlier sketch in SATA 9
Herbert, Frank Patrick
 See Herbert, Frank
Herbert, Helen (Jean) 1947- 57
Herbert, Janis 1956- 139
Herbert, Wally 1934-2007 23
Herbert, Walter William
 See Herbert, Wally
Herbst, Judith 1947- 74
Herda, D.J. 1948- 80
Herge
 See Remi, Georges
Heritage, Martin
 See Horler, Sydney
Herkimer, L(awrence) R(ussell) 1925(?)- 42
Herlihy, Dirlie Anne 1935- 73
Herlong, Madaline
 See Herlong, M.H.
Herlong, M.H. 211
Herman, Charlotte 1937- 203
 Earlier sketches in SATA 20, 99
Hermanson, Dennis (Everett) 1947- 10
Hermes, Jules 1962- 92
Hermes, Patricia 1936- 233
 Earlier sketches in SATA 31, 78, 141, 191
Hermes, Patricia Mary
 See Hermes, Patricia
Hernandez, Natalie Nelson 1929- 123
Herndon, Ernest 91
Herold, Ann Bixby 1937- 72
Herrera, Diego
 See Yayo
Herrera, Juan Felipe 1948- 127
Herrick, Steven 1958- 209
 Earlier sketches in SATA 103, 156
Herriman, George (Joseph) 1880-1944 140
Herriot, James 1916-1995 135
 Brief entry 44
 Earlier sketch in SATA 86
 See also CLR 80
Herrmanns, Ralph 1933- 11
Herrold, Tracey
 See Dils, Tracey E.
Herron, Carolivia 1947- 203
Herron, Edward A(lbert) 1912- 4
Herschler, Mildred Barger 130
Hersey, John 1914-1993 25
 Obituary 76
Hersey, John Richard
 See Hersey, John
Hershberger, Priscilla (Gorman) 1951- 81
Hershenhorn, Esther 1945- 151

Hershey, Kathleen M. 1934- 80
Hershey, Mary 173
Hershey, Mary L.
 See Hershey, Mary
Hersom, Kathleen 1911- 73
Hertz, Grete Janus 1915- 23
Herxheimer, Sophie 1963- 220
Herzig, Alison Cragin 1935- 87
Herzog, Brad 1968- 131
Heshka, Ryan 236
Heslewood, Juliet 1951- 82
Hess, Lilo 1916- ....
Hess, Paul 1961- 134
Hesse, Hermann 1877-1962 50
Hesse, Karen 1952- 215
 Autobiography Feature 113
 Earlier sketches in SATA 74, 103, 158
 See also CLR 141
 See also SAAS 25
Hest, Amy 1950- 193
 Earlier sketches in SATA 55, 82, 129
Heuer, Karsten 1968(?)- 202
Heuer, Kenneth John 1927- 44
Heuman, William 1912-1971 21
Heuston, Kimberley 1960- 167
Heuston, Kimberley Burton
 See Heuston, Kimberley
Heuvel, Eric 1960- 224
Hewes, Agnes Danforth 1874-1963 35
Hewett, Anita 1918-1989 13
Hewett, Joan 1930- 140
 Earlier sketch in SATA 81
Hewett, Richard 1929- 81
Hewitson, Jennifer 1961- 97
Hewitt, Margaret 1961- 84
Hewitt, Sally 1949- 231
 Earlier sketch in SATA 127
Hext, Harrington
 See Phillpotts, Eden
Hey, Nigel 1936- 20
Hey, Nigel Stewart
 See Hey, Nigel
Heyduck-Huth, Hilde 1929- 8
Heyer, Carol 1950- 130
 Earlier sketch in SATA 74
Heyer, Marilee 1942- 102
 Earlier sketch in SATA 64
Heyerdahl, Thor 1914-2002 52
 Earlier sketch in SATA 2
Heyes, (Nancy) Eileen 1956- 150
 Earlier sketch in SATA 80
Heyliger, William 1884-1955
 See YABC 1
Heyman, Ken(neth Louis) 1930- 114
 Earlier sketch in SATA 34
Heyward, (Edwin) DuBose 1885-1940 21
Heywood, Karen 1946- 48
Hezlep, William (Earl) 1936- 88
Hiaasen, Carl 1953- 208
Hiatt, Shelby 226
Hibbert, Arthur Raymond
 See Hibbert, Christopher
Hibbert, Christopher 1924-2008 4
 Obituary 201
Hibbert, Eleanor Alice Burford 1906-1993 2
 Obituary 74
Hickman, Estella (Lee) 1942- 111
Hickman, Janet 1940- 127
 Earlier sketch in SATA 12
Hickman, Martha Whitmore 1925- 26
Hickman, Pamela 1958- 186
 Earlier sketch in SATA 128
Hickock, Will
 See Harrison, C(hester) William
Hickok, Lorena A. 1893-1968 20
Hickox, Rebecca (Ayres) 116
Hicks, Barbara Jean 1953- 165
Hicks, Betty 191
Hicks, Clifford B. 1920- 50
Hicks, Eleanor B.
 See Coerr, Eleanor (Beatrice)

Hicks, Faith Erin 235
Hicks, Harvey
    See Stratemeyer, Edward L.
Hicks, Peter 1952- 111
Hicyilmaz, Gaye 1947- 157
    Earlier sketch in SATA 77
Hieatt, Constance B(artlett) 1928- 4
Hiebert, Ray Eldon 1932- 13
Hierstein, Judith 212
Hierstein, Judy
    See Hierstein, Judith
Higdon, Hal 1931- 4
Higginbottom, David 1923- 87
    Earlier sketch in SATA 25
Higginbottom, J(effrey) Winslow 1945- 29
Higgins, Dalton 223
Higgins, F.E. 219
Higgins, Fiona
    See Higgins, F.E.
Higgins, Joanna 1945- 125
Higgins, Simon (Richard) 1958- 105
Higginsen, Vy 79
High, Linda Oatman 1958- 188
    Autobiography Feature 188
    Earlier sketches in SATA 94, 145
High, Philip E. 1914- 119
High, Philip Empson
    See High, Philip E.
Higham, David 1949- 50
Higham, David Michael
    See Higham, David
Higham, Jon Atlas
    See Higham, Jonathan Huw
Higham, Jonathan Huw 1960- 59
Highet, Helen
    See MacInnes, Helen (Clark)
Hightman, Jason 1971(?)- 189
Hightman, J.P.
    See Hightman, Jason
Hightower, Florence Cole 1916-1981 4
    Obituary 27
Highwater, Jamake (Mamake)
    1942(?)-2001 69
    Brief entry 30
    Earlier sketch in SATA 32
    See also CLR 17
Hilb, Nora 1953- 178
Hildebrandt, Greg, Jr. 1970- 228
Hildebrandt, Greg 1939- 172
    Brief entry 33
    Earlier sketch in SATA 55
Hildebrandt, Tim 1939-2006 55
    Brief entry 33
Hildebrandt, Timothy
    See Hildebrandt, Tim
Hildebrandts, The
    See Hildebrandt, Greg
    and Hildebrandt, Tim
Hilder, Rowland 1905-1993 36
    Obituary 77
Hildick, E. W.
    See Hildick, Wallace
Hildick, Wallace 1925-2001 68
    Earlier sketch in SATA 2
    See also SAAS 6
Hilgartner, Beth 1957- 58
Hill, Alexis
    See Craig, Mary (Francis) Shura
    and Glick, Ruth
Hill, Anthony R. 1942- 164
    Earlier sketch in SATA 91
Hill, Anthony Robert
    See Hill, Anthony R.
Hill, David 1942- 152
    Earlier sketch in SATA 103
Hill, Donna (Marie) 1921- 124
    Earlier sketch in SATA 24
Hill, Douglas 1935-2007 78
    Earlier sketch in SATA 39
Hill, Douglas Arthur
    See Hill, Douglas

Hill, Elizabeth Starr 1925- 143
    Earlier sketch in SATA 24
Hill, Eric 1927- 133
    Brief entry 53
    Earlier sketch in SATA 66
    See also CLR 13
Hill, Gordon
    See Eldin, Peter
Hill, Grace Brooks 67
    Earlier sketch in SATA 1
Hill, Grace Livingston 1865-1947
    See YABC 2
Hill, Helen M(orey) 1915- 27
Hill, Isabel 225
Hill, Isabel T.
    See Hill, Isabel
Hill, John
    See Koontz, Dean
Hill, Johnson
    See Kunhardt, Edith
Hill, Judy I. R.
    See Roberts, Judy I.
Hill, Kathleen Louise 1917- 4
Hill, Kay
    See Hill, Kathleen Louise
Hill, Kirkpatrick 1938- 188
    Earlier sketches in SATA 72, 126
Hill, Laban
    See Hill, Laban Carrick
Hill, Laban Carrick 170
Hill, Lee Sullivan 1958- 96
Hill, Lorna 1902-1991 12
Hill, Margaret (Ohler) 1915- 36
Hill, Meg
    See Hill, Margaret (Ohler)
Hill, Meredith
    See Craig, Mary (Francis) Shura
Hill, Monica
    See Watson, Jane Werner
Hill, Pamela Smith 1954- 112
Hill, Ralph Nading 1917-1987 65
Hill, Robert W(hite) 1919-1982 12
    Obituary 31
Hill, Ruth A.
    See Viguers, Ruth Hill
Hill, Ruth Livingston
    See Munce, Ruth Hill
Hill, Stuart 1958- 186
Hill, Susan 1942- 183
Hill, Susan Elizabeth
    See Hill, Susan
Hill, Susanna Leonard 1965- 193
Hill, Thomas 1960- 82
Hillcourt, William 1900-1992 27
Hillenbrand, Will 1960- 210
    Earlier sketches in SATA 84, 147
Hiller, Ilo (Ann) 1938- 59
Hillerman, Anthony Grove
    See Hillerman, Tony
Hillerman, Tony 1925-2008 6
    Obituary 198
Hillert, Margaret 1920- 91
    Earlier sketch in SATA 8
Hilliard, Richard 183
Hillman, Ben 1957- 202
Hillman, Elizabeth 1942- 75
Hillman, John 1952- 120
Hillman, Martin
    See Hill, Douglas
Hillman, Priscilla 1940- 48
    Brief entry 39
Hillman, Shane 200
Hills, C.A.R. 1955- 39
Hills, Charles Albert Reis
    See Hills, C.A.R.
Hills, Lia 238
Hills, Tad 237
    Earlier sketch in SATA 173
Hilton, Irene Pothus -1979 7
Hilton, James 1900-1954 34

Hilton, Margaret Lynette 1946- 105
    Earlier sketch in SATA 68
    See also CLR 25
    See also SAAS 21
Hilton, Nette
    See Hilton, Margaret Lynette
Hilton, Ralph 1907-1982 8
Hilton, Suzanne 1922- 4
Hilton-Bruce, Anne
    See Hilton, Margaret Lynette
Him, George 1937-1982
    Obituary 30
Himelblau, Linda -2005 179
Himelstein, Shmuel 1940- 83
Himler, Ann 1946- 8
Himler, Ronald 1937- 234
    Earlier sketches in SATA 6, 92, 137, 183
Himler, Ronald Norbert
    See Himler, Ronald
Himmelman, John 1959- 221
    Earlier sketches in SATA 47, 94, 159
Himmelman, John C.
    See Himmelman, John
Hinckley, Helen
    See Jones, Helen Hinckley
Hind, Dolores (Ellen) 1931- 53
    Brief entry 49
Hindin, Nathan
    See Bloch, Robert (Albert)
Hindley, Judy 1940- 179
    Earlier sketch in SATA 120
Hinds, P. Mignon 98
Hinds, Patricia Mignon
    See Hinds, P. Mignon
Hine, Sesyle Joslin 1929- 2
Hines, Anna Grossnickle 1946- 209
    Brief entry 45
    Earlier sketches in SATA 51, 95, 141
    See also SAAS 16
Hines, Gary (Roger) 1944- 136
    Earlier sketch in SATA 74
Hinman, Bonnie 1950- 216
Hinojosa, Maria (de Lourdes) 1961- 88
Hinton, Nigel 1941- 166
Hinton, S. E. 1950- 160
    Earlier sketches in SATA 19, 58, 115
    See also CLR 23
Hinton, Sam 1917-2009 43
Hinton, Susan Eloise
    See Hinton, S. E.
Hintz, Martin 1945- 128
    Brief entry 39
    Earlier sketch in SATA 47
Hintz, Stephen V. 1975- 129
Hippopotamus, Eugene H.
    See Kraus, (Herman) Robert
Hirano, Cathy 1957- 68
Hirao, Amiko 203
Hirsch, Karen 1941- 61
Hirsch, Odo 157
    Earlier sketch in SATA 111
Hirsch, Phil 1926- 35
Hirsch, S. Carl 1913-1990 2
    See also SAAS 7
Hirschfelder, Arlene B. 1943- 227
    Earlier sketches in SATA 80, 138
Hirschi, Ron 1948- 192
    Earlier sketches in SATA 56, 95
Hirschmann, Linda (Ann) 1941- 40
Hirsh, Marilyn 1944-1988 7
    Obituary 58
Hirshberg, Al(bert Simon) 1909-1973 38
Hiscock, Bruce 1940- 204
    Earlier sketch in SATA 57, 137
Hiser, Constance 1950- 71
Hiser, Iona Seibert -1998 4
Hislop, Julia Rose Catherine 1962- 74
Hissey, Jane 1952- 130
    Autobiography Feature 130
    Earlier sketches in SATA 58, 103

Hissey, Jane Elizabeth
See Hissey, Jane
Hitchcock, Alfred (Joseph) 1899-1980 27
Obituary 24
Hite, Sid 1954- 175
Earlier sketches in SATA 75, 136
Hitte, Kathryn 1919- 16
Hitz, Demi
See Demi
Hitzeroth, Deborah L. 1961- 78
Hnizdovsky, Jacques 1915- 32
Ho, Jannie 226
Ho, Louise 185
Ho, Minfong 1951- 151
Earlier sketches in SATA 15, 94
See also CLR 28
Hoagland, Edward (Morley) 1932- 51
Hoare, Robert J(ohn) 1921-1975 38
Hoban, Julia 217
Hoban, Lillian 1925-1998 69
Obituary 104
Earlier sketch in SATA 22
See also CLR 67
Hoban, Russell 1925-2011 136
Earlier sketches in SATA 1, 40, 78
See also CLR 139
Hoban, Russell Conwell
See Hoban, Russell
Hoban, Tana 1917(?)-2006 104
Obituary 173
Earlier sketches in SATA 22, 70
See also CLR 76
See also SAAS 12
Hobart, Lois (Elaine) 7
Hobbie, Holly 1942- 225
Earlier sketch in SATA 178
See also CLR 88
Hobbie, Jocelyn 190
Hobbie, Nathaniel 196
Hobbs, Leigh 1953- 166
Hobbs, Valerie 1941- 193
Autobiography Feature 145
Earlier sketches in SATA 93, 145
See also CLR 148
Hobbs, Will 1947- 177
Autobiography Feature 127
Earlier sketches in SATA 72, 110
See also CLR 59
Hobbs, William Carl
See Hobbs, Will
Hoberman, Mary Ann 1930- 228
Earlier sketches in SATA 5, 72, 111, 158
See also CLR 22
See also SAAS 18
Hobson, Bruce 1950- 62
Hobson, Burton (Harold) 1933- 28
Hobson, Laura Z(ametkin) 1900-1986 52
Hobson, Sally 1967- 172
Earlier sketch in SATA 84
Hoce, Charley E. 174
Hochman, David 202
Hochschild, Arlie Russell 1940- 11
Hockaby, Stephen
See Mitchell, Gladys (Maude Winifred)
Hockenberry, Hope
See Newell, Hope Hockenberry
Hodge, Deborah 1954- 163
Earlier sketch in SATA 122
Hodge, P. W.
See Hodge, Paul W(illiam)
Hodge, Paul W(illiam) 1934- 12
Hodgell, P(atricia) C(hristine) 1951- 42
Hodges, C. Walter 1909-2004 2
Obituary 158
Hodges, Carl G. 1902-1964 10
Hodges, Cyril Walter
See Hodges, C. Walter
Hodges, Elizabeth Jamison 1

Hodges, Margaret 1911-2005 167
Obituary 172
Earlier sketches in SATA 1, 33, 75, 117
See also SAAS 9
Hodges, Margaret Moore
See Hodges, Margaret
Hodgetts, Blake Christopher 1967- 43
Hodgkins, Fran 1964- 199
Hodgkinson, Leigh 1975- 202
Hodgman, Ann 1956- 198
Hodgson, Harriet (W.) 1935- 84
Hoehne, Marcia 1951- 89
Hoellwarth, Cathryn Clinton
See Clinton, Cathryn
Hoestlandt, Jo 1948- 221
Earlier sketch in SATA 94
Hoestlandt, Jocelyne
See Hoestlandt, Jo
Hoexter, Corinne K. 1927- 6
Hoeye, Michael 1947- 136
Hof, Marjolijn 1956- 226
Hoff, Carol 1900-1979 11
Hoff, Mary (King) 1956- 157
Earlier sketch in SATA 74
Hoff, Syd(ney) 1912-2004 138
Obituary 154
Earlier sketches in SATA 9, 72
See also CLR 83
See also SAAS 4
Hoffman, Edwin D. 49
Hoffman, Elizabeth P(arkinson) 1921-2003
Obituary 153
Hoffman, Mary 1945- 211
Earlier sketches in SATA 59, 97, 144
See also SAAS 24
Hoffman, Mat 1972- 150
Hoffman, Nina Kiriki 1955- 160
Hoffman, Phyllis M. 1944- 4
Hoffman, Phyllis Miriam
See Hoffman, Phyllis M.
Hoffman, Rosekrans 1926- 15
Hoffmann, E(rnst) T(heodor) A(madeus)
1776-1822 27
See also CLR 133
Hoffmann, Felix 1911-1975 9
Hoffmann, Heinrich 1809-1894
See CLR 122
Hoffmann, Margaret Jones 1910- 48
Hoffmann, Peggy
See Hoffmann, Margaret Jones
Hofher, Catherine Baxley 1954- 130
Hofher, Cathy
See Hofher, Catherine Baxley
Hofmeyr, Dianne (Louise) 138
Hofsepian, Sylvia A. 1932- 74
Hofsinde, Robert 1902-1973 21
Hogan, Bernice Harris 1929- 12
Hogan, Inez 1895-1973 2
Hogan, James P. 1941-2010 81
Hogan, James Patrick
See Hogan, James P.
Hogan, Jamie 192
Hogan, Linda 1947- 132
Hogan, Mary 1957- 210
Hogarth, Burne 1911-1996 89
Earlier sketch in SATA 63
Hogarth, Grace (Weston Allen) 1905-1995 .. 91
Hogarth, Jr.
See Kent, Rockwell
Hogarth, (Arthur) Paul 1917-2001 41
Hogg, Garry 1902-1976 2
Hogg, Gary 1957- 172
Earlier sketch in SATA 105
Hogner, Dorothy Childs 4
Hogner, Nils 1893-1970 25
Hogrogian, Nonny 1932- 74
Autobiography Feature 127
Earlier sketch in SATA 7
See also CLR 95
See also SAAS 1

Hoh, Diane 1937- 102
Brief entry 48
Earlier sketch in SATA 52
Hoke, Helen
See Watts, Helen L. Hoke
Hoke, Helen L.
See Watts, Helen L. Hoke
Hoke, John 1925-2011 7
Hoke, John Lindsay
See Hoke, John
Hokenson, Terry 1948- 193
Hol, Coby 1943- 126
Holabird, Katharine 1948- 213
Earlier sketches in SATA 62, 135
Holaday, Bobbie 1922- 153
Holbeach, Henry
See Rands, William Brighty
Holberg, Ruth L(angland) 1889-1984 1
Holbrook, Kathy 1963- 107
Holbrook, Peter
See Glick, Carl (Cannon)
Holbrook, Sabra
See Erickson, Sabra Rollins
Holbrook, Sara 131
Holbrook, Stewart Hall 1893-1964 2
Holcomb, Jerry (Leona) Kimble 1927- 113
Holcomb, Nan
See McPhee, Norma H.
Holdcroft, Tina 227
Holden, Elizabeth Rhoda
See Lawrence, Louise
Holder, Jimmy 1962- 234
Holding, James (Clark Carlisle, Jr.)
1907-1997 3
Hole, Stian 1969- 204
Holeman, Linda 1949- 136
Autobiography Feature 136
Earlier sketch in SATA 102
Holgate, Doug 225
Holinger, William (Jacques) 1944- 90
Holisher, Desider 1901-1972 6
Holl, Adelaide Hinkle 1910- 8
Holl, Kristi
See Holl, Kristi D.
Holl, Kristi D. 1951- 51
Holl, Kristi Diane
See Holl, Kristi D.
Holland, Gay W. 1941- 128
Holland, Isabelle (Christian) 1920-2002 70
Autobiography Feature 103
Obituary 132
Earlier sketch in SATA 8
See also CLR 57
Holland, Janice 1913-1962 18
Holland, John L(ewis) 1919- 20
Holland, Joyce
See Morice, Dave
Holland, Julia 1954- 106
Holland, Lynda (H.) 1959- 77
Holland, Lys
See Gater, Dilys
Holland, Marion 1908-1989 6
Obituary 61
Holland, Richard 1976- 216
Holland, Trish 221
Hollander, John 1929- 13
Hollander, Nicole 1940(?)- 101
Hollander, Paul
See Silverberg, Robert
Hollander, Phyllis 1928- 39
Hollander, Zander 1923- 63
Holldobler, Turid 1939- 26
Holliday, Joe
See Holliday, Joseph
Holliday, Joseph 1910- 11
Hollihan, Kerrie Logan 235
Holling, Holling C(lancy) 1900-1973 15
Obituary 26
See also CLR 50
Hollingsworth, Alvin C(arl) 1930- 39

Hollingsworth, Mary 1947- *166*
    Earlier sketch in SATA *91*
Holloway, Teresa (Bragunier) 1906- 26
Hollyer, Beatrice 1957- 226
Hollyer, Belinda 204
Holm, (Else) Anne (Lise) 1922-1998 .... *1*
    See also CLR 75
    See also SAAS 7
Holm, Jennifer L. 1968(?)- 236
    Earlier sketches in SATA *120, 163, 183*
Holm, Matthew 1974- 174
Holm, Sharon Lane 1955- 114
    Earlier sketch in SATA *78*
Holman, Felice 1919- 82
    Earlier sketch in SATA *7*
    See also SAAS *17*
Holm and Hamel
    See Holm, Jennifer L.
Holmberg, Bo R. 1945- 203
Holme, Bryan 1913-1990 26
    Obituary 66
Holmes, Barbara Ware 1945- 127
    Earlier sketch in SATA *65*
Holmes, Elizabeth 1957- 191
Holmes, Elizabeth Ann
    See Holmes, Elizabeth
Holmes, John
    See Souster, (Holmes) Raymond
Holmes, Liz
    See Holmes, Elizabeth
Holmes, Marjorie (Rose) 1910-2002 .... *43*
Holmes, Martha 1961- 72
Holmes, Mary Tavener 1954- 199
Holmes, Mary Z(astrow) 1943- 80
Holmes, Oliver Wendell 1809-1894 34
Holmes, Peggy 1898- 60
Holmes, Raymond
    See Souster, (Holmes) Raymond
Holmes, Rick
    See Hardwick, Richard Holmes, Jr.
Holmes, Sara Lewis 186
Holmgren, Helen Jean 1930- 45
Holmgren, Sister George Ellen
    See Holmgren, Helen Jean
Holmgren, Virginia C(unningham) 1909- 26
Holmquist, Eve 1921- 11
Holt, K.A.
    See Roy, Kari Anne
Holt, Kimberly Willis 1960- 223
    Earlier sketches in SATA *122, 179*
Holt, Margaret 1937- 4
Holt, Margaret Van Vechten (Saunders)
    1899-1963 32
Holt, Michael (Paul) 1929- 13
Holt, Rackham
    See Holt, Margaret Van Vechten (Saunders)
Holt, Rochelle L.
    See DuBois, Rochelle Holt
Holt, Stephen
    See Thompson, Harlan
Holt, Victoria
    See Hibbert, Eleanor Alice Burford
Holtei, Christa 1953- 214
Holton, Leonard
    See Wibberley, Leonard
Holtz, Thomas R., Jr. 1965- 203
Holtze, Sally Holmes 1952- 64
Holtzman, Jerome 1926-2008 57
    Obituary 194
Holub, Joan 1956- 229
    Earlier sketches in SATA *99, 149*
Holub, Josef 1926- 175
Holubitsky, Katherine 1955- 165
    Earlier sketch in SATA *121*
Holyer, Erna Maria 1925- 22
Holyer, Ernie
    See Holyer, Erna Maria
Holyfield, John 1969- 227
Holz, Loretta 1943- 17
Holz, Loretta Marie
    See Holz, Loretta

Homel, David 1952- 97
Homze, Alma C. 1932- 17
Honey, Elizabeth 1947- 137
    Autobiography Feature 137
    Earlier sketch in SATA *112*
Honeycutt, Natalie 1945- 97
Hong, Lily Toy 1958- 76
Hong, Maxine Ting Ting
    See Kingston, Maxine Hong
Honig, Donald 1931- 18
Honig, Donald Martin
    See Honig, Donald
Honness, Elizabeth H. 1904- 2
Hoobler, Dorothy 1941- 161
    Earlier sketches in SATA *28, 109*
Hoobler, Thomas 161
    Earlier sketches in SATA *28, 109*
Hood, Joseph F. 1925- 4
Hood, Robert E. 1926- 21
Hood, Sarah
    See Killough, (Karen) Lee
Hook, Brendan 1963- 105
Hook, Frances 1912-1983 27
Hook, Geoffrey R(aynor) 1928- 103
Hook, Jeff
    See Hook, Geoffrey R(aynor)
Hook, Martha 1936- 27
Hooker, Richard
    See Heinz, W. C.
Hooker, Ruth 1920-1998 21
hooks, bell 1952(?)- 170
    Earlier sketch in SATA *115*
Hooks, William H(arris) 1921- 94
    Earlier sketch in SATA *16*
Hoon, Patricia Easterly 1954- 90
Hooper, Byrd
    See St. Clair, Byrd Hooper
Hooper, Mary 1948- 205
    Earlier sketch in SATA *160*
Hooper, Maureen Brett 1927- 76
Hooper, Meredith 1939- 159
    Earlier sketches in SATA *28, 101*
Hooper, Meredith Jean
    See Hooper, Meredith
Hooper, Patricia 1941- 95
Hoopes, Lyn Littlefield 1953- 49
    Brief entry 44
Hoopes, Ned E(dward) 1932- 21
Hoopes, Roy 1922-2009 11
Hoose, Phillip 1947- 215
    Earlier sketch in SATA *137*
Hoover, H(elen) M(ary) 1935- 132
    Brief entry 33
    Earlier sketches in SATA *44, 83*
    See also SAAS 8
Hoover, Helen (Drusilla Blackburn)
    1910-1984 12
    Obituary 39
Hopcus, Anastasia 234
Hope, Christopher 1944- 62
Hope, Christopher David Tully
    See Hope, Christopher
Hope, Laura Lee
    See Goulart, Ron
    and Stanley, George Edward
Hope Simpson, Jacynth 1930- 12
Hopf, Alice (Martha) L(ightner) 1904-1988 ... *5*
    Obituary 55
Hopgood, Tim 1961- 224
Hopkins, A. T.
    See Turngren, Annette
Hopkins, C. M.
    See Hopkins, Cathy
Hopkins, Cathy 1953- 165
Hopkins, Cathy M.
    See Hopkins, Cathy
Hopkins, Clark 1895-1976
    Obituary 34
Hopkins, Ellen 1955- 128
Hopkins, Ellen L.
    See Hopkins, Ellen

Hopkins, Jackie
    See Hopkins, Jackie Mims
Hopkins, Jackie Mims 1952- 178
    Earlier sketch in SATA *92*
Hopkins, Joseph G(erard) E(dward) 1909- ... *11*
Hopkins, (Hector) Kenneth 1914-1988
    Obituary 58
Hopkins, Lee Bennett 1938- 215
    Earlier sketches in SATA *3, 68, 125, 168*
    See also CLR *44*
    See also SAAS *4*
Hopkins, Lyman
    See Folsom, Franklin (Brewster)
Hopkins, Marjorie 1911-1999 .... *9*
Hopkins, Mary R(ice) 1956- 97
Hopkinson, Amanda 1948- 84
Hopkinson, Deborah 1952- 216
    Autobiography Feature 180
    Earlier sketches in SATA *76, 108, 159, 180*
    See also CLR *118*
Hopman, Philip 1961- 177
Hoppe, Joanne 1932- 42
Hoppe, Matthias 1952- 76
Hoppe, Paul 209
Hopper, Nancy J. 1937- 38
    Brief entry 35
Hoppey, Tim 1958- 225
Hopping, Lorraine Jean
    See Egan, Lorraine Hopping
Horacek, Judy 1961- 211
Horaek, Petr 214
    Earlier sketch in SATA *163*
Horenstein, Henry 1947- 108
Horgan, Paul (George Vincent O'Shaughnessy)
    1903-1995 13
    Obituary 84
Horlak, E.E.
    See Tepper, Sheri S.
Horler, Sydney 1888-1954 102
Horley, Alex 1970- 229
Horn, Sandra Ann 1944- 154
Hornblow, Arthur, Jr. 1893-1976 15
Hornblow, Leonora 1920-2005 18
    Obituary 171
Hornblow, Leonora Schinasi
    See Hornblow, Leonora
Horne, Constance 1927- 149
Horne, Richard 1960-2007 169
    Obituary 180
    Earlier sketch in SATA *111*
Horne, Richard Henry Hengist
    1802(?)-1884 29
Horner, Althea (Jane) 1926- 36
Horner, Dave 1934- 12
Horner, Emily 1982- 233
Horner, Jack 1946- 106
Horner, John R.
    See Horner, Jack
Horner, John Robert
    See Horner, Jack
Hornik, Laurie Miller 159
Horniman, Joanne 1951- 167
    Earlier sketch in SATA *98*
Hornos, Axel 1907-1994 20
Hornstein, Reuben Aaron 1912- 64
Horowitz, Anthony 1955- 236
    Earlier sketches in SATA *137, 195*
Horowitz, Dave 1970- 204
    Earlier sketch in SATA *172*
Horowitz, Eli 230
Horowitz, Ruth 1957- 136
Horrocks, Anita 1958- 169
Horse, Harry
    See Horne, Richard
Horsfield, Alan 1939- 153
Horstman, Lisa 1964- 219
Hort, Lenny 179
Horton, James O. 1943- 173
Horton, James Oliver
    See Horton, James O.
Horton, Joan 217

Horton, Madelyn (Stacey) 1962- *77*
Horvath, Betty 1927- *4*
Horvath, David 1972(?)- *192*
Horvath, Polly 1957- *194*
  Earlier sketches in SATA *85, 140*
  See also CLR *90*
Horwich, Frances R(appaport) 1908-2001 .... *11*
  Obituary *130*
Horwitz, Elinor Lander *45*
  Brief entry *33*
Horwood, William 1944- *85*
Hosford, Dorothy (Grant) 1900-1952 .... *22*
Hosford, Jessie 1892-1990 .... *5*
Hoshi, Shin'ichi 1926- *101*
Hoshino, Felicia 1968- *189*
Hoskyns-Abrahall, Clare (Constance
  Drury) *13*
Hosler, Danamarie 1978- *184*
Hossack, Sylvia 1939- *83*
Hossack, Sylvie Adams
  See Hossack, Sylvia
Hosseini, Khaled 1965- *156*
Hossell, Karen Price
  See Price, Karen
Hosta, Dar *192*
Hostetler, Marian 1932- *91*
Hostetter, Joyce Moyer 1952- *228*
Houck, Carter 1924- *22*
Houck, Colleen 1969- *239*
Hough, Charlotte 1924-2008 .... *9*
  Obituary *202*
Hough, Helen Charlotte
  See Hough, Charlotte
Hough, Judy Taylor 1932- *63*
  Brief entry *51*
  Earlier sketch in SATA *56*
Hough, Richard (Alexander) 1922-1999 ...... *17*
Houghton, Eric 1930- *7*
Houk, Randy 1944- *97*
Houlehen, Robert J. 1918- *18*
Houlton, Peggy Mann 1925(?)-1990 .... *6*
Household, Geoffrey 1900-1988 .... *14*
  Obituary *59*
Housman, Laurence 1865-1959 .... *25*
Houston, Dick 1943- *231*
  Earlier sketch in SATA *74*
Houston, Gloria *138*
  Autobiography Feature *138*
  Earlier sketch in SATA *81*
Houston, James A(rchibald) 1921-2005 .... *74*
  Obituary *163*
  Earlier sketch in SATA *13*
  See also CLR *3*
  See also SAAS *17*
Houston, James D. 1933-2009 .... *78*
  Obituary *203*
Houston, James Dudley
  See Houston, James D.
Houston, James Dudley
  See Houston, James D.
Houston, Jeanne Toyo Wakatsuki
  See Houston, Jeanne Wakatsuki
Houston, Jeanne Wakatsuki 1934- *168*
  Autobiography Feature *168*
  Earlier sketch in SATA *78*
Houston, Juanita C. 1921- *129*
Houtman, Jacqueline 1960- *231*
Houtman, Jacqueline Jaeger
  See Houtman, Jacqueline
Houton, Kathleen
  See Kilgore, Kathleen
Houts, Amy F. *164*
Houts, Michelle *219*
Hovey, Kate *158*
Howard, Alan 1922- *45*
Howard, Alyssa
  See Buckholtz, Eileen (Garber)
  and Glick, Ruth
  and Titchener, Louise
Howard, Arthur 1948- *212*
  Earlier sketch in SATA *165*

Howard, Arthur Charles
  See Howard, Arthur
Howard, Elizabeth Fitzgerald 1927- *119*
  Earlier sketch in SATA *74*
Howard, Ellen 1943- *184*
  Earlier sketches in SATA *67, 99*
Howard, Jane R(uble) 1924- *87*
Howard, Norman Barry 1949- *90*
Howard, P. M.
  See Howard, Pauline Rodriguez
Howard, Paul 1967- *190*
  Earlier sketch in SATA *118*
Howard, Pauline Rodriguez 1951- *124*
Howard, Prosper
  See Hamilton, Charles (Harold St. John)
Howard, Robert West 1908-1988 .... *5*
Howard, Todd 1964- *135*
Howard, Tristan
  See Currie, Stephen
Howard, Vernon (Linwood) 1918-1992 .... *40*
  Obituary *73*
Howard, Warren F.
  See Pohl, Frederik
Howarth, Daniel *222*
  Earlier sketch in SATA *188*
Howarth, David (Armine) 1912-1991 .... *6*
  Obituary *68*
Howarth, Lesley 1952- *94*
Howe, Deborah 1946-1978 .... *29*
Howe, James 1946- *224*
  Earlier sketches in SATA *29, 71, 111, 161*
  See also CLR *9*
Howe, John F. 1957- *79*
Howe, Norma 1930-2011 .... *126*
Howe, Peter 1942- *214*
Howell, Pat 1947- *15*
Howell, S.
  See Styles, (Frank) Showell
Howell, Simmone 1971- *214*
Howell, Virginia
  See Ellison, Virginia H(owell)
Howells, Amanda
  See Gersh, Amanda
Howells, Tania *229*
Howes, Barbara 1914-1996 .... *5*
Howie, Betsy 1962- *215*
Howie, Diana 1945- *122*
Howie, Diana Melson
  See Howie, Diana
Howker, Janni 1957- *72*
  Brief entry *46*
  See also CLR *14*
  See also SAAS *13*
Howland, Ethan 1963- *131*
Howland, Naomi *232*
Hoxter, Holly Nicole 1983- *231*
Hoy, Linda 1946- *65*
Hoy, Nina
  See Roth, Arthur J(oseph)
Hoyle, Geoffrey 1942- *18*
Hoyt, Ard *190*
Hoyt, Edwin P(almer), Jr. 1923- *28*
Hoyt, Erich 1950- *140*
  Earlier sketch in SATA *65*
Hoyt, Olga
  See Gruhzit-Hoyt, Olga (Margaret)
Hrdlitschka, Shelley 1956- *167*
  Earlier sketch in SATA *111*
Hrdlitschka, Shelley Joanne
  See Hrdlitschka, Shelley
Hromic, Alma A.
  See Alexander, Alma
Htin Aung, U.
  See Aung, (Maung) Htin
Hu, Ying-Hwa *173*
Huang, Benrei 1959- *86*
Huang, Nathan 1982(?)- *228*
Hubalek, Linda K. 1954- *111*
Hubbard, Crystal *209*
Hubbard, Jennifer R. *227*

Hubbard, Margaret Ann
  See Priley, Margaret (Ann) Hubbard
Hubbard, Michelle Calabro 1953- *122*
Hubbard, Patricia 1945- *124*
Hubbard, Woodleigh Marx *160*
  Earlier sketch in SATA *98*
Hubbell, Patricia 1928- *186*
  Earlier sketches in SATA *8, 132*
Hubery, Julia *195*
Hubley, Faith Elliot 1924-2001 .... *48*
  Obituary *133*
Hubley, John 1914-1977 .... *48*
  Obituary *24*
Huck, Charlotte S. 1922- *136*
  Earlier sketch in SATA *82*
Hucke, Johannes 1966- *218*
Hudak, Michal 1956- *143*
Hudson, Cheryl Willis 1948- *237*
  Earlier sketches in SATA *81, 160*
Hudson, Jan 1954-1990 .... *77*
  See also CLR *40*
Hudson, Jeffery
  See Crichton, Michael
Hudson, Jeffrey
  See Crichton, Michael
Hudson, (Margaret) Kirsty 1947- *32*
Hudson, Margaret
  See Shuter, Jane (Margaret)
Hudson, W(illiam) H(enry) 1841-1922 .... *35*
Hudson, Wade 1946- *162*
  Earlier sketch in SATA *74*
Huelsmann, Eva 1928- *16*
Huerlimann, Bettina 1909-1983 .... *39*
  Obituary *34*
Huerlimann, Ruth 1939- *32*
  Brief entry *31*
Huff, Barbara A. 1929- *67*
Huff, Tanya 1957- *171*
  Earlier sketch in SATA *85*
Huff, Tanya Sue
  See Huff, Tanya
Huff, T.S.
  See Huff, Tanya
Huff, Vivian 1948- *59*
Huffaker, Sandy 1943- *10*
Huffman, Tom *24*
Huggins, Nathan Irvin 1927-1989 .... *63*
Huggins, Peter 1951- *178*
Hughes, Carol 1955- *217*
  Earlier sketch in SATA *108*
Hughes, Dean 1943- *235*
  Earlier sketches in SATA *33, 77, 139*
  See also CLR *76*
Hughes, D.T.
  See Hughes, Dean
Hughes, Eden
  See Griffin, W. E. B.
Hughes, Edward James
  See Hughes, Ted
Hughes, James Langston
  See Hughes, Langston
Hughes, Langston 1902-1967 .... *33*
  Earlier sketch in SATA *4*
  See also CLR *17*
Hughes, Libby *71*
Hughes, Mark Peter *238*
Hughes, Matilda
  See MacLeod, Charlotte (Matilda)
Hughes, Monica 1925-2003 .... *162*
  Earlier sketches in SATA *15, 70, 119*
  See also CLR *60*
  See also SAAS *11*
Hughes, Monica Ince
  See Hughes, Monica
Hughes, Pat *197*
Hughes, Richard (Arthur Warren)
  1900-1976 .... *8*
  Obituary *25*
Hughes, Sara
  See Saunders, Susan

Hughes, Shirley 1927- *159*
  Earlier sketches in SATA *16, 70, 110*
  See also CLR *15*
Hughes, Susan 1960- *216*
Hughes, Ted 1930-1998 .... *49*
  Brief entry *27*
  Obituary *107*
  See also CLR *131*
Hughes, Thomas 1822-1896 .... *31*
  See also CLR *160*
Hughes, Virginia
  See Campbell, Hope
Hughes, Walter (Llewellyn) 1910-1993 .... *26*
Hughey, Roberta 1942- *61*
Hugo, Pierre Brackers de
  See Brackers de Hugo, Pierre
Hugo, Victor 1802-1885 .... *47*
Hugo, Victor Marie
  See Hugo, Victor
Huline-Dickens, Frank William 1931- *34*
Huling, Jan *172*
Huliska-Beith, Laura *232*
  Earlier sketch in SATA *175*
Hull, Eleanor (Means) 1913- *21*
Hull, Eric Traviss
  See Harnan, Terry
Hull, H. Braxton
  See Jacobs, Helen Hull
Hull, Jesse Redding
  See Hull, Jessie Redding
Hull, Jessie Redding 1932- *51*
Hull, Katharine 1921-1977 .... *23*
Hull, Lise (E.) 1954- *148*
Hull, Maureen 1949- *142*
Hulme, Joy N. 1922- *161*
  Earlier sketches in SATA *74, 112*
Hults, Dorothy Niebrugge 1898-2000 .... *6*
Humble, Richard 1945- *60*
Hume, Lachie *189*
Hume, Lotta Carswell *7*
Hume, Ruth Fox 1922-1980 .... *26*
  Obituary *22*
Hume, Stephen Eaton 1947- *136*
Hummel, Berta 1909-1946 .... *43*
Hummel, Sister Maria Innocentia
  See Hummel, Berta
Hummon, Marcus 1960- *213*
Humphrey, Carol Sue 1956- *167*
Humphrey, Henry (III) 1930- *16*
Humphrey, Kate
  See Forsyth, Kate
Humphrey, Sandra McLeod 1936- *95*
Humphreys, Martha 1943- *71*
Humphreys, Susan L.
  See Lowell, Susan
Humphries, Tudor 1953- *226*
Hundal, Nancy 1957- *128*
Huneck, Stephen 1949- *183*
  Earlier sketch in SATA *129*
Hungerford, Hesba Fay
  See Brinsmead, H(esba) F(ay)
Hungerford, Pixie
  See Brinsmead, H(esba) F(ay)
Hunkin, Tim 1950- *53*
Hunkin, Timothy Mark Trelawney
  See Hunkin, Tim
Hunt, Angela Elwell 1957- *159*
  Earlier sketch in SATA *75*
Hunt, Bernice 1920- *4*
Hunt, Charlotte Dumaresq
  See Demi
Hunt, Francesca
  See Holland, Isabelle (Christian)
Hunt, Irene 1907-2001 .... *91*
  Earlier sketch in SATA *2*
  See also CLR *1*
Hunt, Janie Louise 1963- *102*
Hunt, Jonathan 1966- *84*
Hunt, Joyce 1927- *31*
Hunt, Linda 1940- *39*
Hunt, Lisa B(ehnke) 1967- *84*

Hunt, Mabel Leigh 1892-1971 .... *1*
  Obituary *26*
Hunt, Morton M(agill) 1920- *22*
Hunt, Nigel
  See Greenbank, Anthony Hunt
Hunt, Peter (Leonard) 1945- *76*
Hunter, Anne B. 1966- *118*
Hunter, Bernice Thurman 1922-2002 .... *85*
  Brief entry *45*
Hunter, Bobbi Dooley 1945- *89*
Hunter, Captain Marcy
  See Ellis, Edward S.
Hunter, Chris
  See Fluke, Joanne
Hunter, Clingham M.D.
  See Adams, William Taylor
Hunter, Edith Fisher 1919- *31*
Hunter, Erin
  See Cary, Kate
Hunter, Evan 1926-2005 .... *25*
  Obituary *167*
Hunter, George E.
  See Ellis, Edward S.
Hunter, Hilda 1921- *7*
Hunter, Jana
  See Hunter, Jana Novotny
Hunter, Jana Novotny *190*
Hunter, Jim 1939- *65*
Hunter, Kristin
  See Lattany, Kristin Hunter
Hunter, Leigh
  See Etchison, Birdie L(ee)
Hunter, Lieutenant Ned
  See Ellis, Edward S.
Hunter, Linzie 1979- *227*
Hunter, Mel 1927-2004 .... *39*
Hunter, Mollie 1922- *139*
  Autobiography Feature *139*
  Earlier sketches in SATA *2, 54, 106*
  See also CLR *25*
  See also SAAS *7*
Hunter, Ned
  See Ellis, Edward S.
Hunter, Norman (George Lorimer)
  1899-1995 .... *84*
  Earlier sketch in SATA *26*
Hunter, Ryan Ann
  See Greenwood, Pamela D.
  and Macalaster, Elizabeth G.
Hunter, Sara Hoagland 1954- *98*
Hunter Blair, Pauline
  See Clarke, Pauline
Huntington, Amy 1956- *180*
  Earlier sketch in SATA *138*
Huntington, Geoffrey *145*
Huntington, Harriet E(lizabeth) 1909- *1*
Huntley, Amy *225*
Huntsberry, William E(mery) 1916- *5*
Hurd, Clement (G.) 1908-1988 .... *64*
  Obituary *54*
  Earlier sketch in SATA *2*
  See also CLR *49*
Hurd, Edith Thacher 1910-1997 .... *64*
  Obituary *95*
  Earlier sketch in SATA *2*
  See also CLR *49*
  See also SAAS *13*
Hurd, John Thacher
  See Hurd, Thacher
Hurd, Thacher 1949- *219*
  Autobiography Feature *123*
  Brief entry *45*
  Earlier sketches in SATA *46, 94*
Hurley, Jo
  See Dower, Laura
Hurley, Tonya *207*
Hurlimann, Bettina
  See Huerlimann, Bettina
Hurlimann, Ruth
  See Huerlimann, Ruth

Hurmence, Belinda 1921- *77*
  See also CLR *25*
  See also SAAS *20*
Hurst, Carol Otis 1933-2007 .... *185*
  Earlier sketch in SATA *130*
Hurt-Newton, Tania 1968- *84*
Hurwin, Davida Wills 1950- *180*
Hurwitz, Johanna 1937- *175*
  Earlier sketches in SATA *20, 71, 113*
  See also SAAS *18*
Hurwood, Bernhardt J. 1926-1987 .... *12*
  Obituary *50*
Husain, Shahrukh 1950- *108*
Huser, Glen 1943- *151*
Hutchens, Paul 1902-1977 .... *31*
Hutchins, Carleen M.
  See Hutchins, Carleen Maley
Hutchins, Carleen Maley 1911-2009 .... *9*
  Obituary *206*
Hutchins, Hazel J. 1952- *175*
  Brief entry *51*
  Earlier sketches in SATA *81, 135*
  See also SAAS *24*
Hutchins, Pat 1942- *178*
  Earlier sketches in SATA *15, 70, 111*
  See also CLR *20*
  See also SAAS *16*
Hutchins, Ross Elliott 1906- *4*
Hutchison, Linda 1942- *152*
Huthmacher, J. Joseph 1929- *5*
Hutto, Nelson (Allen) 1904-1985 .... *20*
Hutton, Kathryn 1915- *89*
Hutton, Sam
  See Jones, Allan Frewin
Hutton, Warwick 1939-1994 .... *20*
  Obituary *83*
  See also SAAS *17*
Huxley, Aldous 1894-1963 .... *63*
  See also CLR *151*
Huxley, Aldous Leonard
  See Huxley, Aldous
Huxley, Elspeth (Josceline Grant)
  1907-1997 .... *62*
  Obituary *95*
Hyde, Catherine *232*
Hyde, Catherine R.
  See Hyde, Catherine Ryan
Hyde, Catherine Ryan 1955- *224*
  Earlier sketch in SATA *141*
Hyde, Dayton O(gden) *9*
Hyde, Hawk
  See Hyde, Dayton O(gden)
Hyde, Jeannette
  See Eyerly, Jeannette
Hyde, Margaret O. 1917- *139*
  Earlier sketches in SATA *1, 42, 76*
  See also CLR *23*
  See also SAAS *8*
Hyde, Margaret Oldroyd
  See Hyde, Margaret O.
Hyde, Shelley
  See Reed, Kit
Hyde, Wayne Frederick 1922- *7*
Hylander, Clarence J(ohn) 1897-1964 .... *7*
Hyman, Miles 1962- *210*
Hyman, Paula Chase
  See Chase, Paula
Hyman, Robin 1931- *12*
Hyman, Robin Phiilip
  See Hyman, Robin
Hyman, Trina Schart 1939-2004 .... *95*
  Obituary *158*
  Earlier sketches in SATA *7, 46*
  See also CLR *50*
Hymes, Lucia M(anley) 1907-1998 .... *7*
Hyndman, Jane Andrews Lee 1912-1978 ..... *46*
  Obituary *23*
  Earlier sketch in SATA *1*
Hyndman, Robert Utley 1906-1973 .... *18*
Hynes, Pat *98*

I

Iannone, Jeanne
  See Balzano, Jeanne (Koppel)
Ibatoulline, Bagram 1965(?)- 225
  Earlier sketch in SATA *174*
Ibbitson, John Perrie 1955- 102
Ibbotson, Eva 1925-2010 221
  Earlier sketches in SATA *13, 103, 156*
Ibbotson, M. C(hristine) 1930- 5
Icenoggle, Jodi 1967- 168
Icenoggle, Jodi O.
  See Icenoggle, Jodi
Ichikawa, Satomi 1949- 208
  Brief entry 36
  Earlier sketches in SATA *47, 78, 146*
  See also CLR *62*
Idle, Molly Schaar 223
Iggulden, Hal 1972- 196
Ignatow, Amy 1977- 233
Ignoffo, Matthew 1945- 92
Igus, Toyomi 1953- 112
  Earlier sketch in SATA *76*
Ihimaera, Witi (Tame) 1944- 148
Ikeda, Daisaku 1928- 77
Ilowite, Sheldon A. 1931- 27
Ilsey, Dent
  See Chapman, John Stanton Higham
Ilsley, Dent
  See Chapman, John Stanton Higham
Ilsley, Velma (Elizabeth) 1918- 12
Imai, Ayano 1980- 190
Imai, Miko 1963- 90
Imershein, Betsy 1953- 62
Immel, Mary Blair 1930- 28
Immell, Myra H. 1941- 92
Impey, Rose 1947- 223
  Earlier sketches in SATA *69, 152*
Ingalls, Ann 227
Ingelow, Jean 1820-1897 33
Ingermanson, Randall 1958- 134
Ingermanson, Randy
  See Ingermanson, Randall
Ingersoll, Norman 1928- 79
Ingham, Colonel Frederic
  See Hale, Edward Everett
Ingman, Bruce 1963- 182
  Earlier sketch in SATA *134*
Ingman, Nicholas 1948- 52
Ingold, Jeanette 128
Ingpen, Robert 1936- 166
  Earlier sketch in SATA *109*
Ingpen, Robert Roger
  See Ingpen, Robert
Ingraham, Erick 1950- 145
Ingraham, Leonard W(illiam) 1913-2003 4
Ingram, Scott 1948- 167
  Earlier sketch in SATA *92*
Ingram, W. Scott
  See Ingram, Scott
Ingrams, Doreen 1906-1997 97
  Earlier sketch in SATA *20*
Ingrid, Charles
  See Salsitz, Rhondi Vilott
Ingves, Gunilla 1939- 101
Ingves, Gunilla Anna Maria Folkesdotter
  See Ingves, Gunilla
Inkpen, Mick 1952- 154
  Earlier sketch in SATA *99*
Innerst, Stacy 232
Innes, (Ralph) Hammond
  See Hammond Innes, Ralph
Innes, Ralph Hammond
  See Hammond Innes, Ralph
Innes, Stephanie 220
Innocenti, Roberto 1940- 159
  Earlier sketch in SATA *96*
  See also CLR *126*
Innocenti and Gallaz
  See Gallaz, Christophe
  and Innocenti, Roberto

Inns, Chris 212
Inyart, Gene
  See Namovicz, Gene Inyart
Ionesco, Eugene 1909-1994 7
  Obituary 79
Ipcar, Dahlov (Zorach) 1917- 147
  Autobiography Feature 147
  Earlier sketches in SATA *1, 49*
  See also SAAS *8*
Ireland, Karin 151
  Earlier sketch in SATA *101*
Ironside, Jetske 1940- 60
Irvin, Fred 1914- 15
Irvine, Georgeanne 1955- 72
Irvine, Joan 1951- 80
Irving, Alexander
  See Hume, Ruth Fox
Irving, Robert
  See Adler, Irving
Irving, Washington 1783-1859
  See YABC *2*
  See also CLR *97*
Irwin, Ann(abelle Bowen) 1915-1998 89
  Brief entry 38
  Obituary 106
  Earlier sketch in SATA *44*
  See also CLR *40*
  See also SAAS *14*
Irwin, Constance (H.) Frick 1913-1995 6
Irwin, Hadley
  See Hadley, Lee
  and Irwin, Ann(abelle Bowen)
Irwin, Keith Gordon 1885-1964 11
Isaac, Joanne 1934- 21
Isaacs, Anne 1949- 185
  Earlier sketch in SATA *90*
Isaacs, Jacob
  See Kranzler, George G(ershon)
Isaacson, Philip M(arshal) 1924- 87
Isadora, Rachel 1953(?)- 204
  Brief entry 32
  Earlier sketches in SATA *54, 79, 121, 165*
  See also CLR *7*
Isbell, Rebecca T(emple) 1942- 125
Isham, Charlotte H(ickock) 1912- 21
Ishida, Jui 176
Ish-Kishor, Judith 1892-1972 11
Ish-Kishor, Sulamith 1896-1977 17
Ishmael, Woodi 1914-1995 31
  Obituary 109
Isle, Sue 1963- 105
Isol 1972- 220
Israel, Elaine 1945- 12
Israel, Marion Louise 1882-1973
  Obituary 26
Iterson, S(iny) R(ose) Van
  See Van Iterson, S(iny) R(ose)
Ivanko, John D. 1966- 111
Ivanko, John Duane
  See Ivanko, John D.
Iversen, Jeremy 1980(?)- 174
Iversen, Jeremy Watt
  See Iversen, Jeremy
Iverson, Carol (L.) 1941- 145
Iverson, Diane 1950- 122
Iverson, Eric G.
  See Turtledove, Harry
Ivery, Martha M. 1948- 124
Ives, David 1951- 173
Ives, Morgan
  See Bradley, Marion Zimmer
Ives, Penny 1956- 215
Iwai, Melissa 183
Iwamatsu, Jun Atsushi 1908-1994 81
  Earlier sketch in SATA *14*
  See also CLR *4*
Iwamura, Kazuo 1939- 213
Iwasaki (Matsumoto), Chihiro 1918-1974
  See CLR *18*
Iyengar, Malathi Michelle 1954- 220

J

Jabar, Cynthia 210
Jablonski, Carla 184
Jac, Lee
  See Morton, Lee Jack, Jr.
Jack, Colin 234
Jacka, Martin 1943- 72
Jackson, Alison 1953- 228
  Earlier sketches in SATA *73, 108, 160*
Jackson, Anne 1896(?)-1984
  Obituary 37
Jackson, Barry
  See Jackson, Barry E.
Jackson, Barry E. 200
Jackson, C(aary) Paul 1902-1991 6
Jackson, Caary
  See Jackson, C(aary) Paul
Jackson, Charlotte E. (Cobden) 1903(?)-1989
  Obituary 62
Jackson, Dave
  See Jackson, J. David
Jackson, Donna M. 1959- 206
Jackson, Ellen 1943- 214
  Earlier sketches in SATA *75, 115, 167*
Jackson, Ellen B.
  See Jackson, Ellen
Jackson, Garnet Nelson 1944- 87
Jackson, Geoffrey (Holt Seymour) 1915-1987
  Obituary 53
Jackson, Gina
  See Fluke, Joanne
Jackson, Guida M. 1930- 71
Jackson, J. David 1944- 91
Jackson, Jacqueline 1928- 65
Jackson, Jacqueline Dougan
  See Jackson, Jacqueline
Jackson, Jesse 1908-1983 29
  Obituary 48
  Earlier sketch in SATA *2*
  See also CLR *28*
Jackson, Marjorie 1928- 127
Jackson, Melanie 1956- 141
Jackson, Mike 1946- 91
Jackson, Neta J. 1944- 91
Jackson, O. B.
  See Jackson, C(aary) Paul
Jackson, Rob 1961- 176
Jackson, Robert B(lake) 1926- 8
Jackson, Robert Bradley
  See Jackson, Rob
Jackson, Sally
  See Kellogg, Jean (Defrees)
Jackson, Shirley 1919-1965 2
Jackson, Woody 1948- 92
Jackson Issa, Kai 205
Jacob, Helen Pierce 1927- 21
Jacobin
  See Bisson, Terry
Jacobs, Deborah Lynn 187
Jacobs, Flora Gill 1918-2006 5
  Obituary 178
Jacobs, Francine 1935- 150
  Brief entry 42
  Earlier sketch in SATA *43*
Jacobs, Frank 1929- 30
Jacobs, Helen Hull 1908-1997 12
Jacobs, Joseph 1854-1916 25
Jacobs, Judy 1952- 69
Jacobs, Laurie A. 1956- 89
Jacobs, Leah
  See Gellis, Roberta
Jacobs, Lee
  See Stone, Tanya Lee
Jacobs, Leland Blair 1907-1992 20
  Obituary 71
Jacobs, Linda
  See Altman, Linda Jacobs
Jacobs, Lou(is), Jr. 1921- 2
Jacobs, Paul DuBois 235
Jacobs, Shannon K. 1947- 77

Jacobs, Susan
  See Quinn, Susan
Jacobs, William Jay 1933- 89
  Earlier sketch in SATA 28
Jacobsen, Laura 177
Jacobson, Andrew 235
Jacobson, Daniel 1923- 12
Jacobson, Jennifer
  See Jacobson, Jennifer Richard
Jacobson, Jennifer Richard 1958- 233
  Earlier sketch in SATA 170
Jacobson, Morris K(arl) 1906- 21
Jacobson, Rick 170
Jacobus, Tim 1959- 234
Jacopetti, Alexandra
  See Hart, Alexandra
Jacques, Brian 1939-2011 176
  Earlier sketches in SATA 62, 95, 138
  See also CLR 21
Jacques, Robin 1920-1995 32
  Brief entry 30
  Obituary 86
  See also SAAS 5
Jaekel, Susan M. 1948- 89
Jaffe, Michele 179
Jaffe, Michele Sharon
  See Jaffe, Michele
Jaffee, Al(lan) 1921- 66
  Earlier sketch in SATA 37
Jagendorf, Moritz (Adolf) 1888-1981 2
  Obituary 24
Jago 1979- 216
Jahn, Joseph Michael
  See Jahn, Michael
Jahn, Michael 1943- 28
Jahn, Mike
  See Jahn, Michael
Jahn-Clough, Lisa 1967- 193
  Earlier sketches in SATA 88, 152
Jahsmann, Allan Hart 1916- 28
Jakes, John 1932- 62
Jakes, John William
  See Jakes, John
Jalali, Reza 234
James, Andrew
  See Kirkup, James
James, Ann 1952- 168
  Earlier sketches in SATA 82, 117
James, Betsy 183
James, Bill 1929- 205
James, B.J.
  See James, Brian
James, Brian 1976- 212
  Earlier sketch in SATA 140
James, Bronte
  See Nash, Renea Denise
James, Captain Lew
  See Stratemeyer, Edward L.
James, Charlie 1961- 185
James, Curtis E. 182
James, Dynely
  See Mayne, William
James, Edwin
  See Gunn, James E.
James, Elizabeth 1942- 97
  Earlier sketches in SATA 39, 45, 52
James, Emily
  See Standiford, Natalie
James, Gordon C. 1973- 195
James, Harry Clebourne 1896-1978 11
James, J. Alison 1962- 146
  Earlier sketch in SATA 83
James, Josephine
  See Sterne, Emma Gelders
James, Mary
  See Meaker, Marijane
James, Matt 201
James, Philip
  See del Rey, Lester
  and Moorcock, Michael
James, Rhian Nest 235

James, Robin 1953- 50
James, Robin Irene
  See James, Robin
James, Simon 1961- 202
James, T. F.
  See Fleming, Thomas
James, Tegan
  See Odgers, Sally Farrell
James, Will(iam Roderick) 1892-1942 19
Jameson, W. C. 1942- 93
Jamieson, Ian R.
  See Goulart, Ron
Jamieson, Victoria 218
Jamiolkowski, Raymond M. 1953- 81
Jane, Mary Childs 1909-1991 6
Jane, Pamela 158
Janeczko, Paul B(ryan) 1945- 155
  Earlier sketches in SATA 53, 98
  See also CLR 47
  See also SAAS 18
Janes, Edward C. 1908-1984 25
Janes, Edward Clarence
  See Janes, Edward C.
Janes, J(oseph) Robert 1935- 148
  Brief entry 50
  Earlier sketch in SATA 101
Janeway, Elizabeth (Hall) 1913-2005 19
Janger, Kathleen N. 1940- 66
Jango-Cohen, Judith 1955- 208
Janice
  See Brustlein, Janice Tworkov
Janisch, Heinz 1960- 181
Janni, Rebecca 229
Janosch
  See Eckert, Horst
Janover, Caroline (Davis) 1943- 141
  Earlier sketch in SATA 89
Janovitz, Marilyn 194
Jansen, Jared
  See Cebulash, Mel
Janson, Dora Jane (Heineberg) 1916- 31
Janson, H(orst) W(oldemar) 1913-1982 9
Jansson, Tove (Marika) 1914-2001 41
  Earlier sketch in SATA 3
  See also CLR 125
Janus, Grete
  See Hertz, Grete Janus
Jaques, Faith 1923-1997 97
  Earlier sketches in SATA 21, 69
Jaquith, Priscilla 1908- 51
Jaramillo, Mari-Luci 1928- 139
Jarka, Jeff 221
Jarman, Julia 1946- 198
  Earlier sketch in SATA 133
Jarman, Rosemary Hawley 1935- 7
Jarrell, Mary Von Schrader 1914- 35
Jarrell, Randall 1914-1965 7
  See also CLR 111
Jarrett, Clare 1952- 201
Jarrett, Roxanne
  See Werner, Herma
Jarrie, Martin 1953- 219
Jarrow, Gail 1952- 185
  Earlier sketch in SATA 84
Jarvis, E.K.
  See Ellison, Harlan
  and Silverberg, Robert
Jarvis, Robin 1963- 181
Jarzab, Anna 1984- 227
Jaskol, Julie 1958- 127
Jasner, W. K.
  See Watson, Jane Werner
Jassem, Kate
  See Oppenheim, Joanne
Jauss, Anne Marie 1902(?)-1991 10
  Obituary 69
Javaherbin, Mina 230
Javernick, Ellen 1938- 217
  Earlier sketch in SATA 89
Javins, Marie 1966- 212
Jay, Alison 196

Jay, Stacey 1978(?)- 231
Jayne, Lieutenant R. H.
  See Ellis, Edward S.
Jaynes, Clare
  See Mayer, Jane Rothschild
Jeake, Samuel, Jr.
  See Aiken, Conrad
Jean-Bart, Leslie 1954- 121
Jeapes, Ben 1965- 174
Jecan, Gavriel 1962- 200
Jefferds, Vincent H(arris) 1916- 59
  Brief entry 49
Jefferies, (John) Richard 1848-1887 16
Jeffers, Dawn 189
Jeffers, Oliver 1977- 213
  Earlier sketch in SATA 175
Jeffers, Susan 1942- 202
  Earlier sketches in SATA 17, 70, 129, 137
  See also CLR 30
Jefferson, Sarah
  See Farjeon, (Eve) Annabel
Jeffries, Roderic 1926- 4
Jeffries, Roderic Graeme
  See Jeffries, Roderic
Jenkin-Pearce, Susie 1943- 80
Jenkins, A. M. 1961- 174
Jenkins, Amanda McRaney
  See Jenkins, A. M.
Jenkins, Debra Reid
  See Reid Jenkins, Debra
Jenkins, Emily 1967- 174
  Earlier sketch in SATA 144
Jenkins, Jean 98
Jenkins, Jerry B. 1949- 149
Jenkins, Jerry Bruce
  See Jenkins, Jerry B.
Jenkins, Leonard 189
Jenkins, Marie M(agdalen) 1909- 7
Jenkins, Martin 1959- 216
Jenkins, M.D.
  See Jenkins, Martin
Jenkins, Patrick 1955- 72
Jenkins, Steve 1952- 218
  Earlier sketches in SATA 154, 188
Jenkins, Ward 1968- 238
Jenkins, William A(twell) 1922-1998 9
Jenkyns, Chris 1924- 51
Jennewein, James 215
Jennewein, Jim
  See Jennewein, James
Jennings, Christopher S. 1971(?)- 201
Jennings, Coleman A(lonzo) 1933- 64
Jennings, C.S.
  See Jennings, Christopher S.
Jennings, Dana Andrew 1957- 93
Jennings, Elizabeth (Joan) 1926-2001 66
Jennings, Gary 1928-1999 9
  Obituary 117
Jennings, Gary Gayne
  See Jennings, Gary
Jennings, Linda 1937- 211
Jennings, Linda M.
  See Jennings, Linda
Jennings, Patrick 1962- 205
  Earlier sketches in SATA 96, 160
Jennings, Paul 1943- 165
  Earlier sketch in SATA 88
  See also CLR 40
Jennings, Richard W. 1945- 185
  Earlier sketch in SATA 136
Jennings, Robert
  See Hamilton, Charles (Harold St. John)
Jennings, S. M.
  See Meyer, Jerome Sydney
Jennings, Sharon 1954- 231
  Earlier sketch in SATA 95
Jennings, Sharon Elizabeth
  See Jennings, Sharon
Jennison, C. S.
  See Starbird, Kaye
Jennison, Keith Warren 1911-1995 14

Jensen, Kathryn 1949- *81*
Jensen, Kristine Mary 1961- *78*
Jensen, Niels 1927- *25*
Jensen, Vickie (Dee) 1946- *81*
Jensen, Virginia Allen 1927- *8*
Jenson-Elliott, Cynthia L(ouise) 1962- ... *143*
Jeram, Anita 1965- *219*
  Earlier sketches in SATA *71, 102, 154*
Jerman, Jerry 1949- *89*
Jernigan, E. Wesley 1940- *85*
Jernigan, Gisela (Evelyn) 1948- *85*
Jerome, Elaine *228*
Jeschke, Susan 1942- *42*
  Brief entry *27*
Jessel, Camilla (Ruth) 1937- *143*
  Earlier sketch in SATA *29*
Jessell, Tim *225*
  Earlier sketch in SATA *177*
Jessey, Cornelia
  See Sussman, Cornelia Silver
Jewel
  See Kilcher, Jewel
Jewell, Nancy 1940- *109*
  Brief entry *41*
Jewett, Eleanore Myers 1890-1967 .... *5*
Jewett, Sarah Orne 1849-1909 .... *15*
Jewett, Theodora Sarah Orne
  See Jewett, Sarah Orne
Jezard, Alison 1919- *57*
  Brief entry *34*
Jiang, Cheng An 1943- *109*
Jiang, Ji-li 1954- *101*
Jiang, Zheng An
  See Jiang, Cheng An
Jiler, John 1946- *42*
  Brief entry *35*
Jimenez, Francisco 1943- *219*
  Earlier sketch in SATA *108*
Jinks, Catherine 1963- *207*
  Earlier sketches in SATA *94, 155*
Jobb, Jamie 1945- *29*
Jobling, Curtis *131*
Jocelyn, Ann Henning 1948- *92*
Jocelyn, Marthe 1956- *198*
  Earlier sketches in SATA *118, 163*
Joerns, Consuelo *44*
  Brief entry *33*
Joey D
  See Macaulay, Teresa
Johansen, Krista V.
  See Johansen, K.V.
Johansen, K.V 1968- *186*
Johansen, K.V. 1968- *186*
  Earlier sketch in SATA *129*
Johansson, Philip *163*
John, Antony 1972- *206*
John, Joyce *59*
Johns, Avery
  See Cousins, Margaret
Johns, Elizabeth 1943- *88*
Johns, Janetta
  See Quin-Harkin, Janet
Johns, Linda 1945- *173*
Johns, W(illiam) E(arle) 1893-1968 .... *55*
Johns, Captain W. E.
  See Johns, W(illiam) E(arle)
Johnson, A.
  See Johnson, Annabell
Johnson, A. E.
  See Johnson, Annabell
  and Johnson, Edgar (Raymond)
Johnson, Angela 1961- *188*
  Earlier sketches in SATA *69, 102, 150*
  See also CLR *33*
Johnson, Annabel
  See Johnson, Annabell
Johnson, Annabell 1921- *72*
  Earlier sketch in SATA *2*
Johnson, Art 1946- *123*
Johnson, B. F. 1920- *1*

Johnson, Benjamin F., of Boone
  See Riley, James Whitcomb
Johnson, Bettye 1858-1919
  See Rogers, Bettye
Johnson, Caryn
  See Goldberg, Whoopi
Johnson, Caryn E.
  See Goldberg, Whoopi
Johnson, Caryn Elaine
  See Goldberg, Whoopi
Johnson, Charles R. 1925- *11*
Johnson, Charlotte Buel
  See von Wodtke, Charlotte Buel Johnson
Johnson, Christine 1978- *232*
Johnson, Chuck
  See Johnson, Charles R.
Johnson, Crockett
  See Leisk, David (Johnson)
Johnson, D(ana) William 1945- *23*
Johnson, Daniel Shahid 1954- *73*
Johnson, David
  See Johnson, David A.
Johnson, David A. 1951- *191*
Johnson, D.B. 1944- *183*
  Earlier sketch in SATA *146*
Johnson, Dianne 1960- *130*
  See Johnson, Dinah
Johnson, Dinah *231*
  See Johnson, Dianne
Johnson, Dolores 1949- *69*
Johnson, Donald B.
  See Johnson, D.B.
Johnson, Dorothy M(arie) 1905-1984 ...... *6*
  Obituary *40*
Johnson, E(ugene) Harper *44*
Johnson, Edgar (Raymond) 1912-1990 .... *72*
  Earlier sketch in SATA *2*
Johnson, Eleanor Murdock 1892-1987
  Obituary *54*
Johnson, Elizabeth 1911-1984 .... *7*
  Obituary *39*
Johnson, Eric W(arner) 1918-1994 ....
  Obituary *82*
  Earlier sketch in SATA *8*
Johnson, Evelyne 1922- *20*
Johnson, Fred 19(?)-1982 .... *63*
Johnson, Gaylord 1884-1972 .... *7*
Johnson, Gerald White 1890-1980 .... *19*
  Obituary *28*
Johnson, Gillian 1963- *215*
Johnson, Harper
  See Johnson, E(ugene) Harper
Johnson, Harriett 1908-1987
  Obituary *53*
Johnson, James Ralph 1922- *1*
Johnson, James Weldon 1871-1938 .... *31*
  See also CLR *32*
Johnson, Jane 1951- *48*
Johnson, Jen Cullerton 1972- *230*
Johnson, Joan J. 1942- *59*
Johnson, John E(mil) 1929- *34*
Johnson, Johnny 1901-1995
  See Johnson, (Walter) Ryerson
Johnson, Kathleen Jeffrie 1950- *186*
Johnson, Kathryn
  See Jensen, Kathryn
Johnson, La Verne B(ravo) 1925- *13*
Johnson, Layne *222*
  Earlier sketch in SATA *187*
Johnson, Lee Kaiser 1962- *78*
Johnson, Lissa H(alls) 1955- *65*
Johnson, Lois Smith 1894-1993 .... *6*
Johnson, Lois Walfrid 1936- *130*
  Earlier sketches in SATA *22, 91*
Johnson, Margaret S(weet) 1893-1964 ..... *35*
Johnson, Marguerite Annie
  See Angelou, Maya
Johnson, Mary Frances K. 1929(?)-1979
  Obituary *27*
Johnson, Maud Battle 1918(?)-1985
  Obituary *46*

Johnson, Maureen 1973- *232*
  Earlier sketch in SATA *200*
Johnson, Meredith Merrell 1952- *104*
Johnson, Milton 1932- *31*
Johnson, Mo 1966- *234*
Johnson, Neil 1954- *135*
  Earlier sketch in SATA *73*
Johnson, Pamela 1949- *71*
Johnson, Patricia Polin 1956- *84*
Johnson, Paul Brett 1947- *132*
  Earlier sketch in SATA *83*
Johnson, Rebecca L. 1956- *147*
  Earlier sketch in SATA *67*
Johnson, Rick L. 1954- *79*
Johnson, (Walter) Ryerson 1901-1995 ..... *10*
  Obituary *106*
Johnson, Scott 1952- *119*
  Earlier sketch in SATA *76*
Johnson, Sherrie 1948- *87*
Johnson, Shirley K(ing) 1927- *10*
Johnson, Siddie Joe 1905-1977
  Obituary *20*
Johnson, Spencer 1938- *145*
  Brief entry *38*
Johnson, Stacie
  See Myers, Walter Dean
Johnson, Stephen T. 1964- *189*
  Earlier sketches in SATA *84, 141*
Johnson, Steve 1960- *230*
  Earlier sketch in SATA *177*
Johnson, Sue Kaiser 1963- *78*
Johnson, Sylvia A. *166*
  Brief entry *52*
  Earlier sketch in SATA *104*
Johnson, Varian 1977- *229*
Johnson, William R. *38*
Johnson, William Weber 1909-1992 .... *7*
Johnson-Feelings, Dianne
  See Johnson, Dianne
Johnston, Agnes Christine
  See Dazey, Agnes J(ohnston)
Johnston, Annie Fellows 1863-1931 .... *37*
Johnston, Dorothy Grunbock 1915-1979 ... *54*
Johnston, Ginny 1946- *60*
Johnston, H(ugh) A(nthony) S(tephen)
  1913-1967 .... *14*
Johnston, Janet 1944- *71*
Johnston, Jeffry W. *188*
Johnston, Johanna 1914(?)-1982 .... *12*
  Obituary *33*
Johnston, Julie 1941- *110*
  Autobiography Feature *128*
  Earlier sketch in SATA *78*
  See also CLR *41*
  See also SAAS *24*
Johnston, Lynn 1947- *216*
  Earlier sketch in SATA *118*
Johnston, Lynn Beverley
  See Johnston, Lynn
Johnston, Mark *194*
Johnston, Norma
  See St. John, Nicole
Johnston, Portia
  See Takakjian, Portia
Johnston, Susan Taylor 1942- *180*
  Earlier sketches in SATA *8, 83, 128*
  See Johnston, Tony
Johnston, Tim(othy Patrick) 1962- *146*
Johnston, Tony *226*
  See Johnston, Susan Taylor
Joinson, Carla *160*
Jolin, Paula *186*
Jolivet, Joelle 1965- *221*
Jonas, Ann 1932- *135*
  Brief entry *42*
  Earlier sketch in SATA *50*
  See also CLR *74*
Jonell, Lynne 1956- *196*
  Earlier sketch in SATA *109*

Jones, Adrienne 1915-2000 82
  Earlier sketch in SATA 7
  See also SAAS 10
Jones, Allan Frewin 1954- 204
Jones, Annabel
  See Lewis, Mary
Jones, Betty Millsaps 1940- 54
Jones, Carol 1942- 153
  Earlier sketch in SATA 79
Jones, Carrie 1971- 229
  Earlier sketch in SATA 191
Jones, Charles M.
  See Jones, Chuck
Jones, Charlotte Foltz 1945- 122
  Earlier sketch in SATA 77
Jones, Chuck 1912-2002 53
  Obituary 133
Jones, Constance 112
Jones, Constance A.
  See Jones, Constance
Jones, David 1956- 202
Jones, Diana Wynne 1934-2011 234
  Earlier sketches in SATA 9, 70, 108, 160
  See also CLR 120
  See also SAAS 7
Jones, Douglas B. 202
Jones, Douglas C(lyde) 1924-1998 52
Jones, Elizabeth McDavid 155
Jones, Elizabeth Orton 1910-2005 18
  Obituary 164
Jones, Evan 1915-1996 3
Jones, Frewin
  See Jones, Allan Frewin
Jones, Geraldine
  See McCaughrean, Geraldine
Jones, Gillingham
  See Hamilton, Charles (Harold St. John)
Jones, Gwyneth A. 1952- 159
Jones, Gwyneth Ann
  See Jones, Gwyneth A.
Jones, Harold 1904-1992 14
  Obituary 72
Jones, Helen Hinckley 1903-1991 26
Jones, Helen L(ouise) 1903-1973
  Obituary 22
Jones, Hettie 1934- 42
  Brief entry 27
Jones, Hortense P. 1918- 9
Jones, J. Sydney 1948- 101
Jones, Jasmine
  See Papademetriou, Lisa
Jones, Jennifer (Berry) 1947- 90
Jones, Jessie Mae Orton 1887(?)-1983
  Obituary 37
Jones, John R(obert) 1926- 76
Jones, Jon Sydney
  See Jones, J. Sydney
Jones, Judith
  See James, Bill
Jones, Kimberly K. 1957- 187
Jones, Marcia Thornton 1958- 217
  Earlier sketches in SATA 73, 115
Jones, Martha T(annery) 1931- 130
Jones, Mary Alice 1898(?)-1980 6
Jones, McClure 34
Jones, Noah Z. 182
Jones, Patrick 1961- 210
  Earlier sketch in SATA 136
Jones, Penelope 1938- 31
Jones, Rebecca C(astaldi) 1947- 99
  Earlier sketch in SATA 33
Jones, Robin D(orothy) 1959- 80
Jones, Sanford W.
  See Thorn, John
Jones, Sylvie 185
Jones, Sylvie Michelle
  See Jones, Sylvie
Jones, Terence Graham Parry 1942- 127
  Brief entry 51
  Earlier sketch in SATA 67

Jones, Terry
  See Jones, Terence Graham Parry
Jones, Tim 237
Jones, Tim Wynne
  See Wynne-Jones, Tim
Jones, Traci L. 186
Jones, V. M. 1958- 147
Jones, Veda Boyd 1948- 119
Jones, Victoria Mary
  See Jones, V. M.
Jones, Volcano
  See Mitchell, Adrian
Jones, Weyman (B.) 1928- 4
  See also SAAS 11
Jones, William Glynne
  See Glynne-Jones, William
Jonk, Clarence 1906-1987 10
Jonsberg, Barry 1951- 168
Joos, Francoise 1956- 78
Joos, Frederic 1953- 78
Joosse, Barbara 1949- 220
  Earlier sketches in SATA 52, 96, 164
Joosse, Barbara M.
  See Joosse, Barbara
Joosse, Barbara Monnot
  See Joosse, Barbara
Jordan, Alexis Hill
  See Glick, Ruth
  and Titchener, Louise
Jordan, Anne Devereaux 1943- 80
Jordan, Chris
  See Philbrick, Rodman
Jordan, Deloris 191
Jordan, Devin 221
Jordan, Don
  See Howard, Vernon (Linwood)
Jordan, Hope Dahle 1905-1995 15
Jordan, Jael (Michal) 1949- 30
Jordan, June 1936-2002 136
  Earlier sketch in SATA 4
  See also CLR 10
Jordan, June Meyer
  See Jordan, June
Jordan, Lee
  See Scholefield, Alan
Jordan, Martin George 1944- 84
Jordan, Robert 1948-2007 95
Jordan, Robert K.
  See Jordan, Robert
Jordan, Rosa 1939- 191
Jordan, Roslyn M. 189
Jordan, Sherryl 1949- 122
  Earlier sketch in SATA 71
  See also SAAS 23
Jordan, Shirley 1930- 154
Jordan, Tanis 1946- 84
Jordan-Fenton, Christy 239
Jorgensen, Ivar
  See Ellison, Harlan
  and Garrett, Randall
Jorgensen, Mary Venn -1995 36
Jorgensen, Norman 1954- 157
Jorgenson, Ivar
  See Silverberg, Robert
Jorisch, Stephane 178
Joseph, Anne
  See Coates, Anna
Joseph, Danielle 1973- 235
Joseph, James (Herz) 1924- 53
Joseph, Joan 1939- 34
Joseph, Joseph M(aron) 1903-1979 22
Joseph, Patrick
  See O'Malley, Kevin
Josephs, Rebecca
  See Talbot, Toby
Josephson, Judith Pinkerton 1943- 198
Josh
  See Twain, Mark
Joshua, Peter
  See Stone, Peter
Joslin, Mary 1953- 176

Joslin, Sesyle
  See Hine, Sesyle Joslin
Joubert, Beverly 1957- 204
Joubert, Dereck 204
Journet, Mireille
  See Marokvia, Mireille
Joyce, Bill
  See Joyce, William
Joyce, J(ames) Avery 1902-1987 11
  Obituary 50
Joyce, Peter 1937- 127
Joyce, William 1957- 118
  Brief entry 46
  Earlier sketch in SATA 72
  See also CLR 26
Joyner, Jerry 1938- 34
Juan, Ana 1961- 179
Juarez, Fernando 230
Juarez, Fernando Lopez
  See Juarez, Fernando
Jubb, Sophie 210
Jubert, Herve 185
Juby, Susan 1969- 202
  Earlier sketch in SATA 156
Jucker, Sita 1921- 5
Judah, Aaron 1923- 118
Judd, Cyril
  See Kornbluth, C(yril) M.
  and Merril, Judith
  and Pohl, Frederik
Judd, Denis (O'Nan) 1938- 33
Judd, Frances K.
  See Benson, Mildred
Jude, Conny 81
Judge, Lita 234
  Earlier sketch in SATA 192
Judson, Clara Ingram 1879-1960 38
  Brief entry 27
Judy, Stephen
  See Tchudi, Stephen N.
Judy, Stephen N.
  See Tchudi, Stephen N.
Juhasz, Victor 1954- 177
Jukes, Mavis 1947- 219
  Brief entry 43
  Earlier sketches in SATA 72, 111
  See also SAAS 12
Jules, Jacqueline 1956- 218
  Earlier sketches in SATA 148, 183
Julesberg, Elizabeth Rider Montgomery
  1902-1985 34
  Obituary 41
  Earlier sketch in SATA 3
Julian, Jane
  See Wiseman, David
Julian, Russell 1975- 237
Julian, Sean 236
Jumpp, Hugo
  See MacPeek, Walter G.
Junco, Martha Aviles
  See Aviles, Martha
Jungman, Ann 165
Jupo, Frank J. 1904-1981 7
Jurmain, Suzanne 1945- 169
  Earlier sketch in SATA 72
Jurmain, Suzanne Tripp
  See Jurmain, Suzanne
Juster, Norton 1929- 220
  Earlier sketches in SATA 3, 132
  See also CLR 112
Justus, May 1898-1989 1
  Obituary 106
Jutte, Jan 1953- 231
Juvenilia
  See Taylor, Ann

K

Kaaberbol, Lene
See Kaaberbol, Lene
Kaaberbol, Lene 1960- *159*
Kabdebo, Tamas
See Kabdebo, Thomas
Kabdebo, Thomas 1934- *10*
Kabibble, Osh
See Jobb, Jamie
Kacer, Kathy 1954- *184*
Earlier sketch in SATA *142*
Kaczman, James *156*
Kadair, Deborah Ousley *184*
Kade, Stacey *234*
Kadefors, Sara 1965- *218*
Kadesch, Robert R(udstone) 1922- *31*
Kadohata, Cynthia 1956(?)- *228*
Earlier sketches in SATA *155, 180*
See also CLR *121*
Kadohata, Cynthia L.
See Kadohata, Cynthia
Kaempfert, Wade
See del Rey, Lester
Kaestner, Erich 1899-1974 .... *14*
See also CLR *153*
Kagawa, Julie *228*
Kahl, Jonathan (D.) 1959- *77*
Kahl, M(arvin) P(hilip) 1934- *37*
Kahl, Virginia (Caroline) 1919-2004 .... *48*
Brief entry *38*
Obituary *158*
Kahn, Joan 1914-1994 .... *48*
Obituary *82*
Kahn, Katherine Janus 1942- *220*
Earlier sketches in SATA *90, 167*
Kahn, Peggy
See Katz, Bobbi
Kahn, Roger 1927- *37*
Kahukiwa, Robyn 1940- *134*
Kains, Josephine
See Goulart, Ron
Kaizuki, Kiyonori 1950- *72*
Kajikawa, Kimiko *212*
Kakimoto, Kozo 1915- *11*
Kalashnikoff, Nicholas 1888-1961 .... *16*
Kalb, Jonah 1926- *23*
Kalbacken, Joan 1925- *96*
Kalechofsky, Roberta 1931- *92*
Kaler, James Otis 1848-1912 .... *15*
Kalis, Jennifer *207*
Kalish, Claire M. 1947- *92*
Kallen, Stuart A. 1955- *126*
Earlier sketch in SATA *86*
Kallen, Stuart Arnold
See Kallen, Stuart A.
Kallevig, Christine Petrell 1955- *164*
Kalman, Bobbie 1947- *63*
Kalman, Maira 1949- *137*
Earlier sketch in SATA *96*
See also CLR *32*
Kalnay, Francis 1899-1992 .... *7*
Kaloustian, Rosanne 1955- *93*
Kalow, Gisela 1946- *32*
Kalstein, Dave *175*
Kamara, Mariatu *214*
Kamen, Gloria 1923- *98*
Earlier sketch in SATA *9*
Kamerman, Sylvia E.
See Burack, Sylvia K.
Kamm, Josephine (Hart) 1905-1989 .... *24*
Kammerman, Sylvia K.
See Burack, Sylvia K.
Kandel, Michael 1941- *93*
Kandell, Alice S. 1938- *35*
Kane, Bob 1916-1998 .... *120*
Kane, Henry Bugbee 1902-1971 .... *14*
Kane, Kim 1973(?)- *221*
Kane, L. A.
See Mannetti, Lisa
Kane, Robert W. 1910- *18*

Kane, Wilson
See Bloch, Robert (Albert)
Kanefield, Teri 1960- *135*
Kanell, Beth *215*
Kaner, Etta 1947- *198*
Earlier sketch in SATA *126*
Kanetzke, Howard W(illiam) 1932- *38*
Kangas, Juli 1958- *200*
Kann, Elizabeth *180*
Kann, Victoria *180*
Kanninen, Barbara *196*
Kanninen, Barbara J.
See Kanninen, Barbara
Kanoza, Muriel Canfield
See Canfield, Muriel
Kantner, Seth 1965- *179*
Kanzawa, Toshiko
See Furukawa, Toshi
Kanzler, John 1963- *188*
Kaplan, Andrew 1960- *78*
Kaplan, Anne Bernays
See Bernays, Anne
Kaplan, Bess 1927- *22*
Kaplan, Boche 1926- *24*
Kaplan, Elizabeth 1956- *83*
Kaplan, Elizabeth A.
See Kaplan, Elizabeth
Kaplan, Irma 1900- *10*
Kaplan, Jean Caryl Korn 1926- *10*
Kaplow, Robert 1954- *70*
Karageorge, Michael
See Anderson, Poul
Karas, G. Brian 1957- *222*
Earlier sketch in SATA *178*
Karas, George Brian
See Karas, G. Brian
Karasz, Ilonka 1896-1981
Obituary *29*
Karen, Ruth 1922-1987 .... *9*
Obituary *54*
Kark, Nina Mary
See Bawden, Nina
Karl, Herb 1938- *73*
Karl, Jean E(dna) 1927-2000 .... *122*
Earlier sketch in SATA *34*
See also SAAS *10*
Karlin, Bernie 1927- *68*
Karlin, Eugene 1918- *10*
Karlin, Nurit *103*
Earlier sketch in SATA *63*
Karlins, Mark 1947- *219*
Karnes, Frances A. 1937- *110*
Karp, Naomi J. 1926- *16*
Karpinski, J. Rick
See Karpinski, John Eric
Karpinski, John Eric 1952- *81*
Karpinski, Rick
See Karpinski, John Eric
Karr, Julia *239*
Karr, Kathleen 1946- *212*
Earlier sketches in SATA *82, 127*
Karr, Phyllis Ann 1944- *119*
Karwoski, Gail 1949- *127*
Karwoski, Gail Langer
See Karwoski, Gail
Kashiwagi, Isami 1925- *10*
Kaslik, Ibi
See Kaslik, Ibolya Emma
Kaslik, Ibolya Emma 1973- *185*
Kassem, Lou 1931- *62*
Brief entry *51*
Kastel, Warren
See Silverberg, Robert
Kastner, Erich
See Kaestner, Erich
Kastner, Jill (Marie) 1964- *117*
Earlier sketch in SATA *70*
Kasuya, Masahiro 1937- *51*
Kasza, Keiko 1951- *191*
Earlier sketch in SATA *124*

Kataphusin
See Ruskin, John
Katchen, Carole 1944- *9*
Katcher, Brian 1975- *203*
Kate, Lauren 1981- *237*
Kathryn
See Searle, Kathryn Adrienne
Kato, Aya 1982- *202*
Katona, Robert 1949- *21*
Katsarakis, Joan Harries
See Harries, Joan
Katz, Alan *231*
Earlier sketch in SATA *185*
Katz, Avi 1949- *199*
Katz, Avner 1939- *103*
Katz, Bobbi 1933- *217*
Earlier sketches in SATA *12, 179*
Katz, Fred(eric Phillip) 1938- *6*
Katz, Jane B(resler) 1934- *33*
Katz, Karen 1947- *232*
Earlier sketches in SATA *158, 195*
Katz, Marjorie P.
See Weiser, Marjorie P(hillis) K(atz)
Katz, Susan 1945- *156*
Katz, Welwyn Wilton 1948- *96*
Autobiography Feature *118*
Earlier sketch in SATA *62*
See also CLR *45*
Katz, William 1940- *98*
Katz, William Loren 1927- *13*
Kaufman, Bel *57*
Kaufman, Jeff 1955- *84*
Kaufman, Joe 1911-2001 .... *33*
Kaufman, Joseph
See Kaufman, Joe
Kaufman, Mervyn D. 1932- *4*
Kaufmann, Angelika 1935- *15*
Kaufmann, John 1931- *18*
Kaula, Edna Mason 1906-1987 .... *13*
Kaur Khalsa, Dayal
See Khalsa, Dayal Kaur
Kavaler, Lucy 1930- *23*
Kavanagh, Jack 1920- *85*
Kavanagh, P(atrick) J(oseph Gregory)
1931- *122*
Kavanaugh, Ian
See Webb, Jean Francis (III)
Kay, Alan N. 1965- *144*
Kay, Elizabeth 1949- *165*
Kay, Guy Gavriel 1954- *167*
Earlier sketch in SATA *121*
Kay, Helen
See Goldfrank, Helen Colodny
Kay, Jackie 1961- *165*
Earlier sketch in SATA *97*
Kay, Jacqueline Margaret
See Kay, Jackie
Kay, Julia *205*
Kay, Mara *13*
Kay, Verla 1946- *210*
Earlier sketch in SATA *120*
Kaye, Danny 1913-1987
Obituary *50*
Kaye, Geraldine (Hughesdon) 1925- *85*
Earlier sketch in SATA *10*
Kaye, Judy
See Baer, Judy
Kaye, Marilyn 1949- *230*
Earlier sketches in SATA *56, 110*
Kaye, Mary Margaret
See Kaye, M.M.
Kaye, M.M. 1908-2004 .... *62*
Obituary *152*
Kaye, Mollie
See Kaye, M.M.
Kaye, Peggy 1948- *143*
Keach, James P. 1950- *125*
Keams, Geri 1951- *117*
Keane, Bil 1922- *4*
Keane, Dave 1965- *216*

Keaney, Brian 1954- *188*
  Earlier sketch in SATA *106*
Kearney, Meg 1964- *178*
Kearny, Jillian
  See Goulart, Ron
Keat, Nawuth 1964- *222*
Keating, Bern
  See Keating, Leo Bernard
Keating, Frank 1944- *143*
Keating, Lawrence A. 1903-1966 .... *23*
Keating, Leo Bernard 1915- *10*
Keats, Emma 1899(?)-1979(?) *68*
Keats, Ezra Jack 1916-1983 .... *57*
  Obituary *34*
  Earlier sketch in SATA *14*
  See also CLR *35*
Keefer, Catherine
  See Ogan, George F.
  and Ogan, Margaret E. (Nettles)
Keefer, Janice Kulyk
  See Kulyk Keefer, Janice
Keegan, Marcia 1943- *104*
  Earlier sketch in SATA *9*
Keehn, Sally M. 1947- *165*
  Earlier sketch in SATA *87*
Keel, Frank
  See Keeler, Ronald F(ranklin)
Keeler, Patricia *183*
Keeler, Patricia A.
  See Keeler, Patricia
Keeler, Ronald F(ranklin) 1913-1983 .... *47*
Keely, Jack 1951- *119*
Keen, Martin L. 1913-1992 .... *4*
Keenan, Sheila 1953- *95*
Keene, Ann T. 1940- *86*
Keene, Ann Todd
  See Keene, Ann T.
Keene, Carolyn
  See Benson, Mildred
  and Goulart, Ron
  and Lerangis, Peter
  and McFarlane, Leslie
  and Stanley, George Edward
  and Stratemeyer, Edward L.
Keens-Douglas, Richardo 1953- *154*
  Earlier sketch in SATA *95*
Keep, Linda Lowery
  See Lowery, Linda
Keep, Richard 1949- *170*
Keep, Richard Cleminson
  See Keep, Richard
Keeping, Charles (William James)
  1924-1988 .... *69*
  Obituary *56*
  Earlier sketch in SATA *9*
  See also CLR *34*
Keeshan, Robert J. 1927-2004 .... *32*
  Obituary *151*
Keeter, Susan *237*
Kehlenbeck, Angela 1959- *186*
Kehoe, Tim 1970- *224*
Kehret, Peg 1936- *212*
  Autobiography Feature *149*
  Earlier sketches in SATA *73, 108, 149*
Keillor, Garrison 1942- *58*
Keillor, Gary Edward
  See Keillor, Garrison
Keir, Christine
  See Pullein-Thompson, Christine
Keiser, Paige *220*
Keister, Douglas 1948- *88*
Keith, Doug 1952- *81*
Keith, Eros 1942- *52*
Keith, Hal 1934- *36*
Keith, Harold (Verne) 1903-1998 .... *74*
  Earlier sketch in SATA *2*
Keith, Robert
  See Applebaum, Stan
Keleinikov, Andrei 1924- *65*
Kelemen, Julie 1959- *78*

Kelen, Emery 1896-1978 .... *13*
  Obituary *26*
Kelleam, Joseph E(veridge) 1913-1975 .... *31*
Kelleher, Anne 1959- *97*
Kelleher, Annette 1950- *122*
Kelleher, Daria Valerian 1955- *79*
Kelleher, Victor (Michael Kitchener)
  1939- *129*
  Brief entry *52*
  Earlier sketch in SATA *75*
  See also CLR *36*
Keller, Beverly L(ou) *91*
  Earlier sketch in SATA *13*
Keller, Charles 1942- *82*
  Earlier sketch in SATA *8*
Keller, Debra 1958- *94*
Keller, Dick 1923- *36*
Keller, Emily *96*
Keller, Gail Faithfull
  See Faithfull, Gail
Keller, Holly 1942- *216*
  Brief entry *42*
  Earlier sketches in SATA *76, 108, 157*
  See also CLR *45*
Keller, Irene (Barron) 1927-2002 .... *36*
  Obituary *139*
Keller, Laurie 1961(?)- *196*
Kelley, Ann 1941- *217*
Kelley, Ellen A. *185*
Kelley, Ellen Chavez
  See Kelley, Ellen A.
Kelley, Gary 1945- *217*
  Earlier sketch in SATA *183*
Kelley, J.A.
  See Kelley, Jane
Kelley, Jane 1954- *231*
Kelley, Leo P(atrick) 1928- *32*
  Brief entry *31*
Kelley, Marty 1971- *211*
Kelley, Patrick (G.) 1963- *129*
Kelley, Patte 1947- *93*
Kelley, True 1946- *179*
Kelley, True (Adelaide) 1946- *130*
  Brief entry *39*
  Earlier sketches in SATA *41, 92*
Kelley, True Adelaide
  See Kelley, True
Kellin, Sally Moffet 1932- *9*
Kelling, Furn L. 1914-2000 .... *37*
Kellogg, Gene
  See Kellogg, Jean (Defrees)
Kellogg, Jean (Defrees) 1916-1978 .... *10*
Kellogg, Steven 1941- *177*
  Earlier sketches in SATA *8, 57, 130*
  See also CLR *6*
Kellogg, Steven Castle
  See Kellogg, Steven
Kellow, Kathleen
  See Hibbert, Eleanor Alice Burford
Kelly, C. M. O.
  See Gibbs, (Cecilia) May
Kelly, Clint 1950- *140*
Kelly, Eric P(hilbrook) 1884-1960
  See YABC *1*
Kelly, Fiona
  See Coleman, Michael
  and Hendry, Frances Mary
  and Jones, Allan Frewin
  and Oldfield, Jenny
  and Welford, Sue
Kelly, Irene 1957- *210*
  Earlier sketch in SATA *147*
Kelly, Jacqueline *216*
Kelly, Jeff
  See Kelly, Jeffrey
Kelly, Jeffrey 1946- *65*
Kelly, Jenn 1973- *236*
Kelly, Jenn L.
  See Kelly, Jenn
Kelly, Joanne (W.) 1934- *87*
Kelly, Kate 1958- *91*

Kelly, Kathleen M. 1964- *71*
Kelly, Katy 1955- *215*
  Earlier sketch in SATA *169*
Kelly, Lauren
  See Oates, Joyce Carol
Kelly, Laurene 1954- *123*
Kelly, Martha Rose 1914-1983 .... *37*
Kelly, Marty
  See Kelly, Martha Rose
Kelly, Mij *166*
Kelly, Ralph
  See Geis, Darlene Stern
Kelly, Regina Z(immerman) 1898-1986 .... *5*
Kelly, Rosalie (Ruth) *43*
Kelly, Tara *230*
Kelly, Tom 1961- *191*
Kelly, Walt(er Crawford) 1913-1973 .... *18*
Kelsey, Alice Geer 1896-1982 .... *1*
Kelsey, Elin 1961- *159*
Kelsey, Marybeth *216*
Kemly, Kathleen 1958- *197*
Kemnitz, Thomas Milton, Jr. 1984- *152*
Kemnitz, Tom, Jr.
  See Kemnitz, Thomas Milton, Jr.
Kemp, Gene 1926- *75*
  Earlier sketch in SATA *25*
  See also CLR *29*
Kempner, Mary Jean 1913-1969 .... *10*
Kempter, Christa 1945- *187*
Kempton, Jean Welch 1914- *10*
Kenah, Katharine 1949- *182*
Kenda, Margaret 1942- *71*
Kendall, Carol (Seeger) 1917- *74*
  Earlier sketch in SATA *11*
  See also SAAS *7*
Kendall, Gideon 1966- *215*
Kendall, Katherine
  See Applegate, Katherine
Kendall, Lace
  See Stoutenburg, Adrien (Pearl)
Kendall, Martha E. *87*
Kendall, Russ 1957- *83*
Kenealy, James P. 1927- *52*
  Brief entry *29*
Kenealy, Jim
  See Kenealy, James P.
Kennaway, Adrienne 1945- *171*
  Earlier sketch in SATA *60*
Kennedy, Anne 1955- *198*
Kennedy, Anne Vittur
  See Kennedy, Anne
Kennedy, Brendan 1970- *57*
Kennedy, Dana Forrest 1917- *74*
Kennedy, Dorothy M(intzlaff) 1931- *53*
Kennedy, Doug 1963- *189*
  Earlier sketch in SATA *122*
Kennedy, Frances 1937- *192*
Kennedy, James *214*
Kennedy, John F. 1917-1963 .... *11*
Kennedy, John Fitzgerald
  See Kennedy, John F.
Kennedy, Joseph Charles
  See Kennedy, X. J.
Kennedy, Kim *189*
Kennedy, Marlane 1962- *210*
Kennedy, Pamela (J.) 1946- *87*
Kennedy, Paul E(dward) 1929- *113*
  Earlier sketch in SATA *33*
Kennedy, Richard (Pitt) 1910-1989
  Obituary *60*
Kennedy, (Jerome) Richard 1932- *22*
Kennedy, Robert 1938- *63*
Kennedy, T.A. 1953- *42*
  Brief entry *35*
Kennedy, Teresa
  See Kennedy, T.A.
Kennedy, Teresa A.
  See Kennedy, T.A.
Kennedy, William 1928- *57*
Kennedy, William Joseph
  See Kennedy, William

Kennedy, X. J. 1929- *130*
  Autobiography Feature *130*
  Earlier sketches in SATA *14, 86*
  See also CLR *27*
  See also SAAS *22*
Kennell, Ruth Epperson 1893-1977 .... *6*
  Obituary *25*
Kennemore, Tim 1957- *220*
  Earlier sketch in SATA *133*
Kennen, Ally *190*
Kennett, David 1959- *206*
  Earlier sketch in SATA *121*
Kennison, Ruth *202*
Kenny, Ellsworth Newcomb 1909-1971
  Obituary *26*
Kenny, Herbert Andrew 1912-2002 .... *13*
Kenny, Jude
  See Daly, Jude
Kenny, Kathryn
  See Bowden, Joan Chase
  and Krull, Kathleen
  and Sanderlin, Owenita (Harrah)
  and Stack, Nicolete Meredith
Kenny, Kevin
  See Krull, Kathleen
Kensinger, George
  See Fichter, George S.
Kensington, Kathryn Wesley
  See Rusch, Kristine Kathryn
Kent, Alexander
  See Reeman, Douglas Edward
Kent, David
  See Lambert, David
Kent, Deborah Ann 1948- *155*
  Brief entry *41*
  Earlier sketches in SATA *47, 104*
Kent, Jack
  See Kent, John Wellington
Kent, John Wellington 1920-1985 .... *24*
  Obituary *45*
Kent, Lisa 1942- *90*
Kent, Mallory
  See Lowndes, Robert A(ugustine) W(ard)
Kent, Margaret 1894- *2*
Kent, Rockwell 1882-1971 .... *6*
Kent, Rose *188*
Kent, Sherman 1903-1986 .... *20*
  Obituary *47*
Kenward, Jean 1920- *42*
Kenworthy, Leonard S. 1912-1991 .... *6*
Kenyon, Karen (Smith) 1938- *145*
Kenyon, Kate
  See Adorjan, Carol (Madden)
  and Ransom, Candice
Kenyon, Ley 1913-1990 .... *6*
Keown, Elizabeth *78*
Kepes, Juliet A(ppleby) 1919-1999 .... *13*
Kephart, Beth 1960- *196*
Keplinger, Kody 1991- *237*
Kerby, Johanna *235*
Kerby, Mona 1951- *202*
  Earlier sketch in SATA *75*
Kerigan, Florence 1896-1984 .... *12*
Kerley, Barbara 1960- *191*
  Earlier sketch in SATA *138*
Kerman, Gertrude
  See Furman, Gertrude Lerner Kerman
Kerns, Thelma 1929- *116*
Kerr, Anne Louise
  See Mackey, Weezie Kerr
Kerr, Bob 1951- *120*
Kerr, Jessica 1901-1991 .... *13*
Kerr, (Anne-)Judith 1923-1970 .... *24*
Kerr, M. E.
  See Meaker, Marijane
Kerr, P.B.
  See Kerr, Philip
Kerr, Philip 1956- *168*
Kerr, Phyllis Forbes 1942- *72*
Kerr, Tom 1950- *77*
Kerrin, Jessica Scott *174*

Kerry, Frances
  See Kerigan, Florence
Kerry, Lois
  See Duncan, Lois
Kershen, (L.) Michael 1982- *82*
Kerven, Rosalind 1954- *83*
Ker Wilson, Barbara 1929- *121*
  Earlier sketches in SATA *20, 70*
  See also SAAS *18*
Kerz, Anna 1947- *220*
Keselman, Gabriela 1953- *128*
Kesey, Ken 1935-2001 .... *66*
  Obituary *131*
  See also CLR *170*
Kesey, Ken Elton
  See Kesey, Ken
Kesler, Jay 1935- *65*
Kessel, Joyce Karen 1937- *41*
Kessler, Cristina *190*
Kessler, Ethel 1922- *44*
  Brief entry *37*
Kessler, Leonard P. 1921- *14*
Kessler, Liz 1966- *206*
Kest, Kristin 1967- *168*
  Earlier sketch in SATA *118*
Kesteven, G. R.
  See Crosher, G. R.
Ketcham, Hank
  See Ketcham, Henry King
Ketcham, Henry King 1920-2001 .... *28*
  Brief entry *27*
  Obituary *128*
Ketcham, Sallie 1963- *124*
Ketchum, Liza 1946- *132*
  Earlier sketch in SATA *78*
Ketner, Mary Grace 1946- *75*
Kettelkamp, Larry (Dale) 1933- *2*
  See also SAAS *3*
Ketteman, Helen 1945- *223*
  Earlier sketches in SATA *73, 115, 167*
Kettle, Peter
  See Glover, Denis (James Matthews)
Kevles, Bettyann Holtzmann 1938- *23*
Key, Alexander (Hill) 1904-1979 .... *8*
  Obituary *23*
Key, Samuel M.
  See de Lint, Charles
Key, Watt 1970- *189*
Keyes, Daniel 1927- *37*
Keyes, Diane *207*
Keyes, Fenton 1915-1999 .... *34*
Keyes, Greg 1963- *116*
Keyes, J. Gregory
  See Keyes, Greg
Keyes, Pamela 1962(?)- *238*
Keyser, Marcia 1933- *42*
Keyser, Sarah
  See McGuire, Leslie (Sarah)
Khalid, Mohamed Nor
  See Lat
Khalsa, Dayal Kaur 1943-1989 .... *62*
  See also CLR *30*
Khan, Hena *214*
Khan, Rukhsana 1962- *231*
  Earlier sketches in SATA *118, 165*
Khanshendel, Chiron
  See Rose, Wendy
Kheirabadi, Masoud 1951- *158*
Khemir, Sabiha *87*
Kherdian, David 1931- *74*
  Autobiography Feature *125*
  Earlier sketch in SATA *16*
  See also CLR *24*
Khing, T.T. 1933- *192*
Kibbe, Pat (Hosley) *60*
Kidd, Diana 1933-2000 .... *150*
Kidd, Richard 1952-2008 .... *152*
  Obituary *194*
Kidd, Ronald 1948- *173*
  Earlier sketches in SATA *42, 92*
Kiddell, John 1922- *3*

Kiddell-Monroe, Joan 1908-1972 .... *55*
Kidwell, Carl 1910- *43*
Kiefer, Irene 1926- *21*
Kiefer, Kathleen Balmes 1957- *142*
Kiepper, Shirley Morgan 1933- *10*
Kierstead, Vera M.
  See Kierstead-Farber, Vera M.
Kierstead-Farber, Vera M. 1913- *121*
Kierstead-Farber, Vera May
  See Kierstead-Farber, Vera M.
Kiesel, Stanley 1925- *35*
Kiesler, Kate (A.) 1971- *152*
  Earlier sketch in SATA *90*
Kihn, Greg 1952- *110*
Kikukawa, Cecily H(arder) 1919- *44*
  Brief entry *35*
Kilaka, John 1966- *223*
Kilcher, Jewel 1974- *109*
Kile, Joan 1940- *78*
Kilgore, Kathleen 1946- *42*
Kilian, Crawford 1941- *35*
Killdeer, John
  See Mayhar, Ardath
Killen, Nicola *236*
Killien, Christi 1956- *73*
Killilea, Marie (Lyons) 1913-1991 .... *2*
Killingback, Julia 1944- *63*
Killough, (Karen) Lee 1942- *64*
Kilpatrick, Don *206*
Kilreon, Beth
  See Walker, Barbara (Jeanne) K(erlin)
Kilworth, Garry 1941- *216*
  Earlier sketch in SATA *94*
Kilworth, Garry D.
  See Kilworth, Garry
Kilworth, Garry Douglas
  See Kilworth, Garry
Kim, David 1977- *201*
Kim, Dong-hwa 1950- *225*
Kim, Grace
  See Maccarone, Grace
Kim, Helen 1899-1970 .... *98*
Kim, Joung Un 1970- *205*
Kim, Susan 1958- *232*
Kimball, Gayle 1943- *90*
Kimball, Violet T(ew) 1932- *126*
Kimball, Yeffe 1914-1978 .... *37*
Kimber, Murray 1964- *171*
Kimble, Warren *176*
Kimbrough, Emily 1899-1989 .... *2*
  Obituary *59*
Kimeldorf, Martin 1948- *121*
Kimeldorf, Martin R.
  See Kimeldorf, Martin
Kimenye, Barbara 1940(?)- *121*
Kimmel, Elizabeth Cody *238*
  Earlier sketches in SATA *170, 209*
Kimmel, Eric A. 1946- *208*
  Earlier sketches in SATA *13, 80, 125, 176*
Kimmel, Margaret Mary 1938- *43*
  Brief entry *33*
Kimmelman, Burt 1947- *180*
Kimmelman, Leslie 1958- *211*
  Earlier sketches in SATA *85, 156*
Kincaid, Jamaica 1949-
  See CLR *63*
Kinch, Michael *238*
Kinch, Michael P.
  See Kinch, Michael
Kincher, Jonni 1949- *79*
Kincy, Karen 1986- *234*
Kindl, Patrice 1951- *128*
  Earlier sketch in SATA *82*
  See also CLR *132*
Kindred, Wendy (Good) 1937- *7*
Kinerk, Robert *199*
Kines, Pat Decker 1937- *12*
King, Adam
  See Hoare, Robert J(ohn)
King, Alison
  See Martini, Teri

King, (Maria) Anna 1964- 72
King, A.S. 1970- 217
King, Billie Jean 1943- 12
King, Christine
   See Farris, Christine King
King, Christopher (L.) 1945- 84
King, (David) Clive 1924- 144
   Earlier sketch in SATA 28
King, Colin 1943- 76
King, Cynthia 1925- 7
King, Daniel (John) 1963- 130
King, Daren 1972- 197
King, Elizabeth 1953- 83
King, Frank O. 1883-1969
   Obituary 22
King, Frank R. 1904-1999 127
King, Jane
   See Currie, Stephen
King, Jeanette (Margaret) 1959- 105
King, Larry L. 1929- 66
King, Laurie R. 1952- 88
King, Marian 1900(?)-1986 23
   Obituary 47
King, Martin Luther, Jr. 1929-1968 14
King, Mary Ellen 1958- 93
King, M.G. 1968- 236
King, Paul
   See Drackett, Phil(ip Arthur)
King, Paula
   See Downing, Paula E.
King, Stephen 1947- 161
   Earlier sketches in SATA 9, 55
   See also CLR 124
King, Stephen Edwin
   See King, Stephen
King, Stephen Michael 218
   Earlier sketch in SATA 157
King, Steve
   See King, Stephen
King, Thomas 1943- 96
King, Thomas Hunt
   See King, Thomas
King, Tony 1947- 39
King, Willie Christine
   See Farris, Christine King
Kingfisher, Rupert 209
Kingman, Dong (Moy Shu) 1911-2000 44
Kingman, Lee
   See Natti, Lee
Kingsbury, Evan
   See Walker, Robert W.
Kingsland, Leslie William 1912- 13
Kingsley, Charles 1819-1875
   See YABC 2
   See also CLR 167
Kingsley, Emily Perl 1940- 33
Kingsley, Kaza 193
King-Smith, Dick 1922-2011 192
   Brief entry 38
   Earlier sketches in SATA 47, 80, 135
   See also CLR 40
Kingston, Maxine Hong 1940- 53
Kingston, Maxine Ting Ting Hong
   See Kingston, Maxine Hong
Kinkade, Sheila 1962- 229
Kinnaird, Ross 1954- 236
Kinney, C. Cle(land) 1915- 6
Kinney, Harrison 1921- 13
Kinney, Jean Stout 1912- 12
Kinney, Jeff 1971- 187
Kinsey, Elizabeth
   See Clymer, Eleanor
Kinsey, Helen 1948- 82
Kinsey-Warnock, Natalie 1956- 167
   Earlier sketches in SATA 71, 116
Kinzel, Dorothy 1950- 57
Kinzel, Dottie
   See Kinzel, Dorothy
Kipling, Joseph Rudyard
   See Kipling, Rudyard

Kipling, Rudyard 1865-1936 100
   See also YABC 2
   See also CLR 65
Kippax, Frank
   See Needle, Jan
Kirby, David 1944- 78
Kirby, David K.
   See Kirby, David
Kirby, David Kirk
   See Kirby, David
Kirby, Margaret
   See Bingley, Margaret (Jane Kirby)
Kirby, Pamela F. 1952- 220
Kirby, Susan E. 1949- 62
Kirk, Connie Ann 1957- 167
Kirk, Daniel 1952- 196
   Earlier sketches in SATA 107, 153
Kirk, David 1955- 161
   Earlier sketch in SATA 117
Kirk, Heather 1949- 166
Kirk, Ruth (Kratz) 1925- 5
Kirkham, Dinah
   See Card, Orson Scott
Kirkland, Will
   See Hale, Arlene
Kirkpatrick, Katherine (Anne) 1964- 113
Kirkup, James 1918-2009 12
Kirkus, Virginia
   See Glick, Virginia Kirkus
Kirkwood, Kathryn
   See Fluke, Joanne
Kirsch, Vincent X. 211
Kirshenbaum, Binnie 79
Kirshner, David S. 1958- 123
Kirtland, G. B.
   See Hine, Sesyle Joslin
   and Hine, Al(fred Blakelee)
Kirwan, Wednesday 198
Kish, Eleanor M(ary) 1924- 73
Kish, Ely
   See Kish, Eleanor M(ary)
Kishida, Eriko 1929- 12
Kisinger, Grace Gelvin (Maze) 1913-1965 .. 10
Kissel, Richard 209
Kissin, Eva H. 1923- 10
Kissinger, Rosemary K.
   See Updyke, Rosemary K.
Kistler, John M. 1967- 160
Kitamura, Satoshi 1956- 201
   Earlier sketches in SATA 62, 98, 143
   See also CLR 60
Kitanidis, Phoebe 1977- 230
Kitchen, Bert
   See Kitchen, Herbert Thomas
Kitchen, Herbert Thomas 1940- 70
Kite, L. Patricia
   See Kite, Pat
Kite, Pat 1940- 78
Kitt, Tamara
   See de Regniers, Beatrice Schenk (Freedman)
Kittinger, Jo S(usenbach) 1955- 148
   Earlier sketch in SATA 96
Kittredge, Caitlin 1984- 239
Kituomba
   See Odaga, Asenath (Bole)
Kitzinger, Sheila 1929- 57
Kiwak, Barbara 1966- 103
Kjelgaard, James Arthur 1910-1959 17
   See also CLR 81
Kjelgaard, Jim
   See Kjelgaard, James Arthur
Kjelle, Marylou Morano 1954- 146
Klages, Ellen 1954- 196
Klagsbrun, Francine (Lifton) 36
Klaits, Barrie 1944- 52
Klam, Cheryl 191
Klaperman, Gilbert 1921- 33
Klaperman, Libby Mindlin 1921-1982 33
   Obituary 31
Klass, David 1960- 207
   Earlier sketches in SATA 88, 142

Klass, Morton 1927-2001 11
Klass, Sheila Solomon 1927- 219
   Autobiography Feature 126
   Earlier sketches in SATA 45, 99
   See also SAAS 26
Klassen, Jon 239
Klause, Annette Curtis 1953- 175
   Earlier sketch in SATA 79
   See also CLR 104
Klaveness, Jan O'Donnell 1939- 86
Kleberger, Ilse 1921- 5
Kleeberg, Irene (Flitner) Cumming 1932- 65
Klein, Aaron E. 1930-1998 45
   Brief entry 28
Klein, Bill 1945- 89
Klein, David 1919-2001 59
Klein, Frederick C. 1938- 154
Klein, Gerda Weissmann 1924- 44
Klein, H(erbert) Arthur 8
Klein, James 1932- 115
Klein, Leonore (Glotzer) 1916- 6
Klein, Lisa 1958- 211
Klein, Lisa M.
   See Klein, Lisa
Klein, Mina C(ooper) 1906-1979 8
Klein, Norma 1938-1989 57
   Earlier sketch in SATA 7
   See also CLR 162
   See also SAAS 1
Klein, Rachel S. 1953- 105
Klein, Robin 1936- 164
   Brief entry 45
   Earlier sketches in SATA 55, 80
   See also CLR 21
Klemin, Diana 65
Klemm, Barry 1945- 104
Klemm, Edward G., Jr. 1910-2001 30
Klemm, Roberta K(ohnhorst) 1884-1975 30
Klemstein, Stacey
   See Kade, Stacey
Kleven, Elisa 1958- 217
   Earlier sketches in SATA 76, 173
   See also CLR 85
Klevin, Jill Ross 1935- 39
   Brief entry 38
Kliban, B(ernard) 1935-1990 35
   Obituary 66
Klier, Kimberly Wagner 208
Klimo, Kate 214
Klimowicz, Barbara 1927- 10
Kline, Christina Baker 1964- 101
Kline, James
   See Klein, James
Kline, Jim
   See Kline, Jim
Kline, Lisa Williams 1954- 143
Kline, Suzy 1943- 193
   Autobiography Feature 193
   Brief entry 48
   Earlier sketches in SATA 67, 99, 152
Kling, Heidi R. 233
Klinger, Shula 230
Kliros, Thea 1935- 106
Klise, Kate 221
   Earlier sketch in SATA 181
Klise, M. Sarah 1961- 235
   Earlier sketches in SATA 128, 180
Kloepfer, John 235
Klots, Alexander Barrett 1903-1989
   Obituary 62
Klug, Ron(ald) 1939- 31
Knaak, Richard A. 1961- 166
   Earlier sketch in SATA 86
Knaak, Richard Allen
   See Knaak, Richard A.
Knapman, Timothy 200
Knapp, Edward
   See Kunhardt, Edith
Knapp, Ron 1952- 34
Knebel, Fletcher 1911-1993 36
   Obituary 75

Kneeland, Linda Clarke 1947- 94
Kneen, Maggie 1957- 221
Knickerbocker, Diedrich
    See Irving, Washington
Knifesmith
    See Cutler, Ivor
Knigge, Robert (R.) 1921(?)-1987 50
Knight, Anne (Katherine) 1946- 34
Knight, Brenda 112
Knight, Christopher G. 1943- 96
Knight, Damon (Francis) 1922-2002 9
    Obituary 139
Knight, David C(arpenter) 1925-1984 14
    See also CLR 38
Knight, Eric 1897-1943 18
Knight, Eric Mowbray
    See Knight, Eric
Knight, Francis Edgar 1905- 14
Knight, Frank
    See Knight, Francis Edgar
Knight, Hilary 1926- 132
    Earlier sketches in SATA 15, 69
Knight, Joan
    See Knight, Joan (MacPhail)
Knight, Joan (MacPhail) 159
    Earlier sketch in SATA 82
Knight, Kathryn Lasky
    See Lasky, Kathryn
Knight, Mallory T.
    See Hurwood, Bernhardt J.
Knight, Ruth Adams 1898-1974
    Obituary 20
Knight, Steven 1959- 234
Knight, Theodore O. 1946- 77
Knobloch, Dorothea 1951- 88
Knoepfle, John (Ignatius) 1923- 66
Knorr, Laura 1971- 200
Knott, Bill
    See Knott, William C(ecil, Jr.)
Knott, William C(ecil, Jr.) 1927- 3
Knotts, Howard (Clayton, Jr.) 1922- 25
Knowles, Anne 1933- 37
Knowles, Jo 1970- 197
Knowles, Johanna Beth
    See Knowles, Jo
Knowles, John 1926-2001 89
    Obituary 134
    Earlier sketch in SATA 8
    See also CLR 98
Knox, Calvin M.
    See Silverberg, Robert
Knox, (Mary) Eleanor Jessie 1909-2000 59
    Earlier sketch in SATA 30
Knox, Elizabeth 1959- 176
Knox, Elizabeth Fiona
    See Knox, Elizabeth
Knox, James
    See Brittain, William
Knox, Jolyne 1937- 76
Knudsen, James 1950- 42
Knudsen, Michelle 1974- 220
    Earlier sketch in SATA 171
Knudson, Mike 1965- 209
Knudson, R. R.
    See Knudson, Rozanne
Knudson, Richard L(ewis) 1930- 34
Knudson, Rozanne 1932-2008 79
    Earlier sketch in SATA 7
    See also SAAS 18
Knutson, Barbara 1959-2005 166
Knutson, Kimberley 115
Knye, Cassandra
    See Disch, Thomas M.
Kobayashi, Masako Matsuno 1935- 6
Kober, Shahar 1979- 213
Koch, Dorothy Clarke 1924- 6
Koch, Kenneth 1925-2002 65
Koch, Kenneth Jay
    See Koch, Kenneth
Koch, Phyllis (Mae) McCallum 1911- 10
Kochalka, James 1967- 196

Kocsis, J. C.
    See Paul, James
Koda-Callan, Elizabeth 1944- 140
    Earlier sketch in SATA 67
Kodera, Craig 1956- 222
Kodman, Stanislawa 201
Koehler, Phoebe 1955- 85
Koehler-Pentacoff, Elizabeth 1957- 160
    Earlier sketch in SATA 96
Koehn, Ilse
    See Van Zwienen, Ilse Charlotte Koehn
Koeller, Carol 192
Koenig, Viviane 1950- 80
Koering, Ursula 1921-1976 64
Koerner, W(illiam) H(enry) D(avid)
    1878-1938 21
Koertge, Ron 1940- 209
    Earlier sketches in SATA 53, 92, 131
Koestler-Grack, Rachel A. 1973- 156
Koff, Richard Myram 1926- 62
Koffinke, Carol 1949- 82
Kogan, Deborah
    See Kogan Ray, Deborah
Kogan Ray, Deborah 1940- 203
    Earlier sketches in SATA 8, 50, 161
Kogawa, Joy 1935- 99
Kogawa, Joy Nozomi
    See Kogawa, Joy
Kogler, Jennie
    See Kogler, Jennifer Anne
Kogler, Jennifer Anne 1982(?)- 174
Kohara, Kazuno 207
Kohl, Herbert 1937- 47
Kohl, Herbert R.
    See Kohl, Herbert
Kohl, MaryAnn F(aubion) 1947- 144
    Earlier sketch in SATA 74
Kohler, Dean Ellis 1947- 226
Kohler, Julilly H(ouse) 1908-1976
    Obituary 20
Kohn, Bernice
    See Hunt, Bernice
Kohn, Rita (T.) 1933- 89
Kohner, Frederick 1905-1986 10
    Obituary 48
Koide, Tan 1938-1986 50
Koike, Kay 1940- 72
Koja, Kathe 1960- 199
    Earlier sketch in SATA 155
Koja, Stephan 198
Kolar, Bob 1960(?)- 206
Kolb, Larry J. 1953- 175
Kolba, St. Tamara 22
Kolibalova, Marketa
    See Kolibalova, Marketa
Kolibalova, Marketa 1953- 126
Koller, Jackie French 1948- 157
    Earlier sketches in SATA 72, 109
    See also CLR 68
Kolodny, Nancy J. 1946- 76
Kolosov, Jacqueline 1967- 199
Komaiko, Leah 1954- 164
    Earlier sketch in SATA 97
Komisar, Lucy 1942- 9
Komiya, Teruyuki 239
Komoda, Beverly 1939- 25
Komoda, Kiyo 1937- 9
Kompaneyets, Marc 1974- 169
Komroff, Manuel 1890-1974 2
    Obituary 20
Konigsberg, Bill 1970- 207
Konigsburg, E.L. 1930- 194
    Earlier sketches in SATA 4, 48, 94, 126
    See also CLR 81
Konigsburg, Elaine Lobl
    See Konigsburg, E.L.
Koning, Hans 1921-2007 5
    Obituary 182
Koningsberger, Hans
    See Koning, Hans
Konkle, Janet Everest 1917- 12

Kono, Erin Eitter 1973- 177
Konrad, Marla Stewart 218
Konzak, Burt 1946- 151
Koob, Theodora (J. Foth) 1918- 23
Kooiker, Leonie
    See Kooyker-Romijn, Johanna Maria
Koons, James
    See Pernu, Dennis
Koontz, Dean 1945- 165
    Earlier sketch in SATA 92
    See Koontz, Dean R.
Koontz, Dean R. 225
    See Koontz, Dean
Koontz, Dean Ray
    See Koontz, Dean
Koontz, Robin Michal 1954- 136
    Earlier sketch in SATA 70
Kooyker, Leonie
    See Kooyker-Romijn, Johanna Maria
Kooyker-Romijn, Johanna Maria 1927- 48
Kooyker-Romyn, Johanna Maria
    See Kooyker-Romijn, Johanna Maria
Kopelke, Lisa 1963- 154
Kopper, Lisa 1950- 105
    Brief entry 51
Kopper, Lisa Esther
    See Kopper, Lisa
Koppes, Steven N. 1957- 169
Koppes, Steven Nelson
    See Koppes, Steven N.
Korach, Mimi 1922- 9
Koralek, Jenny 1934- 215
    Earlier sketches in SATA 71, 140
Korczak, Janusz
    See Goldszmit, Henryk
Koren, Edward (Benjamin) 1935- 148
    Earlier sketch in SATA 5
Koren, Edward 1935- 206
Korinets, Iurii Iosifovich
    See Korinetz, Yuri (Iosifovich)
Korinetz, Yuri (Iosifovich) 1923- 9
    See also CLR 4
Korman, Bernice 1937- 78
Korman, Gordon 1963- 226
    Brief entry 41
    Earlier sketches in SATA 49, 81, 119, 167
    See also CLR 25
Korman, Gordon Richard
    See Korman, Gordon
Korman, Justine 1958- 70
Kornblatt, Marc 1954- 147
    Earlier sketch in SATA 84
Kornprobst, Jacques 1937- 177
Korte, Gene J. 1950- 74
Korthues, Barbara 1971- 203
Korty, Carol 1937- 15
Koscielniak, Bruce 1947- 153
    Earlier sketches in SATA 67, 99
Koshin, Alexander (A.) 1952- 86
Kositsky, Lynne 1947- 158
Koskenmaki, Rosalie
    See Maggio, Rosalie
Koss, Amy Goldman 1954- 158
    Earlier sketch in SATA 115
Kossin, Sandy (Sanford) 1926- 10
Kossman, Nina 1959- 84
Kostecki-Shaw, Jenny Sue 203
Kostick, Conor 1964- 186
Kotzwinkle, William 1938- 146
    Earlier sketches in SATA 24, 70
    See also CLR 6
Kouhi, Elizabeth 1917- 54
    Brief entry 49
Kouts, Anne 1945- 8
Koutsky, Jan Dale 1955- 146
Kovacs, Deborah 1954- 132
    Earlier sketch in SATA 79
Kovalski, Maryann 1951- 175
    Earlier sketches in SATA 58, 97
    See also CLR 34
    See also SAAS 21

Kowalski, Kathiann M. 1955- *151*
  Earlier sketch in SATA *96*
Koz, Paula G.
  See Goodman Koz, Paula
Kozjan, Drazen *209*
Kraft, Betsy Harvey 1937- *157*
Kraft, Erik P. *193*
Krahn, Fernando 1935- *49*
  Brief entry *31*
  See also CLR *3*
Krakauer, Hoong Yee Lee 1955- *86*
Krakauer, Jon 1954- *108*
Krall, Dan 1970- *218*
Kramer, Andrew *237*
Kramer, George
  See Heuman, William
Kramer, Nora 1896(?)-1984 .... *26*
  Obituary *39*
Kramer, Remi (Thomas) 1935- *90*
Krantz, Hazel (Newman) *12*
Kranzler, George G(ershon) 1916- *28*
Kranzler, Gershon
  See Kranzler, George G(ershon)
Krasilovsky, Phyllis 1926- *38*
  Earlier sketch in SATA *1*
  See also CLR *83*
  See also SAAS *5*
Krasne, Betty
  See Levine, Betty K(rasne)
Krasner, Steven 1953- *154*
Krasnesky, Thad 1969(?)- *224*
Krasno, Rena 1923- *104*
Kratman, Tom 1956- *175*
Kraus, Joanna Halpert 1937- *87*
Kraus, (Herman) Robert 1925-2001 .... *93*
  Obituary *130*
  Earlier sketches in SATA *4, 65*
  See also SAAS *11*
Krauss, Ruth 1911-1993 .... *30*
  Obituary *75*
  Earlier sketch in SATA *1*
  See also CLR *42*
Krauss, Ruth Ida
  See Krauss, Ruth
Krautter, Elisa (Bialk) 1912(?)-1990 .... *1*
  Obituary *65*
Krautwurst, Terry 1946- *79*
Kray, Robert Clement 1930- *82*
Krech, Bob 1956- *185*
Krech, Robert
  See Krech, Bob
Kredel, Fritz 1900-1973 .... *17*
Kreikemeier, Gregory Scott 1965- *85*
Kreloff, Elliot *189*
Krementz, Jill 1940- *134*
  Earlier sketches in SATA *17, 71*
  See also CLR *5*
  See also SAAS *8*
Kremer, Marcie
  See Sorenson, Margo
Krenina, Katya 1968- *221*
  Earlier sketch in SATA *101*
Krensky, Stephen 1953- *188*
  Brief entry *41*
  Earlier sketches in SATA *47, 93, 136*
Krensky, Stephen Alan
  See Krensky, Stephen
Kresh, Paul 1919-1997 .... *61*
  Obituary *94*
Kress, Nancy 1948- *147*
  Autobiography Feature *147*
  Earlier sketch in SATA *85*
Kricher, John C. 1944- *113*
Krieger, Melanie 1944- *96*
Krinitz, Esther Nisenthal 1927-2001 .... *194*
Kripke, Dorothy Karp *30*
Krisher, Trudy 1946- *160*
  Earlier sketch in SATA *86*
Krisher, Trudy B.
  See Krisher, Trudy

Krishnaswami, Uma 1956- *182*
  Earlier sketch in SATA *144*
Kristiansen, Teddy 1964- *210*
Kristiansen, Teddy H.
  See Kristiansen, Teddy
Kristof, Jane 1932- *8*
Kroeber, Theodora (Kracaw) 1897-1979 .... *1*
Kroeger, Mary Kay 1950- *92*
Krohn, Katherine E(lizabeth) 1961- *125*
  Earlier sketch in SATA *84*
Kroll, Francis Lynde 1904-1973 .... *10*
Kroll, Steven 1941-2011 .... *212*
  Autobiography Feature *135*
  Earlier sketches in SATA *19, 66, 125, 135*
  See also SAAS *7*
Kroll, Virginia L. 1948- *225*
  Earlier sketches in SATA *76, 114, 168*
Kroll, Virginia Louisa
  See Kroll, Virginia L.
Kromhout, Rindert 1958- *189*
Krommes, Beth 1956- *208*
  Earlier sketches in SATA *128, 181*
Kronenwetter, Michael 1943- *62*
Kroniuk, Lisa
  See Berton, Pierre (Francis de Marigny)
Kropp, Paul 1948- *38*
  Brief entry *34*
  See also CLR *96*
Kropp, Paul Stephan
  See Kropp, Paul
Krosoczka, Jarrett J. 1977- *200*
  Earlier sketch in SATA *155*
Krovatin, Christopher 1985- *171*
Krudop, Walter
  See Krudop, Walter Lyon
Krudop, Walter Lyon 1966- *210*
Kruess, James
  See Kruss, James
Kruglik, Gerald *187*
Krull, Kathleen 1952- *229*
  Autobiography Feature *106*
  Brief entry *39*
  Earlier sketches in SATA *52, 80, 149, 184*
  See also CLR *44*
Krumgold, Joseph (Quincy) 1908-1980 .... *48*
  Obituary *23*
  Earlier sketch in SATA *1*
Krupinski, Loretta 1940- *161*
  Earlier sketches in SATA *67, 102*
Krupnick, Karen 1947- *89*
Krupp, E. C. 1944- *123*
  Earlier sketch in SATA *53*
Krupp, Edwin Charles
  See Krupp, E. C.
Krupp, Robin Rector 1946- *53*
Krush, Beth 1918- *18*
Krush, Joe 1918-
  See Krush, Joseph P.
Krush, Joseph P. 1918- *18*
Kruss, James 1926-1997 .... *8*
  See also CLR *9*
Kruusval, Catarina 1951- *201*
Krykorka, Vladyana 1945- *96*
Krystoforski, Andrej 1943- *196*
Kubick, Dana *212*
Kubie, Eleanor Gottheil
  See Kubie, Nora Gottheil Benjamin
Kubie, Nora Benjamin
  See Kubie, Nora Gottheil Benjamin
Kubie, Nora Gottheil Benjamin 1899-1988 . *39*
  Obituary *59*
Kubinyi, Laszlo 1937- *94*
  Earlier sketch in SATA *17*
Kudlinski, Kathleen V. 1950- *213*
  Earlier sketch in SATA *150*
Kuehnert, Stephanie 1979- *205*
Kuenstler, Morton 1927- *10*
Kuh, Charlotte 1892(?)-1985
  Obituary *43*
Kuharski, Janice 1947- *128*
Kuhn, Dwight *199*

Kuijer, Guus 1942- *179*
Kujoth, Jean Spealman 1935-1975
  Obituary *30*
Kuklin, Susan 1941- *163*
  Earlier sketches in SATA *63, 95*
  See also CLR *51*
Kulak, Jeff 1984(?)- *223*
Kulikov, Boris 1966- *205*
  Earlier sketch in SATA *170*
Kulka, Joe *188*
Kulling, Monica 1952- *237*
  Earlier sketch in SATA *89*
Kullman, Harry 1919-1982 .... *35*
Kulyk Keefer, Janice 1952- *132*
Kumin, Maxine 1925- *12*
Kumin, Maxine Winokur
  See Kumin, Maxine
Kunhardt, Dorothy (Meserve) 1901-1979 .... *53*
  Obituary *22*
Kunhardt, Edith 1937- *67*
Kunjufu, Jawanza 1953- *73*
Kunstler, Morton
  See Kuenstler, Morton
Kuntz, J(ohn) L. 1947- *91*
Kuntz, Jerry 1956- *133*
Kupferberg, Herbert 1918-2001 .... *19*
Kuratomi, Chizuko 1939- *12*
  See also CLR *32*
Kurczok, Belinda 1978- *121*
Kurelek, William 1927-1977 .... *8*
  Obituary *27*
  See also CLR *2*
Kurian, George 1928- *65*
Kurilla, Renee 1981- *231*
Kurjian, Judi(th M.) 1944- *127*
Kurland, Gerald 1942- *13*
Kurland, Michael 1938- *118*
  Earlier sketch in SATA *48*
Kurland, Michael Joseph
  See Kurland, Michael
Kuroi, Ken 1947- *120*
Kurokawa, Mitsuhiro 1954- *88*
Kurten, Bjorn (Olof) 1924-1988 .... *64*
Kurtz, Jane 1952- *139*
  Earlier sketch in SATA *91*
  See also CLR *123*
Kurtz, Katherine 1944- *182*
  Earlier sketches in SATA *76, 126*
Kurtz, Katherine Irene
  See Kurtz, Katherine
Kurusa 1942- *226*
Kurz, Rudolf 1952- *95*
Kushner, Donn (J.) 1927- *52*
  See also CLR *55*
Kushner, Ellen 1955- *202*
  Earlier sketch in SATA *98*
Kushner, Ellen Ruth
  See Kushner, Ellen
Kushner, Jill Menkes 1951- *62*
Kushner, Lawrence 1943- *169*
  Earlier sketch in SATA *83*
Kushner, Tony 1956- *160*
Kuskin, Karla 1932-2009 .... *164*
  Obituary *206*
  Earlier sketches in SATA *2, 68, 111*
  See also CLR *4*
  See also SAAS *3*
Kuskin, Karla Seidman
  See Kuskin, Karla
Kusugak, Michael 1948- *143*
Kusugak, Michael Arvaarluk
  See Kusugak, Michael
Kutner, Merrily 1948- *196*
Kuttner, Paul 1922- *18*
Kuyper, Sjoerd 1952- *177*
Kuzma, Kay 1941- *39*
Kvale, Velma R(uth) 1898-1979 .... *8*
Kvasnosky, Laura McGee 1951- *182*
  Earlier sketches in SATA *93, 142*
Kwasney, Michelle D. 1960- *162*
Kyi, Tanya Lloyd 1973- *236*

Kyle, Benjamin
See Gottfried, Theodore Mark
Kyle, Elisabeth
See Dunlop, Agnes M. R.
Kyte, Kathy S. 1946- 50
Brief entry 44

L

L., Barry
See Longyear, Barry B(rookes)
L., Tommy
See Lorkowski, Thomas V(incent)
Labatt, Mary 1944- 215
Labouisse, Eve Curie
See Curie, Eve
Labouisse, Eve Denise
See Curie, Eve
Lacamara, Laura 236
Lace, William W. 1942- 126
Lacey, Joshua
See Doder, Josh
Lachenmeyer, Nathaniel 1969- 221
Lachner, Dorothea
See Knobloch, Dorothea
Lachtman, Ofelia Dumas 1919- 179
Lackey, Mercedes 237
See Lackey, Mercedes R.
Lackey, Mercedes R. 1950- 127
Earlier sketch in SATA *81*
See Lackey, Mercedes
Lackey, Mercedes Ritchie
See Lackey, Mercedes R.
Lacoe, Addie 78
Lacombe, Benjamin 1982- 198
Lacome, Julie 1961- 174
Earlier sketch in SATA *80*
LaCour, Nina 1982- 222
Lacy, Leslie Alexander 1937- 6
Lacy, Rick 231
Ladd, Cheryl (Jean) 1951- 113
Ladd, London 1972(?)- 206
Ladd, Louise 1943- 97
Ladd, Veronica
See Miner, Jane Claypool
Laden, Nina 1962- 148
Earlier sketch in SATA *85*
Lader, Lawrence 1919-2006 6
Obituary 178
LaDoux, Rita C. 1951- 74
Ladwig, Tim 1952- 223
Ladwig, Timothy
See Ladwig, Tim
Lady, A
See Taylor, Ann
Lady Mears
See Tempest, Margaret Mary
Lady of Quality, A
See Bagnold, Enid
La Farge, Oliver 1901-1963 19
La Farge, Oliver Hazard Perry
See La Farge, Oliver
La Farge, Phyllis 14
LaFave, Kim 196
LaFaye, A. 1970- 220
Earlier sketches in SATA *105, 156*
LaFaye, Alexandria R.T.
See LaFaye, A.
LaFevers, R.L. 234
Earlier sketch in SATA *191*
LaFevers, Robin
See LaFevers, R.L.
LaFevers, Robin L.
See LaFevers, R.L.
Lafferty, Mur 1973- 227
Laffin, John (Alfred Charles) 1922- 31
LaFleur, Suzanne 1983- 221
LaFontaine, Bruce 1948- 176
Earlier sketch in SATA *114*

La Fontaine, Jean de 1621-1695 18
Lafrance, Marie 1955- 197
Lager, Claude
See Lapp, Christiane (Germain)
Lager, Marilyn 1939- 52
Lagercrantz, Rose (Elsa) 1947- 39
Lagerloef, Selma
See Lagerlof, Selma
Lagerlof, Selma 1858-1940 15
See also CLR 7
Lagos, Alexander 232
Lagos, Joseph 231
Laguna, Sofie 1968- 158
LaHaye, Tim 1926- 149
LaHaye, Timothy F.
See LaHaye, Tim
Lai, Thanhha 1965- 239
Laidlaw, Rob 205
Laiken, Deirdre S. 1948- 48
Brief entry 40
Laiken, Deirdre Susan
See Laiken, Deirdre S.
Laimgruber, Monika 1946- 11
Lain, Anna
See Lamb, Nancy
Laing, Alexander (Kinnan) 1903-1976 117
Laing, Martha 1951- 39
Lairamore, Dawn 233
Laird, Christa 1944- 108
Autobiography Feature 120
See also SAAS 26
Laird, Elizabeth 1943- 228
Earlier sketches in SATA *77, 114, 159*
See also CLR 65
Laird, Elizabeth Mary Risk
See Laird, Elizabeth
Laird, Jean E(louise) 1930- 38
Laite, Gordon 1925- 31
Lake, Harriet
See Taylor, Paula (Wright)
Lake, Nick 227
Lakeman, Victoria
See Forester, Victoria
Lakin, Patricia 1944- 190
Laklan, Carli 1907-1988 5
Laliberte, Louise-Andree 1958- 169
Lalicki, Barbara 61
Lalicki, Tom 1949- 186
Lally, Soinbhe 1945- 119
LaMarche, Jim 239
Earlier sketch in SATA *162*
Lamb, Albert 187
Lamb, Beatrice Pitney 1904-1997 21
Lamb, Charles 1775-1834 17
Lamb, Elizabeth Searle 1917- 31
Lamb, G(eoffrey) F(rederick) 10
Lamb, Harold (Albert) 1892-1962 53
Lamb, Lynton (Harold) 1907-1977 10
Lamb, Mary Ann 1764-1847 17
Lamb, Nancy 1939- 80
Lamb, Robert (Boyden) 1941- 13
Lamba, Marie 195
Lambert, David 1932- 84
Brief entry 49
Lambert, David Compton
See Lambert, David
Lambert, Janet 1895(?)-1973 25
Lambert, Martha L. 113
Lambert, Saul 1928- 23
Lambert, Stephen 174
Lamburn, Richmal Crompton 1890-1969 5
Lamensdorf, Len 1930- 120
Lamensdorf, Leonard
See Lamensdorf, Len
Laminack, Lester L. 1956- 163
Earlier sketch in SATA *120*
Lammle, Leslie 1965- 213
Lamont, Priscilla 200
Lamorisse, Albert (Emmanuel) 1922-1970 ... 23
Lampert, Emily 1951- 52
Brief entry 49

Lamplugh, Lois 1921- 17
Lampman, Evelyn Sibley 1907-1980 87
Obituary 23
Earlier sketch in SATA *4*
Lamprey, Louise 1869-1951
See YABC 2
Lampton, Chris
See Lampton, Christopher F.
Lampton, Christopher
See Lampton, Christopher F.
Lampton, Christopher F. 67
Brief entry 47
Lamstein, Sarah 1943- 174
Earlier sketch in SATA *126*
Lamstein, Sarah Marwil
See Lamstein, Sarah
Lanagan, Margo 1960- 201
Earlier sketch in SATA *163*
Lancaster, Bruce 1896-1963 9
Lancaster, Matthew 1973(?)-1983
Obituary 45
Lance, Kathryn 1943- 76
Land, Barbara (Neblett) 1923- 16
Land, Jane
See Borland, Kathryn Kilby
and Speicher, Helen Ross S(mith)
Land, Myrick (Ebben) 1922-1998 15
Land, Ross
See Borland, Kathryn Kilby
and Speicher, Helen Ross S(mith)
Landa, Norbert 1952- 218
Landau, Elaine 1948- 141
Earlier sketches in SATA *10, 94*
Landau, Jacob 1917- 38
Landeck, Beatrice 1904-1978 15
Landin, Les 1923- 2
Landis, J. D. 1942- 60
Brief entry 52
Landis, James D.
See Landis, J. D.
Landis, James David
See Landis, J. D.
Landis, Jill Marie 1948- 101
Landman, Tanya 207
Landmann, Bimba 1968- 176
Landon, Dena 1978(?)- 168
Landon, Kristen 1966- 239
Landon, Lucinda 1950- 56
Brief entry 51
Landon, Margaret (Dorothea Mortenson)
1903-1993 50
Landowne, Youme 1970- 211
Landry, Leo 202
Landshoff, Ursula 1908-1989 13
Landstrom, Lena 1943- 206
Earlier sketch in SATA *146*
Landstrom, Olof 1943- 146
Landy, Derek 1974- 210
Lane, Alison Hoffman 215
Lane, Andrew 1963- 239
Lane, Andy
See Lane, Andrew
Lane, Carolyn 1926-1993 10
Lane, Connie
See Laux, Constance
Lane, Dakota 1959- 166
Earlier sketch in SATA *105*
Lane, Jerry
See Martin, Patricia Miles
Lane, John (Richard) 1932- 15
Lane, Leena 199
Lane, Margaret 1907-1994 65
Brief entry 38
Obituary 79
Lane, Rose Wilder 1887-1968 29
Brief entry 28
Lanes, Selma G. 1929- 3
Lanes, Selma Gordon
See Lanes, Selma G.
Lanfredi, Judy 1964- 83

Lang, Andrew 1844-1912 .... *16*
  See also CLR *101*
Lang, Aubrey *169*
Lang, Diane *234*
Lang, Glenna 1951- *221*
Lang, Lang 1982- *208*
Lang, Paul 1948- *83*
Lang, Susan S. 1950- *68*
Lang, T.T.
  See Taylor, Theodore
Langart, Darrell T.
  See Garrett, Randall
Langdo, Bryan 1973- *233*
  Earlier sketches in SATA *138, 191*
Lange, John
  See Crichton, Michael
Lange, Karen E. *190*
Lange, Suzanne 1945- *5*
Langley, Andrew 1949- *166*
  Earlier sketch in SATA *104*
Langley, Charles P(itman) III 1949- *103*
Langley, Jonathan 1952- *122*
Langley, Noel 1911-1980
  Obituary *25*
Langley, Wanda *173*
Langner, Nola
  See Malone, Nola Langner
Langone, John (Michael) 1929- *46*
  Brief entry *38*
Langreuter, Jutta 1944- *122*
Langrish, Katherine *177*
Langsen, Richard C. 1953- *95*
Langstaff, John 1920-2005 .... *68*
  Obituary *172*
  Earlier sketch in SATA *6*
  See also CLR *3*
Langstaff, John Meredith
  See Langstaff, John
Langstaff, Launcelot
  See Irving, Washington
Langston, Laura 1958- *186*
Langton, Jane 1922- *200*
  Autobiography Feature *140*
  Earlier sketches in SATA *3, 68, 129, 140*
  See also CLR *33*
  See also SAAS *5*
Lanier, Sidney 1842-1881 .... *18*
Lanier, Sterling E. 1927-2007 .... *109*
Lanier, Sterling Edmund
  See Lanier, Sterling E.
Lanino, Deborah 1964- *123*
Lankford, Mary D. 1932- *112*
  Earlier sketch in SATA *77*
Lannin, Joanne 1951- *121*
Lannin, Joanne A.
  See Lannin, Joanne
Lansdale, Joe R. 1951- *116*
Lansdale, Joe Richard
  See Lansdale, Joe R.
Lansing, Alfred 1921-1975 .... *35*
Lansing, Karen E. 1954- *71*
Lansky, Vicki 1942- *177*
Lanthier, Jennifer 1964- *204*
Lantier-Sampon, Patricia 1952- *92*
Lantz, Fran
  See Lantz, Francess L(in)
Lantz, Francess L(in) 1952-2004 .... *153*
  Autobiography Feature *153*
  Obituary *159*
  Earlier sketches in SATA *63, 109*
Lantz, Paul 1908- *45*
Lantz, Walter 1900-1994 .... *37*
  Obituary *79*
Lanza, Barbara 1945- *101*
Lapp, Christiane (Germain) 1948- *74*
Lappin, Peter 1911-1999 .... *32*
Larbalestier, Justine *231*
  Earlier sketch in SATA *178*
Lardy, Philippe 1963- *168*
LaReau, Jenna *181*
LaReau, Kara *181*

Larios, Julie 1949- *178*
Larios, Julie Hofstrand
  See Larios, Julie
Larkin, Amy
  See Burns, Olive Ann
Larkin, Maia
  See Wojciechowska, Maia (Teresa)
Larkspur, Penelope
  See Wyatt, Valerie
Laroche, Giles 1956- *221*
  Earlier sketches in SATA *71, 126*
LaRochelle, David 1960- *171*
  Earlier sketch in SATA *115*
Larom, Henry V. 1903(?)-1975
  Obituary *30*
LaRose, Linda *125*
Larrabee, Lisa 1947- *84*
Larranaga, Ana Martin 1969- *229*
Larrecq, John M(aurice) 1926-1980 .... *44*
  Obituary *25*
Larrick (Crosby), Nancy 1910-2004 .... *4*
Larsen, Anita 1942- *78*
Larsen, Egon 1904- *14*
Larsen, Rebecca 1944- *54*
Larson, Eve
  See St. John, Wylly Folk
Larson, Gary 1950- *57*
Larson, Hope 1982- *205*
Larson, Ingrid D(ana) 1965- *92*
Larson, Jean Russell 1930- *121*
Larson, Kirby 1954- *181*
  Earlier sketch in SATA *96*
Larson, Norita D. 1944- *29*
Larson, Norita Dittberner
  See Larson, Norita D.
Larson, William H. 1938- *10*
Larsson, Carl (Olof) 1853-1919 .... *35*
LaSalle, Charles A.
  See Ellis, Edward S.
LaSalle, Charles E.
  See Ellis, Edward S.
Lasell, Elinor H. 1929- *19*
Lasell, Fen H.
  See Lasell, Elinor H.
Lasenby, Jack 1931- *172*
  Earlier sketches in SATA *65, 103*
Laser, Michael 1954- *117*
Lash, Joseph P. 1909-1987 .... *43*
Lasher, Faith B. 1921- *12*
Lasker, David 1950- *38*
Lasker, Joe
  See Lasker, Joseph Leon
Lasker, Joseph Leon 1919- *83*
  Earlier sketch in SATA *9*
  See also SAAS *17*
Laski, Marghanita 1915-1988 .... *55*
Laskin, Pamela L. 1954- *75*
Lasky, Kathryn 1944- *236*
  Earlier sketches in SATA *13, 69, 112, 157,*
  210
  See also CLR *140*
Lasky Knight, Kathryn
  See Lasky, Kathryn
Lass, Bonnie *131*
Lassalle, C. E.
  See Ellis, Edward S.
Lassiter, Mary
  See Hoffman, Mary
Lassiter, Rhiannon 1977- *157*
Lat 1951- *196*
Latham, Barbara 1896- *16*
Latham, Frank B(rown) 1910-2000 .... *6*
Latham, Irene 1971- *228*
Latham, Jean Lee 1902-1995 .... *68*
  Earlier sketch in SATA *2*
  See also CLR *50*
Latham, Mavis
  See Clark, Mavis Thorpe
Latham, Philip
  See Richardson, Robert S(hirley)

Lathrop, Dorothy P(ulis) 1891-1980 .... *14*
  Obituary *24*
Lathrop, Francis
  See Leiber, Fritz (Reuter, Jr.)
Latimer, Jim 1943- *80*
Latimer, Miriam *235*
Latta, Rich
  See Latta, Richard
Latta, Richard 1946- *113*
Latta, Sara L. 1960- *174*
Lattany, Kristin
  See Lattany, Kristin Hunter
Lattany, Kristin (Eggleston) Hunter 1931- . *154*
  Autobiography Feature *154*
  Earlier sketch in SATA *132*
Lattany, Kristin Hunter 1931-2008 .... *132*
  Earlier sketch in SATA *12*
  See also CLR *3*
  See also SAAS *10*
Lattimore, Eleanor Frances 1904-1986 .... *7*
  Obituary *48*
Lattin, Ann
  See Cole, Lois Dwight
Latyk, Olivier 1976- *234*
Lauber, Patricia (Grace) 1924- *138*
  Earlier sketches in SATA *1, 33, 75*
  See also CLR *16*
Laugesen, Malene *207*
Laugesen, Malene Reynolds
  See Laugesen, Malene
Laugesen, Mary E(akin) 1906-1995 .... *5*
Laughbaum, Steve 1945- *12*
Laughlin, Florence Young 1910-2001 .... *3*
Laughlin, Rosemary 1941- *123*
Launder, Sally *206*
Laure, Ettagale
  See Blauer, Ettagale
Laure, Jason 1940- *50*
  Brief entry *44*
Laurence, Ester Hauser 1935- *7*
Laurence, Jean Margaret Wemyss
  See Laurence, Margaret
Laurence, Margaret 1926-1987
  Obituary *50*
Laurie, Rona 1916- *55*
Laurie, Victoria *218*
Laurin, Anne
  See McLaurin, Anne
Lauritzen, Jonreed 1902-1979 .... *13*
Lauscher, Hermann
  See Hesse, Hermann
Lauture, Denize 1946- *86*
Laux, Connie
  See Laux, Constance
Laux, Constance 1952- *97*
Laux, Dorothy 1920- *49*
Lavallee, Barbara 1941- *166*
  Earlier sketch in SATA *74*
Lavender, David (Sievert) 1910-2003 .... *97*
  Obituary *145*
  Earlier sketch in SATA *64*
Lavender, William D. 1921- *143*
Laverne, Christine *175*
Lavert, Gwendolyn Battle 1951-
  See Battle-Lavert, Gwendolyn
Laverty, Donald
  See Blish, James
  and Knight, Damon (Francis)
Lavigne, Louis-Dominique 1949- *107*
Lavine, David 1928- *31*
Lavine, Sigmund Arnold 1908-1986 .... *82*
  Earlier sketch in SATA *3*
  See also CLR *35*
Lavis, Steve *225*
Lavond, Paul Dennis
  See Kornbluth, C(yril) M.
  and Lowndes, Robert A(ugustine) W(ard)
  and Pohl, Frederik
Law, Stephen *225*
Law, Stephen
  See Law, Stephen

Lawford, Paula Jane 1960- 57
Brief entry 53
Lawhead, Stephen R. 1950- 109
Lawhead, Steve
See Lawhead, Stephen R.
Lawler, Janet 222
Lawlor, Laurie 1953- 235
Earlier sketches in SATA 80, 137
Lawlor, William
See Lawlor, William T.
Lawlor, William T. 1951- 183
Lawrence, Ann (Margaret) 1942-1987 41
Obituary 54
Lawrence, Caroline 1954- 203
Lawrence, Iain 1955- 183
Earlier sketch in SATA 135
Lawrence, J. T.
See Rowland-Entwistle, (Arthur) Theodore
(Henry)
Lawrence, Jerome 1915-2004 65
Lawrence, John 1933- 30
Lawrence, Josephine 1890(?)-1978
Obituary 24
Lawrence, Louise 1943- 119
Earlier sketches in SATA 38, 78
Lawrence, Louise de Kiriline 1894-1992 13
Lawrence, Lynn
See Garland, Sherry
Lawrence, Margery H. 1889-1969 120
Lawrence, Michael 1943- 132
Lawrence, Mildred Elwood 1907-1997 3
Lawrence, R(onald) D(ouglas) 1921- 55
Lawrinson, Julia 1969- 141
Lawson, Amy
See Gordon, Amy
Lawson, Carol (Antell) 1946- 42
Lawson, Don(ald Elmer) 1917-1990 9
Lawson, Joan 1906- 55
Lawson, Julie 1947- 126
Earlier sketch in SATA 79
See also CLR 89
Lawson, Marion Tubbs 1896-1994 22
Lawson, Robert 1892-1957 100
See also YABC 2
See also CLR 73
Lawton, Clive A. 1951- 145
Laxdal, Vivienne 1962- 112
Laybourn, Emma 193
Layburn, Joe 228
Laycock, George (Edwin) 1921- 5
Layne, Laura
See Knott, William C(ecil, Jr.)
Layne, Steven L. 171
Layson, Annelex Hofstra 1938(?)- 211
Layton, Neal 1971- 187
Earlier sketch in SATA 152
Layton, Neal Andrew
See Layton, Neal
Lazare, Gerald John 1927- 44
Lazare, Jerry
See Lazare, Gerald John
Lazarevich, Mila 1942- 17
Lazarus, Keo Felker 1913-1993 21
Obituary 129
Lea, Alec 1907- 19
Lea, Bob 1952- 203
Lea, Joan
See Neufeld, John (Arthur)
Leach, Maria 1892-1977 39
Brief entry 28
Leacock, Elspeth 1946- 131
Leacroft, Helen (Mabel Beal) 1919- 6
Leacroft, Richard (Vallance Becher) 1914- 6
Leaf, Margaret P. 1909(?)-1988
Obituary 55
Leaf, (Wilbur) Munro 1905-1976 20
See also CLR 25
Leaf, VaDonna Jean 1929- 26
Leah, Devorah
See Devorah-Leah
Leakey, Richard E(rskine Frere) 1944- 42

Leal, Ann Haywood 216
Leander, Ed
See Richelson, Geraldine
Lear, Edward 1812-1888 100
Earlier sketch in SATA 18
See also CLR 169
Lears, Laurie 1955- 127
Leasor, James 1923-2007 54
Leasor, Thomas James
See Leasor, James
Leavitt, Jerome E(dward) 1916- 23
Leavitt, Martine 1953- 170
LeBar, Mary E(velyn) 1910-1982 35
LeBlanc, Annette M. 1965- 68
LeBlanc, L(ee) 1913- 54
LeBox, Annette 1943- 145
Lebrun, Claude 1929- 66
Le Cain, Errol (John) 1941-1989 68
Obituary 60
Earlier sketch in SATA 6
Lechermeier, Philippe 1968- 235
Lechner, Jack 201
Lechner, John 1966- 200
Leck, James 1973- 229
Lecourt, Nancy (Hoyt) 1951- 73
Ledbetter, Suzann 1953- 119
Leder, Jane Mersky 1945- 61
Brief entry 51
Lederer, Muriel 1929- 48
Lederer, William J. 1912-2009 62
Lederer, William Julius
See Lederer, William J.
Lee, Amanda
See Baggett, Nancy
and Buckholtz, Eileen (Garber)
and Glick, Ruth
Lee, Benjamin 1921- 27
Lee, Betsy 1949- 37
Lee, Carol
See Fletcher, Helen Jill
Lee, Carol Ann 1969- 185
Lee, Chinlun 182
Lee, Cora 223
See Anderson, Catherine Corley
Lee, Dennis (Beynon) 1939- 102
Earlier sketch in SATA 14
See also CLR 3
Lee, Dom 1959- 146
Autobiography Feature 121
Earlier sketch in SATA 83
See also SAAS 26
Lee, Doris Emrick 1905-1983 44
Obituary 35
Lee, Edward
See Lee, J. Edward
Lee, Elizabeth Rogers 1940- 90
Lee, Harper 1926- 11
See also CLR 169
Lee, Hector Viveros 1962- 115
Lee, Howard N.
See Goulart, Ron
Lee, Huy Voun 1969- 217
Earlier sketch in SATA 129
Lee, Insu 213
Lee, J. Edward 1953- 130
Lee, Jared 1943- 215
Lee, Jared D.
See Lee, Jared
Lee, Jeanne M. 1943- 138
Lee, John R(obert) 1923-1976 27
Lee, Jordan
See Scholefield, Alan
Lee, Joseph Edward
See Lee, J. Edward
Lee, Julian
See Latham, Jean Lee
Lee, Linda
See Eyerly, Jeannette
Lee, Liz
See Lee, Elizabeth Rogers

Lee, Lucy
See Talbot, Charlene Joy
Lee, Lyn 1953- 128
Lee, Manning de Villeneuve 1894-1980 37
Obituary 22
Lee, Marian
See Clish, (Lee) Marian
Lee, Marie G. 1964- 178
Earlier sketches in SATA 81, 130
Lee, Marie Myung-Ok
See Lee, Marie G.
Lee, Mary Price 1934- 82
Earlier sketch in SATA 8
Lee, Mildred
See Scudder, Mildred Lee
Lee, Nelle Harper
See Lee, Harper
Lee, Richard S. 1927- 82
Lee, Robert C. 1931- 20
Lee, Robert Edwin 1918-1994 65
Obituary 82
Lee, Robert J. 1921- 10
Lee, Roy
See Hopkins, Clark
Lee, Sally 1943- 67
Lee, Suzy 193
Lee, Tammie
See Townsend, Thomas L.
Lee, Tanith 1947- 185
Earlier sketches in SATA 8, 88, 134
Lee, Virginia 1976- 208
Lee, Y.S. 1974- 232
Leech, Ben
See Bowkett, Stephen
Leeds, Constance 188
Leedy, Loreen 1959- 238
Brief entry 50
Earlier sketches in SATA 54, 84, 128, 175
Leedy, Loreen Janelle
See Leedy, Loreen
Lee-Hostetler, Jeri 1940- 63
Leekley, Thomas B(riggs) 1910-2001 23
Leeming, Jo Ann
See Leeming, Joseph
Leeming, Joseph 1897-1968 26
Leemis, Ralph B. 1954- 72
Leese, Jennifer L.B. 1970- 163
Leeson, Muriel 1920- 54
Leeson, R. A.
See Leeson, Robert (Arthur)
Leeson, Robert (Arthur) 1928- 76
Earlier sketch in SATA 42
Lee Tae-Jun 1904-1956(?) 194
Lee-Tai, Amy 1964- 189
Leffland, Ella 1931- 65
Leffler, Silke 197
Lefler, Irene (Whitney) 1917- 12
LeFrak, Karen 182
Le Gallienne, Eva 1899-1991 9
Obituary 68
Legg, Gerald 1947- 143
Legg, Sarah Martha Ross Bruggeman (?)-1982
Obituary 40
LeGrand
See Henderson, LeGrand
Le Guin, Ursula K. 1929- 194
Earlier sketches in SATA 4, 52, 99, 149
See also CLR 173
Le Guin, Ursula Kroeber
See Le Guin, Ursula K.
Legum, Colin 1919-2003 10
Lehman, Barbara 1963- 170
Earlier sketch in SATA 115
Lehman, Bob 91
Lehman, Elaine 91
Lehmann, Debra Lynn
See Vanasse, Deb
Lehman-Wilzig, Tami 1950- 224
Lehn, Cornelia 1920- 46
Lehne, Judith Logan 1947- 93
Lehr, Delores 1920- 10

Lehr, Norma 1930- 71
Leiber, Fritz (Reuter, Jr.) 1910-1992 45
    Obituary 73
Leibold, Jay 1957- 57
    Brief entry 52
Leichman, Seymour 1933- 5
Leick, Bonnie 205
Leigh, Nila K. 1981- 81
Leigh, Tom 1947- 46
Leigh-Pemberton, John 1911-1997 35
Leighton, Clare (Veronica Hope)
    1899-1989 37
Leighton, Margaret (Carver) 1896-1987 1
    Obituary 52
Leijten, Aileen 216
Leiner, Al(an) 1938- 83
Leiner, Katherine 1949- 93
Leipold, L. Edmond 1902-1983 16
Leisk, David (Johnson) 1906-1975 30
    Obituary 26
    Earlier sketch in SATA 1
    See also CLR 98
Leist, Christina 226
Leister, Mary 1917- 29
Leitch, Patricia 1933- 98
    Earlier sketch in SATA 11
Leitner, Isabella 1924- 86
Lekich, John 202
Leland, Bob 1956- 92
Leland, Robert E.
    See Leland, Bob
Leloup, Genevieve 230
Lematre, Pascal 1967- 225
    Earlier sketch in SATA 176
Lember, Barbara Hirsch 1941- 92
LeMieux, A.C. 1954- 125
    Earlier sketch in SATA 90
LeMieux, Anne
    See LeMieux, A.C.
LeMieux, Anne Connelly
    See LeMieux, A.C.
Lemieux, Michele 1955- 139
Lemke, Horst 1922- 38
Lemna, Don 1936- 216
Lenain, Thierry 1959- 201
Lenanton, Carola Mary Anima Oman
    See Oman, Carola (Mary Anima)
Lenard, Alexander 1910-1972
    Obituary 21
Lendroth, Susan 207
L'Engle, Madeleine 1918-2007 128
    Obituary 186
    Earlier sketches in SATA 1, 27, 75
    See also CLR 172
    See also SAAS 15
L'Engle, Madeleine Camp Franklin
    See L'Engle, Madeleine
Lengyel, Cornel Adam 1915- 27
Lengyel, Emil 1895-1985 3
    Obituary 42
Lennon, John 1940-1980 114
Lennon, John Ono
    See Lennon, John
Leno, Jay 1950- 154
LeNoir, Janice 1941- 89
Lens, Sidney 1912-1986 13
    Obituary 48
Lenski, Lois 1893-1974 100
    Earlier sketches in SATA 1, 26
    See also CLR 26
Lent, Blair 1930-2009 133
    Obituary 200
    Earlier sketch in SATA 2
Lent, Henry Bolles 1901-1973 17
Lent, John 1948- 108
Leodhas, Sorche Nic
    See Alger, Leclaire (Gowans)
Leokum, Arkady 1916(?)- 45
Leon, Carol Boyd 212
Leon, Sharon 1959- 79
Leonard, Alison 1944- 70

Leonard, Anna
    See Gilman, Laura Anne
Leonard, Constance (Brink) 1923- 42
    Brief entry 40
Leonard, Dutch
    See Leonard, Elmore
Leonard, Elmore 1925- 163
Leonard, Elmore John, Jr.
    See Leonard, Elmore
Leonard, Jonathan N(orton) 1903-1975 36
Leonard, Laura 1923- 75
Leonard, Tom 1955- 207
Leonetti, Mike 1958- 202
Leong, Gor Yun
    See Ellison, Virginia H(owell)
Leonhard, Herb 217
Leonhardt, Alice 1950- 234
    Earlier sketch in SATA 152
Lerangis, Peter 1955- 171
    Earlier sketch in SATA 72
Lerman, Josh 215
Lerner, Aaron 1920-2007 35
    Obituary 179
Lerner, Aaron Bunsen
    See Lerner, Aaron
Lerner, Carol 1927- 86
    Earlier sketch in SATA 33
    See also CLR 34
    See also SAAS 12
Lerner, Gerda 1920- 65
Lerner, Harriet 1944- 101
Lerner, Marguerite Rush 1924-1987 11
    Obituary 51
Lerner, Sharon (Ruth) 1938-1982 11
    Obituary 29
Leroe, Ellen 1949- 99
    Brief entry 51
    Earlier sketch in SATA 61
Leroe, Ellen W.
    See Leroe, Ellen
Leroe, Ellen Whitney
    See Leroe, Ellen
Leroux, Gaston 1868-1927 65
Leroux-Hugon, Helene 1955- 132
LeRoy, Gen 52
    Brief entry 36
Lerrigo, Marion Olive 1898-1968
    Obituary 29
LeShan, Eda J(oan) 1922-2002 21
    See also CLR 6
Leshem, Yossi 1947- 222
LeSieg, Theo.
    See Dr. Seuss
Lesinski, Jeanne M. 1960- 120
Leslie, Robert Franklin 1911-1990 7
Leslie, Roger 1961- 168
Leslie, Roger James
    See Leslie, Roger
Leslie, Sarah
    See McGuire, Leslie (Sarah)
LeSourd, Catherine
    See Marshall, (Sarah) Catherine (Wood)
Lessac, Frane
    See Lessac, Frane
Lessac, Frane 1954- 209
    Earlier sketches in SATA 61, 148
Lessem, Dino Don
    See Lessem, Don
Lessem, Don 1951- 182
    Earlier sketches in SATA 97, 155
Lesser, Margaret 1899(?)-1979
    Obituary 22
Lesser, Rika 1953- 53
Lester, Alison 1952- 218
    Earlier sketches in SATA 50, 90, 129
Lester, Helen 1936- 189
    Earlier sketches in SATA 46, 92, 145
Lester, Julius 1939- 157
    Earlier sketches in SATA 12, 74, 112
    See also CLR 143

Lester, Julius Bernard
    See Lester, Julius
Lester, Mike 1955- 206
    Earlier sketch in SATA 131
Le Sueur, Meridel 1900-1996 6
Leszczynski, Diana 211
Lethcoe, Jason 191
Le Tord, Bijou 1945- 95
    Earlier sketch in SATA 49
Letts, Billie 1938- 121
Letts, Elizabeth
    See Alalou, Elizabeth
Leuck, Laura 1962- 192
    Earlier sketches in SATA 85, 146
Leung, Hilary 1975- 225
Leutscher, Alfred (George) 1913- 23
Levai, Blaise 1919- 39
le Vann, Kate 237
Levchuk, Lisa 215
Leveen, Tom 230
Levenkron, Steven 1941- 86
Leverich, Kathleen 1948- 103
LeVert, John 1946- 55
Levert, Mireille 1956- 211
LeVert, William John
    See LeVert, John
Levete, Sarah 1961- 153
Levin, Betty 1927- 201
    Earlier sketches in SATA 19, 84, 137
    See also SAAS 11
Levin, Ira 1929-2007 66
    Obituary 187
Levin, Ira Marvin
    See Levin, Ira
Levin, Marcia Obrasky 1918- 13
Levin, Meyer 1905-1981 21
    Obituary 27
Levin, Miriam (Ramsfelder) 1962- 97
Levine, Abby 1943- 54
    Brief entry 52
Levine, Anna 212
Levine, Betty K(rasne) 1933- 66
Levine, David 1926-2009 43
    Brief entry 35
Levine, Edna S(imon) 35
Levine, Ellen 1939- 190
Levine, Evan 1962- 77
    Earlier sketch in SATA 74
Levine, Gail Carson 1947- 239
    Earlier sketches in SATA 98, 161, 195
    See also CLR 85
Levine, I(srael) E. 1923-2003 12
    Obituary 146
Levine, Joan Goldman 11
Levine, Joseph 1910- 33
Levine, Kristin 1974- 213
Levine, Marge 1934- 81
Levine, Rhoda 14
Levine, Sarah 1970- 57
Levine, Shar 1953- 131
Levine-Freidus, Gail
    See Provost, Gail Levine
Levinson, Nancy Smiler 1938- 211
    Earlier sketches in SATA 33, 80, 140
Levinson, Riki 99
    Brief entry 49
    Earlier sketch in SATA 52
Levithan, David 1972- 235
    Earlier sketch in SATA 166
Levitin, Sonia 1934- 192
    Autobiography Feature 131
    Earlier sketches in SATA 4, 68, 119, 131
    See also CLR 53
    See also SAAS 2
Levitt, Sidney (Mark) 1947- 68
Levon, O. U.
    See Kesey, Ken
Levoy, Myron 1930- 49
    Brief entry 37
Levy, Barrie 112

Levy, Constance 1931- 140
    Earlier sketch in SATA 73
    See also SAAS 22
Levy, Debbie 1957- 232
Levy, Deborah Marian
    See Levy, Debbie
Levy, Elizabeth 1942- 169
    Earlier sketches in SATA 31, 69, 107
    See also SAAS 18
Levy, Janice 172
Levy, Marilyn 1937- 67
Levy, Nathan 1945- 63
Levy, Robert 1945- 82
Lewees, John
    See Stockton, Francis Richard
Lewin, Betsy 1937- 222
    Autobiography Feature 115
    Earlier sketches in SATA 32, 90, 169
Lewin, Hugh 1939- 72
    Brief entry 40
    See also CLR 9
Lewin, Ted 1935- 226
    Autobiography Feature 115
    Earlier sketches in SATA 21, 76, 119, 165,
    195
Lewis, Alice C. 1936- 46
Lewis, Alice Hudson 1895(?)-1971
    Obituary 29
Lewis, Amanda 1955- 80
Lewis, Anthony 1927- 27
Lewis, Anthony 1966- 227
    Earlier sketch in SATA 120
Lewis, Barbara A. 1943- 73
Lewis, Beverly 1949- 80
Lewis, Brenda Ralph 1932- 72
Lewis, Brian 1963- 128
Lewis, C. S. 1898-1963 100
    Earlier sketch in SATA 13
    See also CLR 173
Lewis, Claudia (Louise) 1907-2001 5
Lewis, Clive Staples
    See Lewis, C. S.
Lewis, Cynthia Copeland 1960- 111
Lewis, E. M. 123
    Earlier sketch in SATA 20
Lewis, Earl Bradley
    See Lewis, E.B.
Lewis, E.B. 1956- 211
    Earlier sketches in SATA 93, 124, 168
Lewis, Elizabeth Foreman 1892-1958 121
    See also YABC 2
Lewis, Francine
    See Wells, Helen
Lewis, Harry Sinclair
    See Lewis, Sinclair
Lewis, Hilda (Winifred) 1896-1974
    Obituary 20
Lewis, J. Patrick 1942- 205
    Earlier sketches in SATA 69, 104, 162
Lewis, Jack P(earl) 1919- 65
Lewis, Jean 1924- 61
Lewis, Jon S.
    See Lewis, J.S.
Lewis, Jon Samuel
    See Lewis, J.S.
Lewis, Joseph Anthony
    See Lewis, Anthony
Lewis, J.S. 1972- 238
    Earlier sketch in SATA 203
Lewis, Julinda
    See Lewis-Ferguson, Julinda
Lewis, Kevin 173
Lewis, Kim 1951- 217
    Earlier sketches in SATA 84, 136
Lewis, Linda (Joy) 1946- 67
Lewis, Lucia Z.
    See Anderson, Lucia (Lewis)
Lewis, Marjorie 1929- 40
    Brief entry 35
Lewis, Mary 1907(?)-1988 64
    Obituary 56

Lewis, Mervyn
    See Frewer, Glyn (M.)
Lewis, Michael
    See Untermeyer, Louis
Lewis, Naomi 1911-2009 144
    Earlier sketch in SATA 76
Lewis, Paeony 1960- 173
Lewis, Paul
    See Gerson, Noel Bertram
Lewis, Richard 1935- 3
Lewis, Richard 1956- 209
Lewis, Rob 1962- 72
Lewis, Roger
    See Zarchy, Harry
Lewis, Rose 209
Lewis, Rose A.
    See Lewis, Rose
Lewis, Shannon
    See Llywelyn, Morgan
Lewis, Shari 1934-1998 35
    Brief entry 30
    Obituary 104
Lewis, Sylvan R.
    See Aronson, Virginia
Lewis, Thomas P(arker) 1936- 27
Lewis, Wendy A. 1966- 150
Lewis-Ferguson, Julinda 1955- 85
Lewison, Wendy Cheyette 177
Lewiton, Mina 1904-1970 2
Lew-Vriethoff, Joanne 186
Lexau, Joan M. 130
    Earlier sketches in SATA 1, 36
Ley, Willy 1906-1969 2
Leydon, Rita (Floden) 1949- 21
Leyland, Eric (Arthur) 1911- 37
L'Hommedieu, Dorothy Keasley 1885-1961
    Obituary 29
Li, Xiao Jun 1952- 86
Liao, Jimmy 1958- 202
Liatsos, Sandra Olson 1942- 103
Libby, Alisa M. 189
Libby, Barbara M. 153
Libby, Bill
    See Libby, William M.
Libby, William M. 1927-1984 5
    Obituary 39
Liberty, Gene 1924- 3
Lichtenheld, Tom 208
    Earlier sketch in SATA 152
Lichtman, Wendy 1946- 193
Liddell, Kenneth 1912-1975 63
Liddiment, Carol 224
Lidz, Jane 120
Lieb, Josh 1972- 224
Lieberman, E(dwin) James 1934- 62
Liebers, Arthur 1913-1984 12
Lieblich, Irene 1923- 22
Liers, Emil E(rnest) 1890-1975 37
Lies, Brian 1963- 190
    Earlier sketch in SATA 131
Lieshout, Elle van
    See van Lieshout, Elle
Liestman, Vicki 1961- 72
Lietz, Gerald S. 1918- 11
Liew, Sonny 1974- 219
Life, Kay (Guinn) 1930- 83
Lifton, Betty Jean 1926-2010 118
    Earlier sketch in SATA 6
Lifton, Robert Jay 1926- 66
Light, Steve 237
Lightburn, Ron 1954- 91
Lightburn, Sandra 1955- 91
Lightner, A. M.
    See Hopf, Alice (Martha) L(ightner)
Lightner, Alice
    See Hopf, Alice (Martha) L(ightner)
Lignell, Lois 1911- 37
Liles, Maurine Walpole 1935- 81
Lillegard, Dee 184
Lilley, Stephen R. 1950- 97

Lilley, Stephen Ray
    See Lilley, Stephen R.
Lillington, Kenneth (James) 1916-1998 39
Lilly, Nate 182
Lilly, Ray
    See Curtis, Richard
Lim, John 1932- 43
Liman, Ellen (Fogelson) 1936- 22
Limb, Sue 1946- 203
    Earlier sketch in SATA 158
Limburg, Peter R(ichard) 1929- 13
Lin, Grace 1974- 198
    Earlier sketches in SATA 111, 162
Lincoln, C(harles) Eric 1924-2000 5
Lincoln, Christopher 1952- 208
Lincoln, Hazel 187
Lincoln, James
    See Bates, Katharine Lee
Lindbergh, Anne
    See Sapieyevski, Anne Lindbergh
Lindbergh, Anne Morrow 1906-2001 33
    Obituary 125
Lindbergh, Anne Spencer Morrow
    See Lindbergh, Anne Morrow
Lindbergh, Charles A(ugustus, Jr.)
    1902-1974 33
Lindbergh, Reeve 1945- 163
    Earlier sketch in SATA 116
Lindblom, Steven (Winther) 1946- 94
    Brief entry 39
    Earlier sketch in SATA 42
Linde, Gunnel 1924- 5
Lindenbaum, Pija 1955- 183
    Earlier sketches in SATA 77, 144
Lindgren, Astrid (Anna Emilia Ericsson)
    1907-2002 38
    Obituary 128
    Earlier sketch in SATA 2
    See also CLR 119
Lindgren, Barbro 1937- 207
    Brief entry 46
    Earlier sketches in SATA 63, 120
    See also CLR 86
Lindman, Maj (Jan) 1886-1972 43
Lindner, April 1962- 238
Lindo, Elvira 1962- 219
Lindop, Edmund 1925- 5
Lindquist, Jennie Dorothea 1899-1977 13
Lindquist, Rowena Cory 1958- 98
Lindquist, Willis 1908-1988 20
Lindsay, Nicholas Vachel
    See Lindsay, Vachel
Lindsay, Norman Alfred William
    1879-1969 67
    See also CLR 8
Lindsay, Vachel 1879-1931 40
Lindsey, Kathleen D(orothy) 1949- 153
Line, David
    See Davidson, Lionel
Line, Les 1935-2010 27
Lines, Kathleen Mary 1902-1988
    Obituary 61
Linfield, Esther 40
Lingard, Joan (Amelia) 1932- 130
    Autobiography Feature 130
    Earlier sketches in SATA 8, 74, 114
    See also CLR 89
    See also SAAS 5
Link, Martin 1934- 28
Linn, Margot
    See Ziefert, Harriet
Linnea, Sharon 1956- 82
Lintern, Tom 228
Lion, Melissa 1976- 176
Lionni, Leo(nard) 1910-1999 72
    Obituary 118
    Earlier sketch in SATA 8
    See also CLR 71
Lipinsky de Orlov, Lino S. 1908- 22
Lipkind, William 1904-1974 15
Lipman, David 1931-2008 21

Author Index

Lipman, Matthew 1923-2010 .... *14*
Lipp, Frederick *204*
Lippincott, Bertram 1898(?)-1985
  Obituary *42*
Lippincott, Gary A. 1953- *220*
  Earlier sketches in SATA *73, 119*
Lippincott, Joseph W(harton) 1887-1976 ..... *17*
Lippincott, Sarah Lee 1920- *22*
Lippman, Peter J. 1936- *31*
Lipsyte, Robert 1938- *198*
  Earlier sketches in SATA *5, 68, 113, 161*
  See also CLR *76*
Lipsyte, Robert Michael
  See Lipsyte, Robert
Lisandrelli, Elaine Slivinski 1951- *94*
Lisker, Sonia O. 1933- *44*
Lisle, Holly 1960- *208*
  Earlier sketch in SATA *98*
Lisle, Janet Taylor 1947- *150*
  Brief entry *47*
  Earlier sketches in SATA *59, 96*
  See also SAAS *14*
Lisle, Rebecca *162*
Lisle, Seward D.
  See Ellis, Edward S.
Lisowski, Gabriel 1946- *47*
  Brief entry *31*
Liss, Howard 1922-1995 .... *4*
  Obituary *84*
Lissiat, Amy
  See Thompson, Colin
Lisson, Deborah 1941- *110*
  Earlier sketch in SATA *71*
List, Ilka Katherine 1935- *6*
Liston, Robert A. 1927- *5*
Litchfield, Ada B(assett) 1916-1999 .... *5*
Litchfield, E. 1973- *116*
Lithgow, John 1945- *145*
Lithgow, John Arthur
  See Lithgow, John
Litowinsky, Olga 1936- *26*
Litowinsky, Olga Jean
  See Litowinsky, Olga
Littke, Lael J. 1929- *140*
  Earlier sketches in SATA *51, 83*
Little, A. Edward
  See Klein, Aaron E.
Little, Douglas 1942- *96*
Little, (Flora) Jean 1932- *149*
  Earlier sketches in SATA *2, 68, 106*
  See also CLR *4*
  See also SAAS *17*
Little, Lessie Jones 1906-1986 .... *60*
  Obituary *50*
Little, Mary E. 1912-1999 .... *28*
Littlechild, George 1958- *85*
Littledale, Freya (Lota) 1929-1992 .... *74*
  Earlier sketch in SATA *2*
Littlefield, Bill 1948- *83*
Littlefield, Holly 1963- *97*
Littlesugar, Amy 1953- *176*
  Earlier sketch in SATA *122*
Littleton, Mark R. 1950- *142*
  Earlier sketch in SATA *89*
Littlewood, Karin *211*
Littman, Sarah Darer *221*
  Earlier sketch in SATA *175*
Litty, Julie 1971- *181*
Litwin, Mike *235*
Litzinger, Rosanne 1948- *196*
Liu, Cynthea *221*
Lively, Penelope 1933- *164*
  Earlier sketches in SATA *7, 60, 101*
  See also CLR *159*
Lively, Penelope Margaret
  See Lively, Penelope
Liverakos, L. A.
  See Gilman, Laura Anne
Liversidge, (Henry) Douglas 1913- *8*
Livesey, Claire (Warner) 1927- *127*
Livingston, Carole 1941- *42*

Livingston, (M.) Irene 1932- *150*
Livingston, Myra Cohn 1926-1996 .... *68*
  Obituary *92*
  Earlier sketch in SATA *5*
  See also CLR *7*
  See also SAAS *1*
Livingston, Richard R(oland) 1922- *8*
Livo, Norma J. 1929- *76*
Liwska, Renata *199*
Ljungkvist, Laura *180*
Llerena Aguirre, Carlos 1952- *19*
Llerena Aguirre, Carlos Antonio
  See Llerena Aguirre, Carlos
Llewellyn, Claire 1954- *196*
  Earlier sketches in SATA *77, 143*
Llewellyn, Grace 1964- *110*
Llewellyn, Richard
  See Llewellyn Lloyd, Richard Dafydd Vivian
Llewellyn, Sam 1948- *185*
  Earlier sketch in SATA *95*
Llewellyn, Tom 1964- *234*
Llewellyn Lloyd, Richard Dafydd Vivian
  1906-1983 .... *11*
  Obituary *37*
Llewelyn, T. Harcourt
  See Hamilton, Charles (Harold St. John)
Lloyd, Alan
  See Lloyd, A.R.
Lloyd, Alan Richard
  See Lloyd, A.R.
Lloyd, Alison 1966- *231*
Lloyd, A.R. 1927- *168*
  Earlier sketch in SATA *97*
Lloyd, David
  See Lloyd, David T.
Lloyd, David T. 1954- *167*
Lloyd, E. James
  See James, Elizabeth
Lloyd, Errol 1943- *22*
Lloyd, Hugh
  See Fitzhugh, Percy Keese
Lloyd, James
  See James, Elizabeth
Lloyd, Megan 1958- *239*
  Earlier sketches in SATA *77, 117, 189*
Lloyd, Norman 1909-1980
  Obituary *23*
Lloyd, (Mary) Norris 1908-1993 .... *10*
  Obituary *75*
Lloyd, Saci 1967- *220*
Lloyd, Sam *183*
Lloyd, Tanya
  See Kyi, Tanya Lloyd
Lloyd-Jones, Sally 1960- *179*
Lloyd Webber, Andrew 1948- *56*
Llywelyn, Morgan 1937- *109*
Lo, Ginnie *165*
Lo, Malinda 1974- *222*
Lo, Virginia M.
  See Lo, Ginnie
Lobato, Jose Bento Monteiro 1882-1948 ... *114*
Lobel, Anita (Kempler) 1934- *162*
  Earlier sketches in SATA *6, 55, 96*
Lobel, Arnold (Stark) 1933-1987 .... *55*
  Obituary *54*
  Earlier sketch in SATA *6*
  See also CLR *5*
Lobel, Gillian *181*
Lobsenz, Amelia *12*
Lobsenz, Norman M(itchell) 1919- *6*
Lochak, Michele 1936- *39*
Lochlons, Colin
  See Jackson, C(aary) Paul
Locke, Clinton W. *1*
Locke, Elsie (Violet) 1912-2001 .... *87*
Locke, Gary 1963- *197*
Locke, Lucie 1904-1989 .... *10*
Locke, Robert 1944- *63*
  See also CLR *39*

Locker, Thomas 1937- *109*
  Earlier sketch in SATA *59*
  See also CLR *14*
Lockhart, E.
  See Jenkins, Emily
Lockridge, Hildegarde (Dolson)
  1908-1981 .... *121*
  Earlier sketch in SATA *5*
Lockwood, Mary
  See Spelman, Mary
Lodge, Bernard 1933- *215*
  Earlier sketches in SATA *33, 107*
Lodge, Jo 1966- *173*
  Earlier sketch in SATA *112*
Loeb, Jeffrey 1946- *57*
Loeb, Robert H., Jr. 1917- *21*
Loefgren, Ulf 1931- *3*
Loehfelm, Bill 1969- *153*
Loehr, Mallory *184*
Loehr, Patrick 1968(?)- *194*
Loeper, John J(oseph) 1929- *118*
  Earlier sketch in SATA *10*
Loescher, Ann Dull 1942- *20*
Loescher, Gil 1945- *20*
Loescher, Gilburt Damian
  See Loescher, Gil
Loewer, Jean Jenkins
  See Jenkins, Jean
Loewer, (Henry) Peter 1934- *98*
LoFaro, Jerry 1959- *77*
Lofo
  See Heimann, Rolf
Lofthouse, Liz *199*
Lofting, Hugh (John) 1886-1947 .... *100*
  Earlier sketch in SATA *15*
  See also CLR *143*
Lofts, Norah (Robinson) 1904-1983 .... *8*
  Obituary *36*
Logan, Alysia
  See Divine, L.
Logan, Bob 1968- *238*
Logan, Jake
  See Knott, William C(ecil, Jr.)
  and Krepps, Robert W(ilson)
  and Pearl, Jacques Bain
  and Riefe, Alan
  and Rifkin, Shepard
  and Smith, Martin Cruz
Logan, Laura *237*
Logan, Mark
  See Nicole, Christopher
Logan, Rochelle 1954- *169*
Logsted, Greg *221*
Logston, Anne 1962- *112*
Logue, Christopher 1926-2011 .... *23*
Logue, Mary 1952- *161*
  Earlier sketch in SATA *112*
Logue, Mary Louise
  See Logue, Mary
Loh, Morag 1935- *73*
Lohans, Alison 1949- *101*
Loizeaux, William *185*
Loken, Newton Clayton 1919- *26*
Lomas, Steve
  See Brennan, Joseph Lomas
Lomask, Milton (Nachman) 1909-1991 .... *20*
Lombard, Jenny *178*
Lombino, Salvatore
  See Hunter, Evan
LoMonaco, Palmyra 1932- *102*
London, Jack 1876-1916 .... *18*
  See also CLR *108*
London, Jane
  See Geis, Darlene Stern
London, John Griffith
  See London, Jack
London, Jonathan 1947- *221*
  Earlier sketches in SATA *74, 113, 157*
Lonergan, (Pauline) Joy (MacLean) 1909- ... *10*
Lonette, Reisie (Dominee) 1924- *43*
Long, Cathryn J. 1946- *89*

Long, Earlene (Roberta) 1938- 50
Long, Emmett
    See Leonard, Elmore
Long, Ethan 1968(?)- 223
    Earlier sketch in SATA 182
Long, Helen Beecher 1
Long, Judith Elaine 1953- 20
Long, Judy
    See Long, Judith Elaine
Long, Kim 1949- 69
Long, Laura Mooney 1892-1967
    Obituary 29
Long, Laurel 203
Long, Loren 1966(?)- 188
    Earlier sketch in SATA 151
Long, Melinda 1960- 152
Long, Sylvia 1948- 179
    Earlier sketch in SATA 120
Longbeard, Frederick
    See Longyear, Barry B(rookes)
Longfellow, Henry Wadsworth 1807-1882 ... 19
    See also CLR 99
Longfellow, Layne 1937- 102
Longfellow, Layne A.
    See Longfellow, Layne
Longman, Harold S. 1919- 5
Longsworth, Polly 1933- 28
Longtemps, Kenneth 1933- 17
Longway, A. Hugh
    See Lang, Andrew
Longyear, Barry B(rookes) 1942- 117
Look, Lenore 180
Loomans, Diane 1955- 90
Loomis, Christine 160
    Earlier sketch in SATA 113
Loomis, Jennifer A. 1942- 101
Loomis, Robert D. 5
Lopez, Angelo (Cayas) 1967- 83
Lopez, Antonio Castro
    See Castro L., Antonio
Lopez, Barry 1945- 67
Lopez, Barry Holstun
    See Lopez, Barry
Lopez, Jack 1950- 178
Lopez, Loretta 1963- 190
Lopez, Lorraine 1956- 181
Lopez, Lorraine M.
    See Lopez, Lorraine
Lopez, Mario 1973- 226
Lopez, Rafael 1961(?)- 198
Lopshire, Robert 1927-2002 233
    Earlier sketch in SATA 6
Loraine, Connie
    See Reece, Colleen L.
Lorbiecki, Marybeth 1959- 172
    Earlier sketch in SATA 121
Lord, Athena V. 1932- 39
Lord, Beman 1924-1991 5
    Obituary 69
Lord, Bette Bao 1938- 58
    See also CLR 151
Lord, Cynthia 238
    Earlier sketch in SATA 182
Lord, Doreen Mildred Douglas
    See Lord, Douglas
Lord, Douglas 1904-1992 12
Lord, Janet 204
Lord, John Vernon 1939- 21
Lord, Michele 201
Lord, Nancy J.
    See Titus, Eve
Lord, Patricia C. 1927-1988
    Obituary 58
Lord, Walter 1917-2002 3
Lorde, Diana
    See Reno, Dawn E(laine)
Lorenz, Albert 1941- 115
Lorenzini, Carlo
    See Collodi, Carlo
Lorey, Dean 1967- 193
Lorimer, Janet 1941- 60

Loring, Emilie (Baker) 1864(?)-1951 51
Lorkowski, Thomas V(incent) 1950- 92
Lorkowski, Tom
    See Lorkowski, Thomas V(incent)
Lorraine, Walter (Henry) 1929- 16
Lorrimer, Claire
    See Robins, Patricia
Loss, Joan 1933- 11
Lothrop, Harriet Mulford Stone 1844-1924 . 20
Lottridge, Celia Barker 1936- 157
    Earlier sketch in SATA 112
LoTurco, Laura 1963- 84
Lotz, Wolfgang 1912-1981 65
Loughridge, Stuart 1978- 214
Louie, Ai-Ling 1949- 40
    Brief entry 34
Louis, Catherine 1963- 186
Louis, Pat
    See Francis, Dorothy
Louisburgh, Sheila Burnford
    See Burnford, Sheila (Philip Cochrane Every)
Louise, Anita
    See Riggio, Anita
Louise, Tina 1934- 191
Lourie, Helen
    See Storr, Catherine (Cole)
Lourie, Peter 1952- 183
    Earlier sketches in SATA 82, 142
Lourie, Peter King
    See Lourie, Peter
Love, Ann 1947- 168
    Earlier sketch in SATA 79
Love, D. Anne 1949- 180
    Earlier sketches in SATA 96, 145
Love, Douglas 1967- 92
Love, Judith Dufour
    See Love, Judy
Love, Judy 188
Love, Katherine (Isabel) 1907- 3
Love, Kathleen Ann
    See Love, Ann
Love, Maryann Cusimano 223
Love, Sandra (Weller) 1940- 26
Lovegrove, James 1965- 216
Lovegrove, J.M.H.
    See Lovegrove, James
Lovejoy, Jack 1937- 116
Lovelace, Delos Wheeler 1894-1967 7
Lovelace, Maud Hart 1892-1980 2
    Obituary 23
Lovell, Ingraham
    See Bacon, Josephine Dodge (Daskam)
Lovelock, Brian 1956- 214
Loverseed, Amanda (Jane) 1965- 75
Lovett, Margaret (Rose) 1915- 22
Low, Alice 1926- 156
    Earlier sketches in SATA 11, 76
Low, Elizabeth Hammond 1898-1991 5
Low, Joseph 1911-2007 14
Low, Penelope Margaret
    See Lively, Penelope
Low, William 177
Lowe, Helen 1961- 206
Lowe, Jay, Jr.
    See Loeper, John J(oseph)
Lowell, Pamela 187
Lowell, Susan 1950- 206
    Earlier sketches in SATA 81, 127
Lowenstein, Dyno 1914-1996 6
Lowenstein, Sallie 1949- 116
Lowery, Linda 1949- 151
    Earlier sketch in SATA 74
Lowery, Mike 227
Lowitz, Anson C. 1901(?)-1978 18
Lowitz, Sadyebeth Heath 1901-1969 17
Lowndes, Robert A(ugustine) W(ard)
    1916-1998 117
Lowrey, Janette Sebring 1892-1986 43

Lowry, Lois 1937- 230
    Autobiography Feature 127
    Earlier sketches in SATA 23, 70, 111, 177
    See also CLR 72
    See also SAAS 3
Lowry, Lois Hammersberg
    See Lowry, Lois
Lowry, Peter 1953- 7
Lowther, George F. 1913-1975
    Obituary 30
Loxton, Daniel 1975- 229
Loyie, Larry 1933- 150
Lozansky, Edward D. 1941- 62
Lozier, Herbert 1915- 26
Lubar, David 1954- 190
    Earlier sketch in SATA 133
Lubell, Cecil 1912-2000 6
Lubell, Winifred 1914- 6
Lubell, Winifred A. Milius
    See Lubell, Winifred
Lubin, Leonard
    See Lubin, Leonard B.
Lubin, Leonard B. 1943-1994 45
    Brief entry 37
Lubka, S. Ruth 1948- 154
Lubner, Susan 185
Luby, Thia 1954- 124
Lucado, Max 1955- 104
Lucado, Max Lee
    See Lucado, Max
Lucas, Cedric 1962- 101
Lucas, David 1966- 208
Lucas, E(dward) V(errall) 1868-1938 20
Lucas, Eileen 1956- 113
    Earlier sketch in SATA 76
Lucas, George 1944- 56
Lucas, Jerry 1940- 33
Lucas, Margeaux 186
Lucas, Victoria
    See Plath, Sylvia
Lucashenko, Melissa 1967- 104
Luccarelli, Vincent 1923- 90
Luce, Celia (Geneva Larsen) 1914- 38
Luce, Willard (Ray) 1914-1990 38
Lucht, Irmgard 1937- 82
Lucke, Deb 202
Luckett, Dave 1951- 220
    Earlier sketches in SATA 106, 167
Luckhardt, Mildred Corell 1898-1990 5
Ludden, Allen (Ellsworth) 1918(?)-1981
    Obituary 27
Ludel, Jacqueline 1945- 64
Ludlow, Geoffrey
    See Meynell, Laurence Walter
Ludlum, Mabel Cleland
    See Widdemer, Mabel Cleland
Ludwig, Helen 33
Ludwig, Lyndell 1923- 63
Ludwig, Trudy 1959- 209
    Earlier sketch in SATA 166
Luebs, Robin 1949- 212
Lueders, Edward (George) 1923- 14
Luenn, Nancy 1954- 79
    Earlier sketch in SATA 51
Lufkin, Raymond H. 1897- 38
Lugard, Flora Louisa Shaw 1852-1929 21
Luger, Harriett Mandelay 1914- 23
Luhrmann, Winifred B(ruce) 1934- 11
Luis, Earlene W. 1929- 11
Lujan, Jorge 201
Lukas, Catherine
    See Albee, Sarah
Luke, Pauline 178
Luke, Pauline R.
    See Luke, Pauline
Lum, Bernice 230
Lum, Kate 229
Lum, Peter
    See Crowe, (Bettina) Peter Lum
Lumry, Amanda (R.) 159
Lund, Deb 157

Lund, Doris Herold 1919- *12*
Lunde, Darrin *202*
Lundebrek, Amy 1975- *213*
Lundquist, David R. *239*
Lung, Chang
    See Jordan, Robert
Lunge-Larsen, Lise 1955- *184*
    Earlier sketch in SATA *138*
Lunn, Carolyn (Kowalczyk) 1960- *67*
Lunn, Janet (Louise Swoboda) 1928- *110*
    Earlier sketches in SATA *4, 68*
    See also CLR *18*
    See also SAAS *12*
Lunsford, Cin Forshay
    See Forshay-Lunsford, Cin
Lupica, Michael
    See Lupica, Mike
Lupica, Michael Thomas
    See Lupica, Mike
Lupica, Mike 1952- *236*
    Earlier sketch in SATA *177*
Lupoff, Dick
    See Lupoff, Richard A.
Lupoff, Richard A. 1935- *60*
Lupoff, Richard Allen
    See Lupoff, Richard A.
Lurie, Alison 1926- *112*
    Earlier sketch in SATA *46*
Lurie, Morris 1938- *72*
Lussert, Anneliese 1929- *101*
Lusted, Marcia Amidon 1962- *143*
Lustig, Arnost 1926-2011 .... *56*
Lustig, Loretta 1944- *46*
Lutes, Jason 1967- *210*
Luthardt, Kevin 1973- *172*
Luther, Frank 1905-1980
    Obituary *25*
Luther, Rebekah (Lyn) S(tiles) 1960- *90*
Luttmann, Gail
    See Damerow, Gail
Luttrell, Guy L. 1938- *22*
Luttrell, Ida (Alleene) 1934- *91*
    Brief entry *35*
    Earlier sketch in SATA *40*
Luttrell, William (J. III) 1954- *149*
Lutz, John 1939- *180*
Lutz, John Thomas
    See Lutz, John
Lutz, Norma Jean 1943- *122*
Lutzeier, Elizabeth 1952- *72*
Lutzker, Edythe 1904-1991 .... *5*
Luxbacher, Irene 1970- *219*
    Earlier sketch in SATA *153*
Luzadder, Patrick 1954- *89*
Luzzati, Emanuele 1921-2007 .... *7*
Luzzatto, Paola Caboara 1938- *38*
Ly, Many 1977- *208*
Lybbert, Tyler 1970- *88*
Lydon, Michael 1942- *11*
Lyfick, Warren
    See Reeves, Lawrence F.
Lyle, Katie Letcher 1938- *8*
Lynch, Chris 1962- *209*
    Earlier sketches in SATA *95, 131, 171*
    See also CLR *58*
Lynch, Janet Nichols 1952- *221*
Lynch, Jay 1945- *204*
Lynch, Lorenzo 1932- *7*
Lynch, Marietta 1947- *29*
Lynch, Patricia (Nora) 1898-1972 .... *9*
    See also CLR *167*
Lynch, Patrick James
    See Lynch, P.J.
Lynch, P.J. 1962- *213*
    Earlier sketches in SATA *79, 122*
Lynds, Dennis 1924-2005 .... *47*
    Brief entry *37*
Lyne, Alison Davis *188*
Lyngseth, Joan
    See Davies, Joan
Lynn, Elizabeth A(nne) 1946- *99*

Lynn, Mary
    See Brokamp, Marilyn
Lynn, Patricia
    See Watts, Mabel Pizzey
Lynn, Sarah *237*
Lynn, Tracy *175*
Lyon, Elinor 1921-2008 .... *6*
    Obituary *192*
Lyon, Elinor Bruce
    See Lyon, Elinor
Lyon, George Ella 1949- *207*
    Autobiography Feature *148*
    Earlier sketches in SATA *68, 119, 148*
Lyon, Lea 1945- *212*
Lyon, Lyman R.
    See de Camp, L. Sprague
Lyons, Dorothy M(arawee) 1907-1997 .... *3*
Lyons, Grant 1941- *30*
Lyons, Jayne *226*
Lyons, Marcus
    See Blish, James
Lyons, Mary E. 1947- *195*
    Autobiography Feature *195*
    Earlier sketches in SATA *93, 142*
Lyons, Mary Evelyn
    See Lyons, Mary E.
Lystad, Mary (Hanemann) 1928- *11*
Lytle, Elizabeth Stewart 1949- *79*
Lytle, Robert A. 1944- *119*
Lyttle, Richard B(ard) 1927- *23*
Lytton, Deborah 1966- *218*
Lytton, Edward G.E.L. Bulwer-Lytton Baron
    See Bulwer-Lytton, Edward
Lytton of Knebworth, Baron
    See Bulwer-Lytton, Edward

M

Ma, Wenhai 1954- *84*
Maar, Leonard (Frank, Jr.) 1927- *30*
Maartens, Maretha 1945- *73*
Maas, Selve -1997 .... *14*
Maass, Robert *195*
Mabie, Grace
    See Mattern, Joanne
Mac
    See MacManus, Seumas
    and Maccari, Ruggero
Macalaster, Elizabeth G. 1951- *115*
MacAlister, Katie *159*
MacAlister, V. A.
    See McKernan, Victoria
MacAllan, Andrew
    See Leasor, James
MacAodhagain, Eamon
    See Egan, E. W.
MacArthur-Onslow, Annette Rosemary
    1933- *26*
Macaulay, David (Alexander) 1946- *137*
    Brief entry *27*
    Earlier sketches in SATA *46, 72*
    See also CLR *14*
Macaulay, Teresa 1947- *95*
Macauley, Theresa E.
    See Macaulay, Teresa
Macavinta, Courtney *176*
MacBeth, George (Mann) 1932-1992 .... *4*
    Obituary *70*
MacBride, Roger Lea 1929-1995 .... *85*
Maccarone, Grace *238*
MacCarter, Don 1944- *91*
MacClintock, Dorcas 1932- *8*
MacColl, Michaela *238*
MacCready, Robin Merrow 1959(?)- *190*
MacCullough, Carolyn *174*
MacDonald, Alan 1958- *192*
MacDonald, Amy 1951- *156*
    Autobiography Feature *156*
    Earlier sketches in SATA *76, 136*

MacDonald, Anne Elizabeth Campbell Bard
    -1958
    See MacDonald, Betty
MacDonald, Anne Louise 1955- *217*
MacDonald, Anson
    See Heinlein, Robert A.
MacDonald, Betty 1908-1958
    See YABC *1*
Macdonald, Blackie
    See Emrich, Duncan (Black Macdonald)
Macdonald, Caroline 1948- *86*
    Obituary *111*
    See also CLR *60*
Macdonald, Dwight 1906-1982 .... *29*
    Obituary *33*
MacDonald, George 1824-1905 .... *100*
    Earlier sketch in SATA *33*
    See also CLR *67*
MacDonald, Golden
    See Brown, Margaret Wise
Macdonald, Guy *195*
Macdonald, James D. 1954- *67*
    Earlier sketches in SATA *81, 114, 165, 1*
Macdonald, Marcia
    See Hill, Grace Livingston
MacDonald, Margaret Read 1940- *194*
    Earlier sketches in SATA *94, 164*
Macdonald, Marianne 1934- *113*
Macdonald, Mary
    See Gifford, Griselda
Macdonald, Maryann 1947- *189*
    Earlier sketch in SATA *72*
MacDonald, Ross 1957- *201*
Macdonald, Shelagh 1937- *25*
MacDonald, Suse 1940- *193*
    Brief entry *52*
    Earlier sketches in SATA *54, 109*
Macdonald, Wendy *217*
Macdonald, Wendy M.
    See Macdonald, Wendy
Macdonald, Zillah K(atherine) 1885-1979 ... *11*
MacDonnell, Megan
    See Stevens, Serita
MacDougal, John
    See Blish, James
Mace, Elisabeth 1933- *27*
Mace, Varian 1938- *49*
MacEachern, Stephen *206*
MacEwen, Gwendolyn (Margaret)
    1941-1987 .... *50*
    Obituary *55*
Macfarlan, Allan A. 1892-1982 .... *35*
Macfarlane, Iris 1922- *11*
MacGill-Callahan, Sheila 1926-2000 .... *78*
MacGregor, Carol Lynn *153*
MacGregor, Ellen 1906-1954 .... *39*
    Brief entry *27*
MacGregor-Hastie, Roy (Alasdhair Niall)
    1929- *3*
MacGrory, Yvonne 1948- *142*
Machado, Ana Maria 1941- *150*
MacHale, D.J. 1956- *234*
    Earlier sketch in SATA *175*
MacHale, Donald James
    See MacHale, D.J.
Machetanz, Frederick 1908- *34*
Machin, Sue
    See Williams, Sue
Machin Goodall, Daphne (Edith) *37*
Macht, Norm
    See Macht, Norman L.
Macht, Norman L. 1929- *122*
Macht, Norman Lee
    See Macht, Norman L.
Macht, Norman Lee
    See Macht, Norman L.
MacInnes, Cat *236*
MacInnes, Helen (Clark) 1907-1985 .... *22*
    Obituary *44*
Macintosh, Brownie 1950- *98*
MacIntyre, Elisabeth 1916- *17*

MacIntyre, Rod
  See MacIntyre, R.P.
MacIntyre, R.P. 1947- 203
MacIntyre, R.P. 1947- 203
MacIntyre, Wendy 1947- 196
Mack, Jeff 194
Mack, L.V.
  See Kimmelman, Burt
Mack, Stan(ley) 17
Mack, Todd 168
Mack, Tracy 1968- 183
  Earlier sketch in SATA *128*
Mack, W.C.
  See French, Wendy
Mack, Winnie
  See French, Wendy
Mackall, Dandi D.
  See Mackall, Dandi Daley
Mackall, Dandi Daley 1949- 218
  Earlier sketches in SATA *118, 177, 182*
Mackay, Claire 1930- 97
  Autobiography Feature 124
  Earlier sketch in SATA *40*
  See also CLR *43*
Mackay, Constance D'Arcy (?)-1966 125
Mackay, Donald 1914-2005 81
  Obituary 173
Mackay, Donald Alexander
  See Mackay, Donald
MacKaye, Percy (Wallace) 1875-1956 32
Mackel, Kathryn 1950- 162
Mackel, Kathy
  See Mackel, Kathryn
MacKellar, William 1914- 4
Macken, JoAnn Early 1953- 201
Macken, Walter 1915-1967 36
Mackenzie, Anna 1963- 212
MacKenzie, Jill (Kelly) 1947- 75
Mackenzie, Robert 1974- 204
Mackey, Ernan
  See McInerny, Ralph
Mackey, Weezie Kerr 188
Mackie, Maron
  See McNeely, Jeannette
Mackin, Edward
  See McInerny, Ralph
MacKinnon, Bernie 1957- 69
MacKinnon Groomer, Vera 1915- 57
MacKinstry, Elizabeth 1879-1956 42
Mackler, Carolyn 1973- 231
  Earlier sketch in SATA *156*
MacLachlan, Emily
  See Charest, Emily MacLachlan
MacLachlan, Patricia 1938- 229
  Brief entry 42
  Earlier sketches in SATA *62, 107, 168*
  See also CLR *14*
MacLane, Jack
  See Crider, Bill
MacLean, Alistair 1922(?)-1987 23
  Obituary 50
MacLean, Alistair Stuart
  See MacLean, Alistair
Maclean, Art
  See Shirreffs, Gordon D(onald)
MacLean, Christine Kole 1962- 177
MacLean, Glynne 1964- 150
MacLean, Jill 1941- 211
MacLeod, Beatrice 1910- 162
  Earlier sketch in SATA *10*
MacLeod, Beatrice Beach
  See MacLeod, Beatrice
MacLeod, Charlotte (Matilda) 1922-2005 28
  Obituary 160
MacLeod, Doug 1959- 201
  Earlier sketch in SATA *60*
MacLeod, Elizabeth 184
  Earlier sketch in SATA *158*
MacLeod, Ellen Jane (Anderson) 1916- 14
MacManus, James
  See MacManus, Seumas

MacManus, Seumas 1869-1960 25
MacMaster, Eve (Ruth) B(owers) 1942- 46
MacMillan, Annabelle
  See Quick, Annabelle
MacMillan, Dianne M(arie) 1943- 125
  Earlier sketch in SATA *84*
Macnaughton, Tina 218
  Earlier sketch in SATA *182*
Macneill, Janet
  See McNeely, Jeannette
MacPeek, Walter G. 1902-1973 4
  Obituary 25
MacPhail, Catherine 1946- 197
  Earlier sketch in SATA *130*
MacPherson, Margaret 1908-2001 9
  See also SAAS *4*
MacPherson, Thomas George 1915-1976
  Obituary 30
MacPherson, Winnie 1930- 107
MacRae, Tom 1980- 181
Macrae, Travis
  See Feagles, Anita MacRae
MacRaois, Cormac 1944- 72
Macumber, Mari
  See Sandoz, Mari(e Susette)
Macy, Sue 1954- 227
  Earlier sketches in SATA *88, 134*
Madaras, Lynda 1947- 151
Madden, Colleen 228
Madden, Colleen M.
  See Madden, Colleen
Madden, Don 1927- 3
Madden, Kerry 1961- 168
Madden-Lunsford, Kerry
  See Madden, Kerry
Maddern, Eric 1950- 166
Maddigan, Beth 1967- 174
Maddison, Angela Mary 1923- 10
  See also CLR *24*
Maddock, Reginald (Bertram) 1912-1994 15
Maddox, Jake
  See Trumbauer, Lisa
Madenski, Melissa (Ann) 1949- 77
Madian, Jon 1941- 9
Madigan, Lisa Kay
  See Madigan, L.K.
Madigan, L.K. (?)-2011 224
Madison, Alan 182
Madison, Arnold 1937- 6
Madison, Bennett 220
Madison, Winifred 5
Madonna 1958- 149
Madsen, Gunnar 171
Madsen, Jim 1964- 202
Madsen, Ross Martin 1946- 82
Madsen, Susan A. 1954- 90
Madsen, Susan Arrington
  See Madsen, Susan A.
Maehlqvist, Stefan 1943- 30
Maestro, Betsy (Crippen) 1944- 106
  Brief entry 30
  Earlier sketch in SATA *59*
  See also CLR *45*
Maestro, Giulio 1942- 106
  Earlier sketches in SATA *8, 59*
  See also CLR *45*
Maeterlinck, Maurice 1862-1949 66
Magee, Doug 1947- 78
Magee, Wes 1939- 64
Maggio, Rosalie 1943- 69
Magid, Ken(neth Marshall) 65
Magnus, Erica 1946- 77
Magoon, Kekla 1980- 213
Magoon, Scott 222
  Earlier sketch in SATA *182*
Magorian, James 1942- 92
  Earlier sketch in SATA *32*
Magorian, Michelle 1947- 128
  Earlier sketch in SATA *67*
Magorian, Michelle Jane
  See Magorian, Michelle

Magovern, Peg 103
Magsamen, Sandra 1959- 213
Maguire, Anne
  See Nearing, Penny
Maguire, Eden 232
Maguire, Gregory 1954- 200
  Autobiography Feature 200
  Earlier sketches in SATA *28, 84, 129*
  See also SAAS *22*
Maguire, Gregory Peter
  See Maguire, Gregory
Maguire, Jack 1920-2000 74
Maguire, Jesse
  See Smith, Sherwood
Maguire, Jessie
  See Smith, Sherwood
Maher, Ramona 1934- 13
Mahlqvist, Stefan
  See Maehlqvist, Stefan
Mahon, Julia C(unha) 1916- 11
Mahoney, Karen 239
Mahony, Elizabeth Winthrop
  See Winthrop, Elizabeth
Mahood, Kenneth 1930- 24
Mahy, Margaret 1936- 171
  Earlier sketches in SATA *14, 69, 119*
  See also CLR *155*
Mahy, Margaret May
  See Mahy, Margaret
Maiden, Cecil (Edward) 1902-1981 52
Maidoff, Ilka
  See List, Ilka Katherine
Maifair, Linda Lee 1947- 83
Maik, Henri
  See Hecht, Henri Joseph
Maillu, David G(ian) 1939- 111
Maine, Trevor
  See Catherall, Arthur
Mains, Randolph P. 1946- 80
Maione, Heather 189
Maiorano, Robert 1946- 43
Mair, J. Samia 237
Mair, Julie Samia
  See Mair, J. Samia
Maisner, Heather 1947- 89
Maison, Della
  See Katz, Bobbi
Maitland, Antony Jasper 1935- 25
Maitland, Barbara 102
Mai-Wyss, Tatjana 1972- 187
Maizel, Rebecca 1980- 236
Maizels, Jennie 210
Major, Kevin (Gerald) 1949- 134
  Earlier sketches in SATA *32, 82*
  See also CLR *11*
Majure, Janet 1954- 96
Makhijani, Pooja 188
Makie, Pam 1943- 37
Makowski, Silk
  See Sullivan, Silky
Makowski, Silvia Ann
  See Sullivan, Silky
Malam, John 1957- 152
  Earlier sketch in SATA *89*
Maland, Nick 195
Malaspina, Ann 1957- 222
Malawer, Ted
  See Michael, Ted
Malcolm, Dan
  See Silverberg, Robert
Malcolm, Jahnna N.
  See Beecham, Jahnna
Malcolmson, Anne
  See von Storch, Anne B.
Malcolmson, David 1899-1978 6
Maletta, Dr. Arlene
  See Feltenstein, Arlene
Maley, Carleen
  See Hutchins, Carleen Maley

Mali, Jane Lawrence 1937-1995 .... *51*
  Brief entry *44*
  Obituary *86*
Malkin, Nina 1959(?)- *179*
Mallett, Jerry J. 1939- *76*
Malley, Gemma *198*
Malley, G.R.
  See Malley, Gemma
Mallory, Kenneth 1945- *185*
  Earlier sketch in SATA *128*
Mallowan, Agatha Christie
  See Christie, Agatha
Malmberg, Carl 1904-1979 .... *9*
Malmgren, Dallin 1949- *65*
Malo, John W. 1911-2000 .... *4*
Malone, James Hiram 1930- *84*
Malone, Marianne *229*
Malone, Nola Langner 1930-2003 .... *8*
  Obituary *151*
Malone, Patricia 1932- *155*
Malone, Peter 1953- *191*
Maloney, Pat
  See Markun, Patricia Maloney
Malory, Sir Thomas 1410(?)-1471(?) *59*
  Brief entry *33*
Maltbie, P.I. *237*
Maltbie, Priscilla
  See Maltbie, P.I.
Maltese, Michael 1909(?)-1981
  Obituary *24*
Malvasi, Meg Greene *143*
Malvern, Corinne 1905-1956 .... *34*
Malvern, Gladys (?)-1962 .... *23*
Mama G.
  See Davis, Grania
Mammano, Julie 1962- *202*
  Earlier sketch in SATA *107*
Mamonova, Tatyana 1943- *93*
Manchel, Frank 1935- *10*
Manchess, Gregory 1955- *203*
Manchester, William (Raymond)
  1922-2004 .... *65*
Mandabach, Brian 1962(?)- *197*
Mandel, Brett H. 1969- *108*
Mandel, Peter 1957- *238*
  Earlier sketch in SATA *87*
Mandel, Sally (Elizabeth) 1944- *64*
Mandell, Muriel (Hortense Levin) 1921- *63*
Manders, John 1957- *219*
  Earlier sketch in SATA *175*
Mandine, Selma 1973- *228*
Manes, Stephen 1949- *99*
  Brief entry *40*
  Earlier sketch in SATA *42*
Manfred, Frederick (Feikema) 1912-1994 .... *30*
Mangin, Marie France 1940- *59*
Mangione, Gerlando 1909-1998 .... *6*
  Obituary *104*
Mangione, Jerre
  See Mangione, Gerlando
Mango, Karin N. 1936- *52*
Mangurian, David 1938- *14*
Mania, Cathy 1950- *102*
Mania, Robert 1952- *102*
Mania, Robert C., Jr.
  See Mania, Robert
Maniatty, Taramesha 1978- *92*
Maniscalco, Joseph 1926- *10*
Manivong, Laura 1967- *229*
Manley, Deborah 1932- *28*
Manley, Seon 1921- *15*
  See also CLR *3*
  See also SAAS *2*
Mann, Elizabeth 1948- *153*
Mann, Josephine
  See Pullein-Thompson, Josephine (Mary
    Wedderburn)
Mann, Kenny 1946- *91*
Mann, Pamela 1946- *91*
Mann, Patrick
  See Waller, Leslie

Mann, Peggy
  See Houlton, Peggy Mann
Mannetti, Lisa 1953- *57*
  Brief entry *51*
Mannheim, Grete (Salomon) 1909-1986 ...... *10*
Manniche, Lise 1943- *31*
Manning, Jane *233*
  Earlier sketch in SATA *185*
Manning, Jane K.
  See Manning, Jane
Manning, Maurie
  See Manning, Maurie J.
Manning, Maurie J. *211*
Manning, Maurie Jo
  See Manning, Maurie J.
Manning, Mick 1959- *176*
Manning, Rosemary 1911-1988 .... *10*
Manning, Sarra *162*
Manning-Sanders, Ruth (Vernon)
  1895(?)-1988 .... *73*
  Obituary *57*
  Earlier sketch in SATA *15*
Mannion, Diane
  See Paterson, Diane
Mannis, Celeste Davidson *173*
Mannon, Warwick
  See Hopkins, (Hector) Kenneth
Manos, Helen *199*
Mansir, A. Richard 1932- *170*
Manson, Ainslie Kertland 1938- *115*
Manson, Beverlie 1945- *57*
  Brief entry *44*
Mantchev, Lisa *221*
Mantha, John 1960- *217*
Manthorpe, Helen 1958- *122*
Mantinband, Gerda (B.) 1917- *74*
Manton, Jo
  See Gittings, Jo (Grenville) Manton
Manuel, Lynn 1948- *179*
  Earlier sketch in SATA *99*
Manushkin, Fran 1942- *205*
  Earlier sketches in SATA *7, 54, 93, 166*
Manushkin, Frances
  See Manushkin, Fran
Man Without a Spleen, A
  See Chekhov, Anton
Many, Paul 1947- *210*
Many, Paul A.
  See Many, Paul
Manzano, Sonia 1950- *167*
Mapes, Mary A.
  See Ellison, Virginia H(owell)
Maple, Marilyn 1931- *80*
Mappin, Strephyn 1956- *109*
Mara, Barney
  See Roth, Arthur J(oseph)
Mara, Jeanette
  See Cebulash, Mel
Mara, Rachna
  See Gilmore, Rachna
Marais, Josef 1905-1978
  Obituary *24*
Marasmus, Seymour
  See Rivoli, Mario
Marbach, Ethel
  See Pochocki, Ethel (Frances)
Marcal, Annette B.
  See Callaway, Bernice (Anne)
Marcelino
  See Agnew, Edith J(osephine)
Marcellino, Fred 1939-2001 .... *118*
  Obituary *127*
  Earlier sketch in SATA *68*
March, Carl
  See Fleischman, Sid
Marchant, Bessie 1862-1941
  See YABC *2*
Marchant, Catherine
  See Cookson, Catherine (McMullen)
Marcher, Marion Walden 1890-1987 .... *10*
Marchesi, Stephen 1951- *114*

Marchesi, Steve
  See Marchesi, Stephen
  and Older, Effin
  and Older, Jules
Marchetta, Melina 1965- *170*
Marciano, John Bemelmans 1970- *167*
  Earlier sketch in SATA *118*
  See also CLR *93*
Marco, Lou
  See Gottfried, Theodore Mark
Marcus, Leonard S. 1950- *187*
  Earlier sketch in SATA *133*
Marcus, Paul 1953- *82*
Marcus, Rebecca B(rian) 1907- *9*
Marcuse, Aida E. 1934- *89*
Marek, Margot L. 1934(?)-1987
  Obituary *54*
Maren, Julie 1970- *199*
Margaret, Karla
  See Andersdatter, Karla M.
Margolin, Harriet
  See Ziefert, Harriet
Margolis, Jeffrey A. 1948- *108*
Margolis, Leslie *187*
Margolis, Richard J(ules) 1929-1991 .... *86*
  Obituary *67*
  Earlier sketch in SATA *4*
Margolis, Vivienne 1922- *46*
Mariana
  See Foster, Marian Curtis
Marie, Geraldine 1949- *61*
Mariner, Scott
  See Pohl, Frederik
Marino, Dorothy Bronson 1912- *14*
Marino, Gianna *231*
Marino, Jan 1936- *114*
Marino, Nan *216*
Marino, Nick
  See Deming, Richard
Marino, Peter 1960- *179*
Marinsky, Jane *227*
Mario, Anna
  See Odgers, Sally Farrell
Marion, Henry
  See del Rey, Lester
Maris, Ron *71*
  Brief entry *45*
Mariz, Rae 1981- *237*
Mark, Jan 1943-2006 .... *164*
  Obituary *173*
  Earlier sketches in SATA *22, 69, 114*
  See also CLR *11*
Mark, Janet Marjorie
  See Mark, Jan
Mark, Joan T. 1937- *122*
Mark, Pauline (Dahlin) 1913-1997 .... *14*
Mark, Polly
  See Mark, Pauline (Dahlin)
Mark, Ted
  See Gottfried, Theodore Mark
Markel, Michelle *169*
Marker, Sherry 1941- *76*
Markert, Jennifer 1965- *83*
Markert, Jenny
  See Markert, Jennifer
Markey, Kevin 1965- *215*
Markham, Lynne 1947- *102*
Markham, Marion M. 1929- *60*
Markham, Wendy
  See Staub, Wendy Corsi
Markins, W. S.
  See Jenkins, Marie M(agdalen)
Markle, Sandra 1946- *218*
  Brief entry *41*
  Earlier sketches in SATA *57, 92, 148, 185*
Markle, Sandra L.
  See Markle, Sandra
Marklew, Gilly *211*
Marko, Katherine D(olores) *28*
Markoosie
  See Patsauq, Markoosie

Marks, Alan 1957- *187*
  Earlier sketches in SATA *77, 151*
Marks, Burton 1930- *47*
  Brief entry *43*
Marks, Graham *158*
Marks, Hannah K.
  See Trivelpiece, Laurel
Marks, J.
  See Highwater, Jamake (Mamake)
Marks, J(ames) M(acdonald) 1921- *13*
Marks, Laurie J. 1957- *68*
Marks, Margaret L. 1911(?)-1980
  Obituary *23*
Marks, Mickey Klar -1986 .... *12*
Marks, Peter
  See Smith, Robert Kimmel
Marks, Rita 1938- *47*
Marks, Stan(ley) *14*
Marks-Highwater, J.
  See Highwater, Jamake (Mamake)
Markun, Patricia Maloney 1924- *15*
Markusen, Bruce (Stanley Rodriguez)
  1965- *141*
Marley, Louise 1952- *173*
  Earlier sketch in SATA *120*
Marlin, Hilda
  See Van Stockum, Hilda
Marlow, Layne *204*
Marlow, Max
  See Nicole, Christopher
Marlow, Susan K. 1953- *178*
Marlowe, Amy Bell *67*
  Earlier sketch in SATA *1*
Marlowe, Jack
  See Deary, Terry
Marlowe, Tess
  See Glick, Ruth
Marney, Dean 1952- *90*
Marokvia, Artur 1909- *31*
Marokvia, Mireille 1908-2008 .... *5*
  Obituary *197*
Marokvia, Mireille Journet
  See Marokvia, Mireille
Marol, Jean-Claude 1946- *125*
Marr, John S(tuart) 1940- *48*
Marr, Melissa 1972- *189*
Marric, J. J.
  See Butler, William Vivian
  and Creasey, John
Marrin, Albert 1936- *193*
  Brief entry *43*
  Earlier sketches in SATA *53, 90, 126*
  See also CLR *53*
Marriott, Alice Lee 1910-1992 .... *31*
  Obituary *71*
Marriott, Janice 1946- *134*
Marriott, Pat(ricia) 1920- *35*
Marriott, Zoe 1982- *216*
Marriott, Zoe Davina
  See Marriott, Zoe
Marroquin, Patricio
  See Markun, Patricia Maloney
Mars, W. T.
  See Mars, Witold Tadeusz J.
Mars, Witold Tadeusz J. 1912-1985 .... *3*
Marsden, Carolyn 1950- *212*
  Autobiography Feature *212*
  Earlier sketches in SATA *140, 175*
Marsden, John 1950- *146*
  Earlier sketches in SATA *66, 97*
  See also CLR *34*
  See also SAAS *22*
Marsh, Carole 1946- *127*
Marsh, Dave 1950- *66*
Marsh, J. E.
  See Marshall, Evelyn
Marsh, James 1946- *73*
Marsh, Jean
  See Marshall, Evelyn
Marsh, Joan F. 1923- *83*
Marsh, Katherine 1974- *220*

Marsh, Paul
  See Hopkins, (Hector) Kenneth
Marsh, Valerie 1954- *89*
Marshall, Anthony D(ryden) 1924- *18*
Marshall, Bonnie C. 1941- *141*
  Earlier sketch in SATA *18*
Marshall, Bridget M(ary) 1974- *103*
Marshall, (Sarah) Catherine (Wood)
  1914-1983 .... *2*
  Obituary *34*
Marshall, Douglas
  See McClintock, Marshall
Marshall, Edmund
  See Hopkins, (Hector) Kenneth
Marshall, Edward
  See Marshall, James
Marshall, Evelyn 1897-1991 .... *11*
Marshall, Felicity 1950- *116*
Marshall, Garry 1934- *60*
Marshall, H. H.
  See Jahn, Michael
Marshall, James 1942-1992 .... *75*
  Earlier sketches in SATA *6, 51*
  See also CLR *21*
Marshall, James Edward
  See Marshall, James
Marshall, James Vance
  See Payne, Donald Gordon
Marshall, Janet (Perry) 1938- *97*
Marshall, Jeff
  See Laycock, George (Edwin)
Marshall, Kim
  See Marshall, Michael (Kimbrough)
Marshall, Michael (Kimbrough) 1948- *37*
Marshall, Percy
  See Young, Percy M(arshall)
Marshall, S(amuel) L(yman) A(twood)
  1900-1977 .... *21*
Marsoli, Lisa Ann 1958- *101*
  Brief entry *53*
Marsten, Richard
  See Hunter, Evan
Marston, Elsa 1933- *156*
Marston, Hope Irvin 1935- *127*
  Earlier sketch in SATA *31*
Marszalek, John F. 1939- *167*
Marszalek, John Francis, Jr.
  See Marszalek, John F.
Marszalek, John Francis 1939-
  See Marszalek, John F.
Martchenko, Michael 1942- *154*
  Earlier sketches in SATA *50, 95*
Martel, Aimee
  See Thurlo, Aimee
  and Thurlo, David
Martel, Suzanne 1924- *99*
Martignoni, Margaret E. 1908(?)-1974
  Obituary *27*
Martin, Ann M. 1955- *234*
  Brief entry *41*
  Earlier sketches in SATA *44, 70, 126, 192*
  See also CLR *32*
Martin, Bill, Jr. 1916-2004 .... *145*
  Brief entry *40*
  Earlier sketches in SATA *40, 67*
  See also CLR *97*
Martin, Charles E(lmer)
  See Mastrangelo, Charles E(lmer)
Martin, Christopher
  See Hoyt, Edwin P(almer), Jr.
Martin, C.K. Kelly *207*
Martin, Claire 1933- *76*
Martin, Courtney Autumn 1984- *205*
Martin, David Stone 1913-1992 .... *39*
Martin, Donald
  See Honig, Donald
Martin, Dorothy 1921- *47*
Martin, Dorothy McKay
  See Martin, Dorothy
Martin, Eugene *1*
Martin, Eva M. 1939- *65*

Martin, Frances M(cEntee) 1906-1998 .... *36*
Martin, Francesca 1947- *101*
Martin, Fred 1948- *119*
Martin, Fredric
  See Christopher, Matt(hew Frederick)
Martin, George Raymond Richard
  See Martin, George R.R.
Martin, George R.R. 1948- *118*
Martin, J(ohn) P(ercival) 1880(?)-1966 .... *15*
Martin, Jacqueline Briggs 1945- *188*
  Earlier sketches in SATA *98, 149*
Martin, Jane Read 1957- *84*
Martin, Jeremy
  See Levin, Marcia Obrasky
Martin, Les
  See Schulman, L(ester) M(artin)
Martin, Linda 1961- *82*
Martin, Lynne 1923- *21*
Martin, Marcia
  See Levin, Marcia Obrasky
Martin, Marvin 1926- *126*
Martin, Melanie
  See Pellowski, Michael (Joseph)
Martin, Nancy
  See Salmon, Annie Elizabeth
Martin, Patricia *200*
Martin, Patricia A.
  See Martin, Patricia
Martin, Patricia Miles 1899-1986 .... *43*
  Obituary *48*
  Earlier sketch in SATA *1*
Martin, Peter
  See Chaundler, Christine
Martin, Rafe 1946- *175*
Martin, Rene 1891-1977 .... *42*
  Obituary *20*
Martin, Rupert (Claude) 1905- *31*
Martin, S. R.
  See Mappin, Strephyn
Martin, Stefan 1936- *32*
Martin, Vicky
  See Storey, Victoria Carolyn
Martin, Webber
  See Silverberg, Robert
Martin, Wendy
  See Martini, Teri
Martin, William Ivan, Jr.
  See Martin, Bill, Jr.
Martineau, Diane 1940- *178*
Martineau, Harriet 1802-1876
  See YABC *2*
Martinet, Jeanne 1958- *80*
Martinez, Agnes *167*
Martinez, Arturo O. 1933- *192*
Martinez, Claudia Guadalupe 1978- *214*
Martinez, Ed(ward) 1954- *98*
Martinez, Elizabeth Coonrod 1954- *85*
Martinez, Rueben 1940- *232*
Martinez, Victor 1954-2011 .... *95*
Martini, Angela 1972(?)- *223*
Martini, Teri 1930- *3*
Martini, Therese
  See Martini, Teri
Martino, Alfred C. 1964- *174*
Martinson, Janis
  See Herbert, Janis
Martinusen, Cindy
  See Martinusen-Coloma, Cindy
Martinusen, Cindy McCormick
  See Martinusen-Coloma, Cindy
Martinusen-Coloma, Cindy 1970- *218*
Marton, Jirina 1946- *230*
  Earlier sketches in SATA *95, 144*
Marton, Pierre
  See Stone, Peter
Martson, Del
  See Lupoff, Richard A.
Martyr, Paula (Jane)
  See Lawford, Paula Jane
Maruki, Toshi 1912-2000 .... *112*
  See also CLR *19*

Marvin, Isabel R(idout) 1924- 84
Marx, Patricia Windschill
  See Marx, Trish
Marx, Robert F(rank) 1936- 24
Marx, Trish 1948- 202
  Earlier sketches in SATA *112, 160*
Marzani, Carl (Aldo) 1912-1994 12
Marzollo, Jean 1942- 190
  Autobiography Feature 190
  Earlier sketches in SATA *29, 77, 130*
  See also SAAS *15*
Masefield, John (Edward) 1878-1967 19
  See also CLR *164*
Masiello, Ralph 1961- 214
Masoff, Joy 1951- 118
Mason, Adrienne 1962- 163
Mason, Cherie 170
Mason, Edwin A. 1905-1979
  Obituary 32
Mason, Ernst
  See Pohl, Frederik
Mason, F(rancis) van Wyck 1901-1978 3
  Obituary 26
Mason, Frank W.
  See Mason, F(rancis) van Wyck
Mason, George Frederick 1904-2000 14
Mason, Miriam E(vangeline) 1900-1973 2
  Obituary 26
Mason, Prue 195
Mason, Simon 1962- 178
Mason, Tally
  See Derleth, August (William)
Mason, Van Wyck
  See Mason, F(rancis) van Wyck
Mass, Wendy 1967- 234
  Earlier sketches in SATA *158, 196*
Mass, William
  See Gibson, William
Masse, Josee 221
Masselman, George 1897-1971 19
Massey, Misty 212
Massie, Dianne Redfield 1938- 125
  Earlier sketch in SATA *16*
Massie, Elizabeth 108
Massini, Sarah 213
Masson, Sophie 1959- 179
  Earlier sketch in SATA *133*
Masters, Anthony (Richard) 1940-2003 112
  Obituary 145
Masters, Kelly R(ay) 1897-1987 3
Masters, Mildred 1932- 42
Masters, William
  See Cousins, Margaret
Masters, Zeke
  See Bensen, Donald R.
  and Goulart, Ron
Mastrangelo, Charles E(lmer) 1910-1995 70
  Earlier sketch in SATA *69*
Masuda, Takeshi 1944- 56
Matas, Carol 1949- 194
  Autobiography Feature 112
  Earlier sketch in SATA *93*
  See also CLR *52*
Matchette, Katharine E. 1941- 38
Math, Irwin 1940- 42
Mathabane, Mark 1960- 123
Mather, Kirtley F(letcher) 1888-1978 65
Mathers, Petra 1945- 176
  Earlier sketch in SATA *119*
  See also CLR *76*
Matheson, Richard (Christian) 1953- 119
Matheson, Shirlee Smith 1942- 155
Mathews, Eleanor
  See Mathews, Ellie
Mathews, Ellie 1946(?)- 193
Mathews, Janet 1914-1992 41
Mathews, Judith
  See Goldberger, Judith M.
Mathews, Louise
  See Tooke, Louise Mathews

Mathiesen, Egon 1907-1976
  Obituary 28
Mathieu, Joe 1949- 185
  Brief entry 36
  Earlier sketches in SATA *43, 94*
Mathieu, Joseph P.
  See Mathieu, Joe
Mathis, Sharon Bell 1937- 58
  Earlier sketch in SATA *7*
  See also CLR *147*
  See also SAAS *3*
Matlin, Marlee 1965- 181
Matlin, Marlee Beth
  See Matlin, Marlee
Matloff, Gregory 1945- 73
Matott, Justin 1961- 109
Matranga, Frances Carfi 1922- 78
Matray, James I. 1948- 161
Matray, James Irving
  See Matray, James I.
Matson, Emerson N(els) 1926- 12
Matson, Morgan 230
Matsui, Tadashi 1926- 8
Matsuno, Masako
  See Kobayashi, Masako Matsuno
Matsuoka, Mei 1981- 192
Matte, (Encarnacion) L'Enc 1936- 22
Mattern, Joanne 1963- 122
Mattheson, Jenny 180
Matthew, James
  See Barrie, J. M.
Matthews, Aline
  See De Wire, Elinor
Matthews, Andrew 1948- 138
Matthews, Caitlin 1952- 122
Matthews, Cecily 1945- 221
Matthews, Downs 1925- 71
Matthews, Elizabeth 1978- 194
Matthews, Ellen
  See Bache, Ellyn
Matthews, Ellen 1950- 28
Matthews, Harold Downs
  See Matthews, Downs
Matthews, Jacklyn Meek
  See Meek, Jacklyn O'Hanlon
Matthews, John (Kentigern) 1948- 116
Matthews, L. S. 183
Matthews, Laura S.
  See Matthews, L. S.
Matthews, Liz
  See Pellowski, Michael (Joseph)
Matthews, Morgan
  See Pellowski, Michael (Joseph)
Matthews, Nicola
  See Browne, N.M.
Matthews, Patricia 1927-2006 28
Matthews, Patricia Anne
  See Matthews, Patricia
Matthews, Tina 1961- 190
Matthews, Tom L.
  See Lalicki, Tom
Matthews, William Henry III 1919- 45
  Brief entry 28
Matthiessen, Peter 1927- 27
Mattingley, Christobel (Rosemary) 1931- 85
  Earlier sketch in SATA *37*
  See also CLR *24*
  See also SAAS *18*
Matulay, Laszlo 1912- 43
Matus, Greta 1938- 12
Matzkeit, Philip 220
Maugham, W. S.
  See Maugham, W. Somerset
Maugham, W. Somerset 1874-1965 54
Maugham, William S.
  See Maugham, W. Somerset
Maugham, William Somerset
  See Maugham, W. Somerset
Maurer, Diane Philippoff
  See Maurer-Mathison, Diane V(ogel)

Maurer, Diane Vogel
  See Maurer-Mathison, Diane V(ogel)
Maurer-Mathison, Diane V(ogel) 1944- 89
Mauser, Pat Rhoads
  See McCord, Patricia
Mauser, Patricia Rhoads
  See McCord, Patricia
Maves, Mary Carolyn 1916- 10
Maves, Paul B(enjamin) 1913-1994 10
Mavor, Salley 1955- 125
Mawicke, Tran 1911- 15
Max 1906-1989
  See Diop, Birago (Ismael)
Max, Jill
  See Bennett, Kelly
Max, Peter 1939- 45
Maxon, Anne
  See Best, (Evangel) Allena Champlin
Maxwell, Arthur S. 1896-1970 11
Maxwell, B.E. 1957- 211
Maxwell, Bruce E.
  See Maxwell, B.E.
Maxwell, Edith 1923- 7
Maxwell, Gavin 1914-1969 65
Maxwell, Katie
  See MacAlister, Katie
Maxwell, William (Keepers, Jr.) 1908-2000
  Obituary 128
Maxwell-Hyslop, Miranda 1968- 154
May, Charles Paul 1920- 4
May, Elaine Tyler 1947- 120
May, J. C.
  See May, Julian
May, Julian 1931- 11
May, Katie 225
May, Robert Lewis 1905-1976
  Obituary 27
May, Robert Stephen 1929-1996 46
May, Robin
  See May, Robert Stephen
Mayall, Beth 171
Mayberry, Florence V(irginia) Wilson 10
Maybury, Richard J. 1946- 72
Maybury, Rick
  See Maybury, Richard J.
Maydak, Michael S. 1952- 220
Mayer, Agatha
  See Maher, Ramona
Mayer, Albert Ignatius, Jr. 1906-1994
  Obituary 29
Mayer, Ann M(argaret) 1938- 14
Mayer, Bill 200
Mayer, Danuta 1958- 117
Mayer, Hannelore Valencak 1929- 42
Mayer, Jane Rothschild 1903-2001 38
Mayer, Marianna 1945- 132
  Earlier sketches in SATA *32, 83*
Mayer, Mercer 1943- 137
  Earlier sketches in SATA *16, 32, 73, 129*
  See also CLR *11*
Mayerson, Charlotte Leon 36
Mayerson, Evelyn Wilde 1935- 55
Mayfield, Katherine 1958- 118
Mayfield, Sue 1963- 146
  Earlier sketch in SATA *72*
Mayhar, Ardath 1930- 38
Mayhew, James 1964- 204
  Earlier sketches in SATA *85, 149*
Maynard, Olga 1920- 40
Mayne, William 1928-2010 122
  Earlier sketches in SATA *6, 68*
  See also CLR *123*
  See also SAAS *11*
Mayne, William James Carter
  See Mayne, William
Maynes, J. O. Rocky, Jr.
  See Maynes, J. Oscar, Jr.
Maynes, J. Oscar, Jr. 1929- 38
Mayo, Gretchen Will 1936- 163
  Earlier sketch in SATA *84*

Mayo, Margaret 1935- *165*
    Earlier sketches in SATA *38, 96*
Mayo, Margaret Mary
    See Mayo, Margaret
Mayr, Diane 1949- *197*
Mays, Lucinda L(a Bella) 1924- *49*
Mays, (Lewis) Victor (Jr.) 1927- *5*
Mazellan, Ron *210*
Mazer, Anne 1953- *235*
    Earlier sketches in SATA *67, 105, 192*
Mazer, Harry 1925- *167*
    Earlier sketches in SATA *31, 67, 105*
    See also CLR *16*
    See also SAAS *11*
Mazer, Norma Fox 1931-2009 .... *198*
    Earlier sketches in SATA *24, 67, 105, 168*
    See also CLR *23*
    See also SAAS *1*
Mazille, Capucine 1953- *96*
Mazo, Michael *223*
Mazza, Adriana 1928- *19*
Mazzio, Joann 1926- *74*
Mbugua, Kioi Wa 1962- *83*
McAfee, Carol 1955- *81*
McAlister, Caroline 1960- *235*
McAllister, Amanda
    See Dowdell, Dorothy (Florence) Karns
    and Hager, Jean
    and Meaker, Eloise
McAllister, Angela *225*
    Earlier sketch in SATA *182*
McAllister, Margaret I. 1956- *169*
    Earlier sketch in SATA *117*
McAllister, M.I.
    See McAllister, Margaret I.
McArdle, Paula 1971- *198*
McArthur, Nancy *96*
McAvoy, Jim 1972- *142*
McBain, Ed
    See Hunter, Evan
McBain, Georgina *189*
McBratney, Sam 1943- *203*
    Earlier sketches in SATA *89, 164*
    See also CLR *44*
McBride, Lish *237*
McBrier, Michael
    See Older, Effin
    and Older, Jules
McCafferty, Jim 1954- *84*
McCaffery, Janet 1936- *38*
McCaffrey, Anne 1926-2011 .... *152*
    Autobiography Feature *152*
    Earlier sketches in SATA *8, 70, 116*
    See also CLR *130*
    See also SAAS *11*
McCaffrey, Anne Inez
    See McCaffrey, Anne
McCaffrey, Kate 1970- *228*
McCaffrey, Mary
    See Szudek, Agnes S(usan) P(hilomena)
McCahan, Erin *234*
McCain, Becky Ray 1954- *138*
McCain, Murray (David, Jr.) 1926-1981 .... *7*
    Obituary *29*
McCall, Bruce 1935(?)- *209*
McCall, Edith (Sansom) 1911- *6*
McCall, Virginia Nielsen 1909-2000 .... *13*
McCall, Wendell
    See Pearson, Ridley
McCall Smith, Alexander
    See Smith, Alexander McCall
McCallum, Phyllis
    See Koch, Phyllis (Mae) McCallum
McCallum, Stephen 1960- *91*
McCampbell, Darlene Z. 1942- *83*
McCann, Edson
    See del Rey, Lester
    and Pohl, Frederik
McCann, Gerald 1916- *41*
McCann, Helen 1948- *75*
McCannon, Dindga *41*

McCants, William D. 1961- *82*
McCarter, Neely Dixon 1929- *47*
McCarthy, Agnes 1933- *4*
McCarthy, Colin (John) 1951- *77*
McCarthy, Mary 1951- *203*
McCarthy, Meghan *199*
    Earlier sketch in SATA *168*
McCarthy, Ralph F. 1950- *139*
McCarthy-Tucker, Sherri N. 1958- *83*
McCarty, Peter 1966- *182*
McCarty, Rega Kramer 1904-1986 .... *10*
McCaslin, Nellie 1914-2005 .... *12*
McCaughrean, Geraldine 1951- *173*
    Earlier sketches in SATA *87, 139*
    See also CLR *38*
McCaughren, Tom 1936- *75*
McCauley, Adam 1965- *209*
    Earlier sketch in SATA *128*
McCay, (Zenas) Winsor 1869-1934 .... *134*
    Earlier sketch in SATA *41*
McClafferty, Carla Killough 1958- *137*
McClary, Jane Stevenson 1919-1990
    Obituary *64*
McCleery, Patsy R. 1925- *133*
    Earlier sketch in SATA *88*
McClelland, Susan *214*
McClements, George *196*
McClintock, Barbara 1955- *213*
    Earlier sketches in SATA *57, 95, 146*
McClintock, Marshall 1906-1967 .... *3*
McClintock, May Garelick
    See Garelick, May
McClintock, Mike
    See McClintock, Marshall
McClintock, Norah *226*
    Earlier sketch in SATA *178*
McClintock, Theodore 1902-1971 .... *14*
McClinton, Leon 1933- *11*
McCloskey, Kevin 1951- *79*
McCloskey, (John) Robert 1914-2003 .... *100*
    Obituary *146*
    Earlier sketches in SATA *2, 39*
    See also CLR *7*
McCloy, James F(loyd) 1941- *59*
McClung, Robert M(arshall) 1916- *135*
    Earlier sketches in SATA *2, 68*
    See also CLR *11*
    See also SAAS *15*
McClure, Gillian Mary 1948- *31*
McClure, Nikki *218*
McColley, Kevin 1961- *80*
    See also SAAS *23*
McConduit, Denise Walter 1950- *89*
McConnell, James Douglas Rutherford
    1915-1988 .... *40*
    Obituary *56*
McCord, Anne 1942- *41*
McCord, David (Thompson Watson)
    1897-1997 .... *18*
    Obituary *96*
    See also CLR *9*
McCord, Jean 1924- *34*
McCord, Pat Mauser
    See McCord, Patricia
McCord, Patricia 1943- *159*
    Earlier sketch in SATA *37*
McCord, Patricia Sue Rhoads Mauser
    See McCord, Patricia
McCormack, Caren McNelly *217*
McCormick, Brooks
    See Adams, William Taylor
McCormick, Dell J. 1892-1949 .... *19*
McCormick, (George) Donald (King)
    1911-1998 .... *14*
McCormick, Edith (Joan) 1934- *30*
McCormick, Kimberly A. 1960- *153*
McCormick, Patricia 1956- *181*
    Earlier sketch in SATA *128*
McCourt, Edward (Alexander) 1907-1972
    Obituary *28*

McCourt, Lisa 1964- *214*
    Earlier sketches in SATA *117, 159*
McCourt, Malachy 1931- *126*
McCoy, Glenn 1965- *212*
McCoy, Iola Fuller *3*
McCoy, J(oseph) J(erome) 1917- *8*
McCoy, Karen Kawamoto 1953- *82*
McCoy, Lois (Rich) 1941- *38*
McCrady, Lady 1951- *16*
McCrea, James (Craig, Jr.) 1920- *3*
McCrea, Ruth (Pirman) 1921- *3*
McCreigh, James
    See Pohl, Frederik
McCrumb, Sharyn 1948- *109*
McCue, Lisa 1959- *212*
    Earlier sketches in SATA *65, 177*
McCue, Lisa Emiline
    See McCue, Lisa
McCullen, Andrew
    See Arthur, Robert, (Jr.)
McCullers, Carson 1917-1967 .... *27*
McCullers, Lula Carson Smith
    See McCullers, Carson
McCulloch, Derek (Ivor Breashur) 1897-1967
    Obituary *29*
McCulloch, John Tyler
    See Burroughs, Edgar Rice
McCulloch, Sarah
    See Ure, Jean
McCullough, David 1933- *62*
McCullough, David Gaub
    See McCullough, David
McCullough, Frances Monson 1938- *8*
McCullough, Sharon Pierce 1943- *131*
McCully, Emily Arnold
    See Arnold, Emily
McCune, Dan
    See Haas, Dorothy F.
McCunn, Ruthanne Lum 1946- *63*
McCurdy, Michael 1942- *237*
    Earlier sketches in SATA *13, 82, 147*
McCurdy, Michael Charles
    See McCurdy, Michael
McCusker, Paul 1958- *220*
McCutcheon, Elsie (Mary Jackson) 1937- ... *60*
McCutcheon, John 1952- *97*
McDaniel, Becky Bring 1953- *61*
McDaniel, Lurlene 1944- *218*
    Earlier sketches in SATA *71, 146*
McDaniels, Pellom III 1968- *121*
McDaniels, Preston 1952- *192*
McDearmon, Kay *20*
McDermott, Beverly Brodsky 1941- *11*
McDermott, Eleni *156*
McDermott, Gerald (Edward) 1941- *163*
    Earlier sketches in SATA *16, 74*
    See also CLR *9*
McDermott, Michael 1962- *76*
McDevitt, Jack 1935- *155*
    Earlier sketch in SATA *94*
McDevitt, John Charles
    See McDevitt, Jack
McDole, Carol
    See Farley, Carol (J.)
McDonald, Candice Hartsough 1982- *225*
McDonald, Collin 1943- *79*
McDonald, Gerald D(oan) 1905-1970 .... *3*
McDonald, Jamie
    See Heide, Florence Parry
McDonald, Janet 1953-2007 .... *204*
    Earlier sketch in SATA *148*
McDonald, Jill (Masefield) 1927-1982 .... *13*
    Obituary *29*
McDonald, Joyce 1946- *164*
    Earlier sketch in SATA *101*
McDonald, Lucile Saunders 1898-1992 .... *10*
McDonald, Mary Ann 1956- *84*
McDonald, Megan 1958- *202*
    Autobiography Feature *151*
    Earlier sketches in SATA *67, 99, 148, 151*
    See also CLR *94*

McDonald, Meme 1954- *112*
McDonald, Mercedes 1956- *169*
  Earlier sketch in SATA 97
McDonald, Rae A. 1952- *201*
McDonell, Chris 1960- *138*
McDonnell, Christine 1949- *225*
  Earlier sketches in SATA *34, 115*
McDonnell, Flora (Mary) 1963- *146*
  Earlier sketch in SATA 90
McDonnell, Kathleen 1947- *186*
McDonnell, Lois Eddy 1914-2001 .... *10*
McDonnell, Patrick 1956- *221*
  Earlier sketch in SATA *179*
McDonough, Yona Zeldis 1957- *73*
McDowell, Marilyn Taylor *217*
McElligott, Matt 1968- *196*
  Earlier sketch in SATA *135*
McElligott, Matthew
  See McElligott, Matt
McElmeel, Sharron L. 1942- *128*
McElmurry, Jill *198*
  Earlier sketch in SATA *159*
McElrath, William N. 1932- *65*
McElrath-Eslick, Lori 1960- *204*
  Earlier sketch in SATA 96
McEntee, Dorothy (Layng) 1902- *37*
McEvoy, Anne *214*
McEwen, Katherine *183*
McEwen, Robert (Lindley) 1926-1980
  Obituary *23*
McFadden, Kevin Christopher
  See Pike, Christopher
McFall, Christie 1918- *12*
McFall, Gardner 1952- *183*
McFarlan, Donald M(aitland) 1915- *59*
McFarland, Henry "Hammer"
  See McFarland, Henry O.
McFarland, Henry O. 1934- *143*
McFarland, Kenton D(ean) 1920- *11*
McFarland, Martha
  See Smith-Ankrom, M. E.
McFarlane, Leslie 1902-1977 .... *100*
  Earlier sketches in SATA *31, 1, 65, 67*
  See also CLR *118*
McFarlane, Leslie Charles
  See McFarlane, Leslie
McFarlane, Peter 1940- *95*
McFarlane, Peter William
  See McFarlane, Peter
McFarlane, Sheryl P. 1954- *86*
McFarlane, Todd 1961- *117*
McFerrin, Grady *239*
McGaw, Jessie Brewer 1913-1997 .... *10*
McGee, Barbara 1943- *6*
McGee, Marni *163*
McGhee, Alison 1960- *231*
  Earlier sketch in SATA *196*
McGhee, Alison R.
  See McGhee, Alison
McGhee, Holly M.
  See Durand, Hallie
McGiffin, (Lewis) Lee (Shaffer) 1908-1978 ... *1*
McGill, Alice *159*
McGill, Marci
  See Balterman, Marcia Ridlon
McGill, Marci Ridlon
  See Balterman, Marcia Ridlon
McGill, Ormond 1913- *92*
McGinley, Jerry 1948- *116*
McGinley, Phyllis 1905-1978 .... *44*
  Obituary *24*
  Earlier sketch in SATA 2
McGinnis, Lila S(prague) 1924- *44*
McGinty, Alice B. 1963- *202*
  Earlier sketch in SATA *134*
McGivern, Justin 1985- *129*
McGivern, Maureen Daly
  See Daly, Maureen
McGivern, Maureen Patricia Daly
  See Daly, Maureen
McGough, Elizabeth (Hemmes) 1934- *33*

McGovern, Ann 1930- *132*
  Earlier sketches in SATA *8, 69, 70*
  See also CLR *50*
  See also SAAS *17*
McGowen, Thomas E. 1927- *109*
  Earlier sketch in SATA 2
McGowen, Tom
  See McGowen, Thomas E.
McGrady, Mike 1933- *6*
McGrath, Barbara Barbieri 1953- *230*
  Earlier sketches in SATA *108, 169*
McGrath, Robin 1949- *121*
McGrath, Thomas (Matthew) 1916-1990 ..... *41*
  Obituary *66*
McGraw, Eloise Jarvis 1915-2000 .... *67*
  Obituary *123*
  Earlier sketch in SATA *1*
  See also SAAS 6
McGraw, William Corbin 1916-1999 .... *3*
McGreal, Elizabeth
  See Yates, Elizabeth
McGregor, Barbara 1959- *82*
McGregor, Craig 1933- *8*
McGregor, Iona 1929- *25*
McGrory, Anik *193*
McGuffey, Alexander Hamilton 1816-1896 . *60*
McGuigan, Mary Ann 1949- *228*
  Earlier sketch in SATA *106*
McGuire, Edna 1899- *13*
McGuire, Leslie (Sarah) 1945- *94*
  Brief entry *45*
  Earlier sketch in SATA 52
McGuire, Robert *187*
McGuirk, Leslie (A.) 1960- *152*
McGurk, Slater
  See Roth, Arthur J(oseph)
McHargue, Georgess 1941-2011 .... *77*
  Earlier sketch in SATA *4*
  See also CLR *2*
  See also SAAS *5*
McHenry, E.B. 1963(?)- *193*
McHugh, (Berit) Elisabet 1941- *55*
  Brief entry *44*
McIlvaine, Jane
  See McClary, Jane Stevenson
McIlwraith, Maureen Mollie Hunter
  See Hunter, Mollie
McInerney, Judith W(hitelock) 1945- *49*
  Brief entry *46*
McInerny, Ralph 1929-2010 .... *93*
McInerny, Ralph Matthew
  See McInerny, Ralph
McKaughan, Larry (Scott) 1941- *75*
McKay, Donald 1895- *45*
McKay, Hilary 1959- *208*
  Earlier sketches in SATA *92, 145*
  See also SAAS *23*
McKay, Hilary Jane
  See McKay, Hilary
McKay, Lawrence, Jr. 1948- *114*
McKay, Robert W. 1921- *15*
McKay, Sharon E. 1954- *165*
McKay, Simon
  See Nicole, Christopher
McKean, Dave 1963- *197*
McKean, David Jeff
  See McKean, Dave
McKeating, Eileen 1957- *81*
McKee, David (John) 1935- *158*
  Earlier sketches in SATA *70, 107*
  See also CLR *38*
McKee, Tim 1970- *111*
McKeever, Marcia
  See Laird, Jean E(louise)
McKellar, Danica 1975- *213*
McKelvey, Carole A. 1942- *78*
McKelvy, Charles 1950- *124*
McKendrick, Melveena (Christine) 1941- *55*
McKendry, Joe 1972- *170*
McKenna, Colleen O'Shaughnessy 1948- .. *136*
  Earlier sketch in SATA 76

McKenzie, Dorothy Clayton 1910-1981
  Obituary *28*
McKenzie, Ellen Kindt 1928- *80*
McKernan, Victoria 1957- *171*
McKie, Robin *112*
McKillip, Patricia A. 1948- *174*
  Earlier sketches in SATA *30, 80, 126*
McKillip, Patricia Anne
  See McKillip, Patricia A.
McKim, Audrey Margaret 1909-1999 .... *47*
McKimmie, Chris *194*
McKinley, Jennifer Carolyn Robin
  See McKinley, Robin
McKinley, Robin 1952- *229*
  Brief entry *32*
  Earlier sketches in SATA *50, 89, 130, 195*
  See also CLR *127*
McKinney, Barbara Shaw 1951- *116*
McKinney, Nadine 1938- *91*
McKinty, Adrian *186*
McKissack, Fredrick L. 1939- *162*
  Brief entry *53*
  Earlier sketches in SATA *73, 117*
  See also CLR *55*
McKissack, Fredrick Lemuel
  See McKissack, Fredrick L.
McKissack, Patricia C. 1944- *195*
  Earlier sketches in SATA *51, 73, 117, 162*
  See also CLR *129*
McKissack, Patricia L'Ann Carwell
  See McKissack, Patricia C.
McKissack and McKissack
  See McKissack, Fredrick L.
  and McKissack, Patricia C.
McKown, Robin (?)-1976 .... *6*
McKy, Katie 1956- *184*
McLaren, Chesley *213*
McLaren, Clemence 1938- *158*
  Earlier sketch in SATA *105*
McLaughlin, Frank 1934- *73*
McLaughlin, Julie 1984- *226*
McLaughlin, Lauren *209*
McLaurin, Anne 1953- *27*
McLean, Andrew 1946- *172*
  Earlier sketch in SATA *113*
McLean, Dirk 1956- *236*
McLean, J. Sloan
  See Gillette, Virginia M(ary)
  and Wunsch, Josephine (McLean)
McLean, Jacqueline
  See Kolosov, Jacqueline
McLean, Janet 1946- *113*
McLean, Kathryn (Anderson) 1909-1966 .... *9*
McLean, Virginia Overton 1946- *90*
McLean-Carr, Carol 1948- *122*
McLeish, Kenneth 1940-1997 .... *35*
McLenighan, Valjean 1947- *46*
  Brief entry *40*
McLennan, Connie *171*
McLennan, Will
  See Wisler, G(ary) Clifton
McLeod, Bob 1951- *173*
McLeod, Chum 1955- *95*
McLeod, Emilie Warren 1926-1982 .... *23*
  Obituary *31*
McLeod, Kirsty
  See Hudson, (Margaret) Kirsty
McLeod, Margaret Vail
  See Holloway, Teresa (Bragunier)
McLerran, Alice 1933- *137*
  Earlier sketch in SATA 68
McLimans, David 1949- *182*
McLoughlin, John C. 1949- *47*
McMahon, Bob 1956- *208*
McManus, Patrick F. 1933- *46*
McManus, Patrick Francis
  See McManus, Patrick F.
McMeekin, Clark
  See McMeekin, Isabel McLennan
McMeekin, Isabel McLennan 1895-1973 .... *3*

McMenemy, Sarah 1965- 226
  Earlier sketch in SATA 156
McMillan, Bruce 1947- 192
  Earlier sketches in SATA 22, 70, 129
  See also CLR 47
McMillan, Naomi
  See Grimes, Nikki
McMorey, James L.
  See Moyer, Terry J.
McMorrow, Annalisa 1969- 104
McMullan, Jim 1934- 150
  Earlier sketch in SATA 87
McMullan, K. H.
  See McMullan, Kate
McMullan, Kate 1947- 189
  Brief entry 48
  Earlier sketches in SATA 52, 87, 132
McMullan, Kate Hall
  See McMullan, Kate
McMullan, Margaret 1960- 203
McMurtrey, Martin A(loysias) 1921- 21
McNabb, Linda 1963- 147
McNair, Kate 3
McNair, Sylvia 1924-2002 74
McNamara, Margaret C(raig) 1915-1981
  Obituary 24
McNaught, Harry 32
McNaughton, Colin 1951- 211
  Earlier sketches in SATA 39, 92, 134
  See also CLR 54
McNaughton, Janet 1953- 162
  Earlier sketch in SATA 110
McNeal, Laura 194
McNeal, Tom 194
McNeely, Jeannette 1918- 25
McNeer, May (Yonge) 1902-1994 81
  Earlier sketch in SATA 1
McNeese, Tim 1953- 139
McNeill, Janet
  See Alexander, Janet
McNicholas, Shelagh 191
McNickle, D'Arcy 1904-1977
  Obituary 22
McNickle, William D'Arcy
  See McNickle, D'Arcy
McNicoll, Sylvia (Marilyn) 1954- 113
  See also CLR 99
McNulty, Faith 1918-2005 168
  Earlier sketches in SATA 12, 84, 139
McPhail, David 1940- 219
  Brief entry 32
  Earlier sketches in SATA 47, 81, 140, 183
McPhail, David M.
  See McPhail, David
McPhail, David Michael
  See McPhail, David
McPhee, Norma H. 1928- 95
McPhee, Peter 1957- 214
McPhee, Richard B(yron) 1934- 41
McPherson, James M. 1936- 141
  Earlier sketch in SATA 16
McPherson, James Munro
  See McPherson, James M.
McQueen, Lucinda 1950- 58
  Brief entry 48
McQueen, Mildred Hark 1908-1978 12
McQuillan, Mary 200
McRae, Russell (William) 1934- 63
McShean, Gordon 1936- 41
Mc Swigan, Marie 1907-1962 24
McTavish, Sandy
  See Eyerly, Jeannette
McTighe, Carolyn 238
McVeity, Jen 148
McVey, Vicki 1946- 80
McVicker, Charles (Taggart) 1930- 39
McVicker, Chuck
  See McVicker, Charles (Taggart)
McVoy, Terra Elan 220
McWhirter, A(lan) Ross 1925-1975 37
  Obituary 31

McWhirter, Norris (Dewar) 1925-2004 37
McWilliam, Howard 1977- 219
McWilliams, Karen 1943- 65
Mdurvwa, Hajara E. 1962- 92
Meacham, Margaret 1952- 203
  Earlier sketch in SATA 95
Meachum, Virginia 1918- 133
  Earlier sketch in SATA 87
Mead, Alice 1952- 146
  Earlier sketch in SATA 94
Mead, Margaret 1901-1978
  Obituary 20
Mead, Russell (M., Jr.) 1935- 10
Mead, Stella (?)-1981
  Obituary 27
Meade, Elizabeth Thomasina 1854(?)-1914(?)
  See CLR 163
Meade, Ellen
  See Roddick, Ellen
Meade, Holly 207
Meade, L. T.
  See Meade, Elizabeth Thomasina
Meade, Marion 1934- 127
  Earlier sketch in SATA 23
Meader, Stephen W(arren) 1892-1977 1
Meadmore, Susan
  See Sallis, Susan (Diana)
Meadow, Charles T(roub) 1929- 23
Meadowcroft, Enid LaMonte
  See Wright, Enid Meadowcroft (LaMonte)
Meadows, Daisy
  See Chapman, Linda
Meadows, Graham (W.) 1934- 161
Meadows, Michelle 202
Meaker, M. J.
  See Meaker, Marijane
Meaker, Marijane 1927- 160
  Autobiography Feature 111
  Earlier sketches in SATA 20, 61, 99
  See also CLR 29
  See also SAAS 1
Meaker, Marijane Agnes
  See Meaker, Marijane
Means, Florence Crannell 1891-1980 1
  Obituary 25
  See also CLR 56
Mearian, Judy Frank 1936- 49
Mebus, Scott 1974- 216
Mecca, Judy Truesdell 1955- 127
Mechling, Lauren 1978(?)- 194
Mechling, Lauren 1978(?)- 194
Mechner, Jordan 1964- 205
Medary, Marjorie 1890-1980 14
Meddaugh, Susan 1944- 176
  Earlier sketches in SATA 29, 84, 125
Medearis, Angela Shelf 1956- 123
  Earlier sketch in SATA 72
Medearis, Mary 1915- 5
Medina, Jane 1953- 167
  Earlier sketch in SATA 122
Medina, Meg 1963- 212
Medina, Nico 1982- 193
Medlicott, Mary 1946- 88
Mee, Charles L., Jr. 1938- 72
  Earlier sketch in SATA 8
Meehan, Kierin 218
Meehl, Brian 204
Meek, Jacklyn O'Hanlon 1933- 51
  Brief entry 34
Meek, S(terner St.) P(aul) 1894-1972
  Obituary 28
Meeker, Clare Hodgson 1952- 96
Meeker, Oden 1919(?)-1976 14
Meeker, Richard
  See Brown, Fornan
Meeks, Esther MacBain 1
Meggs, Libby Phillips 1943- 130
Mehdevi, Alexander (Sinclair) 1947- 7
Mehdevi, Anne (Marie) Sinclair 1947- 8
Mehling, Carl 1969(?)- 237
Meidell, Sherry 1951- 73

Meier, Minta 1906- 55
Meighan, Donald Charles 1929- 30
Meigs, Cornelia Lynde 1884-1973 6
  See also CLR 55
Meilach, Dona Z(weigoron) 1926- 34
Meilman, Philip W(arren) 1951- 79
Meinstereifel, Ronald L. 1960- 134
Meisel, Paul 224
  Earlier sketch in SATA 184
Meister, Cari 204
Melanson, Luc 198
Melcher, Daniel 1912-1985
  Obituary 43
Melcher, Frederic Gershom 1879-1963
  Obituary 22
Melcher, Marguerite Fellows 1879-1969 10
Meldrum, Christina 1969(?)- 206
Melendez, Francisco 1964- 72
Melhuish, Eva 199
Melin, Grace Hathaway 1892-1973 10
Mellersh, H(arold) E(dward) L(eslie)
  1897- 10
Melling, David 186
Melmed, Laura Krauss 212
Melmoth, Sebastian
  See Wilde, Oscar
Melnikoff, Pamela (Rita) 97
Melo, Esperanca 239
Meltzer, Amy 1968- 202
Meltzer, Milton 1915-2009 201
  Autobiography Feature 124
  Earlier sketches in SATA 1, 50, 80, 128
  See also CLR 13
  See also SAAS 1
Melville, Anne
  See Potter, Margaret
Melville, Herman 1819-1891 59
Melwood, Mary
  See Lewis, E. M.
Melzack, Ronald 1929- 5
Memling, Carl 1918-1969 6
Menchin, Scott 234
  Earlier sketch in SATA 188
Mendel, Jo
  See Bond, Gladys Baker
  and Gilbertson, Mildred Geiger
Mendelson, Steven T. 1958-1995 86
Mendelson-Stevens, Serita Deborah
  See Stevens, Serita
Mendes, Valerie 1939- 157
Mendez, Raymond A. 1947- 66
Mendez, Simon 1975- 215
Mendonca, Susan
  See Smith, Susan Vernon
Mendoza, George 1934- 41
  Brief entry 39
  See also SAAS 7
Menendez, Shirley (C.) 1937- 146
Meng, Cece 194
Meng, Heinz (Karl) 1924- 13
Mennen, Ingrid 1954- 85
Menotti, Gian Carlo 1911-2007 29
  Obituary 180
Menuhin, Sir Yehudi 1916-1999 40
  Obituary 113
Menville, Douglas 1935- 64
Menzel, Barbara Jean 1946- 63
Menzel, Peter 1948- 207
Mercati, Cynthia 164
Mercati, Cynthia J.
  See Mercati, Cynthia
Mercer, Charles (Edward) 1917-1988 16
  Obituary 61
Mercer, Jessie 21
Mercer, Sienna 192
Meredith, Arnold
  See Hopkins, (Hector) Kenneth
Meredith, David William
  See Miers, Earl Schenck
Meringoff, Laurene Krasny
  See Brown, Laurene Krasny

Meriwether, Louise 1923- 52
  Brief entry 31
Merlin, Arthur
  See Blish, James
Merlin, Christina
  See Heaven, Constance (Christina)
Merola, Caroline 1962- 236
Merrell, Billy 1982- 222
Merriam, Eve 1916-1992 73
  Earlier sketches in SATA *3, 40*
  See also CLR *14*
Merrill, Jane 1946- 42
Merrill, Jane Merrill
  See Merrill, Jane
Merrill, Jean (Fairbanks) 1923- 82
  Earlier sketch in SATA *1*
  See also CLR *52*
Merrill, Phil
  See Merrill, Jane
Merriman, Alex
  See Silverberg, Robert
Merriman, Rachel 1971- 149
  Earlier sketch in SATA *98*
Merrit, Elizabeth
  See Goudge, Eileen
Merski, Patricia K.
  See Merski, P.K.
Merski, P.K. 172
Mertz, Barbara
  See Peters, Elizabeth
Mertz, Barbara Gross
  See Peters, Elizabeth
Merveille, David 200
Merz, Jennifer J. 196
Meschel, Susan V. 1936- 83
Meschenmoser, Sebastian 1980- 229
Meserve, Jessica 211
Messenger, Charles (Rynd Milles) 1942- 59
Messer, Stephen 1972- 231
Messick, Dale 1906-2005 64
  Brief entry 48
Messier, Claire 1956- 103
Messieres, Nicole de
  See de Messieres, Nicole
Messinger, Carla 198
Messmer, Otto 1892(?)-1983 37
Messner, Kate 224
Mesta, Gabriel
  See Anderson, Kevin J.
  and Moesta, Rebecca
Metaxas, Eric 1963- 211
Metcalf, Doris H(unter) 91
Metcalf, Suzanne
  See Baum, L. Frank
Metos, Thomas H(arry) 1932- 37
Metter, Bert(ram Milton) 1927- 56
Metzenthen, David 1958- 167
  Earlier sketch in SATA *106*
Meunier, Brian 1954- 195
Meyer, Barbara 1939- 77
Meyer, Carolyn 1935- 142
  Autobiography Feature 142
  Earlier sketches in SATA *9, 70, 118*
  See also SAAS *9*
Meyer, Carolyn Mae
  See Meyer, Carolyn
Meyer, Edith Patterson 1895-1993 5
Meyer, F(ranklyn) E(dward) 1932- 9
Meyer, Jean Shepherd 11
Meyer, Jerome Sydney 1895-1975 3
  Obituary 25
Meyer, June
  See Jordan, June
Meyer, Kerstin 1966- 190
Meyer, L.A. 1942- 221
  Earlier sketches in SATA *12, 144*
Meyer, Louis A.
  See Meyer, L.A.
Meyer, Renate 1930- 6
Meyer, Stephenie 1973- 193
  See also CLR *142*

Meyer, Susan E. 1940- 64
Meyerhoff, Jenny 1972- 208
Meyers, Susan 1942- 164
  Earlier sketches in SATA *19, 108*
Meynell, Laurence Walter 1899-1989
  Obituary 61
Meynier, Yvonne (Pollet) 1908- 14
Mezey, Robert 1935- 33
Micale, Albert 1913- 22
Michael, James
  See Scagnetti, Jack
Michael, Jan 1947- 216
Michael, Livi 1960- 172
Michael, Manfred
  See Winterfeld, Henry
Michael, Olivia
  See Michael, Livi
Michael, Ted 1984- 234
Michaelis, Antonia 1979- 215
Michaels, Barbara
  See Peters, Elizabeth
Michaels, Jamie 195
Michaels, Joanne Louise
  See Teitelbaum, Michael
Michaels, Kristin
  See Williams, Jeanne
Michaels, Molly
  See Untermeyer, Louis
Michaels, Neal
  See Teitelbaum, Michael
Michaels, Rune 194
Michaels, Ski
  See Pellowski, Michael (Joseph)
Michaels, Steve 1955- 71
Michaels, William M. 1917- 77
Michalak, Jamie 1973- 217
Michel, Anna 1943- 49
  Brief entry 40
Michel, Francois 1948- 82
Michelin, Linda 183
Michelson, Richard 198
  Earlier sketch in SATA *173*
Micich, Paul 74
Mickelson, Scott 1963- 213
Micklish, Rita 1931- 12
Micklos, John, Jr. 1956- 173
  Earlier sketch in SATA *129*
Micklos J., John, Jr. 1956-
  See Micklos, John, Jr.
Micucci, Charles (Patrick, Jr.) 1959- 144
  Earlier sketch in SATA *82*
Middleton, Charlotte 230
Middleton, Haydn 1955- 152
  Earlier sketch in SATA *85*
Miers, Earl Schenck 1910-1972 1
  Obituary 26
Migdale, Lawrence 1951- 89
Miglio, Paige 1966- 201
Mikaelsen, Ben 1952- 173
  Earlier sketches in SATA *73, 107*
Mikaelsen, Benjamin John
  See Mikaelsen, Ben
Miklowitz, Gloria D. 1927- 129
  Earlier sketches in SATA *4, 68*
  See also SAAS *17*
Mikolaycak, Charles 1937-1993 78
  Obituary 75
  Earlier sketch in SATA *9*
  See also SAAS *4*
Mild, Warren (Paul) 1922- 41
Milelli, Pascal 1965- 135
Miles, Betty 1928- 78
  Earlier sketch in SATA *8*
  See also SAAS *9*
Miles, Miska
  See Martin, Patricia Miles
Miles, (Mary) Patricia 1930- 29
Miles, Patricia A.
  See Martin, Patricia Miles
Miles, Victoria 1966- 188
Milford, Kate 1976- 233

Milgrim, David 223
  Earlier sketches in SATA *158, 187*
Milgrom, Harry 1912-1978 25
Milhous, Katherine 1894-1977 15
Milian, Tomaso 238
Milich, Zoran 174
Milios, Rita 1949- 79
Militant
  See Sandburg, Carl
Millais, Raoul 1901- 77
Millar, Barbara F. 1924- 12
Millar, Margaret (Ellis Sturm) 1915-1994 18
  Obituary 79
Millard, Glenda 203
Millard, Kerry 204
Millbank, Captain H. R.
  See Ellis, Edward S.
Millen, C(ynthia) M. 1955- 114
Miller, Albert G(riffith) 1905-1982 12
  Obituary 31
Miller, Alice Ann 1958- 150
Miller, Alice P(atricia McCarthy) 22
Miller, Allan 1978- 216
Miller, Christopher 1976- 215
Miller, Debbie 1951- 160
  Earlier sketch in SATA *103*
  See Miller, Debbie S.
Miller, Debbie S. 232
  See Miller, Debbie
Miller, Deborah Uchill 1944- 61
Miller, Don 1923- 15
Miller, Doris R.
  See Mosesson, Gloria R(ubin)
Miller, Eddie
  See Miller, Edward
Miller, Edna Anita 1920- 29
Miller, Edward 1905-1974 8
Miller, Edward 1964- 218
  Earlier sketch in SATA *183*
Miller, Elizabeth 1933- 41
Miller, Ellanita 1957- 87
Miller, Eugene 1925- 33
Miller, Frances A. 1937- 52
  Brief entry 46
Miller, Heather Lynn 1971- 214
Miller, Helen M(arkley) -1984 5
Miller, Helen Topping 1884-1960
  Obituary 29
Miller, Jane (Judith) 1925-1989 15
Miller, Jewel 1956- 73
Miller, John
  See Samachson, Joseph
Miller, Judi 117
Miller, Karen 1949- 210
Miller, Karen Hokanson
  See Miller, Karen
Miller, Kate 1948- 193
Miller, Kirsten 1973- 185
Miller, Louise (Rolfe) 1940- 76
Miller, M. L. 85
Miller, Madge 1918- 63
Miller, Margaret J.
  See Dale, Margaret J(essy) Miller
Miller, Marilyn (Jean) 1925- 33
Miller, Marvin 65
Miller, Mary
  See Northcott, (William) Cecil
Miller, Mary Beth 1942- 9
Miller, Mary Beth 1964- 185
Miller, Maryann 1943- 73
Miller, Natalie 1917-1976 35
Miller, Pat 1951- 214
Miller, Robert H. 1944- 91
Miller, Ron 1947- 185
Miller, Ruth White
  See White, Ruth
Miller, Sandra
  See Miller, Sandy
Miller, Sandra Peden
  See Miller, Sandy

Miller, Sandy 1948- *41*
  Brief entry *35*
Miller, Sarah 1969- *175*
Miller, Virginia
  See Austin, Virginia
Miller, William R. 1959- *116*
Miller, Woody *236*
Miller Brothers
  See Miller, Allan
Milligan, Bryce 1953- *170*
Milligan, Spike
  See Milligan, Terence Alan
Milligan, Terence Alan 1918-2002 .... *29*
  Obituary *134*
  See also CLR *92*
Millington, Ada
  See Deyneka, Anita
Millman, Isaac 1933- *140*
Mills, Adam
  See Stanley, George Edward
Mills, Claudia 1954- *191*
  Brief entry *41*
  Earlier sketches in SATA *44, 89, 145*
Mills, Elaine (Rosemary) 1941- *72*
Mills, G. Riley *196*
Mills, Joyce C. 1944- *102*
Mills, Judith Christine 1956- *130*
Mills, Yaroslava Surmach 1925-2008 .... *35*
Millspaugh, Ben P. 1936- *77*
Millstead, Thomas E. *30*
Millward, Gwen *202*
Milne, A. A. 1882-1956 .... *100*
  See also YABC *1*
  See also CLR *108*
Milne, Alan Alexander
  See Milne, A. A.
Milne, Lorus J. *5*
  See also CLR *22*
  See also SAAS *18*
Milne, Margery *5*
  See also CLR *22*
  See also SAAS *18*
Milne, Terry
  See Milne, Theresa Ann
Milne, Theresa Ann 1964- *84*
Milnes, Irma McDonough 1924- *101*
Milonas, Rolf
  See Myller, Rolf
Milone, Karen
  See Dugan, Karen
Milone-Dugan, Karen
  See Dugan, Karen
Milord, Susan 1954- *200*
  Earlier sketches in SATA *74, 147*
Milotte, Alfred G(eorge) 1904-1989 .... *11*
  Obituary *62*
Milstein, Linda 1954- *80*
Milton, Ann *134*
Milton, Hilary (Herbert) 1920- *23*
Milton, John R(onald) 1924- *24*
Milton, Joyce 1946- *101*
  Brief entry *41*
  Earlier sketch in SATA *52*
Milusich, Janice *216*
Milverton, Charles A.
  See Penzler, Otto
Milway, Alex 1978- *215*
Milway, Katie Smith 1960- *203*
Minahan, John A. 1956- *92*
Minar, Barbra (Goodyear) 1940- *79*
Minard, Rosemary 1939- *63*
Minarik, Else Holmelund 1920- *127*
  Earlier sketch in SATA *15*
  See also CLR *33*
Miner, Jane Claypool 1933- *103*
  Brief entry *37*
  Earlier sketch in SATA *38*
Miner, Lewis S. 1909-1971 .... *11*
Mines, Jeanette 1948- *61*
Mines, Jeanette Marie
  See Mines, Jeanette

Minier, Nelson
  See Stoutenburg, Adrien (Pearl)
Minnitt, Ronda Jacqueline
  See Armitage, David
Minor, Wendell 1944- *199*
  Earlier sketches in SATA *78, 109, 164*
Minter, Daniel 1961- *176*
Mintonye, Grace *4*
Miranda, Anne 1954- *109*
  Earlier sketch in SATA *71*
Miranda, Inaki 1983(?)- *207*
Mirocha, Paul *192*
Mirsky, Jeannette 1903-1987 .... *8*
  Obituary *51*
Mirsky, Reba Paeff 1902-1966 .... *1*
Misako Rocks! *192*
Misenta, Marisol
  See Innes, Stephanie
Mishica, Clare 1960- *91*
Miskovits, Christine 1939- *10*
Miss Frances
  See Horwich, Frances R(appaport)
Miss Read
  See Saint, Dora Jessie
Mister Rogers
  See Rogers, Fred McFeely
Mitchard, Jacquelyn 1956- *219*
  Earlier sketches in SATA *98, 168*
Mitchell, Adrian 1932-2008 .... *166*
  Obituary *200*
  Earlier sketch in SATA *104*
Mitchell, Allison
  See Griffin, W. E. B.
Mitchell, Betty Jo
  See Mitchell, B.J.
Mitchell, B.J. 1931- *120*
Mitchell, Clyde
  See Ellison, Harlan
  and Silverberg, Robert
Mitchell, Cynthia 1922- *29*
Mitchell, (Sibyl) Elyne (Keith) 1913- *10*
Mitchell, Gladys (Maude Winifred)
  1901-1983 .... *46*
  Obituary *35*
Mitchell, Jay
  See Roberson, Jennifer
Mitchell, Joyce Slayton 1933- *142*
  Brief entry *43*
  Earlier sketch in SATA *46*
Mitchell, K. L.
  See Lamb, Elizabeth Searle
Mitchell, Kathy 1948- *59*
Mitchell, Lori 1961- *128*
Mitchell, Margaree King 1953- *84*
Mitchell, Marianne 1947- *145*
Mitchell, Rhonda *89*
Mitchell, Saundra 1974(?)- *217*
Mitchell, Stephen 1943- *199*
Mitchell, Susan
  See Mitchell, Susan K.
Mitchell, Susan K. 1972- *210*
Mitchell, Todd 1974- *191*
Mitchell, Yvonne 1925-1979
  Obituary *24*
Mitchelson, Mitch
  See Mitchelson, Peter Richard
Mitchelson, Peter Richard 1950- *104*
Mitchison, Naomi (Margaret Haldane)
  1897-1999 .... *24*
  Obituary *112*
Mitchnik, Helen 1901-1982 .... *41*
  Brief entry *35*
Mitchum, Hank
  See Knott, William C(ecil, Jr.)
  and Murray, Stuart A. P.
  and Newton, D(wight) B(ennett)
  and Sherman, Jory (Tecumseh)
Mitgutsch, Ali 1935- *76*
Mitsuhashi, Yoko *45*
  Brief entry *33*

Mitton, Jacqueline 1948- *162*
  Earlier sketches in SATA *66, 115*
Mitton, Simon 1946- *66*
Mitton, Tony 1951- *235*
  Earlier sketches in SATA *104, 149, 203*
Miura, Taro 1968- *181*
Mizner, Elizabeth Howard 1907- *27*
Mizumura, Kazue *18*
Mlynowski, Sarah 1977(?)- *236*
  Earlier sketch in SATA *180*
Mobin-Uddin, Asma *216*
  Earlier sketch in SATA *172*
Mobley, Joe A. 1945- *91*
Moche, Dinah (Rachel) L(evine) 1936- *44*
  Brief entry *40*
Mochi, Ugo (A.) 1889-1977 .... *38*
Mochizuki, Ken 1954- *146*
  Earlier sketch in SATA *81*
  See also SAAS *22*
Modarressi, Mitra 1967- *200*
  Earlier sketch in SATA *126*
Modell, Frank B. 1917- *39*
  Brief entry *36*
Modesitt, Jeanne 1953- *217*
  Earlier sketches in SATA *92, 143*
Modesitt, L.E., Jr. 1943- *164*
  Earlier sketch in SATA *91*
Modesitt, Leland Exton, Jr.
  See Modesitt, L.E., Jr.
Modrell, Dolores 1933- *72*
Moe, Barbara 1937- *20*
Moe, Jorgen (Ingebretsen) 1813-1882
  See CLR *104*
Moed-Kass, Pnina *169*
Moerbeek, Kees 1955- *98*
Moeri, Louise 1924- *93*
  Earlier sketch in SATA *24*
  See also SAAS *10*
Moesta, Rebecca 1956- *182*
Moffett, Jami 1952- *84*
Moffett, Mark W. 1957(?)- *203*
Moffett, Martha (Leatherwood) 1934- *8*
Mogensen, Suzanne A(ncher) 1946- *129*
Mohammed, Khadra *197*
Mohanty, Raja *223*
Mohn, Peter B(urnet) 1934- *28*
Mohn, Viola Kohl 1914- *8*
Mohr, Nicholasa 1938- *97*
  Autobiography Feature *113*
  Earlier sketch in SATA *8*
  See also CLR *22*
  See also SAAS *8*
Mok, Esther 1953- *93*
Molan, Christine 1943- *84*
Molarsky, Osmond 1909- *16*
Moldon, Peter L(eonard) 1937- *49*
Mole, John 1941- *103*
  Earlier sketch in SATA *36*
  See also CLR *61*
Molesworth, Mary Louisa 1839-1921 .... *98*
  See also CLR *166*
Molin, Charles
  See Mayne, William
Molina, Silvia 1946- *97*
Molk, Laurel 1957- *162*
  Earlier sketch in SATA *92*
Mollel, Tololwa M. 1952- *88*
Molloy, Anne Baker 1907-1999 .... *32*
Molloy, Michael (John) 1940- *162*
Molloy, Paul (George) 1924- *5*
Molnar, Haya Leah 1951(?)- *230*
Moloney, James 1954- *202*
  Autobiography Feature *144*
  Earlier sketches in SATA *94, 144*
Molski, Carol *215*
Momaday, N. Scott 1934- *48*
  Brief entry *30*
Momaday, Navarre Scott
  See Momaday, N. Scott
Monaco, Octavia 1963- *169*
Monagle, Bernie 1957- *121*

Moncure, Jane Belk 1926- 23
Monjo, F(erdinand) N(icholas III)
    1924-1978 16
    See also CLR 2
Monk, Isabell 1952- 136
Monks, Lydia 189
Monroe, Chris 1962- 219
Monroe, Christine
    See Monroe, Chris
Monroe, Lyle
    See Heinlein, Robert A.
Monroe, Marion
    See Cox, Marion Monroe
Monroy, Manuel 1970- 196
Monsell, Helen Albee 1895-1971 24
Monson-Burton, Marianne 1975- 139
Montalbano, Andrea 231
Montana, Bob 1920-1975
    Obituary 21
Montanari, Eva 1977- 209
Montecalvo, Janet 177
Montenegro, Laura Nyman 1953- 95
Montero, Gloria 1933- 109
Montes, Marisa 1951- 144
Montgomerie, Norah (Mary) 1913- 26
Montgomery, Constance
    See Cappel, Constance
Montgomery, Elizabeth
    See Julesberg, Elizabeth Rider Montgomery
Montgomery, Elizabeth Rider
    See Julesberg, Elizabeth Rider Montgomery
Montgomery, Hugh (Edward) 1962- 146
Montgomery, L. M. 1874-1942 100
    See also YABC 1
    See also CLR 145
Montgomery, Lucy Maud
    See Montgomery, L. M.
Montgomery, Michael G. 1952- 208
Montgomery, Raymond A. (Jr.) 1936- 39
Montgomery, Rutherford George 1894-1985 . 3
Montgomery, Sy 1958- 184
    Autobiography Feature 132
    Earlier sketches in SATA *114, 132*
Montgomery, Vivian 36
Monthei, Betty 179
Montijo, Rhode 179
Montileaux, Donald F. 1948- 183
Montpetit, Charles 1958- 101
Montresor, Beni 1926-2001 38
    Earlier sketch in SATA 3
    See also SAAS 4
Montserrat, Pep 181
Monty Python
    See Chapman, Graham
    and Cleese, John (Marwood)
    and Gilliam, Terry
    and Idle, Eric
    and Jones, Terence Graham Parry
    and Palin, Michael
Moodie, Craig 1956- 172
Moodie, Fiona 1952- 133
Moody, Minerva
    See Alcott, Louisa May
Moody, Ralph Owen 1898-1982 1
Moon, Carl 1879(?)-1948 25
Moon, Grace (Purdie) 1877(?)-1947 25
Moon, Lily
    See Warnes, Tim
Moon, Nicola 1952- 147
    Earlier sketch in SATA 96
Moon, Pat 1946- 113
Moon, Sheila 1910-1991 5
    Obituary 114
Moon, Sheila Elizabeth
    See Moon, Sheila
Mooney, Bel 1946- 95
Mooney, Bill 1936- 122
Mooney, Elizabeth C(omstock) 1918-1986
    Obituary 48
Mooney, William
    See Mooney, Bill

Moor, Emily
    See Deming, Richard
Moorcock, Michael 1939- 166
    Earlier sketch in SATA 93
Moorcock, Michael John
    See Moorcock, Michael
Moorcock, Michael John
    See Moorcock, Michael
Moore, Anne Carroll 1871-1961 13
Moore, Cheri
    See Ladd, Cheryl (Jean)
Moore, Clement Clarke 1779-1863 18
Moore, Cyd 1957- 233
    Earlier sketches in SATA *83, 133, 186*
Moore, Don W. 1905(?)-1986
    Obituary 48
Moore, Elaine 1944- 86
Moore, Eva 1942- 103
    Earlier sketch in SATA 20
Moore, Ishbel (Lindsay) 1954- 140
Moore, Jack (William) 1941- 46
    Brief entry 32
Moore, Janet Gaylord 1905-1992 18
Moore, Jim 1946- 42
Moore, John Travers 1908- 12
Moore, Lilian 1909-2004 137
    Obituary 155
    Earlier sketch in SATA 52
    See also CLR 15
Moore, Liz
    See Moore, M. Elizabeth
Moore, M. Elizabeth 1959- 156
Moore, Margaret R(umberger) 1903- 12
Moore, Margie 224
    Earlier sketch in SATA 176
Moore, Marianne 1887-1972 20
Moore, Marianne Craig
    See Moore, Marianne
Moore, Patrick (Alfred Caldwell) 1923- 49
    Brief entry 39
    See also SAAS 8
Moore, Patrick 1959- 184
Moore, Perry 1971-2011 193
Moore, Peter 1963- 175
Moore, Peter G.
    See Moore, Peter
Moore, Raina 1970- 212
Moore, Ray (S.) 1905(?)-1984
    Obituary 37
Moore, Regina
    See Dunne, Mary Collins
Moore, Rosalie (Gertrude) 1910-2001 9
Moore, Ruth (Ellen) 1908-1989 23
Moore, Ruth Nulton 1923- 38
Moore, S(arah) E. 23
Moore, Sarah Margaret
    See Hodges, Margaret
Moore, Sean L. 1976- 237
Moore, Stephanie Perry 1969(?)- 214
Moore, Tara 1950- 61
Moore, Yvette 1958- 154
    Earlier sketches in SATA *69, 70*
Moores, Dick
    See Moores, Richard (Arnold)
Moores, Richard (Arnold) 1909-1986
    Obituary 48
Mooser, Stephen 1941- 75
    Earlier sketch in SATA 28
Mora, Francisco X(avier) 1952- 90
Mora, Pat 1942- 232
    Earlier sketches in SATA *92, 134, 186*
    See also CLR 58
Mora, Patricia
    See Mora, Pat
Morais, Flavio 207
Morales, Magaly 225
Morales, Yuyi 180
    Earlier sketch in SATA 154
Moran, Tom 1943- 60
Moranville, Sharelle Byars 196
    Earlier sketch in SATA 152

Moray Williams, Ursula 1911-2006 3
    Obituary 177
    See also SAAS 9
Mordecai, Martin 220
Morden, Simon 1966(?)- 211
Mordhorst, Heidi 1964- 222
Mordvinoff, Nicolas 1911-1973 17
More, Caroline
    See Cone, Molly (Lamken)
    and Strachan, Margaret Pitcairn
Moreau, Jean-Pierre
    See Jarrie, Martin
Moreno, Rene King 190
Moreton, Andrew Esq.
    See Defoe, Daniel
Morey, Charles
    See Fletcher, Helen Jill
Morey, Walt(er Nelson) 1907-1992 51
    Obituary 70
    Earlier sketch in SATA 3
    See also SAAS 9
Morgan, Alfred P(owell) 1889-1972 33
Morgan, Alison (Mary) 1930- 85
    Earlier sketch in SATA 30
Morgan, Anne 1954- 121
Morgan, Christopher 1956- 199
Morgan, Clay 1950- 198
Morgan, Douglas
    See Macdonald, James D.
Morgan, Ellen
    See Bumstead, Kathleen Mary
Morgan, Geoffrey 1916- 46
Morgan, Helen (Gertrude Louise)
    1921-1990 29
Morgan, Jane
    See Cooper, James Fenimore
    and Franklin, Jane (Morgan)
    and Moren, Sally M(oore)
Morgan, Lenore H. 1908-1976 8
Morgan, Mary 1957- 213
    Earlier sketches in SATA *81, 114*
Morgan, McKayla
    See Basile, Gloria Vitanza
Morgan, Michaela
    See Basile, Gloria Vitanza
Morgan, Nicola 1961- 161
Morgan, Nina 1953- 110
Morgan, Pierr 1952- 122
    Earlier sketch in SATA 77
Morgan, Robin (Evonne) 1941- 80
Morgan, Roxanne
    See Gentle, Mary
Morgan, Sarah (Nicola) 1959- 68
Morgan, Shirley
    See Kiepper, Shirley Morgan
Morgan, Stacy T(owle) 1959- 104
Morgan, Stevie
    See Davies, Nicola
Morgan, Tom 1942- 42
Morgan, Wendy
    See Staub, Wendy Corsi
Morgan-Vanroyen, Mary
    See Morgan, Mary
Morgenstern, Susie Hoch 1945- 133
Mori, Hana 1909-1990(?) 88
Mori, Kyoko 1957- 122
    Autobiography Feature 126
    See also CLR 64
    See also SAAS 26
Moriarty, Jaclyn 1968- 239
    Earlier sketch in SATA 162
Moriarty, William J. 1930- 127
Morice, Dave 1946- 93
Morin, Isobel V. 1928- 110
Morine, Hoder
    See Conroy, John Wesley
Morley, Ben 228
Morley, Taia 199
Morley, Wilfred Owen
    See Lowndes, Robert A(ugustine) W(ard)

Morningstar, Mildred (Whaley) 1912-1997 .. *61*
  Obituary *114*
Morozumi, Atsuko *217*
  Earlier sketch in SATA *110*
Morpurgo, Michael 1943- *225*
  Earlier sketches in SATA *93, 143, 184*
  See also CLR *51*
Morrah, Dave
  See Morrah, David Wardlaw, Jr.
Morrah, David Wardlaw, Jr. 1914-1991 .... *10*
Morreale-de la Garza, Phyllis
  See De la Garza, Phyllis
Morressy, John 1930-2006 .... *23*
Morrill, Leslie H(olt) 1934-2003 .... *48*
  Brief entry *33*
  Obituary *148*
  See also SAAS *22*
Morris, Carla *210*
Morris, Carla D.
  See Morris, Carla
Morris, Chris(topher Crosby) 1946- *66*
Morris, Deborah 1956- *91*
Morris, Desmond 1928- *14*
Morris, Desmond John
  See Morris, Desmond
Morris, Don 1954- *83*
Morris, Gerald 1963- *207*
  Earlier sketches in SATA *107, 150*
Morris, Gerald Paul
  See Morris, Gerald
Morris, Gilbert (Leslie) 1929- *104*
Morris, Jackie *202*
  Earlier sketch in SATA *151*
Morris, Janet (Ellen) 1946- *66*
Morris, Jay
  See Tatham, Julie Campbell
Morris, (Margaret) Jean 1924- *98*
Morris, Jeffrey
  See Morris, Jeffrey Brandon
Morris, Jeffrey B.
  See Morris, Jeffrey Brandon
Morris, Jeffrey Brandon 1941- *92*
Morris, Jennifer E. 1969- *179*
Morris, Jill 1936- *165*
  Earlier sketch in SATA *119*
Morris, Juddi *85*
Morris, Judy K. 1936- *61*
Morris, Oradel Nolen *128*
Morris, Richard 1969- *224*
Morris, Robert A(da) 1933- *7*
Morris, William 1913-1994 .... *29*
Morrison, Angela *218*
Morrison, Bill 1935- *66*
  Brief entry *37*
Morrison, Chloe Anthony Wofford
  See Morrison, Toni
Morrison, Dorothy Nafus *29*
Morrison, Frank 1971- *226*
  Earlier sketch in SATA *185*
Morrison, Gordon 1944- *183*
  Earlier sketches in SATA *87, 128*
Morrison, Joan 1922- *65*
Morrison, Lillian 1917- *108*
  Earlier sketch in SATA *3*
Morrison, Lucile Phillips 1896- *17*
Morrison, Martha A. 1948- *77*
Morrison, Meighan 1966- *90*
Morrison, P.R. *196*
Morrison, Richard
  See Lowndes, Robert A(ugustine) W(ard)
Morrison, Robert
  See Lowndes, Robert A(ugustine) W(ard)
Morrison, Roberta
  See Webb, Jean Francis (III)
Morrison, Slade 1964-2010 .... *228*
Morrison, Susan Dudley
  See Gold, Susan Dudley
Morrison, Taylor 1971- *187*
  Earlier sketches in SATA *95, 159*

Morrison, Toni 1931- *235*
  Earlier sketches in SATA *57, 144*
  See also CLR *99*
Morrison, Velma Ford 1909- *21*
Morrison, Wilbur Howard 1915- *64*
Morrison, William
  See Samachson, Joseph
Morriss, James E(dward) 1932- *8*
Morrissey, Dean *183*
Morrow, Barbara Olenyik 1952- *167*
Morrow, Betty
  See Bacon, Elizabeth
Morrow, Sue Anne 1966- *218*
Morse, C. Scott
  See Morse, Scott
Morse, Carol
  See Yeakley, Marjory Hall
Morse, C.S.
  See Morse, Scott
Morse, Dorothy B(ayley) 1906-1979
  Obituary *24*
Morse, Flo 1921- *30*
Morse, Scott 1973- *200*
Morse, Tony 1953- *129*
Morstad, Julie *232*
Mort, Vivian
  See Cromie, Alice Hamilton
Mortensen, Denise Dowling *179*
Mortensen, Lori 1955- *221*
Mortimer, Anne 1958- *206*
  Earlier sketch in SATA *116*
Mortimer, Mary H.
  See Coury, Louise Andree
Morton, Alexandra (Hubbard) 1957- *144*
Morton, Anthony
  See Arthur, Robert, (Jr.)
Morton, Christine
  See Morton-Shaw, Christine
Morton, Jane 1931- *50*
Morton, Joseph C. 1932- *156*
Morton, Lee Jack, Jr. 1928- *32*
Morton, Miriam 1918(?)-1985 .... *9*
  Obituary *46*
Morton-Shaw, Christine 1957- *211*
Mosatche, Harriet 1949- *122*
Mosatche, Harriet S.
  See Mosatche, Harriet
Moscow, Alvin 1925- *3*
Mosel, Arlene (Tichy) 1921-1996 .... *7*
Moseley, James W(illett) 1931- *139*
Moseng, Elisabeth 1967- *90*
Moser, Barry 1940- *185*
  Earlier sketches in SATA *56, 79, 138*
  See also CLR *49*
  See also SAAS *15*
Moser, Don(ald Bruce) 1932- *31*
Moser, Laura *194*
Moser, Lisa *192*
Moses, Sheila P. 1961- *168*
Moses, Will 1956- *178*
  Earlier sketch in SATA *120*
Mosesson, Gloria R(ubin) *24*
Mosher, Richard 1949- *120*
Moskin, Marietta D(unston) 1928- *23*
Moskof, Martin Stephen 1930- *27*
Mosley, Francis 1957- *57*
Moss, Don(ald) 1920- *11*
Moss, Elaine (Dora) 1924- *57*
  Brief entry *31*
Moss, Jeff(rey) 1942-1998 .... *73*
  Obituary *106*
Moss, Marissa 1959- *216*
  Earlier sketches in SATA *71, 104, 163*
  See also CLR *134*
Moss, Miriam 1955- *202*
  Earlier sketches in SATA *76, 140*
Moss, Peggy 1966- *235*
Moss, Thylias 1954- *108*
Moss, Thylias Rebecca Brasier
  See Moss, Thylias

Most, Bernard 1937- *134*
  Brief entry *40*
  Earlier sketches in SATA *48, 91*
Mosz, Gosia 1972- *194*
Mott, Evelyn Clarke 1962- *133*
  Earlier sketch in SATA *75*
Motz, Lloyd 1909-2004 .... *20*
Mould, Chris *205*
Mould, Edwin
  See Whitlock, Ralph
Moulton, Mark Kimball *212*
Mouly, Francoise *155*
Mountain, Robert
  See Montgomery, Raymond A. (Jr.)
Mountfield, David
  See Grant, Neil
Mourlevat, Jean-Claude 1952- *187*
Mourning, Tuesday *206*
Moussard, Jacqueline 1924- *24*
Mowat, Claire 1933- *123*
Mowat, Claire Angel Wheeler
  See Mowat, Claire
Mowat, Farley 1921- *55*
  Earlier sketch in SATA *3*
  See also CLR *20*
Mowat, Farley McGill
  See Mowat, Farley
Mowll, Joshua 1970(?)- *188*
Mowry, Jess 1960- *131*
  Autobiography Feature *131*
  Earlier sketch in SATA *109*
  See also CLR *65*
Moxley, Sheila 1966- *96*
Moyer, Terry J. 1937- *94*
Moyes, Patricia
  See Haszard, Patricia Moyes
Moyler, Alan (Frank Powell) 1926- *36*
Mozelle, Shirley *179*
Mozley, Charles 1915- *43*
  Brief entry *32*
Mphahlele, Es'kia 1919-2008 .... *119*
  Obituary *198*
Mphahlele, Ezekiel
  See Mphahlele, Es'kia
Mphahlele, Zeke
  See Mphahlele, Es'kia
Mr. McGillicuddy
  See Abisch, Roslyn Kroop
Mr. Sniff
  See Abisch, Roslyn Kroop
Mr. Tivil
  See Lorkowski, Thomas V(incent)
Mr. Wizard
  See Herbert, Don
Mraz, David 1947- *219*
Mrs. Fairstar
  See Horne, Richard Henry Hengist
Muchamore, Robert 1972- *175*
Muchmore, Jo Ann 1937- *103*
Mude, O.
  See Gorey, Edward (St. John)
Mudgeon, Apeman
  See Mitchell, Adrian
Mueller, Jorg 1942- *67*
  See also CLR *43*
Mueller, Miranda R. *201*
Mueller, Virginia 1924- *28*
Muggs
  See Watkins, Lois
Muir, Diana
  See Appelbaum, Diana Muir Karter
Muir, Frank (Herbert) 1920-1998 .... *30*
Muir, Helen 1937- *65*
Muirhead, Margaret *220*
Mukerji, Dhan Gopal 1890-1936 .... *40*
  See also CLR *10*
Mulcahy, Lucille Burnett *12*
Muldrow, Diane *229*
Mulford, Philippa G. 1948- *112*
  Earlier sketch in SATA *43*

Mulford, Philippa Greene
   See Mulford, Philippa G.
Mulgan, Catherine 1931- 24
Mulila, Vigad G.
   See Maillu, David G(ian)
Mull, Brandon 1974- 190
Mullen, Michael 1937- 122
Muller, Billex
   See Ellis, Edward S.
Muller, Birte 1973- 214
Muller, Jorg
   See Mueller, Jorg
Muller, (Lester) Robin 1953- 86
Mulligan, Andy 238
Mullin, Caryl Cude 1969- 130
Mullins, Edward S(wift) 1922- 10
Mullins, Hilary 1962- 84
Mulock, Dinah Maria
   See Craik, Dinah Maria (Mulock)
Mulvihill, William Patrick 1923- 8
Mumford, Ruth
   See Dallas, Ruth
Mumy, Bill 1954- 112
Mun
   See Leaf, (Wilbur) Munro
Munari, Bruno 1907-1998 15
   See also CLR 9
Munce, Ruth Hill 1898- 12
Mundy, Simon 1954- 64
Mundy, Simon Andrew James Hainault
   See Mundy, Simon
Munger, Nancy 170
Munowitz, Ken 1935-1977 14
Munoz, Claudio 208
Munoz, William 1949- 92
   Earlier sketch in SATA 42
Munro, Alice 1931- 29
Munro, Alice Anne
   See Munro, Alice
Munro, Eleanor 1928- 37
Munro, Roxie 1945- 223
   Earlier sketches in SATA 58, 136, 184
Munsch, Bob
   See Munsch, Robert (Norman)
Munsch, Robert (Norman) 1945- 120
   Brief entry 48
   Earlier sketches in SATA 50, 83
   See also CLR 19
Munsinger, Lynn 1951- 221
   Earlier sketches in SATA 33, 94, 177
Munson, Derek 1970- 139
Munson, R. W.
   See Karl, Jean E(dna)
Munson-Benson, Tunie 1946- 15
Munsterberg, Peggy 1921- 102
Muntean, Michaela 182
Munthe, Nelly 1947- 53
Munves, James (Albert) 1922- 30
Munzer, Martha E. 1899-1999 4
Murawski, Darlyne A. 193
Murch, Mel
   See Manes, Stephen
Murdoch, David H(amilton) 1937- 96
Murdoch, Patricia 1957- 192
Murdock, Catherine Gilbert 185
Murhall, J(acqueline) J(ane) 1964- 143
Murphy, Barbara Beasley 1933- 130
   Earlier sketch in SATA 5
Murphy, Claire Rudolf 1951- 137
   Earlier sketch in SATA 76
Murphy, E(mmett) Jefferson 1926- 4
Murphy, Elizabeth Ann Maureen
   See Murphy, Liz
Murphy, Jill 1949- 214
   Earlier sketches in SATA 37, 70, 142
   See also CLR 39
Murphy, Jill Frances
   See Murphy, Jill

Murphy, Jim 1947- 224
   Brief entry 32
   Earlier sketches in SATA 37, 77, 124, 185
   See also CLR 53
Murphy, Joseph E., Jr. 1930- 65
Murphy, Kelly 1977- 190
   Earlier sketch in SATA 143
Murphy, Liz 1964- 210
Murphy, Louise 1943- 155
Murphy, Mary 1961- 196
Murphy, Pat
   See Murphy, E(mmett) Jefferson
Murphy, Patricia J. 1963- 132
Murphy, Rita 180
Murphy, Robert (William) 1902-1971 10
Murphy, Shirley Rousseau 1928- 126
   Earlier sketches in SATA 36, 71
   See also SAAS 18
Murphy, Stuart J. 1942- 237
   Earlier sketches in SATA 115, 157
Murphy, Thomas Basil, Jr. 1935- 191
Murphy, Tim
   See Murphy, Jim
Murphy, Tom
   See Murphy, Thomas Basil, Jr.
Murray, John 1923- 39
Murray, Kirsty 1960- 165
   Earlier sketch in SATA 108
Murray, Marguerite 1917- 63
Murray, Marian 5
Murray, Martine 1965- 125
Murray, (Judith) Michele (Freedman)
   1933-1974 7
Murray, Ossie 1938- 43
Murray, Peter
   See Hautman, Pete
Murrow, Liza Ketchum
   See Ketchum, Liza
Musgrave, Florence 1902-1999 3
Musgrove, Margaret W(ynkoop) 1943- 124
   Earlier sketch in SATA 26
Musgrove, Marianne 207
Mussey, Virginia Howell
   See Ellison, Virginia H(owell)
Mussey, Virginia T.H.
   See Ellison, Virginia H(owell)
Mussi, Sarah 206
Mutel, Cornelia F. 1947- 74
Muth, Jon J. 206
   Earlier sketch in SATA 165
Mutz
   See Kuenstler, Morton
Mwangi, Meja 1948- 174
My Brother's Brother
   See Chekhov, Anton
Myers, Anna 220
   Earlier sketch in SATA 160
Myers, Arthur 1917- 91
   Earlier sketch in SATA 35
Myers, Bernice 81
   Earlier sketch in SATA 9
Myers, Caroline Elizabeth Clark
   1887-1980 28
Myers, Christopher 1975- 183
   See also CLR 97
Myers, Edward 1950- 227
   Earlier sketches in SATA 96, 172
Myers, Elisabeth P(erkins) 1918- 36
Myers, (Mary) Hortense (Powner)
   1913-1987 10
Myers, Jack 1913-2006 83
   Obituary 178
Myers, Jack Edgar
   See Myers, Jack
Myers, Laurie 232
Myers, Lou 1915-2005 81
   Obituary 171
Myers, Louis
   See Myers, Lou
Myers, R.E. 1924- 119

Myers, Robert Eugene
   See Myers, R.E.
Myers, Tim 1953- 176
   Earlier sketch in SATA 147
Myers, Timothy Joseph
   See Myers, Tim
Myers, Walter Dean 1937- 229
   Brief entry 27
   Earlier sketches in SATA 41, 71, 109, 157,
   193
   See also CLR 110
   See also SAAS 2
Myers, Walter M.
   See Myers, Walter Dean
Myklusch, Matt 236
Myller, Rolf 1926-2006 27
   Obituary 175
Myra, Harold L(awrence) 1939- 46
   Brief entry 42
Myracle, Lauren 1969- 204
   Earlier sketch in SATA 162
Myrus, Donald (Richard) 1927- 23
Mysterious Traveler, The
   See Arthur, Robert, (Jr.)

N

Na, An 149
Na, Il Sung 231
Naaslund, Goorel Kristina 1940- 170
Nadel, Laurie 1948- 74
Naden, Corinne J. 1930- 166
   Earlier sketch in SATA 79
Nadimi, Suzan 188
Nadin, Joanna 1970- 239
Nadol, Jen 228
Nagda, Ann Whitehead 199
Nagel, Andreas Fischer
   See Fischer-Nagel, Andreas
Nagel, Heiderose Fischer
   See Fischer-Nagel, Heiderose
Nagle, Shane 176
Nahoko, Uehashi
   See Uehashi, Nahoko
Naidoo, Beverley 1943- 180
   Earlier sketches in SATA 63, 135
   See also CLR 29
Nails, Jennifer 213
Naiyomah, Wilson Kimeli 1977- 226
Nakae, Noriko 1940- 59
Nakata, Hiroe 205
Nakatani, Chiyoko 1930-1981 55
   Brief entry 40
   See also CLR 30
Nally, Susan W. 1947- 90
Namioka, Lensey 1929- 157
   Autobiography Feature 116
   Earlier sketches in SATA 27, 89
   See also CLR 48
   See also SAAS 24
Namovicz, Gene Inyart 1927- 6
Nance, Andrew 210
Nanji, Shenaaz 1954- 204
   Earlier sketch in SATA 131
Nanogak Agnes 1925- 61
Napier, Mark
   See Laffin, John (Alfred Charles)
Napoli, Donna Jo 1948- 230
   Autobiography Feature 230
   Earlier sketches in SATA 92, 137, 190
   See also CLR 51
   See also SAAS 23
Napp, Daniel 1974- 204
Narahashi, Keiko 1959- 115
   Earlier sketch in SATA 79
Narayan, R. K. 1906-2001 62
Narayan, Rasipuram Krishnaswami
   See Narayan, R. K.

Nascimbene, Yan 1949- *173*
Earlier sketch in SATA *133*
Nash, Bruce M(itchell) 1947- *34*
Nash, Fredric Ogden
See Nash, Ogden
Nash, Linell
See Smith, Linell Nash
Nash, Mary (Hughes) 1925- *41*
Nash, Ogden 1902-1971 .... *46*
Earlier sketch in SATA *2*
Nash, Renea Denise 1963- *81*
Nast, Elsa Ruth
See Watson, Jane Werner
Nast, Thomas 1840-1902 .... *51*
Brief entry *33*
Nastick, Sharon 1954- *41*
Natale, Vince *196*
Natalini, Sandro 1970- *222*
Natarajan, Srividya *187*
Nathan, Adele (Gutman) 1900(?)-1986
Obituary *48*
Nathan, Amy *155*
Earlier sketch in SATA *104*
Nathan, Dorothy (Goldeen) (?)-1966 .... *15*
Nathan, Robert (Gruntal) 1894-1985 .... *6*
Obituary *43*
Nathanson, Laura Walther 1941- *57*
Nation, Kaleb 1988- *222*
Natti, Lee 1919- *67*
Earlier sketch in SATA *1*
See also SAAS *3*
Natti, Susanna 1948- *125*
Earlier sketch in SATA *32*
Nau, Thomas *186*
Naughtie, Eleanor
See Updale, Eleanor
Naughton, Bill
See Naughton, William John (Francis)
Naughton, James Franklin 1957- *85*
Naughton, Jim
See Naughton, James Franklin
Naughton, William John (Francis)
1910-1992 .... *86*
Navarra, John Gabriel 1927- *8*
Nayeri, Daniel *232*
Nayeri, Dina *226*
Naylor, Penelope 1941- *10*
Naylor, Phyllis 1933-
See Naylor, Phyllis Reynolds
Naylor, Phyllis Reynolds 1933- *209*
Autobiography Feature *152*
See also CLR *135*
See also SAAS *10*
Nazarian, Nikki
See Nichols, Cecilia Fawn
Nazaroff, Alexander I(vanovich) 1898-1981 .. *4*
Nazoa, Aquiles 1920-1976 .... *198*
Neal, Harry Edward 1906-1993 .... *5*
Obituary *76*
Neal, Michael
See Teitelbaum, Michael
Nearing, Penny 1916- *47*
Brief entry *42*
Nebel, Gustave E. *45*
Brief entry *33*
Nebel, Mimouca
See Nebel, Gustave E.
Nee, Kay Bonner *10*
Needham, Kate 1962- *95*
Needle, Jan 1943- *98*
Earlier sketch in SATA *30*
See also CLR *43*
See also SAAS *23*
Needleman, Jacob 1934- *6*
Neel, David 1960- *82*
Neel, Preston 1959- *93*
Neff, Henry H. 1973- *221*
Negri, Rocco 1932- *12*
Negrin, Fabian 1963- *189*
Neidigh, Sherry 1956- *204*
Neier, Aryeh 1937- *59*

Neigoff, Anne *13*
Neigoff, Mike 1920- *13*
Neilan, Eujin Kim 1969- *200*
Neilson, Frances Fullerton (Jones)
1910-2001 .... *14*
Neimark, Anne E. 1935- *145*
Earlier sketch in SATA *4*
Neimark, Paul G. 1934- *80*
Brief entry *37*
Neitzel, Shirley 1941- *134*
Earlier sketch in SATA *77*
Nell
See Hanna, Nell(ie L.)
Nelscott, Kris
See Rusch, Kristine Kathryn
Nelson, Blake 1960- *177*
Nelson, Catherine Chadwick 1926- *87*
Nelson, Cordner 1918-2009 .... *54*
Brief entry *29*
Nelson, Cordner Bruce
See Nelson, Cordner
Nelson, D.A. 1970- *215*
Nelson, Dawn Ann
See Nelson, D.A.
Nelson, Drew 1952- *77*
Nelson, Esther L. 1928- *13*
Nelson, Jandy *229*
Nelson, Jim A.
See Stotter, Mike
Nelson, Julie L. 1970- *117*
Nelson, Kadir *213*
Earlier sketches in SATA *154, 181*
Nelson, Kris
See Rusch, Kristine Kathryn
Nelson, Lawrence E(rnest) 1928-1977
Obituary *28*
Nelson, Marilyn 1946- *60*
Autobiography Feature *180*
Nelson, Mary Carroll 1929- *23*
Nelson, O. Terry 1941- *62*
Nelson, Peter 1953- *73*
Nelson, Peter N.
See Nelson, Peter
Nelson, R. A. *197*
Nelson, Richard K(ing) 1941- *65*
Nelson, Robin Laura 1971- *141*
Nelson, Roy Paul 1923- *59*
Nelson, S.D. *181*
Nelson, Sharlene (P.) 1933- *96*
Nelson, Suzanne 1976- *184*
Nelson, Ted (W.) 1931- *96*
Nelson, Theresa 1948- *143*
Autobiography Feature *143*
Earlier sketch in SATA *79*
Nelson, Vaunda Micheaux 1953- *220*
Nemeth, Sally *187*
Neri, G. *197*
Neri, Greg
See Neri, G.
Neri, Gregory
See Neri, G.
Nerlove, Miriam 1959- *53*
Brief entry *49*
Nesbit, E. 1858-1924 .... *100*
See also YABC *1*
See also CLR *70*
Nesbit, Edith
See Nesbit, E.
Nesbit, Troy
See Folsom, Franklin (Brewster)
Nesbitt, Kenn 1962- *239*
Nespojohn, Katherine V(eronica) 1912-1975 . *7*
Ness, Evaline (Michelow) 1911-1986 .... *26*
Obituary *49*
Earlier sketch in SATA *1*
See also CLR *6*
See also SAAS *1*
Ness, Patrick 1971- *207*
Nestor, Larry 1940- *149*
Nestor, William P(rodromos) 1947- *49*
Nethery, Mary *93*

Neubecker, Robert *214*
Earlier sketch in SATA *170*
Neuberger, Julia (Babette Sarah) 1950- *142*
Earlier sketch in SATA *78*
Neufeld, John (Arthur) 1938- *131*
Autobiography Feature *131*
Earlier sketches in SATA *6, 81*
See also CLR *52*
See also SAAS *3*
Neuhaus, David 1958- *83*
Neumeyer, Peter F(lorian) 1929- *13*
Neurath, Marie (Reidemeister) 1898-1986 ..... *1*
Neuschwander, Cindy 1953- *157*
Earlier sketch in SATA *107*
Neusner, Jacob 1932- *38*
Neville, Charles
See Bodsworth, (Charles) Fred(erick)
Neville, Emily Cheney 1919- *1*
See also SAAS *2*
Neville, Mary
See Woodrich, Mary Neville
Nevins, Albert (Francis) J(erome)
1915-1997 .... *20*
Nevius, Carol 1955- *186*
Newberger, Devra
See Speregen, Devra Newberger
Newberry, Clare Turlay 1903-1970 .... *1*
Obituary *26*
Newbery, John 1713-1767 .... *20*
See also CLR *147*
Newbery, Linda 1952- *184*
Earlier sketch in SATA *142*
Newbigging, Martha *198*
Newbold, Greg *199*
Newcomb, Ellsworth
See Kenny, Ellsworth Newcomb
Newcombe, Eugene A. 1923-1990 .... *45*
Brief entry *33*
Newcombe, Jack
See Newcombe, Eugene A.
Newcome, Robert 1955- *91*
Newcome, Zita 1959- *88*
Newell, Crosby
See Bonsall, Crosby Barbara (Newell)
Newell, Edythe W(eatherford) 1910-1989 .... *11*
Newell, Hope Hockenberry 1896-1965 .... *24*
Newfeld, Frank 1928- *26*
Newgarden, Mark 1959- *194*
Newhouse, Maxwell 1947- *232*
Newland, Gillian *220*
Newlon, (Frank) Clarke 1905(?)-1982 .... *6*
Obituary *33*
Newman, Barbara Johansen *191*
Newman, C.J.
See Newman, Coleman J.
Newman, Coleman J. 1935- *82*
Newman, Daisy 1904-1994 .... *27*
Obituary *78*
Newman, Gerald 1939- *46*
Brief entry *42*
Newman, Jeff 1976- *228*
Newman, Jerry
See Newman, Coleman J.
Newman, Leslea 1955- *234*
Earlier sketches in SATA *71, 128, 134*
Newman, Margaret
See Potter, Margaret
Newman, Marjorie *146*
Newman, Matthew (Harrison) 1955- *56*
Newman, Nanette 1934- *162*
Newman, Robert (Howard) 1909-1988 .... *87*
Obituary *60*
Earlier sketch in SATA *4*
Newman, Shirlee P(etkin) *144*
Earlier sketches in SATA *10, 90*
Newquist, Harvey
See Newquist, H.P.
Newquist, H.P. 1958- *235*
Newsom, Carol 1948- *92*
Earlier sketch in SATA *40*
Newsom, Tom 1944- *80*

Newsome, Richard 1964- 233
Newth, Mette 1942- 140
Newton, David E. 1933- 67
Newton, David Edward
    See Newton, David E.
Newton, James R(obert) 1935- 23
Newton, Jill 1964- 200
Newton, Robert 1965- 191
Newton, Suzanne 1936- 77
    Earlier sketch in SATA 5
Newton, Vanessa
    See Newton, Vanessa Brantley
Newton, Vanessa Brantley 1962(?)- 206
Ney, John 1923- 43
    Brief entry 33
Nez, John 218
    Earlier sketch in SATA 155
Nez, John Abbott
    See Nez, John
Ng, Franklin 82
Ngui, Marc 1972- 229
Nguyen, Vincent 226
    Earlier sketch in SATA 187
Nichol, B(arrie) P(hillip) 1944-1988 66
Nicholas, Louise D.
    See Watkins, Dawn L.
Nicholls, Judith (Ann) 1941- 61
Nicholls, Sally 1983- 209
Nichols, Cecilia Fawn 1906-1987 12
Nichols, Grace 1950- 164
    Earlier sketch in SATA 98
Nichols, Janet (Louise) 1952- 67
Nichols, Judy 1947- 124
Nichols, Leigh
    See Koontz, Dean
Nichols, Michael 1952- 215
Nichols, Nick
    See Nichols, Michael
Nichols, Paul
    See Hawks, Robert
Nichols, Peter
    See Youd, Samuel
Nichols, (Joanna) Ruth 1948- 15
    See also CLR 149
Nichols, Travis 206
Nicholson, C. R.
    See Nicole, Christopher
Nicholson, Christina
    See Nicole, Christopher
Nicholson, Joyce Thorpe 1919-2011 35
Nicholson, Lois P. 1949- 88
Nicholson, Robin
    See Nicole, Christopher
Nicholson, William 239
    Earlier sketch in SATA 180
Nicholson, William 1872-1949
    See CLR 76
Nickel, Barbara 1966- 188
Nickell, Joe 1944- 167
    Earlier sketch in SATA 73
Nickelsburg, Janet 1893-1983 11
Nickerson, Betty 1922- 14
Nickerson, Elizabeth
    See Nickerson, Betty
Nickl, Barbara (Elisabeth) 1939- 56
Nicklaus, Carol 62
    Brief entry 33
Nickle, John 181
Nickless, Will 1902-1979(?) 66
Nic Leodhas, Sorche
    See Alger, Leclaire (Gowans)
Nicol, Ann
    See Turnbull, Ann
Nicolas
    See Mordvinoff, Nicolas
Nicolay, Helen 1866-1954
    See YABC 1
Nicole, Christopher 1930- 5
Nicole, Christopher Robin
    See Nicole, Christopher
Nicoll, Helen 1937- 87

Nicolson, Cynthia Pratt 1949- 141
Ni Dhuibhne, Eilis 1954- 91
Niehaus, Paddy Bouma
    See Bouma, Paddy
Nields, Nerissa 1967- 166
Nielsen, Kay (Rasmus) 1886-1957 16
    See also CLR 16
Nielsen, Laura F. 1960- 93
Nielsen, Laura Farnsworth
    See Nielsen, Laura F.
Nielsen, Nancy J. 1951- 77
Nielsen, Susin 1964- 195
Nielsen, Virginia
    See McCall, Virginia Nielsen
Nielsen-Fernlund, Susin
    See Nielsen, Susin
Nielson, Sheila A. 234
Niemann, Christoph 1970- 238
    Earlier sketch in SATA 191
Nieuwsma, Milton J(ohn) 1941- 142
Nightingale, Sandy 1953- 76
Nikolajeva, Maria 1952- 127
Nikola-Lisa, W. 1951- 180
    Earlier sketch in SATA 71
Niland, Deborah 1951- 172
    Earlier sketch in SATA 27
Niland, Kilmeny 75
Nilsen, Anna 1948- 174
    Earlier sketch in SATA 96
Nilsson, Eleanor 1939- 117
    Earlier sketch in SATA 81
    See also SAAS 23
Nilsson, Per 1954- 159
Nimmo, Jenny 1944- 144
    Earlier sketch in SATA 87
    See also CLR 44
Nishimura, Kae 196
Niven, Larry 1938- 171
    Earlier sketch in SATA 95
Niven, Laurence Van Cott
    See Niven, Larry
Niven, Laurence VanCott
    See Niven, Larry
Nivola, Claire A. 1947- 208
    Earlier sketches in SATA 84, 140
Nix, Garth 1963- 210
    Earlier sketches in SATA 97, 143
    See also CLR 68
Nixon, Hershell Howard 1923- 42
Nixon, Joan Lowery 1927-2003 115
    Obituary 146
    Earlier sketches in SATA 8, 44, 78
    See also CLR 24
    See also SAAS 9
Nixon, K.
    See Nixon, Kathleen Irene (Blundell)
Nixon, Kathleen Irene (Blundell)
    1894-1988(?) 14
    Obituary 59
Nobati, Eugenia 1968- 201
Nobisso, Josephine 1953- 121
    Earlier sketch in SATA 78
Noble, Iris (Davis) 1922-1986 5
    Obituary 49
Noble, Marty 1947- 125
    Earlier sketch in SATA 97
Noble, Trinka Hakes 1944- 197
    Brief entry 37
    Earlier sketch in SATA 123
Nobleman, Marc Tyler 1972- 203
Noda, Takayo 1961- 168
Nodelman, Perry 1942- 101
Nodset, Joan L.
    See Lexau, Joan M.
Noel Hume, Ivor 1927- 65
Noestlinger, Christine
    See Nostlinger, Christine
Noguere, Suzanne 1947- 34
Nolan, Dennis 1945- 166
    Brief entry 34
    Earlier sketches in SATA 42, 92

Nolan, Han 1956- 157
    Earlier sketch in SATA 109
Nolan, Janet 1956- 191
    Earlier sketch in SATA 145
Nolan, Jeannette Covert 1897-1974 2
    Obituary 27
Nolan, Lucy 215
Nolan, Paul T(homas) 1919- 48
Nolan, William F. 1928- 88
    Brief entry 28
Nolan, William Francis
    See Nolan, William F.
Nolen, Jerdine 1953- 157
    Earlier sketch in SATA 105
Noll, Amanda 219
Noll, Sally 1946- 82
Nolte, Jack
    See Carter, Scott William
Noonan, Brandon 1979- 184
Noonan, Diana 1960- 146
Noonan, Julia 1946- 148
    Earlier sketches in SATA 4, 95
Norac, Carl 1960- 166
Norcliffe, James 1946- 234
Norcross, John
    See Conroy, John Wesley
Nordan, Robert W(arren) 1934-2004 133
Nordhoff, Charles Bernard 1887-1947 23
Nordlicht, Lillian 29
Nordstrom, Ursula 1910-1988 3
    Obituary 57
Nordtvedt, Matilda 1926- 67
Norling, Beth 1969- 149
Norman, Charles 1904-1996 38
    Obituary 92
Norman, Geoffrey 223
Norman, Howard
    See Norman, Howard A.
Norman, Howard A. 1949- 81
Norman, James
    See Schmidt, James Norman
Norman, Jay
    See Arthur, Robert, (Jr.)
Norman, Lilith 1927- 120
    Earlier sketch in SATA 86
Norman, Mary 1931- 36
Norman, Steve
    See Pashko, Stanley
Norment, Lisa 1966- 91
Norris, Gunilla Brodde 1939- 20
North, Andrew
    See Norton, Andre
North, Anthony
    See Koontz, Dean
North, Captain George
    See Stevenson, Robert Louis
North, Captain George
    See Stevenson, Robert Louis
North, Howard
    See Trevor, Elleston
North, Joan 1920- 16
North, Milou
    See Erdrich, Louise
North, Robert
    See Withers, Carl A.
North, Sara
    See Bonham, Barbara Thomas
    and Hager, Jean
North, Sherry 201
North, Sterling 1906-1974 45
    Obituary 26
    Earlier sketch in SATA 1
Northcott, (William) Cecil 1902-1987
    Obituary 55
Northeast, Brenda V(ictoria) 1948- 106
Northmore, Elizabeth Florence 1906-1974 . 122
Norton, Alice Mary
    See Norton, Andre
Norton, Andre 1912-2005 91
    Earlier sketches in SATA 1, 43
    See also CLR 50

Norton, Browning
  See Norton, Frank R. B(rowning)
Norton, Frank R. B(rowning) 1909-1989 ..... *10*
Norton, Mary 1903-1992 .... *60*
  Obituary *72*
  Earlier sketch in SATA *18*
  See also CLR *140*
Nosredna, Trebor
  See Anderson, Bob
Nostlinger, Christine 1936- *162*
  Brief entry *37*
  Earlier sketch in SATA *64*
  See also CLR *12*
Noteboom, Erin
  See Bow, Erin
Nourse, Alan E(dward) 1928-1992 .... *48*
  See also CLR *33*
Novak, Matt 1962- *204*
  Brief entry *52*
  Earlier sketches in SATA *60, 104, 165*
Novelli, Luca 1947- *61*
Novgorodoff, Danica 1982(?)- *215*
Nowell, Elizabeth Cameron *12*
Noyes, Deborah 1965- *194*
  Earlier sketch in SATA *145*
Nugent, Cynthia 1954- *205*
Nugent, Nicholas 1949- *73*
Numberman, Neil 1981(?)- *220*
Numeroff, Laura 1953- *206*
  Earlier sketches in SATA *28, 90, 142*
  See also CLR *85*
Numeroff Joffe, Laura
  See Numeroff, Laura
Nunes, Lygia Bojunga 1932- *154*
  Earlier sketch in SATA *75*
Nunn, Laura (Donna) Silverstein 1968- *124*
Nurenberg, Thelma
  See Greenhaus, Thelma Nurenberg
Nurnberg, Maxwell 1897-1984 .... *27*
  Obituary *41*
Nussbaumer, Paul (Edmund) 1934- *16*
Nutt, Ken 1951- *163*
  Earlier sketch in SATA *97*
Nuttall-Smith, Margaret Emily Noel 1919- .. *26*
Nuygen, Mathieu 1967- *80*
Nuzum, K. A. *195*
Nuzum, Kathy A.
  See Nuzum, K. A.
Nwapa, Flora (Nwanzuruaha) 1931-1993
  See CLR *162*
Nyberg, (Everett Wayne) Morgan 1944- *87*
Nyce, (Nellie) Helene von Strecker
  1885-1969 .... *19*
Nyce, Vera 1862-1925 .... *19*
Nye, Naomi Shihab 1952- *198*
  Earlier sketches in SATA *86, 147*
  See also CLR *59*
Nye, Robert 1939- *6*
Nyeu, Tao *206*
Nyikos, Stacy A. 1969- *164*
Nystrom, Carolyn 1940- *130*
  Earlier sketch in SATA *67*

O

O. Henry
  See Henry, O.
Oakes, Elizabeth H. 1964- *132*
Oakes, Vanya 1909-1983 .... *6*
  Obituary *37*
Oakley, Don(ald G.) 1927- *8*
Oakley, Graham 1929- *84*
  Earlier sketch in SATA *30*
  See also CLR *7*
Oakley, Helen (McKelvey) 1906- *10*
Oaks, J. Adams *220*
Oana, Katherine 1929- *53*
  Brief entry *37*
Oates, Eddie H. 1943- *88*

Oates, Joyce Carol 1938- *159*
Oates, Stephen B(aery) 1936- *59*
Obed, Ellen Bryan 1944- *74*
Oberdieck, Bernhard 1949- *230*
Oberle, Joseph 1958- *69*
Oberman, Sheldon 1949-2004 .... *85*
  Autobiography Feature *114*
  Obituary *153*
  See also CLR *54*
  See also SAAS *26*
Obligado, Lilian (Isabel) 1931- *61*
  Brief entry *45*
Obrant, Susan 1946- *11*
O'Brian, E.G.
  See Clarke, Arthur C.
O'Brien, Anne Sibley 1952- *213*
  Brief entry *48*
  Earlier sketches in SATA *53, 80*
O'Brien, Caragh M. *232*
O'Brien, E.G.
  See Clarke, Arthur C.
O'Brien, Esse Forrester 1895(?)-1975
  Obituary *30*
O'Brien, Johnny *222*
O'Brien, Patrick 1960- *193*
O'Brien, Robert C. 1918-1973 .... *23*
  See also CLR *2*
O'Brien, Thomas C. 1938-2010 .... *29*
O'Brien, Thomas Clement
  See O'Brien, Thomas C.
O'Callaghan, Julie 1954- *113*
O'Callahan, Jay 1938- *88*
O'Carroll, Ryan
  See Markun, Patricia Maloney
Ochiltree, Dianne 1953- *117*
Ockham, Joan Price
  See Price, Joan
Ockler, Sarah *239*
O'Connell, Margaret F(orster) 1935-1977 .... *30*
  Obituary *30*
O'Connell, Peg
  See Ahern, Margaret McCrohan
O'Connell, Rebecca 1968- *212*
  Earlier sketch in SATA *130*
O'Connor, Barbara 1950- *193*
  Earlier sketch in SATA *154*
O'Connor, Francine M(arie) 1930- *90*
O'Connor, Genevieve A. 1914- *75*
O'Connor, George *228*
  Earlier sketch in SATA *183*
O'Connor, Ian 1965- *188*
O'Connor, Jane 1947- *186*
  Brief entry *47*
  Earlier sketches in SATA *59, 103, 150*
O'Connor, Karen 1938- *89*
  Earlier sketch in SATA *34*
O'Connor, Patrick
  See Wibberley, Leonard
O'Connor, Richard 1915-1975
  Obituary *21*
O'Conor, Jane 1958- *78*
Odaga, Asenath (Bole) 1937- *130*
  Earlier sketch in SATA *67*
  See also SAAS *19*
O Danachair, Caoimhin
  See Danaher, Kevin
Odanaka, Barbara *159*
O'Daniel, Janet 1921- *24*
O'Day, Cathy
  See Crane, Barbara (Joyce)
O'Dell, Scott 1898-1989 .... *134*
  Earlier sketches in SATA *12, 60*
  See also CLR *126*
Odenwald, Robert P(aul) 1899-1965 .... *11*
Odgers, Sally
  See Odgers, Sally Farrell
Odgers, Sally Farrell 1957- *139*
  Earlier sketch in SATA *72*
Odone, Jamison 1980- *209*

O'Donnell, Dick
  See Lupoff, Richard A.
  and Thompson, Don(ald Arthur)
O'Donnell, Liam 1970- *209*
Odriozola, Elena *186*
Oechsli, Kelly 1918-1999 .... *5*
Oertel, Andreas 1966- *230*
Oesterle, Virginia Rorby
  See Rorby, Ginny
Ofek, Uriel 1926- *36*
  See also CLR *28*
Ofer, Avi 1975- *207*
Offenbacher, Ami 1958- *91*
Offermann, Andrea *231*
Offill, Jenny 1968- *211*
Offit, Sidney 1928- *10*
Ofosu-Appiah, L(awrence) H(enry) 1920- ... *13*
Ogan, George F. 1912-1983 .... *13*
Ogan, M. G.
  See Ogan, George F.
  and Ogan, Margaret E. (Nettles)
Ogan, Margaret E. (Nettles) 1923-1979 ...... *13*
Ogburn, Charlton (Jr.) 1911-1998 .... *3*
  Obituary *109*
Ogburn, Jacqueline K. *162*
Ogilvie, Elisabeth May 1917-2006 .... *40*
  Brief entry *29*
  Obituary *176*
Ogilvy, Gavin
  See Barrie, J. M.
Ogilvy, Ian 1943- *177*
Ogilvy, Ian Raymond
  See Ogilvy, Ian
Ogle, Lucille Edith 1904-1988
  Obituary *59*
Ogletree, Charles J. 1952- *175*
O'Green, Jennifer
  See Roberson, Jennifer
O'Green, Jennifer Roberson
  See Roberson, Jennifer
O'Hagan, Caroline 1946- *38*
O'Hanlon, Jacklyn
  See Meek, Jacklyn O'Hanlon
O'Hara, Elizabeth
  See Ni Dhuibhne, Eilis
O'Hara, Kenneth
  See Morris, (Margaret) Jean
O'Hara, Mary
  See Alsop, Mary O'Hara
O'Hara (Alsop), Mary
  See Alsop, Mary O'Hara
O'Hare, Jeff(rey A.) 1958- *105*
O'hearn, Kate *225*
Ohi, Ruth 1964- *95*
Ohiyesa
  See Eastman, Charles A(lexander)
Ohlsson, Ib 1935- *7*
Ohmi, Ayano 1959- *115*
Ohtomo, Yasuo 1946- *37*
o huigin, sean 1942- *138*
  See also CLR *75*
Oiseau
  See Moseley, James W(illett)
Oke, Janette 1935- *97*
O'Keefe, Susan Heyboer *176*
  Earlier sketch in SATA *133*
O'Keeffe, Frank 1938- *99*
O'Kelley, Mattie Lou 1908-1997 .... *97*
  Earlier sketch in SATA *36*
Okimoto, Jean Davies 1942- *103*
  Earlier sketch in SATA *34*
Okomfo, Amasewa
  See Cousins, Linda
olafsdottir, Gudrun Elin
  See Gunnella
Olaleye, Isaac O. 1941- *96*
  See also SAAS *23*
Olander, Johan 1967- *231*
Olcott, Frances Jenkins 1872(?)-1963 .... *19*
Old, Wendie C(orbin) 1943- *154*

Old Boy
  See Hughes, Thomas
Oldenburg, E(gbert) William 1936-1974 ...... *35*
Older, Effin 1942- *114*
Older, Jules 1940- *156*
  Earlier sketch in SATA *114*
Oldfield, Jenny 1949- *140*
Oldfield, Margaret J(ean) 1932- *56*
Oldfield, Pamela 1931- *86*
Oldham, June *70*
Oldham, Mary 1944- *65*
Oldland, Nicholas 1972- *223*
Olds, Elizabeth 1896-1991 .... *3*
  Obituary *66*
Olds, Helen Diehl 1895-1981 .... *9*
  Obituary *25*
Oldstyle, Jonathan
  See Irving, Washington
O'Leary, Brian (Todd) 1940- *6*
O'Leary, Chris *208*
O'Leary, Patsy B. 1937- *97*
O'Leary, Patsy Baker
  See O'Leary, Patsy B.
Oleynikov, Igor 1953- *202*
Oliphant, B.J.
  See Tepper, Sheri S.
Oliver, Burton
  See Burt, Olive Woolley
Oliver, Chad
  See Oliver, Symmes C.
Oliver, John Edward 1933- *21*
Oliver, Lauren 1982- *228*
Oliver, Lin *202*
Oliver, Marilyn Tower 1935- *89*
Oliver, Mark 1960- *214*
Oliver, Narelle 1960- *197*
  Earlier sketch in SATA *152*
Oliver, Shirley (Louise Dawkins) 1958- *74*
Oliver, Symmes C. 1928-1993 .... *101*
Oliviero, Jamie 1950- *84*
Olmsted, Lorena Ann 1890-1989 .... *13*
Olney, Ross R. 1929- *13*
Olschewski, Alfred (Erich) 1920- *7*
Olsen, Barbara *148*
Olsen, Carol 1945- *89*
Olsen, Ib Spang 1921- *81*
  Earlier sketch in SATA *6*
Olsen, Violet (Mae) 1922-1991 .... *58*
Olson, Arielle North 1932- *67*
Olson, David J. 1974- *198*
Olson, Gene 1922- *32*
Olson, Gretchen *187*
Olson, Helen Kronberg *48*
Olson, Julie 1976- *233*
Olson, Kay Melchisedech 1948- *175*
Olson, Marianne
  See Mitchell, Marianne
Olson-Brown, Ellen 1967- *183*
Olten, Manuela 1970- *197*
Olugebefola, Ademole 1941- *15*
Oluonye, Mary N(kechi) 1955- *111*
Om
  See Gorey, Edward (St. John)
O'Malley, Donough *208*
O'Malley, Kevin 1961- *230*
  Earlier sketches in SATA *157, 191*
Oman, Carola (Mary Anima) 1897-1978 ..... *35*
O'Mara, Carmel 1965- *166*
O'Mara-Horwitz, Carmel
  See O'Mara, Carmel
O'Meara, Walter (Andrew) 1897-1989 .... *65*
Ommanney, F(rancis) D(ownes) 1903-1980 . *23*
Omololu, Cynthia Jaynes *222*
O Mude
  See Gorey, Edward (St. John)
Oneal, Elizabeth 1934- *82*
  Earlier sketch in SATA *30*
  See also CLR *169*
O'Neal, Katherine Pebley 1957- *204*
O'Neal, Reagan
  See Jordan, Robert

O'Neal, Regan
  See Jordan, Robert
Oneal, Zibby
  See Oneal, Elizabeth
O'neill, Alexis 1949- *220*
O'Neill, Amanda 1951- *111*
O'Neill, Catharine *203*
O'Neill, Gerard K(itchen) 1927-1992 .... *65*
O'Neill, Judith (Beatrice) 1930- *34*
O'Neill, Mary L(e Duc) 1908(?)-1990 .... *2*
  Obituary *64*
O'Neill, Reagan
  See Jordan, Robert
Onslow, Annette Rosemary MacArthur
  See MacArthur-Onslow, Annette Rosemary
Onslow, John 1906-1985
  Obituary *47*
Onyefulu, Ifeoma 1959- *157*
  Earlier sketches in SATA *81, 115*
Opie, Iona (Margaret Balfour) 1923- *118*
  Earlier sketches in SATA *3, 63*
  See also SAAS *6*
Opie, Peter (Mason) 1918-1982 .... *118*
  Obituary *28*
  Earlier sketches in SATA *3, 63*
Oppel, Kenneth 1967- *199*
  Earlier sketches in SATA *99, 153*
Oppel, Kenneth Kerry
  See Oppel, Kenneth
Oppenheim, Joanne 1934- *174*
  Earlier sketches in SATA *5, 82, 136*
Oppenheim, Shulamith Levey 1928- *177*
Oppenheimer, Joan L(etson) 1925- *28*
Oppong, Joseph Ransford 1953- *160*
Optic, Oliver
  See Adams, William Taylor
  and Stratemeyer, Edward L.
Oram, Hiawyn 1946- *101*
  Earlier sketch in SATA *56*
Orbach, Ruth Gary 1941- *21*
Orback, Craig *197*
Orczy, Emma
  See Orczy, Baroness Emmuska
Orczy, Emma Magdalena Rosalia Maria Josefa
  See Orczy, Baroness Emmuska
Orczy, Emmuska
  See Orczy, Baroness Emmuska
Orczy, Baroness Emmuska 1865-1947 .... *40*
Orde, A.J.
  See Tepper, Sheri S.
O'Reilly, Jackson
  See Jordan, Robert
Orenstein, Denise Gosliner 1950- *157*
Orgad, Dorit 1936- *199*
Orgel, Doris 1929- *148*
  Earlier sketches in SATA *7, 85*
  See also CLR *48*
  See also SAAS *19*
Orgill, Roxane *198*
Oriolo, Joe
  See Oriolo, Joseph D.
Oriolo, Joseph D. 1913-1985
  Obituary *46*
Orlandelli, Alessandro
  See Horley, Alex
Orlean, Susan 1955- *209*
Orleans, Ilo 1897-1962 .... *10*
Orlev, Uri 1931- *135*
  Earlier sketch in SATA *58*
  See also CLR *30*
  See also SAAS *19*
Orloff, Karen Kaufman *236*
Ormai, Stella *57*
  Brief entry *48*
Ormerod, Jan 1946- *210*
  Brief entry *44*
  Earlier sketches in SATA *55, 70, 132*
  See also CLR *20*
Ormerod, Janette Louise
  See Ormerod, Jan

Ormes, Jackie
  See Ormes, Zelda J.
Ormes, Zelda J. 1914-1986
  Obituary *47*
Ormondroyd, Edward 1925- *14*
Ormsby, Virginia H(aire) 1906-1990 .... *11*
Oron, Judie *239*
Orona-Ramirez, Kristy 1964- *189*
Orozco, Jose-Luis 1948- *179*
Orr, Katherine S(helley) 1950- *72*
Orr, Wendy 1953- *206*
  Earlier sketches in SATA *90, 141*
Orris
  See Ingelow, Jean
Orth, Richard
  See Gardner, Richard (M.)
Ortiz Cofer, Judith
  See Cofer, Judith Ortiz
Orwell, George 1903-1950 .... *29*
  See also CLR *171*
Orwin, Joanna 1944- *141*
Os, Eric van
  See van Os, Erik
Osborn, Elinor 1939- *145*
Osborn, Jacob 1981(?)- *215*
Osborn, Kathy 1955(?)- *199*
Osborn, Lois D(orothy) 1915- *61*
Osborne, Charles 1927- *59*
Osborne, Chester G(orham) 1915-1987 .... *11*
Osborne, David
  See Silverberg, Robert
Osborne, George
  See Silverberg, Robert
Osborne, Leone Neal 1914-1996 .... *2*
Osborne, Linda Barrett 1949- *215*
Osborne, Mary Pope 1949- *144*
  Earlier sketches in SATA *41, 55, 98*
  See also CLR *88*
Osceola
  See Blixen, Karen
Osgood, William E(dward) 1926- *37*
O'Shaughnessy, Darren
  See Shan, Darren
O'Shaughnessy, Ellen Cassels 1937- *78*
O'shaughnessy, Tam 1951- *221*
O'Shea, Catherine Patricia Shiels
  See O'Shea, Pat
O'Shea, Pat 1931-2007 .... *87*
  See also CLR *18*
Osmond, Edward 1900- *10*
Ossoli, Sarah Margaret
  See Fuller, Margaret
Ostendorf, (Arthur) Lloyd, (Jr.) 1921-2000 .. *65*
  Obituary *125*
Osterweil, Adam 1972- *217*
Ostow, Micol 1976- *223*
  Earlier sketch in SATA *170*
Otfinoski, Steven 1949- *116*
  Earlier sketch in SATA *56*
Otis, James
  See Kaler, James Otis
O'Toole, Thomas 1941- *71*
O'Trigger, Sir Lucius
  See Horne, Richard Henry Hengist
Otten, Charlotte
  See Otten, Charlotte F.
Otten, Charlotte F. 1926- *98*
Otten, Charlotte Fennema
  See Otten, Charlotte F.
Ottley, Matt 1962- *171*
  Earlier sketch in SATA *102*
Ottley, Reginald Leslie 1909-1985 .... *26*
  See also CLR *16*
Otto, Margaret Glover 1909-1976
  Obituary *30*
Otto, Svend
  See Soerensen, Svend Otto
Ouellet, Debbie 1954- *219*
Oughton, Jerrie (Preston) 1937- *131*
  Earlier sketch in SATA *76*
Oughton, (William) Taylor 1925- *104*

Ouida
  See De La Ramee, Marie Louise
Ousley, Odille 1896-1976 .... *10*
Outcalt, Todd 1960- *123*
Overmyer, James E. 1946- *88*
Overton, Jenny (Margaret Mary) 1942- *52*
  Brief entry *36*
Owen, Ann
  See Qualey, Marsha
Owen, Annie 1949- *75*
Owen, Caroline Dale
  See Snedeker, Caroline Dale (Parke)
Owen, Clifford
  See Hamilton, Charles (Harold St. John)
Owen, Dilys
  See Gater, Dilys
Owen, (Benjamin) Evan 1918-1984 .... *38*
Owen, (John) Gareth 1936-2002 .... *162*
  Earlier sketch in SATA *83*
  See also CLR *31*
  See also SAAS *14*
Owen, James A. *185*
Owens, Bryant 1968- *116*
Owens, Dana Elaine
  See Queen Latifah
Owens, Gail 1939- *54*
Owens, Mary Beth *191*
Owens, Thomas S(heldon) 1960- *86*
Owens, Tom
  See Owens, Thomas S(heldon)
Oxenbury, Helen 1938- *149*
  Earlier sketches in SATA *3, 68*
  See also CLR *70*
Oxendine, Bess Holland 1933- *90*
Oz, Frank (Richard) 1944- *60*
Ozer, Jerome S. 1927- *59*

P

Paananen, Eloise (Katherine) 1923-1993 .... *9*
Pace, Lorenzo 1943- *131*
Pace, Mildred Mastin 1907- *46*
  Brief entry *29*
Pachter, Hedwig (?)-1988 .... *63*
Pack, Janet 1952- *77*
Pack, Robert 1929- *118*
Packard, Edward 1931- *148*
  Earlier sketches in SATA *47, 90*
Packer, Kenneth L. 1946- *116*
Packer, Vin
  See Meaker, Marijane
Pad, Peter
  See Stratemeyer, Edward L.
Page, Eileen
  See Heal, Edith
Page, Eleanor
  See Coerr, Eleanor (Beatrice)
Page, Gail 1950- *205*
Page, Jake 1936- *81*
Page, James Keena, Jr.
  See Page, Jake
Page, Lou Williams 1912-1997 .... *38*
Page, Mary
  See Heal, Edith
Page, Robin 1943- *154*
Pagliarulo, Antonio 1977(?)- *212*
Pagnucci, Susan 1944- *90*
Pahlen, Kurt 1907-2003
  Obituary *147*
Pahz, Cheryl
  See Pahz, Cheryl Suzanne
Pahz, Cheryl Suzanne 1949- *11*
Pahz, James Alon 1943- *11*
Paice, Margaret 1920- *10*
Paige, Harry W(orthington) 1922- *41*
  Brief entry *35*
Paige, Richard
  See Koontz, Dean

Paige, Robin
  See Albert, Susan Wittig
Paillot, Jim *230*
Paine, Penelope Colville 1946- *87*
Paine, Roberta M. 1925- *13*
Paisley, Tom 1932- *11*
  See also CLR *3*
Pal, Erika *239*
Palatini, Margie *207*
  Earlier sketches in SATA *134, 174*
Palazzo, Anthony D.
  See Palazzo, Tony
Palazzo, Tony 1905-1970 .... *3*
Palder, Edward L. 1922- *5*
Palecek, Josef 1932- *56*
Palecek, Libuse 1937- *89*
Palen, Debbie *195*
Palin, Michael 1943- *67*
Palin, Michael Edward
  See Palin, Michael
Palladini, David (Mario) 1946- *40*
  Brief entry *32*
Pallas, Norvin 1918-1983 .... *23*
Pallister, John C(lare) 1891-1980
  Obituary *26*
Pallotta, Gerard Larry
  See Pallotta, Jerry
Pallotta, Jerry 1953- *186*
Pallotta-Chiarolli, Maria 1960- *117*
Palmer, Bernard (Alvin) 1914-1998 .... *26*
Palmer, C. Everard 1930- *14*
Palmer, (Ruth) Candida 1926- *11*
Palmer, Cyril Everard
  See Palmer, C. Everard
Palmer, Don
  See Benson, Mildred
Palmer, Gary 1968- *231*
Palmer, Hap 1942- *68*
Palmer, Heidi 1948- *15*
Palmer, Helen Marion
  See Geisel, Helen
Palmer, Jessica 1953- *120*
Palmer, Judd 1972- *153*
Palmer, Juliette 1930- *15*
Palmer, Kate Salley 1946- *97*
Palmer, Maria
  See Strachan, Ian
Palmer, Maria
  See Brennan, Herbie
Palmer, Robin 1909-2000 .... *43*
Palmer, Robin 1969- *232*
Palmero Caceres, Ana *198*
Palmisciano, Diane *202*
Paltrowitz, Donna 1950- *61*
  Brief entry *50*
Paltrowitz, Donna Milman
  See Paltrowitz, Donna
Paltrowitz, Stuart 1946- *61*
  Brief entry *50*
Pamela, Todd 1950- *124*
Pamintuan, Macky *214*
  Earlier sketch in SATA *178*
Panagopoulos, Janie Lynn *149*
Panati, Charles 1943- *65*
Panchyk, Richard 1970- *138*
Panetta, George 1915-1969 .... *15*
Panetta, Joseph N. 1953- *96*
Pang, YaWen Ariel *206*
Panik, Sharon 1952- *82*
Panowski, Eileen Thompson 1920- *49*
Pansy
  See Alden, Isabella (Macdonald)
Pantell, Dora (Fuchs) *39*
Panter, Carol 1936- *9*
Paolini, Christopher 1983- *157*
  See also CLR *102*
Papademetriou, Lisa *175*
Paparone, Pam *185*
Paparone, Pamela
  See Paparone, Pam

Papas, Bill
  See Papas, William
Papas, William 1927-2000 .... *50*
Papashvily, George 1898-1978 .... *17*
Papashvily, Helen (Waite) 1906-1996 .... *17*
Pape, D. L.
  See Pape, Donna (Lugg)
Pape, Donna (Lugg) 1930- *82*
  Earlier sketch in SATA *2*
Paperny, Myra (Green) 1932- *51*
  Brief entry *33*
Papineau, Lucie 1962- *224*
Papp, Robert 1967- *205*
Paradis, Adrian A(lexis) 1912- *67*
  Earlier sketch in SATA *1*
  See also SAAS *8*
Paradis, Marjorie Bartholomew
  1886(?)-1970 .... *17*
Paradiz, Valerie 1963- *176*
Paratore, Coleen
  See Paratore, Coleen Murtagh
Paratore, Coleen Murtagh 1958- *200*
Pardo DeLange, Alex *211*
Parenteau, Shirley 1935- *199*
  Brief entry *40*
  Earlier sketch in SATA *47*
Parish, Margaret 1927-1988 .... *73*
  Obituary *59*
  Earlier sketch in SATA *17*
  See also CLR *22*
Parish, Margaret Holt
  See Holt, Margaret
Parish, Peggy
  See Parish, Margaret
Park, Barbara 1947- *123*
  Brief entry *35*
  Earlier sketches in SATA *40, 78*
  See also CLR *34*
Park, Bill
  See Park, W(illiam) B(ryan)
Park, Frances 1955- *171*
Park, Ginger *173*
Park, Janie Jaehyun *150*
Park, Jordan
  See Kornbluth, C(yril) M.
  and Pohl, Frederik
Park, Linda Sue 1960- *200*
  Earlier sketches in SATA *127, 173*
  See also CLR *84*
Park, Nick 1958- *113*
Park, Rosina Ruth Lucia
  See Park, Ruth
Park, Ruth 1917(?)-2010 .... *93*
  Earlier sketch in SATA *25*
  See also CLR *51*
Park, W(illiam) B(ryan) 1936- *22*
Parke, Marilyn 1928- *82*
Parker, Barbara Keevil 1938- *157*
Parker, Daniel
  See Ehrenhaft, Daniel
Parker, Elinor Milnor 1906- *3*
Parker, Jake 1977- *227*
Parker, Julie F. 1961- *92*
Parker, Kim 1963- *174*
Parker, Kristy 1957- *59*
Parker, Lois M(ay) 1912-1996 .... *30*
Parker, Margot M. 1937- *52*
Parker, Marjorie Blain 1960- *205*
  Earlier sketch in SATA *145*
Parker, Mary Jessie 1948- *71*
Parker, Nancy Winslow 1930- *132*
  Earlier sketches in SATA *10, 69*
  See also SAAS *20*
Parker, Richard 1915-1990 .... *14*
Parker, Robert
  See Boyd, Waldo T.
  and Parker, Robert Andrew
Parker, Robert Andrew 1927- *200*
Parker, Steve 1954- *213*
Parker, Tom S. *215*

Parker, Toni Trent 1947-2005 .... *142*
  Obituary *169*
Parker-Rees, Guy *193*
Parker-Rock, Michelle *214*
Parkes, Lucas
  See Harris, John (Wyndham Parkes Lucas) Beynon
Parkhill, John
  See Cox, William R(obert)
Parkins, David 1955- *218*
  Earlier sketch in SATA *176*
Parkinson, Curtis *219*
Parkinson, Ethelyn M(inerva) 1906-1999 ..... *11*
Parkinson, Kathryn N. 1954- *71*
Parkinson, Kathy
  See Parkinson, Kathryn N.
Parkinson, Siobhan
  See Parkinson, Siobhan
Parkinson, Siobhan 1954- *178*
Parks, Deborah A. 1948- *133*
  Earlier sketch in SATA *91*
Parks, Edd Winfield 1906-1968 .... *10*
Parks, Gordon 1912-2006 .... *108*
  Obituary *175*
  Earlier sketch in SATA *8*
Parks, Gordon Roger Alexander
  See Parks, Gordon
Parks, Peggy J. 1951- *143*
Parks, PJ
  See Parks, Peggy J.
Parks, Rosa 1913-2005 .... *83*
  Obituary *169*
Parks, Rosa Louise Lee
  See Parks, Rosa
Parks, Van Dyke 1943- *62*
Parlato, Stephen 1954- *222*
Parley, Peter
  See Goodrich, Samuel Griswold
Parlin, John
  See Graves, Charles Parlin
Parme, Fabrice 1966- *191*
Parnall, Peter 1936- *69*
  Earlier sketch in SATA *16*
  See also SAAS *11*
Paros, Jennifer *210*
Parotti, Phillip (Elliott) 1941- *109*
Parr, Ann 1943- *144*
Parr, Danny
  See Parr, Ann
Parr, Letitia (Evelyn) 1906-1985(?) *37*
Parr, Lucy 1924- *10*
Parr, Todd *179*
  Earlier sketch in SATA *134*
Parra, John 1972- *225*
Parrish, Anne 1888-1957 .... *27*
Parrish, Mary
  See Cousins, Margaret
Parrish, Maxfield
  See Parrish, (Frederick) Maxfield
Parrish, (Frederick) Maxfield 1870-1966 ..... *14*
Parry, Marian 1924- *13*
Parry, Rosanne *212*
Parson Lot
  See Kingsley, Charles
Parsons, Alexandra 1947- *92*
Parsons, Ellen
  See Dragonwagon, Crescent
Parsons, Garry *197*
Parsons, Martin 1951- *116*
Parsons, Martin Leslie
  See Parsons, Martin
Parsons, Tom
  See MacPherson, Thomas George
Parsons-Yazzi, Evangeline *172*
Partch, Virgil Franklin II 1916-1984 .... *39*
  Obituary *39*
Parton, Dolly 1946- *94*
Parton, Dolly Rebecca
  See Parton, Dolly
Partridge, Benjamin W., Jr. 1915-2005 .... *28*
  Obituary *163*

Partridge, Benjamin Waring, Jr.
  See Partridge, Benjamin W., Jr.
Partridge, Cora Cheney
  See Cheney, Cora
Partridge, Elizabeth *216*
  Earlier sketch in SATA *134*
Partridge, Jenny (Lilian) 1947- *52*
  Brief entry *37*
Pasachoff, Naomi 1947- *147*
Pascal, David 1918- *14*
Pascal, Francine 1938- *143*
  Brief entry *37*
  Earlier sketches in SATA *51, 80*
  See also CLR *25*
Paschal, Nancy
  See Trotter, Grace V(iolet)
Paschkis, Julie 1957- *220*
  Earlier sketch in SATA *177*
Pascudniak, Pascal
  See Lupoff, Richard A.
Pashko, Stanley 1913-1982 .... *29*
Pasqualotto, Chiara 1976- *228*
Passailaigue, Thomas E.
  See Paisley, Tom
Pastel, Elyse *201*
Pateman, Robert 1954- *84*
Patent, Dorothy Hinshaw 1940- *162*
  Autobiography Feature *162*
  Earlier sketches in SATA *22, 69, 120*
  See also CLR *19*
  See also SAAS *13*
Paterson, A(ndrew) B(arton) 1864-1941 .... *97*
Paterson, Banjo
  See Paterson, A(ndrew) B(arton)
Paterson, Diane 1946- *177*
  Brief entry *33*
  Earlier sketch in SATA *59*
Paterson, John (Barstow) 1932- *114*
Paterson, Katherine 1932- *204*
  Earlier sketches in SATA *13, 53, 92, 133*
  See also CLR *127*
Paterson, Katherine Womeldorf
  See Paterson, Katherine
Patience, John 1949- *90*
Patneaude, David 1944- *233*
  Earlier sketches in SATA *85, 159*
Paton, Alan 1903-1988 .... *11*
  Obituary *56*
Paton, Alan Stewart
  See Paton, Alan
Paton, Jane (Elizabeth) 1934- *35*
Paton, Priscilla 1952- *98*
Paton Walsh, Gillian
  See Paton Walsh, Jill
Paton Walsh, Jill 1937- *190*
  Autobiography Feature *190*
  Earlier sketches in SATA *4, 72, 109*
  See also CLR *128*
  See also SAAS *3*
Patricelli, Leslie *236*
  Earlier sketch in SATA *207*
Patrick, Susan
  See Robins, Patricia
Patron, Susan 1948- *182*
  Earlier sketch in SATA *76*
Patsauq, Markoosie 1942-
  See CLR *23*
Patschke, Steve 1955- *125*
Patt, Beverly *231*
Patten, Brian 1946- *152*
  Earlier sketch in SATA *29*
Patterson, Charles 1935- *59*
Patterson, Geoffrey 1943- *54*
  Brief entry *44*
Patterson, James 1947- *234*
  Earlier sketches in SATA *164, 197*
Patterson, James B.
  See Patterson, James
Patterson, Lillie G. -1999 .... *88*
  Earlier sketch in SATA *14*

Patterson, Nancy Ruth 1944- *148*
  Earlier sketch in SATA *72*
Patterson, Valerie O. *223*
Pattison, Darcy (S.) 1954- *126*
  Earlier sketch in SATA *72*
Pattou, Edith *164*
Patz (Blaustein), Nancy *154*
Paul, Aileen 1917- *12*
Paul, Alison *196*
Paul, Ann Whitford 1941- *209*
  Earlier sketches in SATA *76, 110, 168*
Paul, Chris 1985- *224*
Paul, David (Tyler) 1934-1988
  Obituary *56*
Paul, Dominique 1973- *184*
Paul, Elizabeth
  See Crow, Donna Fletcher
Paul, Hamish Vigne Christie 1951- *151*
  See also CLR *87*
Paul, James 1936- *23*
Paul, Korky
  See Paul, Hamish Vigne Christie
Paul, Robert
  See Roberts, John G(aither)
Paul, Tessa 1944- *103*
Pauley, Kimberly 1973- *208*
Pauli, Hertha (Ernestine) 1909-1973 .... *3*
  Obituary *26*
Paull, Grace A. 1898- *24*
Paulsen, Gary 1939- *231*
  Earlier sketches in SATA *22, 50, 54, 79, 111, 158, 189*
  See also CLR *82*
Paulson, Jack
  See Jackson, C(aary) Paul
Pauquet, Gina Ruck
  See Ruck-Pauquet, Gina
Pausacker, Jenny 1948- *72*
  See also SAAS *23*
Pausewang, Gudrun 1928- *165*
  Earlier sketch in SATA *104*
Pavel, Frances 1907- *10*
Paver, Michelle *215*
  Earlier sketch in SATA *170*
Paxton
  See Barr, Nevada
Paxton, Thomas R. 1937- *70*
Paxton, Tom
  See Paxton, Thomas R.
Paye, Won-Ldy *185*
Payne, Alan
  See Jakes, John
Payne, Bernal C., Jr. 1941- *60*
Payne, C. Douglas
  See Payne, C.D.
Payne, C.D. 1949- *133*
Payne, C.F. 1956- *179*
Payne, Chris Fox
  See Payne, C.F.
Payne, Donald Gordon 1924- *37*
Payne, Emmy
  See West, Emily Govan
Payne, Nina *135*
Payne, Rachel Ann
  See Jakes, John
Payson, Dale 1943- *9*
Payzant, Charles *18*
Paz, A.
  See Pahz, James Alon
Paz, Natalia Toledo
  See Toledo, Natalia
Paz, Zan
  See Pahz, Cheryl Suzanne
Peace, Mary
  See Finley, Mary Peace
Peacock, Louise *210*
Peacock, Phyllis Hornung 1977- *230*
Peacock, Shane 1957- *192*
Peake, Mervyn 1911-1968 .... *23*
Peale, Norman Vincent 1898-1993 .... *20*
  Obituary *78*

Pearce, Ann Philippa
  See Pearce, Philippa
Pearce, Carl 229
Pearce, Emily Smith 1975- 199
Pearce, Jackson 1984- 235
Pearce, Jacqueline 1962- 146
Pearce, Margaret 104
Pearce, Philippa 1920-2006 129
  Obituary 179
  Earlier sketches in SATA *1, 67*
  See also CLR *9*
Peare, Catherine Owens 1911- 9
Pearle, Ida 207
Pearsall, Shelley 1966- 190
Pearson, Gayle 1947- 119
  Earlier sketch in SATA *53*
Pearson, Jean Mary
  See Gardam, Jane
Pearson, Kit 1947- 77
  Autobiography Feature 117
  See also CLR *26*
Pearson, Mary E. 1955- 211
  Earlier sketch in SATA *134*
Pearson, Michael Parker
  See Pearson, Mike Parker
Pearson, Mike Parker 1957- 228
Pearson, Ridley 1953- 182
Pearson, Susan 1946- 166
  Brief entry 27
  Earlier sketches in SATA *39, 91*
Pearson, Tracey Campbell 1956- 219
  Earlier sketches in SATA *64, 155*
Pease, (Clarence) Howard 1894-1974 2
  Obituary 25
Peavy, Linda 1943- 54
Peck, Anne Merriman 1884-1976 18
Peck, Beth 1957- 190
  Earlier sketch in SATA *79*
Peck, Jan 159
Peck, Jeanie J. 1967- 147
Peck, Marshall III 1951- 92
Peck, Richard 1934- 228
  Autobiography Feature 110
  Earlier sketches in SATA *18, 55, 97, 110, 158,*
  190
  See also CLR *142*
  See also SAAS *2*
Peck, Richard Wayne
  See Peck, Richard
Peck, Robert Newton 1928- 156
  Autobiography Feature 108
  Earlier sketches in SATA *21, 62, 111*
  See also CLR *163*
  See also SAAS *1*
Peck, Sylvia 1953- 133
Peck-Whiting, Jeanie J.
  See Peck, Jeanie J.
Peddicord, Jane Ann 199
Pedersen, Janet 193
Pederson, Sharleen
  See Collicott, Sharleen
Pedler, Caroline 197
Peebles, Anne
  See Galloway, Priscilla
Peek, Merle 1938- 39
Peel, John 1954- 79
Peel, Norman Lemon
  See Hirsch, Phil
Peeples, Edwin A(ugustus, Jr.) 1915-1994 6
Peers, Judi 1956- 119
Peers, Judith May West
  See Peers, Judi
Peet, Bill
  See Peet, William Bartlett
Peet, Creighton B. 1899-1977 30
Peet, Mal 227
  Earlier sketch in SATA *171*
Peet, Malcolm
  See Peet, Mal

Peet, William Bartlett 1915-2002 78
  Obituary 137
  Earlier sketches in SATA *2, 41*
  See also CLR *12*
Peete, Holly Robinson 1964- 229
Peguero, Leone 116
Peirce, Lincoln 232
Pelaez, Jill 1924- 12
Pelham, David 1938- 70
Pelikan, Judy 1941- 219
Pell, Ed(ward) 1950- 157
Pelletier, Andrew T. 195
Pelletier, Andrew Thomas
  See Pelletier, Andrew T.
Pellowski, Anne 1933- 20
Pellowski, Michael (Joseph) 1949- 151
  Brief entry 48
  Earlier sketch in SATA *88*
Pellowski, Michael Morgan
  See Pellowski, Michael (Joseph)
Pelta, Kathy 1928- 18
Peltier, Leslie C(opus) 1900-1980 13
Pemberton, Bonnie 191
Pemberton, John Leigh
  See Leigh-Pemberton, John
Pembury, Bill
  See Groom, Arthur William
Pemsteen, Hans
  See Manes, Stephen
Pendennis, Arthur Esquir
  See Thackeray, William Makepeace
Pender, Lydia Podger 1907- 61
Pendery, Rosemary (Schmitz) 7
Pendle, Alexy 1943- 29
Pendle, George 1906-1977
  Obituary 28
Pendleton, Don
  See Cunningham, Chet
  and Garside, Jack
  and Jagninski, Tom
  and Krauzer, Steven M(ark)
  and Obstfeld, Raymond
Pendleton, Thomas 1965- 206
Pendziwol, Jean E. 1965- 177
Pene du Bois, William (Sherman)
  1916-1993 68
  Obituary 74
  Earlier sketch in SATA *4*
  See also CLR *1*
Penn, Audrey 1947- 212
Penn, Audrey 1950- 22
Penn, Ruth Bonn
  See Rosenberg, Eth Clifford
Pennac, Daniel 1944- 155
Pennage, E. M.
  See Finkel, George (Irvine)
Penner, Fred 1946- 169
  Earlier sketch in SATA *67*
Penner, Frederick Ralph Cornelius
  See Penner, Fred
Penner, Lucille Recht 1942- 226
Penney, Grace Jackson 1904-2000 35
Penney, Ian 1960- 76
Penney, Sue 1957- 152
  Earlier sketch in SATA *102*
Pennington, Eunice 1923- 27
Pennington, Lillian Boyer 1904-2003 45
Pennypacker, Sara 1951- 187
Penrose, Gordon 1925- 66
Penson, Mary E. 1917- 78
Penzler, Otto 1942- 38
Pepe, Phil 1935- 20
Pepe, Philip
  See Pepe, Phil
Peppe, Rodney (Darrell) 1934- 74
  Earlier sketch in SATA *4*
  See also SAAS *10*
Pepper, Frank S. 1910-1988
  Obituary 61
Percy, Charles Henry
  See Smith, Dorothy Gladys

Percy, Rachel 1930- 63
Perdomo, Willie 228
Perdrizet, Marie-Pierre 1952- 79
Perenyi, Constance 1954- 93
Perenyi, Constance Marie
  See Perenyi, Constance
Perera, Hilda 1926- 105
Perera, Thomas Biddle 1938- 13
Peretti, Frank E. 1951- 141
  Earlier sketch in SATA *80*
Perez, L. King 1940- 199
Perez, Lana
  See Perez, Marlene
Perez, Lucia Angela 1973- 182
Perez, Marlene 170
Pericoli, Matteo 1968- 178
Perkins, Al(bert Rogers) 1904-1975 30
Perkins, Dan
  See Tomorrow, Tom
Perkins, Lucy Fitch 1865-1937 72
Perkins, Lynne Rae 1956- 212
  Earlier sketches in SATA *131, 172*
Perkins, (Richard) Marlin 1905-1986 21
  Obituary 48
Perkins, Mitali 1963- 237
  Earlier sketches in SATA *88, 188*
Perks, Anne-Marie 1955- 122
Perl, Erica S. 222
  Earlier sketch in SATA *188*
Perl, Lila 72
  Earlier sketch in SATA *6*
Perl, Susan 1922-1983 22
  Obituary 34
Perlman, Janet 1954- 222
Perlman, Rhea 1948- 183
Perlmutter, O(scar) William 1920-1975 8
Pernu, Dennis 1970- 87
Perrault, Charles 1628-1703 25
  See also CLR *134*
Perret, Delphine 1980- 190
Perret, Gene (Richard) 1937- 76
Perriman, Cole
  See Perrin, Pat
Perriman, Cole
  See Coleman, Wim
  and Perrin, Pat
Perrin, Pat 212
Perrine, Mary 1913-1976 2
Perrins, Lesley 1953- 56
Perro
  See Perro, Bryan
Perro, Bryan 1968- 239
Perrow, Angeli 1954- 121
Perry, Andrea 1956- 190
  Earlier sketch in SATA *148*
Perry, Barbara Fisher
  See Fisher, Barbara
Perry, Elizabeth 1959- 174
Perry, Elizabeth Goodwin
  See Perry, Elizabeth
Perry, John 1967- 223
Perry, M. LaVora 232
Perry, Marie Fritz 165
Perry, Patricia 1949- 30
Perry, Phyllis J(ean) 1933- 152
  Earlier sketches in SATA *60, 101*
Perry, Ritchie (John Allen) 1942- 105
Perry, Roger 1933- 27
Perry, Steve(n Carl) 1947- 76
Pershall, Mary K. 1951- 172
  Earlier sketch in SATA *70*
Pershing, Marie
  See Schultz, Pearle Henriksen
Perske, Robert 1927- 57
Persun, Morgan Reed
  See Watkins, Dawn L.
Perversi, Margaret 213
Petach, Heidi 149
Peter
  See Stratemeyer, Edward L.

Peters, Alexander
  See Hollander, Zander
Peters, Andrew Fusek 1965- 169
  Earlier sketch in SATA 107
Peters, Bernadette 1948- 212
Peters, Caroline
  See Betz, Eva Kelly
Peters, David
  See David, Peter
Peters, Elizabeth 1927- 49
Peters, Emma
  See Price, Karen
Peters, Gabriel
  See Matott, Justin
Peters, Julie Anne 1952- 197
  Earlier sketches in SATA 82, 128
Peters, Linda
  See Catherall, Arthur
Peters, Lisa Westberg 1951- 232
  Earlier sketches in SATA 74, 115, 161
Peters, Patricia 1953- 84
Peters, Russell M. 1929- 78
Peters, S. H.
  See Henry, O.
  and Proffitt, Nicholas
Peters, Stephanie True 1965- 224
Petersen, David 1946- 109
  Earlier sketch in SATA 62
Petersen, Gwenn Boardman 1924- 12
Petersen, P(eter) J(ames) 1941- 118
  Brief entry 43
  Earlier sketches in SATA 48, 83
Petersen, Palle 1943- 85
Petersham, Maud 1890-1971 17
  See also CLR 24
Petersham, Maud Sylvia Fuller
  See Petersham, Maud
Petersham, Miska 1888-1960 17
  See also CLR 24
Peterson, Cris 1952- 174
  Earlier sketches in SATA 84, 145
Peterson, Dawn 1934- 86
Peterson, Esther (Allen) 1934- 35
Peterson, Hans 1922- 8
Peterson, Harold L(eslie) 1922-1978 8
Peterson, Helen Stone 1910- 8
Peterson, Jean Sunde 1941- 108
Peterson, Jeanne Whitehouse 1939- 159
  Earlier sketch in SATA 29
Peterson, John 1924-2002 233
Peterson, Kathleen B. 1951- 119
Peterson, Lorraine 1940- 56
  Brief entry 44
Peterson, Mary 215
Peterson, Shelley 1952- 146
Peterson, Will
  See Cocks, Peter
Petie, Haris
  See Petty, Roberta
Petricic, Dusan 1946- 176
Petrides, Heidrun 1944- 19
Petrie, Catherine 1947- 52
  Brief entry 41
Petrone, Valeria 233
  Earlier sketch in SATA 186
Petrosino, Tamara 193
Petroski, Catherine (Ann Groom) 1939- 48
Petrovich, Michael B(oro) 1922- 40
Petrovskaya, Kyra
  See Wayne, Kyra Petrovskaya
Petruccio, Steven James 1961- 67
Petrucha, Stefan 1959- 213
Petry, Ann 1908-1997 5
  Obituary 94
  See also CLR 12
Petry, Ann Lane
  See Petry, Ann
Pettit, Jayne 1932- 108
Petty, J.T. 1977- 189
Petty, Kate 1951-2007 204
Petty, Roberta 1915- 10

Pevsner, Stella 131
  Earlier sketches in SATA 8, 77
  See also SAAS 14
Peyo
  See Culliford, Pierre
Peyton, K. M.
  See Peyton, Kathleen Wendy
Peyton, Kathleen Wendy 1929- 157
  Earlier sketches in SATA 15, 62
  See also CLR 3
  See also SAAS 17
Pfanner, (Anne) Louise 1955- 68
Pfeffer, Susan Beth 1948- 180
  Earlier sketches in SATA 4, 83
  See also CLR 11
  See also SAAS 17
Pfeffer, Wendy 1929- 204
  Earlier sketches in SATA 78, 142
Pfeiffer, Janet (B.) 1949- 96
Pfister, Marcus 207
  Earlier sketches in SATA 83, 150
  See also CLR 42
Pfitsch, Patricia Curtis 1948- 148
Pfitzenmaier, Audrey 1959- 220
Pflieger, Pat 1955- 84
Pham, LeUyen 1973- 237
  Earlier sketches in SATA 175, 201
Phelan, Mary Kay 1914- 3
Phelan, Matt 1970- 215
  Earlier sketch in SATA 172
Phelan, Terry Wolfe 1941- 56
Phelps, Ethel Johnston 1914-1984 35
Philbrick, Rodman 1951- 163
Philbrick, W. Rodman
  See Philbrick, Rodman
Philbrick, W.R.
  See Philbrick, Rodman
Philbrook, Clem(ent E.) 1917- 24
Phillipps, J.C. 218
Phillipps, Julie Christine
  See Phillipps, J.C.
Phillips, Aileen Paul
  See Paul, Aileen
Phillips, Betty Lou
  See Phillips, Elizabeth Louise
Phillips, Bob 1940- 95
Phillips, Douglas A. 1949- 161
Phillips, Elizabeth Louise 58
  Brief entry 48
Phillips, Gary R. 225
Phillips, Irv(ing W.) 1905-2000 11
  Obituary 125
Phillips, Jack
  See Sandburg, Carl
Phillips, Leon
  See Gerson, Noel Bertram
Phillips, Loretta (Hosey) 1893-1987 10
Phillips, Louis 1942- 102
  Earlier sketch in SATA 8
Phillips, Mark
  See Garrett, Randall
  and Janifer, Laurence M(ark)
Phillips, Mary Geisler 1881-1964 10
Phillips, Michael
  See Nolan, William F.
Phillips, (Woodward) Prentice 1894-1981 10
Phillpotts, Eden 1862-1960 24
Phin
  See Thayer, Ernest Lawrence
Phipson, Joan
  See Fitzhardinge, Joan Margaret
Phiz
  See Browne, Hablot Knight
Phleger, Fred B. 1909-1993 34
Phleger, Marjorie Temple 1908(?)-1986 1
  Obituary 47
Piaget, Jean 1896-1980
  Obituary 23
Piatti, Celestino 1922- 16

Picard, Barbara Leonie 1917- 89
  Earlier sketch in SATA 2
  See also SAAS 10
Pichon, Liz 174
Pickard, Charles 1932- 36
Pickering, James Sayre 1897-1969 36
  Obituary 28
Pickering, Jimmy 195
Pickering, Robert B. 1950- 93
Pielichaty, Helena 1955- 142
Pien, Lark 222
Pienkowski, Jan (Michal) 1936- 131
  Earlier sketches in SATA 6, 58
  See also CLR 6
Pierce, Edith Gray 1893-1977 45
Pierce, Katherine
  See St. John, Wylly Folk
Pierce, Meredith Ann 1958- 127
  Brief entry 48
  Earlier sketch in SATA 67
  See also CLR 20
Pierce, Ruth (Ireland) 1936- 5
Pierce, Sharon
  See McCullough, Sharon Pierce
Pierce, Tamora 1954- 187
  Brief entry 49
  Earlier sketches in SATA 51, 96, 153
Pierce, Terry 178
Pierik, Robert 1921- 13
Piernas-Davenport, Gail 199
Piers, Robert
  See Anthony, Piers
Pig, Edward
  See Gorey, Edward (St. John)
Pignataro, Anna 1965- 223
Pike, Aprilynne 218
Pike, Bob
  See Pike, Robert W.
Pike, Christopher 1954(?)- 239
  Earlier sketches in SATA 68, 156
  See also CLR 29
Pike, Deborah 1951- 89
Pike, E(dgar) Royston 1896-1980 22
  Obituary 56
Pike, R. William 1956- 92
Pike, Robert
  See Pike, Robert W.
Pike, Robert W. 1931- 102
Pike, Robert Wilson
  See Pike, Robert W.
Pilarski, Laura 1926- 13
Pilgrim, Anne
  See Allan, Mabel Esther
Pilkey, Dav 1966- 166
  Earlier sketches in SATA 68, 115
  See also CLR 160
Pilkey, David Murray, Jr.
  See Pilkey, Dav
Pilkington, Francis Meredyth 1907-1993 4
Pilkington, Roger (Windle) 1915-2003 10
  Obituary 144
Pilutti, Deb 208
Pin, Isabel 1975- 183
Pinchot, David 1914(?)-1983
  Obituary 34
Pincus, Harriet 1938- 27
Pinczes, Elinor J(ane) 1940- 81
Pine, Nicholas 1951- 91
Pine, Tillie S(chloss) 1896-1999 13
Pini, Richard (Alan) 1950- 89
Pini, Wendy 1951- 89
Pinkerton, Kathrene Sutherland (Gedney)
  1887-1967
  Obituary 26
Pinkett, Jada
  See Smith, Jada Pinkett
Pinkney, Andrea Davis 1963- 160
  Earlier sketch in SATA 113
Pinkney, Brian 1961- 206
  Earlier sketches in SATA 74, 148
  See also CLR 54

Pinkney, Gloria Jean 1941- *212*
    Earlier sketch in SATA *85*
Pinkney, J. Brian
    See Pinkney, Brian
Pinkney, Jerry 1939- *198*
    Autobiography Feature *198*
    Brief entry *32*
    Earlier sketches in SATA *41, 71, 107, 151*
    See also CLR *43*
    See also SAAS *12*
Pinkney, John *97*
Pinkney, Sandra L. *193*
    Earlier sketch in SATA *128*
Pinkwater, D. Manus
    See Pinkwater, Daniel
Pinkwater, Daniel 1941- *210*
    Earlier sketches in SATA *8, 46, 76, 114, 158*
    See also CLR *4*
    See also SAAS *3*
Pinkwater, Daniel M.
    See Pinkwater, Daniel
Pinkwater, Daniel Manus
    See Pinkwater, Daniel
Pinkwater, Jill *188*
Pinkwater, Manus
    See Pinkwater, Daniel
Pinner, Joma
    See Werner, Herma
Pinto, Sara *200*
Pioneer
    See Yates, Raymond F(rancis)
Piowaty, Kim Kennelly 1957- *49*
Piper, Roger
    See Fisher, John
Pirner, Connie White 1955- *72*
Piro, Richard 1934- *7*
Pirot, Alison Lohans
    See Lohans, Alison
Pirotta, Saviour *184*
Pirsig, Robert M(aynard) 1928- *39*
Pita
    See Rendon, Maria
Pitcher, C.
    See Pitcher, Caroline
Pitcher, Caroline 1948- *214*
    Earlier sketch in SATA *128*
Pitcher, Caroline Nell
    See Pitcher, Caroline
Pitman, (Isaac) James 1901-1985
    Obituary *46*
Pitre, Felix 1949- *84*
Pitrone, Jean Maddern 1920- *4*
Pittman, Helena Clare 1945- *71*
Pitz, Henry C(larence) 1895-1976 .... *4*
    Obituary *24*
Pitzer, Susanna 1958- *181*
Piven, Hanoch 1963- *236*
    Earlier sketch in SATA *173*
Pixley, Marcella *194*
Pizer, Vernon 1918- *21*
Place, Francois 1957- *234*
Place, Marian T(empleton) 1910- *3*
Place, Robin (Mary) 1926- *71*
Plaidy, Jean
    See Hibbert, Eleanor Alice Burford
Plain, Belva 1919-2010 .... *62*
Plaine, Alfred R. 1898(?)-1981
    Obituary *29*
Plant, Andrew *214*
Plath, Sylvia 1932-1963 .... *96*
Platt, Chris 1959- *185*
Platt, Kin 1911- *86*
    Earlier sketch in SATA *21*
    See also SAAS *17*
Platt, Randall 1948- *95*
Platt, Randall Beth
    See Platt, Randall
Platt, Richard 1953- *218*
    Earlier sketches in SATA *120, 166*
Playfellow, Robin
    See Ellis, Edward S.

Playsted, James
    See Wood, James Playsted
Plecas, Jennifer 1966- *229*
    Earlier sketches in SATA *84, 149*
Plimpton, George 1927-2003 .... *10*
    Obituary *150*
Plimpton, George Ames
    See Plimpton, George
Plomer, William Charles Franklin
    1903-1973 .... *24*
Plotz, Helen Ratnoff 1913-2000 .... *38*
Plourde, Lynn 1955- *218*
    Earlier sketches in SATA *122, 168*
Plowden, David 1932- *52*
Plowden, Martha Ward 1948- *98*
Plowhead, Ruth Gipson 1877-1967 .... *43*
Plowman, Stephanie 1922- *6*
Pluckrose, Henry 1931-2011 .... *141*
    Earlier sketch in SATA *13*
Pluckrose, Henry Arthur
    See Pluckrose, Henry
Plum, J.
    See Wodehouse, P. G.
Plum, Jennifer
    See Kurland, Michael
Plumb, Charles P. 1900(?)-1982
    Obituary *29*
Plume, Ilse *170*
    Brief entry *43*
Plumme, Don E.
    See Katz, Bobbi
Plummer, Margaret 1911- *2*
Plum-Ucci, Carol 1957- *184*
Poblocki, Dan 1981- *224*
Pochocki, Ethel (Frances) 1925- *76*
Podendorf, Illa (E.) 1903(?)-1983 .... *18*
    Obituary *35*
Podwal, Mark 1945- *224*
    Earlier sketches in SATA *101, 160*
Podwal, Mark H.
    See Podwal, Mark
Poe, Edgar Allan 1809-1849 .... *23*
Poe, Ty (Christopher) 1975- *94*
Pogany, William Andrew 1882-1955 .... *44*
    Brief entry *30*
Pogany, Willy
    See Pogany, William Andrew
Pogue, Carolyn 1948- *223*
Pogue, David 1963- *231*
Pohl, Frederik 1919- *24*
Pohlmann, Lillian (Grenfell) 1902-1997 .... *11*
Pohrt, Tom 1953- *195*
    Earlier sketches in SATA *67, 152*
Pointon, Robert
    See Rooke, Daphne
Points, Larry G. 1945- *177*
    Earlier sketch in SATA *133*
Points, Larry Gene
    See Points, Larry G.
Pokeberry, P.J.
    See Mitchell, B.J.
Pokiak-Fenton, Margaret *239*
POLA
    See Watson, Pauline
Polacco, Patricia 1944- *212*
    Earlier sketches in SATA *74, 123, 180*
    See also CLR *40*
Polacco, Patricia Ann
    See Polacco, Patricia
Polak, Monique 1960- *230*
    Earlier sketch in SATA *178*
Polatnick, Florence T. 1923- *5*
Polcovar, Jane 1948- *211*
Polder, Markus
    See Kruss, James
Polenghi, Evan 1961- *225*
Polese, Carolyn 1947- *58*
Polese, James 1914- *87*
Polette, Nancy (Jane) 1930- *42*
Polhamus, Jean Burt 1928- *21*
Polhemus, Coleman *210*

Policoff, Stephen Phillip 1948- *77*
Polikoff, Barbara G. 1929- *162*
    Earlier sketch in SATA *77*
Polikoff, Barbara Garland
    See Polikoff, Barbara G.
Polisar, Barry Louis 1954- *134*
    Earlier sketch in SATA *77*
Politi, Leo 1908-1996 .... *47*
    Obituary *88*
    Earlier sketch in SATA *1*
    See also CLR *29*
Polking, Kirk 1925- *5*
Pollack, Jill S. 1963- *88*
Pollack, Merrill S. 1924-1988
    Obituary *55*
Polland, Barbara K(ay) 1939- *44*
Polland, Madeleine A(ngela Cahill) 1918- ... *68*
    Earlier sketch in SATA *6*
    See also SAAS *8*
Pollema-Cahill, Phyllis 1958- *123*
Pollock, Bruce 1945- *46*
Pollock, Mary
    See Blyton, Enid
Pollock, Penny 1935- *137*
    Brief entry *42*
    Earlier sketch in SATA *44*
Pollowitz, Melinda Kilborn 1944- *26*
Polner, Murray 1928- *64*
Polonsky, Arthur 1925- *34*
Polseno, Jo *17*
Pomaska, Anna 1946- *117*
Pomerantz, Charlotte 1930- *177*
    Earlier sketches in SATA *20, 80*
Pomeroy, Pete
    See Roth, Arthur J(oseph)
Pon, Cindy 1973- *216*
Pon, Cynthia *229*
Pond, Alonzo W(illiam) 1894-1986 .... *5*
Pontiflet, Ted 1932- *32*
Poole, Gray Johnson 1906- *1*
Poole, Josephine
    See Helyar, Jane Penelope Josephine
Poole, (Jane Penelope) Josephine
    See Helyar, Jane Penelope Josephine
Poole, Lynn 1910-1969 .... *1*
Poole, Peggy 1925- *39*
Pooler, Paige *235*
Poon, Janice *228*
Poortvliet, Rien 1932- *65*
    Brief entry *37*
Pope, Elizabeth Marie 1917-1992 .... *38*
    Brief entry *36*
Pope, Kevin 1958- *183*
Popescu, Christine
    See Pullein-Thompson, Christine
Poploff, Michelle 1956- *67*
Popp, K. Wendy *91*
Poppel, Hans 1942- *71*
Porfirio, Guy 1958- *197*
Portal, Colette 1936- *6*
Porte, Barbara Ann 1943- *152*
    Brief entry *45*
    Earlier sketches in SATA *57, 93*
Porter, A(nthony) P(eyton) 1945- *68*
Porter, Connie (Rose) 1959(?)- *129*
    Earlier sketch in SATA *81*
Porter, Donald Clayton
    See Gerson, Noel Bertram
Porter, Eleanor H(odgman) 1868-1920
    See CLR *110*
Porter, Gene Stratton
    See Stratton-Porter, Gene
Porter, Janice Lee 1953- *108*
    Earlier sketch in SATA *68*
Porter, Katherine Anne 1890-1980 .... *39*
    Obituary *23*
Porter, Kathryn
    See Swinford, Betty (June Wells)
Porter, Pamela 1956- *193*
Porter, Sheena 1935- *24*
    See also SAAS *10*

Porter, Sue
   See Limb, Sue
Porter, Sue 1951- 213
   Earlier sketch in SATA 76
Porter, Tracey 191
Porter, William Sydney
   See Henry, O.
Portis, Antoinette 189
Porto, Tony 1960- 153
Portteus, Eleanora Marie Manthei (?)-1983
   Obituary 36
Posada, Mia 187
Posell, Elsa Z(eigerman) -1995 3
Posesorski, Sherie 216
Posten, Margaret L(ois) 1915- 10
Postgate, Daniel 1964- 216
Posthuma, Sieb 1960- 150
Postier, Jim 1965- 202
Potok, Chaim 1929-2002 106
   Obituary 134
   Earlier sketch in SATA 33
   See also CLR 92
Potok, Herbert Harold
   See Potok, Chaim
Potok, Herman Harold
   See Potok, Chaim
Potter, Alicia 216
Potter, Beatrix 1866-1943 132
   Earlier sketch in SATA 100
   See also YABC 1
   See also CLR 165
Potter, Ellen 1973- 218
Potter, Giselle 187
   Earlier sketch in SATA 150
Potter, Helen Beatrix
   See Potter, Beatrix
Potter, Katherine 217
Potter, Margaret 1926-1998 21
   Obituary 104
Potter, Marian 1915- 9
Potter, Miriam Clark 1886-1965 3
Potter, Ryan 230
Poulin, Stephane 1961- 98
   See also CLR 28
Poulton, Kimberly 1957(?)- 136
Pournelle, Jerry 1933- 161
   Earlier sketches in SATA 26, 91
Pournelle, Jerry Eugene
   See Pournelle, Jerry
Povelite, Kay 1955- 102
Pow, Tom 1950- 163
Powe-Allred, Alexandra
   See Allred, Alexandra Powe
Powell, A. M.
   See Morgan, Alfred P(owell)
Powell, Consie 174
Powell, E. Sandy 1947- 72
Powell, E.S.
   See Powell, E. Sandy
Powell, Pamela 1960- 78
Powell, Patricia Hruby 1951- 136
Powell, Randy 1956- 118
Powell, Richard Stillman
   See Barbour, Ralph Henry
Powell, Robert (Stephenson Smyth) Baden
   See Baden-Powell, Robert (Stephenson
   Smyth)
Powell, Stephanie 1953- 93
Power, Margaret (M.) 1945- 125
   Earlier sketch in SATA 75
Powers, Anne
   See Schwartz, Anne Powers
Powers, Bill 1931- 52
   Brief entry 31
Powers, Daniel 1959- 164
Powers, J. L. 195
Powers, Jessica
   See Powers, J. L.
Powers, Jessica Lynn
   See Powers, J. L.

Powers, Margaret
   See Heal, Edith
Powers, Tim 1952- 107
Powers, Timothy Thomas
   See Powers, Tim
Powledge, Fred 1935- 37
Poydar, Nancy 190
Poynter, Margaret 1927- 27
Prachaticka, Marketa
   See Kolibalova, Marketa
Prachatika, Marketa
   See Kolibalova, Marketa
Prager, Arthur 44
Prager, Ellen J. 1962- 136
Prange, Beckie 172
Prap, Lila 1955- 177
Praprotnik-Zupancic, Lilijana
   See Prap, Lila
Pratchett, Terence David John
   See Pratchett, Terry
Pratchett, Terry 1948- 185
   Earlier sketches in SATA 82, 139
   See also CLR 64
Prater, John 1947- 149
   Earlier sketches in SATA 72, 103
Prato, Rodica 184
Pratt, Christine Joy 214
Pratt, (Murray) Fletcher 1897-1956 102
Pratt, Kristin Joy 1976- 87
Pratt, Pierre 1962- 208
   Earlier sketches in SATA 95, 166
Preiss, Byron 1953-2005 166
   Brief entry 42
   Earlier sketch in SATA 47
Preiss, Byron Cary
   See Preiss, Byron
Preller, James 1961- 209
   Earlier sketch in SATA 88
Prelutsky, Jack 1940- 171
   Earlier sketches in SATA 22, 66, 118
   See also CLR 115
Prentice, Amy
   See Kaler, James Otis
Prescott, Casey
   See Morris, Chris(topher Crosby)
Presnall, Judith (Ann) Janda 1943- 96
Pressler, Mirjam 1940- 155
Preston, Douglas 1956- 113
Preston, Edna Mitchell 40
Preston, Lillian Elvira 1918- 47
Preus, Margi 209
Preussler, Otfried 1923- 24
Prevert, Jacques 1900-1977
   Obituary 30
Prevert, Jacques Henri Marie
   See Prevert, Jacques
Prevost, Guillaume 1964- 192
Prevost, Mikela 203
Price, Beverley Joan 1931- 98
Price, Charlie 237
   Earlier sketch in SATA 187
Price, Christine (Hilda) 1928-1980 3
   Obituary 23
Price, Garrett 1896-1979
   Obituary 22
Price, Jennifer
   See Hoover, Helen (Drusilla Blackburn)
Price, Joan 1931- 124
Price, Jonathan (Reeve) 1941- 46
Price, Karen 1957- 125
Price, Kathy Z. 1957- 172
Price, Lucie Locke
   See Locke, Lucie
Price, Olive 1903-1991 8
Price, Susan 1955- 128
   Earlier sketches in SATA 25, 85
Price, Willard 1887-1983 48
   Brief entry 38
Price-Groff, Claire 127
Priceman, Marjorie 1958- 234
   Earlier sketches in SATA 81, 120, 168

Prichard, Katharine Susannah 1883-1969 66
Priddy, Roger 227
Prideaux, Tom 1908-1993 37
   Obituary 76
Priestley, Alice 1962- 227
   Earlier sketch in SATA 95
Priestley, Chris 1958- 198
Priestley, Lee (Shore) 1904-1999 27
Priestly, Doug 1954- 122
Priestly, Douglas Michael
   See Priestly, Doug
Prieto, Mariana Beeching 1912-1999 8
Prigmore, Shane 1977- 234
Priley, Margaret (Ann) Hubbard 1909-1992
   Obituary 130
Primavera, Elise 1954- 230
   Brief entry 48
   Earlier sketches in SATA 58, 109, 185
Prime, Derek (James) 1931- 34
Prince, Alison (Mary) 1931- 86
   Earlier sketch in SATA 28
Prince, April Jones 1975- 180
Prince, J(ack) H(arvey) 1908- 17
Prince, Joshua 188
Prince, Maggie 102
Prineas, Sarah 204
Pringle, Eric 138
Pringle, Laurence 1935- 201
   Autobiography Feature 201
   Earlier sketches in SATA 4, 68, 104, 154
   See also CLR 57
   See also SAAS 6
Pringle, Laurence Patrick
   See Pringle, Laurence
Prinz, Yvonne 1960- 175
Prior, Natalie Jane 1963- 106
Pritchett, Elaine H(illyer) 1920- 36
Pritchett, Laura 1971- 178
Pritchett, Laura Rose
   See Pritchett, Laura
Pritts, Kim Derek 1953- 83
Prochazkova, Iva 1953- 68
Proctor, Everitt
   See Montgomery, Rutherford George
Proeysen, Alf 1914-1970 67
   See also CLR 24
Professor Scribbler
   See Hollingsworth, Mary
Proimos, James 1955- 217
   Earlier sketch in SATA 173
Promitzer, Rebecca 229
Prose, Francine 1947- 198
   Earlier sketches in SATA 101, 149
Prosek, James 1975- 216
Protopopescu, Orel 186
Protopopescu, Orel Odinov
   See Protopopescu, Orel
Provensen, Alice 1918- 147
   Earlier sketches in SATA 9, 70
   See also CLR 11
Provensen, Martin 1916-1987 70
   Obituary 51
   Earlier sketch in SATA 9
   See also CLR 11
Provensen, Martin Elias
   See Provensen, Martin
Provenzo, Eugene (F., Jr.) 1949- 142
   Earlier sketch in SATA 78
Provist, d'Alain 1906-1989
   See Diop, Birago (Ismael)
Provost, Gail Levine 1944- 65
Provost, Gary (Richard) 1944-1995 66
Proysen, Alf
   See Proeysen, Alf
Pruett, Candace (J.) 1968- 157
Pryor, Bonnie H. 1942- 69
Pryor, Boori (Monty) 1950- 112
Pryor, Helen Brenton 1897-1972 4
Pryor, Michael 1957- 153
Pucci, Albert John 1920- 44
Pudney, John (Sleigh) 1909-1977 24

Pugh, Ellen (Tiffany) 1920- 7
Pullein-Thompson, Christine 1925-2005 82
    Obituary 172
    Earlier sketch in SATA 3
Pullein-Thompson, Diana
    See Farr, Diana
Pullein-Thompson, Joanna Maxwell
    1898-1961 82
Pullein-Thompson, Josephine (Mary
    Wedderburn) 82
    Earlier sketch in SATA 3
Pullen, Zachary 189
Pullman, Philip 1946- 198
    Earlier sketches in SATA 65, 103, 150
    See also CLR 84
    See also SAAS 17
Pullman, Philip Nicholas
    See Pullman, Philip
Pulver, Harry, Jr. 1960- 129
Pulver, Robin 1945- 208
    Earlier sketches in SATA 76, 133
Puner, Helen W(alker) 1915-1989 37
    Obituary 63
Purdy, Carol 1943- 120
    Earlier sketch in SATA 66
Purdy, Susan G(old) 1939- 8
Purkiss, Diane 1961- 194
Purmell, Ann 1953- 206
    Earlier sketch in SATA 147
Purnell, Idella 1901-1982 120
Purscell, Phyllis 1934- 7
Purtill, Richard L. 1931- 53
Purvis, Leland 232
Pushker, Gloria 1927- 162
    Earlier sketch in SATA 75
Pushker, Gloria Teles
    See Pushker, Gloria
Pushkin, Aleksandr Sergeevich
    See Pushkin, Alexander
Pushkin, Alexander 1799-1837 61
Putnam, Alice 1916- 61
Putnam, Arthur Lee
    See Alger, Horatio, Jr.
Putnam, Peter B(rock) 1920-1998 30
    Obituary 106
Puttapipat, Niroot 199
Puttock, Simon 178
Puvilland, Alex 205
Puvilland, Alexandre
    See Puvilland, Alex
Puybaret, Eric 1976- 299
    Earlier sketch in SATA 195
Pyle, Charles S. 1954(?)- 229
Pyle, Chuck
    See Pyle, Charles S.
Pyle, Howard 1853-1911 100
    Earlier sketch in SATA 16
    See also CLR 117
Pyle, Katharine 1863-1938 66
Pyne, Mable Mandeville 1903-1969 9
Pyrnelle, Louise-Clarke 1850-1907 114

                            Q

Quackenbush, Robert M(ead) 1929- 133
    Autobiography Feature 133
    Earlier sketches in SATA 7, 70
    See also CLR 122
    See also SAAS 7
Qualey, Marsha 1953- 124
    Earlier sketch in SATA 79
Qualls, Sean 233
    Earlier sketch in SATA 177
Quammen, David 1948- 7
Quark, Jason
    See Eldin, Peter
Quarles, Benjamin 1904-1996 12
Quarles, Benjamin Arthur
    See Quarles, Benjamin

Quatermass, Martin
    See Carpenter, John
Quattlebaum, Mary 1958- 185
    Earlier sketches in SATA 88, 134
Quay, Emma 173
    Earlier sketch in SATA 119
Queen, Ellery
    See Deming, Richard
    and Dannay, Frederic
    and Davidson, Avram (James)
    and Fairman, Paul W.
    and Flora, Fletcher
    and Holding, James (Clark Carlisle, Jr.)
    and Hoch, Edward D.
    and Kane, Henry
    and Lee, Manfred B.
    and Marlowe, Stephen
    and Powell, (Oval) Talmage
    and Sheldon, Walter J(ames)
    and Sturgeon, Theodore (Hamilton)
    and Tracy, Don(ald Fiske)
    and Vance, Jack
Queen Latifah 1970- 185
Quennell, Marjorie Courtney 1884-1972 29
Quentin
    See Sheldon, David
Quentin, Brad
    See Bisson, Terry
Quest, (Edna) Olga W(ilbourne) Hall
    See Hall-Quest, (Edna) Olga W(ilbourne)
Quick, Annabelle 1922-1986 2
Quigg, Jane (Hulda) (?)-1986
    Obituary 49
Quigley, Sarah 1976- 220
Quill, Monica
    See McInerny, Ralph
Quimby, Laura 237
Quin-Harkin, Janet 1941- 165
    Earlier sketches in SATA 18, 90, 119
Quin-Harkin, Janet Elizabeth
    See Quin-Harkin, Janet
Quinlan, Susan E. 1954- 88
Quinlan, Susan Elizabeth
    See Quinlan, Susan E.
Quinn, Elisabeth 1881-1962 22
Quinn, Pat 1947- 130
Quinn, Patrick 1950- 73
Quinn, Rob 1972- 138
Quinn, Spencer
    See Abrahams, Peter
Quinn, Susan 1940- 30
Quinn, Susan Taft
    See Quinn, Susan
Quinn, Theodora K.
    See Kroeber, Theodora (Kracaw)
Quinn, Vernon
    See Quinn, Elisabeth
Quintano, D.M.
    See Sheldon, Dyan
Quirk, Anne (E.) 1956- 99
Quixley, Jim 1931- 56
Quyth, Gabriel
    See Jennings, Gary

                            R

Ra, Carol F. 1939- 76
Raab, Evelyn 1951- 129
Rabb, Margo 1972- 188
Rabb, M.E.
    See Rabb, Margo
Rabe, Berniece (Louise) 1928- 148
    Autobiography Feature 148
    Earlier sketches in SATA 7, 77
    See also SAAS 10
Rabe, Olive H(anson) (?)-1968 13
Rabin, Staton 1958- 162
    Earlier sketch in SATA 84
Rabinowich, Ellen 1946- 29

Rabinowitz, Sandy 1954- 52
    Brief entry 39
Rachlin, Carol K(ing) 1919- 64
Rachlin, Harvey 1951- 47
Rachlin, Harvey Brant
    See Rachlin, Harvey
Rachlin, Nahid 64
Rachlis, Eugene (Jacob) 1920-1986
    Obituary 50
Rackham, Arthur 1867-1939 100
    Earlier sketch in SATA 15
    See also CLR 57
Racoma, Robin Yoko 1953- 207
Raczka, Bob 1963- 228
    Earlier sketches in SATA 163, 191
Radencich, Marguerite C. 1952-1998 79
Rader, Laura 197
Radford, Ruby L(orraine) 1891-1971 6
Radin, Ruth Yaffe 1938- 107
    Brief entry 52
    Earlier sketch in SATA 56
Radlauer, David 1952- 28
Radlauer, Edward 1921- 15
Radlauer, Ruth Shaw 1926- 98
    Earlier sketch in SATA 15
Radley, Gail 1951- 112
    Earlier sketch in SATA 25
Radunsky, Vladimir 177
Radzinski, Kandy 1948- 212
Rae, Gwynedd 1892-1977 37
Raebeck, Lois 1921- 5
Rael, Elsa Okon 1927-
    See CLR 84
Raffi
    See Cavoukian, Raffi
Raftery, Gerald (Bransfield) 1905-1986 11
Ragan-Reid, Gale 1956- 90
Rahaman, Vashanti 1953- 98
Rahn, Joan Elma 1929- 27
Rai, Bali 1971- 152
Raible, Alton (Robert) 1918- 35
Raiff, Stan 1930- 11
Railsback, Lisa 230
Raines, Shirley C(arol) 1945- 128
Rainey, W. B.
    See Blassingame, Wyatt Rainey
Rake, Jody 1961- 157
Rallison, Janette 1966- 238
    Earlier sketch in SATA 183
Ralston, Jan
    See Dunlop, Agnes M. R.
Rama, Sue 190
Ramal, Walter
    See de la Mare, Walter (John)
Ramanujan, A(ttipat) K(rishnaswami)
    1929-1993 86
Rame, David
    See Divine, Arthur Durham
Ramirez, Jose 1967- 198
Ramirez, Orlando L. 1972- 194
Ramos, Jorge 1958- 205
Ramsey, Calvin Alexander 239
Ramstad, Ralph L. 1919- 115
Ramthun, Bonnie 214
Rana, Indi
    See Rana, Indira Higham
Rana, Indira Higham 1944- 82
Rana, J.
    See Bhatia, Jamunadevi
Ranadive, Gail 1944- 10
Rand, Ann (Binkley) 30
Rand, Gloria 1925- 156
    Earlier sketch in SATA 101
Rand, Paul 1914-1996 6
Randall, Carrie
    See Ransom, Candice
Randall, David 1972- 167
Randall, Florence Engel 1917-1997 5
Randall, Janet
    See Young, Janet Randall
    and Young, Robert W(illiam)

Randall, Robert
  See Garrett, Randall
  and Silverberg, Robert
Randall, Ruth (Elaine) Painter 1892-1971 ..... *3*
Randell, Beverley
  See Price, Beverley Joan
Randle, Kristen D. 1952- *92*
  Autobiography Feature *119*
  See also SAAS *24*
Randle, Kristen Downey
  See Randle, Kristen D.
Randolph, Boynton M.D.
  See Ellis, Edward S.
Randolph, Ellen
  See Rawn, Melanie
Randolph, Geoffrey
  See Ellis, Edward S.
Randolph, J. H.
  See Ellis, Edward S.
Randolph, Lieutenant J. H.
  See Ellis, Edward S.
Rands, William Brighty 1823-1882 .... *17*
Raney, Ken 1953- *74*
Rania, Queen of Jordan 1970- *233*
Rankin, Joan 1940- *212*
  Earlier sketches in SATA *88, 148*
Rankin, Laura 1953(?)- *236*
  Earlier sketch in SATA *176*
Ranney, Agnes V. 1916-1985 .... *6*
Ransom, Candice 1952- *222*
  Brief entry *49*
  Earlier sketches in SATA *52, 89, 135, 183*
Ransom, Jeanie Franz 1957- *187*
Ransome, Arthur (Michell) 1884-1967 .... *22*
  See also CLR *8*
Ransome, James E. 1961- *227*
  Earlier sketches in SATA *76, 123, 178*
  See also CLR *86*
Rant, Tol E.
  See Longyear, Barry B(rookes)
Rao, Rohitash *218*
Raphael, Elaine
  See Bolognese, Elaine
Raposo, Joseph Guilherme 1938-1989
  Obituary *61*
Rapp, Adam 1968- *148*
Rappaport, Doreen *211*
  Earlier sketch in SATA *151*
Rappaport, Eva 1924- *6*
Rappoport, Ken 1935- *167*
  Earlier sketch in SATA *89*
Rarick, Carrie 1911-2002 .... *41*
Raschka, Chris 1959- *207*
  Earlier sketches in SATA *80, 117, 166*
Raschka, Christopher
  See Raschka, Chris
Rascol, Sabina I. *159*
Rash, Andy *219*
  Earlier sketch in SATA *162*
Raskin, Edith Lefkowitz 1908-1987 .... *9*
Raskin, Ellen 1928-1984 .... *139*
  Earlier sketches in SATA *2, 38*
  See also CLR *12*
Raskin, Joseph 1897-1982 .... *12*
  Obituary *29*
Rathjen, Carl Henry 1909-1984 .... *11*
Rathmann, Peggy 1953- *157*
  Earlier sketch in SATA *94*
  See also CLR *77*
Ratliff, Thomas M. 1948- *118*
Ratner, Sue Lynn
  See Alexander, Sue
Rattigan, Jama Kim 1951- *99*
Ratto, Linda Lee 1952- *79*
Rattray, Simon
  See Trevor, Elleston
Ratz de Tagyos, Paul 1958- *198*
  Earlier sketch in SATA *76*
Rau, Dana Meachen 1971- *218*
  Earlier sketches in SATA *94, 167*

Rau, Margaret 1913- *168*
  Earlier sketch in SATA *9*
  See also CLR *8*
Rauch, Mabel Thompson 1888-1972
  Obituary *26*
Raucher, Herman 1928- *8*
Raude, Karina *199*
Rauh, Sherry
  See North, Sherry
Raum, Elizabeth 1949- *155*
Raut, Radhashyam *222*
Rave, Friederike 1970- *231*
Raven, Margot Theis *184*
RavenWolf, Silver 1956- *155*
Ravielli, Anthony 1916-1997 .... *3*
  Obituary *95*
Ravilious, Robin 1944- *77*
Ravishankar, Anushka 1961- *200*
Rawding, F(rederick) W(illiam) 1930- *55*
Rawlings, Marjorie Kinnan 1896-1953 ...... *100*
  See also YABC *1*
  See also CLR *63*
Rawlins, Donna 1956- *206*
Rawlinson, Julia *212*
  Earlier sketch in SATA *175*
Rawls, (Woodrow) Wilson 1913-1984 .... *22*
  See also CLR *81*
Rawlyk, George Alexander 1935- *64*
Rawn, Melanie 1954- *98*
Rawn, Melanie Robin
  See Rawn, Melanie
Rawson, Katherine 1955- *190*
Ray, Carl 1943-1978 .... *63*
Ray, Deborah
  See Kogan Ray, Deborah
Ray, Delia 1963- *179*
  Earlier sketch in SATA *70*
Ray, Irene
  See Sutton, Margaret Beebe
Ray, Jane 1960- *196*
  Earlier sketches in SATA *72, 152*
Ray, JoAnne 1935- *9*
Ray, Mary (Eva Pedder) 1932- *127*
  Earlier sketch in SATA *2*
Ray, Mary Lyn 1946- *154*
  Earlier sketch in SATA *90*
Rayban, Chloe 1944- *167*
Rayburn, Tricia *234*
Rayevsky, Robert 1955- *190*
  Earlier sketch in SATA *81*
Raymond, James Crossley 1917-1981
  Obituary *29*
Raymond, Robert
  See Alter, Robert Edmond
Rayner, Catherine *204*
Rayner, Hugh *151*
Rayner, Mary 1933- *87*
  Earlier sketch in SATA *22*
  See also CLR *41*
Rayner, Shoo
  See Rayner, Hugh
Rayner, William 1929- *55*
  Brief entry *36*
Raynor, Dorka *28*
Raynor, Gemma 1985- *216*
Rayson, Steven 1932- *30*
Rayyan, Omar 1968- *216*
Razzell, Arthur (George) 1925- *11*
Razzell, Mary (Catherine) 1930- *102*
Razzi, James 1931- *10*
Read, Elfreida 1920- *2*
Read, Nicholas 1956- *146*
Read, Piers Paul 1941- *21*
Reade, Deborah 1949- *69*
Reader, Dennis 1929- *71*
Reading, Richard P(atrick) 1962- *161*
Readman, Jo 1958- *89*
Ready, Kirk L(ewis) 1943- *39*
Reaney, James 1926-2008 .... *43*
Reaney, James Crerar
  See Reaney, James

Reardon, Joyce
  See Pearson, Ridley
Reaver, Chap 1935-1993 .... *69*
  Obituary *77*
Reaver, Herbert R.
  See Reaver, Chap
Reaves, J. Michael
  See Reaves, (James) Michael
Reaves, (James) Michael 1950- *99*
Reber, Deborah *189*
Recorvits, Helen *191*
Redding, Robert Hull 1919- *2*
Redekopp, Elsa *61*
Redlich, Ben 1977- *181*
Redsand, Anna 1948- *184*
Redway, Ralph
  See Hamilton, Charles (Harold St. John)
Redway, Ridley
  See Hamilton, Charles (Harold St. John)
Reece, Colleen L. 1935- *116*
Reece, Gabrielle 1970- *108*
Reed, Amy 1979- *223*
Reed, Betty Jane 1921- *4*
Reed, Dallas
  See Pendleton, Thomas
Reed, E.
  See Evans, Mari
Reed, Gwendolyn E(lizabeth) 1932- *21*
Reed, Kit 1932- *184*
  Autobiography Feature *184*
  Earlier sketches in SATA *34, 116*
Reed, Lynn Rowe *215*
  Earlier sketch in SATA *171*
Reed, Mike 1951- *211*
Reed, Neil 1961- *99*
Reed, Talbot Baines 1852-1893
  See CLR *76*
Reed, Thomas (James) 1947- *34*
Reed, William Maxwell 1871-1962 .... *15*
Reeder, Carolyn 1937- *97*
  Earlier sketch in SATA *66*
  See also CLR *69*
Reeder, Colin (Dawson) 1938- *74*
Reeder, Colonel Red
  See Reeder, Russell P(otter), Jr.
Reeder, Russell P(otter), Jr. 1902-1998 .... *4*
  Obituary *101*
Reeder, Stephanie Owen 1951- *102*
Reed-Jones, Carol 1955- *112*
Reedy, Trent 1979(?)- *239*
Reef, Catherine 1951- *223*
  Earlier sketches in SATA *73, 128, 189*
Reekie, Jocelyn (Margaret) 1947- *145*
Reeman, Douglas Edward 1924- *63*
  Brief entry *28*
Rees, Celia 1949- *124*
Rees, David (Bartlett) 1936-1993 .... *69*
  Obituary *76*
  Earlier sketch in SATA *36*
  See also SAAS *5*
Rees, Douglas 1947- *237*
  Earlier sketch in SATA *169*
Rees, Ennis (Samuel, Jr.) 1925-2009 .... *3*
Rees, (George) Leslie (Clarence)
  1905-2000 .... *105*
  Obituary *135*
Reese, Bob
  See Reese, Robert A.
Reese, Carolyn Johnson 1938- *64*
Reese, Della 1931(?)- *114*
Reese, Lyn
  See Reese, Carolyn Johnson
Reese, Robert A. 1938- *60*
  Brief entry *53*
Reese, (John) Terence 1913-1996 .... *59*
Reeve, Joel
  See Cox, William R(obert)
Reeve, Kirk 1934- *117*
Reeve, Philip 1966- *201*
  Earlier sketch in SATA *170*

Reeve, Rosie 188
  Earlier sketch in SATA 186
Reeves, Dia 1977- 227
Reeves, Faye Couch 1953- 76
Reeves, James
  See Reeves, John Morris
Reeves, Jeni 1947- 111
Reeves, John Morris 1909-1978 87
  Earlier sketch in SATA 15
Reeves, Joyce 1911- 17
Reeves, Lawrence F. 1926- 29
Reeves, Ruth Ellen
  See Ranney, Agnes V.
Regan, Dian Curtis 1950- 224
  Autobiography Feature 149
  Earlier sketches in SATA 75, 133, 149
Regehr, Lydia 1903-1991 37
Reger, James P. 1952- 106
Reger, Rob 1969- 227
Reggiani, Renee 1925- 18
Rehm, Karl M. 1935- 72
Reibstein, Mark 211
Reich, Ali
  See Katz, Bobbi
Reich, Susanna 1954- 214
  Earlier sketch in SATA 113
Reiche, Dietlof 1941- 159
Reichert, Edwin C(lark) 1909-1988
  Obituary 57
Reichert, Mickey Zucker
  See Reichert, Miriam Zucker
Reichert, Miriam Zucker 1962- 85
Reichert, Renee 172
Reichhold, Jane(t E.) 1937- 147
Reid, Alastair 1926- 46
Reid, Barbara 1922- 21
Reid, Barbara (Jane) 1957- 93
  See also CLR 64
Reid, Desmond
  See Moorcock, Michael
  and McNeilly, Wilfred (Glassford)
Reid, Eugenie Chazal 1924- 12
Reid, John Calvin 21
Reid, (Thomas) Mayne 1818-1883 24
Reid, Meta Mayne 1905-1991 58
  Brief entry 36
Reid, Robin (Nicole) 1969- 145
Reid Banks, Lynne 1929- 165
  Earlier sketches in SATA 22, 75, 111
  See also CLR 86
Reider, Katja 1960- 126
Reid Jenkins, Debra 1955- 87
Reidy, Jean 228
Reiff, Stephanie Ann 1948- 47
  Brief entry 28
Reig, June 1933- 30
Reigot, Betty Polisar 1924- 55
  Brief entry 41
Reilly, Joan 195
Reim, Melanie (K.) 1956- 104
Reinach, Jacquelyn (Krasne) 1930-2000 28
Reiner, Carl 1922- 151
Reiner, William B(uck) 1910-1976 46
  Obituary 30
Reinfeld, Fred 1910-1964 3
Reinhardt, Dana 1971- 175
Reinhart, Matthew 1971- 197
  Earlier sketch in SATA 161
Reiniger, Lotte 1899-1981 40
  Obituary 33
Reinsma, Carol 1949- 91
Reinstedt, Randall A. 1935- 101
Reinstedt, Randy
  See Reinstedt, Randall A.
Reisberg, Mira 1955- 82
Reisberg, Veg
  See Reisberg, Mira
Reiser, Lynn 1944- 180
  Earlier sketches in SATA 81, 138
Reiser, Lynn Whisnant
  See Reiser, Lynn

Reisgies, Teresa (Maria) 1966- 74
Reiss, Johanna 1929(?)- 18
  See also CLR 19
Reiss, Johanna de Leeuw
  See Reiss, Johanna
Reiss, John J. 23
Reiss, Kathryn 1957- 144
  Earlier sketch in SATA 76
Reit, Seymour Victory 1918-2001 21
  Obituary 133
Reit, Sy
  See Reit, Seymour Victory
Relf, Patricia 1954- 134
  Earlier sketch in SATA 71
Remark, Erich Paul
  See Remarque, Erich Maria
Remarque, Erich Maria 1898-1970
  See CLR 159
Remi, Georges 1907-1983 13
  Obituary 32
  See also CLR 114
Remington, Frederic S(ackrider)
  1861-1909 41
Remkiewicz, Frank 1939- 217
  Earlier sketches in SATA 77, 152
Rempt, Fiona 1973- 198
Remy, Georges
  See Remi, Georges
Renaud, Anne 1957- 211
Renaud, Bernadette 1945- 66
Renault, Mary 1905-1983 23
  Obituary 36
Rendell, Joan 28
Rendina, Laura (Jones) Cooper 1902- 10
Rendon, Marcie R. 1952- 97
Rendon, Maria 1965- 116
Renee, Janina 1956- 140
Renfro, Ed 1924- 79
Renick, Marion (Lewis) 1905-1983 1
Renier, Aaron 1977- 202
Renken, Aleda 1907- 27
Renlie, Frank H. 1936- 11
Rennert, Laura Joy 224
Rennert, Richard Scott 1956- 67
Rennison, Louise 1951- 149
Reno, Dawn E(laine) 1953- 130
Rensie, Willis
  See Eisner, Will
Renton, Cam
  See Armstrong, Richard
Renvoize, Jean 5
Resau, Laura 1973- 230
  Earlier sketch in SATA 190
Resciniti, Angelo G. 1952- 75
Resnick, Michael David
  See Resnick, Mike
Resnick, Mike 1942- 159
  Earlier sketches in SATA 38, 106
Resnick, Seymour 1920- 23
Retla, Robert
  See Alter, Robert Edmond
Rettig, Liz 199
Rettstatt, Chris
  See Ashland, Monk
Reuter, Bjarne (B.) 1950- 142
  Earlier sketch in SATA 68
Reuter, Carol (Joan) 1931- 2
Revena
  See Wright, Betty Ren
Revsbech, Vicki
  See Liestman, Vicki
Rex, Adam 225
  Earlier sketch in SATA 186
Rex, Michael 191
Rey, H. A. 1898-1977 100
  Earlier sketches in SATA 1, 26, 69
  See also CLR 93
Rey, Hans Augusto
  See Rey, H. A.
Rey, Luis V. 1955- 201

Rey, Margret 1906-1996 86
  Obituary 93
  Earlier sketch in SATA 26
  See also CLR 93
Rey, Margret Elisabeth
  See Rey, Margret
Reyher, Becky
  See Reyher, Rebecca Hourwich
Reyher, Rebecca Hourwich 1897-1987 18
  Obituary 50
Reynish, Jenny 222
Reynold, Ann
  See Bernardo, Anilu
Reynolds, Aaron 1970- 197
Reynolds, Adrian 1963- 192
Reynolds, C. Buck 1957- 107
Reynolds, Dickson
  See Reynolds, Helen Mary Greenwood Campbell
Reynolds, Helen Mary Greenwood Campbell
  1884-1969
  Obituary 26
Reynolds, Jan 1956- 180
Reynolds, John
  See Whitlock, Ralph
Reynolds, Madge
  See Whitlock, Ralph
Reynolds, Malvina 1900-1978 44
  Obituary 24
Reynolds, Marilyn 1935- 121
  See also SAAS 23
Reynolds, Marilyn M.
  See Reynolds, Marilyn
Reynolds, Marilynn 1940- 141
  Earlier sketch in SATA 80
Reynolds, Pamela 1923- 34
Reynolds, Peter H. 1961- 226
  Earlier sketch in SATA 128
Reynolds, Peter J. 1961- 179
Reynolds, Susan 179
Rhine, Richard
  See Silverstein, Alvin
  and Silverstein, Virginia B.
Rhoades, Diane 1952- 90
Rhodes, Bennie (Loran) 1927- 35
Rhodes, Donna McKee 1962- 87
Rhodes, Frank Harold Trevor 1926- 37
Rhuday-Perkovich, Olugbemisola 227
Rhue, Morton
  See Strasser, Todd
Rhyne, Nancy 1926- 66
Rhynes, Martha E. 1939- 141
Ribbons, Ian 1924- 37
  Brief entry 30
  See also SAAS 3
Ricciuti, Edward R(aphael) 1938- 10
Rice, Alice (Caldwell) Hegan 1870-1942 63
Rice, Bebe Faas 1932- 89
Rice, Charles D(uane) 1910-1971
  Obituary 27
Rice, Dale R. 1948- 42
Rice, Dale Richard
  See Rice, Dale R.
Rice, Dick
  See Rice, R. Hugh
Rice, Earle (Wilmont), Jr. 1928- 151
  Earlier sketch in SATA 92
Rice, Edward 1918-2001 47
  Brief entry 42
Rice, Elizabeth 1913-1976 2
Rice, Eve 1951- 91
  Earlier sketch in SATA 34
Rice, Eve Hart
  See Rice, Eve
Rice, Inez 1907- 13
Rice, James 1934- 93
  Earlier sketch in SATA 22
Rice, John F. 1958- 82
Rice, R. Hugh 1929- 115
Rice, Richard H.
  See Rice, R. Hugh

Rich, Anna 1956- 212
Rich, Barbara
　See Graves, Robert
Rich, Elaine Sommers 1926- 6
Rich, Josephine Bouchard 1912- 10
Rich, Louise Dickinson 1903-1991 54
　Obituary 67
Rich, Naomi 217
Richard, Adrienne 1921- 5
　See also SAAS 9
Richard, James Robert
　See Bowen, Robert Sydney
Richards, Chuck 1957- 170
Richards, Frank
　See Hamilton, Charles (Harold St. John)
Richards, Hilda
　See Hamilton, Charles (Harold St. John)
Richards, Jackie 1925- 102
Richards, Jame 230
Richards, Jean 1940- 135
Richards, Justin 169
Richards, Kay
　See Baker, Susan (Catherine)
Richards, Laura E(lizabeth Howe) 1850-1943
　See YABC 1
　See also CLR 54
Richards, Leigh
　See King, Laurie R.
Richards, Marlee
　See Brill, Marlene Targ
Richards, Norman 1932- 48
Richards, R(onald) C(harles) W(illiam)
　1923- 59
　Brief entry 43
Richards, Walter Alden (Jr.) 1907-1988
　Obituary 56
Richardson, Andrew (William) 1986- 120
Richardson, Carol 1932- 58
Richardson, Frank Howard 1882-1970
　Obituary 27
Richardson, Grace Lee
　See Dickson, Naida
Richardson, Jean (Mary) 59
Richardson, Judith Benet 1941- 77
Richardson, Nigel 1957- 187
Richardson, Robert S(hirley) 1902-1981 8
Richardson, Sandy 1949- 116
Richardson, V.A. 189
Richardson, Willis 1889-1977 60
Richelson, Geraldine 1922- 29
Richemont, Enid 1940- 82
Richler, Mordecai 1931-2001 98
　Brief entry 27
　Earlier sketch in SATA 44
　See also CLR 17
Richman, Sophia 1941- 142
Rich-McCoy, Lois
　See McCoy, Lois (Rich)
Richmond, Robin 1951- 75
Richoux, Pat(ricia) 1927- 7
Richter, Alice 1941- 30
Richter, Conrad (Michael) 1890-1968 3
Richter, Hans Peter 1925-1993 6
　See also CLR 21
　See also SAAS 11
Richter, Jutta 1955- 184
Rickard, Graham 1949- 71
Rico, Don(ato) 1917-1985
　Obituary 43
Riddell, Chris 1962- 219
　Earlier sketches in SATA 114, 166
Riddell, Christopher Barry
　See Riddell, Chris
Riddell, Edwina 1955- 82
Ridden, Brian 1934- 123
　See Ridden, Brian John
Riddle, Tohby 1965- 223
　Earlier sketches in SATA 74, 151
Riddleburger, Sam 202
Riddles, Libby 1956- 140
Ride, Sally 1951- 219

Ride, Sally Kristen
　See Ride, Sally
Rideout, Sandy 194
Rider, D. F.
　See Perrin, Pat
Rider, David F.
　See Perrin, Pat
Ridge, Antonia (Florence) (?)-1981 7
　Obituary 27
Ridge, Martin 1923-2003 43
Ridley, Philip 171
　Earlier sketch in SATA 88
Ridlon, Marci
　See Balterman, Marcia Ridlon
Riedman, Sarah R(egal) 1902-1995 1
Riehecky, Janet 1953- 164
Ries, Lori 237
　Earlier sketch in SATA 185
Riesenberg, Felix, Jr. 1913-1962 23
Rieu, E(mile) V(ictor) 1887-1972 46
　Obituary 26
Riffenburgh, Beau 1955- 175
Rigg, Sharon
　See Creech, Sharon
Riggenbach, Holly
　See Black, Holly
Riggio, Anita 1952- 148
　Earlier sketch in SATA 73
Riggs, Shannon 190
Riggs, Sidney Noyes 1892-1975
　Obituary 28
Riggs, Stephanie 1964- 138
Riglietti, Serena 1969- 189
Rigney, James Oliver, Jr.
　See Jordan, Robert
Rikhoff, Jean 1928- 9
Rikki
　See Ducornet, Erica
Riley, James A. 1939- 97
Riley, James Whitcomb 1849-1916 17
Riley, Jocelyn 1949- 60
　Brief entry 50
Riley, Jocelyn Carol
　See Riley, Jocelyn
Riley, Linda Capus 1950- 85
Riley, Martin 1948- 81
Riley-Webb, Charlotte 1948- 235
Rim, Sujean 225
Rimbauer, Steven
　See Pearson, Ridley
Rimes, (Margaret) LeAnn 1982- 154
Rinaldi, Ann 1934- 202
　Brief entry 50
　Earlier sketches in SATA 51, 78, 117, 161
　See also CLR 46
Rinard, Judith E(llen) 1947- 140
　Earlier sketch in SATA 44
Rinck, Maranke 1976- 214
Rinder, Lenore 1949- 92
Ring, Elizabeth 1920- 79
Ringdahl, Mark
　See Longyear, Barry B(rookes)
Ringgold, Faith 1930- 187
　Earlier sketches in SATA 71, 114
　See also CLR 30
Ringi, Kjell (Arne Soerensen) 1939- 12
Rinkoff, Barbara Jean (Rich) 1923-1975 4
　Obituary 27
Rinn, Miriam 1946- 127
Riordan, James 1936- 95
Riordan, Rick 238
　Earlier sketches in SATA 174, 208
Rios, Tere
　See Versace, Marie Teresa Rios
Rioux, Jo 226
Rioux, Jo-Anne
　See Rioux, Jo
Ripken, Cal, Jr. 1960- 215
　Earlier sketch in SATA 114
Ripken, Calvin Edward, Jr.
　See Ripken, Cal, Jr.

Ripley, Catherine 1957- 82
Ripley, Elizabeth Blake 1906-1969 5
Ripper, Charles L(ewis) 1929- 3
Ripper, Chuck
　See Ripper, Charles L(ewis)
Rippin, Sally 220
Riq
　See Atwater, Richard
Rish, David 1955- 110
Riskind, Mary 1944- 60
Rissinger, Matt 1956- 93
Rissman, Art
　See Sussman, Susan
Rissman, Susan
　See Sussman, Susan
Ritchie, Barbara Gibbons 14
Ritchie, Scot 1954- 217
Ritter, Felix
　See Kruss, James
Ritter, John H. 1951- 215
　Earlier sketches in SATA 129, 137
Ritter, Lawrence S(tanley) 1922-2004 58
　Obituary 152
Ritthaler, Shelly 1955- 91
Ritts, Paul 1920(?)-1980
　Obituary 25
Ritz, Karen 1957- 202
　Earlier sketch in SATA 80
Riu, Isabel Ferrer 1969- 222
Rivera, Geraldo (Miguel) 1943- 54
　Brief entry 28
Rivera, Guadalupe
　See Rivera Marin, Guadalupe
Rivera Marin, Guadalupe 1924- 224
Rivers, Elfrida
　See Bradley, Marion Zimmer
Rivers, Karen 1970- 131
Riverside, John
　See Heinlein, Robert A.
Rivkin, Ann 1920- 41
Rivoli, Mario 1943- 10
Roach, Marilynne K. 1946- 9
Roach, Marilynne Kathleen
　See Roach, Marilynne K.
Roach, Portia
　See Takakjian, Portia
Robb, Don 1937- 194
Robb, Laura 1937- 95
Robberecht, Thierry 1960- 182
Robbins, Frank 1917-1994(?) 42
　Brief entry 32
Robbins, Jacqui 221
Robbins, Ken 1945- 219
　Brief entry 53
　Earlier sketches in SATA 94, 147
Robbins, Raleigh
　See Hamilton, Charles (Harold St. John)
Robbins, Ruth 1917(?)- 14
Robbins, Tony
　See Pashko, Stanley
Robbins, Wayne
　See Cox, William R(obert)
Robel, S. L.
　See Fraustino, Lisa Rowe
Roberson, Jennifer 1953- 72
Roberson, John R(oyster) 1930- 53
Robert, Adrian
　See St. John, Nicole
Roberton, Fiona 230
Roberts, Bethany 202
　Earlier sketch in SATA 133
Roberts, Bruce (Stuart) 1930- 47
　Brief entry 39
Roberts, Charles G(eorge) D(ouglas)
　1860-1943 88
　Brief entry 29
　See also CLR 33
Roberts, David
　See Cox, John Roberts
Roberts, David 1970- 191
Roberts, Diane 1937- 184

Roberts, Elizabeth 1944- 80
Roberts, Elizabeth Madox 1886-1941 33
　Brief entry 27
　See also CLR *100*
Roberts, Jim
　See Bates, Barbara S(nedeker)
Roberts, Jody 218
Roberts, John G(aither) 1913-1993 27
Roberts, Judy I. 1957- 93
Roberts, Katherine 1962- 152
Roberts, Ken 223
　See Lake, Kenneth R(obert)
Roberts, Laura Peyton 232
Roberts, M. L.
　See Mattern, Joanne
Roberts, Marion 1966- 212
Roberts, Nancy Correll 1924- 52
　Brief entry 28
Roberts, Priscilla 1955- 184
Roberts, Terence
　See Sanderson, Ivan T(erence)
Roberts, Willo Davis 1928-2004 150
　Autobiography Feature 150
　Obituary 160
　Earlier sketches in SATA *21, 70, 133*
　See also CLR *95*
　See also SAAS *8*
Robertson, Barbara (Anne) 1931- 12
Robertson, Don 1929-1999 8
　Obituary 113
Robertson, Dorothy Lewis 1912- 12
Robertson, Ellis
　See Ellison, Harlan
　and Silverberg, Robert
Robertson, James I., Jr. 1930- 182
Robertson, James Irvin
　See Robertson, James I., Jr.
Robertson, Janet (E.) 1935- 68
Robertson, Jennifer Sinclair 1942-1998 12
Robertson, Jenny
　See Robertson, Jennifer Sinclair
Robertson, Keith (Carlton) 1914-1991 85
　Obituary 69
　Earlier sketch in SATA *1*
　See also SAAS *15*
Robertson, Mark
　See Robertson, M.P.
Robertson, M.P. 1965- 197
Robertson, Stephen
　See Walker, Robert W.
Robertus, Polly M. 1948- 212
　Earlier sketch in SATA *73*
Robeson, Kenneth
　See Dent, Lester
　and Goulart, Ron
Robeson, Kenneth
　See Johnson, (Walter) Ryerson
Robinet, Harriette Gillem 1931- 104
　Earlier sketch in SATA *27*
　See also CLR *64*
Robins, Deri 1958- 166
　Earlier sketch in SATA *117*
Robins, Patricia 1921- 117
Robins, Rollo, Jr.
　See Ellis, Edward S.
Robins, Seelin
　See Ellis, Edward S.
Robinson, Adjai 1932- 8
Robinson, Aminah Brenda Lynn 1940- 159
　Earlier sketch in SATA *77*
Robinson, Barbara (Webb) 1927- 84
　Earlier sketch in SATA *8*
Robinson, C(harles) A(lexander), Jr.
　1900-1965 36
Robinson, Charles 1870-1937 17
Robinson, Charles 1931- 6
Robinson, Dorothy W. 1929- 54
Robinson, Elizabeth Keeler 1959- 204
Robinson, Eve
　See Tanselle, Eve
Robinson, Fiona 1965- 225

Robinson, Glen 1953- 92
Robinson, Glendal P.
　See Robinson, Glen
Robinson, Jan M. 1933- 6
Robinson, Jean O. 1934- 7
Robinson, Joan (Mary) G(ale Thomas)
　1910-1988 7
Robinson, Kim Stanley 1952- 109
Robinson, Lee 1948- 110
Robinson, Lloyd
　See Silverberg, Robert
Robinson, Lynda S(uzanne) 1951- 107
Robinson, Marileta 1942- 32
Robinson, Maudie Millian Oller 1914- 11
Robinson, Maurice R(ichard) 1895-1982
　Obituary 29
Robinson, Nancy K(onheim) 1942-1994 91
　Brief entry 31
　Obituary 79
　Earlier sketch in SATA *32*
Robinson, Ray 1920- 23
Robinson, Raymond Kenneth
　See Robinson, Ray
Robinson, Shari
　See McGuire, Leslie (Sarah)
Robinson, Sharon 1950- 197
　Earlier sketch in SATA *162*
Robinson, Spider 1948- 118
Robinson, Sue
　See Robinson, Susan Maria
Robinson, Susan Maria 1955- 105
Robinson, Susan Patricia
　See Gates, Susan
Robinson, Suzanne
　See Robinson, Lynda S(uzanne)
Robinson, T(homas) H(eath) 1869-1950 17
Robinson, Tim 1963- 205
Robinson, (Wanda) Veronica 1926- 30
Robinson, W(illiam) Heath 1872-1944 17
Robison, Bonnie 1924- 12
Robison, Nancy L(ouise) 1934- 32
Robles, Harold E. 1948- 87
Robottom, John 1934- 7
Robson, Eric 1939- 82
Roca, Francois 1971- 200
Rocco, John 1967- 188
Roche, A. K.
　See Abisch, Roslyn Kroop
　and Kaplan, Boche
Roche, Denis 1967- 196
　Earlier sketch in SATA *99*
Roche, Denis Mary
　See Roche, Denis
Roche, Luane 1937- 170
Roche, P(atricia) K. 1935- 57
　Brief entry 34
Roche, Terry
　See Poole, Peggy
Rochman, Hazel 1938- 105
Rock, Lois
　See Joslin, Mary
Rock, Maxine 1940- 108
Rocker, Fermin 1907- 40
Rockliff, Mara 224
Rocklin, Joanne 1946- 134
　Earlier sketch in SATA *86*
Rockwell, Anne 1934- 235
　Earlier sketches in SATA *33, 71, 114, 162,
　194*
　See also SAAS *19*
Rockwell, Anne F.
　See Rockwell, Anne
Rockwell, Anne Foote
　See Rockwell, Anne
Rockwell, Bart
　See Pellowski, Michael (Joseph)
Rockwell, Harlow 1910-1988 33
　Obituary 56
Rockwell, Lizzy 1961- 233
　Earlier sketch in SATA *185*
Rockwell, Norman (Percevel) 1894-1978 23

Rockwell, Thomas 1933- 231
　Earlier sketches in SATA *7, 70*
　See also CLR *6*
Rockwood, Joyce 1947- 39
Rockwood, Roy
　See McFarlane, Leslie
　and Stratemeyer, Edward L.
Rodanas, Kristina 1952- 155
Rodari, Gianni 1920-1980
　See CLR *24*
Rodd, Kathleen Tennant
　See Rodd, Kylie Tennant
Rodd, Kylie Tennant 1912-1988 57
　Obituary 55
　Earlier sketch in SATA *6*
Rodda, Emily 1948- 230
　Earlier sketches in SATA *97, 146*
　See also CLR *32*
Roddenberry, Eugene Wesley 1921-1991 45
　Obituary 69
Roddenberry, Gene
　See Roddenberry, Eugene Wesley
Roddick, Ellen 1936- 5
Roddie, Shen 153
Roddy, Lee 1921- 57
Rodenas, Paula 73
Rodgers, Frank 1944- 69
Rodgers, Mary 1931- 130
　Earlier sketch in SATA *8*
　See also CLR *20*
Rodman, Emerson
　See Ellis, Edward S.
Rodman, Eric
　See Silverberg, Robert
Rodman, Maia
　See Wojciechowska, Maia (Teresa)
Rodman, Mary Ann 185
Rodman, (Cary) Selden 1909-2002 9
Rodowsky, Colby 1932- 164
　Earlier sketches in SATA *21, 77, 120*
　See also SAAS *22*
Rodowsky, Colby F.
　See Rodowsky, Colby
Rodriguez, Alejo 1941- 83
Rodriguez, Alex 1975- 189
Rodriguez, Beatrice 1969- 230
Rodriguez, Christina 1981- 177
Rodriguez, Edel 1971- 196
Rodriguez, Luis J. 1954- 125
Rodriguez, Rachel 180
Rodriguez, Rachel Victoria
　See Rodriguez, Rachel
Roeder, Virginia Marsh 1926- 98
Roehrig, Catharine H. 1949- 67
Roennfeldt, Robert 1953- 78
Roessel-Waugh, C. C.
　See Waugh, Carol-Lynn Rossel
　and Waugh, Charles G(ordon)
Roets, Lois F. 1937- 91
Roever, J(oan) M(arilyn) 1935- 26
Rofes, Eric 1954-2006 52
Rofes, Eric Edward 1954-2006
　See Rofes, Eric
Roffey, Maureen 1936- 33
Rogak, Lisa 1962- 80
Rogak, Lisa Angowski
　See Rogak, Lisa
Rogan, S. Jones 199
Rogan, Sally Jones
　See Rogan, S. Jones
Rogasky, Barbara 1933- 144
　Earlier sketch in SATA *86*
Roge 1972- 233
Rogers, (Thomas) Alan (Stinchcombe)
　1937- 81
　Earlier sketch in SATA *2*
Rogers, Bettye 1858-1919 103
Rogers, Cindy 1950- 89
Rogers, Emma 1951- 74
Rogers, Frances 1888-1974 10

Rogers, Fred McFeely 1928-2003 .... *33*
  Obituary *138*
Rogers, Gregory 1957- *211*
Rogers, Hal
  See Sirimarco, Elizabeth
Rogers, Jacqueline 1958- *213*
Rogers, Jean 1919- *55*
  Brief entry *47*
Rogers, Matilda 1894-1976 .... *5*
  Obituary *34*
Rogers, Pamela 1927- *9*
Rogers, Paul 1950- *98*
  Earlier sketch in SATA *54*
Rogers, Robert
  See Hamilton, Charles (Harold St. John)
Rogers, Sherry *193*
Rogers, W(illiam) G(arland) 1896-1978 .... *23*
Rohan, M. S.
  See Rohan, Michael Scott
Rohan, Michael Scott 1951- *98*
Rohan, Mike Scott
  See Rohan, Michael Scott
Rohmann, Eric 1957- *239*
  Earlier sketch in SATA *171*
  See also CLR *100*
Rohmer, Harriet 1938- *56*
Rohrer, Doug 1962- *89*
Rojan
  See Rojankovsky, Feodor (Stepanovich)
Rojankovsky, Feodor (Stepanovich)
  1891-1970 .... *21*
Rojany, Lisa *94*
Rokeby-Thomas, Anna E(lma) 1911- *15*
Roland, Albert 1925-2002 .... *11*
Roland, Mary
  See Lewis, Mary
Roleff, Tamara L. 1959- *143*
Rolerson, Darrell A(llen) 1946- *8*
Roll, Winifred 1909-1998 .... *6*
Rollins, Charlemae Hill 1897-1979 .... *3*
  Obituary *26*
Rollins, James 1961- *216*
Rollock, Barbara T(herese) 1924- *64*
Rolston, Steve 1978- *209*
Romack, Janice Reed
  See LeNoir, Janice
Romain, Trevor *134*
Romanenko, Vitaliy 1962- *101*
Romano, Christy
  See Romano, Christy Carlson
Romano, Christy Carlson 1984- *210*
Romano, Clare 1922- *111*
  Earlier sketch in SATA *48*
Romano, Louis G. 1921- *35*
Romano, Melora A. 1966- *118*
Romano, Ray 1957- *170*
Romano, Raymond
  See Romano, Ray
Romijn, Johanna Maria Kooyker
  See Kooyker-Romijn, Johanna Maria
Romyn, Johanna Maria Kooyker
  See Kooyker-Romijn, Johanna Maria
Rong, Yu 1970- *174*
Rongen, Bjoern 1906- *10*
Rongen, Bjorn
  See Rongen, Bjoern
Ronson, Mark
  See Alexander, Marc
Rood, Ronald (N.) 1920- *12*
Rook, Sebastian
  See Jeapes, Ben
Rooke, Daphne 1914-2009 .... *12*
Rooke, Daphne Marie
  See Rooke, Daphne
Rooney, Ronnie 1970- *212*
Roop, Connie 1951- *167*
  Brief entry *49*
  Earlier sketches in SATA *54, 116*
Roop, Constance Betzer
  See Roop, Connie

Roop, Peter 1951- *167*
  Brief entry *49*
  Earlier sketches in SATA *54, 116*
Roop, Peter G.
  See Roop, Peter
Roop, Peter Geiger
  See Roop, Peter
Roos, Maryn *225*
Roos, Stephen 1945- *128*
  Brief entry *41*
  Earlier sketches in SATA *47, 77*
Roosa, Karen 1961- *218*
Roose-Evans, James 1927- *65*
Roosevelt, Eleanor 1884-1962 .... *50*
Root, Barry *232*
  Earlier sketch in SATA *182*
Root, Betty *84*
Root, Kimberly Bulcken *192*
Root, Phyllis 1949- *224*
  Brief entry *48*
  Earlier sketches in SATA *55, 94, 145, 184*
Root, Shelton L., Jr. 1923-1986
  Obituary *51*
Roper, Laura (Newbold) Wood 1911-2003 .. *34*
  Obituary *150*
Roper, Robert 1946- *142*
  Earlier sketch in SATA *78*
Roraback, Robin (Ellan) 1964- *111*
Rorby, Ginny 1944- *238*
  Earlier sketch in SATA *94*
Rorer, Abigail 1949- *85*
Rosaler, Maxine *208*
Rosamel, Godeleine de 1968- *151*
Roscoe, D(onald) T(homas) 1934- *42*
Rose, Anne *8*
Rose, Deborah Lee 1955- *185*
  Earlier sketches in SATA *71, 124*
Rose, Elizabeth (Jane Pretty) 1933- *68*
  Brief entry *28*
Rose, Florella
  See Carlson, Vada F.
Rose, Gerald (Hembdon Seymour) 1935- *68*
  Brief entry *30*
Rose, Malcolm 1953- *168*
  Earlier sketch in SATA *107*
Rose, Nancy A.
  See Sweetland, Nancy A(nn)
Rose, Naomi C. *228*
Rose, Ted 1940- *93*
Rose, Wendy 1948- *12*
Rosen, Elizabeth 1961- *205*
Rosen, Lillian (Diamond) 1928- *63*
Rosen, Marvin 1933- *161*
Rosen, Michael 1946- *229*
  Brief entry *40*
  Earlier sketches in SATA *48, 84, 137, 181*
  See also CLR *45*
Rosen, Michael J. 1954- *199*
  Earlier sketch in SATA *86*
Rosen, Michael Wayne
  See Rosen, Michael
Rosen, Sidney 1916- *1*
Rosen, Winifred 1943- *8*
Rosenbaum, Maurice 1907-1987 .... *6*
Rosenberg, Amye 1950- *74*
Rosenberg, Dorothy 1906- *40*
Rosenberg, Eth Clifford 1915- *92*
  See also SAAS *22*
Rosenberg, Jane 1949- *58*
Rosenberg, Liz 1958- *129*
  Earlier sketch in SATA *75*
Rosenberg, Maxine B(erta) 1939- *93*
  Brief entry *47*
  Earlier sketch in SATA *55*
Rosenberg, Nancy 1931- *4*
Rosenberg, Sharon 1942- *8*
Rosenberry, Vera 1948- *219*
  Earlier sketches in SATA *83, 144*
Rosenblatt, Arthur
  See Rosenblatt, Arthur S.

Rosenblatt, Arthur S. 1938- *68*
  Brief entry *45*
Rosenblatt, Lily 1956- *90*
Rosenbloom, Joseph 1928- *21*
Rosenblum, Richard 1928- *11*
Rosenburg, John M. 1918- *6*
Rosenfeld, Dina 1962- *99*
Rosenstiehl, Agnes 1941- *203*
Rosenstock, Jason 1978- *238*
Rosenthal, Amy Krouse 1965- *222*
  Earlier sketch in SATA *177*
Rosenthal, Betsy R. 1957- *178*
Rosenthal, Eileen *239*
Rosenthal, Harold 1914-1999 .... *35*
Rosenthal, M(acha) L(ouis) 1917-1996 .... *59*
Rosenthal, Marc 1949- *193*
Rosenthal, Mark A(lan) 1946- *64*
Rosing, Norbert 1953- *196*
Rosman, Steven M 1956- *81*
Rosman, Steven Michael
  See Rosman, Steven M
Rosoff, Meg 1956- *209*
  Earlier sketch in SATA *160*
Ross, Alan
  See Warwick, Alan R(oss)
Ross, Christine 1950- *172*
  Earlier sketch in SATA *83*
Ross, Clare
  See Romano, Clare
Ross, Dana Fuller
  See Cockrell, Amanda
  and Gerson, Noel Bertram
Ross, Dave
  See Ross, David
Ross, David 1896-1975 .... *49*
  Obituary *20*
Ross, David 1949- *133*
  Earlier sketch in SATA *32*
Ross, Deborah J.
  See Wheeler, Deborah
Ross, Diana
  See Denney, Diana
Ross, Edward S(hearman) 1915- *85*
Ross, Eileen 1950- *115*
Ross, Frank (Xavier), Jr. 1914- *28*
Ross, Jane 1961- *79*
Ross, John 1921- *45*
Ross, Judy 1942- *54*
Ross, Katharine Reynolds
  See Ross, Kathy
Ross, Kathy 1948- *169*
  Earlier sketch in SATA *89*
Ross, Kent 1956- *91*
Ross, Lillian Hammer 1925- *72*
Ross, Michael Elsohn 1952- *170*
  Earlier sketches in SATA *80, 127*
Ross, Pat(ricia Kienzle) 1943- *53*
  Brief entry *48*
Ross, Ramon R(oyal) 1930- *62*
Ross, Stewart 1947- *134*
  Earlier sketch in SATA *92*
  See also SAAS *23*
Ross, Sylvia 1937- *231*
Ross, Tom 1958- *84*
Ross, Tony 1938- *225*
  Earlier sketches in SATA *17, 65, 130, 176*
Ross, Wilda 1915- *51*
  Brief entry *39*
Rossel, Seymour 1945- *28*
Rossell, Judith 1953- *187*
Rossel-Waugh, C. C.
  See Waugh, Carol-Lynn Rossel
Rossetti, Christina 1830-1894 .... *20*
  See also CLR *115*
Rossetti, Christina Georgina
  See Rossetti, Christina
Rossi, Joyce 1943- *116*
Rossotti, Hazel Swaine 1930- *95*
Rostkowski, Margaret I. 1945- *59*
Rostoker-Gruber, Karen *229*
Roth, Arnold 1929- *21*

Roth, Arthur J(oseph) 1925-1993 .... *43*
  Brief entry *28*
  Obituary *75*
  See also SAAS *11*
Roth, Carol 1940- *222*
Roth, David 1940- *36*
Roth, Julie Jersild *180*
Roth, Matthue 1978(?)- *174*
Roth, R.G.
  See Roth, Robert
Roth, Rob
  See Roth, Robert
Roth, Robert 1965- *230*
Roth, Roger *190*
Roth, Ruby 1983(?)- *216*
Roth, Stephanie
  See Sisson, Stephanie Roth
Roth, Susan L. *181*
  Earlier sketch in SATA *134*
Roth, Ty 1962- *239*
Rothberg, Abraham 1922-2011 .... *59*
Roth-Hano, Renee 1931- *85*
Rothkopf, Carol Z. 1929- *4*
Rothman, Joel 1938- *7*
Rotner, Shelley 1951- *169*
  Earlier sketch in SATA *76*
Rottman, S.L. 1970- *157*
  Earlier sketch in SATA *106*
Rottman, Susan Lynn
  See Rottman, S.L.
Roueche, Berton 1911-1994 .... *28*
Roughsey, Dick 1921(?)-1985 .... *35*
  See also CLR *41*
Roughsey, Goobalathaldin
  See Roughsey, Dick
Rounds, Glen (Harold) 1906-2002 .... *112*
  Obituary *141*
  Earlier sketches in SATA *8, 70*
Rourke, Constance Mayfield 1885-1941
  See YABC *1*
Rouss, Sylvia *211*
Rovetch, Gerda 1925(?)- *202*
Rovetch, L. Bob
  See Rovetch, Lissa
Rovetch, Lissa *201*
Rowan, Deirdre
  See Williams, Jeanne
Rowe, Jennifer
  See Rodda, Emily
Rowe, John A. 1949- *198*
  Earlier sketch in SATA *146*
Rowe, Viola Carson 1903-1969
  Obituary *26*
Rowh, Mark 1952- *90*
Rowland, Florence Wightman 1900-1997 ...... *8*
  Obituary *108*
Rowland-Entwistle, (Arthur) Theodore (Henry)
  1925- *94*
  Earlier sketch in SATA *31*
Rowling, J.K. 1965- *174*
  Earlier sketch in SATA *109*
  See also CLR *112*
Rowling, Joanne Kathleen
  See Rowling, J.K.
Rowsome, Frank (Howard), Jr. 1914-1983 .. *36*
Roy, Gabrielle 1909-1983 .... *104*
Roy, Jacqueline 1954- *74*
Roy, James 1968- *218*
Roy, Jennifer
  See Roy, Jennifer Rozines
Roy, Jennifer Rozines 1967- *178*
Roy, Jessie Hailstalk 1895-1986
  Obituary *51*
Roy, Kari Anne 1977(?)- *221*
Roy, Lena *238*
Roy, Liam
  See Scarry, Patricia (Murphy)
Roy, Ron 1940- *228*
  Brief entry *35*
  Earlier sketches in SATA *40, 110*
Royal, Laura 1956- *85*

Roybal, Laura Husby
  See Roybal, Laura
Royds, Caroline 1953- *55*
Royston, Angela 1945- *230*
  Earlier sketches in SATA *120, 169*
Rozakis, Laurie E. 1952- *84*
Rozen, Anna 1960- *206*
Rubbino, Salvatore 1970- *220*
Rubel, David 1961- *223*
Rubel, Nicole 1953- *181*
  Earlier sketches in SATA *18, 95, 135*
Rubin, Eva Johanna 1925- *38*
Rubin, Susan Goldman 1939- *182*
  Earlier sketches in SATA *84, 132*
Rubin, Vicky 1964- *193*
Rubinetti, Donald 1947- *92*
Rubinger, Ami 1953- *225*
Rubinstein, Gillian 1942- *158*
  Autobiography Feature *116*
  Earlier sketches in SATA *68, 105*
  See also CLR *35*
  See also SAAS *25*
Rubinstein, Gillian Margaret
  See Rubinstein, Gillian
Rubinstein, Patricia -2003
  See Forest, Antonia
Rubinstein, Patricia Giulia Caulfield Kate
  See Forest, Antonia
Rubinstein, Robert E(dward) 1943- *49*
Rublowsky, John M(artin) 1928- *62*
Rubright, Lynn 1936- *171*
Ruby, Laura *227*
  Earlier sketches in SATA *155, 181*
Ruby, Lois 1942- *184*
  Autobiography Feature *105*
  Brief entry *34*
  Earlier sketches in SATA *35, 95*
Ruby, Lois F.
  See Ruby, Lois
Ruchlis, Hy(man) 1913-1992 .... *3*
  Obituary *72*
Ruckdeschel, Liz *214*
Rucker, Mike 1940- *91*
Ruckman, Ivy 1931- *93*
  Earlier sketch in SATA *37*
Ruck-Pauquet, Gina 1931- *40*
  Brief entry *37*
Ruddell, Deborah 1949- *210*
Ruditis, Paul *190*
Rudley, Stephen 1946- *30*
Rudolph, Marguerita 1908- *21*
Rudomin, Esther
  See Hautzig, Esther Rudomin
Rue, Ginger *236*
Rue, Leonard Lee III 1926- *142*
  Earlier sketch in SATA *37*
Rue, Nancy 1951- *233*
Rue, Nancy N.
  See Rue, Nancy
Rue, Nancy Naylor
  See Rue, Nancy
Rueda, Claudia *183*
Ruedi, Norma Paul
  See Ainsworth, Norma
Ruelle, Karen Gray 1957- *209*
  Earlier sketches in SATA *84, 126*
Ruemmler, John D(avid) 1948- *78*
Ruepp, Krista 1947- *143*
Ruffell, Ann 1941- *30*
Ruffins, Reynold 1930- *125*
  Earlier sketch in SATA *41*
Rugg, Jim *206*
Ruggles, Lucy
  See Williams, Kathryn
Rugoff, Milton 1913- *30*
Ruhen, Olaf 1911-1989 .... *17*
Rui, Paolo 1962- *217*
Rukeyser, Muriel 1913-1980
  Obituary *22*
Rumbaut, Hendle 1949- *84*

Rumford, James 1948- *193*
  Earlier sketch in SATA *116*
Rumsey, Marian (Barritt) 1928- *16*
Rumstuckle, Cornelius
  See Brennan, Herbie
Runholt, Susan *216*
Runnerstroem, Bengt Arne 1944- *75*
Runyan, John
  See Palmer, Bernard (Alvin)
Runyon, Brent *217*
Runyon, Catherine 1947- *62*
Ruoff, A. LaVonne Brown 1930- *76*
Rupp, Rebecca *239*
  Earlier sketch in SATA *185*
Rusch, Elizabeth 1966- *198*
Rusch, Kris
  See Rusch, Kristine Kathryn
Rusch, Kristine Kathryn 1960- *113*
Rush, Alison 1951- *41*
Rush, Peter 1937- *32*
Rushdie, Ahmed Salman
  See Rushdie, Salman
Rushdie, Salman 1947-
  See CLR *125*
Rushford, Patricia H(elen) 1943- *134*
Rushmore, Helen 1898-1994 .... *3*
Rushmore, Robert (William) 1926-1986 .... *8*
  Obituary *49*
Ruskin, Ariane
  See Batterberry, Ariane Ruskin
Ruskin, John 1819-1900 .... *24*
Russ, Lavinia (Faxon) 1904-1992 .... *74*
Russell, Charlotte
  See Rathjen, Carl Henry
Russell, Ching Yeung 1946- *107*
Russell, Don(ald Bert) 1899-1986
  Obituary *47*
Russell, Franklin (Alexander) 1926- *11*
Russell, Gertrude Barrer
  See Barrer-Russell, Gertrude
Russell, Helen Ross 1915- *8*
Russell, James 1933- *53*
Russell, Jim
  See Russell, James
Russell, Joan Plummer 1930- *139*
Russell, Natalie 1972- *218*
Russell, P(hilip) Craig 1951- *162*
  Earlier sketch in SATA *80*
Russell, Patrick
  See Sammis, John
Russell, Paul (Gary) 1942- *57*
Russell, Sarah
  See Laski, Marghanita
Russell, Sharman Apt 1954- *123*
Russell, Solveig Paulson 1904-1985 .... *3*
Russo, Marisabina 1950- *188*
  Earlier sketches in SATA *106, 151*
Russo, Monica J. 1950- *83*
Russo, Susan 1947- *30*
Russon, Penni 1974- *179*
Rutgers van der Loeff, An
  See Rutgers van der Loeff-Basenau, An(na)
  Maria Margaretha
Rutgers van der Loeff-Basenau, An(na) Maria
  Margaretha 1910- *22*
Ruth, Rod 1912-1987 .... *9*
Rutherford, Douglas
  See McConnell, James Douglas Rutherford
Rutherford, Meg 1932- *34*
Ruthin, Margaret
  See Catherall, Arthur
Rutkoski, Marie 1977- *219*
Rutland, J. *232*
Rutland, Jarrett
  See Rutland, J.
Rutledge, Jill Zimmerman 1951- *155*
Rutz, Viola Larkin 1932- *12*
Ruurs, Margriet 1952- *215*
  Earlier sketches in SATA *97, 147*
Ruzicka, Rudolph 1883-1978
  Obituary *24*

Ruzzier, Sergio 1966- 210
  Earlier sketch in SATA *159*
Ryan, Betsy
  See Ryan, Elizabeth (Anne)
Ryan, Candace 234
Ryan, Cheli Duran 20
Ryan, Darlene 1958- 176
Ryan, Elizabeth (Anne) 1943- 30
Ryan, Jeanette
  See Mines, Jeanette
Ryan, John 1921-2009 22
Ryan, John Gerald Christopher
  See Ryan, John
Ryan, Margaret 1950- 166
  Earlier sketch in SATA *78*
Ryan, Mary E. 1953- 61
Ryan, Mary Elizabeth
  See Ryan, Mary E.
Ryan, Pam Munoz 1951- 197
  Earlier sketch in SATA *134*
Ryan, Patrick 1957- 138
Ryan, Peter (Charles) 1939- 15
Ryan, Rob 1962- 237
Ryan-Lush, Geraldine 1949- 89
Rybakov, Anatoli (Naumovich) 1911-1998 .. 79
  Obituary 108
Rybakov, Anatolii (Naumovich)
  See Rybakov, Anatoli (Naumovich)
Rybolt, Thomas R. 1954- 62
Rybolt, Thomas Roy
  See Rybolt, Thomas R.
Rybolt, Tom
  See Rybolt, Thomas R.
Rycroft, Nina 228
Rydberg, Ernest E(mil) 1901-1993 21
Rydberg, Lou(isa Hampton) 1908- 27
Rydell, Katy 1942- 91
Rydell, Wendell
  See Rydell, Wendy
Rydell, Wendy 4
Ryden, Hope 91
  Earlier sketch in SATA *8*
Ryder, Joanne 1946- 226
  Brief entry 34
  Earlier sketches in SATA *65, 122, 163*
  See also CLR *37*
Ryder, Pamela
  See Lamb, Nancy
Rye, Anthony
  See Youd, Samuel
Rylander, Chris 239
Rylant, Cynthia 1954- 195
  Brief entry 44
  Earlier sketches in SATA *50, 76, 112, 160*
  See also CLR *86*
  See also SAAS *13*
Rymer, Alta May 1925- 34
Rymond, Lynda Gene 199

S

S. L. C.
  See Twain, Mark
S., Svend Otto
  See Soerensen, Svend Otto
Saaf, Donald W(illiam) 1961- 124
Saal, Jocelyn
  See Sachs, Judith
Sabbeth, Carol (Landstrom) 1957- 125
Saberhagen, Fred 1930-2007 89
  Obituary 184
  Earlier sketch in SATA *37*
Saberhagen, Fred T.
  See Saberhagen, Fred
Saberhagen, Fred Thomas
  See Saberhagen, Fred
Saberhagen, Frederick Thomas
  See Saberhagen, Fred

Sabin, Edwin L(egrand) 1870-1952
  See YABC *2*
Sabin, Francene 27
Sabin, Lou
  See Sabin, Louis
Sabin, Louis 1930- 27
Sabre, Dirk
  See Laffin, John (Alfred Charles)
Sabuda, Robert (James) 1965- 120
  Earlier sketch in SATA *81*
Sabuda, Robert 1965- 170
Sabuda, Robert James
  See Sabuda, Robert
Sachar, Louis 1954- 238
  Brief entry 50
  Earlier sketches in SATA *63, 104, 154*
  See also CLR *161*
Sachs, Elizabeth-Ann 1946- 48
Sachs, Judith 1947- 52
  Brief entry 51
Sachs, Marilyn 1927- 164
  Autobiography Feature 110
  Earlier sketches in SATA *3, 68*
  See also CLR *2*
  See also SAAS *2*
Sachs, Marilyn Stickle
  See Sachs, Marilyn
Sackett, S(amuel) J(ohn) 1928- 12
Sackson, Sid 1920- 16
Sacre, Antonio 1968- 152
Saddler, Allen
  See Richards, R(onald) C(harles) W(illiam)
Saddler, K. Allen
  See Richards, R(onald) C(harles) W(illiam)
Sadie, Stanley 1930-2005 14
Sadie, Stanley John
  See Sadie, Stanley
Sadiq, Nazneen
  See Sheikh, Nazneen
Sadler, Catherine Edwards 1952- 60
  Brief entry 45
Sadler, Marilyn (June) 1950- 79
Sadler, Mark
  See Lynds, Dennis
Sadler, Sonia Lynn 230
Saffer, Barbara 144
Sagan, Carl 1934-1996 58
  Obituary 94
Sagan, Carl Edward
  See Sagan, Carl
Sage, Angie 1952- 197
Sage, Juniper
  See Brown, Margaret Wise
  and Hurd, Edith Thacher
Sagsoorian, Paul 1923- 12
Said, S.F. 1967- 174
Saidman, Anne 1952- 75
Saint, Dora Jessie 1913- 10
St. Anthony, Jane 175
St. Antoine, Sara L. 1966- 84
St. Clair, Byrd Hooper 1905-1976
  Obituary 28
St. Crow, Lili
  See Saintcrow, Lilith
Saintcrow, Lilith 1976- 221
Saint-Exupery, Antoine de 1900-1944 20
  See also CLR *142*
Saint-Exupery, Antoine Jean Baptiste Marie
  Roger de
  See Saint-Exupery, Antoine de
St. George, Judith 1931- 161
  Earlier sketches in SATA *13, 99*
  See also CLR *57*
  See also SAAS *12*
St. George, Judith Alexander
  See St. George, Judith
St. James, Blakely
  See Gottfried, Theodore Mark
  and Platt, Charles
St. James, Blakely
  See Griffin, W. E. B.

St. James, Sierra
  See Rallison, Janette
Saint James, Synthia 1949- 152
  Earlier sketch in SATA *84*
St. John, Lauren 1966- 214
St. John, Nicole 143
  Autobiography Feature 143
  Earlier sketches in SATA *29, 89*
  See also CLR *46*
  See also SAAS *7*
St. John, Patricia Mary 1919-1993
  Obituary 79
St. John, Philip
  See del Rey, Lester
St. John, Wylly Folk 1908-1985 10
  Obituary 45
St. Max, E. S.
  See Ellis, Edward S.
St. Meyer, Ned
  See Stratemeyer, Edward L.
St. Mox, E. A.
  See Ellis, Edward S.
St. Myer, Ned
  See Stratemeyer, Edward L.
St. Tamara
  See Kolba, St. Tamara
Saito, Michiko
  See Fujiwara, Michiko
Sakai, Komako 1966- 213
Sakaki, Ichiro 1969- 192
Sakamoto, Miki 198
Sakers, Don 1958- 72
Sakharnov, S.
  See Sakharnov, Svyatoslav
Sakharnov, Svyatoslav 1923- 65
Sakharnov, Svyatoslav Vladimirovich
  See Sakharnov, Svyatoslav
Saksena, Kate 148
Sakurai, Gail 1952- 153
  Earlier sketch in SATA *87*
Salamanca, Lucy
  See del Barco, Lucy Salamanca
Salas, Laura Purdie 1966- 216
Salassi, Otto R(ussell) 1939-1993 38
  Obituary 77
Salat, Cristina 82
Saldana, Rene, Jr. 186
Saldutti, Denise 1953- 39
Sale, Tim 1956- 153
Salem, Kay 1952- 92
Salerni, Dianne K. 231
Salerno, Steven 176
Salinger, J.D. 1919-2010 67
  See also CLR *18*
Salinger, Jerome David
  See Salinger, J.D.
Salisbury, Graham 1944- 234
  Earlier sketches in SATA *76, 108, 161, 195*
Salisbury, Joyce E(llen) 1944- 138
Salkey, (Felix) Andrew (Alexander)
  1928-1995 118
  Earlier sketch in SATA *35*
Salley, Coleen 166
Sallis, Susan (Diana) 1929- 55
Salmieri, Daniel 1983- 208
Salmon, Annie Elizabeth 1899- 13
Salmon, Dena K. 1959(?)- 219
Salonen, Roxane Beauclair 1968- 184
Salsi, Lynn 1947- 130
Salsitz, R. A. V.
  See Salsitz, Rhondi Vilott
Salsitz, Rhondi Vilott 115
Salten, Felix
  See Salzmann, Siegmund
Salter, Cedric
  See Knight, Francis Edgar
Salter, Sydney 220
Saltman, Judith 1947- 64
Saltzberg, Barney 1955- 233
  Earlier sketches in SATA *135, 194*

Saltzman, David (Charles Laertes)
  1967-1990 86
Salvadori, Mario (George) 1907-1997 97
  Earlier sketch in SATA 40
Salwood, F.K.
  See Kilworth, Garry
Salzer, L. E.
  See Wilson, Lionel
Salzman, Marian 1959- 77
Salzmann, Siegmund 1869-1945 25
Samachson, Dorothy (Mirkin) 1914-1997 3
Samachson, Joseph 1906-1980 3
  Obituary 52
Sammis, John 1942- 4
Sampson, Emma (Keats) Speed 1868-1947 . 68
Sampson, Fay 1935- 151
  Brief entry 40
  Earlier sketch in SATA 42
Sampson, Fay Elizabeth
  See Sampson, Fay
Sampson, Jeff 1982- 232
Sampson, Michael 1952- 143
  Earlier sketch in SATA 95
Samson, Anne S(tringer) 1933- 2
Samson, Joan 1937-1976 13
Samson, Suzanne M. 1959- 91
Samuels, Barbara 199
Samuels, Charles 1902-1982 12
Samuels, Cynthia K(alish) 1946- 79
Samuels, Gertrude 1910(?)-2003 17
  Obituary 147
Sanborn, Duane 1914-1996 38
Sancha, Sheila 1924- 38
Sanchez, Alex 1957- 151
Sanchez, Anita 1956- 209
Sanchez, Sonia 1934- 136
  Earlier sketch in SATA 22
  See also CLR 18
Sanchez-Silva, Jose Maria 1911- 132
  Earlier sketch in SATA 16
  See also CLR 12
Sand, George X. 45
Sandak, Cass R(obert) 1950-2001 51
  Brief entry 37
Sandberg, (Karin) Inger 1930- 15
Sandberg, Karl C. 1931- 35
Sandberg, Lasse (E. M.) 1924- 15
Sandburg, Carl 1878-1967 8
  See also CLR 67
Sandburg, Carl August
  See Sandburg, Carl
Sandburg, Charles
  See Sandburg, Carl
Sandburg, Charles A.
  See Sandburg, Carl
Sandburg, Helga 1918- 3
  See also SAAS 10
Sandell, Lisa Ann 1977- 175
Sandemose, Iben 1950- 211
Sander, Heather L. 1947- 157
Sanderlin, George 1915- 4
Sanderlin, Owenita (Harrah) 1916- 11
Sanders, Betty Jane
  See Monthei, Betty
Sanders, Nancy I. 1960- 141
  Earlier sketch in SATA 90
Sanders, Scott Russell 1945- 109
  Earlier sketch in SATA 56
Sanders, Winston P.
  See Anderson, Poul
Sanderson, Irma 1912- 66
Sanderson, Ivan T(erence) 1911-1973 6
Sanderson, Margaret Love
  See Keats, Emma
  and Sampson, Emma (Keats) Speed
Sanderson, Ruth 1951- 224
  Earlier sketches in SATA 41, 109, 172
Sanderson, Ruth L.
  See Sanderson, Ruth
Sanders-Wells, Linda 220
Sand-Eveland, Cyndi 211

Sandin, Joan 1942- 197
  Earlier sketches in SATA 12, 94, 153
Sandison, Janet
  See Cameron, Elizabeth Jane
Sandler, Martin W. 216
  Earlier sketch in SATA 160
Sandom, J. Gregory
  See Welsh, T.K.
Sandom, J.G.
  See Welsh, T.K.
Sandoz, Mari(e Susette) 1900-1966 5
Sanford, Agnes (White) 1897-1976 61
Sanford, Doris 1937- 69
Sanford, Rose
  See Simmonds, Posy
Sanger, Amy Wilson 1967- 205
Sanger, Marjory Bartlett 1920- 8
San Jose, Christine 1929- 167
Sankey, Alice (Ann-Susan) 1910- 27
Sansone, Adele 1953- 230
San Souci, Daniel 192
  Earlier sketch in SATA 96
San Souci, Robert D. 1946- 220
  Earlier sketches in SATA 40, 81, 117, 158
  See also CLR 43
Santamaria, Benjamin 1955- 184
Santat, Dan 224
  Earlier sketch in SATA 188
Santesson, Hans Stefan 1914(?)-1975
  Obituary 30
Santiago, Esmeralda 1948- 129
Santopolo, Jill 214
Santore, Charles 1935- 200
Santoro, C.
  See Santoro, Christopher
Santoro, Christopher 218
Santoro, Scott 1956- 236
Santos, Helen
  See Griffiths, Helen
Santrey, Louis
  See Sabin, Louis
Santucci, Barbara 1948- 130
Sapergia, Barbara 1943- 181
Sapet, Kerrily 1972- 214
Sapieyevski, Anne Lindbergh 1940-1993 81
  Brief entry 32
  Earlier sketches in SATA 35, 78
Saport, Linda 1954- 123
Sapp, Allen 1929- 151
Sarac, Roger
  See Caras, Roger A(ndrew)
Sarah, Duchess of York
  See Ferguson, Sarah
Sarasin, Jennifer
  See Sachs, Judith
Sarcone-Roach, Julia 215
Sardinha, Rick 192
Sarg, Anthony Frederick
  See Sarg, Tony
Sarg, Tony 1882-1942
  See YABC 1
Sargent, Pamela 1948- 78
  Earlier sketch in SATA 29
Sargent, Robert 1933- 2
Sargent, Sarah 1937- 44
  Brief entry 41
Sargent, Shirley 1927-2004 11
Sarnoff, Jane 1937- 10
Saroff, Phyllis V. 202
Saroyan, William 1908-1981 23
  Obituary 24
Sartell, Debra 229
Sarton, Eleanor May
  See Sarton, May
Sarton, May 1912-1995 36
  Obituary 86
Sasaki, Chris 182
Sasaki, Ellen Joy 206
Saseen, Sharon (Dillon) 1949- 59

Sasek, Miroslav 1916-1980 16
  Obituary 23
  See also CLR 4
Sasso, Sandy Eisenberg 1947- 162
  Earlier sketches in SATA 86, 116
Sathre, Vivian 1952- 133
  Earlier sketch in SATA 79
Satterfield, Charles
  See del Rey, Lester
  and Pohl, Frederik
Sattgast, L. J.
  See Sattgast, Linda J.
Sattgast, Linda J. 1953- 91
Sattler, Helen Roney 1921-1992 74
  Earlier sketch in SATA 4
  See also CLR 24
Sattler, Jennifer
  See Sattler, Jennifer Gordon
Sattler, Jennifer Gordon 218
Sauer, Julia Lina 1891-1983 32
  Obituary 36
Sauer, Tammi 1972- 223
Sauerwein, Leigh 1944- 155
Saul, Carol P. 1947- 117
  Earlier sketch in SATA 78
Saul, John 1942- 98
Saul, John W.
  See Saul, John
Saul, John Woodruff III
  See Saul, John
Saul, (Ellen) Wendy 1946- 42
Saulnier, Karen Luczak 1940- 80
Saunders, Caleb
  See Heinlein, Robert A.
Saunders, Dave 1939- 85
Saunders, Julie 1939- 85
Saunders, (William) Keith 1910-1994 12
Saunders, Rubie (Agnes) 1929- 21
Saunders, Steven
  See Jones, Allan Frewin
Saunders, Susan 1945- 96
  Brief entry 41
  Earlier sketch in SATA 46
Saunders-Smith, Gail 1952- 169
Sauvain, Philip Arthur 1933- 111
Savadier, Elivia 1950- 228
  Earlier sketches in SATA 79, 164
Savage, Alan
  See Nicole, Christopher
Savage, Blake
  See Goodwin, Harold L(eland)
Savage, Candace 1949- 142
Savage, Deborah 1955- 76
Savage, Jeff 1961- 97
Savage, Katharine James 1905-1989
  Obituary 61
Savage, Stephen 1965- 194
Savage, Thomas 1915-2003
  Obituary 147
Savageau, Cheryl 1950- 96
Savery, Constance (Winifred) 1897-1999 1
Saville, Andrew
  See Taylor, Andrew
Saville, (Leonard) Malcolm 1901-1982 23
  Obituary 31
Saviozzi, Adriana
  See Mazza, Adriana
Savitt, Sam 1917-2000 8
  Obituary 126
Savitz, Harriet May 1933-2008 72
  Earlier sketch in SATA 5
  See also SAAS 26
Sawicki, Mary 1950- 90
Sawyer, (Frederick) Don(ald) 1947- 72
Sawyer, Kem Knapp 1953- 84
Sawyer, Kim Vogel 233
Sawyer, Robert J. 1960- 149
  Earlier sketch in SATA 81
Sawyer, Robert James
  See Sawyer, Robert J.

Sawyer, Ruth 1880-1970 .... *17*
  See also CLR 36
Saxby, H.M.
  See Saxby, (Henry) Maurice
Saxby, (Henry) Maurice 1924- *71*
Saxon, Andrew
  See Arthur, Robert, (Jr.)
Saxon, Antonia
  See Sachs, Judith
Say, Allen 1937- *161*
  Earlier sketches in SATA *28, 69, 110*
  See also CLR *135*
Sayers, Frances Clarke 1897-1989 .... *3*
  Obituary *62*
Sayles, Elizabeth 1956- *220*
  Earlier sketches in SATA *108, 163*
Saylor-Marchant, Linda 1963- *82*
Sayre, April Pulley 1966- *233*
  Earlier sketches in SATA *88, 131, 191*
Sazer, Nina 1949- *13*
Scabrini, Janet 1953- *13*
Scagell, Robin 1946- *107*
Scagnetti, Jack 1924- *7*
Scaletta, Kurtis 1968- *215*
Scalora, Suza *224*
Scamander, Newt
  See Rowling, J.K.
Scamell, Ragnhild 1940- *180*
  Earlier sketch in SATA *77*
Scandiffio, Laura *227*
Scanlon, Elizabeth Garton
  See Scanlon, Liz Garton
Scanlon, Liz Garton *226*
Scanlon, Marion Stephany *11*
Scannel, John Vernon
  See Scannell, Vernon
Scannell, Vernon 1922-2007 .... *59*
  Obituary *188*
Scarborough, Elizabeth
  See Scarborough, Elizabeth Ann
Scarborough, Elizabeth Ann 1947- *171*
  Earlier sketch in SATA *98*
Scarf, Maggi
  See Scarf, Maggie
Scarf, Maggie 1932- *5*
Scariano, Margaret M. 1924- *86*
Scarlett, Susan
  See Streatfeild, Noel
Scarrow, Alex 1966- *236*
Scarry, Huck
  See Scarry, Richard McClure, Jr.
Scarry, Patricia (Murphy) 1924- *2*
Scarry, Patsy
  See Scarry, Patricia (Murphy)
Scarry, Richard (McClure) 1919-1994 .... *75*
  Obituary *90*
  Earlier sketches in SATA *2, 35*
  See also CLR *41*
Scarry, Richard McClure, Jr. 1953- *35*
Schachner, Judith Byron 1951- *178*
  Earlier sketch in SATA *88*
Schachner, Judy
  See Schachner, Judith Byron
Schachtel, Roger 1949- *38*
Schachtel, Roger Bernard
  See Schachtel, Roger
Schade, Susan *189*
Schaedler, Sally *116*
Schaefer, Carole Lexa *173*
Schaefer, Jack (Warner) 1907-1991 .... *66*
  Obituary *65*
  Earlier sketch in SATA *3*
Schaefer, Lola M. 1950- *183*
  Earlier sketches in SATA *91, 144*
Schaeffer, Mead 1898- *21*
Schaeffer, Susan Fromberg 1940-2011 .... *22*
Schaer, Brigitte 1958- *112*
Schallau, Daniel 1966- *222*
Schaller, George
  See Schaller, George B.
Schaller, George B. 1933- *30*

Schaller, George Beals
  See Schaller, George B.
Schanzer, Rosalyn (Good) 1942- *138*
  Earlier sketch in SATA *77*
Schatell, Brian *66*
  Brief entry *47*
Schechter, Betty (Goodstein) 1921- *5*
Schechter, Simone
  See Elkeles, Simone
Schecter, Ellen 1944- *85*
Scheeder, Louis 1946- *141*
Scheer, Julian (Weisel) 1926-2001 .... *8*
Scheerger, Sarah Lynn
  See Lynn, Sarah
Scheffer, Victor B(lanchard) 1906- *6*
Scheffler, Axel 1957- *230*
  Earlier sketch in SATA *180*
Scheffler, Ursel 1938- *81*
Scheffrin-Falk, Gladys 1928- *76*
Scheidl, Gerda Marie 1913- *85*
Scheier, Michael 1943- *40*
  Brief entry *36*
Schell, Mildred 1922- *41*
Schell, Orville (Hickok) 1940- *10*
Scheller, Melanie 1953- *77*
Schellie, Don 1932- *29*
Schembri, Jim 1962- *124*
Schembri, Pamela 1969- *195*
Schemm, Mildred Walker 1905-1998 .... *21*
  Obituary *103*
Schenker, Dona 1947- *133*
  Earlier sketch in SATA *68*
Scher, Paula 1948- *47*
Scherer, Jeffrey *194*
Scherf, Margaret 1908-1979 .... *10*
Schermer, Judith (Denise) 1941- *30*
Schertle, Alice 1941- *231*
  Earlier sketches in SATA *36, 90, 145, 192*
Schick, Alice 1946- *27*
Schick, Eleanor 1942- *144*
  Earlier sketches in SATA *9, 82*
Schick, Joel 1945- *31*
  Brief entry *30*
Schields, Gretchen 1948- *75*
Schiff, Ken(neth Roy) 1942- *7*
Schiller, Andrew 1919- *21*
Schiller, Barbara (Heyman) 1928- *21*
Schiller, Pamela (Byrne) *127*
Schindel, John 1955- *213*
  Earlier sketches in SATA *77, 115*
Schindelman, Joseph 1923- *67*
  Brief entry *32*
Schindler, S.D. 1952- *198*
  Brief entry *50*
  Earlier sketches in SATA *75, 118, 171*
Schindler, Steven D.
  See Schindler, S.D.
Schinto, Jeanne 1951- *93*
Schisgall, Oscar 1901-1984 .... *12*
  Obituary *38*
Schlaepfer, Gloria G. 1931- *154*
Schlee, Ann 1934- *44*
  Brief entry *36*
Schleichert, Elizabeth 1945- *77*
Schlein, Miriam 1926-2004 .... *130*
  Obituary *159*
  Earlier sketches in SATA *2, 87*
  See also CLR *41*
Schlesinger, Arthur M., Jr. 1917-2007 .... *61*
  Obituary *181*
  See Schlesinger, Arthur Meier
Schlesinger, Arthur Meier 1888-1965
Schlessinger, Laura (Catherine) 1947- *160*
  Earlier sketch in SATA *110*
Schlitz, Laura Amy *232*
  Earlier sketch in SATA *184*
Schloat, G. Warren, Jr. 1914-2000 .... *4*
Schlossberg, Elisabeth *221*
Schmais, Libby *227*
Schmatz, Pat *197*

Schmid, Eleonore 1939- *126*
  Earlier sketches in SATA *12, 84*
Schmid, Paul *231*
Schmid, Susan Maupin *208*
Schmiderer, Dorothy 1940- *19*
Schmidt, Annie M. G. 1911-1995 .... *67*
  Obituary *91*
  See also CLR *22*
Schmidt, C.A. *196*
Schmidt, Diane 1953- *70*
Schmidt, Elizabeth 1915- *15*
Schmidt, Gary D. 1957- *193*
  Earlier sketches in SATA *93, 135*
Schmidt, James Norman 1912-1983 .... *21*
Schmidt, Karen Lee 1953- *185*
  Earlier sketch in SATA *94*
Schmidt, Lynette 1952- *76*
Schmitz, Tamara *207*
Schneider, Antonie 1954- *167*
  Earlier sketch in SATA *89*
Schneider, Christine M. 1972(?)- *171*
  Earlier sketch in SATA *120*
Schneider, Dick
  See Schneider, Richard H.
Schneider, Elisa
  See Kleven, Elisa
Schneider, Herman 1905-2003 .... *7*
  Obituary *148*
Schneider, Howie -2007 .... *181*
Schneider, Josh 1980- *196*
Schneider, Katy *237*
Schneider, Laurie
  See Adams, Laurie
Schneider, Nina 1913-2007 .... *2*
  Obituary *186*
Schneider, Nina Zimet
  See Schneider, Nina
Schneider, Rex 1937- *44*
Schneider, Richard H. 1922- *171*
Schneider, Richard Henry
  See Schneider, Richard H.
Schneider, Robyn 1986- *187*
Schnirel, James R. 1931- *14*
Schnitter, Jane T. 1958- *88*
Schnitzlein, Danny *134*
Schnur, Steven 1952- *144*
  Earlier sketch in SATA *95*
Schnurre, Wolfdietrich 1920-1989
  Obituary *63*
Schoberle, Cecile 1949- *80*
Schock, Pauline 1928- *45*
Schoell, William 1951- *160*
Schoen, Barbara (Taylor) 1924-1993 .... *13*
Schoenherr, Ian *235*
  Earlier sketch in SATA *177*
Schoenherr, John 1935-2010 .... *66*
  Earlier sketch in SATA *37*
  See also SAAS *13*
Schoenherr, John Carl
  See Schoenherr, John
Schofield, Sandy
  See Rusch, Kristine Kathryn
Scholastica, Sister Mary
  See Jenkins, Marie M(agdalen)
Scholefield, A. T.
  See Scholefield, Alan
Scholefield, Alan 1931- *66*
Scholefield, Edmund O.
  See Griffin, W. E. B.
Scholey, Arthur 1932- *28*
Scholz, Jackson Volney 1897-1986
  Obituary *49*
Schon, Nick 1955- *223*
Schone, Virginia *22*
Schongut, Emanuel 1936- *184*
  Brief entry *36*
  Earlier sketch in SATA *52*
Schoonmaker, Elizabeth *239*
Schoonover, Frank (Earle) 1877-1972 .... *24*
Schoor, Gene 1921- *3*

Schories, Pat 1952- 232
  Earlier sketches in SATA *116, 164*
Schorr, Melissa 1972- 194
Schorr, Melissa Robin
  See Schorr, Melissa
Schott, Jane A. 1946- 172
Schotter, Roni 190
  Earlier sketches in SATA *105, 149*
Schrader, Dave 1967(?)- 225
Schraff, Anne E(laine) 1939- 92
  Earlier sketch in SATA *27*
Schram, Penninah 1934- 219
  Earlier sketch in SATA *119*
Schrank, Joseph 1900-1984
  Obituary 38
Schrecengost, Maity 1938- 118
Schrecengost, S. Maitland
  See Schrecengost, Maity
Schreck, Karen
  See Schreck, Karen Halvorsen
Schreck, Karen Halvorsen 1962- 185
Schrecker, Judie 1954- 90
Schreiber, Elizabeth Anne (Ferguson)
  1947- 13
Schreiber, Ralph W(alter) 1942- 13
Schreiner, Samuel A(gnew), Jr. 1921- 70
Schroades, John 214
Schroder, Monika 1965- 229
Schroeder, Alan 1961- 98
  Earlier sketch in SATA *66*
Schroeder, Binette
  See Nickl, Barbara (Elisabeth)
Schroeder, Russell (K.) 1943- 146
Schroeder, Ted 1931(?)-1973
  Obituary 20
Schubert, Dieter 1947- 217
  Earlier sketches in SATA *62, 101*
Schubert, Ingrid 1953- 217
Schubert, Leda 1945(?)- 232
  Earlier sketch in SATA *181*
Schubert, Leda Deirdre
  See Schubert, Leda
Schubert-Gabrys, Ingrid 1953- 101
  Earlier sketch in SATA *62*
Schuelein-Steel, Danielle
  See Steel, Danielle
Schuelein-Steel, Danielle Fernande
  See Steel, Danielle
Schuerger, Michele R. 110
Schuett, Stacey 1960- 168
  Earlier sketch in SATA *75*
Schulke, Flip Phelps Graeme 1930- 57
Schulman, Arlene 1961- 105
Schulman, Janet 1933- 208
  Earlier sketches in SATA *22, 137*
Schulman, L(ester) M(artin) 1934- 13
Schulte, Elaine L(ouise) 1934- 36
Schultz, Betty K(epka) 1932- 125
Schultz, Gwendolyn 21
Schultz, James Willard 1859-1947
  See YABC *1*
Schultz, Pearle Henriksen 1918- 21
Schulz, Charles M. 1922-2000 10
  Obituary 118
Schulz, Charles Monroe
  See Schulz, Charles M.
Schumacher, Julie 1958- 191
Schumaker, Ward 1943- 96
Schuman, Michael A. 1953- 134
  Earlier sketch in SATA *85*
Schur, Maxine
  See Schur, Maxine Rose
Schur, Maxine Rose 1948- 135
  Autobiography Feature 135
  Brief entry 49
  Earlier sketches in SATA *53, 98*
Schurfranz, Vivian 1925- 13
Schutzer, A. I. 1922- 13
Schuyler, Pamela R. 1948- 30
Schwabach, Karen 185
Schwager, Tina 1964- 110

Schwandt, Stephen (William) 1947- 61
Schwark, Mary Beth 1954- 51
Schwartz, Alvin 1927-1992 56
  Obituary 71
  Earlier sketch in SATA *4*
  See also CLR *89*
Schwartz, Amy 1954- 189
  Brief entry 41
  Earlier sketches in SATA *47, 83, 131*
  See also CLR *25*
  See also SAAS *18*
Schwartz, Anne Powers 1913-1987 10
Schwartz, Carol 1954- 77
Schwartz, Charles W(alsh) 1914- 8
Schwartz, David M. 1951- 239
  Earlier sketches in SATA *59, 110*
Schwartz, David Martin
  See Schwartz, David M.
Schwartz, Elizabeth Reeder 1912- 8
Schwartz, Ellen 1949- 117
Schwartz, Howard 1945- 238
Schwartz, Jerome L.
  See Lawrence, Jerome
Schwartz, Joanne 1960- 220
Schwartz, Joel L. 1940- 54
  Brief entry 51
Schwartz, John 1957- 232
Schwartz, Joyce R. 1950- 93
Schwartz, Julius 1907-2004 45
Schwartz, Perry 1942- 75
Schwartz, Sheila (Ruth) 1929- 27
Schwartz, Stephen (Lawrence) 1948- 19
Schwartz, Virginia Frances 1950- 184
  Earlier sketch in SATA *131*
Schwarz, Silvia Tessa Viviane
  See Schwarz, Viviane
Schwarz, Viviane 1977- 204
Schwarz, (Silvia Tessa) Viviane 1977- 141
Schweitzer, Byrd Baylor
  See Baylor, Byrd
Schweitzer, Iris 59
  Brief entry 36
Schweninger, Ann 1951- 168
  Earlier sketches in SATA *29, 98*
Schwerin, Doris H(alpern) 1922- 64
Schy, Yael 197
Scieszka, Jon 1954- 238
  Earlier sketches in SATA *68, 105, 160, 199*
  See also CLR *107*
Scillian, Devin 199
  Earlier sketch in SATA *128*
Scioscia, Mary (Hershey) 1926- 63
Sciurba, Katie 1957- 196
Scofield, Penrod 1933- 62
  Obituary 78
Scoggin, Margaret C(lara) 1905-1968 47
  Brief entry 28
Scoltock, Jack 1942- 141
  Earlier sketch in SATA *72*
Scoppettone, Sandra 1936- 92
  Earlier sketch in SATA *9*
Scot, Michael
  See Rohan, Michael Scott
Scot-Bernard, P.
  See Bernard, Patricia
Scotland, Jay
  See Jakes, John
Scott, Alastair
  See Allen, Kenneth S.
Scott, Ann Herbert 1926- 140
  Autobiography Feature 140
  Brief entry 29
  Earlier sketches in SATA *56, 94*
Scott, Bill
  See Scott, William N(eville)
Scott, Bill 1920(?)-1985
  Obituary 46
Scott, Cora Annett (Pipitone) 1931- 11
Scott, Dan
  See Barker, S. Omar

Scott, Elaine 1940- 198
  Earlier sketches in SATA *36, 90, 164*
Scott, Elizabeth 1972- 194
Scott, Inara 236
Scott, Jack Denton 1915-1995 83
  Earlier sketch in SATA *31*
  See also CLR *20*
  See also SAAS *14*
Scott, Jane (Harrington) 1931- 55
Scott, Jane Wooster 1939- 226
Scott, Jennifer Power 1968- 230
Scott, Jessica
  See De Wire, Elinor
Scott, John 1912-1976 14
Scott, John Anthony 1916- 23
Scott, John M(artin) 1913- 12
Scott, Mary
  See Mattern, Joanne
Scott, Melissa 1960- 109
Scott, Michael 1959- 211
Scott, Michael Peter
  See Scott, Michael
Scott, Mike
  See Scott, Michael
Scott, Richard
  See Rennert, Richard Scott
Scott, Roney
  See Gault, William Campbell
Scott, Sally 1909-1978 43
Scott, Sally 1948- 44
Scott, Sally Elisabeth
  See Scott, Sally
Scott, W. N.
  See Scott, William N(eville)
Scott, Sir Walter 1771-1832
  See YABC *2*
  See also CLR *154*
Scott, Warwick
  See Trevor, Elleston
Scott, William N(eville) 1923- 87
Scotti, Anna
  See Coates, Anna
Scotton, Rob 1960- 214
  Earlier sketch in SATA *177*
Scribner, Charles, Jr. 1921-1995 13
  Obituary 87
Scribner, Joanne L. 1949- 33
Scribner, Kimball 1917- 63
Scrimger, Richard 1957- 164
  Earlier sketch in SATA *119*
Scrimsher, Lila Gravatt 1897-1974
  Obituary 28
Scroder, Walter K. 1928- 82
Scroggs, Kirk 187
Scruggs, Sandy 1961- 89
Scudder, Brooke 1959- 154
Scudder, Mildred Lee 1908- 6
  See also SAAS *12*
Scull, Marie-Louise 1943-1993 77
Scuro, Vincent 1951- 21
Seabrooke, Brenda 1941- 148
  Earlier sketches in SATA *30, 88*
Seagraves, D.B.
  See Seagraves, Donny Bailey
Seagraves, Donny
  See Seagraves, Donny Bailey
Seagraves, Donny Bailey 1951- 224
Seaman, Augusta Huiell 1879-1950 31
Seamands, Ruth 1916- 9
Searcy, Margaret Zehmer 1926- 54
  Brief entry 39
Searight, Mary W(illiams) 1918- 17
Searle, Kathryn Adrienne 1942- 10
Searle, Ronald 1920- 70
  Earlier sketch in SATA *42*
Searle, Ronald William Fordham
  See Searle, Ronald
Sears, Stephen W. 1932- 4
Seaskull, Cecil
  See Castellucci, Cecil

Sebastian, Lee
See Silverberg, Robert
Sebestyen, Igen
See Sebestyen, Ouida
Sebestyen, Ouida 1924- *140*
Earlier sketch in SATA *39*
See also CLR *17*
See also SAAS *10*
Sebrey, Mary Ann 1951- 62
Sechrist, Elizabeth Hough 1903-1991 2
Sederman, Marty *211*
Sedges, John
See Buck, Pearl S.
Sedgwick, Marcus 1968- *197*
Earlier sketch in SATA *160*
Sedita, Francesco 1974- 235
Seed, Cecile Eugenie 1930- 86
Earlier sketch in SATA *8*
See also CLR *76*
Seed, Jenny
See Seed, Cecile Eugenie
Seed, Sheila Turner 1937(?)-1979
Obituary 23
Seeger, Elizabeth 1889-1973
Obituary 20
Seeger, Laura Vaccaro 200
Earlier sketch in SATA *172*
Seeger, Pete 1919- *139*
Earlier sketch in SATA *13*
Seeger, Peter R.
See Seeger, Pete
Seeley, Laura L. 1958- 71
Seever, R.
See Reeves, Lawrence F.
Sefozo, Mary 1925- 82
Sefton, Catherine
See Waddell, Martin
Segal, John *178*
Segal, Joyce 1940- 35
Segal, Lore 1928- 228
Autobiography Feature 228
Earlier sketches in SATA *4, 66, 163*
See also SAAS *11*
Segal, Lore Groszmann
See Segal, Lore
Segar, E(lzie) C(risler) 1894-1938 .... *61*
Segovia, Andres 1893(?)-1987
Obituary 52
Seguin, Marilyn W(eymouth) 1951- *91*
Seguin-Fontes, Marthe 1924- *109*
Seibold, J. Otto 1960- *196*
Earlier sketches in SATA *83, 149*
See also SAAS *22*
Seidel, Ross 95
Seidelman, James Edward 1926- 6
Seiden, Art(hur) *107*
Brief entry 42
Seidensticker, John 1944- 200
Seidler, Ann (G.) 1925- *131*
Seidler, Tor 1952- *149*
Brief entry 46
Earlier sketches in SATA *52, 98*
Seidman, Karla
See Kuskin, Karla
Seidman, Laurence Ivan 1925- 15
Seigel, Kalman 1917-1998 12
Obituary 103
Seignobosc, Francoise 1897-1961 21
Seinfeld, Jerry 1954- *146*
Seitz, Jacqueline 1931- 50
Seixas, Judith S. 1922- 17
Sejima, Yoshimasa 1913- 8
Selberg, Ingrid (Maria) 1950- 68
Selden, George
See Thompson, George Selden
Selden, Neil R(oy) 1931- *61*
Self, Margaret Cabell 1902-1996 24
Selfors, Suzanne 1963- *193*
Selick, Henry 1952- *183*
Selig, Sylvie 1942- *13*

Selkirk, Jane
See Chapman, John Stanton Higham
Sellers, Naomi
See Flack, Naomi John White
Sellier, Marie 1953- *212*
Selman, LaRue W. 1927- 55
Selsam, Millicent E(llis) 1912-1996 29
Obituary 92
Earlier sketch in SATA *1*
See also CLR *1*
Seltzer, Meyer 1932- 17
Seltzer, Richard 1946- 41
Seltzer, Richard Warren, Jr.
See Seltzer, Richard
Selvadurai, Shyam 1965(?)- *171*
Selway, Martina 1940- *169*
Earlier sketch in SATA *74*
Selzer, Adam 1980- 229
Earlier sketch in SATA *192*
Selznick, Brian 1966- 210
Earlier sketches in SATA *79, 117, 171*
Semel, Nava 1954- *107*
Semloh
See Holmes, Peggy
Sendak, Jack 1924(?)-1995 28
Sendak, Maurice 1928- *165*
Earlier sketches in SATA *1, 27, 113*
See also CLR *131*
Sendak, Maurice Bernard
See Sendak, Maurice
Sender, Ruth M(insky) 1926- 62
Sengler, Johanna 1924- 18
Senir, Mirik
See Snir, Mirik
Senisi, Ellen B. 1951- *116*
Senisi, Ellen Babinec
See Senisi, Ellen B.
Senn, J(oyce) A(nn) 1941- *115*
Senn, Steve 1950- 60
Brief entry 48
Sensel, Joni 1962- 204
Senzai, N.H. 233
Serafini, Frank 201
Serage, Nancy 1924- 10
Seredy, Kate 1899-1975 .... *1*
Obituary 24
See also CLR *10*
Serfozo, Mary 1925- *194*
Serlin, Andra
See Abramson, Andra Serlin
Seroff, Victor I(lyitch) 1902-1979 12
Obituary 26
Serra, Sebastia 1966- 202
Serraillier, Ian (Lucien) 1912-1994 73
Obituary 83
Earlier sketch in SATA *1*
See also CLR *2*
See also SAAS *3*
Serres, Alain 1956- 239
Serros, Michele 175
Serros, Michele M.
See Serros, Michele
Servello, Joe 1932- 10
Service, Pamela F. 1945- 222
Earlier sketch in SATA *64*
Service, Robert
See Service, Robert W.
Service, Robert W. 1874(?)-1958 20
Serwadda, W(illiam) Moses 1931- 27
Serwer-Bernstein, Blanche L(uria)
1910-1997 10
Sescoe, Vincent E. 1938- 123
Seskin, Steve 1953- *211*
Seth, Mary
See Lexau, Joan M.
Seton, Anya 1904(?)-1990 .... *3*
Obituary 66
Seton, Ernest (Evan) Thompson 1860-1946 . 18
See also CLR *59*
Seton-Thompson, Ernest
See Seton, Ernest (Evan) Thompson

Seuling, Barbara 1937- 220
Autobiography Feature 220
Earlier sketches in SATA *10, 98, 145, 193*
See also SAAS *24*
Seuss, Dr.
See Dr. Seuss
Severn, Bill
See Severn, William Irving
Severn, David
See Unwin, David S.
Severn, William Irving 1914- *1*
Sewall, Marcia 1935- *119*
Earlier sketches in SATA *37, 69*
Seward, Prudence 1926- 16
Sewell, Anna 1820-1878 .... *100*
Earlier sketch in SATA *24*
See also CLR *17*
Sewell, Helen (Moore) 1896-1957 38
Sexton, Anne 1928-1974 10
Sexton, Anne Harvey
See Sexton, Anne
Sexton, Brenda 1957- 237
Seymour, Alta Halverson 10
Seymour, Jane 1951- *139*
Seymour, Tres 1966- *164*
Earlier sketch in SATA *82*
Sfar, Joann 1971- *182*
Shachtman, Tom 1942- 49
Shackleton, C.C.
See Aldiss, Brian W.
Shader, Rachel
See Sofer, Barbara
Shadow, Jak
See Sutherland, Jon
Shadyland, Sal
See Cooper, Louise
Shafer, Audrey *183*
Shafer, Robert E(ugene) 1925- 9
Shaffer, Terea 1968- 79
Shahan, Sherry 1949- 216
Earlier sketches in SATA *92, 134*
Shahn, Ben(jamin) 1898-1969
Obituary 21
Shahn, Bernarda Bryson
See Bryson, Bernarda
Shaik, Fatima *114*
Shalant, Phyllis 1949- *150*
Shan, Darren 1972- 239
Earlier sketches in SATA *129, 168, 199*
Shan, D.B.
See Shan, Darren
Shanahan, Lisa *199*
Shanberg, Karen
See Shragg, Karen (I.)
Shane, Harold Gray 1914-1993 36
Obituary 76
Shange, Ntozake 1948- *157*
Shanks, Ann Zane (Kushner) 10
Shannon, David 1959- 228
Earlier sketches in SATA *107, 152*
See also CLR *87*
Shannon, George 1952- 202
Earlier sketches in SATA *35, 94, 143*
Shannon, George William Bones
See Shannon, George
Shannon, Jacqueline 63
Shannon, Margaret
See Silverwood, Margaret Shannon
Shannon, Monica 1905(?)-1965 28
Shannon, Terry
See Mercer, Jessie
Shannon, Terry Miller 1951- *148*
Shapiro, Irwin 1911-1981 32
Shapiro, Jody Fickes 1940- *193*
Shapiro, Karen Jo 1964- *186*
Shapiro, Michelle 1961- *196*
Shapiro, Milton J. 1926- 32
Shapiro, Tricia
See Andryszewski, Tricia
Shapiro, Zachary 1970- *213*

Shapp, Charles M(orris) 1906-1989
   Obituary *61*
Shapp, Martha Glauber 1910- *3*
Sharenow, Robert *193*
Sharfman, Amalie *14*
Sharkey, Niamh *213*
Sharma, Partap 1939- *15*
Sharma, Rashmi
   See Singh, Rashmi Sharma
Sharman, Alison
   See Leonard, Alison
Sharmat, Marjorie Weinman 1928- *133*
   Earlier sketches in SATA *4, 33, 74*
Sharmat, Mitchell 1927- *127*
   Earlier sketch in SATA *33*
Sharp, Anne Wallace 1947- *144*
Sharp, Luke
   See Alkiviades, Alkis
Sharp, Margery 1905-1991 .... *29*
   Obituary *67*
   Earlier sketch in SATA *1*
   See also CLR 27
Sharp, Zerna A. 1889-1981
   Obituary *27*
Sharpe, Jon
   See Duncan, Alice
   and Knott, William C(ecil, Jr.)
   and Messman, Jon
Sharpe, Mitchell R(aymond) 1924- *12*
Sharpe, Susan 1946- *71*
Sharratt, Nick 1962- *199*
   Earlier sketches in SATA *104, 153*
Shasha, Mark 1961- *80*
Shattuck, Roger 1923-2005 .... *64*
   Obituary *174*
Shattuck, Roger Whitney
   See Shattuck, Roger
Shaw, Arnold 1909-1989 .... *4*
   Obituary *63*
Shaw, Carolyn V. 1934- *91*
Shaw, Charles (Green) 1892-1974 .... *13*
Shaw, Evelyn S. 1927- *28*
Shaw, Flora Louisa
   See Lugard, Flora Louisa Shaw
Shaw, Hannah 1982(?)- *227*
Shaw, Janet 1937- *146*
   Earlier sketch in SATA *61*
   See also CLR 96
Shaw, Janet Beeler
   See Shaw, Janet
Shaw, Liane 1959- *222*
Shaw, Lisa
   See Rogak, Lisa
Shaw, Margret 1940- *68*
Shaw, Mary 1965- *180*
Shaw, Nancy 1946- *162*
   Earlier sketch in SATA *71*
Shaw, Ray *7*
Shaw, Richard 1923- *12*
Shawn, Frank S.
   See Goulart, Ron
Shay, Art
   See Shay, Arthur
Shay, Arthur 1922- *4*
Shay, Lacey
   See Shebar, Sharon Sigmond
Shea, Bob *231*
   Earlier sketch in SATA *188*
Shea, George 1940- *54*
   Brief entry *42*
Shea, Pegi Deitz 1960- *172*
   Earlier sketches in SATA *77, 137*
Shearer, Alex 1949- *204*
Shearer, John 1947- *43*
   Brief entry *27*
   See also CLR 34
Shearer, Ted 1919- *43*
Shearing, Leonie 1972- *184*
Sheban, Chris *182*
Shebar, Sharon Sigmond 1945- *36*
Shecter, Ben 1935- *16*

Shecter, Vicky Alvear 1961- *234*
Shedd, Warner 1934- *147*
   Earlier sketch in SATA *87*
Sheedy, Alexandra Elizabeth 1962- *39*
   Earlier sketch in SATA *19*
Sheehan, Ethna 1908-2000 .... *9*
Sheehan, Patty 1945- *77*
Sheehan, Sean 1951- *154*
   Earlier sketch in SATA *86*
Sheen, Barbara 1949- *143*
Shefelman, Janice 1930- *205*
   Earlier sketches in SATA *58, 129*
Shefelman, Janice Jordan
   See Shefelman, Janice
Shefelman, Tom 1927- *204*
   Earlier sketch in SATA *58*
Sheffer, H. R.
   See Abels, Harriette S(heffer)
Sheffield, Charles 1935-2002 .... *109*
Sheffield, Janet N. 1926- *26*
Sheikh, Nazneen 1944- *101*
Sheinkin, Steve 1968- *204*
Sheinmel, Alyssa B. *233*
Sheinmel, Courtney 1977- *211*
Shekerjian, Regina Tor *16*
Shelby, Anne 1948- *85*
   Autobiography Feature *121*
   See also SAAS 26
Sheldon, Ann
   See Antle, Nancy
Sheldon, Ann *67*
   Earlier sketch in SATA *1*
Sheldon, Aure 1917-1976 .... *12*
Sheldon, David *185*
Sheldon, Deyan *181*
Sheldon, Dyan *238*
Sheldon, John
   See Bloch, Robert (Albert)
Sheldon, Muriel 1926- *45*
   Brief entry *39*
Shell, Barry 1951- *176*
Shelley, Frances
   See Wees, Frances Shelley
Shelley, John 1959- *202*
Shelley, Mary
   See Shelley, Mary Wollstonecraft
Shelley, Mary Wollstonecraft 1797-1851 ..... *29*
   See also CLR 133
Shelton, Paula Young 1961- *227*
Shelton, William Roy 1919-1995 .... *5*
   Obituary *129*
Shemie, Bonnie (Jean Brenner) 1949- *96*
Shemin, Margaretha (Hoeneveld) 1928- *4*
Shen, Michele 1953- *173*
Shenker, Michele
   See Shen, Michele
Shenton, Edward 1895-1977 .... *45*
Shepard, Aaron 1950- *187*
   Earlier sketches in SATA *75, 113*
Shepard, Ernest Howard 1879-1976 .... *100*
   Obituary *24*
   Earlier sketches in SATA *3, 33*
   See also CLR 27
Shepard, James R.
   See Shepard, Jim
Shepard, Jim 1956- *164*
   Earlier sketch in SATA *90*
Shepard, Mary
   See Knox, (Mary) Eleanor Jessie
Shephard, Esther 1891-1975 .... *5*
   Obituary *26*
Shepherd, Amanda *201*
Shepherd, Donna Walsh
   See Walsh Shepherd, Donna
Shepherd, Elizabeth *4*
Shepherd, Irana *173*
Shepherd, Roni
   See Shepherd, Irana
Sheppard, Kate *195*
Shepperson, Rob *178*

Sherburne, Zoa (Lillian Morin) 1912-1995 .... *3*
   See also SAAS *18*
Sherk-Savage, Candace
   See Savage, Candace
Sherlock, Patti *71*
Sherman, D(enis) R(onald) 1934- *48*
   Brief entry *29*
Sherman, Diane (Finn) 1928- *12*
Sherman, Elizabeth
   See Friskey, Margaret (Richards)
Sherman, Harold (Morrow) 1898-1987 .... *37*
   Obituary *137*
Sherman, Josepha *163*
   Earlier sketch in SATA *75*
Sherman, Michael
   See Lowndes, Robert A(ugustine) W(ard)
Sherman, Nancy
   See Rosenberg, Nancy
Sherman, Pat *174*
Sherman, Peter Michael
   See Lowndes, Robert A(ugustine) W(ard)
Sherrard, Valerie 1957- *141*
Sherrard, Valerie Anne
   See Sherrard, Valerie
Sherrod, Jane
   See Singer, Jane Sherrod
Sherry, Clifford J. 1943- *84*
Sherry, (Dulcie) Sylvia 1932- *122*
   Earlier sketch in SATA *8*
Sherwan, Earl 1917- *3*
Sherwood, Jonathan
   See London, Jonathan
Sheth, Kashmira *186*
Shetterly, Will 1955- *78*
   Autobiography Feature *106*
Shetterly, William Howard
   See Shetterly, Will
Shiefman, Vicky 1942- *22*
Shields, Brenda Desmond (Armstrong)
   1914- *37*
Shields, Carol Diggory *174*
Shields, Charles 1944- *10*
Shields, Gillian *203*
Shiels, Barbara
   See Adams, Barbara Johnston
Shiffman, Lena 1957- *101*
Shiga, Jason 1976- *228*
Shiina, Makoto 1944- *83*
Shimin, Symeon 1902-1984 .... *13*
Shimko, Bonnie 1941- *191*
Shine, Andrea 1955- *104*
Shine, Deborah 1932- *71*
Shinn, Everett 1876-1953 .... *21*
Shinn, Sharon 1957- *229*
   Earlier sketches in SATA *110, 164*
Shipp, Josh 1982- *236*
Shippen, Katherine B(inney) 1892-1980 .... *1*
   Obituary *23*
   See also CLR 36
Shippey, T. A. 1943- *143*
Shippey, Thomas Alan
   See Shippey, T. A.
Shipton, Eric Earle 1907-1977 .... *10*
Shipton, Jonathan 1948- *215*
Shipton, Paul 1963- *196*
Shiraz, Yasmin *173*
Shirer, William L. 1904-1993 .... *45*
   Obituary *78*
   See Shirer, William Lawrence
Shirley, Debra *203*
Shirley, Gayle C 1955- *96*
Shirley, Gayle Corbett
   See Shirley, Gayle C
Shirley, Jean 1919- *70*
Shirreffs, Gordon D(onald) 1914-1996 .... *11*
Shirts, Morris A(lpine) 1922- *63*
Shlichta, Joe 1968- *84*
Shmurak, Carole B. 1944- *118*
Sholokhov, Mikhail 1905-1984
   Obituary *36*

Sholokhov, Mikhail Aleksandrovich
See Sholokhov, Mikhail
Shore, Diane Z. 215
Earlier sketch in SATA 179
Shore, Diane ZuHone
See Shore, Diane Z.
Shore, June Lewis 30
Shore, Nancy 1960- 124
Shore, Robert 1924- 39
Short, Michael 1937- 65
Short, Roger
See Arkin, Alan
Shortall, Leonard W. 19
Shortt, Tim(othy Donald) 1961- 96
Shotwell, Louisa Rossiter 1902-1993 3
Shoulders, Michael 1954- 216
Shoup, Barbara 1947- 156
Earlier sketch in SATA 86
See also SAAS 24
Shoveller, Herb 184
Showalter, Jean B(reckinridge) 12
Showell, Ellen Harvey 1934- 33
Showers, Paul C. 1910-1999 92
Obituary 114
Earlier sketch in SATA 21
See also CLR 6
See also SAAS 7
Shpakow, Tanya 1959(?)- 94
Shpitalnik, Vladimir 1964- 83
Shragg, Karen (I.) 1954- 142
Shreeve, Elizabeth 1956- 156
Shreve, Susan
See Shreve, Susan Richards
Shreve, Susan Richards 1939- 152
Brief entry 41
Earlier sketches in SATA 46, 95
Shriver, Jean Adair 1932- 75
Shriver, Maria 1955- 134
Shriver, Maria Owings
See Shriver, Maria
Shrode, Mary
See Hollingsworth, Mary
Shtainmets, Leon 32
Shub, Elizabeth 1915(?)-2004 5
Shuken, Julia 1948- 84
Shulevitz, Uri 1935- 165
Earlier sketches in SATA 3, 50, 106
See also CLR 61
Shulman, Alix Kates 1932- 7
Shulman, Dee 1957- 146
Shulman, Irving 1913-1995 13
Shulman, Lisa 202
Shulman, Mark 1962- 184
Shulman, Max 1919-1988
Obituary 59
Shulman, Milton 1913-2004
Obituary 154
Shulman, Neil B(arnett) 1945- 89
Shulman, Polly 235
Shumsky, Zena
See Collier, Zena
Shura, Mary Francis
See Craig, Mary (Francis) Shura
Shusterman, Neal 1962- 201
Autobiography Feature 140
Earlier sketches in SATA 85, 121, 140
Shuter, Jane (Margaret) 1955- 151
Earlier sketch in SATA 90
Shuttlesworth, Dorothy Edwards 3
Shwartz, Susan (Martha) 1949- 94
Shyer, Christopher 1961- 98
Shyer, Marlene Fanta 13
Siberell, Anne 29
Sibley, Don 1922- 12
Siburt, Ruth 1951- 121
Siculan, Daniel 1922- 12
Siddals, Mary McKenna 232
Siddon, Barbara
See Bradford, Barbara Taylor
Sidgwick, Ethel 1877-1970 116
Sidjakov, Nicolas 1924- 18

Sidman, Joyce 1956- 236
Earlier sketches in SATA 145, 181
Sidney, Frank
See Warwick, Alan R(oss)
Sidney, Margaret
See Lothrop, Harriet Mulford Stone
Siebert, Diane 1948- 189
Siegal, Aranka 1930- 88
Brief entry 37
Siegel, Beatrice 36
Siegel, Helen
See Siegl, Helen
Siegel, Randolph
See Siegel, Randy
Siegel, Randy 234
Siegel, Robert 1939- 39
Siegel, Robert Harold
See Siegel, Robert
Siegel, Siena Cherson 1967(?)- 185
Siegelson, Kim L. 1962- 114
Sieger, Ted 1958- 189
Siegl, Helen 1924- 34
Siepmann, Mary Aline
See Wesley, Mary (Aline)
Sierra, Judy 1945- 239
Earlier sketches in SATA 104, 162, 195
Sieswerda, Paul L. 1942- 147
Sievert, Terri
See Dougherty, Terri (L.)
Sigsawa, Keiichi 1972- 211
Silas
See McCay, (Zenas) Winsor
Silcock, Sara Lesley 1947- 12
Silin-Palmer, Pamela 184
Sill, Cathryn 1953- 221
Earlier sketches in SATA 74, 141
Sill, John 1947- 222
Earlier sketches in SATA 74, 140
Sillitoe, Alan 1928-2010 61
Sills, Leslie (Elka) 1948- 129
Silly, E. S.
See Kraus, (Herman) Robert
Silsbe, Brenda 1953- 73
Silva, Joseph
See Goulart, Ron
Silvano, Wendi 1962- 223
Silver, Jago
See Jago
Silver, Maggie 216
Silver, Ruth
See Chew, Ruth
Silverberg, Robert 1935- 91
Autobiography Feature 104
Earlier sketch in SATA 13
See also CLR 59
Silverman, Erica 1955- 222
Earlier sketches in SATA 78, 112, 165
Silverman, Janis L. 1946- 127
Silverman, Mel(vin Frank) 1931-1966 9
Silverman, Robin L. 1954- 96
Silverman, Robin Landew
See Silverman, Robin L.
Silverstein, Alvin 1933- 124
Earlier sketches in SATA 8, 69
See also CLR 25
Silverstein, Herma 1945- 106
Silverstein, Robert Alan 1959- 124
Earlier sketch in SATA 77
Silverstein, Shel 1932-1999 92
Brief entry 27
Obituary 116
Earlier sketch in SATA 33
See also CLR 96
Silverstein, Sheldon Allan
See Silverstein, Shel
Silverstein, Virginia B. 1937- 124
Earlier sketches in SATA 8, 69
See also CLR 25
Silverstein, Virginia Barbara Opshelor
See Silverstein, Virginia B.
Silverthorne, Elizabeth 1930- 35

Silverwood, Margaret Shannon 1966- 137
Earlier sketch in SATA 83
Silvey, Diane F. 1946- 135
Sim, David 1953- 162
Sim, Dorrith M. 1931- 96
Simak, Clifford D(onald) 1904-1988
Obituary 56
Simard, Remy 1959- 168
Siminovich, Lorena 1976(?)- 219
Simmie, Lois (Ann) 1932- 106
Simmonds, Posy 1945- 130
See also CLR 23
Simmonds, Rosemary Elizabeth
See Simmonds, Posy
Simmons, Andra 1939- 141
Simmons, Elly 1955- 134
Simmons, Michael 1970- 185
Simms, Laura 1947- 117
Simner, Janni Lee 113
Simon, Charlie May
See Fletcher, Charlie May Hogue
Simon, Francesca 1955- 111
Simon, Gabriel 1972- 118
Simon, Hilda Rita 1921- 28
See also CLR 39
Simon, Howard 1903-1979 32
Obituary 21
Simon, Joe
See Simon, Joseph H.
Simon, Joseph H. 1913-2011 7
Simon, Martin P(aul William) 1903-1969 12
Simon, Mina Lewiton
See Lewiton, Mina
Simon, Norma (Feldstein) 1927- 129
Earlier sketches in SATA 3, 68
Simon, Seymour 1931- 202
Earlier sketches in SATA 4, 73, 138
See also CLR 63
Simon, Shirley (Schwartz) 1921- 11
Simon, Solomon 1895-1970 40
Simonetta, Linda 1948- 14
Simonetta, Sam 1936- 14
Simons, Barbara B(rooks) 1934- 41
Simont, Marc 1915- 126
Earlier sketches in SATA 9, 73
Simpson, Colin 1908-1983 14
Simpson, Harriette
See Arnow, Harriette (Louisa) Simpson
Simpson, Jacynth Hope
See Hope Simpson, Jacynth
Simpson, Lesley 1963- 150
Simpson, Margaret 1943- 128
Simpson, Myrtle L(illias) 1931- 14
Sims, Blanche 168
Earlier sketch in SATA 75
Sims, Blanche L.
See Sims, Blanche
Sims, Rudine
See Bishop, Rudine Sims
Simundsson, Elva 1950- 63
Sinclair, Clover
See Gater, Dilys
Sinclair, Emil
See Hesse, Hermann
Sinclair, Jeff 1958- 77
Sinclair, Olga 1923- 121
Sinclair, Rose
See Smith, Susan Vernon
Sinclair, Upton 1878-1968 9
Sinclair, Upton Beall
See Sinclair, Upton
Singer, A.L.
See Lerangis, Peter
Singer, Arthur 1917-1990 64
Singer, Isaac
See Singer, Isaac Bashevis
Singer, Isaac Bashevis 1904-1991 27
Obituary 68
Earlier sketch in SATA 3
See also CLR 1

Singer, Jane Sherrod 1917-1985 .... *4*
  Obituary *42*
Singer, Julia 1917- *28*
Singer, Kurt D. 1911-2005 .... *38*
  Obituary *172*
Singer, Marilyn 1948- *234*
  Autobiography Feature *158*
  Brief entry *38*
  Earlier sketches in SATA *48, 80, 125, 158, 201*
  See also CLR *48*
  See also SAAS *13*
Singer, Muff 1942-2005 .... *104*
  Obituary *160*
Singer, Nicky 1956- *194*
Singer, Susan (Mahler) 1941- *9*
Singh, Rashmi Sharma 1952- *90*
Singleton, Linda Joy 1957- *166*
  Earlier sketch in SATA *88*
Singleton, L.J.
  See Singleton, Linda Joy
Singleton, Sarah 1966- *214*
Sinykin, Sheri
  See Sinykin, Sheri Cooper
Sinykin, Sheri Cooper 1950- *142*
  Autobiography Feature *142*
  Earlier sketches in SATA *72, 133*
Sinykin, Sheril Terri Cooper
  See Sinykin, Sheri Cooper
Siomades, Lorianne *217*
Sipiera, Paul P., (Jr.) 1948- *144*
  Earlier sketch in SATA *89*
Siracusa, Catherine (Jane) 1947- *82*
Sirett, Dawn (Karen) 1966- *88*
Sirimarco, Elizabeth 1966- *158*
Sirof, Harriet 1930- *94*
  Earlier sketch in SATA *37*
Sirois, Allen L. 1950- *76*
Sirvaitis (Chernyaev), Karen (Ann) 1961- ... *79*
Sis, Peter 1949- *192*
  Earlier sketch in SATA *149*
  See also CLR *110*
Sisson, Rosemary Anne 1923- *11*
Sisson, Stephanie Roth *237*
  Earlier sketch in SATA *202*
Sister Mary Terese
  See Donze, Mary Terese
Sita, Lisa 1962- *87*
Sitarski, Anita *200*
Sitomer, Alan Lawrence *174*
Sitomer, Harry 1903-1985 .... *31*
Sitomer, Mindel 1903-1987 .... *31*
Sittenfeld, Curtis 1975(?)- *164*
Sive, Helen R(obinson) 1951- *30*
Sivulich, Sandra (Jeanne) Stroner 1941- *9*
Siy, Alexandra *193*
Skarmeta, Antonio 1940- *57*
Skeers, Linda 1958- *207*
Skelly, James R(ichard) 1927- *17*
Skelton, Matthew 1971- *185*
Skinner, Constance Lindsay 1877-1939
  See YABC *1*
Skinner, Cornelia Otis 1901-1979 .... *2*
Skipper, G. C. 1939- *46*
  Brief entry *38*
Sklansky, Amy E(dgar) 1971- *145*
Sklansky, Amy E. 1971- *204*
Skofield, James *95*
  Brief entry *44*
Skold, Betty Westrom 1923- *41*
Skorpen, Liesel Moak 1935- *3*
Skott, Maria
  See Nikolajeva, Maria
Skovron, Jon 1976- *229*
Skrypuch, Marsha Forchuk 1954- *134*
Skultety, Nancy Laney 1960- *175*
Skurzynski, Gloria 1930- *145*
  Autobiography Feature *145*
  Earlier sketches in SATA *8, 74, 122*
  See also SAAS *9*

Skurzynski, Gloria Joan
  See Skurzynski, Gloria
Skutch, Robert 1925- *89*
Skye, Maggie
  See Werner, Herma
Skye, Obert *200*
  Earlier sketch in SATA *170*
Slack, Michael 1969- *189*
Slackman, Charles B. 1934- *12*
Slade, Arthur G. 1967- *221*
  Earlier sketches in SATA *106, 149*
Slade, Arthur Gregory
  See Slade, Arthur G.
Slade, Christian 1974- *238*
  Earlier sketch in SATA *193*
Slade, Richard 1910-1971 .... *9*
Slade, Suzanne 1964- *226*
Slangerup, Erik Jon 1969- *130*
Slate, Joseph 1928- *174*
  Earlier sketches in SATA *38, 122*
Slate, Joseph Frank
  See Slate, Joseph
Slater, Dashka 1963- *179*
Slater, David Michael 1970- *212*
Slater, Ray
  See Lansdale, Joe R.
Slaughter, Hope 1940- *84*
Slaughter, Jean
  See Doty, Jean Slaughter
Slaughter, Tom 1955- *152*
Slavicek, Louise Chipley 1956- *144*
Slavin, Bill 1959- *199*
  Earlier sketches in SATA *76, 148*
Slaymaker, Melissa Eskridge 1958- *158*
Slayton, Fran Cannon *221*
Sleator, William 1945-2011 .... *208*
  Earlier sketches in SATA *3, 68, 118, 161*
  See also CLR *128*
Sleator, William Warner III
  See Sleator, William
Slegers, Liesbet 1975- *154*
Sleigh, Barbara 1906-1982 .... *86*
  Obituary *30*
  Earlier sketch in SATA *3*
Slepian, Jan 1921- *85*
  Brief entry *45*
  Earlier sketch in SATA *51*
  See also SAAS *8*
Slepian, Janice B.
  See Slepian, Jan
Slicer, Margaret O. 1920- *4*
Slier, Debby
  See Shine, Deborah
Sloan, Brian 1966- *172*
Sloan, Carolyn 1937- *116*
  Earlier sketch in SATA *58*
Sloan, Glenna 1930- *120*
Sloan, Glenna Davis
  See Sloan, Glenna
Sloane, Eric 1910(?)-1985 .... *52*
  Obituary *42*
Sloane, Todd 1955- *88*
Sloat, Teri 1948- *164*
  Earlier sketches in SATA *70, 106*
Slobodkin, Florence Gersh 1905-1994 .... *5*
  Obituary *107*
Slobodkin, Louis 1903-1975 .... *26*
  Earlier sketch in SATA *1*
Slobodkina, Esphyr 1908-2002 .... *1*
  Obituary *135*
  See also SAAS *8*
Sloggett, Nellie 1851-1923 .... *44*
Slonim, David 1966- *207*
Sloss, Lesley Lord 1965- *72*
Slote, Alfred 1926- *72*
  Earlier sketch in SATA *8*
  See also CLR *4*
  See also SAAS *21*
Slote, Elizabeth 1956- *80*
Small, Charlie
  See Ward, Nick

Small, David 1945- *216*
  Brief entry *46*
  Earlier sketches in SATA *50, 95, 126, 183*
  See also CLR *53*
Small, Ernest
  See Lent, Blair
Small, Mary 1932- *165*
Small, Terry 1942- *75*
Smallcomb, Pam 1954- *159*
Smallman, Steve *227*
  Earlier sketch in SATA *197*
Smalls, Irene
  See Smalls-Hector, Irene
Smalls-Hector, Irene 1950- *146*
  Earlier sketch in SATA *73*
  See also CLR *103*
Smallwood, Norah (Evelyn) 1910(?)-1984
  Obituary *41*
Smaridge, Norah (Antoinette) 1903-1994 ...... *6*
Smath, Jerry 1933- *198*
Smee, Nicola 1948- *167*
  Earlier sketch in SATA *76*
Smiley, Virginia Kester 1923- *2*
Smit, Noelle 1972- *199*
Smith, Alexander McCall 1948- *179*
  Earlier sketch in SATA *73*
Smith, Andrew 1959- *209*
Smith, Andrew Anselmo
  See Smith, Andrew
Smith, Andy J. 1975- *207*
Smith, Anne Warren 1938- *41*
  Brief entry *34*
Smith, Barry (Edward Jervis) 1943- *75*
Smith, Beatrice S(chillinger) *12*
Smith, Betsy Covington 1937- *55*
  Earlier sketch in SATA *43*
Smith, Betty (Wehner) 1904-1972 .... *6*
Smith, Bradford 1909-1964 .... *5*
Smith, Brenda 1946- *82*
Smith, C. Pritchard
  See Hoyt, Edwin P(almer), Jr.
Smith, Caesar
  See Trevor, Elleston
Smith, Cat Bowman 1939- *201*
Smith, Charles R., Jr. 1969- *203*
  Earlier sketch in SATA *159*
Smith, Craig 1955- *172*
  Earlier sketches in SATA *81, 117*
Smith, Cynthia Leitich 1967- *215*
  Earlier sketch in SATA *152*
Smith, D. James 1955- *176*
Smith, Danna *216*
Smith, Danna Kessimakis
  See Smith, Danna
Smith, Datus C(lifford), Jr. 1907-1999 .... *13*
  Obituary *116*
Smith, Debra 1955- *89*
Smith, Derek 1943- *141*
Smith, Dick King
  See King-Smith, Dick
Smith, D.J.
  See Smith, D. James
Smith, Dodie
  See Smith, Dorothy Gladys
Smith, Doris Buchanan 1934-2002 .... *75*
  Obituary *140*
  Earlier sketch in SATA *28*
  See also SAAS *10*
Smith, Dorothy Gladys 1896-1990 .... *82*
  Obituary *65*
Smith, Dorothy Stafford 1905- *6*
Smith, Duane 1974- *202*
Smith, E(lmer) Boyd 1860-1943
  See YABC *1*
Smith, E(dric) Brooks 1917- *40*
Smith, Elwood H. 1941- *236*
  Earlier sketch in SATA *203*
Smith, Emily Wing 1980- *215*
Smith, Emma 1923- *52*
  Brief entry *36*

Smith, (Katherine) Eunice (Young)
1902-1993 5
Smith, Frances C(hristine) 1904-1986 3
Smith, Gary R. 1932- 14
Smith, Geof 1969- 102
Smith, George Harmon 1920- 5
Smith, Gordon 1951- 184
Smith, Greg Leitich 152
Smith, H(arry) Allen 1907-1976
Obituary 20
Smith, Helene 1937- 142
Smith, Hope Anita 202
Smith, Howard E(verett), Jr. 1927- 12
Smith, Hugh L(etcher) 1921-1968 5
Smith, Icy 1966- 228
Smith, Imogene Henderson 1922- 12
Smith, Jacqueline B. 1937- 39
Smith, Jada Pinkett 1971- 161
Smith, James Noel 1950- 193
Smith, Janet (Buchanan) Adam
See Adam Smith, Janet (Buchanan)
Smith, Janice Lee 1949- 155
Earlier sketch in SATA 54
Smith, Jean
See Smith, Frances C(hristine)
Smith, Jean Pajot 1945- 10
Smith, Jeff 1958- 161
Earlier sketch in SATA 93
Smith, Jeff Allen
See Smith, Jeff
Smith, Jeffrey Alan
See Smith, Jeff
Smith, Jenny 1963- 90
Smith, Jessie
See Kunhardt, Edith
Smith, Jessie Willcox 1863-1935 21
See also CLR 59
Smith, Jim W.W. 231
Smith, Joan (Mary) 1933- 54
Brief entry 46
Smith, Johnston
See Crane, Stephen
Smith, Jos A. 1936- 181
Earlier sketches in SATA 73, 120
Smith, Joseph Arthur
See Smith, Jos A.
Smith, Judie R. 1936- 80
Smith, Kirsten 1970- 210
Smith, Lafayette
See Higdon, Hal
Smith, Lane 1959- 224
Earlier sketches in SATA 76, 131, 179
See also CLR 47
Smith, Lee
See Albion, Lee Smith
Smith, Lendon H(oward) 1921- 64
Smith, Lillian H(elena) 1887-1983
Obituary 32
Smith, Linda 1949- 177
Smith, Linell Nash 1932- 2
Smith, Lucia B. 1943- 30
Smith, Maggie 1965- 235
Earlier sketch in SATA 190
Smith, Margaret Emily Noel Nuttall
See Nuttall-Smith, Margaret Emily Noel
Smith, Marion Hagens 1913- 12
Smith, Marion Jaques 1899-1987 13
Smith, Mary Ellen 10
Smith, Marya 1945- 78
Smith, Mike
See Smith, Mary Ellen
Smith, Nancy Covert 1935- 12
Smith, Norman F. 1920- 70
Earlier sketch in SATA 5
Smith, Patricia Clark 1943- 96
Smith, Pauline C.
See Arthur, Robert, (Jr.)
Smith, Pauline C(oggeshall) 1908-1994 27
Smith, Philip Warren 1936- 46
Smith, R. Alexander McCall
See Smith, Alexander McCall

Smith, Rebecca 1946- 123
Smith, Robert Kimmel 1930- 77
Earlier sketch in SATA 12
Smith, Robert Paul 1915-1977 52
Obituary 30
Smith, Roland 1951- 193
Earlier sketches in SATA 115, 161
Smith, Rosamond
See Oates, Joyce Carol
Smith, Ruth Leslie 1902- 2
Smith, Samantha 1972-1985
Obituary 45
Smith, Sandra Lee 1945- 75
Smith, Sarah Stafford
See Smith, Dorothy Stafford
Smith, Sharon 1947- 82
Smith, Sherri L. 1971- 156
Smith, Sherwood 1951- 206
Autobiography Feature 206
Earlier sketches in SATA 82, 140
Smith, Shirley Raines
See Raines, Shirley C(arol)
Smith, Susan Carlton 1923- 12
Smith, Susan Mathias 1950- 43
Brief entry 35
Smith, Susan Vernon 1950- 48
Brief entry 45
Smith, Tim(othy R.) 1945- 151
Smith, Ursula 1934- 54
Smith, Vian (Crocker) 1920-1969 11
Smith, Wanda VanHoy 1926- 65
Smith, Ward
See Goldsmith, Howard
Smith, Wendy
See French, Wendy
Smith, William A. 1918- 10
Smith, William Jay 1918- 154
Autobiography Feature 154
Earlier sketches in SATA 2, 68
See also SAAS 22
Smith, Winsome 1935- 45
Smith, Z.Z.
See Westheimer, David
Smith-Ankrom, M. E. 1942- 130
Smith-Griswold, Wendy 1955- 88
Smith Hernandez, Duncan Tonatiuh
See Tonatiuh, Duncan
Smith-Rex, Susan J. 1950- 94
Smithsen, Richard
See Pellowski, Michael (Joseph)
Smithson, Ryan 1985- 216
Smits, Teo
See Smits, Theodore R(ichard)
Smits, Theodore R(ichard) 1905-1996 45
Brief entry 28
Smolinski, Dick 1932- 86
Smothers, Ethel Footman 1944- 149
Earlier sketch in SATA 76
Smucker, Anna Egan 1948- 209
Smucker, Barbara 1915-2003 130
Earlier sketches in SATA 29, 76
See also CLR 10
See also SAAS 11
Smucker, Barbara Claassen
See Smucker, Barbara
Smyth, Iain 1959- 105
Snedeker, Caroline Dale (Parke) 1871-1956
See YABC 2
Sneed, Brad 191
Sneider, Marian 1932-2005 197
Snell, Gordon 1933(?)- 228
Snell, Nigel (Edward Creagh) 1936- 57
Brief entry 40
Snellgrove, L(aurence) E(rnest) 1928- 53
Snelling, Dennis (Wayne) 1958- 84
Sneve, Virginia Driving Hawk 1933- 95
Earlier sketch in SATA 8
See also CLR 2
Snicket, Lemony 1970- 215
Earlier sketches in SATA 126, 187
See also CLR 79

Sniegoski, Thomas E. 1962- 195
Sniegoski, Tom
See Sniegoski, Thomas E.
Snir, Eleyor 225
Snir, Mirik 1948- 226
Snodgrass, Mary Ellen 1944- 75
Snodgrass, Quentin Curtius
See Twain, Mark
Snodgrass, Thomas Jefferson
See Twain, Mark
Snook, Barbara (Lillian) 1913-1976 34
Snow, Alan 1959- 190
Snow, Carol 1965- 208
Snow, Donald Clifford 1917-1979 16
Snow, Dorothea J(ohnston) 1909- 9
Snow, Richard F. 1947- 52
Brief entry 37
Snow, Richard Folger
See Snow, Richard F.
Snow, Sarah 229
Snyder, Anne 1922-2001 4
Obituary 125
Snyder, Bernadette McCarver 1930- 97
Snyder, Betsy 230
Snyder, Carol 1941- 35
Snyder, Gerald S(eymour) 1933- 48
Brief entry 34
Snyder, Jerome 1916-1976
Obituary 20
Snyder, Laurel 1974- 209
Snyder, Midori 1954- 106
Snyder, Paul A. 1946- 125
Snyder, Zilpha Keatley 1927- 226
Autobiography Feature 163
Earlier sketches in SATA 1, 28, 75, 110, 163
See also CLR 121
See also SAAS 2
Snyderman, Reuven K. 1922- 5
So, Meilo 162
Sobel, June 1950- 149
Soble, Jennie
See Cavin, Ruth
Sobol, Donald J. 1924- 132
Earlier sketches in SATA 1, 31, 73
See also CLR 4
Sobol, Harriet Langsam 1936- 47
Brief entry 34
Sobol, Richard 211
Sobol, Rose 1931- 76
Sobott-Mogwe, Gaele 1956- 97
Soderberg, Erin Kate
See Downing, Erin
Soderlind, Arthur E(dwin) 1920- 14
Soentpiet, Chris K. 1970- 159
Earlier sketch in SATA 97
Soerensen, Svend Otto 1916- 67
Sofer, Barbara 1949- 109
Sofer, Rachel
See Sofer, Barbara
Softly, Barbara Frewin 1924- 12
Sogabe, Aki 207
Soglow, Otto 1900-1975
Obituary 30
Sohl, Frederic J(ohn) 1916- 10
Sohr, Daniel 1973- 190
Sokol, Bill
See Sokol, William
Sokol, William 1923- 37
Sokolov, Kirill 1930- 34
Solbert, Romaine G. 1925- 2
Solbert, Ronni
See Solbert, Romaine G.
Solheim, James 233
Earlier sketch in SATA 133
Solomon, Heather M. 188
Solomon, Joan 1930- 51
Brief entry 40
Solomons, Ikey Esquir
See Thackeray, William Makepeace
Solonevich, George 1915-2003 15
Solot, Mary Lynn 1939- 12

Solov'ev, Mikhail
   See Soloviov, Michael
Soloviov, Michael 1972- 222
Soman, David 1965- 200
Somerlott, Robert 1928-2001 62
Somers, Kevin 205
Somervill, Barbara A(nn) 1948- 140
Sommer, Angela
   See Sommer-Bodenburg, Angela
Sommer, Carl 1930- 175
   Earlier sketch in SATA 126
Sommer, Elyse 1929- 7
Sommer, Robert 1929- 12
Sommer-Bodenburg, Angela 1948- 113
   Earlier sketch in SATA 63
Sommerdorf, Norma 1926- 131
Sommerdorf, Norma Jean
   See Sommerdorf, Norma
Sommerfelt, Aimee 1892-1975 5
Son, John 160
Sones, Sonya 131
Sonneborn, Ruth (Cantor) 1899-1974 4
   Obituary 27
Sonnenblick, Jordan 1969- 223
   Earlier sketch in SATA 185
   See also CLR 144
Sonnenmark, Laura A. 1958- 73
Soo, Kean 201
Sopko, Eugen 1949- 58
Sorel, Edward 1929- 126
   Brief entry 37
   Earlier sketch in SATA 65
Sorensen, Henri 1950- 115
   Earlier sketch in SATA 77
Sorensen, Svend Otto
   See Soerensen, Svend Otto
Sorensen, Virginia 1912-1991 2
   Obituary 72
   See also SAAS 15
Sorenson, Jane 1926- 63
Sorenson, Margo 1946- 96
Sorley Walker, Kathrine 41
Sorra, Kristin 185
Sorrells, Walter 177
Sorrentino, Joseph N. 1937- 6
Sortor, June Elizabeth 1939- 12
Sortor, Toni
   See Sortor, June Elizabeth
Sosa, Hernan 1977- 203
Soskin, V. H.
   See Ellison, Virginia H(owell)
Soto, Gary 1952- 174
   Earlier sketches in SATA 80, 120
   See also CLR 38
Sotomayor, Antonio 1902-1985 11
Souci, Robert D. San
   See San Souci, Robert D.
Souders, Taryn 1977- 237
Soudley, Henry
   See Wood, James Playsted
Souhami, Jessica 176
Soule, Gardner (Bosworth) 1913-2000 14
Soule, Jean Conder 1919- 10
Soup, Cuthbert
   See Swallow, Gerry
Souster, (Holmes) Raymond 1921- 63
South, Sheri Cobb 1959- 82
Southall, Ivan 1921-2008 134
   Autobiography Feature 134
   Earlier sketches in SATA 3, 68
   See also CLR 165
   See also SAAS 3
Southall, Ivan Francis
   See Southall, Ivan
Southey, Robert 1774-1843 54
Southgate, Vera 54
Souza, Janet
   See Tashjian, Janet
Sovak, Jan 1953- 115
Sowden, Celeste
   See Walters, Celeste

Sowter, Nita 69
Spafford, Suzy 1945- 160
Spagnoli, Cathy 1950- 134
   Earlier sketch in SATA 79
Spain, Sahara Sunday 1991- 133
Spain, Susan Rosson 185
Spalding, Andrea 1944- 150
   Earlier sketch in SATA 101
Spalenka, Greg 1958- 198
Spanfeller, James J. 1930- 19
   See also SAAS 8
Spanfeller, Jim
   See Spanfeller, James J.
Spangenberg, Judith Dunn 1942- 5
Spangler, Brie 212
Spanyol, Jessica 1965- 206
   Earlier sketch in SATA 137
Spar, Jerome 1918- 10
Sparks, Barbara 1942- 78
Sparks, Beatrice (Mathews) 1918- 44
   Brief entry 28
   See also CLR 139
Sparks, Mary W. 1920- 15
Spaulding, Douglas
   See Bradbury, Ray
Spaulding, Leonard
   See Bradbury, Ray
Spaulding, Norma 107
Speare, Elizabeth George 1908-1994 62
   Obituary 83
   Earlier sketch in SATA 5
   See also CLR 8
Spearing, Craig J. 228
Spearing, Judith (Mary Harlow) 1922- 9
Spears, Rick 182
Speck, Katie 196
Speck, Nancy 1959- 104
Specking, Inez 1890-1960(?) 11
Speed, Nell
   See Keats, Emma
   and Sampson, Emma (Keats) Speed
Speed, Nell (Ewing) 1878-1913 68
Speer, Bonnie Stahlman 1929- 113
Speer-Lyon, Tammie L. 1965- 89
Speicher, Helen Ross S(mith) 1915- 8
Speir, Nancy 1958- 210
   Earlier sketch in SATA 81
Spelling, Tori 1973- 236
Spelling, Victoria Davey
   See Spelling, Tori
Spellman, John W(illard) 1934- 14
Spellman, Roger G.
   See Cox, William R(obert)
Spelman, Cornelia Maude 1946- 144
   Earlier sketch in SATA 96
Spelman, Mary 1934- 28
Spelvin, George
   See Lerangis, Peter
   and Phillips, David Atlee
Spence, Cynthia
   See Eble, Diane
Spence, Eleanor (Rachel) 1928- 21
   See also CLR 26
Spence, Geraldine 1931- 47
Spencer, Ann 1918- 10
Spencer, Britt 206
Spencer, Cornelia
   See Yaukey, Grace S(ydenstricker)
Spencer, Donald D(ean) 1931- 41
Spencer, Elizabeth 1921- 14
Spencer, Leonard G.
   See Garrett, Randall
   and Silverberg, Robert
Spencer, William 1922- 9
Spencer, Zane A(nn) 1935- 35
Spengler, Margaret 223
Sper, Emily 1957- 142
Speregen, Devra Newberger 1964- 84
Sperling, Dan(iel Lee) 1949- 65
Sperry, Armstrong W. 1897-1976 1
   Obituary 27

Sperry, Raymond
   See Garis, Howard R.
Sperry, Raymond, Jr. 1
Spetter, Jung-Hee 1969- 134
Spicer, Dorothy Gladys -1975 32
Spiegel, Beth 184
Spiegelman, Art 1948- 158
   Earlier sketch in SATA 109
Spiegelman, Judith M. 5
Spielberg, Steven 1947- 32
Spier, Peter (Edward) 1927- 54
   Earlier sketch in SATA 4
   See also CLR 5
Spilhaus, Athelstan (Frederick) 1911-1998 .. 13
   Obituary 102
Spilka, Arnold 1917- 6
Spillane, Frank Morrison
   See Spillane, Mickey
Spillane, Mickey 1918-2006 66
   Obituary 176
Spillebeen, Geert 1956- 225
Spinelli, Eileen 1942- 225
   Earlier sketches in SATA 38, 101, 150, 186
Spinelli, Jerry 1941- 195
   Earlier sketches in SATA 39, 71, 110, 158
   See also CLR 82
Spink, Reginald (William) 1905-1994 11
Spinka, Penina Keen 1945- 72
Spinner, Stephanie 1943- 234
   Earlier sketches in SATA 38, 91, 132
Spinossimus
   See White, William, Jr.
Spiotta-DiMare, Loren 173
Spires, Ashley 1978- 183
Spires, Elizabeth 1952- 215
   Earlier sketches in SATA 71, 111
Spiridellis, Gregg 1971(?)- 199
Spirin, Gennadii
   See Spirin, Gennady
Spirin, Gennadij
   See Spirin, Gennady
Spirin, Gennady 1948- 204
   Earlier sketches in SATA 95, 134
   See also CLR 88
Spiro, Ruth 208
Spivak, Dawnine 101
Spizman, Robyn Freedman 194
Spohn, David 1948- 72
Spohn, Kate 1962- 147
   Earlier sketch in SATA 87
Spollen, Christopher 1952- 12
Spooner, Michael (Tim) 1954- 92
Spoor, Mike 218
Spowart, Robin 1947- 177
   Earlier sketch in SATA 82
Spradlin, Michael P. 235
   Earlier sketch in SATA 204
Sprague, Gretchen 1926-2003 27
Spranger, Nina 1969- 203
Spratt, R.A. 235
Spratt, Rachel
   See Spratt, R.A.
Sprengel, Artie
   See Lerangis, Peter
Sprigge, Elizabeth (Miriam Squire)
   1900-1974 10
Spring, (Robert) Howard 1889-1965 28
Springer, Kristina 226
Springer, Margaret 1941- 78
Springer, Marilyn Harris 1931- 47
Springer, Nancy 1948- 222
   Earlier sketches in SATA 65, 110, 172
Springstubb, Tricia 1950- 78
   Brief entry 40
   Earlier sketch in SATA 46
Spudvilas, Anne 1951- 199
   Earlier sketch in SATA 94
Spurll, Barbara 1952- 78
Spurr, Elizabeth 172
Spykman, E(lizabeth) C(hoate) 1896-1965 .. 10
   See also CLR 35

Spyri, Johanna (Heusser) 1827-1901 .... *100*
  Earlier sketch in SATA *19*
  See also CLR *115*
Squires, Janet *215*
Squires, Phil
  See Barker, S. Omar
Srba, Lynne *98*
Sreenivasan, Jyotsna 1964- *101*
S-Ringi, Kjell
  See Ringi, Kjell (Arne Soerensen)
Staake, Bob 1957- *209*
Stacey, Cherylyn 1945- *96*
Stacy, Donald
  See Pohl, Frederik
Stadler, John *204*
Stadtler, Bea 1921- *17*
Stafford, Jean 1915-1979
  Obituary *22*
Stafford, Liliana 1950- *141*
Stafford, Paul 1966- *116*
Stahl, Ben(jamin) 1910-1987 .... *5*
  Obituary *54*
Stahl, Hilda 1938-1993 .... *48*
  Obituary *77*
Stahler, David, Jr. *218*
  Earlier sketch in SATA *162*
Staib, Walter *233*
Staines, Bill 1949- *213*
Stainton, Sue *187*
Stair, Gobin (John) 1912- *35*
Stalder, Valerie *27*
Stamaty, Mark Alan 1947- *230*
  Earlier sketch in SATA *12*
Stambler, Irwin 1924- *5*
Stamp, Jorgen 1969- *225*
Stampler, Ann Redisch *209*
Standiford, Natalie 1961- *169*
  Earlier sketch in SATA *81*
Stanek, Lou Willett 1931- *63*
Stang, Judit 1921-1977 .... *29*
Stang, Judy
  See Stang, Judit
Stangl, (Mary) Jean 1928- *67*
Stanhope, Eric
  See Hamilton, Charles (Harold St. John)
Stankevich, Boris 1928- *2*
Stanley, Diane 1943- *213*
  Brief entry *32*
  Earlier sketches in SATA *37, 80, 115, 164*
  See also CLR *46*
  See also SAAS *15*
Stanley, Elizabeth 1947- *206*
Stanley, George Edward 1942-2011 .... *228*
  Earlier sketches in SATA *53, 111, 157, 1, 67*
Stanley, Jerry 1941- *127*
  Earlier sketch in SATA *79*
Stanley, Mandy *165*
Stanley, Robert
  See Hamilton, Charles (Harold St. John)
Stanley, Sanna 1962- *145*
Stanli, Sue
  See Meilach, Dona Z(weigoron)
Stanstead, John
  See Groom, Arthur William
Stanton, Karen 1960- *190*
Stanton, Schuyler
  See Baum, L. Frank
Staples, Suzanne Fisher 1945- *207*
  Earlier sketches in SATA *70, 105, 151*
  See also CLR *137*
Stapleton, Marjorie (Winifred) 1932- *28*
Stapp, Arthur D(onald) 1906-1972 .... *4*
Starbird, Kaye 1916- *6*
  See also CLR *60*
Stark, Evan 1942- *78*
Stark, James
  See Goldston, Robert (Conroy)
Stark, Ken 1943- *199*
Stark, Ulf 1944- *124*
Starke, Ruth (Elaine) 1946- *129*
Starkey, Marion L(ena) 1901-1991 .... *13*

Starmer, Aaron 1976- *226*
Starr, Ward
  See Manes, Stephen
Starret, William
  See McClintock, Marshall
Starr Taylor, Bridget 1959- *99*
Stasiak, Krystyna *49*
Staub, Frank 1949- *116*
Staub, Frank Jacob
  See Staub, Frank
Staub, Wendy Corsi 1964- *114*
Stauffacher, Sue 1961- *236*
  Earlier sketches in SATA *155, 199*
Stauffer, Don
  See Berkebile, Fred D(onovan)
Staunton, Schuyler
  See Baum, L. Frank
Staunton, Ted 1956- *167*
  Earlier sketch in SATA *112*
Stead, Erin E. 1982- *232*
Stead, Judy *210*
Stead, Philip C.
  See Stringer, Helen
Stead, Philip Christian *225*
Stead, Rebecca 1968(?)- *228*
  Earlier sketch in SATA *188*
Steadman, Ralph 1936- *123*
  Earlier sketch in SATA *32*
Steadman, Ralph Idris
  See Steadman, Ralph
Stearman, Kaye 1951- *118*
Stearn, Ted 1961- *218*
Stearns, Monroe (Mather) 1913-1987 .... *5*
  Obituary *55*
Steckler, Arthur 1921-1985 .... *65*
Steding, Laurie 1953- *119*
Steel, Danielle 1947- *66*
Steel, Danielle Fernande
  See Steel, Danielle
Steele, Addison II
  See Lupoff, Richard A.
Steele, Alexander 1958- *116*
Steele, Henry Maxwell
  See Steele, Max
Steele, Mary 1930- *94*
Steele, Mary Q(uintard Govan) 1922-1992 .. *51*
  Obituary *72*
  Earlier sketch in SATA *3*
Steele, Max 1922-2005 .... *168*
  Earlier sketch in SATA *10*
Steele, Philip 1948- *140*
  Earlier sketch in SATA *81*
Steele, William O(wen) 1917-1979 .... *51*
  Obituary *27*
  Earlier sketch in SATA *1*
Steelhammer, Ilona 1952- *98*
Steelsmith, Shari 1962- *72*
Stefanik, Alfred T. 1939- *55*
Steffanson, Con
  See Cassiday, Bruce (Bingham)
  and Goulart, Ron
Steffens, Bradley 1955- *166*
  Earlier sketch in SATA *77*
Steffensmeier, Alexander 1977- *195*
Stegeman, Janet Allais 1923- *49*
  Brief entry *49*
Steggall, Susan 1967- *182*
Steig, William 1907-2003 .... *111*
  Obituary *149*
  Earlier sketches in SATA *18, 70*
  See also CLR *103*
Steig, William H.
  See Steig, William
Stein, David Ezra *211*
  Earlier sketch in SATA *180*
Stein, Janet 1955- *218*
Stein, M(eyer) L(ewis) 1920- *6*
Stein, Mathilde 1969- *195*
Stein, Mini *2*
Stein, R(ichard) Conrad 1937- *154*
  Earlier sketches in SATA *31, 82*

Stein, Wendy 1951- *77*
Steinbeck, John 1902-1968 .... *9*
  See also CLR *172*
Steinbeck, John Ernst
  See Steinbeck, John
Steinberg, Alfred 1917-1995 .... *9*
Steinberg, David 1962- *200*
Steinberg, D.J.
  See Steinberg, David
Steinberg, Don 1962- *239*
Steinberg, Fannie 1899-1990 .... *43*
Steinberg, Fred J. 1933- *4*
Steinberg, Phillip Orso 1921- *34*
Steinberg, Rafael (Mark) 1927- *45*
Steinberg, Saul 1914-1999 .... *67*
Steincrohn, Maggie
  See Davis, Maggie S.
Steiner, Barbara A(nnette) 1934- *83*
  Earlier sketch in SATA *13*
  See also SAAS *13*
Steiner, Charlotte 1900-1981 .... *45*
Steiner, George 1929- *62*
Steiner, Joan *199*
  Earlier sketch in SATA *110*
Steiner, Jorg
  See Steiner, Jorg
Steiner, Jorg 1930- *35*
Steiner, K. Leslie
  See Delany, Samuel R., Jr.
Steiner, Stan(ley) 1925-1987 .... *14*
  Obituary *50*
Steinmetz, Karen *235*
Steins, Richard 1942- *79*
Stem, Jacqueline 1931- *110*
Stemple, Heidi E.Y. 1966- *214*
Stemple, Jason *179*
Steneman, Shep 1945- *132*
Stengel, Joyce A. 1938- *158*
Stephanie, Gordon
  See Gordon, Stephanie Jacob
Stephens, Alice Barber 1858-1932 .... *66*
Stephens, Casey
  See Wagner, Sharon B.
Stephens, Helen 1972- *234*
Stephens, Henrietta Henkle 1909-1993 .... *6*
Stephens, J.B.
  See Lynn, Tracy
Stephens, Mary Jo 1935- *8*
Stephens, Rebecca 1961- *141*
Stephens, Reed
  See Donaldson, Stephen R.
Stephens, Suzanne
  See Kirby, Susan E.
Stephens, William M(cLain) 1925- *21*
Stephensen, A. M.
  See Manes, Stephen
Stephenson, Kristina *224*
Stephenson, Lynda 1941- *179*
Stephenson, Lynda A.
  See Stephenson, Lynda
Stepp, Ann 1935- *29*
Stepto, Michele 1946- *61*
Steptoe, Javaka 1971- *213*
  Earlier sketch in SATA *151*
Steptoe, John (Lewis) 1950-1989 .... *63*
  Earlier sketch in SATA *8*
  See also CLR *12*
Sterling, Brett
  See Bradbury, Ray
  and Hamilton, Edmond
  and Samachson, Joseph
Sterling, Dorothy 1913-2008 .... *83*
  Autobiography Feature *127*
  Obituary *200*
  Earlier sketch in SATA *1*
  See also CLR *1*
  See also SAAS *2*
Sterling, Helen
  See Watts, Helen L. Hoke
Sterling, Philip 1907-1989 .... *8*
  Obituary *63*

Sterling, Shirley (Anne) 1948- *101*
Stern, Ellen Norman 1927- *26*
Stern, Judith M. 1951- *75*
Stern, Madeleine
   See Stern, Madeleine B.
Stern, Madeleine B. 1912-2007 .... *14*
Stern, Madeleine Bettina
   See Stern, Madeleine B.
Stern, Maggie 1953- *156*
Stern, Philip Van Doren 1900-1984 .... *13*
   Obituary *39*
Stern, Simon 1943- *15*
Sterne, Emma Gelders 1894- *6*
Steurt, Marjorie Rankin 1888-1978 .... *10*
Stevens, April 1963- *208*
Stevens, Bryna 1924- *65*
Stevens, Carla M(cBride) 1928- *13*
Stevens, Chambers 1968- *128*
Stevens, Diane 1939- *94*
Stevens, Franklin 1933- *6*
Stevens, Greg
   See Cook, Glen
Stevens, Gwendolyn 1944- *33*
Stevens, Helen 1953- *209*
Stevens, Jan Romero 1953- *95*
Stevens, Janet 1953- *193*
   Earlier sketches in SATA *90, 148*
Stevens, Kathleen 1936- *49*
Stevens, Leonard A. 1920- *67*
Stevens, Lucile Vernon 1899-1994 .... *59*
Stevens, Margaret Dean
   See Aldrich, Bess Streeter
Stevens, Patricia Bunning 1931- *27*
Stevens, Peter
   See Geis, Darlene Stern
Stevens, Serita 1949- *70*
Stevens, Serita Deborah
   See Stevens, Serita
Stevens, Serita Mendelson
   See Stevens, Serita
Stevens, Shira
   See Stevens, Serita
Stevenson, Anna (M.) 1905- *12*
Stevenson, Augusta 1869(?)-1976 .... *2*
   Obituary *26*
Stevenson, Burton Egbert 1872-1962 ..... *25*
Stevenson, Drew 1947- *60*
Stevenson, Emma *207*
Stevenson, Harvey 1960- *148*
   Earlier sketch in SATA *80*
Stevenson, James 1929- *195*
   Brief entry *34*
   Earlier sketches in SATA *42, 71, 113, 161*
   See also CLR *17*
Stevenson, Janet 1913- *8*
Stevenson, Robert Louis 1850-1894 .... *100*
   See also YABC *2*
   See also CLR *107*
Stevenson, Robert Louis Balfour
   See Stevenson, Robert Louis
Stevenson, Sucie
   See Stevenson, Sucie
Stevenson, Sucie 1956- *194*
   Earlier sketch in SATA *104*
Stewart, A(gnes) C(harlotte) *15*
Stewart, Amber *181*
Stewart, Chantal 1945- *173*
   Earlier sketch in SATA *121*
Stewart, Charles
   See Zurhorst, Charles (Stewart, Jr.)
Stewart, Eleanor
   See Porter, Eleanor H(odgman)
Stewart, Elisabeth J(ane) 1927- *93*
Stewart, Elizabeth Laing 1907- *6*
Stewart, Gail B. 1949- *141*
Stewart, George Rippey 1895-1980 .... *3*
   Obituary *23*
Stewart, Jennifer J. 1960- *128*
Stewart, Jennifer Jenkins
   See Stewart, Jennifer J.

Stewart, Joel *211*
   Earlier sketch in SATA *151*
Stewart, John 1920- *14*
Stewart, Mary (Florence Elinor) 1916- *12*
Stewart, Mary Rainbow
   See Stewart, Mary (Florence Elinor)
Stewart, Melissa 1968- *209*
   Earlier sketches in SATA *111, 167*
Stewart, Paul 1955- *199*
   Earlier sketches in SATA *114, 163*
Stewart, Robert Neil 1891-1972 .... *7*
Stewart, Sarah *143*
Stewart, Scott
   See Zaffo, George J.
Stewart, Trenton Lee 1970- *216*
Stewart, W(alter) P. 1924- *53*
Stewart, Whitney 1959- *167*
   Earlier sketch in SATA *92*
Stewig, John Warren 1937- *162*
   Earlier sketches in SATA *26, 110*
Stickler, Soma Han 1942- *128*
Stidworthy, John 1943- *63*
Stiefvater, Maggie 1981- *237*
Stiegemeyer, Julie *180*
Stier, Catherine *198*
Stiles, Martha Bennett *108*
   Earlier sketch in SATA *6*
Still, James 1906-2001 .... *29*
   Obituary *127*
Stille, Darlene R. 1942- *170*
   Earlier sketch in SATA *126*
Stille, Darlene Ruth
   See Stille, Darlene R.
Stillerman, Marci *104*
Stillerman, Robbie 1947- *12*
Stilley, Frank 1918- *29*
Stilton, Geronimo *158*
Stimpson, Gerald
   See Mitchell, Adrian
Stimson, James 1964- *213*
Stine, Catherine *165*
Stine, G(eorge) Harry 1928-1997 .... *136*
   Earlier sketch in SATA *10*
Stine, Jovial Bob
   See Stine, R.L.
Stine, R.L. 1943- *194*
   Earlier sketches in SATA *31, 76, 129*
   See also CLR *111*
Stine, Robert Lawrence
   See Stine, R.L.
Stinetorf, Louise (Allender) 1900-1992 .... *10*
Stinson, Kathy 1952- *98*
Stirling, Arthur
   See Sinclair, Upton
Stirling, Ian 1941- *77*
Stirling, Nora B(romley) 1900-1997 ..... *3*
Stirnweis, Shannon 1931- *10*
Stobbs, William 1914-2000 .... *17*
   Obituary *120*
Stock, Carolmarie 1951- *75*
Stock, Catherine 1952- *214*
   Earlier sketches in SATA *65, 114, 158*
Stockdale, Susan 1954- *206*
   Earlier sketch in SATA *98*
Stockham, Peter (Alan) 1928- *57*
Stockton, Francis Richard 1834-1902 .... *44*
   Brief entry *32*
Stockton, Frank R.
   See Stockton, Francis Richard
Stockwell-Moniz, Marc J. 1954- *164*
Stoddard, Edward G. 1923- *10*
Stoddard, Hope 1900-1987 .... *6*
Stoddard, Sandol 1927- *98*
   Earlier sketch in SATA *14*
Stoehr, Shelley 1969- *107*
Stoeke, Janet Morgan 1957- *202*
   Earlier sketches in SATA *90, 136*
Stohl, Margaret *227*
Stohner, Anu 1952- *179*
Stoiko, Michael 1919- *14*
Stojic, Manya 1967- *156*

Stoker, Abraham
   See Stoker, Bram
Stoker, Bram 1847-1912 .... *29*
Stokes, Cedric
   See Beardmore, George
Stokes, Jack (Tilden) 1923- *13*
Stokes, Olivia Pearl 1916- *32*
Stolarz, Laurie Faria 1972- *203*
Stolz, Mary 1920-2006 .... *133*
   Obituary *180*
   Earlier sketches in SATA *10, 71*
   See also SAAS *3*
Stolz, Mary Slattery
   See Stolz, Mary
Stone, Alan
   See Svenson, Andrew E(dward)
Stone, David K(arl) 1922- *9*
Stone, David Lee 1978- *166*
Stone, Eugenia 1879-1971 .... *7*
Stone, Gene
   See Stone, Eugenia
Stone, Helen V(irginia) *6*
Stone, Idella Purnell
   See Purnell, Idella
Stone, Ikey
   See Purnell, Idella
Stone, Irving 1903-1989 .... *3*
   Obituary *64*
Stone, Jeff *178*
Stone, Jon 1931-1997 .... *39*
   Obituary *95*
Stone, Josephine Rector
   See Dixon, Jeanne
Stone, Kyle M. 1972- *202*
Stone, Lesley
   See Trevor, Elleston
Stone, Mary Hanlon *231*
Stone, Peter 1930-2003 .... *65*
   Obituary *143*
Stone, Phoebe *205*
   Earlier sketch in SATA *134*
Stone, Raymond *1*
Stone, Rosetta
   See Dr. Seuss
Stone, Tanya Lee 1965- *217*
   Earlier sketch in SATA *182*
Stonehouse, Bernard 1926- *140*
   Earlier sketches in SATA *13, 80*
Stones, (Cyril) Anthony 1934- *72*
Stong, Phil(ip Duffield) 1899-1957 ...... *32*
Stoops, Erik D(aniel) 1966- *142*
   Earlier sketch in SATA *78*
Stoppelmoore, Cheryl Jean
   See Ladd, Cheryl (Jean)
Stops, Sue 1936- *86*
Storace, Patricia *193*
Storad, Conrad J. 1957- *119*
Storey, Margaret 1926- *9*
Storey, Victoria Carolyn 1945- *16*
Stork, Francisco
   See Stork, Francisco X.
Stork, Francisco X. 1953- *210*
Storme, Peter
   See Stern, Philip Van Doren
Storms, Patricia 1963- *217*
Storr, Catherine (Cole) 1913-2001 .... *87*
   Obituary *122*
   Earlier sketch in SATA *9*
Story, Josephine
   See Loring, Emilie (Baker)
Stotko, Mary-Ann 1960- *154*
Stott, Ann *219*
Stott, Dorothy (M.) 1958- *99*
   Earlier sketch in SATA *67*
Stott, Dot
   See Stott, Dorothy (M.)
Stotter, Mike 1957- *108*
Stotts, Stuart *227*
Stout, Shawn K. *226*
Stout, William 1949- *132*
Stoutenburg, Adrien (Pearl) 1916-1982 .... *3*

Stoutland, Allison 1963- *130*
Stover, Allan C(arl) 1938- *14*
Stover, Jill (Griffin) 1958- *82*
Stover, Marjorie Filley 1914- *9*
Stowe, Harriet Beecher 1811-1896
    See YABC *1*
    See also CLR *131*
Stowe, Harriet Elizabeth Beecher
    See Stowe, Harriet Beecher
Stowe, Leland 1899-1994 .... *60*
    Obituary *78*
Stowe, Rosetta
    See Ogan, George F.
    and Ogan, Margaret E. (Nettles)
Stower, Adam *229*
    Earlier sketch in SATA *195*
Strachan, Bruce 1959- *205*
Strachan, Ian 1938- *85*
Strachan, Linda *167*
Strachan, Margaret Pitcairn 1908-1998 .... *14*
Strahinich, H. C.
    See Strahinich, Helen C.
Strahinich, Helen C. 1949- *78*
Strait, Treva Adams 1909-2002 .... *35*
Strand, Mark 1934- *41*
Strange, Philippa
    See Coury, Louise Andree
Stranger, Joyce
    See Wilson, Joyce M.
Strangis, Joel 1948- *124*
Strannigan, Shawn 1956- *93*
Strannigan, Shawn Alyne
    See Strannigan, Shawn
Strasnick, Lauren *222*
Strasser, Todd 1950- *215*
    Earlier sketches in SATA *41, 45, 71, 107, 153*
    See also CLR *11*
Stratemeyer, Edward L. 1862-1930 .... *100*
    Earlier sketches in SATA *1, 67*
    See also CLR *166*
    See Adams, Harrison
Stratford, Philip 1927- *47*
Stratton, Allan 1951- *178*
Stratton, J. M.
    See Whitlock, Ralph
Stratton, Thomas
    See Coulson, Robert S(tratton)
    and DeWeese, Thomas Eugene
Stratton-Porter, Gene 1863-1924 .... *15*
    See also CLR *87*
Strauss, Gwen 1963- *77*
Strauss, Joyce 1936- *53*
Strauss, Linda Leopold 1942- *127*
Strauss, Susan (Elizabeth) 1954- *75*
Strayer, E. Ward
    See Stratemeyer, Edward L.
Streano, Vince(nt Catello) 1945- *20*
Streatfeild, Mary Noel
    See Streatfeild, Noel
Streatfeild, Noel 1897(?)-1986 .... *20*
    Obituary *48*
    See also CLR *83*
Street, Janet Travell 1959- *84*
Street, Julia Montgomery 1898-1993 .... *11*
Streissguth, Thomas 1958- *116*
Strelkoff, Tatiana 1957- *89*
Stren, Patti 1949- *88*
    Brief entry *41*
    See also CLR *5*
Strete, Craig Kee 1950- *96*
    Earlier sketch in SATA *44*
Stretton, Barbara (Humphrey) 1936- *43*
    Brief entry *35*
Strevens-Marzo, Bridget *238*
Strickland, Brad 1947- *200*
    Earlier sketches in SATA *83, 137, 142*
Strickland, Craig (A.) 1956- *102*
Strickland, Dorothy S(alley) 1933- *89*
Strickland, Michael R. 1965- *144*
    Earlier sketch in SATA *83*
Strickland, Shadra *209*

Strickland, Tessa *173*
Strickland, William Bradley
    See Strickland, Brad
Striegel, Jana 1955- *140*
Striegel-Wilson, Jana
    See Striegel, Jana
Striker, Lee
    See Clark, Margaret (D.)
Striker, Susan 1942- *63*
Stringam, Jean 1945- *233*
Stringer, Helen *225*
Stringer, Lauren 1957- *183*
    Earlier sketch in SATA *129*
Stroeyer, Poul 1923- *13*
Stromoski, Rick 1958- *111*
Strong, Charles
    See Epstein, Beryl
    and Epstein, Samuel
Strong, David
    See McGuire, Leslie (Sarah)
Strong, Jeremy 1949- *175*
    Earlier sketches in SATA *36, 105*
Strong, J.J.
    See Strong, Jeremy
Strong, Pat
    See Hough, Richard (Alexander)
Strong, Stacie 1965- *74*
Stroud, Bettye 1939- *165*
    Earlier sketch in SATA *96*
Stroud, Jonathan 1970- *213*
    Earlier sketches in SATA *102, 159*
    See also CLR *134*
Stroyer, Poul
    See Stroeyer, Poul
Strug, Kerri 1977- *108*
Stryer, Andrea Stenn 1938- *192*
Stryker, Daniel
    See Morris, Chris(topher Crosby)
    and Stump, Jane Barr
Stuart, David
    See Hoyt, Edwin P(almer), Jr.
Stuart, Derek
    See Foster, John L(ouis)
Stuart, Forbes 1924- *13*
Stuart, Ian
    See MacLean, Alistair
Stuart, Jesse (Hilton) 1906-1984 .... *2*
    Obituary *36*
Stuart, Ruth McEnery 1849(?)-1917 .... *116*
Stuart, Sheila
    See Baker, Mary Gladys Steel
Stuart-Clark, Christopher (Anthony) 1940- .. *32*
Stuber, Barbara 1951- *234*
Stubis, Talivaldis 1926- *5*
Stubley, Trevor (Hugh) 1932- *22*
Stuchner, Joan Betty *209*
Stucky, Naomi R. 1922- *72*
Stucley, Elizabeth
    See Northmore, Elizabeth Florence
Stultifer, Morton
    See Curtis, Richard
Sture-Vasa, Mary
    See Alsop, Mary O'Hara
Sturges, Philemon *174*
Sturman, Jennifer *237*
Sturtevant, Katherine 1950- *180*
    Earlier sketch in SATA *130*
Sturton, Hugh
    See Johnston, H(ugh) A(nthony) S(tephen)
Sturtzel, Howard A(llison) 1894-1985 .... *1*
Sturtzel, Jane Levington 1903-1996 .... *1*
Stutley, D(oris) J(ean) 1959- *142*
Stutson, Caroline 1940- *234*
    Earlier sketch in SATA *104*
Stuve-Bodeen, Stephanie
    See Bodeen, S. A.
Stux, Erica 1929- *140*
Styles, (Frank) Showell 1908- *10*
Stynes, Barbara White *133*
Suarez, Maribel 1952- *201*
Suba, Susanne *4*

Suber, Melissa *213*
Subond, Valerie
    See Grayland, Valerie (Merle Spanner)
Sudbery, Rodie 1943- *42*
Sudyka, Diana *208*
Sue, Majella Lue *209*
Suen, Anastasia 1956(?)- *157*
Sufrin, Mark 1925- *76*
Sugarman, Joan G. 1917- *64*
Sugarman, Tracy 1921- *37*
Sugita, Yutaka 1930- *36*
Suhl, Yuri (Menachem) 1908-1986 .... *8*
    Obituary *50*
    See also CLR *2*
    See also SAAS *1*
Suhr, Joanne *129*
Suid, Murray 1942- *27*
Sullivan, Edward T. *206*
Sullivan, George (Edward) 1927- *147*
    Earlier sketches in SATA *4, 89*
Sullivan, Jacqueline Levering *203*
Sullivan, Jody
    See Rake, Jody
Sullivan, Kathryn A. 1954- *141*
Sullivan, Mary Ann 1954- *63*
Sullivan, Mary W(ilson) 1907- *13*
Sullivan, Pat
    See Messmer, Otto
Sullivan, Paul 1939- *106*
Sullivan, Sarah G. 1953- *179*
Sullivan, Silky 1940- *101*
Sullivan, Sue
    See Sullivan, Susan E.
Sullivan, Susan E. 1962- *123*
Sullivan, Thomas Joseph, Jr. 1947- *16*
Sullivan, Tom
    See Sullivan, Thomas Joseph, Jr.
Sully, Tom 1959- *104*
Suma, Nova Ren *223*
Sumichrast, Jozef 1948- *29*
Sumiko
    See Davies, Sumiko
Summerforest, Ivy B.
    See Kirkup, James
Summers, Barbara 1944- *182*
Summers, Cassia Joy
    See Cowley, Joy
Summers, James L(evingston) 1910-1973 .... *57*
    Brief entry *28*
Summertree, Katonah
    See Windsor, Patricia
Summy, Barrie *208*
Sumner, William 1971- *229*
Sun, Chyng Feng 1959- *90*
Sunderlin, Sylvia (S.) 1911-1997 .... *28*
    Obituary *99*
Sung, Betty Lee *26*
Supeene, Shelagh Lynne 1952- *153*
Supplee, Suzanne *204*
Supraner, Robyn 1930- *101*
    Earlier sketch in SATA *20*
Supree, Burt(on) 1941-1992 .... *73*
Surface, Mary Hall 1958- *126*
Surge, Frank 1931- *13*
Susac, Andrew 1929- *5*
Susi, Geraldine Lee 1942- *98*
Sussman, Cornelia Silver 1914-1999 .... *59*
Sussman, Irving 1908-1996 .... *59*
Sussman, Michael 1953- *217*
Sussman, Michael B.
    See Sussman, Michael
Sussman, Susan 1942- *48*
Sutcliff, Rosemary 1920-1992 .... *78*
    Obituary *73*
    Earlier sketches in SATA *6, 44*
    See also CLR *138*
Sutcliffe, Jane 1957- *138*
Sutherland, Colleen 1944- *79*
Sutherland, Efua (Theodora Morgue)
    1924-1996 .... *25*
Sutherland, Jon 1958- *167*

Sutherland, Jonathan D.
   See Sutherland, Jon
Sutherland, Jonathan David
   See Sutherland, Jon
Sutherland, Margaret 1941- 15
Sutherland, Zena Bailey 1915-2002 37
   Obituary 137
Suttles, Shirley (Smith) 1922- 21
Sutton, Ann (Livesay) 1923- 31
Sutton, Eve(lyn Mary) 1906-1992 26
Sutton, Felix 1910(?)-1973 31
Sutton, Jane 1950- 52
   Brief entry 43
Sutton, Larry M(atthew) 1931- 29
Sutton, Margaret Beebe 1903-2001 1
   Obituary 131
Sutton, Myron Daniel 1925- 31
Sutton, Roger 1956- 93
Sutton, Sally 1973- 214
Suzanne, Jamie
   See Hawes, Louise
   and Lantz, Francess L(in)
   and Singleton, Linda Joy
   and Zach, Cheryl (Byrd)
Suzuki, David 1936- 138
Suzuki, David Takayoshi
   See Suzuki, David
Svendsen, Mark 1962- 181
   Earlier sketch in SATA *120*
Svendsen, Mark Nestor
   See Svendsen, Mark
Svenson, Andrew E(dward) 1910-1975 2
   Obituary 26
Swaab, Neil 1978- 191
Swaim, Jessica 1950- 202
Swain, Carol 1962- 172
Swain, Gwenyth 1961- 134
   Earlier sketch in SATA *84*
Swain, Ruth
   See Swain, Ruth Freeman
Swain, Ruth Freeman 1951- 161
   Earlier sketch in SATA *119*
Swain, Su Zan (Noguchi) 1916- 21
Swain, Wilson 1976- 225
Swallow, Gerry 227
Swallow, Pamela Curtis 178
Swamp, Jake 1941- 98
Swan, Susan 1944- 108
   Earlier sketch in SATA *22*
Swann, Brian (Stanley Frank) 1940- 116
Swann, E.L.
   See Lasky, Kathryn
Swann, Ruth Rice 1920- 84
Swanson, Diane 1944- 203
Swanson, Helen M(cKendry) 1919- 94
Swanson, June 1931- 76
Swanson, Susan Marie 209
Swanson, Wayne 1942- 167
Swarner, Kristina 1965- 215
Swarthout, Glendon (Fred) 1918-1992 26
Swarthout, Kathryn 1919- 7
Swayne, Sam(uel F.) 1907- 53
Swayne, Zoa (Lourana) 1905- 53
Swearingen, Greg 1976- 225
Sweat, Lynn 1934- 168
   Earlier sketch in SATA *57*
Swede, George 1940- 67
Sweeney, James B(artholomew) 1910-1999 . 21
Sweeney, Joyce 1955- 167
   Earlier sketches in SATA *65, 68, 108*
Sweeney, Joyce Kay
   See Sweeney, Joyce
Sweeney, Karen O'Connor
   See O'Connor, Karen
Sweeney, Matthew (Gerard) 1952- 156
Sweet, Melissa 1956- 211
   Earlier sketch in SATA *172*
Sweet, Sarah C.
   See Jewett, Sarah Orne
Sweetland, Nancy A(nn) 1934- 48
Swender, Jennifer 235

Swenson, Allan A(rmstrong) 1933- 21
Swenson, May 1919-1989 15
Swentzell, Rina 1939- 79
Swiatkowska, Gabi 1971(?)- 180
Swift, Bryan
   See Knott, William C(ecil, Jr.)
Swift, David
   See Kaufmann, John
Swift, Hildegarde Hoyt 1890(?)-1977
   Obituary 20
Swift, Jonathan 1667-1745 19
   See also CLR *161*
Swift, Merlin
   See Leeming, Joseph
Swiger, Elinor Porter 1927- 8
Swinburne, Laurence (Joseph) 1924- 9
Swinburne, Stephen R. 1952- 231
   Earlier sketches in SATA *150, 188*
Swinburne, Steve
   See Swinburne, Stephen R.
Swindells, Robert (Edward) 1939- 150
   Brief entry 34
   Earlier sketches in SATA *50, 80*
   See also SAAS *14*
Swinford, Betty (June Wells) 1927- 58
Swinford, Bob
   See Swinford, Betty (June Wells)
Swithen, John
   See King, Stephen
Switzer, Ellen 1923- 48
Swope, Sam 156
Swope, Samuel
   See Swope, Sam
Sybesma, Jetske
   See Ironside, Jetske
Sydney, Frank
   See Warwick, Alan R(oss)
Sydor, Colleen 1960- 207
Sykes, Julie 1963- 202
Sylvada, Peter 1964- 202
Sylver, Adrienne 230
Sylvester, Natalie G(abry) 1922- 22
Syme, (Neville) Ronald 1913-1992 87
   Earlier sketch in SATA *2*
Symes, R. F. 77
Symes, Ruth Louise 1962- 179
Symons, (Dorothy) Geraldine 1909- 33
Symons, Stuart
   See Stanley, George Edward
Symynkywicz, Jeffrey B. 1954- 87
Symynkywicz, Jeffrey Bruce
   See Symynkywicz, Jeffrey B.
Synge, (Phyllis) Ursula 1930- 9
Sypher, Lucy Johnston 1907- 7
Szasz, Suzanne (Shorr) 1915-1997 13
   Obituary 99
Szekeres, Cyndy 1933- 157
   Autobiography Feature 157
   Earlier sketches in SATA *5, 60, 131*
   See also SAAS *13*
Szekessy, Tanja 98
Szpura, Beata 1961- 93
Szuc, Jeff 1975- 220
Szudek, Agnes S(usan) P(hilomena) 57
   Brief entry 49
Szulc, Tad 1926-2001 26
Szydlow, Jarl
   See Szydlowski, Mary Vigliante
Szydlowski, Mary Vigliante 1946- 94
Szymanski, Lois 1957- 91

T

Taback, Simms 1932- 170
   Brief entry 36
   Earlier sketches in SATA *40, 104*
   See also CLR *100*
Taber, Gladys (Bagg) 1899-1980
   Obituary 22

Tabor, Nancy Maria Grande 1949- 161
   Earlier sketch in SATA *89*
Tabrah, Ruth Milander 1921- 14
Tacang, Brian 213
Tackach, James 1953- 123
Tackach, James M.
   See Tackach, James
Tadgell, Nicole 1969- 220
   Earlier sketch in SATA *177*
Tafolla, Carmen 1951- 220
Tafolla, Mary Carmen
   See Tafolla, Carmen
Tafuri, Nancy 1946- 192
   Autobiography Feature 192
   Earlier sketches in SATA *39, 75, 130*
   See also CLR *74*
   See also SAAS *14*
Tagg, Christine Elizabeth 1962- 138
Tagliaferro, Linda 173
Taha, Karen T(erry) 1942- 156
   Earlier sketch in SATA *71*
Tai, Sharon O. 1963- 153
Tait, Douglas 1944- 12
Takabayashi, Mari 1960- 156
   Earlier sketch in SATA *115*
Takahashi, Hideko 209
Takahashi, Rumiko 1957- 163
Takakjian, Portia 1930- 15
Takashima, Misako
   See Misako Rocks!
Takashima, Shizuye 1928- 13
Takayama, Sandi 1962- 106
Takeda, Pete(r M.) 1964- 148
Tal, Eve 1947- 176
Talbert, Marc (Alan) 1953- 154
   Autobiography Feature 154
   Earlier sketches in SATA *68, 99*
Talbot, Charlene Joy 1928- 10
Talbot, Toby 1928- 14
Talbott, Hudson 1949- 212
   Earlier sketches in SATA *84, 131*
Talifero, Gerald 1950- 75
Talker, T.
   See Rands, William Brighty
Tallarico, Tony 1933- 116
Tallcott, Emogene 10
Tallec, Olivier 1970- 197
Tallis, Robyn
   See Smith, Sherwood
Tallon, Robert 1939- 43
   Brief entry 28
Talmadge, Marian 14
Tamaki, Jillian 1980- 201
Tamar, Erika 1934- 150
   Earlier sketches in SATA *62, 101*
Tamarin, Alfred H. 1913-1980 13
Tamburine, Jean 1930- 12
Tames, Richard (Lawrence) 1946- 102
   Earlier sketch in SATA *67*
Tamminga, Frederick W(illiam) 1934- 66
Tammuz, Benjamin 1919-1989
   Obituary 63
Tan, Amy 1952- 75
Tan, Amy Ruth
   See Tan, Amy
Tan, Shaun 1974- 198
Tanaka, Beatrice 1932- 76
Tanaka, Shelley 214
   Earlier sketch in SATA *136*
Tanaka, Yoko 1947- 215
Tang, Charles 1948- 81
Tang, Greg 172
Tang, You-Shan 1946- 53
Tania B.
   See Blixen, Karen
Tankard, Jeremy 1973- 191
Tannen, Mary 1943- 37
Tannenbaum, Beulah Goldstein 1916- 3
Tannenbaum, D(onald) Leb 1948- 42
Tanner, Jane 1946- 74
Tanner, Lian 1951- 237

Tanner, Louise S(tickney) 1922-2000 9
Tanobe, Miyuki 1937- 23
Tanselle, Eve 1933- 125
Tapio, Pat Decker
   See Kines, Pat Decker
Tapp, Kathy Kennedy 1949- 88
   Brief entry 50
Tarbescu, Edith 1939- 107
Tarkington, (Newton) Booth 1869-1946 17
Tarpley, Natasha A(nastasia) 1971- 147
Tarr, Judith 1955- 237
   Earlier sketches in SATA *64, 149*
Tarry, Ellen 1906-2008 16
   See also CLR 26
   See also SAAS 16
Tarshis, Jerome 1936- 9
Tarshis, Lauren 187
Tarsky, Sue 1946- 41
Taschek, Karen 1956- 185
Tashjian, Jake 1994- 234
Tashjian, Janet 1956- 238
   Earlier sketches in SATA *102, 151*
Tashjian, Virginia A. 1921-2008 3
Tasker, James 1908- 9
Tate, Don(ald E.) 159
Tate, Eleanora E. 1948- 191
   Earlier sketches in SATA *38, 94*
   See also CLR 37
Tate, Eleanora Elaine
   See Tate, Eleanora E.
Tate, Ellalice
   See Hibbert, Eleanor Alice Burford
Tate, Joan 1922- 86
   Earlier sketch in SATA *9*
   See also SAAS 20
Tate, Mary Anne
   See Hale, Arlene
Tate, Nikki 134
Tate, Richard
   See Masters, Anthony (Richard)
Tate, Suzanne 1930- 91
Tatham, Betty 142
Tatham, Campbell
   See Elting, Mary
Tatham, Julie
   See Tatham, Julie Campbell
Tatham, Julie Campbell 1908-1999 80
Tavares, Matt 198
   Earlier sketch in SATA *159*
Tavares, Victor 1971- 176
Taves, Isabella 1915- 27
Taxali, Gary 1968- 234
Tayleur, Karen 1961- 213
Taylor, Alastair 1959- 130
Taylor, Andrew 1951- 70
Taylor, Andrew John Robert
   See Taylor, Andrew
Taylor, Ann 1782-1866 41
   Brief entry 35
Taylor, Audilee Boyd 1931- 59
Taylor, Barbara J. 1927- 10
Taylor, Ben
   See Strachan, Ian
Taylor, Brooke 205
Taylor, Carl 1937-2010 14
Taylor, Carrie-Jo
   See Taylor, C.J.
Taylor, Cheryl Munro 1957- 96
Taylor, C.J. 1952- 224
Taylor, Cora (Lorraine) 1936- 103
   Earlier sketch in SATA *64*
   See also CLR 63
Taylor, Dave 1948- 78
Taylor, David
   See Taylor, Dave
Taylor, David 1900-1965 10
Taylor, Debbie A. 1955- 169
Taylor, Eleanor 1969- 206
Taylor, Elizabeth 1912-1975 13
Taylor, Florance Walton 9

Taylor, Florence M(arian Tompkins)
   1892-1983 9
Taylor, Gage 1942-2000 87
Taylor, Geoff 1946- 204
Taylor, G.P. 1958(?)- 216
   Earlier sketch in SATA *156*
Taylor, Graham Peter
   See Taylor, G.P.
Taylor, Greg 1951- 221
Taylor, Herb(ert Norman, Jr.) 1942-1987 22
   Obituary 54
Taylor, J. David
   See Taylor, Dave
Taylor, Jane 1783-1824 41
   Brief entry 35
Taylor, Jerry D(uncan) 1938- 47
Taylor, John Robert
   See Taylor, Andrew
Taylor, Judy
   See Hough, Judy Taylor
Taylor, Kenneth N. 1917-2005 26
Taylor, Kenneth Nathaniel
   See Taylor, Kenneth N.
Taylor, Kim 180
Taylor, L(ester) B(arbour), Jr. 1932- 27
Taylor, Lois Dwight Cole
   See Cole, Lois Dwight
Taylor, Louise Todd 1939- 47
Taylor, Margaret 1950- 106
Taylor, Mark 1927- 32
   Brief entry 28
Taylor, Mildred D. 1943- 135
   See also CLR 144
   See also SAAS 5
Taylor, Mildred Delois
   See Taylor, Mildred D.
Taylor, Paula (Wright) 1942- 48
   Brief entry 33
Taylor, Peter Lane 210
Taylor, Robert Lewis 1912-1998 10
Taylor, Sean 1965- 192
Taylor, Susan Champlin
   See Champlin, Susan
Taylor, Sydney (Brenner) 1904(?)-1978 28
   Obituary 26
   Earlier sketch in SATA *1*
Taylor, Theodore 1921-2006 128
   Obituary 177
   Earlier sketches in SATA *5, 54, 83*
   See also CLR 30
   See also SAAS 4
Taylor, William 1938- 164
   Earlier sketches in SATA *78, 113*
   See also CLR 63
Taylor-Butler, Christine 1959- 218
Tazewell, Charles 1900-1972 74
Tchana, Katrin
   See Tchana, Katrin Hyman
Tchana, Katrin H.
   See Tchana, Katrin Hyman
Tchana, Katrin Hyman 1963- 177
   Earlier sketch in SATA *125*
Tchekhov, Anton
   See Chekhov, Anton
Tchen, Richard 120
Tchudi, Stephen N. 1942- 55
Teague, Bob
   See Teague, Robert
Teague, David 235
Teague, Mark 1963- 205
   Earlier sketches in SATA *68, 99, 170*
Teague, Mark Christopher
   See Teague, Mark
Teague, Robert 1929- 32
   Brief entry 31
Teal, Val 1902-1997 10
   Obituary 114
Teal, Valentine M.
   See Teal, Val
Teale, Edwin Way 1899-1980 7
   Obituary 25

Teasdale, Sara 1884-1933 32
Tebbel, John (William) 1912-2004 26
Teckentrup, Britta 1969- 200
Tedesco, P.R.
   See Naylor, Phyllis Reynolds
Teensma, Lynne Bertrand
   See Bertrand, Lynne
Tee-Van, Helen Damrosch 1893-1976 10
   Obituary 27
Teevee, Ningeokuluk 1963- 223
Tegner, Bruce 1928- 62
Teitelbaum, Michael 1953- 116
   Earlier sketch in SATA *59*
Tejima
   See Tejima, Keizaburo
Tejima, Keizaburo 1931- 139
   See also CLR 20
Telander, Todd (G.) 1967- 88
Teleki, Geza 1943- 45
Telemaque, Eleanor Wong 1934- 43
Telescope, Tom
   See Newbery, John
Telgemeier, Raina 1977- 228
Tellegen, Toon 1941- 229
Teller, Janne 1964- 230
Tellis, Annabel 1967- 191
Temkin, Sara Anne Schlossberg 1913-1996 . 26
Temko, Florence 13
Tempest, Margaret Mary 1892-1982
   Obituary 33
Templar, Maurice
   See Groom, Arthur William
Temple, Arthur
   See Northcott, (William) Cecil
Temple, Charles 1947- 79
Temple, Frances (Nolting) 1945-1995 85
Temple, Herbert 1919- 45
Temple, Paul
   See McConnell, James Douglas Rutherford
Temple, William F(rederick) 1914-1989 107
Tenggren, Gustaf 1896-1970 18
   Obituary 26
Tennant, Kylie
   See Rodd, Kylie Tennant
Tennant, Veronica 1947- 36
TenNapel, Doug 1966- 234
Tenneshaw, S.M.
   See Beaumont, Charles
   and Garrett, Randall
   and Silverberg, Robert
Tenniel, John 1820-1914 74
   Brief entry 27
   See also CLR 146
Teplin, Scott 231
Tepper, Sheri S. 1929- 113
Tepper, Yona 1941- 228
Terada, Alice M. 1928- 90
Terban, Marvin 1940- 54
   Brief entry 45
Teresi, Judith M.
   See Goldberger, Judith M.
ter Haar, Jaap 1922- 6
   See also CLR 15
Terhune, Albert Payson 1872-1942 15
Terkel, Susan N(eiburg) 1948- 103
   Earlier sketch in SATA *59*
Terlouw, Jan (Cornelis) 1931- 30
Terrazzini, Daniela Jaglenka 218
Terrell, John Upton 1900-1988
   Obituary 60
Terrill, Beth 198
Terrill, Elizabeth
   See Terrill, Beth
Terris, Susan 1937- 77
   Earlier sketch in SATA *3*
Terry, Luther L(eonidas) 1911-1985 11
   Obituary 42
Terry, Margaret
   See Dunnahoo, Terry Janson
Terry, Michael 1947- 233
Terry, Walter 1913-1982 14

Terry, Will 1966- 205
Terzian, James P. 1915- 14
Tessendorf, K(enneth) C(harles) 1925-2003 . 75
   Obituary 142
Tessler, Manya 200
Tessler, Stephanie Gordon
   See Gordon, Stephanie Jacob
Testa, Dom 208
Tester, Sylvia Root 1939- 64
   Brief entry 37
Tether, (Cynthia) Graham 1950- 46
   Brief entry 36
Tetzner, Lisa 1894-1963 169
Thach, James Otis 1969- 195
Thacher, Mary McGrath 1933- 9
Thackeray, William Makepeace 1811-1863 .. 23
Thake, Richard 1938- 237
Thaler, Michael C.
   See Thaler, Mike
Thaler, Mike 1936- 215
   Brief entry 47
   Earlier sketches in SATA *56, 93*
Thaler, Shmuel 1958- 126
   Earlier sketch in SATA *72*
Thamer, Katie 1955- 42
Thane, Elswyth 1900-1984(?) 32
Tharp, Louise (Marshall) Hall 1898-1992 3
   Obituary 129
Tharp, Tim 1957- 189
Thayer, Ernest Lawrence 1863-1940 60
Thayer, Jane
   See Woolley, Catherine
Thayer, Marjorie 1908-1992 74
   Brief entry 37
Thayer, Peter
   See Wyler, Rose
Thelwell, Norman 1923-2004 14
Themerson, Stefan 1910-1988 65
Thermes, Jennifer 1966- 155
Theroux, Paul 1941- 109
   Earlier sketch in SATA *44*
Theroux, Paul Edward
   See Theroux, Paul
Thesman, Jean 124
   Earlier sketch in SATA *74*
The Tjong-Khing
   See Khing, T.T.
Thieda, Shirley Ann 1943- 13
Thiele, Colin 1920-2006 125
   Earlier sketches in SATA *14, 72*
   See also CLR 27
   See also SAAS 2
Thiele, Colin Milton
   See Thiele, Colin
Thiesing, Lisa 1958- 159
   Earlier sketch in SATA *95*
Thimmesh, Catherine 189
Thiry, Joan (Marie) 1926- 45
Thisdale, Francois 1964- 222
Thistlethwaite, Miles 1945- 12
Thollander, Earl 1922- 22
Thomas, Abigail 1941- 112
Thomas, Andrea
   See Hill, Margaret (Ohler)
Thomas, Art(hur Lawrence) 1952- 48
   Brief entry 38
Thomas, Carroll
   See Ratliff, Thomas M.
   and Shmurak, Carole B.
Thomas, Cassia 236
Thomas, Dylan 1914-1953 60
Thomas, Dylan Marlais
   See Thomas, Dylan
Thomas, Egbert S.
   See Ellis, Edward S.
Thomas, Estelle Webb 1899-1982 26
Thomas, Frances 1943- 171
   Earlier sketch in SATA *92*
Thomas, Garen 213
Thomas, H. C.
   See Keating, Lawrence A.

Thomas, Ianthe 1951- 139
   Brief entry 42
   See also CLR 8
Thomas, J. F.
   See Fleming, Thomas
Thomas, Jan 1958- 226
   Earlier sketch in SATA *197*
Thomas, Jane Resh 1936- 171
   Earlier sketches in SATA *38, 90*
Thomas, Jerry D. 1959- 91
Thomas, Joan Gale
   See Robinson, Joan (Mary) G(ale Thomas)
Thomas, Joyce Carol 1938- 210
   Autobiography Feature 137
   Earlier sketches in SATA *40, 78, 123, 137*
   See also CLR 19
   See also SAAS 7
Thomas, Lee
   See Floren, Lee
   and Pendleton, Thomas
Thomas, Lowell Jackson, Jr. 1923- 15
Thomas, Margaret
   See Thomas, Peggy
Thomas, Meredith 1963- 119
Thomas, Michael
   See Wilks, Michael Thomas
Thomas, Middy 1931- 191
Thomas, Patricia 1934- 199
   Earlier sketch in SATA *51*
Thomas, Peggy 174
Thomas, Rob 1965- 97
Thomas, Scott 1959- 147
Thomas, Velma Maia 1955- 171
Thomas, Vernon (Arthur) 1934- 56
Thomas, Victoria
   See DeWeese, Thomas Eugene
   and Kugi, Constance Todd
Thomasma, Kenneth R. 1930- 90
Thomason, Mark 215
Thomassie, Tynia 1959- 92
Thompson, Alicia 1984- 224
Thompson, Brenda 1935- 34
Thompson, Carol 1951- 189
   Earlier sketch in SATA *85*
Thompson, China
   See Lewis, Mary
Thompson, Colin 1942- 198
   Earlier sketches in SATA *95, 163*
Thompson, David H(ugh) 1941- 17
Thompson, Eileen
   See Panowski, Eileen Thompson
Thompson, George Selden 1929-1989 73
   Obituary 63
   Earlier sketch in SATA *4*
   See also CLR 8
Thompson, Harlan 1894-1987 10
   Obituary 53
Thompson, Hilary 1943- 56
   Brief entry 49
Thompson, Holly 1959- 239
Thompson, Joanna Maxwell Pullein
   See Pullein-Thompson, Joanna Maxwell
Thompson, Julian F(rancis) 1927- 155
   Brief entry 40
   Earlier sketches in SATA *55, 99*
   See also CLR 24
   See also SAAS 13
Thompson, K(athryn Carolyn) Dyble
   1952- 82
Thompson, Kate 1956- 204
Thompson, Kay 1912(?)-1998 16
   See also CLR 22
Thompson, Keith 1982- 238
Thompson, Lauren 1962- 200
   Earlier sketches in SATA *132, 174*
Thompson, Lauren Stevens
   See Thompson, Lauren
Thompson, Megan Lloyd
   See Lloyd, Megan
Thompson, Richard 1951- 184
Thompson, Ruth Plumly 1891-1976 66

Thompson, Sharon 1952- 119
Thompson, Sharon Elaine
   See Thompson, Sharon
Thompson, Stith 1885-1976 57
   Obituary 20
Thompson, Vivian L(aubach) 1911- 3
Thomson, Bill 1963- 187
Thomson, Celia
   See Lynn, Tracy
Thomson, David (Robert Alexander)
   1914-1988 40
   Obituary 55
Thomson, Melissa 1979- 205
Thomson, Pat 1939- 122
   Earlier sketch in SATA *77*
Thomson, Peggy 1922- 31
Thomson, Sarah L. 212
   Earlier sketch in SATA *178*
Thon, Melanie Rae 1957- 132
Thong, Roseanne 174
Thor, Annika 1950- 222
Thorburn, John
   See Goldsmith, John Herman Thorburn
Thorn, John 1947- 59
Thorndyke, Helen Louise
   See Benson, Mildred
Thorne, Ian
   See May, Julian
Thorne, Jean Wright
   See May, Julian
Thornhill, Jan 1955- 148
   Earlier sketch in SATA *77*
Thornton, Hall
   See Silverberg, Robert
Thornton, W. B.
   See Burgess, Thornton Waldo
Thornton, Yvonne S. 1947- 96
Thornton, Yvonne Shirley
   See Thornton, Yvonne S.
Thorpe, E(ustace) G(eorge) 1916- 21
Thorpe, J. K.
   See Nathanson, Laura Walther
Thorvall, Kerstin 1925- 13
Thorvall-Falk, Kerstin
   See Thorvall, Kerstin
Thrasher, Crystal (Faye) 1921- 27
Threadgall, Colin 1941- 77
Three Little Pigs
   See Lantz, Francess L(in)
Thum, Gladys 1920- 26
Thum, Marcella 28
   Earlier sketch in SATA *3*
Thundercloud, Katherine
   See Witt, Shirley Hill
Thurber, James 1894-1961 13
Thurber, James Grover
   See Thurber, James
Thurlo, Aimee 161
Thurlo, David 161
Thurman, Judith 1946- 33
Thurman, Mark (Gordon Ian) 1948- 63
Thwaite, Ann (Barbara Harrop) 1932- 14
Tibbetts, Peggy 127
Tibbles, Jean-Paul 1958- 115
Tibo, Gilles 1951- 107
   Earlier sketch in SATA *67*
Tiburzi, Bonnie 1948- 65
Ticheburn, Cheviot
   See Ainsworth, William Harrison
Tichenor, Tom 1923-1992 14
Tichnor, Richard 1959- 90
Tichy, William 1924- 31
Tickle, Jack
   See Chapman, Jane
Tidholm, Anna-Clara 1946- 223
Tiegreen, Alan F. 1935- 94
   Brief entry 36
Tierney, Fiona 229
Tierney, Frank M. 1930- 54
Tierney, Tom 1928- 113
Tiffault, Benette W. 1955- 77

Tildes, Phyllis Limbacher 1945- 210
Tiller, Ruth L. 1949- 83
Tilley, Debbie 190
Tillman, Nancy 211
Tillotson, Katherine 224
Tilly, Nancy 1935- 62
Tilton, Madonna Elaine 1929- 41
Tilton, Rafael
  See Tilton, Madonna Elaine
Timberlake, Amy 156
Timberlake, Carolyn
  See Dresang, Eliza (Carolyn Timberlake)
Timmers, Leo 1970- 190
Timmins, Jeffrey Stewart 1979- 227
Timmins, William F(rederick) 10
Tinbergen, Niko(laas) 1907-1988
  Obituary 60
Tincknell, Cathy 194
Tiner, John Hudson 1944- 32
Tingle, Dolli (?)-
  See Brackett, Dolli Tingle
Tingle, Rebecca 174
Tingle, Tim 208
Tingum, Janice 1958- 91
Tinkelman, Murray 1933- 12
Tinkham, Kelly A. 188
Tinkle, (Julien) Lon 1906-1980 36
Tinling, Marion (Rose) 1904- 140
Tipene, Tim 1972- 141
Tippett, James S(terling) 1885-1958 66
Tirone Smith, Mary-Ann 1944- 143
Titcomb, Gordon 237
Titlebaum, Ellen 195
Titler, Dale M(ilton) 1926- 35
  Brief entry 28
Titmarsh, Michael Angelo
  See Thackeray, William Makepeace
Titus, Eve 1922- 2
Tjia, Sherwin 1975- 204
Tjong Khing, The 1933- 76
Tobias, Katherine
  See Gottfried, Theodore Mark
Tobias, Tobi 1938- 82
  Earlier sketch in SATA 5
  See also CLR 4
Tobin, James 226
Tocci, C. Lee 1958- 220
Tocci, Cynthia Lee
  See Tocci, C. Lee
Tocher, Timothy 228
Todd, Anne Ophelia
  See Dowden, Anne Ophelia Todd
Todd, Barbara 1961- 173
Todd, Barbara K(eith) 1917- 10
Todd, Chuck 195
Todd, H(erbert) E(atton) 1908-1988 84
  Earlier sketch in SATA 11
Todd, Loreto 1942- 30
Todd, Pamela 212
Todd, Peter
  See Hamilton, Charles (Harold St. John)
Toews, Miriam 1964- 165
Tofel, Richard J. 1957- 140
Toffler-Corrie, Laura 237
Toft, Di 1958- 233
Toft, Kim Michelle 1960- 170
Tokunbo, Dimitrea 187
Tolan, Stephanie S. 1942- 142
  Earlier sketches in SATA 38, 78
Toland, John (Willard) 1912-2004 38
Tolbert, Steve 1944- 143
Toledo, Francisco 1940- 198
Toledo, Natalia 1967- 197
Tolkien, J. R. R. 1892-1973 100
  Obituary 24
  Earlier sketches in SATA 2, 32
  See also CLR 152
Tolkien, John Ronald Reuel
  See Tolkien, J. R. R.
Toll, Emily
  See Cannon, Eileen E(mily)

Toll, Nelly S. 1935- 78
Tolland, W. R.
  See Heitzmann, William Ray
Tolles, Martha 1921- 76
  Earlier sketch in SATA 8
Tolliver, Ruby C(hangos) 1922- 110
  Brief entry 41
  Earlier sketch in SATA 55
Tolmie, Kenneth Donald 1941- 15
Tolstoi, Lev
  See Tolstoy, Leo
Tolstoy, Leo 1828-1910 26
Tolstoy, Count Leo
  See Tolstoy, Leo
Tolstoy, Leo Nikolaevich
  See Tolstoy, Leo
Tomalin, Ruth 29
Tomaselli, Rosa
  See Pausacker, Jenny
Tomecek, Steve 172
Tomes, Margot (Ladd) 1917-1991 70
  Brief entry 27
  Obituary 69
  Earlier sketch in SATA 36
Tomey, Ingrid 1943- 77
Tomfool
  See Farjeon, Eleanor
Tomic, Tomislav 1977- 202
Tomkins, Jasper
  See Batey, Tom
Tomline, F. Latour
  See Gilbert, W(illiam) S(chwenck)
Tomlinson, Heather 192
Tomlinson, Jill 1931-1976 3
  Obituary 24
Tomlinson, Reginald R(obert) 1885-1979(?)
  Obituary 27
Tomlinson, Theresa 1946- 165
  Earlier sketch in SATA 103
  See also CLR 60
Tommaso, Rich 1970(?)- 200
Tomorrow, Tom 1961- 223
Tompert, Ann 1918- 139
  Earlier sketches in SATA 14, 89
Tompkins, Troy
  See Cle, Troy
Tonatiuh, Duncan 231
Toner, Raymond John 1908-1986 10
Tong, Gary S. 1942- 66
Tong, Paul 188
Took, Belladonna
  See Chapman, Vera (Ivy May)
Tooke, Louise Mathews 1950- 38
Tooke, Susan 173
Toonder, Martin
  See Groom, Arthur William
Toothaker, Roy Eugene 1928- 18
Tooze, Ruth (Anderson) 1892-1972 4
Topaz, Ksenia 212
Topek, Susan Remick 1955- 78
Topping, Audrey R(onning) 1928- 14
Tor, Regina
  See Shekerjian, Regina Tor
Torbert, Floyd James 1922- 22
Torgersen, Don Arthur 1934- 55
  Brief entry 41
Torley, Luke
  See Blish, James
Torrecilla, Pablo 1967- 206
Torres, Andres Segovia
  See Segovia, Andres
Torres, Daniel 1958- 102
Torres, J. 1969- 230
Torres, John A. 1965- 163
  Earlier sketch in SATA 94
Torres, John Albert
  See Torres, John A.
Torres, Joseph
  See Torres, J.
Torres, Laura 1967- 146
  Earlier sketch in SATA 87

Torres, Leyla 1960- 155
Torrey, Michele 1960(?)- 238
Torrey, Rich
  See Torrey, Richard
Torrey, Richard 189
Torrie, Malcolm
  See Mitchell, Gladys (Maude Winifred)
Toten, Teresa 1955- 99
Totham, Mary
  See Breinburg, Petronella
Touponce, William F. 1948- 114
Tournier, Michel 1924- 23
Tournier, Michel Edouard
  See Tournier, Michel
Towle, Ben 1970- 228
Towle, Wendy 1963- 79
Towne, Mary
  See Spelman, Mary
Townley, Rod
  See Townley, Roderick
Townley, Roderick 1942- 177
Townsend, Brad W. 1962- 91
Townsend, John Rowe 1922- 132
  Autobiography Feature 132
  Earlier sketches in SATA 4, 68
  See also CLR 2
  See also SAAS 2
Townsend, Michael 1981- 231
  Earlier sketch in SATA 194
Townsend, Sue 1946- 93
  Brief entry 48
  Earlier sketch in SATA 55
Townsend, Susan Lilian
  See Townsend, Sue
Townsend, Thomas L. 1944- 59
Townsend, Tom
  See Townsend, Thomas L.
Townsend, Wendy 1962- 201
Townson, Hazel 134
Toye, William Eldred 1926- 8
Trafton, Jennifer 239
Traherne, Michael
  See Watkins-Pitchford, Denys James
Trahey, Jane 1923-2000 36
  Obituary 120
Trapani, Iza 1954- 214
  Earlier sketches in SATA 80, 116
Trapp, Maria Augusta von
  See von Trapp, Maria Augusta
Travers, P(amela) L(yndon) 1899-1996 100
  Obituary 90
  Earlier sketches in SATA 4, 54
  See also CLR 93
  See also SAAS 2
Travis, Lucille 133
  Earlier sketch in SATA 88
Treadgold, Mary 1910-2005 49
Trease, (Robert) Geoffrey 1909-1998 60
  Obituary 101
  Earlier sketch in SATA 2
  See also CLR 42
  See also SAAS 6
Treat, Lawrence 1903-1998 59
Tredez, Alain 1926- 17
Tredez, Denise 1930- 50
Treece, Henry 1912-1966 2
  See also CLR 2
Tregarthen, Enys
  See Sloggett, Nellie
Tregaskis, Richard 1916-1973 3
  Obituary 26
Treherne, Katie Thamer 1955- 76
Trell, Max 1900-1996 14
  Obituary 108
Tremain, Ruthven 1922- 17
Trembath, Don 1963- 168
  Earlier sketch in SATA 96
Tremens, Del
  See MacDonald, Amy
Trent, Robbie 1894-1988 26

Trent, Timothy
　See Malmberg, Carl
Treseder, Terry Walton 1956- 68
Tresilian, (Cecil) Stuart 1891-(?) 40
Tresselt, Alvin 1916-2000 7
　See also CLR 30
Trevino, Elizabeth B(orton) de 1904- 29
　Earlier sketch in SATA 1
　See also SAAS 5
Trevor, Elleston 1920-1995 28
Trevor, Frances
　See Teasdale, Sara
Trevor, Glen
　See Hilton, James
Trevor, (Lucy) Meriol 1919-2000 113
　Obituary 122
　Earlier sketch in SATA 10
Trewellard, J.M. 195
Trewellard, Juliet
　See Trewellard, J.M.
Trez, Alain
　See Tredez, Alain
Trez, Denise
　See Tredez, Denise
Trezise, Percy 1923-
　See CLR 41
Trezise, Percy James
　See Trezise, Percy
Triggs, Tony D. 1946- 70
Trimble, Marshall I(ra) 1939- 93
Trimby, Elisa 1948- 47
　Brief entry 40
Trine, Greg 238
Tring, A. Stephen
　See Meynell, Laurence Walter
Triplett, Gina 229
Tripp, Eleanor B(aldwin) 1936- 4
Tripp, Janet 1942- 108
Tripp, Jenny 188
Tripp, John
　See Moore, John Travers
Tripp, Nathaniel 1944- 101
Tripp, Paul 1916-2002 8
　Obituary 139
Tripp, Valerie 1951- 168
　Earlier sketch in SATA 78
Tripp, Wallace (Whitney) 1940- 31
Trivelpiece, Laurel 1926- 56
　Brief entry 46
Trivett, Daphne Harwood 1940- 22
Trivizas, Eugene 1946- 84
Trnka, Jiri 1912-1969 43
　Brief entry 32
Trollope, Anthony 1815-1882 22
Trost, Lucille W(ood) 1938- 149
　Earlier sketch in SATA 12
Trott, Betty 1933- 91
Trotter, Deborah W. 184
Trotter, Grace V(iolet) 1900-1991 10
Trottier, Maxine 1950- 175
　Earlier sketch in SATA 131
Troughton, Joanna (Margaret) 1947- 37
Trout, Kilgore
　See Farmer, Philip Jose
Trout, Richard E. 123
Trudeau, Garretson Beekman
　See Trudeau, G.B.
Trudeau, Garry
　See Trudeau, G.B.
Trudeau, Garry B.
　See Trudeau, G.B.
Trudeau, G.B. 1948- 168
　Earlier sketch in SATA 35
Trueit, Trudi
　See Trueit, Trudi Strain
Trueit, Trudi Strain 1963- 179
Trueman, Matthew 183
Trueman, Terry 1947- 178
　Earlier sketch in SATA 132
Truesdell, Judy
　See Mecca, Judy Truesdell

Truesdell, Sue
　See Truesdell, Susan G.
Truesdell, Susan G. 212
　Brief entry 45
　Earlier sketch in SATA 108
Trumbauer, Lisa 1963- 228
　Earlier sketch in SATA 149
Trumbauer, Lisa Trutkoff
　See Trumbauer, Lisa
Truss, Jan 1925- 35
Truss, Lynne 1955(?)- 194
Tryon, Leslie 194
　Earlier sketch in SATA 139
Tsiang, Sarah 239
Tsiang, Yi-Mei
　See Tsiang, Sarah
Tubb, Jonathan N. 1951- 78
Tubb, Kristin O'Donnell 1971- 209
Tubby, I. M.
　See Kraus, (Herman) Robert
Tucker, Allan James
　See James, Bill
Tucker, Caroline
　See Nolan, Jeannette Covert
Tucker, James
　See James, Bill
Tudor, Edward
　See Browne, Anthony
Tudor, Tasha 1915-2008 160
　Obituary 205
　Earlier sketches in SATA 20, 69
　See also CLR 13
Tuerk, Hanne 1951- 71
Tugeau, Jeremy 199
Tulloch, Richard 1949- 180
　Earlier sketch in SATA 76
Tulloch, Richard George
　See Tulloch, Richard
Tulloch, Shirley 169
Tully, John (Kimberley) 1923- 14
Tumanov, Vladimir A. 1961- 138
Tung, Angela 1972- 109
Tunis, Edwin (Burdett) 1897-1973 28
　Obituary 24
　Earlier sketch in SATA 1
　See also CLR 2
Tunis, John R(oberts) 1889-1975 37
　Brief entry 30
Tunnell, Michael
　See Tunnell, Michael O.
Tunnell, Michael O. 1950- 157
　Earlier sketch in SATA 103
Tunnell, Michael O'Grady
　See Tunnell, Michael O.
Tunnicliffe, C(harles) F(rederick)
　1901-1979 62
Turck, Mary C. 1950- 144
Turk, Hanne
　See Tuerk, Hanne
Turk, Ruth 1917- 82
Turkle, Brinton 1915- 79
　Earlier sketch in SATA 2
Turlington, Bayly 1919-1977 5
　Obituary 52
Turnbull, Agnes Sligh 1888-1982 14
Turnbull, Ann 1943- 160
　Earlier sketch in SATA 18
Turnbull, Ann Christine
　See Turnbull, Ann
Turnbull, Susan 222
Turner, Alice K. 1940- 10
Turner, Ann 1945- 188
　Autobiography Feature 188
　Earlier sketches in SATA 14, 77, 113, 178
Turner, Ann Warren
　See Turner, Ann
Turner, Bonnie 1932- 75
Turner, Elizabeth 1774-1846
　See YABC 2
Turner, Glennette Tilley 1933- 183
　Earlier sketch in SATA 71

Turner, Josie
　See Crawford, Phyllis
Turner, Megan Whalen 1965- 174
　Earlier sketch in SATA 94
Turner, Pamela S. 1957- 211
Turner, Philip (William) 1925- 83
　Earlier sketch in SATA 11
　See also CLR 89
　See also SAAS 6
Turner, Robyn 1947- 77
Turner, Sheila R.
　See Seed, Sheila Turner
Turngren, Annette 1902(?)-1980
　Obituary 23
Turngren, Ellen (?)-1964 3
Turska, Krystyna (Zofia) 1933- 31
　Brief entry 27
Turteltaub, H. N.
　See Turtledove, Harry
Turtledove, Harry 1949- 166
　Earlier sketch in SATA 116
Turtledove, Harry Norman
　See Turtledove, Harry
Tusa, Tricia 1960- 207
　Earlier sketches in SATA 72, 111
Tusiani, Joseph 1924- 45
Tutt, Keith 1959- 238
Tuttle, Cameron 237
Tuxbury, Larry 1969- 235
Twain, Mark 1835-1910 100
　See also YABC 2
　See also CLR 156
Tweit, Susan J 1956- 94
Tweit, Susan Joan
　See Tweit, Susan J
Tweton, D. Jerome 1933- 48
Twinem, Neecy 1958- 92
Twohill, Maggie
　See Angell, Judie
Tworkov, Jack 1900-1982 47
　Obituary 31
Tyche
　See Papademetriou, Lisa
Tyers, Jenny 1969- 89
Tyers, Kathy 1952- 82
Tyler, Anne 1941- 173
　Earlier sketches in SATA 7, 90
Tyler, Linda
　See Tyler, Linda W(agner)
Tyler, Linda W(agner) 1952- 65
Tyler, Vicki 1952- 64
Tyne, Joel
　See Schembri, Jim
Tyrrell, Frances 1959- 107

U

Ubell, Earl 1926-2007 4
　Obituary 182
Uchida, Yoshiko 1921-1992 53
　Obituary 72
　Earlier sketch in SATA 1
　See also CLR 56
　See also SAAS 1
Udall, Jan Beaney 1938- 10
Uden, (Bernard Gilbert) Grant 1910- 26
Uderzo, Albert 1927-
　See CLR 37
Udovic, David 1950- 189
Udovic, Jane Morris 1947- 224
Udry, Janice May 1928- 152
　Earlier sketch in SATA 4
Uegaki, Chieri 1969- 211
　Earlier sketch in SATA 153
Uehashi, Nahoko 1962- 215
Ueno, Noriko
　See Nakae, Noriko
Ugliano, Natascia 196
Uhlberg, Myron 174

Uhlig, Richard 1970- *195*
Uhlig, Susan 1955- *129*
Ulam, S(tanislaw) M(arcin) 1909-1984 .... *51*
Ullman, Barb Bentler *210*
Ullman, James Ramsey 1907-1971 .... *7*
Ulm, Robert 1934-1977 .... *17*
Ulmer, Louise 1943- *53*
Ulmer, Wendy K. 1950- *201*
Ulrich, Maureen 1958- *206*
Ulriksen, Mark 1957- *210*
Ulyatt, Kenneth 1920- *14*
Umansky, Kaye 1946- *224*
    Earlier sketches in SATA *158, 188*
Unada
    See Gliewe, Unada (Grace)
Uncle Carter
    See Boucher, (Clarence) Carter
Uncle Eric
    See Maybury, Richard J.
Uncle Gus
    See Rey, H. A.
Uncle Mac
    See McCulloch, Derek (Ivor Breashur)
Uncle Ray
    See Coffman, Ramon Peyton
Uncle Shelby
    See Silverstein, Shel
Underhill, Alice Mertie (Waterman)
    1900-1971 .... *10*
Underhill, Liz 1948- *53*
    Brief entry *49*
Underwood, Deborah 1962- *206*
Unger, Harlow G. 1931- *75*
Unger, Harlow Giles
    See Unger, Harlow G.
Unger, Jim 1937- *67*
Ungerer, (Jean) Thomas 1931- *106*
    Earlier sketches in SATA *5, 33*
    See also CLR *77*
Ungerer, Tomi 1931-
    See Ungerer, (Jean) Thomas
Unkelbach, Kurt 1913-1992 .... *4*
Unnerstad, Edith (Totterman) 1900-1982 .... *3*
    See also CLR *36*
Unobagha, Uzo *139*
Unrau, Ruth 1922- *9*
Unstead, R(obert) J(ohn) 1915-1988 .... *12*
    Obituary *56*
Unsworth, Walt(er) 1928- *4*
Untermeyer, Bryna Ivens 1909-1985 .... *61*
Untermeyer, Louis 1885-1977 .... *37*
    Obituary *26*
    Earlier sketch in SATA *2*
Unwin, David S. 1918-2010 .... *14*
Unwin, David Storr
    See Unwin, David S.
Unwin, Nora S(picer) 1907-1982 .... *3*
    Obituary *49*
Unzner, Christa 1958- *230*
    Earlier sketches in SATA *80, 141*
Unzner-Fischer, Christa
    See Unzner, Christa
Updale, Eleanor 1953- *175*
Updyke, Rosemary K. 1924- *103*
Upitis, Alvis *109*
Upjohn, Rebecca 1962- *238*
Urbain, Cat 1956- *211*
Urbain, Catherine
    See Urbain, Cat
Urban, Helle (Denise) 1957- *149*
Urban, Linda *199*
Urbanovic, Jackie *189*
Urberuaga, Emilio 1954- *219*
Urbigkit, Cat 1965- *196*
Urdahl, Catherine *215*
Ure, Jean 1943- *192*
    Autobiography Feature *192*
    Earlier sketches in SATA *48, 78, 129*
    See also CLR *34*
    See also SAAS *14*

U'Ren, Andrea 1968- *213*
    Earlier sketch in SATA *142*
Uris, Leon 1924-2003 .... *49*
    Obituary *146*
Uris, Leon Marcus
    See Uris, Leon
Ursu, Anne *177*
Ury, Allen B. 1954- *98*
Uschan, Michael V. 1948- *129*
Usher, Margo Scegge
    See McHargue, Georgess
Usher, Mark David
    See Usher, M.D.
Usher, M.D. 1966- *221*
Uslan, Michael E. 1951- *169*
Uston, Ken(neth Senzo) 1935-1987 .... *65*
Uttley, Alice Jane 1884-1976 .... *88*
    Obituary *26*
    Earlier sketch in SATA *3*
Uttley, Alison
    See Uttley, Alice Jane
Utz, Lois (Marie) 1932-1986 .... *5*
    Obituary *50*

V

Vaeth, J. Gordon 1921- *17*
Vaeth, Joseph Gordon
    See Vaeth, J. Gordon
Vagin, Vladimir (Vasilevich) 1937- *142*
Vail, Rachel 1966- *201*
    Earlier sketches in SATA *94, 163*
Vainio, Pirkko 1957- *123*
    Earlier sketch in SATA *76*
Valen, Nanine 1950- *21*
Valencak, Hannelore
    See Mayer, Hannelore Valencak
Valens, Amy 1946- *70*
Valens, E(vans) G(ladstone), Jr. 1920-1992 ... *1*
Valentine, Johnny *72*
Valentine, Madeline *236*
Valerio, Geraldo 1970- *180*
Valgardson, W. D. 1939- *151*
    Earlier sketch in SATA *101*
Valgardson, William Dempsey
    See Valgardson, W. D.
Valleau, Emily 1925- *51*
Vamos, Samantha R. *215*
Van Abbe, Salaman 1883-1955 .... *18*
Van Allsburg, Chris 1949- *156*
    Earlier sketches in SATA *37, 53, 105*
    See also CLR *113*
Van Anrooy, Francine 1924- *2*
Van Anrooy, Frans
    See Van Anrooy, Francine
Vanasse, Deb 1957- *170*
Van Buren, David *203*
Van Camp, Katie 1981- *222*
Vance, Cynthia *207*
Vance, Eleanor Graham 1908-1985 .... *11*
Vance, Gerald
    See Garrett, Randall
    and Silverberg, Robert
Vance, Marguerite 1889-1965 .... *29*
Vance-Abrams, Cynthia
    See Vance, Cynthia
VanCleave, Janice 1942- *116*
    Autobiography Feature *123*
    Earlier sketch in SATA *75*
Vandenburg, Mary Lou 1943- *17*
Vander Boom, Mae M. *14*
Vander-Els, Betty 1936- *63*
van der Heide, Iris 1970- *183*
van der Linde, Laurel 1952- *78*
van der Linden, Martijn 1979- *214*
van der Meer, Ron 1945- *98*
Vanderpool, Clare 1964- *232*
van de Ruit, John 1975- *199*

Van der Veer, Judy 1912-1982 .... *4*
    Obituary *33*
Vanderwal, Andrew H. 1956- *219*
Vanderwerff, Corrine 1939- *117*
Vander Zee, Ruth *199*
    Earlier sketch in SATA *159*
Vande Velde, Vivian 1951- *211*
    Earlier sketches in SATA *62, 95, 141*
    See also CLR *145*
Vandivert, Rita (Andre) 1905-1986 .... *21*
Van Draanen, Wendelin *207*
    Earlier sketch in SATA *122*
Van Dusen, Chris *228*
    Earlier sketch in SATA *173*
Van Duyn, Janet 1910- *18*
Van Dyne, Edith
    See Baum, L. Frank
    and Sampson, Emma (Keats) Speed
    and van Zantwijk, Rudolf (Alexander
    Marinus)
Vane, Mitch
    See Vane, Mitchelle
Vane, Mitchelle *176*
van Eekhout, Greg *232*
van Etten, David
    See Levithan, David
van Frankenhuyzen, Gijsbert 1951- *132*
Van Genechten, Guido 1957- *165*
van Haeringen, Annemarie *193*
Van Hook, Beverly 1941- *99*
Van Hook, Beverly H.
    See Van Hook, Beverly
Van Hook, Beverly Hennen
    See Van Hook, Beverly
Van Horn, William 1939- *43*
van Hout, Mies 1962- *178*
Van Iterson, S(iny) R(ose) *26*
Van Kampen, Vlasta 1943- *163*
    Earlier sketch in SATA *54*
Van Laan, Nancy 1939- *214*
    Earlier sketch in SATA *105*
van Lawick-Goodall, Jane
    See Goodall, Jane
Van Leeuwen, Jean 1937- *211*
    Autobiography Feature *141*
    Earlier sketches in SATA *6, 82, 132, 141*
    See also SAAS *8*
van Lhin, Erik
    See del Rey, Lester
van Lieshout, Elle 1963- *217*
van Lieshout, Maria *201*
Van Loon, Hendrik Willem 1882-1944 .... *18*
van Ommen, Sylvia 1978- *186*
VanOosting, James 1951- *170*
Van Orden, M(erton) D(ick) 1921- *4*
van Os, Erik 1963- *217*
Van Patter, Bruce *183*
Van Reek, Wouter *204*
Van Rensselaer, Alexander (Taylor Mason)
    1892-1962 .... *14*
Van Riper, Guernsey, Jr. 1909-1995 .... *3*
van Rossum, Heleen 1962- *174*
Van Rynbach, Iris 1952- *102*
Vansant, Rhonda Joy Edwards 1950- *92*
Van Steenwyk, Elizabeth (Ann) 1928- *89*
    Earlier sketch in SATA *34*
Van Stockum, Hilda 1908-2006 .... *5*
    Obituary *179*
van Straaten, Harmen 1961- *218*
    Earlier sketch in SATA *195*
Van Tuyl, Barbara 1940- *11*
van Vogt, A(lfred) E(lton) 1912-2000 .... *14*
    Obituary *124*
Van Wassenhove, Sue 1951- *202*
Van Woerkom, Dorothy (O'Brien)
    1924-1996 .... *21*
Van Wormer, Joe
    See Van Wormer, Joseph Edward
Van Wormer, Joseph Edward 1913-1998 .... *35*
Van Wright, Cornelius *173*

Van Zwienen, Ilse Charlotte Koehn
  1929-1991 .... *34*
  Brief entry *28*
  Obituary *67*
Van Zyle, Jon 1942- *176*
  Earlier sketch in SATA *84*
Varela, Barry *180*
Varga, Judy
  See Stang, Judit
Varley, Dimitry V. 1906-1984 .... *10*
Varley, Susan 1961- *134*
  Earlier sketch in SATA *63*
Varon, Sara *195*
Vasileva, Tatiana
  See Wassiljewa, Tatjana
Vasiliev, Valery 1949- *80*
Vasilieva, Tatiana
  See Wassiljewa, Tatjana
Vasiliu, Mircea 1920- *2*
Vass, George 1927- *57*
  Brief entry *31*
Vaughan, Carter A.
  See Gerson, Noel Bertram
Vaughan, Harold Cecil 1923- *14*
Vaughan, Marcia (K.) 1951- *159*
  Earlier sketches in SATA *60, 95*
Vaughan, Richard 1947- *87*
Vaughan, Sam 1928- *14*
Vaughn, Ruth 1935- *14*
Vaught, Susan 1965- *195*
Vaupel, Robin *198*
Vautier, Ghislaine 1932- *53*
Vavra, Robert James 1935- *8*
Vecsey, George Spencer 1939- *9*
Vedral, Joyce L(auretta) 1943- *65*
Vega, Denise *216*
  Earlier sketch in SATA *174*
Vega, Denise B.
  See Vega, Denise
Vega, Diego
  See Adkins, Jan
Veglahn, Nancy (Crary) 1937- *5*
Vejjajiva, Jane 1963- *189*
Velasquez, Crystal *228*
Velasquez, Eric *226*
  Earlier sketch in SATA *192*
Velasquez, Gloria 1949- *229*
  Earlier sketch in SATA *113*
Velthuijs, Max 1923-2005 .... *110*
  Obituary *160*
  Earlier sketch in SATA *53*
Venable, Alan (Hudson) 1944- *8*
Venable, Colleen A.F. 1980- *233*
Venezia, Mike 1945- *150*
Venner, Grace Chang
  See Chang, Grace
Ventura, Anthony
  See Pellowski, Michael (Joseph)
Ventura, Piero (Luigi) 1937- *61*
  Brief entry *43*
  See also CLR *16*
Venuti, Kristin Clark *237*
Vequin, Capini
  See Quinn, Elisabeth
Verba, Joan Marie 1953- *78*
Verboven, Agnes 1951- *103*
verDorn, Bethea (Stewart) 1952- *76*
Vere, Ed *197*
Verissimo, Erico (Lopes) 1905-1975 .... *113*
Verne, Jules 1828-1905 .... *21*
  See also CLR *88*
Verne, Jules Gabriel
  See Verne, Jules
Verner, Gerald 1897(?)-1980
  Obituary *25*
Verney, John 1913-1993 .... *14*
  Obituary *75*
Verniero, Joan C. 1949- *181*
Vernon, (Elda) Louise A(nderson) 1914- *14*
Vernon, Rosemary
  See Smith, Susan Vernon

Vernon, Ursula *204*
Vernor, D.
  See Casewit, Curtis W(erner)
Verr, Harry Coe
  See Kunhardt, Edith
Verral, Charles Spain 1904-1990 .... *11*
  Obituary *65*
Verrillo, Erica 1953- *199*
Verrillo, Erica F.
  See Verrillo, Erica
Verroken, Sarah 1982- *223*
Verrone, Robert J. 1935(?)-1984
  Obituary *39*
Versace, Marie Teresa Rios 1917- *2*
Vertreace, Martha M(odena) 1945- *78*
Vesey, A(manda) 1939- *62*
Vesey, Mark (David) 1958- *123*
Vesey, Paul
  See Allen, Samuel W(ashington)
Vess, Charles 1951- *215*
Vestergaard, Hope *178*
Vestly, Anne-Cath(arina) 1920-2008 .... *14*
  See also CLR *99*
Vevers, (Henry) Gwynne 1916-1988 .... *45*
  Obituary *57*
Viator, Vacuus
  See Hughes, Thomas
Viau, Nancy *208*
Vicar, Henry
  See Felsen, Henry Gregor
Vick, Helen Hughes 1950- *88*
Vicker, Angus
  See Felsen, Henry Gregor
Vickers, Sheena 1960- *94*
Vickery, Kate
  See Kennedy, T.A.
Victor, Edward 1914- *3*
Victor, Joan Berg 1942- *30*
Vidrine, Beverly Barras 1938- *188*
  Earlier sketch in SATA *103*
Vieceli, Emma 1979- *210*
Viereck, Ellen K. 1928- *14*
Viereck, Phillip 1925- *3*
Viergutz, Dina Nayeri
  See Nayeri, Dina
Viertel, Janet 1915- *10*
Vigan, Delphine de 1966- *236*
Vigliante, Mary
  See Szydlowski, Mary Vigliante
Vigna, Judith 1936- *102*
  Earlier sketch in SATA *15*
Viguers, Ruth Hill 1903-1971 .... *6*
Vila, Laura *207*
Vilela, Fernando 1973- *216*
Villareal, Ray *187*
Villasenor, Edmund
  See Villasenor, Victor E.
Villasenor, Edmundo
  See Villasenor, Victor E.
Villasenor, Victor
  See Villasenor, Victor E.
Villasenor, Victor E. 1940- *171*
Villasenor, Victor Edmundo
  See Villasenor, Victor E.
Villeneuve, Anne *230*
Villiard, Paul 1910-1974 .... *51*
  Obituary *20*
Villiers, Alan (John) 1903-1982 .... *10*
Vilott, Rhondi
  See Salsitz, Rhondi Vilott
Vincent, Amy
  See Gray, Claudia
Vincent, Eric Douglas 1953- *40*
Vincent, Erin 1969- *188*
Vincent, Felix 1946- *41*
Vincent, Gabrielle 1928-2000 .... *121*
  Earlier sketch in SATA *61*
  See also CLR *13*
Vincent, Mary Keith
  See St. John, Wylly Folk
Vincent, Rachel 1978- *222*

Vincent, William R.
  See Heitzmann, William Ray
Vinegar, Tom
  See Gregg, Andrew K.
Vinest, Shaw
  See Longyear, Barry B(rookes)
Vinge, Joan (Carol) D(ennison) 1948- *113*
  Earlier sketch in SATA *36*
Vining, Elizabeth Gray 1902-1999 .... *6*
  Obituary *117*
Vinson, Kathryn 1911-1995 .... *21*
Vinton, Iris 1906(?)-1988 .... *24*
  Obituary *55*
Viola, Herman J(oseph) 1938- *126*
Viorst, Judith 1931- *172*
  Earlier sketches in SATA *7, 70, 123*
  See also CLR *90*
Vip
  See Partch, Virgil Franklin II
Vipont, Charles
  See Foulds, Elfrida Vipont
Vipont, Elfrida
  See Foulds, Elfrida Vipont
Viramontes, Helena Maria 1954-
  See CLR *285*
Viscott, David S(teven) 1938-1996 .... *65*
Visser, W(illem) F(rederik) H(endrik)
  1900-1968 .... *10*
Vitale, Stefano 1958- *225*
  Earlier sketches in SATA *114, 180*
Vivas, Julie 1947- *96*
Vivelo, Jackie 1943- *63*
Vivelo, Jacqueline J.
  See Vivelo, Jackie
Vivelo, Jacqueline Jean
  See Vivelo, Jackie
Vivian, Siobhan 1979(?)- *215*
Vizzini, Ned 1981- *179*
  Earlier sketch in SATA *125*
Vlahos, Olivia 1924- *31*
Vlasic, Bob
  See Hirsch, Phil
Voake, Charlotte *180*
  Earlier sketch in SATA *114*
Voake, Steve 1961- *178*
Vo-Dinh, Mai 1933- *16*
Voelkel, J&P
  See Voelkel, Jon
Voelkel, Jon *239*
Vogel, Carole Garbuny 1951- *231*
  Earlier sketches in SATA *70, 105*
Vogel, Ilse-Margret 1914-2001 .... *14*
  See also CLR *170*
Vogel, John H., Jr. 1950- *18*
Vogt, Esther Loewen 1915-1999 .... *14*
Vogt, Gregory L. *94*
Vogt, Marie Bollinger 1921- *45*
Vohwinkel, Astrid 1969- *207*
Voight, Virginia Frances 1909-1989 .... *8*
Voigt, Cynthia 1942- *160*
  Brief entry *33*
  Earlier sketches in SATA *48, 79, 116*
  See also CLR *141*
Voigt, Erna 1925- *35*
Voigt-Rother, Erna
  See Voigt, Erna
Vojtech, Anna 1946- *108*
  Earlier sketch in SATA *42*
Vollstadt, Elizabeth Weiss 1942- *121*
Volponi, Paul *228*
  Earlier sketch in SATA *175*
Volting, Dr. R.E.
  See Lerangis, Peter
Von Ahnen, Katherine 1922- *93*
von Buhler, Cynthia *185*
Vondra, J. Gert
  See Vondra, Josef
Vondra, Josef 1941- *121*
Vondra, Josef Gert
  See Vondra, Josef
Von Gunden, Kenneth 1946- *113*

Von Hagen, Victor Wolfgang 1908-1985 ...... *29*
von Klopp, Vahrah
  See Malvern, Gladys
von Schmidt, Eric 1931-2007 .... *50*
  Brief entry *36*
  Obituary *181*
von Storch, Anne B. 1910- *1*
von Trapp, Maria Augusta 1905-1987 .... *16*
von Wodtke, Charlotte Buel Johnson
  1918-1982 .... *46*
von Ziegesar, Cecily 1970- *161*
Vos, Ida 1931-2006 .... *121*
  Earlier sketch in SATA *69*
  See also CLR *85*
Vosburgh, Leonard (W.) 1912- *15*
Votaw, Carol 1961- *201*
Voyle, Mary
  See Manning, Rosemary
Vrettos, Adrienne Maria *187*
Vriens, Jacques 1946- *151*
Vugteveen, Verna Aardema
  See Aardema, Verna
Vulture, Elizabeth T.
  See Gilbert, Suzie
Vuong, Lynette Dyer 1938- *110*
  Earlier sketch in SATA *60*
Vyner, Tim 1963- *228*

W

Waas, Uli
  See Waas-Pommer, Ulrike
Waas-Pommer, Ulrike 1949- *85*
Waber, Bernard 1924- *155*
  Brief entry *40*
  Earlier sketches in SATA *47, 95*
  See also CLR *55*
Waber, Paulis *231*
Wachtel, Shirley Russak 1951- *88*
Wachter, Oralee (Roberts) 1935- *61*
  Brief entry *51*
Waddell, Evelyn Margaret 1918- *10*
Waddell, Martin 1941- *232*
  Autobiography Feature *129*
  Earlier sketches in SATA *43, 81, 127, 129*
  See also CLR *31*
  See also SAAS *15*
Waddy, Lawrence 1912-2010 .... *91*
Waddy, Lawrence Heber
  See Waddy, Lawrence
Wade, Mary Dodson 1930- *151*
  Earlier sketch in SATA *79*
Wade, Suzanne
  See Kirby, Susan E.
Wade, Theodore E., Jr. 1936- *37*
Wademan, Peter John 1946- *122*
Wademan, Spike
  See Wademan, Peter John
Wadsworth, Ginger 1945- *223*
  Earlier sketches in SATA *103, 157*
Wagenheim, Kal 1935- *21*
Wagner, Hilary *237*
Wagner, Michele R. 1975- *157*
Wagner, Sharon B. 1936- *4*
Wagoner, David (Russell) 1926- *14*
Wahl, Jan (Boyer) 1933- *132*
  Earlier sketches in SATA *2, 34, 73*
  See also SAAS *3*
Wahl, Mats 1945- *186*
Wahman, Wendy *218*
Waide, Jan 1952- *29*
Wainscott, John Milton 1910-1981 .... *53*
Wainwright, Debra *218*
Wainwright, Richard M. 1935- *91*
Wainwright, Ruth
  See Symes, Ruth Louise
Wait, Lea 1946- *137*
Waite, Judy *174*

Waite, Judy Bernard
  See Bernard, Patricia
Waite, Michael
  See Waite, Michael P.
Waite, Michael P. 1960- *101*
Waite, P(eter) B(usby) 1922- *64*
Waites, Joan C. *187*
Waitley, Douglas 1927- *30*
Wakefield, Jean L.
  See Laird, Jean E(louise)
Wakin, Daniel (Joseph) 1961- *84*
Wakin, Edward 1927- *37*
Wakiyama, Hanako 1966- *192*
Walck, Henry Z. 1908(?)-1984
  Obituary *40*
Walden, Amelia Elizabeth *3*
Walden, Mark *188*
Waldherr, Kris 1963- *76*
Waldman, Bruce 1949- *15*
Waldman, Neil 1947- *203*
  Earlier sketches in SATA *51, 94, 142*
Waldrep, Richard *198*
Waldron, Ann Wood 1924-2010 .... *16*
Waldron, Kathleen Cook *176*
Waldron, Kevin 1979- *230*
Wales, Dirk 1931- *205*
Walgren, Judy 1963- *118*
Walker, Addison
  See Walker, Mort
Walker, Addison Mort
  See Walker, Mort
Walker, Alice 1944- *31*
Walker, Alice Malsenior
  See Walker, Alice
Walker, Anna *223*
Walker, Barbara (Jeanne) K(erlin) 1921- *80*
  Earlier sketch in SATA *4*
Walker, Barbara M(uhs) 1928- *57*
Walker, (James) Braz(elton) 1934-1983 .... *45*
Walker, David 1965- *197*
Walker, David G(ordon) 1926- *60*
Walker, David Harry 1911-1992 .... *8*
  Obituary *71*
Walker, Diana 1925- *9*
Walker, Diane Marie Catherine
  See Walker, Kate
Walker, Dick
  See Pellowski, Michael (Joseph)
Walker, Frank 1931-2000 .... *36*
Walker, Holly Beth
  See Bond, Gladys Baker
Walker, Kate 1950- *165*
  Earlier sketch in SATA *82*
Walker, Kathrine Sorley
  See Sorley Walker, Kathrine
Walker, Kristin *228*
Walker, Lou Ann 1952- *66*
  Brief entry *53*
Walker, Louise Jean 1891-1976
  Obituary *35*
Walker, Mary Alexander 1927- *61*
Walker, Mildred
  See Schemm, Mildred Walker
Walker, Mort 1923- *8*
Walker, Pamela 1948- *142*
  Earlier sketch in SATA *24*
Walker, Paul Robert 1953- *154*
Walker, Robert W. 1948- *66*
Walker, Robert Wayne
  See Walker, Robert W.
Walker, Sally M. 1954- *221*
  Earlier sketch in SATA *135*
Walker, Stephen J. 1951- *12*
Walker, Steve *232*
Walker-Blondell, Becky 1951- *89*
Wallace, Barbara Brooks 1922- *136*
  Earlier sketches in SATA *4, 78*
  See also CLR *150*
  See also SAAS *17*
Wallace, Beverly Dobrin 1921- *19*

Wallace, Bill 1947- *169*
  Brief entry *47*
  Earlier sketches in SATA *53, 101*
Wallace, Carol 1948- *218*
Wallace, Chad *229*
Wallace, Daisy
  See Cuyler, Margery
Wallace, Ian 1950- *219*
  Earlier sketches in SATA *53, 56, 141*
  See also CLR *37*
Wallace, John 1966- *155*
  Earlier sketch in SATA *105*
Wallace, John A(dam) 1915-2004 .... *3*
  Obituary *155*
Wallace, Karen 1951- *188*
  Earlier sketches in SATA *83, 139*
Wallace, Nancy Elizabeth 1948- *222*
  Earlier sketches in SATA *141, 186*
Wallace, Nigel
  See Hamilton, Charles (Harold St. John)
Wallace, Paula S. *153*
Wallace, Rich 1957- *233*
  Earlier sketches in SATA *117, 158, 196*
Wallace, Robert 1932-1999 .... *47*
  Brief entry *37*
Wallace, Ruby Ann 1923(?)- *77*
Wallace, Sandra Neil *236*
Wallace, William Keith
  See Wallace, Bill
Wallace-Brodeur, Ruth 1941- *169*
  Brief entry *41*
  Earlier sketches in SATA *51, 88*
Wallenfels, Stephen *232*
Wallenta, Adam 1974- *123*
Waller, Leslie 1923-2007 .... *20*
Walley, Byron
  See Card, Orson Scott
Walliams, David 1971- *227*
Wallis, Diz 1949- *77*
Wallis, G. McDonald
  See Campbell, Hope
Wallner, Alexandra 1946- *156*
  Brief entry *41*
  Earlier sketches in SATA *51, 98*
Wallner, John C. 1945- *133*
  Earlier sketches in SATA *10, 51*
Wallower, Lucille *11*
Walrod, Amy 1973(?)- *182*
Walsh, Ann 1942- *176*
  Earlier sketch in SATA *62*
Walsh, Ellen Stoll 1942- *194*
  Earlier sketches in SATA *49, 99, 147*
Walsh, George Johnston 1889-1981 .... *53*
Walsh, Gillian Paton
  See Paton Walsh, Jill
Walsh, Jill Paton
  See Paton Walsh, Jill
Walsh, Joanna 1970- *182*
Walsh, Lawrence 1942- *170*
Walsh, Marissa 1972- *195*
Walsh, Mary Caswell 1949- *118*
Walsh, Mitzy
  See Walsh, Marissa
Walsh, Pat 1954- *237*
Walsh, Rebecca *217*
Walsh, Suella *170*
Walsh, V. L.
  See Walsh, Vivian
Walsh, Vivian 1960- *120*
Walsh Shepherd, Donna 1948- *78*
Walter, Frances V. 1923- *71*
Walter, Mildred Pitts 1922- *133*
  Brief entry *45*
  Earlier sketch in SATA *69*
  See also CLR *61*
  See also SAAS *12*
Walter, Villiam Christian
  See Andersen, Hans Christian
Walter, Virginia
  See Walter, Virginia A.
Walter, Virginia A. *134*

Walters, Audrey 1929- *18*
Walters, Celeste 1938- *126*
Walters, Eric 1957- *205*
　Earlier sketches in SATA *99, 155*
Walters, Eric Robert
　See Walters, Eric
Walters, Gregory 1964- *213*
Walters, Helen B. (?)-1987
　Obituary *50*
Walters, Hugh
　See Hughes, Walter (Llewellyn)
Walther, Thomas A. 1950- *31*
Walther, Tom
　See Walther, Thomas A.
Waltner, Elma 1912-1987 .... *40*
Waltner, Willard H. 1909- *40*
Walton, Darwin McBeth 1926- *119*
Walton, Fiona L. M. 1959- *89*
Walton, Richard J. 1928- *4*
Walton, Rick 1957- *204*
　Earlier sketches in SATA *101, 151*
Waltrip, Lela (Kingston) 1904-1995 .... *9*
Waltrip, Mildred 1911- *37*
Waltrip, Rufus (Charles) 1898-1988 .... *9*
Walworth, Nancy Zinsser 1917- *14*
Wang, Gabrielle *212*
Wang, Lin 1973- *221*
Wang, Shaoli *216*
Wangerin, Walter, Jr. 1944- *98*
　Brief entry *37*
　Earlier sketch in SATA *45*
Waniek, Marilyn
　See Nelson, Marilyn
Waniek, Marilyn Nelson 1946-
　See Nelson, Marilyn
Wannamaker, Bruce
　See Moncure, Jane Belk
Warbler, J. M.
　See Cocagnac, Augustin Maurice(-Jean)
Warburg, Sandol Stoddard
　See Stoddard, Sandol
Warburton, Tom 1968(?)- *218*
Ward, David 1967- *213*
Ward, E. D.
　See Gorey, Edward (St. John)
　and Lucas, E(dward) V(errall)
Ward, Ed
　See Stratemeyer, Edward L.
Ward, Helen 1962- *206*
　Earlier sketches in SATA *72, 144*
Ward, Jay 1920-1989
　Obituary *63*
Ward, Jennifer 1963- *226*
　Earlier sketch in SATA *146*
Ward, John (Stanton) 1917- *42*
Ward, Jonas
　See Ard, William
　and Cox, William R(obert)
　and Garfield, Brian (Francis Wynne)
Ward, Lindsay M. *236*
Ward, Lynd (Kendall) 1905-1985 .... *36*
　Obituary *42*
　Earlier sketch in SATA *2*
Ward, Martha (Eads) *5*
Ward, Melanie
　See Curtis, Richard
　and Lynch, Marilyn
Ward, Nicholas John
　See Ward, Nick
Ward, Nick 1955- *190*
Ward, Rachel 1964- *229*
Ward, Tom
　See Stratemeyer, Edward L.
Wardell, Dean
　See Prince, J(ack) H(arvey)
Wardlaw, Lee 1955- *115*
　Earlier sketch in SATA *79*
Ware, Cheryl 1963- *101*
Ware, Chris 1967- *140*
Ware, Leon (Vernon) 1909-1976 .... *4*

Wargin, Kathy-jo 1964- *210*
　Earlier sketch in SATA *145*
Warhola, James 1955- *187*
Waring, Geoff *238*
Warman, Jessica 1981- *225*
Warner, Frank A. *67*
　Earlier sketch in SATA *1*
Warner, Gertrude Chandler 1890-1979 .... *9*
　Obituary *73*
Warner, J(ohn) F. 1929- *75*
Warner, Lucille Schulberg *30*
Warner, Marsha *232*
Warner, Matt
　See Fichter, George S.
Warner, Oliver (Martin Wilson) 1903-1976 . *29*
Warner, Sally 1946- *214*
　Earlier sketch in SATA *131*
Warner, Sunny (B.) 1931- *108*
Warnes, Tim 1971- *216*
　Earlier sketches in SATA *116, 166*
Warnes, Timothy
　See Warnes, Tim
Warnick, Elsa 1942- *113*
Warren, Andrea 1946- *98*
Warren, Betsy
　See Warren, Elizabeth Avery
Warren, Billy
　See Warren, William Stephen
Warren, Cathy 1951- *62*
　Brief entry *46*
Warren, Elizabeth
　See Supraner, Robyn
Warren, Elizabeth Avery 1916- *46*
　Brief entry *38*
Warren, Jackie M. 1953- *135*
Warren, Joshua P(aul) 1976- *107*
Warren, Joyce W(illiams) 1935- *18*
Warren, Mary Phraner 1929- *10*
Warren, Robert Penn 1905-1989 .... *46*
　Obituary *63*
Warren, Scott S. 1957- *79*
Warren, William Stephen 1882-1968 .... *9*
Warrick, Patricia Scott 1925- *35*
Warriner, John 1907(?)-1987
　Obituary *53*
Warsh
　See Warshaw, Jerry
Warshaw, Jerry 1929- *30*
Warshaw, Mary 1931- *89*
Warshofsky, Fred 1931- *24*
Warshofsky, Isaac
　See Singer, Isaac Bashevis
Wartski, Maureen (Ann Crane) 1940- *50*
　Brief entry *37*
Warwick, Alan R(oss) 1900-1973 .... *42*
Wa-Sha-Quon-Asin
　See Belaney, Archibald Stansfeld
Wa-sha-quon-asin
　See Belaney, Archibald Stansfeld
Washburn, Bradford 1910-2007 .... *38*
　Obituary *181*
Washburn, Henry Bradford, Jr.
　See Washburn, Bradford
Washburn, Jan(ice) 1926- *63*
Washburn, Lucia *193*
Washburne, Carolyn Kott 1944- *86*
Washburne, Heluiz Chandler 1892-1970 ...... *10*
　Obituary *26*
Washington, Booker T. 1856-1915 .... *28*
Washington, Donna L. 1967- *159*
　Earlier sketch in SATA *98*
Wasserman, Robin 1978- *207*
Wasserstein, Wendy 1950-2006 .... *94*
　Obituary *174*
Wassiljewa, Tatjana 1928- *106*
Watanabe, Etsuko 1968- *219*
Watanabe, Shigeo 1928- *131*
　Brief entry *32*
　Earlier sketch in SATA *39*
　See also CLR *8*
Waters, John F(rederick) 1930- *4*

Waters, Summer
　See Sykes, Julie
Waters, Tony 1958- *75*
Waterton, Betty 1923- *99*
　Brief entry *34*
　Earlier sketch in SATA *37*
Waterton, Betty Marie
　See Waterton, Betty
Watkins, Angela Farris *239*
Watkins, Dawn L. *126*
Watkins, Gloria Jean
　See hooks, bell
Watkins, Lis
　See Watkins, Liselotte
Watkins, Liselotte 1971- *215*
Watkins, Lois 1930- *88*
Watkins, Peter 1934- *66*
Watkins, Yoko Kawashima 1933- *93*
Watkins-Pitchford, Denys James
　1905-1990 .... *87*
　Obituary *66*
　Earlier sketch in SATA *6*
　See also SAAS *4*
Watling, James 1933- *117*
　Earlier sketch in SATA *67*
Watson, Aldren A(uld) 1917- *42*
　Brief entry *36*
Watson, Amy Zakrzewski 1965- *76*
Watson, B. S.
　See Teitelbaum, Michael
Watson, Carol 1949- *78*
Watson, C.G. *193*
Watson, Clyde 1947- *68*
　Earlier sketch in SATA *5*
　See also CLR *3*
Watson, Geoff 1978- *237*
Watson, Helen Orr 1892-1978
　Obituary *24*
Watson, James 1936- *106*
　Earlier sketch in SATA *10*
Watson, Jane Werner 1915- *54*
　Earlier sketch in SATA *3*
Watson, Jesse Joshua *199*
Watson, John H.
　See Farmer, Philip Jose
Watson, Mary 1953- *117*
Watson, N. Cameron 1955- *81*
Watson, Nancy Dingman *32*
Watson, Pauline 1925- *14*
Watson, Renee 1978- *233*
Watson, Richard F.
　See Silverberg, Robert
Watson, Richard Jesse 1951- *211*
　Earlier sketch in SATA *62*
Watson, Sally (Lou) 1924- *3*
Watson, Sasha *211*
Watson, Stephanie 1979- *237*
Watson, Wendy (McLeod) 1942- *142*
　Earlier sketches in SATA *5, 74*
Watson Taylor, Elizabeth 1915- *41*
Watt, Melanie 1975- *193*
　Earlier sketch in SATA *136*
Watt, Thomas 1935- *4*
Wattenberg, Jane *174*
Watterson, Bill 1958- *66*
Watt-Evans, Lawrence 1954- *121*
Watts, Bernadette 1942- *230*
　Earlier sketches in SATA *4, 103*
Watts, Ephraim
　See Horne, Richard Henry Hengist
Watts, Franklin (Mowry) 1904-1978 .... *46*
　Obituary *21*
Watts, Helen L. Hoke 1903-1990
　Obituary *65*
Watts, Irene N(aemi) 1931- *111*
　Earlier sketch in SATA *56*
Watts, Isaac 1674-1748 .... *52*
Watts, James K(ennedy) M(offitt) 1955- *59*
Watts, Jeri Hanel 1957- *170*
Watts, Julia 1969- *103*
Watts, Leander 1956- *146*

Watts, Leslie Elizabeth 1961- *168*
Watts, Mabel Pizzey 1906-1994 .... *11*
Watts, Nigel 1957-1999 .... *121*
Watts, Sarah 1986- *234*
Waugh, C. C. Roessel
    See Waugh, Carol-Lynn Rossel
    and Waugh, Charles G(ordon)
Waugh, Carol-Lynn Rossel 1947- *41*
Waugh, Dorothy -1996 .... *11*
Waugh, Sylvia 1935- *169*
Waugh, Virginia
    See Sorensen, Virginia
Wax, Wendy A. 1963- *219*
    Earlier sketches in SATA *73, 163*
Wayland, April Halprin 1954- *143*
    Earlier sketch in SATA *78*
    See also SAAS *26*
Wayland, Patrick
    See O'Connor, Richard
Wayne, (Anne) Jenifer 1917-1982 .... *32*
Wayne, Kyra Petrovskaya 1918- *8*
Wayne, Richard
    See Decker, Duane
Wayshak, Deborah Noyes
    See Noyes, Deborah
Waystaff, Simon
    See Swift, Jonathan
Weales, Gerald (Clifford) 1925- *11*
Weary, Ogdred
    See Gorey, Edward (St. John)
Weatherford, Carole Boston 1956- *226*
    Earlier sketches in SATA *138, 181*
Weatherill, Cat *203*
Weatherly, Lee 1967- *192*
Weatherly, Myra 1926- *130*
Weatherly, Myra S.
    See Weatherly, Myra
Weaver, Brian M.
    See Numberman, Neil
Weaver, Harriett E. 1908-1993 .... *65*
Weaver, Janice *236*
Weaver, John L. 1949- *42*
Weaver, Robyn
    See Conley, Robyn
Weaver, Robyn M.
    See Conley, Robyn
Weaver, Tess *197*
Weaver, Ward
    See Mason, F(rancis) van Wyck
Weaver, Will 1950- *217*
    Earlier sketches in SATA *88, 109, 161*
Weaver, William Weller
    See Weaver, Will
Weaver-Gelzer, Charlotte 1950- *79*
Webb, Christopher
    See Wibberley, Leonard
Webb, Jacqueline
    See Pearce, Margaret
Webb, Jacquelyn
    See Pearce, Margaret
    and Pearce, Margaret
Webb, Jean Francis (III) 1910-1991 .... *35*
Webb, Kaye 1914- *60*
Webb, Lois Sinaiko 1922- *82*
Webb, Margot 1934- *67*
Webb, Sarah *235*
Webb, Sharon 1936-2010 .... *41*
Webb, Sophie 1958- *135*
Webber, Andrew Lloyd
    See Lloyd Webber, Andrew
Webber, Desiree Morrison 1956- *170*
Webber, Irma E(leanor Schmidt)
    1904-1995 .... *14*
Weber, Alfons 1921- *8*
Weber, Bruce 1942- *120*
    Earlier sketch in SATA *73*
Weber, Debora 1955- *58*
Weber, Dennis J. 1951- *234*
Weber, EdNah New Rider 1919(?)- *168*
Weber, Elka 1968- *219*

Weber, Jill 1950- *209*
    Earlier sketch in SATA *127*
Weber, Judith E(ichler) 1938- *64*
Weber, Ken(neth J.) 1940- *90*
Weber, Lenora Mattingly 1895-1971 .... *2*
    Obituary *26*
Weber, Lisa K. *217*
Weber, Lori 1959- *220*
Weber, Michael 1945- *87*
Weber, Penny *235*
Weber, Sandra 1961- *158*
Weber, William J(ohn) 1927- *14*
Webster, Alice Jane Chandler 1876-1916 ..... *17*
Webster, David 1930- *11*
Webster, Frank V. *67*
    Earlier sketch in SATA *1*
Webster, Gary
    See Garrison, Webb B(lack)
Webster, James 1925-1981 .... *17*
    Obituary *27*
Webster, Jean
    See Webster, Alice Jane Chandler
Wechsler, Doug *189*
Wechsler, Herman J. 1904-1976
    Obituary *20*
Wechter, Nell (Carolyn) Wise 1913-1989 .. *127*
    Earlier sketch in SATA *60*
Weck, Thomas L. 1942- *62*
Wedd, Kate
    See Gregory, Philippa
Weddle, Ethel Harshbarger 1897-1996 .... *11*
Wedekind, Annie *204*
Weeks, Sarah *194*
    Earlier sketch in SATA *158*
Weems, David B(urnola) 1922- *80*
Wees, Frances Shelley 1902-1982 .... *58*
Weevers, Peter 1944- *59*
Wegen, Ronald 1946-1985 .... *99*
Wegman, William (George) 1943- *135*
    Earlier sketches in SATA *78, 129*
Wegner, Fritz 1924- *20*
Wehrman, Vicki *223*
Weidhorn, Manfred 1931- *60*
Weidt, Maryann N. 1944- *85*
Weigel, Jeff 1958- *170*
Weigelt, Udo 1960- *201*
    Earlier sketch in SATA *168*
Weihs, Erika 1917-2010 .... *107*
    Earlier sketch in SATA *15*
Weik, Mary Hays 1898(?)-1979 .... *3*
    Obituary *23*
Weil, Ann Yezner 1908-1969 .... *9*
Weil, Lisl 1910- *7*
Weilerstein, Sadie Rose 1894-1993 .... *3*
    Obituary *75*
Weill, Cynthia 1959- *167*
Wein, Elizabeth E. 1964- *151*
    Earlier sketch in SATA *82*
Wein, Elizabeth Eve
    See Wein, Elizabeth E.
Wein, Hallie
    See Zobel Nolan, Allia
Weinberg, Larry
    See Weinberg, Lawrence (E.)
Weinberg, Lawrence (E.) *92*
    Brief entry *48*
Weinberger, Tanya 1939- *84*
Weiner, Sandra 1922- *14*
Weingarten, Lynn *217*
Weingarten, Violet (Brown) 1915-1976 .... *3*
    Obituary *27*
Weingartner, Charles 1922- *5*
Weinheimer, Beckie 1958- *186*
Weinstein, Bruce 1960- *220*
Weinstein, Bruce M.
    See Weinstein, Bruce
Weinstein, Ellen Slusky 1959- *200*
Weinstein, Muriel Harris *215*
Weinstein, Nina 1951- *73*
Weinstock, Robert 1967- *204*
Weir, Bob 1947- *76*

Weir, Diana (R.) Loiewski 1958- *111*
Weir, Joan S(herman) 1928- *99*
Weir, LaVada *2*
Weir, Rosemary (Green) 1905-1994 .... *21*
Weir, Wendy 1949- *76*
Weis, Margaret 1948- *164*
    Earlier sketches in SATA *38, 92*
Weisberger, Bernard A(llen) 1922- *21*
Weisburd, Stefi 1957- *202*
Weise, Patty *236*
Weiser, Marjorie P(hillis) K(atz) 1934- *33*
Weisgard, Leonard (Joseph) 1916-2000 .... *85*
    Obituary *122*
    Earlier sketches in SATA *2, 30*
    See also SAAS *19*
Weiss, Adelle 1920- *18*
Weiss, Ann E(dwards) 1943- *69*
    Earlier sketch in SATA *30*
    See also SAAS *13*
Weiss, Edna
    See Barth, Edna
Weiss, Ellen 1953- *44*
Weiss, Harvey 1922- *76*
    Earlier sketches in SATA *1, 27*
    See also CLR *4*
    See also SAAS *19*
Weiss, Jaqueline Shachter 1926- *65*
Weiss, Malcolm E. 1928- *3*
Weiss, Margaret Edith
    See Weis, Margaret
Weiss, Miriam
    See Schlein, Miriam
Weiss, Mitch 1951- *183*
    Earlier sketch in SATA *123*
Weiss, Nicki 1954- *86*
    Earlier sketch in SATA *33*
Weiss, Renee Karol 1923- *5*
Weissberger, Ela 1930- *181*
Weissberger, Ela Stein
    See Weissberger, Ela
Weissenborn, Hellmuth 1898-1982
    Obituary *31*
Weissman, Elissa Brent *217*
Weitzman, David L. 1936- *172*
    Earlier sketch in SATA *122*
Wekesser, Carol A. 1963- *76*
Welber, Robert *26*
Welch, Amanda (Jane) 1945- *75*
Welch, D'Alte Aldridge 1907-1970
    Obituary *27*
Welch, Holly *206*
Welch, Jean-Louise
    See Kempton, Jean Welch
Welch, Pauline
    See Bodenham, Hilda Morris
Welch, Ronald
    See Felton, Ronald Oliver
Welch, Sheila Kelly 1945- *130*
Welch, Willy 1952- *93*
Weldin, Frauke 1969- *188*
Welford, Sue 1942- *75*
Weller, George 1907-2002 .... *31*
    Obituary *140*
Weller, George Anthony
    See Weller, George
Welling, Peter J. 1947- *135*
Wellington, Monica 1957- *222*
    Earlier sketches in SATA *67, 99, 157*
Wellman, Alice 1900-1984 .... *51*
    Brief entry *36*
Wellman, Manly Wade 1903-1986 .... *6*
    Obituary *47*
Wellman, Paul I. 1898-1966 .... *3*
Wellman, Paul Iselin
    See Wellman, Paul I.
Wellman, Sam 1939- *122*
Wellman, Samuel
    See Wellman, Sam
Wells, H. G. 1866-1946 .... *20*
    See also CLR *133*

Wells, Helen
  See Campbell, Hope
Wells, Helen 1910-1986 .... *49*
  Earlier sketch in SATA *2*
Wells, Herbert George
  See Wells, H. G.
Wells, J. Wellington
  See de Camp, L. Sprague
Wells, June
  See Swinford, Betty (June Wells)
Wells, Robert
  See Welsch, Roger L(ee)
Wells, Robert E. *239*
  Earlier sketch in SATA *184*
Wells, Rosemary 1943- *237*
  Earlier sketches in SATA *18, 69, 114, 156,*
  207
  See also CLR *69*
  See also SAAS *1*
Wells, Susan (Mary) 1951- *78*
Wels, Byron G(erald) 1924-1993 .... *9*
Welsbacher, Anne 1955- *89*
Welsch, Roger L(ee) 1936- *82*
Welsh, C.E.L. *234*
Welsh, Chris
  See Welsh, C.E.L.
Welsh, David
  See Hills, C.A.R.
Welsh, Mary Flynn 1910(?)-1984
  Obituary *38*
Welsh, T.K. 1956- *184*
Weltevrede, Pieter 1957- *228*
Weltner, Linda R(iverly) 1938- *38*
Welton, Jude 1955- *143*
  Earlier sketch in SATA *79*
Welty, S. F.
  See Welty, Susan F.
Welty, Susan F. 1905- *9*
Wemmlinger, Raymond *190*
Wendelin, Rudolph 1910-2000 .... *23*
Weninger, Brigitte 1960- *189*
Wensell, Ulises 1945- *229*
Wentworth, Robert
  See Hamilton, Edmond
Werlin, Nancy 1961- *161*
  Earlier sketches in SATA *87, 119*
Werner, Elsa Jane
  See Watson, Jane Werner
Werner, Herma 1926- *47*
  Brief entry *41*
Werner, Jane
  See Watson, Jane Werner
Werner, K.
  See Casewit, Curtis W(erner)
Wersba, Barbara 1932- *58*
  Autobiography Feature *103*
  Earlier sketch in SATA *1*
  See also CLR *78*
  See also SAAS *2*
Werstein, Irving 1914(?)-1971 .... *14*
Werth, Kurt 1896-1983 .... *20*
Wesley, Alison
  See Barnes, Michael
Wesley, Kathryn
  See Rusch, Kristine Kathryn
Wesley, Mary (Aline) 1912-2002 .... *66*
Wesley, Valerie Wilson 1947- *168*
  Earlier sketch in SATA *106*
Wesselhoeft, Conrad 1953- *237*
West, Andrew
  See Arthur, Robert, (Jr.)
West, Anna 1938- *40*
West, Barbara
  See Price, Olive
West, Betty 1921- *11*
West, Bruce 1951- *63*
West, C. P.
  See Wodehouse, P. G.
West, Dorothy
  See Benson, Mildred
West, Emily Govan 1919- *38*

West, Emmy
  See West, Emily Govan
West, Jacqueline 1979- *235*
West, James
  See Withers, Carl A.
West, Jerry
  See Svenson, Andrew E(dward)
West, (Mary) Jessamyn 1902-1984
  Obituary *37*
West, John
  See Arthur, Robert, (Jr.)
West, Owen
  See Koontz, Dean
West, Ward
  See Borland, Harold Glen
Westall, Robert (Atkinson) 1929-1993 .... *69*
  Obituary *75*
  Earlier sketch in SATA *23*
  See also CLR *13*
  See also SAAS *2*
Westaway, Jane 1948- *121*
Westcott, Nadine Bernard 1949- *130*
Westera, Marleen 1962- *187*
Westerberg, Christine 1950- *29*
Westerduin, Anne 1945- *105*
Westerfeld, Scott 1963- *230*
  Earlier sketch in SATA *161*
Westervelt, Virginia Veeder 1914-2005 .... *10*
Westheimer, David 1917-2005 .... *14*
  Obituary *170*
Westheimer, David Kaplan
  See Westheimer, David
Westmacott, Mary
  See Christie, Agatha
Westman, Barbara *70*
Westman, Paul (Wendell) 1956- *39*
Westmoreland, William C. 1914-2005 .... *63*
Westmoreland, William Childs
  See Westmoreland, William C.
Weston, Allen
  See Hogarth, Grace (Weston Allen)
  and Norton, Andre
Weston, Carol 1956- *135*
Weston, Carrie *190*
Weston, John (Harrison) 1932- *21*
Weston, Martha 1947- *119*
  Earlier sketch in SATA *53*
Weston, Robert Paul *209*
Westphal, Arnold Carl 1897- *57*
Westrup, Hugh *102*
Westwood, Jennifer 1940-2008 .... *10*
  Obituary *192*
Wexler, Jerome (LeRoy) 1923- *14*
Weyland, Jack 1940- *81*
Weyn, Suzanne 1955- *220*
  Earlier sketches in SATA *63, 101, 164*
Weyr, Garret
  See Freymann-Weyr, Garret
Wezyk, Joanna 1966- *82*
Whaley, Joyce Irene 1923- *61*
Whalin, W. Terry 1953- *93*
Whamond, Dave *222*
Wharf, Michael
  See Weller, George
Wharmby, Margot *63*
Wharton, Edith 1862-1937
  See CLR *136*
Wharton, Edith Newbold Jones
  See Wharton, Edith
Wharton, Thomas 1963- *223*
Whatley, Bruce 1954- *213*
  Earlier sketch in SATA *177*
Wheat, Chris 1949- *238*
Wheatley, Arabelle 1921- *16*
Wheatley, Nadia 1949- *147*
Wheeler, Cindy 1955- *49*
  Brief entry *40*
Wheeler, Deborah 1947- *83*
Wheeler, Janet D. *1*
Wheeler, Jill C. 1964- *136*
  Earlier sketch in SATA *86*

Wheeler, Jody 1952- *148*
  Earlier sketch in SATA *84*
Wheeler, Lisa 1963- *237*
  Earlier sketches in SATA *162, 200*
Wheeler, Opal 1898- *23*
Whelan, Elizabeth M(urphy) 1943- *14*
Whelan, Gloria 1923- *224*
  Earlier sketches in SATA *85, 128, 178*
  See also CLR *90*
Whelan, Gloria Ann
  See Whelan, Gloria
Whelan, Kat *238*
Whinnem, Reade Scott *224*
Whipple, A(ddison) B(eecher) C(olvin)
  1918- *64*
Whipple, Cal
  See Whipple, A(ddison) B(eecher) C(olvin)
Whisp, Kennilworthy
  See Rowling, J.K.
Whistler, Reginald John 1905-1944 .... *30*
Whistler, Rex
  See Whistler, Reginald John
Whitaker, Zai *183*
Whitcher, Susan (Godsil) 1952- *96*
Whitcomb, Jon 1906-1988 .... *10*
  Obituary *56*
Whitcomb, Laura 1958- *214*
  Earlier sketch in SATA *171*
White, Amy Brecount *228*
White, Anne Terry 1896-1980 .... *2*
White, Bessie (Felstiner) 1892(?)-1986
  Obituary *50*
White, Carolyn 1948- *130*
White, Dale
  See Place, Marian T(empleton)
White, Dori 1919- *10*
White, E. B. 1899-1985 .... *100*
  Obituary *44*
  Earlier sketches in SATA *2, 29*
  See also CLR *107*
White, Eliza Orne 1856-1947
  See YABC *2*
White, Elwyn Brooks
  See White, E. B.
White, Florence M(eiman) 1910- *14*
White, Kathryn 1956- *234*
White, Kathryn Ivy
  See White, Kathryn
White, K.I.
  See White, Kathryn
White, Laurence B(arton), Jr. 1935- *10*
White, Lee *223*
  Earlier sketch in SATA *176*
White, Linda
  See White, Linda Arms
White, Linda Arms *238*
White, Martin 1943- *51*
White, Nancy 1942- *126*
White, Ramy Allison *67*
  Earlier sketch in SATA *1*
White, Robb 1909-1990 .... *83*
  Earlier sketch in SATA *1*
  See also CLR *3*
  See also SAAS *1*
White, Ruth 1942- *186*
  Autobiography Feature *186*
  Earlier sketches in SATA *39, 117, 165*
White, Ruth C.
  See White, Ruth
White, T(erence) H(anbury) 1906-1964 .... *12*
  See also CLR *139*
White, Tekla N. 1934- *115*
White, Timothy (Thomas Anthony)
  1952-2002 .... *60*
White, Tom 1923- *148*
White, Tracy *235*
White, Tracy A.
  See White, Tracy
White, William, Jr. 1934- *16*
Whitehead, Don(ald) F. 1908-1981 .... *4*
Whitehead, Jenny 1964- *191*

Whitehead, Kathy 1957- *176*
Whitehouse, Arch
    See Whitehouse, Arthur George Joseph
Whitehouse, Arthur George Joseph
    1895-1979 .... *14*
    Obituary *23*
Whitehouse, Elizabeth S(cott) 1893-1968 .... *35*
Whitehouse, Jeanne
    See Peterson, Jeanne Whitehouse
Whitelaw, Nancy 1933- *166*
    Earlier sketch in SATA *76*
Whitesel, Cheryl Aylward *162*
Whiting, Sue 1960- *205*
Whiting, Susan Allana
    See Whiting, Sue
Whitinger, R. D.
    See Place, Marian T(empleton)
Whitley, David 1984- *225*
Whitley, Mary Ann
    See Sebrey, Mary Ann
Whitley, Peggy 1938- *140*
    Obituary *31*
Whitlock, Pamela 1921(?)-1982
    Obituary *31*
Whitlock, Ralph 1914-1995 .... *35*
Whitman, Alice
    See Marker, Sherry
Whitman, Candace 1958- *208*
Whitman, Emily *238*
Whitman, Sylvia (Choate) 1961- *135*
    Earlier sketch in SATA *85*
Whitman, Walt 1819-1892 .... *20*
Whitman, Walter
    See Whitman, Walt
Whitmore, Arvella 1922- *125*
Whitmore, Benette 1955- *203*
Whitney, Alex(andra) 1922- *14*
Whitney, David C(harles) 1921- *48*
    Brief entry *29*
Whitney, Kim Ablon *162*
Whitney, Phyllis A. 1903-2008 .... *30*
    Obituary *189*
    Earlier sketch in SATA *1*
    See also CLR *59*
Whitney, Phyllis Ayame
    See Whitney, Phyllis A.
Whitney, Sharon 1937- *63*
Whitney, Thomas P. 1917-2007 .... *25*
    Obituary *189*
Whitney, Thomas Porter
    See Whitney, Thomas P.
Whittington, Mary K(athrine) 1941- *75*
Whitworth, John 1945- *123*
Whybrow, Ian *202*
    Earlier sketch in SATA *132*
Whyte, Mal(colm Kenneth, Jr.) 1933- *62*
Whyte, Mary 1953- *148*
    Earlier sketch in SATA *94*
Whyte, Ron 1942(?)-1989
    Obituary *63*
Whytock, Cherry *177*
Wiater, Stanley 1953- *84*
Wibbelsman, Charles J(oseph) 1945- *59*
Wibberley, Leonard 1915-1983 .... *45*
    Obituary *36*
    Earlier sketch in SATA *2*
    See also CLR *3*
Wibberley, Leonard Patrick O'Connor
    See Wibberley, Leonard
Wiberg, Harald (Albin) 1908- *93*
    Brief entry *40*
Wick, Walter 1953- *148*
Wickberg, Susan
    See Rottman, S.L.
Wickens, Elaine *86*
Wicker, Ireene 1905(?)-1987
    Obituary *55*
Wickstrom, Sylvie 1960- *169*
Wickstrom, Thor 1960- *200*
Widdemer, Mabel Cleland 1902-1964 .... *5*
Widener, Terry 1950- *209*
    Earlier sketch in SATA *105*

Widerberg, Siv 1931- *10*
Wiebe, Rudy 1934- *156*
Wiebe, Rudy Henry
    See Wiebe, Rudy
Wieler, Diana (Jean) 1961- *109*
Wiener, Lori 1956- *84*
Wier, Ester (Alberti) 1910-2000 .... *3*
Wiese, Kurt 1887-1974 .... *36*
    Obituary *24*
    Earlier sketch in SATA *3*
    See also CLR *86*
Wiesel, Elie 1928- *56*
Wiesel, Eliezer
    See Wiesel, Elie
Wiesner, David 1956- *181*
    Earlier sketches in SATA *72, 117, 139*
    See also CLR *84*
Wiesner, Portia
    See Takakjian, Portia
Wiesner, William 1899-1984 .... *5*
Wiewandt, Thomas 1945- *231*
Wiggers, Raymond 1952- *82*
Wiggin, Eric E. 1939- *167*
    Earlier sketch in SATA *88*
Wiggin, Eric Ellsworth 1939-
    See Wiggin, Eric E.
Wiggin (Riggs), Kate Douglas (Smith)
    1856-1923
    See YABC *1*
    See also CLR *52*
Wiggins, VeraLee (Chesnut) 1928-1995 .... *89*
Wight, Eric 1974- *232*
    Earlier sketch in SATA *218*
Wight, James Alfred
    See Herriot, James
Wignell, Edel 1936- *69*
Wijnberg, Ellen *85*
Wijngaard, Juan 1951- *230*
Wikland, Ilon 1930- *93*
    Brief entry *32*
Wikler, Madeline 1943- *114*
Wilber, Donald N(ewton) 1907-1997 .... *35*
Wilbur, C. Keith 1923- *27*
Wilbur, Frances 1921- *107*
Wilbur, Helen L. 1948- *204*
Wilbur, Richard 1921- *108*
    Earlier sketch in SATA *9*
Wilbur, Richard Purdy
    See Wilbur, Richard
Wilburn, Kathy 1948- *68*
Wilcox, Charlotte 1948- *72*
Wilcox, Leah 1975(?)- *207*
Wilcox, R(uth) Turner 1888-1970 .... *36*
Wilcox, Roger
    See Collins, Paul
Wild, Jocelyn 1941- *46*
Wild, Kate 1954- *192*
Wild, Margaret 1948- *197*
    Earlier sketch in SATA *151*
Wild, Robin (Evans) 1936- *46*
Wild, Robyn 1947- *117*
Wilde, D. Gunther
    See Hurwood, Bernhardt J.
Wilde, Oscar 1854(?)-1900 .... *24*
    See also CLR *114*
Wilde, Oscar Fingal O'Flahertie Willis
    See Wilde, Oscar
Wilder, Buck
    See Smith, Tim(othy R.)
Wilder, Laura Elizabeth Ingalls
    See Wilder, Laura Ingalls
Wilder, Laura Ingalls 1867-1957 .... *100*
    Earlier sketches in SATA *15, 29*
    See also CLR *111*
Wildish, Lee *231*
Wildsmith, Brian 1930- *124*
    Earlier sketches in SATA *16, 69*
    See also CLR *52*
    See also SAAS *5*
Wiles, Deborah *171*
Wilhelm, Doug 1952- *190*

Wilhelm, Hans 1945- *196*
    Autobiography Feature *196*
    Earlier sketches in SATA *58, 135*
    See also CLR *46*
    See also SAAS *21*
Wilkie, Katharine E(lliott) 1904-1980 .... *31*
Wilkin, Eloise 1904-1987 .... *49*
    Obituary *54*
Wilkins, Ebony Joy *234*
Wilkins, Frances 1923- *14*
Wilkins, Kim *147*
Wilkins, Marilyn (Ruth) 1926- *30*
Wilkins, Marne
    See Wilkins, Marilyn (Ruth)
Wilkins, Mary Huiskamp 1926- *2*
    See also CLR *42*
Wilkins, Mary Huiskamp Calhoun
    See Wilkins, Mary Huiskamp
Wilkins, Rose *180*
Wilkinson, (Thomas) Barry 1923- *50*
    Brief entry *32*
Wilkinson, Beth 1925- *80*
Wilkinson, Brenda 1946- *91*
    Earlier sketch in SATA *14*
    See also CLR *20*
Wilkinson, (John) Burke 1913-2000 .... *4*
Wilkinson, Carole 1950- *210*
Wilkinson, Sylvia 1940- *56*
    Brief entry *39*
Wilkon, Jozef 1930- *133*
    Earlier sketches in SATA *31, 71*
Wilkowski, Sue *193*
Wilks, Michael Thomas 1947- *44*
    See Wilks, Mike
Wilks, Mike *224*
    See Wilks, Michael Thomas
Will
    See Lipkind, William
Willard, Barbara (Mary) 1909-1994 .... *74*
    Earlier sketch in SATA *17*
    See also CLR *2*
    See also SAAS *5*
Willard, Elizabeth Kimmel
    See Kimmel, Elizabeth Cody
Willard, Mildred Wilds 1911-1978 .... *14*
Willard, Nancy 1936- *191*
    Brief entry *30*
    Earlier sketches in SATA *37, 71, 127*
    See also CLR *5*
Willcox, Isobel 1907-1996 .... *42*
Willems, Mo *228*
    Earlier sketches in SATA *154, 180*
    See also CLR *114*
Willett, Edward 1959- *115*
Willett, Edward C.
    See Willett, Edward
Willey, Bee *184*
Willey, Margaret 1950- *226*
    Earlier sketch in SATA *86*
Willey, Robert
    See Ley, Willy
Willhoite, Michael A. 1946- *71*
William, Kate
    See Armstrong, Jennifer
Williams, Alex 1969- *209*
Williams, Arlene *171*
Williams, Barbara 1925- *107*
    Earlier sketch in SATA *11*
    See also CLR *48*
    See also SAAS *16*
Williams, Barbara 1937- *62*
Williams, Beryl
    See Epstein, Beryl
Williams, Brian (Peter) 1943- *54*
Williams, Carol Lynch 1959- *212*
    Earlier sketch in SATA *110*
Williams, Charles
    See Collier, James Lincoln
Williams, Clyde C. 1881-1974 .... *8*
    Obituary *27*

Williams, Coe
 See Harrison, C(hester) William
Williams, Colleen Madonna Flood 1963- .. *156*
Williams, Cynthia G. 1958- *123*
Williams, Dar 1967- *168*
Williams, Donna Reilly 1945- *83*
Williams, Dorothy
 See Williams, Marcia
Williams, Dorothy Snowden
 See Williams, Dar
Williams, Eric (Ernest) 1911-1983 .... *14*
 Obituary *38*
Williams, Ferelith Eccles
 See Eccles Williams, Ferelith
Williams, Frances B.
 See Browin, Frances Williams
Williams, Gabrielle *238*
Williams, Garth (Montgomery) 1912-1996 .. *66*
 Obituary *90*
 Earlier sketch in SATA *18*
 See also CLR *57*
 See also SAAS *7*
Williams, Guy R(ichard) 1920- *11*
Williams, Hawley
 See Heyliger, William
Williams, Helen 1948- *77*
Williams, J. R.
 See Williams, Jeanne
Williams, J. Walker
 See Wodehouse, P. G.
Williams, Jay 1914-1978 .... *41*
 Obituary *24*
 Earlier sketch in SATA *3*
 See also CLR *8*
Williams, Jeanne 1930- *5*
Williams, Jenny 1939- *60*
Williams, Karen Lynn 1952- *224*
 Earlier sketches in SATA *66, 99*
Williams, Kathryn 1981- *222*
Williams, Katie 1978- *235*
Williams, Kit 1946(?)- *44*
 See also CLR *4*
Williams, L. E.
 See Williams, Laura E.
Williams, Laura E.
 See Williams, Laura Ellen
Williams, Laura Ellen *180*
Williams, Leslie 1941- *42*
Williams, Linda 1948- *59*
Williams, Louise Bonino 1904(?)-1984
 Obituary *39*
Williams, Lynn
 See Hale, Arlene
Williams, Maiya 1962- *230*
Williams, Marcia 1945- *159*
 Earlier sketches in SATA *71, 97*
Williams, Marcia Dorothy
 See Williams, Marcia
Williams, Margery
 See Bianco, Margery Williams
Williams, Mark
 See Arthur, Robert, (Jr.)
Williams, Mark London 1959- *140*
Williams, Maureen 1951- *12*
Williams, Michael
 See St. John, Wylly Folk
Williams, Patrick J.
 See Griffin, W. E. B.
Williams, Paulette Linda
 See Shange, Ntozake
Williams, Pete
 See Faulknor, Cliff(ord Vernon)
Williams, Richard Treat
 See Williams, Treat
Williams, S. P.
 See Hart, Virginia
Williams, Sam *177*
 Earlier sketch in SATA *124*
Williams, Selma R(uth) 1925- *14*
Williams, Sherley Anne 1944-1999 .... *78*
 Obituary *116*

Williams, Sheron 1955- *77*
Williams, Shirley
 See Williams, Sherley Anne
Williams, Slim
 See Williams, Clyde C.
Williams, Sophy 1965- *135*
Williams, Sue 1948-2007 .... *208*
Williams, Susan
 See Beckhorn, Susan Williams
Williams, Suzanne
 See Williams, Suzanne Morgan
Williams, Suzanne 1953- *202*
 Earlier sketch in SATA *71*
Williams, Suzanne M.
 See Williams, Suzanne Morgan
Williams, Suzanne Morgan 1949- *207*
Williams, Treat 1951- *234*
Williams, Ursula Moray
 See Moray Williams, Ursula
Williams, Vera B(aker) 1927- *102*
 Brief entry *33*
 Earlier sketch in SATA *53*
 See also CLR *9*
Williams-Andriani, Renee 1963- *98*
Williams-Ellis, (Mary) Amabel (Nassau
 Strachey) 1894-1984 .... *29*
 Obituary *41*
Williams-Garcia, Rita 1957- *160*
 Earlier sketch in SATA *98*
 See also CLR *36*
Williamson, Gwyneth 1965- *109*
Williamson, Henry (William) 1895-1977 ..... *37*
 Obituary *30*
Williamson, Joanne S(mall) 1926- *122*
 Earlier sketch in SATA *3*
Williamson, Kate T. 1979- *215*
Williamson, Melanie *196*
Willis, Charles
 See Clarke, Arthur C.
Willis, Connie 1945- *110*
 See also CLR *66*
Willis, Cynthia Chapman *215*
Willis, Jeanne 1959- *237*
 Earlier sketches in SATA *61, 123, 195*
Willis, Jeanne Mary
 See Willis, Jeanne
Willis, Meredith Sue 1946- *101*
Willis, Nancy Carol 1952- *139*
 Earlier sketch in SATA *93*
Willis, Paul J. 1955- *113*
Willms, Russ *95*
Willner-Pardo, Gina 1957- *235*
Willoughby, Lee Davis
 See Avallone, Michael (Angelo, Jr.)
 and Brandner, Gary (Phil)
 and Deming, Richard
 and DeAndrea, William L(ouis)
 and Laymon, Richard (Carl)
 and Streib, Dan(iel Thomas)
 and Toombs, John
 and Webb, Jean Francis (III)
Willson, Robina Beckles
 See Beckles Willson, Robina
Willson, Sarah
 See Albee, Sarah
Wilma, Dana
 See Faralla, Dana
Wilsdorf, Anne 1954- *191*
Wilson, Anne 1974- *224*
Wilson, April *80*
Wilson, Barbara Ker
 See Ker Wilson, Barbara
Wilson, Beth P(ierre) *8*
Wilson, Budge 1927- *55*
 Brief entry *51*
Wilson, Carletta 1951- *81*
Wilson, Carter 1941- *6*
Wilson, Charles Morrow 1905-1977 .... *30*
Wilson, Christopher B. 1910(?)-1985
 Obituary *46*
Wilson, Daniel H. 1978- *239*

Wilson, Darryl B(abe) 1939- *90*
Wilson, Diane Lee *172*
Wilson, Dirk
 See Pohl, Frederik
Wilson, Dorothy Clarke 1904-2003 .... *16*
Wilson, Edward A(rthur) 1886-1970 .... *38*
Wilson, Ellen (Janet Cameron) (?)-1976 .... *9*
 Obituary *26*
Wilson, Eric (H.) 1940- *34*
 Brief entry *32*
Wilson, Erica 1928-2011 .... *51*
Wilson, Forrest 1918- *27*
Wilson, Gahan 1930- *35*
 Brief entry *27*
Wilson, Gina 1943- *85*
 Brief entry *34*
 Earlier sketch in SATA *36*
Wilson, (Leslie) Granville 1912- *14*
Wilson, Hazel (Hutchins) 1898-1992 .... *3*
 Obituary *73*
Wilson, J(erry) M. 1964- *121*
Wilson, Jacqueline 1945- *199*
 Brief entry *52*
 Earlier sketches in SATA *61, 102, 153*
Wilson, John 1922- *22*
Wilson, John 1951- *227*
 Earlier sketch in SATA *182*
Wilson, John Alexander
 See Wilson, John
Wilson, Johnniece Marshall 1944- *75*
Wilson, Jonathan 1950- *181*
Wilson, Joyce M. *84*
 Earlier sketch in SATA *21*
 See also SAAS *24*
Wilson, Karma *221*
 Earlier sketch in SATA *174*
Wilson, Leslie 1952- *166*
Wilson, Linda Miller 1936- *116*
Wilson, Lionel 1924-2003 .... *33*
 Brief entry *31*
 Obituary *144*
Wilson, Marjorie
 See Wilson, Budge
Wilson, Martin 1973- *205*
Wilson, Maurice (Charles John) 1914- *46*
Wilson, Nancy Hope 1947- *138*
 Earlier sketch in SATA *81*
Wilson, Nathan D.
 See Wilson, N.D.
Wilson, N.D. 1978- *194*
Wilson, Nick
 See Ellis, Edward S.
Wilson, Phil 1948- *181*
Wilson, Ron(ald William) 1941- *38*
Wilson, Sarah 1934- *208*
 Earlier sketches in SATA *50, 142*
Wilson, Tom 1931-2011 .... *33*
 Brief entry *30*
Wilson, Troy 1970- *169*
Wilson, Walt(er N.) 1939- *14*
Wilson-Max, Ken 1965- *170*
 Earlier sketch in SATA *93*
Wilton, Elizabeth 1937- *14*
Wilton, Hal
 See Pepper, Frank S.
Wilwerding, Walter Joseph 1891-1966 .... *9*
Wimmer, Mike 1961- *194*
 Earlier sketch in SATA *70*
Winborn, Marsha (Lynn) 1947- *75*
Winch, John 1944- *165*
 Earlier sketch in SATA *117*
Winchester, James H(ugh) 1917-1985 .... *30*
 Obituary *45*
Winchester, Stanley
 See Youd, Samuel
Windawi, Thura al- 1983(?)- *165*
Winders, Gertrude Hecker -1987 .... *3*
Windham, Basil
 See Wodehouse, P. G.
Windham, Kathryn T. 1918-2011 .... *14*

Windham, Kathryn Tucker
See Windham, Kathryn T.
Windham, Sophie 184
Windling, Terri 1958- 233
Earlier sketch in SATA 151
Windrow, Martin
See Windrow, Martin Clive
Windrow, Martin C.
See Windrow, Martin Clive
Windrow, Martin Clive 1944- 68
Windsor, Claire
See Hamerstrom, Frances
Windsor, Linda 1950- 124
Windsor, Patricia 1938- 78
Earlier sketch in SATA 30
See also SAAS 19
Wineman-Marcus, Irene 1952- 81
Winer, Yvonne 1934- 120
Winerip, Michael 175
Winfield, Arthur M.
See Stratemeyer, Edward L.
Winfield, Edna
See Stratemeyer, Edward L.
Winfield, Julia
See Armstrong, Jennifer
Wing, Natasha 1960- 200
Earlier sketch in SATA 82
Wingerter, Linda S. 1973(?)- 207
Winget, Susan 211
Winick, Judd 1970- 124
Winks, Robin William 1930-2003 61
Winn, Alison
See Wharmby, Margot
Winn, Chris 1952- 42
Winn, Janet Bruce 1928- 43
Winn, Marie 1936(?)- 38
Winnick, Karen B. 1946- 211
Winnick, Karen B(eth) B(inkoff) 1946- 51
Winn-Lederer, Ilene 198
Winslow, Barbara 1947- 91
Winstead, Rosie 180
Winston, Clara 1921-1983 54
Obituary 39
Winston, Richard 1917-1979 54
Winston, Sherri 1964(?)- 201
Winter, Janet 1926- 126
Winter, Jeanette 1939- 184
Earlier sketch in SATA 151
Winter, Jonah 1962- 225
Earlier sketch in SATA 179
Winter, Milo (Kendall) 1888-1956 21
Winter, Paula Cecelia 1929- 48
Winter, R. R.
See Winterbotham, R(ussell) R(obert)
Winter, Susan 182
Winterbotham, R(ussell) R(obert)
1904-1971 10
Winterbotham, Russ
See Winterbotham, R(ussell) R(obert)
Winterfeld, Henry 1901-1990 55
Winters, J. C.
See Cross, Gilbert B.
Winters, Jon
See Cross, Gilbert B.
Winters, Katherine
See Winters, Kay
Winters, Kay 1936- 153
Earlier sketch in SATA 103
Winters, Nina 1944- 62
Winters, Paul A. 1965- 106
Winterson, Jeanette 1959- 190
Winterton, Gayle
See Adams, William Taylor
Winthrop, Elizabeth 1948- 164
Autobiography Feature 116
Earlier sketches in SATA 8, 76
See also CLR 89
Winton, Ian (Kenneth) 1960- 76
Winton, Tim 1960- 98
Wintz-Litty, Julie
See Litty, Julie
Wirt, Ann
See Benson, Mildred

Wirt, Mildred A.
See Benson, Mildred
Wirtenberg, Patricia Z. 1932-2007 10
Wirtenberg, Patricia Zarrella
See Wirtenberg, Patricia Z.
Wirth, Beverly 1938- 63
Wirths, Claudine (Turner) G(ibson)
1926-2000 104
Earlier sketch in SATA 64
Wise, Bill 1958- 191
Wise, Lenny
See Wise, Leonard
Wise, Leonard 1940- 167
Wise, Leonard A.
See Wise, Leonard
Wise, Leonard Allan
See Wise, Leonard
Wise, William 1923- 163
Earlier sketch in SATA 4
Wise, Winifred E. 2
Wiseman, Ann (Sayre) 1926- 31
Wiseman, B(ernard) 1922-1995 4
Wiseman, David 1916- 43
Brief entry 40
Wiseman, Eva 1947- 210
Wishinsky, Frieda 1948- 166
Earlier sketches in SATA 70, 112
Wisler, G(ary) Clifton 1950- 103
Brief entry 46
Earlier sketch in SATA 58
Wismer, Donald (Richard) 1946- 59
Wisner, Bill
See Wisner, William L.
Wisner, William L. 1914(?)-1983 42
Wisnewski, Andrea 234
Wisnewski, David 1953-2002
See Wisniewski, David
Wisniewski, David 1953-2002 95
Obituary 139
See also CLR 51
Wister, Owen 1860-1938 62
Witham, (Phillip) Ross 1917- 37
Withers, Carl A. 1900-1970 14
Withers, Pam 1956- 182
Withrow, Sarah 1966- 199
Earlier sketch in SATA 124
Witt, Dick 1948- 80
Witt, Shirley Hill 1934- 17
Wittanen, Etolin 1907- 55
Wittels, Harriet Joan 1938- 31
Wittenstein, Vicki Oransky 1954- 228
Wittig, Susan
See Albert, Susan Wittig
Wittlinger, Ellen 1948- 189
Autobiography Feature 128
Earlier sketches in SATA 83, 122
Wittman, Sally (Anne Christensen) 1941- 30
Witty, Paul 1898-1976 50
Obituary 30
Wodehouse, P. G. 1881-1975 22
Wodehouse, Pelham Grenville
See Wodehouse, P. G.
Wodge, Dreary
See Gorey, Edward (St. John)
Woelfle, Gretchen 1945- 145
Wohlberg, Meg 1905-1990 41
Obituary 66
Wohlrabe, Raymond A. 1900-1977 4
Wohnoutka, Mike 230
Earlier sketch in SATA 195
Wojciechowska, Maia (Teresa) 1927-2002 ... 83
Autobiography Feature 104
Obituary 134
Earlier sketches in SATA 1, 28
See also CLR 1
See also SAAS 1
Wojciechowski, Susan 126
Earlier sketch in SATA 78
Wojnarowski, Adrian 1970- 190
Wojtowycz, David 1969- 236
Wojtusik, Elizabeth 208
Wolcott, Patty 1929- 14
Wold, Allen L. 1943- 64

Wold, Jo Anne 1938- 30
Woldin, Beth Weiner 1955- 34
Wolf, Allan 1963- 192
Wolf, Bernard 1930- 102
Brief entry 37
Wolf, Erica (Van Varick) 1978- 156
Wolf, Gita 1956- 238
Earlier sketch in SATA 101
Wolf, J. M.
See Wolf, Joan M.
Wolf, Janet 1957- 78
Wolf, Joan M. 1966- 193
Wolf, Sallie 1950- 205
Earlier sketch in SATA 80
Wolfe, Art 1952- 76
Wolfe, Burton H. 1932- 5
Wolfe, Frances 216
Wolfe, Gene 1931- 165
Earlier sketch in SATA 118
Wolfe, Gene Rodman
See Wolfe, Gene
Wolfe, Gillian 199
Wolfe, Louis 1905-1985 8
Obituary 133
Wolfe, Rinna (Evelyn) 1925- 38
Wolfenden, George
See Beardmore, George
Wolfer, Dianne 1961- 167
Autobiography Feature 117
Earlier sketch in SATA 104
Wolff, Alexander (Nikolaus) 1957- 137
Earlier sketch in SATA 63
Wolff, Ashley 1956- 203
Earlier sketches in SATA 50, 81, 155
Wolff, Diane 1945- 27
Wolff, Ferida 1946- 164
Earlier sketch in SATA 79
Wolff, Jason 1972- 213
Wolff, Jennifer Ashley
See Wolff, Ashley
Wolff, Nancy 202
Wolff, Robert Jay 1905-1977 10
Wolff, Sonia
See Levitin, Sonia
Wolff, Virginia Euwer 1937- 137
Earlier sketch in SATA 78
See also CLR 62
Wolfhard, Steve 235
Wolfman, Judy 1933- 138
Wolf-Sampath, Gita
See Wolf, Gita
Wolfson, Evelyn 1937- 62
Wolitzer, Hilma 1930- 31
Wolkoff, Judie (Edwards) 93
Brief entry 37
Wolkstein, Diane 1942- 138
Earlier sketches in SATA 7, 82
Wollheim, Donald A(llen) 1914-1990
Obituary 69
Wolny, P.
See Janeczko, Paul B(ryan)
Wolters, Richard A. 1920-1993 35
Wondriska, William 1931- 6
Wong, Jade Snow 1922-2006 112
Obituary 175
Wong, Janet S. 1962- 210
Earlier sketches in SATA 98, 148
See also CLR 94
Wong, Marissa Lopez 226
Wong, Nicole 214
Woo, Howie 1974- 207
Wood, Addie Robinson
See Wiggin, Eric E.
Wood, Anne (Savage) 1937- 64
Wood, Audrey 198
Brief entry 44
Earlier sketches in SATA 50, 81, 139
See also CLR 26
Wood, Catherine
See Etchison, Birdie L(ee)
Wood, David 1944- 212
Earlier sketch in SATA 87

Wood, Don 1945- *50*
  Brief entry *44*
  See also CLR 26
Wood, Douglas 1951- *234*
  Earlier sketches in SATA *81, 132, 180*
Wood, Douglas Eric
  See Wood, Douglas
Wood, Edgar A(llardyce) 1907-1998 .... *14*
Wood, Esther
  See Brady, Esther Wood
Wood, Frances Elizabeth *34*
Wood, Frances M. 1951- *97*
Wood, Jacqueline
  See Wood, Jakki
Wood, Jakki 1957- *211*
Wood, James Playsted 1905- *1*
Wood, Jenny 1955- *88*
Wood, John Norris 1930- *85*
Wood, June Rae 1946- *120*
  Earlier sketch in SATA *79*
  See also CLR 82
Wood, Kerry
  See Wood, Edgar A(llardyce)
Wood, Kim Marie *134*
Wood, Laura N.
  See Roper, Laura (Newbold) Wood
Wood, Linda C(arol) 1945- *59*
Wood, Marcia 1956- *80*
Wood, Marcia Mae
  See Wood, Marcia
Wood, Michele *239*
Wood, Nancy
  See Wood, Nancy C.
Wood, Nancy C. 1936- *178*
  Earlier sketch in SATA *6*
Wood, Nuria
  See Nobisso, Josephine
Wood, Owen 1929- *64*
Wood, Phyllis Anderson 1923- *33*
  Brief entry *30*
Wood, Richard 1949- *110*
Wood, Tim(othy William Russell) 1946- *88*
Wood, Wallace 1927-1981
  Obituary *33*
Woodard, Carol 1929- *14*
Woodburn, John Henry 1914- *11*
Woodbury, David Oakes 1896-1981 .... *62*
Woodford, Peggy 1937- *25*
Woodhouse, Barbara (Blackburn)
  1910-1988 .... *63*
Woodhull, Ann Love *194*
Wooding, Chris 1977- *166*
Wooding, Sharon
  See Wooding, Sharon L(ouise)
Wooding, Sharon L(ouise) 1943- *66*
Woodman, Allen 1954- *76*
Woodrich, Mary Neville 1915- *2*
Woodruff, Elvira 1951- *211*
  Earlier sketches in SATA *70, 106, 162*
Woodruff, Joan Leslie 1953- *104*
Woodruff, Liza 1971(?)- *182*
Woodruff, Marian
  See Goudge, Eileen
Woodruff, Noah 1977- *86*
Woods, George A(llan) 1926-1988 .... *30*
  Obituary *57*
Woods, Geraldine 1948- *111*
  Brief entry *42*
  Earlier sketch in SATA *56*
Woods, Harold 1945- *56*
  Brief entry *42*
Woods, Lawrence
  See Lowndes, Robert A(ugustine) W(ard)
Woods, Margaret 1921- *2*
Woods, Nat
  See Stratemeyer, Edward L.
Woods, Titania
  See Weatherly, Lee
Woodson, Jack
  See Woodson, John Waddie Jr.
Woodson, Jacqueline 1964- *189*
  Earlier sketches in SATA *94, 139*
  See also CLR 49

Woodson, Jacqueline Amanda
  See Woodson, Jacqueline
Woodson, John Waddie Jr. 1913- *10*
Woodtor, Dee
  See Woodtor, Delores Parmer
Woodtor, Dee Parmer 1945(?)-2002
  See Woodtor, Delores Parmer
Woodtor, Delores Parmer 1945-2002 .... *93*
Wood-Trost, Lucille
  See Trost, Lucille W(ood)
Woodward, (Landon) Cleveland 1900-1986 . *10*
  Obituary *48*
Woodworth, Chris 1957- *168*
Woodworth, Viki 1952- *127*
Woody, Regina Jones 1894-1983 .... *3*
Woodyadd, Charlotte
  See Hough, Charlotte
Woog, Adam 1953- *125*
  Earlier sketch in SATA *84*
Wooldridge, Connie Nordhielm 1950- *143*
  Earlier sketch in SATA *92*
Wooldridge, Frosty 1947- *140*
Wooldridge, Rhoda 1906-1988 .... *22*
Wooley, Susan Frelick 1945- *113*
Woolf, Paula 1950- *104*
Woolfe, Angela 1976- *169*
Woolley, Catherine 1904-2005 .... *3*
  Obituary *166*
Woolman, Steven 1969-2004 .... *163*
  Earlier sketch in SATA *90*
Woolsey, Janette 1904-1989 .... *3*
  Obituary *131*
Worcester, Donald E(mmet) 1915- *18*
Word, Reagan 1944- *103*
Work, Virginia 1946- *57*
  Brief entry *45*
Worline, Bonnie Bess 1914- *14*
Wormell, Christopher 1955- *154*
  Earlier sketch in SATA *103*
Wormell, Mary 1959- *96*
Wormser, Richard 1933- *106*
  Autobiography Feature *118*
  See also SAAS 26
Wormser, Sophie 1897-1979 .... *22*
Worth, Richard
  See Wiggin, Eric E.
Worth, Richard 1945- *59*
  Brief entry *46*
Worth, Valerie 1933-1994 .... *81*
  Earlier sketches in SATA *8, 70*
  See also CLR 21
Worthington, Leonie 1956- *200*
Wortis, Avi
  See Avi
Wortis, Edward Irving
  See Avi
Wosmek, Frances 1917- *29*
Woychuk, Denis 1953- *71*
Wrede, Patricia C(ollins) 1953- *146*
  Earlier sketch in SATA *67*
Wriggins, Sally Hovey 1922- *17*
Wright, Alexandra 1979- *103*
Wright, Betty Ren 1927- *109*
  Brief entry *48*
  Earlier sketch in SATA *63*
Wright, Cliff 1963- *168*
  Earlier sketch in SATA *76*
Wright, Courtni
  See Wright, Courtni C(rump)
Wright, Courtni C(rump) 1950- *84*
Wright, Courtni Crump
  See Wright, Courtni C(rump)
Wright, Dare 1914(?)-2001 .... *21*
  Obituary *124*
Wright, David K. 1943- *112*
  Earlier sketch in SATA *73*
Wright, Elinor
  See Lyon, Elinor
Wright, Enid Meadowcroft (LaMonte)
  1898-1966 .... *3*
Wright, Esmond 1915-2003 .... *10*
Wright, Frances Fitzpatrick 1897-1982 .... *10*

Wright, J. B.
  See Barkan, Joanne
Wright, Johanna *220*
Wright, Judith 1915-2000 .... *14*
  Obituary *121*
Wright, Judith Arundell
  See Wright, Judith
Wright, Katrina
  See Gater, Dilys
Wright, Kenneth
  See del Rey, Lester
Wright, Kit 1944- *87*
Wright, Leslie B(ailey) 1959- *91*
Wright, Maureen 1961- *233*
Wright, Michael 1954- *198*
Wright, Nancy Means *38*
Wright, R(obert) H(amilton) 1906- *6*
Wright, Rachel *220*
  Earlier sketch in SATA *134*
Wright, Simeon 1942- *232*
Wright, Susan Kimmel 1950- *97*
Wrightfrierson
  See Wright-Frierson, Virginia (Marguerite)
Wright-Frierson, Virginia (Marguerite)
  1949- *110*
  Earlier sketch in SATA *58*
Wrightson, Alice Patricia
  See Wrightson, Patricia
Wrightson, Patricia 1921-2010 .... *112*
  Obituary *215*
  Earlier sketches in SATA *8, 66*
  See also CLR 154
  See also SAAS 4
Wroble, Lisa A. 1963- *134*
Wrongo, I.B.
  See Katz, Alan
Wronker, Lili
  See Wronker, Lili Cassel
Wronker, Lili Cassel 1924- *10*
Wryde, Dogear
  See Gorey, Edward (St. John)
Wu, Donald *212*
Wu, Elizabeth
  See Wu, Liz
Wu, Liz *184*
Wu, Norbert 1961- *155*
  Earlier sketch in SATA *101*
Wulf, Linda Press *205*
Wulffson, Don 1943- *155*
  Earlier sketches in SATA *32, 88*
Wulffson, Don L.
  See Wulffson, Don
Wummer, Amy 1955- *201*
Wunderli, Stephen 1958- *79*
Wunsch, Josephine (McLean) 1914- *64*
Wunsch, Marjory 1942- *220*
  Earlier sketch in SATA *82*
Wuorio, Eva-Lis 1918- *34*
  Brief entry *28*
Wurts, Janny 1953- *98*
Wyatt, B. D.
  See Robinson, Spider
Wyatt, David 1968- *185*
Wyatt, Jane
  See Bradbury, Bianca (Ryley)
Wyatt, Melissa 1963- *177*
Wyatt, Valerie *209*
Wyeth, Betsy James 1921- *41*
Wyeth, N(ewell) C(onvers) 1882-1945 .... *17*
  See also CLR 106
Wyler, Rose 1909-2000 .... *18*
  Obituary *121*
Wylie, Betty Jane *48*
Wylie, Laura
  See Matthews, Patricia
Wylie, Laurie
  See Matthews, Patricia
Wyllie, Stephen *86*
Wyman, Andrea *75*
Wyman, Carolyn 1956- *83*
Wymer, Norman (George) 1911- *25*
Wynard, Talbot
  See Hamilton, Charles (Harold St. John)

Wyndham, John
    See Harris, John (Wyndham Parkes Lucas)
    Beynon
Wyndham, Lee
    See Hyndman, Jane Andrews Lee
Wyndham, Robert
    See Hyndman, Robert Utley
Wynne, Patricia J. 210
Wynne-Jones, Tim 1948- 186
    Autobiography Feature 136
    Earlier sketches in SATA *67, 96, 136*
    See also CLR *58*
Wynne-Jones, Timothy
    See Wynne-Jones, Tim
Wynter, Edward (John) 1914- 14
Wynyard, Talbot
    See Hamilton, Charles (Harold St. John)
Wyshynski, Sue 233
Wyss, Johann David Von 1743-1818 29
    Brief entry 27
    See also CLR *92*
Wyss, Thelma Hatch 1934- 202
    Earlier sketches in SATA *10, 140*

X

Xavier, Father
    See Hurwood, Bernhardt J.
Xuan, YongSheng 1952- 226
    Autobiography Feature 226
    Earlier sketch in SATA *116*

Y

Yaccarino, Dan 192
    Earlier sketch in SATA *141*
Yadin, (Rav-Aloof) Yigael 1917-1984 55
Yaffe, Alan
    See Yorinks, Arthur
Yagher, Kevin 1962- 143
Yakovetic, (Joseph Sandy) 1952- 59
Yakovetic, Joe
    See Yakovetic, (Joseph Sandy)
Yamada, Utako 1963- 188
Yamaguchi, Marianne (Illenberger) 1936- 7
Yamaka, Sara 1978- 92
Yamanaka, Lois-Ann 1961- 166
Yamasaki, Katie 206
Yancey, Diane 1951- 138
    Earlier sketch in SATA *81*
Yancey, Richard
    See Yancey, Rick
Yancey, Rick 193
Yang, Belle 1960- 170
Yang, Dori Jones 1954- 239
Yang, James 1960- 190
Yang, Jay 1941- 12
Yang, Mingyi 1943- 72
Yankovic, Al 1959- 239
Yankovic, Weird Al
    See Yankovic, Al
Yanok, Johnny 236
Yarbrough, Camille 1938- 79
    See also CLR *29*
Yarbrough, Ira 1910(?)-1983
    Obituary 35
Yaroslava
    See Mills, Yaroslava Surmach
Yarrow, Peter 1938- 195
Yashima, Taro
    See Iwamatsu, Jun Atsushi
Yates, Elizabeth 1905-2001 68
    Obituary 128
    Earlier sketch in SATA *4*
    See also SAAS *6*
Yates, Janelle K(aye) 1957- 77
Yates, John 1939- 74
Yates, Kelly 1971- 208
Yates, Louise 1983(?)- 218

Yates, Philip 1956- 212
    Earlier sketches in SATA *92, 149*
Yates, Raymond F(rancis) 1895-1966 31
Yaukey, Grace S(ydenstricker) 1899-1994 ... 80
    Earlier sketch in SATA *5*
Yayo 1961- 226
Yazzie, Johnson 1946- 205
Ye, Ting-xing 1952- 106
Yeahpau, Thomas M. 1975- 187
Yeakley, Marjory Hall 1908- 21
Yeates, Thomas 1955- 230
Yeatman, Linda 1938- 42
Yeatts, Tabatha 1970- 215
Yee, Brenda Shannon 133
Yee, Lisa 1959- 218
    Earlier sketch in SATA *160*
Yee, Paul 1956- 211
    Earlier sketches in SATA *67, 96, 143*
    See also CLR *44*
Yee, Tammy 206
Yee, Wong Herbert 1953- 172
    Earlier sketches in SATA *78, 115*
Yee, Ying S.
    See Lee, Y.S.
Yeh, Chun-Chan 1914- 79
Ye Junjian
    See Yeh, Chun-Chan
Yelchin, Eugene 1956- 232
    Earlier sketch in SATA *196*
Yenawine, Philip 1942- 85
Yensid, Retlaw
    See Disney, Walt(er Elias)
Yeo, Wilma (Lethem) 1918-1994 81
    Earlier sketch in SATA *24*
Yeoman, John 1934- 80
    Earlier sketch in SATA *28*
    See also CLR *46*
Yep, Kathleen S. 203
Yep, Laurence 1948- 213
    Earlier sketches in SATA *7, 69, 123, 176*
    See also CLR *132*
Yep, Laurence Michael
    See Yep, Laurence
Yepsen, Roger B(ennet), Jr. 1947- 59
Yerian, Cameron John 21
Yerian, Margaret A. 21
Yerxa, Leo 1947- 181
Yetska
    See Ironside, Jetske
Yezerski, Thomas F. 1969- 190
Yin 194
Ylvisaker, Anne 1965(?)- 172
Yoder, Carolyn P. 1953- 149
Yoder, Carolyn Patricia
    See Yoder, Carolyn P.
Yoder, Dorothy Meenen 1921- 96
Yoder, Dot
    See Yoder, Dorothy Meenen
Yoder, Walter D. 1933- 88
Yohalem, Eve 219
Yolen, Jane 1939- 230
    Autobiography Feature 111
    Earlier sketches in SATA *4, 40, 75, 112, 158,
    194*
    See also CLR *149*
    See also SAAS *1*
Yolen, Jane Hyatt
    See Yolen, Jane
Yonezu, Yusuke 196
Yonge, Charlotte 1823-1901 17
Yonge, Charlotte Mary
    See Yonge, Charlotte
Yoo, Paula 1969(?)- 174
Yoo, Taeeun 191
Yoon, Salina 1972- 204
Yorinks, Adrienne 1956- 171
Yorinks, Arthur 1953- 200
    Earlier sketches in SATA *33, 49, 85, 144*
    See also CLR *20*
York, Alison
    See Nicole, Christopher
York, Andrew
    See Nicole, Christopher

York, Carol Beach 1928- 77
    Earlier sketch in SATA *6*
York, Rebecca
    See Buckholtz, Eileen (Garber)
    and Glick, Ruth
York, Simon
    See Heinlein, Robert A.
Yoshida, Toshi 1911- 77
Yoshikawa, Sachiko 181
Yost, Edna 1889-1971
    Obituary 26
Youd, C. S.
    See Youd, Samuel
Youd, Samuel 1922- 135
    Brief entry 30
    Earlier sketch in SATA *47*
    See also CLR *2*
    See also SAAS *6*
Youme
    See Landowne, Youme
Young, Amy L. 185
Young, Anne Mortimer
    See Mortimer, Anne
Young, Bob
    See Young, Robert W(illiam)
    and Young, James Robert
Young, Carol 1945- 102
Young, Catherine
    See Olds, Helen Diehl
Young, Clarence
    See Garis, Howard R.
    and Stratemeyer, Edward L.
Young, Collier
    See Bloch, Robert (Albert)
Young, Dan 1952- 126
Young, Dianne 1959- 88
Young, Dorothea Bennett 1924- 31
Young, Ed 1931- 211
    Earlier sketches in SATA *10, 74, 122, 173*
    See also CLR *27*
Young, Ed Tse-chun
    See Young, Ed
Young, Edward
    See Reinfeld, Fred
Young, E.L. 1973- 219
Young, Elaine L.
    See Schulte, Elaine L(ouise)
Young, Emma L.
    See Young, E.L.
Young, James
    See Graham, Ian
Young, Jan
    See Young, Janet Randall
Young, Janet 1957- 188
Young, Janet Randall 1919-1994 3
Young, Janet Ruth
    See Young, Janet
Young, Jeff C. 1948- 132
Young, John
    See Macintosh, Brownie
Young, Judy 1956- 207
    Earlier sketch in SATA *155*
Young, Judy (Elaine) Dockrey 1949- 72
Young, Karen Romano 1959- 237
    Earlier sketches in SATA *116, 168*
Young, Ken 1956- 86
Young, Lois Horton 1911-1981 26
Young, Louisa 161
Young, Louise B. 1919- 64
Young, Margaret B. 1922-2009 2
Young, Margaret Buckner
    See Young, Margaret B.
Young, Mary 1940- 89
Young, Miriam 1913-1974 7
Young, Ned 233
Young, Noela 1930- 89
Young, (Rodney Lee) Patrick (Jr.) 1937- 22
Young, Percy M(arshall) 1912-2004 31
    Obituary 154
Young, Richard Alan 1946- 72
Young, Robert W(illiam) 1916-1969 3
Young, Ross B. 1955- 150
Young, Ruth 1946- 67

Young, Sara
   See Pennypacker, Sara
Young, Scott A. 1918-2005 5
Young, Scott Alexander
   See Young, Scott A.
Young, Selina 1971-2006 201
Young, Vivien
   See Gater, Dilys
Younger, Barbara 1954- 108
Youngs, Betty 1934-1985 53
   Obituary 42
Younkin, Paula 1942- 77
Yount, Lisa (Ann) 1944- 124
   Earlier sketch in SATA 74
Yourgrau, Barry 179
Yovanoff, Brenna 1979- 239
Yuditskaya, Tatyana 1964- 75
Yue, Stephanie 1984- 231
Yum, Hyewon 211
Yumoto, Kazumi 1959- 153

Z

Zach, Cheryl (Byrd) 1947- 98
   Brief entry 51
   Earlier sketch in SATA 58
   See also SAAS 24
Zacharias, Gary L. 1946- 153
Zadoff, Allen 1967- 224
Zaffo, George J. (?)-1984 42
Zagarenski, Pamela 1969(?)- 183
Zagwyn, Deborah Turney 1953- 138
   Earlier sketch in SATA 78
Zahares, Wade 193
Zahedi, Morteza 1978- 233
Zahidi, Murtiza
   See Zahedi, Morteza
Zahler, Diane 228
Zahn, Timothy 1951- 156
   Earlier sketch in SATA 91
Zaid, Barry 1938- 51
Zaidenberg, Arthur 1908(?)-1990 34
   Obituary 66
Zakanitch, Robert Rahway 1935- 231
Zakanitch, Robert S.
   See Zakanitch, Robert Rahway
Zalben, Jane Breskin 1950- 170
   Earlier sketches in SATA 7, 79, 120
   See also CLR 84
Zallinger, Jean (Day) 1918- 115
   Earlier sketches in SATA 14, 80
Zallinger, Peter Franz 1943- 49
Zambreno, Mary Frances 1954- 140
   Earlier sketch in SATA 75
Zanderbergen, George
   See May, Julian
Zappa, Ahmet 1974- 180
Zappa, Ahmet Emuukha Rodan
   See Zappa, Ahmet
Zappitello, Beth 237
Zappler, Lisbeth 1930- 10
Zarchy, Harry 1912-1987 34
Zarin, Cynthia 1959- 192
   Earlier sketch in SATA 108
Zaring, Jane (Thomas) 1936- 40
Zarins, Joyce Audy
   See dos Santos, Joyce Audy
Zaslavsky, Claudia 1917- 36
Zaugg, Sandra L. 1938- 118
Zaugg, Sandy
   See Zaugg, Sandra L.
Zaunders, Bo 1939- 137
Zawadzki, Marek 1958- 97
Zebra, A.
   See Scoltock, Jack
Zebrowski, George 1945- 67
Zebrowski, George T.
   See Zebrowski, George

Zecca, Katherine 207
Zeck, Gerald Anthony 1939- 40
Zeck, Gerry
   See Zeck, Gerald Anthony
Zed, Dr.
   See Penrose, Gordon
Zei, Alki 1925- 24
   See also CLR 6
Zeier, Joan T(heresa) 1931- 81
Zeinert, Karen 1942-2002 137
   Earlier sketch in SATA 79
Zeises, Lara M. 1976- 184
   Earlier sketch in SATA 145
Zelazny, Roger 1937-1995 57
   Brief entry 39
Zelazny, Roger Joseph
   See Zelazny, Roger
Zeldis, Malcah 1931- 146
   Earlier sketch in SATA 86
Zelinsky, Paul O. 1953- 154
   Brief entry 33
   Earlier sketches in SATA 49, 102
   See also CLR 55
Zellan, Audrey Penn
   See Penn, Audrey
Zemach, Harve
   See Fischtrom, Harvey
Zemach, Kaethe 1958- 149
   Brief entry 39
   Earlier sketch in SATA 49
Zemach, Margot 1931-1989 70
   Obituary 59
   Earlier sketch in SATA 21
Zemach-Bersin, Kaethe
   See Zemach, Kaethe
Zeman, Ludmila 1947- 153
Zepeda, Gwendolyn 1971- 206
Zephaniah, Benjamin 1958- 189
   Earlier sketches in SATA 86, 140
Zephaniah, Benjamin Obadiah Iqbal
   See Zephaniah, Benjamin
Zephaniah, Benjamin Pbadiah Iqubal
   See Zephaniah, Benjamin
Zerman, Melvyn Bernard 1930-2010 46
Zettner, Pat 1940- 70
Zevin, Gabrielle 1977- 176
Zhang, Christopher Zhong-Yuan 1954- 91
Zhang, Song Nan 1942- 170
   Earlier sketch in SATA 85
Ziefert, Harriet 1941- 205
   Earlier sketches in SATA 101, 154
Ziegler, Jack (Denmore) 1942- 60
Ziemienski, Dennis (Theodore) 1947- 10
Ziliox, Marc
   See Fichter, George S.
Zillah
   See Macdonald, Zillah K(atherine)
Zim, Herbert S(pencer) 1909-1994 30
   Obituary 85
   Earlier sketch in SATA 1
   See also CLR 2
   See also SAAS 2
Zim, Sonia Bleeker 1909-1971 2
   Obituary 26
Zima, Gordon 1920- 90
Zimelman, Nathan 1921- 65
   Brief entry 37
Zimmer, Dirk 1943- 147
   Earlier sketch in SATA 65
Zimmer, Tracie Vaughn 169
Zimmerman, Andrea 1950- 192
   Earlier sketch in SATA 123
Zimmerman, Andrea Griffing
   See Zimmerman, Andrea
Zimmerman, H. Werner 1951- 101
Zimmerman, Heinz Werner
   See Zimmerman, H. Werner
Zimmerman, Naoma 1914-2004 10
Zimmermann, Arnold E. 1909- 58

Zimmermann, Karl 1943- 211
Zimmermann, Karl R.
   See Zimmermann, Karl
Zimmett, Debbie
   See Becker, Deborah Zimmett
Zimmy
   See Stratemeyer, Edward L.
Zimnik, Reiner 1930- 36
   See also CLR 3
Zindel, Bonnie 1943- 34
Zindel, Lizabeth 187
Zindel, Paul 1936-2003 102
   Obituary 142
   Earlier sketches in SATA 16, 58
   See also CLR 85
Ziner, Feenie
   See Ziner, Florence
Ziner, Florence 1921- 5
Zingara, Professor
   See Leeming, Joseph
Zinger, Yitskhok
   See Singer, Isaac Bashevis
Zink, Michelle 1969- 220
Zion, Eugene 1913-1975 18
Zion, Gene
   See Zion, Eugene
Zobel, Allia
   See Zobel Nolan, Allia
Zobel Nolan, Allia 218
Zoehfeld, Kathleen Weidner 1954- 193
Zohorsky, Janet R. 1958- 148
Zolkower, Edie Stoltz 171
Zolkowski, Cathy (A.) 1969- 121
Zollars, Jaime 191
Zolotow, Charlotte 1915- 138
   Earlier sketches in SATA 1, 35, 78
   See also CLR 77
Zolotow, Charlotte Gertrude Shapiro
   See Zolotow, Charlotte
Zolotow, Ellen
   See Dragonwagon, Crescent
Zonderman, Jon 1957- 92
Zonia, Dhimitri 1921- 20
Zonta, Pat 1951- 143
Zubrowski, Bernard 1939- 90
   Earlier sketch in SATA 35
Zubrowski, Bernie
   See Zubrowski, Bernard
Zucker, Jonny 228
Zucker, Miriam S.
   See Reichert, Miriam Zucker
Zuckerman, Amy 217
Zuckerman, Andrew 1977- 224
Zuckerman, Linda 190
Zudeck, Darryl 1961- 61
Zug, Mark 204
Zulkey, Claire 1979- 225
Zupa, G. Anthony
   See Zeck, Gerald Anthony
Zupancic, Lilijana Praprotnik
   See Prap, Lila
Zurbo, Matt(hew) 1967- 98
Zurhorst, Charles (Stewart, Jr.) 1913-1989 .. 12
Zurlo, Tony 1941- 145
Zuromskis, Diane
   See Stanley, Diane
Zuromskis, Diane Stanley
   See Stanley, Diane
Zusak, Markus 1975- 149
Zwahlen, Diana 1947- 88
Zweifel, Frances W. 1931- 14
Zwerger, Lisbeth 1954- 194
   Earlier sketches in SATA 66, 130
   See also CLR 46
   See also SAAS 13
Zwinger, Ann (H.) 1925- 46
Zymet, Cathy Alter 1965- 121